BUSINESS ANALYTICS

Data Analysis and Decision Making

SEVENTH EDITION

S. Christian Albright
*Kelly School of Business,
Indiana University, Emeritus*

Wayne L. Winston
*Kelly School of Business,
Indiana University, Emeritus*

Cengage

Australia • Brazil • Canada • Mexico • Singapore • United Kingdom • United States

Business Analytics: Data Analysis and Decision Making, 7e

S. Christian Albright and Wayne L. Winston

Senior Vice President, Higher Ed Product, Content, and Market Development: Erin Joyner

Product Director: Jason Fremder

Senior Product Manager: Aaron Arnsparger

Senior Learning Designer: Brandon Foltz

Content Manager: Conor Allen

Digital Delivery Lead: Mark Hopkinson

Product Assistant: Christian Wood

Marketing Manager: Chris Walz

Production Service: Lumina Datamatics Ltd.

Designer, Creative Studio: Erin Griffin

Text Designer: Erin Griffin

Cover Designer: Erin Griffin

Cover Image(s): Ron Dale/ShutterStock.com

Intellectual Property Analyst: Reba Frederics

Intellectual Property Project Manager: Nick Barrows

For product information and technology assistance, contact us at
Cengage Customer & Sales Support, 1-800-354-9706 or support.cengage.com.
For permission to use material from this text or product, submit all requests online at **www.copyright.com**.

Library of Congress Control Number: 2019935644

Student Edition:
ISBN: 978-0-357-10995-3

Loose-leaf Edition:
ISBN: 978-0-357-10996-0

Cengage
200 Pier 4 Boulevard
Boston, MA 02210
USA

Cengage is a leading provider of customized learning solutions with employees residing in nearly 40 different countries and sales in more than 125 countries around the world. Find your local representative at: **www.cengage.com**.

To learn more about Cengage platforms and services, register or access your online learning solution, or purchase materials for your course, visit **www.cengage.com**.

Printed in the United States of America
Print Number: 04   Print Year: 2022

To my wonderful wife Mary—my best friend and companion; and to Sam, Lindsay, Teddy, and Archie   S.C.A

To my wonderful family   W.L.W.

ABOUT THE AUTHORS

S. Christian Albright got his B.S. degree in Mathematics from Stanford in 1968 and his PhD in Operations Research from Stanford in 1972. He taught in the Operations & Decision Technologies Department in the Kelley School of Business at Indiana University (IU) for close to 40 years, before retiring from teaching in 2011. While at IU, he taught courses in management science, computer simulation, statistics, and computer programming to all levels of business students, including undergraduates, MBAs, and doctoral students. In addition, he taught simulation modeling at General Motors and Whirlpool, and he taught database analysis for the Army. He published over 20 articles in leading operations research journals in the area of applied probability, and he has authored the books *Statistics for Business and Economics, Practical Management Science, Spreadsheet Modeling and Applications, Data Analysis for Managers*, and *VBA for Modelers*. He worked for several years after "retirement" with the Palisade Corporation developing training materials for its software products, he has developed a commercial version of his Excel® tutorial, called ExcelNow!, and he continues to revise his textbooks.

On the personal side, Chris has been married for 47 years to his wonderful wife, Mary, who retired several years ago after teaching 7th grade English for 30 years. They have one son, Sam, who lives in Philadelphia with his wife Lindsay and their two sons, Teddy and Archie. Chris has many interests outside the academic area. They include activities with his family, traveling with Mary, going to cultural events, power walking while listening to books on his iPod, and reading. And although he earns his livelihood from quantitative methods, his *real* passion is for playing classical piano music.

Wayne L. Winston taught in the Operations & Decision Technologies Department in the Kelley School of Business at Indiana University for close to 40 before retiring a few years ago. Wayne received his B.S. degree in Mathematics from MIT and his PhD in Operations Research from Yale. He has written the successful textbooks *Operations Research: Applications and Algorithms, Mathematical Programming: Applications and Algorithms, Simulation Modeling Using @RISK, Practical Management Science, Data Analysis and Decision Making, Financial Models Using Simulation and Optimization*, and *Mathletics*. Wayne has published more than 20 articles in leading journals and has won many teaching awards, including the school-wide MBA award four times. He has taught classes at Microsoft, GM, Ford, Eli Lilly, Bristol-Myers Squibb, Arthur Andersen, Roche, PricewaterhouseCoopers, and NCR, and in "retirement," he is currently teaching several courses at the University of Houston. His current interest is showing how spreadsheet models can be used to solve business problems in all disciplines, particularly in finance and marketing.

Wayne enjoys swimming and basketball, and his passion for trivia won him an appearance several years ago on the television game show *Jeopardy!*, where he won two games. He is married to the lovely and talented Vivian. They have two children, Gregory and Jennifer.

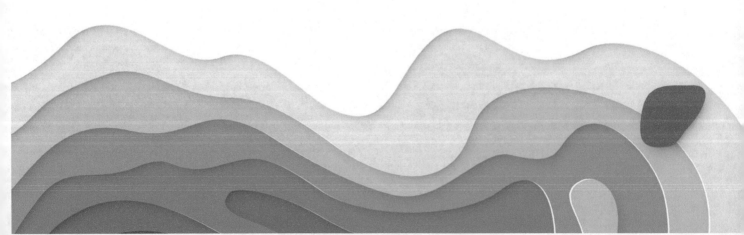

BRIEF CONTENTS

CONTENTS

PREFACE

With today's technology, companies are able to collect tremendous amounts of data with relative ease. Indeed, many companies now have more data than they can handle. However, before the data can be useful, they must be analyzed for trends, patterns, and relationships. This book illustrates in a practical way a variety of methods, from simple to complex, to help you analyze data sets and uncover important information. In many business contexts, data analysis is only the first step in the solution of a problem. Acting on the solution and the information it provides to make good decisions is a critical next step. Therefore, there is a heavy emphasis throughout this book on analytical methods that are useful in decision making. The methods vary considerably, but the objective is always the same—to equip you with decision-making tools that you can apply in your business careers.

We recognize that the majority of students in this type of course are *not* majoring in a quantitative area. They are typically business majors in finance, marketing, operations management, or some other business discipline who will need to analyze data and make quantitative-based decisions in their jobs. We offer a hands-on, example-based approach and introduce fundamental concepts as they are needed. Our vehicle is spreadsheet software—specifically, Microsoft Excel®. This is a package that most students already know and will almost surely use in their careers. Our MBA students at Indiana University have been so turned on by the required course that is based on this book that *almost all* of them (mostly finance and marketing majors) have taken at least one of our follow-up elective courses in spreadsheet modeling. We are convinced that students see value in quantitative analysis when the course is taught in a practical and example-based approach.

Rationale for Writing This Book

Business Analytics: Data Analysis and Decision Making is different from other textbooks written for statistics and management science. Our rationale for writing this book is based on four fundamental objectives.

- **Integrated coverage and applications.** The book provides a unified approach to business-related problems by integrating methods and applications that have been traditionally taught in separate courses, specifically statistics and management science.
- **Practical in approach.** The book emphasizes realistic business examples and the processes managers actually use to analyze business problems. The emphasis is *not* on abstract theory or computational methods.
- **Spreadsheet-based teaching.** The book provides students with the skills to analyze business problems with tools they have access to and will use in their careers. To this end, we have adopted Excel and commercial spreadsheet add-ins.
- **Latest tools.** This is not a static field. The software keeps changing, and even the mathematical algorithms behind the software continue to evolve. Each edition of this book has presented the most recent tools in Excel and the accompanying Excel add-ins, and the current edition is no exception.

Integrated Coverage and Applications

In the past, many business schools have offered a required statistics course, a required decision-making course, and a required management science course—or some subset of these. The current trend, however, is to have only one required course that covers the basics of statistics, some regression analysis, some decision making under uncertainty, some linear programming, some simulation, and some advanced data analysis methods. Essentially, faculty in the quantitative area get one opportunity to teach all business students, so we attempt to cover a variety of useful quantitative methods. We are not necessarily arguing that this trend is ideal, but rather that it is a reflection of the reality at our university and, we suspect, at many others. After several years of teaching this course, we have found it to be a great opportunity to attract students to the subject and to more advanced study.

The book is also integrative in another important aspect. It not only integrates a number of analytical methods, but it also applies them to a wide variety of business problems—that is, it analyzes realistic examples from many business disciplines. We include examples, problems, and cases that deal with portfolio optimization, workforce scheduling, market share analysis, capital budgeting, new product analysis, and many others.

Practical in Approach

This book has been designed to be very example-based and practical. We strongly believe that students learn best by working through examples, and they appreciate the material most when the examples are realistic and interesting. Therefore, our approach in the book differs in two important ways from many competitors. First, there is just enough conceptual development to give students an understanding and appreciation for the issues raised in the examples. We often introduce important concepts, such as standard deviation as a measure of variability, in the context of examples rather than discussing them in the abstract. Our experience is that students gain greater intuition and understanding of the concepts and applications through this approach.

Second, we place virtually no emphasis on hand calculations. We believe it is more important for students to understand why they are conducting an analysis and to interpret the results than to emphasize the tedious calculations associated with many analytical techniques. Therefore, we illustrate how powerful software can be used to create graphical and numerical outputs in a matter of seconds, freeing the rest of the time for in-depth interpretation of the results, sensitivity analysis, and alternative modeling approaches.

Spreadsheet-based Teaching

We are strongly committed to teaching spreadsheet-based, example-driven courses, regardless of whether the basic area is data analysis or management science. We have found tremendous enthusiasm for this approach, both from students and from faculty around the world who have used our books. Students learn and remember more, and they appreciate the material more. In addition, instructors typically enjoy teaching more, and they usually receive immediate reinforcement through better teaching evaluations. We were among the first to move to spreadsheet-based teaching about two decades ago, and we have never regretted the move.

What We Hope to Accomplish in This Book

Condensing the ideas in the previous paragraphs, we hope to:

- continue to make quantitative courses attractive to a wide audience by making these topics real, accessible, and interesting;
- give students plenty of hands-on experience with real problems and challenge them to develop their intuition, logic, and problem-solving skills;
- expose students to real problems in many business disciplines and show them how these problems can be analyzed with quantitative methods; and
- develop spreadsheet skills, including experience with powerful spreadsheet add-ins, that add immediate value to students' other courses and for their future careers.

New in the Seventh Edition

There are several important changes in this edition.

- *New introductory material on Excel:* Chapter 1 now includes an introductory section on spreadsheet modeling. This provides business examples for getting students up to speed in Excel and covers such Excel tools as IF and VLOOKUP functions, data tables, goal seek, range names, and more.
- *Reorganization of probability chapters:* Chapter 4, Probability and Probability Distributions, and Chapter 5, Normal, Binomial, Poisson, and Exponential Distributions, have been shortened slightly and combined into a single Chapter 5, Probability and Probability Distributions. This created space for the new Chapter 4 discussed next.
- *New material on "Power BI" tools and data visualization:* The previous chapters on Data Mining and Importing Data into Excel have been reorganized and rewritten to include an increased focus on the tools commonly included under the Business Analytics umbrella. There is now a new Chapter 4, Business Intelligence Tools for Data Analysis, which includes Excel's Power Query tools for importing data into Excel, Excel's Power Pivot add-in (and the DAX language) for even more powerful data analysis with pivot tables, and Tableau Public for data visualization. The old online Chapter 18, Importing Data into Excel, has been eliminated, and its material has been moved to this new Chapter 4.

- *Updated for Office 365, Windows or Mac:* The 7th Edition is completely compatible with the latest version of Excel, and all screenshots in the book are from the latest version. However, because the changes from previous versions are not that extensive for Business Analytics purposes, the 7th Edition also works well even if you are still using Microsoft Office 2013, 2010, or 2007. Also, recognizing that many students are now using Macs, we have attempted to make the material compatible with Excel for Mac whenever possible.

- *Updated Problems:* Numerous problems have been modified to include the most updated data available. In addition, the **DADM 7e Problem Database.xlsx** file provides instructors with an entire database of problems. This file indicates the context of each of the problems and shows the correspondence between problems in this edition and problems in the previous edition.

- *Less emphasis on add-ins (when possible):* There is more emphasis in this edition on implementing spreadsheet calculations, especially statistical calculations, with built-in Excel tools rather than with add-ins. For example, there is no reliance on Palisade's StatTools add-in in the descriptive statistics chapters 2 and 3 or in the confidence interval and hypothesis testing chapters 8 and 9. Nevertheless, Palisade's add-ins are still relied on in chapters where they are really needed: PrecisionTree for decision trees in Chapter 6; StatTools for regression and time series analysis in Chapters 10, 11, and 12; @RISK for simulation in Chapters 15 and 16; and StatTools and NeuralTools for logistic regression and neural networks in Chapter 17.

- *New optional add-in:* Although it is not an "official" part of the book, Albright wrote a DADM_Tools add-in for Excel (Windows or Mac), with tools for creating summary stats, histograms, correlations and scatterplots, regression, time series analysis, decision trees, and simulation. This add-in provides a "lighter" alternative to the Palisade add-ins and is freely available at https://kelley.iu.edu/albrightbooks/free_downloads.htm.

Software

This book is based entirely on Microsoft Excel, the spreadsheet package that has become the standard analytical tool in business. Excel is an extremely powerful package, and one of our goals is to convert *casual* users into *power* users who can take full advantage of its features. If you learn no more than this, you will be acquiring a valuable skill for the business world. However, Excel has some limitations. Therefore, this book relies on several Excel add-ins to enhance Excel's capabilities. As a group, these add-ins comprise what is arguably the most impressive assortment of spreadsheet-based software accompanying any book on the market.

DecisionTools® Suite Add-in

The textbook website for *Business Analytics: Data Analysis and Decision Making* provides a link to the powerful DecisionTools® Suite by Palisade Corporation. This suite includes seven separate add-ins:

- **@RISK**, an add-in for simulation
- **StatTools**, an add-in for statistical data analysis
- **PrecisionTree**, a graphical-based add-in for creating and analyzing decision trees
- **TopRank**, an add-in for performing what-if analyses
- **NeuralTools®**, an add-in for estimating complex, nonlinear relationships
- **Evolver**™, an add-in for performing optimization (an alternative to Excel's Solver)
- **BigPicture**, a smart drawing add-in, useful for depicting model relationships

We use @RISK and PrecisionTree extensively in the chapters on simulation and decision making under uncertainty, and we use StatTools as necessary in the data analysis chapters. We also use BigPicture in the optimization and simulation chapters to provide a "bridge" between a problem statement and an eventual spreadsheet model.

Online access to the DecisionTools Suite, available with new copies of the book and for MindTap adopters, is an academic version, slightly scaled down from the professional version that sells for hundreds of dollars and is used by many leading companies. It functions for one year when properly installed, and it puts only modest limitations on the size of data sets or models that can be analyzed.

SolverTable Add-in

We also include SolverTable, a supplement to Excel's built-in Solver for optimization.[1] If you have ever had difficulty understanding Solver's sensitivity reports, you will appreciate SolverTable. It works like Excel's data tables, except that for each input (or pair of inputs), the add-in runs Solver and reports the *optimal* output values. SolverTable is used extensively in the optimization chapters.

Windows versus Mac

We have seen an increasing number of students using Macintosh laptops rather than Windows laptops. These students have two basic options when using our book. The first option is to use the latest version of Excel for Mac. Except for a few advanced tools such as Power Pivot (discussed in Chapter 4), the Mac version of Excel is very similar to the Windows version. However, the Palisade and SolverTable add-ins will not work with Excel for Mac. Therefore, the second option, the preferable option, is to use a Windows emulation program (Bootcamp and Parallels are good candidates), along with Office for Windows. Students at Indiana have used this second option for years and have had no problems.

Software Calculations by Chapter

This section indicates how the various calculations are implemented in the book. Specifically, it indicates which calculations are performed with built-in Excel tools and which require Excel add-ins.

Important note: The Palisade add-ins used in several chapters do *not* work in Excel for Mac. This is the primary reason Albright developed his own DADM_Tools add-in, which works in Excel for Windows *and* Excel for Mac. This add-in is freely available at the author's website (https://kelley.iu.edu/albrightbooks/free_downloads.htm), together with a Word document on how to use it. However, it is optional and is not used in the book.

Chapter 1 – Introduction to Business Analytics

- The section on basic spreadsheet modeling is implemented with built-in Excel functions.

Chapter 2 – Describing the Distribution of a Variable

- Everything is implemented with built-in Excel functions and charts.

  o Summary measures are calculated with built-in functions AVERAGE, STDEV.S, etc.
  o Histograms and box plots are created with the Excel chart types introduced in 2016.
  o Time series graphs are created with Excel line charts.

- Palisade's StatTools add-in can do all of this. It isn't used in the chapter, but it is mentioned in a short appendix, and an Intro to StatTools video is available.
- Albright's DADM_Tools add-in can do all of this except for time series graphs.

Chapter 3 – Finding Relationships among Variables

- Everything is implemented with built-in Excel functions and charts.

  o Summary measures of numeric variables, broken down by categories of a categorical variable, are calculated with built-in functions AVERAGE, STDEV.S, etc. (They are embedded in array formulas with IF functions.)
  o Side-by-side box plots are created with the Excel box plot chart type introduced in 2016.
  o Scatterplots are created with Excel scatter charts.
  o Correlations are calculated with Excel's CORREL function. A combination of the CORREL and INDIRECT functions is used to create tables of correlations.

- StatTools can do all of this. It isn't used in the chapter, but it is mentioned in a short appendix.
- DADM_Tools can do all of this.

[1] SolverTable is available on this textbook's website and on Albright's website, www.kelley.iu.edu/albrightbooks.

Chapter 4 - Business Intelligence (BI) Tools for Data Analysis

- Queries are implemented with Excel's Power Query tools (available only in Excel for Windows).
- Pivot table analysis is implemented with a combination of Excel's Data Model and the Power Pivot add-in (available only in Excel for Windows).
- Tableau Public (a free program for Windows or Mac) is used for data visualization.

Chapter 5 – Probability and Probability Distributions

- All calculations are performed with built-in Excel functions.

Chapter 6 – Decision Making Under Uncertainty

- Decision trees are implemented with Palisade's PrecisionTree add-in.
- DADM_Tools implements decision trees.

Chapter 7 – Sampling and Sampling Distributions

- All calculations are performed with built-in Excel functions.

Chapter 8 – Confidence Interval Estimation

- Everything is implemented with Excel functions, which are embedded in a **Confidence Interval Template.xlsx** file developed by Albright. This isn't an add-in; it is a regular Excel file where the confidence interval formulas have already been created, and users only need to enter their data.
- StatTools can do all of this, but it isn't used in the chapter.
- DADM_Tools doesn't perform confidence interval calculations.

Chapter 9 – Hypothesis Testing

- Everything is implemented with Excel functions, which are embedded in **Hypothesis Test Template.xlsx** and **Normality Tests Template.xlsx** files developed by Albright. These aren't add-ins; they are regular Excel files where the hypothesis test formulas have already been created, and users only need to enter their data.
- StatTools can do all of this, but it isn't used in the chapter.
- DADM_Tools doesn't perform hypothesis test calculations.

Chapters 10, 11 – Regression Analysis

- StatTools is used throughout to perform the regression calculations.
- Excel's built-in regression functions (SLOPE, INTERCEPT, etc.) are illustrated for simple linear regression, but they are used sparingly.
- Excel's Analysis ToolPak add-in is mentioned, but it isn't used.
- DADM_Tools implements regression calculations.

Chapter 12 – Time Series Analysis and Forecasting

- Autocorrelations and the runs test for randomness are implemented with Excel functions, which are embedded in **Autocorrelation Template.xlsx** and **Runs Test Template.xlsx** files developed by Albright. These aren't add-ins; they are regular Excel files where the relevant formulas have already been created, and users only need to enter their data.
- Moving averages and exponential smoothing are implemented in StatTools.
- DADM_Tools implements moving averages and exponential smoothing calculations.

Chapters 13, 14 – Optimization

- The optimization is performed with Excel's Solver add-in.
- Albright's SolverTable add-in performs sensitivity analysis on optimal solutions. It works in Excel for Windows but *not* in Excel for Mac.

Chapters 15, 16 – Simulation

- Built-in Excel functions for generating random numbers from various distributions are illustrated, and the Excel-only way of running simulations with data tables is shown in an introductory example.
- Palisade's @RISK add-in is used in the rest of the examples.
- DADM_Tools implements simulation.

Chapter 17 – Data Mining

- Logistic regression is implemented with StatTools.
- Neural networks are implemented with Palisade's NeuralTools add-in.
- Other calculations are implemented with Excel functions.

Chapter 18 – Analysis of Variance and Experimental Design (online)

- Most of the chapter is implemented with StatTools.
- DADM_Tools doesn't perform ANOVA calculations.

Chapter 19 – Statistical Process Control

- All control charts are implemented with StatTools.
- DADM_Tools doesn't implement control charts.

Potential Course Structures

Although we have used the book for our own required one-semester course, there is admittedly much more material than can be covered adequately in one semester. We have tried to make the book as modular as possible, allowing an instructor to cover, say, simulation before optimization or vice-versa, or to omit either of these topics. The one exception is statistics. Due to the natural progression of statistical topics, the basic topics in the early chapters should be covered before the more advanced topics (regression and time series analysis) in the later chapters. With this in mind, there are several possible ways to cover the topics.

- **One-semester Required Course, with No Statistics Prerequisite** (or where MBA students need a refresher for whatever statistics they learned previously): If data analysis is the primary focus of the course, then Chapters 2–3, 5, 7–11 should be covered. Depending on the time remaining, any of the topics in Chapters 4 and 17 (advanced data analysis tools), Chapters 6 (decision making under uncertainty), 12 (time series analysis), 13–14 (optimization), or 15–16 (simulation) can be covered in practically any order.

- **One-semester Required Course, with a Statistics Prerequisite**: Assuming that students know the basic elements of statistics (up through hypothesis testing), the material in Chapters 2–3, 5, and 7–9 can be reviewed quickly, primarily to illustrate how Excel and add-ins can be used to do the number crunching. The instructor can then choose among any of the topics in Chapters 4, 6, 10–11, 12, 13–14, 15–16 (in practically any order), or 17 to fill the remainder of the course.

- **Two-semester Required Sequence**: Given the luxury of spreading the topics over two semesters, the entire book, or at least most of it, can be covered. The statistics topics in Chapters 2–3 and 7–9 should be covered in chronological order before other statistical topics (regression and time series analysis), but the remaining chapters can be covered in practically any order.

Instructor Supplements

Textbook Website: www.cengage.com/decisionsciences/albright/ba/7e

The companion website provides immediate access to an array of teaching resources—including data and solutions files for all of the Examples, Problems, and Cases in the book, Test Bank files, PowerPoint slides, and access to the DecisionTools® Suite by Palisade Corporation and the SolverTable add-in. Instructors who want to compare the problems in the previous edition of this text to the problems in this edition can also download the file **DADM 7e Problem Database.xlsx** which details that correlation. You can easily download the instructor resources you need from the password-protected, instructor-only section of the site.

Test Bank

Cengage Learning Testing Powered by Cognero® is a flexible, online system that allows you to import, edit, and manipulate content from the text's *Test Bank* or elsewhere, including your own favorite test questions; create multiple test versions in an instant; and deliver tests from your LMS, your classroom, or wherever you want.

Student Supplements

Textbook Website: www.cengage.com/decisionsciences/albright/ba/7e

Every new student edition of this book comes with access to the *Business Analytics: Data Analysis and Decision Making, 7e* textbook website that links to the following files and tools:

- Excel files for the examples in the chapters (usually two versions of each—a template, or data-only version, and a finished version)
- Data files required for the Problems and Cases
- **Excel Tutorial for Windows.xlsx**, which contains a useful tutorial for getting up to speed in Excel (**Excel Tutorial for the Mac.xlsx** is also available)
- DecisionTools® Suite software by Palisade Corporation
- SolverTable add-in

Acknowledgements

We are also grateful to many of the professionals who worked behind the scenes to make this book a success: Aaron Arnsparger, Senior Product Manager; Brandon Foltz, Senior Learning Designer; Conor Allen, Content Manager; Project Manager, Anubhav Kaushal; and Marketing Manager, Chris Walz.

We also extend our sincere appreciation to the reviewers who provided feedback on the authors' proposed changes that resulted in this seventh edition:

John Aloysius, *Walton College of Business, University of Arkansas*

Henry F. Ander, *Arizona State University*

Dr. Baabak Ashuri, *School of Building Construction, Georgia Institute of Technology*

James Behel, *Harding University*

Robert H. Burgess, *Scheller College of Business, Georgia Institute of Technology*

Paul Damien, *McCombs School of Business, University of Texas in Austin*

Parviz Ghandforoush, *Virginia Tech*

Betsy Greenberg, *University of Texas*

Anissa Harris, *Harding University*

Tim James, *Arizona State University*

Norman Johnson, *C.T. Bauer College of Business, University of Houston*

Shivraj Kanungo, *The George Washington University*

Miguel Lejeune, *The George Washington University*

José Lobo, *Arizona State University*

Stuart Low, *Arizona State University*

Lance Matheson, *Virginia Tech*

Patrick R. McMullen, *Wake Forest University*

Barbara A. Price, PhD, *Georgia Southern University*

Laura Wilson-Gentry, *University of Baltimore*

Toshiyuki Yuasa, *University of Houston*

S. Christian Albright
Wayne L. Winston
April 2019

CHAPTER 1
Introduction to Business Analytics

StockLite/Shutterstock.com

BUSINESS ANALYTICS PROVIDES INSIGHTS AND IMPROVES PERFORMANCE

This book is about analyzing data and using quantitative modeling to help companies understand their business, make better decisions, and improve performance. We have been teaching the methods discussed in this book for decades, and companies have been using these methods for decades to improve performance and save millions of dollars. Therefore, we were a bit surprised when a brand new term, Business Analytics (BA), became hugely popular several years ago. All of a sudden, BA promised to be the road to success. By using quantitative BA methods—data analysis, optimization, simulation, prediction, and others—companies could drastically improve business performance. Haven't those of us in our field been doing this for years? What is different about BA that has made it so popular, both in the academic world and even more so in the business world?

The truth is that BA *does* use the same quantitative methods that have been used for years, the same methods you will learn in this book. BA has not all of a sudden invented brand new quantitative methods to eclipse traditional methods. The main difference is that BA uses *big data* to solve business problems and provide insights. Companies now have access to huge sources of data, and the technology is now available to use huge data sets for quantitative analysis, predictive modeling, optimization, and simulation. In short, the same quantitative methods that have been used for years can now be even more effective by utilizing big data and the corresponding technology.

For a quick introduction to BA, you should visit the BA Wikipedia site (search the Web for "business analytics"). Among other things, it lists areas where BA plays a prominent role, including the following: retail sales analytics; financial services analytics; risk and credit analytics; marketing analytics; pricing analytics; supply chain analytics; and transportation analytics. If you glance through the examples and problems in this book, you will see that most of them come from these same areas. Again, the difference is that we use relatively small data sets to get you started—we do not want to overwhelm you with gigabytes of data—whereas real applications of BA use huge data sets to advantage.

A more extensive discussion of BA can be found in the Fall 2011 research report, *Analytics: The Widening Divide*, published in the MIT Sloan Management Review in collaboration with IBM, a key developer of BA software (search the Web for the article's title). This 22-page article discusses what BA is and provides several case studies. In addition, it lists three key competencies people need to compete successfully in the BA world—and hopefully you will be one of these people.

- **Competency 1: Information management skills to manage the data.** This competency involves expertise in a variety of techniques for managing data. Given the key role of data in BA methods, data quality is extremely important. With data coming from a number of disparate sources, both internal and external to an organization, achieving data quality is no small feat.

- **Competency 2: Analytics skills and tools to understand the data.** We were not surprised, but rather very happy, to see this competency listed among the requirements because these skills are exactly the skills we cover throughout this book—optimization with advanced quantitative algorithms, simulation, and others.
- **Competency 3: Data-oriented culture to act on the data.** This refers to the culture within the organization. Everyone involved, especially top management, must believe strongly in fact-based decisions arrived at using analytical methods.

The article argues persuasively that the companies that have these competencies and have embraced BA have a distinct competitive advantage over companies that are just starting to use BA methods or are not using them at all. This explains the title of the article. The gap between companies that embrace BA and those that do not will only widen in the future.

This field of BA and, more specifically, data analysis is progressing very quickly, not only in academic areas but also in many applied areas. By analyzing big data sets from various sources, people are learning more and more about the way the world works. One recent book, *Everybody Lies: Big Data New Data, and What the Internet Can Tell Us About Who We Really Are,* by Stephens-Davidowitz (2017), is especially interesting. The title of the book suggests that people lie to themselves, friends, Facebook, and surveys, but they don't lie on Google searches. The author, a social scientist, has focused on the data from Google searches to study wide-ranging topics, including economics, finance, education, sports, gambling, racism, and sex. Besides his insightful and often unexpected findings, the author presents several general conclusions about analysis with big data:

- Not surprisingly, insights are more likely to be obtained when analyzing data in novel ways, such as analyzing the organ sizes of race horses instead of their pedigrees. (A data analyst used data on race horse heart size to predict that American Pharaoh would be great. The horse went on to win the Triple Crown in 2015, the first horse to do so since 1978.) On the other hand, if all available data have been analyzed in every conceivable way, as has been done with stock market data, even analysis with big data is unlikely to produce breakthroughs.
- Huge data sets allow analysts to zoom in on smaller geographical areas or smaller subsets of a population for keener insights. For example, when analyzing why some areas of the U.S. produce more people who warrant an entry on Wikipedia, you might find that richer and more educated states have more success. However, with a data set of more than 150,000 Americans of Wikipedia fame, the author was able to pinpoint that a disproportionate number were born in college towns. Traditional small data sets don't allow drilling down to this level of detail.
- Companies are increasingly able to run controlled experiments, usually on the Web, to learn the causes of behavior. The new term for these experiments is *A/B testing*. The purpose of a test is to determine whether a person prefers A or B. For example, Google routinely runs A/B tests, showing one randomly selected group of customers one thing and a second randomly selected group another. The difference could be as slight as the presence or absence of an arrow link on a Web page. Google gets immediate results from such tests by studying the customers' clicking behavior. The company can then use the results of one test to lead to another follow-up test. A/B testing is evidently happening all the time, whether or not we're aware of it.
- A potential drawback of analyzing big data is dimensionality, where there are so many potential explanatory variables that one will almost surely look like a winner—even though it isn't. The author illustrates this by imagining daily coin flips of 1000 coins and tracking which of them comes up heads on days when the stock market is up. One of these coins, just by chance, is likely to correlate highly with the stock market, but this coin is hardly a useful predictor of *future* stock market movement.

The analysis of big data will not solve all the world's problems, and there are ethical issues about studying people's behavior—and acting on the findings—from Web-based data such as Google searches. However, the potential for new and important insights into human behavior is enormous.

1-1 Introduction

We are living in the age of technology. This has two important implications for everyone entering the business world. First, technology has made it possible to collect huge amounts of data. Technology companies like Google and Amazon capture click data from websites, retailers collect point-of-sale data on products and customers every time a transaction occurs; credit agencies collect data on people who have or would like to obtain credit; investment companies have a limitless supply of data on the historical patterns of stocks, bonds, and other securities; and government agencies have data on economic trends, the environment, social welfare, consumer product safety, and virtually everything else imaginable. It has become relatively *easy* to collect the data. As a result, data are plentiful. However, as many organizations have discovered, it is a challenge to make sense of the data they have collected.

A second important implication of technology is that it has given many more people the power and responsibility to analyze data and make decisions on the basis of quantitative analysis. People entering the business world can no longer pass all the quantitative analysis to the "quant jocks," the technical specialists who have traditionally done the number crunching. The vast majority of employees now have a computer at their disposal, access to relevant data, and training in easy-to-use software, particularly spreadsheet and database software. For these employees, quantitative methods are no longer forgotten topics they once learned in college. Quantitative analysis is now an essential part of their daily jobs.

A large amount of data already exists, and it will only increase in the future. Many companies already complain of swimming in a sea of data. However, enlightened companies are seeing this expansion as a source of competitive advantage. In fact, one of the hottest topics in today's business world is **business analytics**, also called **data analytics**. These terms have been created to encompass the types of analysis discussed in this book, so they aren't really new; we have been teaching them for years. The new aspect of business analytics is that it typically implies the analysis of very *large* data sets, the kind that companies currently encounter. For this reason, the term **big data** has also become popular. By using quantitative methods to uncover the *information* from the data and then act on this information—again guided by quantitative analysis—companies are able to gain advantages over their less enlightened competitors. Here are several pertinent examples.

- Direct marketers analyze enormous customer databases to see which customers are likely to respond to various products and types of promotions. Marketers can then target different classes of customers in different ways to maximize profits—and give their customers what they want.
- Hotels and airlines also analyze enormous customer databases to see what their customers want and are willing to pay for. By doing this, they have been able to devise very clever pricing strategies, where different customers pay different prices for the same accommodations. For example, a business traveler typically makes a plane reservation closer to the time of travel than a vacationer. The airlines know this. Therefore, they reserve seats for these business travelers and charge them a higher price for the same seats. The airlines profit from clever pricing strategies, and the customers are happy.
- Financial planning services have a virtually unlimited supply of data about security prices, and they have customers with widely differing preferences for various types of investments. Trying to find a match of investments to customers is a very

challenging problem. However, customers can easily take their business elsewhere if good decisions are not made on their behalf. Therefore, financial planners are under extreme competitive pressure to analyze masses of data so that they can make informed decisions for their customers.[1]

- We all know about the pressures U.S. manufacturing companies have faced from foreign competition in the past few decades. The automobile companies, for example, have had to change the way they produce and market automobiles to stay in business. They have had to improve quality and cut costs by orders of magnitude. Although the struggle continues, much of the success they have had can be attributed to data analysis and wise decision making. Starting on the shop floor and moving up through the organization, these companies now measure almost everything, analyze these measurements, and then act on the results of their analysis.

We talk about companies analyzing data and making decisions. However, *companies* don't really do this; *people* do it. And who will these people be in the future? They will be *you*! We know from experience that students in all areas of business, at both the undergraduate and graduate level, will be *required* to analyze large complex data sets, run regression analyses, make quantitative forecasts, create optimization models, and run simulations. You are the person who will be analyzing data and making important decisions to help your company gain a competitive advantage. And if you are *not* willing or able to do so, there will be plenty of other technically trained people who will be more than happy to do it.

The goal of this book is to teach you how to use a variety of quantitative methods to analyze data and make decisions in a very hands-on way. We discuss a number of quantitative methods and illustrate their use in a large variety of realistic business situations. As you will see, this book includes many examples from finance, marketing, operations, accounting, and other areas of business. To analyze these examples, we take advantage of the Microsoft Excel® spreadsheet software, together with several powerful Excel add-ins. In each example we provide step-by-step details of the method and its implementation in Excel.

This is *not* a "theory" book. It is also not a book where you can lean comfortably back in your chair and read about how *other* people use quantitative methods. It is a "get your hands dirty" book, where you will learn best by actively following the examples throughout the book on your own computer. By the time you have finished, you will have acquired some very useful skills for today's business world.

1-2 Overview of the Book

This section provides an overview of the methods covered in this book and the software that is used to implement them. Then the rest of the chapter illustrates how some of Excel's basic tools can be used to solve quantitative problems.

1-2a The Methods

This book is rather unique in that it combines topics from two separate fields: statistics and management science. Statistics is the area of data analysis, whereas management science is the area of model building, optimization, and decision making. In the academic arena these two fields have traditionally been separated, sometimes widely. Indeed, they are often housed in separate academic departments. However, both are useful in accomplishing what the title of this book promises: data analysis and decision making.

Therefore, we do not distinguish between the statistics and the management science parts of this book. Instead, we view the entire book as a collection of useful quantitative methods for analyzing data and helping to make business decisions. In addition, our

1 For a great overview of how quantitative techniques have been used in the financial world, read the book *The Quants*, by Scott Patterson. It describes how quantitative models made millions for a lot of bright young analysts, but it also describes the dangers of relying totally on quantitative models, at least in the complex world of global finance.

choice of software helps to integrate the various topics. By using a single package, Excel, together with several Excel add-ins, you will see that the methods of statistics and management science are similar in many important respects.

Three important themes run through this book. Two of them are in the title: data analysis and decision making. The third is *dealing with uncertainty*.[2] Each of these themes has subthemes. Data analysis includes data description, data visualization, data inference, and the search for relationships in data. Decision making includes *optimization* techniques for problems with no uncertainty, *decision analysis* for problems with uncertainty, and structured *sensitivity analysis*. Dealing with uncertainty includes measuring uncertainty and modeling uncertainty explicitly. There are obvious overlaps between these themes and subthemes. When you make inferences from data and search for relationships in data, you must deal with uncertainty. When you use *decision trees* to help make decisions, you must deal with uncertainty. When you use *simulation models* to help make decisions, you must deal with uncertainty, and then you often make inferences from the simulation results.

Figure 1.1 shows where these themes and subthemes are discussed in the book. The next few paragraphs discuss the book's contents in more detail.

Figure 1.1 Themes and Subthemes

We begin in Chapters 2, 3, and 4 by illustrating a number of ways to summarize the information in data sets. These include graphical and tabular summaries, as well as numeric summary measures such as means, medians, and standard deviations. As stated earlier, organizations are now able to collect huge amounts of raw data, but what does it all mean? Although there are very sophisticated methods for analyzing data, some of which are covered in later chapters, the "simple" methods in Chapters 2, 3, and 4 are crucial for obtaining an initial understanding of the data. Fortunately, Excel and available add-ins now make this quite easy. For example, Excel's pivot table tool for "slicing and dicing" data is an analyst's dream come true. You will be amazed at the insights you can gain from pivot tables—with very little effort.

Uncertainty is a key aspect of most business problems. To deal with uncertainty, you need a basic understanding of probability. We discuss the key concepts in Chapter 5. This chapter covers basic rules of probability and then discusses the extremely important concept of probability distributions, with emphasis on two of the most important probability distributions, the normal and binomial distributions.

---

2 The fact that the uncertainty theme did not find its way into the title of this book does not detract from its importance. We just wanted to keep the title reasonably short.

In Chapter 6 we apply probability to decision making under uncertainty. These types of problems—faced by all companies on a continual basis—are characterized by the need to make a decision *now*, even though important information, such as demand for a product or returns from investments, will not be known until later. The methods in Chapter 6 provide a rational basis for making such decisions.

In Chapters 7, 8, and 9 we discuss sampling and statistical inference. Here the basic problem is to estimate one or more characteristics of a population. If it is too expensive or time-consuming to learn about the *entire* population—and it usually is—it is instead common to select a random sample from the population and then use the information in the sample to *infer* the characteristics of the population.

In Chapters 10 and 11 we discuss the extremely important topic of regression analysis, which is used to study relationships between variables. The power of regression analysis is its generality. Every part of a business has variables that are related to one another, and regression can often be used to estimate relationships between these variables.

From regression, we move to time series analysis and forecasting in Chapter 12. This topic is particularly important for providing inputs into business decision problems. For example, manufacturing companies must forecast demand for their products to make sensible decisions about order quantities from their suppliers. Similarly, fast-food restaurants must forecast customer arrivals, sometimes down to the level of 15-minute intervals, so that they can staff their restaurants appropriately. Chapter 12 illustrates some of most frequently used forecasting methods.

Chapters 13 and 14 are devoted to spreadsheet optimization. We assume a company must make several decisions, and there are constraints that limit the possible decisions. The job of the decision maker is to choose the decisions such that all the constraints are satisfied and an objective, such as total profit or total cost, is optimized. The solution process consists of two steps. The first step is to build a spreadsheet model that relates the decision variables to other relevant quantities by means of logical formulas. The second step is then to find the optimal solution. Fortunately, Excel contains a Solver add-in that performs the optimization. All you need to do is specify the objective, the decision variables, and the constraints; Solver then uses powerful algorithms to find the optimal solution. As with regression, the power of this approach is its generality.

Chapters 15 and 16 illustrate a number of computer simulation models. As mentioned earlier, most business problems have some degree of uncertainty. The demand for a product is unknown, future interest rates are unknown, the delivery lead time from a supplier is unknown, and so on. Simulation allows you to build this uncertainty *explicitly* into spreadsheet models. Some cells in the model contain random values with given probability distributions. Every time the spreadsheet recalculates, these random values change, which causes "bottom-line" output cells to change as well. The trick then is to force the spreadsheet to recalculate many times and keep track of interesting outputs. In this way you can see an entire distribution of output values that might occur, not just a single best guess.

Chapter 17 then returns to data analysis. It provides an introduction to data mining, a topic of increasing importance in today's data-driven world. Data mining is all about exploring data sets, especially large data sets, for relationships and patterns that can help companies gain a competitive advantage. It employs a number of relatively new technologies to implement various algorithms, several of which are discussed in this chapter.

Finally, there are two online chapters, 18 and 19, that complement topics included in the book itself. Chapter 18 discusses analysis of variance (ANOVA) and experimental design. Chapter 19 discusses quality control and statistical process control. These two online chapters follow the same structure as the chapters in the book, complete with many examples and problems.

1-2b The Software

The methods in this book can be used to analyze a wide variety of business problems. However, they are not of much practical use unless you have the software to implement them. Very few business problems are small enough to be solved with pencil and paper. They require powerful software.

The software available with this book, together with Microsoft Excel, provides you with a powerful combination. This software is being used—and will continue to be used—by leading companies all over the world to analyze large, complex problems. We firmly believe that the experience you obtain with this software, through working the examples and problems in the book, will give you a key competitive advantage in the business world.

It all begins with Excel. Almost all the quantitative methods discussed in the book are implemented in Excel. We cannot forecast the state of computer software in the long-term future, but Excel is currently *the* most heavily used spreadsheet package on the market, and there is every reason to believe that this state will persist for many years. Most companies use Excel, most employees and most students have been trained in Excel, and Excel is a *very* powerful, flexible, and easy-to-use package.

It helps to understand Microsoft's versions of Excel. Until recently, we referred to Excel 2007, Excel 2010, and so on. Every few years, Microsoft released a new version of Office, and hence Excel. The latest was Excel 2016, and the next is going to be Excel 2019, which might be out by the time you read this. Each of these versions is basically fixed. For example, if you had Excel 2013, you had to wait for Excel 2016 to get the newest features. However, within the past few years, Microsoft has offered a subscription service, Office 365, which allows you to install free updates about once per month. Will Microsoft eventually discontinue the fixed versions and push everyone to the subscription service? We don't know, but it would be nice. Then we could assume that everyone had the same version of Excel, with all the latest features. Actually, this isn't quite true. There are different levels of Microsoft Office 365, some less expensive but with fewer features. You can find details on Microsoft's website. This book assumes you have the features in Excel 2016 or the ProPlus version of Office 365. You can see your version by opening Excel and selecting Account from the File menu.

We also realize that many of you are using Macs. There is indeed a version of Office 365 for the Mac, but its version of Excel doesn't yet have all the features of Excel for Windows. For example, we discuss two of Microsoft's "power" tools, Power Query and Power Pivot, in Chapter 4. At least as of this writing, these tools are not available in Excel for Mac. On the other hand, some features, including pivot charts, histograms, and box plots, were not in Office 365 for Mac until recently, when they suddenly appeared. So Microsoft is evidently catching up. In addition, some third-party add-ins for Excel, notably the Palisade DecisionTools Suite used in some chapters, are not available for Macs and probably never will be. If you really need these features and want to continue using your Mac, your best option is to install Windows emulation software such as Boot Camp or Parallels. Our students at Indiana have been doing this successfully for years.

Built-in Excel Features

Virtually everyone in the business world knows the basic features of Excel, but relatively few know some of its more powerful features. In short, relatively few people are the "power users" we expect you to become by working through this book. To get you started, the files **Excel Tutorial for Windows.xlsx** and **Excel Tutorial for the Mac.xlsx** explain some of the "intermediate" features of Excel—features that we expect you to be able to use. (See the Preface for instructions on how to access the resources that accompany this textbook.) These include the **SUMPRODUCT**, **VLOOKUP**, **IF**, **NPV**, and **COUNTIF**, functions. They also include range names, data tables, Paste Special, Goal Seek, and many others. Finally, although we assume you can perform routine spreadsheet tasks such as copying and pasting, the tutorial provides many tips to help you perform these tasks more efficiently.[3]

In addition to this tutorial, the last half of this chapter presents several examples of modeling quantitative problems in Excel. These examples provide a head start in using Excel tools you will use in the rest of the book. Then later chapters will introduce other useful Excel tools as they are needed.

---

3 Albright and several colleagues have created a more robust commercial version of this tutorial called **ExcelNow!**. The Excel Tutorial files explain how you can upgrade to this commercial version.

Analysis ToolPak

All versions of Excel, extending back at least two decades, have included an add-in called Analysis ToolPak. It has several tools for data analysis, including correlation, regression, and inference. Unfortunately, Microsoft hasn't updated Analysis ToolPak for years, so it is not as good as it could be. We will mention Analysis ToolPak a few times throughout the book, but we will use other Excel tools whenever they are available.

Solver Add-in

Chapters 13 and 14 make heavy use of Excel's Solver add-in. This add-in, developed by Frontline Systems®, not Microsoft, uses powerful algorithms to perform spreadsheet optimization. Before this type of spreadsheet optimization add-in was available, specialized (nonspreadsheet) software was required to solve optimization problems. Now you can do it all within the familiar Excel environment.

SolverTable Add-in

An important theme throughout this book is sensitivity analysis: How do outputs change when inputs change? Typically these changes are made in spreadsheets with a data table, a built-in Excel tool. However, data tables don't work in optimization models, where the goal is to see how the *optimal* solution changes when certain inputs change. Therefore, we include an Excel add-in called SolverTable, which works almost exactly like Excel's data tables. (This add-in was developed for Excel for Windows by Albright. Unfortunately, it doesn't work for Excel for Mac.) Chapters 13 and 14 illustrate the use of SolverTable.

Palisade DecisionTools Suite

In addition to SolverTable and built-in Excel add-ins, an educational version of Palisade Corporation's powerful DecisionTools® Suite is available. All programs in this suite are Excel add-ins, so the learning curve isn't very steep. There are seven separate add-ins in this suite: @RISK, BigPicture, StatTools, PrecisionTree, NeuralTools, TopRank, and Evolver. The add-ins we will use most often are StatTools (for data analysis), Precision-Tree (for decision trees), and @RISK (for simulation). These add-ins will be discussed in some detail in the chapters where they are used.

DADM_Tools Add-In

We realize that some of you prefer not to use the Palisade software because it might not be available in companies where your students are eventually employed. Nevertheless, some of the methods discussed in the book, particularly decision trees and simulation, are difficult to implement with Excel tools only. Therefore, Albright recently developed an add-in called DADM_Tools that implements decision trees and simulation, as well as forecasting and several basic data analysis tools. This add-in is freely available from the author's website at https://kelley.iu.edu/albrightbooks/free_downloads.htm, and students can continue to use it after the course is over, even in their eventual jobs, for free. You can decide whether you want to use the Palisade software, the DADM_Tools add-in, or neither.

1-3 Introduction to Spreadsheet Modeling[4]

A common theme in this book is spreadsheet modeling, where the essential elements of a business problem are entered and related in an Excel spreadsheet for further analysis. This section provides an introduction to spreadsheet modeling with some relatively simple models. Together with the Excel tutorial mentioned previously, the goal of this section is to get you "up to speed" in using Excel effectively for the rest of the book.

---

4 If you (or your students) are already proficient in basic Excel tools, you can skip this section, which is new to this edition of the book.

1-3a Basic Spreadsheet Modeling: Concepts and Best Practices

Most spreadsheet models involve *inputs*, *decision variables*, and *outputs*. The **inputs** have given fixed values, at least for the purposes of the model. The **decision variables** are those a decision maker controls. The **outputs** are the ultimate values of interest; they are determined by the inputs and the decision variables.

Spreadsheet modeling is the process of entering the inputs and decision variables into a spreadsheet and then relating them appropriately, by means of formulas, to obtain the outputs. After you have done this, you can then proceed in several directions. You might want to perform a sensitivity analysis to see how one or more outputs change as selected inputs or decision variables change. You might want to find the values of the decision variable(s) that minimize or maximize a particular output, possibly subject to certain constraints. You might also want to create charts that show graphically how certain parameters of the model are related.

Getting all the spreadsheet logic correct and producing useful results is a big part of the battle. However, it is also important to use good spreadsheet modeling *practices*. You probably won't be developing spreadsheet models for your sole use; instead, you will be sharing them with colleagues or even a boss (or an instructor). The point is that other people will be reading and trying to make sense out of your spreadsheet models. Therefore, you should construct your spreadsheet models with *readability* in mind. Features that can improve readability include the following:[5]

- A clear, logical layout to the overall model
- Separation of different parts of a model, possibly across multiple worksheets
- Clear headings for different sections of the model and for all inputs, decision variables, and outputs
- Use of range names
- Use of boldface, italics, larger font size, coloring, indentation, and other formatting features
- Use of cell comments
- Use of text boxes for assumptions and explanations

The following example illustrates the process of building a spreadsheet model according to these guidelines. We build this model in stages. In the first stage, we build a model that is correct, but not very readable. At each subsequent stage, we modify the model to enhance its readability.

EXAMPLE

1.1 ORDERING NCAA T-SHIRTS

It is March, and the annual NCAA Basketball Tournament is down to the final four teams. Randy Kitchell is a T-shirt vendor who plans to order T-shirts with the names of the final four teams from a manufacturer and then sell them to the fans. The fixed cost of any order is $750, the variable cost per T-shirt to Randy is $8, and Randy's selling price is $18. However, this price will be charged only until a week after the tournament. After that time, Randy figures that interest in the T-shirts will be low, so he plans to sell all remaining T-shirts, if any, at $6 each. His best guess is that demand for the T-shirts during the full-price period will be 1500. He is thinking about ordering 1450 T-shirts, but he wants to build a spreadsheet model that will let him experiment with the uncertain demand and his order quantity. How should he proceed?

Objective

To build a spreadsheet model in a series of stages, with all stages being correct but each stage being more readable and flexible than the previous stages.

---

[5] For further guidelines that attempt to make spreadsheet models more flexible and less prone to errors, see the article by LeBlanc et al. (2018).

Solution

The logic behind the model is fairly simple, but the model is built for generality. Specifically, the formulas allow for the order quantity to be less than, equal to, or greater than demand. If demand is greater than the order quantity, Randy will sell all the T-shirts ordered for $18 each. If demand is less than the order quantity, Randy will sell as many T-shirts as are demanded at the $18 price and all leftovers at the $6 price. You can implement this logic in Excel with an IF function.

A first attempt at a spreadsheet model appears in Figure 1.2. (See the file **TShirt Sales Finished.xlsx**, where each stage appears on a separate worksheet.) You enter a possible demand in cell B3, a possible order quantity in cell B4, and then calculate the profit in cell B5 with the formula

=−750−8*B4+IF(B3>B4,18*B4,18*B3+6*(B4−B3))

This formula subtracts the fixed and variable costs and then adds the revenue according to the logic just described.

Figure 1.2 Base Model

▲	A	B
1	NCAA t-shirt sales	
2		
3	Demand	1500
4	Order	1450
5	Profit	13750

Excel Function

IF

Excel's IF function has the syntax =IF(*condition, result_if_True,result_if_False*). The *condition* is any expression that is either true or false. The two expressions *result_if_True* and *result_if_False* can be any expressions you would enter in a cell: numbers, text, or other Excel functions (including other IF functions). If either expression is text, it must be enclosed in double quotes, such as **=IF(Score>590,"A","B")**. Also, the condition can be complex combinations of conditions, using the keywords AND or OR. Then the syntax is, for example, **=IF(AND(Score1<60,Score2<60),"Fail","Pass")**.

This model in Figure 1.2 is entirely correct, but it isn't very readable or flexible because it breaks a rule that you should never break: It *hard codes* input values into the profit formula. A spreadsheet model should *never* include input numbers in formulas. Instead, it should store input values in separate cells and then use *cell references* to these inputs in its formulas. A remedy appears in Figure 1.3, where the inputs have been entered in the range B3:B6, and the profit formula in cell B10 has been changed to

Never hard code numbers into Excel formulas. Use cell references instead.

=−B3−B4*B9+IF(B8>B9,B5*B9,B5*B8+B6*(B9−B8))

Figure 1.3 Model with Input Cells

▲	A	B
1	NCAA t-shirt sales	
2		
3	Fixed order cost	$750
4	Variable cost	$8
5	Selling price	$18
6	Discount price	$6
7		
8	Demand	1500
9	Order	1450
10	Profit	$13,750

This is exactly the same formula as before, but it is now more flexible. If an input changes, the profit recalculates automatically. Most important, the inputs are no longer buried in the formula.

Still, the profit formula is not very readable as it stands. You can make it more readable by using range names. The mechanics of range names are covered in detail later in this section. For now, the results of using range names for cells

B3 through B6, B8, and B9 are shown in Figure 1.4. This model looks exactly like the previous model, but the formula in cell B10 is now

=−Fixed_order_cost−Variable_cost*Order+IF(Demand>Order, Selling_price*Order,Selling_price*Demand +Discount_Price*(Order−Demand))

This formula is admittedly more long-winded, but it is easier to read.

Figure 1.4 Model with Range Names in Profit Formula

◢	A	B	C	D	E	F
1	NCAA t-shirt sales					
2						
3	Fixed order cost	$750		Range names used		
4	Variable cost	$8		Demand	='Model 3'!$B$8	
5	Selling price	$18		Discount_price	='Model 3'!$B$6	
6	Discount price	$6		Fixed_order_cost	='Model 3'!$B$3	
7				Order	='Model 3'!$B$9	
8	Demand	1500		Selling_price	='Model 3'!$B$5	
9	Order	1450		Variable_cost	='Model 3'!$B$4	
10	Profit	$13,750				

Figure 1.5 Model with Intermediate Outputs

◢	A	B	C	D	E	F
1	NCAA t-shirt sales					
2						
3	Fixed order cost	$750		Range names used		
4	Variable cost	$8		Demand	='Model 4'!$B$8	
5	Selling price	$18		Discount_price	='Model 4'!$B$6	
6	Discount price	$6		Fixed_order_cost	='Model 4'!$B$3	
7				Order	='Model 4'!$B$9	
8	Demand	1500		Selling_price	='Model 4'!$B$5	
9	Order	1450		Variable_cost	='Model 4'!$B$4	
10						
11	Costs					
12	Fixed cost	$750				
13	Variable costs	$11,600				
14	Revenues					
15	Full-price shirts	$26,100				
16	Discount-price shirts	$0				
17	Profit	$13,750				

Next, Randy might like to have profit broken down into various costs and revenues as shown in Figure 1.5, rather than one single profit cell. The formulas in cells B12, B13, B15, and B16 are straightforward, so they are not repeated here. You can then accumulate these to get profit in cell B17 with the formula

=−(B12+B13)+(B15+B16)

Of course, range names could be used for these intermediate output cells, but this is probably more work than it's worth. You should always use discretion when deciding how many range names to use.

If you see the model in Figure 1.5, how do you know which cells contain inputs or decision variables or outputs? Labels and/or color coding can help to distinguish these types. A blue/red/gray color-coding style has been applied in Figure 1.6, along with descriptive labels in boldface. The blue cells at the top are input cells, the red cell in the middle is a decision variable, and the gray cell at the bottom is the key output. There is nothing sacred about this particular convention. Feel free to adopt your own convention and style, but use it consistently.

Fundamental Insight

Spreadsheet Layout and Documentation

If you want your spreadsheets to be used (and you want your value in your company to rise), think carefully about your spreadsheet layout and then document your work carefully. For layout, consider whether certain data are best oriented in rows or columns, whether your work is better placed in a single sheet or in multiple sheets, and so on. For documentation, use descriptive labels and headings, color coding, cell comments, and text boxes to make your spreadsheets more readable. It takes time and careful planning to design and then document your spreadsheet models, but the time is well spent. And if you come back in a few days to a spreadsheet model you developed and you can't make sense of it, don't be afraid to redesign your work completely—from the ground up.

The model in Figure 1.6 is still not the last word on this example. As shown in later examples, you can create data tables to see how sensitive profit is to the inputs, the demand, and the order quantity. You can also create charts to show results graphically. But this is enough for now. You can see that the model in Figure 1.6 is now much more readable and flexible than the original model in Figure 1.2.

Figure 1.6 Model with Category Labels and Color Coding

⊿	A	B	C	D	E	F
1	NCAA t-shirt sales					
2						
3	Input variables			Range names used		
4	Fixed order cost	$750		Demand	='Model 5'!$B$10	
5	Variable cost	$8		Discount_price	='Model 5'!$B$7	
6	Selling price	$18		Fixed_order_cost	='Model 5'!$B$4	
7	Discount price	$6		Order	='Model 5'!$B$13	
8				Selling_price	='Model 5'!$B$6	
9	Uncertain variable			Variable_cost	='Model 5'!$B$5	
10	Demand	1500				
11						
12	Decision variable					
13	Order	1450				
14						
15	Output variables					
16	Costs					
17	Fixed cost	$750				
18	Variable costs	$11,600				
19	Revenues					
20	Full-price shirts	$26,100				
21	Discount-price shirts	$0				
22	Profit	$13,750				

1-3b Cost Projections

In the following example, a company wants to project its costs of producing products, given that material and labor costs are likely to increase through time. We build a simple model and then use Excel's charting capabilities to obtain a graphical image of projected costs.

EXAMPLE

1.2 PROJECTING THE COSTS OF BOOKSHELVES AT WOODWORKS

The Woodworks Company produces a variety of custom-designed wood furniture for its customers. One favorite item is a bookshelf, made from either cherry or oak. The company knows that wood prices and labor costs are likely to increase in the future. Table 1.1 shows the number of board-feet and labor hours required for a bookshelf, the current costs per board-foot and labor hour, and the anticipated annual increases in these costs. (The top row indicates that either type of bookshelf requires 30 board-feet of wood and 16 hours of labor.) Build a spreadsheet model that enables the company to experiment with the growth rates in wood and labor costs so that a manager can see, both numerically and graphically, how the costs of the bookshelves increase in the next few years.

Table 1.1 Input Data for Manufacturing a Bookshelf

Resource	Cherry	Oak	Labor
Required per bookshelf	30	30	16
Current unit cost	$5.50	$4.30	$18.50
Anticipated annual cost increase	2.4%	1.7%	1.5%

Objective
To learn good spreadsheet practices, to create copyable formulas with the careful use of relative and absolute addresses, and to create line charts from multiple series of data.

Solution

The completed spreadsheet model appears in Figure 1.7 and in the file **Bookshelf Costs Finished.xlsx**. You can develop it with the following steps.

1. **Inputs.** You should usually enter the inputs for a model in the upper-left corner of a worksheet as you can see in the shaded ranges in Figure 1.7. We have used our standard convention of coloring inputs—the numbers from the statement of the problem—blue. You can develop your own convention, but the input cells should be distinguished in some way. Note that the inputs are grouped logically and are explained with appropriate labels. You should always document your spreadsheet model with descriptive labels. Also, note that by entering inputs explicitly in input cells, you can *refer* to them later in Excel formulas.

Always enter input values in input cells and then refer to them in Excel formulas. Do not bury input values in formulas.

Figure 1.7 Bookshelf Cost Model

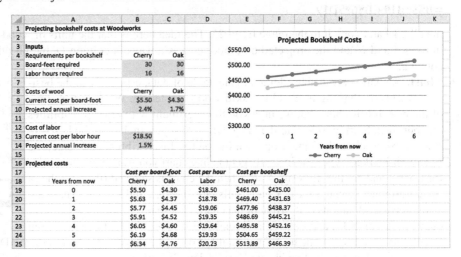

2. **Design output table.** Plan ahead for how you want to structure your outputs. We created a table where there is a row for every year in the future (year 0 corresponds to the current year), there are three columns for projected unit costs (columns B–D), and there are two columns for projected total bookshelf costs (columns E and F). The headings reflect this design. This isn't the only possible design, but it works well. The important point is that you should have some logical design in mind before you dive in.

3. **Projected unit costs of wood.** The dollar values in the range B19:F25 are calculated from Excel formulas. Although the logic in this example is straightforward, it is still important to have a strategy in mind before you enter formulas. In particular, you should always try to design your spreadsheet so that you can enter a single formula and then copy it. This saves work and avoids errors. For the costs per board-foot in columns B and C, enter the formula

Always try to organize your spreadsheet model so that you can copy formulas across multiple cells.

=B9

in cell B19 and copy it to cell C19. Then enter the general formula

=B19*(1+B$10)

in cell B20 and copy it to the range B20:C25. We assume you know the rules for absolute and relative addresses (dollar sign for absolute, no dollar sign for relative), but it takes some planning to use these so that copying is possible. Make sure you understand why we made row 10 absolute but column B relative.

Typing dollar signs in formulas for absolute references is inefficient. Press the F4 key instead.

Excel Tip

 Press the Fn key and the F4 key (together) on Mac keyboards.

Relative and Absolute Addresses in Formulas

Relative and absolute addresses are used in Excel formulas to facilitate copying. A dollar sign next to a column or row address indicates that the address is absolute and will not change when copying. The lack of a dollar sign indicates that the address is relative and will change when copying. After you select a cell in a formula, you can press the F4 key repeatedly to cycle through the relative/absolute possibilities: =B4 (both column and row relative); =$B$4 (both column and row absolute); =B$4 (column relative, row absolute); and =$B4 (column absolute, row relative).

4 Projected unit labor costs. To calculate projected hourly labor costs, enter the formula

=B13

in cell D19. Then enter the formula

=D19*(1+B$14)

in cell D20 and copy it down column D.

5 Projected bookshelf costs. Each bookshelf cost is the sum of its wood and labor costs. By a careful use of absolute and relative addresses, you can enter a single formula for these costs—for all years and for both types of wood. To do this, enter the formula

=B$5*B19+B$6*$D19

in cell E19 and copy it to the range E19:F25. The idea here is that the units of wood and labor per bookshelf are always in rows 5 and 6, and the projected unit labor cost is always in column D, but all other references are relative to allow copying.

6 Chart. A chart is a valuable addition to any table of data, especially in the business world, so charting in Excel is a skill worth mastering. We illustrate some of the possibilities here, but we urge you to experiment with other possibilities on your own. Start by selecting the range E18:F25—yes, including the labels in row 18. Next, click the Line dropdown list on the Insert ribbon and select the Line with Markers type. You instantly get the line chart you want, with one series for Cherry and another for Oak. Also, when the chart is selected (that is, it has a border around it), you see two Chart Tools tabs, Design and Format. There are also three useful buttons to the right of the chart. (These three buttons were introduced in Excel 2013, and the two tabs condense the tools in the three tabs from Excel 2007 and 2010.) The most important button is the Select Data button on the Design ribbon. It lets you choose the ranges of the data for charting in case Excel's default choices aren't what you want. (The default choices are based on the selected range when you create the chart.)

The many chart options are easily accessible from the Chart Tools tabs that are visible when a chart is selected. Don't be afraid to experiment with them to produce professional-looking charts.

 The three buttons to the right of the chart don't appear in Excel for Mac.

Click Select Data now to obtain the dialog box in Figure 1.8. On the left, you control the series (one series or multiple series) being charted; on the right, you control the data used for the horizontal axis. By selecting E18:F25, you have the series on the left correct, including the names of these series (Cherry and Oak), but if you didn't, you could select one of the series and click the Edit button to change it. The data on the horizontal axis are currently the default 1, 2, and so on. To use the data in column A, click the Edit button on the right and select the range A19:A25. Then you can experiment with various formatting options to make the chart even better. For example, we rescaled the vertical axis to start at $300 rather than $0 (right-click any of the numbers on the vertical axis and select Format Axis), and we added a chart title at the top and a title for the horizontal axis at the bottom.

Figure 1.8 Select Data Source Dialog Box

 The Select Data Source dialog box in Excel for Mac has a different layout, but the options are basically the same.

Using the Model for What-If Questions

The model in Figure 1.7 can now be used to answer many what-if questions. In fact, many models are built for the purpose of permitting experimentation with various scenarios. The important point is that the model has been built in such a way that a manager can enter any desired values in the input cells, and all outputs, including the chart, will update automatically.

1-3c Breakeven Analysis

Many business problems require you to find the appropriate level of some activity. This might be the level that maximizes profit (or minimizes cost), or it might be the level that allows a company to break even—no profit, no loss. The following example illustrates a typical breakeven analysis.

EXAMPLE

1.3 BREAKEVEN ANALYSIS AT QUALITY SWEATERS

The Quality Sweaters Company sells hand-knitted sweaters. The company is planning to print a catalog of its products and undertake a direct mail campaign. The cost of printing the catalog is $20,000 plus $0.10 per catalog. The cost of mailing each catalog (including postage, order forms, and buying names from a mail-order database) is $0.15. In addition, the company plans to include direct reply envelopes in its mailings and incurs $0.20 in extra costs for each direct mail envelope used by a respondent. The average size of a customer order is $40, and the company's variable cost per order (primarily due to labor and material costs) averages about 80% of the order's value—that is, $32. The company plans to mail 100,000 catalogs. It wants to develop a spreadsheet model to answer the following questions:

1. How does a change in the response rate affect profit?
2. For what response rate does the company break even?

Objective

To learn how to work with range names, to learn how to answer what-if questions with one-way data tables, to introduce Excel's Goal Seek tool, and to learn how to document and audit Excel models with cell comments and Excel's formula auditing tools.

Solution

The completed spreadsheet model appears in Figure 1.9. (See the file **Breakeven Analysis Finished.xlsx**.) First, note the clear layout of the model. The input cells are colored blue, they are separated from the outputs, headings are boldfaced, several headings are indented, numbers are formatted appropriately, and a list to the right spells out all range names we have used. (See the next Excel Tip on how to create this list.) Also, following the convention we use throughout the book, the decision variable (number mailed) is colored red, and the bottom-line output (profit) is colored gray.

Adopt some layout and formatting conventions, even if they differ from ours, to make your spreadsheets readable and easy to follow.

Excel Tip

Creating Range Names

To create a range name for a range of cells (which could be a single cell), highlight the cell(s), click in the Name Box just to the left of the Formula Bar, and type a range name. Alternatively, if a column (or row) of labels appears next to the cells to be range-named, you can use these labels as the range names. To do this, highlight the labels and the cells to be named (for example, A4:B5 in Figure 1.9), click Create from Selection on the Formulas ribbon, and make sure the appropriate box in the resulting dialog box is checked. The labels in our example are to the left of the cells to be named, so the Left column box should be checked. This is a quick way to create range names, and we did it for all range names in the example. Note that if a label contains any "illegal" range-name characters, such as a space, the illegal characters are converted to underscores.

Figure 1.9 Quality Sweaters Model

	A	B	C	D	E	F	G	H	I
1	Quality Sweaters direct mail model						Range names used		
2							Average_order		=Model!$B$11
3	Catalog inputs			Model of responses			Fixed_cost_of_printing		=Model!$B$4
4	Fixed cost of printing	$20,000		Response rate	8%		Number_mailed		=Model!$B$8
5	Variable cost of printing mailing	$0.25		Number of responses	8000		Number_of_responses		=Model!$E$5
6							Profit		=Model!$E$13
7	Decision variable			Model of revenue, costs, and profit			Response_rate		=Model!$E$4
8	Number mailed	100000		Total Revenue	$320,000		Total_cost		=Model!$E$12
9				Fixed cost of printing	$20,000		Total_Revenue		=Model!$E$8
10	Order inputs			Total variable cost of printing mailing	$25,000		Variable_cost_of_printing_mailing		=Model!$B$5
11	Average order	$40		Total variable cost of orders	$257,600		Variable_cost_per_order		=Model!$B$12
12	Variable cost per order	$32.20		Total cost	$302,600				
13				Profit	$17,400				

Excel Tip

This option to paste a list of range names is evidently not available in Excel for Mac.

Pasting Range Names

Including a list of the range names in your spreadsheet is useful for documentation. To do this, select a cell (such as cell G2 in Figure 1.9), select the Use in Formula dropdown list from the Formulas ribbon, and then click the Paste List option. You get a list of all range names and their cell addresses. However, if you change any of these range names (delete one, for example), the paste list does not update automatically; you have to create it again.

To create this model, you can proceed through the following steps.

1. **Headings and range names.** We have named a lot of cells, more than you might want to name, but you will see their value when you create formulas.
2. **Values of input variables and the decision variable.** Enter these values and format them appropriately. As usual, we have used our blue/red/gray color-coding scheme. Note that the number mailed has been designated as a *decision* variable, not as an input variable (and it is colored red, not blue). This is because the company gets to choose the value of this variable. Finally, some of the values have been combined in the statement of the problem. For example, the $32.20 in cell B12 is really 80% of the $40 average order size, plus the $0.20 per return envelope. To document this, comments appear in a few cells, as shown in Figure 1.10.

Excel Tip

Inserting Cell Comments

Inserting comments in cells is a great way to document non-obvious aspects of your spreadsheet models. To enter a comment in a cell, right-click the cell, select the Insert Comment item, and type your comment. This creates a little red mark in the cell, indicating a comment, and you can see the comment by moving the cursor over the cell. When a cell contains a comment, you can edit or delete the comment by right-clicking the cell and selecting the appropriate item.

Figure 1.10 Cell Comments in Model

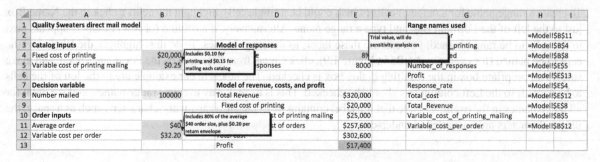

3. **Model the responses.** Enter any reasonable value, such as 8%, in the Response_rate cell. You will perform sensitivity on this value later on. Then enter the formula

=**Number_mailed*Response_rate**

in cell E5. (Are you starting to see the advantage of range names?)

4. **Model the revenue, costs, and profits.** Enter the following formulas in cells E8 through E13:

=**Number_of_responses*Average_order**
=**Fixed_cost_of_printing**
=**Variable_cost_of_printing_mailing*Number_mailed**
=**Number_of_responses*Variable_cost_per_order**
=**SUM(E9:E11)**
=**Total_revenue-Total_cost**

These formulas should all be self-explanatory because of the range names used.

Excel Tip

The second option below doesn't appear to work in Excel for Mac.

Entering Formulas with Range Names

To enter a formula that contains range names, you do not have to type the full range names. You actually have two options. First, you can click or drag the cells, and range names will appear in your formulas. Second, you can start typing the range name in the formula and, after a few letters, Excel will show you a list you can choose from.

Forming a One-Way Data Table

Now that a basic model has been created, the questions posed by the company can be answered. For question 1, you can form a one-way data table to show how profit varies with the response rate as shown in Figure 1.11. Data tables are used often in this book, so make sure you understand how to create them. First, enter a sequence of trial values of the response rate in column A, and enter a link to profit in cell B17 with the formula =**Profit**. This cell is shaded for emphasis, but this isn't necessary. (In general, other outputs could be part of the table, and they would be placed in columns C, D, and so on. There would be a link to each output in row 17.) Finally, highlight the entire table range, A17:B27, and select Data Table from the What-If Analysis dropdown list on the Data ribbon to bring up the dialog box in Figure 1.12. Fill it in as shown to indicate that the only input, Response_rate, is listed along a column. (You can enter either a range name or a cell address in this dialog box. The easiest way is to point to the cell.)

Data tables are also called what-if tables. They let you see what happens to selected outputs as selected inputs change.

When you click OK, Excel substitutes each response rate value in the table into the Response_rate cell, recalculates profit, and reports it in the table. For a final touch, you can create a chart of the values in the data table. To do this, select the A18:B27 range and select the type of chart you want from the Insert ribbon. Then you can fix it up by adding titles and making other modifications to suit your taste.

Figure 1.11 Data Table and Chart for Profit

	A	B	C	D	E	F
15	Question 1 - sensitivity of profit to response rate					
16	Response rate	Profit				
17		$17,400				
18	1%	−$37,200				
19	2%	−$29,400				
20	3%	−$21,600				
21	4%	−$13,800				
22	5%	−$6,000				
23	6%	$1,800				
24	7%	$9,600				
25	8%	$17,400				
26	9%	$25,200				
27	10%	$33,000				

Figure 1.12 Data Table
Dialog Box

Excel Tool

One-Way Data Table

A one-way data table allows you to see how one or more outputs vary as a single input varies over a selected range of values. These input values can be arranged vertically in a column or horizontally in a row. We explain only the vertical arrangement because it is the most common. To create the table, enter the input values in a column range, such as A18:A27 of Figure 1.11, and enter links to one or more output cells in columns to the right and one row above the inputs, as in cell B17. Then select the entire table, beginning with the upper-left blank cell (A17), select Data Table from the What-If Analysis dropdown list on the Data ribbon, and fill in the resulting dialog box as in Figure 1.12. Leave the Row Input cell blank and use the cell where the original value of the input lives as the Column Input cell. When you click OK, each value in the left column of the table is substituted into the column input cell, the spreadsheet recalculates, and the resulting value of the output is placed in the table. Also, if you click anywhere in the body of the table (B18:B27 in the figure), you will see that Excel has entered the TABLE function to remind you that a data table lives here. Note that the column input cell must be on the same worksheet as the table itself; otherwise, Excel issues an error.

Fundamental Insight

The Power of Data Tables

Unfortunately, many Excel users are unaware of data tables, which are among the most powerful and useful tools Excel has to offer. After you have developed a model that relates inputs to outputs, you can then build data tables in a matter of seconds to see how the outputs vary as key inputs vary over some range. Data tables are perfect for answering a large number of what-if questions quickly and easily.

As the chart indicates, profit increases in a linear manner as the response rate varies. More specifically, each percentage point increase in the response rate increases profit by $7800. Here is the reasoning. Each percentage point increase in response rate results in 100,000(0.01) = 1000 more orders. Each order yields a revenue of $40, on average, but incurs a variable cost of $32.20. The net gain in profit is $7.80 per order, or $7800 for 1000 orders.

Using Goal Seek

From the data table, you can see that profit changes from negative to positive when the response rate is somewhere between 5% and 6%. Question 2 asks for the exact breakeven point. You could find this by trial and error, but it is easier to use Excel's Goal Seek tool. Essentially, Goal Seek is used to solve a *single* equation in a *single* unknown. Here, the equation is Profit = 0, and the unknown is the response rate. To implement Goal Seek, select Goal Seek from the What-If Analysis dropdown list on the Data ribbon and fill in the resulting dialog box as shown in Figure 1.13. (Range names or cell addresses can be used in the top and bottom boxes, but a *number* must be entered in the middle box.) After you click OK, the Response_rate and Profit cells have values 5.77% and $0. In words, if the response rate is 5.77%, Quality Sweaters breaks even. If the response rate is greater than 5.77%, the company makes money; if the rate is less than 5.77%, the company loses money. However, this assumes that the company mails 100,000 catalogs. If it sends more or fewer catalogs, the breakeven response rate will change.

The purpose of the Goal Seek tool is to solve one equation in one unknown. It is used here to find the response rate that makes profit equal to 0.

Figure 1.13 Goal Seek
Dialog Box

Excel Tool

Change the Goal Seek accuracy in Excel for Mac by selecting Preferences from the Excel menu and then choosing the Calculation group.

Goal Seek

The purpose of the Goal Seek tool is to solve one equation in one unknown. Specifically, Goal Seek allows you to vary a single input cell to force a single output cell to a selected value. To use it, select Goal Seek from the What-If Analysis dropdown list on the Data ribbon and fill in the resulting dialog box in Figure 1.13. Enter a reference to the output cell in the Set cell box, enter the numeric value you want the output cell to equal in the To value box, and enter a reference to the input cell in the By changing cell box. Note that Goal Seek sometimes stops when the Set cell is close, but not exactly equal to, the desired value. To improve Goal Seek's accuracy, you can select Options from the File menu and then the Formulas link. Then you can check the Enable iterative calculation box and reduce Maximum Change to any desired level of precision. We chose a precision level of 0.000001. For this level of precision, Goal Seek searches until profit is within 0.000001 of the desired value, $0.

Using the Formula Auditing Tool

The model in this example is fairly small and simple. Even so, you can use a handy Excel tool to see how all the parts are related. This is the Formula Auditing tool, which is available on the Formulas ribbon. See Figure 1.14.

The Trace Precedents and Trace Dependents buttons are probably the most useful buttons in this group. To see which formulas have direct links to the Number_of_ responses cell, select this cell and click the Trace Dependents button. Arrows are drawn to each cell that directly depends on the number of responses, as shown in Figure 1.15. Alternatively, to see which cells are used to create the formula in the Total_ revenue cell, select this cell and click the Trace Precedents button. Now you see that the Average_order and Number_of_responses cells are used directly to calculate revenue, as shown in Figure 1.16. Using these two buttons, you can trace your logic (or someone else's logic) as far backward or forward as you like. When you are finished, just click the Remove Arrows button.

The Formula Auditing tool is indispensable for untangling the logic in a spreadsheet, especially if someone else developed it and you are trying to figure out what they did.

Figure 1.14 Formula
Auditing Group

Trace Precedents   Show Formulas
Trace Dependents   Error Checking
Remove Arrows   Evaluate Formula   Watch Window

Formula Auditing

Figure 1.15 Dependents of
Number_of_responses Cell

	A	B	C	D	E
1	Quality Sweaters direct mail model				
2					
3	Catalog inputs			Model of responses	
4	Fixed cost of printing	$20,000		Response rate	8%
5	Variable cost of printing mailing	$0.25		Number of responses	8000
6					
7	Decision variable			Model of revenue, costs, and profit	
8	Number mailed	100000		Total Revenue	$320,000
9				Fixed cost of printing	$20,000
10	Order inputs			Total variable cost of printing mailing	$25,000
11	Average order	$40		Total variable cost of orders	$257,600
12	Variable cost per order	$32.20		Total cost	$302,600
13				Profit	$17,400

Figure 1.16 Precedents of
Total_revenue Cell

	A	B	C	D	E
1	**Quality Sweaters direct mail model**				
2					
3	**Catalog inputs**			**Model of responses**	
4	Fixed cost of printing	$20,000		Response rate	8%
5	Variable cost of printing mailing	$0.25		Number of responses	8000
6					
7	**Decision variable**			**Model of revenue, costs, and profit**	
8	Number mailed	100000		Total Revenue	$320,000
9				Fixed cost of printing	$20,000
10	**Order inputs**			Total variable cost of printing mailing	$25,000
11	Average order	$40		Total variable cost of orders	$257,600
12	Variable cost per order	$32.20		Total cost	$302,600
13				Profit	$17,400

Excel Tool

Formula Auditing Toolbar

The formula auditing toolbar allows you to see dependents of a selected cell (which cells have formulas that reference this cell) or precedents of a given cell (which cells are referenced in this cell's formula). You can even see dependents or precedents that reside on a different worksheet. In this case, the auditing arrows appear as dashed lines and point to a small spreadsheet icon. By double-clicking the dashed line, you can see a list of dependents or precedents on other worksheets. These tools are especially useful for understanding how someone else's spreadsheet works.

1-3d Ordering with Quantity Discounts and Demand Uncertainty

In the following example, we again attempt to find the appropriate level of some activity: how much of a product to order when customer demand for the product is uncertain. Two important features of this example are the presence of quantity discounts and the explicit use of probabilities to model uncertain demand.

EXAMPLE

1.4 ORDERING WITH QUANTITY DISCOUNTS AT SAM'S BOOKSTORE

Sam's Bookstore, with many locations across the United States, places orders for all of the latest books and then distributes them to its individual bookstores. Sam's needs a model to help it order the appropriate number of any title. For example, Sam's plans to order a popular new hardback novel, which it will sell for $30. It can purchase any number of this book from the publisher, but due to quantity discounts, the unit cost for all books it orders depends on the number ordered. If the number ordered is less than 1000, the unit cost is $24. After each 1000, the unit cost drops: to $23 for at least 1000 copies; to $22.25 for at least 2000; to $21.75 for at least 3000; and to $21.30 (the lowest possible unit cost) for at least 4000. For example, if Sam's orders 2500 books, its total cost is $22.25(2500) = $55,625. Sam's is uncertain about the demand for this book—it estimates that demand could be anywhere from 500 to 4500. Also, as with most hardback novels, this one will eventually come out in paperback. Therefore, if Sam's has any hardbacks left when the paperback comes out, it will put them on sale for $10, at which price it believes all leftovers will be sold. How many copies of this hardback novel should Sam's order from the publisher?

Objective

To learn how to build in complex logic with IF formulas, to get help about Excel functions, to learn how to use lookup functions, to see how two-way data tables provide answers to more extensive what-if questions, and to learn about Excel's SUMPRODUCT function.

Solution

The profit model appears in Figure 1.17. (See the file **Quantity Discounts Finished.xlsx**.) The order quantity and demand in the Order_quantity and Demand cells are trial values. (Comments in these cells are a reminder of this.) You can enter any values in these cells to test the logic of the model. The Order_quantity cell is colored red because the company can choose its value. In contrast, the Demand cell is colored green to indicate that this input value is uncertain and is being treated explicitly as such. Also, a table is used to indicate the quantity discounts cost structure. You can use the following steps to build the model.

Figure 1.17 Sam's Profit Model

	A	B	C	D	E	F	G	H	I	J	K
1	Ordering decision with quantity discounts							Range names used:			
2								Cost			=Model!$B$18
3	Inputs			Quantity discount structure				CostLookup			=Model!$D$5:$E$9
4	Unit cost - see table to right			At least	Unit cost			Demand			=Model!$B$12
5	Regular price	$30		0	$24.00			Leftover_price			=Model!$B$6
6	Leftover price	$10		1000	$23.00			Order_quantity			=Model!$B$9
7				2000	$22.25			Probabilities			=Model!$B$35:$J$35
8	Decision variable			3000	$21.75			Profit			=Model!$B$19
9	Order quantity	2500		4000	$21.30			Regular_price			=Model!$B$5
10								Revenue			=Model!$B$17
11	Uncertain quantity							Units_sold_at_leftover_price			=Model!$B$16
12	Demand	2000						Units_sold_at_regular_price			=Model!$B$15
13											
14	Profit model										
15	Units sold at regular price	2000									
16	Units sold at leftover price	500									
17	Revenue	$65,000									
18	Cost	$55,625									
19	Profit	$9,375									

1. **Inputs and range names.** Enter all inputs and name the ranges as indicated. The Create from Selection shortcut was used to name all ranges except for CostLookup and Probabilities. For these latter two, you can select the ranges and enter the names in the Name Box—the "manual" method.

2. **Revenues.** The company can sell only what it has, and it sells any leftovers at the discounted sale price. Therefore, enter the following formulas in cells B15, B16, and B17:

   =MIN(Order_quantity,Demand)

   =IF(Order_quantity>Demand, Order_quantity-Demand,0)

   =Units_sold_at_regular_price*Regular_price+Units_sold_at_leftover_price*Leftover_price

   The logic in the first two of these cells is necessary to account correctly for the cases when the order quantity is greater than demand and when it is less than or equal to demand. You could use the following equivalent alternative to the IF function in cell B16:

   =MAX(Order_quantity-Demand,0)

Excel Tool

The f_x button in Excel for Mac opens a Formula Builder pane to the right, but the functionality is essentially the same as in Excel for Windows.

f_x Button and Function Library Group

To learn more about an Excel function, click the f_x button next to the Formula bar. This is called the Insert Function button, although some people call it the Function Wizard. If there is already a function, such as an IF function, in a cell and you then click the f_x button, you will get help on this function. If you select an empty cell and then click the f_x button, you can choose a function to get help on. (The same help is available from the Function Library group on the Formulas ribbon.)

3. **Total ordering cost.** Depending on the order quantity, you can find the appropriate unit cost from the unit cost table and multiply it by the order quantity to obtain the total ordering cost. This can be accomplished with a complex nested IF formula, but a better way is to use the VLOOKUP function. Specifically, enter the formula

=VLOOKUP(Order_quantity,CostLookup,2)*Order_quantity

in cell B18. The VLOOKUP part of this formula says to compare the order quantity to the first (leftmost) column of the table in the CostLookup range and return the corresponding value in the second column (because the third argument is 2).

Excel Function

VLOOKUP

The VLOOKUP function is one of Excel's most useful functions. To use it, first create a vertical lookup table, with values to use for comparison listed in the left column of the table and corresponding output values in as many columns to the right as you like. (See the CostLookup range in Figure 1.17 for an example.) Then the VLOOKUP function takes three or four arguments: (1) the value you want to compare to the values in the left column of the table; (2) the lookup table range; (3) the index of the column you want the returned value to come from, where the index of the left column is 1, the index of the next column is 2, and so on; and optionally (4) TRUE (for an approximate match, the default) or FALSE (for an exact match). If you omit the last argument, the values in the left column of the table must be entered in ascending order. (See online help for more details.) If the last argument is TRUE or is omitted, Excel scans down the leftmost column of the table and finds the last entry less than or equal to the first argument. (In this sense, it finds an approximate match.) There is also an HLOOKUP function that works exactly the same way, except that the lookup table is arranged in rows, not columns.

---

4. **Profit.** Calculate the profit with the formula

=Revenue-Cost

Two-Way Data Table

The next step is to create a two-way data table for profit as a function of the order quantity and demand (see Figure 1.18). To create this table, first enter a link to the profit with the formula **=Profit** in cell A22, and enter possible order quantities and possible demands in column A and row 22, respectively. (We used the same values for both order quantity and demand, from 500 to 4500 in increments of 500. This is not necessary—the demand could change in increments of 100 or even 1—but it is reasonable. Perhaps Sam's is required by the publisher to order in multiples of 500.) Then select Data Table from the What-If Analysis dropdown list on the Data ribbon, and enter the Demand cell as the Row Input cell and the Order_quantity cell as the Column Input cell.

A two-way data table allows you to see how a single output varies as two inputs vary simultaneously.

Figure 1.18 Profit as a Function of Order Quantity and Demand

	A	B	C	D	E	F	G	H	I	J
21	Data table of profit as a function of order quantity (along side) and demand (along top)									
22	$9,375	500	1000	1500	2000	2500	3000	3500	4000	4500
23	500	$3,000	$3,000	$3,000	$3,000	$3,000	$3,000	$3,000	$3,000	$3,000
24	1000	-$3,000	$7,000	$7,000	$7,000	$7,000	$7,000	$7,000	$7,000	$7,000
25	1500	-$9,500	$500	$10,500	$10,500	$10,500	$10,500	$10,500	$10,500	$10,500
26	2000	-$14,500	-$4,500	$5,500	$15,500	$15,500	$15,500	$15,500	$15,500	$15,500
27	2500	-$20,625	-$10,625	-$625	$9,375	$19,375	$19,375	$19,375	$19,375	$19,375
28	3000	-$25,250	-$15,250	-$5,250	$4,750	$14,750	$24,750	$24,750	$24,750	$24,750
29	3500	-$31,125	-$21,125	-$11,125	-$1,125	$8,875	$18,875	$28,875	$28,875	$28,875
30	4000	-$35,200	-$25,200	-$15,200	-$5,200	$4,800	$14,800	$24,800	$34,800	$34,800
31	4500	-$40,850	-$30,850	-$20,850	-$10,850	-$850	$9,150	$19,150	$29,150	$39,150

Excel Tool

Two-Way Data Table

A two-way data table allows you to see how a single output cell varies as you vary two input cells. Unlike a one-way data table, only a single output cell can be used. To create this type of table, enter a reference to the output cell in the top-left corner of the table, enter possible values of the two inputs below and to the right of this corner cell, and select the entire table. Then select Data Table from the What-If Analysis dropdown on the Data ribbon, and enter references to the cells where the original two input variables live. The Row Input cell corresponds to the values along the top row of the table, and the Column Input cell corresponds to the values along the left-most column of the table. When you click OK, Excel substitutes each pair of input values into these two input cells, recalculates the spreadsheet, and enters the corresponding output value in the table.

The resulting data table shows that profit depends heavily on both order quantity and demand and (by scanning across rows) how higher demands lead to larger profits. But it is still unclear which order quantity Sam's should select. Remember that Sam's can choose the order quantity (the *row* of the data table), but it has no direct control over demand (the *column* of the table).

This is actually a preview of decision making under uncertainty. To calculate an expected profit, you multiply each profit by its probability and add the products.

The ordering decision depends not only on which demands are *possible* but also on which demands are *likely* to occur. The usual way to express this information is with a set of probabilities that sum to 1. Suppose Sam's estimates these as the values in row 35 of Figure 1.19. These estimates are probably based on other similar books it has sold in the past. The most likely demands are 2000 and 2500, with other values on both sides less likely. You can use these probabilities to find an *expected* profit for each order quantity. This expected profit is a weighted average of the profits in any row in the data table, using the probabilities as the weights. The easiest way to do this is to enter the formula

=SUMPRODUCT(B23:J23,Probabilities)

in cell B38 and copy it down to cell B46. You can also create a chart of these expected profits, as shown in Figure 1.19. (Excel refers to these as *column charts*. The height of each bar is the expected profit for that particular order quantity.)

Excel Function

SUMPRODUCT

The SUMPRODUCT function takes two range arguments, which must be exactly the same size and shape, and it sums the products of the corresponding values in these two ranges. For example, the formula **=SUMPRODUCT(A10:B11,E12:F13)** is a shortcut for a formula involving the sum of four products: **=A10*E12+A11*E13+B10*F12+B11*F13**. This is an extremely useful function, especially when the ranges involved are large, and it is used repeatedly throughout the book. (Actually, the SUMPRODUCT function can have more than two range arguments, all the same size and shape, but the most common use of SUMPRODUCT is when only two ranges are involved.)

The largest of the expected profits, $12,250, corresponds to an order quantity of 2000, so we would recommend that Sam's order 2000 copies of the book. This does not guarantee that Sam's will make a profit of $12,250—the actual profit depends on the eventual demand—but it represents a reasonable way to proceed in the face of uncertain demand.

Figure 1.19 Comparison of Expected Profits

	A	B	C	D	E	F	G	H	I	J	K
33	Model of expected demands										
34	Demand	500	1000	1500	2000	2500	3000	3500	4000	4500	
35	Probability	0.025	0.05	0.15	0.25	0.25	0.15	0.07	0.04	0.015	
36								Sum of probabilities -->		1	
37	Order quantity	Expected profit									
38	500	$3,000									
39	1000	$6,750									
40	1500	$9,500									
41	2000	$12,250									
42	2500	$11,375									
43	3000	$9,500									
44	3500	$4 875									
45	4000	$1,350									
46	4500	-$4,150									
47											
48											
49											
50											
51											

Order 2000 to maximize the expected profit.

Expected Profit versus Order Quantity

1-3e Estimating the Relationship Between Price and Demand

The following example illustrates a very important modeling concept: estimating relationships between variables by **curve fitting.** The ideas can be illustrated at a relatively low level by taking advantage of some useful Excel tools.

EXAMPLE

1.5 ESTIMATING SENSITIVITY OF DEMAND TO PRICE AT THE LINKS COMPANY

The Links Company sells its golf clubs at golf outlet stores throughout the United States. The company knows that demand for its clubs varies considerably with price. In fact, the price has varied over the past 12 months, and the demand at each price level has been observed. The data are in the data sheet of the file **Golf Club Demand.xlsx** (see Figure 1.20). For example, during month 12, when the price was $390, 6800 sets of clubs were sold. (The demands in column C are in hundreds of units. The cell comment in cell C3 is a reminder of this.) The company wants to estimate the relationship between demand and price and then use this estimated relationship to answer the following questions:

1. Assuming the unit cost of producing a set of clubs is $250 and the price must be a multiple of $10, what price should Links charge to maximize its profit?
2. How does the optimal price depend on the unit cost of producing a set of clubs?

Figure 1.20 Demand and Price Data for Golf Clubs

	A	B	C
1	Demand for golf clubs		
2			
3	Month	Price	Demand
4	1	450	45
5	2	300	103
6	3	440	49
7	4	360	86
8	5	290	125
9	6	450	52
10	7	340	87
11	8	370	68
12	9	500	45
13	10	490	44
14	11	430	58
15	12	390	68

Objective

To illustrate Excel's Trendline tool, and to illustrate conditional formatting.

Solution

This example is divided into two parts: estimating the relationship between price and demand, and creating the profit model. (Both can be found in the file **Golf Club Demand Finished.xlsx.**)

Estimating the Relationship Between Price and Demand

A scatterplot of demand versus price appears in Figure 1.21. (This can be created in the usual way as an Excel chart of the scatter type.) Obviously, demand decreases as price increases, but the goal is to quantify this relationship. Therefore, after creating this chart, right-click any point on the chart and select Add Trendline to see the pane in Figure 1.22. This allows you to superimpose several different curves (including a straight line) on the chart. We consider three possibilities, the **linear, power,** and **exponential** curves, defined by the following general equations (where y and x, a general output and a general input, correspond to demand and price for this example):

- Linear: $y = a + bx$
- Power: $y = ax^b$
- Exponential: $y = ae^{bx}$

Figure 1.21 Scatterplot of Demand Versus Price

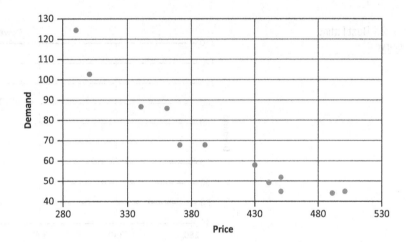

Figure 1.22 Trendline Options Dialog Box

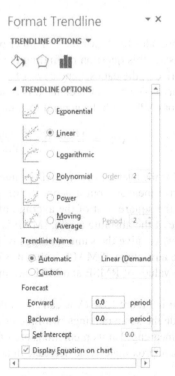

Before proceeding, we describe some general properties of these three functions because of their widespread applicability. The linear function is the easiest. Its graph is a straight line. When x changes by 1 unit, y changes by b units. The constant a is called the intercept, and b is called the slope.

The power function is a curve except in the special case where the exponent b is 1. (Then it is a straight line.) Assuming that a is positive, the shape of this curve depends on the exponent b. If $b > 1$, y increases at an increasing rate as x increases. If $0 < b < 1$, y increases, but at a decreasing rate, as x increases. Finally, if $b < 0$, y decreases as x increases. An important property of the power curve is that when x changes by 1%, y changes by a constant percentage, and this percentage is approximately equal to b%. For example, if $y = 100x^{-2.35}$, then every 1% increase in x leads to an approximate 2.35% decrease in y.

The exponential function also represents a curve whose shape depends on the constant b in the exponent. Again, assume that a is positive. Then if $b > 0$, y increases as x increases; if $b < 0$, y decreases as x increases. An important property of the exponential function is that if x changes by 1 unit, y changes by a constant percentage, and this percentage is approximately equal to $100 \times b$%. For example, if $y = 100e^{-0.014x}$, then whenever x increases by 1 unit, y decreases by approximately 1.4%. Here, e is the special number $2.7182\ldots$, and e to any power can be calculated in Excel with the EXP function. For example, you can calculate $e^{-0.014}$ with the formula **=EXP(−0.014)**.

Returning to the example, if you superimpose any of these curves on the chart of demand versus price, Excel chooses the best-fitting curve of that type. In addition, if you check the Display Equation on Chart option, you see the equation of this best-fitting curve. For example, the best-fitting power curve appears in Figure 1.23. (The equation might not appear exactly as in the figure. However, it can be resized and reformatted to appear as shown.)

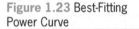
Figure 1.23 Best-Fitting Power Curve

Each of these curves provides the best-fitting member of its "family" to the demand/price data, but which of these three is best overall? You can answer this question by finding the **mean absolute percentage error** (MAPE) for each of the three curves. To do so, for any price in the data set and any of the three curves, first predict demand by substituting the given price into the equation for the curve. The predicted demand is typically not the same as the observed demand, so you can calculate the absolute percentage error (APE) with the general formula:

$$\text{APE} = \frac{|\text{Observed demand} - \text{Predicted demand}|}{\text{Observed demand}} \tag{1.1}$$

Then for any curve, MAPE is the average of these APE values. The curve with the smallest MAPE is the best fit overall.

MAPE is a popular error measure, but it is not the only error measure used. Another popular error measure is RMSE (root mean square error), the square root of the average of the squared errors. Another possible measure is MAE (mean absolute error), the average of the absolute errors. (MAE is sometimes called MAD, mean absolute deviation.) These three measures often, but not always, give the same rankings of fits, so any of them can be used, and all three are calculated in this example. However, the advantage of MAPE is that it is easy to interpret a value such as 5.88%: the fitted values are off, on average, by 5.88%. The values of RMSE and MAE are more difficult to interpret because they depend on the units of the observations.

The calculations appear in Figure 1.24. (You can check the formulas in the finished version of the file.) As you can see, the three error measures provide the same rankings, with the power fit being best according to all three. In particular, MAPE for the power curve is 5.88%, meaning that its predictions are off, on average, by 5.88%. This power curve predicts that each 1% increase in price leads to an approximate 1.9% decrease in demand.

Figure 1.24 Finding the Best-Fitting Curve Overall

	A	B	C	D	E	F	G	H	I	J	K	L	M	N	O	P
17	Parameters of best-fitting curves					Prediction			Absolute percentage error			Squared error			Absolute error	
18	Linear				Linear	Power	Exponential	Linear	Power	Exponential	Linear	Power	Exponential	Linear	Power	Exponential
19	Intercept	211.31			51.74	50.80	51.20	14.98%	12.89%	13.78%	45.43	33.63	38.47	6.74	5.80	6.20
20	Slope	-0.3546			104.93	110.12	106.94	1.87%	6.91%	3.83%	3.72	50.72	15.53	1.93	7.12	3.94
21	Power				55.29	53.02	53.78	12.83%	8.21%	9.75%	39.51	16.20	22.84	6.29	4.02	4.78
22	Constant	5871064			83.65	77.76	79.65	2.73%	9.58%	7.38%	5.50	67.83	40.28	2.35	8.24	6.35
23	Exponent	-1.9082			108.48	117.48	112.32	13.22%	6.01%	10.14%	273.04	56.53	160.70	16.52	7.52	12.68
24	Exponential				51.74	50.80	51.20	0.50%	2.31%	1.53%	0.07	1.44	0.64	0.26	1.20	0.80
25	Constant	466.51			90.75	86.73	87.87	4.31%	0.32%	1.00%	14.03	0.08	0.76	3.75	0.27	0.87
26	Exponent	-0.00491			80.11	73.80	75.84	17.81%	8.53%	11.52%	146.60	33.68	61.41	12.11	5.80	7.84
27					34.01	41.55	40.06	24.42%	7.67%	10.99%	120.78	11.92	24.44	10.99	3.45	4.94
28					37.56	43.18	42.07	14.65%	1.86%	4.38%	41.53	0.67	3.72	6.44	0.82	1.93
29					58.83	55.40	56.49	1.43%	4.48%	2.61%	0.69	6.75	2.29	0.83	2.60	1.51
30					73.02	66.75	68.74	7.38%	1.84%	1.09%	25.16	1.56	0.55	5.02	1.25	0.74
31									MAPE			RMSE			MAE	
32								9.68%	5.88%	6.50%	7.72	4.84	5.57	6.10	4.01	4.38

Developing the Profit Model

Now we move to the profit model, which assumes the company produces exactly enough sets of clubs to meet demand. This model, shown in Figure 1.25, is straightforward to develop; you can see the details in the finished version of the file.

Maximizing Profit

To see which price maximizes profit, you can build the data table shown in Figure 1.26. Here, the column input cell is B11 and the linking formula in cell B25 is =B17. The corresponding chart shows that profit first increases and then decreases. You can find the maximum profit and corresponding price in at least three ways. First, you can estimate them from the chart. Second, you can scan down the data table for the maximum profit, which is shown in the figure. The following Excel Tip describes a third method that uses some of Excel's more powerful features.

Figure 1.25 Profit Model

	A	B	C	D	E
1	Profit model, using best fitting power curve for estimating demand				
2					
3	Parameters of best-fitting power curve (from Estimation sheet)				
4	Constant	5871064			
5	Exponent	−1.9082			
6					
7	Monetary inputs				
8	Unit cost to produce	$250			
9					
10	Decision variable				
11	Unit price (trial value)	$400			
12					
13	Profit model				
14	Predicted demand	63.601			
15	Total revenue	$25,441			
16	Total cost	$15,900			
17	Profit	$9,540			

Excel Tip

Conditional Formatting

Cell B39 in Figure 1.26 is colored because it corresponds to the maximum profit in the column, but Excel's Conditional Formatting tool can do this for you—automatically. To color the maximum profit, select the range of profits, B26:B47, click the Conditional Formatting dropdown arrow on the Home ribbon, then Top/Bottom Rules, and then Top 10 Items to bring up the dialog box in Figure 1.27. By asking for the top 1 item, the maximum value in the range is colored. You can experiment with the many other Conditional Formatting options. This is a great tool.

Figure 1.26 Profit as a
Function of Price

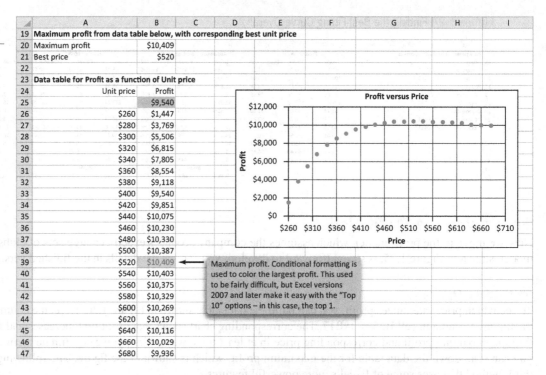

	A	B	C	D	E	F	G	H	I
19	**Maximum profit from data table below, with corresponding best unit price**								
20	Maximum profit	$10,409							
21	Best price	$520							
22									
23	**Data table for Profit as a function of Unit price**								
24	Unit price	Profit							
25		$9,540							
26	$260	$1,447							
27	$280	$3,769							
28	$300	$5,506							
29	$320	$6,815							
30	$340	$7,805							
31	$360	$8,554							
32	$380	$9,118							
33	$400	$9,540							
34	$420	$9,851							
35	$440	$10,075							
36	$460	$10,230							
37	$480	$10,330							
38	$500	$10,387							
39	$520	$10,409							
40	$540	$10,403							
41	$560	$10,375							
42	$580	$10,329							
43	$600	$10,269							
44	$620	$10,197							
45	$640	$10,116							
46	$660	$10,029							
47	$680	$9,936							

Maximum profit. Conditional formatting is used to color the largest profit. This used to be fairly difficult, but Excel versions 2007 and later make it easy with the "Top 10" options – in this case, the top 1.

Figure 1.27 Conditional
Formatting Dialog Box

What about the corresponding best price, shown in cell B21 of Figure 1.26? You could enter this manually, but wouldn't it be nice if you could get Excel to find the maximum profit in the data table, determine the price in the cell to its left, and report it in cell B21, all automatically? This is indeed possible. Enter the formula

=INDEX(A26:A47,MATCH(B20,B26:B47,0),1)

in cell B21, and the best price appears. This formula uses two Excel functions, MATCH and INDEX. MATCH compares the first argument (the maximum profit in cell B20) to the range specified in the second argument (the range of profits) and returns the index of the cell where a match appears. (The third argument, 0, specifies that you want an *exact* match.) In this case, the MATCH function returns 14 because the maximum profit is in the 14th cell of the profits range. Then the INDEX function is called effectively as =INDEX(A26:A47,14,1). The first argument is the range of prices, the second is a row index, and the third is a column index. Very simply, this function says to return the value in the 14th row and first column of the prices range.

Sensitivity to Variable Cost

We now return to question 2 in the example: How does the best price change as the unit variable cost changes? You can answer this question with a two-way data table. Remember that this is a data table with two inputs—one along the left side and the other across the top row—and a single output. The two inputs for this problem are unit variable cost and unit price, and the single output is profit. The corresponding data table is in the range A55:F83, shown in Figure 1.28. To develop this table, enter desired inputs in column A and row 55, enter the linking formula **=B17** in cell A55 (it always goes in the top-left corner of a two-way data table), select the entire table, select Data Table from the What-If Analysis dropdown list, and enter **B8** as the Row Input cell and **B11** as the Column Input cell.

As before, you can scan the columns of the data table for the maximum profits and enter them (manually) in rows 51 and 52. (Alternatively, you can use the Excel features described in the previous Excel Tip to accomplish these tasks. Take a look at the finished version of the file for details. This file also explains how conditional formatting is used to color the maximum profit in *each* column of the table.) Then you can create a chart of maximum profit (or best price) versus unit cost. The chart in Figure 1.28 shows that the maximum profit decreases at a decreasing rate as the unit cost increases.

Figure 1.28 Profit as a Function of Unit Cost and Unit Price

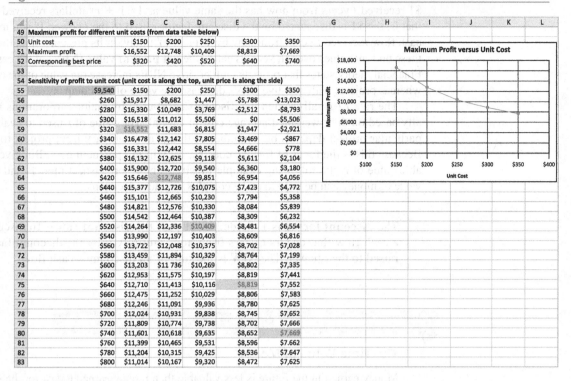

	A	B	C	D	E	F
49	Maximum profit for different unit costs (from data table below)					
50	Unit cost	$150	$200	$250	$300	$350
51	Maximum profit	$16,552	$12,748	$10,409	$8,819	$7,669
52	Corresponding best price	$320	$420	$520	$640	$740
53						
54	Sensitivity of profit to unit cost (unit cost is along the top, unit price is along the side)					
55	$9,540	$150	$200	$250	$300	$350
56	$260	$15,917	$8,682	$1,447	-$5,788	-$13,023
57	$280	$16,330	$10,049	$3,769	-$2,512	-$8,793
58	$300	$16,518	$11,012	$5,506	$0	-$5,506
59	$320	$16,552	$11,683	$6,815	$1,947	-$2,921
60	$340	$16,478	$12,142	$7,805	$3,469	-$867
61	$360	$16,331	$12,442	$8,554	$4,666	$778
62	$380	$16,132	$12,625	$9,118	$5,611	$2,104
63	$400	$15,900	$12,720	$9,540	$6,360	$3,180
64	$420	$15,646	$12,748	$9,851	$6,954	$4,056
65	$440	$15,377	$12,726	$10,075	$7,423	$4,772
66	$460	$15,101	$12,665	$10,230	$7,794	$5,358
67	$480	$14,821	$12,576	$10,330	$8,084	$5,839
68	$500	$14,542	$12,464	$10,387	$8,309	$6,232
69	$520	$14,264	$12,336	$10,409	$8,481	$6,554
70	$540	$13,990	$12,197	$10,403	$8,609	$6,816
71	$560	$13,722	$12,048	$10,375	$8,702	$7,028
72	$580	$13,459	$11,894	$10,329	$8,764	$7,199
73	$600	$13,203	$11,736	$10,269	$8,802	$7,335
74	$620	$12,953	$11,575	$10,197	$8,819	$7,441
75	$640	$12,710	$11,413	$10,116	$8,819	$7,552
76	$660	$12,475	$11,252	$10,029	$8,806	$7,583
77	$680	$12,246	$11,091	$9,936	$8,780	$7,625
78	$700	$12,024	$10,931	$9,838	$8,745	$7,652
79	$720	$11,809	$10,774	$9,738	$8,702	$7,666
80	$740	$11,601	$10,618	$9,635	$8,652	$7,669
81	$760	$11,399	$10,465	$9,531	$8,596	$7,662
82	$780	$11,204	$10,315	$9,425	$8,536	$7,647
83	$800	$11,014	$10,167	$9,320	$8,472	$7,625

Other Modeling Issues

The layout of the **Golf Club Demand.xlsx** file is fairly straightforward. However, note that instead of a single worksheet, there are two worksheets, partly for logical purposes and partly to reduce clutter. There is one worksheet for estimation of the demand function and the various scatterplots, and there is another for the profit model.

One last issue is the placement of the data tables for the sensitivity analysis. You might be inclined to put these on a separate Sensitivity worksheet. However, Excel does not allow you to build a data table on one worksheet that uses a row or column input cell from *another* worksheet. Therefore, you are forced to put the data tables on the same worksheet as the profit model.

1-3f Decisions Involving the Time Value of Money

In many business situations, cash flows are received at different points in time, and a company must determine a course of action that maximizes the "value" of cash flows. Here are some examples:

- Should a company buy a more expensive machine that lasts for 10 years or a less expensive machine that lasts for 5 years?
- What level of plant capacity is best for the next 20 years?
- A company must market one of several midsize cars. Which car should it market?

To make decisions when cash flows are received at different points in time, the key concept is that the later a dollar is received, the less valuable the dollar is. For example, suppose you can invest money at a 5% annual interest rate. Then $1.00 received now is essentially equivalent to $1.05 a year from now. The reason is that if you have $1.00 now, you can invest it and gain $0.05 in interest in one year. If $r = 0.05$ is the interest rate (expressed as a decimal), we can write this as

$$\$1.00 \text{ now} = \$1.05 \text{ a year from now} = \$1.00(1 + r) \tag{1.2}$$

Dividing both sides of Equation (1.2) by $1 + r$, this can be rewritten as

$$\$1.00 \times 1/(1 + r) \text{ now} = \$1.00 \text{ a year from now} \tag{1.3}$$

The value $1/(1 + r)$ in Equation (1.3) is called the **discount factor,** and it is always less than 1. The quantity on the left, which evaluates to $0.952 for $r = 0.05$, is called the **present value** of $1.00 received a year from now. The idea is that if you had $0.952 now, you could invest it at 5% and have it grow to $1.00 in a year.

In general, if money can be invested at annual rate r compounded each year, then $1 received t years from now has the same value as $1/(1 + r)^t$ dollars received today—that is, the $1 is discounted by the discount factor raised to the t power. If you multiply a cash flow received t years from now by $1/(1 + r)^t$ to obtain its present value, the total of these present values over all years is called the **net present value (NPV)** of the cash flows. Financial theory states that projects with positive NPVs increase the value of the company, whereas projects with negative NPVs decrease the value of the company.

The rate r (usually called the **discount rate**) used by major corporations is generally based on their weighted average cost of capital. The value of r used to evaluate any particular project depends on a number of things and can vary from project to project. Because this is the focus of finance courses, we will not pursue it here. But given a suitable value of r, the following example illustrates how spreadsheet models and the time value of money can be used to make complex business decisions.

> The **discount factor** is 1 divided by (1 plus the **discount rate**). To discount a cash flow that occurs t years from now, multiply it by the discount factor raised to the t power. The **NPV** is the sum of all discounted cash flows.

Fundamental Insight

The Time Value of Money

Money earned in the future is less valuable than money earned today, for the simple reason that money earned today can be invested to earn interest. Similarly, costs incurred in the future are less "costly" than costs incurred today. This is why you typically don't simply sum up revenues and costs in a multiperiod model. You instead *discount* future revenues and costs for a fair comparison with revenues and costs incurred today. The resulting sum of discounted cash flows is the net present value (NPV), and it forms the cornerstone of much of financial theory and applications.

EXAMPLE

1.6 CALCULATING NPV AT ACRON

Acron is a large drug company. At the current time, the beginning of year 0, Acron is trying to decide whether one of its new drugs, Niagra, is worth pursuing. Niagra is in the final stages of development and will be ready to enter the market one year from now. The final cost of development, to be incurred at the beginning of year 1, is $15 million. Acron estimates that the demand for Niagra will gradually grow and then decline over its useful lifetime of 20 years. Specifically, the company expects its gross margin (revenue minus cost) to be $1.5 million in year 1, then to increase at an annual rate of 6% through year 8, and finally to decrease at an annual rate of 5% through year 20. Acron wants to develop a spreadsheet model of its 20-year cash flows, assuming its cash flows, other than the initial development cost, are incurred at the *ends* of the respective years. (To simplify the model, taxes are ignored.) Using an annual discount rate of 7.5% for the purpose of calculating NPV, the drug company wants to answer the following questions:

1. Is the drug worth pursuing, or should Acron abandon it now and not incur the $15 million development cost?
2. How do changes in the model inputs change the answer to question 1?

Objective
To illustrate efficient selection and copying of large ranges and to learn Excel's NPV function.

Solution
The model of Acron's cash flows appears in Figure 1.29. As with many financial spreadsheet models that extend over a multi-year period, you enter "typical" formulas in the first year or two and then copy this logic down to all years. (We could make the years go across, not down. In that case, splitting the screen is useful so that you can see the first and last years of data. Splitting the screen is explained in the following Excel Tip.)

Excel Tip

Splitting the Screen

To split the screen horizontally and vertically, select the cell where you want the split to occur and click Split on the View ribbon. This creates horizontal and vertical split lines that you can move if you like.

Figure 1.29 Acron's Model of 20-Year NPV

▲	A	B	C	D	E	F	G
1	Calculating NPV at Acron				Range names used:		
2					Development_cost	=Model!$B$4	
3	Inputs				Discount_rate	=Model!$B$9	
4	Development cost	15			Gross_margin	=Model!$B$13:$B$32	
5	Gross margin year 1	1.2			Gross_margin_year_1	=Model!$B$5	
6	Peak year	8			Peak_year	=Model!$B$6	
7	Rate of increase	6%	(through peak year)		Rate_of_decrease	=Model!$B$8	
8	Rate of decrease	5%	(after peak year)		Rate_of_increase	=Model!$B$7	
9	Discount rate	7.5%					
10							
11	Cash flows						
12	End of year	Gross margin					
13	1	1.2000					
14	2	1.3200					
15	3	1.4520					
16	4	1.5972					
17	5	1.7569					
18	6	1.9326					
19	7	2.1259					
20	8	2.3385					
21	9	2.2215					
22	10	2.1105					
23	11	2.0049					
24	12	1.9047					
25	13	1.8095					
26	14	1.7190					
27	15	1.6330					
28	16	1.5514					
29	17	1.4738					
30	18	1.4001					
31	19	1.3301					
32	20	1.2636					
33	NPV	2.3961					

To create the model, complete the following steps. (See the file **Calculating NPV Finished.xlsx**.)

1. **Inputs and range names.** Enter the given input data in the blue cells, and name the ranges as shown. As usual, the range names for cells B4 through B9 can be created all at once with the Create from Selection shortcut, as can the range name for the gross margins in column B. In the latter case, select the range B12:B32 and then use the Create from Selection shortcut.
2. **Cash flows.** Start by entering the formula

   =Gross_margin_year_1

   in cell B13 for the year 1 gross margin. Then enter the general formula

   =IF(A14<=Peak_year,B13*(1+Rate_of_increase),B13*(1−Rate_of_decrease))

   in cell B14 and copy it down to cell B32 to calculate the other yearly gross margins. Note how this IF function checks the year index in column A to see whether sales are still increasing or have started to decrease. By using the (range-named) input cells in this formula, you can change any of these inputs in cells B6 through B8, and the calculated cells will automatically update. This is a *much* better practice than embedding the numbers in the formula itself.

Excel Tip

Efficient Selection

An easy way to select a large range, assuming that the first and last cells of the range are visible, is to select the first cell and then, with your finger on the Shift key, select the last cell. (Don't forget that you can split the screen to make these first and last cells visible when the range is large.) This selects the entire range and is easier than scrolling.

Excel Tip

The shortcut for copying in Excel for Mac is command+enter.

Efficient Copying with Ctrl+Enter

An easy way to enter the same formula in a range all at once is to select the range (as in the preceding Excel Tip), type the formula, and press Ctrl+Enter (both keys at once). After you get used to this shortcut, you will probably use it all the time.

---

3. **Net present value.** The NPV is based on the sequence of cash flows in column B. From the general discussion of NPV, to discount everything back to the beginning of year 1, the value in cell B13 should be multiplied by $1/(1 + r)^1$, the value in cell B14 should be multiplied by $1/(1 + r)^2$, and so on, and these quantities should be summed to obtain the NPV. (Here, $r = 0.075$ is the discount rate.) Fortunately, however, Excel has a built-in NPV function to accomplish this calculation. To use it, enter the formula

Use the Ctrl+Enter shortcut to enter a formula in a range all at once. It is equivalent to copying.

=−Development_cost+NPV(Discount_rate,Gross_margin)

in cell B33. The NPV function takes two arguments: the discount rate and a range of cash flows. It assumes that the first cell in this range is the cash flow at the end of year 1, the second cell is the cash flow at the end of year 2, and so on. This explains why the development cost is subtracted *outside* the NPV function—it is incurred at the *beginning* of year 1. In general, any cash flow incurred at the beginning of year 1 must be placed outside the NPV function so that it won't be discounted.

The stream of cash flows in the NPV function must occur at the ends of year 1, year 2, and so on. If the timing is irregular, you can discount "manually" or you can use Excel's XNPV function.

   Note that the *sum* of the cash flows in column B is slightly more than $34.54 million, but the NPV (aside from the development cost) is only about $18.06 million. This is because values farther into the future are discounted so heavily. At the extreme, the $1.2188 million cash flow in year 20 is equivalent to only $1.2188[1/(1 + 0.075)^{20}] = $0.287 million now.

Excel Function

NPV

The NPV function takes two arguments, the discount rate (entered as a decimal, such as 0.075 for 7.5%) and a stream of cash flows. These cash flows are assumed to occur in consecutive years, starting at the end of year 1. If there is an initial cash flow at the beginning of year 1, such as an initial investment, it should be entered outside the NPV function. (There is also an XNPV function that has three arguments: a discount rate, a series of cash flows, and a series of dates when the cash flows occur. Because these dates do not have to be equally spaced through time, this function is more flexible than the NPV function. We will not use the XNPV function in this book, but you can learn more about it in Excel's online help.)

Deciding Whether to Continue with the Drug

NPV calculations are typically used to see whether a certain project should be undertaken. If the NPV is positive, the project is worth pursuing. If the NPV is negative, the company should look for other places to invest its money. Figure 1.29 shows that the NPV for this drug is positive, over $3.06 million. Therefore, if Acron is comfortable with its predictions of future cash flows, it should continue with the development and marketing of the drug. However, Acron might first want to see how sensitive the NPV is to changes in the sales predictions. After all, these predictions are intelligent guesses at best.

One possible sensitivity analysis appears in Figure 1.30. This shows a one-way data table to see how the NPV changes when the number of years of increase (the input in cell B6) changes. Again, the important question is whether the NPV stays positive. It certainly does when the input variable is greater than its current value of 8. However, if sales start decreasing soon enough—that is, if the value in B6 is 4 or less—the NPV turns negative. This should probably not concern Acron, because its best guess for the years of increase is considerably greater than 4.

Another possibility is to see how long *and* how good the good years are. To do this, you can create the two-way data table shown in Figure 1.31, where cell B7 is the row input cell and cell B6 is the column input cell. Now you can see that if sales increase through year 6, all reasonable yearly increases result in a positive NPV. However, if sales increase only through year 5, then a low enough yearly increase can produce a negative NPV. Acron might want to step back and estimate how likely these bad scenarios are before proceeding with the drug.

Figure 1.30 Sensitivity of NPV to Years of Sales Increase

	D	E
11	**Sensitivity to peak year (cell B6)**	
12		6.7451
13	3	−0.9700
14	4	0.5688
15	5	2.1146
16	6	3.6629
17	7	5.2084
18	8	6.7451
19	9	8.2657
20	10	9.7616

Figure 1.31 Sensitivity of NPV to Years of Increase and Yearly Increase

	D	E	F	G	H	I	J
22	**Sensitivity to rate of increase in early years (cell B7) and peak year (cell B6)**						
23	6.7451	5%	6%	7%	8%	9%	10%
24	3	−2.0305	−1.8221	−1.6119	−1.3998	−1.1858	−0.9700
25	4	−1.0958	−0.7742	−0.4470	−0.1142	0.2244	0.5688
26	5	−0.1995	0.2401	0.6911	1.1537	1.6281	2.1146
27	6	0.6574	1.2191	1.8000	2.4006	3.0214	3.6629
28	7	1.4739	2.1609	2.8768	3.6227	4.3995	5.2084
29	8	2.2489	3.0633	3.9183	4.8156	5.7573	6.7451
30	9	2.9809	3.9237	4.9206	5.9746	7.0886	8.2657
31	10	3.6682	4.7393	5.8798	7.0940	8.3864	9.7616

1-4 Conclusion

In this chapter we have tried to convince you that the skills in this book are important for *you* as you enter the business world. The methods we discuss are no longer the sole province of the "quant jocks." By having a computer loaded with powerful software, you incur a responsibility to use this software to analyze business problems effectively. We have also given you a taste of the spreadsheet modeling process you will see in much of the rest of the book, and you have learned a number of useful Excel tools for analyzing spreadsheet models. You will get to use these and other Excel tools in the next few chapters as you enter the exciting world of data analysis.

Summary of Key Terms

TERM	EXPLANATION	EXCEL	PAGES
Model inputs	The given numeric values in any problem statement		21
Decision variables	The variables a decision maker has control over to obtain the best solutions		21
Model outputs	The numeric values that result from combinations of inputs and decision variables through the use of logical formulas		21
IF function	Useful for implementing logic	=IF(condition,result_If_True, result_If_False)	23
Relative, absolute cell addresses	Useful for copying formulas; absolute row or column stays fixed, relative row or column "moves"	A1 (relative), $A1 or A$1 (mixed), $A$1 (absolute); press F4 to cycle through possibilities	28
Range names	Useful for making formulas more readable	Type name in Name box, or use Create from Selection shortcut on Formulas ribbon	31
Pasting range names	Provides a list of all range names in the current workbook	Use Paste List from Use in Formula dropdown list on Formulas ribbon	32
Cell comments	Useful for documenting contents of cells	Right-click cell, select Insert Comment menu item	33
One-way data table	Shows how one or more outputs vary as a single input varies	Use Data Table from What-If Analysis dropdown list on Data ribbon	35
Goal Seek	Solves one equation in one unknown	Use Goal Seek from What-If Analysis dropdown list on Data ribbon	36
Formula Auditing toolbar	Useful for checking which cells are related to other cells through formulas	Use Formula Auditing buttons on Formulas ribbon	38
f_x button	Useful for getting help on Excel functions	On Formulas ribbon	41
VLOOKUP function	Useful for finding a particular value based on a comparison	=VLOOKUP(valueToCompare, lookupTable,columnToReturn,True/False)	41
Two-way data table	Shows how a single output varies as two inputs vary	Use Data Table from What-If Analysis dropdown list on Data ribbon	42
SUMPRODUCT function	Calculates the sum of products of values in two (or more) same-sized ranges	=SUMPRODUCT(range1,range2)	43
Trendline tool	Superimposes the best-fitting line or curve of a particular type on a scatter chart or time series graph	With chart selected, right-click any point and select Add Trendline	45
Conditional formatting	Formats cells depending on whether specified conditions hold	Use Conditional Formatting on Home ribbon	50
Net present value (NPV)	The current worth of a stream of cash flows that occur in the future		54
Discount rate	Interest rate used for discounting future cash flows to calculate present values		54
Splitting screen	Useful for separating the screen horizontally and/or vertically	Select Split from View ribbon	56
Efficient selection	Useful for selecting a large rectangular range	While pressing the Shift key, select the upper-left and bottom-right cells of the range	57
Efficient copying	Shortcut for copying a formula to a range	Select the range, enter the formula, and press Ctrl+Enter	57
NPV function	Calculates NPV of a stream of cash flows at the ends of consecutive years, starting in year 1	=NPV(discountRate,cashFlows)	57

Problems

Solutions for problems whose numbers appear within a colored box can be found in the Student Solution Files.

Level A

1. The sensitivity analysis in Example 1.3 was on the response rate. Suppose now that the response rate is *known* to be 8%, and the company wants to perform a sensitivity analysis on the number mailed. After all, this is a variable under direct control of the company. Create a one-way data table and a corresponding line chart of profit versus the number mailed, where the number mailed varies from 80,000 to 150,000 in increments of 10,000. Does it appear, from the results you see here, that there is an optimal number to mail, from all possible values, that maximizes profit?

2. Continuing the previous problem, use Goal Seek for *each* value of number mailed (once for 80,000, once for 90,000, and so on). For each, find the response rate that allows the company to break even. Then chart these values, where the number mailed is on the horizontal axis, and the breakeven response rate is on the vertical axis. Explain the behavior in this chart.

3. In Example 1.3, the range E9:E11 does not have a range name. Open your completed Excel file and name this range **Costs**. Then look at the formula in cell E12. It does *not* automatically use the new range name. Modify the formula so that it does. Then select cell G4 and paste the new list of range names over the previous list.

4. In some ordering problems, like the one in Example 1.4, whenever demand exceeds existing inventory, the excess demand is not lost but is filled by expedited orders—at a premium cost to the company. Change Sam's model to reflect this behavior. Assume that the unit cost of expediting is $40, well above the highest regular unit cost.

5. The spreadsheet model for Example 1.4 contains a two-way data table for profit versus order quantity and demand. Experiment with Excel's chart types to create a chart that shows this information graphically in an intuitive format. (Choose the format you would choose to give a presentation to your boss.)

6. In Example 1.4, the quantity discount structure is such that *all* the units ordered have the same unit cost. For example, if the order quantity is 2500, then each unit costs $22.25. Sometimes the quantity discount structure is such that the unit cost for the first so many items is one value, the unit cost for the next so many units is a slightly lower value, and so on. Modify the model so that Sam's pays $24 for units 1 to 1500, $23 for units 1501 to 2500, and $22 for units 2501 and above. For example, the total cost for an order quantity of 2750 is 1500(24) + 1000(23) + 250(22). (*Hint:* Use IF functions, not VLOOKUP.)

7. Suppose you have an extra six months of data on demands and prices, in addition to the data in Example 1.5. These extra data points are (350,84), (385,72), (410,67), (400,62), (330,92), and (480,53). (The price is shown first and then the demand at that price.) After adding these points to the original data, use Excel's Trendline tool to find the best-fitting linear, power, and exponential trend lines. Then calculate the MAPE for each of these, based on all 18 months of data. Does the power curve still have the smallest MAPE?

8. Consider the power curve $y = 10000x^{-22.35}$. Calculate y when $x = 5$; when $x = 10$; and when $x = 20$. For each of these values of x, find the percentage change in y when x increases by 1%. That is, find the percentage change in y when x increases from 5 to 5.05; when it increases from 10 to 10.1; and when it increases from 20 to 20.2. Is this percentage change constant? What number is it very close to? Write a brief memo on what you have learned about power curves from these calculations.

9. Consider the exponential curve $y = 1000e^{-0.014x}$. Calculate y when $x = 5$; when $x = 10$; and when $x = 20$. For each of these values of x, find the percentage change in y when x increases by one unit. That is, find the percentage change in y when x increases from 5 to 6; when it increases from 10 to 11; and when it increases from 20 to 21. Is this percentage change constant? When expressed as a decimal, what number is it very close to? Write a brief memo on what you have learned about exponential curves from these calculations.

10. Modify the model in Example 1.6 so that development lasts for an extra year. Specifically, assume that development costs of $12 million and $3 million are incurred at the beginnings of years 1 and 2, and then the sales in the current model occur one year later, that is, from year 2 until year 21. Again, calculate the NPV discounted back to the beginning of year 1, and perform the same sensitivity analyses. Comment on the effects of this change in timing.

11. Modify the model in Example 1.6 so that sales increase, then stay steady, and finally decrease. Specifically, assume that the gross margin is $1.5 million in year 1, then increases by 10% annually through year 6, then stays constant through year 10, and finally decreases by 5% annually through year 20. Perform a sensitivity analysis with a two-way data table to see how NPV varies with the length of the increase period (currently 6 years) and the length of the constant period (currently 4 years). Comment on whether the company should pursue the drug, given your results.

12. Create a one-way data table in the model in Example 1.6 to see how the NPV varies with discount rate, which is allowed to vary from 6% to 10% in increments of 0.5%. Explain intuitively why the results go in the direction they go—that is, the NPV decreases as the discount

rate increases. Should the company pursue the drug for all of these discount rates?

13. Julie James is opening a lemonade stand. She believes the fixed cost per week of running the stand is $50.00. Her best guess is that she can sell 300 cups per week at $0.50 per cup. The variable cost of producing a cup of lemonade is $0.20.

   a. Given her other assumptions, what level of sales volume will enable Julie to break even?

   b. Given her other assumptions, discuss how a change in sales volume affects profit.

   c. Given her other assumptions, discuss how a change in sales volume and variable cost jointly affect profit.

   d. Use Excel's Formula Auditing tools to show which cells in your spreadsheet affect profit directly.

14. You are thinking of opening a small copy shop. It costs $5000 to rent a copier for a year, and it costs $0.03 per copy to operate the copier. Other fixed costs of running the store will amount to $400 per month. You plan to charge an average of $0.10 per copy, and the store will be open 365 days per year. Each copier can make up to 100,000 copies per year.

   a. For one to five copiers rented and daily demands of 500, 1000, 1500, and 2000 copies per day, find annual profit. That is, find annual profit for *each* of these combinations of copiers rented and daily demand.

   b. If you rent three copiers, what daily demand for copies will allow you to break even?

   c. Graph profit as a function of the number of copiers for a daily demand of 500 copies; for a daily demand of 2000 copies. Interpret your graphs.

15. Dataware is trying to determine whether to give a $10 rebate, cut the price $6, or have no price change on a software product. Currently, 40,000 units of the product are sold each week for $45 apiece. The variable cost of the product is $5. The most likely case appears to be that a $10 rebate will increase sales 30%, and half of all people will claim the rebate. For the price cut, the most likely case is that sales will increase 20%.

   a. Given all other assumptions, what increase in sales from the rebate would make the rebate and price cut equally desirable?

   b. Dataware does not really know the increase in sales that will result from a rebate or price cut. However, the company is sure that the rebate will increase sales

by between 15% and 40% and that the price cut will increase sales by between 10% and 30%. Perform a sensitivity analysis that could be used to help determine Dataware's best decision.

16. A company manufacturers a product in the United States and sells it in England. The unit cost of manufacturing is $50. The current exchange rate (dollars per pound) is 1.221. The demand function, which indicates how many units the company can sell in England as a function of price (in pounds) is of the power type, with constant 27556759 and exponent -2.4.

   a. Develop a model for the company's profit (in dollars) as a function of the price it charges (in pounds). Then use a data table to find the profit-maximizing price to the nearest pound.

   b. If the exchange rate varies from its current value, does the profit-maximizing price increase or decrease? Does the maximum profit increase or decrease?

17. The yield of a chemical reaction is defined as the ratio (expressed as a percentage) of usable output to the amount of raw material input. Suppose the yield of a chemical reaction depends on the length of time the process is run and the temperature at which the process is run. The yield can be expressed as follows:

$$\text{Yield} = 90.79 - 1.095x_1 - 1.045x_2 - 2.781x_1^2 \\ -2.524x_2^2 - 0.775x_1x_2$$

Here $x_1 =$ (Temperature $- 125)/10$ and $x_2 =$ (Time $- 300)/30$, where temperature is measured in degrees Fahrenheit, and time is measured in seconds. Use a data table to find the temperature and time settings that maximize the yield of this process.

18. The payback of a project is the number of years it takes before the project's total cash flow is positive. Payback ignores the time value of money. It is interesting, however, to see how differing assumptions on project growth impact payback. Suppose, for example, that a project requires a $300 million investment right now. The project yields cash flows for 10 years, and the year 1 cash flow will be between $30 million and $100 million. The annual cash flow growth will be between 5% and 25% per year. (Assume that this growth is the *same* each year.) Use a data table to see how the project payback depends on the year 1 cash flow and the cash flow growth rate.

PART 1
DATA ANALYSIS

CHAPTER 2

Describing the Distribution of a Variable

Scott Olson/Getty Images News/Getty Images

RECENT PRESIDENTIAL ELECTIONS

Presidential elections in the United States are scrutinized more than ever. It hardly seems that one is over before we start hearing plans and polls for the next. There is thorough coverage of the races leading up to the elections, but it is also interesting to analyze the results after the elections have been held. This is not difficult, given the many informative websites that appear immediately with election results. For example, a Web search for "2016 presidential election results" finds many sites with in-depth results, interactive maps, and more. In addition, the resulting data can often be imported into Excel® for further analysis.

The file **Presidential Elections.xlsx** contains such downloaded data for the 2000 (Bush versus Gore), 2004 (Bush versus Kerry), 2008 (Obama versus McCain), 2012 (Obama versus Romney), and 2016 (Trump versus Clinton) elections. The results of the 2000 election are particularly interesting. As you might remember, this was one of the closest elections of all time, with Bush defeating Gore by a very narrow margin in the electoral vote, 271 to 266, following a disputed recount in Florida. In fact, Gore actually beat Bush in the total count of U.S. votes, 50,999,897 to 50,456,002. However, because of the all-or-nothing nature of electoral votes in each state, Bush's narrow margin of victory in many closely contested states won him a lot of electoral votes. In contrast, Gore outdistanced Bush by a wide margin in several large states, winning him the same electoral votes he would have won even if these races had been much closer.

A closer analysis of the state-by-state results shows how this actually happened. The Excel file contains two new columns: **Bush Votes minus Gore Votes** and **Pct for Bush minus Pct for Gore**, with a value for each state (including the District of Columbia). We then created column charts of these two variables, as shown in Figures 2.1 and 2.2.

Each of these charts tells the same story, but in slightly different ways. From Figure 2.1, you can see how Gore won big (large vote difference) in several large states, most notably California, Massachusetts, and New York. Bush's only comparable margin of victory was in his home state of Texas. However, Bush won a lot of close races in states with relatively few electoral votes—but enough to add up to an overall win. As Figure 2.2 indicates, many of these "close" races, such as Alaska and Idaho for Bush and District of Columbia for Gore, were not that close after all, at least not from a percentage standpoint. This is one case of many where multiple charts can be created to "tell a story." Perhaps an argument can be made that Figure 2.1 tells the story best, but Figure 2.2 is also interesting.

Figure 2.1 Chart of Vote Differences

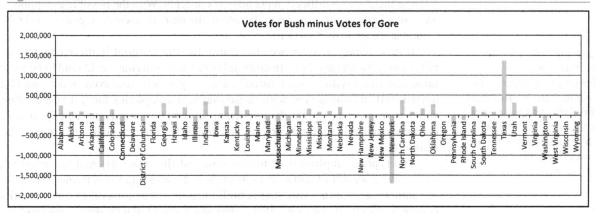

Figure 2.2 Chart of Percent Differences

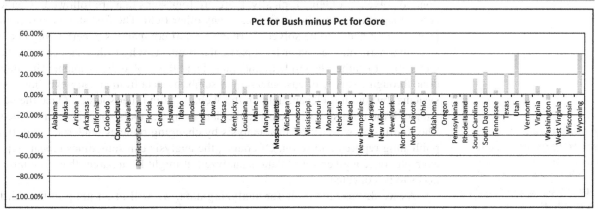

The bottom line is that the election could easily have gone the other way. With one more swing state, particularly Florida, Al Gore would have been president. On the other hand, Gore won some very close races as well, particularly in Iowa, Minnesota, New Mexico, and Oregon. If these had gone the other way, the popular vote would still have been very close, but Bush's victory in the electoral vote would have been more impressive.

2-1 Introduction

The goal of this chapter and the next two chapters is very simple: to make sense of data by constructing appropriate summary measures, tables, and graphs. The purpose here is to present the data in a form that makes sense to people. There are numerous ways to do this, limited only by your imagination (and the software you are using), but there are several tools used most often: (1) a variety of graphs, including bar charts, pie charts, histograms, scatterplots, and time series graphs; (2) numeric summary measures such as counts, percentages, averages, and measures of variability; and (3) tables of summary measures such as totals, averages, and counts, grouped by categories. These terms might not all be familiar to you at this point, but you have undoubtedly seen examples of them in newspapers, magazine articles, and books.

The material in these three chapters is *simple, complex*, and *important*. It is simple because there are no difficult mathematical concepts. With the possible exception of variance, standard deviation, and correlation, all the numeric measures, graphs, and tables are natural and easy to understand.

It is customary to refer to the raw numbers as data and the output of data analysis as information. You start with the data, and your goal is to end with information that an organization can use for competitive advantage.

If it is so easy, why do we also claim that the material in these chapters is complex? The data sets available to companies in today's digital world tend to be extremely large and filled with "unstructured" data. As you will see, even in data sets that are quite small in comparison with those that real companies face, it is a challenge to summarize the data so that the important *information* stands out clearly. It is easy to produce summary measures, graphs, and tables, but the real goal is to produce the most *insightful* ones.

The typical employees of today—not just the managers and technical specialists—have a wealth of software tools at their disposal, and it is frequently up to them to summarize data in a way that is both meaningful and useful to their constituents: people within their company, their company's stockholders, their company's suppliers, and their company's customers. It takes some training and practice to do this effectively.

Data analysis in the real world is almost never done in a vacuum. It is almost always done to solve a problem. Typically, there are four steps that are followed, whether the context is business, medical science, or any other field. The first step is to recognize a problem that needs to be solved. Perhaps a retail company is experiencing decreased sales in a particular region or for a particular product. Why is this happening? The second step is to gather data to help understand and then solve the problem. This might be done through a survey of customers, by assembling data from already-existing company systems, by finding relevant data on the Web, or from other sources. Once the data are gathered, the third step is to analyze the data using the tools you will learn in the book. The fourth step is to act on this analysis by changing policies, undertaking initiatives, publishing reports, and so on. Of course, the analysis can sometimes repeat steps. For example, once a given set of data is analyzed, it might be apparent that even more data needs to be collected.

Use your imagination to ask interesting questions about the many data sets available to you. This book will supply you with the tools to answer these questions.

As we discuss the tools for analyzing data, we will often jump to the third step directly, providing you with a data set to analyze. Although this data set may not be directly connected to the goal of solving a company's problem, you should still strive to ask interesting questions of the data. (We have tried to include interesting data sets, often containing real data, that make this possible.) If the data set contains salaries, you might ask what drives these salaries. Does it depend on the industry a person is in? Does it depend on gender? Does it depend on educational background? Is the salary structure, whatever it is, changing over time? If the data set contains cost-of-living indexes, there are also a lot of interesting questions you can ask. How are the indexes changing over time? Does this behavior vary in different geographical regions? Does this behavior vary across different items such as housing, food, and automobiles? These early chapters provide you with many tools to answer such questions, but it is up to you to ask good questions—and then take advantage of the most appropriate tools to answer them.

The material in these chapters is organized as follows. This chapter discusses a number of ways to analyze one variable at a time. Chapter 3 discusses ways to discover relationships between variables. Finally, Chapter 4, a new chapter in this edition of the book, takes data analysis to a higher level. It first discusses two relatively new tools in Excel, Power

Query and Power Pivot, for importing and analyzing data. It then discusses Tableau Public, a free non-Microsoft software package for creating insightful visualizations of data.

2-2 Basic Concepts

We begin with a short discussion of several important concepts: populations and samples, data sets, variables and observations, and types of data.

2-2a Populations and Samples

First, we distinguish between a population and a sample. A **population** includes all of the entities of interest: people, households, machines, or whatever. The following are three typical populations:

- All potential voters in a presidential election
- All subscribers to a cable television provider
- All invoices submitted for Medicare reimbursement by nursing homes

In these situations and many others, it is virtually impossible to obtain information about all members of the population. For example, it is far too costly to ask all potential voters which presidential candidates they prefer. Therefore, we often try to gain insights into the characteristics of a population by examining a **sample**, or subset, of the population. In later chapters, we examine populations and samples in some depth, but for now it is enough to know that samples should be *representative* of the population so that observed characteristics of the sample can be generalized to the population as a whole.

> A **population** includes all of the entities of interest in a study. A **sample** is a subset of the population, often randomly chosen and preferably representative of the population as a whole.

We use the terms *population* and *sample* a few times in this chapter, which is why we have defined them here. However, the distinction is not really important until later chapters. Our intent in this chapter is to focus entirely on the data in a given data set, not to generalize beyond it. Therefore, the given data set could be a population or a sample from a population. For now, the distinction is irrelevant. (Sampling is discussed in more detail in Chapter 7.)

2-2b Data Sets, Variables, and Observations

We now discuss the types of data sets we will examine. Although the focus of this book is Excel, virtually all statistical software packages use the same concept of a data set: A **data set** is generally a rectangular table of data where the columns contain **variables**, such as height, gender, and income, and each row contains an **observation**. Each observation includes the attributes of a particular member of the population: a person, a company, a city, a machine, or whatever. This terminology is common, but other terms are often used. A variable (column) is often called a **field** or an **attribute**, and an observation (row) is often called a **case** or a **record**. Also, data sets are occasionally rearranged, so that the variables are in rows and the observations are in columns. However, the most common arrangement by far is to have variables in columns, with variable names in the top row, and observations in the remaining rows.

A **data set** is usually a rectangular table of data, with variables in columns and observations in rows. A **variable** (or **field** or **attribute**) is a characteristic of members of a population, such as height, gender, or salary. An **observation** (or **case** or **record**) is a list of all variable values for a single member of a population.

In anticipation of Chapter 4, this definition of "data set" as a single table of data is often expanded to several *related* tables of data. However, for this chapter and the next chapter, each data set will be restricted to a single table of data.

EXAMPLE

2.1 DATA FROM AN ENVIRONMENTAL SURVEY

The data set in Figure 2.3 shows a few of the 30 responses from a questionnaire concerning the president's environmental policies. (See the file **Questionnaire Data.xlsx**.)

Figure 2.3 Environmental Survey Data

	A	B	C	D	E	F	G
1	Person	Age	Gender	State	Children	Salary	Opinion
2	1	35	Male	Minnesota	1	$65,400	5
3	2	61	Female	Texas	2	$62,000	1
4	3	35	Male	Ohio	0	$63,200	3
5	4	37	Male	Florida	2	$52,000	5
6	5	32	Female	California	3	$81,400	1
7	6	33	Female	New York	3	$46,300	5
8	7	65	Female	Minnesota	2	$49,600	1
9	8	45	Male	New York	1	$45,900	5
10	9	40	Male	Texas	3	$47,700	4
11	10	32	Female	Texas	1	$59,900	4

Objective

To illustrate variables and observations in a typical data set.

Solution

Each observation lists the person's age, gender, state of residence, number of children, annual salary, and opinion of the president's environmental policies. These six pieces of information represent the variables. It is customary to include a row (row 1 in this case) that lists variable names. These variable names should be concise but meaningful. Note that an index of the observation is often included in column A. If you sort on other variables, you can always sort on the index to get back to the original sort order.

2-2c Data Types

There are several ways to categorize data, as we explain in the context of Example 2.1. A basic distinction is between **numeric** and **categorical** data. The distinction is whether you intend to do any arithmetic on the data. It makes sense to do arithmetic on numeric data, but not on categorical data. Actually, there is a third **data type**, a **date** variable. As you may know, Excel stores dates as numbers, but for obvious reasons, dates are treated differently from typical numbers.

Three types of variables that appear to be numeric but are usually treated as categorical are phone numbers, zip codes, and Social Security numbers. Do you see why? Can you think of others?

A variable is **numeric** if meaningful arithmetic can be performed on it. Otherwise, the variable is **categorical**.

In the questionnaire data set, Age, Children, and Salary are clearly numeric. For example, it makes perfect sense to sum or average any of these. In contrast, Gender and State are clearly categorical because they are expressed as text, not numbers.

The Opinion variable is less obvious. It is expressed numerically, on a 1-to-5 scale. However, these numbers are really only *codes* for the categories "strongly disagree," "disagree," "neutral," "agree," and "strongly agree." There is never any intent to perform arithmetic on these numbers; in fact, it is not really appropriate to do so. Therefore, it is most appropriate to treat the Opinion variable as categorical. Note, too, that there is a definite ordering of its categories, whereas there is no natural ordering of the categories for the Gender or State variables. When there is a natural ordering of categories, the variable is classified as **ordinal**. If there is no natural ordering, as with the Gender or State variables, the variable is classified as **nominal**.

A categorical variable is **ordinal** if there is a natural ordering of its possible categories. If there is no natural ordering, the variable is **nominal**.

Excel Tip

Horizontal Alignment Conventions

Excel automatically right-aligns numbers and left-aligns text. We use this automatic formatting, but we add our own. Specifically, we right-align all numbers that are available for arithmetic; we left-align all text such as Male, Female, Yes, and No; and we center-align everything else, including dates, indexes such as the Person column, numbers that are indicators of categories such as in the Opinion column, and numbers such as phone numbers that aren't available for arithmetic. You don't need to follow this convention, but it helps to identify the appropriate roles of variables.

Excel Tip

Documenting with Cell Comments

To remember, for example, that "1" stands for "strongly disagree" in the Opinion variable, you can enter a comment—a reminder to yourself and others—in any cell. To do so, right-click a cell and select Insert Comment. A small red tag appears in any cell with a comment. Moving the cursor over that cell causes the comment to appear. You will see numerous comments in the files that accompany the book.

Categorical variables can be coded numerically. In Figure 2.3, Gender has not been coded, whereas Opinion has been coded. This is largely a matter of taste—so long as you realize that coding a categorical variable does not make it numeric and appropriate for arithmetic operations. An alternative way of displaying the data set appears in Figure 2.4. Now Opinion has been replaced by text, and Gender has been coded as 1 for males and 0 for females. This 0−1 coding for a categorical variable is very common. Such a variable is usually called a **dummy variable**, and it often simplifies the analysis. You will see dummy variables throughout the book.

A **dummy variable** is a 0−1 coded variable for a specific category. It is coded as 1 for all observations in that category and 0 for all observations not in that category.

Figure 2.4 Environmental Data Using a Different Coding

	A	B	C	D	E	F	G	H	I	J	K	L
1	Person	Age	Gender	State	Children	Salary	Opinion					
2	1	Middle-aged	1	Minnesota	1	$65,400	Strongly agree					
3	2	Elderly	0	Texas	2	$62,000	Strongly disagree		Note the formulas in columns B, C, and			
4	3	Middle-aged	1	Ohio	0	$63,200	Neutral		G that generate this recoded data. The			
5	4	Middle-aged	1	Florida	2	$52,000	Strongly agree		formulas in columns B and G are based			
6	5	Young	0	California	3	$81,400	Strongly disagree		on the lookup tables below.			
7	6	Young	0	New York	3	$46,300	Strongly agree					
8	7	Elderly	0	Minnesota	2	$49,600	Strongly disagree					
9	8	Middle-aged	1	New York	1	$45,900	Strongly agree		Age lookup table (range name AgeLookup)			
10	9	Middle-aged	1	Texas	3	$47,700	Agree		0	Young		
11	10	Young	0	Texas	1	$59,900	Agree		35	Middle-aged		
12	11	Middle-aged	1	New York	1	$48,100	Agree		60	Elderly		
13	12	Middle-aged	0	Virginia	0	$58,100	Neutral					
14	13	Middle-aged	0	Illinois	2	$56,000	Strongly disagree		Opinion lookup table (range name OpinionLookup)			
15	14	Middle-aged	0	Virginia	2	$53,400	Strongly disagree		1	Strongly disagree		
16	15	Middle-aged	0	New York	2	$39,000	Disagree		2	Disagree		
17	16	Middle-aged	1	Michigan	2	$61,500	Disagree		3	Neutral		
18	17	Middle-aged	1	Ohio	0	$37,700	Strongly disagree		4	Agree		
19	18	Middle-aged	0	Michigan	2	$36,700	Agree		5	Strongly agree		
28	27	Young	1	Illinois	3	$45,400	Disagree					
29	28	Elderly	1	Michigan	2	$53,900	Strongly disagree					
30	29	Middle-aged	1	California	1	$44,100	Neutral					
31	30	Middle-aged	0	New York	2	$31,000	Agree					

In addition, the Age variable has been categorized as "young" (34 years or younger), "middle-aged" (from 35 to 59 years), and "elderly" (60 years or older). This method of categorizing a numeric variable is called **binning** (putting the data into discrete bins), and it is also common. (It is also called **discretizing**.) The purpose of the study dictates whether age should be treated numerically or categorically; there is no absolute right or wrong way.

A **binned** (or **discretized**) **variable** corresponds to a numeric variable that has been categorized into discrete categories. These categories are usually called **bins**.

Excel Tip

VLOOKUP Function

As Figure 2.4 indicates, we used lookup tables, along with the very important VLOOKUP function, to transform the data set from Figure 2.3 to Figure 2.4. Take a look at these functions in the questionnaire file. There is arguably no more important Excel function than VLOOKUP, so you should definitely learn how to use it. If you need help, consult the Excel Tutorial files that accompany the book.

Numeric variables can be classified as **discrete** or **continuous**. The basic distinction is whether the data arise from counts or continuous measurements. The variable Children is clearly a count (discrete), whereas the variable Salary is best treated as continuous. This distinction between discrete and continuous variables is often important because it dictates the most natural type of analysis.

A numeric variable is **discrete** if it results from a count, such as the number of children. A **continuous** variable is the result of an essentially continuous measurement, such as weight or height.

Data sets can also be categorized as cross-sectional or time series. The opinion data set in Example 2.1 is **cross-sectional**. A pollster evidently sampled a cross section of people at one particular point in time. In contrast, a **time series** data set tracks one or more variables through time. A typical time series variable is the series of daily closing values of the Dow Jones Industrial Average (DJIA). Very different types of analyses are appropriate for cross-sectional and time series data, as will become apparent in this and later chapters.

Cross-sectional data are data on a cross section of a population at a distinct point in time. **Time series** data are data collected over time.

A time series data set generally has the same layout—variables in columns and observations in rows—but now each variable is a time series. Also, one of the columns usually indicates the time period. A typical example appears in Figure 2.5. (See the file **Toy Revenues.xlsx**.) It has quarterly observations on revenues from toy sales over a four-year period in column B, with the time periods listed chronologically in column A.

Figure 2.5 Typical Time Series Data Set

	A	B	C
1	Quarter	Revenue	
2	Q1-2015	$1,026,000	
3	Q2-2015	$1,056,000	
4	Q3-2015	$1,182,000	
5	Q4-2015	$2,861,000	
6	Q1-2016	$1,172,000	
7	Q2-2016	$1,249,000	
8	Q3-2016	$1,346,000	
9	Q4-2016	$3,402,000	
10	Q1-2017	$1,286,000	
11	Q2-2017	$1,317,000	
12	Q3-2017	$1,449,000	
13	Q4-2017	$3,893,000	
14	Q1-2018	$1,462,000	
15	Q2-2018	$1,452,000	
16	Q3-2018	$1,631,000	
17	Q4-2018	$4,200,000	

2-3 Summarizing Categorical Variables

This section discusses methods for summarizing a categorical variable. Because it is not appropriate to perform arithmetic on the values of the variable, there are only a few possibilities for summarizing the variable, and these are all based on *counting*. First, you can count the *number* of categories. Many categorical variables such as Gender have only two categories. Others such as Region can have more than two categories. As you count the categories, you can also give the categories *names*, such as Male and Female. Keep in mind that categorical variables, such as Opinion in Example 2.1, can be coded numerically. In these cases, it is still a good idea to supply text descriptions of the categories, such as "strongly agree," and it is often useful to substitute these meaningful descriptions for the numeric codes, as in Figure 2.4. This is especially useful for statistical reports.

Once you know the number of categories and their names, you can count the number of observations in each category. The resulting counts can be reported as "raw counts" or as percentages of totals. For example, if there are 1000 observations, you can report that there are 560 males and 440 females, or you can report that 56% of the observations are males and 44% are females. Actually, it is often useful to report the counts in both ways. Finally, once you have the counts, you can display them graphically, usually in a column chart or possibly a pie chart. The following example illustrates how to do this in Excel.

The only meaningful way to summarize categorical data is with counts of observations in the categories.

EXAMPLE

2.2 SUPERMARKET SALES

The file **Supermarket Transactions.xlsx** contains over 14,000 transactions made by supermarket customers over a period of approximately two years. (The data are not real, but real supermarket chains have huge data sets similar to this one.) A small sample of the data appears in Figure 2.6. Column B contains the date of the purchase, column C is a unique identifier for each customer, columns D–H contain information about the customer, columns I–K contain the location of the store, columns L–N (hidden to conserve space) contain information about the product purchased, and the last two columns indicate the number of items purchased and the amount paid.

Figure 2.6 Supermarket Data Set

◢	A	B	C	D	E	F	G	H	I	J	K	O	P
1	Transaction	Purchase Date	Customer ID	Gender	Marital Status	Homeowner	Children	Annual Income	City	State or Province	Country	Units Sold	Revenue
2	1	12/18/2016	7223	F	S	Y	2	$30K - $50K	Los Angeles	CA	USA	5	$27.38
3	2	12/20/2016	7841	M	M	Y	5	$70K - $90K	Los Angeles	CA	USA	5	$14.90
4	3	12/21/2016	8374	F	M	N	2	$50K - $70K	Bremerton	WA	USA	3	$5.52
5	4	12/21/2016	9619	M	M	Y	3	$30K - $50K	Portland	OR	USA	4	$4.44
6	5	12/22/2016	1900	F	S	Y	3	$130K - $150K	Beverly Hills	CA	USA	4	$14.00
7	6	12/22/2016	6696	F	M	Y	3	$10K - $30K	Beverly Hills	CA	USA	3	$4.37
8	7	12/23/2016	9673	M	S	Y	2	$30K - $50K	Salem	OR	USA	4	$13.78
9	8	12/25/2016	354	F	M	Y	2	$150K +	Yakima	WA	USA	6	$7.34
10	9	12/25/2016	1293	M	M	Y	3	$10K - $30K	Bellingham	WA	USA	1	$2.41
11	10	12/25/2016	7938	M	S	N	1	$50K - $70K	San Diego	CA	USA	2	$8.96

Objective

To summarize categorical variables in a large data set.

Solution

Most of the variables in this data set are categorical. Only Children, Units Sold, and Revenue are numeric. Purchase Date is a date variable, and Transaction and Customer ID are used only to identify transactions and customers. All other variables are categorical, including Annual Income, which has been binned into categories. Three of the categorical variables—Gender, Marital Status, and Homeowner—have only two categories. The others have more than two categories.

The first question is how you can discover all of the categories for a variable such as State or Province. Without good tools, this is not a trivial problem. One option is to sort on this variable and then manually go through the list, looking for the different categories. Another possibility is to copy the categorical column to a blank area of the worksheet and then use the Remove Duplicates item on Excel's Data ribbon. (Try it!) Fortunately, there are easier ways, using Excel's built-in table and pivot table tools. We postpone these for later and deal for now only with the categorical variables with obvious categories.

Figure 2.7 displays summaries of Gender, Marital Status, Homeowner, and Annual Income, along with several corresponding charts for Gender. Each of the counts in column S can be obtained with Excel's COUNTIF function. For example, the formula in cell S3 is **=COUNTIF($D$2:$D$14060,R3)**. This function takes two arguments, the data range and a criterion, so it is perfect for counting observations in a category. Then the percentages in column T are the counts divided by the total number of observations. (As a check, it is a good idea to sum these percentages. They should sum to 100% for each variable.)

Figure 2.7 Summaries of Categorical Variables

As the charts indicate, you get essentially the same chart whether you graph the counts or the percentages. However, be careful with misleading scales. If you select the range R2:S4 and then insert a column chart, you get the top left chart by default. Its vertical scale starts well above 6000, which makes it appear that there are *many* more females than males. By resetting the vertical scale to start at 0, as in the two middle charts, you see more accurately that there are almost as many males as females. Finally, you can decide whether you prefer a column chart or a pie chart. We tend to prefer column charts, but this is a matter of taste. (We also tend to prefer column charts to horizontal bar charts, but this is also a matter of taste.) Our only recommendation in general is to keep charts *simple* so that the information they contain emerges as clearly as possible.

When you have a choice between a "simple" chart and a "fancier" chart, keep it simple. Simple charts tend to reveal the information in the data more clearly.

Excel Tip

Creating and Modifying an Excel Chart

If you are new to Excel charts, you should try creating the charts in Figure 2.7 on your own. One way is to select a blank cell, select a desired chart type from the Insert ribbon, and then designate the data to be included in the chart. However, it is usually simpler and more efficient to select the data to be charted and then insert the chart. For example, try highlighting the range R2:S4 and then inserting a column chart. Except for a little cleanup (changing the chart title, and possibly changing the vertical scale), you get almost exactly what you want with very little work. Don't be afraid to right-click for context-sensitive chart menus or to use the special ribbons that appear when a chart is selected. You can learn a lot by experimenting with these tools.

If this example of summarizing categorical variables appears to be overly tedious, be patient. As indicated earlier, Excel has powerful tools, especially pivot tables, that make this summarization much easier. We discuss pivot tables in depth in the next chapter. For now, just remember that the only meaningful way to summarize a categorical variable is to count observations in its categories.

Before leaving this section, we mention one other efficient way to find counts for a categorical variable. This method uses dummy (0–1) variables. To see how it works, focus on any category of a categorical variable, such as M for Gender. Recode the variable so that each M is replaced by a 1 and all other values are replaced by 0. (This can be done in Excel in a new column, using a simple IF formula. See column E of Figure 2.8.) Now you can find the count of males by *summing* the 0's and 1's, and you can find the percentage of males by *averaging* the 0's and 1's. That is, the formulas in cells E14061 and E14062 use the SUM and AVERAGE functions on the data in column E. You should convince yourself why this works (for example, what arithmetic are you really doing when you average 0's and 1's?), and you should remember this method. It is one reason why dummy variables are used so frequently in data analysis.

Figure 2.8 Summarizing a Category with a Dummy Variable

	A	B	C	D	E
1	Transaction	Purchase Date	Customer ID	Gender	Gender Dummy for M
2	1	12/18/2016	7223	F	0
3	2	12/20/2016	7841	M	1
4	3	12/21/2016	8374	F	0
5	4	12/21/2016	9619	M	1
6	5	12/22/2016	1900	F	0
7	6	12/22/2016	6696	F	0
14058	14057	12/31/2018	250	M	1
14059	14058	12/31/2018	6153	F	0
14060	14059	12/31/2018	3656	M	1
14061				Count	6889
14062				Percent	49.0%

Problems

Solutions for problems whose numbers appear within a colored box can be found in the Student Solution Files.

Level A

1. The file **P02_01.xlsx** indicates the gender and nationality of the MBA incoming class in two successive years at the Kelley School of Business at Indiana University.
   a. For each year, create tables of counts of gender and of nationality. Then create column charts of these counts. Do they indicate any noticeable change in the composition of the two classes?
   b. Repeat part **a** for nationality, but recode this variable so that all nationalities that have counts of 1 or 2 are classified as Other.

2. The file **P02_02.xlsx** contains information on 256 movies that grossed at least $1 million in 2017.
   a. Create two column charts of counts, one of the different genres and one of the different distributors.
   b. Recode the Genre column so that all genres with a count of 10 or less are lumped into a category called Other. Then create a column chart of counts for this recoded variable. Repeat similarly for the Distributor variable.

3. The file **P02_03.xlsx** contains data from a survey of 399 people regarding a government environmental policy.
   a. Which of the variables in this data set are categorical? Which of these are nominal; which are ordinal?
   b. For each categorical variable, create a column chart of counts.

c. Recode the data into a new data set, making four transformations: (1) change Gender to list "Male" or "Female"; (2) change Children to list "No children" or "At least one child"; (3) change Salary to be categorical with categories "Less than $40K," "Between $40K and $70K," "Between $70K and $100K," and "Greater than $100K " (where you can treat the breakpoints however you like); and (4) change Opinion to be a numeric code from 1 to 5 for Strongly Disagree to Strongly Agree. Then create a column chart of counts for the new Salary variable.

4. The file **P02_04.xlsx** contains salary data on all Major League Baseball players for each year from 2012 to 2018. For any three selected years, create a table of counts of the various positions, expressed as percentages of all players for the year. Then create a column chart of these percentages for these years. Do they remain fairly constant from year to year?

Level B

5. The file **P02_05.xlsx** contains monthly values of the Dow Jones Industrial Average from 1950 until recently. It also contains the percentage changes from month to month. (This file is used in an example later in this chapter.) Create a new column for recoding the percentage changes into six categories: Large negative ($<-3\%$), Medium negative ($<-1\%$, $\geq-3\%$), Small negative ($<0\%$, $\geq-1\%$), Small positive ($<1\%$, $\geq0\%$), Medium positive ($<3\%$, $\geq1\%$), and Large positive ($\geq3\%$). Then create a column chart of the counts of this categorical variable. Comment on its shape.

2-4   Summarizing Numeric Variables

There are many ways to summarize numeric variables, both with numeric summary measures and with charts, and we discuss the most common ways in this section. But before getting into details, it is important to understand the basic goal of this section. Starting with a numeric variable such as Salary, where there is one observation for each person, the basic goal is to learn how these salaries are distributed across people. To do this, we can ask a number of questions, including the following: (1) What are the most "typical" salaries? (2) How spread out are the salaries? (3) What are the "extreme" salaries on either end? (4) Is a chart of the salaries symmetric about some middle value, or is it skewed in one direction? (5) Does the chart of salaries have any other peculiar features besides possible skewness? In the next chapter, we explore methods for checking whether a variable such as Salary is related to *other* variables, but for now the goal is simply to explore the distribution of values in the Salary column.

2-4a   Numeric Summary Measures

Throughout this section, we focus on a Salary variable. Specifically, we examine the 2018 salaries for Major League Baseball players, as described in the following extended example.

Excel Tip

Statistical Functions

Microsoft introduced a number of new or modified statistical functions in Excel 2010, but for backward compatibility, it also retained the older versions. You can recognize the new functions with periods, such as NORM.DIST (new) versus NORMDIST (old). Because these new functions have now existed for nearly a decade, we usually use them in this book, but if you are used to the older versions, you can continue to use them.

EXAMPLE

2.3 BASEBALL SALARIES

The file **Baseball Salaries.xlsx** contains data on 877 Major League Baseball (MLB) players in the 2018 season. (The file also contains similar data for each of the years 2012 to 2017.) There are four variables, as shown in Figure 2.9: the player's name, team, position, and salary. How can these 877 salaries be summarized?

Figure 2.9 Baseball Salaries

	A	B	C	D
1	Name	Team	Position	Salary
2	Mike Trout	Los Angeles Angels	Outfielder	$34,083,333
3	Clayton Kershaw	Los Angeles Dodgers	Pitcher	$34,000,000
4	Zack Greinke	Arizona Diamondbacks	Pitcher	$31,954,483
5	Miguel Cabrera	Detroit Tigers	First Baseman	$30,000,000
6	David Price	Boston Red Sox	Pitcher	$30,000,000
7	Jake Arrieta	Philadelphia Phillies	Pitcher	$30,000,000
8	Yoenis Cespedes	New York Mets	Outfielder	$29,000,000
9	Justin Verlander	Houston Astros	Pitcher	$28,000,000
10	Jon Lester	Chicago Cubs	Pitcher	$27,500,000
11	Albert Pujols	Los Angeles Angels	First Baseman	$27,000,000
12	Felix Hernandez	Seattle Mariners	Pitcher	$26,857,143
13	Jason Heyward	Chicago Cubs	Outfielder	$26,055,288
14	Giancarlo Stanton	New York Yankees	Outfielder	$25,000,000

Objective

To learn how salaries are distributed across all 2018 MLB players.

Solution

The various numeric summary measures can be categorized into several groups: measures of central tendency; minimum, maximum, percentiles, and quartiles; measures of variability; and measures of shape. We explain each of these in this extended example.

Measures of Central Tendency

There are three common measures of central tendency, all of which try to answer the basic question of which value is most "typical." These are the mean, the median, and the mode.

The **mean** is the average of all values. If the data set represents a sample from some larger population, this measure is called the **sample mean** and is usually denoted by $\overline{X}$ (pronounced "X-bar"). If the data set represents the entire population, it is called the **population mean** and is usually denoted by μ (the Greek letter *mu*). This distinction is not important in this chapter, but it will become relevant in later chapters on statistical inference. In either case, the formula for the mean is given by Equation (2.1).

Formula for the Mean

$$\text{Mean} = \frac{\sum_{i=1}^{n} X_i}{n} \tag{2.1}$$

Here, n is the number of observations and X_i is the value of observation i. Equation (2.1) says to add all the observations and divide by n, the number of observations. The Σ (Greek capital *sigma*) symbol means to sum from $i = 1$ to $i = n$, that is, to sum over all observations.

For Excel data sets, you can calculate the mean with the AVERAGE function. This is shown for the baseball data, along with many other summary measures discussed shortly, in Figure 2.10. Specifically, the average salary for all players is $4,512,768. Is this a "typical" salary? Keep reading.

The **median** is the middle observation when the data are sorted from smallest to largest. If the number of observations is odd, the median is literally the middle observation. For example, if there are nine observations, the median is the fifth smallest (or fifth largest). If the number of observations is even, the median is usually defined as the average of the two middle observations, although there are some slight variations of this definition. For example, if there are 10 observations, the median is usually defined as the average of the fifth and sixth smallest values.

For highly skewed data, the median is typically a better measure of central tendency. The median is unaffected by the extreme values, whereas the mean can be very sensitive to extreme values.

The median can be calculated in Excel with the MEDIAN function. Figure 2.10 shows that the median salary is $1,450,000. In words, half of the players make less than this, and half make more. Why is the median in this example so much smaller than the mean, and which is more appropriate? These are relevant questions for many real-world data sets. In this case, the vast majority of baseball players have relatively modest salaries that are dwarfed by the huge salaries of a few stars. Because it is an average, the mean is strongly influenced by these really large values, so it is quite large. In contrast, the median is completely unaffected by the magnitude of the really large salaries, so it is much smaller. (For example, the median would not change by a single cent if the highest paid player made $34 *billion* instead of his $34 million, but the mean would increase to more than $43 million.)

Figure 2.10 Summary Measures of Baseball Salaries

▲	A	B	C	D	E	F
1	**Measures of central tendency**				**Measures of variability**	
2	Mean	$4,512,768			Range	$33,538,333
3	Median	$1,450,000	Mode count		Interquartile range	$5,442,529
4	Mode	$545,000	44		Variance	38,845,755,393,289
5					Standard deviation	$6,232,636
6	**Min, max, percentiles, quartiles**				Mean absolute deviation	$4,553,478
7	Min	$545,000				
8	Max	$34,083,333			**Measures of shape**	
9	Q1	$557,471	1		Skewness	2.0663
10	Q2	$1,450,000	2		Kurtosis	4.1060
11	Q3	$6,000,000	3			
12	P01	$545,000	0.01		**Percentages of values <= given values**	
13	P05	$545,320	0.05		Value	Percentage <=
14	P10	$547,560	0.10		$1,000,000	45.38%
15	P20	$554,640	0.20		$1,500,000	51.20%
16	P50	$1,450,000	0.50		$2,000,000	55.53%
17	P80	$7,733,333	0.80		$2,500,000	59.29%
18	P90	$13,050,000	0.90		$3,000,000	62.94%
19	P95	$19,520,000	0.95			
20	P99	$27,120,000	0.99			

In many situations like this, where the data are skewed to the right (a few extremely large salaries not balanced by any extremely small salaries), most people would argue that the median is a more representative measure of central tendency than the mean. However, for variables that are *not* skewed in one direction or the other, the mean and median are often quite close to one another.

The **mode** is the value that appears most often, and it can be calculated in Excel with the MODE function. In most cases where a variable is essentially continuous, the mode is not very interesting because it is often the result of a few lucky ties. However, the mode for the salary data in Figure 2.10 is not the result of luck. Its value, $545,000, is the minimum possible salary set by the league. As shown in cell C4 (with a COUNTIF formula), this value occurred 44 times. In other words, close to 5% of the players earn the minimum possible salary. This is a good example of learning something you might not have known simply by exploring the data.

Minimum, Maximum, Percentiles, and Quartiles

Given a certain percentage such as 25%, what is the salary value such that this percentage of salaries is below it? This type of question leads to **percentiles** and **quartiles**. Specifically, for any percentage p, the pth percentile is the value such that a percentage p of all values are less than or equal to it. Similarly, the first, second, and third quartiles are the percentiles corresponding to $p = 25\%$, $p = 50\%$, and $p = 75\%$. These three values divide the data into four groups, each with (approximately) a quarter of all observations. Note that the second quartile is equal to the median by definition. To complete this group of descriptive measures, we add the **minimum** and **maximum** values, with the obvious meanings.

You are probably aware of percentiles from standardized tests. For example, if you learn that your score in the verbal SAT test is at the 93rd percentile, this means that you scored better than 93% of those taking the test.

The minimum and maximum can be calculated with Excel's MIN and MAX functions. For the percentiles and quartiles, you can use Excel's PERCENTILE and QUARTILE functions. The PERCENTILE function takes two arguments: the data range and a value of p between 0 and 1. (It has to be between 0 and 1. For example, if you want the 95th percentile, you must enter the second argument as 0.95, not as 95.) The QUARTILE function also takes two arguments: the data range and 1, 2, or 3, depending on which quartile you want. Figure 2.10 shows the minimum, maximum, the three quartiles, and several commonly requested percentiles for the baseball data. As you can see, 25% of the players make no more than $557,471 (very close to the league minimum) and 25% of all players make more than $6,000,000. In fact, more than 1% of the players make more than $27 million, with Mike Trout topping the list at about $34 million.

Excel Tip

Entering Arguments for Copying

Note the values in column C of Figure 2.10 for percentiles and quartiles. These allow you to enter one formula for the percentiles and one for quartiles that can then be copied down. Specifically, the formulas in cells B12 and B9 are

=PERCENTILE('Salaries 2018'!$D$2:$D$878,C12)

and

= QUARTILE('Salaries 2018'!$D$2:$D$878,C9)

(Here, 'Salaries 2018'! is a reference to the worksheet that contains the data.) Always look for ways to make your Excel formulas copyable. It saves time and it avoids errors. And if you don't want the values in column C to be visible, just color them white.

Excel Tip

Minimum and Maximum as Quartiles

Following up on the previous tip, the minimum and maximum can be calculated with Excel's QUARTILE function by using 0 and 4 as the last argument. This means that if you enter 0 and 4 in cells C7 and C8 of Figure 2.10, the QUARTILE formula in cell B9 can be copied to cells B7 and B8.

Excel Tip

New PERCENTILE and QUARTILE Functions

Microsoft introduced four new functions, PERCENTILE.EXC, PERCENTILE.INC, QUARTILE.EXC, and QUARTILE.INC, in Excel 2010. The INC (inclusive) versions work just like the "old" PERCENTILE and QUARTILE functions. The EXC (exclusive) versions are recommended for small data sets. However, the differences are minor, and the "old" PERCENTILE and QUARTILE functions work fine.

If you are given a salary figure such as $1 million, you might want to find the percentage of all salaries less than or equal to this. This is essentially the opposite of a percentile question. In a percentile question, you are given a percentage and you want to find a value. Now you are given a value and you want to find a percentage. You can find this percentage in Excel by dividing a COUNTIF function by the total number of observations. A few such values are shown in the bottom right of Figure 2.10. The typical formula in cell F14, which is then copied down, is

=COUNTIF('Salaries 2018'!$D$2:$D$878,"<="&E14)/COUNT('Salaries 2018'!$D$2:$D$878)

The following Excel tip explains this formula in more detail.

Excel Tip

Creating a Condition with Concatenation

The condition in this COUNTIF formula is a bit tricky. You literally want it to be "<=1000000", but you want the formula to refer to the value in column E to enable copying. Therefore, you can **concatenate** (string together) the literal part, "<=", and the variable part, the reference to cell E14. The ampersand symbol (&) in the middle is the symbol used to concatenate in Excel. This use of concatenation to join literal and variable parts is especially useful in functions like COUNTIF that require a condition, so you should learn how to use it.

Measures of Variability

In this subsection, we list a few other measures that summarize variability, that is, how much the data values are spread out. These include the range, the interquartile range, the variance and standard deviation, and the mean absolute deviation.

The **range** is a crude measure of variability. It is defined as the maximum value minus the minimum value. For the baseball salaries, this range is $33,538,333. This value certainly indicates how spread out the salaries are, but it is too sensitive to the extremes. For example, if Mike Trout's salary increased by $10 million, the range would increase by $10 million—just because of one player.

A less sensitive measure is the **interquartile range** (abbreviated **IQR**). It is defined as the third quartile minus the first quartile, so it is really the range of the middle 50% of the data. For the baseball data, the IQR is $5,442,529. If you excluded the 25% of players with the lowest salaries and the 25% with the highest salaries, this IQR would be the range of the remaining salaries.

The range or a modified range such as the IQR probably seems like a natural measure of variability, but there is another measure that is quoted much more frequently: standard deviation. Actually, there are two related measures, variance and standard deviation, and we begin with a definition of variance. The **variance** is essentially the average of the squared deviations from the mean, where if X_i is a typical observation, its squared deviation from the mean is $(X_i - \text{mean})^2$. As in the discussion of the mean, there is a **sample variance**, usually denoted by s^2, and a **population variance**, usually denoted by σ^2 (where σ is the Greek letter *sigma*). They are defined as follows:

Formula for Sample Variance

$$s^2 = \frac{\sum_{i=1}^{n}(X_i - \text{mean})^2}{n-1}$$

(2.2)

Formula for Population Variance

$$\sigma^2 = \frac{\sum_{i=1}^{n}(X_i - \text{mean})^2}{n}$$

(2.3)

Technical Note

Denominators of Variance Formulas

It is traditional to use the capital letter N for the population size and lowercase n for the sample size, but this distinction is not important in this chapter. Furthermore, there is a technical reason why the sample variance uses $n - 1$ in the denominator, not n, and this is explained in a later chapter. In any case, the difference is negligible when n is large. Excel implements both of these formulas. You can use the VAR.S function to obtain the sample variance (denominator $n - 1$), and you can use the VAR.P function to obtain the population variance (denominator n).

To understand why the variance is indeed a measure of variability, look closely at either formula. If all observations are close to the mean, their squared deviations from the mean will be relatively small, and the variance will be relatively small. On the other hand, if at least a few of the observations are far from the mean, their squared deviations from the mean will be large, and this will cause the variance to be large. Note that because deviations from the mean are *squared*, an observation a certain amount *below* the mean contributes the same to variance as an observation that same amount *above* the mean.

The fundamental problem with variance as a measure of variability is that it is in *squared* units. For example, if the observations are measured in dollars, the variance is in squared dollars. A more natural measure is the square root of variance. This is called the **standard deviation**. Again, there are two versions of standard deviation. The **sample standard deviation**, usually denoted by s, is the square root of the quantity in Equation (2.2). The **population standard deviation**, usually denoted by σ, is the square root of the quantity in Equation (2.3).

To calculate either standard deviation in Excel, you can first find the variance with the VAR.S or VAR.P function and then take its square root. Alternatively, you can find it directly with the STDEV.S (sample) or STDEV.P (population) function.

We used these functions, actually the sample versions, in cells F4 and F5 of Figure 2.10 for the baseball salaries. The huge value for variance is in dollars squared, whereas the standard deviation is in dollars, about $6.233 million. By the way, you might argue that the *population* versions of these parameters should be used instead, and you would have a point. After all, the data set includes *all* 2018 baseball players. However, you can check that with 877 players, the difference between the sample and population measures is negligible.

Excel Tip

New VAR and STDEV Functions

Microsoft added four new functions, VAR.S, VAR.P, STDEV.S, and STDEV.P, in Excel 2010. These are identical to the "old" VAR, VARP, STDEV, and STDEVP functions, and you can use either the old or the new versions.

The data in Figure 2.11 help clarify these concepts. It is in the file **Variability.xlsx**. (It will help if you open this file and look at its formulas as you read this.) The variable Diameter1 on the left has relatively low variability; its 10 values vary closely around its mean of approximately 100, found in cell A16 with the AVERAGE function. To show how variance is calculated, we explicitly calculated the 10 squared deviations from the mean in column B. Then either variance, sample or population, can be calculated (in cells A19 and A22) as the sum of squared deviations divided by 9 or 10. Alternatively, they can be calculated more directly (in cells B19 and B22) with Excel's VAR.S and VAR.P functions. Next, either standard deviation, sample or population, can be calculated as the square root of the corresponding variance or with Excel's STDEV.S or STDEV.P functions.

The calculations are exactly the same for Diameter2 on the right. This variable also has mean approximately equal to 100, but its observations vary much more around 100 than the observations for Diameter1. As expected, this increased variability is obvious in a comparison of the variances and standard deviations for the two suppliers.

This example also indicates why variability is important. Imagine that you are about to buy 10 parts from one of two suppliers, and you want each part's diameter to be close to 100 centimeters. Furthermore, suppose that Diameter1 in the example represents 10 randomly selected parts from supplier 1, whereas Diameter2 represents 10 randomly selected parts from Supplier 2. You can see that both suppliers are very close to the target of 100 *on average*, but the increased

Variability is usually the enemy. Being close to a target value on average is not good enough if there is a lot of variability around the target.

Figure 2.11 Calculating Variance and Standard Deviation

	A	B	C	D	E	F
1	Low variability supplier				High variability supplier	
2						
3	Diameter1	Sq dev from mean			Diameter2	Sq dev from mean
4	102.61	6.610041			103.21	9.834496
5	103.25	10.310521			93.66	41.139396
6	96.34	13.682601			120.87	432.473616
7	96.27	14.205361			110.26	103.754596
8	103.77	13.920361			117.31	297.079696
9	97.45	6.702921			110.23	103.144336
10	98.22	3.308761			70.54	872.257156
11	102.76	7.403841			39.53	3665.575936
12	101.56	2.313441			133.22	1098.657316
13	98.16	3.530641			101.91	3.370896
14						
15	Mean				Mean	
16	100.039				100.074	
17						
18	Sample variance				Sample variance	
19	9.1098	9.1098			736.3653	736.3653
20						
21	Population variance				Population variance	
22	8.1988	8.1988			662.7287	662.7287
23						
24	Sample standard deviation				Sample standard deviation	
25	3.0182	3.0182			27.1361	27.1361
26						
27	Population standard deviation				Population standard deviation	
28	2.8634	2.8634			25.7435	25.7435

variability for Supplier 2 makes this supplier much less attractive. There is a famous saying in operations management: *Variability is the enemy.* This example illustrates exactly what this saying means.

Empirical Rules for Interpreting Standard Deviation

Now you know how to *calculate* the standard deviation, but there is a more important question: How do you interpret its value? Fortunately, the standard deviation often has a very natural interpretation, which is why it is quoted so frequently. This interpretation can be stated as three **empirical rules**. ("Empirical" means that they are based on commonly observed data, as opposed to theoretical mathematical arguments.) Specifically, if the values of this variable are approximately *normally* distributed (symmetric and bell-shaped), then the following rules hold:

• Approximately 68% of the observations are within one standard deviation of the mean, that is, within the interval $\overline{X} \pm s$.
• Approximately 95% of the observations are within two standard deviations of the mean, that is, within the interval $\overline{X} \pm 2s$.
• Approximately 99.7% of the observations—almost all of them—are within three standard deviations of the mean, that is, within the interval $\overline{X} \pm 3s$.

Fortunately, many variables in real-world data are approximately normally distributed, so these empirical rules correctly apply. (The normal distribution is discussed in depth in Chapter 5.)

These empirical rules give a concrete meaning to standard deviation for symmetric, bell-shaped distributions. However, they tend to be less accurate for skewed distributions.

Fundamental Insight

Usefulness of Standard Deviation

Variability is an important property of any numeric variable, and there are several measures for quantifying the amount of variability. Of these, standard deviation is by far the most frequently quoted measure. It is measured in the same units as the variable, it has a long tradition, and, at least for many data sets, it obeys the empirical rules discussed here. These empirical rules give a very specific meaning to standard deviation.

As an example, if the parts supplied by the suppliers in Figure 2.11 have diameters that are approximately normally distributed, then the intervals in the empirical rules for supplier 1 are about 100 ± 3, 100 ± 6, and 100 ± 9. Therefore, about 68% of this supplier's parts will have diameters from 97 to 103, 95% will have diameters from 94 to 106, and almost none will have diameters below 91 or above 109. Obviously, the situation for supplier 2 is much worse. With a standard deviation slightly larger than 25, the second empirical rule implies that about 1 out of every 20 of this supplier's parts will be below 50 or above 150. It is clear that supplier 2 has to reduce its variability. In fact, this is exactly what almost all suppliers are continuously trying to do: reduce variability.

Returning to the baseball data, Figure 2.10 indicates that the standard deviation of salaries is about $6.233 million. (The variance is shown, but because it is in squared dollars, it is a huge value with no meaningful interpretation.) Can the empirical rules be applied to these baseball salaries? The answer is that you can always try, but if the salaries are not at least approximately normally distributed, the rules won't be very accurate. And because of obvious skewness in the salary data, due to the stars with huge salaries, the assumption of a normal distribution is not a good one.

Nevertheless, the rules are checked in Figure 2.12. For each of the three rules, the lower and upper endpoints of the corresponding interval are found in columns I and J. Right away there are problems. Because the standard deviation is *larger* than the mean, all three lower endpoints are *negative*, which automatically means that there can be no salaries below them. But continuing anyway, the COUNTIF was used, again with concatenation, to find the number of salaries above the upper endpoints in column L, and the corresponding percentages appear in column N. Finally, subtracting columns M and N from 100% in column O gives the percentages between the endpoints. These three percentages, according to the empirical rules, should be about 68%, 95%, and 99.7%. Rules 2 and 3 are not way off, but rule 1 isn't even close.

Figure 2.12 Empirical Rules for Baseball Salaries

◢	H	I	J	K	L	M	N	O
1	**Do empirical rules apply?**							
2		Lower endpoint	Upper endpoint	# below lower	# above upper	% below lower	% above upper	% between
3	Rule 1	−$1,719,868	$10,745,405	0	121	0%	14%	86.20%
4	Rule 2	−$7,952,504	$16,978,041	0	61	0%	7%	93.04%
5	Rule 3	−$14,185,141	$23,210,677	0	18	0%	2%	97.95%

The point of these calculations is that even though the empirical rules give substantive meaning to the standard deviation for many variables, they should be applied with caution, especially when the data are clearly skewed.

Before leaving variance and standard deviation, you might ask why the deviations from the mean are *squared* in the definition of variance. Why not simply take *absolute* deviations from the mean? For example, if the mean is 100 and two observations have values 95 and 105, then each has a *squared* deviation of 25, but each has an *absolute* deviation of only 5. Wouldn't this latter value be a more natural measure of variability? Intuitively, it would, but there is a long history of using squared deviations. They have many attractive theoretical properties that are not shared by absolute deviations. Still, some analysts quote the **mean absolute deviation** (abbreviated as **MAD**) as another measure of variability, particularly in time series analysis. It is defined as the average of the absolute deviations.

Don't be surprised if the empirical rules don't hold for skewed data. The rules are based on the normal distribution, which is symmetric and bell-shaped.

Formula for Mean Absolute Deviation

$$\text{MAD} = \frac{\sum_{i=1}^{n} |X_i - \text{mean}|}{n} \tag{2.4}$$

There is another empirical rule for MAD: For many (but not all) variables, the standard deviation is approximately 25% larger than MAD, that is, $s \approx 1.25*MAD$. Fortunately, Excel has a function, AVEDEV, that performs the calculation in Equation (2.4). Using it for the baseball salaries in Figure 2.10, you can see that MAD is about \$4.553 million. If this is multiplied by 1.25, the result is slightly over \$5.69 million, which is not too far from the standard deviation.

Measures of Shape

There are two final measures of a distribution you will hear occasionally: **skewness** and **kurtosis**. Each of these has not only an intuitive meaning but also a specific numeric measure. We have already mentioned skewness in terms of the baseball salaries. It occurs when there is a lack of symmetry. A few stars have really large salaries, and no players have really small salaries. More specifically, the largest salaries are much farther to the right of the mean than the smallest salaries are to the left of the mean. This lack of symmetry is usually apparent from a histogram of the salaries, discussed in the next section. We say that these salaries are **skewed to the right** (or **positively skewed**) because the skewness is due to the really *large* salaries. If the skewness were due to really small values, as might occur with temperature lows in Antarctica, then we would call it **skewness to the left** (or **negatively skewed**).

In either case, a measure of skewness can be calculated with Excel's SKEW function. For the baseball data, it is approximately 2.1, as shown in Figure 2.10. You don't need to know exactly what this value means. Simply remember that (1) it is positive when there is skewness to the right, (2) it is negative when there is skewness to the left, (3) it is approximately zero when the data are symmetric, and (4) its magnitude increases as the degree of skewness increases.

The other measure, kurtosis, has to do with the "fatness" of the tails of the distribution relative to the tails of a normal distribution. Remember from the third empirical rule that a normal distribution has almost all of its observations within three standard deviations of the mean. In contrast, a distribution with high kurtosis has many more extreme observations. In reality, this is much more important than you might imagine. For example, many researchers believe the Wall Street meltdown in late 2008 was at least partly due to financial analysts relying on the normal distribution, whereas in reality the actual distribution had much fatter tails. More specifically, financial analysts followed complex mathematical models that indicated really extreme events would virtually never occur. Unfortunately, a number of extreme events *did* occur, and they sent the economy into a deep recession.[1]

Kurtosis is all about extreme events—the kind that occurred in late 2008 and sent Wall Street into a panic.

Although kurtosis can be calculated in Excel with the KURT function (it is about 4.1 for the baseball salaries), we won't have any use for this measure in the book. Nevertheless, when you hear the word kurtosis, think of fat tails and extreme events. And if you plan to work on Wall Street, you should definitely learn more about kurtosis.

Numeric Summary Measures in the Status Bar

You might have noticed that summary measures sometimes appear automatically in the status bar at the bottom of your Excel window. The rule is that if you select multiple cells (in a single column or even in multiple columns), selected summary measures appear for the selected cells. (Nothing appears if only a single cell is selected.) These can be very handy for quick lookups. Also, you can choose the summary measures that appear by right-clicking the status bar and selecting your favorites.

Numeric Summary Measures with Add-Ins

All the summary measure just discussed can be calculated with built-in Excel functions such as AVERAGE and STDEV.S. However, Excel add-ins can be used to speed up the process. Specifically, Palisade's StatTools add-in, part of their Decision Tools Suite, is discussed in an appendix to this chapter. StatTools can generate summary measures for one or more numeric variables in seconds, and it is also capable of more advanced statistical analysis, such as regression and time series analysis, topics of later chapters.

2-4b Charts for Numeric Variables

There are many graphical ways to indicate the distribution of a numeric variable, but the two we prefer and discuss in this subsection are **histograms** and **box plots** (also called **box-whisker plots**). Each of these is useful primarily for cross-sectional variables. If they are used for time series variables, the time dimension is lost. Therefore, we discuss **time series graphs** for time series variables separately in the next section.

---

1 The popular book *The Black Swan*, by Nassim Nicholas Taleb, is all about extreme events and the trouble they can cause.

Histograms

A histogram is the most common type of chart for showing the distribution of a numeric variable. It is based on binning the variable—that is, dividing it up into discrete categories. The histogram is then a column chart of the counts in the various categories, usually with no gaps between the vertical bars. In general, a histogram is useful for showing the shape of a distribution. Of particular interest is whether the distribution is symmetric or skewed.

Fundamental Insight

Histograms Versus Summary Measures

It is important to remember that each of the summary measures we have discussed for a numeric variable—mean, median, standard deviation, and others—describes only one aspect of a numeric variable. In contrast, a histogram provides the complete picture. It indicates the "center" of the distribution, the variability, the skewness, and other aspects, all in one chart.

The steps for creating a histogram are straightforward:

1. Decide how many bins to use and what the endpoints of the bins should be. For example, with exam scores between 51 and 100, you might choose 10 bins: 51 to 55, 56 to 60, 61 to 65, and so on.
2. Count the number of observations in each bin. There are Excel functions for doing this, including COUNTIFS and FREQUENCY. (We prefer COUNTIFS. The FREQUENCY function is an array function and is tricky to use.)
3. Create a column chart of these counts and remove the gaps between the bars.

The steps are fairly easy, but the whole process is tedious, and it is easy to make mistakes. Therefore, numerous tools have been developed for creating histograms quickly and easily. For Excel users, these include the following:

1. Microsoft added histograms to its list of chart types in Excel 2016. (It was recently added to the latest version of Excel for the Mac as well.) You can find this in the Statistics Chart group (the icon looks like a mini-histogram) on the Insert ribbon. Just select any cell in the data column, click the Histogram button in this group, and you get an automatic histogram.
2. The Analysis ToolPak add-in includes a histogram tool. Just be warned that its results are not very pretty.

Each of these requires a choice of bins: how many and which endpoints. Fortunately, researchers have devised good rules of thumb for bin selection, so that you don't have to worry about the details. For example, Excel's built-in histogram chooses the bins automatically, but then you can right-click the horizontal axis and choose Format Axis to modify the bins, at least to some extent. Fortunately, the bin selection is usually not crucial. The real purpose of a histogram is show the shape of the distribution of data values, and the same basic shape emerges with any reasonable set of bins.

Figure 2.13 shows a histogram of the 2018 baseball salaries. It was created with Excel's fairly new histogram chart type. (To create it, select any cell in the Salary column and then click the histogram chart type on the Insert ribbon.) The bins are selected automatically, but this makes little difference for the salary data. You can see exactly what you need to see: The baseball salaries are heavily skewed to the right. Nevertheless, if you right-click the horizontal axis and choose Format Axis, the pane in Figure 2.14 opens. This allows you to change the bins, at least to some extent.

Figure 2.13 Histogram of 2018 Baseball Salaries

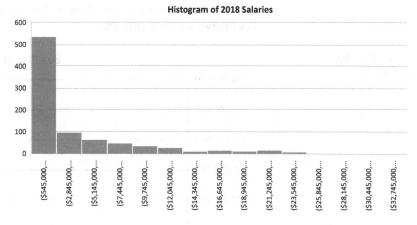

Figure 2.14 Options for Changing Bins

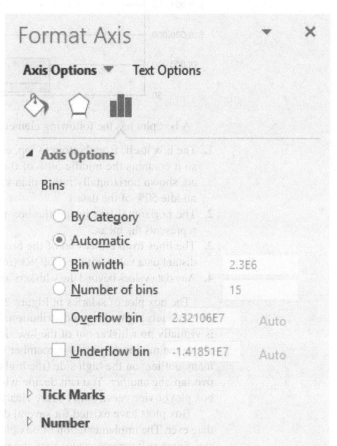

Box Plots

A **box plot** (also called a **box-whisker plot**) is an alternative type of chart for showing the distribution of a variable. For the distribution of a single variable, a box plot is not nearly as popular as a histogram, but as you will see in the next chapter, side-by-side box plots are very useful for *comparing* distributions, such as salaries for men versus salaries for women. As with histograms, box plots are "big picture" charts. They show you at a glance some of the key features of a distribution.

Like histograms, box plots were added to Excel in Excel 2016, and they are now available in Excel for Windows and Excel for Mac. They are in the same chart group as histograms on the Insert ribbon. The box plot of 2018 baseball salaries appears in Figure 2.15. To create it, select the entire Salary column before clicking the box plot option on the Insert ribbon. (If you select only a single cell, you will get box plots broken down by Position, the type illustrated in the next chapter.) You can also delete the horizontal axis label. The label shown has no significance.

Figure 2.15 Box Plot of Baseball Salaries

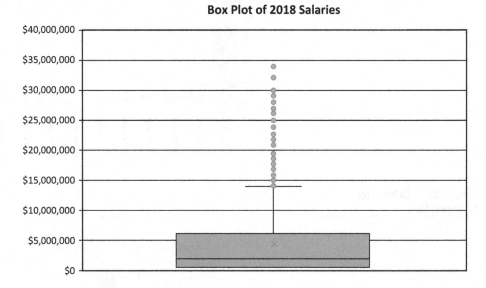

A box plot has the following elements:

1. The box itself, from bottom to top, extends from the first quartile to the third quartile, so it contains the middle 50% of the data. (Box plots from some software packages are shown horizontally rather than vertically. Then the *width* of the box indicates the middle 50% of the data.)
2. The horizontal line inside the box represents the median, and the x inside the box represents the mean.
3. The lines from either end of the box, also called whiskers, extend as far as the most distant data value within 1.5 IQRs (interquartile ranges) of the box.
4. Any data values beyond the whiskers are called outliers and are shown as individual points.

The box plot of salaries in Figure 2.15 should now make more sense. It is typical of an extremely right-skewed distribution. The mean is much larger than the median, there is virtually no whisker out of the low side of the box (because the first quartile is barely above the minimum value—remember all the players earning $545,000?), and there are many outliers on the high side (the highest paid players). In fact, many of these outliers overlap one another. You can decide whether you prefer the histogram of salaries to the box plot or vice versa, but both are clearly telling the same story.

Box plots have existed for several decades, and they are probably more popular now than ever. The implementation of box plots in Excel is just one version of what you might see. Some software packages vary the width of the box to indicate some other feature of the distribution. (The width of the box is irrelevant in Excel's box plots.) Nevertheless, they all follow the same basic rules and provide the same basic information.

Fundamental Insight

Box Plots Versus Histograms

Box plots and histograms are complementary ways of displaying the distribution of a numeric variable. Although histograms are much more popular and are argu-ably more intuitive, box plots are still very informative. Besides, side-by-side box plots are very useful for comparing two or more populations, as illustrated in the next chapter.

Problems

Solutions for problems whose numbers appear within a colored box can be found in the Student Solution Files.

Level A

6. The file **P02_06.xlsx** lists the average time (in minutes) it takes citizens of 379 metropolitan areas to travel to work and back home each day.
   a. Create a histogram of the daily commute times.
   b. Find the most representative average daily commute time across this distribution.
   c. Find a useful measure of the variability of these average commute times around the mean.
   d. The empirical rule for standard deviations indicates that approximately 95% of these average travel times will fall between which two values? For this particular data set, is this empirical rule at least approximately correct?

7. The file **P02_07.xlsx** includes data on 204 employees at the (fictional) company Beta Technologies.
   a. Indicate the data type for each of the six variables included in this data set.
   b. Create a histogram of the Age variable. How would you characterize the age distribution for these employees?
   c. What proportion of these full-time Beta employees are female?
   d. Find appropriate summary measures for each of the numeric variables in this data set.
   e. For the Salary variable, explain why the empirical rules for standard deviations do or do not apply.

8. The file **P02_08.xlsx** contains data on 500 shipments of one of the computer components that a company manufactures. Specifically, the proportion of items that are defective is listed for each shipment.
   a. Create a histogram that will help a production manager understand the variation of the proportion of defective components in the company's shipments.
   b. Is the mean or median the most appropriate measure of central location for this data set? Why?
   c. Do the empirical rules for standard deviations apply? Can you tell, or at least make an educated guess, by looking at the shape of the histogram? Why?

9. The file **P02_09.xlsx** lists the times required to service 200 consecutive customers at a (fictional) fast-food restaurant.
   a. Create a histogram of the customer service times. How would you characterize the distribution of service times?
   b. Calculate the mean, median, and first and third quartiles of this distribution.
   c. Which measure of central tendency, the mean or the median, is more appropriate in describing this distribution? Explain your reasoning.
   d. Find and interpret the variance and standard deviation of these service times.

   e. Are the empirical rules for standard deviations applicable for these service times? If not, explain why. Can you tell whether they apply, or at least make an educated guess, by looking at the shape of the histogram? Why?

10. The file **P02_10.xlsx** contains midterm and final exam scores for 96 students in a corporate finance course.
    a. Create a histogram for each of the two sets of exam scores.
    b. What are the mean and median scores on each of these exams?
    c. Explain why the mean and median values are different for these data.
    d. Based on your previous answers, how would you characterize this group's performance on the midterm and on the final exam?
    e. Create a new column of differences (final exam score minus midterm score). A positive value means the student improved, and a negative value means the student did the opposite. What are the mean and median of the differences? What does a histogram of the differences indicate?

11. The file **P02_11.xlsx** contains data on 148 houses that were recently sold in a (fictional) suburban community. The data set includes the selling price of each house, along with its appraised value, square footage, number of bedrooms, and number of bathrooms.
    a. Which of these variables are continuous? Which are discrete?
    b. Create histograms for the appraised values and selling prices of the houses. How are these two distributions similar? How are they different?
    c. Find the maximum and minimum sizes (measured in square footage) of all sample houses.
    d. Find the house(s) at the 80th percentile of all sample houses with respect to appraised value. Find the house(s) at the 80th percentile of all sample houses with respect to selling price.
    e. What are the typical number of bedrooms and the typical number of bathrooms in this set of houses? How do you interpret the word "typical"?

12. The file **P02_12.xlsx** includes data on the 50 top graduate programs in the United States, according to a 2009 *U.S. News & World Report* survey.
    a. Indicate the type of data for each of the 10 variables considered in the formulation of the overall ranking.
    b. Create a histogram for each of the numeric variables in this data set. Indicate whether each of these distributions is approximately symmetric or skewed. Which, if any, of these distributions are skewed to the right? Which, if any, are skewed to the left?
    c. Identify the schools with the largest and smallest annual out-of-state tuition and fee levels.
    d. Find the annual out-of-state tuition and fee levels at each of the 25th, 50th, and 75th percentiles for these schools.

e. (Requires Excel version 2016 or later) Create a box plot to characterize this distribution of these MBA salaries. Is this distribution essentially symmetric or skewed? If there are any outliers on either end, which schools do they correspond to?

13. The file **P02_13.xlsx** contains the thickness (in centimeters) of 252 mica pieces. A piece meets specifications if its thickness is between 7 and 15 centimeters.
   a. What fraction of mica pieces meets specifications?
   b. Are the empirical rules for standard deviations at least approximately valid for these data? Can you tell, or at least make an educated guess, by looking at a histogram of the data?
   c. If the histogram of the data is approximately bell-shaped and you want about 95% of the observations to meet specifications, is it sufficient for the average and standard deviation to be, at least approximately, 11 and 2 centimeters, respectively?

14. (Requires Excel version 2016 or later) Recall that the file **Supermarket Transactions.xlsx** contains over 14,000 transactions made by super-market customers over a period of approximately two years. Using these data, create side-by-side box plots for revenues broken down by state or province. Are these distributions essentially symmetric or skewed? Note that these box plots include revenues from countries besides the United States. Do whatever it takes to create side-by-side box plots of revenue for only states within the United States.

15. (Requires Excel version 2016 or later) Recall that the file **Baseball Salaries.xlsx** contains data on 877 MLB players in the 2018 season. Using these data, create side-by-side box plots to characterize the distribution of salaries of all pitchers versus all non-pitchers. Summarize your findings.

16. The file **P02_16.xlsx** contains traffic data from 256 weekdays on four variables. Each variable lists the number of vehicle arrivals to a tollbooth during a specific five-minute period of the day.
   a. Create a histogram of each variable. How would you characterize and compare these distributions?
   b. Find a table of summary measures for these variables that includes (at least) the means, medians, standard

deviations, first and third quartiles, and 5th and 95th percentiles. Use these to compare the arrival process at the different times of day.

Level B

17. The file **P02_17.xlsx** contains salaries of 200 recent graduates from a (fictional) MBA program.
   a. What salary level is most indicative of those earned by students graduating from this MBA program this year?
   b. Do the empirical rules for standard deviations apply to these data? Can you tell, or at least make an educated guess, by looking at the shape of the histogram? Why?
   c. If the empirical rules apply here, between which two numbers can you be about 68% sure that the salary of any one of these 200 students will fall?
   d. If the MBA program wants to make a statement such as "Some of our recent graduates started out making X dollars or more, and almost all of them started out making at least Y dollars" for their promotional materials, what values of X and Y would you suggest they use? Defend your choice.
   e. As an admissions officer of this MBA program, how would you proceed to use these findings to market the program to prospective students?

18. The file **P02_18.xlsx** contains daily values of the Standard & Poor's 500 Index for a five-year period. It also contains percentage changes in the index from each day to the next.
   a. Create a histogram of the percentage changes and describe its shape.
   b. Check the percentage of these percentage changes that are more than k standard deviations from the mean for $k = 1, 2, 3, 4,$ and 5. Are these approximately what the empirical rules indicate or are there "fat" tails? Do you think this has any real implications for the financial markets? (Note that we have discussed the empirical rules only for $k = 1, 2,$ and 3. For $k = 4$ and 5, they indicate that only 0.006% and 0.0001% of the observations should be this distant from the mean.)

2-5 Time Series Data

When we analyze time series variables, summary measures such as means and standard deviations and charts such as histograms and box plots are often inappropriate. Our main interest in time series variables is how they change over time, and this information is lost in traditional summary measures, histograms, and box plots. Imagine, for example, that you are interested in daily closing prices of a stock that has historically been between 20 and 60. If you create a histogram with a bin such as 45 to 50, you will get a count of all daily closing prices in this interval—but you won't know when they occurred. The histogram is missing a key feature: time. Similarly, if you report the *mean* of a time series such as the monthly Dow Jones average over the past 40 years, you will get a measure that is not relevant for the current and future values of the Dow.

Therefore, we turn to a different but very intuitive type of graph called a **time series graph**. This is a graph of the values of one or more time series, using time on the horizontal axis, and it is always the place to start a time series analysis. We illustrate some possibilities in the following example.

EXAMPLE

2.4 CRIME IN THE UNITED STATES

The file **Crime in US.xlsx** contains annual data on violent and property crimes for the years 1960 to 2010. Part of the data is listed in Figure 2.16. This shows the number of crimes. The rates per 100,000 population are not shown, but they can be calculated easily. Are there any apparent trends in this data? If so, are the trends the same for the different types of crime?

Figure 2.16 Crime Data

	A	B	C	D	E	F	G	H	I	J	K
1	Year	Population	Violent crime total	Murder and nonnegligent manslaughter	Forcible rape	Robbery	Aggravated assault	Property crime total	Burglary	Larceny-theft	Motor vehicle theft
2	1960	179,323,175	288,460	9,110	17,190	107,840	154,320	3,095,700	912,100	1,855,400	328,200
3	1961	182,992,000	289,390	8,740	17,220	106,670	156,760	3,198,600	949,600	1,913,000	336,000
4	1962	185,771,000	301,510	8,530	17,550	110,860	164,570	3,450,700	994,300	2,089,600	366,800
5	1963	188,483,000	316,970	8,640	17,650	116,470	174,210	3,792,500	1,086,400	2,297,800	408,300
6	1964	191,141,000	364,220	9,360	21,420	130,390	203,050	4,200,400	1,213,200	2,514,400	472,800
7	1965	193,526,000	387,390	9,960	23,410	138,690	215,330	4,352,000	1,282,500	2,572,600	496,900
8	1966	195,576,000	430,180	11,040	25,820	157,990	235,330	4,793,300	1,410,100	2,822,000	561,200
9	1967	197,457,000	499,930	12,240	27,620	202,910	257,160	5,403,500	1,632,100	3,111,600	659,800
10	1968	199,399,000	595,010	13,800	31,670	262,840	286,700	6,125,200	1,858,900	3,482,700	783,600

Excel Tip

Formatting Long Variable Names

Note the format of the variable names in row 1. If you have long variable names, one possibility is to align them vertically and check the Wrap Text option. (These are both available through the Format Cells command, which can be accessed by right-clicking any cell or pressing Ctrl+1.) With these changes, the row 1 labels are neither too tall nor too wide.

Objective

To see how time series graphs help to detect trends in crime data.

Solution

It is easy to create a time series graph in Excel. Here are the steps:

1. Select one or more columns with time series data.
2. Optionally, select a column with dates if there is one. These dates are used to label the horizontal axis.
3. Select one of the line chart types, such as the line chart with markers, from the Insert ribbon.

This procedure will usually get you nearly what you want, and then you can modify the chart to suit your needs, such as adding a title.

Excel Tip

Date variable

When you proceed as above, the date variable is sometimes treated as another time series variable, with a line of its own. The happens, for example, in the crime data set with the Year variable. It looks numeric, so Excel treats it as another time series variable. In this case, select the chart, click Select Data on the Chart Tools Design ribbon, delete the date series in the left pane, and edit the right pane, selecting the date variable range for the horizontal axis.

Excel Tip

Secondary axis

If you select two time series variables with very different magnitudes, the smaller will get swamped by the larger in the time series graph. In this case, right-click the smaller series, select Format Data Series, and check Secondary Axis. This allows you to see the smaller series on a separate scale.

These steps were used to create the time series graphs in Figures 2.17, 2.18, and 2.19. The graph in Figure 2.17 shows that violent and property crimes both increased sharply until the early 1990s and have gradually decreased since then. However, the time series population series in Figure 2.18 indicates that the U.S. population has increased steadily since 1960, so it is possible that the trend in crime *rates* is different than the trends in Figure 2.17. This is indeed true, as seen in Figure 2.19. It shows the good news that the crime rate has been falling since its peak in the early 1990s.[2]

The whole purpose of time series graphs is to detect historical patterns in the data. In this crime example, you are looking for broad trends.

Figure 2.17 Total Violent and Property Crimes

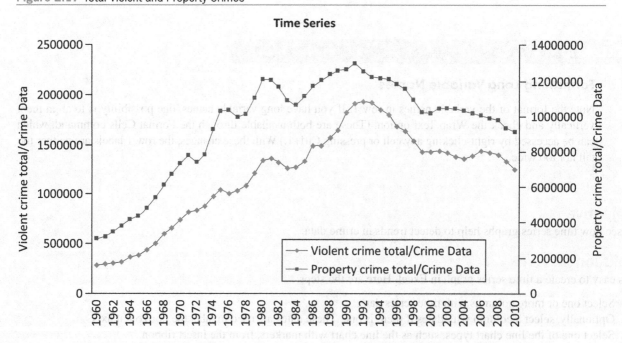

[2] Why did this occur? One compelling reason was suggested by Levitt and Dubner in their popular book *Freakonomics*. You can read their somewhat controversial analysis to see if you agree.

Figure 2.18 Population Totals

Figure 2.19 Violent and Property Crime Rates

We also created two more time series graphs that appear in Figures 2.20 and 2.21. The first shows the crime rates for the various types of violent crimes, and the second does the same for property crimes. The patterns (up, then down) are similar for each type of crime, but they are certainly not identical. For example, the larceny-theft and motor vehicle theft rates both peaked in the early 1990s, but the burglary rate was well in decline by this time. Finally, Figure 2.20 indicates one problem with having multiple time series variables on a single graph—any variable with small values can be dominated by variables with much larger values. It might be a good idea to create two separate graphs for these four variables, with murder and rape on one and robbery and aggravated assault on the other. Then you could see the murder and rape patterns more clearly, and each of the graphs would be less cluttered.

Figure 2.20 Rates of Violent Crime Types

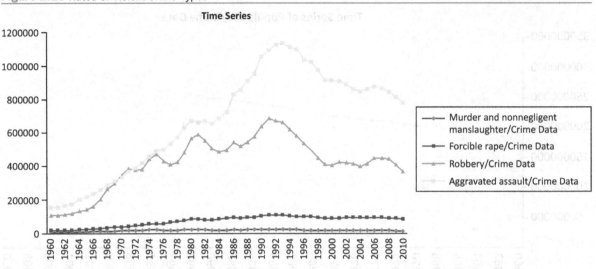

Figure 2.21 Rates of Property Crime Types

Excel Tool

Sparklines

One feature introduced in Excel 2010 is the *sparkline*. This is a mini-chart embedded in a cell. Although it applies to any kind of data, it is especially useful for time series data. Try the following. Open a file, such as the problem file P03_30.xlsx, that has multiple time series—one per column. Highlight the cell below the last time series value of the first time series and click the Line button in the Sparklines group on the Insert ribbon. In the resulting dialog box, select the data in the first time series. You will get a mini-time-series graph in the cell. Now copy this cell across for the other time series, and increase the row height to expand the graphs. Change any of the time series values to see how the sparklines change automatically. We suspect that these instant sparkline graphs are becoming quite popular.

As mentioned earlier, traditional summary measures such as means, medians, and standard deviations are often not very meaningful for time series data, at least not for the original data. However, it is often useful to find differences or percentage changes in the data from period to period and then report traditional summary measures of these. The following example illustrates these ideas.

EXAMPLE

2.5 THE DOW JONES INDEX

The Dow Jones Industrial Average (DJIA or simply "the Dow") is an index of 30 large publicly traded U.S. stocks and is one of the most quoted stock indexes. The file **DJIA Monthly Close.xlsx** contains monthly values of the Dow from 1950 through early 2018. What is a useful way to summarize the data in this file?

Objective

To find useful ways to summarize the monthly Dow data.

Solution

A time series graph and a few summary measures of the Dow appear in Figure 2.22. The graph clearly shows a gradual increase through the early 1990s (except for Black Monday in 1987), a sharp increase through the rest of the 1990s, some huge swings through 2008, and a sharp increase since then. The mean (4781), the median (1210), and any of the other traditional summary measures are of historical interest at best.

Figure 2.22 Summary Measures and Graph of the Dow

In situations like this, it is useful to look at percentage changes in the Dow. These have been calculated in the file and have been used to create the summary measures and time series graph in Figure 2.23. The graph shows that these percentage changes have fluctuated around zero, sometimes with wild swings (like Black Monday). Actually, the mean and median of the percentage changes are slightly positive, about 0.67% and 0.85%, respectively. In addition, the quartiles show that 25% of the changes have been less than −1.61% and 25% have been greater than 3.22%. Finally, the empirical rules indicate, for example, that about 95% of the percentage changes over this period should be no more than two standard deviations (8.18%) from the mean. You can check that the actual percentage within two standard deviations of the mean is close to 95%, so this empirical rule applies very well.[3]

---

3 One of the problems asks you to check whether all three of the empirical rules apply to similar stock price data. The extreme tails are where there are some surprises.

Figure 2.23 Summary Measures and Graph of Percentage Changes of the Dow

Summary measures	
Mean	0.67%
Std. Dev.	4.09%
Median	0.85%
Quartile 1	−1.61%
Quartile 3	3.22%

Problems

Solutions for problems whose numbers appear within a colored box can be found in the Student Solution Files.

Level A

19. The file **P02_19.xlsx** lists annual percentage changes in the Consumer Price Index (CPI) from 1914 through 2017. Find and interpret the first and third quartiles and the interquartile range for these annual percentage changes. Discuss whether these are meaningful summary measures for this time series data set. Suppose that the data set listed the actual CPI values, not percentage changes, for each year. Would the quartiles and interquartile range be meaningful in this case? Why or why not?

20. The Consumer Confidence Index (CCI) attempts to measure people's feelings about general business conditions, employment opportunities, and their own income prospects. Monthly average values of the CCI are listed in the file **P02_20.xlsx**.
   a. Create a time series graph of the CCI values.
   b. Have U.S. consumers become more or less confident through time?
   c. How would you explain recent variations in the overall trend of the CCI?

21. The file **P02_21.xlsx** contains monthly interest rates on 30-year and 15-year fixed-rate mortgages in the United States from 1991 to 2017. What conclusion(s) can you draw from a time series graph of these mortgage rates? Specifically, what has been happening to mortgage rates in general, and how does the behavior of the 30-year rates compare to the behavior of the 15-year rates?

22. The file **P02_22.xlsx** contains annual trade balances (exports minus imports) from 1980 to 2017.
   a. Create a times series graph for each of the three time series in this file.

   b. Characterize recent trends in the U.S. balance of trade figures using your time series graphs.

23. What has happened to the total number and average size of farms in the U.S. since the middle of the 20th century? Answer this question by creating a time series graph of the data from the U.S. Department of Agriculture in the file **P02_23.xlsx**. Is the observed result consistent with your knowledge of the structural changes within the U.S. farming economy?

24. Is educational attainment in the United States on the rise? Explore this question by creating time series graphs for each of the variables in the file **P02_24.xlsx**. Comment on any observed trends in the annual educational attainment of the general U.S. population over the given period.

25. The monthly averages of the federal funds rate and the bank prime loan rate are listed in the file **P02_25.xlsx**.
   a. Describe the time series behavior of these two variables. Can you discern any cyclical or other patterns in the times series graphs of these key interest rates?
   b. Discuss whether it would make much sense, especially to a person at the present time, to quote traditional summary measures such as means or percentiles of these series.

Level B

26. In which months of the calendar year do U.S. gasoline service stations typically have their *lowest* retail sales levels? In which months of the calendar year do the service stations typically have their *highest* retail sales levels? Create time series graphs for the monthly data in the file **P02_26. xlsx** to respond to these two questions. There are really two series, one of actual values and one of seasonally adjusted values. The latter adjusts for any possible seasonality, such as higher values in June and lower values in January, so that any trends are more apparent.

27. The file **P02_27.xlsx** contains monthly data for total U.S. electronic and appliance store sales. There are really two series, one of actual values and one of seasonally adjusted values. The latter adjusts for any possible seasonality, such as higher values in June and lower values in January, so that any trends are more apparent.
  a. Is there an observable trend in these data? That is, do the values of the series tend to increase or decrease over time?
  b. Is there a seasonal pattern in these data? If so, what is the seasonal pattern?
28. The file **P02_28.xlsx** contains total monthly U.S. retail sales data for a number of years. There are really two series, one of actual sales and one of seasonally adjusted sales. The latter adjusts for any possible seasonality, such as higher sales in December and lower sales in February, so that any trends are more apparent.
  a. Create a graph of both time series and comment on any observable trends, including a possible seasonal pattern, in the data. Does seasonal adjustment make a difference? How?
  b. Based on your time series graph of actual sales, make a qualitative projection about the total retail sales levels for the next 12 months. Specifically, in which months of the subsequent year do you expect retail sales levels to be *highest?* In which months of the subsequent year do you expect retail sales levels to be *lowest?*

2-6 Outliers and Missing Values

Most textbooks on data analysis, including this one, tend to use example data sets that are "cleaned up." Unfortunately, the data sets you are likely to encounter in your job are often not so clean. Two particular problems you will encounter are outliers and missing data, the topics of this section. There are no easy answers for dealing with these problems, but you should at least be aware of the issues.

Outliers

An **outlier** is literally a value or an entire observation (row) that lies well outside of the norm. For the baseball data, Mike Trout's salary of $34 million is definitely an outlier. This is indeed his correct salary—the number wasn't entered incorrectly—but it is way beyond what most players make. Actually, statisticians disagree on an exact definition of an outlier. Going by the third empirical rule, you might define an outlier as any value more than three standard deviations from the mean, but this is only a rule of thumb. Let's just agree to define outliers as *extreme* values, and then for any particular data set, you can decide how extreme a value needs to be to qualify as an outlier.

Sometimes an outlier is easy to detect and deal with. For example, this is often the case with data entry errors. Suppose a data set includes a Height variable, a person's height measured in inches, and you see a value of 720. This is certainly an outlier—and it is certainly an error. Once you spot it, you can go back and check this observation to see what the person's height should be. Maybe an extra 0 was accidentally appended and the true value is 72. In any case, this type of outlier is usually easy to discover and fix.

Sometimes a careful check of the variable values, one variable at a time, will not reveal any outliers, but there still might be unusual *combinations* of values. For example, it would be strange to find a person with Age equal to 10 and Height equal to 72. Neither of these values is unusual by itself, but the combination is certainly unusual. Again, this would probably be a result of a data entry error, but it would be harder to spot. (The scatterplots discussed in the next chapter are useful for spotting unusual combinations.)

It isn't always easy to detect outliers, but an even more important issue is what to do about them when they are detected. Of course, if they are due to data entry errors, they can be fixed, but what if they are legitimate values like Mike Trout's salary? One or a few wild outliers like this one can dominate a statistical analysis. For example, they can make a mean or standard deviation much different than if the outliers were not present.

For this reason, some people argue, possibly naïvely, that outliers should be eliminated before running statistical analyses. However, it is *not* appropriate to eliminate outliers simply to produce "nicer" results. There has to be a legitimate reason for eliminating outliers, and such a reason sometimes exists. For example, suppose you want to analyze salaries of "typical" managers at your company. Then it is probably appropriate to eliminate the CEO and possibly other high-ranking executives from the analysis, arguing that they aren't really part of the population of interest and would just skew the results. Or if you are interested in the selling prices of "typical" homes in your community, it is probably appropriate to eliminate the few homes that sell for over $2 million, again arguing that these are not the types of homes you are interested in.

Probably the best advice for dealing with outliers is to run the analyses two ways: with the outliers and without them. This way, you can report the results both ways—and you are being honest.

One good way of dealing with outliers is to report results with the outliers and without them.

Missing Values

There are no missing data in the baseball salary data set. All 877 observations have a value for each of the four variables. For real data sets, however, this is probably the exception rather than the rule. Unfortunately, most real data sets have missing values in the data. This could be because a person didn't want to provide all the requested personal information (what business is it of yours how old I am or how much alcohol I drink?), it could be because data doesn't exist (stock prices in the 1990s for companies that went public after 2000), or it could be because some values are simply unknown. Whatever the reason, you will undoubtedly encounter data sets with varying degrees of missing values.

As with outliers, there are two issues: how to detect missing values and what to do about them. The first issue isn't as simple as you might imagine. For an Excel data set, you might expect missing data to be obvious from blank cells. This is certainly one possibility, but there are others. Missing data are coded in a variety of strange ways. One common method is to code missing values with an unusual number such as −9999 or 9999. Another method is to code missing values with a symbol such as − or *. If you know the code (and it is often supplied in a footnote), then it is usually a good idea, at least in Excel, to perform a global search and replace, replacing all of the missing value codes with blanks.

The more important issue is what to do about missing values. One option is to ignore them. Then you will have to be aware of how the software deals with missing values. For example, if you use Excel's AVERAGE function on a column of data with missing values, it reacts the way you would hope and expect—it adds all the nonmissing values and divides by the number of nonmissing values. Most statistical software reacts this same way.

Because this is such an important topic in real-world data analysis, researchers have studied many ways of filling in the gaps so that the missing data problem goes away (or is at least disguised). One possibility is to fill in all of the missing values in a column with the average of the nonmissing values in that column. Indeed, this is an option in some software packages, but it is often not a very good option. (Is there any reason to believe that missing values would be *average* values if they were known? Probably not.) Another possibility is to examine the nonmissing values in the *row* of any missing value. It is possible that they provide some clues on what the missing value should be. For example, if a person is male, is 55 years old, has an MBA degree from Harvard, and has been a manager at an oil company for 25 years, this should probably help to predict his missing salary. (It probably isn't below $100,000.) We will not discuss this issue any further here because it is quite complex, and there are no easy answers. But be aware that you will undoubtedly have to deal with missing data at some point in your job, either by ignoring the missing values or by filling in the gaps in some way.

Problems

Solutions for problems whose numbers appear within a colored box can be found in the Student Solution Files.

Level A

29. The file **P02_29.xlsx** contains monthly percentages of on-time arrivals at several of the largest U.S. airports and all of the major airlines from 1988 to 2008. The "By Airline" sheet contains a lot of missing data, presumably because some of the airlines were not in existence in 1988 and some went out of business before 2008. The "By Airport" sheet contains missing data only for Atlantic City International Airport (and we're not sure why).

a. Calculate summary measures (means, medians, standard deviations, and any other measures you would like to report) for each airline and each airport. How do these deal with missing data?

b. Create histograms for a few of the airports and a few of the airlines, including Atlantic City International. How do these deal with missing data?

c. Create time series graphs for a few of the airports and a few of the airlines, including Atlantic City International. How do these deal with missing data?

d. Which airports and which airlines have done a good job? Which would you like to avoid?

30. (Requires Excel 2016 or later.) *The Wall Street Journal CEO Compensation Study* analyzed CEO pay for many U.S. companies with fiscal year 2008 revenue of at least $5 billion that filed their proxy statements between October 2008 and March 2009. The data are in the file **P02_30.xlsx**.

a. Create a new variable that is the sum of salary and bonus, and create a box plot of this new variable.

b. As the box plot key indicates, mild outliers are observations between 1.5 IQR (interquartile range) and 3.0 IQR from the edge of the box, whereas extreme outliers are greater than 3 IQR from the edge of the box. Use these definitions to identify the names of all CEOs who are mild outliers and all those who are extreme outliers.

Level B

31. There is no consistent way of defining an outlier that everyone agrees upon. For example, some people refer to an outlier that is any observation more than three standard deviations from the mean. Other people use the box plot definition, where an outlier (moderate or extreme) is any observation more than 1.5 IQR from the edges of the box, and some people care only about the *extreme* box plot-type outliers, those that are 3.0 IQR from the edges of the box. The file **P02_18.xlsx** contains daily percentage changes in the S&P 500 index over several years. Identify outliers—days when the percentage change was unusually large in either a negative or positive direction—according to each of these three definitions. Which definition produces the most outliers?

32. Sometimes it is possible that missing data are predictive in the sense that rows with missing data are somehow different from rows without missing data. Check this with the file **P02_32.xlsx**, which contains blood pressures for 1000 (fictional) people, along with variables that can be related to blood pressure. These other variables have a number of missing values, presumably because the people didn't want to report certain information.

a. For each of these other variables, find the mean and standard deviation of blood pressure for all people without missing values and for all people with missing values. Can you conclude that the presence or absence of data for any of these other variables has anything to do with blood pressure?

b. Some analysts suggest filling in missing data for a variable with the *mean* of the nonmissing values for that variable. Do this for the missing data in the blood pressure data. In general, do you think this is a valid way of filling in missing data? Why or why not?

2-7 Excel Tables for Filtering, Sorting, and Summarizing

This section discusses a great tool that was introduced in Excel 2007: tables. It is useful to begin with some terminology and history. Earlier in this chapter, we discussed data arranged in a rectangular range of rows and columns, where each row is an observation and each column is a variable, with variable names at the top of each column. In pre-2007 versions of Excel, data sets of this form were called *lists*, and Excel provided several tools for dealing with lists. In Excel 2007, recognizing the importance of data sets, Microsoft made them much more prominent and provided better tools for analyzing them. Specifically, you now have the ability to designate a rectangular data set as a table and then employ a number of powerful tools for analyzing their data. These tools include filtering, sorting, and summarizing. We illustrate Excel tables in the following example.

EXAMPLE

2.6 HYTEX'S CUSTOMER DATA

The file **Catalog Marketing.xlsx** contains data on 1000 customers of HyTex, a (fictional) direct marketing company, for the current year. A sample of the data appears in Figure 2.24. The definitions of the variables are fairly straightforward, but details about several of them are listed in cell comments in row 1. HyTex wants to find some useful and quick information about its customers by using an Excel table. How can it proceed?

Figure 2.24 HyTex Customer Data

	A	B	C	D	E	F	G	H	I	J	K	L	M	N	O
1	Person	Age	Gender	Own Home	Married	Close	Salary	Children	History	Catalogs	Region	State	City	First Purchase	Amount Spent
2	1	1	0	0	0	1	$16,400	1	1	12	South	Florida	Orlando	10/23/2011	$218
3	2	2	0	1	1	0	$108,100	3	3	18	Midwest	Illinois	Chicago	5/25/2009	$2,632
4	3	2	1	1	1	1	$97,300	1	NA	12	South	Florida	Orlando	8/18/2015	$3,048
5	4	3	1	1	1	1	$26,800	0	1	12	East	Ohio	Cleveland	12/26/2012	$435
6	5	1	1	0	0	1	$11,200	0	NA	6	Midwest	Illinois	Chicago	8/4/2015	$106
7	6	2	0	0	0	1	$42,800	0	2	12	West	Arizona	Phoenix	3/4/2013	$759
8	7	2	0	0	0	1	$34,700	0	NA	18	Midwest	Kansas	Kansas City	6/11/2015	$1,615
9	8	3	0	1	1	0	$80,000	0	3	6	West	California	San Francisco	8/17/2009	$1,985
10	9	2	1	1	0	1	$60,300	0	NA	24	Midwest	Illinois	Chicago	5/29/2015	$2,091
11	10	3	1	1	1	0	$62,300	0	3	24	South	Florida	Orlando	6/9/2011	$2,644

Objective

To illustrate Excel tables for analyzing the HyTex data.

Solution

The range A1:O1001 is in the form of a data set—it is a rectangular range bounded by blank rows and columns, where each row is an observation, each column is a variable, and variable names appear in the top row. Therefore, it is a candidate for an Excel table. However, it doesn't benefit from Excel's table tools until you actually *designate* it as a table. To do so, select *any* cell in the data set, click the Table button in the left part of the Insert ribbon, and accept the default options. Or as a quicker alternative, use the Ctrl+t key combination. In either case, two things happen. First, the data set is designated as a table, it is formatted nicely, and a dropdown arrow appears next to each variable name, as shown in Figure 2.25. Second, a new Table Tools Design ribbon becomes available (see Figure 2.26). This ribbon is available any time the active cell is inside a table. Note that the table has a generic name like Table1 by default, but you can change this to a more descriptive name if you like.

You can also designate a table by selecting any option on the Format as Table dropdown on the Home ribbon. A third alternative is even easier: select any cell in the data set and press Ctrl + t.

Figure 2.25 Table with Dropdown Arrows Next to Variable Names

	A	B	C	D	E	F	G	H	I	J	K	L	M	N	O
1	Person	Age	Gender	Own Home	Married	Close	Salary	Children	History	Catalogs	Region	State	City	First Purchase	Amount Spent
2	1	1	0	0	0	1	$16,400	1	1	12	South	Florida	Orlando	10/23/2011	$218
3	2	2	0	1	1	0	$108,100	3	3	18	Midwest	Illinois	Chicago	5/25/2009	$2,632
4	3	2	1	1	1	1	$97,300	1	NA	12	South	Florida	Orlando	8/18/2015	$3,048
5	4	3	1	1	1	1	$26,800	0	1	12	East	Ohio	Cleveland	12/26/2012	$435
6	5	1	1	0	0	1	$11,200	0	NA	6	Midwest	Illinois	Chicago	8/4/2015	$106
7	6	2	0	0	0	1	$42,800	0	2	12	West	Arizona	Phoenix	3/4/2013	$759
8	7	2	0	0	0	1	$34,700	0	NA	18	Midwest	Kansas	Kansas City	6/11/2015	$1,615
9	8	3	0	1	1	0	$80,000	0	3	6	West	California	San Francisco	8/17/2009	$1,985
10	9	2	1	1	0	1	$60,300	0	NA	24	Midwest	Illinois	Chicago	5/29/2015	$2,091
11	10	3	1	1	1	0	$62,300	0	3	24	South	Florida	Orlando	6/9/2011	$2,644

Figure 2.26 Table Tools Design Ribbon

One handy feature of Excel tables is that the variable names remain visible even when you scroll down the screen. Try it to see how it works. When you scroll down far enough that the variable names would disappear, the column headers, A, B, C, etc., change to the variable names. Therefore, you no longer need to freeze panes or split the screen to see the variable names. However, this works only when the active cell is within the table. If you click outside the table, the column headers revert back to A, B, C, etc.

The dropdown arrows next to the variable names allow you to filter in many different ways. For example, click the Own Home dropdown list, uncheck Select All, and check the 1 box. This filters out all customers except those who own their own home. Filtering is discussed in more detail later on, but at this point, just be aware that filtering does not *delete* any observations; it only hides them. There are three indications that the table has been filtered: (1) the row numbers are colored blue and some are missing; (2) a message appears at the bottom of the screen indicating that only 516 out of 1000 records are visible; and (3) there is a filter icon next to the Own Home dropdown arrow. It is easy to remove this filter by opening the Own Home dropdown list and selecting Clear Filter, but don't do so yet.

As illustrated in Figure 2.26, there are various options you can apply to tables, including the following:

- A number of table styles are available for making the table attractive. You can experiment with these, including the various table styles and table style options. Note the dropdown list in the Table Styles group. It gives you many more styles than the ones originally visible. There is even a "no color" style you might prefer.
- In the Tools group, you can click Convert to Range. This undesignates the range as a table (and the dropdown arrows disappear).
- In the Properties group, you can change the name of the table. You can also click the Resize Table button to expand or contract the table's data range.
- A particularly useful option is the Total Row in the Table Style Options group. If you check this, a new row is appended to the bottom of the table (see Figure 2.27). It creates a sum formula in the rightmost column.[4] This sum includes *only* the non-hidden rows. To prove this to yourself, clear the Own Home filter and check the sum. It increases to $1,216,768. This total row is quite flexible. First, you can summarize the last column by a number of summary measures, such as Average, Max, Min, Count, and others. To do so, select cell O1002 and click the dropdown list that appears. Second, you can summarize any other column in the table in the same way. For example, if you select cell G1002, a dropdown list appears for Salary, and you can then summarize Salary with the same summarizing options.

Figure 2.27 Total Violent and Property Crimes

	Person	Age	Gender	Own Home	Married	Close	Salary	Children	History		Region	State	City	First Purchase	Amount Spent
993	992	2	1	1	1	1	$65,900	1	2	12	Midwest	Kansas	Kansas City	12/26/2011	$1,081
994	993	3	1	1	1	0	$59,700	0	3	18	Midwest	Ohio	Cincinnati	10/23/2012	$1,857
996	995	3	1	1	0	1	$41,900	0	2	6	South	Florida	Miami	7/7/2013	$654
997	996	2	0	1	0	1	$53,800	0	2	12	West	Washington	Seattle	8/14/2015	$843
999	998	2	1	1	1	1	$102,600	0	3	18	East	Pennsylvania	Philadelphia	8/9/2013	$2,546
1001	1000	2	1	1	1	1	$102,500	1	3	24	West	Utah	Salt Lake City	3/9/2012	$2,464
1002	Total														$796,260

Excel tables have a lot of built-in intelligence. Although there is not enough space here to explain all possibilities, try the following to see what we mean:

The Total row in an Excel table summarizes only the visible data. The data that has been filtered out is ignored.

- In cell R2, enter a formula by typing an equals sign, pointing to cell O2, typing a divide sign (/), and pointing to cell G2. You do *not* get the usual formula **=O2/G2**.
- Instead you get **=Table1[[#This Row],[AmountSpent]]/Table1[[#This Row],[Salary]]**. This is certainly not the Excel syntax you are used to, but it makes perfect sense.[5]
- Similarly, you can expand the table with a new variable, such as the ratio of Amount Spent to Salary. Start by typing the variable name Ratio in cell P1. Then in cell P2, enter a formula exactly as you did in the previous bullet. You will notice two things. First, as soon as you enter the Ratio label, column P becomes part of the table. Second, as soon as you enter the new formula in one cell, it is automatically copied to all of column P. This is what we mean by table intelligence.
- Excel tables expand automatically as new rows are added to the bottom or new columns are added to the right. (You saw this latter behavior in the previous bullet.) To appreciate the benefit of this, suppose you have a monthly time series data set. You designate it as a table and then build a line chart from it to show the time series behavior. Later on, if you add new data to the bottom of the table, the chart will *automatically* update to include the new data. This is a great feature. In fact, when we discuss pivot tables in the next chapter, we will recommend basing them on tables, not ranges, whenever possible. Then they too will update automatically when new data are added to the table.

Filtering

We now discuss ways of filtering data sets—that is, finding records that match particular criteria. One way to filter is to create an Excel table, as indicated in the previous subsection. This automatically provides the dropdown arrows next to the field names that provide many filter options. Indeed, this is the way we will filter in this section: on an existing table. However, a designated table is not required for filtering. You can filter on any rectangular data set with variable names. There are actually three ways to do so. For each method, the active cell should be a cell inside the data set.

Filtering is possible without using Excel tables, but there are definitely advantages to filtering with Excel tables.

---

4 The actual formula is =**SUBTOTAL(109,[AmountSpent])**, where 109 is a code for summing. However, you never need to type any such formula; you can choose the summary function you want from the dropdown list.

5 If you don't like this type of formula, you can go to Options under the File menu and uncheck the "Use table names in formulas" option in the Formulas group.

- Use the Filter button from the Sort & Filter dropdown list on the Home ribbon.
- Use the Filter button from the Sort & Filter group on the Data ribbon.
- Right-click any cell in the data set and select Filter. You get several options, the most popular of which is Filter by Selected Cell's Value. For example, if the selected cell has value 1 and is in the Children column, then only customers with a single child will remain visible.

The point is that Microsoft realizes how important filtering is to Excel users. Therefore, they have made filtering a very prominent and powerful Excel tool.

As far as we can tell, the two main advantages of filtering on a table, as opposed to the three options just listed, are the nice formatting (banded rows, for example) provided by tables, and, more importantly, the total row. If this total row is showing, it summarizes *only* the visible records; the rows hidden by filters are ignored.

We now illustrate a number of filtering possibilities for the HyTex data. We won't lead you through a lot of descriptions and screenshots. Once you know the possibilities that are available, you should find them quite easy to use.

- **Filter on one or more values in a field.** Click the Catalogs dropdown arrow. You will see five checkboxes, all checked: Select All, 6, 12, 18, and 24. To select one or more values, uncheck Select All and then check any values you want to filter on, such as 6 and 24. In this case, only customers who received 6 or 24 catalogs will remain visible.
- **Filter on more than one field.** With the Catalogs filter still in place, create a filter on some other field, such as customers with one child. When there are filters on multiple fields, only records that meet *all* of the criteria are visible, in this case customers with one child who received 6 or 24 catalogs.
- **Filter on a continuous numeric field.** The Salary and Amount Spent fields are essentially continuous fields, so it would not make much sense to filter on one or a few particular values. However, it does make sense to filter on *ranges* of values, such as all salaries greater than $75,000. This is easy. Click the drop-down arrow next to Salary and select Number Filters. You will see a number of obvious possibilities, including Greater Than.

The number of ways you can filter in Excel tables is virtually unlimited. Don't be afraid to experiment. You can always clear filters to get back to where you started.

- **Top 10 and Above/Below Average filters.** Continuing the previous bullet, the Number Filters include Top 10, Above Average, and Below Average options. These are particularly useful if you like to see the highs and the lows. The Above Average and Below Average filters do exactly what their names imply. The Top 10 filter is actually more flexible than its name implies. It can be used to select the top *n* items (where you can choose *n*), the bottom *n* items, the top *n* percent of items, or the bottom *n* percent of items. Note that if a Top 10 filter is used on a text field, the ordering is alphabetical. If it is used on a date field, the ordering is chronological.
- **Filter on a text field.** If you click the dropdown arrow for a text field such as Region, you can choose one or more of its values, such as East and South, to filter on. You can also select the Text Filters item, which provides a number of choices, including Begins With, Ends With, Contains, and others. For example, if there were an Address field, you could use the Begins With option to find all addresses that begin with P.O. Box.
- **Filter on a date field.** Excel has great built-in intelligence for filtering on dates. If you click the First Purchase dropdown arrow, you will see an item for each year in the data set with plus signs next to them. By clicking on the plus signs, you can drill down to months and then days for as much control as you need. Figure 2.28 shows one possibility, where we have filtered out all dates except the first part of July 2015. In addition, if you select the Date Filters item, you get a number of possibilities, such as Yesterday, Next Week, Last Month, and many others.
- **Filter on color or icon.** Excel has many ways to color cells or enter icons in cells. Often the purpose is to denote the sizes of the numbers in the cells, such as red for small numbers and green for large numbers. We won't cover the possibilities in this book, but you can experiment with Conditional Formatting on the Home ribbon. The point is that cells are often colored in certain ways or contain certain icons. Therefore, Excel allows you to filter on background color, font color, or icon. For example, if certain salaries are colored yellow, you can isolate them by filtering on yellow.
- **Use a custom filter.** If nothing else works, you can try a custom filter, available at the bottom of the Number Filters, Text Filters, and Date Filters lists. Figures 2.29 and 2.30 illustrate two possibilities. The first of these filters out all salaries between $25,000 and $75,000. Without a custom filter, this wouldn't be possible. The second filter uses the * wildcard to find regions ending in *est* (West and Midwest). Admittedly, this is an awkward way to perform this filter, but it indicates how flexible custom filters can be.

We remind you once again that if you filter on an Excel table and you have summary measures in a total row at the bottom of the table, these summary measures are based *only* on the filtered data; they ignore the hidden rows.

One final comment about filters is that when you click the dropdown arrow for any variable, you always get three items at the top for *sorting*, not filtering (see Figure 2.28, for example). These allow you to perform the obvious sorts, from high to low

Figure 2.28 Filtering on a Date Variable

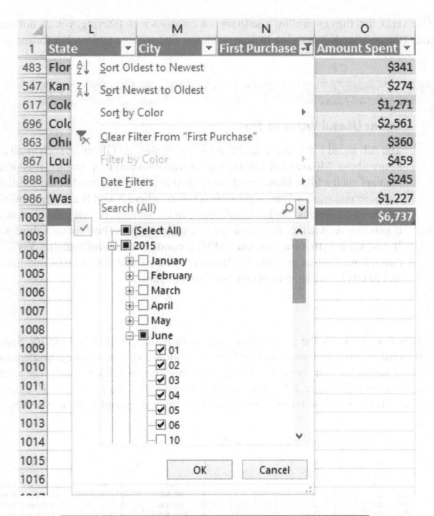

Figure 2.29 Custom Filter for Salary

or vice versa, and they even allow you to sort on color. As with filtering, you do not need to designate an Excel table to perform sorting (the popular A-Z and Z-A buttons work just fine without tables), but sorting is made even easier with tables.

Excel Tip

Other Useful Ways to Filter

The Advanced Filter tool is useful for implementing an OR filter, such as all customers who are either male with salary above $40,000 OR female with at least two children. In fact, it is probably the most natural way to implement such a filter. However, there is another way that is used in the solutions of a few problems in Chapter 2. Suppose you want a filter of the type A OR B, where A and B are any conditions, maybe even AND conditions. Create two columns labeled Condition A and Condition B. Fill each with an IF formula that returns Yes or No, depending on whether the condition holds in that row. Then create a third new column labeled Condition A or B, and fill it with a formula like **=IF(OR(conditionA, conditionB), "Yes", "No")**, where conditionA and conditionB are references to the Yes/No values in the Condition A and Condition B columns. Then you can filter on Yes in this last column to obtain the desired results.

Now that you know the possibilities, here is one particular filter you can try. Suppose HyTex wants information about all middle-aged married customers with at least two children who have above average salaries, own their own home, and live in Indiana or Kentucky. You should be able to create this filter in a few seconds. The result, sorted in decreasing order of Amount Spent and shown in Figure 2.31, indicates that the average salary for these 10 customers is $84,750, and their total amount spent at HyTex is $14,709. (We summarized Salary by average and Amount Spent by sum in the total row.)

Figure 2.31   Results from a Typical Filter

	A	B	C	D	E	F	G	H	I	J	K	L	M	N	O
1	Person	Age	Gender	Own Home	Married	Close	Salary	Children	History	Catalogs	Region	State	City	First Purchase	Amount Spent
155	154	2	1	1	1	1	$70,400	2	NA	12	Midwest	Indiana	Indianapolis	4/28/2015	$1,127
163	162	2	0	1	1	1	$85,500	2	2	18	Midwest	Kentucky	Louisville	6/7/2011	$895
370	369	2	1	1	1	0	$82,400	2	3	24	Midwest	Indiana	Indianapolis	11/25/2014	$2,035
430	429	2	1	1	1	0	$113,400	3	3	18	Midwest	Kentucky	Louisville	6/15/2014	$1,790
570	569	2	1	1	1	1	$74,500	2	2	12	Midwest	Indiana	Indianapolis	4/12/2010	$824
742	741	2	0	1	1	1	$72,200	2	2	18	Midwest	Kentucky	Louisville	10/1/2011	$715
764	763	2	1	1	1	1	$77,100	2	2	6	Midwest	Indiana	Indianapolis	7/3/2014	$568
790	789	2	0	1	1	0	$96,800	3	NA	24	Midwest	Kentucky	Louisville	3/7/2015	$3,082
838	837	2	1	1	1	1	$113,000	2	2	18	Midwest	Kentucky	Louisville	3/3/2015	$1,554
851	850	2	0	1	1	1	$62,200	3	NA	24	Midwest	Indiana	Indianapolis	6/17/2015	$2,119
1002	Total														$14,709

Problems

Solutions for problems whose numbers appear within a colored box can be found in the Student Solution Files.

Level A

33. The file **P02_03.xlsx** contains data from a survey of 399 people regarding an environmental policy. Use filters for each of the following.

a. Identify all respondents who are female, middle-aged, and have two children. What is the average salary of these respondents?

b. Identify all respondents who are elderly and strongly disagree with the environmental policy. What is the average salary of these respondents?

c. Identify all respondents who strongly agree with the environmental policy. What proportion of these individuals are young?

d. Identify all respondents who are either (1) middle-aged men with at least one child and an annual salary of at least $50,000, or (2) middle-aged women with two or fewer children and an annual salary of at least $30,000. What are the mean and median salaries of the respondents who meet these conditions? What proportion of the respondents who satisfy these conditions agree or strongly agree with the environmental policy?

34. The file **P02_07.xlsx** includes data on 204 employees at the (fictional) company Beta Technologies. Use filters for each of the following.

a. Identify all employees who are male and have exactly 4 years of post-secondary education. What is the average salary of these employees?

b. Find the average salary of all female employees who have exactly 4 years of post-secondary education. How does this mean salary compare to the one obtained in part **a**?

c. Identify all employees who have more than 4 years of post-secondary education. What proportion of these employees are male?

d. Identify all full-time employees who are either (1) females between the ages of 30 and 50 (inclusive) with at least 5 years of prior work experience, at least 10 years of prior work experience at Beta, and at least 4 years of post-secondary education; or (2) males between the ages of 40 and 60 (inclusive) with at least 6 years of prior work experience, at least 12 years of prior work experience at Beta, and at least 4 years of post-secondary education.

e. For those employees who meet the conditions specified in part **d**, compare the mean salary of the females with that of the males. Also, compare the median salary of the female employees with that of the male employees.

f. What proportion of the full-time employees identified in part **d** earns less than $50,000 per year?

35. The file **P02_35.xlsx** contains data from a survey of 500 randomly selected households. Use Excel filters to answer the following questions.

a. What are the average monthly home mortgage payment, average monthly utility bill, and average total debt (excluding the home mortgage) of all homeowners residing in the southeast part of the city?

b. What are the average monthly home mortgage payment, average monthly utility bill, and average total debt (excluding the home mortgage) of all homeowners residing in the northwest part of the city? How do these results compare to those found in part **a**?

c. What is the average annual income of the first household wage earners who rent their home (house or apartment)? How does this compare to the average annual income of the first household wage earners who own their home?

d. What proportion of the surveyed households contains a single person who owns his or her home?

36. Recall that the file **Supermarket Transactions.xlsx** contains over 14,000 transactions made by supermarket customers over a period of approximately two years. Use Excel filters to answer the following questions.

a. What proportion of these transactions are made by customers who are married?

b. What proportion of these transactions are made by customers who do not own a home?

c. What proportion of these transactions are made by customers who have at least one child?

d. What proportion of these supermarket customers are single and own a home?

Level B

37. The file **P02_35.xlsx** contains data from a survey of 500 randomly selected households. Use Excel filters to answer the following questions.

a. Identify households that own their home and have a monthly home mortgage payment in the top quartile of the monthly payments for all households.

b. Identify households with monthly expenditures on utilities that are within two standard deviations of the mean monthly expenditure on utilities for all households.

c. Identify households with total indebtedness (excluding home mortgage) less than 10% of the household's primary annual income level.

2-8 Conclusion

The summary measures, charts, and tables discussed in this chapter are extremely useful for describing variables in data sets. The methods in this chapter (and the next two chapters) are often called *exploratory* methods because they allow you to explore the characteristics of the data and at least tentatively answer interesting questions. Most of these tools have been available for many years, but with the powerful software now accessible to virtually everyone, the tools can be applied quickly and easily to gain insights. We can promise that you will be using many if not all of these tools in your job. Indeed, the knowledge you gain from these early chapters is arguably the most valuable knowledge you will gain from the book.

To help you remember which analyses are appropriate for different questions and different data types, and which tools are useful for performing the various analyses, we have created a taxonomy in the file **Data Analysis Taxonomy.xlsx**. (It isn't shown here because it doesn't fit nicely on the printed page.) Feel free to refer back to the diagram in this file as you apply the tools in this chapter and the next chapter.

Summary of Key Terms

TERM	EXPLANATION	EXCEL	PAGES	EQUATION
Population	Includes all objects of interest in a study—people, households, machines, etc.		22	
Sample	Representative subset of population, usually chosen randomly		22	
Variable (or field or attribute)	Attribute or measurement of members of a population, such as height, gender, or salary		23	
Observation (or case or record)	List of all variable values for a single member of a population		23	
Data set	(Usually) a rectangular array of data, with variables in columns, observations in rows, and variable names in the top row		23	
Data types	Several categorizations are possible: numeric versus categorical, discrete versus continuous, cross-sectional versus time series; categorical can be nominal or ordinal		24	
Dummy variable	A variable coded 1 or 0: 1 for observations in the category, 0 for observations not in the category		25	
Binned (or discretized) variable	Numeric variable that has been categorized into discrete categories called bins		25	
Mean	Average of observations	AVERAGE	32	2.1
Median	Middle observation after sorting	MEDIAN	32	
Mode	Most frequent observation	MODE	32	
Percentiles	Values that have specified percentages of observations below them	PERCENTILE	33	
Quartiles	Values that have 25%, 50%, or 75% of observations below them	QUARTILE	33	
Minimum	Smallest observation	MIN	33	
Maximum	Largest observation	MAX	33	
Concatenate	String together two or more pieces of text	& character (or CONCATENATE function)	35	
Range	Difference between largest and smallest observations	MAX, MIN	35	
Interquartile range (IQR)	Difference between first and third quartiles	QUARTILE	35	
Variance	Measure of variability; essentially the average of squared deviations from the mean	VAR.S (or VAR.P)	35	2.2, 2.3
Standard deviation	Measure of variability in same units as observations; square root of variance	STDEV.S (or STDEV.P)	36	
Empirical rules	Rules that specify approximate percentage observations within one, two, or three standard deviations of mean for symmetric, bell-shaped distributions		37	
Mean absolute Deviation (MAD)	Another measure of variability; average of absolute deviations from the mean	AVEDEV	39	2.4
Skewness	When one tail of a distribution is longer than the other	SKEW	39	
Kurtosis	Measure of "fatness" of tails of a distribution (relative to a normal distribution)	KURT	39	

TERM	EXPLANATION	EXCEL	PAGES	EQUATION
Histogram	Chart of bin counts for a numeric variable; shows shape of the distribution	Excel 2016 or later	45	
Box plots	Alternative chart that shows the distribution of a numeric variable	Excel 2016 or later	45	
Time series graph	Graph showing behavior through time of one or more time series variables	Excel line chart	45	
Outlier	Observation that lies outside of the general range of observations in a data set		61	
Missing values	Values that are not reported in a data set		62	
Excel table	Rectangular range specified as a table; especially useful for sorting, filtering, and summarizing	Table from Insert ribbon (or Ctrl+t)	63	

Problems

Conceptual Questions

C.1. An airline analyst wishes to estimate the proportion of all American adults who are afraid to fly because of potential terrorist attacks. To estimate this percentage, the analyst decides to survey 1500 Americans from across the nation. Identify the relevant sample and population in this situation.

C.2. The number of children living in each of a large number of randomly selected households is an example of which data type? Be specific.

C.3. Does it make sense to construct a histogram for the state of residence of randomly selected individuals in a sample? Explain why or why not.

C.4. Characterize the likely shape of a histogram of the distribution of scores on a midterm exam in a graduate statistics course.

C.5. A researcher is interested in determining whether there is a relationship between the weekly number of room air-conditioning units sold and the time of year. What type of descriptive chart would be most useful in performing this analysis? Explain your choice.

C.6. Suppose that the histogram of a given income distribution is positively skewed. What does this fact imply about the relationship between the mean and median of this distribution?

C.7. "The midpoint of the line segment joining the first quartile and third quartile of any distribution is the median." Is this statement true or false? Explain your answer.

C.8. Explain why the standard deviation would likely *not* be a reliable measure of variability for a distribution of data that includes at least one extreme outlier.

C.9. Explain how a box plot can be used to determine whether a distribution of values is essentially symmetric.

C.10. Suppose that you collect a random sample of 250 salaries for the salespersons employed by a large PC manufacturer. Furthermore, assume that you find that two of these salaries are considerably higher than the others in the sample. Before analyzing this data set, should you delete the unusual observations? Explain why or why not.

Solutions for problems whose numbers appear within a colored box can be found in the Student Solution Files.

Level A

38. The file **P02_35.xlsx** contains data from a survey of 500 randomly selected households.
   a. Indicate the type of data for each of the variables included in the survey.
   b. For each of the categorical variables in the survey, indicate whether the variable is nominal or ordinal, and why.
   c. Create a histogram for each of the numeric variables in this data set. Indicate whether each of these distributions is approximately symmetric or skewed. Which, if any, of these distributions are skewed to the right? Which, if any, are skewed to the left?
   d. Find the maximum and minimum debt levels for the households in this sample.
   e. Find the indebtedness levels at each of the 25th, 50th, and 75th percentiles.
   f. Find and interpret the interquartile range for the indebtedness levels of these households.

39. The file **P02_39.xlsx** contains SAT and ACT test scores by state for high school graduates of the 2016–2017 school year. These are broken down by reading/writing and math/science scores. The file also lists the percentages of students taking these two tests by state.
   a. Create a histogram for each of the numeric variables. Are these distributions essentially symmetric or are they skewed?
   b. Compare the two "Pct taking" columns. Does anything stand out?
   c. Find summary statistics for each of the variables. Which is the most appropriate measure of central tendency? Why?
   d. For the SAT, the Total score is the sum of the ERW and Math scores. How does the mean of the Total

variable relate to the means of the ERW and Math variables? Is the same true for medians?

40. *The Wall Street Journal CEO Compensation Study* analyzed CEO pay from many U.S. companies with fiscal year 2008 revenue of at least $5 billion that filed their proxy statements between October 2008 and March 2009. The data are in the file **P02_30.xlsx**.

a. Create histograms to gain a clearer understanding of the distributions of annual base salaries and bonuses earned by the surveyed CEOs in fiscal 2008. How would you characterize these histograms?

b. Find the annual salary below which 75% of all given CEO salaries fall.

c. Find the annual bonus above which 55% of all given CEO bonuses fall.

d. Determine the range of the middle 50% of all given total direct compensation figures. For the 50% of the executives that do not fall into this middle 50% range, is there more variability in total direct compensation to the right than to the left? Explain.

41. The file **P02_41.xlsx** contains monthly returns on American Express stock for several years. As the formulas in the file indicate, each return is the percentage change in the adjusted closing price from one month to the next. Do monthly stock returns appear to be skewed or symmetric? On average, do they tend to be positive, negative, or zero?

42. The file **P02_42.xlsx** contains monthly returns on Mattel stock for several years. As the formulas in the file indicate, each return is the percentage change in the adjusted closing price from one month to the next. Create a histogram of these returns and summarize what you learn from it. On average, do the returns tend to be positive, negative, or zero?

43. The file **P02_43.xlsx** contains U.S. Bureau of Labor Statistics data on the monthly unemployment percentage among people 25 years old or older, broken down by education level. Use box plots and time series graphs to compare the unemployment levels in the different education groups. What are the advantages of box plots? What are the advantages of time series graphs?

44. The file **P02_44.xlsx** contains annual data on the percentage of people in the United States living below the poverty level.

a. In which years of the sample has the poverty rate exceeded the rate that defines the third quartile of these data?

b. In which years of the sample has the poverty rate fallen below the rate that defines the first quartile of these data?

c. What is the typical poverty rate during this period?

d. Create and interpret a time series graph for these data. How successful have Americans been recently in their efforts to win "the war against poverty"?

e. Given that this data set is a time series, discuss whether the measures requested in parts **a-c** are very meaningful at the current time.

Level B

45. The file **P02_45.xlsx** contains the salaries of 135 business school professors at a (fictional) large state university.

a. If you increased every professor's salary by $1000, what would happen to the mean and median salary?

b. If you increased every professor's salary by $1000, what would happen to the standard deviation of the salaries?

c. If you increased every professor's salary by 5%, what would happen to the standard deviation of the salaries?

46. The file **P02_46.xlsx** lists the fraction of U.S. men and women of various heights and weights. Use these data to estimate the mean and standard deviation of the height of American men and women. (*Hint*: Assume all heights in a group are concentrated at the group's midpoint.) Do the same for weights.

47. Recall that HyTex Company is a direct marketer of technical products and that the file **Catalog Marketing.xlsx** contains recent data on 1000 HyTex customers.

a. Identify all customers in the data set who are 55 years of age or younger, female, single, and who have had at least some dealings with HyTex before this year. Find the average number of catalogs sent to these customers and the average amount spent by these customers this year.

b. Do any of the customers who satisfy the conditions stated in part **a** have salaries that fall in the bottom 10% of all 1000 combined salaries in the data set? If so, how many?

c. Identify all customers in the sample who are more than 30 years of age, male, homeowners, married, and who have had little if any dealings with HyTex before this year. Find the average combined household salary and the average amount spent by these customers this year.

d. Do any of the customers who satisfy the conditions stated in part **c** have salaries that fall in the top 10% of all 1000 combined salaries in the data set? If so, how many?

48. Recall that the file **Baseball Salaries.xlsx** contains data on 877 MLB players in the 2018 season. Using this data set, answer the following questions:

a. Find the mean and median of the salaries of all shortstops. Are any of these measures influenced significantly by one or more unusual observations?

b. Find the standard deviation, first and third quartiles, and 5th and 95th percentiles for the salaries of all shortstops. Are any of these measures influenced significantly by one or more unusual observations?

c. Create a histogram of the salaries of all shortstops. Are any of these measures influenced significantly by one or more unusual observations?

49. (Requires Excel 2016 or later) In 1969 and again in 1970, a lottery was held to determine who would be drafted and sent to Vietnam in the following year. For each date of the year, a ball was put into an urn. For example, in the first lottery, January 1 was number 305 and February 14 was number 4. This means that a person born on February 14 would be drafted before a person born on January 1. The file **P02_49.xlsx** contains the "draft number" for each date for the two lotteries. Do you notice anything unusual about the results of either lottery? What do you think might have caused this result? (*Hint*: Create a box plot for each month's numbers.)

50. The file **P02_50.xlsx** contains the average price of gasoline in each of the 50 states for each of several years. (*Note*: You will need to manipulate the data to some extent before performing the analyses requested below.)
  a. Compare the distributions of gasoline price data (one for each year) across states. Specifically, did the mean and standard deviation of these distributions change over time? If so, how do you explain the trends?
  b. In which regions of the country did gasoline prices change the most?
  c. In which regions of the country did gasoline prices remain relatively stable?

51. The file **P02_51.xlsx** contains data on U.S. home-ownership rates by state for each of several years.
  a. Employ numeric summary measures to characterize the changes in home ownership rates across the country during this period.
  b. Do the trends appear to be uniform across the United States or are they unique to certain regions of the country? Explain.

52. Recall that HyTex Company is a direct marketer of technical products and that the file **Catalog Marketing.xlsx** contains recent data on 1000 HyTex customers.
  a. Identify all customers who are either (1) home-owners between the ages of 31 and 55 who live reasonably close to a shopping area that sells similar merchandise, and have a combined salary between $40,000 and $90,000 (inclusive) and a history of being a medium or high spender at HyTex; or (2) homeowners greater than the age of 55 who live reasonably close to a shopping area that sells similar merchandise and have a combined salary between $40,000 and $90,000 (inclusive) and a history of being a medium or high spender at HyTex.
  b. Characterize the subset of customers who satisfy the conditions specified in part **a**. In particular, what proportion of these customers are women? What proportion of these customers are married? On average, how many children do these customers have? Finally, how many catalogs do these customers typically receive, and how much do they typically spend each year at HyTex?
  c. In what ways are the customers who satisfy condition 1 in part **a** different from those who satisfy condition 2 in part **a**? Be specific.

53. Recall that the file **Supermarket Transactions.xlsx** contains data on over 14,000 transactions. There are two numeric variables, Units Sold and Revenue. The first of these is discrete and the second is continuous. For each of the following, do whatever it takes to create a bar chart of counts for Units Sold and a histogram of Revenue for the given subpopulation of purchases.
  a. All purchases made during January and February of 2016.
  b. All purchase made by married female homeowners.
  c. All purchases made in the state of California.
  d. All purchases made in the Produce product department.

54. The file **P02_54.xlsx** contains daily values of an EPA air quality index in Washington DC and Los Angeles from January 1980 through April 2009. For some unknown reason, the source provides slightly different dates for the two cities.
  a. Starting in column G, create three new columns: Date, Wash DC Index, and LA Index. Fill the new date column with *all* dates from 1/1/1980 to 4/30/2009. Then use lookup functions to fill in the two new index columns, entering the observed index if available or a blank otherwise. (*Hint*: Use a combination of the VLOOKUP function with False as the last argument and the IFERROR function. Look up the latter in online help if you have never seen it before.)
  b. Create a separate time series graph of each new index column. Because there are so many dates, it is difficult to see how the graph deals with missing data, but see if you can determine this (maybe by expanding the size of the graph or trying a smaller example). In spite of the few missing points, explain the patterns in the graphs and how Washington DC compares to Los Angeles.

55. The file **P02_55.xlsx** contains monthly sales (in millions of dollars) of beer, wine, and liquor. The data have not been seasonally adjusted, so there might be seasonal patterns that can be discovered. For any month in any year, define that month's seasonal index as the ratio of its sales value to the average sales value over all months of that year.
  a. Calculate these seasonal indexes, one for each month in the series. Do you see a consistent pattern from year to year? If so, what is it?
  b. To "deseasonalize" the data and get the seasonally adjusted series often reported, divide each monthly sales value by the corresponding seasonal index from part **a**. Then create a time series graph of both series, the actual sales and the seasonally adjusted sales. Explain how they are different and why the seasonally adjusted series might be of interest.

56. The file **P02_56.xlsx** contains monthly values of indexes that measure the amount of energy necessary to heat or cool buildings due to outside temperatures. (See the explanation in the Source sheet of the file.)

These are reported for each state in the United States and also for several regions, as listed in the Locations sheet, from 1931 to 2000. Create summary measures and/or charts to see whether there is any indication of temperature changes (global warming?) through time, and report your findings.

57. The file **P02_57.xlsx** contains data on mortgage loans in 2008 for each state in the United States. The file is different from similar ones in this chapter in that each state has its own sheet with the same data laid out in the same format. Each state sheet breaks down all mortgage applications by loan purpose, applicant race, loan type, outcome, and denial reason (for those that were denied).

The question is how a *single* data set for all states can be created for analysis. The Typical Data Set sheet indicates a simple way of doing this, using the powerful but little-known INDIRECT function. This sheet is basically a template for bringing in any pieces of data from the state sheet you would like to examine.

a. Create histograms and summary measures for the example data given in the Typical Data Set sheet and write a short report on your findings.

b. Create a copy of the Typical Data Set sheet and repeat part **a** on this copy for at least one other set of variables (of your choice) from the state sheets.

CASE 2.1 Correct Interpretation of Means

A mean, as defined in this chapter, is a simple concept—it is the average of a set of numbers. But even this simple concept can cause confusion if you aren't careful. The data in Figure 2.32 are typical of data presented by marketing researchers for a type of product, in this case beer. (See the file **C02_01.xlsx**.)

Each value is an average of the number of sixpacks of beer purchased per customer during a month. For the individual brands, the value is the average only for the customers who purchased at least one six-pack of that brand. For example, the value for Miller is the average number of six-packs purchased of *all* of these brands for customers who purchased at least one six-pack of Miller. In contrast, the "Any" average is the average number of six-packs purchased of these brands for all customers in the population.

Is there a paradox in these averages? On first glance, it might appear unusual, or even impossible, that the "Any" average is less than each brand average. Make up your own (small) data set, where you list a number of customers, along with the number of six-packs of each brand of beer each customer purchased, and calculate the averages for your data that correspond to those in Figure 2.32. Do you get the same result (that the "Any" average is lower than all of the others)? Are you *guaranteed* to get this result? Does it depend on the amount of brand loyalty in your population, where brand loyalty is greater when customers tend to stick to the same brand, rather than buying multiple brands? Write up your results in a concise report.

Figure 2.32 Average Beer Purchases

▲	A	B	C	D	E	F	G	H
1	Miller	Budweiser	Coors	Michelob	Heineken	Old Milwaukee	Rolling Rock	Any
2	6.77	6.66	6.64	7.11	7.29	7.3	7.17	4.71

CASE 2.2 The Dow Jones Industrial Average

The monthly closing values of the Dow Jones Industrial Average (DJIA) for the period beginning in January 1950 are given in the file **C02_02.xlsx**. According to Wikipedia, the Dow Jones Industrial Average, also referred to as the Industrial Average, the Dow Jones, the Dow 30, or simply the Dow, is one of several stock market indices created by Charles Dow. The average is named after Dow and one of his business associates, statistician Edward Jones. It is an index that shows how 30 large, publicly owned companies based in the United States have traded during a standard trading

session in the stock market. It is the second oldest U.S. market index after the Dow Jones Transportation Average, which Dow also created.

The *Industrial* portion of the name is largely historical, as many of the modern 30 components have little or nothing to do with traditional heavy industry. The average is price-weighted, and to compensate for the effects of stock splits and other adjustments, it is currently a scaled average. The value of the Dow is not the actual average of the prices of its component stocks, but rather the sum of the component prices divided by a *divisor*, which changes whenever one of the component stocks has a stock split or stock dividend, so as to generate a consistent value for the index.

Along with the NASDAQ Composite, the S&P 500 Index, and the Russell 2000 Index, the Dow is among the most closely watched benchmark indices for tracking stock market activity. Although Dow compiled the index to gauge the performance of the industrial sector within the U.S. economy, the index's performance continues to be influenced not only by corporate and economic reports, but also by domestic and foreign political events such as war and terrorism, as well as by natural disasters that could potentially lead to economic harm.

Using the summary measures and graphical tools from this chapter, analyze this important time series over the given period. Summarize in detail the behavior of the monthly closing values of the Dow and the associated monthly percentage changes in the closing values of the Dow.

CASE 2.3 Home and Condo Prices

The file **C02_03.xlsx** contains an index of home prices and a seasonally adjusted (SA) version of this index for several large U.S. cities. It also contains a condo price index for several large cities and a national index. (The data are explained in the Source sheet.) Use the tools in this chapter to explore these data, and write a report of your findings.

Some important questions you can answer are the following: Are there trends over time? Are there differences across cities? Are there differences across different months of the year? Do condo prices mirror home prices? Why are *seasonally adjusted* (SA) indexes published?

APPENDIX Introduction to StatTools

StatTools is a statistical add-in developed by Palisade as part of their DecisionTools Suite.[6] StatTools contains many procedures discussed in this chapter and later chapters of the book. Most of these procedures, including the summary stats, histograms, box plots, and time series graph procedures discussed in this chapter, can be implemented with Excel's built-in tools, but StatTools can perform them more quickly. Later chapter will make further comments about StatTools procedures relevant to those chapters.

Rather than fill this appendix with a lot of explanations and screenshots, we created an **Introduction to StatTools** video. This video shows the StatTools ribbon, so that you can see the types of procedures StatTools can perform. StatTools is very easy to learn once you know the basics explained in this video. Therefore, if you decide to use StatTools for the statistical procedures discussed in this chapter and later chapters, we strongly recommend you watch this video first.

---

6 StatTools was originally based on StatPro, an add-in developed by Albright in the 1990s. A free version of StatPro is still available at https://kelley.iu.edu/albrightbooks/Free_downloads.htm, but Albright no longer supports it.

CHAPTER 3

Finding Relationships among Variables

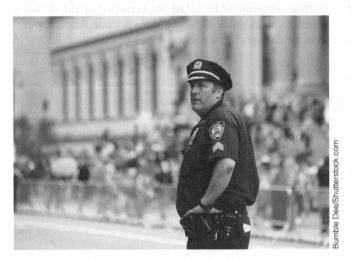

Bumble Dee/Shutterstock.com

DATA ANALYTICS AT NYPD

If your impression of the New York Police Department (NYPD) is based on the hit TV show *NYPD Blue* (1993 to 2005), think again. The NYPD has a history of applying analytics to make its 36,000 uniformed officers more effective and efficient at their jobs. As described in Levine et al. (2017), the NYPD developed CompStat in 1993, a structured process for examining crime statistics. Then on the heels of the terrorism attack on September 11, 2001, they created a Counterterrorism Bureau, the first of its kind in a U.S. municipal police department. Their latest use of analytics, begun in 2008, is the Domain Awareness System (DAS), a network of sensors, databases, devices, software, and infrastructure that delivers up-to-date information and analytics to mobile devices and precinct desktops. This system is now deployed across every police precinct in the city, on all officers' smartphones, and on the tablets in all police vehicles. It provides officers with the timely information they need to respond quickly and appropriately to situations as they arise.

Before DAS, the NYPD had a tremendous amount of information about crimes and offenders, but it didn't have the means to get this information to the officers who needed it in a timely manner. For example, suppose a 911 call about a domestic disturbance was received. Before DAS, the caller spoke to an operator, whose transcription of the call was passed to a dispatcher. The dispatcher then assigned the job to officers in the vicinity, telling them there was a domestic incident at a stated address. With this limited information, the officers had to manage the situation as well as possible, often having to make life-or-death decisions without any historical context. Imagine how much better the officers could react if they knew ahead of time that there was a warrant for the arrest of the person at this address or that this was the fifth such call from this address in the past few months. With DAS, this type of information is immediately available from one of the officer's phones. (The officer in the passenger seat looks up the information on the phone; the officer driving is instructed to keep his eyes on the road.) In fact, the officers can now access the caller's statements as transcribed by the operator, information they never had before DAS.

DAS also implements predictive analytics for more strategic decisions, such as where a precinct commanding officer should place units on patrol. Before DAS, this decision was made by marking locations of crimes in the past month on a map, circling "hot spots" on the map where most crimes seemed to occur, and positioning units at the hot spots. Predictive analytics can improve on this process by predicting where *future* crimes are likely to occur.

Prior to DAS, there was a weekly CompStat meeting about strategic decisions that revolved around a static piece of paper listing the numbers of crimes of various types for the week, the last 28 days, and year-to-date. There was some summarization on this sheet, such as how this week's numbers compared to the numbers from a year ago, but not very much. There was almost no way for those at the meeting to use these numbers for strategic decisions because they couldn't see the patterns that led to the numbers. This is now possible with DAS. Each number is now presented in an interactive form on a computer screen. If a user clicks on a number, DAS shows all the records included in that number and marks them on a map. Data visualization software then enables the user to explore trends and patterns with bar charts or time series charts, for example. This information, formerly available only to headquarters staff, is now available to commanding officers and their crime analysts.

The Data system has created a "big data" problem for the NYPD. Audio gunshot detectors, 911 calls, license plate readers (LPRs), closed-circuit television cameras, and environmental sensors all feed real-time data into DAS. As of 2016, it also contains two billion readings from license plates (with photos), 54 million 911 calls, 15 million complaints, 12 million detective reports, 11 million arrests, 2 million warrants, and 30 days of video from 9000 cameras. How can all this data be analyzed? Much of the analysis is based on pattern recognition. For example, pattern recognition is implemented on the LPR data. Predictive analytics inform officers where and when a specific license plate is likely to be scanned in the next few minutes. (This is performed only on vehicles on an NYPD watch list.) Time-and-place patterns occur when a vehicle passes the *same* LPR multiple times on a specific day of the week and a specific time of day, such as every Tuesday at 2 PM. Routing patterns occur when a vehicle passes a fixed LPR and then later passes a second fixed LPR, such as entering the Queensboro Bridge and then driving south on FDR Drive, and it does this on multiple days. These types of patterns give officers a better chance of finding suspected vehicles by focusing their searches.

The DAS system has been a huge success. NYPD officers tend to be skeptical of new systems involving technology, but DAS was designed for cops by cops. Therefore, they appear to trust it and use it. As a measure of its popularity with NYPD officers, there were 100,000 mobile job clicks per week by the end of 2015.

3-1 Introduction

The previous chapter introduced a number of summary measures, graphs, and tables to describe the distribution of a single variable. For a variable such as baseball salary, the entire focus was on how salaries were distributed over some range. This is an important first step in any exploratory data analysis—to look closely at variables one at a time—but it is almost never the *last* step. The primary interest is usually in *relationships* between variables. For example, it is natural to ask what drives baseball salaries. Does it depend on qualitative factors, such as the player's team or position? Does it depend on quantitative factors, such as the number of hits the player gets or the number of strikeouts? To answer these questions, you have to examine relationships between various variables and salary.

This chapter again discusses numerical summary measures, graphs, and tables, but they now involve at least two variables at a time. The most useful numeric summary measure is correlation, a measure that applies primarily to numeric variables. The most useful graph is a scatterplot, which again applies primarily to numeric variables. Other tools are used for relationships involving categorical variables. For example, to break down a numeric variable by a categorical variable, it is often useful to create side-by-side box plots. Finally, we discuss Excel®'s arguably most powerful tool, the pivot table. A pivot table enables you to break down one variable by others so that relationships can be uncovered quickly.

A key issue in this chapter is that different tools should be used to examine relationships, depending on whether the variables involved are numeric or categorical.

As you read this chapter, remember that the diagram in the file **Data Analysis Taxonomy.xlsx** is available. This diagram gives you the big picture of which analyses are appropriate for which data types and which tools are best for performing the various analyses.

3-2 Relationships among Categorical Variables

Consider a data set with at least two categorical variables, Smoking and Drinking. Each person is categorized into one of three smoking categories: nonsmoker (NS), occasional smoker (OS), and heavy smoker (HS). Similarly, each person is categorized into one of three drinking categories: nondrinker (ND), occasional drinker (OD), and heavy drinker (HD). Do the data indicate that smoking and drinking habits are related? For example, do nondrinkers tend to be nonsmokers? Do heavy smokers tend to be heavy drinkers?

Use a crosstabs, a table of counts of joint categories, to discover relationships between two categorical variables.

As discussed in the previous chapter, the most meaningful way to describe a categorical variable is with counts, possibly expressed as percentages of totals, and corresponding charts of the counts. The same is true of examining relationships between two categorical variables. You can find the counts of the categories of either variable separately, and more importantly, you can find counts of the *joint* categories of the two variables, such as the count of all nondrinkers who are also nonsmokers. Again, corresponding percentages of totals and charts help tell the story.

It is customary to display all such counts in a table called a **crosstabs** (for cross-tabulations). This is also sometimes called a **contingency table**. Example 3.1 illustrates these tables.

EXAMPLE

3.1 RELATIONSHIP BETWEEN SMOKING AND DRINKING

The file **Smoking Drinking.xlsx** lists the smoking and drinking habits of 8761 adults. (This is fictional data.) The categories have been coded so that "N," "O," and "H" stand for "Non," "Occasional," and "Heavy," and "S" and "D" stand for "Smoker" and "Drinker." Is there any indication that smoking and drinking habits are related? If so, how are they related?

Objective

To use a crosstabs to explore the relationship between smoking and drinking.

Solution

The first question is the data format. If you are lucky, you will be given a table of counts. However, it is also possible that you will have to create these counts. In the file for this example, the data are in long columns, part of which is shown in Figure 3.1. Presumably, there could be other variables describing these people, but only the Smoking and Drinking variables are relevant here.

Figure 3.1 Smoking and Drinking Data

	A	B	C
1	Person	Smoking	Drinking
2	1	NS	OD
3	2	NS	HD
4	3	OS	HD
5	4	HS	ND
6	5	NS	OD
7	6	NS	ND
8	7	NS	OD
9	8	NS	ND
10	9	OS	HD
11	10	HS	HD

Figure 3.2 Crosstabs of Smoking and Drinking

	E	F	G	H	I
1	Crosstabs from COUNTIFS formulas				
2					
3		NS	OS	HS	Total
4	ND	2118	435	163	2716
5	OD	2061	1067	552	3680
6	HD	733	899	733	2365
7	Total	4912	2401	1448	8761
8					
9	Shown as percentages of row totals				
10		NS	OS	HS	Total
11	ND	78.0%	16.0%	6.0%	100.0%
12	OD	56.0%	29.0%	15.0%	100.0%
13	HD	31.0%	38.0%	31.0%	100.0%
14					
15	Shown as percentages of column totals				
16		NS	OS	HS	
17	ND	43.1%	18.1%	11.3%	
18	OD	42.0%	44.4%	38.1%	
19	HD	14.9%	37.4%	50.6%	
20	Total	100.0%	100.0%	100.0%	

To create the crosstabs, start by entering the category headings in row 3 and column E of Figure 3.2. The goal is to fill the table in rows 4–6 with counts of joint categories, along with row and column sums. If you are thinking about using the COUNTIF function to obtain the joint counts, you are close. However, the COUNTIF function lets you specify only a single criterion, and there are now *two* criteria, one for smoking and one for drinking. Fortunately, Excel has a function designed exactly for this: COUNTIFS. It enables you to specify any number of range-criterion pairs. In fact, you can fill the entire table with a single formula entered in cell F4 and copied to the range F4:H6:

=COUNTIFS($B$2:$B$8762,F$3,$C$2:$C$8762,$E4)

The first two arguments are for the condition on smoking; the last two are for the condition on drinking. You can then sum across rows and down columns to get the totals.

The resulting counts appear in the top table in Figure 3.2. For example, among the 8761 people, 4912 are nonsmokers, 2365 are heavy drinkers, and 733 are nonsmokers *and* heavy drinkers. Because the totals are far from equal (there are many more nonsmokers than heavy smokers, for example), any relationship between smoking and drinking is difficult to detect in these raw counts. Therefore, it is useful to express the counts as percentages of row totals in the middle table and as percentages of column totals in the bottom table.

The latter two tables indicate, in complementary ways, that there is definitely a relationship between smoking and drinking. If there were no relationship, the rows in the middle table would be practically identical, as would the columns in the bottom table. (Make sure you understand why this is true.) But they are far from identical. For example, the middle table indicates that only 6% of the nondrinkers are heavy smokers, whereas 31% of the heavy drinkers are heavy smokers. Similarly, the bottom table indicates that 43.1% of the nonsmokers are nondrinkers, whereas only 11.3% of the heavy smokers are nondrinkers. In short, these tables indicate that smoking and drinking habits tend to go with one another. These tendencies are reinforced by the column charts of the two percentage tables in Figure 3.3.

Relationships between the two variables are usually more evident when the counts are expressed as percentages of row totals or percentages of column totals.

Figure 3.3 Column Charts of Smoking and Drinking Percentages

Fundamental Insight

Counts Versus Percentages

There is no single correct way to display the data in a crosstabs. Ultimately, the data are always counts, but they can be shown as raw counts, percentages of row totals, percentages of column totals, or even percentages of the overall total. Nevertheless, when you are looking for relationships between two categorical variables, showing the counts as percentages of row totals or percentages of column totals usually makes any relationships emerge more clearly. Corresponding charts are also very useful.

Excel Tip

Creating Charts from Crosstabs

It takes almost no work to create these charts. To get the one on the left, highlight the range E10:H13 and insert a column chart from the Insert ribbon. Do the same with the range E16:H19 to get the chart on the right, except that it will have smoking on the horizontal axis and drinking in the legend. To reverse their roles, click the Switch Row/Column button on the Chart Tools Design ribbon.

Although this example illustrates that it doesn't take too much work to create crosstabs and corresponding charts, you will see a much quicker and easier way when pivot tables are discussed later in this chapter.

Problems

Solutions for problems whose numbers appear within a colored box can be found in the Student Solution Files.

Level A

1. The file **P02_01.xlsx** indicates the gender and nationality of the MBA incoming class in two successive years at the Kelley School of Business at Indiana University.

a. For each year separately, recode Nationality so that all nationalities with a count of 1 or 2 are listed as Other.

b. For each year, create a crosstabs of Gender versus the recoded Nationality and an associated column chart. Does there seem to be any relationship between Gender and the recoded Nationality? Is the pattern about the same in the two years?

2. The file **P02_03.xlsx** contains data from a survey of 399 people regarding a government environmental policy.

a. Create a crosstabs and an associated column chart for Gender versus Opinion. Express the counts as percentages so that for either gender, the percentages add to 100%. Discuss your findings. Specifically, do the two genders tend to differ in their opinions about the environmental policy?

b. Repeat part **a** with Age versus Opinion.

c. Recode Salary to be categorical with categories "Less than $40K," "Between $40K and $70K," "Between $70K and $100K," and "Greater than $100K" (where you can treat the breakpoints however you like). Then repeat part **a** with this new Salary variable versus Opinion.

3. The file **P02_02.xlsx** contains data on 256 movies that grossed at least $1 million in 2017.

a. Recode Distributor so that all distributors with fewer than 10 movies are listed as Other. Similarly, recode Genre so that all genres with fewer than 10 movies are listed as Other.

b. Create a crosstabs and an associated column chart for these two recoded variables. Express the counts as percentages so that for any distributor, the percentages add to 100%. Discuss your findings.

4. Recall from Chapter 2 that the file **Supermarket Transactions.xlsx** contains over 14,000 transactions made by supermarket customers over a period of approximately two years. To understand which customers purchase which products, create a crosstabs and an associated column chart for each of the following. For each, express the counts as percentages so that for any value of the first variable listed, the percentages add to 100%. Do any patterns stand out?

a. Gender versus Product Department

b. Marital Status versus Product Department

c. Annual Income versus Product Department

Level B

5. Recall from Chapter 2 that HyTex Company is a direct marketer of technical products and that the file **Catalog Marketing.xlsx** contains recent data on 1000 HyTex customers. To understand these customers, first recode Salary and Amount Spent as indicated in part **a**, and then create each of the requested crosstabs and an associated column chart in parts **b** to **e**. Express each count as a percentage, so that for any value of the first variable listed, the percentages add up to 100%. Do any patterns stand out?

a. Find the first, second, and third quartiles of Salary, and then recode Salary as 1 to 4, depending on which quarter of the data each value falls into. For example, the first salary, $16,400, is recoded as 1 because $16,400 is less than the first quartile, $29,975. Recode Amount Spent similarly, based on its quartiles. (*Hint*: The recoding can be done most easily with lookup tables.)

b. Age versus the recoded Amount Spent

c. Own Home versus the recoded Amount Spent

d. History versus the recoded Amount Spent

e. The recoded Salary versus the recoded Amount Spent

6. The smoking/drinking example in this section used the function COUNTIFS function to find the counts of the joint categories. Without using this function (or pivot tables), devise another way to get the counts. The raw data are in the file **Smoking Drinking.xlsx**. (*Hint*: One possibility is to concatenate the values in columns B and C into a new column D. But feel free to find the counts in any way you like.)

3-3 Relationships among Categorical Variables and a Numeric Variable

The comparison problem, where a numeric variable is compared across two or more subpopulations, is one of the most important problems faced by data analysts in all fields of study.

This section describes a very common situation where the goal is to break down a numeric variable such as salary by a categorical variable such as gender. This is precisely what pivot tables were built for, as you will see later in the chapter. For now, however, Excel's numeric and graphical tools will be used. This general problem, typically referred to as the **comparison problem**, is one of the most important problems in data analysis. It occurs whenever you want to compare a numeric variable across two or more subpopulations. Here are some examples:

- The subpopulations are males and females, and the numeric variable is salary.
- The subpopulations are different regions of the country, and the numeric variable is the cost of living.
- The subpopulations are different days of the week, and the numeric variable is the number of customers going to a particular fast-food chain.
- The subpopulations are different machines in a manufacturing plant, and the numeric variable is the number of defective parts produced per day.
- The subpopulations are patients who have taken a new drug and those who have taken a placebo, and the numeric variable is the recovery rate from a particular disease.
- The subpopulations are undergraduates with various majors (business, English, history, and so on), and the numeric variable is the starting salary after graduating.

The list could continue. The discussion of the comparison problem begins in this chapter, where methods are used to investigate whether there appear to be differences across the subpopulations on the numeric variable of interest. In later chapters, inferential methods—confidence intervals and hypothesis tests—are used to see whether the differences in *samples* from the subpopulations can be generalized to the subpopulations as a whole.

Fundamental Insight

Breaking Down by Category

There is arguably no more powerful data analysis technique than breaking down a numeric variable by a categorical variable. The methods in this chapter, especially side-by-side box plots and pivot tables, get you started with this general comparison problem. They allow you to see quickly, with charts and/or numeric summary measures, how two or more categories compare. More advanced techniques for comparing across categories are discussed in later chapters.

Stacked and Unstacked Formats

The stacked format is by far the most common. There are one or more long numeric variables and another long variable that specifies which category each observation is in.

There are two possible **data formats** you might see, stacked and unstacked. Consider salary data on males and females. (There could be other variables in the data set, but they aren't relevant here.) The data are **stacked** if there are two "long" variables, Gender and Salary, as indicated in Figure 3.4. The idea is that the male salaries are stacked in with the female salaries. This is the format you will see in the majority of data sets. However, you will occasionally see data in **unstacked** format, as shown in Figure 3.5. (Note that both

Figure 3.4 Stacked Data

	A	B
1	**Gender**	**Salary**
2	Male	81600
3	Female	61600
4	Female	64300
5	Female	71900
6	Male	76300
7	Female	68200
8	Male	60900
9	Female	78600
10	Female	81700
11	Male	60200
12	Female	69200
13	Male	59000
14	Male	68600
15	Male	51900
16	Female	64100
17	Male	67600
18	Female	81100
19	Female	77000
20	Female	58800
21	Female	87800
22	Male	78900

Figure 3.5 Unstacked Data

	A	B
1	Female Salary	Male Salary
2	61600	81600
3	64300	76300
4	71900	60900
5	68200	60200
6	78600	59000
7	81700	68600
8	69200	51900
9	64100	67600
10	81100	78900
11	77000	
12	58800	
13	87800	

tables list exactly the same data. See the file **Stacked Unstacked Data.xlsx**.) Now there are two "short" variables, Female Salary and Male Salary. In addition, it is very possible that the two variables have different lengths. This is the case here because there are more females than males.

Keep this distinction in mind. Some statistical software packages require that the data for a comparison problem be in one of these formats, usually the stacked format. In any case, it is fairly easy to rearrange unstacked data into stacked format or vice versa.

We now return to the baseball data, which is in stacked format, to see which, if any, of the categorical variables makes a difference in player salaries.

EXAMPLE

3.2 BASEBALL SALARIES

The file **Baseball Salaries Extra.xlsx** contains the same 2018 baseball data examined in the previous chapter. In addition, several extra categorical variables are included:

• Pitcher (Yes for all pitchers, No for the others)
• League (American or National)
• Division (National West, American East, and so on)
• Yankees (Yes if team is New York Yankees, No otherwise)
• Playoff 2017 Team (Yes for the eight teams that made it to the 2017 playoffs, No for the others)
• World Series 2017 Team (Yes for Houston Astros and Los Angeles Dodgers, No for others)

Do pitchers (or any other positions) earn more than others? Does one league pay more than the other, or do any divisions pay more than others? How does the notoriously high Yankees payroll compare to the others? Do the successful teams from 2017 tend to have larger 2018 payrolls?

Objective

To learn methods for breaking down baseball salaries by various categorical variables.

Solution

It is useful to look first at some numeric summary measures for salary. These are the same summary measures from the previous chapter, but now we want to break them down by position or by one of the other categorical variables. You could do this with Excel formulas, but they are not quite as straightforward as before. If you want to create counts or averages, you can use Excel's COUNTIF and AVERAGEIF functions. However, there are no MEDIANIF, MINIF, MAXIF, STDEVIF functions or others you might need. Still, there is a way, using array formulas.

The results appear in Figure 3.6. This table lists selected summary measures for each of the positions in the data set. A typical formula, the standard deviation for catchers, is shown at the bottom. It uses the STDEV.S function but with an IF function inside. This IF function is essentially a filter on catchers, so the function takes the standard deviation of catcher salaries only. However, this is an array formula, so after you type it, you must press Ctrl + Shift + Enter (all three keys at once). This puts curly brackets around the formula, but you do *not* actually type these curly brackets. If you want to see salaries broken down by team or any other categorical variable, you can easily run this analysis again with a different categorical variable.

Figure 3.6 Summary Measures of Salary by Position

	A	B	C	D	E	F	G	H	I	J
1		Summary stats for Salary broken down by categories of Position								
2										
3		Position	Catcher	Designated Hitter	First Baseman	Outfielder	Pitcher	Second Baseman	Shortstop	Third Baseman
4		Mean	$3,511,360	$12,460,183	$8,737,151	$5,130,183	$3,829,218	$4,928,349	$3,570,414	$6,029,821
5		Median	$1,250,000	$13,262,214	$5,333,333	$1,675,000	$1,100,000	$2,400,000	$1,025,000	$2,916,666
6		Min	$545,000	$570,000	$545,000	$545,000	$545,000	$546,900	$545,000	$545,000
7		Max	$22,177,778	$18,666,667	$30,000,000	$34,083,333	$34,000,000	$24,000,000	$20,000,000	$23,000,000
8		Quartile 1	$557,471	$11,318,607	$585,000	$561,500	$555,000	$657,000	$564,125	$565,000
9		Quartile 3	$3,975,000	$17,062,500	$14,333,333	$6,450,000	$5,000,000	$8,500,000	$5,112,500	$12,000,000
10		1st percentile	$545,000	$1,091,500	$545,336	$545,000	$545,000	$547,008	$545,000	$546,100
11		5th percentile	$546,240	$3,177,500	$546,880	$546,275	$545,000	$547,960	$546,305	$548,300
12		95th percentile	$14,675,000	$18,500,000	$24,200,000	$21,375,000	$16,000,000	$16,108,674	$15,286,666	$19,319,795
13		99th percentile	$22,049,778	$18,633,334	$28,560,000	$27,674,880	$27,700,000	$20,880,000	$18,120,000	$21,504,000
14		Std Dev	$5,009,483	$6,572,010	$8,977,109	$6,978,709	$5,650,088	$5,489,065	$4,837,949	$6,896,281
15		Mean Abs Dev	$3,430,724	$4,512,040	$7,670,583	$5,217,029	$3,880,380	$4,327,677	$3,617,415	$5,900,264
16										
17		Typical formula								
18		Cell C14	=STDEV.S(IF('Salaries 2018'!$C$2:$C$878=C3,'Salaries 2018'!$J$2:$J$878))							

There are a lot of numbers to digest in Figure 3.6, so it is difficult to get a clear picture of differences across positions. It is more enlightening to see a graphical summary of this information. There are several types of graphs you can use. Our favorite way, discussed shortly, is to create side-by-side box plots. A second possibility is to use pivot tables and corresponding pivot charts, as discussed later in this chapter.

Side-by-side box plots are our favorite graphical way of comparing the distribution of a numeric variable across categories of some categorical variable.

For now, we illustrate side-by-side box plots. Assuming you have Excel 2016 or later, you can create box plots of Salary by Position. First, select the two columns of data, Position and Salary. Then select a box plot from the Statistical charts list on the Insert ribbon. Excel automatically uses the distinct categories in the Position variable to create a separate box plot for each position. You can interpret each of these box plots as explained in the previous chapter. More importantly, you can compare them.

The results appear in Figure 3.7. Now the differences between positions emerge fairly clearly. A few of the conclusions that can be made follow.

Figure 3.7 Box Plots of Salary by Position

- The salaries for all positions except designated hitter are skewed to the right (mean greater than median, long lines and outliers to the right).
- As a whole, first basemen tend to be the highest paid players, followed by third basemen. The designated hitters also make a lot, but there are only a few of them in the data set.
- As a whole, pitchers don't make as much as first basemen and third basemen, but there are a lot of pitchers who are high-earning outliers.
- Except for a few notable exceptions, catchers receive the lowest salaries.

Because these side-by-side box plots are so easy to obtain, you can generate a lot of them to provide insights into the salary data. Several interesting examples appear in Figures 3.8–3.10. These box plots lead to the following conclusions:

- Pitchers make somewhat less than other players, although there are many outliers in each group.
- The Yankees payroll is indeed *much* larger than the payrolls for the rest of the teams. In fact, it is so large that its stars' salaries aren't even considered outliers relative to the rest of the team.
- Aside from the many outliers, the playoff teams from 2017 tend to have slightly larger payrolls than the non-playoff teams. The one question we cannot answer, however, at least not without additional data, is whether these larger payrolls are a cause or an effect of being successful.

You can often create a categorical variable on the fly with an IF formula and then use it for side-by-side box plots. We did this with the Yankees, for example.

Figure 3.8 Box Plots of Salary by Pitcher/Non-Pitcher

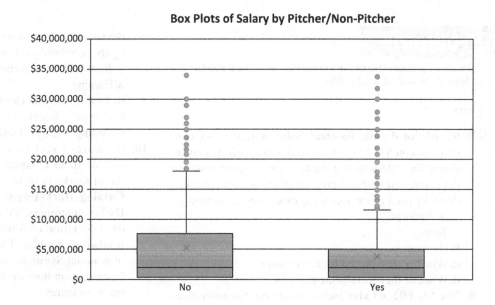

Figure 3.9 Box Plots of Salary by Yankees/Non-Yankees

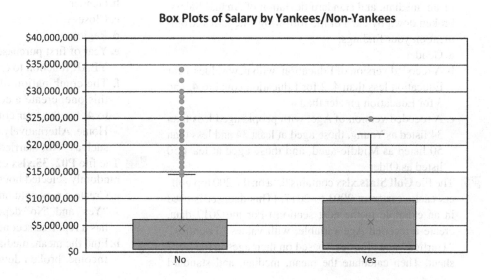

Figure 3.10 Box Plots of Salary by Playoff Team/Non-Playoff Team

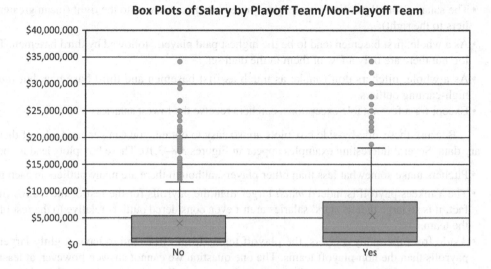

Problems

Solutions for problems whose numbers appear within a colored box can be found in the Student Solution Files.

Level A

7. Recall that the file **Baseball Salaries Extra.xlsx** contains data on 877 Major League Baseball (MLB) players during the 2018 season. Find the mean, median, standard deviation, and first and third quartiles of Salary, broken down by each of the following categories. Comment on your findings.
   a. Team
   b. Division
   c. Whether they played for the Yankees
   d. Whether they were in the playoffs

8. The file **P02_07.xlsx** includes data on 204 employees at the (fictional) company Beta Technologies. Find the mean, median, and standard deviation of Annual Salary, broken down by each of the following categories. Comment on your findings.
   a. Gender
   b. A recoded version of Education, with new values 1 for Education less than 4, 2 for Education equal to 4, and 3 for Education greater than 4
   c. A recoded version of Age, with people aged less than 34 listed as Young, those aged at least 34 and less than 50 listed as Middle-aged, and those aged at least 50 listed as Older

9. The file **Golf Stats.xlsx** contains data on the 200 top golfers each year from 2003 to 2017. (This data set is used in an example in the next section.) For the 2017 data, create a recoded Age variable, with values "Twenties," "Thirties," and "Forties," based on their ages in the 2017 sheet. Then calculate the mean, median, and standard deviation of the following 2017 variables, broken down by the recoded Age. Comment on whether it appears that golfers peak in their thirties.
   a. Earnings
   b. Yards/Drive and Driving Accuracy
   c. Greens in Regulation
   d. Putting Average (Golfers want this to be small.)

10. (Requires Excel version 2016 or later for box plots) Recall from Chapter 2 that HyTex Company is a direct marketer of technical products and that the file **Catalog Marketing.xlsx** contains recent data on 1000 HyTex customers. Find the mean, median, and standard deviation of Amount Spent, broken down by the following variables. Then create side-by-side box plots of Amount Spent, broken down by the same variables. Comment on how the box plots complement the summary measures.
   a. Age
   b. Gender
   c. Close
   d. Region
   e. Year of first purchase. (*Hint*: For this one, use Excel's YEAR function to create a Year column.)
   f. The combination of Married and Own Home. (For this one, create a code variable, with values from 1 to 4, for the four combinations of Married and Own Home. Alternatively, create a text variable with values such as "Not married, Owns home.")

11. The file **P02_35.xlsx** contains data from a survey of 500 randomly selected households.
   a. Create a new column Has Second Income with values "Yes" and "No" depending on whether the household has a reported second income.
   b. Find the mean, median, and standard deviation of First Income, broken down by the variable you created in

part **a**. Is there any indication that first income tends to be any larger or smaller, or has more or less variation, depending on whether there is a second income?

c. Repeat part **b** for each of the Monthly Payment and Debt variables.

12. (Requires Excel version 2016 or later for box plots) The file **P02_02.xlsx** contains data about 256 movies that grossed at least $1 million in 2017.

a. Recode Genre so that all genres with fewer than 10 movies are listed as Other.

b. Find the mean, median, and standard deviation of Total US Gross, broken down by the recoded Genre variable. Also, create side-by-side box plots of Total US Gross, again broken down by the recoded Genre variable. Comment on what the results say about the popularity of different genres.

13. (Requires Excel version 2016 or later for box plots) *The Wall Street Journal CEO Compensation Study* analyzed chief executive officer (CEO) pay from many U.S. companies with fiscal year 2008 revenue of at least $5 billion that filed their proxy statements between October 2008 and March 2009. The data are in the file **P02_30.xlsx**.

a. Create a new variable Total 2008, the sum of Salary 2008 and Bonus 2008. (Actually, this is not "total" compensation because it omits the very lucrative compensation from stock options.) Also, recode Company Type so that the Technology and Telecommunications are collapsed into a Tech/Telecomm category.

b. Find the mean, median, and standard deviation of Total 2008, broken down by the recoded Company Type. Also, create side-by-side box plots of Total 2008, again broken down by the recoded Company Type. What do the results tell you about differences in level or variability across company types?

14. (Requires Excel version 2016 or later for box plots) The file **P02_55.xlsx** contains monthly sales (in millions of dollars) of beer, wine, and liquor. The data have not been seasonally adjusted, so there might be seasonal patterns that can be discovered.

a. Create a new Month Name variable with values Jan, Feb, and so on. (Use Excel's MONTH function and then a lookup table.)

b. Create side-by-side box plots of Total Sales, broken down by Month Name. Is there any evidence of differences across months for either the level of sales or the variability of sales?

15. (Requires Excel version 2016 or later for box plots) The file **P03_15.xlsx** contains monthly data on the various components of the Consumer Price Index (CPI). The source claims that these data have not been seasonally adjusted. The following parts ask you to check this claim.

a. Create a new Month Name variable with values Jan, Feb, and so on. (Use Excel's MONTH function and then a lookup table.)

b. Create side-by-side box plots of each component of the CPI (including the All Items variable), broken

down by the Month Name variable from part **a**. What results would you expect for "not seasonally adjusted" data? Are your results in line with this?

16. (Requires Excel version 2016 or later for box plots) The file **P02_11.xlsx** contains data on 148 houses that were recently sold in a (fictional) suburban community. The data set includes the selling price of each house, along with its appraised value, square footage, number of bedrooms, and number of bathrooms.

a. Create two new variables, Ratio 1 and Ratio 2. Ratio 1 is the ratio of Appraised Value to Selling Price, and Ratio 2 is the ratio of Selling Price to Square Feet. Identify any obvious outliers in these two Ratio variables.

b. Find the mean, median, and standard deviation of each Ratio variable, broken down by Bedrooms. Also, create side-by-side box plots of each Ratio variable, again broken down by Bedrooms. Comment on the results.

c. Repeat part **b** with Bedrooms replaced by Bathrooms.

d. If you repeat parts **b** and **c** with any obvious outlier(s) from part **a** removed, do the conclusions change in any substantial way?

Level B

17. The file **P02_32.xlsx** contains blood pressures for 1000 people, along with variables that can be related to blood pressure. These other variables have a number of missing values, probably because some people didn't want to report certain information. For each of the Alcohol, Exercise, and Smoke variables, use StatTools to find the mean, median, and standard deviation of Blood Pressure, broken down by whether the data for that variable are missing. For example, there should be one set of statistics for people who reported their alcohol consumption and another for those who didn't report it. Based on your results, does it appear that there is any difference in blood pressure between those who reported and those who didn't?

18. The file **P03_18.xlsx** contains the times in the Chicago marathon for the top runners each year (the top 10,000 in 2006 and the top 20,000 in 2007 and 2008).

a. Merge the top 1,000 values (that is, the lowest 1,000 times) from each year into a new Combined sheet, and in the new sheet, create a variable Year that lists the year.

b. The Time variable, shown as something like 2:16:12, is really stored as a time, the fraction of day starting from midnight. So 2:16:12, for example, which means 2 hours, 16 minutes, and 12 seconds, is stored as 0.0946, meaning that 2:16:12 AM is really 9.46% of the way from midnight to the next midnight. This isn't very useful. Do whatever it takes to recode the times into a new Minutes variable with two decimals, so that 2:16:12 becomes 136.20 minutes. (*Hint*: Look up Time functions in Excel's online help.)

c. Create a new variable Nationality to recode Country as "KEN, ETH," "USA," or "Other," depending on whether the runner is from Kenya/Ethiopia (the usual winners), the USA, or some other country.

  d. Find the mean, median, standard deviation, and first and third quartiles of Minutes, broken down by Nationality. Also, create side-by-side box plots of Minutes, again broken down by Nationality. Comment on the results.

  e. Repeat part **d**, replacing Nationality by Gender.

19. (Requires Excel version 2016 or later for box plots) The file **P03_19.xlsx** contains daily values of the S&P Index from 1970 to mid-2015. It also contains percentage changes in the index from each day to the next.

  a. Create a new variable President that lists the U.S. presidents Nixon through Obama on each date. You can look up the presidents and dates online.

  b. Find the mean, median, standard deviation, and first and third quartiles of % Change, broken down by President. Also, create side-by-side box plots of % Change, again broken down by President. Comment on the results.

20. The file **P02_56.xlsx** contains monthly values of indexes that measure the amount of energy necessary to heat or cool buildings due to outside temperatures. (See the explanation in the Source sheet of the file.) These are reported for each state in the United States and also for several regions, as listed in the Locations sheet, from 1931 to 2000.

  a. For each of the Heating Degree Days and Cooling Degree Days sheets, create a new Season variable with values "Winter," "Spring," "Summer," and "Fall." Winter consists of December, January, and February; Spring consists of March, April, and May; Summer consists of June, July, and August; and Fall consists of September, October, and November.

  b. Find the mean, median, and standard deviation of Heating Degree Days (HDD), broken down by Season, for the 48 contiguous states location (code 5999). (Ignore the first and last rows for the given location, the ones that contain -9999, the code for missing values.) Also, create side-by-side box plots of HDD, broken down by season. Comment on the results. Do they go in the direction you would expect? Do the same for Cooling Degree Days (which has no missing data).

  c. Repeat part **b** for California (code 0499).

  d. Repeat part **b** for the New England group of states (code 5801).

3-4 Relationships Among Numeric Variables

This section discusses methods for finding relationships among numeric variables. For example, you might want to examine the relationship between heights and weights of people, or between salary and years of experience of employees. To study such relationships, we introduce two new summary measures, correlation and covariance, and a type of chart called a scatterplot.

In general, don't use correlations that involve coded categorical variables such as 0–1 dummies. The methods from the previous two sections are more appropriate.

Note that these measures can be applied to *any* variables that are displayed numerically. However, they are appropriate only for truly numeric variables, not for categorical variables that have been coded numerically. In particular, many people create dummy (0–1) variables for categorical variables such as Gender and then include these dummies in a table of correlations. This is certainly possible, and it is not really "wrong." However, if you want to investigate relationships involving categorical variables, it is better to employ the tools in the previous two sections.

3-4a Scatterplots

We first discuss scatterplots, a graphical method for detecting relationships between two numeric variables.[1] Then we will discuss the numeric summary measures, correlation and covariance, in the next subsection. (We do it in this order because correlation and covariance make more sense once you understand scatterplots.) A **scatterplot** is a scatter of points, where each point denotes the values of an observation for two selected variables. The two variables are often labeled generically as X and Y, so a scatterplot is sometimes called an **X-Y chart**. The whole purpose of a scatterplot is to make a relationship (or the lack of it) apparent. Do the points tend to rise upward from left to right? Do they tend to fall downward from left to right? Does the pattern tend to be linear, nonlinear, or no particular shape? Do any points fall outside the general pattern? The answers to these questions provide information about the possible relationship between the two variables. The process is illustrated in Example 3.3.

---

1 Various terms are used for this type of graph. We use the term scatterplot. You might also see the terms scatter plot (two words), scatter chart, scatter diagram, or scattergram. They all mean exactly the same thing.

EXAMPLE

3.3 GOLF STATS ON THE PGA TOUR

For over a decade, the Professional Golf Association (PGA) has kept statistics on all PGA Tour players, and these stats are published on the Web. We imported yearly data from 2003–2017 into the file **Golf Stats.xlsx**. The file includes an observation for each of the top 200 earners for each year, including age, earnings, events played, rounds played, 36-hole cuts made (only the top scorers on Thursday and Friday get to play on the weekend; the others don't make the cut), top 10s, and wins. It also includes stats about efficiency in the various parts of the game (driving, putting, greens in regulation, and sand saves), as well as good holes (eagles and birdies) and bad holes (bogies). A sample of the data for 2017 appears in Figure 3.11, with the data sorted in decreasing order of earnings and a few variables not shown. What relationships can be uncovered in these data for any particular year?

Figure 3.11   Golf Stats

	A	B	C	D	E	F	G	H	I	J	K	L	M	N
1	Rank	Player	Age	Events	Rounds	Cuts Made	Top 10s	Wins	Earnings	Yards/Drive	Driving Accuracy	Greens in Regulation	Putting Average	Sand Save Pct
2	1	Justin Thomas	24	25	79	18	12	5	$9,921,560	309.7	55.1	67.2	1.694	48.2
3	2	Jordan Spieth	24	23	78	19	12	3	$9,433,033	295.6	60.0	70.0	1.711	55.8
4	3	Dustin Johnson	33	20	70	17	8	4	$8,732,193	315.0	57.0	69.5	1.755	44.3
5	4	Hideki Matsuyama	26	22	76	19	7	3	$8,380,570	303.3	58.6	69.0	1.739	50.9
6	5	Jon Rahm	23	23	83	21	11	1	$6,123,248	305.8	58.7	68.6	1.761	59.1
7	6	Rickie Fowler	29	21	77	18	10	1	$6,083,198	300.3	63.9	67.0	1.721	68.7
8	7	Marc Leishman	34	25	90	22	7	2	$5,866,391	298.6	57.9	67.0	1.759	53.0
9	8	Brooks Koepka	27	24	80	19	7	1	$5,612,397	311.1	55.8	63.5	1.721	48.2
10	9	Kevin Kisner	34	28	98	24	8	1	$4,766,936	289.5	67.8	66.4	1.785	52.1
11	10	Brian Harman	31	30	100	21	7	1	$4,396,470	289.9	62.8	63.8	1.738	58.7

Objective

To use scatterplots to search for relationships in the golf data.

Solution

This example is typical in that there are many numeric variables, and it is up to you to search for possible relationships. A good first step is to ask some interesting questions and then try to answer them with scatterplots. For example, do younger players play more events? Are earnings related to age? Which is related most strongly to earnings: driving, putting, or greens in regulation? Do the answers to these questions remain the same from year to year? This example is all about *exploring* the data, and we will answer only a few of the questions that could be asked. Fortunately, scatterplots are easy to create, so you can do a lot of exploring very quickly.

Scatterplots are great for initial exploration of the data. If a scatterplot suggests a relationship between two variables, other methods can then be used to examine this relationship in more depth.

To create a scatterplot, you highlight any two variables of interest and select a scatter chart of the top left type from the Insert ribbon. At this point, you will probably want to modify the chart by deleting the legend, inserting some titles, and possibly changing some formatting. Also, you might want to swap the roles of the *X* and *Y* variables.

Excel Tip

Selecting Multiple Ranges Efficiently

How do you select two long variables such as Age and Earnings? Here are the steps that make it easy. (1) Select the Age label in cell B1. (2) Hold down the Shift and Ctrl keys and press the down arrow key. This selects the Age column. (3) Hold down the Ctrl key and select the Earnings label in cell H1. (4) Hold down the Shift and Ctrl keys and press the down arrow key. Now both columns are selected.

Several scatterplots appear in Figures 3.12 through 3.15. The scatterplots in Figure 3.12 indicate the possibly surprising results that age is practically unrelated to the number of events played and earnings. Each scatter is basically a shapeless swarm of points, and a shapeless swarm always indicates "no relationship." The scatterplots in Figure 3.13 confirm what you would expect. Specifically, players who play in more events tend to earn more, although there are a number of exceptions to this pattern. Also, players who make more 36-hole cuts tend to earn more.

Figure 3.12 Scatterplots of Age Versus Events and Earnings

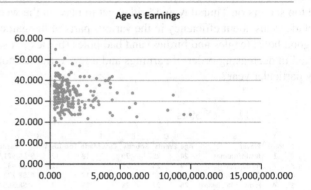

Figure 3.13 Scatterplots of Earnings Versus Events and Cuts Made

Excel Tip

Data Labels in Scatterplots

Unfortunately, there is no automatic way to enter a label such as "Dustin Johnson" next to a point in a scatterplot. If you click twice on a point (don't double-click, but slowly click twice), you can select this point. Then if you right-click, you have the option of adding a data label. However, this data label is always the value of the *Y* variable. In this case, it would be Dustin's earnings, not his name.

Golfers will be particularly interested in the scatterplots in Figures 3.14 and 3.15. The scatterplots in Figure 3.14 indicate a slight positive relationship between earnings and driving length (yards per drive) but almost no relationship between earnings and driving accuracy (percentage of fairways hit). The scatterplots in Figure 3.15 indicate a slight positive relationship between earnings and greens hit in regulation and a *negative* relationship between earnings and putting average. Does this mean that better putters earn *less*? Absolutely not! The putting stat is the average number of putts per hole, so a *lower* value is better. Therefore, the downward relationship indicated in the chart is expected. In fact, the driving and putting scatterplots tend to confirm the old saying in golf: Drive for show, putt for dough.

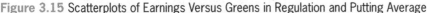

Figure 3.14 Scatterplots of Earnings Versus Driving Length and Driving Accuracy

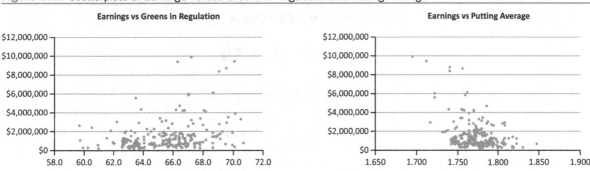

Figure 3.15 Scatterplots of Earnings Versus Greens in Regulation and Putting Average

You could obviously ask many more questions about the relationships in this golf data set and then attempt to answer them with scatterplots. For example, are the relationships (or lack of them) in the scatterplots consistent through the years? Or would it be better to use Earnings per Round instead of Earnings as the *Y* variable? Or are there other variables not shown here, such as the percentage of holed putts of less than 10 feet, that are more highly related to Earnings? You now have a powerful tool, scatterplots, for examining relationships, and the tool is easy to implement. We urge you to use it—a lot.

Trend Lines in Scatterplots

Excel allows you to superimpose a trend line, linear or curved, on a scatterplot. It is an easy way to quantify the relationship apparent in the scatterplot.

Chapters 10 and 11 discuss regression, a method for quantifying relationships between variables. We can provide a brief introduction to regression at this point by discussing the very useful Trendline tool in Excel. Once you have a scatterplot, Excel enables you to superimpose one of several trend lines on the scatterplot. Essentially, a **trend line** is a line or curve that "fits" the scatter as well as possible. This could indeed be a straight line, or it could be one of several types of curves. (By the way, you can also superimpose a trend line on a time series graph, exactly as described here for scatterplots.)

To illustrate the Trendline option, we created the scatterplot of driving length versus driving accuracy in Figure 3.16. If you are a golfer, you are probably not surprised to see

Figure 3.16 Scatterplot with Trendline Superimposed

that the longest hitters tend to be less accurate. This scatterplot is definitely downward sloping, and it appears to follow a straight line reasonably well.

Therefore, it is reasonable to fit a linear trend line to this scatterplot, as you see in the figure. To do this, right-click any point on the chart, select Add Trendline, and fill out the resulting dialog box as shown in Figure 3.17. Note that we have checked the Display Equation on Chart option. The equation you see is a regression equation. It states that driving length (y) is 358.56 minus 1.0704 times driving accuracy (x). This line is certainly not a perfect fit because there are many points well above the line and others below the line. Still, it quantifies the downward relationship reasonably well.

Figure 3.17 Trendline Options Dialog Box

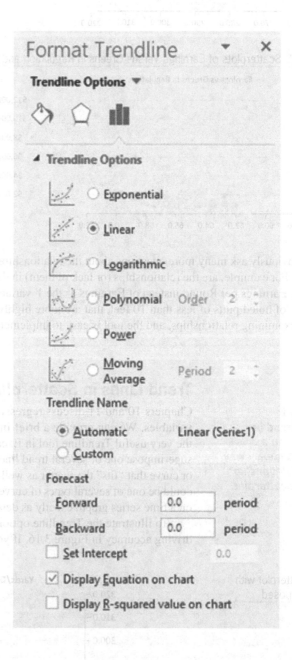

The tools in this subsection, scatterplots and trend lines superimposed on scatterplots, are among the most valuable tools you will learn in the book. When you are interested in a possible relationship between two numeric variables, these are the tools you should use first.

3-4b Correlation and Covariance

Many numeric summary measures for a *single* variable were discussed in Chapter 2. The two measures discussed in this section, correlation and covariance, involve *two* variables. Specifically, each measures the strength and direction of a *linear* relationship between two numeric variables. Intuitively, the relationship is "strong" if the points in a scatterplot cluster tightly around some straight line. If this straight line rises from left to right, the relationship is *positive* and the measures will be positive numbers. If it falls from left to right, the relationship is *negative* and the measures will be negative numbers.

To measure the covariance or correlation between two numerical variables X and Y— indeed, to form a scatterplot of X versus Y—X and Y must be "paired" variables. That is, they must have the same number of observations, and the X and Y values for any observation should be naturally paired. For example, each observation could be the height and weight for a particular person, the time in a store and the amount purchased for a particular customer, and so on.

With this in mind, let X_i and Y_i be the paired values for observation i, and let n be the number of observations. Then the **covariance** between X and Y, denoted by Covar(X, Y), is given by the following formula.

Formula for Covariance

$$\text{Covar}(X, Y) = \frac{\sum_{i=1}^{n}(X_i - \overline{X})(Y_i - \overline{Y})}{n - 1} \tag{3.1}$$

You will probably never have to use Equation (3.1) directly—Excel has a built-in COVAR function that does it for you—but the formula does indicate what covariance is all about. It is essentially an average of products of deviations from means. If X and Y vary in the *same* direction, then when X is above its mean, Y will tend to be above its mean, and when X is below its mean, Y will tend to be below its mean. In either case, the product of deviations will be positive—a positive times a positive or a negative times a negative—so the covariance will be positive. The opposite is true when X and Y vary in *opposite* directions. Then the covariance will be negative.

Covariance is too sensitive to the measurement scales of X and Y to make it interpretable, so it is better to rely on correlation, which is unaffected by measurement scales.

Covariance has a serious limitation as a descriptive measure because it is very sensitive to the *units* in which X and Y are measured. For example, the covariance can be inflated by a factor of 1000 simply by measuring X in dollars rather than thousands of dollars. This limits the usefulness of covariance as a descriptive measure, and we will use it very little in the book.[2]

In contrast, the **correlation**, denoted by Correl(X, Y), remedies this problem. It is a *unitless* quantity that is unaffected by measurement scales. For example, the correlation is the same regardless of whether the variables are measured in dollars, thousands of dollars, or millions of dollars. The correlation is defined by Equation (3.2), where Stdev(X) and Stdev(Y) denote the standard deviations of X and Y. Again, you will probably never have to use this formula for calculations—Excel does it for you with the built-in CORREL function—but it does show how correlation and covariance are related to one another.

Formula for Correlation

$$\text{Correl}(X, Y) = \frac{\text{Covar}(X, Y)}{\text{Stdev}(X) \times \text{Stdev}(Y)} \tag{3.2}$$

---

2 Don't write off covariance too quickly, however. If you plan to take a finance course in investments, you will see plenty of covariances.

Correlation is useful only for measuring the strength of a linear relationship. Strongly related variables can have correlation close to 0 if the relationship is nonlinear.

The correlation is not only unaffected by the units of measurement of the two variables, but it is *always* between -1 and $+1$. The closer it is to either of these two extremes, the closer the points in a scatterplot are to a straight line, either in the negative or positive direction. On the other hand, if the correlation is close to 0, the scatterplot is typically a "cloud" of points with no apparent relationship. However, although it is not common, it is also *possible* that the points are close to a curve and have a correlation close to 0. This is because correlation is relevant only for measuring *linear* relationships.

When there are several numeric variables in a data set, it is useful to create a table of covariances and/or correlations. Each value in the table then corresponds to a particular pair of variables. However, we first make three important points about the roles of scatterplots, correlations, and covariances.

- **A correlation is a single-number summary of a scatterplot.** It never conveys as much information as the full scatterplot; it only summarizes the information in the scatterplot. Still, it is often more convenient to report a table of correlations for many variables than to report an unwieldy number of scatterplots.
- **You are usually on the lookout for large correlations, those near -1 or $+1$.** But how large is "large"? There is no generally agreed-upon cutoff, but by looking at a number of scatterplots and their corresponding correlations, you will start to get a sense of what a correlation such as -0.5 or $+0.7$ really means in terms of the strength of the linear relationship between the variables. (In addition, a concrete meaning will be given to the *square* of a correlation in Chapters 10 and 11.)
- **Do not even try to interpret covariances numerically except possibly to check whether they are positive or negative.** For interpretive purposes, concentrate on correlations.

Fundamental Insight

Scatterplots Versus Correlations

It is important to remember that a correlation is a single-number measure of the linear relationship between two numeric variables. Although a correlation is a very useful measure, it is hard to imagine exactly what a correlation such as 0.3 or 0.8 actually means. In contrast, a scatterplot of two numeric variables indicates the relationship between the two variables very clearly. In short, a scatterplot conveys *much* more information than the corresponding correlation.

EXAMPLE

3.3 GOLF STATS (CONTINUED)

In the previous subsection, you saw how relationships between several of the golf variables can be detected with scatterplots. What further insights are possible by looking at correlations between these variables?

Objective
To use correlations to understand relationships in the golf data.

Solution
With the many numeric variables in the golf data set, it is indeed unwieldy to create scatterplots for all pairs of variables (unless you have an add-in like StatTools), but it is fairly easy to create a table of correlations. You could use Excel's CORREL function to calculation each correlation, but if there are many variables, the following steps allow you to fill a table of correlations much more quickly. (Refer to Figure 3.18 as you read this.)

1. Highlight all columns of variables to be correlated, including their variable names at the top, and create range names for them with the Create from Selection button on the Formulas ribbon.
2. Copy the variable names to the top row and left column of your correlation table.
3. Create a copyable formula involving the CORREL and INDIRECT functions to calculate all correlations in the table.

The resulting table of correlations appears in Figure 3.18. The typical formula shown at the bottom was copied to the entire table. The INDIRECT function refers to the range names created in step 1 to get the ranges for the CORREL function. However, note that range names replace illegal characters like / and spaces with underscores. Therefore, the corresponding changes had to be made to the variable names in the table. Also, there are missing data in some of the variables. When calculating the correlation between any two variables, the CORREL function ignores any rows with missing data for these two variables.

Figure 3.18 Correlations for Golf Data

	A	B	C	D	E	F	G	H	I	J	K	L
1	Table of correlations											
2												
3			Age	Events	Rounds	Cuts_Made	Earnings	Yards_Drive	Driving_Accuracy	Greens_in_Regulation	Putting_Average	Sand_Save_Pct
4		Age	1.000	−0.085	−0.098	−0.105	−0.191	−0.381	0.341	0.020	0.226	−0.071
5		Events	−0.085	1.000	0.943	0.698	0.156	−0.036	−0.002	0.035	0.095	−0.128
6		Rounds	−0.098	0.943	1.000	0.888	0.334	0.124	0.045	0.241	−0.045	−0.041
7		Cuts_Made	−0.105	0.698	0.888	1.000	0.546	0.272	0.058	0.367	−0.179	0.058
8		Earnings	−0.191	0.156	0.334	0.546	1.000	0.387	−0.081	0.308	−0.438	0.130
9		Yards_Drive	−0.381	−0.036	0.124	0.272	0.387	1.000	−0.590	0.330	−0.044	−0.089
10		Driving_Accuracy	0.341	−0.002	0.045	0.058	−0.081	−0.590	1.000	0.233	0.167	−0.085
11		Greens_in_Regulation	0.020	0.035	0.241	0.367	0.308	0.330	0.233	1.000	0.228	−0.160
12		Putting_Average	0.226	0.095	−0.045	−0.179	−0.438	−0.044	0.167	0.228	1.000	−0.267
13		Sand_Save_Pct	−0.071	−0.128	−0.041	0.058	0.130	−0.089	−0.085	−0.160	−0.267	1.000
14												
15		Typical formula										
16		Cell C5	=CORREL(INDIRECT($B5),INDIRECT(C$3))									

You can ignore the 1.000 values along the diagonal because a variable is always perfectly correlated with itself. Besides these, you are typically looking for relatively large values, either positive or negative. When the table is fairly large, conditional formatting is useful. For example, you can format all correlations between 0.6 and 0.999 as red and all correlations between −0.999 and −0.5 as green, as has been done here. There are three large positive values, all above 0.69, involving events, rounds, and cuts made. None of these should come as a surprise. There is only one large negative correlation, the one between driving length and driving accuracy, and you already saw the corresponding scatterplot in Figure 3.16. So if you want to know what a correlation of approximately −0.6 really means, you can look at the scatterplot in this figure. It indicates a definite downward trend, but there is still quite a lot of variability around the best-fitting straight line.

You typically scan a table of correlations for the large correlations, either positive or negative. Conditional formatting is useful, especially if the table is a large one.

Again, a correlation is only a summary of a scatterplot. Therefore, you can learn more about any interesting-looking correlations by creating the corresponding scatterplot. For example, the scatterplot corresponding to the 0.888 correlation between Cuts Made and Rounds appears in Figure 3.19. (We also superimposed a trend line.) This chart shows the strong linear relationship between cuts made and rounds played, but it also shows that there is still considerable variability around the best-fitting straight line, even with a correlation as large as 0.888.

Figure 3.19 Scatterplot of Rounds Versus Cuts Made

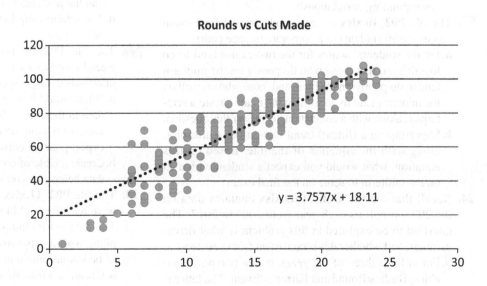

Rounds vs Cuts Made

$y = 3.7577x + 18.11$

Problems

Level A

21. The file **P02_07.xlsx** includes data on 204 employees at the (fictional) company Beta Technologies.
  a. Create a table of correlations between the variables Age, Prior Experience, Beta Experience, Education, and Annual Salary. Which of the first four of these variables is most highly correlated (in a positive direction) with Annual Salary?
  b. Create scatterplots of Annual Salary (Y axis) versus each of Age, Prior Experience, Beta Experience, and Education.
  c. For the variable from part **a** most highly correlated with Annual Salary, create a (linear) trend line in its scatterplot with the corresponding equation shown in the chart. What does this equation imply about the relationship between the two variables? Be specific.

22. The file **P03_22.xlsx** lists financial data on movies released from 1980 to 2011 with budgets of at least $20 million.
  a. Reduce the size of this data set by deleting all movies with a budget of more than $100 million. Also, delete all movies where US Gross and/or Worldwide Gross is listed as Unknown.
  b. For the remaining movies, create a table of correlations between the variables Budget, US Gross, and Worldwide Gross. Comment on the results. Are there any surprises?
  c. For the movies remaining after part **a**, create a scatterplot of Worldwide Gross (Y axis) versus US Gross and another scatterplot of US Gross (Y axis) versus Budget. Briefly explain any patterns you see in these scatterplots. Do they seem to be consistent with the corresponding correlations?

23. The file **P02_10.xlsx** contains midterm and final exam scores for 96 students in a corporate finance course.
  a. Do the students' scores for the two exams tend to go together, so that those who do poorly on the midterm tend to do poorly on the final, and those who do well on the midterm tend to do well on the final? Create a scatterplot, along with a correlation, to answer this question.
  b. Superimpose a (linear) trend line on the scatterplot, along with the equation of the line. Based on this equation, what would you expect a student with a 75 on the midterm to score on the final exam?

24. Recall that the file **Golf Stats.xlsx** contains data on the 200 top golfers each year from 2003 to 2017. The question to be explored in this problem is what drives earnings, and whether this is consistent from year to year.
  a. For at least three of the years, create two new variables, Birdies/Round and Earnings/Event. The latter is potentially a better measure of earnings because some players enter more events than others.

  b. Create a separate table of correlations for each of the selected years that includes Earnings/Event, Yards/Drive, Driving Accuracy, Greens in Regulation, Putting Average, Sand Save Pct, and Birdies/Round. Explain whether these correlations help answer the questions posed above.
  c. There is a saying in golf: "Drive for show, putt for dough." Create a separate set of scatterplots for each of the selected years of Earnings/Event (Y axis) versus each of Yards/Drive, Driving Accuracy, and Putting Average. Discuss whether these scatterplots tend to support the saying.

25. The file **P03_25.xlsx** contains data about 211 movies released in 2006 and 2007. The question to be explored in this problem is whether the total gross for a movie can be predicted from how it does in its first week or two.
  a. Create a table of correlations between the five variables 7-day Gross, 14-day Gross, Total US Gross, International Gross, and US DVD Sales. Does it appear that the last three variables are related to either of the first two?
  b. Explore the basic question further by creating a scatterplot of each of Total US Gross, International Gross, and US DVD Sales (Y axis) versus each of 7-day Gross and 14-day Gross (X axis)—six scatterplots in all. Do these support the claim that you can tell how well a movie will do by seeing how it does in its first week or two?

26. The file **P02_39.xlsx** contains SAT and ACT test scores by state for high school graduates of the 2016–2017 school year. These are broken down by reading/writing and math/science scores. The file also lists the percentages of students taking these two tests by state. Create correlations and scatterplots to explore the following relationships and comment on the results.
  a. The relationship between the total SAT score and the percentage taking the SAT exam.
  b. The relationship between the ERW and Math components of the SAT exam.
  c. The relationship between the composite ACT score and the percentage taking the ACT exam.
  d. The relationship between the four components of the ACT exam.

27. The file **P02_16.xlsx** contains traffic data from 256 weekdays on four variables. Each variable lists the number of arrivals during a specific 5-minute period of the day.
  a. What would it mean, in the context of traffic, for the data in the four columns to be positively correlated? Based on your observations of traffic, would you expect positive correlations?
  b. Create a table of correlations and check whether these data behave as you would expect.

28. The file **P02_11.xlsx** contains data on 148 houses that were recently sold in a (fictional) suburban community. The data set includes the selling price of each house, along with its appraised value, square footage, number of bedrooms, and number of bathrooms.
  a. Create a table of correlations between all of the variables. Comment on the magnitudes of the correlations. Specifically, which of the last three variables,

Square Feet, Bedrooms, and Bathrooms, are highly correlated with Selling Price?

b. Create four scatterplots to show how the other four variables are related to Selling Price. In each, Selling Price should be on the Y axis. Are these in line with the correlations in part **a**?

c. You might think of the difference, Selling Price minus Appraised Value, as the "error" in the appraised value, in the sense that this difference is how much more or less the house sold for than the appraiser expected. Find the correlation between this difference and Selling Price, and find the correlation between the *absolute value* of this difference and Selling Price. If either of these correlations is reasonably large, what is it telling us?

Level B

29. The file **P03_29.xlsx** contains daily prices of four precious metals: gold, silver, platinum, and palladium. The question to be explored here is whether changes in these commodities move together through time.

a. Create time series graphs of the four series. Do the series appear to move together?

b. Create four new difference variables, one for each metal. Each should list this month's price minus the previous month's price. Then create time series graphs of the differences.

c. Create a table of correlations between the differences created in part **b**. Based on this table, comment on whether the changes in the prices of these metals tend to move together over time.

d. For all correlations in part **c** above 0.6, create the corresponding scatterplots of the differences (for example, gold differences versus silver differences). Do these, along with the time series graphs from parts **a** and **b**, provide a clearer picture of how these series move together over time?

30. The file **P03_30.xlsx** contains daily data on exchange rates of various currencies versus the U.S. dollar. It is of interest to financial analysts and economists to see whether exchange rates move together through time. You could find the correlations between the exchange rates themselves, but it is often more useful with time series data to check for correlations between *differences* from day to day.

a. Create a column of differences for each currency.

b. Create a table of correlations between all of the *original* variables. Then on the same sheet, create a second table of correlations between the difference variables. On this same sheet, enter two cutoff values, one positive such as 0.6 and one negative such as −0.5, and use conditional formatting to color all correlations (in both tables) above the positive cutoff green and all correlations below the negative cutoff red. Do it so that the 1's on the diagonal are not colored.

c. Based on the second table and your coloring, can you conclude that these currencies tend to move together in the same direction? If not, what can you conclude?

31. The file **P02_35.xlsx** contains data from a survey of 500 randomly selected (fictional) households.

a. Create a table of correlations between the last five variables (First Income to Debt). On the sheet with these correlations, enter a "cutoff" correlation such as 0.5 in a blank cell. Then use conditional formatting to color green all correlations in the table at least as large as this cutoff, but don't color the 1's on the diagonal. The coloring should change automatically as you change the cutoff. This is always a good idea for highlighting the "large" correlations in a correlations table.

b. Do some investigation to see how missing values are handled when calculating correlations. There are two basic possibilities (and both of these are options in some software packages). First, it could delete all rows that have missing values for *any* variables and then calculate all of the correlations based on the remaining data. Second, when it creates the correlation for any *pair* of variables, it could (temporarily) delete only the rows that have missing data for these two variables and then calculate the correlation on what remains for these two variables. Why would you prefer the second option?

32. We have indicated that if you have two categorical variables and you want to check whether they are related, the best method is to create a crosstabs, possibly with the counts expressed as percentages. But suppose both categorical variables have only two categories and these variables are coded as dummy 0–1 variables. Then there is nothing to prevent you from finding the correlation between them with the same Equation (3.2) from this section, that is, with Excel's CORREL function. However, if we let $C(i, j)$ be the count of observations where the first variable has value i and the second variable has value j, there are only four joint counts that can have any bearing on the relationship between the two variables: $C(0,0)$, $C(0,1)$, $C(1,0)$, and $C(1,1)$. Let $C_1(1)$ be the count of 1s for the first variable and let $C_2(1)$ be the count of 1s for the second variable. Then it is clear that $C_1(1) = C(1,0) + C(1,1)$ and $C_2(1) = C(0,1) + C(1,1)$, so $C_1(1)$ and $C_2(1)$ are determined by the joint counts. It can be shown algebraically that the correlation between the two 0–1 variables is

$$\frac{nC(1,1) - C_1(1)C_2(1)}{\sqrt{C_1(1)(n - C_1(1))}\sqrt{C_2(1)(n - C_2(1))}}$$

To illustrate this, the file **P03_32.xlsx** contains two 0–1 variables. (The values were generated randomly.) Create a crosstabs to find the required counts, and use the above formula to calculate the correlation. Then use StatTools (or Excel's CORREL function) to find the correlation in the usual way. Do your two results match? (Again, we do not necessarily recommend finding correlations between 0–1 variables. A crosstabs is more meaningful and easier to interpret.)

3-5 Pivot Tables

We now discuss one of Excel's most powerful—and easy-to-use—tools, **pivot tables**. Pivot tables allow you to break the data down by categories so that you can see, for example, average sales by gender, by region of country, by time of day, or any combination of these. Sometimes pivot tables are used to display counts, such as the number of customers broken down by gender and region of country. These tables of counts, often called crosstabs or contingency tables, have been used by statisticians for years. However, crosstabs typically list only counts, whereas pivot tables can list counts, sums, averages, and other summary measures.

It is easiest to understand pivot tables by means of examples, so we illustrate several possibilities in the following example.

EXAMPLE

3.4 CUSTOMER ORDERS AT ELECMART

The file **Elecmart Sales.xlsx** (see Figure 3.20) contains data on 400 customer orders during a period of several months for the fictional Elecmart company.[3] There are several categorical variables and several numeric variables. The categorical variables include the day of week, time of day, region of country, type of credit card used, gender of customer, and buy category of the customer (high, medium, or low) based on previous behavior. The numeric variables include the number of items ordered, the total cost of the order, and the price of the highest-priced item purchased. How can the manager of Elecmart use pivot tables to summarize the data so that she can understand the buying patterns of her customers?

Objective

To use pivot tables to break down the customer order data by a number of categorical variables.

Figure 3.20 Elecmart Data

	A	B	C	D	E	F	G	H	I	J
1	Date	Day	Time	Region	Card Type	Gender	Buy Category	Items Ordered	Total Cost	High Item
2	4-Mar	Sun	Morning	West	ElecMart	Female	High	4	$136.97	$79.97
3	4-Mar	Sun	Morning	West	Other	Female	Medium	1	$25.55	$25.55
4	4-Mar	Sun	Afternoon	West	ElecMart	Female	Medium	5	$113.95	$90.47
5	4-Mar	Sun	Afternoon	Northeast	Other	Female	Low	1	$6.82	$6.82
6	4-Mar	Sun	Afternoon	West	ElecMart	Male	Medium	4	$147.32	$83.21
7	4-Mar	Sun	Afternoon	Northeast	Other	Female	Medium	5	$142.15	$50.90
8	5-Mar	Mon	Evening	West	Other	Male	Low	1	$18.65	$18.65
9	5-Mar	Mon	Evening	South	Other	Male	High	4	$178.34	$161.93
10	5-Mar	Mon	Evening	West	Other	Male	Low	2	$25.83	$15.91
11	6-Mar	Tue	Morning	Midwest	Other	Female	Low	1	$18.13	$18.13
12	6-Mar	Tue	Morning	Northeast	ElecMart	Female	Medium	2	$54.52	$54.38
13	6-Mar	Tue	Afternoon	South	Other	Male	Medium	2	$61.93	$56.32
14	7-Mar	Wed	Morning	Northeast	ElecMart	Male	High	3	$147.68	$96.64
15	7-Mar	Wed	Afternoon	Northeast	Other	Male	Low	1	$27.24	$27.24

---

[3] Users of previous editions of the book will notice that the dates have been changed. This changes a few values in the reported pivot tables.

Solution

First, we preview the results you can obtain. Pivot tables are useful for breaking down numeric variables by categories, or for counting observations in categories and possibly expressing the counts as percentages. So, for example, you might want to see how the average total cost for females differs from the similar average for males. Or you might simply want to see the percentage of the 400 sales made by females. Pivot tables allow you to find such averages and percentages easily.

Pivot tables are perfect for breaking down data by categories. Many people refer to this as "slicing and dicing" the data.

Actually, you could find such averages or percentages without using pivot tables. For example, you could sort on gender and then find the average of the Female rows and the average of the Male rows. However, this takes time, and more complex breakdowns are even more difficult and time-consuming. They are all easy and quick with pivot tables. Besides that, the resulting tables can be accompanied with corresponding charts that require virtually no extra effort to create. Pivot tables are a manager's dream. Fortunately, Excel makes them a manager's *reality*.

We begin by building a pivot table to find the sum of Total Cost broken down by time of day and region of country. Although we show this in a number of screen shots, just to help you get the knack of it, the process takes only a few seconds after you gain some experience with pivot tables.

Beginning in Excel 2013, there is a Recommended Pivot Tables option. It guesses which pivot tables you might want.

To start, click the PivotTable button at the far left on the Insert ribbon (see Figure 3.21). This produces the dialog box in Figure 3.22. The top section allows you to specify the table or range that contains the data. (You can also specify an external data source, but we will not cover this option here.) The bottom section allows you to select the location where you want the results to be placed. If you start by selecting any cell inside the data set, Excel's guess for the table or range is usually correct, although you can override it if necessary. Make sure the

Figure 3.21 PivotTable Button on Insert Ribbon

Figure 3.22 Create PivotTable Dialog Box

range selected for this example is A1:J401. This selected range should include the variable names at the top of each column. Then click OK. Note that with these settings, the pivot table will be placed in a new worksheet with a generic name such as Sheet1. You will probably want to rename it something like Pivot Table.

This produces a blank pivot table, as shown in Figure 3.23. Also, assuming any cell inside this blank pivot table is selected, the PivotTable Tools "super tab" is visible. This super tab has two ribbons, Analzye and Design. (The Analyze ribbon was named Options in Excel 2007 and 2010.) The Analyze ribbon appears in Figure 3.24, and the Design ribbon appears in Figure 3.25. Each of these has a variety of buttons for manipulating pivot tables, some of which we will explore shortly. Finally, the PivotTable Fields pane in Figure 3.26 is visible. By default, it is docked at the right of the screen, but you can move it if you like.

Figure 3.23 Blank Pivot Table

Figure 3.24 PivotTable Analyze Ribbon

Figure 3.25 PivotTable Design Ribbon

Figure 3.26 PivotTable Fields
Pane

Note that the two pivot table ribbons and the PivotTable Fields pane are visible only when the active cell is inside a pivot table. If you click outside the pivot table, say, in cell D1, all three of these will disappear. Don't worry. You can get them back by selecting any cell inside the pivot table.

The PivotTable Fields pane indicates that a pivot table has four areas. These are for Filters, Rows, Columns, and Values. They correspond to the four areas in Figure 3.26 where you can put fields.[4]

A Rows field has categories that go down the left side of a pivot table, a Columns field has categories that go across the top of a pivot table, a Filters field lets you filter the pivot table by its categories, and a Values field contains the data you want to summarize. Typically (but not always), you will place categorical variables in the Filters, Rows, and/or Columns areas, and you will place numeric variables in the Values area.

In the present example, check the Time, Region, and Total Cost boxes in the upper half of the PivotTable Fields pane. You immediately get the pivot table in Figure 3.27. It shows the sum of Total Cost, broken down by time of day and region of country. For example, the total cost of orders in the morning in the South was $3835.86, and the total cost of orders in the morning (over all regions) was $18,427.31.

Excel applies two rules to variables checked at the top of the PivotTable Fields pane:

• When you check a text variable or a date variable in the field list, it is added to the Rows area.
• When you check a numeric variable in the field list, it is added to the Values area and summarized with the Sum function.

This is exactly what happens when you check Time, Region, and Total Cost. However, this is just the beginning. With very little work, you can do a lot more. Some of the many possibilities are explained in the remainder of this example.

First, notice that the pivot table in Figure 3.27 has *both* Rows fields, Time and Region, in column A. This is one of three possible layouts: Compact, Outline, or Tabular. These are available from the Report Layout dropdown list on the Design ribbon. When you create a

There are three different layouts for pivot tables, but the differences are relatively minor. Ultimately, it is a matter of taste.

---

4 In discussing pivot tables, Microsoft uses the term *field* rather than *variable*, so we will do so as well.

Figure 3.27 Sum of Total Cost by Time and Region (Compact Layout)

	A	B
1		
2		
3	**Row Labels** ▼	**Sum of Total Cost**
4	⊟**Afternoon**	**24265.6**
5	Midwest	3187.16
6	Northeast	8159.78
7	South	5729.72
8	West	7188.94
9	⊟**Evening**	**18834.3**
10	Midwest	2552.89
11	Northeast	5941.49
12	South	3864.12
13	West	6475.8
14	⊟**Morning**	**18427.31**
15	Midwest	3878.22
16	Northeast	5084.57
17	South	3835.86
18	West	5628.66
19	**Grand Total**	**61527.21**

pivot table (in an .xlsx file), you get the compact layout by default. If you would rather have the tabular or outline layout, it is easy to switch to them. In particular, the tabular layout, shown in Figure 3.28, is closer to what was used in pre-2007 versions of Excel. (Outline layout, not shown here, is very similar to tabular layout except for the placement of its subtotals.)

Figure 3.28 Sum of Total Cost by Time and Region (Tabular Layout)

	A	B	C
1			
2			
3	**Time** ▼	**Region** ▼	**Sum of Total Cost**
4	⊟**Afternoon**	Midwest	3187.16
5		Northeast	8159.78
6		South	5729.72
7		West	7188.94
8	**Afternoon Total**		**24265.6**
9	⊟**Evening**	Midwest	2552.89
10		Northeast	5941.49
11		South	3864.12
12		West	6475.8
13	**Evening Total**		**18834.3**
14	⊟**Morning**	Midwest	3878.22
15		Northeast	5084.57
16		South	3835.86
17		West	5628.66
18	**Morning Total**		**18427.31**
19	**Grand Total**		**61527.21**

One significant advantage to using tabular (or outline) layout instead of compact layout is that you can see which fields are in the Rows and Columns areas. Take another look at the pivot table in Figure 3.27. It is fairly obvious that categories such as Afternoon and Morning have to do with time of day and that categories such as Midwest and South have to do with region of country. However, there are no labels that explicitly name the Rows fields. In contrast, the tabular layout in Figure 3.28 names them explicitly, and it makes filtering more transparent. Some critics have been very vocal about their dislike for compact layout due to the lack of meaningful labels, and we tend to agree. Therefore, the remaining screenshots in this chapter show tabular layout.

Changing Locations of Fields

Starting with the pivot table in Figure 3.28, you can choose where to place either Time or Region; it does *not* have to be in the Rows area. To place the Region variable in the Columns area, for example, drag the Region button from the Rows area of the PivotTable Fields pane to the Columns area. The pivot table changes automatically, as shown in Figure 3.29. (This is called pivoting.)

Figure 3.29 Placing Region in the Columns Area

	A	B	C	D	E	F
1						
2						
3	Sum of Total Cost	Region				
4	Time	Midwest	Northeast	South	West	Grand Total
5	Morning	3878.22	5084.57	3835.86	5628.66	18427.31
6	Afternoon	3187.16	8159.78	5729.72	7188.94	24265.6
7	Evening	2552.89	5941.49	3864.12	6475.8	18834.3
8	Grand Total	9618.27	19185.84	13429.7	19293.4	61527.21

Note that times of day in column A are now in chronological order, not in alphabetical order as they were by default. It is easy to make this change. Select the top of the Morning cell (A7) until the cursor becomes a four-way arrow and drag it above Afternoon.

You can also categorize by a third field such as Gender. As before, if you check Gender in the PivotTable Fields pane, it goes to the Rows area by default, but you could then drag it to another area. The pivot table in Figure 3.30 shows the result of placing Gender in the Rows area. For example, the sum of Total Cost for morning orders by females in the West is 4211.19. You can place as many fields as you like in any area. The only downside is that the pivot table starts to get cluttered. If you want to remove a field from the pivot table, just uncheck its its item in the top part of the PivotTable Fields pane or drag it off from the bottom part of the pane.

Changing the locations of fields in pivot tables is easy. We favor dragging the fields to the various areas, but you can experiment with the other options.

Figure 3.30 Adding a Second Field to the Rows Area

	A	B	C	D	E	F	G
1							
2							
3	Sum of Total Cost		Region				
4	Time	Gender	Midwest	Northeast	South	West	Grand Total
5	⊟ Morning	Female	2880.13	2864.79	2774.01	4211.19	12730.12
6		Male	998.09	2219.78	1061.85	1417.47	5697.19
7	Morning Total		3878.22	5084.57	3835.86	5628.66	18427.31
8	⊟ Afternoon	Female	2092.39	6206.8	5073.03	5210.59	18582.81
9		Male	1094.77	1952.98	656.69	1978.35	5682.79
10	Afternoon Total		3187.16	8159.78	5729.72	7188.94	24265.6
11	⊟ Evening	Female	1411.32	1103.44	1181.66	1885.91	5582.33
12		Male	1141.57	4838.05	2682.46	4589.89	13251.97
13	Evening Total		2552.89	5941.49	3864.12	6475.8	18834.3
14	Grand Total		9618.27	19185.84	13429.7	19293.4	61527.21

If you checked the Gender field to get Figure 3.30, you'll notice that Gender is *below* Time in the Rows box. This makes Time the "outer" Rows field and Gender the "inner" Rows field in the pivot table. To reverse their roles, drag Gender above Time in the Rows box. This leads to the pivot table in Figure 3.31. The two pivot tables provide slightly different views of the same summarization, and you can choose the one you like best. This ability to categorize by multiple fields and rearrange the fields as you like is a big reason why pivot tables are so powerful and useful—and easy to use.

Changing Field Settings

You can change various settings in the Field Settings dialog box. You can get to this dialog box in at least two ways. First, there is a Field Setting button on the Analyze ribbon. Second, you can right-click any of the pivot table cells and select Field Settings. The field settings are particularly useful for fields in the Values area.

For now, right-click any number in the pivot table in Figure 3.31 and select Value Field Settings to obtain the dialog box in Figure 3.32. This allows you to choose how you want to summarize the Total Cost variable—by Sum, Average, Count,

Figure 3.31 Pivot Table with Rows Fields Reversed

	A	B	C	D	E	F	G
1							
2							
3	Sum of Total Cost		Region ⌄				
4	Gender ⌄	Time ⌄	Midwest	Northeast	South	West	Grand Total
5	⊟ Female	Morning	2880.13	2864.79	2774.01	4211.19	12730.12
6		Afternoon	2092.39	6206.8	5073.03	5210.59	18582.81
7		Evening	1411.32	1103.44	1181.66	1885.91	5582.33
8	**Female Total**		**6383.84**	**10175.03**	**9028.7**	**11307.69**	**36895.26**
9	⊟ Male	Morning	998.09	2219.78	1061.85	1417.47	5697.19
10		Afternoon	1094.77	1952.98	656.69	1978.35	5682.79
11		Evening	1141.57	4838.05	2682.46	4589.89	13251.97
12	**Male Total**		**3234.43**	**9010.81**	**4401**	**7985.71**	**24631.95**
13	**Grand Total**		**9618.27**	**19185.84**	**13429.7**	**19293.4**	**61527.21**

The key to summarizing the data the way you want it summarized is the Value Field Settings dialog box. Get used to it because you will use it often.

or several others. You can also click the Number Format button to choose from the usual number formatting options, and you can click the Show Values As tab to display the data in various ways (more on this later). If you choose Average and format as currency with two decimals, the resulting pivot table appears as in Figure 3.33. Now each number is the average of Total Cost for all orders in its combination of categories. For example, the average of Total Cost for all morning orders by females in the South is $146.00, and the average of *all* orders by females in the South is $143.31.

Figure 3.32 Value Field Settings Dialog Box

Value Field Settings

Source Name: Total Cost

Custom Name: Average of Total Cost

Summarize Values By | Show Values As

Summarize value field by

Choose the type of calculation that you want to use to summarize data from the selected field

Sum
Count
Average
Max
Min
Product

Number Format   OK   Cancel

Figure 3.33 Pivot Table with Average of Total Cost

	A	B	C	D	E	F	G
1							
2							
3	Average of Total C		Region ⌄				
4	Gender ⌄	Time ⌄	Midwest	Northeast	South	West	Grand Total
5	⊟ Female	Morning	$160.01	$143.24	$146.00	$150.40	$149.77
6		Afternoon	$123.08	$172.41	$153.73	$192.98	$164.45
7		Evening	$176.42	$183.91	$107.42	$171.45	$155.06
8	**Female Total**		**$148.46**	**$164.11**	**$143.31**	**$171.33**	**$157.67**
9	⊟ Male	Morning	$124.76	$170.75	$132.73	$141.75	$146.08
10		Afternoon	$121.64	$162.75	$109.45	$141.31	$138.60
11		Evening	$103.78	$172.79	$167.65	$148.06	$154.09
12	**Male Total**		**$115.52**	**$170.02**	**$146.70**	**$145.19**	**$148.39**
13	**Grand Total**		**$135.47**	**$166.83**	**$144.41**	**$159.45**	**$153.82**

Filtering

When you place a categorical field in the Rows, Columns, or Filters area, all its categories show by default. But it is often useful to filter out, or hide, some of these categories. This lets you focus on the categories of most interest. There are several ways to filter; you can choose the method you prefer.

1. Click the dropdown arrow next to any Rows or Columns field in the pivot table and check the categories you want to show. Alternatively, choose Label Filters from the dropdown list, which provide several useful options.
2. Add a field to the Filters area. Then filter with its dropdown arrow.
3. Add a **slicer** (or a **timeline** for date fields) from the Filters group on the Analyze ribbon. These are graphical items for making filters more transparent. (Slicers were introduced in Excel 2010. Timelines were introduced in Excel 2013.)

Figures 3.34, 3.35, and 3.36 illustrate these three options. Figure 3.34 uses filters on Time and Region to hide the Afternoon, South, and West categories. Note that the grand totals are only for the filtered data. For example, $142.91 in cell B7 is the average of Total Cost only for the morning and evening orders in the Midwest. Also note the filter signs on the Time and Region dropdown arrows. You can click either of these to change or remove the filters.

Figure 3.34 Filtering on the Fields in the Rows and Columns Areas

	A	B	C	D
1				
2				
3	Average of Total Cost	Region ▾⊤		
4	Time ▾⊤	Midwest	Northeast	Grand Total
5	Morning	$149.16	$154.08	$151.91
6	Evening	$134.36	$174.75	$160.27
7	Grand Total	$142.91	$164.57	$155.87

Figure 3.35 uses a filter for Day in the Filters area. It indicates that multiple categories were checked in the Day dropdown list. However, without opening this list, you can't tell which days were selected. (They are Friday and Saturday.) This lack of transparency is a drawback of filters in the Filters area.

Figure 3.35 Using a Day Filter in the Filters Area

	A	B	C	D	E	F
1	Day	(Multiple Items) ▾⊤				
2						
3	Average of Total Cost	Region ▾				
4	Time ▾	Midwest	Northeast	South	West	Grand Total
5	Morning	$175.20	$172.40	$151.51	$162.39	$166.50
6	Afternoon	$133.13	$200.93	$167.23	$182.74	$173.95
7	Evening	$144.21	$161.78	$138.82	$133.56	$144.15
8	Grand Total	$149.93	$182.85	$153.05	$159.96	$163.52

Figure 3.36 illustrates a slicer on Day and a timeline on Date. When you select Insert Slicer from the Analyze ribbon, you can check as many fields as you like. You get a slicer for each field you check. (For a timeline, you are likely to select only a single date variable.) To choose categories from a slicer, select as many as you want in the usual way: hold down the Ctrl key to select multiple items or the Shift key to select contiguous items. It is clear from this slicer and this timeline that only orders on Fridays and Saturdays during March and April are summarized. This is the advantage of slicers and timelines. They make filters transparent. By the way, to create Figure 3.36, starting from Figure 3.35, we unchecked the Day field in the PivotTable Fields pane. However, this did not remove the filter on Day. When we inserted the slicer on Day, Friday and Saturday were already selected. Just keep this in mind. When you delete a filtered field from a pivot table, the filter is still remembered.

Slicers and timelines aren't really part of a pivot table in the sense that when they are selected, the PivotTable Fields pane isn't opened. However, they each have their own ribbon. For example, when you select a slicer, a Slicer Tools Options tab appears, with an associated ribbon. This lets you make several cosmetic changes to the slicer.

Sorting

You can sort by categories or values in a pivot table. We already mentioned one sort, where Morning was moved above Afternoon by dragging. However, dragging was required only because the "natural" order Morning, Afternoon, Evening is not

Figure 3.36 Filtering with a Slicer and a Timeline

	A	B	C	D	E	F	G	H	I
1									
2									
3	Average of Total Cost	Region					**Day**		
4	Time	Midwest	Northeast	South	West	Grand Total	Sun		
5	Morning	$167.57	$113.10	$161.47	$119.90	$135.61	Mon		
6	Afternoon	$93.57	$101.05	$143.65	$86.22	$111.34			
7	Evening	$218.29	$94.31	$148.04	$149.87	$139.91	Tue		
8	Grand Total	$131.62	$105.13	$147.72	$134.26	$127.45	Wed		
9							Thu		
10									
11		Date					Fri		
12		Mar - Apr 2018			MONTHS ▾		Sat		
13		2018							
14		JAN FEB MAR APR MAY JUN JUL							
15									
16									
17		◀			▶				
18									

alphabetical or reverse alphabetical order. More commonly, you will sort by clicking the dropdown arrow next to a Rows or Columns field and using one of the Sort options at the top. These include A-Z, Z-A, and More Sort Options. You can experiment with the latter.

Sorting by values— the values in the body of the pivot table—is also possible. For example, if you select cell E5 in Figure 3.36 and click the A-Z button on the Data ribbon, not only will cells E5, E6, and E7 will be sorted in increasing order, but (as you would hope) the entire range A5:F7 will be rearranged as well. This is just one possibility. You can also right-click a value in the pivot table, select Sort and then More Sort Options to get the dialog box in Figure 3.37. This lets you sort in increasing or decreasing order from top to bottom or from left to right. Don't be afraid to experiment with these options. You can always press Ctrl+z to undo your sort.

Figure 3.37 More Sort Options for Values

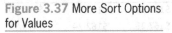

Sort By Value   ?   ✕

Sort options   Sort direction

◉ Smallest to Largest   ◉ Top to Bottom

◯ Largest to Smallest   ◯ Left to Right

Summary

Sort Time by Average of Total Cost in ascending order using values in this column:
West

OK   Cancel

Pivot Charts

It is easy to accompany pivot tables with **pivot charts**. These charts are really Excel charts, but they are better because they adapt automatically to the underlying pivot table. If you make a change to the pivot table, such as pivoting the Rows and Columns fields, the pivot chart makes the same change automatically. To create a pivot chart, click anywhere inside the pivot table, select the PivotChart button on the Analyze ribbon, and select a chart type. That's all there is to it. The resulting pivot chart (using the default column chart option) for the pivot table in Figure 3.36 appears in Figure 3.38. If you decide to pivot the Rows and Columns fields, the pivot chart changes automatically, as shown in Figure 3.39. Note that the categories on the horizontal axis are always based on the Rows field, and the categories in the legend are always based on the Columns field.

Figure 3.38 Pivot Chart Based on Pivot Table

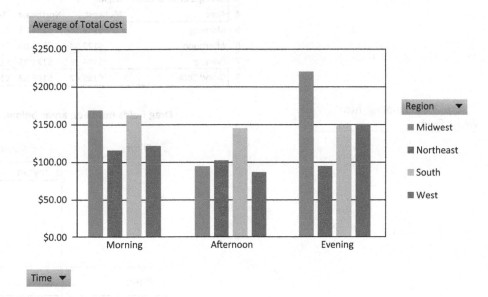

Figure 3.39 Pivot Chart after Pivoting Rows and Columns Fields

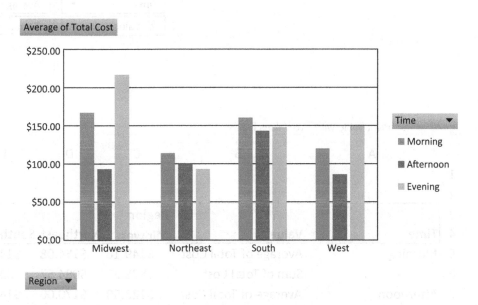

Note that when you activate a pivot chart, the PivotTable Tools "super tab" changes to PivotChart Tools. This super tab includes three ribbons for manipulating pivot charts: Analyze, Design, and Format. There is not enough space here to discuss the many options on these ribbons, but they are intuitive and easy to use. As usual, don't be afraid to experiment.

Multiple Variables in the Values Area

Multiple variables can be placed in the Values area. In addition, a given variable in the Values area can be summarized by more than one summarizing function. This can create a rather busy pivot table, so we indicate our favorite way of doing it. Starting with the pivot table in Figure 3.40, drag Total Cost in the top of the PivotTable Fields pane (the item that is already checked) to the Values area. The bottom part of the PivotTable Fields pane should now appear as in Figure 3.41, and the pivot table should now appear as in Figure 3.42. Note in particular the Values button in the Rows area of Figure 3.41. This button controls the placement of the data in the pivot table. You have a number of options for this button: (1) leave it where it is, (2) drag it above the Time button, (3) drag it to the Columns area, below the Region button, or (4) drag it to the Columns area, above the Region button. You can experiment with these options, but we tend to prefer option (2), which leads to the pivot table in Figure 3.43.

Figure 3.40   Basic Pivot Table

	A	B	C	D	E	F
1						
2						
3	Average of Total Cost	Region ▾				
4	Time ▾	Midwest	Northeast	South	West	Grand Total
5	Morning	$149.16	$154.08	$142.07	$148.12	$148.61
6	Afternoon	$122.58	$170.00	$146.92	$175.34	$157.57
7	Evening	$134.36	$174.75	$143.12	$154.19	$154.38
8	Grand Total	$135.47	$166.83	$144.41	$159.45	$153.82

Figure 3.41 Choosing Two Values Fields

Drag fields between areas below:

▼ Filters

▥ Columns

Region ▾

☰ Rows

Time ▾

Σ Values ▾

Σ Values

Average of To... ▾

Sum of Total ... ▾

Figure 3.42   Pivot Table with Two Values Fields

	A	B	C	D	E	F	G
1							
2							
3			Region ▾				
4	Time ▾	Values	Midwest	Northeast	South	West	Grand Total
5	Morning	Average of Total Cost	$149.16	$154.08	$142.07	$148.12	$148.61
6		Sum of Total Cost	3878.22	5084.57	3835.86	5628.66	18427.31
7	Afternoon	Average of Total Cost	$122.58	$170.00	$146.92	$175.34	$157.57
8		Sum of Total Cost	3187.16	8159.78	5729.72	7188.94	24265.6
9	Evening	Average of Total Cost	$134.36	$174.75	$143.12	$154.19	$154.38
10		Sum of Total Cost	2552.89	5941.49	3864.12	6475.8	18834.3
11	Total Average of Total Cost		$135.47	$166.83	$144.41	$159.45	$153.82
12	Total Sum of Total Cost		9618.27	19185.84	13429.7	19293.4	61527.21

In a similar manner, you can experiment with the buttons in the Values area. However, the effect here is less striking. If you drag the Sum of Total Cost button *above* the Average of Total Cost button in the field list, the effect is simply to switch the ordering of these summaries in the pivot table.

Summarizing by Count

The field in the Values area, whatever it is, can be summarized by the Count function. This is useful when you want to know, for example, how *many* of the orders were placed by females in the South. When summarizing by Count, the key is to understand that the field placed in the Values area is *irrelevant*, so long as you summarize it by the Count function. To illustrate, start

Figure 3.43   Rearranged Pivot Table with Two Values Fields

	A	B	C	D	E	F	G
1							
2							
3			Region ▼				
4	Values	Time ▼	Midwest	Northeast	South	West	Grand Total
5	Average of Total Cost	Morning	$149.16	$154.08	$142.07	$148.12	$148.61
6		Afternoon	$122.58	$170.00	$146.92	$175.34	$157.57
7		Evening	$134.36	$174.75	$143.12	$154.19	$154.38
8	Sum of Total Cost	Morning	3878.22	5084.57	3835.86	5628.66	18427.31
9		Afternoon	3187.16	8159.78	5729.72	7188.94	24265.6
10		Evening	2552.89	5941.49	3864.12	6475.8	18834.3
11	Total Average of Total Cost		$135.47	$166.83	$144.41	$159.45	$153.82
12	Total Sum of Total Cost		9618.27	19185.84	13429.7	19293.4	61527.21

with the pivot table in Figure 3.40, where Total Cost is summarized with the Average function. Next, right-click any number in the pivot table, select Value Field Settings, and select the Count from the Summarize Values By options. The default Custom Name you will see in this dialog box, Count of Total Cost, is misleading, because Total Cost has nothing to do with the counts obtained. Therefore, we like to change this Custom Name label to Count. While in the Value Field Settings dialog box, change the number format to Number with zero decimals. The resulting pivot table appears in Figure 3.44. For example, 27 of the 400 orders were placed in the morning in the South, and 115 of the 400 orders were placed in the Northeast. (Do you now see why the counts have nothing to do with Total Cost?) This type of pivot table, with counts for various categories, is the same as the *crosstabs* discussed in Section 3-2. However, these counts can be created much more quickly with a pivot table.

When data are summarized by counts, there are a number of ways they can be displayed. The pivot table in Figure 3.44 shows "raw counts." Depending on the type of information you want, it might be more useful to display the counts as percentages. Three particular options are typically chosen: as percentages of total, as percentages of row totals, and as percentages of column totals. When shown as percentages of total, the percentages in the table sum to 100%; when shown as percentages of row totals, the percentages in *each* row sum to 100%; when shown as percentages of column totals, the percentages in *each* column sum to 100%. Each of these options can be useful, depending on the question you are trying to answer. For example, if you want to know whether the daily pattern of orders varies from region to region, showing the counts as percentages of column totals is useful so that you can compare columns. But if you want to see whether the regional ordering pattern varies by time of day, showing the counts as percentages of row totals is useful so that you can compare rows.

Counts can be displayed in a number of ways. You should choose the way that best answers the question you are asking.

Figure 3.44 Pivot Table with Counts

	A	B	C	D	E	F
1						
2						
3	Count	Region ▼				
4	Time ▼	Midwest	Northeast	South	West	Grand Total
5	Morning	26	33	27	38	124
6	Afternoon	26	48	39	41	154
7	Evening	19	34	27	42	122
8	Grand Total	71	115	93	121	400

To display the counts as percentages, right-click any number in the pivot table, select **Show Values As**, and select the option you want. (You can also get to these options from the **Show Values As** tab in the Value Field Settings dialog box.) For example, if you choose % of Column Totals, the resulting pivot table and corresponding pivot chart appear in Figure 3.45. As you can see by comparing columns, the pattern of regional orders varies somewhat by time of day.

Figure 3.45 Pivot Table and
Pivot Chart with Counts As
Percentages of Column Totals

Count	Region				
Time	Midwest	Northeast	South	West	Grand Total
Morning	36.62%	28.70%	29.03%	31.40%	31.00%
Afternoon	36.62%	41.74%	41.94%	33.88%	38.50%
Evening	26.76%	29.57%	29.03%	34.71%	30.50%
Grand Total	100.00%	100.00%	100.00%	100.00%	100.00%

Sometimes it is useful to see the raw counts *and* the percentages. This can be done easily by dragging any variable to the Values area, summarizing it by Count, and displaying it as "Normal." Figure 3.46 shows one possibility, where we have changed the custom names of the two Count variables to make them more meaningful. Alternatively, the counts and percentages could be shown in two separate pivot tables.

Pivot Table Tip

Right-Clicking to Choose Options

We keep saying to make changes in the Value Field Settings dialog box. However, you can also make changes directly by right-clicking a value in the pivot table. For example, when you right-click a number in the Values area, you see Number Format, Summarize Values By, and Show Values As menu items, among others.

Grouping

Finally, categories in a Rows or Columns variable can be grouped. This is especially useful when a Rows or Columns variable has many distinct values. Because a pivot table creates a row or column for each distinct value, the results can be unwieldy. We present two possibilities. First, suppose you want to summarize Sum of Total Cost by Date. If you have Excel 2016 or later, the dates will automatically be grouped in some way, probably by month or by quarter. (Prior to Excel 2016, they weren't grouped at all. You saw a row for each separate date.) In any case, you can right-click any date and select Group. Then you can choose the grouping you prefer.

For example, starting with a blank pivot table, we dragged Date to the Rows area and Total Cost to the Values area to get the pivot table in Figure 3.47 (shown in compact layout). By right-clicking any of the month labels and selecting Group, the dialog box in Figure 3.48 opens. The dates are currently grouped by Month and Day, meaning that if you expand any month in column A, you will see a row for each day in that month. If you select Quarter, Month, and Day in Figure 3.48, you will see the pivot table in Figure 3.49 (after collapsing the months).

Figure 3.46 Pivot Table with Raw Counts and Percentages of Column Totals

		Region				
Values	Time	Midwest	Northeast	South	West	Grand Total
Count	Morning	26	33	27	38	124
	Afternoon	26	48	39	41	154
	Evening	19	34	27	42	122
% of column	Morning	40.32%	26.50%	28.56%	29.17%	29.95%
	Afternoon	33.14%	42.53%	42.66%	37.26%	39.44%
	Evening	26.54%	30.97%	28.77%	33.56%	30.61%
Total Count		71	115	93	121	400
Total % of column		100.00%	100.00%	100.00%	100.00%	100.00%

Figure 3.47 Default Grouping on Date

Row Labels	Average of Total Cost
⊞ Mar	$102.97
⊞ Apr	$146.79
⊞ May	$174.89
⊞ Jun	$191.51
Grand Total	$153.82

Figure 3.48 Grouping Dialog Box

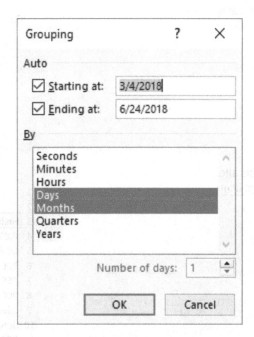

Figure 3.49 Another Grouping
on Date

	A	B
1		
2		
3	**Row Labels** ▼	**Average of Total Cost**
4	⊟ **Qtr1**	
5	⊞ Mar	$102.97
6	**Qtr1 Total**	$102.97
7	⊟ **Qtr2**	
8	⊞ Apr	$146.79
9	⊞ May	$174.89
10	⊞ Jun	$191.51
11	**Qtr2 Total**	$170.54
12	**Grand Total**	**$153.82**

Pivot Table Tip

Grouping on Dates

Suppose you have multiple years of data and you would like a monthly grouping such as January 2017 through December 2019. If you simply select Months in the Grouping dialog box, all of the Januaries, for example, will be lumped together. The trick is to select both Months and Years in the dialog box.

As a second possibility for grouping, suppose you want to see how the average of Total Cost varies by the amount of the highest priced item in the order. You can drag Total Cost to the Values area, summarized by Average, and drag High Item to the Rows area. Because High Item has nearly 400 distinct values, the resulting pivot table is virtually worthless. Therefore, grouping is useful. This time there are no natural groupings as there are for a date variable, so it is up to you to create the groupings. Excel provides the suggested grouping in Figure 3.50, but you can override it. For example, changing the bottom entry to 50 leads to the pivot table in Figure 3.51. Some experimentation is typically required to obtain the grouping that presents the results in the most appropriate way.

Figure 3.50 Grouping Dialog
Box for a Non-Date Variable

Figure 3.51 Pivot Table after
Grouping by 50 on High Item

	A	B
1		
2		
3	**High Item** ▼	**Average of Total Cost**
4	6.82-56.82	$72.78
5	56.82-106.82	$139.66
6	106.82-156.82	$172.71
7	156.82-206.82	$253.55
8	206.82-256.82	$324.26
9	256.82-306.82	$328.92
10	306.82-356.82	$361.53
11	356.82-406.82	$415.17
12	**Grand Total**	**$153.82**

By now, we have illustrated the pivot table features that are most commonly used. Be aware, however, that there are *many* more features available. These include, but are not limited to, the following:

- Showing/hiding subtotals and grand totals (check the Layout options on the Design ribbon)
- Dealing with blank rows, that is, categories with no data (right-click any number, choose PivotTable Options, and check the options on the Layout & Format tab)
- Displaying the data behind a given number in a pivot table (double-click any number in the Values area to get a new worksheet)
- Formatting a pivot table with various styles (check the style options on the Design ribbon)
- Moving or renaming pivot tables (check the PivotTable and Action groups on the Analyze ribbon)
- Refreshing pivot tables as the underlying data changes (check the Refresh dropdown list on the Analyze ribbon)
- Creating pivot table formulas for calculated fields or calculated items (check the Formulas dropdown list on the Analyze ribbon)
- Basing pivot tables on external databases (see the next chapter)

Not only are these (and other) features available, but Excel usually provides more than one way to implement them. The suggestions given here are just some of the ways they can be implemented. The key to learning pivot table features is to *experiment*. There are entire books written about pivot tables, but we don't recommend them. You can learn a lot more, and a lot more quickly, by experimenting with data such as the Elecmart data. Don't be afraid to mess up. Pivot tables are very forgiving, and you can always start over.

Excel Tip

How Excel Stores Pivot Table Data

When you create a pivot table, Excel stores a snapshot of your source data in memory in a pivot cache. The amount of memory depends on the size of the data source, but it can be large. Fortunately, if you create another pivot table based on the same data source, Excel is intelligent enough to use the same pivot cache, thus conserving memory. (This sharing behavior began with Excel 2010. There is a way to mimic the pre-2010 behavior, that is, to create a separate pivot cache for each pivot table, but it is not discussed here.)

We complete this section by providing one last example to illustrate how pivot tables can answer business questions quickly.

EXAMPLE

3.5 FROZEN LASAGNA DINNERS

The file **Lasagna Triers.xlsx** contains data on over 800 potential customers being tracked by a (fictional) company that has been marketing a frozen lasagna dinner. The file contains a number of demographics on these customers, as indicated in Figure 3.52: their age, weight, income, pay type, car value, credit card debt, gender, whether they live alone, dwelling type, monthly number of trips to the mall, and neighborhood. It also indicates whether they have tried the company's frozen lasagna. The company wants to understand why some potential customers are triers and others are not. Does gender make a difference? Does income make a difference? In general, what distinguishes triers from nontriers? How can the company use pivot tables to explore these questions?

Figure 3.52 Lasagna Trier Data

	A	B	C	D	E	F	G	H	I	J	K	L	M
1	Person	Age	Weight	Income	Pay Type	Car Value	CC Debt	Gender	Live Alone	Dwell Type	Mall Trips	Nbhd	Have Tried
2	1	48	175	65500	Hourly	2190	3510	Male	No	Home	7	East	No
3	2	33	202	29100	Hourly	2110	740	Female	No	Condo	4	East	Yes
4	3	51	188	32200	Salaried	5140	910	Male	No	Condo	1	East	No
5	4	56	244	19000	Hourly	700	1620	Female	No	Home	3	West	No
6	5	28	218	81400	Salaried	26620	600	Male	No	Apt	3	West	Yes
7	6	51	173	73000	Salaried	24520	950	Female	No	Condo	2	East	No
8	7	44	182	66400	Salaried	10130	3500	Female	Yes	Condo	6	West	Yes
9	8	29	189	46200	Salaried	10250	2860	Male	No	Condo	5	West	Yes
10	9	28	200	61100	Salaried	17210	3180	Male	No	Condo	10	West	Yes
11	10	29	209	9800	Salaried	2090	1270	Female	Yes	Apt	7	East	Yes

Objective

To use pivot tables to explore which demographic variables help to distinguish lasagna triers from nontriers.

Pivot tables, with counts in the Values area, are a great way to discover which variables have the largest effect on a Yes/No variable.

Solution

The key is to set up a pivot table that shows counts of triers and nontriers for different categories of any of the potential explanatory variables. For example, one such pivot table shows the percentages of triers and nontriers for males and females separately. If the percentages are different for males than for females, the company will know that gender has an effect. On the other hand, if the percentages for males and females are about the same, the company will know that gender does not make much of a difference.

The typical pivot table should be set up as shown in Figure 3.53. The Rows variable is any demographic variable you want to investigate—in this case, Gender. The Columns variable is Have Tried (Yes or No). The Values variable can be *any* variable, as long as it is expressed as a count. Finally, it is useful to show these counts as percentage of row totals. This way you can easily look down column C to see whether the percentage in one category (Female) who have tried the product is any different from the percentage in another category (Male) who have tried the product. As you can see, males are somewhat more likely to try the product than females: 60.92% versus 54.27%. This is also apparent from the associated pivot chart.

Figure 3.53 Pivot Table and Pivot Chart for Examining the Effect of Gender

Once this generic pivot table and associated pivot chart are set up, you can easily explore other demographic variables by swapping them for Gender. For example, Figure 3.54 indicates that people who live alone are (not surprisingly) *much* more likely to try this frozen microwave product than people who don't live alone.

As another example, Figure 3.55 indicates that people with larger incomes are slightly more likely to try the product. There are two things to note about this income pivot table. First, because there are so many individual income values, grouping is useful. You can experiment with the grouping to get the most meaningful results. Second, you should be a bit skeptical about the last group, which has 100% triers. It is possible that there are only one or two people in this group. (It turns out that there are four.) For this reason, it is a good idea to create two pivot tables of the counts, one showing percentage of row totals and one showing the raw counts. This second pivot table is shown at the bottom of Figure 3.55.

Figure 3.54 Pivot Table and Pivot Chart for Examining the Effect of Live Alone

	A	B	C	D
3	Count	Have Tried ▼		
4	Live Alone ▼	No	Yes	Grand Total
5	No	45.57%	54.43%	100.00%
6	Yes	25.52%	74.48%	100.00%
7	Grand Total	42.17%	57.83%	100.00%

Figure 3.55 Pivot Table and Pivot Chart for Examining the Effect of Income

	A	B	C	D
3	Count	Have Tried ▼		
4	Income ▼	No	Yes	Grand Total
5	0-49999	45.47%	54.53%	100.00%
6	50000-99999	37.45%	62.55%	100.00%
7	100000-149999	30.43%	69.57%	100.00%
8	150000-199999	0.00%	100.00%	100.00%
9	Grand Total	42.17%	57.83%	100.00%

	A	B	C	D
14	Count	Have Tried ▼		
15	Income ▼	No	Yes	Grand Total
16	0-49999	256	307	563
17	50000-99999	91	152	243
18	100000-149999	14	32	46
19	150000-199999		4	4
20	Grand Total	361	495	856

The problem posed in this example is a common one in real business situations. One variable indicates whether people are in one group or another (triers or nontriers), and there are a lot of other variables that could potentially explain why some people are in one group and others are in the other group. There are a number of sophisticated techniques for attacking this *classification* problem, and some of these are discussed in Chapter 17. However, you can go a long way toward understanding which variables are important by the simple pivot table method illustrated here.

Problems

Solutions for problems whose numbers appear within a colored box can be found in the Student Solution Files.

Level A

33. Solve problem 1 with pivot tables and create corresponding pivot charts. Express the counts as percentages of row totals. What do these percentages indicate about this particular data set? Then repeat, expressing the counts as percentages of column totals.

34. Solve problem 2 with pivot tables and create corresponding pivot charts. Express the counts as percentages of row totals. What do these percentages indicate about this particular data set? Then repeat, expressing the counts as percentages of column totals.

35. Solve problem 3 with pivot tables and create corresponding pivot charts. Express the counts as percentages of row totals. What do these percentages indicate about this particular data set? Then repeat, expressing the counts as percentages of columns totals.

36. Solve problem 4 with pivot tables and create corresponding pivot charts. Express the counts as percentage of row totals. What do these percentages indicate about this particular data set? Then repeat, expressing the counts as percentages of column totals.

37. Solve problem 7 with pivot tables and create corresponding pivot charts. However, find only means and standard deviations, not medians or quartiles. (This is one drawback of pivot tables. Medians, quartiles, and percentiles are not in the list of summary measures.)

38. Solve problem 8 with pivot tables and create corresponding pivot charts. However, find only means and standard deviations, not medians. (This is one drawback of pivot tables. Medians are not among their summary measures.)

39. Solve problem 9 with pivot tables and create corresponding pivot charts. However, find only means and standard deviations, not medians. (This is one drawback of pivot tables. Medians are not among their summary measures.)

40. The file **P03_40.xlsx** contains monthly data on the number of vehicles crossing the border from Mexico into four southwestern states.
   a. Restructure this data set on a new sheet so that there are three long columns: Month, State, and Crossings. Essentially, you should stack the original columns B through E on top of one another to get the Crossings column, and you should also indicate which state each row corresponds to in the State column. The Month column should have four replicas of the original Month column.
   b. Create a pivot table and corresponding pivot table chart based on the restructured data. It should break down the average of Crossings by Year and State. Comment on any patterns you see in the chart.

41. *The Wall Street Journal CEO Compensation Study* analyzed CEO pay from many U.S. companies with fiscal year 2008 revenue of at least $5 billion that filed their proxy statements between October 2008 and March 2009. The data are in the file **P02_30.xlsx**.
   a. Create a pivot table and a corresponding pivot chart that simultaneously shows average of Salary 2008 and average of Bonus 2008, broken down by Company Type. Comment on any striking results in the chart.
   b. In the Data sheet, create a new column, Total 2008, which is the sum of Salary 2008 and Bonus 2008. Then create two pivot tables and corresponding pivot charts on a single sheet. The first should show the counts of CEOs broken down by Company Type, and the second should simultaneously show the average of Total 2008, the minimum of Total 2008, and the maximum of Total 2008, all broken down by Company Type. Comment on any striking results in these charts.

42. One pivot table element we didn't explain is a **calculated item**. This is usually a new category for some categorical variable that is created from existing categories. It is easiest to learn from an example. Open the file **Elecmart Sales.xlsx** from this section, create a pivot table, and put Day in the Rows area. Proceed as follows to create two new categories, Weekday and Weekend.
   a. Select any day and select Calculated Item from the Formulas dropdown list on the PivotTable Tools Options ribbon. This will open a dialog box. Enter Weekend in the Name box and enter the formula =**Sat** + **Sun** in the formula box. (You can double-click the items in the Items list to help build this formula.) When you click OK, you will see Weekend in the pivot table.
   b. Do it yourself. Create another calculated item, Weekday, for Mon through Fri.
   c. Filter out all of the individual days from the row area, so that only Weekday and Weekend remain, and then find the sum of Total Cost for these two new categories. How can you check whether these sums are what you think they should be? (Notes about calculated items: First, if you have Weekend, Weekday, and some individual days showing in the Rows area, the sum of Total Cost will double-count these individual days, so be careful about this. Second, be aware that if you create a calculated item from some variable such as Day, you are no longer allowed to drag that variable to the Filters area.)

43. Building on the previous problem, another pivot table element we didn't explain is a **calculated field**. This is usually a new numerical variable built from numerical variables that can be summarized in the Values area. It acts somewhat like a new column in the spreadsheet data, but there is an important difference. Again, it is easiest to learn from an example. Open the file **Elecmart Sales.xlsx** and follow the instructions below.

a. Create a new column in the data, CostPerItem, which is Total Cost divided by Items Ordered. Then create a pivot table and find the average of CostPerItem, broken down by Region. Explain exactly how this value was calculated. Would such an average be of much interest to a manager at Elecmart? Why or why not?

b. Select any average in the pivot table and then select Calculated Field from the Formulas dropdown list on the Analyze ribbon. This will open a dialog box. Enter CF_CostPerItem in the name box (we added CF, for calculated field, because we are not allowed to use the CostPerItem name that already exists), enter the formula =**TotalCost/ItemsOrdered**, and click OK. You should now see a new column in the pivot table, Sum of CF_CostPerItem, with *different* values than in the Average of CostPerItem column. Do some investigation to understand how each "sum" was calculated. From a manager's point of view, does it make any sense? (Note on calculated fields: When you summarize a calculated field, it doesn't matter whether you express it as sum, average, max, or any other summary measure. It is calculated in exactly the same way in each case.)

44. The file **P02_18.xlsx** contains daily values of the S&P Index from 1970 to mid-2015. It also contains percentage changes in the index from each day to the next. Create a pivot table with average of % Change in the Values area and Date in the Rows area. You will see every single date, with no real averaging taking place. This problem lets you explore how you can group naturally on a date variable. For each part below, explain the result briefly. (Note that if you are using Excel 2016, grouping by date will be done automatically.)

a. Group by Month.

b. Group by Year.

c. Group by Month and Year (select both in the Group dialog box). Can you make it show the year averages from part **b**?

d. Group by Quarter.

e. Group by Month and Quarter. Can you make it show the averages from part **c**?

f. Group by Quarter and Year.

g. Group by Month, Quarter, and Year.

45. Using the **Elecmart Sales.xlsx** file from this section, experiment with slicers as follows.

a. Create a pivot table that shows the average of Total Cost, broken down by Region in the Rows area and Time in the Columns area. Then insert two slicers, one for Region and one for Time. Select the West and Northeast buttons on the Region slicer and the Morning and Afternoon buttons on the Time slicer. Explain what happens in the pivot table.

b. Create a pivot table that shows the average of Total Cost, broken down by Region in the Rows area and

Time in the Columns area. Insert a Day slicer and select the Sat and Sun buttons. Explain what averages are now showing in the pivot table. Verify this by deleting the slicer and placing Days in the Filters area, with Sat and Sun selected.

46. We used the **Lasagna Triers.xlsx** file in this section to show how pivot tables can help explain which variables are related to the buying behavior of customers. Illustrate how the same information could be obtained with slicers. Specifically, set up the pivot table as in the example, but use a slicer instead of a Rows variable. Then set it up exactly as in the example, *with* a Rows variable, but include a slicer for some other variable. Comment on the type of results you obtain with these two versions. Do slicers appear to provide any advantage in this type of problem?

Level B

47. Solve problem 5 with pivot tables and create corresponding pivot charts. If you first find the quartiles of Salary and Amount Spent (by any method), is it possible to create the desired crosstabs by grouping, *without* recoding these variables?

48. Solve problem 17 with pivot tables. However, find only means and standard deviations, not medians. This is one drawback of pivot tables. Medians are not among their summary measures. Can you think of a way to calculate medians by category?

49. The file **P03_22.xlsx** lists financial data on movies released from 1980 to 2011 with budgets of at least $20 million.

a. Create three new variables, Ratio1, Ratio2, and Decade. Ratio1 should be US Gross divided by Budget, Ratio2 should be Worldwide Gross divided by Budget, and Decade should list 1980s, 1990s, or 2000s, depending on the year of the release date. If either US Gross or Worldwide Gross is listed as "Unknown," the corresponding ratio should be blank. (*Hint*: For Decade, use the YEAR function to fill in a new Year column. Then use a lookup table to populate the Decade column.)

b. Use a pivot table to find counts of movies by various distributors. Then go back to the data and create one more column, Distributor New, which lists the distributor for distributors with at least 30 movies and lists Other for the rest. (*Hint*: Use a lookup table to populate Distributor New, but also use an IF to fill in Other where the distributor is missing.)

c. Create a pivot table and corresponding pivot chart that shows average and standard deviation of Ratio1, broken down by Distributor New, with Decade in the Filters area. Comment on any striking results.

d. Repeat part **c** for Ratio2.

50. The file **P03_50.xlsx** lists NBA salaries for five seasons. (Each NBA season straddles two calendar years.)
    a. Merge all of the data into a single new sheet called All Data. In this new sheet, add a new column Season that lists the season, such as 2006–2007.
    b. Note that many of the players list a position such as C–F or F–C. Presumably, the first means the player is primarily a center but sometimes plays forward, whereas the second means the opposite. Recode these so that only the primary position remains (C in the first case, F in the second). To complicate matters further, the source lists positions differently in 2007–2008 than in other years. It lists PG and SG (point guard and shooting guard) instead of just G, and it lists SF and PF (small forward and power forward) instead of just F. Recode the positions for this season to be consistent with the other seasons (so that there are only three positions: G, F, and C).
    c. Note that many players have (p) or (t) in their Contract Thru value. The Source sheet explains this. Create two new columns in the All Data sheet, Years Remaining and Option. The Years Remaining column should list the years remaining in the contract. For example, if the season is 2004–2005 and the contract is through 2006–2007, years remaining should be 2. The Option column should list Player if there is a (p), Team if there is a (t), and blank if neither.
    d. Use a pivot table to find the average Salary by Season. Change it to show average Salary by Team. Change it to show average Salary by Season and Team. Change it to show average Salary by Primary Position. Change it to show average Salary by Team and Primary Position, with filters for Season, Contract Years, Years Remaining, and Option. Comment on any striking findings.

51. The file **P02_29.xlsx** contain monthly percentages of on-time arrivals at several of the largest U.S. airports.
    a. Explain why the current format of either data set limits the kind of information you can obtain with a pivot table. For example, does it allow you find the average on-time arrival percentage by year for any selected subset of airports, such as the average for O'Hare, Los Angeles International, and La Guardia?
    b. Restructure the data appropriately and then use a pivot table to answer the specific question in part **a**.

3-6 Conclusion

Finding relationships among variables is arguably the most important task in data analysis. This chapter has equipped you with some very powerful tools for detecting relationships. As we have discussed, the tools vary depending on whether the variables are categorical or numerical. (Again, refer to the diagram in the **Data Analysis Taxonomy.xlsx** file.) Tables and charts of counts are useful for relationships among categorical variables. Summary measures broken down by categories and side-by-side box plots are useful for finding relationships between a categorical and a numerical variable. Scatterplots and correlations are useful for finding relationships among numerical variables. Finally, pivot tables are useful for all types of variables.

Summary of Key Terms

TERM	EXPLANATION	EXCEL	PAGES	EQUATION
Crosstabs (or contingency table)	Table of counts of joint categories of two categorical variables	COUNTIFS function or pivot table	82	
Comparison problem	Comparing a numeric variable across two or more subpopulations		86	
Stacked or unstacked data formats	Stacked means long columns, one for categories and another for values; unstacked means a separate values column for each category		86	
Scatterplot (or X-Y chart)	Chart for detecting a relationship between two numeric variables; one point for each observation	Scatter from Insert ribbon	95	
Trend line	Line or curve fit to scatterplot (or time series graph)	Right-click on chart point, select Add Trendline	99	

Key Terms (continued)

TERM	EXPLANATION	EXCEL	PAGES	EQUATION
Covariance	Measure of linear relationship between two numeric variables, but affected by units of measurement	COVAR function	101	3.1
Correlation	Measure of linear relationship between two numeric variables, always from −1 to +1	CORREL function	102	3.2
Pivot table	Table for breaking down data by category; can show counts, averages, or other summary measures	PivotTable from Insert ribbon	108	
Pivot chart	Chart corresponding to a pivot table	PivotTable Tools Analyze ribbon	117	
Slicers, timelines	Graphical elements for filtering in pivot tables	PivotTable Tools Analyze ribbon	127	

Problems

Conceptual Questions

C.1. When you are trying to discover whether there is a relationship between two categorical variables, why is it useful to transform the counts in a crosstabs to percentages of row or column totals? Once you do this, how can you tell if the variables are related?

C.2. Suppose you have a crosstabs of two "Yes/No" categorical variables, with the counts shown as percentages of row totals. What will these percentages look like if there is absolutely no relationship between the variables? Besides this case, list all possible *types* of relationships that could occur. (There aren't many.)

C.3. If you suspect that a company's advertising expenditures in a given month affect its sales in *future* months, what correlations would you look at to confirm your suspicions? How would you find them?

C.4. Suppose you have customer data on whether they have bought your product in a given time period, along with various demographics on the customers. Explain how you could use pivot tables to see which demographics are the primary drivers of their "yes/no" buying behavior.

C.5. Suppose you have data on student achievement in high school for each of many school districts. In spreadsheet format, the school district is in column A, and various student achievement measures are in columns B, C, and so on. If you find fairly low correlations (magnitudes from 0 to 0.4, say) between the variables in these achievement columns, what exactly does this mean?

C.6. In the final round of most professional golf tournaments, two players play together in a "twosome." It often appears that good play or bad play is contagious. That is, if one player in the twosome plays well, the other plays well, and if one player plays badly, the other player plays badly. What data would you collect,

and how would you use the data, to check whether this "contagious" property is true?

C.7. Suppose you have a large data set for some sport. Each row might correspond to a particular team (as in the file **P03_57.xlsx** on football outcomes, for example) or it might even correspond to a given play. Each row contains one or more measures of success as well as many pieces of data that could be drivers of success. How might you find the most important drivers of success if the success measure is categorical (such as Win or Lose)? How might you find the most important drivers of success if the success measure is numerical and basically continuous (such as Points Scored in basketball)?

C.8. If two variables are highly correlated, does this imply that changes in one *cause* changes in the other? If not, give at least one example from the real world that illustrates what else could cause a high correlation.

C.9. Suppose there are two commodities A and B with strongly negatively correlated daily returns, such as a stock and gold. Is it possible to find another commodity with daily returns that are strongly negatively correlated with *both* A and B?

C.10. In checking whether several times series, such as monthly exchange rates of various currencies, move together, why do most analysts look at correlations between their *differences* rather than correlations between the original series?

Solutions for problems whose numbers appear within a colored box can be found in the Student Solution Files.

Level A

52. Suppose you would like to create a separate table of correlations for each category of a categorical variable. The only alternative, at least with the software you have, is to sort on the categorical variable, insert some blank rows between values of different categories, copy the headings to each section, and then ask for correlations from each. Do this with the movie data in the file **P03_25.xlsx**. Specifically, separate the data into three data sets based on Genre: one for Comedy, one for Drama, and one for all the rest. For this problem, you can ignore the third group. For each of Comedy and Drama, create a table of correlations between 7-day Gross, 14-day Gross, Total US Gross, International Gross, and US DVD Sales. Comment on whether the correlation structure is much different for these two popular genres.

53. The file **P03_53.xlsx** lists campaign contributions, by number of contributors and contribution amount, by state (including Washington DC) for the four leading contenders in the 2008 presidential race. Create a scatterplot and corresponding correlation between Dollar Amount (Y axis) and Contributors for each of the four contenders. For each scatterplot, superimpose a linear trend line and show the corresponding equation. Interpret each equation and compare them across candidates. Finally, identify the state for any points that aren't on or very close to the corresponding trend line.

54. The file **P03_54.xlsx** lists data for 593 movies released in 2011. Obviously, some movies are simply more popular than others, but success in 2011, measured by 2011 gross or 2011 tickets sold, could also be influenced by the release date. To check this, create a new variable, Days Out, which is the number of days the movie was out during 2011. For example, a movie released on 12/15 would have Days Out equal to 17 (which includes the release day). Create two scatterplots and corresponding correlations, one of 2011 Gross (Y axis) versus Days Out and one of 2011 Tickets Sold (Y axis) versus Days Out. Describe the behavior you see. Do you think a movie's success can be predicted very well just by knowing how many days it has been out?

55. The file **P03_55.xlsx** lists the average salary for each MLB team from 2004 to 2011, along with the number of team wins in each of these years.
   a. Create a table of correlations between the Wins columns. What do these correlations indicate? Are they higher or lower than you expected?
   b. Create a table of correlations between the Salary columns. What do these correlations indicate? Are they higher or lower than you expected?
   c. For each year, create a scatterplot and the associated correlations between Wins for that year (Y axis) and Salary for that year. Does it appear that teams are buying their way to success?
   d. The coloring in the Wins columns indicates the playoff teams. Create a new Yes/No column for each year, indicating whether the team made it to the playoffs that year. Then create a pivot table for each year showing average of Salary for that year, broken down by the Yes/No column for that year. Do these pivot tables indicate that teams are buying their way into the playoffs?

56. The file **P03_56.xlsx** lists the average salary for each NBA team from the 2004–2005 season to the

2009–2010 season, along with the number of team wins each of these years. Answer the same questions as in the previous problem for this basketball data.

57. The file **P03_57.xlsx** lists the average salary for each NFL team from 2002 to 2009, along with the number of team wins each of these years. Answer the same questions as in problem 55 for this football data.

58. The file **P03_58.xlsx** lists salaries of MLB players in the years 2007 to 2009. Each row corresponds to a particular player. As indicated by blank salaries, some players played in one of these years, some played in two of these years, and the rest played in all three years.
   a. Create a new Yes/No variable, All 3 Years, that indicates which players played all three years.
   b. Create two pivot tables and corresponding pivot charts. The first should show the count of players by position who played all three years. The second should show the average salary each year, by position, for all players who played all three years. (For each of these, put the All 3 Years variable in the Filters area.) Explain briefly what these two pivot tables indicate.
   c. Consider the data set consisting of only the players who played all three years. Using this data set, create a table of correlations of the three salary variables. What do these correlations indicate about player salaries?

59. The file **P03_59.xlsx** lists the results of about 20,000 runners in the 2008 New York Marathon.
   a. For all runners who finished in 3.5 hours or less, create a pivot table and corresponding pivot chart of average of Time by Gender. (To get a fairer comparison in the chart, change it so that the vertical axis starts at zero.) For the same runners, and on the same sheet, create another pivot table and pivot chart of counts by Gender. Comment on the results.
   b. For all runners who finished in 3.5 hours or less, create a pivot table and corresponding pivot chart of average of Time by Age. Group by Age so that the teens are in one category, those in their twenties are in another category, and so on. For the same runners, and on the same sheet, create another pivot table and pivot chart of counts of these age groups. Comment on the results.
   c. For all runners who finished in 3.5 hours or less, create a single pivot table of average of Time and of counts, broken down by Country. Then filter so that only the 10 countries with the 10 lowest average times appear. Finally, sort on average times so that the fastest countries rise to the top. Guess who the top two are! (*Hint*: Try the Value Filters for the Country variable.) Comment on the results.

60. The file **P02_12.xlsx** includes data on the 50 top graduate programs in the United States, according to a *U.S. News & World Report* survey.
   a. Create a table of correlations between all of the numerical variables. Discuss which variables are highly correlated with which others.

b. The Overall score is the score schools agonize about. Create a scatterplot and corresponding correlation of each of the other variables versus Overall, with Overall always on the Y axis. What do you learn from these scatterplots?

61. Recall from an example in the previous chapter that the file **Supermarket Transactions.xlsx** contains over 14,000 transactions made by supermarket customers over a period of approximately two years. Set up a single pivot table and corresponding pivot chart, with some instructions to a user (like the supermarket manager) in a text box, on how the user can get answers to any typical question about the data. For example, one possibility (of many) could be total revenue by product department and month, for any combination of gender, marital status, and homeowner. (The point is to get you to explain pivot table basics to a nontechnical user.)

62. The file **P03_15.xlsx** contains monthly data on the various components of the Consumer Price Index.
  a. Use Excel formulas to create differences for each of the variables.
  b. Create a times series graph for each CPI component, including the All Items component. Then create a time series graph for each difference variable. Comment on any patterns or trends you see.
  c. Create a table of correlations between the differences. Comment on any large correlations (or the lack of them).
  d. Create a scatterplot for each difference variable versus the difference for All Items (Y axis). Comment on any patterns or outliers you see.

Level B

63. The file **P03_63.xlsx** contains financial data on 85 U.S. companies in the Computer and Electronic Product Manufacturing sector (NAICS code 334) with 2009 earnings before taxes of at least $10,000. Each of these companies listed R&D (research and development) expenses on its income statement. Create a table of correlations between all of the variables and use conditional formatting to color green all correlations involving R&D that are strongly positive or negative. (Use cutoff values of your choice to define "strongly.") Then create scatterplots of R&D (Y axis) versus each of the other most highly correlated variables. Comment on any patterns you see in these scatterplots, including any obvious outliers, and explain why (or if) it makes sense that these variables are highly correlated with R&D. If there are highly correlated variables with R&D, can you tell which way the causality goes?

64. The file **P03_64.xlsx** lists monthly data since 1950 on the well-known Dow Jones Industrial Average (DJIA), as well as the less well-known Dow Jones Transportation Average (DJTA) and Dow Jones Utilities Average (DJUA). Each of these is an index based on 20 to 30 leading companies (which change over time).

a. Create monthly differences in three new columns. The Jan-50 values will be blank because there are no Dec-49 values. Then, for example, the Feb-50 difference is the Feb-50 value minus the Jan-50 value.
  b. Create a table of correlations of the three difference columns. Does it appear that the three Dow indexes tend to move together through time?
  c. It is possible (and has been claimed) that one of the indexes is a "leading indicator" of another. For example, a change in the DJUA in September might predict a similar change in the DJIA in the following December. To check for such behavior, create four "lags" of the difference variables. Do this for each of the three difference variables. You should end up with 12 lag variables. Explain in words what these lag variables contain. For example, what is the Dec-50 lag 3 of the DJIA difference?
  d. Create a table of correlations of the three differences and the 12 lags. Use conditional formatting to color green all correlations greater than 0.5 (or any other cutoff you choose). Does it appear that any index is indeed a leading indicator of any other? Explain.

65. The file **P03_65.xlsx** lists a lot of data for each NBA team for the seasons 2004–2005 to 2008–2009. The variables are divided into groups: (1) Overall success, (2) Offensive, and (3) Defensive. The basic question all basketball fans (and coaches) ponder is what causes success or failure.
  a. Explore this question by creating a correlation matrix with the variable Wins (the measure of success) and all of the variables in groups (2) and (3). Based on these correlations, which five variables appear to be the best predictors of success? (Keep in mind that negative correlations can also be important.)
  b. Explore this question in a different way, using the Playoff Team column as a measure of success. Here, it makes sense to proceed as in the Lasagna Triers example in Section 3-5, using the variables in groups (2) and (3) as the predictors. However, these predictors are all basically continuous, so grouping would be required for all of them in the pivot table, and grouping is always somewhat arbitrary. Instead, create a copy of the Data sheet. Then for each variable in groups (2) to (13), create a formula that returns 1, 2, 3, or 4, depending on which quarter of that variable the value falls in (1 if it is less than or equal to the first quartile, and so on). (This sounds like a lot of work, but a *single* copyable formula will work for the entire range.) Now use these discrete variables as predictors and proceed as in the Lasagna Triers example. List the five variables that appear to be the best (or at least good) predictors of making the playoffs.

66. The file **P03_66.xlsx** lists a lot of data for each NFL team for the years 2004 to 2009. The variables are divided into groups: (1) Overall success, (2) Team Offense, (3) Passing Offense, (4) Rushing Offense, (5) Turnovers Against,

(6) Punt Returns, (7) Kick Returns, (8) Field Goals, (9) Punts, (10) Team Defense, (11) Passing Defense, (12) Rushing Defense, and (13) Turnovers Caused. The basic question all football fans (and coaches) ponder is what causes success or failure. Answer the same questions as in the previous problem for this football data, but use all of the variables in groups (2) to (13) as possible predictors.

67. The file **P02_57.xlsx** contains data on mortgage loans in 2008 for each state in the United States. The file is different from others in this chapter in that each state has its own sheet with the same data in the same format. Each state sheet breaks down all mortgage applications by loan purpose, applicant race, loan type, outcome, and denial reason (for those that were denied). The question is how a *single* data set for all states can be created for analysis. The Typical Data Set sheet indicates a simple way of doing this, using the powerful but little-known INDIRECT function. This sheet is basically a template for bringing in any pieces of data from the state sheets you would like to examine.

   a. Do whatever it takes to populate the Typical Data Set sheet with information in the range B7:D11 and B14:D14 (18 variables in all) of each state sheet. Add appropriate labels in row 3, such as Asian Dollar Amount Applied For.
   b. Create a table of correlations between these variables. Color yellow all correlations between a given applicant race, such as those between Asian Mortgage Application, Asian Dollar Amount Applied For, and Asian Average Income. Comment on the magnitudes of these. Are there any surprises?
   c. Create scatterplots of White Dollar Amount Applied For (X axis) versus the similar variable for each of the other five applicant races. Comment on any patterns in these scatterplots, and identify any obvious outliers.

CASE 3.1 Customer Arrivals at Bank98

Bank98 operates a main location and three branch locations in a medium-size city. All four locations perform similar services, and customers typically do business at the location nearest them. The bank has recently had more congestion—longer waiting lines—than it (or its customers) would like. As part of a study to learn the causes of these long lines and to suggest possible solutions, all locations have kept track of customer arrivals during one-hour intervals for the past 10 weeks. All branches are open Monday through Friday from 9 A.M. until 5 P.M. and on Saturday from 9 A.M. until noon. For each location, the file **C03_01.xlsx** contains the number of customer arrivals during each hour of a 10-week period.

The manager of Bank98 has hired you to make some sense of these data. Specifically, your task is to present charts and/or tables that indicate how customer traffic into the bank locations varies by day of week and hour of day. There is also interest in whether any daily or hourly patterns you observe are stable across weeks. Although you don't have full information about the way the bank currently runs its operations—you know only its customer arrival pattern and the fact that it is currently experiencing long lines—you are encouraged to append any suggestions for improving operations, based on your analysis of the data.

CASE 3.2 Saving, Spending, and Social Climbing

The best-selling book *The Millionaire Next Door* by Thomas J. Stanley and William D. Danko (Longstreet Press, 1996) presents some very interesting data on the characteristics of millionaires. We tend to believe that people with expensive houses, expensive cars, expensive clothes, country club memberships, and other outward indications of wealth are the millionaires. The authors define wealth, however, in terms of savings and investments, not consumer items. In this sense, they argue that people with a lot of expensive *things* and even large incomes often have surprisingly little wealth. These people tend to spend much of what they make on consumer items, often trying to keep up with, or impress, their peers.

In contrast, the real millionaires, in terms of savings and investments, frequently come from "unglamorous"

professions (particularly teaching), own unpretentious homes and cars, dress in inexpensive clothes, and otherwise lead rather ordinary lives.

Consider the (fictional) data in the file **C03_02.xlsx**. For several hundred couples, it lists their education level, their annual combined salary, the market value of their home and cars, the amount of savings they have accumulated (in savings accounts, stocks, retirement accounts, and so on), and a self-reported "social climber index" on a scale of 1 to 10 (with 1 being very unconcerned about social status and material items and 10 being very concerned about these). Prepare a report based on these data, supported by relevant charts and/or tables, that could be used in a book such as *The Millionaire Next Door*. Your conclusions can either support or contradict those of Stanley and Danko.

CASE 3.3 Churn in the Cellular Phone Market

The term **churn** is very important to managers in the cellular phone business. Churning occurs when a customer stops using one company's service and switches to another company's service. Obviously, managers try to keep churning to a minimum, not only by offering the best possible service, but by trying to identify conditions that lead to churning and taking steps to stop churning before it occurs. For example, if a company learns that customers tend to churn at the end of their two-year contract, they could offer customers an incentive to stay a month or two before the end of their two-year contract. The file **C03_03.xlsx** contains data on over 2000 customers of a particular cellular phone company. Each row contains the activity of a particular customer for a given time period, and the last column indicates whether the customer churned during this time period. Use the tools in this chapter (and possibly the previous chapter) to learn (1) how these variables are distributed, (2) how the variables in columns B–R are related to each other, and (3) how the variables in columns B–R are related to the Churn variable in column S. Write a short report of your findings, including any recommendations you would make to the company to reduce churn.

CASE 3.4 Southwest Border Apprehensions and Unemployment

Illegal immigration across the southwest border of the United States has been a hotly debated topic in recent years. Many people argue that illegal immigration is related to the U.S. unemployment rate: when the unemployment rate is up, there are more attempts to cross the border illegally. The file **C03_04.xlsx** contains data on the number of apprehensions on the southwest border and the U.S. unemployment rate. There are both yearly data since 1981 and monthly data since 2000. Using these data, make an argument, one way or the other, for whether apprehensions are related to the unemployment rate.

APPENDIX Using StatTools to Find Relationships

The StatTools add-in from Palisade can be used to speed up several procedures discussed in this chapter:

- It can calculate a table of summary measures of a numeric variable, broken down by a categorical variable. (This is illustrated in the **Introduction to StatTools** video that accompanies the book.)
- It can create one or more scatterplots from its list of Summary Graphs on the StatTools ribbon. It can even color the points in a scatterplot based on the category of a categorical variable.
- It can create a table of correlations (or covariances) from the Summary Statistics dropdown list on the StatTools ribbon.

Note, however, that StatTools doesn't do pivot tables. There is no need because Excel does them very nicely.

CHAPTER 4

Business Intelligence (BI) Tools for Data Analysis

Rep. Mark Takano

NurPhoto/Getty Images

INTERNATIONAL CHART DAY

Charts have been an important part of data analysis for well over a century, but with the increasing emphasis on data visualization, there is now an official International Chart Day as of April 26, 2018. It is sponsored by Tumblr (software) and the Society for New Design in collaboration with the Office of United States Representative Mark Takano from California. In their website at https://www.internationalchartday.com/, they describe their purpose as follows:

Charts and other variations of information graphics have been around for hundreds of years, and are an important tool for making complex information easier to understand. However, not all charts are created equal: they can sometimes be too complicated or convey false and/or misleading information if not executed correctly.

On April 26, chart lovers will unite to celebrate the first-ever "International Chart Day," an opportunity for the infographic creating community to engage the public by sharing their favorite examples, further explaining the history and value of charts, and sharing insight in to how to create high-quality, visually engaging, informative visualizations.

The goal is to assist the public in becoming better consumers of data, information and news.

TO THIS END WE SHALL:

1. Celebrate charts and infographics of all types;
2. Help the public understand how to read charts and gain useful insights from them;
3. Help chart makers of all levels understand the necessary components of a truthful chart;
4. Encourage the wider usage and adoption of charts;
5. Combat the spread of fake news by making the public smarter consumers of information.

The organizers of the first International Chart Day invited everyone to share their favorite data visualizations online. Therefore, Tableau Software, the developer of Tableau Public discussed in this chapter, shared five of its recent "Viz of the Day" winners. (See the Blog section at https://public.tableau.com/s/.) These five illustrate the immense variety of data visualizations:

1. **Women's Representation in Politics**, by Yvette Kovacs of Starschema in Budapest, Hungary, shows the degree to which women are represented in parliaments around the world. She uses the same small chart type for each country, listed in decreasing order of women's representation and color coded to show women's representation in parliament. When you hover over any of these, you see a line chart of women's representation through time in that country.
2. **The Best Way to Get Around Austin TX**, by Xeomatrix, is a multi-faceted data dashboard that shows the hotspots for bike share usage in Austin by time of day. The dashboard contains three charts and a filter pane on the left. The first chart is a map of different bicycle start stations with bubbles sized and colored to reflect the number of

trips from that station. The second chart is a bar chart of the trips to the most popular bicycle end stations. The third chart is a colored-coded grid showing the number of trips by day and hour of day.

3. **Ratios of Inequity**, by Nai Louza of UBS in London, uses a map to show the states in the United States and Puerto Rico with the highest and lowest ratios of high-income households to low-income households. The map uses a color-coded (but same-sized) hexagon for each state, along with a few text boxes to add commentary. When you hover over any state's hexagon, you see a line chart of how the inequity ratio has changed over time. (As of 2016, New Jersey had the highest inequity ratio, 1.97, and Puerto Rico had the lowest, 0.02.)

4. **Explore European Cities on a Budget**, by Sarah Bartlett of Slalom Consulting, uses a graphics-packed visualization to describe the five cheapest European cities to visit: Kiev, Krakow, Belgrade, Bucharest, and Sofia. It begins with a bar chart of dollars per day for these cities. Then it has a separate section for each of the five cities, showing costs broken down for accommodations, attractions, meals, drinks, and transportation, as well rainy days per month, some city facts, and a link to explore the city further.

5. **The State of the World's Children**, by Simon Beaumont of UNICEF, uses a world map in the top section where you can select a country and a health theme (Adolescents, Basic Indicators, Child Protection, Demographics, Economics, Education, Health, HIV AIDS, Nutrition, Residence, and Women). Then in the bottom section, you can see how the selected country compares to regions of the world on different components of the selected health theme. For example, if you choose United States and Demographics, you can see how the United States compares to Western Europe on life expectancy. (Western Europe is slightly ahead.)

It is unlikely that International Chart Day will become another Fourth of July, but its significance is that it underscores the importance of data visualization in today's world.[1] The visualizations described here provide insights, tell stories, and can be addictive. Fortunately, as you will see later in this chapter, the visualization software now available allows everyone to display data in creative ways.

4-1 Introduction

As data analysis has become more important in the business world, Microsoft and other software companies have created better tools for analyzing data—or, to use a popular term, for creating **business intelligence (BI)**. This chapter discusses some of these tools, tools that didn't even exist 10 or 15 years ago. Our primary focus is on a set of Microsoft add-ins for Excel sometimes called the Power BI suite. They include Power Query and Power Pivot, which we will discuss in some detail, plus two others, Power View and Power Map, that aren't discussed here. Microsoft refers to the role of these add-ins as **self-service BI**. The meaning is that the people who need to analyze data for their jobs—financial analysts, marketing analysts, cost accountants, and so on—no longer need to rely on IT departments (and the long wait time this often requires). Instead, they can use these "power" tools themselves to get the results they need—right away. The power tools for Excel are not the only self-service BI tools Microsoft offers. Many companies use the analysis tools in Microsoft's SQL Service database software, called SQL Service Analysis Services (SSAS), and Microsoft also offers a stand-alone package called Power BI. The latter has tools like those we will discuss for Excel, but it is a separate package. In addition, other software companies offer similar BI software; the term "BI" is not used only by Microsoft.

When you think of data analysis, you probably think of numbers, whether they reside in a large table or a summary report. However, we humans tend to gain more insights when we see graphs of the numbers. Several types of graphs, including histograms,

---

1 For an elementary but insightful discussion of the difference between effective and ineffective visualizations, we recommend the article by Camm et al. (2017).

scatterplots, and others illustrated in the previous two chapters, have been used for over a century. Recently, however, there has been an emphasis on **data visualization**, where data are shown graphically in new and imaginative ways. We discuss a popular non-Microsoft software package, Tableau Public. We chose to include Tableau Public for three reasons: It is powerful, it is quite easy to learn, and it is free.

Finally, you cannot always assume that the data you obtain are clean. There can be—and often are—many instances of wrong values, which can occur for many reasons. Unless you fix these at the beginning, the resulting data analysis can be seriously flawed. Therefore, we conclude this chapter by discussing a few techniques for cleansing data.

4-2 Importing Data into Excel with Power Query

Power Query refers to Excel's improved tools for importing data from various sources into Excel.

Excel is not the only software that can be used to analyze data, but it is almost certainly the most popular. Unfortunately, the data sets to be analyzed are often stored somewhere else, *not* in Excel workbooks. Therefore, if you want to use Excel for data analysis, you must learn methods for importing data into Excel. This is not a new topic. Technologies for importing external data into Excel have existed for years, and they continue to evolve. The good news is that the most recent tools are better and easier to use than ever. This section illustrates these tools, often referred to as **Power Query**.[2] Be aware, however, that this section is aimed at Excel for Windows users (or Mac users with Windows emulation software). The Power Query tools have not yet been included in Excel for Mac, and we have no way of knowing when they will be. (A Web search will quickly show that Mac users are clamoring for these tools, so hopefully Microsoft is listening.) Excel for Mac does have some tools for importing data, but they are older tools and will be discussed here only briefly.

4-2a Introduction to Relational Databases

The data sets discussed in the previous two chapters can also be called databases, but they are a special type of database, a **single-table database**. Traditionally, these have been called **flat files**. Many of the databases you analyze will indeed be single-table databases, where all the data are held in a single rectangular table. More generally, however, a database is a set of *related* tables, where each table is a data set of the type discussed in the previous two chapters. Because the tables are related, this type of database is called a **relational database**.

This raises two questions: (1) Why are data often stored in multiple tables rather in a single large table, and (2) how are the tables related? The answer to the first question is to avoid redundancy. Suppose you want to create a database of donors and donations to a charitable organization. For the donors, you want to store their name, their address, their email address, their phone number, and possibly more. For the donations, you want to store the donor's name, the date of the donation, the amount, and possibly more. Now imagine that Carol Wilkinson is a frequent donor. If you store *everything* in a single table, there will be a row for each donation, and each such row for Carol will repeat her address, email address, phone number, and possibly other personal information. Not only does this inflate the size of the database, but it introduces the possibility of errors. If Carol moves to a new home, you must then be careful to change her address in each of her donation rows. This is not a good way to manage data.

The solution is to split the donors and donations into separate tables. The Donors table will include a single row for each person who has ever donated. All addresses, email addresses, and phone numbers will be listed in this table exactly once, making them easy to modify if someone moves, for example. The Donations table will include a single row for each donation, including the date and amount of the donation and possibly

---

2 There is no mention of the term Power Query in any Excel ribbon, but the term is still used in discussions of Excel's newest query tools.

other information. The result is exactly what is required: two relatively small tables with no redundant information.

But this brings us to the second question: How are the tables related? For example, if you want information about the donor who donated $1500 on May 21, 2018, how do you know which donor this is? The answer is to use *keys*. In the Donors table, there will be a **primary key** column that is a unique identifier of the donor.[3] There are multiple ways to create primary keys. One possibility is to use an existing unique identifier, such as a social security number. Another possibility is to use a last name with a numeric suffix, such as wilkinson1. (Then the next Wilkinson donor would be wilkinson2, and so on.) Finally, it is always possible to use an **autonumber key**, where the first donor has key 1, the second has key 2, and so on. Then if there are already 783 donors in the database and another is added, that donor's key is automatically 784. It really doesn't matter what primary key is used, so long as it is unique for each donor.

The actual values in primary and key fields are often meaningless, but they serve their purpose of relating tables.

Now suppose an autonumber primary key is used, and Carol's key is 241. This is listed in the Donors table. Then a **foreign key** column is appended to the Donations table. Each time Carol donates, this foreign key value will be 241. The actual number has no intrinsic meaning; it is used only for lookup purposes. If you want to see all Carol's donations, you go to the Donations table and search for foreign key 241. Note that a foreign key is *not* unique. Carol can make several donations, so her foreign key 241 can appear multiple times in the Donations table. In the other direction, if you see a donation with foreign key 137, you can search the Donors table for the unique primary key 137 to see who made this donation.

Fundamental Insight

The whole purpose of separating data into separate tables in a relational database is to avoid redundancy. Each table contains data about a specific entity, such as customers, products, orders, and so on. However, primary and foreign keys are then necessary to relate the tables. For example, these keys let you look up information about all orders made by a specific customer for a specific product.

The relationship between the Donors and Donations table is called a **one-to-many** relationship. Each donation corresponds to exactly one donor, but one donor can make many donations. In this case, the primary key resides in the "one" table, and the foreign key resides in the "many" table.

Tables in a relational database are related through primary and foreign keys. A primary key is a unique identifier, whereas a foreign key is used for lookup purposes and is not necessarily unique. A primary key resides in the "one" side of a one-to-many relationship; a foreign key resides in the "many" side.

There can also be **many-to-many** relationships. A typical example is of orders and products from an online store. A specific order can be for many products, and a specific product can be part of many orders. Then there will be an Orders table and a Products table, each with a primary key. The usual way to relate them is with a **linking** table (also called a bridge table) that might be called Order Details. This will be a long thin table with a row for each product in each order. For example, if an order is for five products, this will add five rows to the Order Details table. This linking table will have at least two foreign

3 As we have mentioned before, the term "field" is often used instead of "column," especially in database discussions. We will use the two terms interchangeably.

keys, one for the order and one for the product, and possibly nothing else. These keys let you look up all orders that contain a specific product or all products in a specific order. Note that the relationship between Orders and Order Details is one-to-many, as is the relationship between Products and Order Details.

Tables and relationships between them are usually shown in a relationships diagram. The relationship between Donors and Donations appears in Figure 4.1. The relationship between Orders, Order Details, and Products appears in Figure 4.2. In each case, the "ID" fields are the key fields. Key fields do not have to have "ID" in their names, and primary/foreign key pairs do not even have to have the same names, but these customs are often used. Note the "1" next to the "one" side of each relationship and "*" next to the "many" side. (These diagrams are from Power Pivot, discussed later in the chapter. Diagrams in other software packages often use the infinity symbol, ∞, for the many side.)

Figure 4.1 Relationship between Donors and Donations

Figure 4.2 Relationship between Orders, Order Details, and Products

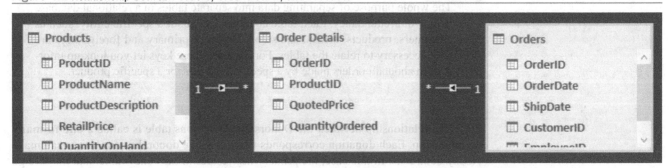

Until recently, all multi-table relational databases were stored in a **relational database management system (RDBMS)**. This is software that creates and manages databases. Microsoft Access, part of the Office suite, is one such system. Access is a desktop system where your database files can reside locally on your hard drive. (They have an extension .mdb or .accdb.) Server-based systems are more common in corporate settings, where the databases are stored on a server and are usually managed by a database administrator (DBA). To access the data, you typically need to log in with appropriate credentials. Some of the most popular server-based systems are Microsoft SQL Server, Oracle Database, IBM Db2, and MySQL.

Data are usually stored in a RDBMS, but data analysts typically want to perform their analyses in Excel. Therefore, several technologies have been developed in the past few decades to import data from a RDBMS into Excel. All these technologies involve one or more queries, where a **query** specifies exactly which data you want to import. At the very least, the query must specify the table or tables that contain the data you want, the columns you want, and the rows you want. Queries are so common that a language for queries was developed about 30 years ago. This language is called **Structured Query Language (SQL)**, and it continues to be used today. The power of SQL is that, with minor modifications, it can be used to query *any* RDBMS. However, it presents a hurdle for the many Excel users who do not know SQL. Therefore, Microsoft and other companies have been trying to make querying easier by creating more transparent tools. In Microsoft's case,

SQL is the traditional language for specifying a query.

the result is Power Query, as we will discuss shortly. However, it is useful to discuss other possibilities.

First, it has always been possible to create multi-table relational databases directly in Excel. Each table is of the type discussed in the previous two chapters. They could all be in the same worksheet or in separate worksheets. To be relatable, they must have primary and foreign key columns as discussed earlier. Then to relate them, you can use VLOOKUP functions. Figure 4.3 illustrates a simple example, where the primary key in column A is an autonumber key, and the formula in cell K4, copied down, is **=VLOOKUP(G12,$A$3:$E$10,2)**. (You can find this example in the **Multi-Table Query in Excel Finished.xlsx** file.) This VLOOKUP method is frequently used, but it is cumbersome. Besides, the tables involved might be too large to fit into Excel's (approximately) one-million row limit.

Figure 4.3 Multi-Table Query in an Excel Worksheet

	A	B	C	D	E	F	G	H	I	J	K	L	M
1	Donors table						Donations table				Query: donations after May		
2													
3	DonorID	Name	Other info...				DonorID	Date	Donation		Name	Date	Donation
4	1	Bob Hanson					1	01/22/18	$525		Candy Entson	06/01/18	$200
5	2	Cheryl Jones					7	01/28/18	$475		Tim Jenkins	06/20/18	$900
6	3	Tim Jenkins					5	02/15/18	$25		Candy Entson	08/11/18	$25
7	4	Pat McCain					2	03/11/18	$1,100		Cheryl Jones	08/12/18	$650
8	5	Don Lemon					4	04/11/18	$550		Tim Jenkins	08/14/18	$950
9	6	Bill Paxon					6	04/22/18	$250		Pat McCain	09/11/18	$975
10	7	Candy Entson					1	05/16/18	$325		Tim Jenkins	09/16/18	$650
11							4	05/26/18	$50		Bob Hanson	09/17/18	$1,175
12							7	06/01/18	$200		Tim Jenkins	10/02/18	$150
13							3	06/20/18	$900				
14							7	08/11/18	$25				
15							2	08/12/18	$650				
16							3	08/14/18	$950				
17							4	09/11/18	$975				
18							3	09/16/18	$650				
19							1	09/17/18	$1,175				
20							3	10/02/18	$150				

Second, the Power Query tools are only the latest in the evolution of Microsoft's tools for importing data into Excel. Depending on your version of Excel, you might have to use older (and less friendly) tools. Figure 4.4 shows the tools in Excel 2010 for Windows. They are in the Get External Data group on the Data ribbon.

Here are a few comments about these 2010 tools:

Excel's older tools, before Power Query, are still available, but they are not nearly as good as the newer tools.

- The From Access tool allows you to import data from one table only or from a saved query in Access. The latter is useful, but it means you must first create a query within Access.
- The From Web tool allows you to import data from the Web, but it doesn't work on many Web data sets. The similar Web tool in Power Query, discussed later in this section, is *much* better.
- The From SQL Server and From Analysis Services tools require you to have a SQL Server account.
- The From Microsoft Query tool was probably the most popular query tool in Excel before Power Query. It still works fine, but Power Query is more powerful and easier to use.

Excel 2016 for Mac (at least as of this writing) is another story altogether. It has the Get External Data tools shown in Figure 4.5. The New Database Query has only two items in its dropdown list: SQL Server ODBC and From Database. The former requires a SQL Server account. The latter returns an alert that you must first install an ODBC Driver Manager, and it provides almost no guidance on how to do so. Also, it is not at all clear how the From HTML tool works. (Do a Web search for this HTML tool for the Mac. No one seems

Figure 4.4 Get External Data Tools in Excel 2010 for Windows

Figure 4.5 Get External Data Tools in Excel 2016 for Mac

to understand how it works.) Let's just say that until improvements are made, Excel for Mac is not set up for importing external data.

From here on, the discussion and screenshots will focus on Excel that is part of Office 365 for Windows, which contains all the Power BI tools, including Power Query. (Even this isn't quite true. See the following box.)

It is virtually impossible to keep track of all the versions of Excel and which versions contain which features. Besides, subscribers to Office 365 get monthly updates, often with *new* features. Excel's Power BI tools are included in most versions of Office 365 for Windows, but not all. See https://powerpivotpro .com/2015/10/what-versions-of-office-2016-contain-power-pivot/ for details. Also, these tools were available in one form or another in Excel 2013 and even Excel 2010. (They still aren't available in Excel for Mac.) There is not enough space here to list all the differences, and such a discussion would be hopelessly confusing.[4] If you are using a pre-2016 version of Excel for Windows, perform a Web search for, say, "Power Query Excel 2013" or "Power BI Excel 2010." Eventually, we expect that almost all Excel users will have an Office 365 subscription, so that the differences between old versions of Excel will be irrelevant. We also expect that the Power BI tools will eventually be included in Excel for Mac, but there is no way to tell when this will occur.

---

4 When we tried to learn Power Query in 2016, we bought a book on the subject that was published less than a year before. Even so, most of its explanations and screenshots were already out of date. This is common in today's software world, so get used to it!

4-2b Excel's Data Model

When you run a query to import external data into Excel, you must decide where you want to store the data. Until recently, there were two basic options: (1) into an Excel table, as discussed in Chapter 2, or (2) into a pivot table (or pivot chart) report, as discussed in Chapter 3. The first option is often a good one unless the size of the imported data is larger than the size of an Excel worksheet—which is sometimes the case. The second option makes sense if your eventual goal is to analyze the data with pivot tables or pivot charts. In this case, the data won't be directly visible but will instead be stored in a pivot cache, the source for pivot tables and pivot charts.

There is now a third option, a **Data Model** in Excel. A Data Model essentially mimics the behavior of a RDBMS, but all within Excel. A Data Model stores related tables in a special type of compressed format—not in an Excel worksheet—for use in creating pivot table reports. This is extremely important. It means that you can store your data, even millions of rows of data, inside an Excel workbook and then use Excel's powerful tools to analyze the data. No VLOOKUPs are necessary, and once the data are in Excel, there is no further need for Access or any other RDBMS. However, the Data Model can keep a link to the source data set, so that if the source data set changes, you can refresh your Data Model with the newest data.

> **Fundamental Insight**
>
> Before Excel's relatively new Data Model, relational data had to be imported from Access or other relational database packages into Excel for analysis. Now relational databases can be stored in Excel directly, where they can then be analyzed. In short, a Data Model is a relational database that is stored in Excel.

The following example illustrates one way to create a Data Model in Excel.

EXAMPLE

4.1 IMPORTING RELATED DATABASE TABLES

The Contoso database stored in the file **Contoso Sales.accdb** is a "practice" Access database Microsoft created a few years ago. It contains 2007–2009 sales data from the fictional Contoso Company in five related tables: Dates, Products, Product-Categories, ProductSubcategories, and Sales. For illustration, there are two other files, **Geography.csv** and **Stores.xlsx**. The Stores file contains data on the stores where Contoso sells its products, and the Geography file contains data (for mapping purposes) about the locations of the stores. These latter two files aren't currently related to one another or to the Contoso data, but the files contain key fields that can be used to relate them. How can data from Contoso be imported into a Data Model in Excel?

Objective

To use Power Query to import the Contoso tables and the Stores and Geography files into a Data Model in Excel.

Solution

The following steps can be used to obtain the results in the **Contoso Import Finished.xlsx** file. (We again warn you that these are based on Excel in Office 365 for Windows.)

1. Open a new workbook in Excel. If the Developer tab isn't visible, right-click any ribbon, select Customize the Ribbon, and check the Developer item in the right pane of the resulting dialog box. The Developer ribbon has useful tools for programmers, but it also provides an easy way to get to Excel's add-ins lists.

2. Click COM Add-Ins on the Developer ribbon and check the Microsoft Power Pivot for Excel item. This creates a Power Pivot tab and associated ribbon. You will need Power Pivot to "see" the imported data in the following steps.

Power Pivot must be loaded to "see" the data in a Data Model.

3. On the Data ribbon, click Get Data, then From Database, and then From Microsoft Access Database. Maneuver to the **Contoso.accdb** file and click Import.
4. This opens the Navigator window in Figure 4.6. Fill it in as shown, checking the Select multiple items option and checking all five tables. When any table is selected, you see a preview of its data in the right pane.

Figure 4.6 Navigator Window

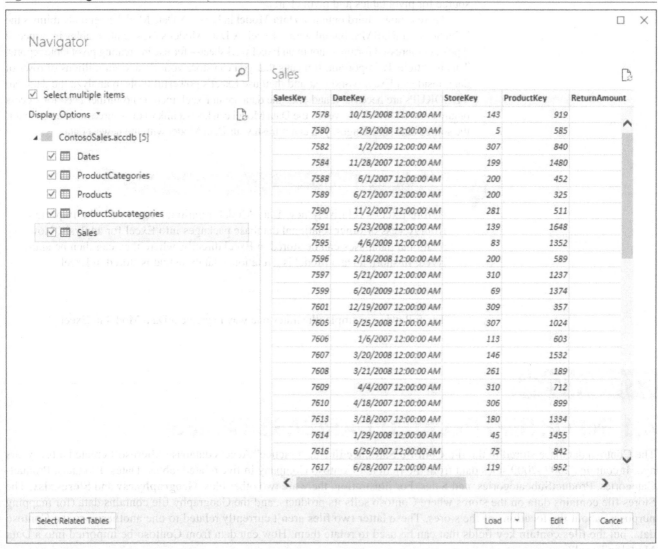

5. From the Load dropdown list, select Load To. This opens the Import Data dialog box in Figure 4.7. Fill it out as shown, selecting Only Create Connection and checking the bottom Data Model option, and click OK.
6. A Query & Connections pane with five queries, one for each table, will open in Excel, but when the data have finished downloading, you won't see any data. Read on.
7. Because you filled out the Import Data dialog box as shown in Figure 4.7, the data don't appear in an Excel table or pivot table. Instead, they are stored in a Data Model. To see the Data Model, select Manage from the Power Pivot ribbon. This opens the Power Pivot window in Figure 4.8, where you can see the imported data. This looks like an Excel workbook, with a tab for each of the five tables, but it is quite different, as we will discuss shortly. Note the two buttons circled at the bottom right. These are toggles between data and diagram views. Figure 4.8 shows the data view.

Figure 4.7 Import Data Dialog
Box

Figure 4.8 Power Pivot Window: Data Model in Data View

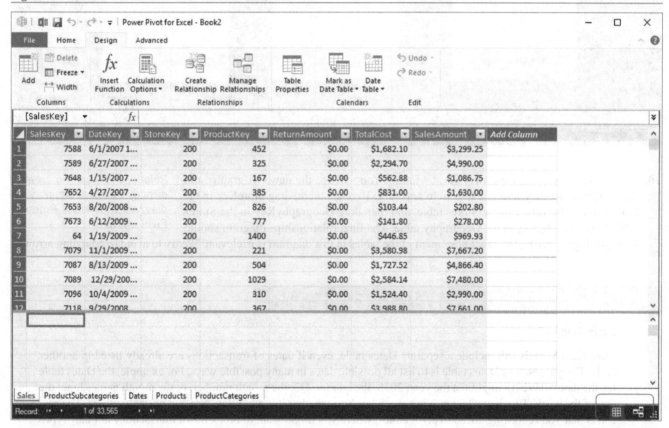

8. Click the diagram button at the bottom right and then move/resize the tables appropriately to see the relationships diagram in Figure 4.9. Although these tables are related in the Access source file through primary and foreign keys, they aren't automatically linked with the arrows shown in the figure.[5] However, you can drag from the obvious key fields to create these arrows and hence relate the tables. For example, drag from DateKey in the Dates table to DateKey in the Sales table to relate these two tables.

9. Back in the Excel window, click From Text/CSV on the Data ribbon, maneuver to the **Geography.csv** file, click Load To, and again fill out the dialog box as in Figure 4.7. Then repeat with the Stores data. This time, select From File from the Get Data dropdown list, choose From Workbook, and maneuver to the **Sales.xlsx** file. Once again, fill out the dialog box as in Figure 4.7.

---

5 We're not sure why Power Pivot doesn't "inherit" the relations from the Access file. It does for some Access databases but not for this one. In any case, it's easy to create the relationships, as explained here.

Figure 4.9 Power Pivot Window: Data Model in Diagram View

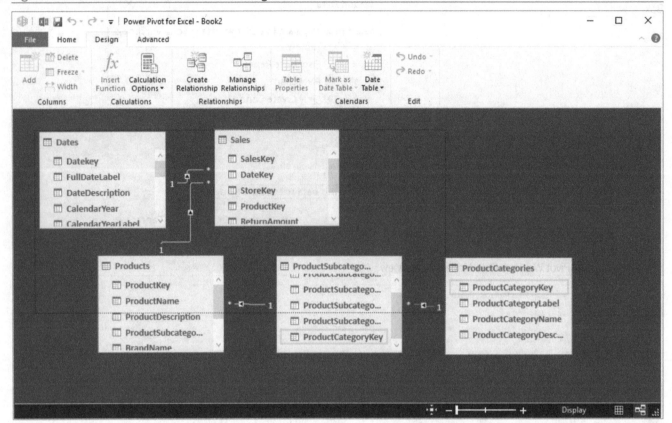

10. Open diagram view in the Power Pivot window. You will see the new Geography and Stores tables, but they won't be related to anything. To relate them, drag StoreKey in the Sales table to StoreKey in the Stores table, and then drag GeographyKey in the Stores table to GeographyKey in the Geography table. The final relationships diagram should look like Figure 4.10. (The exact placement of the tables in this diagram is irrelevant. We try to avoid overlapping arrows.)

Relationships can be created directly by dragging in diagram view of the Power Pivot window.

Data Model Tip

Date Table

Most Data Models will include a separate Dates table, even if dates of transactions are already listed in another table. The purpose of a Dates table is to list all possible dates in many possible ways. For example, the Dates table for the date 6/19/2018 might list the year, 2018; the quarter, Q2; the month number, 6; the month name, June; the day of the week, Tuesday; whether it is a weekday, Yes; whether it is a holiday, No; and possibly others. The reason is that you're looking ahead to pivot tables, where you might want to break down transactions in many types of date-related ways. By creating all these date fields right away, you save yourself a lot of work later.

You have just seen how a small subset of the Power Query tools can be used to import related data into an Excel Data Model, where they can then be analyzed with pivot tables. If you compare the size of the original blank Excel file with the size of the finished file, you will see that the size increased from about 8 KB to about 2.5 MB. Although you can't see the data in any Excel worksheets, the data *are* stored with the workbook in the compressed Data Model format.

Figure 4.10 Final Contoso Relationships Diagram

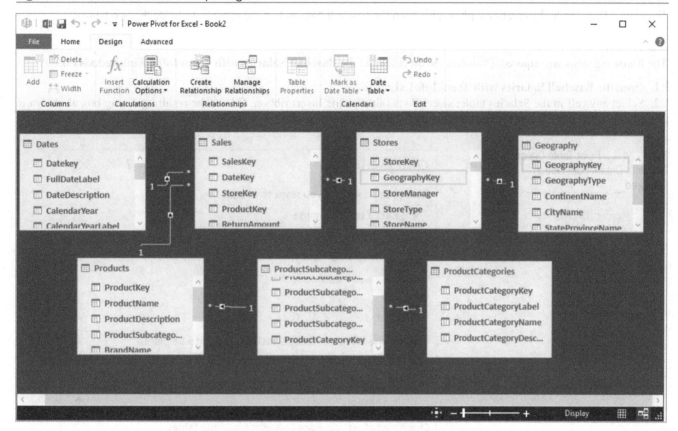

There is no need to store data in worksheets if the data are already stored in a Data Model.

By the way, suppose you select the Table option in Figure 4.7 *and* you check the Data Model option. This inflates your Excel workbook for no good reason. Each of the five Contoso tables is imported into a separate worksheet, and the same Data Model is created as before. Therefore, the *same* data are being stored twice, once in worksheets and once in the Data Model. It's best to store the data just once, and the Data Model is often the better choice. Also, as you will see shortly, it doesn't make sense to select the Pivot Table (or Pivot Chart) option *and* check the Data Model option. If you eventually want pivot tables, you can create them directly from the Data Model.

Importing multiple related tables is just one way of creating an Excel Data Model. The following example illustrates another possibility.

EXAMPLE

4.2 CREATING A DATA MODEL WITH A PIVOT TABLE

The file **Baseball Salaries with Team Info1.xlsx** is similar to the file used in Chapter 2, but now there is only one Salaries sheet (for 2018 players), and there is an extra Teams sheet. The tables on the two sheets have been designated as Excel tables, with table names Salary_Table and Team_Table. The Team table has a row for each of the 30 teams, listing the team's name, the team's division (such as National East), and the team's league (American or National). The Salary table has a row for each player, which includes the player's team, his position, and his salary. In database terms, the Team field is a primary key for the Teams table and a foreign key for the Salaries table. However, these tables are not yet related; they haven't yet been linked through their key fields. How can you use a pivot table to create a Data Model from the Teams and Salaries tables?

Objective

To create a Data Model by creating a pivot table from the baseball data and, in the process, to relate the two tables.

Solution

The following steps are required. (You can see the results in the **Baseball Salaries with Team Info1 Finished.xlsx** file.)

1. Open the **Baseball Salaries with Team Info1.xlsx** file.
2. Select any cell in the Salaries table; select PivotTable on the Insert ribbon; fill out the resulting dialog box as shown in Figure 4.11, making sure to check the Data Model option near the bottom; and click OK.

Figure 4.11 Pivot Table Dialog Box with Data Model Option Checked

3. As usual, a new sheet with a blank pivot table will open, but something else happens. If you open the Power Pivot window as in Example 4.1, you will see that the table from the Salaries sheet has been added to a new Data Model.

You can start a Data Model by creating a pivot table from existing worksheet data.

4. Back in the pivot table sheet in Excel, drag Salary to the Values area.
5. At this point, the "Active" link at the top of the PivotTable Fields pane is active (bold-faced), and only the fields in the Salary_Table are listed. But now click the "All" link. All fields in both tables are then listed. (See Figure 4.12.)
6. Expand the Team_Table list and check the Division field, the goal being to find the sum of salaries in each of the six divisions. However, because the two tables are not yet related, you will see the warning in yellow in Figure 4.12. Also, the pivot table values will be wrong because Excel is unable to combine data from two tables that aren't related.
7. To fix the problem, click the Auto-Detect button. In this case, Excel has the intelligence to recognize that the Team fields in the two tables serve as key fields, so it uses them to relate the tables. Nevertheless, it lets you examine the relationship. To do this, click the Manage Relationships button on the resulting dialog box and then click Edit to see the dialog box in Figure 4.13. This has indeed been filled in correctly, and it is exactly how you would fill it in if you clicked the CREATE button instead of the Auto-Detect button in Figure 4.12. The point is that the two tables are now related based on their Team key fields—and the pivot table values are now correct.

If you drag fields from unrelated tables to a pivot table, you will be warned about a missing relationship.

Figure 4.12 PivotTable Field
Pane with Multiple Tables

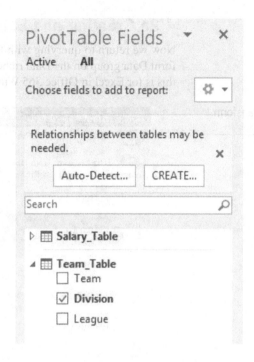

Figure 4.13 Edit Relationship Dialog Box

8. To see what else has happened, open the Power Pivot window again. In diagram view, you will see both tables, linked by their key fields. That is, both tables are now part of the workbook's Data Model. The only difference between this example and the previous Contoso example is that the Data Model has now been created through pivot table operations, not through importing external data.

9. Want a surprise? To be safe, save your work. Then delete the Salaries and Teams sheets. Now manipulate the pivot table any way you like. The pivot table will still work fine! This is because the pivot table's source is the Data Model, and the original data sheets are no longer necessary.

The title of this subsection is Excel's Data Model, but the two examples have discussed pivot tables and the Power Pivot window, the subjects of Section 4-3. It is difficult to disentangle the Data Model and Power Pivot, and many users evidently think they are the same thing. They are not. The purpose of a Data Model is to store related tables in a compressed format so that relational databases that have typically been stored in a RDBMS can now be stored in Excel. Power Pivot provides a window for viewing and managing the data in a Data Model, and it contains advanced tools, some discussed in Section 4-3, that go well beyond Excel's "regular" pivot table functionality. In short, the Data Model and Power Pivot are not the same, but they work hand in hand.

4-2c Creating and Editing Queries

Now we return to querying with Power Query. The tools to do so are in the Get & Transform Data group on the Data ribbon, as shown in Figure 4.14. (Again, we remind you that this is for Excel in Office 365 Windows.)

Figure 4.14 Get & Transform Data Group

There are three important strengths of Power Query relative to previous Excel importing tools:

1. You can import data from more sources than before. The Get Data dropdown list in Figure 4.14 shows some of these sources, including the many RDBMS sources, and the three buttons to the right of Get Data show that you can import data from a text file, the Web, and a table/range in Excel. The list of sources will almost certainly grow in the future.

The Query Editor is essentially a user-friendly substitute for the SQL query language. It lets you choose the rows and columns to include—and much more.

2. Once you locate data of interest, you can use the new Query Editor to "shape" the data to be imported. For example, you can specify the columns and rows of interest. The Query Editor provides a friendly graphical user interface for building a query, replacing the need for a complex SQL statement.

3. Your queries are stored in step-by-step fashion so that they can be modified and reused later. This is important if you make frequent queries from the same basic data source. It means you don't have start over with each query.

A complete discussion of Power Query's feature would require an entire book, so we will only lead you through two examples to illustrate some possibilities. Be aware that the query tools continue to evolve, so the details shown here may have changed by the time you read this. (Try the following: From Excel's File menu, click Feedback and then the Send a Suggestion button. This opens a Web page of suggestions by users. If you scroll through the list, you will see quite a few about Power Query. This is a very popular tool, and users want it to be even better.)

EXAMPLE

4.1 IMPORTING RELATED DATABASE TABLES (CONTINUED)

When you imported the Contoso data earlier, you imported *all* of the five selected tables, that is, all the rows and all the columns. What other importing options does Power Query provide?

Objective

To learn how to "shape" a query with Power Query.

Solution

If you select From Microsoft Access Database in Figure 4.14 and then maneuver to the **Contoso.accdb** file, you get the Navigator window in Figure 4.6, where you can select the tables of interest. For now, select all five tables as before. However, instead of loading the data right way, click the Edit button. This opens the Query Editor in Figure 4.15. This lets you preview the data, but, more importantly, it lets you "shape" the data to be imported.

Figure 4.15 Query Editor

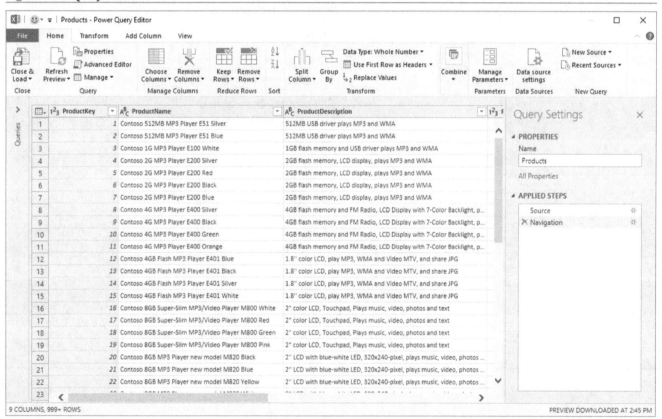

For example, if you click the Choose Columns button, you see a list of all columns in the selected table, and you can decide which columns you want to keep. As for rows, the dropdown arrow next to each column opens a window, just like you saw for tables in Chapter 2, where you can filter the rows to be returned. You can also transform the data in various ways. For example, the Split Column button lets you separate names like Wilson, John into two separate columns, based on the comma delimiter. For advanced users, the Advanced Editor button lets you see and manipulate the query command used behind the scenes to retrieve the data. (This is written a new query language called M, not SQL.) As you choose columns, filter rows, and so on, watch the Applied Steps to the right. All your actions are "recorded" as steps in the query, and you can later modify any of these steps as necessary.

This just scratches the surface of the Query Editor. We haven't discussed all the buttons on the its Home ribbon, and we haven't even shown its Transform, Add Column, and View ribbons. The Query Editor is a very powerful tool. If you plan to perform frequent queries in your eventual job, you will want to master this tool.

When you are finished shaping the data with the Query Editor, click the Close & Load dropdown arrow. This presents two options:

• The Close & Load option uses the current default setting to return the data to Excel in some way. This default setting seems to change, depending on your recent queries, so we don't recommend it.
• The second option, Close & Load To, is safer. It opens the Import Data dialog box in Figure 4.7, where you can decide how you want the data imported.

By double-clicking any query in the Queries & Connection pane, you can return to the Query Editor and modify the query.

For either option, the Queries & Connections pane in Figure 4.16 opens on the right side of the Excel window. (You can then close it or reopen it with the Queries & Connections button, a toggle, on Excel's Data ribbon.) This pane is very handy. For example, if you double-click any item, the Query Editor opens, where you can modify your query if necessary.

Figure 4.16 Queries & Connections Pane

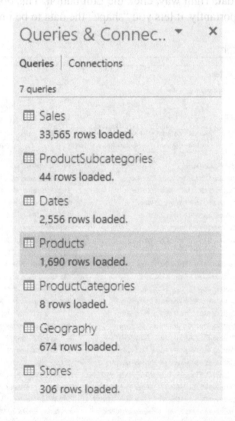

The next example involves a Web query. Obviously, Web pages have a variety of structures, but many have data in some type of tabular form. When you find a Web page with interesting data, you can try to import the data into Excel with the From Web button on the Data ribbon. Not all Web queries will succeed—this depends on how the Web page was created—but many more succeed with Power Query than with Excel's older Web query tool.

The newer Web query tool is much better—that is, much more likely to succeed—than the original Web query tool.

EXAMPLE

4.3 IMPORTING BASEBALL SALARY DATA FROM THE WEB

We first searched the Web for baseball salaries and found promising 2018 salary data at https://www.usatoday.com/sports/mlb/salaries/2018/player/all/. How can you import these data into Excel?

Objective

To use Power Query's new and improved Web query tool to import baseball salary data into Excel.

Solution

To import the data into Excel, do the following:

1. Click the From Web button on the Data ribbon, paste this URL into the resulting dialog box, and click OK.
2. The Navigator window in Figure 4.17 opens with two items on the left: Document and Table 0. In general, more items might be listed, and you can click any of them to see a preview on the right. In this case, Document has nothing interesting, but Table 0 appears to have the desired salary data, so select it and click Edit.

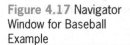

Figure 4.17 Navigator Window for Baseball Example

3. The Query Editor open, exactly as in the previous example. At this point, you can delete "junk" columns or rows and eventually use the Close & Load To option to return the data to Excel.

As these two examples illustrate, the basic sequence for all data imports is the following: (1) select the type of data source; (2) choose the tables of interest in the Navigator window; (3) use the Query Editor to shape the query; and (4) use a Close & Load To option to import the data into Excel. In this sense, Power Query is consistent across different types of data sources, and it is quite easy to learn.

As a final note, keep in mind that when you import data from an external source such as an Access file or the Web, the imported data remain linked to the source. This means that if the source data change, you can click the Refresh button on Excel's Data ribbon to update your imported data. If, for whatever reason, you want to sever the link, you can right-click the query in the Query & Connections pane and select Delete. Your imported data won't disappear; it just won't be refreshable.

Problems

Solutions for problems whose numbers appear within a colored box can be found in the Student Solution Files.

Level A

1. The **P04_01.mdb** file is an Access database file with two related tables about classical musicians. Use Power Query to import the data into a Data Model and then create a pivot table that shows the number of musicians for each instrument, sorted in decreasing order of the count.

2. The **P04_02.mdb** file is an Access database file with several related tables about food recipes. Use Power Query to import all tables and fields into a Data Model. Using Design view in the Power Pivot window as a guide, indicate the following types of relationships: (1) between Ingredient_Classes and Ingredients, (2) between Ingredients and Recipes, (3) between Measurements and Recipes, and (4) between Recipe_Classes and Recipes. If there are any linking tables, what role do they play? Finally, use a pivot table based on the Data Model to find, for each ingredient, the number of recipes that use that ingredient.

3. The **P04_03.xlsx** file contains four tables on four separate sheets with information about a company's sales in the latter part of 2018. These tables are not currently related, but they are relatable through key "ID" fields. Create a pivot table based on any of the tables—you can decide which—and check the option to add this to a Data Model. Then add fields from all the tables to the pivot table, creating relationships when necessary. (That is, mimic Example 4.2.) Manipulate the pivot table to find the Sum of QuantityOrdered, broken down by month of OrderDate and ProductName, but only for products in the Clothing category. Finally, after checking in the Power Pivot window that the tables are related correctly, delete the original four sheets. Your pivot table should still work fine.

4. The **P04_04.mdb** file is an Access database file with several related tables created by an entertainment agency. Use Power Query to import three of these tables, Entertainers, Entertainer_Members, and Members, into a Data Model. Is the relationship between Entertainers and Members one-to-many? What role does the Entertainer_Members play? Which, if any, of the members are in at least two entertainer groups?

5. The **P04_05.mdb** file is an Access database file with several related tables on college courses that students just completed. Use Power Query to import all tables and fields into a Data Model. Which of the tables, if any, are linking tables, and why are they required? By examining only the tables in the Power Pivot window (that is, not using pivot tables), find the following information about Steven Buchanan's schedule: the sections of the courses he took, the rooms and buildings of these sections, the days and times of these sections, and his grades in these sections.

6. Search the Web for NBA Salaries HoopsHype. (NBA stands for National Basketball Association.) Unless the site has changed, you should find a list of all NBA player salaries for the current season and several future seasons. Copy the URL and use it with Power Query to import the salaries for the current season only. (This was the 2017–2018 season as of this writing.) Create a histogram and box plot of these salaries. Is the salary distribution what you'd expect? Explain.

7. The **P04_07.txt** file is a text file listing the number of mobile subscriptions in four years for several countries. (You can view the data in NotePad if you like.) Use Power Query to import the data into an Excel table, using the Query Editor to delete the first and last columns and the last four rows. The result should be a table with three columns and four rows for each country, one for each year. An alternative arrangement has five columns (Country, 2002, 2003, 2004, 2005) and one row per country. Show that you can create this alternative arrangement with a pivot table based on the imported data.

Level B

8. Visit the website https://finance.yahoo.com/quote/YHOO/history?p=YHOO (or search the Web for Yahoo historical stock prices if this link no longer works) to find historical stock prices for any specified stock symbol, such as MSFT for Microsoft. Use this website to find all daily stock price data for Microsoft for 2017. Copy the URL and use it with Power Query to import the Microsoft 2017 data into a table in Excel. Delete the rows that have to do with dividends and sort in chronological order. Finally, create a line chart of the adjusted closing prices. (Note: There are two quirks about importing from this Yahoo site. First, Yahoo lets you import only 100 rows at a time. This means you will have to perform multiple queries to get all the 2017 data. Second, it imports the stock price data as text, not numeric, evidently because of the dividend rows. However, you can change this in the Query Editor with the Data Type dropdown on the Transform ribbon.)

9. The **P04_09.mdb** file is an Access database file for a fictional bowling league. This league consists of teams that play matches—one team against another—in various tournaments. Use Power Query to import all the tables into a Data Model. Then use the Power Pivot window to view the data and relationships. There are problems with the relationships, which you would find if you started creating pivot tables—the structure of this database is complex. However, using only the tables themselves in the Power Pivot window, not pivot tables, answer the following questions:

a. There are 20 tournaments listed in the Tournaments table. How many of these have been played?

b. How many matches are there per tournament?

c. How many games are there per match?

d. How many players are on a team?

e. Who is the team captain of the Terrapins?

f. Where was match 8 played, which teams played in match 8, and what was the total handicapped score of each of these teams in game 2 of this match?

10. The **P04_10.mdb** file is an Access database file created by a classical music CD collector (when CDs were "in"). Keep in mind that a classical CD can have multiple works by multiple composers, played or sung by multiple artists of various types or groups. Use Power Query to import all tables and fields into a Data Model. Then browse the tables and view the relationships diagram in the Power Pivot window. Explain the relationships between tables, with emphasis of the role of the CDs_Works table. (Move the tables around in Design view to get a clearer picture of the relationships.) Then use a pivot table to find the count of works, by composer, and sort them in decreasing order of count. (Note that these counts will often include different recordings of the same work, such as Beethoven's Fifth Symphony.)

11. The **srn_tmp.txt** file is a text file that contains monthly temperature from 1895 through January 2005. The **srn_data.txt** is a "data dictionary" that explains the temperature file. (The data dictionary mentions two other files, **srn_pcp.txt** and **srn_pdsi.txt**. These files have been provided, but they aren't used here.) Proceed as follows:

a. Use Power Query to import the temperature data into an Excel table (not a Data Model). Use the Query Editor for only one purpose: to change the data type for column 1 to text. (You can do this with the Data Type dropdown on the Transform ribbon.)

b. In Excel, change the column headings for columns 2 to 13 to month names: Jan, Feb, etc. Also, delete the last column, which is empty.

c. Create two new columns to the right of column 1: Code and Year. Fill the Code column with the first three digits of the column 1 value, using Excel's LEFT function, and fill the Year column with the last four digits of the column 1 value, using Excel's RIGHT function. Then copy the Code and Year columns, paste them over themselves as values, and delete column 1, which is no longer necessary.

d. Scan down to any year 2005 row. Only January's temperature is listed. The rest are missing, denoted by the code -99.9. Perform a search and replace for -99.9, replacing each with a blank.

e. The codes in the Code column are 001 to 048 for the contiguous 48 states. The other codes, above 100, are for regions. Delete all rows with these region codes.

f. The **State Codes.xlsx** file contains a table of codes and the corresponding states. Copy its data somewhere to the right of the imported temperature data. Then insert a new column, State, to the right of the temperature data Code column and use a VLOOKUP function to fill it with the state names.

g. Add three new columns to the right of the Year column: Low, High, and Average. Low and High should be the minimum and maximum monthly temperature for that year, respectively, and Average should be the average over all 12 months of that year.

h. Create a pivot table and pivot chart, based on the temperature data, where you can see a line chart of the Low, High, and Average values across years for any selected state. Filter out the year 2005 and use a slicer for the State filter.

12. The **P04_12.txt** file is a text file with data about uninsured people in each state for the years 2003–2007. Use Power Query to import this data into an Excel table (not a Data Model) and sort in increasing order of Year. As you will see, this is a wide table, with four columns for every state and only five rows, and it isn't very useful for analysis. It would be better to have a narrow, tall table with columns for Year, State, and the four uninsured numbers/percentages reported. Do whatever it takes to rearrange the data this way. Then create a pivot table where you can see any of the numbers/percentages across years for any selected state. (Hint: You could do this with a lot of cutting and pasting. However, a better way is to use Excel's INDEX function with clever row and column indexes. For example, the number of uninsured females in Alaska in 2004 can be found with =**INDEX**(*range,2,5*), where *range* is the range of the imported numbers/percentages.)

13. You have been hired to create a relational database for a regional soccer league. Each team in the league has players, and the teams play one another, maybe multiple times, during the soccer season. How would you structure this database? Would you use a single-table database? If so, what fields would the table include? Would it be a multi-table database? If so, what tables would be included, how would they be related, and what fields would each table include? As you develop this structure, think about the questions you might want to ask of the database, probably with pivot tables. There is clearly no single correct structure, but there are structures that are better than others.

4-3 Data Analysis with Power Pivot

This section discusses the most publicized member of Microsoft's Power BI tools, **Power Pivot**. This add-in was introduced as a free add-in for Excel 2010 and is now an integral part of Excel.[6] The first question you probably have is a natural one: With the pivot table functionality discussed in the previous chapter already in Excel—without Power Pivot— why is Power Pivot needed? This is not an easy question to answer, at least not before you have seen what Power Pivot provides. Hopefully, by the end of this section, you will have some appreciation for why many data analysts, those who have used pivot tables for years, love Power Pivot.

We mentioned earlier that although the Data Model and Power Pivot are *not* the same thing, they work hand in hand for powerful data analysis. To convince you that they are not the same thing, try the following:

The Power Pivot add-in is now part of Excel, but it still must be added in through the COM add-ins list.

1. Click the COM Add-ins button on the Developer ribbon and make sure the Microsoft Power Pivot for Excel item is *not* checked.
2. Open the result of Example 4.1, where a seven-table Data Model has been created from the Contoso database. You can't "see" the data, but the seven tables are stored in the Data Model.
3. Select Pivot Table from the Insert ribbon and make sure the Use this workbook's Data Model option is checked, as shown in Figure 4.18.

Figure 4.18 Basing a Pivot Table on the Data Model

4. A blank pivot table will appear, and all fields from all seven imported tables will be available for the pivot table. You can create a few example pivot tables to confirm that everything works correctly.

The point here is that you do *not* need Power Pivot to create pivot tables from an existing Data Model. Also, as you saw in the previous section, Power Pivot is not needed to *create* a Data Model. However, it helps to have both. To get a sense of this, click the Manage Data Model button on the Data ribbon. Assuming Power Pivot isn't checked in the COM Add-ins list, you will see the dialog box in Figure 4.19. If you click Enable, Power Pivot is automatically checked in the COM Add-ins list, and the **Power Pivot window** opens so that you can see and manage the data in the Data Model.

---

6 We remind you again that Power Pivot is not included in all versions of Office 365. You can check your own version by viewing the COM add-ins list on the Developer ribbon. Unless Power Pivot is on the list, your version doesn't have it.

Figure 4.19 Enabling the Data Analysis Add-ins

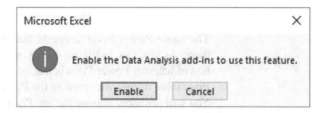

For the rest of this section, we will be using the Power Pivot add-in, so make sure it is loaded by checking its item in the COM Add-ins list. You will know Power Pivot is loaded when there is a Power Pivot tab and associated ribbon in Excel, as shown in Figure 4.20. If you click its Manage button, the Power Pivot window in Figure 4.21 appears. This is where you can see your Data Model, if there is one, and manage it as discussed in this section. You can close the Power Pivot window at any time, and Excel will remain open. Alternatively, you can leave the Power Pivot window open and switch between it and the Excel window in the usual way. (If they are not both visible, click the Excel button, second from left at the top of the Power Pivot window, to go from Power Pivot to Excel. In the other direction, click the Manage button on Excel's Power Pivot ribbon to go from Excel to Power Pivot.) Note the Save button and the Save options in the File menu in the Power Pivot window. These work exactly like the usual Excel Save options—that is, they save the active workbook, along with its Data Model, if any. This enables you to save from either the Power Pivot window or the Excel window.

It is easy to go back and forth between the Excel window and the Power Pivot window. Both can be open at the same time.

Figure 4.20 Power Pivot Ribbon

Figure 4.21 Power Pivot Window (with No Data Model Yet)

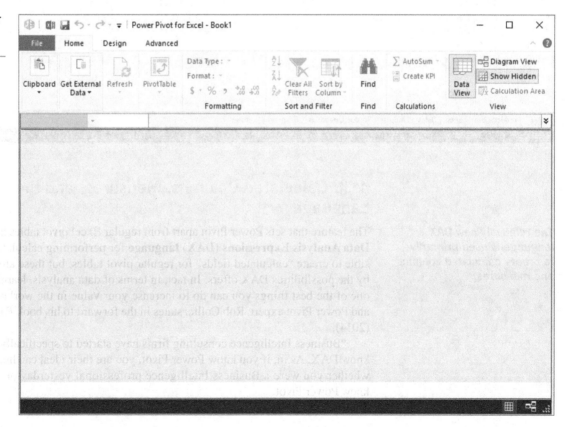

4-3a Basing Pivot Tables on a Data Model

The name Power Pivot suggests that it can be used to create pivot tables, so let's start there. As you saw in Figure 4.18, you can create a pivot table from a Data Model regardless of whether Power Pivot is loaded. However, if Power Pivot is loaded, you can click the PivotTable dropdown arrow in the Power Pivot window to see the options in Figure 4.22. You will probably choose the top PivotTable option to get the usual blank pivot table, but you can experiment with the other options. For example, the Two Charts options provide two pivot charts, both based on the Data Model, and you can then populate them in different and independent ways. So, Power Pivot does indeed provide options for creating pivot tables and pivot charts, but it provides much more.

Figure 4.22 Pivot Table Options in Power Pivot Window

4-3b Calculated Columns, Measures, and the DAX Language

The relatively new DAX language is used primarily to create calculated columns and measures.

The feature that sets Power Pivot apart from regular Excel pivot tables is the relatively new **Data Analysis Expressions (DAX) language** for performing calculations. It is still possible to create "calculated fields" for regular pivot tables, but these are totally outclassed by the possibilities DAX offers. In fact, in terms of data analysis, learning DAX might be one of the best things you can do to increase your value in the workplace. As one DAX and Power Pivot expert, Rob Collie, states in the forward to his book *Power Pivot Alchemy* (2014),

"Business Intelligence consulting firms have started to specifically target people who know DAX. As in, if you know Power Pivot, you are their ideal candidate. Doesn't matter whether you were a Business Intelligence professional yesterday or not – just that you know Power Pivot."

This section provides an overview of DAX, but it illustrates only a few of the many possibilities. If you want to learn more, you should read a book on DAX such as Rob Collie's or either of the books listed in the references by Ferrari and Russo. DAX is built around formulas and functions. Some of these are very similar to Excel formulas and functions, but some have no Excel counterparts. There are well over 100 DAX functions.

To get started, take another look at the Power Pivot window in Figure 4.22. This looks like a regular Excel workbook, with rows, columns, and table tabs at the bottom. However, there are important differences. The main difference is that you *cannot* edit individual cells. The data you see—the data in the Data Model—are linked to a data source and cannot be changed except by changing the source data. The two main things you *can* do in the Power Pivot window is add calculated columns and add measures, and you do each of these with DAX formulas. A **calculated column** is basically like a new column in Excel, based on data from other columns in the selected table or even columns in related tables. A **measure** is a summary function of some type.[7] Measures are intended for use in the Values area of pivot tables.

> A calculated column is a new column in a table of a Data Model. It is based on fields in the current table or related tables. A measure is a summarization of columns in a Data Model, or a function of other measures, that is intended for use in the Values area of pivot tables. Both are created with DAX formulas.

Referring to the data in Figure 4.22, one simple measure, the type you saw in the previous chapter, is "Sum of SalesAmount." For example, this could be used in a pivot table to break down the sum of sales amount by product and/or order date. However, DAX allows you to create measures that are considerably more complex than simple sums. The following extended example illustrates several possibilities.

EXAMPLE

4.4 USING DAX ON THE CONTOSO DATA

Starting with the results in the file **Contoso Import Finished.xlsx** (from Example 4.1), where seven tables were imported into an Excel Data Model, create some useful calculated columns and measures with DAX and use them to create insightful pivot tables.

Objective
To see what DAX calculated columns and measures look like and how they can be used in pivot tables.

Solution
For illustration, we will create two types of calculated columns. (You can see the results in the **Contoso Pivot Table Finished .xlsx** file.) The first is like a typical new column in Excel. We'll call it Profit, calculated as SalesAmount minus ReturnAmount minus TotalCost. To create it, do the following:

1. Referring to Figure 4.22, click anywhere in the right blank column, the column with the *Add Column* heading.
2. Type an equals sign (which you'll see in the formula bar), click the SalesAmount heading, type a minus sign, click the ReturnAmount heading, type another minus sign, click the TotalCost heading, and press Enter. As you do this, you will

---

7 When the Power Pivot add-in was introduced for Excel 2010, the term "measure" was used. Then Microsoft decided to change it to "calculated field" for Excel 2013. Based on user complaints, the term has been changed back to "measure."

see your DAX formula being created in the formula bar. The final formula should be **=Sales[SalesAmount]-Sales[Retur-nAmount]-Sales[TotalCost]**. Although this looks like an Excel formula (the type you'd create from an Excel table), it is really a DAX formula. The syntax is that column names are in square brackets, preceded by table names. (The table names can be omitted if there is no ambiguity, but it is good practice to include them.)

3. The default heading for the new column is Calculated Column 1. This is too generic, so right-click the heading, select Rename Column, and type Profit.

Alternatively, you can combine steps 2 and 3 by typing **Profit:= Sales[SalesAmount]-Sales[ReturnAmount]-Sales[TotalCost]** in the formula bar. You type the name of the calculated column, then colon equals (:=), and then the formula.

With a calculated column, each row's value in the column must be calculated.

When you type the formula and then press Enter, the entire column fills with the profit calculations. This illustrates that you can't create a partial column with DAX; you must fill an entire column. Also, because there are 33,565 rows in this table, DAX must calculate Profit for each of these rows. This is a critical distinction between a calculated column and a measure.

The second example of a calculated column uses a DAX function, RELATED, that has no counterpart in Excel. It is used to get data into one table from another related table. To use this function, select the Products table, click anywhere in the first blank column, and type **ProductCategory:=RELATED(** to see the list in Figure 4.23. It shows all columns from all tables. Choose ProductCategoryName from the ProductCategories table, type), and press Enter. Then repeat, creating a ProductSubcategory calculated column from the ProductSubcategoryName field in the ProductSubcategories table.

Figure 4.23 Using the RELATED Function

You now have information on product category and product subcategory in the Products table. But why would you want this, given that this information already exists in two related tables? After all, relational database tables are structured specifically to avoid redundancy. There are two reasons. First, you can now hide the ProductCategories and ProductSubcategories tables (by right-clicking their sheet tabs and selecting Hide from Client Tools). Then when you use the Data Model to create pivot tables, all information about products will be in a single Products table, which is less confusing to a user.

The RELATED function is used to bring data from a related table into a table.

The second reason is that you can now build a **hierarchy** in the Products table. Do this as follows:

1. Switch to diagram view in the Power Pivot window.
2. Move the cursor over the Products table. You will see two buttons at the top right, Create Hierarchy and Maximize. Click Maximize to expand the table and then click Create Hierarchy.
3. You will see a new Hierarchy field in the list, which you can rename Product Structure. Then drag the fields ProductCategory, ProductSubcategory, BrandName, and ProductName, in that order, slightly below the hierarchy name, each slightly below the previous field. (This might take a little practice.) The result should look like Figure 4.24.

A hierarchy allows you to drill down in a pivot table, such as from country to state to city to ZIP code.

Figure 4.24 Creating a Product Structure Hierarchy

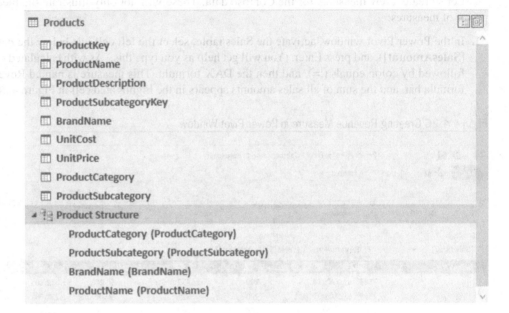

4. Click the Maximize button—it's now a Restore button—to restore the table to its original size.

You will soon see how useful this product hierarchy is for drilling down in pivot tables.

DAX offers many more functions for creating calculated columns, such as date functions for manipulating dates. Also, you can experiment with formulas that look like Excel formulas. For example, you can use IF formulas just like in Excel to create calculated columns. But this is enough to get you started.

We now turn to measures, which are arguably even more important than calculated columns. As stated earlier, a measure is any summarization of the data in the Data Model that can be placed in the Values area of pivot tables. Measures can be created implicitly or explicitly. Given the Contoso Data Model developed so far, suppose you create the usual type of pivot table by dragging the new Profit field to the Values area. This will automatically use the Sum summarization; that is, you will see the sum of Profit broken down by any Row or Column fields. Behind the scenes, however, a measure, Sum of Profit, is created implicitly, and

A measure is a summarization of data intended for the Values area of a pivot table. The flexibility of measures created by DAX is the real "power" in Power Pivot.

this sum is calculated on the fly, depending on how you break it down. For example, if you drag ProductName to the Rows area of the pivot table, Sum of Profit will be calculated for each product and for all products combined (the grand total). The point here is that you are using measures in pivot tables, even if you aren't aware of it.

However, measures can also be created *explicitly*, and the only limit is your imagination and your expertise in DAX. There are two ways you can create a measure explicitly:

1. You can type a DAX formula in the Power Pivot window. You can enter it in *any* table of the Data Model, but you normally select the table most closely associated with the measure.
2. You can click the Measures dropdown arrow on the Power Pivot ribbon in the Excel window, as shown in Figure 4.25. These two items allow you to create new measures or edit existing measures.

Figure 4.25
Measures
Dropdown List
for Power Pivot

Let's create a few measures for the Contoso data. These will not only illustrate the mechanics, but they will show the power of measures:

1. In the Power Pivot window, activate the Sales table, select the left cell just below the data, type **Revenue:=SUM(Sales [SalesAmount])**, and press Enter. (You will get help as you type this.) As with calculated columns, you name the measure, followed by colon equals (:=), and then the DAX formula. This measure is named Revenue. The formula shows in the formula bar, and the sum of all sales amounts appears in the highlighted cell in Figure 4.26.

Figure 4.26 Creating Revenue Measure in Power Pivot Window

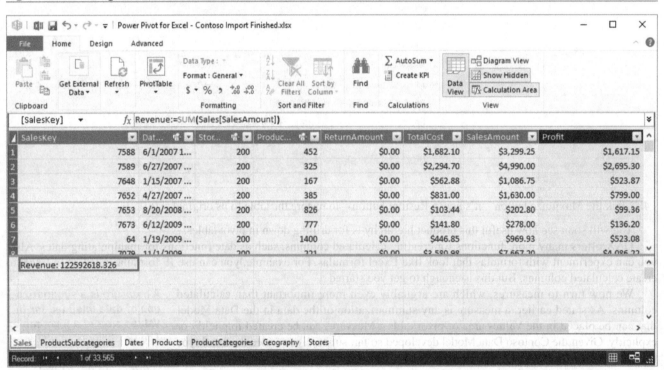

2. Repeat in the cell below, typing **Cost:=SUM(Sales[TotalCost])** to create another measure called Cost.
3. For variety, create another measure called Ratio with the New Measure item in Figure 4.25. When you click this item, a dialog box appears. Fill it in as shown in Figure 4.27. (The format at the bottom is used for displaying values of the measure in pivot tables.) This measure is associated with the Sales table, its name is Ratio, and its formula, **=[Revenue]/[Cost]**, is based on the existing Revenue and Cost measures (inside required square brackets), not original data columns. That is, you can create measures from other measures. This has an important advantage, as you will see in step 5. *A new measure can be defined in terms of existing measures. If those existing measures change, the new measure updates automatically.*
4. Create a pivot table based on the Data Model. The field list under the Sales table will include the original Sales fields *plus* the three measures you just created. (They have an *fx* symbol next to them to remind you that they are measures.) For now, drag the Ratio measure to the Values area and the Product Structure hierarchy from the Products table to the Rows area. This illustrates the value of a hierarchy. It allows you to drill down, such as shown in Figure 4.28. The numbers in this pivot table are calculated exactly as you'd want them to be. For example, for all sales in the VCD & DVD subcategory of the TV and Video category, the sum of all revenues is 214.2% of the sum of all costs. In other words, each ratio is a ratio of sums.

Figure 4.27 Creating Ratio
Measure

Figure 4.28 Pivot Table with
Ratio Measure and Product
Hierarchy

	A	B	C
1	ProductCategory	ProductSubcategory	Ratio
2	⊞ Audio		237.7%
3	⊞ Cameras and camcorders		249.4%
4	⊞ Cell phones		225.1%
5	⊞ Computers		231.4%
6	⊞ Music, Movies and Audio Books		256.3%
7	⊟ TV and Video	⊞ Car Video	212.1%
8		⊞ Home Theater System	217.9%
9		⊞ Televisions	236.7%
10		⊞ VCD & DVD	214.2%
11	TV and Video Total		220.4%
12	Grand Total		234.4%

5. To see the flexibility of measures, suppose your boss now tells you that you calculated the Revenue and Cost measures incorrectly. Revenue should be the sum of SalesAmount *minus* the sum of ReturnAmount. Also, 5% of all costs are considered overhead costs, and this 5% should not be included in the Cost measure. Fortunately, you do *not* have to start over. You can simply edit the Revenue and Cost measures in the obvious way, using the Manage Measures item in Figure 4.26. Then because Ratio is the ratio of these measures, it updates automatically, as does the pivot table. Try it. You should see that the ratio for VCD & DVD changes to 222.8%.

6. This step goes beyond the level of the book, but it shows how powerful DAX can be. (You can see the details in the finished version of the file.) We hope it will motivate you to look up and learn the functions involved, especially the complex but powerful CALCULATE function:

a. Create the "correct" revenue measure with the formula

   Net Revenue:=[Revenue]-SUM(Sales[ReturnAmount])

b. Create the year-to-date net revenue in any year with the formula

   Net Revenue YTD:=CALCULATE([Net Revenue],DATESYTD(Dates[DateKey]))

c. Create the year-to-date net revenue for the previous year with the formula

   Net Revenue YTD-1:=CALCULATE([Net Revenue YTD],DATEADD(Dates[DateKey],-1,YEAR))

Date-related measures are especially useful, such as for comparing year-to-date revenue this year versus last year.

d. Create the percentage change from one year to the next with the formula

Percent Change YTD YOY:=([Net Revenue YTD]-[Net Revenue YTD-1])/[Net Revenue YTD-1]

Then, using a slicer for CalendarYear, the pivot table in Figure 4.29 is easy to create. It shows, for example, that net revenue through October 2008 was $30,743,029, whereas net revenue through October 2009 was $30,309,555, 1.41% lower than in 2008. If you change the slicer year to 2008, the comparison will be between 2007 and 2008—and you will see that the percentage changes are considerably *more* negative. Evidently, Contoso tried to correct the downward slide in 2009. In contrast, if you change the slicer year to 2010, column C will be blank because there are no data for 2010 in the database.

Figure 4.29 Year-to-Date Measures

	A	B	C	D	E	F	G	H
1	CalendarMonthLabel ▼	Net Revenue YTD-1	Net Revenue YTD	Percent Change YTD YOY	CalendarYear			
2	January	$2,774,510	$2,713,037	-2.22%	2007			
3	February	$5,683,470	$5,242,963	-7.75%				
4	March	$8,127,843	$8,109,508	-0.23%	2008			
5	April	$11,279,806	$11,146,191	-1.18%				
6	May	$14,877,739	$14,325,849	-3.71%	2009			
7	June	$17,774,831	$17,732,692	-0.24%	2010			
8	July	$21,266,356	$20,959,554	-1.44%				
9	August	$24,294,299	$24,225,011	-0.29%	2005			
10	September	$27,522,393	$27,141,076	-1.39%	2006			
11	October	$30,743,029	$30,309,555	-1.41%				
12	Novemeber	$34,545,456	$33,620,194	-2.68%	2011			
13	December	$38,398,111	$36,733,274	-4.34%				
14	Grand Total	$38,398,111	$36,733,274	-4.34%				

An important aspect of measures is that they are calculated only when they are required in a pivot table. For example, before the Product Structure hierarchy was added to the pivot table in Figure 4.28, there was just one calculation, the ratio for all sales, that is, the sum of sales amounts for all sales divided by the sum of costs for all sales. *The values of a measure are calculated only as they are needed in a pivot table.* Then when the Product Structure hierarchy was added, the Ratio measure had to be calculated only for the members of the hierarchy. If you then added another field such as Continent (from the Geography table) to the pivot table, the Ratio measure would have to be calculated again, but only for combinations of product hierarchy items and continents. Contrast this with the calculated Profit column that had to be calculated over 33,000 times when it was created.

There is one common error made by DAX beginners when they create measures. Suppose you create a measure in the Sales table with the formula **Profit:=[SalesAmount]-[Return Amount]-[TotalCost]**. You will almost surely wonder why this produces an error. It is *not* a syntax error. The problem is that SalesAmount, ReturnAmount, and TotalCost are columns in the Sales table, not measures, and a measure must be a summarization. There is no summarizing in this formula. In contrast, the formula **Total Profit:=Sum[SalesAmount]-Sum[Return Amount]-Sum[TotalCost]** works fine. *A measure must be a summarization. For example, it can't be a simple addition or subtraction of individual fields.*

Now, suppose you drag this Total Profit measure to the Values area of a pivot table. Then you have no choice of how it is summarized; its definition indicates that it is summarized by Sum. If you wanted it to be summarized by Average, you should use the Average function instead of the Sum function in the definition of the measure.

One last simple thing you can do with Power Pivot is *hide* individual columns (or entire tables). To do so, right-click any column (or table tab) in the Power Pivot window and choose Hide from Client Tools. This is especially useful if you are designing the file for others to use and there are certain columns (or tables) that would never be needed in pivot tables. By hiding them, your users won't ever see them in the PivotTable Fields list, so they won't be tempted to use them in pivot tables, and there will be less confusion. As an example, key fields are good candidates for hiding. They serve their purpose in relating tables, and they continue to serve this purpose even when they are hidden, but they are usually meaningless in pivot tables.

This section has presented a *brief* introduction to calculated columns, measures, and the DAX language. As you will find if you explore these topics further on your own, some of the things you can do with DAX are quite complex, and they take time and practice to master. This is the reason Rob Collie, the author mentioned earlier, states that people with these skills are in great demand. To gain insights, companies need to break down massive amounts of data in all sorts of ways, and, at least in the Microsoft world, DAX is the key to doing this successfully.

Fundamental Insight

The pivot table functionality that has been part of Excel for decades is great, but it has its limits in terms of generating the reports that businesspeople need. With Power Pivot and its DAX language, these limits are expanded significantly. It takes a lot of work to learn and master DAX, but this work is well worth the effort. DAX experts are in high demand.

Problems

Solutions for problems whose numbers appear within a colored box can be found in the Student Solution Files.

Level A

14. The **P04_14.xlsx** file contains the Contoso Data Model discussed in Example 4.4, but without any calculated columns, measures, or hierarchies:
    a. In the Sales table, create two calculated columns: Net Revenue as SalesAmount minus ReturnAmount and Cost without Overhead as 0.95 times TotalCost. Then create a pivot table with ProductCategoryName in the Rows area and the two calculated columns in the Values area, each summarized by Sum.
    b. In the Sales table, create two measures: Total Net Revenue as Sum of Net Revenue and Total Cost without Overhead as Sum of Cost without Overhead. Then create a pivot table (on a new sheet) with ProductCategoryName in the Rows area and the two measures in the Values area.
    c. Do these two pivot tables give the same results? Are there any differences between them? Which requires more calculations? Explain.

15. The **P04_14.xlsx** file contains the Contoso Data Model discussed in Example 4.4, but without any calculated columns, measures, or hierarchies:
    a. In the Stores table, create a calculated column named Large Store, which is 1 for all stores with at least 800 square feet and 0 for others. You can do this with an IF formula just like in Excel.
    b. In the Stores table, hide all columns except the calculated column.
    c. In the Stores table, create a hierarchy called Store Location, using the fields ContinentName, RegionCountryName, StateProvinceName, and CityName from the Geography table, and then hide the Geography table.
    d. In the Sales table, create a calculated column called Return, which is 1 if ReturnAmount is positive and 0

otherwise. Then create a measure called Total Returns as Sum of Return.
    e. Create a pivot table with Total Returns in the Values area, Large Store in the Columns area, and the Store Location hierarchy in the Rows area. Discuss what the numbers mean.

16. The **P04_14.xlsx** file contains the Contoso Data Model discussed in Example 4.4, but without any calculated columns, measures, or hierarchies. Create a Product Structure hierarchy in the Products table, but when you drag the fields to the hierarchy, drag them in the wrong order, such as ProductSubcategory, then BrandName, then ProductCategory, and then ProductName. Does Power Pivot allow this? What happens?

17. The **P04_14.xlsx** file contains the Contoso Data Model discussed in Example 4.4, but without any calculated columns, measures, or hierarchies. The question here is whether you can have two different hierarchies in the same table:
    a. In the Stores table, create a hierarchy called Store Location 1, using the fields RegionCountryName and StateProvinceName from the Geography table.
    b. In the Stores table, try to create a second hierarchy called Store Location 2, using the fields Continent, RegionCountryName, and CityName. Are you allowed to do so?
    c. Create two pivot tables on separate worksheets, one summarizing SalesAmount by the first hierarchy and the other summarizing SalesAmount by the second hierarchy (if it's allowed).

18. The **P04_18.xlsx** file contains a single-table Data Model on a company's sales and a single blank worksheet:
    a. Create a pivot table on the worksheet, based on the Data Model, and drag Revenue to the Values area and Date to the Rows area.
    b. Create a measure, **Total Revenue:=Sum([Revenue])**, and add it to Values area of the existing pivot table. Do you get the same results as in part a? Explain.

19. The **P04_19.xlsx** file contains a Data Model with four related tables about a company's sales and a single blank worksheet:

a. Create two calculated TRUE/FALSE columns, **Data Error:=[ShipDate]<[OrderDate]** and **Shipped Late:=[ShipDate]>[OrderDate]+3**.

b. Create a pivot table based on the Data Model to find the number of data errors and the number of orders that were shipped late.

Level B

20. The **P04_18.xlsx** file contains a single-table Data Model on a company's sales and a single blank worksheet. The goal is to create a pivot table that shows the ratio of average revenue per transaction in the Charleston store to average revenue per transaction in all other stores combined, broken down by month:

a. Create the calculated columns **RevenueCharleston:=[Revenue]*(Sales[Store]="Charleston")** and **RevenueOther:=[Revenue]*(Sales[Store]<>"Charleston")**. Then create the measure **Ratio1:=Average([RevenueCharleston])/Average([RevenueOther])** and use it in a pivot table, broken down by month. Explain why you don't get the desired ratios.

b. Modify the Data Model to get the desired ratios.

21. Before Power Pivot, you could create "calculated fields" for pivot tables. This problem explores calculated fields versus Power Pivot's measures for ratios. The **P04_21.xlsx** file contains a list of transactions for a specific product at various stores for the last several months. Each transaction lists the revenue from the transaction and the number of units of the product sold in the transaction. The ratio of these, also listed, is the unit price at the time the product was sold:

a. Create a pivot table but do *not* add it to a Data Model. Drag Unit Price to the Values area and Store to the Rows area. Are the values in the pivot table meaningful? Does it help if you summarize by Average rather than Sum? Explain.

b. With this same pivot table selected, choose Calculated Field from the Fields, Items, & Sets dropdown list on the PivotTable Tools Analyze ribbon. In the resulting dialog box, provide the name Unit Price1 and the formula **=Revenue/Units Sold**. Click Add and then OK. Explain exactly how the calculation in the Sum of Unit Price1 column is made. Which column is better to report, the Average of Unit Price in part a or the Sum of Unit Price1 calculated here?

c. Go back to the Data sheet. Insert another pivot table, place it on a new worksheet, and check the Add to Data Model option.

d. Open the Power Pivot window. In the rows below the data, create four measures: **Unit Price2:=[Revenue]/[Units Sold]**, **Unit Price3:=Sum([Revenue])/Sum([Units Sold])**, **Unit Price4:=Sum([Revenue]/[Units Sold])**, and **Unit Price5:=Average([Price per unit])**. Two of these should produce errors. Which ones, and why? Then in the pivot table, drag each of the other two to the Values area and drag Store to the Rows area. How do the results compare to the results in parts a and b?

22. The **P04_19.xlsx** file contains a Data Model with four related tables about a company's sales and a single blank worksheet. This problem illustrates a potential problem with pivot tables when there is a many-to-many relationship, in this case between Products and Orders. (The "fix" to this problem is beyond the level of this book, but the issue is indicated here.) Suppose you are asked to find the number of orders that contain a specific product such as Dog Ear Cyclecomputer.

a. The natural way is to create a pivot table with OrderID from the Orders table in the Values area, summarized by Count, and ProductName from the Products table in the Rows area. When you create this pivot table, you should see that the counts are wrong. They show 944, the total number of orders, for *each* product.

b. Try instead putting OrderID from the Order_Details table in the Values area of the pivot table, again summarized by Count. Provide a convincing argument why these counts are correct. For example, check the records for Dog Ear Cyclecomputer in the Order_Details table.

4-4 Data Visualization with Tableau Public

As stated in the introduction, visualizing data with various types of graphs is not new. Analysts have been using standard graphs such as histograms and scatterplots for over a century. However, there has recently been an increased emphasis on visualizing data with imaginative types of graphs, and software has been developed to create these visualizations.[8] In this section, we will discuss a popular non-Microsoft software package called **Tableau Public**. This is the free version of the commercial Tableau product developed by Tableau Software, a company that has specialized in visualization techniques since

8 In the introduction to this chapter, we mentioned Microsoft's stand-alone software package Power BI. If you search the Web for Power BI, you will find "Microsoft Power BI—Data Visualization Software." This is one more confirmation of the importance of data visualization in today's business world.

its founding in 2003. You can download Tableau Public—for free—for Windows or Mac from https://public.tableau.com/en-us/s/ (or search for Tableau Public in case this link has changed). We will lead you through an example of using Tableau Public, but we also recommend the Resources link at this website. It has over 20 "how to" videos on using the software.

Tableau Public is not an Excel add-in or even a Microsoft product. However, it can import data from Excel worksheets.

Remember that Tableau Public is stand-alone software; it is *not* an Excel add-in. To use Tableau Public, you will typically go through the following steps to create and publish what Tableau calls a "viz" (plural "vizzes"):

1. Connect to external data. For our purposes, this will be data from an Excel workbook, but other data sources are possible.
2. If necessary, manipulate the data into a useful form for visualizations.
3. Create one or more charts based on the data.
4. Optionally, combine charts into a **dashboard** (a set of related charts) or a **story** (somewhat like a PowerPoint presentation).
5. Publish your viz to the Web.

This last step means that you can view many visualizations—created by other users or even by yourself—on the Web. From the https://public.tableau.com/en-us/s/ site, click the Gallery tab. This lists the "Viz of the Day" for many days and is probably the best way to see what the software can do. Besides, many of these provide interesting examples of current news stories. For example, the Viz of the Day on the day this section was written was about World Cub 2018 soccer match between Tunisia and England. All these visualizations are intended to tell a story by visual means. The authors started with data and then probably made a few false starts in Tableau Public before they got the viz that told their story best. You will probably go through this same process in creating your own visualizations. The mechanics are fairly straightforward, but imagination is required to produce *insightful* visualizations.

The following extended example takes you through the process of creating a viz from the same baseball salary data you have seen before.

EXAMPLE

4.5 USING TABLEAU PUBLIC WITH BASEBALL SALARY DATA

The file **Baseball Salaries with Team Info2.xlsx** contains a sheet for each year from 2012 to 2018 listing each player, his team, his position, and his salary for that year. It also contains a Teams sheet that lists each team, the division and league of the team, and the team's city, state/province, and country. (One team, the Toronto Blue Jays, is in Canada.) How can Tableau Public be used to create insightful charts and a dashboard of team salaries?

Objective
To learn the mechanics of Tableau Public for creating a viz of baseball team salaries.

Solution
We will go through the basic steps listed earlier. The first step is to connect to the Excel file. To do this, open Tableau Public. You will see a Connect pane on the left where you can select Microsoft Excel and then navigate to the baseball salaries file. Keep in mind that this only creates a connection to the Excel file. Anything you do to the data in Tableau Public will *not* be reflected in the Excel source file, which doesn't change at all.

You will see the Excel sheets listed on the left of the Tableau Public window. We want all the Salary 201x sheets to be joined with the Teams sheet. To do this, select all Salary 201x sheets (select the first, then, while holding the Shift key, select the last) and drag them to the *Drag sheets here* section on the right. This creates a union of all the Salary 201x sheets, where the data from all years are stacked on top of one another. Then drag the Teams sheet to the right of the Salary 201x union.

This joins them through the Team key fields on all sheets. (Yes, Tableau Public knows about relating tables with primary and foreign keys.) The result appears as in Figure 4.30, where you see a preview of the single combined table of data.

Figure 4.30 Imported Data in Tableau Public

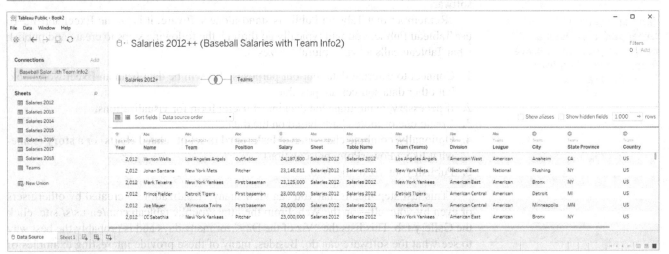

For the second step, manipulating the imported data, there is very little to do in this example. There is a row for each player in each year, exactly what you want. However, there are a couple minor changes you can make:

1. The symbol above each field name indicates the data type, but these can be changed. Specifically, the Year field's data type is currently numeric (the # sign), but to create line charts, it needs to be a date, so click the # sign and change the data type to Date.
2. Several columns won't be used for any charts, so they can be hidden. To do so, click the dropdown arrow above any field name and select Hide. Do this for the Name, Sheet, Table Name, and Team (Teams) fields.

Tableau tip

Undoing or Redoing

The left and right arrows at the top left of the Tableau Public window let you undo or redo actions. The same keystroke combinations as for Excel, Ctrl+z and Ctrl+y, can also be used.

Now it's time to create some charts. You can create the first one by clicking the Sheet 1 tab in Figure 4.30. This sheet starts as shown in Figure 4.31. All fields appear on the left, and these can be dragged to the various areas on the right: Pages, Filters, Marks of different types, Columns and Rows fields, and the Sheet 1 area.

Each "worksheet" in Tableau Public contains some type of chart.

Figure 4.31 Blank Tableau Public Worksheet

Tableau tip

Dimensions and Measures

Tableau Public uses terminology that has become common in data analysis: *dimensions* and *measures*. Essentially, measures are numeric fields you want to summarize, and dimensions are fields you can break measures down by. In terms of pivot tables, measures are fields you typically drag to the Values area, and dimensions are fields you typically drag to the Rows, Columns, or Filters areas. In the current example, Tableau Public has created a hierarchy (Country, StateProvince, City) for the team location dimension. It has also automatically generated the Latitude and Longitude measures from the location dimension for use in maps.

Fundamental Insight

The concepts of dimensions and measures have become very common, and if you plan to be a data analyst, you will see them a lot. This is because you frequently need to break down numeric variables (measures) by categorical variables (dimensions). In Excel, you typically do this with pivot tables, but this is not exclusively a Microsoft tool. Many other software packages have similar functionality, even though the terminology used may differ.

The first chart will be a map of the United States and lower Canada with a bubble for each team. Each bubble will be sized and colored to indicate the team's relative total salary. There will be filters for Division and Year. To create this chart, do the following:

1. Drag Country, then StateProvince, then City, then Team to the Detail button. This creates a map, and the Longitude and Latitude measures are automatically added to the Columns and Rows areas.
2. Drag Salary to the Color button. Then click the Color button, reduce the opacity to about 50%, click the Edit Colors button, and choose a color theme you like. (We chose Red, with darker shades of red indicating larger salaries.) You will see a color pane on the right. This isn't needed, so right-click it and select Hide Card to make it disappear.
3. Drag Salary to the Size button. Then click the Size button and increase or decrease the size if you like. Again, you can hide its card on the right as in step 2.
4. Drag Division to the Filters area. In the resulting dialog box, click the All button to show teams in all divisions. Then click the dropdown arrow for Division in the Filters area and check the Show Filter option. This creates a list of checkboxes in the right pane of the window.
5. Drag Year to the Filters area. You will see two dialog boxes. In the first, select Years; in the second, select All. Then, as in step 4, select the Show Filter option. Finally, click the dropdown arrow at the top of the filter box, select Edit Title, and change the title to Year.
6. Click the Show Me button at the top right. This is always available for displaying the possible types of charts. (Those not possible are grayed out.) For now, click the Show Me button again to hide the list of chart types. By the way, if you start experimenting with the chart types and make a mess of things, you can always "undo" multiple times to return to the original map.
7. Right-click the Sheet 1 tab and rename it Team Salary Map.

The finished version should look like Figure 4.32, where the filters have been applied to show only American League team salaries for 2018. If you hover the cursor over any bubble on the map, you will see information about that team.

Figure 4.32 Map of Team Salaries

The next chart will include a series of line charts, one for each team, that show total team salary through the years. To create it, do the following:

1. Click the button to the right of the Team Salary Map tab to get a new blank worksheet. Rename this worksheet Team Salaries by Year.
2. Drag Year to the Columns area and Salary to the Rows area. This creates a line chart of the total salary of all teams by year. (You could click the Show Me button to change the chart type if you wanted.)
3. Drag Team to the Detail area. Now you see a line chart for each team.
4. Drag Salary to the Color area and change the color to match the color in the previous chart. (All the charts will eventually be included in a dashboard, so consistent coloring is recommended.)
5. As in the map chart, create filters for Division and Position.
6. Right-click the Year label above the chart and select the Hide option. Then double-click the Salary label on the vertical axis to get a dialog box where you can change the axis title from Salary to Total Team Salary.

The finished version should look like Figure 4.33, where filters have been applied to show only National West teams and non-pitchers. In addition, if you click any line, that team's line will be highlighted, as shown in the figure.

Figure 4.33 Line Charts of Team Salaries

The final chart will be series of column charts, one for each year, showing the average salary for each position. To create it, do the following:

1. Open another new worksheet and rename it Average Salary by Position, Year.
2. Drag Year to the Columns area and then drag Position to the right of Year in the Columns area.
3. Drag Salary to the Rows area. Then right-click the Salary button in the Rows area and change the Measure summarization to Average.

4. Drag Salary to the Color area, change the color to match the color in the previous two charts, change the Measure summarization to Average, and hide the card in the right pane.
5. Create a filter for Position.
6. Right-click the Year/Position label above the chart and select the Hide option.

The finished version should look like Figure 4.33, where a filter has been applied to show everyone except the few (highly paid) designated hitters. One thing becomes evident immediately: It pays to be a first baseman!

Figure 4.34 Average Salary by Position and Year

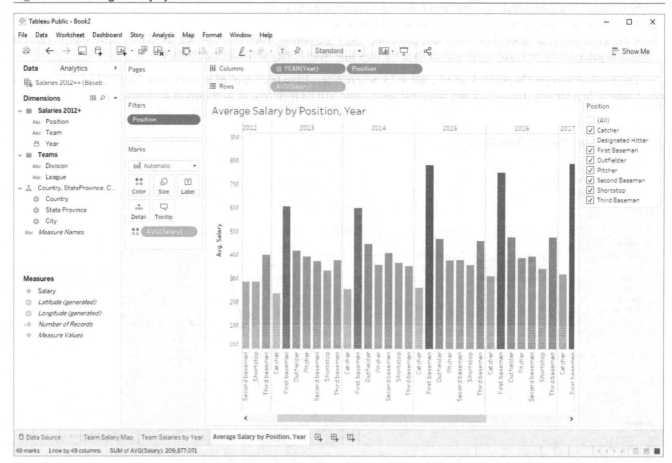

The final step in this example, before publishing to the Web, is to combine the three charts into a dashboard. To do this, do the following:

1. Click the middle "plus sign" button next to the sheet tabs. This opens a blank dashboard, with the existing charts listed in the left pane. Rename this dashboard sheet MLB Salaries 2012–2018.

   A dashboard in Tableau Public is a set of related charts.

2. Drag Team Salary Map in this list to the open space in the dashboard.
3. Drag Team Salaries by Year in this list below Team Salary Map. (As you drag, you will see gray sections where you are allowed to drop.)
4. Drag Average Salary by Position, Year in this list just to the right of Team Salaries by Year. You should now have an arrangement with a large map chart on top and two smaller charts below it. Of course, you could rearrange these if you wanted.
5. In the left pane, there is a Size dropdown arrow. This lets you fit the dashboard to your device: desktop, laptop, or phone. Use the dropdown arrows to select the Automatic option.
6. The chart titles are not needed, so right-click each of them and either select the Hide option or select Edit Title and change the title to a single space. (The latter option provides blank space on the chart for the filters in the next step.)
7. The five filters created earlier are listed along the right side of the dashboard. It will take less space to compress them and float them inside the respective charts. To do this, click the name of any filter, such as Division, to see a dropdown arrow

in a gray box. Click it and select Multiple Values (dropdown). Then click it again and select Floating. Now you can drag the filter (by the gray area with two white lines at the top) to a blank space on the appropriate chart. Of course, you can also change or clear the filter if you like. After doing this for all filters and clearing the filters, the dashboard should look approximately like Figure 4.35.

Figure 4.35 Dashboard with Floating Filters

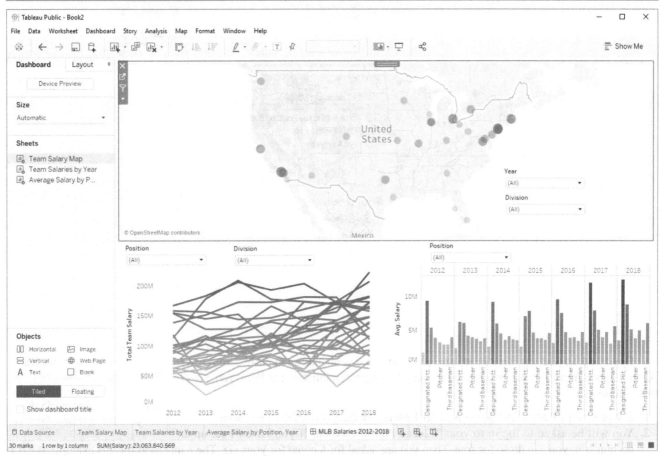

8. When a chart is selected, as the map chart is selected in Figure 4.35, you see options in gray at the top left (or right). Click third button, the filter symbol, to make it white. Then click any team's bubble on the map. The other two charts automatically filter for this team. By holding down the Ctrl key, you can select multiple teams in this way, and the rest will be filtered out. For now, click the filter symbol again to remove the filter.
9. You can also create a "highlight" action. To do so, select Actions from the Dashboard menu at the top of the window, and in the Actions dialog box, select Highlight from the Add Action list. Then fill out the resulting dialog box as shown in Figure 4.36, click OK, and click OK once more to back out. Now select any team's bubble in the map, and that team's line chart will be highlighted. This is slightly different from the filter in step 8. With a filter, the other teams' line charts are completely hidden. With a highlight, they are just grayed out. By the way, if you add the filter in step 8 *and* this highlight action, the filter action takes precedence.

Figure 4.36 Creating a Highlight Action

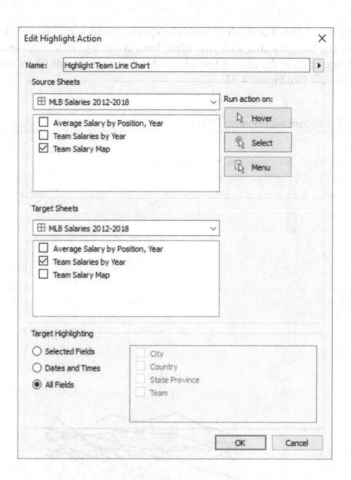

Obviously, as with any work of art, you could fine-tune your charts and dashboard forever. At some point, however, you will decide it is good enough to publish to the Web. You can do this as follows:

When you "save" a Tableau Public project, you are publishing it to the Web. You need an account to do this, but you can get one for free.

1. Select Save to Tableau Public (or Save to Tableau Public As) from the File menu.
2. You will be asked to log in to your Tableau Public account. If you haven't set up an account yet, you can do so for free. Then you are asked for a name for your viz. The name used for this example is MLB Salaries 2012–2018. (It can be the same as the dashboard name, but it doesn't have to be the same.)
3. Your viz will open in your default browser, where you can edit it slightly if necessary. Then a button below the viz allows you to share its URL with others (like your instructor) or copy its embed code for use in your own Web pages. For more details, watch the publishing video at https://public.tableau.com/en-us/s/resources.

The final viz for this example is available at https://public.tableau.com/profile/dadm#!/vizhome/MLBSalaries2012-2018/MLBSalaries2012–2018. It is interactive, so try it out. (Make sure you copy and paste the entire URL.)

If you make changes to your work and you try to close Tableau Public, you will be asked if you want to save your "workbook." Just be aware that this means saving your changes to the Web, not to a file on your hard drive.

This has been a very brief tour of Tableau Public. To learn more, you can view the videos on Tableau Public's Resource page or you can experiment on your own. To say the least, Tableau Public is feature-rich, and you might want to try a few options we haven't illustrated here. For example, you might have noticed the Analytics tab near the top left when creating charts. (See Figure 4.33, for example.) Its options depend on the type of chart, but for the line charts in Figure 4.33, it provides the option of including box-whisker plots on the chart, as shown in Figure 4.37. We will close by letting you decide whether these box-whisker plots add insights to the chart or just clutter it up. With data visualizations, there is bound to be plenty of subjectivity.

Figure 4.37 Box-Whisker Plots Added with Analytics Option

Problems

Solutions for problems whose numbers appear within a colored box can be found in the Student Solution Files.

Level A

23. The **P04_23.xlsx** file contains annual CO_2 emissions data for world countries. (This is basically the same data set used in the training videos on the Tableau Public website.) Use Tableau Public to create at least two charts of the data. Then integrate these charts into a dashboard and publish your results to the Web.

24. The **P04_24.xlsx** file contains data on over 6000 Airbnb listings in New York City. Use Tableau Public to create at least two charts of the data. Then integrate these charts into a dashboard and publish your results to the Web.

25. The **P04_25.xlsx** file lists the top finishers in the last five Boston marathons, grouped by age and type.
   a. The times are listed as 2:33:53, for example, meaning 2 hours, 33 minutes, and 53 seconds, but they are entered and formatted as clock times. Do whatever it takes to express them as minutes. (Hint: A clock time is really a number, the fraction of time from midnight to the next midnight, so simply multiply this by the number of minutes in a day to convert to minutes.)
   b. Import the data into Tableau Public.
   c. Create at least two charts of the data. Then integrate these charts into a dashboard and publish your results to the Web.

Level B

26. Tableau Public can also import table data from pdf files. The **P04_26.pdf** file (from the Bureau of Labor Statistics) contains two tables. We are interested only in the first table, which contains monthly values of the Consumer Price Index for all urban consumers (the CPI-U index) from 1913 to mid-2018. Proceed as follows:
   a. Import the data in Table 1 into Tableau Public. (When you connect to the pdf source file, ask it to scan for All. You will see several items in the left pane. Experiment to see which union of them you need.) There should be 14 columns: Year, a column for each month, and a Table Name column. Hide this last column.
   b. It would be better to have only three columns: Year, Month, and CPI. Tableau Public lets you restructure the data in this way with its "pivot" tool. To use it, highlight all month columns and select Pivot from the dropdown arrow above any month heading. The month columns will be collapsed into two long columns, which you can rename Month and CPI.
   c. Change the data type of the Year column to Number (whole).
   d. Change the data type of CPI to Number (decimal).
   e. Dates are tricky to work with in Tableau Public. (See https://onlinehelp.tableau.com/current/pro/desktop/en-us/functions_functions_date.html for help.) The

goal here is to calculate a date field called Date, which will be used in a line chart. First, change the data type of Month to Date. Second, click the dropdown arrow above Month and select Create Calculated Field to open a dialog box. Enter MonthNumber for the name of the field, enter the formula **Month([Month])** in the body—no equals sign is needed—and click OK. For example, this returns 4 for April. Finally, create another calculated field named Date with the formula **MakeDate([Year],[MonthNumber],1)**. (This is like Excel's Date function, which also takes three integer arguments.)

f. Create a line chart of CPI. To do so, first drag CPI from the Dimensions list to the Measures list. (We're not sure why it is in the Dimensions list.) Then drag Date to the Columns area and CPI to the Rows area and create a Filter for Date on Year. You should see a line chart of CPI by year, but you should then be able to expand the Year(Date) button to Year(Quarter) and then to Year(Month). This is the advantage of having a Date field.

g. Create a dashboard that looks approximately like Figure 4.38, where each chart has its own Year filter.

27. Visit https://www.olympic.org/olympic-results, where you can search for all kinds of Olympics results. Find data of interest to you, import (or type) the data into Excel, use the data to create a viz in Tableau Public, and publish your results to the Web.

Figure 4.38 Dashboard of CPI Time Series Charts

4-5 Data Cleansing

When you study statistics in a course, the data sets you analyze have usually been carefully prepared by the textbook author or your instructor. For that reason, they are usually in good shape—they contain exactly the data you need, there are no missing data, and there are no "bad" entries (caused by typographical errors, for example). Unfortunately, you cannot count on real-world data sets to be so perfect. This is especially the case when you obtain data from external sources such as the Web. There can be all sorts of problems with the data, and it is your responsibility to correct these problems before you do any serious analysis. This initial step, called **cleansing data**, can be tedious, but it can prevent totally misleading results later on.

In this section we examine one data set that has a number of errors, all of which could very possibly occur in real data sets. We discuss methods for *finding* the problems and for *correcting* them. However, you should be aware of two things. First, the errors in this example are only a few of those that could occur. Cleansing data requires careful detective work to uncover all possible errors that might be present. Second, once an error is found, it is not always clear how to correct it. A case in point is missing data. For example, some respondents to a questionnaire, when asked for their annual income, might leave this box blank. How should you treat these questionnaires when you perform the eventual data analysis? Should you delete them entirely, should you replace their blank incomes with the *average* income of all who responded to this question, or should you use a more complex rule to estimate the missing incomes? All three of these options have been suggested by analysts, and all of them have their pros and cons. Perhaps the safest method is to delete any questionnaires with missing data, so that you don't have to guess at the missing values, but this could mean throwing away a lot of potentially useful data. The point is that some subjectivity and common sense must be used when cleansing data sets.

Again, cleansing data typically involves careful detective work and some common sense. The process is tedious but often necessary. Fortunately, you can use powerful Excel tools to search for suspicious data values and then fix them.

EXAMPLE

4.6 CUSTOMER DATA WITH ERRORS

The **Data Cleansing.xlsx** file has data on 1500 customers of a particular company. A portion of these data appears in Figure 4.39, where many of the rows have been hidden. How much of this data set is usable? How much needs to be cleansed?

Figure 4.39 Data Set with Bad Data

	A	B	C	D	E	F	G	H	I
1	Customer	SSN	Birthdate	Age	Region	Cred Card User	Income	Purchases	Amount Spent
2	1	539-84-9599	10/26/44	70	East	0	62900	4	2080
3	2	444-05-4079	01/01/32	67	West	1	23300	0	0
4	3	418-18-5649	08/17/73	25	East	1	48700	8	3990
5	4	065-63-3311	08/02/47	51	West	1	137600	2	920
6	5	059-58-9566	10/03/48	50	East	0	101400	2	1000
7	6	443-13-8685	03/24/60	39	East	0	139700	1	550
8	7	638-89-7231	12/02/43	55	South	1	50900	3	1400
9	8	202-94-6453	11/08/74	24	South	1	50500	0	0
10	9	266-29-0308	09/28/67	31	North	0	151400	2	910
11	10	943-85-8301	07/05/65	33	West	0	88300	2	1080
12	11	047-07-5332	11/13/64	34	North	0	120300	3	1390
1498	1497	638-19-2849	07/31/30	68	South	0	121100	5	2540
1499	1498	670-57-4549	07/21/54	44	North	1	64000	4	2160
1500	1499	166-84-2698	10/30/66	32	South	0	91000	6	2910
1501	1500	366-03-5021	09/23/34	64	South	0	121400	1	530

Objective

To find and fix errors in this company's data set.

Solution

We purposely constructed this data set to have a number of problems, all of which you might encounter in real data sets. We begin with the Social Security Number (SSN). Presumably, all 1500 customers are distinct people, so all 1500 SSNs should be different. How can you tell if they are? One simple way is as follows.

1. Sort on the SSN column.
2. Once the SSNs are sorted, enter the formula **=If(B3=B2,1,0)** in cell J3 and copy this formula down column J. This formula checks whether two adjacent SSNs are equal.

3. Enter the formula **=SUM(J3:J501)** in cell J2 to see if there are any duplicate SSNs (see Figure 4.40). As you can see, there are two pairs of duplicate SSNs.

Figure 4.40 Checking for Duplicate SSNs

	A	B	C	D	E	F	G	H	I	J
1	Customer	SSN	Birthdate	Age	Region	Cred Card User	Income	Purchases	Amount Spent	Duplicates
2	681	001-05-3748	03/24/36	63	North	0	159700	1	530	2
3	685	001-43-2336	08/21/63	35	North	0	149300	4	1750	0
4	62	001-80-6937	12/27/54	44	West	1	44000	4	2020	0
5	787	002-23-4874	01/31/76	23	North	0	153000	3	1330	0
6	328	004-10-8303	10/19/76	22	West	1	49800	4	1940	0
7	870	004-39-9621	10/13/57	41	South	0	138900	2	1010	0

4. To find the duplicates, select the range from cell J3 down and select Find from the Find & Select dropdown menu on the Home ribbon, with the resulting dialog box filled in as shown in Figure 4.41. In particular, make sure the bottom box has Values selected.

Figure 4.41 Dialog Box for Locating Duplicates

5. Click the Find Next button twice to find the offenders. Customers 369 and 618 each have SSN 283-42-4994, and customers 159 and 464 each have SSN 680-00-1375.

At this point, the company should check the SSNs of these four customers, which are hopefully available from another source, and enter them correctly here. (You can then delete column J and sort on column A to bring the data set back to its original form.)

The Birthdate and Age columns present two interesting problems. When the birthdates were entered, they were entered in exactly the form shown (10/26/44, for example). Then the age was calculated by a somewhat complex formula, just as you would calculate your own age.[9] Are there any problems? First, sort on Birthdate. You will see that the first 18 customers all have birthdate 05/17/27—quite a coincidence (see Figure 4.42). As you may know, Excel's dates are stored internally as integers (the number of days since January 1, 1900), which you can see by formatting dates as numbers. So highlight these 18 birthdates and format them with the Number option (zero decimals) to see which number they correspond to. It turns out to be 9999, the code often used for a missing value. Therefore, it is likely that these 18 customers were not born on 05/17/27 after all. Their birthdates were probably *missing* and simply entered as 9999, which were then formatted as dates. If birthdate is important for further analysis, these 18 customers should probably be deleted from the data set or their birthdates should be changed to blanks if the true values cannot be found.

---

9 In case you are interested in some of Excel's date functions, we left the formula for age in cell D2. (We replaced this formula by its values in the rest of column D; otherwise, Excel takes quite a while to recalculate it 1500 times.) This formula uses Excel's TODAY, YEAR, MONTH, and DAY functions. Check online help to learn more about these functions.

Figure 4.42 Suspicious
Duplicate Birthdates

	A	B	C	D	E	F	G	H	I
1	Customer	SSN	Birthdate	Age	Region	Cred Card User	Income	Purchases	Amount Spent
2	64	205-84-3572	05/17/27	71	East	0	50500	1	490
3	429	279-23-7773	05/17/27	71	South	0	120300	4	2100
4	463	619-94-0553	05/17/27	71	East	0	62300	2	930
5	466	365-18-7407	05/17/27	71	East	0	155400	4	1900
6	486	364-94-9180	05/17/27	71	West	0	116500	2	1040
7	494	085-32-5438	05/17/27	71	East	0	103700	1	480
8	607	626-04-1182	05/17/27	71	South	1	75900	3	1540
9	645	086-39-4715	05/17/27	71	North	0	155300	5	2480
10	661	212-01-7062	05/17/27	71	West	0	147900	5	2450
11	730	142-06-2339	05/17/27	71	West	1	38200	1	510
12	754	891-12-9133	05/17/27	71	North	0	77300	4	1980
13	782	183-25-0406	05/17/27	71	West	0	51600	0	0
14	813	338-58-7652	05/17/27	71	East	1	47500	2	1020
15	1045	715-28-2884	05/17/27	71	South	0	82400	4	1850
16	1068	110-67-7322	05/17/27	71	North	0	138500	3	1400
17	1131	602-63-2343	05/17/27	71	North	1	67800	3	1520
18	1179	183-40-5102	05/17/27	71	East	0	44800	4	1940
19	1329	678-19-0332	05/17/27	71	West	0	83900	5	2710
20	174	240-78-9827	01/09/30	69	East	0	29900	2	960

It gets even more interesting if you sort on the Age variable. You will see that the first 12 customers after sorting have *negative* ages (see Figure 4.43). You have just run into a Y2K (year 2000) problem. These 12 customers were all born before 1930. Excel guesses that any two-digit year from 00 to 29 corresponds to the 21st century, whereas those from 30 to 99 correspond to the 20th century.[10] This guess was obviously a bad one for these 12 customers, and you should change their birthdates to the 20th century. An easy way to do this is to highlight these 12 birthdates, select Replace from the Find & Select dropdown list, fill out the resulting dialog box as shown in Figure 4.44, and click the Replace All button. This replaces any year that begins with 202, as in 2028, with a year that begins with 192. (Always be careful with the Replace All option. For example, if you enter /20 and /19 in the "Find what:" and "Replace with:" boxes, you will not only replace the years, but the 20th *day* of any month will also be replaced by the 19th day.) If you copy the formula for Age that was originally in cell D2 to all of column D, the ages should recalculate automatically as *positive* numbers.

Figure 4.43 Negative Ages: A
Y2K Problem

	A	B	C	D	E	F	G	H	I
1	Customer	SSN	Birthdate	Age	Region	Cred Card User	Income	Purchases	Amount Spent
2	148	237-88-3817	08/11/29	−31	South	0	63800	8	3960
3	324	133-99-5496	05/13/28	−30	North	0	142500	2	1000
4	426	968-16-0774	09/29/28	−30	North	0	68400	2	1100
5	440	618-84-1169	10/19/28	−30	West	1	113600	1	470
6	1195	806-70-0226	10/14/28	−30	West	0	40600	4	1960
7	1310	380-84-2860	10/17/28	−30	West	0	91800	2	980
8	589	776-44-8345	04/16/27	−29	West	1	59300	2	1030
9	824	376-25-7809	11/02/27	−29	North	0	9999	2	1070
10	922	329-51-3208	03/21/28	−29	East	1	35400	6	3000
11	229	964-27-4755	01/29/27	−28	East	0	26700	1	450
12	1089	808-29-7482	02/28/27	−28	South	0	90000	5	2580
13	1037	594-47-1955	08/10/25	−27	East	1	128300	3	1510

The Region variable presents a problem that can be very hard to detect—because you usually are not looking for it. There are four regions: North, South, East, and West. If you sort on Region and scroll down, you will find a few East values, a few North values, a few South values, and a few West values, and then the East values start again. Why aren't the East values all together? If you look closely, you will see that a few of the labels in these cells—those at the top after sorting—begin with a space. The person who entered them inadvertently entered a space before the name. Does this matter? It certainly can. Suppose you create a pivot table, for example, with Region in the Rows area. You will get eight row categories, not four. Therefore, you should delete the extra spaces. The most straightforward way is to use Replace from the Find & Select dropdown menu in the obvious way. (Excel also has a handy TRIM function that removes any leading or trailing spaces from a label.)

A slightly different problem occurs in the Cred Card User column, where 1 corresponds to credit card users and 0 corresponds to nonusers. A typical use of these numbers might be to find the proportion of credit card users, which you can find by entering the formula **=AVERAGE(F2:F1501)** in some blank cell. This *should* give the proportion of 1's, but instead it gives an

---

10 To make matters even worse, a different rule was used in earlier versions of MS Office. There is no guarantee that Microsoft will continue to use this same rule in future editions of Office. However, if you enter four-digit years from now on, as you should, it won't make any difference.

error (#DIV/0!). What is wrong? A clue is that the numbers in column F are left-justified, whereas numbers in Excel are usually *right*-justified. Here is what might have happened. Data on credit card users and nonusers might initially have been entered as the labels Yes and No. Then to convert them to 1 and 0, someone might have entered the formula **IF(F4="Yes","1","0")**. The double quotes around 1 and 0 cause them to be interpreted as *text*, not *numbers*, and no arithmetic can be done on them. (In addition, text is typically left-justified, the telltale sign seen here.) Fortunately, Excel has a VALUE function that converts text entries that look like numbers to numbers. So you should form a new column that uses this VALUE function on the entries in column F to convert them to numbers. (Specifically, you can create these VALUE formulas in a new column, then do a Copy and Paste Special as Values to replace the formulas by their values, and finally cut and paste these values over the original text in column F.)

Next consider the Income column. If you sort on it, you will see that most incomes are from $20,000 to $160,000. However, there are a few at the top that are much smaller, and there are a few 9999s (see Figure 4.45). By this time, you can guess that the 9999's correspond to missing values, so unless these true values can be found, these customers should probably be deleted if Income is crucial to the analysis (or their incomes should be changed to blanks). The small numbers at the top take some educated guesswork. Because they range from 22 to 151, a reasonable guess, and hopefully one that can be confirmed, is that the person who entered these incomes thought of them as "thousands" and simply omitted the trailing three zeroes. If this is indeed correct, you can fix them by multiplying each by 1000. (There is an easy way to do this. Enter the multiple 1000 in some blank cell, and press Ctrl+c to copy it. Next, highlight the range G2:G12, click the Paste dropdown menu, select Paste Special, and check the Multiply option. Remember this trick. You can use it often.)

Figure 4.45 Suspicious
Incomes

	A	B	C	D	E	F	G	H	I
1	Customer	SSN	Birthdate	Age	Region	Cred Card User	Income	Purchases	Amount Spent
2	439	390-77-9781	06/03/70	28	West	0	22	8	4160
3	593	744-30-0499	05/04/60	38	East	0	25	5	2460
4	1343	435-02-2521	08/24/42	56	West	1	43	5	2600
5	925	820-65-4438	11/12/32	66	North	0	55	6	2980
6	1144	211-02-9333	08/13/34	64	North	0	71	9999	9999
7	460	756-41-9393	05/14/71	27	East	0	81	3	1500
8	407	241-86-3823	07/03/59	39	East	1	88	4	2000
9	833	908-76-1846	09/17/60	38	West	0	104	4	1970
10	233	924-59-1581	05/12/31	67	South	0	138	6	2950
11	51	669-39-4544	10/05/33	65	West	0	149	2	1010
12	816	884-27-5089	03/05/62	37	North	1	151	2	900
13	824	376-25-7809	11/02/27	−29	North	1	9999	2	1070
14	518	378-83-7998	11/02/74	24	West	1	9999	2	940
15	570	758-72-4033	11/07/70	28	South	1	9999	3	1520
16	605	600-05-9780	07/10/58	40	North	1	9999	0	0
17	796	918-32-8454	03/22/54	45	North	0	9999	3	1570

Finally, consider the Purchases (number of separate purchases by a customer) and Amount Spent (total spent on all purchases) columns. First, sort on Purchases. You will see the familiar 9999s at the bottom. In fact, each 9999 for Purchases has a corresponding 9999 for Amount Spent. This makes sense. If the number of purchases is unknown, the total amount spent is probably also unknown. You can effectively delete these 9999 rows by inserting a blank row right above them. Excel then automatically senses the boundary of the data. Essentially, a blank row or column imposes a separation from the "active" data.

Now we examine the remaining data for these two variables. Presumably, there is a relationship between these variables, where the amount spent increases with the number of purchases. You can check this with a scatterplot of the (nonmissing) data, which is shown in Figure 4.46. There is a clear upward trend for most of the points, but there are some suspicious outliers at the bottom of the plot. Again, you might take an educated guess. Perhaps the *average* spent per purchase, rather than the total amount spent, was entered for a few of the customers. This would explain the abnormally small values. (It would also explain why these outliers are all at about the same height in the plot.) If you can locate these outliers in the data set, you can multiply each by the corresponding number of purchases (if your educated guess is correct). How do you locate them in the data set? First, sort on Amount Spent, then sort on Purchases. This will arrange the amounts spent in increasing order for each value of Purchases. Then, using the scatterplot as a guide, scroll through each value of Purchases (starting with 2) and locate the abnormally low values of Amount Spent, which are all together. This procedure is a bit tedious, but it is better than working with invalid data.

Figure 4.46 Scatterplot with Suspicious Outliers

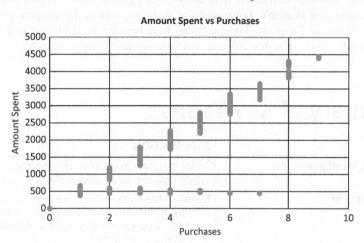

Again, cleansing data typically involves careful detective work and some common sense. The bad news is that it is tedious. The good news is that you can use the powerful Excel tools we have discussed to search for suspicious data values and then fix them.

Problems

Solutions for problems whose numbers appear within a colored box can be found in the Student Solution Files.

Level A

28. The file **P04_28.xlsx** contains a data set that represents 30 responses from a questionnaire concerning the president's environmental policies. Each observation lists the person's age, gender, state of residence, number of children, annual salary, and opinion of the president's environmental policies. Check for bad or suspicious values and change them appropriately.

29. The file **P04_29.xlsx** contains the following data on movie stars: the name of each star, the star's gender, domestic gross (average domestic gross of the star's last few movies), foreign gross (average foreign gross of the star's last few movies), and income (current amount the star asks for a movie). Check for bad or suspicious values (including names) and change them appropriately.

30. The file **P04_30.xlsx** contains data on a bank's employees. Check for bad or suspicious values and change them appropriately.

31. The file **P04_31.xlsx** contains data on 500 randomly selected households. Check for bad or suspicious values and change them appropriately.

Level B

32. The file **P04_32.xlsx** contains data imported into Excel from Microsoft's Northwind database. There are worksheets for the company's customers, products, product categories, and transactions. Each transaction is for a product purchased by a customer, but if a customer purchases multiple products at the same time, there are several corresponding rows in the Transactions table, one for each product purchased. The ID columns allow you to look up names of customers, products, and product categories. However, some of the IDs in the Transactions sheet have purposely been corrupted. There can be three reasons. First, an ID in the Transactions sheet might not correspond to any customer, product, or product category. Second, because each order is by a single customer, a given OrderID should correspond to only one CustomerID. Third, a given product ID should *always* correspond to the same product category ID. Besides the corrupted IDs, there is one other potential type of error, concerning dates. Shipping dates can be blank (for orders that haven't yet shipped), but they shouldn't be *before* the corresponding order dates. Find all corrupted IDs and shipping dates in the Transactions sheet. Highlight all bad data in yellow. You don't need to change them (because in most cases there is no way of knowing the correct values).

4-6 Conclusion

The material in the previous two chapters represents the bare minimum people who analyze data should know. Most of these concepts and methods have existed for many years. Even pivot tables, arguably the most important method in these chapters, have existed for over two decades. In contrast, the material in sections 4-2, 4-3, and 4-4 of this chapter is relatively new and represents the foreseeable future of data analysis. The goal is always to gain important, often hidden insights from the massive amount of data now available. Fortunately, as you have seen in this chapter, powerful and user-friendly software such as the "Power" add-ins for Excel and Tableau Public have become available and will continue to be developed. There is little doubt that the people who master this software will become increasingly valuable.

Summary of Key Terms

TERM	EXPLANATION	EXCEL	PAGES
Business intelligence (BI)	An increasingly popular term referring to the insights gained from data analysis		
Self-service BI	Refers to business intelligence that can be generated by employees in all areas of business, without need for IT department help, by using powerful, user-friendly software		
Data visualization	Imaginative graphs for providing insights not immediately obvious from numbers alone		
Power Query	A recent set of Excel tools for importing external data into Excel from a variety of sources	Get & Transform Data group on Data ribbon	
Single-table database	A database with all data in a single table		
Flat file	An older name for a single-table database		
Relational database	A database with multiple tables related by key fields, structured to avoid redundancy		
Primary key	A field in a database table that serves as a unique identifier		
Autonumber key	A primary key that automatically assigns consecutive integer values		
Foreign key	A field in a database table that is related to a primary key in another table		
One-to-many relationship	A relationship between two tables where each record in the "one" table can be associated with many records in the "many" table but where each record in the "many" table can be associated with only one record in the "one" table		
Many-to-many relationship	A relationship between two tables where each record in each table can be associated with many records in the other table		
Linking table	A table used to transform a many-to-many relationship between two tables into two one-to-many relationships; usually composed mostly of foreign keys		
Relational database management system (RDBMS)	A complete system, often server-based, for managing one or more corporate relational databases (Microsoft SQL Server, Oracle Database, IBM Db2, MySQL, and others)		
Query	A statement that specifies exactly which data a user requires from a database		
Structured Query Language (SQL)	A language developed to express queries that can be used (with minor modifications) for all RDBMS		

Key Terms (continued)

TERM	EXPLANATION	EXCEL	PAGES
Excel Data Model	A recent Microsoft technology used to mimic relational databases, but all within Excel	Visible in Power Pivot window	
Power Pivot	A recent Excel add-in for creating more powerful pivot table reports than are possible with "regular" pivot tables	Load through COM add-ins list	
Power Pivot window	A window for viewing and managing the data in an Excel Data Model	Open with Manage button on Power Pivot ribbon	
Data Analysis Expressions (DAX) language	A language recently developed to create calculated columns and measures in Power Pivot		
Calculated column	A new column created in the Data Model by using a DAX formula	Power Pivot window	
Measure	A summarization of data in a Data Model created with a DAX formula and used in the Values area of a pivot table	Power Pivot window	
Hierarchy	A natural sequence of fields such as Country, State, City that can be used to drill down in a pivot table	Power Pivot window	
Tableau Public	A free software package developed by Tableau Software for creating data visualizations		
Dimensions and Measures	General terms used by Tableau Public and others, where measures are numeric fields to be summarized and dimensions are usually categorical fields used to break measures down by		
Dashboard	As used by Tableau Public, a collection of related charts used to tell different aspects of the same basic story		
Story	As used by Tableau Public, a sequence of visualizations that tell a data narrative, somewhat like a sequence of PowerPoint slides		
Viz	Short for visualization, any workbook created in Tableau Public containing charts, dashboards, and/ or stories		
Cleansing data	Process of removing errors from a data set		

Conceptual Questions

C.1. What does the term "self-service BI" mean, and why is it important in today's business world?

C.2. Explain how primary and foreign key fields work and why they are needed in a relational database.

C.3. Suppose your company takes orders for its products, which are supplied to your company by vendors. You want to create a relational database of this information. Discuss the relationship between orders and products and between products and vendors. What tables would you create for this database, and what would you include in these tables?

C.4. A linking table is required for a many-to-many relationship, like between orders and products. Explain what fields a linking table must include at the very least. Give examples of other fields it might also include.

C.5. What is the role of an Excel Data Model?

C.6. Can you *see* data in an Excel Data Model if Power Pivot is not loaded? Can you *use* data in an Excel Data Model in a pivot table if Power Pivot is not loaded?

C.7. When you want to filter data for import into Excel, you could filter in the Query Editor, or you could import all the data and then filter inside Excel? What are the pros and cons of these two approaches?

C.8. Suppose you try to create a measure called Profit with the formula =**[Revenue]-[Cost]**, where Revenue and

Cost are columns in one of your tables. Why will this produce an error? What should you do to fix it?

C.9. What is the role of a hierarchy in an Excel Data Model? Could you have created something similar in Excel before Data Models and Power Pivot?

C.10. Tableau Public uses the terms "dimensions" and "measures." What do these correspond to (at least usually) in Excel pivot tables? Why are they so important to data analysis in general?

C.11. What is the "Y2K" problem with dates in Excel (and other software)? What should you do to avoid the problem?

Problems

Solutions for problems whose numbers appear within a colored box can be found in the Student Solution Files.

Level A

Problems 33 to 37 ask you to import data from the **Shirt Orders.mdb** *file into Excel. This is an Access database file with three related tables: Customers, Orders, and Products.*

33. Find all records from the Orders table where the order was placed in 2015 or 2016, the product ID is from 1 to 5, the customer ID is not 7, and the number of units ordered is at least 75. Import all fields in the Orders table for each of these records into an Excel table (not a Data Model).

34. Find all records from the Orders table that correspond to orders for between 50 and 100 items (inclusive) made by the customer Rags to Riches for the product Short-sleeve Polo. Import the dates, units ordered, and discounts for each of these orders into an Excel table (not a Data Model).

35. The goal here is to create a table in Excel that contains the order date, customer name, and product description for all orders that satisfy conditions on orders, products, and customers. Proceed as follows:
  a. Use Power Query to import all three tables into Excel as tables (not a Data Model). The only use for Query Editor is to remove the columns not used for this problem: Street, City, State, Zip, Phone for customers, Discount for orders, and UnitPrice for products.
  b. Add three new fields, Customer, Product, and Gender, to the Orders table in Excel and use VLOOKUP functions to fill them.
  c. Filter the Orders table as necessary. For this problem, use a ">75" filter for units ordered, "Both" for gender, and both "Threads" and "Shirts R Us" for customer.

36. Solve the previous problem a different way. Use Power Query to import the same data but load the data into a Data Model. Then use the RELATED function to bring the customer, product, and gender information into the Orders table and finally apply the same filters as in the previous problem.

37. The company would like to know how many units of its products designed for each gender category (men,

women, and both genders) were sold to each customer during each quarter of the past five years (Q1 of 2012 through Q4 of 2016). Use Power Query to import the appropriate data into an Excel pivot table report (not a Data Model or a table) and then manipulate the pivot table to show the required information.

Problems 38 to 42 ask you to import and then analyze data from the **Foodmart.mdb** *file. This is an Access database file, another "practice" Microsoft database, with five related tables: Customers, Dates, Facts, Products, and Stores. The Facts table, with over 250,000 rows, has a row for each sale of a product during part of 1997 and 1998. Four of its fields are foreign keys relating the sale to the other four tables. Its other two fields, the "facts," are Revenue and UnitsSold from the sale.*

38. Use Power Query to create a Data Model consisting of relevant fields from the Facts and Products tables, where "relevant" means they are needed for the following. Use a pivot table to find the top three products in terms of the highest number of sales transactions.

39. Do the same as in the previous problem but now include the Dates table in the import and find the top four products in terms of the highest number of sales transactions in 1998.

40. Use Power Query to create a Data Model consisting of relevant fields from the Facts, Products, and Customers tables. The latter should include at least the Country and City fields. In the Power Pivot window, create a hierarchy called Country-City consisting of the Country and City fields. Then create a pivot table based on the Data Model to find the three cities that have generated the most revenue in the Beverages product department in their respective countries.

41. Use Power Query to create a Data Model consisting of relevant fields from the Facts, Products, Stores, and Dates tables. Then create two hierarchies, Product Structure and Store Location. The first should contain the fields ProductFamily, ProductDepartment, ProductCategory, and ProductSubcategory. The second should contain the fields Country, Region, StateProvince, and City. Use this to create a pivot table and accompanying pivot chart that breaks down total revenue by the two hierarchies, the first in the Rows area and the second in the Columns area. Also, include a slicer for the day of the week (Monday, Tuesday, etc.). Do whatever it takes to produce a pivot chart like in Figure 4.47, which shows total revenue on the weekends.

42. Use Power Query to create a Data Model consisting of relevant fields from the Facts and Products tables. Because you don't plan to use the various "ID" key fields in any pivot table, use the Query Editor to remove them. Then create a pivot table of total revenue for each product family. What can you say about this pivot table, and why? What could you do instead to make sure that the ID key fields are never part of any pivot table?

43. The **P04_43.txt** file is a text file that contains yearly data for the number of licensed drivers (those under 18, those over 85, and total) by gender and state. Use Power

Figure 4.47 Total Revenue on Weekends

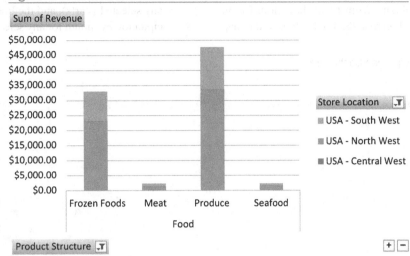

Query to import the data into Excel and then save the Excel file. Use appropriate text functions (unless you want to do it manually) to shorten the variable names to names like Arizona Females Young, Arizona Females Old, and Arizona Females All. Explain briefly what the presence of consecutive commas in the text file indicates. How are these imported into Excel?

44. The **P04_44.txt** file is a text file that lists daily values of an air quality index for Los Angeles. The first value in each row is a date such as 20070322. This means March 22, 2007. Use Power Query to import the data into Excel and then save the Excel file. Use appropriate Excel functions to transform the text values such as 20070322 into dates and format them as "mm/dd/yyyy." Then use Tableau Public to create a line chart of the air quality index by month and publish your results to the Web.

Level B

45. The **srn_pcp.txt** file is a text file that contains monthly precipitation from 1895 through January 2005. The **srn_data.txt** is a "data dictionary" that explains the precipitation file. (The data dictionary mentions two other files, **srn_tmp.txt** and **srn_pdsi.txt**. These files are available but they aren't used here.) Proceed as follows. (Note: You could import the text data directly into Tableau Public, avoiding Excel altogether. However, we find it easier to manipulate the data in Excel than in Tableau Public—except for the pivot tool in step i.)
   a. Use Power Query to import the precipitation data into an Excel table (not a Data Model). Use the Query Editor for only one purpose, to change the data type for column 1 to text. (You can do this with the Data Type dropdown on the Transform ribbon.)
   b. In Excel, change the column headings for columns 2 to 13 to month names: Jan, Feb, etc. Also, delete the last column, which is empty.

   c. Create two new columns to the right of column 1: Code and Year. Fill the Code column with the first three digits of the column 1 value, using Excel's LEFT function, and fill the Year column with the last four digits of the column 1 value, using Excel's RIGHT function. Then copy the Code and Year columns, paste them over themselves as values, and delete column 1, which is no longer necessary.
   d. Scan down to any year 2005 row. Only January's precipitation is listed. The rest are missing, denoted by the code -99.9. Perform a search and replace for -99.9, replacing each with a blank.
   e. The codes in the Code column are 001 to 048 for the contiguous 48 states. The other codes, above 100, are for regions. Delete all rows with these region codes.
   f. The **State Codes.xlsx** file contains a table of codes and the corresponding states. Copy its data somewhere to the right of the imported precipitation data. Then insert a new column, State, to the right of the precipitation Code column and use a VLOOKUP function to fill it with the state names. Copy the State column and paste it over itself as values. Then the columns you copied from the State Codes file are no longer needed, so you can delete them. You can also delete the Code column.
   g. Save this Excel file as **Precip Data.xlsx**. It should have 14 columns: State, Year, and a column for each month.
   h. Open Tableau Public and import the data from the Excel file you just created.
   i. The data aren't structured well for analysis. It would be better to have four columns: State, Year, Month, and Precip. Tableau Public has a "pivot" tool for restructuring. Highlight all month columns and select Pivot from the dropdown arrow above any month's heading. This collapses the month columns into two long columns, which you can rename Month and Precip.

j. Now that the data are in the proper form, create two charts and a dashboard from them that should look approximately like Figure 4.48. The bubbles in the map are sized and colored according to total precipitation in any selected year(s), and the line chart shows total precipitation by month for any selected year(s) and state(s).

Figure 4.48 Finished Precipitation Dashboard

PART 2
PROBABILITY AND DECISION MAKING UNDER UNCERTAINTY

CHAPTER 5

Probability and Probability Distributions

Sorbis/Shutterstock.com

GAME AT MCDONALD'S

Several years ago, McDonald's ran a campaign in which it gave game cards to its customers. These game cards made it possible for customers to win hamburgers, french fries, soft drinks, and other fast-food items, as well as cash prizes. Each card had 10 covered spots that could be uncovered by rubbing them with a coin. Beneath three of these spots were "zaps." Beneath the other seven spots were names of prizes, two of which were identical. For example, one card might have two pictures of a hamburger, one picture of a Coke, one of french fries, one of a milk shake, one of $5, one of $1000, and three zaps. For this card the customer could win a hamburger. To win on any card, the customer had to uncover the two matching spots (which showed the potential prize for that card) before uncovering a zap; any card with a zap uncovered was automatically void. Assuming that the two matches and the three zaps were arranged randomly on the cards, what is the probability of a customer winning?

We label the two matching spots M_1 and M_2, and the three zaps Z_1, Z_2, and Z_3. Then the probability of winning is the probability of uncovering M_1 *and* M_2 before uncovering Z_1, Z_2, or Z_3. In this case the relevant set of outcomes is the set of all orderings of M_1, M_2, Z_1, Z_2, and Z_3, shown in the order they are uncovered. As far as the outcome of the game is concerned, the other five spots on the card are irrelevant. Thus, an outcome such as M_2, M_1, Z_3, Z_1, Z_2 is a winner, whereas M_2, Z_2, Z_1, M_1, Z_3 is a loser. Actually, the first of these would be declared a winner as soon as M_1 was uncovered, and the second would be declared a loser as soon as Z_2 was uncovered. However, we show the whole sequence of M's and Z's so that we can count outcomes correctly. We then find the probability of winning using an equally likely argument. Specifically, we divide the number of outcomes that are winners by the total number of outcomes. It can be shown that the number of outcomes that are winners is 12, whereas the total number of outcomes is 120. Therefore, the probability of a winner is $12/120 = 0.1$.

This calculation, which shows that, on average, 1 out of 10 cards could be winners was obviously important for McDonald's. Actually, this provides only an upper bound on the fraction of cards where a prize was awarded. Many customers threw their cards away without playing the game, and even some of the winners neglected to claim their prizes. So, for example, McDonald's knew that if they made 50,000 cards where a milk shake was the winning prize, somewhat less than 5000 milk shakes would be given away. Knowing approximately what their expected "losses" would be from winning cards, McDonald's was able to design the game (how many cards of each type to print) so that the expected extra revenue (from customers attracted to the game) would cover the expected losses.

5-1 Introduction

A key aspect of solving real business problems is dealing appropriately with uncertainty. This involves recognizing explicitly that uncertainty exists and using quantitative methods to model uncertainty. If you want to develop realistic business models, you cannot simply act as if uncertainty doesn't exist. For example, if you don't know next month's demand, you shouldn't build a model that assumes next month's demand is a sure 1500 units. This is only wishful thinking. You should instead incorporate demand uncertainty explicitly into your model. To do this, you need to know how to deal quantitatively with uncertainty. This involves probability and probability distributions. We introduce these topics in this chapter and then use them in a number of later chapters.

There are many sources of uncertainty. Demands for products are uncertain, times between arrivals to a supermarket are uncertain, stock price returns are uncertain, changes in interest rates are uncertain, and so on. In many situations, the uncertain quantity—demand, time between arrivals, stock price return, change in interest rate—is a numerical quantity. In the language of probability, it is called a **random variable**. More formally, a random variable associates a numerical value with each possible random outcome.

Associated with each random variable is a **probability distribution** that lists all of the possible values of the random variable and their corresponding probabilities. A probability distribution provides very useful information. It not only indicates the possible values of the random variable but it also indicates how likely they are. For example, it is useful to know that the possible demands for a product are, say, 100, 200, 300, and 400, but it is even more useful to know that the probabilities of these four values are, say, 0.1, 0.2, 0.4, and 0.3. This implies, for example, that there is a 70% chance that demand will be at least 300.

It is often useful to summarize the information from a probability distribution with numerical summary measures. These include the mean, variance, and standard deviation. As their names imply, these summary measures are much like the corresponding summary measures in Chapters 2 and 3. However, they are *not* identical. The summary measures in this chapter are based on probability distributions, not an observed data set. We will use numerical examples to explain the difference between the two—and how they are related.

The purpose of this chapter is to explain the basic concepts and tools necessary to work with probability distributions and their summary measures. The chapter then discusses several important probability distributions, particularly the normal distribution and the binomial distribution, in some detail.

Modeling uncertainty, as we will be doing in the next chapter and later in Chapters 15 and 16, is sometimes difficult, depending on the complexity of the model, and it is easy to get so caught up in the details that you lose sight of the big picture. For this reason, the flow chart in Figure 5.1 is useful. (A colored version of this chart is available in the file **Modeling Uncertainty Flow Chart.xlsx**.) Take a close look at the middle row of this chart. You begin with inputs, some of which are uncertain quantities, you use Excel® formulas to incorporate the logic of the model, and the result is probability distributions of important outputs. Finally, you use this information to make decisions. (The abbreviation EMV stands for expected monetary value. It is discussed extensively in Chapter 6.) The other boxes in the chart deal with implementation issues, particularly with the software you can use to perform the analysis. Study this chart carefully and return to it as you proceed through the next few chapters and Chapters 15 and 16.

Before proceeding, we discuss two terms you often hear in the business world: *uncertainty* and *risk*. They are sometimes used interchangeably, but they are not really the same. You typically have no control over uncertainty; it is something that simply exists. A good example is the uncertainty in exchange rates. You cannot be sure what the exchange rate between the U.S. dollar and the euro will be a year from now. All you can try to do is *measure* this uncertainty with a probability distribution.

Figure 5.1 Flow Chart for Modeling Uncertainty

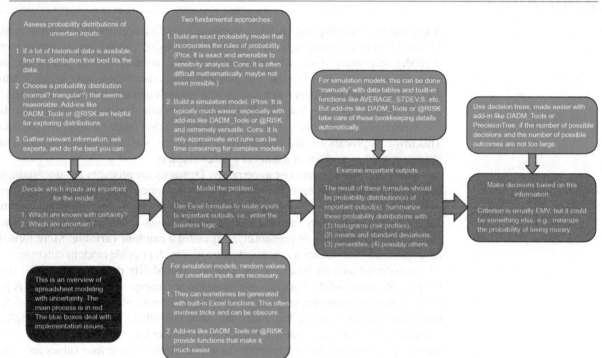

In contrast, risk depends on your position. Even though you don't know what the exchange rate will be, it makes no difference to you—there is no risk to you—if you have no European investments, you aren't planning a trip to Europe, and you don't have to buy or sell anything in Europe. You have risk only when you stand to gain or lose money depending on the eventual exchange rate. Of course, the type of risk you face depends on your position. If you are holding euros in a money market account, you are hoping that euros gain value relative to the dollar. But if you are planning a European vacation, you are hoping that euros lose value relative to the dollar.

Uncertainty and risk are inherent in many of the examples in this book. By learning about probability, you will learn how to measure uncertainty, and you will also learn how to measure the risks involved in various decisions. One important topic you will *not* learn much about is risk *mitigation* by various types of hedging. For example, if you know you have to purchase a large quantity of some product from Europe a year from now, you face the risk that the value of the euro could increase dramatically, thus costing you a lot of money. Fortunately, there are ways to hedge this risk, so that if the euro does increase relative to the dollar, your hedge minimizes your losses. Hedging risk is an extremely important topic, and it is practiced daily in the real world, but it is beyond the scope of this book.

5-2 Probability Essentials

We begin with a brief discussion of probability. The concept of probability is one that you all encounter in everyday life. When a weather forecaster states that the chance of rain is 70%, he or she is making a probability statement. When a sports commentator states that the odds against the Golden State Warriors winning the NBA Championship are 3 to 1, he or she is also making a probability statement. The *concept* of probability is quite intuitive. However, the *rules* of probability are not always as intuitive or easy to master. We examine the most important of these rules in this section.

A **probability** is a number between 0 and 1 that measures the likelihood that some event will occur. An event with probability 0 cannot occur, whereas an event with probability 1 is certain to occur. An event with probability greater than 0 and less than 1 involves uncertainty. The closer its probability is to 1, the more likely it is to occur.

As the examples in the preceding paragraph illustrate, probabilities are sometimes expressed as percentages or odds. However, these can easily be converted to probabilities on a 0-to-1 scale. If the chance of rain is 70%, then the probability of rain is 0.7. Similarly, if the odds against the Warriors winning are 3 to 1, then the probability of the Warriors winning is 1/4 (or 0.25).

There are only a few probability rules you need to know, and they are discussed in the next few subsections. Surprisingly, these are the *only* rules you need to know. Probability is not an easy topic, and a more thorough discussion of it would lead to considerable mathematical complexity, well beyond the level of this book. However, it is all based on the few relatively simple rules discussed next.

5-2a Rule of Complements

The simplest probability rule involves the *complement* of an event. If A is any event, then the **complement of A**, denoted by $\overline{A}$ (or in some books by A^c), is the event that A does *not* occur. For example, if A is the event that the Dow Jones Industrial Average will finish the year at or above the 25,000 mark, then the complement of A is that the Dow will finish the year below 25,000.

If the probability of A is $P(A)$, then the probability of its complement, $P(\overline{A})$, is given by Equation (5.1). Equivalently, the probability of an event and the probability of its complement sum to 1. For example, if you believe that the probability of the Dow finishing at or above 25,000 is 0.25, then the probability that it will finish the year below 25,000 is $1 - 0.25 = 0.75$.

Rule of Complements

$$P(\overline{A}) = 1 - P(A) \tag{5.1}$$

5-2b Addition Rule

Events are **mutually exclusive** if at most one of them can occur. That is, if one of them occurs, then none of the others can occur. For example, consider the following three events involving a company's annual revenue for the coming year: (1) revenue is less than $1 million, (2) revenue is at least $1 million but less than $2 million, and (3) revenue is at least $2 million. Clearly, only one of these events can occur. Therefore, they are mutually exclusive. They are also **exhaustive events**, which means that they exhaust all possibilities— one of these three events *must* occur. Let A_1 through A_n be any n events. Then the *addition rule* of probability involves the probability that at least one of these events will occur. In general, this probability is quite complex, but it simplifies considerably when the events are mutually exclusive. In this case the probability that at least one of the events will occur is the sum of their individual probabilities, as shown in Equation (5.2). Of course, when the events are mutually exclusive, "at least one" is equivalent to "exactly one." In addition, if the events A_1 through A_n are exhaustive, then the probability is 1 because one of the events is certain to occur.

Addition Rule for Mutually Exclusive Events

$$P(\text{at least one of } A_1 \text{ through } A_n) = P(A_1) + P(A_2) + \cdots + P(A_n) \qquad (5.2)$$

In a typical application, the events A_1 through A_n are chosen to partition the set of all possible outcomes into a number of mutually exclusive events. For example, in terms of a company's annual revenue, define A_1 as "revenue is less than \$1 million," A_2 as "revenue is at least \$1 million but less than \$2 million," and A_3 as "revenue is at least \$2 million." Then these three events are mutually exclusive and exhaustive. Therefore, their probabilities must sum to 1. Suppose these probabilities are $P(A_1) = 0.5$, $P(A_2) = 0.3$, and $P(A_3) = 0.2$. (Note that these probabilities *do* sum to 1.) Then the additive rule enables you to calculate other probabilities. For example, the event that revenue is at least \$1 million is the event that either A_2 or A_3 occurs. From the addition rule, its probability is

$$P(\text{revenue is at least \$1 million}) = P(A_2) + P(A_3) = 0.5$$

Similarly,

$$P(\text{revenue is less than \$2 million}) = P(A_1) + P(A_2) = 0.8$$

and

$$P(\text{revenue is less than \$1 million } or \text{ at least \$2 million}) = P(A_1) + P(A_3) = 0.7$$

Again, the addition rule works only for mutually exclusive events. If the events overlap, the situation is more complex. For example, suppose you are dealt a bridge hand (13 cards from a 52-card deck). Let H, D, C, and S, respectively, be the events that you get at least 5 hearts, at least 5 diamonds, at least 5 clubs, and at least 5 spades. What is the probability that at least one of these four events occurs? It is not the sum of their individual probabilities because they are not mutually exclusive. For example, you could get a hand with 5 hearts *and* 5 spades. Probabilities such as this one are actually quite difficult to calculate, and we will not pursue them here. Just be aware that the addition rule does not apply unless the events are mutually exclusive.

5-2c Conditional Probability and the Multiplication Rule

Probabilities are always assessed relative to the information currently available. As new information becomes available, probabilities can change. For example, if you read that Steph Curry suffered a season-ending injury, your assessment of the probability that the Warriors will win the NBA Championship would obviously change. (It would probably become 0!) A formal way to revise probabilities on the basis of new information is to use *conditional probabilities*.

Let A and B be any events with probabilities $P(A)$ and $P(B)$. Typically, the probability $P(A)$ is assessed without knowledge of whether B occurs. However, if you are *told* that B has occurred, then the probability of A might change. The new probability of A is called the **conditional probability** of A given B, and it is denoted by $P(A|B)$. Note that there is still uncertainty involving the event to the left of the vertical bar in this notation; you do not know whether it will occur. However, there is no uncertainty involving the event to the right of the vertical bar; you *know* that it has occurred. The conditional probability can be calculated with the following formula.

Conditional Probability

$$P(A|B) = \frac{P(A \text{ and } B)}{P(B)} \qquad \textbf{(5.3)}$$

The numerator in this formula is the probability that *both* A and B occur. This probability must be known to find $P(A|B)$. However, in some applications $P(A|B)$ and $P(B)$ are known. Then you can multiply both sides of Equation (5.3) by $P(B)$ to obtain the following **multiplication rule** for $P(A \text{ and } B)$.

Multiplication Rule

$$P(A \text{ and } B) = P(A|B)\,P(B) \qquad \textbf{(5.4)}$$

The conditional probability formula and the multiplication rule are both valid; in fact, they are equivalent. The one you use depends on which probabilities you know and which you want to calculate, as illustrated in Example 5.1.

EXAMPLE

5.1 ASSESSING UNCERTAINTY AT BENDER COMPANY

Bender Company supplies contractors with materials for the construction of houses. The company currently has a contract with one of its customers to fill an order by the end of July. However, there is some uncertainty about whether this deadline can be met, due to uncertainty about whether Bender will receive the materials it needs from one of its suppliers by the middle of July. Right now it is July 1. How can the uncertainty in this situation be assessed?

Objective
To apply probability rules to calculate the probability that Bender will meet its end-of-July deadline, given the information the company has at the beginning of July.

Solution
Let A be the event that Bender meets its end-of-July deadline, and let B be the event that Bender receives the materials from its supplier by the middle of July. The probabilities Bender is best able to assess on July 1 are probably $P(B)$ and $P(A|B)$. At the beginning of July, Bender might estimate that the chances of getting the materials on time from its supplier are 2 out of 3, so that $P(B) = 2/3$. Also, thinking ahead, Bender estimates that *if* it receives the required materials on time, the chances of meeting the end-of-July deadline are 3 out of 4. This is a conditional probability statement that $P(A|B) = 3/4$. Then the multiplication rule implies that

$$P(A \text{ and } B) = P(A|B)P(B) = (3/4)(2/3) = 0.5$$

That is, there is a fifty–fifty chance that Bender will get its materials on time *and* meet its end-of-July deadline.

This uncertain situation is depicted graphically in the form of a **probability tree** in Figure 5.2. Note that Bender initially faces (at the leftmost branch of the tree) the uncertainty of whether event B or its complement will occur. Regardless of whether event B occurs, Bender must next confront the uncertainty regarding event A. This uncertainty is reflected in the set of two pairs of branches in the right half of the tree. Hence, there are four mutually exclusive outcomes regarding the two uncertain events, as listed to the right of the tree. Initially, Bender is interested in the first possible outcome, the joint occurrence of events A and B, the top probability in the figure. Another way to compute this probability is to multiply the probabilities associated with the branches leading to this outcome, that is, the probability of B times the probability of A given B. As the figure indicates, this is (3/4)(2/3), or 0.5.

Figure 5.2 Probability Tree for
Bender Example

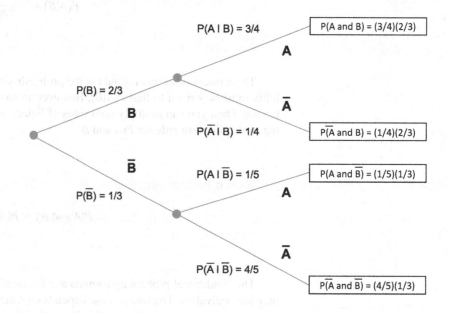

There are several other probabilities of interest in this example. First, let $\overline{B}$ be the complement of B; it is the event that the materials from the supplier do *not* arrive on time. We know that $P(\overline{B}) = 1 - P(B) = 1/3$ from the rule of complements. However, we do not yet know the conditional probability $P(A|\overline{B})$, the probability that Bender will meet its end-of-July deadline, given that it does not receive the materials from the supplier on time. In particular, $P(A|\overline{B})$ is *not* equal to $1 - P(A|B)$. (Can you see why?) Suppose Bender estimates that the chances of meeting the end-of-July deadline are 1 out of 5 if the materials do not arrive on time, so that $P(A|\overline{B}) = 1/5$. Then a second use of the multiplication rule gives

$$P(A \text{ and } \overline{B}) = P(A|\overline{B})P(\overline{B}) = (1/5)(1/3) = 0.0667$$

In words, there is only 1 chance out of 15 that the materials will not arrive on time *and* Bender will meet its end-of-July deadline. This is the third (from the top) probability listed at the right of the tree.

The bottom line for Bender is whether it will meet its end-of-July deadline. After mid-July, this probability is either $P(A|B) = 3/4$ or $P(A|\overline{B}) = 1/5$ because by this time, Bender will *know* whether the materials arrived on time. But on July 1, the relevant probability is $P(A)$—there is still uncertainty about whether B or $\overline{B}$ will occur. Fortunately, you can calculate $P(A)$ from the probabilities you already know. The logic is that A consists of the two mutually exclusive events (A and B) and (A and $\overline{B}$). That is, if A is to occur, it must occur with B or with $\overline{B}$. Therefore, the *addition* rule for mutually exclusive events implies that

$$P(A) = P(A \text{ and } B) + P(A \text{ and } \overline{B}) = 1/2 + 1/15 = 17/30 = 0.5667$$

The chances are 17 out of 30 that Bender will meet its end-of-July deadline, given the information it has at the beginning of July.

5-2d Probabilistic Independence

A concept that is closely tied to conditional probability is probabilistic independence. You just saw that the probability of an event A can depend on whether another event B has occurred. Typically, the probabilities $P(A)$, $P(A|B)$, and $P(A|\overline{B})$ are all different, as in Example 5.1. However, there are situations where all of these probabilities are equal. In this case, A and B are **probabilistically independent events**. This does *not* mean they are mutually exclusive. Rather, probabilistic independence means that knowledge of one event is of no value when assessing the probability of the other.

When two events are probabilistically independent, the multiplication rule simplifies to Equation (5.5). This follows by substituting $P(A)$ for $P(A|B)$ in the multiplication rule, which is allowed because of independence. In words, the probability that both events occur is the product of their individual probabilities.

Multiplication Rule for Independent Events

$$P(A \text{ and } B) = P(A)P(B) \qquad \qquad \textbf{(5.5)}$$

How can you tell whether events *are* probabilistically independent? Unfortunately, this issue usually cannot be settled with mathematical arguments. Typically, you need actual data to decide whether independence is reasonable. As a simple example, let A be the event that a family's first child is male, and let B be the event that its second child is male. Are A and B independent? You could argue that they aren't independent if you believe, say, that a boy is more likely to be followed by another boy than by a girl. You could argue that they are independent if you believe the chances of the second child being a boy are the same, regardless of the gender of the first child. (Note that neither argument requires that boys and girls are equally likely.)

In any case, the only way to settle the argument is to observe many families with at least two children. If you observe, say, that 55% of all families with first child male also have the second child male, and only 45% of all families with first child male have the second child female, then you can make a good case that A and B are *not* independent.

The concept of independence carries over to random variables. Two random variables, X and Y, are independent if any two events, one involving only X and the other involving only Y, are independent. The idea is that knowledge of X is of no help in predicting Y, and vice versa. For example, if X is the amount of rain in Seattle in March and Y is the amount of rain in Seattle in June, it might be realistic to assume that X and Y are independent random variables. March weather probably doesn't have much effect on June weather. On the other hand, if X and Y are the changes in stock prices of two companies in the same industry from one day to the next, it might not be realistic to assume that X and Y are independent. The reason is that they might both be subject to the same economic influences.

Note that the multiplication rule applies to events involving independent random variables. For example, if X and Y are independent, then $P(X = 10 \text{ and } Y = 15)$ equals the product $P(X = 10)P(Y = 15)$.

It is probably fair to say that most events in the real world are not truly independent. However, because of the simplified multiplication rule for independent events, many mathematical models assume that events are independent; the math is much easier with this assumption. The question then is whether the results from such a model are believable. This depends on how unrealistic the independence assumption really is.

5-2e Equally Likely Events

Much of what you know about probability is probably based on situations where outcomes are equally likely. These include flipping coins, throwing dice, drawing balls from urns, and other random mechanisms that are often discussed in introductory probability books. For example, suppose an urn contains 20 red marbles and 10 blue marbles. You plan to randomly select five marbles from the urn, and you are interested, say, in the probability of selecting at least three red marbles. To find this probability, you argue that every possible set of five marbles is equally likely to be chosen. Then you *count* the number of sets of five marbles that contain at least three red marbles, you count the total number of sets of five marbles that could be selected, and you set the desired probability equal to the ratio of these two counts.

It is true that many probabilities, particularly in games of chance, *can* be calculated by using an equally likely argument. It is also true that probabilities calculated in this way satisfy all of the rules of probability. However, many probabilities, especially those in business situations, *cannot* be calculated by equally likely arguments for the simple reason that the possible outcomes are not equally likely. For example, just because you are able to identify five possible scenarios for a company's future, there is probably no reason whatsoever to conclude that each scenario has probability 1/5.

The bottom line is that there is no need in this book to discuss complex counting rules for equally likely outcomes because most outcomes in the business world are not equally likely.

5-2f Subjective Versus Objective Probabilities

We now ask a very basic question: Where do the probabilities in a probability distribution come from? A complete answer to this question could lead to a chapter by itself, so we only briefly discuss the issues involved. There are essentially two distinct ways to assess probabilities, objectively and subjectively. **Objective probabilities** are those that can be estimated from long-run proportions, whereas **subjective probabilities** cannot be estimated from long-run proportions. Some examples will clarify this distinction.

Consider throwing two dice and observing the sum of the two sides that face up. What is the probability that the sum of these two sides is 7? You might argue as follows. Because there are $6 \times 6 = 36$ ways the two dice can fall, and because exactly 6 of these result in a sum of 7, the probability of a 7 is 6/36 = 1/6. This is the equally likely argument and it reduces probability to counting.

What if the dice are weighted in some way? Then the equally likely argument is no longer valid. You can, however, toss the dice many times and record the proportion of tosses that result in a sum of 7. This proportion is called a *relative frequency*.

> The **relative frequency** of an event is the proportion of times the event occurs out of the number of times the random experiment is run.

A famous result called the *law of large numbers* states that this relative frequency, in the long run, will get closer and closer to the "true" probability of a 7. This is exactly what we mean by an objective probability. It is a probability that can be estimated as the long-run proportion of times an event occurs in a sequence of many identical experiments.

If you are flipping coins, throwing dice, or spinning roulette wheels, objective probabilities are certainly relevant. You don't need a person's *opinion* of the probability that a roulette wheel, say, will end up pointing to a red number; you can simply spin it many times and keep track of the proportion of times it points to a red number. However, there are many situations, particularly in business, that cannot be repeated many times—or even more than once—under identical conditions. In these situations objective probabilities make no sense (and equally likely arguments usually make no sense either), so you must use subjective probabilities. A subjective probability is one person's assessment of the likelihood that a certain event will occur. We assume that the person making the assessment uses all of the information available to make the most rational assessment possible.

This definition of subjective probability implies that one person's assessment of a probability can differ from another person's assessment of the *same* probability. For example, consider the probability that the New England Patriots will win the next Super Bowl. If you ask a casual football observer to assess this probability, you will get one answer, but if you ask a person with a lot of inside information about injuries, team cohesiveness, and so on, you might get a very different answer. Because these probabilities are *subjective,* people with different information typically assess probabilities in different ways.

Subjective probabilities are usually relevant for unique, one-time situations. However, most situations are not completely unique; you often have some history to guide you. That is, historical relative frequencies can be factored into subjective probabilities. For example, suppose a company is about to market a new product. This product might be different in some ways from any products the company has marketed before, but it might also share some features with the company's previous products. If the company wants to assess the probability that the new product will be a success, it will certainly analyze the unique features of this product and the current state of the market to obtain a subjective assessment. However, the company will also look at its past successes and failures with reasonably similar products. If the proportion of successes with past products was 20%, say, then this value might be a starting point in the assessment of *this* product's probability of success.

All of the "given" probabilities in this chapter and later chapters can be placed somewhere on the objective-to-subjective continuum, usually closer to the subjective end. An important implication of this is that these probabilities are not cast in stone; they are usually only educated guesses. Therefore, it is always a good idea to run a *sensitivity analysis* (especially in Excel, where this is easy to do) to see how "bottom-line" results depend on the given probabilities. Sensitivity analysis is especially important in Chapter 6, when we study decision making under uncertainty.

Problems

Solutions for problems whose numbers appear within a colored box can be found in the Student Solution Files.

Level A

1. In a particular suburb, 30% of the households have installed electronic security systems.
   a. If a household is chosen at random from this suburb, what is the probability that this household has *not* installed an electronic security system?
   b. If two households are chosen at random from this suburb, what is the probability that *neither* has installed an electronic security system?

2. Several major automobile producers are competing to have the largest market share for sport utility vehicles (SUVs) in the coming quarter. A professional automobile market analyst assesses that the odds of General Motors *not* being the market leader are 6 to 1. The odds against Toyota and Ford having the largest market share in the coming quarter are similarly assessed to be 12 to 5 and 8 to 3, respectively.
   a. Find the probability that General Motors will have the largest market share for SUVs in the coming quarter.
   b. Find the probability that Toyota will have the largest market share for SUVs in the coming quarter.
   c. Find the probability that Ford will have the largest market share for SUVs in the coming quarter.
   d. Find the probability that some other automobile manufacturer will have the largest market share for SUVs in the coming quarter.

3. The publisher of a popular financial periodical has decided to undertake a campaign in an effort to attract new subscribers. Market research analysts in this company believe that there is a 1 in 4 chance that the increase in the number of new subscriptions resulting from this campaign will be less than 3000, and there is a 1 in 3 chance that the increase in the number of new subscriptions resulting from this campaign will be between 3000 and 5000. What is the probability that the increase in the number of new subscriptions resulting from this campaign will be less than 3000 *or* more than 5000?

4. Suppose that you draw a single card from a standard deck of 52 playing cards.
   a. What is the probability that this card is a diamond *or* club?
   b. What is the probability that this card is not a 4?
   c. Given that this card is a black card, what is the probability that it is a spade?
   d. Let E_1 be the event that this card is a black card. Let E_2 be the event that this card is a spade. Are E_1 and E_2 independent events? Why or why not?
   e. Let E_3 be the event that this card is a heart. Let E_4 be the event that this card is a 3. Are E_3 and E_4 independent events? Why or why not?

Level B

5. In a large accounting firm, the proportion of accountants with MBA degrees and at least five years of professional experience is 75% as large as the proportion of accountants with no MBA degree and less than five years of professional experience. Furthermore, 35% of the accountants in this firm have MBA degrees, and 45% have fewer than five years of professional experience. If one of the firm's accountants is selected at random, what is the probability that this accountant has an MBA degree or at least five years of professional experience, but not both?

6. A local beer producer sells two types of beer, a regular brand and a light brand with 30% fewer calories. The company's marketing department wants to verify that its traditional approach of appealing to local white-collar workers with light beer commercials and appealing to local blue-collar workers with regular beer commercials is indeed a good strategy. A randomly selected group of 400 local workers are questioned about their beer-drinking preferences, and the data in the file **P05_06. xlsx** are obtained.

   a. If a blue-collar worker is chosen at random from this group, what is the probability that he/she prefers light beer (to regular beer or no beer at all)?

   b. If a white-collar worker is chosen at random from this group, what is the probability that he/she prefers light beer (to regular beer or no beer at all)?

   c. If you restrict your attention to workers who like to drink beer, what is the probability that a randomly selected blue-collar worker prefers to drink light beer?

   d. If you restrict your attention to workers who like to drink beer, what is the probability that a randomly selected white-collar worker prefers to drink light beer?

   e. Does the company's marketing strategy appear to be appropriate? Explain why or why not.

7. Suppose that two dice are tossed. For each die, it is equally likely that 1, 2, 3, 4, 5, or 6 dots will turn up. Let S be the sum of the two dice.

   a. What is the probability that S will be 5 or 7?

   b. What is the probability that S will be some number other than 4 or 8?

   c. Let E_1 be the event that the first die shows a 3. Let E_2 be the event that S is 6. Are E_1 and E_2 independent events?

   d. Again, let E_1 be the event that the first die shows a 3. Let E_3 be the event that S is 7. Are E_1 and E_3 independent events?

   e. Given that S is 7, what is the probability that the first die showed 4 dots?

   f. Given that the first die shows a 3, what is the probability that S is an even number?

5-3 Probability Distribution of a Random Variable

We now discuss one of the most important concepts in this book, the probability distribution of a random variable.

There are really two types of random variables: discrete and continuous. A **discrete** random variable has only a finite number of possible values, whereas a **continuous** random variable has a continuum of possible values.[1] Usually a discrete distribution results from a count, whereas a continuous distribution results from a measurement. For example, the number of children in a family is clearly discrete, whereas the amount of rain this year in San Francisco is clearly continuous.

Fundamental Insight

Concept of Probability Distribution

A probability distribution describes the uncertainty of a numerical outcome. It is *not* based, at least not directly, on a data set of the type discussed in the previous chapters. Instead, it is a list of all possible outcomes and their corresponding probabilities.

Mathematically, there is an important difference between discrete and continuous probability distributions. Specifically, a proper treatment of continuous distributions, analogous to the treatment we provide in this section, requires calculus—which we do not presume for this book. Therefore, we discuss only discrete distributions in this section. Later in the book, we often *use* continuous distributions, particularly the bell-shaped normal distribution, but we simply state their properties without deriving them mathematically.

---

1 Actually, a more rigorous discussion allows a discrete random variable to have an infinite number of possible values, such as all positive integers.

The essential properties of a discrete random variable and its associated probability distribution are quite simple. We discuss them in general and then analyze a numerical example.

Usually, capital letters toward the end of the alphabet, such as X, Y, and Z, are used to denote random variables.

Let X be a random variable. To specify the probability distribution of X, we need to specify its possible values and their probabilities. We assume that there are k possible values, denoted $x_1, x_2, ..., x_k$. The probability of a typical value x_i is denoted in one of two ways, either $P(X = x_i)$ or $p(x_i)$. The first is a reminder that this probability involves the random variable X, whereas the second is a shorthand notation. Probability distributions must satisfy two criteria: (1) the probabilities must be nonnegative, and (2) they must sum to 1. In symbols, we must have

$$\sum_{i=1}^{k} p(x_i) = 1, \quad p(x_i) \geq 0$$

A discrete probability distribution is a set of possible values and a corresponding set of probabilities that sum to 1.

This is basically all there is to it: a list of possible values and a list of associated probabilities that sum to 1. It is also sometimes useful to calculate *cumulative* probabilities. A **cumulative probability** is the probability that the random variable is *less than or equal to* some particular value. For example, assume that 10, 20, 30, and 40 are the possible values of a random variable X, with corresponding probabilities 0.15, 0.25, 0.35, and 0.25. Then a typical cumulative probability is $P(X \leq 30)$. From the addition rule it can be calculated as

$$P(X \leq 30) = P(X = 10) + P(X = 20) + P(X = 30) = 0.75$$

The point is that the cumulative probabilities are determined by the individual probabilities.

5-3a Summary Measures of a Probability Distribution

It is often convenient to summarize a probability distribution, discrete or continuous, with two or three well-chosen numbers. The first of these is the **mean**, often denoted μ. It is also called the **expected value** of X and denoted $E(X)$ (for expected X). The mean of a discrete distribution is a weighted sum of the possible values, weighted by their probabilities, as shown in Equation (5.6). In much the same way that an average of a set of numbers indicates "central location," the mean indicates the "center" of the probability distribution.

Mean of a Probability Distribution, μ

$$\mu = E(X) = \sum_{i=1}^{k} x_i p(x_i) \qquad \textbf{(5.6)}$$

To measure the variability in a distribution, we calculate its variance or standard deviation. The **variance** of a discrete distribution, denoted by σ^2 or $Var(X)$, is a weighted sum of the squared deviations of the possible values from the mean, where the weights are again the probabilities. This is shown in Equation (5.7). As in Chapter 2, the variance is expressed in the *square* of the units of X, such as dollars squared. Therefore, a more natural measure of variability is the **standard deviation**, denoted by σ or Stdev(X). It is the square root of the variance, as indicated by Equation (5.8).

Variance of a Probability Distribution, σ^2

$$\sigma^2 = Var(X) = \sum_{i}^{k} [x_i - E(X)]^2 p(x_i) \qquad \textbf{(5.7)}$$

> **Standard Deviation of a Probability Distribution, σ**
>
> $$\sigma = \text{Stdev}(X) = \sqrt{\text{Var}(X)} \qquad (5.8)$$

Equation (5.7) is useful for understanding variance as a weighted average of squared deviations from the mean. However, the following is an equivalent formula for variance and is somewhat easier to implement in Excel. (It can be derived with straightforward algebra.) In words, you find the weighted average of the squared values, weighted by their probabilities, and then subtract the square of the mean.

> **Variance (computing formula)**
>
> $$\sigma^2 = \sum_{i=1}^{k} x_i^2 \, p(x_i) - \mu^2 \qquad (5.9)$$

We now consider a typical example.

EXAMPLE

5.2 MARKET RETURN SCENARIOS FOR THE NATIONAL ECONOMY

An investor is concerned with the market return for the coming year, where the market return is defined as the percentage gain (or loss, if negative) over the year. The investor believes there are five possible scenarios for the national economy in the coming year: rapid expansion, moderate expansion, no growth, moderate contraction, and serious contraction. Furthermore, she has used all of the information available to her to estimate that the market returns for these scenarios are, respectively, 23%, 18%, 15%, 9%, and 3%. That is, the possible returns vary from a high of 23% to a low of 3%. Also, she has assessed that the probabilities of these outcomes are 0.12, 0.40, 0.25, 0.15, and 0.08. Use this information to describe the probability distribution of the market return.

In reality, there is a continuum of possible returns. The assumption of only five possible returns is clearly an approximation to reality, but such an approximation is often useful.

Objective

To compute the mean, variance, and standard deviation of the probability distribution of the market return for the coming year.

Solution

To make the connection between the general notation and this particular example, let X denote the market return for the coming year. Then each possible economic scenario leads to a possible value of X. For example, the first possible value is $x_1 = 23\%$, and its probability is $p(x_1) = 0.12$. These values and probabilities appear in columns B and C of Figure 5.3. (See the file **Market Return Finished.xlsx**.) Note that the five probabilities sum to 1, as they should. This probability distribution implies, for example, that the probability of a market return at least as large as 18% is 0.12 + 0.40 = 0.52 because it could occur as a result of rapid or moderate expansion of the economy. Similarly, the probability that the market return is 9% or less is 0.15 + 0.08 = 0.23 because this could occur as a result of moderate or serious contraction of the economy.

The summary measures of this probability distribution appear in the range B11:B13. They can be calculated with the following steps. (Note that the formulas make use of the range names listed in the figure.)

Figure 5.3 Probability Distribution of Market Returns

	A	B	C	D	E	F	G
1	Mean, variance, and standard deviation of the market return					Range names used	
2						Market_return	=$C$4:$C$8
3	Economic outcome	Probability	Market return	Sq dev from mean		Mean	=$B$11
4	Rapid Expansion	0.12	0.23	0.005929		Probability	=$B$4:$B$8
5	Moderate Expansion	0.40	0.18	0.000729		Sq_dev_from_mean	=$D$4:$D$8
6	No Growth	0.25	0.15	0.000009		Stdev	=$B$13
7	Moderate Contraction	0.15	0.09	0.003969		Variance	=$B$12
8	Serious Contraction	0.08	0.03	0.015129			
9							
10	Summary measures of return						
11	Mean	15.3%					
12	Variance	0.002811	0.002811	←———— Quick alternative formula			
13	Stdev	5.3%	5.3%				

Procedure for Calculating Summary Measures

1. **Mean return.** Calculate the mean return in cell B11 with the formula

=SUMPRODUCT(Market_return,Probability)

This formula illustrates the general rule in Equation (5.6): The mean is the sum of products of possible values and probabilities.
2. **Squared deviations.** To get ready to compute the variance from Equation (5.7), calculate the squared deviations from the mean by entering the formula

=(C4-Mean)^2

in cell D4 and copying it down through cell D8.
3. **Variance.** Calculate the variance of the market return in cell B12 with the formula

=SUMPRODUCT(Sq_dev_from_mean,Probability)

This illustrates the general formula for variance in Equation (5.7). The variance is always a sum of products of squared deviations from the mean and probabilities. Alternatively, you can skip the calculation of the squared deviations from the mean and use Equation (5.9) directly. This is done in cell C12 with the formula

As always, range names are not required, but they make the Excel formulas easier to read. You can use them or omit them, as you wish.

=SUMPRODUCT(Market_return,Market_return,Probability)-Mean^2

By entering the Market_return range twice in this SUMPRODUCT formula, you get the squares. From now on, we will use this simplified formula for variance and dispense with squared deviations from the mean. But regardless of how it is calculated, you should remember the essence of variance: It is a weighted average of squared deviations from the mean.
4. **Standard deviation.** Calculate the standard deviation of the market return in cell B13 with the formula

=SQRT(Variance)

You can see that the mean return is 15.3% and the standard deviation is 5.3%. What do these measures really mean? First, the mean, or *expected,* return does not imply that the most likely return is 15.3%, nor is this the value that the investor "expects" to occur. In fact, the value 15.3% is not even a possible market return, at least not according to the model. You can understand these measures better in terms of long-run averages. Specifically, if you could imagine the coming year being repeated many times, each time using the probability distribution in columns B and C to generate a market return, then the average of these market returns would be close to 15.3%, and their standard deviation—calculated as in Chapter 2—would be close to 5.3%.

Before leaving this section, we emphasize a key point, a point that is easy to forget with all the details. The whole point of discussing probability and probability distributions, especially in the context of business problems, is that uncertainty is often a key factor, and you cannot simply ignore it. The mean return in this example is 15.3%. However, it would be far from realistic to treat the actual return as a sure 15.3%, with no uncertainty. If you did this, you would be ignoring the uncertainty completely, and it is often the uncertainty that makes business problems interesting—and adds risk. Therefore, to model such problems in a realistic way, you must deal with probability and probability distributions.

5-3b Conditional Mean and Variance[2]

There are many situations where the mean and variance of a random variable depend on some external event. In this case, you can *condition* on the outcome of the external event to find the overall mean and variance (or standard deviation) of the random variable.

It is best to motivate this with an example. Consider the random variable X, representing the percentage change in the price of stock A from now to a year from now. This change is driven partly by circumstances specific to company A, but it is also driven partly by the economy as a whole. In this case, the outcome of the economy is the external event. Let's assume that the economy in the coming year will be awful, stable, or great with probabilities 0.20, 0.50, and 0.30, respectively. (Of course, these are subjective probabilities.) In addition, we make the following assumptions.

- Given that the economy is awful, the mean and standard deviation of X are -20% and 30%.
- Given that the economy is stable, the mean and standard deviation of X are 5% and 20%.
- Given that the economy is great, the mean and standard deviation of X are 25% and 15%.

Each of these statements is a statement about X *conditional* upon the economy. What can we say about the *unconditional* mean and standard deviation of X? That is, what are the mean and standard deviation of X *before* we learn the state of the economy? The answers come from Equations (5.10) and (5.11). In the context of the example, p_i is the probability of economy state i, and $E_i(X)$ and $Var_i(X)$ are the mean and variance of X, given that economy state i occurs.

Conditional Mean Formula

$$E(X) = \sum_{i=1}^{k} E_i(X)p_i \qquad (5.10)$$

Conditional Variance Formula

$$Var(X) = \sum_{i=1}^{k} \{Var_i(X) + [E_i(X)]^2\}p_i - [E(X)]^2 \qquad (5.11)$$

---

2 This section is somewhat advanced and can be omitted. It won't be used in the rest of the book.

In the example, the mean percentage change in the price of stock A, from Equation (5.10), is

$$E(X) = 0.2(-20\%) + 0.5(5\%) + 0.3(25\%) = 6\%$$

To calculate the standard deviation of X, first use Equation (5.11) to calculate the variance, and then take its square root. The variance is

$$Var(X) = \{0.2[(30\%)^2 + (-20\%)^2] + 0.5[(20\%)^2 + (5\%)^2]$$

$$+ 0.3[(15\%)^2 + (25\%)^2]\} - (6\%)^2 = 0.06915$$

Taking the square root gives

$$Stdev(X) = \sqrt{0.06915} = 26.30\%$$

Of course, these calculations can be done easily in Excel. See the file **Stock Price and Economy Finished.xlsx** for details.

The point of this example is that it is often easier to assess the uncertainty of some random variable X by conditioning on every possible outcome of some external event like the economy. However, *before* that outcome is known, the relevant mean and standard deviation of X are those calculated from Equations (5.10) and (5.11). In this particular example, *before* you know the state of the economy, the relevant mean and standard deviation of the change in the price of stock A are 6% and 26.3%, respectively.

Problems

Solutions for problems whose numbers appear within a colored box can be found in the Student Solution Files.

Level A

8. Consider a random variable with the following probability distribution: $P(X = 0) = 0.1$, $P(X = 1) = 0.2$, $P(X = 2) = 0.3$, $P(X = 3) = 0.3$, and $P(X = 4) = 0.1$.
a. Find $P(X \le 2)$.
b. Find $P(1 < X \le 3)$.
c. Find $P(X > 0)$.
d. Find $P(X > 3 | X > 2)$.
e. Find the expected value of X.
f. Find the standard deviation of X.

9. A study has shown that the probability distribution of X, the number of customers in line (including the one being served, if any) at a checkout counter in a department store, is given by $P(X = 0) = 0.25$, $P(X = 1) = 0.25$, $P(X = 2) = 0.20$, $P(X = 3) = 0.20$, and $P(\ge 4) = 0.10$. Consider a newly arriving customer to the checkout line.
a. What is the probability that this customer will not have to wait behind anyone?
b. What is the probability that this customer will have to wait behind at least one customer?
c. On average, the newly arriving customer will have to wait behind how many other customers?

10. A construction company has to complete a project no later than three months from now or there will be significant cost overruns. The manager of the construction company believes that there are four possible values for the random variable X, the number of months from now it will take to complete this project: 2, 2.5, 3, and 3.5. The manager currently thinks that the probabilities of these four possibilities are in the ratio 1 to 2 to 4 to 2. That is, $X = 2.5$ is twice as likely as $X = 2$, $X = 3$ is twice as likely as $X = 2.5$, and $X = 3.5$ is half as likely as $X = 3$.
a. Find the probability distribution of X.
b. What is the probability that this project will be completed in less than three months from now?
c. What is the probability that this project will *not* be completed on time?
d. What is the expected completion time (in months) of this project from now?
e. How much variability (in months) exists around the expected value you found in part **d**?

Level B

11. The National Football League playoffs are just about to begin. Because of their great record in the regular season, the Steelers get a bye in the first week of the playoffs. In the second week, they will play the winner of the game between the Ravens and the Patriots. A football expert estimates that the Ravens will beat the Patriots with probability 0.45. This same expert estimates that if the Steelers play the Ravens, the mean and standard deviation of the point spread (Steelers points minus Ravens points) will be 6.5 and 10.5, whereas if the Steelers play the Patriots, the mean and standard deviation of the point spread (Steelers points minus Patriots points) will be 3.5 and 12.5. Find the mean and standard deviation of the point spread (Steelers points minus their opponent's points) in the Steelers game.

12. The "house edge" in any game of chance is defined as

$$\frac{E(\text{player's loss on a bet})}{\text{Size of player's loss on a bet}}$$

For example, if a player wins \$10 with probability 0.48 and loses \$10 with probability 0.52 on any bet, the house edge is

$$\frac{-[10(0.48) - 10(0.52)]}{10} = 0.04$$

Give an interpretation to the house edge that relates to how much money the house is likely to win on average. Which do you think has a larger house edge: roulette or sports gambling? Why?

5-4 The Normal Distribution

In the rest of this chapter, we discuss specific probability distributions, starting with the single most important distribution in statistics, the normal distribution. It is a continuous distribution and is the basis of the familiar symmetric bell-shaped curve. Any particular normal distribution is specified by its mean and standard deviation. By changing the mean, the normal curve shifts to the right or left. By changing the standard deviation, the curve becomes more or less spread out. Therefore, there are really many normal distributions, not just a single one. We say that the normal distribution is a *two-parameter family*, where the two parameters are the mean and the standard deviation.

5-4a Continuous Distributions and Density Functions

We first take a moment to discuss continuous probability distributions in general. In the previous section we discussed discrete distributions, characterized by a list of possible values and their probabilities. The same basic idea holds for continuous distributions such as the normal distribution, but the mathematics is more complex. Now instead of a list of possible values, there is a *continuum* of possible values, such as all values between 0 and 100 or all values greater than 0. Instead of assigning probabilities to each individual value in the continuum, the total probability of 1 is spread over this continuum. The key to this spreading is called a *density function*, which acts like a histogram. The higher the value of the density function, the more likely this region of the continuum is.

A **density function**, usually denoted by $f(x)$, specifies the probability distribution of a continuous random variable X. The higher $f(x)$ is, the more likely x is. Also, the total area between the graph of $f(x)$ and the horizontal axis, which represents the total probability, is equal to 1. Finally, $f(x)$ is nonnegative for all possible values of X.

As an example, consider the density function shown in Figure 5.4. (This is *not* a normal density function.) It indicates that all values in the continuum from 25 to 100 are possible, but that the values near 70 are most likely. (This density function might correspond to scores on an exam.) More specifically, because the height of the density at 70 is approximately twice the height of the curve at 84 or 53, a value near 70 is approximately twice as likely as a value near 84 or a value near 53. In this sense, the height of the density function indicates *relative* likelihoods.

For continuous distributions, probabilities are areas under the density function. These probabilities can often be calculated with Excel functions.

Probabilities are found from a density function as areas under the curve. For example, the area of the designated region in Figure 5.5 represents the probability of a score between 65 and 75. Also, the area under the *entire* curve is 1 because the total probability of all possible values is always 1. Fortunately, Excel functions have been developed to find these areas—without the need for bulky tables. We take advantage of these Excel functions in the rest of this chapter and in later chapters.

Figure 5.4 A Skewed Density Function

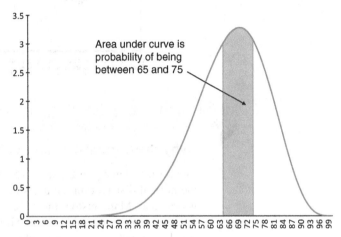

Figure 5.5 Probability as the Area Under the Density

Area under curve is probability of being between 65 and 75

As in the previous chapter, the mean is a measure of central tendency of the distribution, and the standard deviation (or variance) measures the variability of the distribution. We will list their values for the normal distribution and any other continuous distributions where we need them. By the way, the mean for the (nonnormal) density in Figure 5.4 is slightly *less* than 70—it is always to the left of the peak for a left-skewed distribution and to the right of the peak for a right-skewed distribution—and the standard deviation is approximately 15.

5-4b The Normal Density Function

The **normal distribution** is a continuous distribution with possible values ranging over the *entire* number line—from "minus infinity" to "plus infinity." However, only a relatively small range has much chance of occurring. The normal density function is actually quite complex, in spite of its "nice" bell-shaped appearance. For the sake of completeness, we list the formula for the normal density function in Equation (5.12). Here, μ and σ are the mean and standard deviation of the distribution.

Normal Density Function

$$f(x) = \frac{1}{\sqrt{2\pi}\sigma}e^{-(x-\mu)^2/(2\sigma^2)} \quad \text{for} \quad -\infty < x < +\infty \qquad (5.12)$$

The curves in Figure 5.6 illustrate several normal density functions for different values of μ and σ. The mean μ can be any number: negative, positive, or zero. As you can see, the effect of increasing or decreasing the mean μ is to shift the curve to the right or the left. On the other hand, the standard deviation σ must be a *positive* number. It controls the spread of the normal curve. When σ is small, the curve is more peaked; when σ is large, the curve is more spread out. For shorthand, we use the notation $N(\mu, \sigma)$ to refer to the normal distribution with mean μ and standard deviation σ. For example, $N(-2, 1)$ refers to the normal distribution with mean -2 and standard deviation 1.

Figure 5.6 Several Normal Density Functions

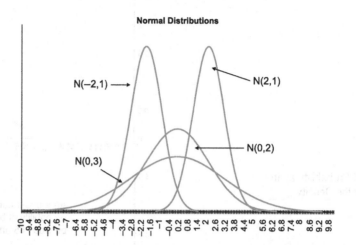

Fundamental Insight

Why the Normal Distribution?

The normal density in Equation (5.12) is certainly not very intuitive, so why is the normal distribution the basis for so much of statistical theory? One reason is practical. Many histograms based on real data resemble the bell-shaped normal curve to a remarkable extent. Granted, not all histograms are symmetric and bellshaped, but a surprising number are. Another reason is theoretical. In spite of the complexity of Equation (5.12), the normal distribution has many appealing properties that have enabled researchers to build the rich statistical theory that finds widespread use in business, the sciences, and other fields.

5-4c Standardizing: Z-Values

There are infinitely many normal distributions, one for each pair μ and σ. We single out one of these for special attention, the *standard* normal distribution. The **standard normal** distribution has mean 0 and standard deviation 1, so we denote it by $N(0, 1)$. It is also commonly referred to as the Z distribution. Suppose the random variable X is normally distributed with mean μ and standard deviation σ. We define the random variable Z by Equation (5.13). This operation is called *standardizing*. That is, to **standardize** a variable, you subtract its mean and then divide the difference by the standard deviation. When X is normally distributed, the standardized variable is $N(0, 1)$.

Standardizing a Normal Random Variable

$$Z = \frac{X - \mu}{\sigma} \qquad (5.13)$$

One reason for standardizing is to measure variables with different means and/or standard deviations on a single scale. For example, suppose several sections of a college course are taught by different instructors. Because of differences in teaching methods and grading procedures, the distributions of scores in these sections might differ. However, if each instructor calculates his or her mean and standard deviation and then calculates a Z-value for each student, the distributions of the Z-values should be approximately the same in each section.

It is easy to interpret a Z-value. It is the number of standard deviations to the right or the left of the mean. If Z is positive, the original value (in this case, the original score) is to the *right* of the mean; if Z is negative, the original score is to the *left* of the mean. For example, if the Z-value for some student is 2, then this student's score is two standard deviations above the mean. If the Z-value for another student is -0.5, then this student's score is half a standard deviation below the mean. We illustrate Z-values in Example 5.1.

EXAMPLE

5.3 STANDARDIZING RETURNS FROM MUTUAL FUNDS

The annual returns for 30 mutual funds appear in Figure 5.7. (See the file **Standardizing Finished.xlsx**.) Find and interpret the Z-values of these returns.

Objective
To use Excel to standardize annual returns of various mutual funds.

Figure 5.7 Mutual Fund Returns and Z-Values

	A	B	C	D	E	F
1	Standardizing mutual fund returns				Range names used	
2					Mean	=$B$4
3	Summary statistics from values below				Stdev	=$B$5
4	Mean		0.091	0.000		
5	Stdev		0.047	1.000		
6						
7	Fund		Annual return	Z value		
8	1		0.007	−1.8047		
9	2		0.080	−0.2363		
10	3		0.082	−0.1934		
11	4		0.123	0.6875		
12	5		0.022	−1.4824		
13	6		0.054	−0.7949		
35	28		0.094	0.0645		
36	29		0.078	−0.2793		
37	30		0.066	−0.5371		

Solution
The 30 annual returns appear in column B of Figure 5.7. Their mean and standard deviation are calculated in cells B4 and B5 with the AVERAGE and STDEV.S functions. The corresponding Z-values are calculated in column C by entering the formula

=(B8-Mean)/Stdev

in cell C8 and copying it down column C. (Note that Mean and Stdev are range names for cells B4 and B5.)

The Z-values in Figure 5.7 range from a low of -1.80 to a high of 2.19. Specifically, the return for stock 1 is about 1.80 standard deviations below the mean, whereas the return for fund 17 is about 2.19 standard deviations above the mean. As you will see shortly, these values are typical: Z-values are usually in the range from -2 to $+2$ and values beyond -3 or $+3$ are very uncommon. (Recall the *empirical rules* for interpreting standard deviation discussed in Chapter 2.) Also, the Z-values automatically have mean 0 and standard deviation 1, as you can see in cells C4 and C5 by using the AVERAGE and STDEV.S functions on the Z-values in column C.

5-4d Normal Tables and Z-Values[3]

A common use for Z-values and the standard normal distribution is in calculating probabilities and percentiles by the traditional method. This method is based on a table of the standard normal distribution found in many statistics textbooks. Such a table is given in Figure 5.8. The body of the table contains probabilities. (The entire body of this table was generated by the single copyable formula shown.) The left and top margins contain possible values. Specifically, suppose you want to find the probability that a standard normal random variable is less than 1.35. You locate 1.3 along the left and 0.05—the second decimal in 1.35—along the top, and then read into the table to find the probability 0.9115. In words, the probability is about 0.91 that a standard normal random variable is less than 1.35.

Figure 5.8 Table of Normal Probabilities

	A	B	C	D	E	F	G	H	I	J	K
1	z	0.00	0.01	0.02	0.03	0.04	0.05	0.06	0.07	0.08	0.09
2	0.0	0.5000	0.5040	0.5080	0.5120	0.5160	0.5199	0.5239	0.5279	0.5319	0.5359
3	0.1	0.5398	0.5438	0.5478	0.5517	0.5557	0.5596	0.5636	0.5675	0.5714	0.5753
4	0.2	0.5793	0.5832	0.5871	0.5910	0.5948	0.5987	0.6026	0.6064	0.6103	0.6141
5	0.3	0.6179	0.6217	0.6255	0.6293	0.6331	0.6368	0.6406	0.6443	0.6480	0.6517
6	0.4	0.6554	0.6591	0.6628	0.6664	0.6700	0.6736	0.6772	0.6808	0.6844	0.6879
7	0.5	0.6915	0.6950	0.6985	0.7019	0.7054	0.7088	0.7123	0.7157	0.7190	0.7224
8	0.6	0.7257	0.7291	0.7324	0.7357	0.7389	0.7422	0.7454	0.7486	0.7517	0.7549
9	0.7	0.7580	0.7611	0.7642	0.7673	0.7704	0.7734	0.7764	0.7794	0.7823	0.7852
10	0.8	0.7881	0.7910	0.7939	0.7967	0.7995	0.8023	0.8051	0.8078	0.8106	0.8133
11	0.9	0.8159	0.8186	0.8212	0.8238	=NORM.S.DIST($A11+F$1, TRUE)				0.8365	0.8389
12	1.0	0.8413	0.8438	0.8461	0.8485	NORM.S.DIST(z, cumulative)	54	0.8577	0.8599	0.8621	
13	1.1	0.8643	0.8665	0.8686	0.8708	0.8729	0.8749	0.8770	0.8790	0.8810	0.8830
14	1.2	0.8849	0.8869	0.8888	0.8907	0.8925	0.8944	0.8962	0.8980	0.8997	0.9015
15	1.3	0.9032	0.9049	0.9066	0.9082	0.9099	0.9115	0.9131	0.9147	0.9162	0.9177
16	1.4	0.9192	0.9207	0.9222	0.9236	0.9251	0.9265	0.9279	0.9292	0.9306	0.9319
17	1.5	0.9332	0.9345	0.9357	0.9370	0.9382	0.9394	0.9406	0.9418	0.9429	0.9441
18	1.6	0.9452	0.9463	0.9474	0.9484	0.9495	0.9505	0.9515	0.9525	0.9535	0.9545
19	1.7	0.9554	0.9564	0.9573	0.9582	0.9591	0.9599	0.9608	0.9616	0.9625	0.9633
20	1.8	0.9641	0.9649	0.9656	0.9664	0.9671	0.9678	0.9686	0.9693	0.9699	0.9706
21	1.9	0.9713	0.9719	0.9726	0.9732	0.9738	0.9744	0.9750	0.9756	0.9761	0.9767
22	2.0	0.9772	0.9778	0.9783	0.9788	0.9793	0.9798	0.9803	0.9808	0.9812	0.9817
23	2.1	0.9821	0.9826	0.9830	0.9834	0.9838	0.9842	0.9846	0.9850	0.9854	0.9857
24	2.2	0.9861	0.9864	0.9868	0.9871	0.9875	0.9878	0.9881	0.9884	0.9887	0.9890
25	2.3	0.9893	0.9896	0.9898	0.9901	0.9904	0.9906	0.9909	0.9911	0.9913	0.9916
26	2.4	0.9918	0.9920	0.9922	0.9925	0.9927	0.9929	0.9931	0.9932	0.9934	0.9936
27	2.5	0.9938	0.9940	0.9941	0.9943	0.9945	0.9946	0.9948	0.9949	0.9951	0.9952
28	2.6	0.9953	0.9955	0.9956	0.9957	0.9959	0.9960	0.9961	0.9962	0.9963	0.9964
29	2.7	0.9965	0.9966	0.9967	0.9968	0.9969	0.9970	0.9971	0.9972	0.9973	0.9974
30	2.8	0.9974	0.9975	0.9976	0.9977	0.9977	0.9978	0.9979	0.9979	0.9980	0.9981
31	2.9	0.9981	0.9982	0.9982	0.9983	0.9984	0.9984	0.9985	0.9985	0.9986	0.9986
32	3.0	0.9987	0.9987	0.9987	0.9988	0.9988	0.9989	0.9989	0.9989	0.9990	0.9990
33	3.1	0.9990	0.9991	0.9991	0.9991	0.9992	0.9992	0.9992	0.9992	0.9993	0.9993
34	3.2	0.9993	0.9993	0.9994	0.9994	0.9994	0.9994	0.9994	0.9995	0.9995	0.9995
35	3.3	0.9995	0.9995	0.9995	0.9996	0.9996	0.9996	0.9996	0.9996	0.9996	0.9997
36	3.4	0.9997	0.9997	0.9997	0.9997	0.9997	0.9997	0.9997	0.9997	0.9997	0.9998

---

3 If you intend to rely on Excel functions for normal calculations (and we hope you do!), you can skip this subsection.

Alternatively, if you are given a probability, you can use the table to find the value with this much probability to the left of it under the standard normal curve. This is called a *percentile* calculation. For example, if the probability is 0.75, you can find the 75th percentile by locating the probability in the table closest to 0.75 and then reading to the left and up. With interpolation, the required value is approximately 0.675. In words, the probability of being to the left of 0.675 under the standard normal curve is approximately 0.75.

There are some obvious drawbacks to using the standard normal table for probability calculations. The first is that there are holes in the table—interpolation is often necessary. A second drawback is that the standard normal table takes different forms in different textbooks. These differences are rather minor, but they can easily cause confusion. Finally, the table requires you to perform calculations, where errors are easy to make.

The Excel functions discussed next make the whole procedure much easier and less error-prone.

5-4e Normal Calculations in Excel

Two types of calculations are typically made with normal distributions: finding probabilities and finding percentiles. Excel has functions for both of these. The functions used for normal probability calculations are NORM.DIST and NORM.S.DIST. The main difference between these is that the one with the "S" (for standard) applies only to $N(0, 1)$ calculations, whereas NORM.DIST applies to *any* normal distribution. On the other hand, percentile calculations that take a probability and return a value are often called *inverse* calculations. Therefore, the Excel functions for these are named NORM.INV and NORM.S.INV. Again, the "S" in the second of these indicates that it applies to the standard normal distribution.

The NORM.DIST and NORM.S.DIST functions return left-tail probabilities, such as the probability that a normally distributed variable is *less than* 35. The syntax for these functions is

=NORM.DIST(x,μ,σ,TRUE)

and

=NORM.S.DIST (x,TRUE)

Here, x is a number you supply, and μ and σ are the mean and standard deviation of the normal distribution. The last argument in the NORM.DIST function, TRUE (or 1), is used to obtain the *cumulative* normal probability, the type usually required. (This TRUE/FALSE argument is a nuisance to remember, but it is necessary. If the last argument is FALSE, or 0, the function returns the height of the density at x, which is not usually what you want.) The NORM.S.DIST function takes only two arguments (because μ and σ are known to be 0 and 1), so it is easier to use—when it applies. (Note that the "old" NORMSDIST function doesn't require the last TRUE/FALSE argument, but the newer NORM.S.DIST function, introduced in Excel 2010, does.)

The NORM.INV and NORM.S.INV functions return values for user-supplied probabilities. For example, if you supply the probability 0.95, these functions return the 95 th percentile. Their syntax is

=NORM.INV(p,μ,σ)

and

=NORM.S.INV(p)

where p is a probability you supply. These are analogous to the NORM.DIST and NORM.S.DIST functions except there is no final TRUE/FALSE argument in the "INV" functions.

Old Normal Functions

Prior to Excel 2010, the normal functions were NORMDIST, NORMSDIST, NORMINV, and NORMSINV. They are almost the same as the new functions, the ones with periods in their names, except that NORMSDIST does not take a last TRUE/FALSE argument. Microsoft kept these old functions for backward compatibility, so you can continue to use them if you prefer.

Fundamental Insight

Probability and Percentile Calculations

There are two basic types of calculations involving probability distributions, normal or otherwise. In a probability calculation, you provide a possible value, and you ask for the probability of being less than or equal to this value. In a percentile calculation, you provide a probability, and you ask for the value that has this probability to the left of it. Excel's statistical functions use DIST functions to perform probability calculations and INV (for inverse) functions to perform percentile calculations.

We illustrate these Excel functions in the following example.[4]

EXAMPLE

5.4 NORMAL CALCULATIONS IN EXCEL

Use Excel to calculate the following probabilities and percentiles for the standard normal distribution: (a) $P(Z < -2)$, (b) $P(Z > 1)$, (c) $P(-0.4 < Z < 1.6)$, (d) the 5th percentile, (e) the 75th percentile, and (f) the 99th percentile. Then for the $N(75, 8)$ distribution, find the following probabilities and percentiles: (a) $P(X < 70)$, (b) $P(X > 73)$, (c) $P(75 < X < 85)$, (d) the 5th percentile, (e) the 60th percentile, and (f) the 97th percentile.

Objective

To calculate probabilities and percentiles for standard normal and general normal distributions in Excel.

Solution

The solution appears in Figure 5.9. (See the file **Normal Calculations Finished.xlsx**.) The $N(0, 1)$ calculations are in rows 7 through 14; the $N(75, 8)$ calculations are in rows 23 through 30. For your convenience, the formulas used in column B are spelled out in column D (as labels). Note that the standard normal calculations use the normal functions with the "S" in the middle; the rest use the normal functions without the "S"—and require more arguments.

Note the following for normal *probability* calculations:

- For "less than" probabilities, use NORM.DIST or NORM.S.DIST directly. (See rows 7 and 23.)
- For "greater than" probabilities, subtract the NORM.DIST or NORM.S.DIST function from 1. (See rows 8 and 24.)
- For "between" probabilities, subtract the two NORM.DIST or NORM.S.DIST functions. For example, in row 9 the probability of being between −0.4 and 1.6 is the probability of being less than 1.6 minus the probability of being less than −0.4.

---

4 Actually, we already illustrated the NORM.S.DIST function; it was used to create the body of Figure 5.8. In other words, you can use it to build your own normal probability table.

Figure 5.9 Normal Calculations with Excel Functions

	A	B	C	D
1	Normal probability calculations			
2				
3	Examples with standard normal			
4				
5	Probability calculations			
6	Range	Probability		
7	Less than −2	0.0228		=NORM.S.DIST(−2,TRUE)
8	Greater than 1	0.1587		=1-NORM.S.DIST(1,TRUE)
9	Between −0.4 and 1.6	0.6006		=NORM.S.DIST(1.6,TRUE)-NORM.S.DIST(−0.4,TRUE)
10				
11	Percentiles			
12	5th	−1.645		=NORM.S.INV(0.05)
13	75th	0.674		=NORM.S.INV(0.75)
14	99th	2.326		=NORM.S.INV(0.99)
15				
16	Examples with nonstandard normal			
17				Range names used:
18	Mean	75		Mean = $B$18
19	Stdev	8		Stdev = $B$19
20				
21	Probability calculations			
22	Range	Probability		
23	Less than 70	0.2660		=NORM.DIST(70,Mean,Stdev,TRUE)
24	Greater than 73	0.5987		=1-NORM.DIST(73,Mean,Stdev,TRUE)
25	Between 75 and 85	0.3944		=NORM.DIST(85,Mean,Stdev,TRUE)-NORM.DIST(75,Mean,Stdev,TRUE)
26				
27	Percentiles			
28	5th	61.841		=NORM.INV(0.05,Mean,Stdev)
29	60th	77.027		=NORM.INV(0.6,Mean,Stdev)
30	97th	90.046		=NORM.INV(0.97,Mean,Stdev)

The percentile calculations are even more straightforward. In most percentile problems you want to find the value with a certain probability to the *left* of it. In this case you use the NORM.INV or NORM.S.INV function with the specified probability as the first argument. See rows 12 through 14 and 28 through 30.

Note that when you are calculating probabilities for *any* continuous distribution, including the normal distribution, there is no need to distinguish between "less than" and "less than or equal to" events, or between "greater than" and "greater than or equal to" events. The reason is that there is no *positive* probability of being equal to any particular value. However, as you will see when we discuss the binomial distribution, this is not true of discrete distributions.

There are a couple of variations of percentile calculations. First, suppose you want the value with probability 0.05 to the *right* of it. This is the same as the value with probability 0.95 to the left of it, so you use NORM.INV or NORM.S.INV with probability argument 0.95. For example, the value with probability 0.4 to the right of it in the N(75, 8) distribution is the 60th percentile, 77.027. (See cell B29 in Figure 5.6.)

As a second variation, suppose you want to find an interval of the form −x to x, for some positive number x, with (1) probability 0.025 to the left of −x, (2) probability 0.025 to the right of x, and (3) probability 0.95 between −x and x. This is a very common problem in statistical inference. In general, you want a probability (such as 0.95) to be in the middle of the interval so that half of the remaining probability (0.025) is in each of the tails. (See Figure 5.10.) Then the required x

Figure 5.10 Typical Normal Probabilities

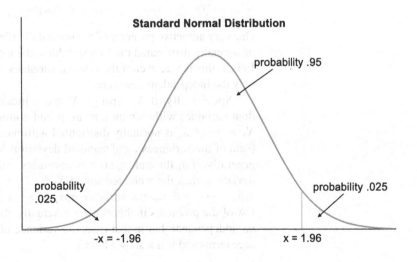

can be found with NORM.INV or NORM.S.INV, using probability argument 0.975, because there must be a total probability of 0.975 to the left of x.

For example, if the relevant distribution is the standard normal, the required value of x is 1.96, found with the function NORM.S.INV(0.975). Similarly, if you want probability 0.90 in the middle and probability 0.05 in each tail, the required x is 1.645, found with the function NORM.S.INV(0.95). Remember these two numbers, 1.96 and 1.645. They occur frequently in statistical applications.

5-4f Empirical Rules Revisited

We introduced three empirical rules in Chapter 2 that apply to many data sets. Namely, about 68% of the data fall within one standard deviation of the mean, about 95% fall within two standard deviations of the mean, and almost all fall within three standard deviations of the mean. For these rules to hold with real data, the distribution of the data must be at least approximately symmetric and bell-shaped. Let's look at these rules more closely.

The normal distribution is the basis for the empirical rules introduced in Chapter 2.

Suppose X is normally distributed with mean μ and standard deviation σ. To perform a probability calculation on X, it is useful to first standardize X and then perform the calculation on the standardized variable Z. Specifically, we will find the probability that X is within k standard deviations of its mean for $k = 1$, $k = 2$, and $k = 3$. In general, this probability is $P(\mu - k\sigma < X < \mu + k\sigma)$. But by standardizing the values $\mu - k\sigma$ and $\mu + k\sigma$, we obtain the equivalent probability $P(-k < Z < k)$, where Z has a $N(0, 1)$ distribution. This latter probability can be calculated in Excel with the formula

=NORM.S.DIST(k, TRUE)−NORM.S.DIST(−k, TRUE)

By substituting the values 1, 2, and 3 for k, we find the following probabilities:

$P(-1 < Z < 1) = 0.6827$
$P(-2 < Z < 2) = 0.9545$
$P(-3 < Z < 3) = 0.9973$

As you can see, there is virtually no chance of being beyond three standard deviations from the mean, the chances are about 19 out of 20 of being within two standard deviations of the mean, and the chances are about 2 out of 3 of being within one standard deviation of the mean. These probabilities are the basis for the empirical rules in Chapter 2. These rules more closely approximate reality as the histograms of observed data become more symmetric and bell-shaped.

5-4g Weighted Sums of Normal Random Variables

One very attractive property of the normal distribution is that if you create a weighted sum of normally distributed random variables, the weighted sum is also normally distributed. In fact, this is true even if the random variables are *not* independent, but we will examine only the independent case here.

Specifically, if X_1 through X_n are n independent and normally distributed random variables with common mean μ and common standard deviation σ, then the sum $X_1 + \cdots + X_n$ is normally distributed with mean $n\mu$ (sum of the means), variance $n\sigma^2$ (sum of the variances), and standard deviation $\sqrt{n}\sigma$ (square root of the variance). More generally, if a_1 through a_n are any constants and each X has its own mean and standard deviation, then the weighted sum $a_1 X_1 + \cdots + a_n X_n$ is normally distributed with mean $a_1\mu_1 + \cdots + a_n\mu_n$ and variance $a_1^2\sigma_1^2 + \cdots + a_n^2\sigma_n^2$. You will need this fact to solve a few of the problems in this chapter. (Actually, this is the correct mean even if the X's are *not* independent, but in that case, the variance of the weighted sum also includes covariance terms and is not shown here.)

5-4h Normal Distribution Examples

In this section we apply the normal distribution to several business problems.

EXAMPLE

5.5 PERSONNEL TESTING AT ZTEL

The personnel department of ZTel, a large communications company, is reconsidering its hiring policy. Each applicant for a job must take a standard exam, and the hire or no-hire decision depends at least in part on the result of the exam. The scores of all applicants have been examined closely. They are approximately normally distributed with mean 525 and standard deviation 55.

The current hiring policy occurs in two phases. The first phase separates all applicants into three categories: automatic accepts, automatic rejects, and maybes. The automatic accepts are those whose test scores are 600 or above. The automatic rejects are those whose test scores are 425 or below. All other applicants (the maybes) are passed on to a second phase where their previous job experience, special talents, and other factors are used as hiring criteria. The personnel manager at ZTel wants to calculate the percentage of applicants who are automatic accepts or rejects, given the current standards. She also wants to know how to change the standards to automatically reject 10% of all applicants and automatically accept 15% of all applicants.

Objective

To determine test scores that can be used to accept or reject job applicants at ZTel.

Solution

Let X be the test score of a typical applicant. Then historical data suggest that the distribution of X is $N(525, 55)$. A probability such as $P(X \leq 425)$ can be interpreted as the probability that a typical applicant is an automatic reject, or it can be interpreted as the percentage of *all* applicants who are automatic rejects. Given this observation, the solution to ZTel's problem appears in Figure 5.11. (See the file **Personnel Decisions Finished.xlsx**.) The probability that a typical applicant is automatically accepted is 0.0863, found in cell B10 with the formula

=1–NORM.DIST(B7,Mean,Stdev,TRUE)

Similarly, the probability that a typical applicant is automatically rejected is 0.0345, found in cell B11 with the formula

Figure 5.11 Calculations for Personnel Example

	A	B	C	D	E	F
1	**Personnel Decisions**					
2				Range names used:		
3	Mean of test scores	525		Mean	=$B$3	
4	Stdev of test scores	55		Stdev	=$B$4	
5						
6	**Current Policy**					
7	Automatic accept point	600				
8	Automatic reject point	425				
9						
10	Percent accepted	8.63%		=1-NORM.DIST(B7,Mean,Stdev,TRUE)		
11	Percent rejected	3.45%		=NORM.DIST(B8,Mean,Stdev,TRUE)		
12						
13	**New Policy**					
14	Percent accepted	15%				
15	Percent rejected	10%				
16						
17	Automatic accept point	582		=NORM.INV(1-B14,Mean,Stdev)		
18	Automatic reject point	455		=NORM.INV(B15,Mean,Stdev)		

=NORM.DIST(B8,Mean,Stdev,TRUE)

Therefore, ZTel automatically accepts about 8.6% and rejects about 3.5% of all applicants under the current policy.

To find new cutoff values that reject 10% and accept 15% of the applicants, we need the 10th and 85th percentiles of the $N(525, 55)$ distribution. These are 455 and 582 (rounded to the nearest integer), respectively, found in cells B17 and B18 with the formulas

=NORM.INV(1–B14,Mean,Stdev)

and

=NORM.INV(B15,Mean,Stdev)

To accomplish its objective, ZTel needs to raise the automatic rejection point from 425 to 455 and lower the automatic acceptance point from 600 to 582.

EXAMPLE

5.6 QUALITY CONTROL AT PAPERSTOCK

PaperStock Company runs a manufacturing facility that produces a paper product. The fiber content of this product is supposed to be 20 pounds per 1000 square feet. (This is typical for the type of paper used in grocery bags, for example.) Because of random variations in the inputs to the process, however, the fiber content of a typical 1000-square-foot roll varies according to a $N(\mu, \sigma)$ distribution. The mean fiber content (μ) can be controlled—that is, it can be set to any desired level by adjusting an instrument on the machine. The variability in fiber content, as measured by the standard deviation σ, is 0.10 pound when the process is "good," but it sometimes increases to 0.15 pound when the machine goes "bad." A given roll of this product must be rejected if its actual fiber content is less than 19.8 pounds or greater than 20.3 pounds. Calculate the probability that a given roll is rejected, for a setting of $\mu = 20$, when the machine is "good" and when it is "bad."

Objective

To determine the machine settings that result in paper of acceptable quality at PaperStock Company.

Solution

Let X be the fiber content of a typical roll. The distribution of X will be either $N(20, 0.10)$ or $N(20, 0.15)$, depending on the status of the machine. In either case, the probability that the roll must be rejected can be calculated as shown in Figure 5.12. (See the file **Paper Machine Settings Finished.xlsx**.) The formula for rejection in the "good" case appears in cell B12 and is spelled out to its right.

This is the sum of two probabilities: the probability of being to the left of the lower limit and the probability of being to the right of the upper limit. (See Figure 5.13.) A similar formula for the "bad" case appears in cell B13, using Stdev_bad in place of Stdev_good.

You can see that the probability of a rejected roll in the "good" case is 0.024; in the "bad" case it is 0.114. That is, when the standard deviation increases by 50% from 0.10 to 0.15, the percentage of rolls rejected more than quadruples, from 2.4% to 11.4%.

It is certainly possible that the true process mean and "good" standard deviation will not always be equal to the values in cells B3 and B4. Therefore, it is useful to see how sensitive the rejection probability is to these two parameters. You can do this with a two-way data table, as shown in Figure 5.12. The tabulated values show that the probability of rejection varies greatly even for small changes in the key inputs. In particular, a combination of a badly centered mean and a large standard deviation can make the probability of rejection quite large.

To form this data table, enter the formula = B12 in cell B17, highlight the range B17:H25, and create a data table with row input cell B4 and column input cell B3.

Figure 5.12 Calculations for Paper Quality Example

	A	B	C	D	E	F	G	H	I	J	K
1	**Paper Machine Settings**			**Range names used:**							
2				Mean	=$B$3						
3	Mean	20		Stdev_bad	=$B$5			The point of this example is that the			
4	Stdev in good case	0.1		Stdev_good	=$B$4			probability of a reject, i.e., falling outside			
5	Stdev in bad case	0.15						the allowed limits, can vary greatly, not only			
6								when the mean is off target, but also when			
7	Reject region							the standard deviation increases. The			
8	Lower limit	19.8						illustrates the famous line that "variability is			
9	Upper limit	20.3						the enemy."			
10											
11	Probability of reject										
12	in good case	0.024		=NORM.DIST(B8,Mean,Stdev_good,TRUE)+(1-NORM.DIST(B9,Mean,Stdev_good,TRUE))							
13	in bad case	0.114		=NORM.DIST(B8,Mean,Stdev_bad,TRUE)+(1-NORM.DIST(B9,Mean,Stdev_bad,TRUE))							
14											
15	**Data table of rejection probability as a function of the mean and good standard deviation**										
16					Standard deviation						
17		0.024	0.1	0.11	0.12	0.13	0.14	0.15			
18		19.7	0.841	0.818	0.798	0.779	0.762	0.748			
19		19.8	0.500	0.500	0.500	0.500	0.500	0.500			
20		19.9	0.159	0.182	0.203	0.222	0.240	0.256			
21	Mean	20	0.024	0.038	0.054	0.072	0.093	0.114			
22		20.1	0.024	0.038	0.054	0.072	0.093	0.114			
23		20.2	0.159	0.182	0.203	0.222	0.240	0.256			
24		20.3	0.500	0.500	0.500	0.500	0.500	0.500			
25		20.4	0.841	0.818	0.798	0.779	0.762	0.748			

Figure 5.13 Rejection Regions for Paper Quality Example

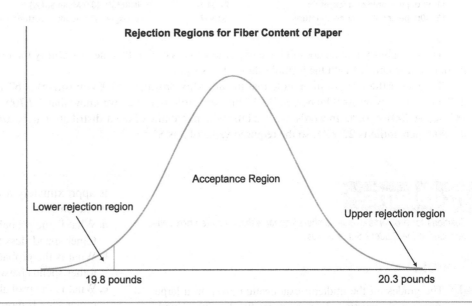

Rejection Regions for Fiber Content of Paper

Acceptance Region

Lower rejection region

Upper rejection region

19.8 pounds

20.3 pounds

EXAMPLE

5.7 ANALYZING AN INVESTOR'S AFTER-TAX PROFIT

Howard Davis invests $10,000 in a certain stock on January 1. By examining past movements of this stock and consulting with his broker, Howard estimates that the annual return from this stock, X, is normally distributed with mean 5% and standard deviation 14%. Here X (when expressed as a decimal) is the profit Howard receives per dollar invested. It means that on December 31, his $10,000 will have grown to $10,000 (1 + X)$ dollars. Because Howard is in the 33% tax bracket, he will then have to pay the Internal Revenue Service 33% of his profit, if he makes a profit. However, he doesn't have to pay any tax if he loses money. Calculate the probability that Howard will have to pay the IRS at least $400, and calculate the probability that he won't have to pay any tax. Also, calculate the dollar amount such that Howard's after-tax profit is 90% certain to be less than this amount; that is, calculate the 90th percentile of his after-tax profit.

Objective

To determine the after-tax profit Howard Davis can be 90% certain of earning.

Solution

Howard's before-tax profit is $10,000X$ dollars, so the amount he pays the IRS is $0.33(10,000X)$, or $3300X$ dollars. We want the probability that this is at least $400. Because $3300X > 400$ is the same as $X > 4/33$, the probability of this outcome can be found as in Figure 5.14. (See the file **Tax on Stock Return Finished.xlsx**.) It is calculated in cell B8 with the formula spelled out to its right. As you can see, Howard has about a 30% chance of paying at least $400 in taxes.

Figure 5.14   Calculations for Taxable Returns Example

	A	B	C	D	E	F	G	H	I
1	Tax on Stock Return								
2				Range names used:					
3	Amount invested	$10,000		Amount_invested	=$B$3				
4	Mean	5%		Mean	=$B$4				
5	Stdev	14%		Stdev	=$B$5				
6	Tax rate	33%		Tax_rate	=$B$6				
7									
8	Probability he pays at least $400 in taxes	0.305		=1-NORM.DIST(400/(Amount_invested*Tax_rate),Mean,Stdev,TRUE)					
9	Probability of no tax	0.360		=NORM.DIST(0,Mean,Stdev,TRUE)					
10									
11	90th percentile of stock return	22.94%		=NORM.INV(0.9,Mean,Stdev)					
12	90th percentile of after-tax return	$1,537		=(1-Tax_rate)*Amount_invested*B10					

The probability that he doesn't have to pay any tax is easier. It is the probability the return on the stock is negative. This is 0.36, found in cell B9 with the formula shown to its right.

To answer the last question, note that the after-tax profit (when X is positive) is 67% of the before-tax profit, or $6700X$ dollars, and we want its 90th percentile. If this percentile is x, then we know that $P(6700X < x) = 0.90$, which is the same as $P(X < x/6700) = 0.90$. In words, we want the 90th percentile of the X distribution to be $x/6700$. From cell B11 of Figure 5.14, the 90th percentile is 22.94%, so the required value of x is $1,537.

Problems

Solutions for problems whose numbers appear within a colored box can be found in the Student Solution Files.

Level A

13. The grades on the midterm examination given in a large managerial statistics class are normally distributed with mean 75 and standard deviation 9. The instructor of this class wants to assign an A grade to the top 10% of the scores, a B grade to the next 10% of the scores, a C grade to the next 10% of the scores, a D grade to the next 10% of the scores, and an F grade to all scores below the 60th percentile of this distribution. For each possible letter grade, find the lowest acceptable score within the established range. For example, the lowest acceptable score for an A is the score at the 90th percentile of this normal distribution.

14. Suppose it is known that the distribution of purchase amounts by customers entering a popular retail store

is approximately normal with mean $75 and standard deviation $20.

a. What is the probability that a randomly selected customer spends less than $85 at this store?

b. What is the probability that a randomly selected customer spends between $65 and $85 at this store?

c. What is the probability that a randomly selected customer spends more than $45 at this store?

d. Find the dollar amount such that 75% of all customers spend no more than this amount.

e. Find the dollar amount such that 80% of all customers spend at least this amount.

f. Find two dollar amounts, equidistant from the mean, such that 90% of all customer purchases are between these values.

15. A machine used to regulate the amount of a certain chemical dispensed in the production of a particular type of cough syrup can be set so that it discharges an average of μ milliliters (ml) of the chemical in each bottle of cough syrup. The amount of chemical placed into each bottle of cough syrup is known to have a normal distribution with a standard deviation of 0.250 ml. If this machine discharges more than 2 ml of the chemical when preparing a given bottle of this cough syrup, the bottle is considered to be unacceptable by industry standards. Determine the setting for μ so that no more than 1% of the bottles of cough syrup prepared by this machine will be rejected.

16. Assume that the monthly sales for Toyota passenger cars follow a normal distribution with mean 5000 cars and standard deviation 1400 cars.

    a. There is a 1% chance that Toyota will sell more than what number of passenger cars during the next year? (You can assume that sales in different months are probabilistically independent.)

    b. What is the probability that Toyota will sell between 55,000 and 65,000 passenger cars during the next year?

17. An investor has invested in nine different investments. The dollar returns on the different investments are probabilistically independent, and each return follows a normal distribution with mean $50,000 and standard deviation $10,000.

    a. There is a 1% chance that the total return on the nine investments is less than what value?

    b. What is the probability that the investor's total return is between $400,000 and $520,000?

18. Suppose that the weight of a typical American male follows a normal distribution with $\mu = 180$ lb and $\sigma = 30$ lb. Also, suppose 91.92% of all American males weigh more than I weigh.

    a. What fraction of American males weigh more than 225 pounds?

    b. How much do I weigh?

    c. If I weighed 20 pounds more than I do, what percentile would I be in?

19. Assume that the length of a typical televised baseball game, including all the commercial timeouts, is normally distributed with mean 2.45 hours and standard deviation 0.37 hour. Consider a televised baseball game that begins at 2:00 in the afternoon. The next regularly scheduled broadcast is at 5:00.

    a. What is the probability that the game will cut into the next show, that is, go past 5:00?

    b. If the game is over before 4:30, another half-hour show can be inserted into the 4:30–5:00 slot. What is the probability of this occurring?

20. The amount of a soft drink that goes into a typical 12-ounce can varies from can to can. It is normally distributed with an adjustable mean μ and a fixed standard deviation of 0.05 ounce. (The adjustment is made to the filling machine.)

    a. If regulations require that cans have at least 11.9 ounces, what is the smallest mean μ that can be used so that at least 99.5% of all cans meet the regulation?

    b. If the mean setting from part a is used, what is the probability that a typical can has at least 12 ounces?

21. Suppose that the demands for a company's product in weeks 1, 2, and 3 are each normally distributed. The means are 50, 45, and 65. The standard deviations are 10, 5, and 15. Assume that these three demands are probabilistically independent.

    a. Suppose that the company currently has 180 units in stock, and it will not be receiving any more shipments from its supplier for at least three weeks. What is the probability that stock will run out during this three-week period?

    b. How many units should the company currently have in stock so that it can be 98% certain of not running out during this three-week period? Again, assume that it won't receive any more shipments during this period.

Level B

22. Matthew's Bakery prepares peanut butter cookies for sale every morning. It costs the bakery $0.50 to bake each peanut butter cookie, and each cookie is sold for $1.25. At the end of the day, leftover cookies are discounted and sold the following day at $0.40 per cookie. The daily demand (in dozens) for peanut butter cookies at this bakery is known to be normally distributed with mean 200 and standard deviation 60. The manager of Matthew's Bakery is trying to determine how many dozen peanut butter cookies to make each morning to maximize the product's contribution to bakery profits. Use simulation to find a very good, if not optimal, production plan.

23. The manufacturer of a particular bicycle model has the following costs associated with the management of this product's inventory. In particular, the company currently maintains an inventory of 1000 units of this bicycle model at the beginning of each year. If X units are demanded each year and X is less than 1000, the excess supply, $1000 - X$ units, must be stored until next year at a cost of $50 per unit. If X is greater than 1000 units, the excess demand, $X - 1000$ units, must be produced separately at an extra cost of $80 per unit. Assume that the annual demand (X) for this bicycle model is normally distributed with mean 1000 and standard deviation 75.

    a. Find the expected annual cost associated with managing potential shortages or surpluses of this product. (*Hint*: Use simulation to approximate the answer. An exact solution using probability arguments is beyond the level of this book.)

    b. Find two annual total cost levels, equidistant from the expected value found in part a, such that 95% of all costs associated with managing potential shortages or surpluses of this product are between these values. (Continue to use simulation.)

    c. Comment on this manufacturer's annual production policy for this bicycle model in light of your findings in part b.

24. It is widely known that many drivers on interstate highways in the United States do not observe the posted speed limit. Assume that the actual rates of speed driven by U.S. motorists are normally distributed with mean μ mph and standard deviation 5 mph. Given this information, answer each of the following independent questions. (*Hint*: Use Goal Seek in parts **a** and **b**, and use the Solver add-in with no objective in part **c**. Solver is usually used to optimize, but it can also be used to solve equations with multiple unknowns.)

   a. If 40% of all U.S. drivers are observed traveling at 65 mph or more, what is the mean μ?

   b. If 25% of all U.S. drivers are observed traveling at 50 mph or less, what is the mean μ?

   c. Suppose now that the mean μ and standard deviation σ of this distribution are both unknown. Furthermore, it is observed that 40% of all U.S. drivers travel at less than 55 mph and 10% of all U.S. drivers travel at more than 70 mph. What must μ and σ be?

25. The lifetime of a certain manufacturer's washing machine is normally distributed with mean 4 years. Only 15% of all these washing machines last at least 5 years. What is the standard deviation of the lifetime of a washing machine made by this manufacturer?

26. A fast-food restaurant sells hamburgers and chicken sandwiches. On a typical weekday the demand for hamburgers is normally distributed with mean 313 and standard deviation 57; the demand for chicken sandwiches is normally distributed with mean 93 and standard deviation 22.

   a. How many hamburgers must the restaurant stock to be 98% sure of not running out on a given day?

   b. Answer part **a** for chicken sandwiches.

   c. If the restaurant stocks 400 hamburgers and 150 chicken sandwiches for a given day, what is the probability that it will run out of hamburgers or chicken sandwiches (or both) that day? Assume that the demand for hamburgers and the demand for chicken sandwiches are probabilistically independent.

   d. Why is the independence assumption in part **c** probably not realistic? Using a more realistic assumption, do you think the probability requested in part **c** would increase or decrease?

27. Referring to the box plots introduced in Chapter 2, the sides of the "box" are at the first and third quartiles, and the difference between these (the length of the box) is called the interquartile range (IQR). Some implementations of box plots define a *mild* outlier as an observation that is between 1.5 and 3 IQRs from the box, and an *extreme* outlier as an observation that is more than 3 IQRs from the box.

   a. If the data are normally distributed, what percentage of values will be mild outliers? What percentage will be extreme outliers? Why don't the answers depend on the mean and/or standard deviation of the distribution?

   b. Check your answers in part **a** with simulation. Simulate a large number of normal random numbers (you can choose any mean and standard deviation), and count the number of mild and extreme outliers with appropriate formulas. Do these match, at least approximately, your answers to part **a**?

5-5 The Binomial Distribution

The normal distribution is undoubtedly the most important probability distribution in statistics. Not far behind, however, is the *binomial* distribution. The **binomial distribution** is a discrete distribution that can occur in two situations: (1) when sampling from a population with only two types of members (males and females, for example), and (2) when performing a sequence of identical experiments, each of which has only two possible outcomes.

Fundamental Insight

What the Binomial Distribution Describes

Unlike the normal distribution, which can describe many types of random phenomena, the binomial distribution is relevant for a very common and specific situation: the number of *successes* in a fixed number of *trials*, where the trials are probabilistically independent and the probability of success remains constant across trials. Whenever this situation occurs, the binomial distribution is the relevant distribution for the number of successes.

For the latter case, imagine any experiment that can be repeated many times under identical conditions. It is common to refer to each repetition of the experiment as a *trial*.

We assume that the outcomes of successive trials are probabilistically independent of one another and that each trial has only two possible outcomes. We label these two possibilities generically as *success* and *failure*. In any particular application the outcomes might be Democrat/Republican, defective/nondefective, went bankrupt/remained solvent, and so on. We label the probability of a success on each trial as p, and the probability of a failure as $1 - p$. We let n be the number of trials.

Consider a situation where there are n independent, identical trials, where the probability of a success on each trial is p and the probability of a failure is $1 - p$. Define X to be the random number of successes in the n trials. Then X has a **binomial distribution** with parameters n and p.

For example, the binomial distribution with parameters 100 and 0.3 is the distribution of the number of successes in 100 trials when the probability of success is 0.3 on each trial. A simple example that you can keep in mind throughout this section is the number of heads you would see if you flipped a coin n times. Assuming the coin is well balanced, the relevant distribution is binomial with parameters n and $p = 0.5$. This coin-flipping example is often used to illustrate the binomial distribution because of its simplicity, but you will see that the binomial distribution also applies to many important business situations.

To understand how the binomial distribution works, consider the coin-flipping example with $n = 3$. If X represents the number of heads in three flips of the coin, then the possible values of X are 0, 1, 2, and 3. You can find the probabilities of these values by considering the eight possible outcomes of the three flips: (T,T,T), (T,T,H), (T,H,T), (H,T,T), (T,H,H), (H,T,H), (H,H,T), and (H,H,H). Because of symmetry (the well-balanced property of the coin), each of these eight possible outcomes must have the same probability, so each must have probability 1/8. Next, note that one of the outcomes has $X = 0$, three outcomes have $X = 1$, three outcomes have $X = 2$, and one outcome has $X = 3$. Therefore, the probability distribution of X is

$$P(X = 0) = 1/8, \quad P(X = 1) = 3/8, \quad P(X = 2) = 3/8, \quad P(X = 3) = 1/8$$

This is a special case of the binomial distribution, with $n = 3$ and $p = 0.5$. In general, where n can be any positive integer and p can be any probability between 0 and 1, there is a rather complex formula for calculating $P(X = k)$ for any integer k from 0 to n. Instead of presenting this formula, we will discuss how to calculate binomial probabilities in Excel. You do this with the BINOM.DIST function. The general form of this function is

=BINOM.DIST(k,n,p,cum)

The middle two arguments are the number of trials n and the probability of success p on each trial. The first parameter k is an integer number of successes that you specify. The last parameter, *cum*, is either TRUE or FALSE. It is TRUE (or 1) if you want the probability of *less than or equal to* k successes, and it is FALSE (or 0) if you want the probability of *exactly* k successes. We illustrate typical binomial calculations, including those involving the BINOM.INV function for percentile calculations, in Example 5.8.

Excel Tip

Old Binomial Functions

Prior to Excel 2010, the binomial functions were BINOMDIST and CRITBINOM. They are exactly the same as the new BINOM.DIST and BINOM.INV functions. Microsoft kept these old functions for backward compatibility, so you can continue to use them if you prefer.

EXAMPLE

5.8 BINOMIAL CALCULATIONS IN EXCEL

Suppose that 100 identical batteries are inserted in identical flashlights. Each flashlight takes a single battery. After eight hours of continuous use, a given battery is still operating with probability 0.6 or has failed with probability 0.4. Let X be the number of successes in these 100 trials, where a success means that the battery is still functioning. Find the probabilities of the following events: (a) exactly 58 successes, (b) no more than 65 successes, (c) less than 70 successes, (d) at least 59 successes, (e) greater than 65 successes, (f) between 55 and 65 successes (inclusive), (g) exactly 40 failures, (h) at least 35 failures, and (i) less than 42 failures. Then find the 95th percentile of the distribution of X.

Objective

To use Excel's BINOM.DIST and BINOM.INV functions for calculating binomial probabilities and percentiles.

Solution

Figure 5.15 shows the solution to all of these problems. (See the file **Binomial Calculations Finished.xlsx**.) The probabilities requested in parts (a) through (f) all involve the number of successes X. The key to these is the wording of phrases such as "no more than," "greater than," and so on. In particular, you have to be careful to distinguish between probabilities such as $P(X < k)$ and $P(X \le k)$. The latter includes the possibility of having $X = k$ and the former does not.

Figure 5.15 Typical Binomial Calculations

◢	A	B	C	D	E	F	G	H
1	Binomial Probability Calculations							
2				Range names used:				
3	Number of trials	100		n	=$B$3			
4	Probability of success on each trial	0.6		p	=$B$4			
5								
6	Event	Probability						
7	Exactly 58 successes	0.0742		=BINOM.DIST(58,n,p,FALSE)				
8	No more than 65 successes	0.8697		=BINOM.DIST(65,n,p,TRUE)				
9	Less than 70 successes	0.9752		=BINOM.DIST(69,n,p,TRUE)				
10	At least 59 successes	0.6225		=1-BINOM.DIST(58,n,p,TRUE)				
11	Greater than 65 successes	0.1303		=1-BINOM.DIST(65,n,p,TRUE)				
12	Between 55 and 65 successes (inclusive)	0.7386		=BINOM.DIST(65,n,p,TRUE)-BINOM.DIST(54,n,p,TRUE)				
13								
14	Exactly 40 failures	0.0812		=BINOM.DIST(40,n,1-p,FALSE)				
15	At least 35 failures	0.8697		=1-BINOM.DIST(34,n,1-p,TRUE)				
16	Less than 42 failures	0.6225		=BINOM.DIST(41,n,1-p,TRUE)				
17								
18	Finding the 95th percentile (trial and error)							
19		Trial values	CumProb					
20		65	0.8697		=BINOM.DIST(A20,n,p,TRUE)			
21		66	0.9087		(Copy down)			
22		67	0.9385					
23		68	0.9602					
24		69	0.9752					
25		70	0.9852					
26								
27		68	0.95		=BINOM.INV(n,p,B27)			

With this in mind, the probabilities requested in (a) through (f) become:

a. $P(X = 58)$

b. $P(X \le 65)$

c. $P(X < 70) = P(X \le 69)$

d. $P(X \ge 59) = 1 - P(X < 59) = 1 - P(X \le 58)$

e. $P(X > 65) = 1 - P(X \le 65)$

f. $P(55 \le X \le 65) = P(X \le 65) - P(X < 55) = P(X \le 65) - P(X \le 54)$

Note how we have manipulated each of these so that it includes only terms of the form $P(X = k)$ or $P(X \le k)$ for appropriate values of k. These are the types of probabilities that can be handled directly by the BINOM.DIST function. The answers appear in the range B7:B12, and the corresponding formulas are shown (as labels) to their right.

The probabilities requested in (g) through (i) involve *failures* rather than successes. But because each trial results in either a success or a failure, the number of failures is also binomially distributed, with parameters n and $1 - p = 0.4$. So in rows 14 through 16 the requested probabilities are calculated in exactly the same way, except that $1-p$ is substituted for p in the third argument of the BINOM.DIST function.

Finally, to calculate the 95th percentile of the distribution of X, you can proceed by trial and error. For each value k from 65 to 70, the probability $P(X \leq k)$ is calculated in column B with the BINOM.DIST function. As you can see, there is no value k such that $P(X \leq k) = 0.95$ exactly. Specifically, $P(X \leq 67)$ is slightly less than 0.95 and $P(X \leq 68)$ is slightly greater than 0.95. Therefore, the meaning of the "95th percentile" is somewhat ambiguous. If you want the largest value k such that $P(X \leq k) \leq 0.95$, then this k is 67. If instead you want the smallest value k such that $P(X \leq k) \geq 0.95$, then this value is 68. The latter interpretation is the one usually accepted for binomial percentiles.

In fact, Excel has another built-in function, BINOM.INV for finding this value of k. This function is illustrated in row 27 of Figure 5.15 in cell A27. This BINOM.INV function returns 68, the smallest value k such that $P(X \leq k) \geq 0.95$ for this binomial distribution.

5-5a Mean and Standard Deviation of the Binomial Distribution

It can be shown that the mean and standard deviation of a binomial distribution with parameters n and p are given by the following equations.

Mean and Standard Deviation of the Binomial Distribution

$$E(X) = np \qquad (5.14)$$

$$\text{Stdev}(X) = \sqrt{np(1 - p)} \qquad (5.15)$$

The formula for the mean is quite intuitive. For example, if you observe 100 trials, each with probability of success 0.6, your best guess for the number of successes is $100(0.6) = 60$. The standard deviation is less obvious but still very useful. It indicates how far the actual number of successes is likely to deviate from the mean. In this case the standard deviation is $\sqrt{100(0.6)(0.4)} = 4.90$.

Fortunately, the empirical rules discussed in Chapter 2 also apply, at least approximately, to the binomial distribution. That is, there is about a 95% chance that the actual number of successes will be within two standard deviations of the mean, and there is almost no chance that the number of successes will be more than three standard deviations from the mean. So for this example, it is very likely that the number of successes will be in the range of approximately 50 to 70, and it is very unlikely that there will be fewer than 45 or more than 75 successes.

This reasoning is extremely useful. It provides a rough estimate of the number of successes you are likely to observe. Suppose 1000 parts are sampled randomly from an assembly line and, based on historical performance, the percentage of parts with some type of defect is about 5%. Translated into a binomial model, each of the 1000 parts, independently of the others, has some type of defect with probability 0.05. Would it be surprising to see, say, 75 parts with a defect? The mean is $1000(0.05) = 50$ and the standard deviation is $\sqrt{1000(0.05)(0.95)} = 6.89$. Therefore, the number of parts with defects is approximately 95% certain to be within $50 \pm 2(6.89)$, or approximately from 36 to 64. Because 75 is slightly beyond three standard deviations from the mean, it is highly unlikely that there would be 75 (or more) defective parts.

5-5b The Binomial Distribution in the Context of Sampling

The binomial distribution also applies to sampling from a population with two types of members. Let's say these two types are men and women, although in applications they might be Democrats and Republicans, users of our product and nonusers, and so on. We assume that the population has N members, of whom N_M are men and N_W are women (where $N_M + N_W = N$). If you sample n of these randomly, you are typically interested in the composition of the sample. You might expect the number of men in the sample to be binomially distributed with parameters n and $p = N_M/N$, the fraction of men in the population. However, this depends on how the sampling is performed.

If sampling is done **without replacement**, each member of the population can be sampled only once. That is, once a person is sampled, his or her name is struck from the list and cannot be sampled again. If sampling is done **with replacement**, then it is possible, although maybe not likely, to select a given member of the population more than once. Most real-world sampling is performed *without* replacement. There is no point in obtaining information from the same person more than once. However, *the binomial model applies only to sampling with replacement.* Because the composition of the remaining population keeps changing as the sampling progresses, the binomial model provides only an approximation if sampling is done without replacement. If there is no replacement, the value of p, the proportion of men in this case, does *not* stay constant, a requirement of the binomial model. The appropriate distribution for sampling without replacement is called the **hypergeometric** distribution, a distribution we will not discuss here.[5]

If n is small relative to N, however, the binomial distribution is a very good approximation to the hypergeometric distribution and can be used even if sampling is performed without replacement. A rule of thumb is that if n is no greater than 10% of N, that is, no more than 10% of the population is sampled, then the binomial model can be used safely. Of course, most national polls sample considerably less than 10% of the population. In fact, they often sample only about a thousand people from the hundreds of millions in the entire population. The bottom line is that in most real-world sampling contexts, the binomial model is perfectly adequate.

5-5c The Normal Approximation to the Binomial

If n is large and p is not too close to 0 or 1, the binomial distribution is bell-shaped and can be approximated well by the normal distribution.

If you graph the binomial probabilities, you will see an interesting phenomenon—namely, the graph begins to look symmetric and bell-shaped when n is fairly large and p is not too close to 0 or 1. An example is illustrated in Figure 5.16 with the parameters $n = 30$ and $p = 0.4$. Generally, if $np > 5$ and $n(1 - p) > 5$, the binomial distribution can be approximated well by a normal distribution with mean np and standard deviation $\sqrt{np(1 - p)}$. Before Excel functions were available, this fact was used to find approximate binomial probabilities from normal tables. Although this is no longer necessary, it is still useful to know that a binomial distribution resembles a normal distribution for large n.

Excel Tip

Continuity Correction

Because the normal distribution is continuous and the binomial distribution is discrete, the normal approximation to the binomial can be improved slightly with a continuity correction. If you want to approximate a binomial probability such as $P(36 \leq X \leq 45)$, expand the interval by 0.5 on each end in the normal approximation. That is, approximate with the normal probability $P(35.5 \leq X \leq 45.5)$. Similarly, approximate binomial $P(X \leq 45)$ with normal $P(X \leq 45.5)$, or binomial $P(X \geq 36)$ with normal $P(X \geq 35.5)$. Admittedly, this continuity correction is mostly of historical interest. With Excel's binomial functions, there is no need to resort to a normal approximation.

One practical consequence of the normal approximation to the binomial is that the empirical rules can be applied. That is, when the binomial distribution is approximately symmetric and bell-shaped, there is about a 68% chance that the number of successes will

---

5 Excel has a function **HYPGEOM.DIST** for sampling without replacement that works much like the BINOM. DIST function. You can look it up under the Statistical category of Excel functions.

Figure 5.16 Bell-shaped
Binomial Distribution

Relationship Between Normal and Binomial Distributions

If you look at a graph of a binomial distribution when n is fairly large and p is
not too close to 0 or 1, you will see that the distribution is bell-shaped. This is no
accident. It can be proven mathematically that the normal distribution provides a
very good approximation to the binomial under these conditions (n large, p not
too close to 0 or 1). One implication is that the empirical rules from Chapter 2
apply very well to binomial distributions, using the mean and standard deviation
in Equations (5.14) and (5.15). For example, there is about a 95% chance that the
number of successes will be within two standard deviations of the mean.

be within one standard deviation of the mean. Similarly, there is about a 95% chance that
the number of successes will be within two standard deviations of the mean, and the number of successes will almost surely be within three standard deviations of the mean. Here,
the mean is np and the standard deviation is $\sqrt{np(1 - p)}$.

5-5d Binomial Distribution Examples

The binomial distribution finds many applications in the business world and elsewhere.
We discuss a few typical applications in this section.

EXAMPLE

5.9 IS THIS MUTUAL FUND REALLY A WINNER?

An investment broker at the Michaels & Dodson Company claims that he has found a real winner. He has tracked a mutual
fund that has beaten a standard market index in 37 of the past 52 weeks. Could this be due to chance, or has he *really* found a
winner?

Objective

To determine the probability of a mutual fund outperforming a standard market index at least 37 out of 52 weeks.

Solution

The broker is no doubt tracking a lot of mutual funds, and he is probably reporting only the best of these. Therefore, we will check whether the best of *many* mutual funds could do at least this well purely by chance. To do this, we first specify what we mean by "purely by chance." This means that each week, a given fund has a fifty-fifty chance of beating the market index, independently of performance in other weeks. In other words, the number of weeks where a given fund outperforms the market index is binomially distributed with $n = 52$ and $p = 0.5$. With this in mind, cell B6 of Figure 5.17 shows the probability that a given fund does at least as well—beats the market index at least 37 out of 52 weeks—as the reported fund. (See the **Beating the Market Finished.xlsx** file.) Because $P(X \geq 37) = 1 - P(X \leq 36)$, the relevant formula is

=1–BINOM.DIST(B3–1,B4,0.5,TRUE)

Obviously, this probability, 0.00159, is quite small. A single fund isn't likely to beat the market this often purely by chance.

Figure 5.17 Binomial Calculations for Investment Example

	A	B	C	D	E	F	G
1	Beating the market						
2							
3	Weeks beating market index	37					
4	Total number of weeks	52					
5							
6	Probability of doing at least this well by chance	0.00159		=1-BINOM.DIST(B3-1,B4,0.5,TRUE)			
7							
8	Number of mutual funds	400					
9	Probability of at least one doing at least this well	0.471		=1-BINOM.DIST(0,B8,B6,TRUE)			
10							
11	Two-way data table of the probability in B9 as a function of values in B3 and B8						
12			Number of weeks beating the market index				
13		0.471	36	37	38	39	40
14	Number of mutual funds	200	0.542	0.273	0.113	0.040	0.013
15		300	0.690	0.380	0.164	0.060	0.019
16		400	0.790	0.471	0.213	0.079	0.025
17		500	0.858	0.549	0.258	0.097	0.031
18		600	0.904	0.616	0.301	0.116	0.038

However, the probability that the *best* of many mutual funds does at least this well is much larger. To calculate this probability, assume that 400 funds are being tracked, and let Y be the number of these that beat the market at least 37 of 52 weeks. Then Y is also binomially distributed, with parameters $n = 400$ and $p = 0.00159$, the probability calculated previously. To see whether *any* of the 400 funds beats the market at least 37 of 52 weeks, calculate $P(Y \geq 1) = 1 - P(Y = 0)$ in cell B9 with the formula

=1–BINOM.DIST(0,B8,B7,TRUE)

(Can you see why the fourth argument could be TRUE *or* FALSE?) The resulting probability is nearly 0.5—that is, there is nearly a fifty-fifty chance that at least one of 400 funds will do as well as the reported fund. This certainly casts doubt on the broker's claim that he has found a real winner. It is more likely that his star fund just got lucky and will perform no better than average in succeeding weeks.

To see how the probability in cell B9 depends on the level of success of the reported fund (the value in cell B3) and the number of mutual funds being tracked (in cell B8), a two-way data table has been created in the range B13:G18. (The formula in cell B13 is =B9, the row input cell is B3, and the column input cell is B8.) As you saw, beating the market 37 times out of 52 is no big deal with 400 funds, but beating it 40 times out of 52, even with 600 funds, is something worth reporting. The probability of this happening purely by chance is only 0.038, or less than 1 out of 25.

The next example requires a normal calculation to find a probability p, which is then used in a binomial calculation.

EXAMPLE

5.10 DAILY SALES AT A SUPERMARKET

Customers at a supermarket spend varying amounts. Historical data indicate that the amount spent per customer is normally distributed with mean $85 and standard deviation $30. If 500 customers shop in a given day, calculate the mean and standard deviation of the number who spend at least $100. Then calculate the probability that at least 30% of all customers spend at least $100.

Objective

To use the normal *and* binomial distributions to calculate the typical number of customers who spend at least $100 per day and the probability that at least 30% of all 500 daily customers spend at least $100.

Solution

Both questions involve the number of customers who spend at least $100. Because the amounts spent are normally distributed, the probability that a typical customer spends at least $100 is found with the NORM.DIST function. This probability, 0.309, appears in cell B7 of Figure 5.18. (See the file **Supermarket Spending Finished.xlsx**.) It is calculated with the formula

=1-NORM.DIST(100,B4,B5,TRUE)

This probability is then used as the parameter p in a binomial model. The mean and standard deviation of the number who spend at least $100 are calculated in cells B13 and B14 as np and $\sqrt{np(1-p)}$ using $n = 500$, the number of shoppers, and $p = 0.309$. The expected number who spend at least $100 is slightly greater than 154, and the standard deviation of this number is slightly greater than 10.

To answer the second question, note that 30% of 500 customers is 150 customers. Then the probability that at least 30% of the customers spend at least $100 is the probability that a binomially distributed random variable, with $n = 500$ and $p = 0.309$, is at least 150. This binomial probability, which turns out to be about $2/3$, is calculated in cell B16 with the formula

=1-BINOM.DIST(0.3*B10-1,B10,B7,TRUE)

Note that the first argument evaluates to 149. This is because the probability of *at least* 150 customers is one minus the probability of less than or equal to 149 customers.

Figure 5.18 Calculations for Supermarket Example

	A	B	C	D	E	F
1	**Supermarket spending**					
2						
3	Amount spent per customer (normally distributed)					
4	Mean	$85				
5	StDev	$30				
6						
7	Probability that a customer spends at least $100	0.309		=1-NORM.DIST(100,B4,B5,TRUE)		
8						
9						
10	Number of customers	500				
11						
12	Mean and stdev of number who spend at least $100					
13	Mean	154.27		=B10*B7		
14	StDev	10.33		=SQRT(B10*B7*(1-B7))		
15						
16	Probability at least 30% spend at least $100	0.676		=1-BINOM.DIST(0.3*B10-1,B10,B7,TRUE)		

EXAMPLE

5.11 OVERBOOKING BY AIRLINES

This example presents a simplified version of calculations used by airlines when they overbook flights. They realize that a certain percentage of ticketed passengers will cancel at the last minute. Therefore, to avoid empty seats, they sell more tickets than there are seats, hoping that just about the right number of passengers show up. We assume that the no-show rate is 10%. In binomial terms, we assume that each ticketed passenger, independently of the others, shows up with probability 0.90 and cancels with probability 0.10.

For a flight with 200 seats, the airline wants to see how sensitive various probabilities are to the number of tickets it issues. In particular, it wants to calculate (a) the probability that more than 205 passengers show up, (b) the probability that more than 200 passengers show up, (c) the probability that at least 195 seats are filled, and (d) the probability that at least 190 seats are filled. The first two of these are "bad" events from the airline's perspective; they mean that some customers will be bumped from the flight. The last two events are "good" in the sense that the airline wants most of the seats to be occupied.

Objective

To assess the benefits and drawbacks of airline overbooking.

Solution

To solve the airline's problem, we use the BINOM.DIST function and a data table. The solution appears in Figure 5.19. (See the file **Airline Overbooking Finished.xlsx**.) For any number of tickets issued in cell B6, the required probabilities are calculated in row 10. For example, the formulas in cells B10 and D10 are

=1-BINOM.DIST(205,NTickets,1-PNoShow,TRUE)

Figure 5.19 Binomial Calculations for Overbooking Example

	A	B	C	D	E
1	Airline overbooking			Range names used:	
2				NTickets	=$B$6
3	Number of seats	200		PNoShow	=$B$4
4	Probability of no-show	0.1			
5					
6	Number of tickets issued	215			
7					
8	Required probabilities				
9		More than 205 show up	More than 200 show up	At least 195 seats filled	At least 190 seats filled
10		0.001	0.050	0.421	0.820
11					
12	Data table showing sensitivity of probabilities to number of tickets issued				
13	Number of tickets issued	More than 205 show up	More than 200 show up	At least 195 seats filled	At least 190 seats filled
14		0.001	0.050	0.421	0.820
15	206	0.000	0.000	0.012	0.171
16	209	0.000	0.001	0.064	0.384
17	212	0.000	0.009	0.201	0.628
18	215	0.001	0.050	0.421	0.820
19	218	0.013	0.166	0.659	0.931
20	221	0.064	0.370	0.839	0.978
21	224	0.194	0.607	0.939	0.995
22	227	0.406	0.802	0.981	0.999
23	230	0.639	0.920	0.995	1.000
24	233	0.822	0.974	0.999	1.000

and

=1-BINOM.DIST(194,NTickets,1-PNoShow,TRUE)

Note that the condition "more than" requires a slightly different calculation from "at least." The probability of more than 205 is one minus the probability of less than or equal to 205, whereas the probability of at least 195 is one minus the probability of less than or equal to 194. Also, note that a passenger who shows up is called a success. Therefore, the third argument of each BINOM.DIST function is one minus the no-show probability.

To see how sensitive these probabilities are to the number of tickets issued, a one-way data table was created at the bottom of the spreadsheet. It is *one-way* because there is only one *input,* the number of tickets issued, even though four output probabilities are tabulated. (To create the data table, list several possible numbers of tickets issued along the side in column A and create links in row 14 to the probabilities in row 10. That is, enter the formula =B10 in cell B14 and copy it across row 14. Then form a data table using the range A14:E24, no row input cell, and column input cell B6.)

The results are as expected. As the airline issues more tickets, there is a larger chance of having to bump passengers from the flight, but there is also a larger chance of filling most seats. In reality, the airline has to make a trade-off between these two, taking its various costs and prices into account.

The following example concerns a real problem that occurs every time you watch election returns on TV. This problem is of particular interest in light of the highly unusual events that took place during election night television coverage of the U.S. presidential election in 2000, where the networks declared Al Gore an early winner in at least one state that he eventually lost. The basic question is how soon the networks can declare one of the candidates the winner, based on early voting returns. Our example is somewhat unrealistic because it ignores the possibility that early tabulations can be biased one way or the other. For example, the earliest reporting precincts might be known to be more heavily in favor of the Democrat than the population in general. Nevertheless, the example indicates, at least approximately, why the networks are able to make early conclusions based on such seemingly small amounts of data.

EXAMPLE

5.12 PROJECTING ELECTION WINNERS FROM EARLY RETURNS

We assume that there are N voters in the population, of whom N_R will vote for the Republican and N_D will vote for the Democrat. The eventual winner will be the Republican if $N_R > N_D$ and will be the Democrat otherwise, but we won't know which until all of the votes are tabulated. (To simplify the example, we assume there are only two candidates and that the election will *not* end in a tie.) Let's suppose that a small percentage of the votes have been counted and the Republican is currently ahead 540 to 460. On what basis can the networks declare the Republican the winner, especially if there are millions of voters in the population?

Objective

To use a binomial model to determine whether early returns reflect the eventual winner of an election between two candidates.

Solution

Let $n = 1000$ be the total number of votes that have been tabulated. If X is the number of Republican votes so far, we are given that $X = 540$. Now we pose the following question. If the Democrat were going to be the eventual winner, that is, $N_D > N_R$, and we randomly sampled 1000 voters from the population, how likely is it that at least 540 of these voters would be in favor of the Republican? If this is very *unlikely*, then the only reasonable conclusion is that the Democrat will *not* be the eventual winner. This is the reasoning the networks might use to declare the Republican the winner so early in the tabulation.

We use a binomial model to see how unlikely the event "at least 540 out of 1000" is, assuming that the Democrat will be the eventual winner. We need a value for p, the probability that a typical vote is for the Republican. This probability should be the proportion of voters in the entire population who favor the Republican. All we know is that this probability is less than 0.5, because we have *assumed* that the Democrat will eventually win. In Figure 5.20, we show how the probability of at least 540 out of 1000 varies with values of p less than, but close to, 0.5. (See the file **Election Returns Finished.xlsx**.)

Figure 5.20
Binomial
Calculations for
Voting Example

	A	B	C	D	E	F
1	**Election returns**					
2						
3	Population proportion for Republican	0.49				
4						
5	Votes tabulated so far	1000				
6	Votes for Republican so far	540				
7						
8	P(at least this many R votes) - binomial	0.0009		=1-BINOM.DIST(B6-1,B5,B3,TRUE)		
9						
10	Data table showing sensitivity of this probability to population proportion for Republican					
11	Population proportion for Republican	Probability				
12		0.0009				
13	0.490	0.0009				
14	0.492	0.0013				
15	0.494	0.0020				
16	0.496	0.0030				
17	0.498	0.0043				
18	0.499	0.0052				

We enter a trial value of 0.49 for p in cell B3 and then calculate the required probability in cell B9 with the formula

=1-BINOM.DIST(B6-1,B5,B3,TRUE)

Then we use this to create the data table at the bottom of the spreadsheet. This data table tabulates the probability of the given lead (at least 540 out of 1000) for various values of p less than 0.5. As shown in the last few rows, even if the eventual outcome were going to be a virtual tie—with the Democrat slightly ahead—there would still be *very* little chance of the Republican being at least 80 votes ahead so far. But because the Republican *is* currently ahead by 80 votes, the networks feel safe in declaring the Republican the winner. Admittedly, the probability model they use is more complex than our simple binomial model, but the idea is the same.

Problems

Solutions for problems whose numbers appear within a colored box can be found in the Student Solution Files.

Level A

28. Many vehicles used in space travel are constructed with redundant systems to protect flight crews and their valuable equipment. In other words, backup systems are included within many vehicle components so that if one or more systems fail, backup systems will assure the safe operation of the given component and thus the entire vehicle. For example, consider one particular component of the U.S. space shuttle that has n duplicated systems (i.e., one original system and $n - 1$ backup systems). Each of these systems functions, independently of the others, with probability 0.98. This shuttle component functions successfully provided that *at least* one of the n systems functions properly.

a. Find the probability that this shuttle component functions successfully if $n = 2$.

b. Find the probability that this shuttle component functions successfully if $n = 4$.

c. What is the minimum number n of duplicated systems that must be incorporated into this shuttle component to ensure at least a 0.9999 probability of successful operation?

29. Suppose that a popular hotel for vacationers in Orlando, Florida, has a total of 300 identical rooms. As many major airline companies do, this hotel has adopted an overbooking policy in an effort to maximize the usage of its available lodging capacity. Assume that each potential hotel customer holding a room reservation, independently of other customers, cancels the reservation or simply does not show up at the hotel on a given night with probability 0.15.

a. Find the largest number of room reservations that this hotel can book and still be at least 95% sure that everyone who shows up at the hotel will have a room on a given night.

b. Given that the hotel books the number of reservations found in part **a**, find the probability that at least 90% of the available rooms will be occupied on a given night.

c. Given that the hotel books the number of reservations found in part **a**, find the probability that at most 80% of the available rooms will be occupied on a given night.

d. How does your answer to part **a** change as the required assurance rate increases from 95% to 97%? How does your answer to part **a** change as the required assurance rate increases from 95% to 99%?

e. How does your answer to part **a** change as the cancellation rate varies between 5% and 25% (in increments of 5%)? Assume now that the required assurance rate remains at 95%.

30. A production process manufactures items with weights that are normally distributed with mean 15 pounds and standard deviation 0.1 pound. An item is considered to be defective if its weight is less than 14.8 pounds or greater than 15.2 pounds. Suppose that these items are currently produced in batches of 1000 units.

a. Find the probability that at most 5% of the items in a given batch will be defective.

b. Find the probability that at least 90% of the items in a given batch will be acceptable.

c. How many items would have to be produced in a batch to guarantee that a batch consists of no more than 1% defective items?

31. Past experience indicates that 30% of all individuals entering a certain store decide to make a purchase. Using (a) the binomial distribution and (b) the normal approximation to the binomial, find that probability that 10 or more of the 30 individuals entering the store in a given hour will decide to make a purchase. Compare the results obtained using the two different approaches. Under what conditions will the normal approximation to this binomial probability become even more accurate?

32. Suppose that the number of ounces of soda put into a soft-drink can is normally distributed with $\mu = 12.05$ ounces and $\sigma = 0.03$ ounce.

a. Legally, a can must contain at least 12 ounces of soda. What fraction of cans will contain at least 12 ounces of soda?

b. What fraction of cans will contain less than 11.9 ounces of soda?

c. What fraction of cans will contain between 12 and 12.08 ounces of soda?

d. One percent of all cans will weigh more than what value?

e. Ten percent of all cans will weigh less than what value?

f. The soft-drink company controls the mean weight in a can by setting a timer. For what mean should the timer be set so that only 1 in 1000 cans will be underweight?

g. Every day the company produces 10,000 cans. The government inspects 10 randomly chosen cans each day. If at least two are underweight, the company is fined $10,000. Given that $\mu = 12.05$ ounces and $\sigma = 0.03$ ounce, what is the probability that the company will be fined on a given day?

33. Suppose that 53% of all registered voters prefer presidential candidate Smith to presidential candidate Jones. (You can substitute the names of the most recent presidential candidates.)

a. In a random sample of 100 voters, what is the probability that the sample will indicate that Smith will win the election (that is, there will be more votes in the sample for Smith)?

b. In a random sample of 100 voters, what is the probability that the sample will indicate that Jones will win the election?

c. In a random sample of 100 voters, what is the probability that the sample will indicate a dead heat (fifty-fifty)?

d. In a random sample of 100 voters, what is the probability that between 40 and 60 (inclusive) voters will prefer Smith?

34. Assume that, on average, 95% of all ticket holders show up for a flight. If a plane seats 200 people, how many tickets should be sold to make the chance of an overbooked flight as close as possible to 5%?

35. Suppose that 55% of all people prefer Coke to Pepsi. We randomly choose 500 people and ask them if they prefer Coke to Pepsi. What is the probability that our survey will (erroneously) indicate that Pepsi is preferred by more people than Coke? Does this probability increase or decrease as we take larger and larger samples? Why?

36. Suppose that 4% of all tax returns are audited. In a group of n tax returns, consider the probability that at most two returns are audited. How large must n be before this probability is less than 0.01?

37. Suppose that the height of a typical American female is normally distributed with $\mu = 64$ inches and $\sigma = 4$ inches. We observe the height of 500 American females.

a. What is the probability that fewer than 35 of the 500 women will be less than 58 inches tall?

b. Let X be the number of the 500 women who are less than 58 inches tall. Find the mean and standard deviation of X.

Level B

38. Many firms utilize sampling plans to control the quality of manufactured items ready for shipment. To illustrate the use of a sampling plan, suppose that a particular company produces and ships electronic computer chips in lots, each lot consisting of 1000 chips. This company's sampling plan specifies that quality control personnel should randomly sample 50 chips from each lot and accept the lot for shipping if the number of defective chips is four or fewer. The lot will be rejected if the number of defective chips is five or more.

a. Find the probability of accepting a lot as a function of the actual fraction of defective chips. In particular, let the actual fraction of defective chips in a given lot equal any of 0.02, 0.04, 0.06, 0.08, 0.10, 0.12, 0.14, 0.16, 0.18. Then compute the lot acceptance probability for each of these lot defective fractions.

b. Construct a graph showing the probability of lot acceptance for each of the lot defective fractions, and interpret your graph.

c. Repeat parts **a** and **b** under a revised sampling plan that calls for accepting a given lot if the number of defective chips found in the random sample of 50 chips is *five* or fewer. Summarize any notable differences between the two graphs.

39. A standardized test consists entirely of multiple-choice questions, each with five possible choices. You want to ensure that a student who randomly guesses on each question will obtain an expected score of zero. How can you accomplish this?

40. In the current tax year, suppose that 5% of the millions of individual tax returns are fraudulent. That is, they contain errors that were purposely made to cheat the government.

a. Although these errors are often well concealed, let's suppose that a thorough IRS audit will uncover them. If a random 250 tax returns are audited, what is the probability that the IRS will uncover at least 15 fraudulent returns?

b. Answer the same question as in part **a**, but this time assume there is only a 90% chance that a given fraudulent return will be spotted as such if it is audited.

41. Suppose you work for a survey research company. In a typical survey, you mail questionnaires to 150 companies. Of course, some of these companies might decide not to respond. Assume that the nonresponse rate is 45%; that is, each company's probability of not responding, independently of the others, is 0.45.

a. If your company requires at least 90 responses for a valid survey, find the probability that it will get this

many. Use a data table to see how your answer varies as a function of the nonresponse rate (for a reasonable range of response rates surrounding 45%).

b. Suppose your company does this survey in two "waves." It mails the 150 questionnaires and waits a certain period for the responses. As before, assume that the nonresponse rate is 45%. However, after this initial period, your company follows up (by telephone, say) on the nonrespondents, asking them to please respond. Suppose that the nonresponse rate on this second wave is 70%; that is, each original nonrespondent now responds with probability 0.3, independently of the others. Your company now wants to find the probability of obtaining at least 110 responses total. It turns out that this is a difficult probability to calculate directly. So instead, approximate it with simulation.

42. Suppose you are sampling from a large population, and you ask the respondents whether they believe men should be allowed to take paid paternity leave from their jobs when they have a new child. Each person you sample is equally likely to be male or female. The population proportion of females who believe males should be granted paid paternity leave is 56%, and the population proportion of males who favor it is 48%. If you sample 200 people and count the number who believe males should be granted paternity leave, is this number binomially distributed? Explain why or why not. Would your answer change if you knew your sample was going to consist of exactly 100 males and 100 females?

43. A woman claims that she is a fortune-teller. Specifically, she claims that she can predict the direction of the change (up or down) in the Dow Jones Industrial Average for the next 10 days. For example, one possible prediction might be U, U, D, U, D, U, U, D, D, D. (You can assume that she makes all 10 predictions right now, although that does not affect your answer to the question.) Obviously, you are skeptical, thinking that she is just guessing, so you would be surprised if her predictions are accurate. Which would surprise you more: (1) she predicts at least 8 out of 10 correctly, or (2) she predicts at least 6 out of 10 correctly on each of four separate occasions? Answer by assuming that (1) she is really guessing and (2) each day the Dow is equally likely to go up or down.

5-6 The Poisson and Exponential Distributions

The final two distributions in this chapter are called the Poisson and exponential distributions. In most statistical applications, including those in the rest of this book, these distributions play a much less important role than the normal and binomial distributions. For this reason, we will not analyze them in much detail. However, in many applied management science models, the Poisson and exponential distributions are key distributions.

For example, much of the study of probabilistic inventory models, queueing models, and reliability models relies heavily on these two distributions.

5-6a The Poisson Distribution

The **Poisson distribution** is a discrete distribution. It usually applies to the *number* of events occurring within a specified period of time or space. Its possible values are all of the nonnegative integers: 0, 1, 2, and so on—there is no upper limit. Even though there is an infinite number of possible values, this causes no real problems because the probabilities of all sufficiently large values are essentially 0.

The Poisson distribution is characterized by a single parameter, usually labeled λ (Greek lambda), which must be positive. By adjusting the value of λ, we are able to produce different Poisson distributions, all of which have the same basic shape as in Figure 5.21. That is, they first increase and then decrease. It turns out that λ is easy to interpret. It is both the mean and the variance of the Poisson distribution. Therefore, the standard deviation is $\sqrt{\lambda}$.

Figure 5.21 Typical Poisson Distribution

Typical Examples of the Poisson Distribution

- A bank manager is studying the arrival pattern to the bank. The events are customer arrivals, the number of arrivals in an hour is Poisson distributed, and λ represents the expected number of arrivals per hour.
- An engineer is interested in the lifetime of a type of battery. A device that uses this type of battery is operated continuously. When the first battery fails, it is replaced by a second; when the second fails, it is replaced by a third, and so on. The events are battery failures, the number of failures that occur in a month is Poisson distributed, and λ represents the expected number of failures per month.
- A retailer is interested in the number of customers who order a particular product in a week. Then the events are customer orders for the product, the number of customer orders in a week is Poisson distributed, and λ is the expected number of orders per week.
- In a quality control setting, the Poisson distribution is often relevant for describing the number of defects in some unit of space. For example, when paint is applied to the body of a new car, any minor blemish is considered a defect. Then the number of defects on the hood, say, might be Poisson distributed. In this case, λ is the expected number of defects per hood.

These examples are representative of the many situations where the Poisson distribution has been applied. The parameter λ is often called a *rate*—arrivals per hour, failures per month, and so on. If the unit of time (or space) is changed, the rate must be modified accordingly. For example, if the number of arrivals to a bank in a single hour is Poisson distributed with rate $\lambda = 30$, then the number of arrivals in a half-hour period is Poisson distributed with rate $\lambda = 15$.

You can use Excel to calculate Poisson probabilities much as you did with binomial probabilities. The relevant function is the POISSON function. It takes the form

=POISSON.DIST *(k,λ,cum)*

The third argument *cum* works exactly as in the binomial case. If it is FALSE (or 0), the function returns $P(X = k)$; if it is TRUE (or 1), the function returns $P(X \leq k)$. As examples, if $\lambda = 5$ **=POISSON.DIST(7,5,FALSE)** returns the probability of exactly 7, **=POISSON.DIST(7,5,TRUE)** returns the probability of less than or equal to 7, and **= 1-POISSON.DIST(3,5,TRUE)** returns the probability of greater than 3.

The next example shows how a manager or consultant could use the Poisson distribution.

EXAMPLE

5.13 MANAGING TV INVENTORY AT KRIEGLAND

Kriegland is a department store that sells various brands of plasma screen TVs. One of the manager's biggest problems is to decide on an appropriate inventory policy for stocking TVs. He wants to have enough in stock so that customers receive their requests right away, but he does not want to tie up too much money in inventory that sits on the storeroom floor.

Most of the difficulty results from the unpredictability of customer demand. If this demand were constant and known, the manager could decide on an appropriate inventory policy fairly easily. But the demand varies widely from month to month in a random manner. All the manager knows is that the historical average demand per month is approximately 17. Therefore, he decides to call in a consultant. The consultant immediately suggests using a probability model. Specifically, she attempts to find the probability distribution of demand in a typical month. How might she proceed?

Objective

To model the probability distribution of monthly demand for plasma screen TVs with a particular Poisson distribution.

Solution

Let X be the demand in a typical month. The consultant knows that there are many possible values of X. For example, if historical records show that monthly demands have always been between 0 and 40, the consultant knows that almost all of the probability should be assigned to the values 0 through 40. However, she does not relish the thought of finding 41 probabilities, $P(X = 0)$ through $P(X = 40)$, that sum to 1 and reflect historical frequencies. Instead, she discovers from the manager that the histogram of demands from previous months is shaped much like the graph in Figure 5.21. That is, it rises to some peak and then falls.

Knowing that a Poisson distribution has this same basic shape, the consultant decides to model the monthly demand with a Poisson distribution. To choose a particular Poisson distribution, all she has to do is choose a value of λ, the mean demand per month. Because the historical average is approximately 17, she chooses $\lambda = 17$. Now she can test the Poisson model by calculating probabilities of various events and asking the manager whether these probabilities are reasonable approximations to reality.

For example, the Poisson probability that monthly demand is less than or equal to 20, $P(X \leq 20)$, is 0.805 [using the Excel function **POISSON.DIST(20,17,TRUE)**], and the probability that demand is between 10 and 15 inclusive, $P(10 \leq X \leq 15)$, is 0.345 [using **POISSON.DIST(15,17,TRUE)-POISSON.DIST(9,17,TRUE)**]. Figure 5.22 illustrates various probability calculations and shows the graph of the individual Poisson probabilities. (See the file **Poisson Demand Distribution Finished.xlsx**.)

Figure 5.22 Poisson Calculations for TV Example

▲	A	B	C	D	E	F	G	H	I	J
1	Poisson distribution for monthly demand									
2				Range name used:						
3	Mean monthly demand	17		Mean	=$B$3					
4										
5	Representative probability calculations									
6	Less than or equal to 20	0.805		=POISSON.DIST(20,Mean,TRUE)						
7	Between 10 and 15 (inclusive)	0.345		=POISSON.DIST(15,Mean,TRUE)-POISSON.DIST(9,Mean,TRUE)						
8										
9	Individual probabilities									
10	Value	Probability								
11	0	0.000		=POISSON.DIST(A11,Mean,FALSE)						
12	1	0.000		copy down						
13	2	0.000								
14	3	0.000								
15	4	0.000								
16	5	0.000								
17	6	0.001								
18	7	0.003								
19	8	0.007								
20	9	0.014								
21	10	0.023								
22	11	0.036								
23	12	0.050								
24	13	0.066								
25	14	0.080								
26	15	0.091								
27	16	0.096								
28	17	0.096								
29	18	0.091								
30	19	0.081								
31	20	0.069								

Poisson Distribution with Mean 17

If the manager believes that these probabilities and other similar probabilities are reasonable, then the *statistical* part of the consultant's job is finished. Otherwise, she must try a different Poisson distribution—a different value of λ—or perhaps a different type of distribution altogether.

5-6b The Exponential Distribution

Suppose that a bank manager is studying the pattern of customer arrivals at her branch location. As indicated previously in this section, the number of arrivals in an hour at a facility such as a bank is often well described by a Poisson distribution with parameter λ, where λ represents the expected number of arrivals per hour. An alternative way to view the uncertainty in the arrival process is to consider the *times* between customer arrivals. The most common probability distribution used to model these times, often called *interarrival times,* is the *exponential* distribution.

In general, the *continuous* random variable X has an **exponential distribution** with parameter λ (with λ > 0) if the density function of X has the form $f(x) = \lambda e^{-\lambda x}$ for $x > 0$. This density function has the shape shown in Figure 5.23. Because this density function decreases continuously from left to right, its most likely value is $x = 0$. Alternatively, if you collect many observations from an exponential distribution and draw a histogram of the observed values, you should expect it to resemble the smooth curve shown in Figure 5.23, with the tallest bars to the left. The mean and standard deviation of this distribution are easy to remember. They are both equal to the *reciprocal* of the parameter λ. For example, an exponential distribution with parameter λ = 0.1 has mean and standard deviation both equal to 10.

Figure 5.23 Exponential
Density Function

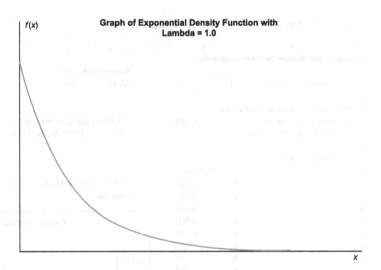

As with the normal distribution, you usually want probabilities to the left or right of a given value. For any exponential distribution, the probability to the left of a given value $x > 0$ can be calculated with Excel's EXPON.DIST function. This function takes the form

=EXPON.DIST(x,λ,TRUE)

For example, if $x = 0.5$ and $\lambda = 5$ (so that the mean equals $1/5 = 0.2$), the probability of being less than 0.5 can be found with the formula

=EXPON.DIST(0.5,5,TRUE)

This returns the probability 0.918. Of course, the probability of being greater than 0.5 is then $1 - 0.918 = 0.082$.

Returning to the bank manager's analysis of customer arrival data, when the times between arrivals are exponentially distributed, you sometimes hear that "arrivals occur according to a Poisson process." This is because there is a close relationship between the exponential distribution, which measures *times* between events such as arrivals, and the **Poisson distribution**, which counts the *number* of events in a certain length of time. The details of this relationship are beyond the level of this book, so we will not explore the topic further. But if you hear, for example, that customers arrive at a facility according to a Poisson process at the rate of six per hour, then the corresponding times between arrivals are exponentially distributed with mean 1/6 hour.

Problems

Solutions for problems whose numbers appear within a colored box can be found in the Student Solution Files.

Level A

44. The annual number of industrial accidents occurring in a particular manufacturing plant is known to follow a Poisson distribution with mean 12.
 a. What is the probability of observing exactly 12 accidents during the coming year?
 b. What is the probability of observing no more than 12 accidents during the coming year?
 c. What is the probability of observing at least 15 accidents during the coming year?
 d. What is the probability of observing between 10 and 15 accidents (inclusive) during the coming year?

 e. Find the smallest integer k such that we can be at least 99% sure that the annual number of accidents occurring will be less than k.

45. Suppose the number of baskets scored by the Indiana University basketball team in one minute follows a Poisson distribution with $\lambda = 1.5$. In a 10-minute span of time, what is the probability that Indiana University scores exactly 20 baskets; at most 20 baskets? (Use the fact that if the rate per minute is λ, then the rate in t minutes is λt.)

46. Suppose that the times between arrivals at a bank during the peak period of the day are exponentially distributed with a mean of 45 seconds. If you just observed an arrival, what is the probability that you will need to wait for more than a minute before observing the next arrival? What is the probability you will need to wait at least two minutes?

Level B

47. Consider a Poisson random variable X with parameter $\lambda = 2$.

a. Find the probability that X is within one standard deviation of its mean.

b. Find the probability that X is within two standard deviations of its mean.

c. Find the probability that X is within three standard deviations of its mean.

d. Do the empirical rules we learned previously seem to be applicable in working with the Poisson distribution where $\lambda = 2$? Explain why or why not.

e. Repeat parts **a** through **d** for the case of a Poisson random variable where $\lambda = 20$.

48. Based on historical data, the probability that a major league pitcher pitches a no-hitter in a game is about 1/1300.

a. Use the binomial distribution to determine the probability that in 650 games 0, 1, 2, or 3 no-hitters will be pitched. (Find the separate probabilities of these four events.)

b. Repeat part **a** using the Poisson approximation to the binomial. This approximation says that if n is large and p is small, a binomial distribution with parameters n and p is approximately the same as a Poisson distribution with $\lambda = np$.

5-7 Conclusion

We have covered a lot of ground in this chapter, and much of the material, especially that on the normal distribution, will be used in later chapters. The normal distribution is the cornerstone for much of statistical theory. As you will see in later chapters on statistical inference and regression, an assumption of normality is behind most of the procedures we use. Therefore, it is important for you to understand the properties of the normal distribution and how to work with it in Excel. The binomial, Poisson, and exponential distributions, although not used as frequently as the normal distribution in this book, are also extremely important. The examples we have discussed indicate how these distributions can be used in a variety of business situations. Finally, whenever a situation involves uncertainty, the rules of probability are relevant. Although we haven't discussed the mathematical details of probability in much depth, you should at least be familiar with the basic rules of probability discussed here.

Summary of Key Terms

TERM	EXPLANATION	EXCEL	PAGE	EQUATION
Random variable	Associates a numeric value with each possible outcome in a situation involving uncertainty		140	
Probability	A number between 0 and 1 that measures the likelihood that some event will occur		142	
Rule of complements	The probability of any event and the probability of its complement sum to 1	Basic formulas	142	5.1
Mutually exclusive events	Events where only one of them can occur		142	
Exhaustive events	Events where at least one of them must occur		143	
Addition rule for mutually exclusive events	The probability that at least one of a set of mutually exclusive events will occur is the sum of their probabilities	Basic formulas	143	5.2
Conditional probability formula	Updates the probability of an event, given the knowledge that another event has occurred	Basic formulas	144	5.3
Multiplication rule	Formula for the probability that two events both occur	Basic formulas	144	5.4
Probability tree	A graphical representation of how events occur through time, useful for calculating probabilities of multiple events		145	
Probabilistically independent events	Events where knowledge that one of them has occurred is of no value in assessing the probability that the other will occur		146	5.5

Key Terms (continued)

TERM	EXPLANATION	EXCEL	PAGE	EQUATION
Relative frequency	The proportion of times the event occurs out of the number of times a random experiment is performed		147	
Cumulative probability	"Less than or equal to" probabilities associated with a random variable		150	
Mean (or expected value) of a probability distribution	A measure of central tendency—the weighted sum of the possible values, weighted by their probabilities	Basic formulas	151	5.6
Variance of a probability distribution	A measure of variability: the weighted sum of the squared deviations of the possible values from the mean, weighted by the probabilities	Basic formulas	151	5.7, 5.9
Standard deviation of a probability distribution	A measure of variability: the square root of the variance	Basic formulas	151	5.8
Density function	Specifies the probability distribution of a continuous random variable		168	
Normal distribution	A continuous distribution with possible values ranging over the *entire* number line; its density function is a symmetric bell-shaped curve		169	5.1
Standardizing a normal random variable	Transforms any normal distribution with mean μ and standard deviation σ to the *standard* normal distribution with mean 0 and standard deviation 1		170	5.2
Normal calculations in Excel	Useful for finding probabilities and percentiles for non-standard and standard normal distributions	NORM.DIST, NORM.S.DIST, NORM.INV, NORM.S.INV	175	
Empirical rules for normal distribution	About 68% of the data fall within one standard deviation of the mean, about 95% of the data fall within two standard deviations of the mean, and almost all fall within three standard deviations of the mean		177	
Binomial distribution	The distribution of the number of successes in n independent, identical trials, where each trial has probability p of success	BINOM.DIST BINOM.INV	190	
Mean and standard deviation of a binomial distribution	The mean and standard deviation of a binomial distribution with parameters n and p are np and $\sqrt{np(1-p)}$, respectively		193	5.3, 5.4
Sampling without replacement	Sampling where no member of the population can be sampled more than once		194	
Hypergeometric distribution	Relevant when sampling without replacement, especially when the fraction of the population sampled is large	HYPGEOM.DIST		
Sampling with replacement	Sampling where any member of the population can be sampled more than once		194	
Normal approximation to the binomial distribution	If $np > 5$ and $n(1-p) > 5$, the binomial distribution can be approximated well by a normal distribution with mean np and standard deviation $\sqrt{np(1-p)}$		194	
Poisson distribution	A discrete probability distribution that often describes the number of events occurring within a specified period of time or space; mean and variance both equal the parameter λ	POISSON.DIST	207	
Exponential distribution	A continuous probability distribution useful for measuring *times* between events, such as customer arrivals to a service facility; mean and standard deviation both equal the reciprocal of the parameter	EXPON.DIST	210	

Problems

Conceptual Questions

C.1. Suppose that you want to find the probability that event *A* or event *B* will occur. If these two events are *not* mutually exclusive, explain how you would proceed.

C.2. "If two events are mutually exclusive, they must *not* be independent events." Is this statement true or false? Explain your choice.

C.3. Is the number of passengers who show up for a particular commercial airline flight a discrete or a continuous random variable? Is the time between flight arrivals at a major airport a discrete or a continuous random variable? Explain your answers.

C.4. Suppose that officials in the federal government are trying to determine the likelihood of a major smallpox epidemic in the United States within the next 12 months. Is this an example of an objective probability or a subjective probability? How might the officials assess this probability?

C.5. Consider the statement, "When there are a finite number of outcomes, then all probability is just a matter of counting. Specifically, if *n* of the outcomes are favorable to some event *E*, and there are *N* outcomes total, then the probability of *E* is *n/N*." Is this statement always true? Is it always false?

C.6. If there is uncertainty about some monetary outcome and you are concerned about return and risk, then all you need to see are the mean and standard deviation. The entire distribution provides no extra useful information. Do you agree or disagree? Provide an example to back up your argument.

C.7. Choose at least one uncertain quantity of interest to you. For example, you might choose the highest price of gas between now and the end of the year, the highest point the Dow Jones Industrial Average will reach between now and the end of the year, the number of majors Tiger Woods will win in his career, and so on. Using all of the information and insight you have, assess the probability distribution of this uncertain quantity. Is there one "right answer?"

C.8. Historically, the most popular measure of variability has been the standard deviation, the square root of the weighted sum of *squared* deviations from the mean, weighted by their probabilities. Suppose analysts had always used an alternative measure of variability, the weighted sum of the *absolute* deviations from the mean, again weighted by their probabilities. Do you think this would have made a big difference in the theory and practice of probability and statistics?

C.9. Suppose a person flips a coin, but before you can see the result, the person puts her hand over the coin. At this point, does it make sense to talk about the *probability* that the result is heads? Is this any different from the probability of heads *before* the coin was flipped?

C.10. Consider an event that will either occur or not. For example, the event might be that California will experience a major earthquake in the next five years. You let *p* be the probability that the event will occur. Does it make any sense to have a probability distribution of *p*? Why or why not? If so, what might this distribution look like? How would you interpret it?

C.11. Suppose a couple is planning to have two children. Let B1 be the event that the first child is a boy, and let B2 be the event that the second child is a boy. You and your friend get into an argument about whether B1 and B2 are *independent* events. You think they are independent and your friend thinks they aren't. Which of you is correct? How could you settle the argument?

C.12 For each of the following uncertain quantities, discuss whether it is reasonable to assume that the probability distribution of the quantity is normal. If the answer isn't obvious, discuss how you could discover whether a normal distribution is reasonable.
  a. The change in the Dow Jones Industrial Average between now and a year from now
  b. The length of time (in hours) a battery that is in continuous use lasts
  c. The time between two successive arrivals to a bank
  d. The time it takes a bank teller to service a random customer
  e. The length (in yards) of a typical drive on a par 5 by Phil Michelson
  f. The amount of snowfall (in inches) in a typical winter in Minneapolis
  g. The average height (in inches) of all boys in a randomly selected seventh-grade middle school class
  h. Your bonus from finishing a project, where your bonus is $1000 per day under the deadline if the project is completed before the deadline, your bonus is $500 if the project is completed right on the deadline, and your bonus is $0 if the project is completed after the deadline
  i. Your gain on a call option on a stock, where you gain nothing if the price of the stock a month from now is less than or equal to $50 and you gain $(P - 50)$ dollars if the price *P* a month from now is greater than $50

C.13 For each of the following uncertain quantities, discuss whether it is reasonable to assume that the probability distribution of the quantity is binomial. If you think it is, what are the parameters *n* and *p*? If you think it isn't, explain your reasoning.
  a. The number of wins the Boston Red Sox baseball team has next year in its 81 home games
  b. The number of free throws Kobe Bryant misses in his next 250 attempts
  c. The number of free throws it takes Kobe Bryant to achieve 100 successes

d. The number out of 1000 randomly selected customers in a supermarket who have a bill of at least $150

e. The number of trading days in a typical year where Microsoft's stock price increases

f. The number of spades you get in a 13-card hand from a well-shuffled 52-card deck

g. The number of adjacent 15-minute segments during a typical Friday where at least 10 customers enter a McDonald's restaurant

h. The number of pages in a 500-page book with at least one misprint on the page

C.14 One disadvantage of a normal distribution is that there is always some probability that a quantity is negative, even when this makes no sense for the uncertain quantity. For example, the time a light bulb lasts cannot be negative. In any particular situation, how would you decide whether you could ignore this disadvantage for all practical purposes?

C.15 For real applications, the normal distribution has two potential drawbacks: (1) it can be negative, and (2) it isn't symmetric. Choose some continuous random numeric outcomes of interest to you. Are either potential drawbacks really drawbacks for your random outcomes? If so, which is the more serious drawback?

C.16 Many basketball players and fans believe strongly in the "hot hand." That is, they believe that players tend to shoot in streaks, either makes or misses. If this is the case, why does the binomial distribution not apply, at least not exactly, to the number of makes in a given number of shots? Which assumption of the binomial model is violated, the independence of successive shots or the constant probability of success on each shot? Or can you tell?

Solutions for problems whose numbers appear within a colored box can be found in the Student Solution Files.

Level A

49. A business manager who needs to make many phone calls has estimated that when she calls a client, the probability that she will reach the client right away is 60%. If she does not reach the client on the first call, the probability that she will reach the client with a subsequent call in the next hour is 20%.

a. Find the probability that the manager reaches her client in two or fewer calls.

b. Find the probability that the manager reaches her client on the second call but not on the first call.

c. Find the probability that the manager is unsuccessful on two consecutive calls.

50. Suppose that a marketing research firm sends questionnaires to two different companies. Based on historical evidence, the marketing research firm believes that each company, independently of the other, will return the questionnaire with probability 0.40.

a. What is the probability that *both* questionnaires are returned?

b. What is the probability that *neither* of the questionnaires is returned?

c. Now, suppose that this marketing research firm sends questionnaires to *ten* different companies. Assuming that each company, independently of the others, returns its completed questionnaire with probability 0.40, how do your answers to parts **a** and **b** change?

51. Based on past sales experience, an appliance store stocks five window air conditioner units for the coming week. No orders for additional air conditioners will be made until next week. The weekly consumer demand for this type of appliance has the probability distribution given in the file **P05_51.xlsx**.

a. Let X be the number of window air conditioner units left at the end of the week (if any), and let Y be the number of special stockout orders required (if any), assuming that a special stockout order is required each time there is a demand and no unit is available in stock. Find the probability distributions of X and Y.

b. Find the expected value of X and the expected value of Y.

c. Assume that this appliance store makes a $60 profit on each air conditioner sold from the weekly available stock, but the store loses $20 for each unit sold on a special stockout order basis. Let Z be the profit that the store earns in the coming week from the sale of window air conditioners. Find the probability distribution of Z.

d. Find the expected value of Z.

52. A roulette wheel contains the numbers 0, 00, and 1 to 36. If you bet $1 on a single number coming up, you earn $35 if the number comes up and lose $1 otherwise. Find the mean and standard deviation of your winnings on a single bet. Then find the mean and standard deviation of your net winnings if you make 100 bets. You can assume (realistically) that the results of the 100 spins are independent. Finally, provide an interval such that you are 95% sure your net winnings from 100 bets will be inside this interval.

53. You are involved in a risky business venture where three outcomes are possible: (1) you will lose not only your initial investment ($5000) but an additional $3000; (2) you will just make back your initial investment (for a net gain of $0); or (3) you will make back your initial investment plus an extra $10,000.

The probability of (1) is half as large as the probability of (2), and the probability of (3) is one-third as large as the probability of (2).

a. Find the individual probabilities of (1), (2), and (3). (They should sum to 1.)

b. Find the expected value and standard deviation of your net gain (or loss) from this venture.

54. Suppose the annual return on XYZ stock follows a normal distribution with mean 12% and standard deviation 30%.

a. What is the probability that XYZ's value will decrease during a year?

b. What is the probability that the return on XYZ during a year will be at least 20%?

c. What is the probability that the return on XYZ during a year will be between −6% and 9%?

d. There is a 5% chance that the return on XYZ during a year will be greater than what value?

e. There is a 1% chance that the return on XYZ during a year will be less than what value?

f. There is a 95% chance that the return on XYZ during a year will be between which two values (equidistant from the mean)?

55. A family is considering a move from a midwestern city to a city in California. The distribution of housing costs where the family currently lives is normal, with mean $105,000 and standard deviation $18,200. The distribution of housing costs in the California city is normal with mean $235,000 and standard deviation $30,400. The family's current house is valued at $110,000.

a. What percentage of houses in the family's current city cost less than theirs?

b. If the family buys a $200,000 house in the new city, what percentage of houses there will cost less than theirs?

c. What price house will the family need to buy to be in the same percentile (of housing costs) in the new city as they are in the current city?

56. The number of traffic fatalities in a typical month in a given state has a normal distribution with mean 125 and standard deviation 31.

a. If a person in the highway department claims that there will be at least m fatalities in the next month with probability 0.95, what value of m makes this claim true?

b. If the claim is that there will be no more than n fatalities in the next month with probability 0.98, what value of n makes this claim true?

57. It can be shown that a sum of normally distributed random variables is also normally distributed. Do *all* functions of normal random variables lead to normal random variables? Consider the following. SuperDrugs is a chain of drugstores with three similar-size stores in a given city. The sales in a given week for any of these stores is normally distributed with mean $15,000 and standard deviation $3000. At the end of each week, the sales figure for the store with the largest sales among the three stores is recorded. Is this maximum value normally distributed? To answer this question, simulate a weekly sales figure at each of the three stores and calculate the maximum. Then replicate this maximum 500 times and create a histogram of the 500 maximum values. Does it appear to be normally shaped? Whatever this distribution looks like, use your simulated values to estimate the mean and standard deviation of the maximum.

58. In the financial world, there are many types of complex instruments called derivatives that *derive* their value from the value of an underlying asset. Consider the following simple derivative. A stock's current price is $80 per share. You purchase a derivative whose value to you becomes known a month from now. Specifically, let P be the price of the stock in a month. If P is between $75 and $85, the derivative is worth nothing to you. If P is less than $75, the derivative results in a loss of 100*(75 − P) dollars to you. (The factor of 100 is because many derivatives involve 100 shares.) If P is greater than $85, the derivative results in a gain of 100*(P − 85) dollars to you. Assume that the distribution of the *change* in the stock price from now to a month from now is normally distributed with mean $1 and standard deviation $8. Let P (big loss) be the probability that you lose at least $1000 (that is, the price falls below $65), and let P (big gain) be the probability that you gain at least $1000 (that is, the price rises above $95). Find these two probabilities. How do they compare to one another?

Level B

59. Equation (5.7) for variance indicates exactly what variance is: the weighted average of squared deviations from the mean, weighted by the probabilities. However, the computing formula for variance, Equation (5.9), is more convenient for spreadsheet calculations. Show algebraically that the two formulas are equivalent.

60. The basic game of craps works as follows. You throw two dice. If the sum of the two faces showing up is 7 or 11, you win and the game is over. If the sum is 2, 3, or 12, you lose and the game is over. If the sum is anything else (4, 5, 6, 8, 9, or 10), that value becomes your "point." You then keep throwing the dice until the sum matches your point or equals 7. If your point occurs first, you win and the game is over. If 7 occurs first, you lose and the game is over. What is the probability that you win the game?

61. Consider an individual selected at random from a sample of 750 married women (see the data in the file **P05_61.xlsx**) in answering each of the following questions.

a. What is the probability that this woman does not work outside the home, given that she has at least one child?

b. What is the probability that this woman has no children, given that she works part time?

c. What is the probability that this woman has at least two children, given that she does not work full time?

62. Suppose that 8% of all managers in a given company are African American, 13% are women, and 17% have earned an MBA degree from a top-10 graduate business school. Let A, B, and C be, respectively, the events that a randomly selected individual from this population is African American, is a woman, and has earned an MBA from a top-10 graduate business school.

a. Do you believe that A, B, and C are independent events? Explain why or why not.

b. Assuming that *A*, *B*, and *C are* independent events, find the probability that a randomly selected manager from this company is a white male and has earned an MBA degree from a top-10 graduate business school.

c. If *A*, *B*, and *C* are *not* independent events, can you calculate the probability requested in part **b** from the information given? What further information would you need?

63. Two gamblers play a version of roulette with a wheel as shown in the file **P05_63.xlsx**. Each gambler places four bets, but their strategies are different, as explained below. For each gambler, use the rules of probability to find the distribution of their net winnings after four bets. Then find the mean and standard deviation of their net winnings. The file gets you started.

a. Player 1 always bets on red. On each bet, he either wins or loses what he bets. His first bet is for $10. From then on, he bets $10 following a win, and he doubles his bet after a loss. (This is called a martingale strategy and is used frequently at casinos.) For example, if he spins red, red, not red, and not red, his bets are for $10, $10, $10, and $20, and he has a net loss of $10. Or if he spins not red, not red, not red, and red, then his bets are for $10, $20, $40, and $80, and he has a net gain of $10.

b. Player 2 always bets on black and green. On each bet, he places $10 on black and $2 on green. If red occurs, he loses all $12. If black occurs, he wins a net $8 ($10 gain on black, $2 loss on green). If green occurs, he wins a net $50 ($10 loss on black, $60 gain on green).

64. Suppose the New York Yankees and Philadelphia Phillies (two Major League Baseball teams) are playing a best-of-three series. The first team to win two games is the winner of the series, and the series ends as soon as one team has won two games. The first game is played in New York, the second game is in Philadelphia, and if necessary the third game is in New York. The probability that the Yankees win a game in their home park is 0.55. The probability that the Phillies win a game in their home park is 0.53. You can assume that the outcomes of the games are probabilistically independent.

a. Find the probability that the Yankees win the series.

b. Suppose you are a Yankees fan, so you place a bet on each game played where you win $100 if the Yankees win the game and you lose $105 if the Yankees lose the game. Find the distribution of your net winnings. Then find the mean and standard deviation of this distribution. Is this betting strategy favorable to you?

c. Repeat part **a**, but assume that the games are played in Philadelphia, then New York, then Philadelphia. How much does this "home field advantage" help the Phillies?

d. Repeat part **a**, but now assume that the series is a best-of-five series, where the first team that wins three games wins the series. Assume that games alternate between New York and Philadelphia, with the first game in New York.

65. Have you ever watched the odds at a horse race? You might hear that the odds against a given horse winning are 9 to 1, meaning that the horse has probability $1/(1 + 9) = 1/10$ of winning. However, these odds, after being converted to probabilities, typically sum to something greater than one. Why is this? Suppose you place a bet of $10 on this horse. It seems that it is a fair bet if you lose your $10 if the horse loses, but you win $90 if the horse wins. However, argue why this isn't really fair to you, that is, argue why your expected winnings are negative.

66. When you sum 30 or more independent random variables, the sum of the random variables will usually be approximately normally distributed, even if each individual random variable is not normally distributed. Use this fact to estimate the probability that a casino will be behind after 90,000 roulette bets, given that it wins $1 or loses $35 on each bet with probabilities 37/38 and 1/38.

67. Many companies use sampling to determine whether a batch should be accepted. An (n, c) sampling plan consists of inspecting n randomly chosen items from a batch and accepting the batch if c or fewer sampled items are defective. Suppose a company uses a $(100, 5)$ sampling plan to determine whether a batch of 10,000 computer chips is acceptable.

a. The "producer's risk" of a sampling plan is the probability that an acceptable batch will be rejected by the sampling plan. Suppose the customer considers a batch with 3% defectives acceptable. What is the producer's risk for this sampling plan?

b. The "consumer's risk" of a sampling plan is the probability that an unacceptable batch will be accepted by the sampling plan. Our customer says that a batch with 9% defectives is unacceptable. What is the consumer's risk for this sampling plan?

68. Suppose that if a presidential election were held today, 53% of all voters would vote for candidate Smith over candidate Jones. (You can substitute the names of the most recent presidential candidates.) This problem shows that even if there are 100 million voters, a sample of several thousand is enough to determine the outcome, even in a fairly close election.

a. If 1500 voters are sampled randomly, what is the probability that the sample will indicate (correctly) that Smith is preferred to Jones?

b. If 6000 voters are sampled randomly, what is the probability that the sample will indicate (correctly) that Smith is preferred to Jones?

69. A company assembles a large part by joining two smaller parts together. Assume that the smaller parts are normally distributed with a mean length of 1 inch and a standard deviation of 0.01 inch.
    a. What fraction of the larger parts are longer than 2.05 inches?
    b. What fraction of the larger parts are between 1.96 inches and 2.02 inches long?

70. (Suggested by Sam Kaufmann, Indiana University MBA, who has run Harrah's Lake Tahoe Casino.) A high roller has come to the casino to play 300 games of craps. For each game of craps played there is a 0.493 probability that the high roller will win $1 and a 0.507 probability that the high roller will lose $1. After 300 games of craps, what is the probability that the casino will be behind more than $10?

71. (Suggested by Sam Kaufmann, Indiana University MBA, who has run Harrah's Lake Tahoe Casino.) A high roller comes to the casino intending to play 500 hands of blackjack for $1 a hand. On each hand, the high roller will win $1 with probability 0.48 and lose $1 with probability 0.52. After the 500 hands, what is the probability that the casino has lost more than $40?

72. The weekly demand for TVs at Lowland Appliance is normally distributed with mean 400 and standard deviation 100. Each time an order for TVs is placed, it arrives exactly four weeks later. That is, TV orders have a four-week lead time. Lowland doesn't want to run out of TVs during any more than 1% of all lead times. How low should Lowland let its TV inventory drop before it places an order for more TVs? (Hint: How many standard deviations above the mean lead-time demand must the reorder point be for there to be a 1% chance of a stockout during the lead time?)

73. An elevator rail is assumed to meet specifications if its diameter is between 0.98 and 1.01 inches. Each year a company produces 100,000 elevator rails. For a cost of $10/\sigma^2$ per year the company can rent a machine that produces elevator rails whose diameters have a standard deviation of σ. (The idea is that the company must pay more for a smaller variance.) Each such machine will produce rails having a mean diameter of one inch. Any rail that does not meet specifications must be reworked at a cost of $12. Assume that the diameter of an elevator rail follows a normal distribution.
    a. What standard deviation (within 0.001 inch) minimizes the annual cost of producing elevator rails? You do not need to try standard deviations in excess of 0.02 inch.
    b. For your answer in part a, one elevator rail in 1000 will be at least how many inches in diameter?

74. What caused the crash of TWA Flight 800 in 1996? Physics professors Hailey and Helfand of Columbia University believe there is a reasonable possibility that a meteor hit Flight 800. They reason as follows. On a given day, 3000 meteors of a size large enough to destroy an airplane hit the earth's atmosphere. Approximately 50,000 flights per day, averaging two hours in length, have been flown from 1950 to 1996. This means that at any given point in time, planes in flight cover approximately two-billionths of the world's atmosphere. Determine the probability that at least one plane in the last 47 years has been downed by a meteor. (Hint: Use the Poisson approximation to the binomial. This approximation says that if n is large and p is small, a binomial distribution with parameters n and p is approximately Poisson distributed with $\lambda = np$.)

75. In the decade 1982 through 1991, 10 employees working at the Amoco Company chemical research center were stricken with brain tumors. The average employment at the center was 2000 employees. Nationwide, the average incidence of brain tumors in a single year is 20 per 100,000 people. If the incidence of brain tumors at the Amoco chemical research center were the same as the nationwide incidence, what is the probability that at least 10 brain tumors would have been observed among Amoco workers during the decade 1982 through 1991? What do you conclude from your analysis? (Source: AP wire service report, March 12, 1994)

76. Claims arrive at random times to an insurance company. The daily amount of claims is normally distributed with mean $1570 and standard deviation $450. Total claims on different days each have this distribution, and they are probabilistically independent of one another.
    a. Find the probability that the amount of total claims over a period of 100 days is at least $150,000.
    b. If the company receives premiums totaling $165,000, find the probability that the company will net at least $10,000 for the 100-day period.

77. Your company is running an audit on Sleaze Company. Because Sleaze has a bad habit of overcharging its customers, the focus of your audit is on checking whether the billing amounts on its invoices are correct. Assume that each invoice is for too high an amount with probability 0.06 and for too low an amount with probability 0.01 (so that the probability of a correct billing is 0.93). Also, assume that the outcome for any invoice is probabilistically independent of the outcomes for other invoices.
    a. If you randomly sample 200 of Sleaze's invoices, what is the probability that you will find at least 15 invoices that overcharge the customer? What is the probability you won't find any that undercharge the customer?
    b. Find an integer k such that the probability is at least 0.99 that you will find at least k invoices that overcharge the customer. (Hint: Use trial and error with the BINOM.DIST function to find k.)

78. Continuing the previous problem, suppose that when Sleaze overcharges a customer, the distribution of the amount overcharged (expressed as a percentage of the correct billing amount) is normally distributed with mean 15% and standard deviation 4%.
  a. What percentage of overbilled customers are charged at least 10% more than they should pay?
  b. What percentage of *all* customers are charged at least 10% more than they should pay?
  c. If your auditing company samples 200 randomly chosen invoices, what is the probability that it will find at least five where the customer was overcharged by at least 10%?

79. As any credit-granting agency knows, there are always some customers who default on credit charges. Typically, customers are grouped into relatively homogeneous categories, so that customers within any category have approximately the same chance of defaulting on their credit charges. Here we will look at one particular group of customers. We assume each of these customers has (1) probability 0.07 of defaulting on his or her current credit charges, and (2) total credit charges that are normally distributed with mean $350 and standard deviation $100. We also assume that if a customer defaults, 20% of his or her charges can be recovered. The other 80% are written off as bad debt.
  a. What is the probability that a typical customer in this group will default and produce a write-off of more than $250 in bad debt?
  b. If there are 500 customers in this group, what are the mean and standard deviation of the number of customers who will meet the description in part **a**?
  c. Again assuming there are 500 customers in this group, what is the probability that at least 25 of them will meet the description in part **a**?
  d. Suppose now that nothing is recovered from a default—the whole amount is written off as bad debt. Show how to simulate the total amount of bad debt from 500 customers in just two cells, one with a binomial calculation, the other with a normal calculation.

80. The Excel functions discussed in this chapter are useful for solving a lot of probability problems, but there are other problems that, even though they are similar to normal or binomial problems, cannot be solved with these functions. In cases like this, simulation can often be used. Here are a couple of such problems for you to simulate. For each example, simulate 500 replications of the experiment.
  a. You observe a sequence of parts from a manufacturing line. These parts use a component that is supplied by one of two suppliers. Each part made with a component from supplier 1 works properly with probability 0.95, and each part made with a component from supplier 2 works properly with probability 0.98. Assuming that 100 of these parts are made, 60 from supplier 1 and 40 from supplier 2, you want the probability that at least 97 of them work properly.
  b. Here we look at a more generic example such as coin flipping. There is a sequence of trials where each trial is a success with probability *p* and a failure with probability $1 - p$. A run is a sequence of consecutive successes or failures. For most of us, intuition says that there should not be long runs. Test this by finding the probability that there is at least one run of length at least six in a sequence of 15 trials. (The run could be of 0s or 1s.) You can use any value of *p* you like—or try different values of *p*.

81. In the game of soccer, players are sometimes awarded a penalty kick. The player who kicks places the ball 12 yards from the 24-foot-wide goal and attempts to kick it past the goalie into the net. (The goalie is the only defender.) The question is where the player should aim. Make the following assumptions. (1) The player's kick is off target from where he aims, left or right, by a normally distributed amount with mean 0 and some standard deviation. (2) The goalie typically guesses left or right and dives in that direction at the moment the player kicks. If the goalie guesses wrong, he won't block the kick, but if he guesses correctly, he will be able to block a kick that would have gone into the net as long as the kick is within a distance *d* from the middle of the goal. The goalie is equally likely to guess left or right. (3) The player never misses high, but he can miss to the right of the goal (if he aims to the right) or to the left (if he aims to the left). For reasonable values of the standard deviation and *d*, find the probability that the player makes a goal if he aims at a point *t* feet inside the goal. (By symmetry, you can assume he aims to the right, although the goalie doesn't know this.) What value of *t* seems to maximize the probability of making a goal?

82. In the 2012 Major League Baseball season, the Baltimore Orioles were ahead after the 7th inning in 74 games, and they won all 74 games. Use an appropriate model to explore how unusual such a streak is. Would you place it in the same category as the famous 56-game hitting streak (at least one hit per game) by Joe DiMaggio in 1941? Discuss the differences, including those that are caused by pressure.

CASE 5.1 Simpson's Paradox

The results we obtain with conditional probabilities can be quite counterintuitive, even paradoxical. This case is similar to one described in an article by Blyth (1972), and is usually referred to as Simpson's paradox. [Two other examples of Simpson's paradox are described in articles by Westbrooke (1998) and Appleton et al. (1996).] Essentially, Simpson's paradox says that even if one treatment has a better effect than another on *each* of two separate subpopulations, it can have a *worse* effect on the population as a whole.

Suppose that the population is the set of managers in a large company. We categorize the managers as those with an MBA degree (the Bs) and those without an MBA degree (the $\bar{B}$s). These categories are the two "treatment" groups. We also categorize the managers as those who were hired directly out of school by this company (the Cs) and those who worked with another company first (the $\bar{C}$s). These two categories form the two "subpopulations." Finally, we use as a measure of effectiveness those managers who have been promoted within the past year (the As).

Assume the following conditional probabilities are given:

$$P(A|B \text{ and } C) = 0.10, P(A|\bar{B} \text{ and } C) = 0.05 \qquad \textbf{(5.16)}$$

$$P(A|B \text{ and } \bar{C}) = 0.35, P(A|\bar{B} \text{ and } \bar{C}) = 0.20 \qquad \textbf{(5.17)}$$

$$P(C|B) = 0.90, P(C|\bar{B}) = 0.30 \qquad \textbf{(5.18)}$$

Each of these can be interpreted as a proportion. For example, the probability $P(A|B \text{ and } C)$ implies that 10% of all

managers who have an MBA degree and were hired by the company directly out of school were promoted last year. Similar explanations hold for the other probabilities.

Joan Seymour, the head of personnel at this company, is trying to understand these figures. From the probabilities in Equation (5.16), she sees that among the subpopulation of workers hired directly out of school, those with an MBA degree are twice as likely to be promoted as those without an MBA degree. Similarly, from the probabilities in Equation (5.17), she sees that among the subpopulation of workers hired after working with another company, those with an MBA degree are *almost* twice as likely to be promoted as those without an MBA degree. The information provided by the probabilities in Equation (5.18) is somewhat different. From these, she sees that employees with MBA degrees are three times as likely as those without MBA degrees to have been hired directly out of school.

Joan can hardly believe it when a whiz-kid analyst uses these probabilities to show—correctly—that

$$P(A|B) = 0.125, P(A|\bar{B}) = 0.155 \qquad \textbf{(5.19)}$$

In words, those employees *without* MBA degrees are more likely to be promoted than those with MBA degrees. This appears to go directly against the evidence in Equations (5.16) and (5.17), both of which imply that MBAs have an advantage in being promoted. Can you derive the probabilities in Equation (5.19)? Can you shed any light on this "paradox"?

CASE 5.2 EuroWatch Company

EuroWatch Company assembles expensive wristwatches and then sells them to retailers throughout Europe. The watches are assembled at a plant with two assembly lines. These lines are intended to be identical, but line 1 uses somewhat older equipment than line 2 and is typically less reliable. Historical data have shown that each watch coming off line 1, independently of the others, is free of defects with probability 0.98. The similar probability for line 2 is 0.99. Each line produces 500 watches per hour. The production manager has asked you to answer the following questions.

1. She wants to know how many defect-free watches each line is likely to produce in a given hour. Specifically, find the smallest integer k (for each line separately) such that you can be 99% sure that the line will not produce more than k defective watches in a given hour.
2. EuroWatch currently has an order for 500 watches from an important customer. The company plans to fill this

order by packing slightly more than 500 watches, all from line 2, and sending this package off to the customer. Obviously, EuroWatch wants to send as few watches as possible, but it wants to be 99% sure that when the customer opens the package, there are at least 500 defect-free watches. How many watches should be packed?
3. EuroWatch has another order for 1000 watches. Now it plans to fill this order by packing slightly more than one hour's production from each line. This package will contain the *same* number of watches from each line. As in the previous question, EuroWatch wants to send as few watches as possible, but it again wants to be 99% sure that when the customer opens the package, there are at least 1000 defect-free watches. The question of how many watches to pack is unfortunately quite difficult because the total number of defect-free watches is *not* binomially distributed. (Why not?) Therefore, the

manager asks you to solve the problem with simulation (and some trial and error). (*Hint*: It turns out that it is much faster to simulate small numbers than large numbers, so simulate the number of watches with defects, not the number without defects.)

4. Finally, EuroWatch has a third order for 100 watches. The customer has agreed to pay $50,000 for the order—that is, $500 per watch. If EuroWatch sends more than 100 watches to the customer, its revenue doesn't increase; it can never exceed $50,000. Its unit cost of producing a watch is $450, regardless of which line it is assembled on. The order will be filled entirely from a single line, and EuroWatch plans to send slightly more than 100 watches to the customer.

If the customer opens the shipment and finds that there are fewer than 100 defect-free watches (which we assume the customer has the ability to do), then he will pay only for the defect-free watches—EuroWatch's revenue will decrease by $500 per watch short of the 100 required—and on top of this, EuroWatch will be required to make up the difference at an expedited cost of $1000 per watch. The customer won't pay a dime for these expedited watches. (If expediting is required, EuroWatch will make sure that the expedited watches are defect-free. It doesn't want to lose this customer entirely.)

You have been asked to develop a spreadsheet model to find EuroWatch's expected profit for any number of watches it sends to the customer. You should develop it so that it responds correctly, regardless of which assembly line is used to fill the order and what the shipment quantity is. (*Hints*: Use the BINOM.DIST function, with last argument 0, to fill up a column of probabilities for each possible number of defective watches. Next to each of these, calculate EuroWatch's profit. Then use a SUM-PRODUCT to obtain the expected profit. Finally, you can assume that EuroWatch will never send more than 110 watches. It turns out that this large a shipment is not even close to optimal.)

CASE   5.3 Cashing in on the Lottery

Many states supplement their tax revenues with state-sponsored lotteries. Most of them do so with a game called lotto. Although there are various versions of this game, they are all basically as follows. People purchase tickets that contain r distinct numbers from 1 to m, where r is generally 5 or 6 and m is generally around 50. For example, in Virginia, the state discussed in this case, $r = 6$ and $m = 44$. Each ticket costs $1, about 39 cents of which is allocated to the total jackpot.[6] There is eventually a drawing of $r = 6$ distinct numbers from the $m = 44$ possible numbers. Any ticket that matches these 6 numbers wins the jackpot.

There are two interesting aspects of this game. First, the current jackpot includes not only the revenue from this round of ticket purchases but also any jackpots carried over from previous drawings because of no winning tickets. Therefore, the jackpot can build from one drawing to the next, and in celebrated cases it has become huge. Second, if there is more than one winning ticket—a distinct possibility—the winners share the jackpot equally. (This is called *parimutuel* betting.) So, for example, if the current jackpot is $9 million and there are three winning tickets, then each winner receives $3 million.

It can be shown that for Virginia's choice of r and m, there are approximately 7 million possible tickets (7,059,052 to be exact). Therefore, any ticket has about one chance out of 7 million of being a winner. That is, the probability of winning with a single ticket is $p = 1/7,059,052$—not very good odds. If n people purchase tickets, then the number of winners is binomially distributed with parameters n and p. Because n is typically very large and p is small, the number of winners has approximately a Poisson distribution with rate $\lambda = np$. (This makes ensuing calculations somewhat easier.) For example, if 1 million tickets are purchased, then the number of winning tickets is approximately Poisson distributed with $\lambda = 1/7$.

In 1992, an Australian syndicate purchased a huge number of tickets in the Virginia lottery in an attempt to assure itself of purchasing a winner. It worked! Although the syndicate wasn't able to purchase all 7 million possible tickets (it was about 1.5 million shy of this), it did purchase a winning ticket, and there were no other winners. Therefore, the syndicate won a 20-year income stream worth approximately $27 million, with a net present value of approximately $14 million. This made the syndicate a big profit over the cost of the tickets it purchased. Two questions come to mind: (1) Is this hogging of tickets unfair to the rest of the public? (2) Is it a wise strategy on the part of the syndicate (or did it just get lucky)?

To answer the first question, consider how the lottery changes for the general public with the addition of the syndicate. To be specific, suppose the syndicate can invest $7 million and obtain *all* of the possible tickets, making itself a sure winner. Also, suppose n people from the general public purchase tickets, each of which has 1 chance out of 7 million of being a winner. Finally, let R be the jackpot carried

---

6 Of the remaining 61 cents, the state takes about 50 cents. The other 11 cents is used to pay off lesser prize winners whose tickets match some, but not all, of the winning 6 numbers. To keep this case relatively simple, however, we ignore these lesser prizes and concentrate only on the jackpot.

over from any previous lotteries. Then the total jackpot on this round will be $[R + 0.39\,(7{,}000{,}000 + n)]$ because 39 cents from every ticket goes toward the jackpot. The number of winning tickets for the public will be Poisson distributed with $\lambda = n/7{,}000{,}000$. However, any member of the public who wins will *necessarily* have to share the jackpot with the syndicate, which is a sure winner. Use this information to calculate the expected amount the public will win. Then do the same calculation when the syndicate does *not* play. (In this case the jackpot will be smaller, but the public won't have to share any winnings with the syndicate.) For values of n and R that you can select, is the public better off with or without the syndicate? Would you, as a general member of the public, support a move to outlaw syndicates from hogging the tickets?

The second question is whether the syndicate is wise to buy so many tickets. Again assume that the syndicate can spend \$7 million and purchase each possible ticket. (Would this be possible in reality?) Also, assume that n members of the general public purchase tickets, and that the carryover from the previous jackpot is R. The syndicate is thus assured of having a winning ticket, but is it assured of covering its costs? Calculate the expected net benefit (in terms of net present value) to the syndicate, using any reasonable values of n and R, to see whether the syndicate can expect to come out ahead.

Actually, the analysis suggested in the previous paragraph is not complete. There are at least two complications to consider. The first is the effect of taxes. Fortunately for the Australian syndicate, it did not have to pay federal or state taxes on its winnings, but a U.S. syndicate wouldn't be so lucky. Second, the jackpot from a \$20 million jackpot, say, is actually paid in 20 annual \$1 million payments. The Lottery Commission pays the winner \$1 million immediately and then purchases 19 "strips" (bonds with the interest not included) maturing at 1-year intervals with face value of \$1 million each. Unfortunately, the lottery prize does not offer the liquidity of the Treasury issues that back up the payments. This lack of liquidity could make the lottery less attractive to the syndicate.

CHAPTER 6

Decision Making Under Uncertainty

wavebreakmedia/Shutterstock.com

COST-EFFECTIVE HEPATITIS B INTERVENTIONS

Hepatitis B is a viral disease that can lead to death and liver cancer if not treated. It is especially prevalent in Asian populations. The disease chronically infects approximately 8% to 10% of people in China and a similar percentage of Americans of Asian descent. It often infects newborns and children, in which case it is likely to become a lifelong infection. Chronic infection is often asymptomatic for decades, but if left untreated, about 25% of the chronically infected will die of liver diseases such as cirrhosis or liver cancer.

A hepatitis B vaccine became available in the 1980s, but it is costly (thousands of dollars per year) and it does not *cure* the disease. Vaccination of children in the United States is widespread, and only about 0.5% of the general population is infected. This percentage, however, jumps to about 10% for U.S. adult Asian and Pacific Islanders, where the rate of liver cancer is more than three times that of the general U.S. population. The situation is even worse in China, where it is estimated that approximately 300,000 die each year from liver disease caused by hepatitis B. Although rates of newborn vaccination in China have increased in recent years, about 20% of 1- to 4-year olds and 40% of 5- to 19-year olds still remain unprotected. In a pilot program in the Qinghai province, the feasibility of a vaccination "catch-up" program was demonstrated, but China's public health officials worried about the cost effectiveness of a country-wide catch-up program.

The article by Hutton et al. (2011) reports the results of the work his team carried out over several years with the Asian Liver Center at Stanford University. They used decision analysis and other quantitative methods to analyze the cost effectiveness of several interventions to combat hepatitis B in the United States and China. They addressed two policy questions in the study: (1) What combination of screening, treatment, and vaccination is most cost effective for U.S. adult Asian and Pacific Islanders; and (2) Is it cost effective to provide hepatitis B catch-up vaccination for children and adolescents in China?

For the first question, the team first considered the approach usually favored by the medical community, clinical trials, but they decided it was infeasible because of expense and the time (probably decades) required. Instead, they used decision analysis with a decision tree very much like those in this chapter. The initial decision is whether to screen people for the disease. If this initial decision is no, the next decision is whether to vaccinate. If this decision is no, they wait to see whether infection occurs. On the other side, if the initial decision to screen is yes, there are three possible outcomes: infected, immune, or susceptible. If infected, the next decision is whether to treat. If immune, no action is necessary. If susceptible, the sequence is the same as after the "no screen" decision. At end nodes with a possibility (or certainty) of being infected, the team used a probabilistic "Markov" model to determine future health states.

The various decision strategies were compared in terms of incremental cost to gain an incremental unit of health, with units of health expressed in quality-adjusted life years (QALYs). Interventions are considered cost effective if they cost less per QALY gained than three times a country's per capita GDP; they are considered *very* cost effective if they cost less than a country's per capita GDP.

The study found that it is cost effective to screen Asian and Pacific Islanders so that they can receive treatment, and it is also cost effective to vaccinate those in close contact with infected individuals so that they can be protected from infection. Specifically, they estimated that this policy costs from $36,000 to $40,000 per QALY gained, whereas an intervention that costs $50,000 per QALY gained is considered cost effective in the United States. However, they found that it is not cost effective to provide universal vaccination for *all* U.S. adult Asian and Pacific Islanders, primarily because the risk of being exposed to hepatitis B for U.S. adults is low.

For the second question, the team used a similar decision analysis to determine that providing catch-up vaccination for children up to age 19 not only improves health outcomes but saves costs. Using sensitivity analysis, they found that catch-up vaccination might not be cost saving if the probability of a child becoming infected is one-fifth as high as the base-case estimate of 100 out of 100,000 per year. This is due to the high level of newborn vaccination coverage already achieved in some urban areas of China. They also found if treatment becomes cheaper, the cost advantages of vaccination decrease. However, treatment costs would have to be halved and infection risk would have to be five times lower than in their base case before the cost of providing catch-up vaccination would exceed $2500 per QALY gained (roughly equal to per capita GDP in China).

In any case, their analysis influenced China's 2009 decision to expand free catch-up vaccination to all children in China under the age of 15. This decision could result in about 170 million children being vaccinated, and it could prevent hundreds of thousands of chronic infections and close to 70,000 deaths from hepatitis B.

6-1 Introduction

This chapter provides a formal framework for analyzing decision problems that involve uncertainty. Our discussion includes the following:

- criteria for choosing among alternative decisions
- how probabilities are used in the decision-making process
- how early decisions affect decisions made at a later stage
- how a decision maker can quantify the value of information
- how attitudes toward risk can affect the analysis

Throughout, we employ a powerful graphical tool—a decision tree—to guide the analysis. A decision tree enables a decision maker to view all important aspects of the problem at once: the decision alternatives, the uncertain outcomes and their probabilities, the economic consequences, and the chronological order of events. Although decision trees have been used for years, often created with paper and pencil, we show how they can be implemented in Excel with the PrecisionTree add-in from Palisade.

Many examples of decision making under uncertainty exist in the business world, including the following:

- Companies routinely place bids for contracts to complete a certain project within a fixed time frame. Often these are sealed bids, where each company presents a bid for completing the project in a sealed envelope. Then the envelopes are opened, and the low bidder is awarded the bid amount to complete the project. Any particular company in the bidding competition must deal with the uncertainty of the other companies' bids, as well as possible uncertainty regarding their cost to complete the project if they win the bid. The trade-off is between bidding low to win the bid and bidding high to make a larger profit.
- Whenever a company contemplates introducing a new product into the market, there are a number of uncertainties that affect the decision, probably the most important being the customers' reaction to this product. If the product generates high customer demand, the company will make a large profit. But if demand is low—and the vast majority of new products do poorly—the company could fail to recoup its development costs. Because the level of customer demand is critical, the company might try to gauge this level by

test marketing the product in one region of the country. If this test market is a success, the company can then be more optimistic that a full-scale national marketing of the product will also be successful. But if the test market is a failure, the company can cut its losses by abandoning the product.

- Whenever manufacturing companies make capacity expansion decisions, they face uncertain consequences. First, they must decide whether to build new plants. If they don't expand and demand for their products is higher than expected, they will lose revenue because of insufficient capacity. If they do expand and demand for their products is lower than expected, they will be stuck with expensive underutilized capacity. Companies also need to decide *where* to build new plants. This decision involves a whole new set of uncertainties, including exchange rates, labor availability, social stability, competition from local businesses, and others.

- Banks must continually make decisions on whether to grant loans to businesses or individuals. Many banks made many very poor decisions, especially on mortgage loans, during the years leading up to the financial crisis in 2008. They fooled themselves into thinking that housing prices would only increase, never decrease. When the bottom fell out of the housing market, banks were stuck with loans that could never be repaid.

- Utility companies must make many decisions that have significant environmental and economic consequences. For these companies it is not necessarily enough to conform to federal or state environmental regulations. Recent court decisions have found companies liable—for huge settlements—when accidents occurred, even though the companies followed all existing regulations. Therefore, when utility companies decide whether to replace equipment or mitigate the effects of environmental pollution, they must take into account the possible environmental consequences (such as injuries to people) as well as economic consequences (such as lawsuits). An aspect of these situations that makes decision analysis particularly difficult is that the potential "disasters" are often extremely unlikely; hence, their probabilities are difficult to assess accurately.

- Sports teams continually make decisions under uncertainty. Sometimes these decisions involve long-run consequences, such as whether to trade for a promising but as yet untested pitcher in baseball. Other times these decisions involve short-run consequences, such as whether to go for a fourth down or kick a field goal late in a close football game. You might be surprised at the level of quantitative sophistication in today's professional sports. Management and coaches typically do *not* make important decisions by gut feeling. They employ many of the tools in this chapter and in other chapters of this book.

Although the focus of this chapter is on *business* decisions, the approach discussed in this chapter can also be used in important personal decisions you have to make. As an example, if you are just finishing an undergraduate degree, should you go immediately into a graduate program, or should you work for several years and then decide whether to pursue a graduate degree? As another example, if you currently have a decent job but you have the option to take another possibly more promising job that would require you and your family to move to another part of the country, should you stay or move?

You might not have to make too many life-changing decisions like these, but you will undoubtedly have to make a few. How will you make them? You will probably not use all the formal methods discussed in this chapter, but the discussion provided here should at least motivate you to think in a structured way before making your final decisions.

6-2 Elements of Decision Analysis

Although decision making under uncertainty occurs in a wide variety of contexts, the problems we discuss in this chapter are alike in the following ways:

1. A problem has been identified that requires a solution.
2. A number of possible decisions have been identified.
3. Each decision leads to a number of possible outcomes.

4. There is uncertainty about which outcome will occur, and probabilities of the possible outcomes are assessed.
5. For each decision and each possible outcome, a payoff is received or a cost is incurred.
6. A "best" decision must be chosen using an appropriate decision criterion.

We now discuss these elements in some generality.[1]

Identifying the Problem

When something triggers the need to solve a problem, you should think carefully about the problem that needs to be solved before diving in. Perhaps you are just finishing your undergraduate degree (the trigger), and you want to choose the Business School where you should get your MBA degree. You could define the problem as which MBA program you should attend, but maybe you should define it more generally as what you should do next now that you have your undergraduate degree. You don't necessarily have to enter an MBA program right away. You could get a job and then get an MBA degree later, or you could enter a graduate program in some area other than Business. Maybe you could even open your own business and forget about graduate school. The point is that by changing the problem from deciding which MBA program to attend to deciding what to do next, you change the decision problem in a fundamental way.

Possible Decisions

The possible decisions depend on the previous step: how the problem is specified. But after you identify the problem, all possible decisions for this problem should be listed. Keep in mind that if a potential decision isn't in this list, it won't have a chance of being chosen as the best decision later, so this list should be as comprehensive as possible. Some problems are of a multistage nature, as discussed in Section 6.6. In such problems, a first-stage decision is made, then an uncertain outcome is observed, then a second-stage decision is made, then a second uncertain outcome is observed, and so on. (Often there are only two stages, but there could be more.) In this case, a "decision" is really a "strategy" or "contingency plan" that prescribes what to do at each stage, depending on prior decisions and observed outcomes. These ideas are clarified in Section 6.6.

Possible Outcomes

One of the main reasons why decision making under uncertainty is difficult is that decisions have to be made *before* uncertain outcomes are revealed. For example, you must place your bet at a roulette wheel *before* the wheel is spun. Or you must decide what type of auto insurance to purchase *before* you find out whether you will be in an accident. However, before you make a decision, you must at least list the possible outcomes that might occur. In some cases, the outcomes will be a small set of discrete possibilities, such as the 11 possible sums (2 through 12) of the roll of two dice. In other cases, the outcomes will be a continuum of possibilities, such as the possible damage amounts to a car in an accident. In this chapter, we generally allow only a small discrete set of possible outcomes. If the actual set of outcomes is a continuum, we typically choose a small set of representative outcomes from this continuum.

Probabilities of Outcomes

A list of all possible outcomes is not enough. As a decision maker, you must also assess the likelihoods of these outcomes with probabilities. These outcomes are generally *not* equally likely. For example, if there are only two possible outcomes, rain or no rain, when you are deciding whether to carry an umbrella to work, there is no generally no reason to assume that each of these outcomes has a 50-50 chance of occurring. Depending on the weather report, they might be 80-20, 30-70, or any of many other possibilities.

There is no easy way to assess the probabilities of the possible outcomes. Sometimes they will be determined at least partly by historical data. For example, if demand for your

---

1 For an interesting discussion of decision making at a very nontechnical level, we recommend the book by Hammond et al. (2015).

product is uncertain, with possible outcomes "low," "medium," and "high," you might assess their probabilities as 0.5, 0.3, and 0.2 because past demands have been low about 50% of the time, medium about 30% of the time, and high about 20% of the time.[2] However, this product might be a totally new product, unlike any of your previous products. Then data on past demands will probably not be relevant, and your probability assessments for demand of the new product will necessarily contain a heavy subjective component—your best guesses based on your experience and possibly the inputs of the marketing experts in your company. In fact, probabilities in most real business decision-making problems are of the subjective variety, so managers must make the probability assessments most in line with the data available and their gut feeling.

To complicate matters, probabilities sometimes *change* as more information becomes available. For example, suppose you assess the probability that the Golden State Warriors will win the NBA championship this year. Will this assessment change if you hear later that Steph Curry has suffered a season-ending injury? It almost surely will, probably quite a lot. Sometimes, as in this basketball example, you will change your probabilities in an *informal* way when you get new information. However, in Section 6.6, we show how probabilities can be updated in a *formal* way by using an important law of probabilities called Bayes' rule.

Payoffs and Costs

Decisions and outcomes have consequences, either good or bad. These must be assessed before intelligent decisions can be made. In our problems, these will be *monetary* payoffs or costs, but in many real-world decision problems, they can be nonmonetary, such as environmental damage or loss of life. Nonmonetary consequences can be very difficult to quantify, but an attempt must be made to do so. Otherwise, it is impossible to make meaningful trade-offs.

Decision Criterion

Once all of these elements of a decision problem have been specified, you must make some difficult trade-offs. For example, would you rather take a chance at receiving $1 million, with the risk of losing $2 million, or would you rather play it safer? Of course, the answer depends on the probabilities of these two outcomes, but as you will see later in the chapter, if very large amounts of money are at stake (relative to your wealth), your attitude toward risk can also play a key role in the decision-making process.

In any case, for each possible decision, you face a number of uncertain outcomes with given probabilities, and each of these leads to a payoff or a cost. The result is a probability distribution of payoffs and costs. For example, one decision might lead to the following: a payoff of $50,000 with probability 0.1, a payoff of $10,000 with probability 0.2, and a cost of $5000 with probability 0.7. (The three outcomes are mutually exclusive; their probabilities sum to 1.) Another decision might lead to the following: a payoff of $5000 with probability 0.6 and a cost of $1000 with probability 0.4. Which of these two decisions do you favor? The choice is not obvious. The first decision has more upside potential but more downside risk, whereas the second decision is safer.

In situations like this—the same situations faced throughout this chapter—you need a *decision criterion* for choosing between two or more probability distributions of payoff/ cost outcomes. Several methods have been proposed:

- Look at the worst possible outcome for each decision and choose the decision that has the least bad of these. This is relevant for an extreme pessimist.
- Look at the 5th percentile of the distribution of outcomes for each decision and choose the decision that has the best of these. This is also relevant for a pessimist—or a company that wants to limit its losses. (Any percentile, not just the 5th, could be chosen.)

---

2 As discussed in the previous chapter, there are several equivalent ways to express probabilities. As an example, you can state that the probability of your team winning a basketball game is 0.6. Alternatively, you can say that the probability of them winning is 60%, or that the odds of them winning are 3 to 2. These are all equivalent. We will generally express probabilities as decimal numbers between 0 and 1, but we will sometimes quote percentages.

- Look at the best possible outcome for each decision and choose the decision that has the best of these. This is relevant for an extreme optimist.
- Look at the variance (or standard deviation) of the distribution of outcomes for each decision and choose the decision that has the smallest of these. This is relevant for minimizing risk but it treats upside risk and downside risk in the same way.
- Look at the downside risk (however you want to define it) of the distribution of outcomes for each decision and choose the decision with the smallest of these. Again, this is relevant for minimizing risk, but now it minimizes only the part of the risk you really want to avoid.

The point here is that a probability distribution of payoffs and costs has several summary measures that *could* be used a decision criterion, and you could make an argument for any of the measures just listed. However, the measure that has been used most often, and the one that will be used for most of this chapter, is the *mean* of the probability distribution, also called its *expected value*. Because we are dealing with monetary outcomes, this criterion is generally known as the **expected monetary value**, or **EMV criterion**. The EMV criterion has a long-standing tradition in decision-making analysis, both at a theoretical level (hundreds of scholarly journal articles) and at a practical level (used by many businesses). It provides a rational way of making decisions, at least when the monetary payoffs and costs are of "moderate" size relative to the decision maker's wealth. (Section 6.7 presents another decision criterion when the monetary values are not "moderate.")

> The expected monetary value, or EMV, for any decision is a weighted average of the possible payoffs/costs for this decision, weighted by the probabilities of the outcomes. Using the EMV criterion, you choose the decision with the largest EMV. This is sometimes called "playing the averages."

The EMV criterion is also easy to operationalize. For each decision, you take a weighted sum of the possible monetary outcomes, weighted by their probabilities, to find the EMV. Then you identify the largest of these EMVs. For the two decisions listed earlier, their EMVs are as follows:

- Decision 1: EMV $= 50000(0.1) + 10000(0.3) + (-5000)(0.6) = \$3500$
- Decision 2: EMV $= 5000(0.6) + (-1000)(0.4) = \$2600$

Therefore, according to the EMV criterion, you should choose decision 1.

6-3 EMV and Decision Trees

Because the EMV criterion plays such a crucial role in decision making under uncertainty, it is worth exploring in more detail.

First, if you are acting according to the EMV criterion, you value a decision with a given EMV the *same* as a sure monetary outcome with the same EMV. To see how this works, suppose there is a third decision in addition to the previous two. If you choose this decision, there is no risk at all; you receive a sure $3000. Should you make this decision, presumably to avoid risk? According to the EMV criterion, the answer is no. Decision 1, with an EMV of $3500, is equivalent (for an EMV maximizer) to a sure $3500 payoff. Hence, it is favored over the new riskless decision. (Read this paragraph several times and think about its consequences. It is sometimes difficult to accept this logic in real decision-making problems, which is why not everyone uses the EMV criterion in every situation.)

Second, the EMV criterion doesn't *guarantee* good outcomes. Indeed, no criterion can guarantee good outcomes. If you make decision 1, for example, you might get lucky and make $50,000, but there is a 70% chance that you will lose $5000. This is the very nature of decision making under uncertainty: you make a decision and then you wait to see the consequences. They might be good and they might be bad, but at least by using the EMV criterion, you know that you have proceeded rationally.

Third, the EMV criterion is easy to operationalize in a spreadsheet. This is shown in Figure 6.1. (See the file **Simple Decision Problem Finished.xlsx**.) For any decision, you list the possible payoff/cost values and their probabilities. Then you calculate the EMV with a SUMPRODUCT function. For example, the formula in cell B7 is

=SUMPRODUCT(A3:A5,B3:B5)

Figure 6.1 EMV Calculations in Excel

	A	B	C	D	E	F	G	H
1	Decision 1			Decision 2			Decision 3	
2	Payoff/Cost	Probability		Payoff/Cost	Probability		Payoff/Cost	Probability
3	$50,000	0.1		$5,000	0.6		$3,000	1
4	$10,000	0.2		−$1,000	0.4			
5	−$5,000	0.7						
6								
7	EMV	$3,500		EMV	$2,600		EMV	$3,000

Usually, the most important information from a sensitivity analysis is whether the best decision continues to be best as one or more inputs change.

The advantage to calculating EMVs in a spreadsheet is that you can easily perform sensitivity analysis on any of the inputs. For example, Figure 6.2 shows what happens when the good outcome for decision 2 becomes more probable (and the bad outcome becomes less probable). Now the EMV for decision 2 is the largest of the three EMVs, so it is the best decision.

Figure 6.2 EMV Calculations with Different Inputs

	A	B	C	D	E	F	G	H
1	Decision 1			Decision 2			Decision 3	
2	Payoff/Cost	Probability		Payoff/Cost	Probability		Payoff/Cost	Probability
3	$50,000	0.1		$5,000	0.8		$3,000	1
4	$10,000	0.2		−$1,000	0.2			
5	−$5,000	0.7						
6								
7	EMV	$3,500		EMV	$3,800		EMV	$3,000

You might still be wondering why we choose the EMV criterion in the first place. One way of answering this is that EMV represents a long-run average. If—and this is a big if—the decision could be repeated many times, all with the same monetary values and probabilities, the EMV is the long-run average of the outcomes you would observe. For example, by making decision 1, you would gain $50,000 about 10% of the time, you would gain $10,000 about 20% of the time, and you would lose $5000 about 70% of the time. In the long run, your average net gain would be about $3500.

This argument might or might not be relevant. For a company that routinely makes many decisions of this type, even though they are not identical, long-term averages make sense. Sometimes they win, and sometimes they lose, but it makes sense for them to be concerned only with long-term averages. However, a particular decision problem is often a "one-shot deal." It won't be repeated many times in the future; in fact, it won't be repeated at all. In this case, you might argue that a long-term average criterion makes no sense and that some other criterion should be used instead. This has been debated by decision analysts, including many academics, for years, and the arguments continue. Nevertheless, most analysts agree that when "moderate" amounts of money are at stake, the EMV criterion provides a rational way of making decisions, even for one-shot deals. Therefore, we use the EMV criterion in most of this chapter.

A decision problem evolves through time. A decision is made, then an uncertain outcome is observed, then another decision might need to be made, then another uncertain outcome might be observed, and so on. All the while, payoffs are being received or costs are being incurred. It is useful to show all these elements of the decision problem, including the timing, in a type of graph called a **decision tree**. A decision tree not only allows everyone involved to *see* the elements of the decision problem in an intuitive format, but it also provides a straightforward way of making the necessary EMV calculations.

The decision tree for the simple decision problem discussed earlier appears in Figure 6.3.

Figure 6.3 Simple Decision Tree

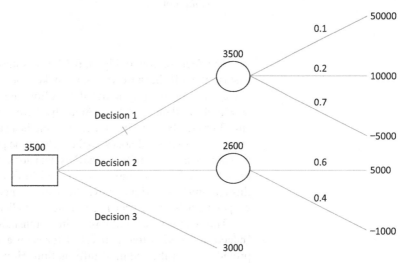

This decision tree was actually created in Excel by using its built-in shape tools on a blank worksheet, but you could just as well draw it on a piece of paper. Alternatively, you could use the Palisade PrecisionTree add-in that we discuss later in the chapter. The important thing for now is how you interpret this decision tree. It is important to realize that decision trees such as this one have been used for over 50 years. They all use the following basic conventions:

Decision Tree Conventions

1. Decision trees are composed of *nodes* (circles, squares, and triangles) and *branches* (lines).
2. The nodes represent points in time. A *decision node* (a square) represents a time when you make a decision. A *probability node* (a circle) represents a time when the result of an uncertain outcome becomes known. An *end node* (a triangle) indicates that the problem is completed—all decisions have been made, all uncertainty has been resolved, and all payoffs and costs have been incurred. (When people draw decision trees by hand, they often omit the actual triangles, as we have done in Figure 6.3. However, we still refer to the right-hand tips of the branches as the end nodes.)

3. Time proceeds *from left to right*. This means that any branches leading into a node (from the left) have already occurred. Any branches leading out of a node (to the right) have not yet occurred.
4. Branches leading out of a decision node represent the possible decisions; you get to choose the branch you prefer. Branches leading out of probability nodes represent the possible uncertain outcomes; you have no control over which of these will occur.
5. Probabilities are listed on probability branches. These probabilities are *conditional* on the events that have already been observed (those to the left). Also, the probabilities on branches leading out of any probability node must sum to 1.
6. Monetary values are shown to the right of the end nodes. (As we discuss shortly, some monetary values can also be placed under the branches where they occur in time.)
7. EMVs are calculated through a "folding-back" process, discussed next. They are shown above the various nodes. It is then customary to mark the optimal decision branch(es) in some way. We have marked ours with a small notch.

The decision tree in Figure 6.3 follows these conventions. The decision node comes first (to the left) because you must make a decision *before* observing any uncertain outcomes. The probability nodes then follow the decision branches, and the probabilities appear above their branches. (Actually, there is no need for a probability node after decision 3 branch because its monetary value is a sure $3000.) The ultimate payoffs or costs appear next to the end nodes, to the right of the probability branches. The EMVs above the probability nodes are for the various decisions. For example, the EMV for the decision 1 branch is $3500. The maximum of the EMVs corresponds to the decision 1 branch, and this maximum is written above the decision node. Because it corresponds to decision 1, we put a notch on the decision 1 branch to indicate that this decision is best.

This decision tree is almost a direct translation of the spreadsheet model in Figure 6.1. Indeed, a decision tree is overkill for such a simple problem; the spreadsheet model provides all of the required information. However, as you will see later, especially in Section 6.6, decision trees provide a useful view of more complex problems. In addition, decision trees provides a framework for doing all of the EMV calculations. They allow you to use the following **folding-back procedure** to find the EMVs and the best decision.

Folding-Back Procedure

Starting from the right of the decision tree and working back to the left:

1. At each probability node, calculate an EMV—a sum of products of monetary values and probabilities.
2. At each decision node, take a maximum of EMVs to identify the optimal decision.[3]

This is exactly what we did in Figure 6.3. At each probability node, we calculated EMVs in the usual way (sums of products) and wrote them above the nodes. Then at the decision node, we took the maximum of the three EMVs and wrote it above this node.

3 Some decision problems involve only costs. In that case it is more convenient to label the tree with positive costs and take *minimums* of expected costs at the decision nodes.

The folding-back process is a systematic way of calculating EMVs in a decision tree and thereby identifying the best decision strategy.

Although this procedure requires more work for more complex decision trees, the same two steps—taking EMVs at probability nodes and taking maximums at decision nodes—are the only arithmetic operations required. In addition, the PrecisionTree add-in discussed later in the chapter performs the folding-back calculations for you.

Problems

Solutions for problems whose numbers appear within a colored box can be found in the Student Solution Files.

Level A

1. Several decision criteria besides EMV are suggested in the section. For each of the following criteria, rank all three decisions in Figure 6.1 from best to worst.
   a. Look only at the worst possible outcome for each decision.
   b. Look only at the best possible outcome for each decision.
   c. Look at the variance of the distribution of outcomes for each decision, which you want to be small. (The variance of a probability distribution is the weighted sum of squared differences from the mean, weighted by the probabilities.)

2. For the decision problem in Figure 6.1, use data tables to perform the following sensitivity analyses. The goal in each is to see whether decision 1 continues to have the largest EMV. In each part, provide a brief explanation of the results.
   a. Let the payoff from the best outcome, the value in cell A3, vary from $30,000 to $50,000 in increments of $2500.

b. Let the probability of the worst outcome for the first decision, the value in cell B5, vary from 0.7 to 0.9 in increments of 0.025, and use *formulas* in cells B3 and B4 to ensure that they remain in the ratio 1 to 2 and the three probabilities for decision 1 continue to sum to 1.
   c. Use a two-way data table to let the inputs in parts **a** and **b** vary simultaneously over the indicated ranges.

Level B

3. Some decision makers prefer decisions with low risk, but this depends on how risk is measured. As we mentioned in this section, variance (see the definition in problem 1) is one measure of risk, but it includes both upside and downside risk. That is, an outcome with a large positive payoff contributes to variance, but this type of "risk" is good. Consider a decision with some possible payoffs and some possible costs, with given probabilities. How might you develop a measure of *downside* risk for such a decision? With your downside measure of risk, which decision in Figure 6.1 do you prefer, decision 1 or decision 2? (There is no single correct answer.)

6-4 One-Stage Decision Problems

Many decision problems are similar to the simple decision problem discussed in the previous section. You make a decision, then you wait to see an uncertain outcome, and a payoff is received or a cost is incurred. We refer to these as **single-stage decision problems** because you make only one decision, the one right now. They all unfold in essentially the same way, as indicated by the spreadsheet model in Figure 6.1 or the decision tree in Figure 6.3. The following example is typical of one-stage decision problems. This example is used as a starting point for more complex examples in later sections.

EXAMPLE

6.1 NEW PRODUCT DECISIONS AT ACME

The Acme Company must decide whether to market a new product. As in many new-product situations, there is considerable uncertainty about the eventual success of the product. The product is currently part way through the development process, and some fixed development costs have already been incurred. If the company decides to continue development and then market the product, there will be additional fixed costs, and they are estimated to be $6 million. If the product is marketed, its unit margin (selling price minus variable cost) will be $18. Acme classifies the possible market results as "great," "fair," and "awful," and it estimates the probabilities of these outcomes to be 0.45, 0.35, and 0.20, respectively. Finally, the company estimates that the corresponding sales volumes (in thousands of units sold) from these three outcomes are 600, 300, and 90, respectively. Assuming that Acme is an EMV maximizer, should it finish development and then market the product, or should it stop development at this point and abandon the product?[4]

Objective

To use the EMV criterion to help Acme decide whether to go ahead with the product.

Where Do the Numbers Come From?

Acme's cost accountants should be able to estimate the monetary inputs: the fixed costs and the unit margin. (Any fixed costs already incurred are sunk and therefore have no relevance to the current decision.) The uncertain sales volume is really a continuous variable but, as in many decision problems, Acme has replaced the continuum by three representative possibilities. The assessment of the probabilities and the sales volumes for these three possibilities might be based partly on historical data and market research, but they almost surely have a subjective component.

Solution

The elements of the decision problem appear in Figure 6.4. (See the files **New Product Decisions - Single-Stage 1a Finished.xlsx** and **New Product Decisions - Single-Stage 1b Finished.xlsx**.) If the company decides to stop development and abandon the product, there are no payoffs, costs, or uncertainties; the EMV is $0. (Actually, this isn't really an *expected* value; it is a sure $0.) On the other hand, if the company proceeds with the product, it incurs the fixed cost and receives $18 for every unit it sells. The probability distribution of sales volume given in the problem statement appears in columns A to C, and each sales volume is multiplied by the unit margin to obtain the net revenues in column D. Finally, the formula for the EMV in cell B12 is

=SUMPRODUCT(D8:D10,B8:B10)-B4

Because this EMV is positive, slightly over $1 million, the company is better off marketing the product than abandoning it.

Figure 6.4 Spreadsheet Model for Single-Stage New Product Decision

	A	B	C	D	E	F	G
1	Acme single-stage new product decision						
2							
3	Decision 1: Continue development and market the new product					% decrease in all sales volumes	0%
4	Fixed cost	$6,000,000				EMV for decision 1	$1,074,000
5	Unit margin	$18					
6						Sensitivity analysis to percentage decrease in all sales volumes	
7	Market	Probability	Sales volume	Net revenue		% decrease	EMV for decision 1
8	Great	0.45	600,000	$10,800,000			$1,074,000
9	Fair	0.35	300,000	$5,400,000		5%	$720,300
10	Awful	0.20	90,000	$1,620,000		10%	$366,600
11						15%	$12,900
12	EMV	$1,074,000				20%	-$340,800
13							
14	Decision 2: Stop development and abandon product						
15	No payoffs, no costs, no uncertainty						
16	EMV	$0					

As before, a decision tree is probably overkill for this problem, but it is shown in Figure 6.5. (All monetary and sales volumes are shown in thousands.) This tree indicates one of at least two equivalent ways to show the EMV calculations. The values at the end nodes ignore the fixed cost, which is instead shown under the decision branch as a negative number. Therefore, the 7074 value above the probability node is the expected net revenue, not including the fixed cost. Then the fixed cost is subtracted from this to obtain the 1074 value above the decision node.

Figure 6.6 shows an equivalent tree, where the fixed cost is still shown under the decision branch but is subtracted from each end node. Now the EMV above the probability node is after subtraction of the fixed cost. The two trees are equivalent and either is perfectly acceptable. However, the second tree provides the insight that two of the three outcomes result in a net *loss* to Acme, even though the weighted average, the EMV, is well in the positive range. (Besides, as you will see in the next section, the second tree is the way the PrecisionTree add-in does it.)

---

4 To keep the model simple, we ignore taxes and the time value of money.

Using the spreadsheet model in Figure 6.4, it is easy to perform a sensitivity analysis. Usually, the main purpose of such an analysis is to see whether the best decision changes as one or more inputs change. As an example, we will see whether the best decision continues to be "proceed with marketing" if the total market decreases. Specifically, we let each of the potential sales volumes decrease by the *same* percentage and we keep track of the EMV from marketing the product. The results appear in Figure 6.7. For any percentage decrease in cell G3, the EMV from marketing is calculated in cell G4 with the formula

$$=(1-G3)*SUMPRODUCT(D8:D10,B8:B10)-B4$$

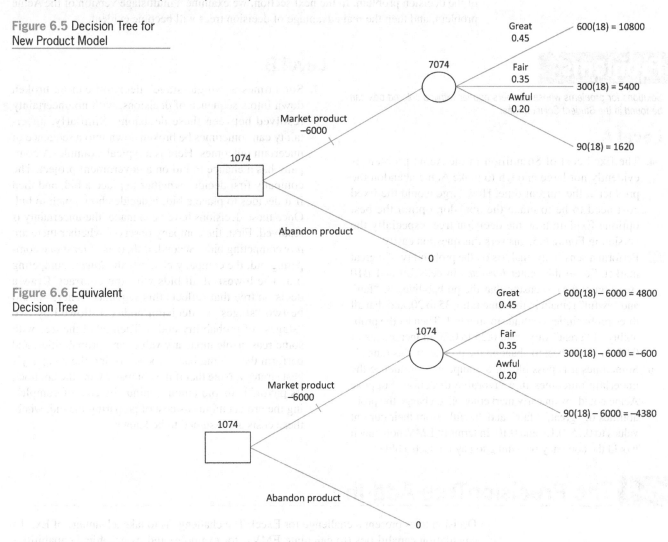

Figure 6.5 Decision Tree for New Product Model

Figure 6.6 Equivalent Decision Tree

Then a data table is used in the usual way, with cell G3 as the column input cell, to calculate the EMV for various percentage decreases. As you can see, the EMV stays positive, so that marketing remains best, for decreases up to 15%. But if the decrease is 20%, the EMV becomes negative, meaning that the best decision is to abandon the product. In this case, the possible gains from marketing are not large enough to offset the fixed cost.

Figure 6.7 Sensitivity Analysis

	F	G
3	% decrease in all sales volumes	0%
4	EMV for decision 1	$1,074,000
5		
6	Sensitivity analysis to percentage decrease in all sales volumes	
7	% decrease	EMV for decision 1
8		$1,074,000
9	5%	$720,300
10	10%	$366,600
11	15%	$12,900
12	20%	−$340,800

The Acme problem is a prototype for all single-stage decision problems. When only a single decision needs to be made, and all of the elements of the decision problem have been specified, it is easy to calculate the required EMVs for the possible decisions and hence determine the EMV-maximizing decision in a spreadsheet model. The problem and the calculations can also be shown in a decision tree, although this doesn't really provide any new information except possibly to give everyone involved a better "picture" of the decision problem. In the next section, we examine a multistage version of the Acme problem, and then the real advantage of decision trees will become evident.

Problems

Solutions for problems whose numbers appear within a colored box can be found in the Student Solution Files.

Level A

4. The fixed cost of $6 million in the Acme problem is evidently not large enough to make Acme abandon the product at the current time. How large would the fixed cost need to be to make the abandon option the best option? Explain how the decision tree, especially the version in Figure 6.5, answers this question easily.

5. Perform a sensitivity analysis on the probability of a great market. To do this, enter *formulas* in cells B9 and B10 (see Figure 6.4) to ensure that the probabilities of "fair" and "awful" remain in the same ratio, 35 to 20, and that all three probabilities continue to sum to 1. Then let the probability of "great" vary from 0.25 to 0.50 in increments of 0.05. Is it ever best to abandon the product in this range?

6. Sometimes it is possible for a company to influence the uncertain outcomes in a favorable direction. Suppose Acme could, by an early marketing blitz, change the probabilities of "great," "fair," and "awful" from their current values to 0.75, 0.15, and 0.10. In terms of EMV, how much would the company be willing to pay for such a blitz?

Level B

7. Sometimes a "single-stage" decision can be broken down into a sequence of decisions, with no uncertainty resolved between these decisions. Similarly, uncertainty can sometimes be broken down into a sequence of uncertain outcomes. Here is a typical example. A company has a chance to bid on a government project. The company first decides whether to place a bid, and then if it decides to place a bid, it decides how much to bid. Once these decisions have been made, the uncertainty is resolved. First, the company observes whether there are *any* competing bids. Second, if there is at least one competing bid, the company observes the *lowest* competing bid. The lowest of all bids wins the contract. Draw a decision tree that reflects this sequence. There should be two "stages" of decision nodes, followed by two "stages" of probability nodes. Then label the tree with some reasonable monetary values and probabilities, and perform the folding back process to find the company's best strategy. Note that if the company wins the contract, its payoff is its bid amount minus its cost of completing the project minus its cost of preparing the bid, where these costs are assumed to be known.

6-5 The PrecisionTree Add-In

Decision trees present a challenge for Excel. The challenge is to take advantage of Excel's calculation capabilities (to calculate EMVs, for example) and its graphical capabilities (to draw the decision tree). Using only Excel's built-in tools, this is virtually impossible (or at least very painful) to do. Fortunately, Palisade has developed an Excel add-in called **PrecisionTree** that makes the process relatively straightforward. This add-in not only enables you to draw and label a decision tree, but it also performs the folding-back procedure automatically and then allows you to perform sensitivity analysis on key input parameters.

The first thing you must do to use PrecisionTree is to "add it in." We assume you have already installed the Palisade DecisionTools Suite. Then to run PrecisionTree, you have two options:

- If Excel is not currently running, you can open Excel *and* PrecisionTree by selecting PrecisionTree from the Palisade group in the list of programs on your computer.
- If Excel is currently running, the first option will open PrecisionTree on top of Excel.

In either case, you will see the Welcome screen in Figure 6.8. Note the Quick Start link. We will come back to this shortly.

Once you click OK to dismiss the Welcome screen, you will know that PrecisionTree is loaded because of the new PrecisionTree tab and associated ribbon shown in Figure 6.9.

Figure 6.8 PrecisionTree
Welcome Screen

Figure 6.9 PrecisionTree Ribbon

Although PrecisionTree is quite easy to use once you are familiar with it, you have to learn the basics. The easiest way to do this is to run a series of Quick Start videos. To do this, you can bring up the Welcome screen in Figure 6.8 at any time through the Precision-Tree Help dropdown list. Then you can click the Quick Start link on the Welcome screen. This opens an example file shown in Figure 6.10. The five buttons on the left each launch a video that explains the basic features of PrecisionTree. Rather than repeat this information here, we urge you to watch the videos and practice the steps—as often as you like. From here on, we assume that you have done so.

Figure 6.10 PrecisionTree Quick Start Buttons

*single-stage_decision_
tree video.*

It is instructive to examine PrecisionTree's decision tree for Acme's single stage problem. The completed tree appears in Figure 6.11. (See the file **New Product Decisions - Single-Stage - 1c Finished.xlsx**.) It is essentially a mixture of the trees in Figures 6.4 and 6.5, and it is equivalent to each of them. As in Figure 6.4, the fixed cost is entered as a negative number below the decision branch, and the net revenues are entered below the probability branches. Then PrecisionTree calculates the net value—the sum of the monetary values on any path through the tree—to the right of the corresponding triangle end nodes. For the folding back process, it uses these net values. Specifically, the 1074 value to the right of the probability node is calculated (automatically) as $(4800)(0.45) + (-600)(0.35) + (-4380)(0.20)$.[5] Then the 1074 value to the right of the decision node is calculated as the maximum of 1074 and 0.

In other words, PrecisionTree draws essentially the same tree and makes the same calculations that you could do by hand. Its advantages are that (1) it generates a nice-looking tree with all of the relevant inputs displayed, (2) it performs the folding-back calculations automatically, and (3) it permits quick sensitivity analyses on any of the model inputs. Also, you can easily identify the best decisions by following the TRUE branches. We will continue to use PrecisionTree in the rest of the chapter for trees that are considerably more complex than the one in Figure 6.11.

PrecisionTree Tip

Formatting Numbers

If you are careful about formatting numbers in Excel, you might spend a lot of time formatting all of the numbers in a decision tree just the way you like them. However, there is a much quicker way in PrecisionTree. From the Settings dropdown on the PrecisionTree ribbon, select Model Settings and then the Format tab. By entering the formats you prefer here, the entire tree is formatted appropriately.

Figure 6.11
Decision Tree from
PrecisionTree

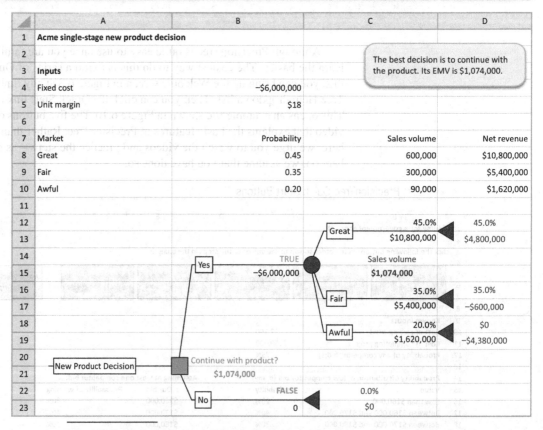

5 PrecisionTree refers to the "probability" nodes and branches as "chance" nodes and branches. The terms are equivalent.

We finish this section with one important reminder discussed in the Quick Start videos. PrecisionTree reserves the cells with colored font (green, red, and blue) for *its* special formulas, so you should not change these cells. Your entries—probabilities and monetary values—should all be in the cells with black font, and it is a good practice to cell reference these inputs whenever possible. For example, we didn't enter 45% in cell C12; we entered a link to cell B8.

Problems

Solutions for problems whose numbers appear within a colored box can be found in the Student Solution Files.

Level A

8. Explain in some detail how the PrecisionTree calculations in Figure 6.11 for the Acme problem are exactly the same as those for the hand-drawn decision tree in Figure 6.6. In other words, explain exactly how PrecisionTree gets the monetary values in the colored cells in Figure 6.11.

9. Use PrecisionTree's Sensitivity Analysis tools to perform the sensitivity analysis requested in problem 5 of the previous section. (Watch the Step 5 video in Figure 6.10 if necessary.)

Level B

10. Use PrecisionTree to solve problem 7 of the previous section.

6-6 Multistage Decision Problems

Many real-world decision problems evolve through time in stages. A company first makes a decision. Then it observes an uncertain outcome that provides some information. Based on this information, the company then makes another decision. Then it observes another uncertain outcome. This process could continue for more stages, but we will limit the number of stages to two: a first decision, a first uncertain outcome, a second decision, and a second uncertain outcome. As time unfolds, payoffs are received and costs are incurred, depending on the decisions made and the uncertain outcomes observed. The objective is again to maximize EMV, but now we are searching for an EMV-maximizing *strategy*, often called a **contingency plan**, that specifies which decision to make at each stage.

As you will see shortly, a contingency plan tells the company which decision to make at the first stage, but the company won't know which decision to make at the second stage until the information from the first uncertain outcome is known. For example, if the information is bad news about a product, then the company might decide at the second stage to abandon the product, but if the news is good, the company might decide to continue with the product. This is the essence of a contingency plan: it specifies what do for each possible uncertain outcome.

An important aspect of multistage decision problems is that probabilities can change through time. After you receive the information from the first-stage uncertain outcome, you might need to reassess the probabilities of future uncertain outcomes. As an example, if a new product is observed to do very poorly in a regional test market, your assessment of the probability that it will do well in a national market will almost surely decrease. Sometimes this reassessment of probabilities can be done in an informal subjective manner. But whenever possible, it should be done with a probability law called Bayes' rule. This rule provides a mathematical way of updating probabilities as new information becomes available. We explain how it works in this section.

Another important aspect of multistage decision problems is the value of information. Sometimes the first-stage decision is to buy information that will help in making the second-stage decision. The question then is how much this information is worth. If you *knew* what the information would be, there would be no point in buying it. However, you virtually never know what the information will be; you can only assess the probabilities of various information outcomes. In such cases, the goal is to calculate the *expected value* of the information—how much better you would be with the information than without it—and then compare this to the actual cost of buying the information to see whether it is worth buying. Again, we explain how it works in this section.

We now show one way the Acme decision problem can be extended to two stages. Later in this section, we examine another multistage version of Acme's problem.

EXAMPLE

6.2 NEW PRODUCT DECISIONS AT ACME WITH TECHNOLOGICAL UNCERTAINTY

In this version of the example, we assume as before that the new product is still in the development stage. However, we now assume that there is a chance that the product will be a failure for technological reasons, such as a new drug that fails to meet FDA approval. At this point in the development process, Acme assesses the probability of technological failure to be 0.2. The $6 million fixed cost from before is now broken down into two components: $4 million for addition development costs and $2 million for fixed costs of marketing, the latter to be incurred only if the product is a technological success and the company decides to market it. The unit margin and the probability distribution of the product's sales volume if it is marketed are the same as before. How should Acme proceed?

Objective

To use a decision tree to find Acme's EMV-maximizing strategy for this two-stage decision problem.

Where Do the Numbers Come From?

The probability of technological failure might be based partly on historical data—the technological failure rate of similar products in the past—but it is probably partly subjective, based on how the product's development has proceeded so far. The probability distribution of sales volume is a more difficult issue. When Acme makes its first decision, right now, it must look ahead to see how the market might look in the future, after the development stage, which could be quite a while from now. (The same issue is relevant in Example 6.1, although we didn't discuss it there.) This a difficult assessment, and it is an obvious candidate for an eventual sensitivity analysis.[6]

Solution

The reason this is a two-stage decision problem is that Acme can decide right away to stop development and abandon the product, thus saving further fixed costs of development. However, if Acme decides to continue development and the product turns out to be a technological success, a second decision on whether to market the product must still be made.

A spreadsheet model such as in Figure 6.1 for the single-stage problem could be developed to calculate the relevant EMVs, but this isn't as easy as it sounds. A much better way is to use a decision tree, using the PrecisionTree add-in. The finished tree appears in Figure 6.12. (See the file **New Product Decisions - Technological Uncertainty Finished.xlsx**.) The first decision is whether to continue development. If "Yes," the fixed development cost is incurred, so it is entered on this branch. Then there is a probability node for the technological success or failure. If it's a failure, there are no further costs, but the fixed development cost is lost. If it's a success, Acme must decide whether to market the product. From this point, the tree is exactly like the single-stage tree, except that the fixed development cost has been incurred.

By following the TRUE branches, you can see Acme's best strategy. The company *should* continue development, and if the product is a technological success, it *should* be marketed. The EMV, again the weighted average of all possible monetary outcomes with this strategy, is $59,200. However, this is only the *expected* value, or mean, of the probability distribution of monetary outcomes. You can see the full probability distribution by requesting a risk profile from PrecisionTree (through the Decision Analysis dropdown). This appears, both in graphical and tabular form, in Figure 6.13. Note that Acme has a 64% chance of incurring a net loss with this strategy, including a possible loss of $4.38 million. This doesn't sound good. However, the company has a 36% chance of a net gain of $4.8 million and, in an expected value sense, this more than offsets the possible losses.

---

6 We have purposely avoided the use of Bayes' rule for now. It will be used in the next version of the Acme problem.

Figure 6.12 Decision Tree with Possible Technological Failure

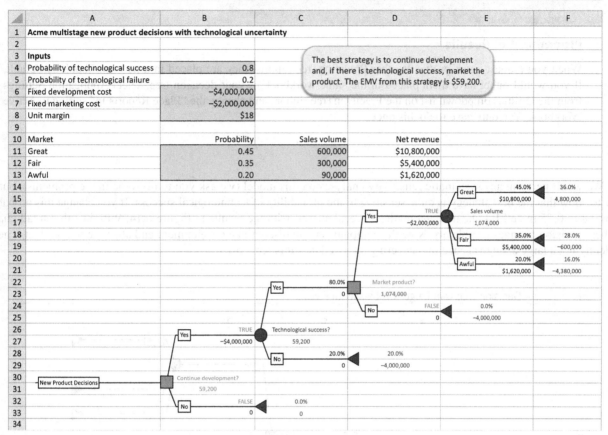

Figure 6.13 Risk Profile from Best Strategy

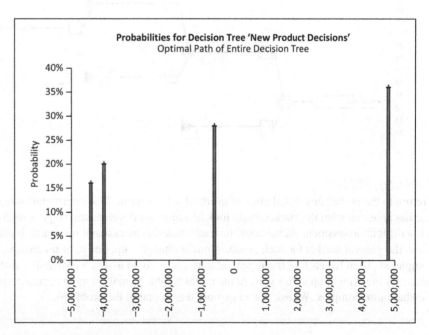

Chart Data		
	Optimal Path	
	Value	Probability
#1	−4,380,000	16.0000%
#2	−4,000,000	20.0000%
#3	−600,000	28.0000%
#4	4,800,000	36.0000%

Placement of Results

When you request a risk profile or other PrecisionTree reports, they are placed in a new workbook by default. If you would rather have them placed in the same workbook as your decision tree, select Application Settings from the Utilities dropdown list on the PrecisionTree ribbon, and change the "Place Reports In" setting to Active Workbook. You only have to do this once.

We won't perform any systematic sensitivity analyses on this model (we ask you to do some in the problems), but it is easy to show that the best strategy is quite sensitive to the probability of technological success. If you change this probability from 0.8 to 0.75 in cell B4, the tree automatically recalculates, with the results in Figure 6.14. With just this small change, the best decision changes completely. Now the company should discontinue development and abandon the product. There is evidently not a large enough chance of recovering the fixed development cost.

Figure 6.14 Decision Tree with Larger Probability of Failure

Modeling Issues

We return to the probability distribution of eventual sales volume. The interpretation here is that at the time of the first decision, Acme has assessed what the market might look like after the development stage, which could be quite a while from now. Again, this is a difficult assessment. Acme could instead break this assessment into parts. It could first assess a probability distribution for how the general market for such products might change—up, down, or no change, for example—by the time development is completed. Then for each of these general markets, it could assess a probability distribution for the sales volume of its new product. By breaking it up in this way, Acme might be able to make a more accurate assessment, but the decision tree would be somewhat more complex. We ask you to explore this in one of the problems.

The next example illustrates another possible multistage extension of the Acme decision problem. This example provides an opportunity to introduce two important topics discussed earlier: Bayes' rule for updating probabilities and the value of information.

EXAMPLE

6.3 NEW PRODUCT DECISIONS AT ACME WITH AN OPTION TO BUY INFORMATION

Suppose now that Acme has just about finished the development process on the new product, so that fixed development costs are no longer an issue, and technological failure is no longer a possibility. The only question is whether Acme should market the product, given the uncertainty about the eventual sales volume. If the company decides to market the product, it will incur fixed marketing costs of $4 million. To keep the model simple, we now assume that there are only two possible market outcomes, good or bad. The sales volumes for these two possible outcomes are 600,000 units and 100,000 units, and Acme assesses that their probabilities are 0.4 and 0.6. However, before making the ultimate decision, Acme has the option to hire a well-respected marketing research firm for $150,000. If Acme decides to use this option, the result will be a *prediction* of good or bad. That is, the marketing research firm will predict that either "We think the market for this product will be good" or "We think the market for this product will be bad." Acme has used this firm before, so it has a sense of the prediction accuracy, as indicated in Table 6.1. Each row in this table indicates the actual market outcome, and each column indicates the prediction. If the actual market is good, the prediction will be good with probability 0.8 and bad with probability 0.2. If the actual market is bad, the prediction will be bad with probability 0.7 and good with probability 0.3. What should Acme do to maximize its EMV?

Table 6.1 Prediction Accuracy of Marketing Research Firm

Actual/Predicted	Good	Bad
Good	0.8	0.2
Bad	0.3	0.7

Objective

To use a decision tree to see whether the marketing research firm is worth its cost and whether the product should be marketed.

Where Do the Numbers Come From?

The main question here concerns the probabilities. Acme's assessment of the probabilities of good or bad markets, 0.4 and 0.6, would be assessed as in earlier examples, probably subjectively. The probabilities in Table 6.1 are probably based partly on historical dealings with the marketing research firm—perhaps they have been right in about 75% of their predictions, give or take a bit—and some subjectivity. In any case, all of these probabilities are prime candidates for sensitivity analysis.

Solution

Acme must first decide whether to hire the marketing research firm. If it decides not to, it can then immediately decide whether to market the product. On the other hand, if it decides to hire the firm, it must then wait for the firm's prediction. After the prediction is received, Acme can then make the ultimate decision on whether to market the product. However, when making this ultimate decision, Acme should definitely take the firm's prediction into account.

A "skeleton" for the appropriate decision tree, without any of the correct probabilities or monetary values, appears in Figure 6.15. For now, just focus on the structure of the tree, and how time flows from left to right. The tree is not symmetric. If Acme doesn't hire the firm, this "No" decision branch is followed immediately by another decision node for whether to market the product. However, if Acme does hire the firm, this "Yes" decision branch is followed by a probability node for the firm's prediction. Then after a good or a bad prediction, there is a decision node for whether to market the product.

multistage_ decision_tree video.

Now it is time to label the tree with probabilities and monetary values. The monetary values present no problems, as will be seen shortly. However, the probabilities require a digression so that we can discuss Bayes' rule. The problem is that the given probabilities in Table 6.1 are not the probabilities required in the tree. After we discuss Bayes' rule, we will return to Acme's decision problem.

Figure 6.15 Skeleton of Decision Tree with Option to Buy Information

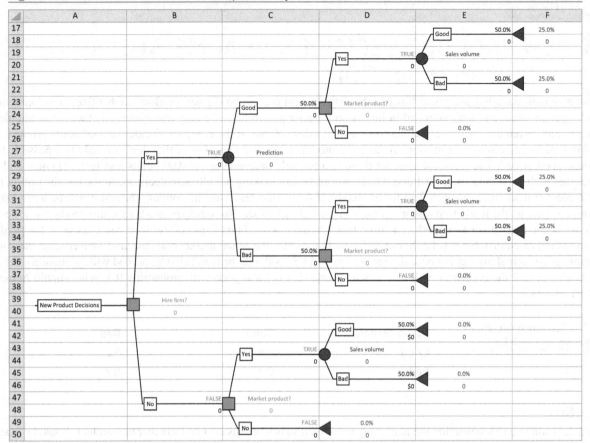

6.6a Bayes' Rule

Bayes' rule, named after the Reverend Thomas Bayes from the 1700s, is a formal mathematical mechanism for updating probabilities as new information becomes available. The general idea is simple, as illustrated in Figure 6.16. The original probabilities are called **prior probabilities**. Then information is observed and Bayes' rule is used to update the prior probabilities to **posterior probabilities**. As the diagram indicates, the terms prior and posterior are relative. If later information is observed, the posterior probabilities in the middle play the role of priors. They are used, along with Bayes' rule, to calculate new posterior probabilities.

The actual updating mechanism can be done in two ways: with frequencies (counts) or with probabilities. We (and our students) believe that the frequency approach is much easier to understand, so we will present it first. But because the probability approach is useful for spreadsheet calculations, we will present it as well.

Figure 6.16 Bayesian Updating Process

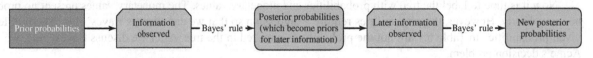

Bayes' Rule: Frequency Approach

Consider the following situation. During a routine physical exam, a middle-aged man named Joe tests positive for a certain disease. There were previously no indications that Joe had this disease, but the positive test sends him into a panic. He "knows" now that he has the disease. Or does he? Suppose that only 1% of all undiagnosed middle-aged men have this disease. Also, suppose the test Joe took is not entirely accurate. For middle-aged men who don't have the disease, there is a 10% chance they will test positive (the false positive rate). For middle-aged men who have the disease, there is a 5% chance they will test negative (the false negative rate). So with a positive test result, what is the probability that Joe has the disease?

A frequency approach starts with a large number, say 10,000, of middle-aged men and follows them according to the stated percentages. A diagram of this appears in Figure 6.17. The percentages on the links are the given percentages, and the number in each box is the percentage times the number in the box above it. We know that Joe's status is in one of the two gray boxes because he tested positive. Therefore, the probability that he has the disease, that is, the probability that his status is in the leftmost gray box, is $95/(95 + 990)$, or about 8.75%.

Figure 6.17 Frequency Approach for Updating Probabilities

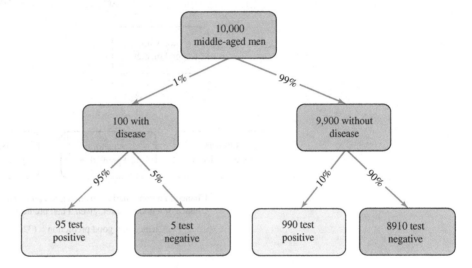

Joe's chance of having the disease, given a positive test = 95/(95+990) = 8.75%
Joe's chance of having the disease, given a negative test = 5/(5+8910) = 0.056%

Joe's chance of testing positive = (95+990)/10000 = 10.9%

We suspect that you are surprised by this low posterior probability. If so, you're not alone. Highly trained physicians, when posed with this same problem, have given widely ranging answers—almost the entire range from 0% to 100%. The problem is that we humans don't have very good intuition about probabilities. However, there are two simple reasons why Joe's posterior probability of having the disease is as low as it is. First, not many men in his age group, only 1%, have the disease. Therefore, we tend to believe that *Joe* doesn't have the disease unless we see convincing evidence to the contrary. The second reason is that this test has fairly large error rates, 10% false positives and 5% false negatives. Therefore, the evidence from the test is *not* entirely convincing.

What if Joe tested negative? Then using the same numbers in the diagram, his posterior probability of having the disease would drop quite a lot from the prior of 1%; it would be $5/(5 + 8910)$, or about 0.06%. We were fairly sure he didn't have the disease before the test (because only 1% of his age group has it), and a negative test result convinces us even more that he doesn't have the disease.

One final calculation that will become useful in Acme's problem appears at the bottom of Figure 6.17. This is the probability that Joe tests positive in the first place. (In general, it is the probability of any potential piece of information.) Of the 10,000 men, 95 + 990 test positive, so this probability is $(95 + 990)/10000$, or about 10.9%. Most of these are *false* positives.

This frequency approach is quite straightforward, even though it often yields surprising and unintuitive results. You are asked to apply it to several other scenarios in the problems. For now, we apply it to Acme's problem in Example 6.3. The prior probabilities of good or bad markets are 40% and 60%. The probabilities for the accuracy of the predictions are given in Table 6.1. From these, we can follow 1000 similar products and predictions, exactly as we did with Joe's disease. (We use 1000 rather than 10,000 for variety. The number chosen doesn't influence the results at all.) The diagram appears in Figure 6.18. The probability of a good market increases from 40% to 64% with a good prediction, and it decreases to 16% with a bad prediction. Also, the probability that the prediction will be good is 50%.

Figure 6.18 Frequencies for Updating Probabilities in Acme Problem

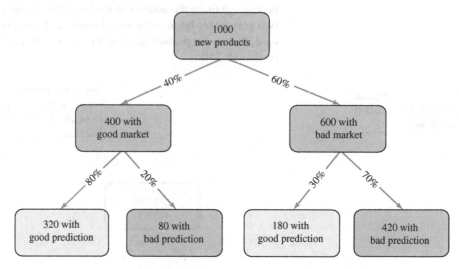

Chance of a good market, given a good prediction = 320/(320+180) = 64%
Chance of a good market, given a bad prediction = 80/(80+420) = 16%

Chance of a good prediction = (320+180)/1000 = 50%

You should be aware that three complementary probabilities are implied by the probabilities shown. After a good prediction, the market will be either good or bad, so the posterior probability of a bad market is 36%. Similarly, the posterior probability of a bad market after a bad prediction is 84%, and the probability of a bad prediction is 50%.

If you like this frequency approach for updating probabilities, you can keep using it. It is a perfectly acceptable way to update probabilities as information is received, and it is equivalent to a more formal use of Bayes' rule, which we now present.

Bayes' Rule: Probability Approach

For any possible outcome O, let $P(O)$ be the probability of O. This implicitly indicates the probability of O occurring, given all the information currently available. If we want to indicate that new information, I, is available, we write the probability as $P(O|I)$. This is called a **conditional probability**. The vertical bar is read "given that," so this is the probability of O, given that we have information I.

The typical situation is that there are several outcomes such as "good market" and "bad market." In general, denote these outcomes as O_1 to O_n, assuming there are n possibilities. Then we start with n prior probabilities, $P(O_1)$ to $P(O_n)$, that sum to 1. Next, we observe new information, I, such as a market prediction, and we want the n updated posterior probabilities, $P(O_1|I)$ to $P(O_n|I)$, that sum to 1. We assume the "opposite" conditional probabilities, $P(I|O_1)$ to $P(I|O_n)$, are given. In Bayesian terminology, these are called **likelihoods**. These likelihoods are the accuracy probabilities in Table 6.1. For example, one of these is the probability of seeing a good prediction, *given* that the market will be good.

However, these likelihoods are not what we need in the decision tree. Because time goes from left to right, we first need the (unconditional) probabilities of possible predictions and then we need the posterior probabilities of market outcomes, given the predictions (see Figure 6.15). So Bayes' rule is a formal rule for turning these conditional probabilities around. It is given in Equation (6.1) for any i from 1 to n.

Bayes' Rule

$$P(O_i|I) = \frac{P(I|O_i)P(O_i)}{P(I|O_1)P(O_1) + \cdots + P(I|O_n)P(O_n)} \qquad (6.1)$$

In words, Bayes' rule says that the posterior is the likelihood times the prior, divided by a sum of likelihoods times priors. As a side benefit, the denominator in Bayes' rule is also useful in multistage decision trees. It is the probability $P(I)$ of the information outcome.

Denominator of Bayes' Rule (Law of Total Probability)

$$P(I) = P(I|O_1)P(O_1) + \cdots + P(I|O_n)P(O_n) \qquad (6.2)$$

This formula is important in its own right. For I to occur, it must occur along with one of the O's. Equation (6.2) decomposes the probability of I into all of these possibilities. It is sometimes called the **law of total probability**.

In the special case where there are only two O's, labeled as O and Not O, Bayes' rule takes the following form:

Bayes' Rule for Two Outcomes

$$P(O|I) = \frac{P(I|O)P(O)}{P(I|O)P(O) + P(I|\text{Not } O)P(\text{Not } O)} \qquad (6.3)$$

Implementing Bayes' Rule for Acme

These formulas are actually fairly easy to implement in Excel, as shown in Figure 6.19 for the Acme problem. (See the file **New Product Decisions – Information Option Finished. xlsx**.) It is important to be consistent in the use of rows and columns for the outcomes (the O's) and the predictions (the I's). If you examine Figure 6.19 closely, we have always put the Good/Bad labels for market outcomes *down* columns, and we have always put the Good/Bad labels for predictions *across* rows. You could do it in the opposite way, but you should be consistent. This allows you to copy formulas. The given probabilities, the priors and the likelihoods, are in the left section, columns B and C. The Bayes' rule calculations are in the right section, columns G and H.

We first implement Equation (6.2) in cells G7 and H7. The formula in cell G7, a sum of likelihoods times priors, is

=SUMPRODUCT(B14:B15,$B$9:$B$10)

and this can be copied to cell H7. Next, we implement Equation (6.3) in the range G11:H12 to calculate the posteriors. Each is a likelihood times a prior, divided by one of the sums in row 7. The formula in cell G11 is

=B14*$B$9/G$7

bayesian_revision video.

Figure 6.19 Bayes' Rule Calculations for Acme Problem

	A	B	C	D	E	F	G	H	I
1	Acme multistage new product decisions with an option to buy information								
2									
3	**Inputs**								
4	Cost of market research	−$150,000				**Bayes' rule calculations**			
5	Fixed marketing cost	−$4,000,000				Probabilities of predictions			
6	Unit margin	$18					Good	Bad	Sum check
7							0.5	0.5	1
8	Market	Prior probability	Sales volume	Net revenue					
9	Good	0.40	600,000	$10,800,000		Posterior probabilities, given predictions			
10	Bad	0.60	100,000	$1,800,000		Actual\Predicted	Good	Bad	
11						Good	0.64	0.16	
12	Probabilities that indicate the accuracy of the predictions					Bad	0.36	0.84	
13	Actual\Predicted	Good	Bad	Sum check		Sum check	1	1	
14	Good	0.8	0.2	1					
15	Bad	0.3	0.7	1					

and because of the careful use of relative/absolute addresses, this can be copied to the range G11:H12. (The "Sum checks" indicate which probabilities should sum to 1.) Fortunately, this procedure is perfectly general. If you always enter outcomes down columns and information across rows, the same essential formulas given here will always work. Of course, you can check that these Bayes' rule calculations give the same results as the frequency approach in Figure 6.18.

Completing the Acme Decision Tree

Now that we have the required probabilities, we can label Acme's decision tree from Figure 6.15 with monetary values and probabilities. The completed tree appears in Figure 6.20. You should examine this tree carefully. The cost of hiring the marketing research firm is entered when the hiring takes place, in cell B28, the fixed cost of marketing the product is entered when the decision to market occurs, in cells D20, D32, and C44, and the net revenues are enter in the branches to the right as before. As for probabilities, the priors are entered in the bottom section of the tree, the part where the marketing research firm is not hired. Then the probabilities of the predictions are entered in column C (they just happen to be 50-50), and the posterior probabilities are entered in column E. Of course, all of these entries are cell references to the inputs and calculations in Figure 6.19.

As before, once all of the monetary values and probabilities are entered in the tree, PrecisionTree automatically performs all the folding-back calculations, as you can see in Figure 6.20. Then you can follow the TRUEs. In this case, the marketing research firm should be hired. If its prediction is "good," Acme should market the product. If its prediction is "bad," Acme should abandon the product. The EMV from this strategy is $1.63 million.

Fundamental Insight

Making Sequential Decisions

Whenever you have a chance to make several sequential decisions and you will learn useful information between decision points, the decision you make initially depends on the decisions you plan to make in the future, and these depend on the information you will learn in the meantime. In other words, when you decide what to do initially, you should look ahead to see what your future options will be, and what your decision will be under each option. Such a contingency plan is typically superior to a *myopic* (short-sighted) plan that doesn't take into account future options in the initial decision making.

Figure 6.20 Completed Decision Tree for Acme Problem

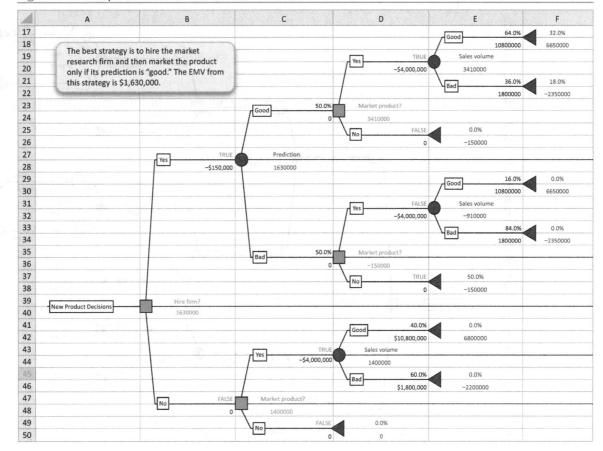

6-6b The Value of Information

In a decision-making context, information is usually bought to reduce the uncertainty about some outcome. The information always comes with a price tag, in this case $150,000, and the question is whether the information is worth this much. Alternatively, the question is how much you would be willing to pay for the information. In some situations the answer is clear. To see such a situation, change the fixed marketing cost from $4 million to $2 million to get the decision tree in Figure 6.21. Then the marketing research is worth *nothing* to Acme. It is not even worth $1, let alone $150,000. Do you see why? The key is that Acme should now make the *same* decision, market the product, regardless of the prediction the marketing research firm makes. Essentially, Acme will now ignore the firm's prediction, so it makes no sense for Acme to pay for a prediction it intends to ignore.

The reason the marketing research firm's prediction is worthless is partly because it's inaccurate and partly because marketing continues to be better than not marketing even when the probability of a bad market is high. In other words, it would take a *really* bad market prediction to persuade to Acme not to market.

However, the behavior is different in Figure 6.20, where the fixed marketing cost is $4 million. Now the fixed cost more than offsets the possible gain from a good market unless the probability of a good market is fairly high—64% and 40% are high enough, but 16% isn't. In this case, the marketing research firm *should* be hired for $150,000, and then Acme should market the product only if it hears a good prediction.

In this case, we know that the marketing research firm is worth its $150,000 price, but how much would Acme be willing to pay to hire the firm. This amount is called the **expected value of information**, or **EVI**, and it is given by Equation (6.4).[7]

---

7 The traditional term is EVSI, where S stands for "sample," meaning "imperfect." We think "sample" has too much of a statistical connotation, so we omit it.

Figure 6.21 Completed Tree with a Smaller Fixed Marketing Cost

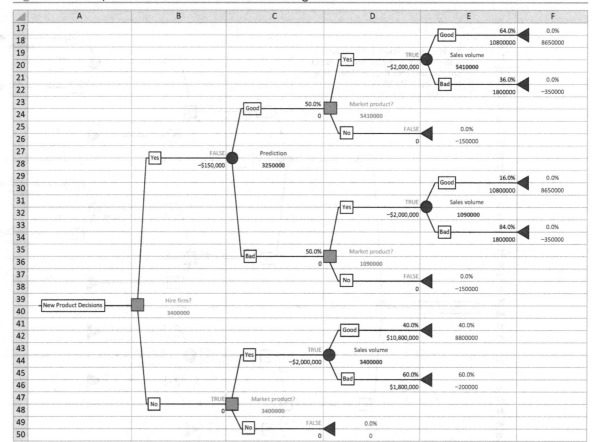

The **EVI** is the most you would be willing to pay for the sample information.

Equation for EVI

EVI = EMV with (free) information − EMV without information   **(6.4)**

The calculation of EVI is quite easy, given the completed decision tree in Figure 6.20. The $1.63 million value in cell C28 is Acme's net EMV after paying $150,000 to the firm. If Acme could get this information for free, its EMV would be 1.630 + 0.150, or $1.78 million. On the other hand, the bottom section of the tree shows that Acme's EMV with no information is $1.4 million. Therefore, according to Equation (6.4), EVI is

EVI = 1.78 − 1.4 = $380,000

In other words, the marketing research firm could charge up to $380,000, and Acme would still be willing to hire them. You can prove this to yourself. With the fixed marketing cost at $4 million, change the cost of the hiring the firm to $379,000. The decision tree should still have a TRUE for the hiring decision. Then change the cost to $381,000. Now there should be a FALSE for the hiring decision.

Although the calculation of EVI is straightforward once the decision tree has been created, the decision tree itself requires a lot of probability assessments and Bayes' rule calculations. These can be difficult, depending on the type of information available. There-fore, it is sometimes useful to ask how much *any* information could be worth, regardless of its form or accuracy. The result is called the **expected value of perfect information**, or **EVPI**, and it is given by Equation (6.5).

The **EVPI** is the most you would be willing to pay for perfect information.

Equation for EVPI

EVPI = EMV with (free) perfect information − EMV without information **(6.5)**

To calculate EVPI for the Acme problem, forget about the marketing research firm and its possible prediction. All you have is the bottom of the tree in Figure 6.20, which uses Acme's prior probabilities of market outcomes. So Acme's EMV with no infor-mation is $1.4 million. To find the EMV with free perfect information, imagine that Acme will be told, truthfully, whether the market will be good or bad before the mar-keting decision has to be made. With probability 0.4, the prior probability, it will be told "good," and with probability 0.6, it will be told "bad." If it knows the market will be good, it should market the product because the net payoff is $10.8 million from sales minus $4 million for the fixed cost, or $6.8 million, a positive value. On the other hand, if it knows the market will be bad, it should not market the product because this would lead to a net payoff of $1.8 million from sales minus $4 million for the fixed cost, which is less than the 0 value it could get from not marketing the product. Therefore, according to Equation (6.5), EVPI is

$$EVPI = (0.4)(6.8) + (0.6)(0) - 1.4 = \$1.32 \text{ million}$$

In words, no information, regardless of its form or accuracy, could be worth more than $1.32 million to Acme. This calculation is often performed because it is easy and it provides an upper limit on the value of *any* information. As we saw, however, some infor-mation, such as the marketing research firm's prediction, can be worth considerably less than $1.32 million. This is because the firm's predictions are not perfect.

Let's make the EVPI calculation once more, for the problem where the fixed market-ing cost is reduced to $2 million. In this case, the value of the market research firm was 0, but will EVPI also be 0? The answer is no. Referring to the bottom section of Figure 6.21, the calculation is

$$EVPI = (0.4)*\text{Max}(10.8-2,0) + (0.6)*\text{Max}(1.8-2,0) - 3.4$$

$$= (0.4)(8.8) + (0.6)(0) - 3.4 = \$0.12 \text{ million}$$

Each "Max" in this equation indicates the best of marketing and not marketing, and the second max is 0 because the fixed marketing cost is greater than the sales revenue if the market is bad.

In this case, Acme shouldn't pay anything for the marketing research firm's infor-mation, but *other* types of information could be worth up to $0.12 million. The intuition here is the following. The marketing research firm's information is worthless because Acme will ignore it, marketing the product regardless of the information. But perfect information is worth something because Acme will act one way, market the product, if the information is good, and it will act another way, don't market the product, if the infor-mation is bad. Presumably, other types of *imperfect* information could have the same effect and hence be worth something, but they can't be worth more than $0.12 million.

> ### Fundamental Insight
>
> #### The Value of Information
>
> The amount you should be willing to spend for information is the expected increase in EMV you can obtain from having the information. If the actual price of the information is less than or equal to this amount, you should purchase it; otherwise, the information is not worth its price. In addition, information that never affects your decision is worthless, and it should not be purchased at any price. Finally, the value of *any* information can never be greater than the value of perfect information that would eliminate all uncertainty.

6-6c Sensitivity Analysis

We have already performed one sensitivity analysis, simply by changing the fixed marketing cost in cell B5 from $4 million to $2 million and seeing how the tree changes. You can perform any number of similar "ad hoc" sensitivity analyses in this way, provided that the entries in the tree are linked to the input section of your worksheet. But you might also like to perform a more formal sensitivity analysis with PrecisionTree's powerful tools. We will show the results of several such sensitivity analyses, each with the fixed marketing cost set to $4 million. (We won't provide the step-by-step details of how to perform these in PrecisionTree, but if you need help, you can watch the Quick Start step 5 video we referenced earlier.)

The first sensitivity analysis is on the prior probability, currently 0.4, of a good market. To do this, you should make sure cell B10 contains a formula, **=1−B9**. The reason is that as the probability in cell B9 varies, we want probability in cell B10 to vary accordingly. (In general, if you want to perform a sensitivity analysis on a probability, you should use formulas to guarantee that the relevant probabilities continue to sum to 1. In the file for this example, you will see that there are also formulas in cells C14 and C15 for this same purpose.)

The **strategy region graph** in Figure 6.22 shows how Acme's EMVs from hiring and not hiring the firm vary as the prior probability of a good market varies from 0.2 to 0.6. Acme wants the largest EMV, which corresponds to the Yes line for small probabilities (up to about 0.48) and the No line for large probabilities. Why would Acme hire the firm only when the prior probability of a good market is small? The reason is that this is when

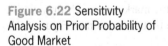

Figure 6.22 Sensitivity Analysis on Prior Probability of Good Market

the firm's predictions are most helpful. On the right side of the graph, Acme is already fairly sure that the market is good, so the marketing research firm's predictions in this case are less useful. Of course, the value of a sensitivity analysis such as this is that your intuition might not be so good. It tells you what you might not have been able to figure out on your own.

If you don't want to use PrecisionTree's Sensitivity Analysis, which is admittedly a bit confusing, you can use data tables that capture the TRUE/FALSE values on decision branches. One of these is illustrated in Figure 6.23. It tells exactly the same story as Figure 6.22.

Figure 6.23 Sensitivity Analysis with a Data Table

	H	I	J	K	L	M
16	Sensitivity of hiring decision to prior probability of Good					
17	P(Good)	Hire?				
18		TRUE	←	Link to cell B27		
19	0.38	TRUE				
20	0.39	TRUE				
21	0.40	TRUE				
22	0.41	TRUE				
23	0.42	TRUE				
24	0.43	TRUE				
25	0.44	TRUE				
26	0.45	TRUE				
27	0.46	TRUE				
28	0.47	TRUE				
29	0.48	FALSE				
30	0.49	FALSE				
31	0.50	FALSE				
32	0.51	FALSE				
33	0.52	FALSE				
34	0.53	FALSE				

When you fill out PrecisionTree's Sensitivity Analysis dialog box, you can choose a "starting node" other than the "Entire Model." We repeated the analysis by choosing cell D36 as the starting node. (See Figure 6.20.) The idea here is that Acme has already decided to hire the firm and has then seen a bad prediction. The strategy region graph in Figure 6.24 shows the EMVs from marketing and not marketing the product, from this point on, as the prior probability of a good market varies as before.

Figure 6.24 Sensitivity Analysis for Marketing Decision after a Bad Prediction

As you can see, Acme should *not* market the product after a bad prediction unless the prior probability of a good market is approximately 0.55 or higher. This makes intuitive sense.

In one final sensitivity analysis, a two-way analysis, we let the prior probability of a good market vary as before, and we let the fixed marketing cost vary from 25% below to 25% above its current value of $4 million. Also, we choose "Entire Model" as the starting node. The results are shown in Figure 6.25. The diamonds correspond to input values where Acme should hire the firm, and the triangles correspond to input values where Acme shouldn't hire the firm. The pattern indicates that hiring is best only when the fixed marketing cost is high and/or the prior probability of a good market is low. For example, if the prior probability of a good market is 0.5, the Acme should hire the firm only if its fixed marketing cost is $4.2 million or above. As another example, if Acme's fixed marketing cost is $3.8 million, it should hire the firm only if the prior probability of a good market is 0.4 or below.

Figure 6.25 Two-Way Sensitivity Analysis

One of the most important benefits of using PrecisionTree (or Excel data tables) is that once you have built the decision tree, you can quickly run any number of sensitivity analyses such as the ones shown. They often provide important insights that help you better understand the decision problem. You are asked to perform other sensitivity analyses on this example (and Example 6.2) in the problems.

Problems

Solutions for problems whose numbers appear within a colored box can be found in the Student Solution Files.

Level A

11. In Example 6.2, Acme's probability of technological success, 0.8, is evidently large enough to make "continue development" the best decision. How low would this probability have to be to make the opposite decision best?

12. In Example 6.2, the fixed costs are split $4 million for development and $2 million for marketing. Perform a sensitivity analysis where the sum of these two fixed costs remains at $6 million but the split changes. Specifically, let the fixed cost of development vary from $1 million to $5 million in increments of $0.5 million. Does Acme's best strategy change in this range? Use either a data table or PrecisionTree's Sensitivity Analysis tools to answer this question.

13. In Example 6.2, use a two-way PrecisionTree sensitivity analysis to examine the changes in both of the two previous problems simultaneously. Let the probability of technological success vary from 0.6 to 0.9 in increments of 0.05, and let the fixed cost of development vary as indicated in the previous problem. Explain in a short memo exactly what the results of the sensitivity analysis imply about Acme's best strategy.

14. In the file **Bayes Rule for Disease.xlsx**, explain why the probabilities in cells B9 and B10 (or those in cells C9 and C10) do **not** necessarily sum to 1, but why the probabilities in cells B9 and C9 (or those in cells B10 and C10) *do* necessarily sum to 1.

15. In using Bayes' rule for the presence of a disease (see Figure 6.17 and the file **Bayes Rule for Disease.xlsx**), we assumed that there are only two test results, positive or negative. Suppose there is another possible test result, "maybe." The 2×2 range B9:C10 in the file should now be replaced by a 2×3 range, B9:D10, for positive, maybe, and negative (in that order). Let the corresponding probabilities in row 9 be 0.85, 0.10, and 0.05, and let those in row 10 be 0.05, 0.15, and 0.80. Redo the Bayes' rule calculations with both the frequency approach and the probability approach.

16. The finished version of the file for Example 6.3 contains two "Strategy B9" sheets. Explain what each of them indicates and how they differ.

17. Starting with the finished version of the file for Example 6.3, get back into PrecisionTree's One-Way Sensitivity Analysis dialog box and add three more inputs. (These will be in addition to the two inputs already there, cells B9 and B5.) The first should be the unit margin in cell B6, varied from $15 to $21 in increments of $1, the second should be the sales volume from a good market in cell C9, varied from 400 to 700 in increments of 50, and the third should be the probability of a good prediction, given a good market, in cell B14, varied from 0.7 to 0.9 in increments of 0.05. Make sure the analysis type is one-way, all five of the inputs are checked, and the starting node is "Entire Model." In the "Include Results" section, check the Strategy Region, Tornado Graph, and Spider Graph options, and then run the analysis. Interpret the resulting outputs. Specifically, what do the tornado and spider graphs indicate?

18. Starting with the finished version of the file for Example 6.3, change the probabilities in cells B9 (make it smaller), B14 (make it larger), and B15 (make it smaller) in some systematic way (you can choose the details) and, for each combination, calculate the EVI. Does EVI change in the way you'd expect? Why?

19. Suppose you are a heterosexual white male and are going to be tested to see if you are HIV positive. Assume that if you are HIV positive, your test will always come back positive. Assume that if you are not HIV positive, there is still a 0.001 chance that your test will indicate that you are HIV positive. In reality, 1 of 10,000 heterosexual white males is HIV positive. Your doctor calls and says that you have tested HIV positive. He is sorry but there is a 99.9% $(1 - 0.001)$ chance that you have HIV. Is he correct? What is the actual probability that you are HIV positive?

Level B

20. If you examine the decision tree in Figure 6.12 (or any other decision trees from PrecisionTree), you will see *two* numbers (in blue font) to the right of each end node. The bottom number is the combined monetary value from following the corresponding path through the tree. The top number is the probability that this path will be followed, given that the *best* strategy is used. With this in mind, explain (1) how the positive probabilities following the end nodes are calculated, (2) why some of the probabilities following the end nodes are 0, and (3) why the sum of the probabilities following the end nodes is necessarily 1.

21. In Example 6.2, a technological failure implies that the game is over—the product must be abandoned. Change the problem so that there are two levels of technological failure, each with probability 0.1. In the first level, Acme can pay a further development cost D to fix the product and make it a technological success. Then it can decide whether to market the product. In the second level, the product must be abandoned. Modify the decision tree as necessary. Then answer the following questions.
   a. For which values of D should Acme fix the product and then market it, given that the first level of technological failure occurs?
   b. For which values of D is Acme's best *first* decision still to "continue development"?
   c. Explain why these two questions are asking different things and can have different answers.

22. The model in Example 6.3 has only two market outcomes, good and bad, and two corresponding predictions, good and bad. Modify the decision tree by allowing three outcomes and three predictions, good, fair, and bad. You can change the inputs to the model (monetary values and probabilities) in any reasonable way you like. Then you will also have to modify the Bayes' rule calculations. You can decide whether it is easier to modify the existing tree or start from scratch with a new tree.

23. The terms *prior* and *posterior* are relative. Assume that the test in Figure 6.17 (and in the file **Bayes Rule for Disease.xlsx**) has been performed, and the outcome is positive, which leads to the posterior probabilities shown. Now assume there is a *second* test, independent of the first, that can be used as a follow-up. Assume that its false-positive and false-negative rates are 0.02 and 0.06.
   a. Use the posterior probabilities as *prior* probabilities in a second Bayes' rule calculation. (Now *prior* means

prior to the second test.) If Joe also tests positive in this second test, what is the posterior probability that he has the disease?

b. We assumed that the two tests are independent. Why might this not be realistic? If they are not independent, what kind of additional information would you need about the likelihoods of the test results?

24. In the OJ Simpson trial it was accepted that OJ had battered his wife. OJ's lawyer tried to negate the impact of this information by stating that in a one-year period, only 1 out of 2500 battered women are murdered, so the fact that OJ battered his wife does not give much evidence that he was the murderer. The prosecution (foolishly!) let this go unchallenged. Here are the relevant statistics: In a typical year 6.25 million women are battered, 2500 are battered and murdered, and 2250 of the women who were battered and murdered were killed by the batterer. How should the prosecution have refuted the defense's argument?

6-7 The Role of Risk Aversion

Rational decision makers are sometimes willing to violate the EMV maximization criterion when large amounts of money are at stake. These decision makers are willing to sacrifice some EMV to reduce risk. Are you ever willing to do so personally? Consider the following scenarios.

- You have a chance to enter a lottery where you will win $100,000 with probability 0.1 or win nothing with probability 0.9. Alternatively, you can receive $5000 for certain. Would you take the certain $5000, even though the EMV of the lottery is $10,000? Or change the $100,000 to $1,000,000 and the $5000 to $50,000 and ask yourself whether you'd prefer the sure $50,000.
- You can buy collision insurance on your expensive new car or not buy it. The insurance costs a certain premium and carries some deductible provision. If you decide to pay the premium, then you are essentially paying a certain amount to avoid a gamble: the possibility of wrecking your car and not having it insured. You can be sure that the premium is greater than the expected cost of damage; otherwise, the insurance company would not stay in business. Therefore, from an EMV standpoint you should not purchase the insurance. But would you drive without this type of insurance?

These examples, the second of which is certainly realistic, illustrate situations where rational people do not behave as EMV maximizers. Then how do they act? This question has been studied extensively by many researchers, both mathematically and behaviorally. Although there is still not perfect agreement, most researchers believe that if certain basic behavioral assumptions hold, people are **expected utility** maximizers—that is, they choose the alternative with the largest expected utility. Although we will not go deeply into the subject of expected utility maximization, the discussion in this section presents the main ideas.

Fundamental Insight

Risk Aversion

When large amounts of money are at stake, most of us are risk averse, at least to some extent. We are willing to sacrifice some EMV to avoid risk. The exact way this is done, using utility functions and expected utility, can be difficult to implement in real situations, but the idea is simple. If you are an EMV maximizer, you are indifferent between a gamble with a given EMV and a sure dollar amount equal to the EMV of the gamble. However, if you are risk averse, you prefer the sure dollar amount to the gamble. That is, you are willing to accept a sure dollar amount that is somewhat *less than* the EMV of the gamble, just to avoid risk. The more EMV you are willing to give up, the more risk averse you are.

6-7a Utility Functions

We begin by discussing an individual's **utility function**. This is a mathematical function that transforms monetary values—payoffs and costs—into *utility values*. Essentially, an individual's utility function specifies the individual's preferences for various monetary payoffs and costs and, in doing so, it automatically encodes the individual's attitudes toward risk. Most individuals are *risk averse*. Intuitively, this means they are willing to sacrifice some EMV to avoid risky gambles. In terms of the utility function, this means that every extra dollar of payoff is worth slightly less than the previous dollar, and every extra dollar of cost is considered slightly more costly (in terms of utility) than the previous dollar. The resulting utility functions are shaped as in Figure 6.26. Mathematically, these functions are said to be *increasing* and *concave*. The increasing part means that they go uphill—everyone prefers more money to less money. The concave part means that they increase at a decreasing rate. This is the risk-averse behavior.

Figure 6.26 Risk-Averse Utility Function

There are two aspects of implementing **expected utility maximization** in a real decision analysis. First, an individual's (or company's) utility function must be assessed. This is a time-consuming task that typically involves many trade-offs. It is usually carried out by experts in the field, and we do not discuss the details of the process here. Second, the resulting utility function is used to find the best decision. This second step is relatively straightforward. You substitute utility values for monetary values in the decision tree and then fold back as usual. That is, you calculate expected *utilities* at probability branches and take maximums of expected *utilities* at decision branches. We will look at a numerical example later in this section.

6-7b Exponential Utility

Utility assessment is not easy. Even in the best of circumstances, when a trained consultant attempts to assess the utility function of a single person, the process requires the person to make a series of choices between hypothetical alternatives involving uncertain outcomes. Unless the person has some training in probability, these choices will probably be difficult to understand, let alone make, and it is unlikely that the person will answer *consistently* as the questioning proceeds. The process is even more difficult when a *company's* utility function is being assessed. Because different company executives typically have different attitudes toward risk, it can be difficult for these people to reach a consensus on a common utility function.

For these reasons, classes of ready-made utility functions are available. One important class is called *exponential utility* and has been used in many financial investment decisions. An exponential utility function has only one adjustable numerical parameter, called the *risk tolerance*, and there are straightforward ways to discover an appropriate value of this parameter for a particular individual or company. So the advantage of using an exponential utility function is that it is relatively easy to assess. The drawback is that exponential utility functions do not capture all types of attitudes toward risk. Nevertheless, their ease of use has made them popular.

An **exponential utility function** has the following form:

Exponential utility

$$U(x) = 1 - e^{-x/R} \tag{6.6}$$

Here x is a monetary value (a payoff if positive, a cost if negative), $U(x)$ is the utility of this value, and $R > 0$ is the risk tolerance. As the name suggests, the risk tolerance measures how much risk the decision maker will accept. The larger the value of R, the *less* risk averse the decision maker is. That is, a person with a large value of R is more willing to take risks than a person with a small value of R. In the limit, a person with an extremely large value of R is an EMV maximizer.

> The **risk tolerance** for an exponential utility function is a single number that specifies an individual's aversion to risk. The higher the risk tolerance, the less risk averse the individual is.

To assess a person's (or company's) exponential utility function, only one number, the value of R, needs to be assessed. There are two tips for doing this. First, it has been shown that the risk tolerance is approximately equal to the dollar amount R such that the decision maker is indifferent between the following two options:

- Option 1: Receive no payoff at all.
- Option 2: Receive a payoff of R dollars or incur a cost of $R/2$ dollars, depending on the flip of a fair coin.

For example, if you are indifferent between a bet where you win $1000 or lose $500, with probability 0.5 each, and not betting at all, your R is approximately $1000. From this criterion it certainly makes intuitive sense that a wealthier person (or company) ought to have a larger value of R. This has been found in practice.

A second tip for finding R is based on empirical evidence found by Ronald Howard, a prominent decision analyst. Through his consulting experience with large companies, he discovered tentative relationships between risk tolerance and several financial variables: net sales, net income, and equity. [See Howard (1988).] Specifically, he found that R was approximately 6.4% of net sales, 124% of net income, and 15.7% of equity for the companies he studied. For example, according to this prescription, a company with net sales of $30 million should have a risk tolerance of approximately $1.92 million. Howard admits that these percentages are only guidelines. However, they do indicate that larger and more profitable companies tend to have larger values of R, which means that they are more willing to take risks involving large dollar amounts.

We illustrate the use of the expected utility criterion, and exponential utility in particular, in the following version of the Acme decision problem.

Finding the appropriate risk tolerance value for any company or individual is not necessarily easy, but it is easier than assessing an entire utility function.

EXAMPLE

6.4 NEW PRODUCT DECISIONS WITH RISK AVERSION

This example is the same as Acme's single-stage decision problem in Example 6.1, but we now assume that Acme is risk averse and that it assesses its utility function as exponential with risk tolerance $5 million. How does this risk aversion affect its decision-making progress?

Objective

To see how risk aversion affects Acme's decision-making process.

Where Do the Numbers Come From?

The only new number is the risk tolerance. According to the earlier discussion, this value implies that Acme is indifferent between entering a gamble where it could win $5 million or lose $2.5 million on the flip of a fair coin, or not enter the gamble at all. Because the risk tolerance is a difficult number to assess, it is a good candidate for a sensitivity analysis.

Solution

Starting with the decision tree from the previous example (see Figure 6.11), there are only two changes to make. First, it is useful to add the risk tolerance as a new input, as shown in cell B12 of Figure 6.27. Second, you must tell PrecisionTree that you want to use expected utility. To do so, select Model Settings from the PrecisionTree Settings dropdown list, select the Utility Function tab, and fill it in as shown in Figure 6.28. The most important part is to check the "Use Utility Function" option. Then you can choose any of three display options. If you choose Expected Value, you will see EMVs on the tree (in the colored cells), but expected utility will actually be maximized in the background. This is useful if you want to see how much EMV you are sacrificing by being risk-averse. Alternatively, if you choose Expected Utility, as is done here, you will see utility values rather than monetary values. The Certainty Equivalent option will be discussed shortly.

Figure 6.27 Risk Tolerance as an Extra Input

▲	A	B	C	D
1	**Acme single-stage new product decision with risk aversion**			
2				
3	**Inputs**			
4	Fixed cost	−$6,000,000		
5	Unit margin	$18		
6				
7	Market	Probability	Sales volume	Net revenue
8	Great	0.45	600000	$10,800,000
9	Fair	0.35	300000	$5,400,000
10	Awful	0.20	90000	$1,620,000
11				
12	Risk tolerance	$5,000,000		

Figure 6.28 PrecisionTree Utility Function Dialog Box

The resulting tree that displays expected utilities appears in Figure 6.29. If you compare this tree to the EMV tree in Figure 6.11, you will see that Acme's best strategy has been reversed. As an EMV maximizer, Acme should market the product. As a risk-averse expected utility maximizer, it should not market the product. The expected utility from marketing the product is negative, −0.047, and the utility from not marketing the product is 0. (We formatted these as decimal numbers in the tree.

They are *not* expressed in dollars.) Neither of these expected utilities is meaningful in an absolute sense; only their relative values are important. The larger corresponds to the best decision.

Figure 6.29 Decision Tree Displaying Expected Utilities

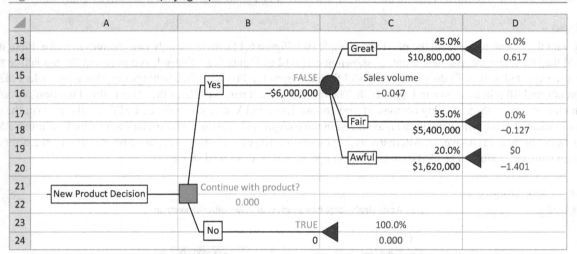

6-7c Certainty Equivalents

The reversal in Acme's decision can be understood better by looking at certainty equivalents. For a risk-averse person, the **certainty equivalent** of a gamble is the *sure* dollar amount the person would accept to avoid the gamble. In other words, the person is indifferent between taking this sure amount and taking the gamble. By selecting Certainty Equivalent in Figure 6.28, you can see the certainty equivalents in the tree, as shown in Figure 6.30. (We formatted the certainty equivalents as currencies because that's what they really are.)

Recall from Figure 6.11 that the EMV for marketing the product is $1.074 million. However, this is not how the risk-averse Acme sees the decision to market the product. Acme now sees this gamble as equivalent to a *loss* of approximately $230,000. In other words, Acme would *pay* up to $230,000 to avoid this gamble. Of course, it doesn't have to pay anything. The company can simply decide to abandon the product and receive a sure payoff of $0; hence, TRUE on the bottom branch indicates the best decision.

Again, risk aversion is all about giving up some EMV to avoid a gamble. In this case, Acme is able to obtain an EMV of $1.074 million by marketing the product, but the company is willing to trade this for a sure $0 payoff because of its aversion to risk.

What happens if Acme is less risk-averse, with a larger risk tolerance? You can check, for example, that if the company's risk tolerance doubles from $5 million to $10 million, the best decision reverts back to the original "market the product" decision, and the certainty equivalent of this decision increases to about $408,000. That is, Acme would be willing to accept a sure $408,000 to avoid a gamble with EMV $1.074 million. Only when the company's risk tolerance becomes huge will the certainty equivalent be near the original EMV of $1.074 million.

Figure 6.30 Decision Tree Displaying Certainty Equivalents

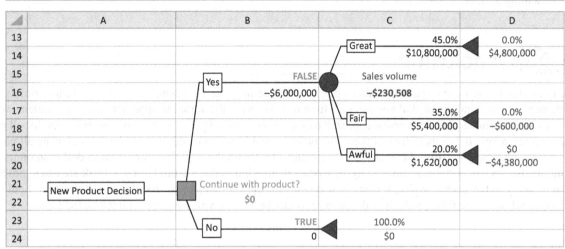

6-7d Is Expected Utility Maximization Used?

The previous discussion indicates that expected utility maximization is a somewhat involved task. The question, then, is whether the effort is justified. Theoretically, expected utility maximization might be interesting to researchers, but is it really used in the business world? The answer appears to be: not very often. For example, one article on the practice of decision making [see Kirkwood (1992)] quotes Ronald Howard—the same person we quoted previously—as having found risk aversion to be of practical concern in only 5% to 10% of business decision analyses. This same article quotes the president of a Fortune 500 company as saying, "Most of the decisions we analyze are for a few million dollars. It is adequate to use expected value (EMV) for these."

Problems

Level A

25. Explain what it means in general when we say a risk-averse decision maker is willing to give up some EMV to avoid risk? How is this apparent in certainty equivalents of gambles?
26. Using the finished version of the file for Example 6.4, use a data table to perform a sensitivity analysis on the risk tolerance. Specifically, let the risk tolerance in cell B12 vary from $5 million to $20 million and keep track of two outputs in the data table, the TRUE/FALSE value in cell B14 and the certainty equivalent in cell C15. Interpret the results.
27. You saw in Example 6.4 how Acme prefers to abandon the product when the risk tolerance in cell B12 is $5 million. This is despite the fact that the EMV from

continuing with the product is well above 0. Using this same risk tolerance, experiment with the sales volume from a great market in cell C8 to see approximately how large it has to be for Acme to prefer the "continue with product" decision. (One way to do this is with a data table, using the TRUE/FALSE value in cell B14 as the single output.) With this sales volume, what is the certainty equivalent of the "continue with product" decision? How does it compare to the decision's EMV? Explain the difference between the two.

Level B

28. Starting with the finished version of Example 6.2, change the decision criterion to "maximize expected utility," using an exponential utility function with risk tolerance $5 million. Display certainty equivalents on the tree.

a. Keep doubling the risk tolerance until the company's best strategy is the same as with the EMV criterion—continue with development and then market if successful. Comment on the implications of this.

b. With this final risk tolerance, explain exactly what the certainty equivalents in cells B31, C27, D23, and E17 (that is, those to the right of the various nodes) really mean. You might phrase these explanations something like, "If Acme were at the point where …, they would be willing to trade … for …."

29. Starting with the finished version of Example 6.3, change the decision criterion to "maximize expected utility," using an exponential utility function with risk tolerance $5 million. Display certainty equivalents on the tree. Is the company's best strategy the same as with the EMV criterion? What is the EVI? (*Hint*: EVI is still the most Acme would be willing to pay in dollars for the marketing research firm's predictions, and it can be calculated from certainty equivalents.)

6-8 Conclusion

In this chapter we have discussed methods that can be used in decision-making problems where uncertainty is a key element. Perhaps the most important skill you can gain from this chapter is the ability to approach decision problems with uncertainty in a systematic manner. This systematic approach requires you to list all possible decisions or strategies, list all possible uncertain outcomes, assess the probabilities of these outcomes (possibly with the aid of Bayes' rule), calculate all necessary monetary values, and finally perform the necessary calculations to obtain the best decision. If large dollar amounts are at stake, you might also need to perform a utility analysis, where the decision maker's attitudes toward risk are taken into account. Once the basic analysis has been completed, using best guesses for the various parameters of the problem, you should perform a sensitivity analysis to see whether the best decision continues to be best within a range of input parameters.

Summary of Key Terms

TERM	EXPLANATION	EXCEL	PAGES	EQUATION
Expected monetary value (EMV)	The weighted average of the possible payoffs from a decision, weighted by their probabilities		228	
EMV criterion	Choose the decision with the maximum EMV		228	
Decision tree	A graphical device for illustrating all of the aspects of the decision problem and for finding the optimal decision (or decision strategy)		230	
Folding-back procedure	Calculation method for decision tree; starting at the right, take EMVs at probability nodes, maximums of EMVs at decision nodes		231	
PrecisionTree	Excel add-in developed by Palisade for building and analyzing decision trees	Has its own ribbon	236	
Contingency plan	A decision strategy where later decisions depend on earlier decisions and outcomes observed in the meantime		240	
Risk profile	Chart that represents the probability distribution of monetary outcomes for any decision		242	
Bayes' rule	Formula for updating probabilities as new information becomes available; *prior probabilities* are transformed into *posterior probabilities*		248	6.1
Law of total probability	The denominator in Bayes' rule, for calculating the (unconditional) probability of an information outcome		248	6.2
Expected value of information (EVI)	The most the (imperfect) information (such as the results of a test market) would be worth		252	6.4
Expected value of perfect information (EVPI)	The most perfect information on some uncertain outcome would be worth; represents an upper bound on *any* EVI		252	6.5

Key Terms (continued)

TERM	EXPLANATION	EXCEL	PAGES	EQUATION
Strategy region graph	Useful for seeing how the optimal decision changes as selected inputs vary	PrecisionTree	254	
Tornado and spider graphs	Useful for seeing which inputs affect a selected EMV the most	PrecisionTree	256	
Expected utility maximization	Choosing the decision that maximizes the *expected utility;* typically sacrifices EMV to avoid risk when large monetary amounts are at stake		258	
Utility function	A mathematical function that encodes an individual's (or company's) attitudes toward risk		258	
Exponential utility function, risk tolerance	A popular class of utility functions, where only a single parameter, the *risk tolerance,* has to be specified		259	6.6
Certainty equivalent	The sure dollar value equivalent to the expected utility of a gamble		262	

Problems

Solutions for problems whose numbers appear within a colored box can be found in the Student Solution Files.

Conceptual Questions

C.1. Your company needs to make an important decision that involves large monetary consequences. You have listed all of the possible outcomes and the monetary payoffs and costs from all outcomes and all potential decisions. You want to use the EMV criterion, but you realize that this requires probabilities and you see no way to find the required probabilities. What can you do?

C.2. If your company makes a particular decision in the face of uncertainty, you estimate that it will either gain $10,000, gain $1000, or lose $5000, with probabilities 0.40, 0.30, and 0.30, respectively. You (correctly) calculate the EMV as $2800. However, you distrust the use of this EMV for decision-making purposes. After all, you reason that you will never receive $2800; you will receive $10,000, $1000, or lose $5000. Discuss this reasoning.

C.3. In the previous question, suppose you have the option of receiving a check for $2700 instead of making the risky decision described. Would you make the risky decision, where you *could* lose $5000, or would you take the sure $2700? What would influence your decision?

C.4. In a classic oil-drilling example, you are trying to decide whether to drill for oil on a field that might or might not contain any oil. Before making this decision, you have the option of hiring a geologist to perform some seismic tests and then predict whether there is any oil or not. You assess that if there is actually oil, the geologist will predict there is oil with probability 0.85. You also assess that if there is no oil, the geologist will predict there is no oil with probability 0.90.

Why will these two probabilities *not* appear on the decision tree? Which probabilities *will* be on the decision tree?

C.5. Your company has signed a contract with a good customer to ship the customer an order no later than 20 days from now. The contract indicates that the customer will accept the order even if it is late, but instead of paying the full price of $10,000, it will be allowed to pay 10% less, $9000, due to lateness. You estimate that it will take anywhere from 17 to 22 days to ship the order, and each of these is equally likely. You believe you are in good shape, reasoning that the expected days to ship is the average of 17 through 22, or 19.5 days. Because this is less than 20, you will get your full $10,000. What is wrong with your reasoning?

C.6. You must make one of two decisions, each with possible gains and possible losses. One of these decisions is much riskier than the other, having much larger possible gains but also much larger possible losses, and it has a larger EMV than the safer decision. Because you are risk averse and the monetary values are large relative to your wealth, you base your decision on expected utility, and it indicates that you should make the safer decision. It also indicates that the certainty equivalent for the risky decision is $210,000, whereas its EMV is $540,000. What do these two numbers mean? What do you know about the certainty equivalent of the safer decision?

C.7. A potentially huge hurricane is forming in the Caribbean, and there is some chance that it might make a direct hit on Hilton Head Island, South Carolina, where you are in charge of emergency preparedness. You have made plans for evacuating everyone from the island, but such an evacuation is obviously costly and upsetting for all involved, so the decision to evacuate shouldn't be made lightly. Discuss how you would make such a decision. Is EMV a relevant concept in this situation? How would you evaluate the consequences of uncertain outcomes?

C.8. It seems obvious that if you can purchase information before making an ultimate decision, this information should generally be worth something, but explain exactly why (and when) it is sometimes worth nothing.

C.9. Insurance companies wouldn't exist unless customers were willing to pay the price of the insurance and the insurance companies were making a profit. So explain how insurance is a win-win proposition for customers and the company.

C.10. You often hear about the trade-off between risk and reward. Is this trade-off part of decision making under uncertainty when the decision maker uses the EMV criterion? For example, how does this work in investment decisions?

C.11. Can you ever use the material in this chapter to help you make your own real-life decisions? Consider the following. You are about to take an important and difficult exam in one of your MBA courses, and you see an opportunity to cheat. Obviously, from an ethical point of view, you shouldn't cheat, but from a purely monetary point of view, could it also be the wrong decision? To model this, consider the long-term monetary consequences of all possible outcomes.

Level A

30. The SweetTooth Candy Company knows it will need 10 tons of sugar six months from now to implement its production plans. The company has essentially two options for acquiring the needed sugar. It can either buy the sugar at the going market price when it is needed, six months from now, or it can buy a futures contract now. The contract guarantees delivery of the sugar in six months but the cost of purchasing it will be based on today's market price. Assume that possible sugar futures contracts available for purchase are for five tons or ten tons only. No futures contracts can be purchased or sold in the intervening months. Thus, SweetTooth's possible decisions are to (1) purchase a futures contract for ten tons of sugar now, (2) purchase a futures contract for five tons of sugar now and purchase five tons of sugar in six months, or (3) purchase all ten tons of needed sugar in six months. The price of sugar bought now for delivery in six months is $0.0851 per pound. The transaction costs for five-ton and ten-ton futures contracts are $65 and $110, respectively. Finally, the company has assessed the probability distribution for the possible prices of sugar six months from now (in dollars per pound). The file **P06_30.xlsx** contains these possible prices and their corresponding probabilities.
a. Identify the decision that minimizes SweetTooth's expected cost of meeting its sugar demand.

b. Perform a sensitivity analysis on the optimal decision, letting each of the three currency inputs vary one at a time plus or minus 25% from its base value, and summarize your findings. Which of the inputs appears to have the largest effect on the best decision?

31. Carlisle Tire and Rubber, Inc., is considering expanding production to meet potential increases in the demand for one of its tire products. Carlisle's alternatives are to construct a new plant, expand the existing plant, or do nothing in the short run. The market for this particular tire product may expand, remain stable, or contract. Carlisle's marketing department estimates the probabilities of these market outcomes to be 0.25, 0.35, and 0.40, respectively. The file **P06_31.xlsx** contains Carlisle's payoffs and costs for the various combinations of decisions and outcomes.
a. Identify the strategy that maximizes this tire manufacturer's expected profit.
b. Perform a sensitivity analysis on the optimal decision, letting each of the monetary inputs vary one at a time plus or minus 10% from its base value, and summarize your findings. Which of the inputs appears to have the largest effect on the best solution?

32. A local energy provider offers a landowner $180,000 for the exploration rights to natural gas on a certain site and the option for future development. This option, if exercised, is worth an additional $1,800,000 to the landowner, but this will occur only if natural gas is discovered during the exploration phase. The landowner, believing that the energy company's interest in the site is a good indication that gas is present, is tempted to develop the field herself. To do so, she must contract with local experts in natural gas exploration and development. The initial cost for such a contract is $300,000, which is lost forever if no gas is found on the site. If gas is discovered, however, the landowner expects to earn a net profit of $6,000,000. The landowner estimates the probability of finding gas on this site to be 60%.
a. Identify the strategy that maximizes the landowner's expected net earnings from this opportunity.
b. Perform a sensitivity analysis on the optimal decision, letting each of the inputs vary one at a time plus or minus 25% from its base value, and summarize your findings. Which of the inputs appears to have the largest effect on the best solution?

33. Techware Incorporated is considering the introduction of two new software products to the market. The company has four options regarding these products: introduce neither product, introduce product 1 only, introduce product 2 only, or introduce both products. Research and development costs for products 1 and 2 are $180,000 and $150,000, respectively. Note that the first option entails no costs because research and development efforts have not yet begun. The success of these software products depends on the national economy in the coming year. The company's revenues, depending on its decision and the state of the economy, are given in the file **P06_33.xlsx**. The probabilities of a strong, fair, or weak economy in the coming year are assessed to be 0.30, 0.50, and 0.20, respectively.

a. Identify the strategy that maximizes Techware's expected net revenue.

b. Perform a sensitivity analysis on the optimal decision, letting each of the inputs vary one at a time plus or minus 25% from its base value, and summarize your findings. Which of the inputs appears to have the largest effect on the best solution?

34. An investor with $10,000 available to invest has the following options: (1) he can invest in a risk-free savings account with a guaranteed 3% annual rate of return; (2) he can invest in a fairly safe stock, where the possible annual rates of return are 6%, 8%, or 10%; or (3) he can invest in a more risky stock, where the possible annual rates of return are 1%, 9%, or 17%. The investor can place all of his available funds in any one of these options, or he can split his $10,000 into two $5000 investments in any two of these options. The joint probability distribution of the possible return rates for the two stocks is given in the file **P06_34.xlsx**.

a. Identify the strategy that maximizes the investor's expected one-year earnings.

b. Perform a sensitivity analysis on the optimal decision, letting the amount available to invest and the risk-free return both vary, one at a time, plus or minus 100% from their base values, and summarize your findings.

35. A buyer for a large department store chain must place orders with an athletic shoe manufacturer six months prior to the time the shoes will be sold in the department stores. The buyer must decide on November 1 how many pairs of the manufacturer's newest model of tennis shoes to order for sale during the coming summer season. Assume that each pair of this new brand of tennis shoes costs the department store chain $45 per pair. Furthermore, assume that each pair of these shoes can then be sold to the chain's customers for $70 per pair. Any pairs of these shoes remaining unsold at the end of the summer season will be sold in a closeout sale next fall for $35 each. The probability distribution of consumer demand for these tennis shoes during the coming summer season has been assessed by market research specialists and is provided in the file **P06_35.xlsx**. Finally, assume that the department store chain must purchase these tennis shoes from the manufacturer in lots of 100 pairs.

a. Identify the strategy that maximizes the department store chain's expected profit earned by purchasing and subsequently selling pairs of the new tennis shoes. Is a decision tree really necessary? If so, what does it add to the analysis? If not, why not?

b. Perform a sensitivity analysis on the optimal decision, letting the three monetary inputs vary one at a time over reasonable ranges, and summarize your findings.

Which of the inputs appears to have the largest effect on the best solution?

36. Two construction companies are bidding against one another for the right to construct a new community center building. The first construction company, Fine Line Homes, believes that its competitor, Buffalo Valley Construction, will place a bid for this project according to the distribution shown in the file **P06_36.xlsx**. Furthermore, Fine Line Homes estimates that it will cost $160,000 for its own company to construct this building. Given its fine reputation and long-standing service within the local community, Fine Line Homes believes that it will likely be awarded the project in the event that it and Buffalo Valley Construction submit exactly the same bids. Find the bid that maximizes Fine Line's expected profit. Is a decision tree really necessary? If so, what does it add to the analysis? If not, why not?

37. You have sued your employer for damages suffered when you recently slipped and fell on an icy surface that should have been treated by your company's physical plant department. Your injury was sufficiently serious that you, in consultation with your attorney, decided to sue your company for $500,000. Your company's insurance provider has offered to settle this suit with you out of court. If you decide to reject the settlement and go to court, your attorney is confident that you will win the case but is uncertain about the amount the court will award you in damages. He has provided his assessment of the probability distribution of the court's award to you in the file **P06_37.xlsx**. In addition, there are extra legal fees of $10,000 you will have to pay if you go to court. Let S be the insurance provider's proposed out-of-court settlement (in dollars). For which values of S will you decide to accept the settlement? For which values of S will you choose to take your chances in court? Assume that your goal is to maximize the expected net payoff from this litigation.

38. Consider a population of 2000 people, 800 of whom are women. Assume that 300 of the women in this population earn at least $60,000 per year, and 200 of the men earn at least $60,000 per year.

a. What is the probability that a randomly selected person from this population earns less than $60,000 per year?

b. If a randomly selected person is observed to earn less than $60,000 per year, what is the probability that this person is a man?

c. If a randomly selected person is observed to earn at least $60,000 per year, what is the probability that this person is a woman?

39. Yearly automobile inspections are required for residents of the state of Pennsylvania. Suppose that 18% of all inspected cars in Pennsylvania have problems that need to be corrected. Unfortunately, Pennsylvania state inspections fail to detect these problems 12% of the time. On the other hand, assume that an inspection never detects a problem when there is no problem. Consider a car that is inspected and is found to be free of problems. What is the probability that there is indeed something wrong that the inspection has failed to uncover?

40. Referring to the landowner's decision problem in Problem 32, suppose now that, at a cost of $90,000, the landowner can request a soundings test on the site where natural gas is believed to be present. The company that conducts the soundings concedes that the test has a 30% false-negative rate (it indicates no gas when gas is present) and a 10% false-positive rate (it indicates gas when no gas is present).

a. If the landowner pays for the soundings test and the test indicates that gas is present, what is the landowner's revised probability that the site contains gas?

b. If the landowner pays for the soundings test and the test indicates that gas is not present, what is the landowner's revised probability that there is no gas on the site?

c. Should the landowner request the soundings test at a cost of $90,000? Why or why not? If not, at what price (if any) would the landowner be willing to pay for the soundings test?

41. A customer has approached a bank for a $100,000 one-year loan at an 8% interest rate. If the bank does not approve this loan application, the $100,000 will be invested in bonds that earn a 6% annual return. Without additional information, the bank believes that there is a 4% chance that this customer will default on the loan, assuming that the loan is approved. If the customer defaults on the loan, the bank will lose $100,000. At a cost of $1000, the bank can thoroughly investigate the customer's credit record and supply a favorable or unfavorable recommendation. Past experience indicates that the probability of a favorable recommendation for a customer who will eventually not default is 0.80, and the chance of a favorable recommendation for a customer who will eventually default is 0.15.

a. Use a decision tree to find the strategy the bank should follow to maximize its expected profit.

b. Calculate and interpret the expected value of information (EVI) for this decision problem.

c. Calculate and interpret the expected value of perfect information (EVPI) for this decision problem.

d. How sensitive are the results to the accuracy of the credit record recommendations? Are there any "reasonable" values of the error probabilities that change the optimal strategy?

42. A company is considering whether to market a new product. Assume, for simplicity, that if this product is marketed, there are only two possible outcomes: success or failure. The company assesses that the probabilities of these two outcomes are p and $1-p$, respectively. If the product is marketed and it proves to be a failure, the company will have a net loss of $450,000. If the product is marketed and it proves to be a success, the

company will have a net gain of $750,000. If the company decides not to market the product, there is no gain or loss. The company can first survey prospective buyers of this new product. The results of the consumer survey can be classified as favorable, neutral, or unfavorable. Based on similar surveys for previous products, the company assesses the probabilities of favorable, neutral, and unfavorable survey results to be 0.6, 0.3, and 0.1 for a product that will eventually be a success, and it assesses these probabilities to be 0.1, 0.2, and 0.7 for a product that will eventually be a failure. The total cost of administering this survey is C dollars.

a. Let $p = 0.4$. For which values of C, if any, would this company choose to conduct the survey?

b. Let $p = 0.4$. What is the largest amount this company would be willing to pay for perfect information about the potential success or failure of the new product?

c. Let $p = 0.5$ and $C = \$15,000$. Find the strategy that maximizes the company's expected net earnings. Does the optimal strategy involve conducting the survey? Explain why or why not.

43. The U.S. government wants to determine whether immigrants should be tested for a contagious disease, and it is planning to base this decision on financial considerations. Assume that each immigrant who is allowed to enter the United States and has the disease costs the country $100,000. Also, assume that each immigrant who is allowed to enter the United States and does not have the disease will contribute $10,000 to the national economy. Finally, assume that $x\%$ of all potential immigrants have the disease. The U.S. government can choose to admit all immigrants, admit no immigrants, or test immigrants for the disease before determining whether they should be admitted. It costs T dollars to test a person for the disease, and the test result is either positive or negative. A person who does not have the disease *always* tests negative. However, 10% of all people who *do* have the disease test negative. The government's goal is to maximize the expected net financial benefits per potential immigrant.

a. If $x = 5$, what is the largest value of T at which the U.S. government will choose to test potential immigrants for the disease?

b. How does your answer to the question in part **a** change if x increases to 10?

c. If $x = 5$ and $T = \$500$, what is the government's optimal strategy?

44. The senior executives of an oil company are trying to decide whether to drill for oil in a particular field in the Gulf of Mexico. It costs the company $600,000 to drill in the selected field. Company executives believe that if oil is found in this field its estimated value will be $3,400,000. At present, this oil company believes that there is a 45% chance that the selected field actually contains oil. Before drilling, the company can hire a geologist at a cost of $55,000 to perform seismographic tests. Based on similar tests in other fields, the tests have a 25% false negative rate (no oil predicted when oil is present) and a 15% false positive rate (oil predicted when no oil is present).

a. Assuming that this oil company wants to maximize its expected net earnings, use a decision tree to determine its optimal strategy.

b. Calculate and interpret EVI for this decision problem. Experiment with the accuracy probabilities of the geologist to see how EVI changes as they change.

c. Calculate and interpret EVPI for this decision problem.

45. A product manager at Clean & Brite (C&B) wants to determine whether her company should market a new brand of toothpaste. If this new product succeeds in the marketplace, C&B estimates that it could earn $1,800,000 in future profits from the sale of the new toothpaste. If this new product fails, however, the company expects that it could lose approximately $750,000. If C&B chooses not to market this new brand, the product manager believes that there would be little, if any, impact on the profits earned through sales of C&B's other products. The manager has estimated that the new toothpaste brand will succeed with probability 0.50. Before making her decision regarding this toothpaste product, the manager can spend $75,000 on a market research study. Based on similar studies with past products, C&B believes that the study will predict a successful product, given that product would actually be a success, with probability 0.75. It also believes that the study will predict a failure, given that the product would actually be a failure, with probability 0.65.

a. To maximize expected profit, what strategy should the C&B product manager follow?

b. Calculate and interpret EVI for this decision problem.

c. Calculate and interpret EVPI for this decision problem.

46. Ford is going to produce a new vehicle, the Pioneer, and wants to determine the amount of annual capacity it should build. Ford's goal is to maximize the profit from this vehicle over the next five years. Each vehicle will sell for $19,000 and incur a variable production cost of $16,000. Building one unit of annual capacity will cost $2000. Each unit of capacity will also cost $1000 per year to maintain, even if the capacity is unused. Demand for the Pioneer is unknown but marketing estimates the distribution of annual demand to be as shown in the file **P06_46.xlsx**. Assume that the number of units sold during a year is the minimum of capacity and annual demand. Which capacity level should Ford choose? Do you think EMV is the appropriate criterion?

47. Many decision problems have the following simple structure. A decision maker has two possible decisions, 1 and 2. If decision 1 is made, a *sure* cost of c is incurred. If decision 2 is made, there are two possible outcomes, with costs c_1 and c_2 and probabilities p and $1 - p$. We

assume that $c_1 < c < c_2$. The idea is that decision 1, the riskless decision, has a moderate cost, whereas decision 2, the risky decision, has a low cost c_1 or a high cost c_2.

a. Calculate the expected cost from the risky decision.

b. List as many scenarios as you can think of that have this structure. (Here's an example to get you started. Think of insurance, where you pay a sure premium to avoid a large possible loss.) For each of these scenarios, indicate whether you would base your decision on EMV or on expected utility.

48. A nuclear power company is deciding whether to build a nuclear power plant at Diablo Canyon or at Roy Rogers City. The cost of building the power plant is $10 million at Diablo and $20 million at Roy Rogers City. If the company builds at Diablo, however, and an earthquake occurs at Diablo during the next five years, construction will be terminated and the company will lose $10 million (and will still have to build a power plant at Roy Rogers City). Without further expert information the company believes there is a 20% chance that an earthquake will occur, at Diablo during the next five years. For $1 million, a geologist can be hired to analyze the fault structure at Diablo Canyon. She will predict either that an earthquake will occur or that an earthquake will not occur. The geologist's past record indicates that she will predict an earthquake with probability 0.95 if an earthquake will occur, and she will predict no earthquake with probability 0.90 if an earthquake will not occur. Should the power company hire the geologist? Also, calculate and interpret EVI and EVPI.

49. Referring to Techware's decision problem in Problem 33, suppose now that Techware's utility function of net revenue x (measured in dollars) is $U(x) = 1 - e^{-x/350000}$.

a. Find the decision that maximizes Techware's expected utility. How does this optimal decision compare to the optimal decision with an EMV criterion? Explain any difference between the two optimal decisions.

b. Repeat part **a** when Techware's utility function is $U(x) = 1 - e^{-x/50000}$.

50. Referring to the bank's customer loan decision problem in Problem 41, suppose now that the bank's utility function of profit x (in dollars) is $U(x) = 1 - e^{-x/150000}$. Find the strategy that maximizes the bank's expected utility. How does this optimal strategy compare to the optimal decision with an EMV criterion? Explain any difference between the two optimal strategies.

51. A television network earns an average of $25 million each season from a hit program and loses an average of $8 million each season on a program that turns out to be a flop. Of all programs picked up by this network in recent years, 25% turn out to be hits and 75% turn out to be flops. At a cost of C dollars, a market research firm will analyze a pilot episode of a prospective program and issue a report predicting whether the given program will end up being a hit. If the program is actually going to be a hit, there is a 75% chance that the market

researchers will predict the program to be a hit. If the program is actually going to be a flop, there is only a 30% chance that the market researchers will predict the program to be a hit.

    a. What is the maximum value of C that the network should be willing to pay the market research firm?

    b. Calculate and interpret EVPI for this decision problem.

52. [Based on Balson et al. (1992).] An electric utility company is trying to decide whether to replace its PCB transformer in a generating station with a new and safer transformer. To evaluate this decision, the utility needs information about the likelihood of an incident, such as a fire, the cost of such an incident, and the cost of replacing the unit. Suppose that the total cost of replacement as a present value is $75,000. If the transformer is replaced, there is virtually no chance of a fire. However, if the current transformer is retained, the probability of a fire is assessed to be 0.0025. If a fire occurs, the cleanup cost could be high ($80 million) or low ($20 million). The probability of a high cleanup cost, given that a fire occurs, is assessed at 0.2.

    a. If the company uses EMV as its decision criterion, should it replace the transformer?

    b. Perform a sensitivity analysis on the key parameters of the problem that are difficult to assess, namely, the probability of a fire, the probability of a high cleanup cost, and the high and low cleanup costs. Does the optimal decision from part **a** remain optimal for a wide range of these parameters?

    c. Do you believe EMV is the correct criterion to use in this type of problem involving environmental accidents?

53. The Indiana University basketball team trails by two points with eight seconds to go and has the ball. Should it attempt a two-point shot or a three-point shot? Assume that the Indiana shot will end the game and that no foul will occur on the shot. Assume that a three-point shot has a 30% chance of success, and a two-point shot has a 45% chance of success. Finally, assume that Indiana has a 50% chance of winning in overtime.

Level B

54. Mr. Maloy has just bought a new $30,000 sport utility vehicle. As a reasonably safe driver, he believes there is only about a 5% chance of being in an accident in the coming year. If he is involved in an accident, the damage to his new vehicle depends on the severity of the accident. The probability distribution of damage amounts (in dollars) is given in the file **P06_54.xlsx**. Mr. Maloy is trying to decide whether to pay $170 each year for collision insurance with a $300 deductible. Note that with this type of insurance, he pays the *first* $300 in damages if he causes an accident and the insurance company pays the remainder.

    a. Identify the decision that minimizes Mr. Maloy's annual expected cost.

    b. Perform a sensitivity analysis on the best decision with respect to the probability of an accident, the premium, and the deductible amount, and summarize your findings. (You can choose the ranges to test.)

55. The purchasing agent for a PC manufacturer is currently negotiating a purchase agreement for a particular electronic component with a given supplier. This component is produced in lots of 1000, and the cost of purchasing a lot is $30,000. Unfortunately, past experience indicates that this supplier has occasionally shipped defective components to its customers. Specifically, the proportion of defective components supplied by this supplier has the probability distribution given in the file **P06_55.xlsx**. Although the PC manufacturer can repair a defective component at a cost of $20 each, the purchasing agent learns that this supplier will now assume the cost of replacing defective components in excess of the first 100 faulty items found in a given lot. This guarantee may be purchased by the PC manufacturer prior to the receipt of a given lot at a cost of $1000 per lot. The purchasing agent wants to determine whether it is worthwhile to purchase the supplier's guarantee policy.

    a. Identify the strategy that minimizes the expected total cost of achieving a complete lot of satisfactory microcomputer components.

    b. Perform a sensitivity analysis on the optimal decision with respect to the number of components per lot and the three monetary inputs, and summarize your findings. (You can choose the ranges to test.)

56. A home appliance company is interested in marketing an innovative new product. The company must decide whether to manufacture this product in house or employ a subcontractor to manufacture it. The file **P06_56.xlsx** contains the estimated probability distribution of the cost of manufacturing one unit of this new product (in dollars) if the home appliance company produces the product in house. This file also contains the estimated probability distribution of the cost of purchasing one unit of the product if from the subcontractor. There is also uncertainty about demand for the product in the coming year, as shown in the same file. The company plans to meet all demand, but there is a capacity issue. The subcontractor has unlimited capacity, but the home appliance company has capacity for only 5000 units per year. If it decides to make the product in house and demand is greater than capacity, it will have to purchase the excess demand from an external source at a premium: $225 per unit. Assuming that the company wants to minimize the expected cost of meeting demand in the coming year, should it make the new product in house or buy it from the subcontractor? Do you need a decision tree, or can you perform the required EMV calculations without one? (You can assume that neither the company nor the subcontractor will ever produce *more* than demand.)

57. A grapefruit farmer in central Florida is trying to decide whether to take protective action to limit damage to his crop in the event that the overnight temperature falls to a level well below freezing. He is concerned that if the temperature falls sufficiently low and he fails to make an effort to protect his grapefruit trees, he runs the risk of losing his entire crop, which is worth approximately $75,000. Based on the latest forecast issued by the National Weather Service, the farmer estimates that there is a 60% chance that he will lose his entire crop if it is left unprotected. Alternatively, the farmer can insulate his fruit by spraying water on all of the trees in his orchards. This action, which would likely cost the farmer C dollars, would prevent total devastation but might not completely protect the grapefruit trees from incurring some damage as a result of the unusually cold overnight temperatures. The file **P06_57.xlsx** contains the assessed distribution of possible damages (in dollars) to the insulated fruit in light of the cold weather forecast. The farmer wants to minimize the expected total cost of coping with the threatening weather.

a. Find the maximum value of C below which the farmer should insulate his crop to limit the damage from the unusually cold weather.

b. Set C equal to the value identified in part **a.** Perform sensitivity analysis to determine under what conditions, if any, the farmer would be better off not spraying his grapefruit trees and taking his chances in spite of the threat to his crop.

c. Suppose that C equals $25,000, and in addition to this protection, the farmer can purchase insurance on the crop. Discuss possibilities for reasonable insurance policies and how much they would be worth to the farmer. You can assume that the insurance is relevant only if the farmer purchases the protection, and you can decide on the terms of the insurance policy.

58. A retired partner from a large brokerage firm has one million dollars available to invest in particular stocks or bonds. Each investment's annual rate of return depends on the state of the economy in the coming year. The file **P06_58.xlsx** contains the distribution of returns for these stocks and bonds as a function of the economy's state in the coming year. As this file indicates, the returns from stocks and bonds in a fair economy are listed as X and Y. This investor wants to allocate her one million dollars to maximize her expected value of the portfolio one year from now.

a. If $X = Y = 15\%$ find the optimal investment strategy for this investor. (*Hint*: You could try a decision tree approach, but it would involve a massive tree. It is much easier to find an algebraic expression for the expected final value of the investment when a percentage p is put in stocks and the remaining percentage is put in bonds.)

b. For which values of X (where $10\% < X < 20\%$) and Y (where $12.5\% < Y < 17.5\%$), if any, will this investor prefer to place all of her available funds in stocks? Use the same method as in part **a** for each combination of X and Y.

59. A city in Ohio is considering replacing its fleet of gasoline-powered automobiles with electric cars. The manufacturer of the electric cars claims that this municipality will experience significant cost savings over the life of the fleet if it chooses to pursue the conversion. If the manufacturer is correct, the city will save about $1.5 million dollars. If the new technology employed within the electric cars is faulty, as some critics suggest, the conversion to electric cars will cost the city $675,000. A third possibility is that less serious problems will arise and the city will break even with the conversion. A consultant hired by the city estimates that the probabilities of these three outcomes are 0.30, 0.30, and 0.40, respectively. The city has an opportunity to implement a pilot program that would indicate the potential cost or savings resulting from a switch to electric cars. The pilot program involves renting a small number of electric cars for three months and running them under typical conditions. This program would cost the city $75,000. The city's consultant believes that the results of the pilot program would be significant but not conclusive; she submits the values in the file **P06_59.xlsx**, a compilation of probabilities based on the experience of other cities, to support her contention. For example, the first row of her table indicates that if a conversion to electric cars will actually result in a savings of $1.5 million, the pilot program will indicate that the city saves money, loses money, and breaks even with probabilities 0.6, 0.1, and 0.3, respectively. What actions should the city take to maximize its expected savings? When should it run the pilot program, if ever?

60. Sharp Outfits is trying to decide whether to ship some customer orders now via UPS or wait until after the threat of another UPS strike is over. If Sharp Outfits decides to ship the requested merchandise now and the UPS strike takes place, the company will incur $60,000 in delay and shipping costs. If Sharp Outfits decides to ship the customer orders via UPS and no strike occurs, the company will incur $4000 in shipping costs. If Sharp Outfits decides to postpone shipping its customer orders via UPS, the company will incur $10,000 in delay costs regardless of whether UPS goes on strike. Let p represent the probability that UPS will go on strike and impact Sharp Outfits's shipments.

a. For which values of p, if any, does Sharp Outfits minimize its expected total cost by choosing to postpone shipping its customer orders via UPS?

b. Suppose now that, at a cost of $1000, Sharp Outfits can purchase information regarding the likelihood of a UPS strike in the near future. Based on similar strike threats in the past, the company assesses that if there will be a strike, the information will predict a strike with probability 0.75, and if there will not be a strike, the information will predict no strike with probability 0.85. Provided that $p = 0.15$, what strategy should Sharp Outfits pursue to minimize its expected total cost?

c. Using the analysis from part **b**, find the EVI when $p = 0.15$. Then use a data table to find EVI for p from 0.05 to 0.30 in increments of 0.05, and chart EVI versus p.

d. Continuing part **b**, calculate and interpret the EVPI when $p = 0.15$.

61. A homeowner wants to decide whether he should install an electronic heat pump in his home. Given that the cost of installing a new heat pump is fairly large, the homeowner wants to do so only if he can count on being able to recover the initial expense over *five* consecutive years of cold winter weather. After reviewing historical data on the operation of heat pumps in various kinds of winter weather, he computes the expected annual costs of heating his home during the winter months with and without a heat pump in operation. These cost figures are shown in the file **P06_61.xlsx**. The probabilities of experiencing a mild, normal, colder than normal, and severe winter are $0.2(1 - x)$, $0.5(1 - x)$, $0.3(1 - x)$, and x, respectively. In words, as the last probability varies, the first three probabilities remain in the ratios 2 to 5 to 3, and all probabilities continue to sum to 1.

a. Given that $x = 0.1$, what is the most that the homeowner is willing to pay for the heat pump?

b. If the heat pump costs $500, how large must x be before the homeowner decides it is economically worthwhile to install the heat pump?

c. Given that $c = 0.1$, calculate and interpret EVPI when the heat pump costs $500.

62. Suppose an investor has the opportunity to buy the following contract, a stock call option, on March 1. The contract allows him to buy 100 shares of ABC stock at the end of March, April, or May at a guaranteed price of $50 per share. He can exercise this option at most once. For example, if he purchases the stock at the end of March, he can't purchase more in April or May at the guaranteed price. The current price of the stock is $50. Each month, assume that the stock price either goes up by a dollar (with probability 0.55) or goes down by a dollar (with probability 0.45). If the investor buys the contract, he is hoping that the stock price will go up. The reasoning is that if he buys the contract, the price goes up to $51, and he buys the stock (that is, he exercises his option) for $50, he can then sell the stock for $51 and make a profit of $1 per share. On the other hand, if the stock price goes down, he doesn't have to exercise his option; he can just throw the contract away.

a. Use a decision tree to find the investor's optimal strategy—that is, when he should exercise the option— *assuming* that he purchases the contract.

b. How much should he be willing to pay for such a contract?

63. (This problem assumes knowledge of the basic rules of football.) The ending of the game between the Indianapolis Colts and the New England Patriots (NFL teams) in Fall 2009 was quite controversial. With about two minutes left in the game, the Patriots were ahead 34 to 28 and had the ball on their *own* 28-yard line with fourth down and two yards to go. In other words, they were 72 yards from a touchdown. Their coach, Bill Belichick, decided to go for the first down rather than punt, contrary to conventional wisdom. They didn't make the first down, so possession went to the Colts, who then scored a touchdown to win by a point. Belichick was harshly criticized by most of the media, but was his unorthodox decision really a bad one?

a. Use a decision tree to analyze the problem. You can make some simplifying decisions: (1) the game would essentially be over if the Patriots made a first down, and (2) at most one score would occur after a punt or a failed first down attempt. (There are no monetary values. However, you can assume the Patriots receive $1 for a win and $0 for a loss, so that maximizing EMV is equivalent to maximizing the probability that the Patriots win.)

b. Show that the Patriots should go for the first down if $p > 1 - q/r$. Here, p is the probability the Patriots make the first down, q is the probability the Colts score a touchdown after a punt, and r is the probability the Colts score a touchdown after the Patriots fail to make a first down. What are your best guesses for these three probabilities? Based on them, was Belichick's decision justified?

64. (This problem assumes knowledge of the basic rules of baseball.) George Lindsey (1959) looked at box scores of more than 1000 baseball games and found the expected number of runs scored in an inning for each on-base and out situation to be as listed in the file **P06_64.xlsx**. For example, if a team has a man on first base with one out, it scores 0.5 run on average until the end of the inning. You can assume throughout this problem that the team batting wants to maximize the expected number of runs scored in the inning.

a. Use this data to explain why, in most cases, bunting with a man on first base and no outs is a bad decision. In what situation might bunting with a man on first base and no outs be a good decision?

b. Assume there is a man on first base with one out. What probability of stealing second makes an attempted steal a good idea?

65. (This problem assumes knowledge of the basic rules of basketball.) One controversial topic in basketball (college or any other level) is whether to foul a player deliberately with only a few seconds left in the game. Consider the following scenario. With about 10 seconds left in the game, team A is ahead of team B by three points, and team B is just about to inbound the ball. Assume team A has committed enough fouls so that future fouls result in team B going to the free-throw line. If team A purposely commits a foul as soon as possible, team B will shoot two foul shots (a point apiece). The thinking is that this is better than letting team B shoot a three-point shot, which would be their best way to tie the game and send it into overtime. However, there is a downside to fouling. Team B could make the first free throw, purposely miss the second, get the rebound, and score a two-point shot to tie the game, or it could even score a three-point shot to win the game. Examine this decision, using reasonable input parameters. It doesn't appear that this deliberate fouling strategy is used very often, but do you think it should be used?

66. (This problem assumes knowledge of the basic rules of football.) The following situation actually occurred in a 2009 college football game between Washington and Notre Dame. With about 3.5 minutes left in the game, Washington had fourth down and one yard to go for a touchdown, already leading by two points. Notre Dame had just had two successful goal-line stands from in close, so Washington's coach decided not to go for the touchdown and the virtually sure win. Instead, Washington kicked a field goal, and Notre Dame eventually won in overtime. Use a decision tree, with some reasonable inputs, to see whether Washington made a wise decision or should have gone for the touchdown. Note that the only "monetary" values here are 1 and 0. You can think of Washington getting $1 if they win and $0 if they lose. Then the EMV is $1*P(\text{Win}) + 0*P(\text{lose}) = P(\text{Win})$, so maximizing EMV is equivalent to maximizing the probability of winning.

CASE 6.1 Jogger Shoe Company

The Jogger Shoe Company is trying to decide whether to make a change in its most popular brand of running shoes. The new style would cost the same to produce and be priced the same, but it would incorporate a new kind of lacing system that (according to its marketing research people) would make it more popular.

There is a fixed cost of $300,000 for changing over to the new style. The unit contribution to before-tax profit for either style is $8. The tax rate is 35%. Also, because the fixed cost can be depreciated and will therefore affect the after-tax cash flow, a depreciation method is needed. You can assume it is straight-line depreciation.

The current demand for these shoes is 190,000 pairs annually. The company assumes this demand will continue for the next three years if the current style is retained. However, there is uncertainty about demand for the new style, if it is introduced. The company models this uncertainty by assuming a normal distribution in year 1, with mean 220,000 and standard deviation 20,000. The company also assumes that this demand, whatever it is, will remain constant for the next three years. However, if demand in year 1 for the new style is sufficiently low, the company can always switch back to the current style and realize an annual demand of 190,000. The company wants a strategy that will maximize the expected net present value (NPV) of total cash flow for the next three years, where a 10% interest rate is used for the purpose of calculating NPV.

Realizing that the continuous normal demand distribution doesn't lend itself well to decision trees that require a discrete set of outcomes, the company decides to replace the normal demand distribution with a discrete distribution with five "typical" values. Specifically, it decides to use the 10th, 30th, 50th, 70th, and 90th percentiles of the given normal distribution. Why is it reasonable to assume that these five possibilities are equally likely? With this discrete approximation, how should the company proceed?

CASE 6.2 Westhouser Paper Company

The Westhouser Paper Company in the state of Washington currently has an option to purchase a piece of land with good timber forest on it. It is now May 1, and the current price of the land is $2.2 million. Westhouser does not actually need the timber from this land until the beginning of July, but its top executives fear that another company might buy the land between now and the beginning of July. They assess that there is a 5% chance that a competitor will buy the land during May. If this does not occur, they assess that there is a 10% chance that the competitor will buy the land during June. If Westhouser does not take advantage of its current option, it can attempt to buy the land at the beginning of June or the beginning of July, provided that it is still available.

Westhouser's incentive for delaying the purchase is that its financial experts believe there is a good chance that the price of the land will fall significantly in one or both of the next two months. They assess the possible price decreases and their probabilities in Tables 6.2 and 6.3. Table 6.2 shows the probabilities of the possible price decreases during May. Table 6.3 lists the *conditional* probabilities of the possible price decreases in June, *given* the price decrease in May. For example, it indicates that if the price decrease in May is $60,000, then the possible price decreases in June are $0, $30,000, and $60,000 with respective probabilities 0.6, 0.2, and 0.2.

If Westhouser purchases the land, it believes that it can gross $3 million. (This does not count the cost of purchasing the land.) But if it does not purchase the land, Westhouser believes that it can make $650,000 from alternative investments. What should the company do?

Table 6.2 Distribution of Price Decrease in May

Price Decrease	Probability
$0	0.5
$60,000	0.3
$120,000	0.2

Table 6.3 Distribution of Price Decrease in June

Price Decrease in May					
$0		$60,000		$120,000	
June Decrease	Probability	June Decrease	Probability	June Decrease	Probability
$0	0.3	$0	0.6	$0	0.7
$60,000	0.6	$30,000	0.2	$20,000	0.2
$120,000	0.1	$60,000	0.2	$40,000	0.1

CASE 6.3 Electronic Timing System for Olympics

Sarah Chang is the owner of a small electronics company. In six months, a proposal is due for an electronic timing system for the next Olympic Games. For several years, Chang's company has been developing a new microprocessor, a critical component in a timing system that would be superior to any product currently on the market. However, progress in research and development has been slow, and Chang is unsure whether her staff can produce the microprocessor in time. If they succeed in developing the microprocessor (probability p_1), there is an excellent chance (probability p_2) that Chang's company will win the $1 million Olympic contract. If they do not, there is a small chance (probability p_3) that she will still be able to win the same contract with an alternative but inferior timing system that has already been developed.

If she continues the project, Chang must invest $200,000 in research and development. In addition, making a proposal (which she will decide whether to do after seeing whether the R&D is successful) requires developing a prototype timing system at an additional cost. This additional cost is $50,000 if R&D is successful (so that she can develop the new timing system), and it is $40,000 if R&D is unsuccessful (so that she needs to go with the older timing system).

Finally, if Chang wins the contract, the finished product will cost an additional $150,000 to produce.

a. Develop a decision tree that can be used to solve Chang's problem. You can assume in this part of the problem that she is using EMV (of her net profit) as a decision criterion. Build the tree so that she can enter any values for p_1, p_2, and p_3 (in input cells) and automatically see her optimal EMV and optimal strategy from the tree.

b. If $p_2 = 0.8$ and $p_3 = 0.1$, what value of p_1 makes Chang indifferent between abandoning the project and going ahead with it?

c. How much would Chang benefit if she knew for certain that the Olympic organization would guarantee her the contract? (This guarantee would be in force only if she were successful in developing the product.) Assume $p_1 = 0.4$, $p_2 = 0.8$, and $p_3 = 0.1$.

d. Suppose now that this is a relatively big project for Chang. Therefore, she decides to use expected utility as her criterion, with an exponential utility function. Using some trial and error, see which risk tolerance changes her initial decision from "go ahead" to "abandon" when $p_1 = 0.4$, $p_2 = 0.8$, and $p_3 = 0.1$.

CASE 6.4 Developing a Helicopter Component for the Army

The Ventron Engineering Company has just been awarded a $2 million development contract by the U.S. Army Aviation Systems Command to develop a blade spar for its Heavy Lift Helicopter program. The blade spar is a metal tube that runs the length of and provides strength to the helicopter blade. Due to the unusual length and size of the Heavy Lift Helicopter blade, Ventron is unable to produce a single-piece blade spar of the required dimensions using existing extrusion

equipment and material. The engineering department has prepared two alternatives for developing the blade spar: (1) sectioning or (2) an improved extrusion process. Ventron must decide which process to use. (Backing out of the contract at any point is not an option.) The risk report has been prepared by the engineering department. The information from this report is explained next.

The sectioning option involves joining several shorter lengths of extruded metal into a blade spar of sufficient length. This work will require extensive testing and rework over a 12-month period at a total cost of $1.8 million. Although this process will definitely produce an adequate blade spar, it merely represents an extension of existing technology.

To improve the extrusion process, on the other hand, it will be necessary to perform two steps: (1) improve the material used, at a cost of $300,000, and (2) modify the extrusion press, at a cost of $960,000. The first step will require six months of work, and if this first step is successful, the second step will require another six months of work. If both steps are successful, the blade spar will be available at that time, that is, a year from now. The engineers estimate that the probabilities of succeeding in steps 1 and 2 are 0.9 and 0.75, respectively. However, if either step is unsuccessful (which will be known only in six months for step 1 and in a year for step 2), Ventron will have no alternative but to switch to the sectioning process—and incur the sectioning cost on top of any costs already incurred.

Development of the blade spar must be completed within 18 months to avoid holding up the rest of the contract. If necessary, the sectioning work can be done on an accelerated basis in a six-month period, but the cost of sectioning will then increase from $1.8 million to $2.4 million. The director of engineering, Dr. Smith, wants to try developing the improved extrusion process. He reasons that this is not only cheaper (if successful) for the current project, but its expected side benefits for future projects could be sizable. Although these side benefits are difficult to gauge, Dr. Smith's best guess is an additional $2 million. (These side benefits are obtained only if both steps of the modified extrusion process are completed successfully.)

a. Develop a decision tree to maximize Ventron's EMV. This includes the revenue from this project, the side benefits (if applicable) from an improved extrusion process, and relevant costs. You don't need to worry about the time value of money; that is, no discounting or net present values are required. Summarize your findings in words in the spreadsheet.

b. What value of side benefits would make Ventron indifferent between the two alternatives?

c. How much would Ventron be willing to pay, right now, for perfect information about both steps of the improved extrusion process? (This information would tell Ventron, right now, the ultimate success or failure outcomes of both steps.)

APPENDIX | Decision Trees with DADM_Tools

When this edition of the book was being developed, we weren't sure whether we would be able to offer Palisade's DecisionTools Suite as in previous editions. If Palisade's PrecisionTree add-in were not available, there wouldn't be any feasible way to create complex decision trees—there are no built-in Excel tools for doing so. Therefore, Albright developed his own decision tree program, the first in a series of programs that eventually became the DADM_Tools add-in. This add-in, along with a help file, is freely available at his website https://kelley.iu.edu/albrightbooks/Free_downloads.htm.

There are several differences between the DADM_Tools decision tree program and Palisade's PrecisionTree add-in:

- DADM_Tools is free.
- The DADM_Tools decision tree program works on a Mac; PrecisionTree doesn't.

- The DADM_Tools decision tree program doesn't have the sensitivity analysis tools available in PrecisionTree. However, the same sensitivity analyses can be performed with Excel data tables.
- PrecisionTree uses its own functions in the colored cells for the folding back process. The DADM_Tools decision tree program uses regular Excel formulas to accomplish the same thing. The difference is that the latter are more transparent; you can understand the folding back process better by studying these formulas.
- The DADM_Tools decision tree program uses diamonds instead of triangles for end nodes—a purely cosmetic difference.

Many of the solutions to the problems in this chapter are available in two versions: one with DADM_Tools and one with PrecisionTree.

PART 3
STATISTICAL INFERENCE

CHAPTER 7

Sampling and Sampling Distributions

Geniyrocka/Shutterstock.com

SAMPLE SIZE SELECTION IN A LEGAL CASE

This chapter introduces the important problem of estimating an unknown population quantity by randomly sampling from the population. Sampling is often expensive and/or time-consuming, so a key step in any sampling plan is to determine the sample size that produces a prescribed level of accuracy. Some of the issues in finding an appropriate sample size are discussed in Afshartous (2008). The author was involved as an expert statistical witness for the plaintiff in a court case. Over a period of several years, a service company had collected a flat "special service handling fee" from its client during any month in which a special service request was made. The plaintiff claimed that many of these fees had been charged erroneously and sought to recover all the money collected from such erroneous fees. The statistical question concerns either the *proportion* of all monthly billing records that were erroneous or the *total number* of all erroneous billing records. Both sides had to agree on a sampling method for sampling through the very large population of billing records. They eventually agreed to *simple* random sampling, as discussed in this chapter. However, there was some contention (and confusion) regarding the appropriate sample size.

Their initial approach was to find a sample size n sufficiently large to accurately estimate p, the unknown proportion of all monthly billing records in error. Specifically, if they wanted to be 95% confident that the error in their estimate of p would be no more than 5%, then a standard sample size formula (provided in Chapter 8) requires n to be 385. (This number is surprisingly independent of the total number of billing records.) Then, for example, if the sample discovered 77 errors, or 20% of the sampled items, they would be 95% confident that between 15% and 25% (20% plus or minus 5%) of *all* billing records were in error.

The author argued that this "plus or minus 5%" does not necessarily provide the desired level of accuracy for the quantity of most interest, the total number of erroneously charged fees. A couple of numerical examples illustrate his point. Let's suppose that there were 100,000 billing records total and that 20%, or 20,000, were billed erroneously. Then the plus or minus 5% interval translates to an interval from 15,000 to 25,000 bad billings. That is, we are 95% confident that the estimate is not off by more than 5000 billing records on either side. The author defines the *relative error* in this case to be 0.25: the potential error, 5000, divided by the number to be estimated, 20,000. Now change the example slightly so that 60%, or 60,000, were billed erroneously. Then plus or minus 5% translates to the interval from 55,000 to 65,000, and the relative error is 5000/60,000, or 0.083. The point is that the same plus or minus 5% *absolute* error for p results in a much smaller *relative* error in the second example.

Using this reasoning, the author suggested that they should choose the sample size to achieve a prescribed *relative* error in the number of bad billings. This can change the magnitude of the sample size considerably. For example, the author demonstrated by means of a rather complicated sample size formula that if a relative error of 0.10 is desired and the value of p is somewhere around 0.10, a sample size of about 3600 is required. On the other hand, if a relative error of 0.10 is still desired but the value of p is somewhere around 0.5, then the required sample size is only about 400.

Sample size formulas, and statistical arguments that lead to them, are far from intuitive. In this legal case, by keeping the math to a minimum and using simple terminology like *relative error*, the author eventually convinced the others to use his approach, even though it led to a considerably larger sample size than the 385 originally proposed.

7-1 Introduction

This chapter sets the stage for statistical inference, a topic that is explored in the following two chapters. In a typical statistical inference problem, you want to discover one or more characteristics of a given population. For example, you might want to know the proportion of toothpaste customers who have tried, or intend to try, a particular brand. Or you might want to know the average amount owed on credit card accounts for a population of customers at a shopping mall. Generally, the population is large and/or spread out, and it is difficult, maybe even impossible, to contact each member. Therefore, you identify a sample of the population and then obtain information from the members of the sample.

There are two main objectives of this chapter. The first is to discuss the sampling schemes that are generally used in real sampling applications. We focus on several types of *random* samples and see why these are preferable to nonrandom samples. The second objective is to see how the information from a sample of the population—for example, 1% of the population—can be used to infer the properties of the entire population. The key here is the concept of a *sampling distribution*. In this chapter we focus on the sampling distribution of the sample mean, and we discuss the role of a famous mathematical result called the *central limit theorem*. Specifically, we discuss how the central limit theorem is the reason for the importance of the *normal* distribution in statistical inference.

7-2 Sampling Terminology

We begin by introducing some terminology that is used in sampling. In any sampling problem there is a relevant *population*. The **population** is the set of all members about which a study intends to make inferences, where an *inference* is a statement about a numerical characteristic of the population, such as an average income or the proportion of incomes below $50,000. It is important to realize that a population is defined in relationship to any particular study. Any analyst planning a survey should first decide which population the conclusions of the study will concern, so that a sample can be chosen from *this* population.

> The relevant population contains all members about which a study intends to make inferences.

For example, if a marketing researcher plans to use a questionnaire to infer consumers' reactions to a new product, she must first decide which population of consumers is of interest—all consumers, consumers over 21 years old, consumers who do most of their shopping online, or others. Once the relevant consumer population has been designated, a sample from this population can then be surveyed. However, it is important to remember that inferences made from the study pertain only to this *particular* population.

Before you can choose a sample from a given population, you typically need a list of all members of the population. In sampling terminology, this list is called a **frame**, and the potential sample members are called **sampling units**. Depending on the context, sampling units could be individual people, households, companies, cities, or others.

> A frame is a list of all members, called sampling units, in the population.

It is customary in virtually all statistical literature to let uppercase N be the population size and lowercase n be the sample size. We follow this convention as well.

In this chapter we assume that the population is finite and consists of N sampling units. We also assume that a frame of these N sampling units is available. Unfortunately, there are many situations where a complete frame is practically impossible to obtain. For example, if the purpose of a study is to survey the attitudes of all unemployed teenagers in Chicago, it is practically impossible to obtain a complete frame of them. In this situation the best alternative is to obtain a partial frame from which the sample can be selected. If the partial frame omits any significant segments of the population that a complete frame would include, then the resulting sample could be biased. For instance, if you use a restaurant guide to choose a sample of restaurants, you automatically omit all restaurants that do not advertise in the guide. Depending on the purposes of the study, this could be a serious omission.

There are two basic types of samples: *probability samples* and *judgmental samples*. A **probability sample** is a sample in which the sampling units are chosen from the population according to a random mechanism. In contrast, no formal random mechanism is used to select a **judgmental sample**. In this case the sampling units are chosen according to the sampler's judgment.

> The members of a probability sample are chosen according to a random mechanism, whereas the members of a judgmental sample are chosen according to the sampler's judgment.

We will not discuss judgmental samples. The reason is very simple—there is no way to measure the accuracy of judgmental samples because the rules of probability do not apply to them. In other words, if a population characteristic is estimated from the observations in a judgmental sample, there is no way to measure the accuracy of this estimate. In addition, it is very difficult to choose a representative sample from a population *without* using some random mechanism. Because our judgment is usually not as good as we think, judgmental samples are likely to contain our own built-in biases. Therefore, we focus exclusively on probability samples from here on.

Fundamental Insight

Why Random Sampling?

One reason for sampling randomly from a population is to avoid biases (such as choosing mainly stay-at-home mothers because they are easier to contact). An equally important reason is that random sampling allows you to use probability to make inferences about unknown population parameters. If sampling were not random, there would be no basis for using probability to make such inferences.

7-3 | Methods for Selecting Random Samples

This section discusses the types of random samples that are used in real sampling applications. Different types of sampling schemes have different properties. There is typically a trade-off between cost and accuracy. Some sampling schemes are cheaper and easier to administer, whereas others are more costly but provide more accurate information. Some of these issues are discussed here. However, anyone who intends to make a living in survey sampling needs to learn much more about the topic than we can cover here.

7-3a Simple Random Sampling

The simplest type of sampling scheme is appropriately called *simple random sampling*. Suppose you want to sample n units from a population of size N. Then a **simple random sample** of size n has the property that every possible sample of size n has the same probability of being chosen. Simple random samples are the easiest to understand, and their statistical properties are the most straightforward. Therefore, we will focus primarily on simple random samples in the rest of this book. However, as we discuss shortly, more complex random samples are often used in real applications.

> A simple random sample of size n is one where each possible sample of size n has the same chance of being chosen.

Let's illustrate the concept with a simple random sample for a small population. Suppose the population size is $N = 5$, and the five members of the population are labeled a, b, c, d, and e. Also, suppose the sample size is $n = 2$. Then the possible samples are $(a, b), (a, c), (a, d), (a, e), (b, c), (b, d), (b, e), (c, d), (c, e)$, and (d, e). That is, there are 10 possible samples—the number of ways two members can be chosen from five members. Then a *simple* random sample of size $n = 2$ has the property that each of these 10 possible samples has the same probability, $1/10$, of being chosen.

One other property of simple random samples can be seen from this example. If you focus on any member of the population, such as member b, you will see that b is a member of 4 of the 10 samples. Therefore, the probability that b is chosen in a simple random sample is $4/10$, or $2/5$. In general, any member has the same probability n/N of being chosen in a simple random sample. If you are one of 100,000 members of a population, then the probability that you will be selected in a simple random sample of size 100 is $100/100,000$, or 1 out of 1000.

There are several ways simple random samples can be chosen, all of which involve random numbers. One approach that works well for the small example with $N = 5$ and $n = 2$ is to generate a single random number with the RAND function in Excel®. You divide the interval from 0 to 1 into 10 equal subintervals of length $1/10$ each and see which of these subintervals the random number falls into. You then choose the corresponding sample. For example, suppose the random number is 0.465. This is in the fifth subinterval, that is, the interval from 0.4 to 0.5, so you choose the fifth sample, (b, c).

The RAND function in Excel generates numbers that are distributed randomly and uniformly between 0 and 1.

This method is clearly consistent with simple random sampling—each of the samples has the same chance of being chosen—but it is prohibitive when n and N are large. In this case there are too many possible samples to list. Fortunately, there is another method that can be used. The idea is simple. You sort the N members of the population randomly, using Excel's RAND function to generate random numbers for the sort. Then you include the first n members from the sorted sequence in the random sample. This procedure is illustrated in Example 7.1.

EXAMPLE

7.1 SAMPLING FAMILIES TO ANALYZE ANNUAL INCOMES

Consider the frame of 40 families with annual incomes shown in column B of Figure 7.1, with several rows hidden. (See the file **Random Sampling.xlsm**. The extension is .xlsm because this file contains a macro. When you open it, you will need to enable the macro.) We want to choose a simple random sample of size 10 from this frame. How can this be done? And how do summary statistics of the chosen families compare to the corresponding summary statistics of the population?

Figure 7.1 Population Income
Data

	A	B	C	D
1	Simple random sampling			
2				
3	Summary statistics			
4		Mean	Median	Stdev
5	Population	$39,985	$38,500	$7,377
6	Sample			
7				
8	Population			
9	Family	Income		
10	1	$43,300		
11	2	$44,300		
12	3	$34,600		
13	4	$38,000		
47	38	$46,900		
48	39	$37,300		
49	40	$41,000		

Objective

To illustrate how Excel's random number function, RAND, can be used to generate simple random samples.

Solution

The idea is very simple. You first generate a column of random numbers next to the data. Then you sort the rows according to the random numbers and choose the first 10 families in the sorted rows. The following procedure produces the results in Figure 7.2. (See the first sheet in the finished version of the file.)

1. **Random numbers next to a copy.** Copy the original data to columns D and E. Then enter the formula

   = RAND()

   in cell F10 and copy it down column F.
2. **Replace with values.** To enable sorting, you must first "freeze" the random numbers—that is, replace their formulas with values. To do this, copy the range F10:F49 and select Paste Values from the Paste dropdown menu on the Home ribbon.
3. **Sort.** Sort on column F in ascending order. Then the 10 families with the 10 smallest random numbers are the ones in the sample. These are shaded in the figure. (Note that you could instead have chosen the 10 families with the 10 *largest* random numbers. This would be equally valid.)
4. **Means.** Use the AVERAGE, MEDIAN, and STDEV.S functions in row 6 to calculate summary statistics of the first 10 incomes in column E. Similar summary statistics for the population have already been calculated in row 5. (Cell D5 uses the STDEV.P function because this is the *population* standard deviation.)

To obtain more random samples of size 10 (for comparison), you would need to go through this process repeatedly. To save you the trouble of doing so, we wrote a macro to automate the process. (See the Automated sheet in the finished version of the file.) This sheet looks essentially the same as the sheet in Figure 7.2, except that there is a button to run the macro, and only the required data remain on the spreadsheet. Try clicking this button. Each time you do so, you will get a different random sample—and different summary measures in row 6. By doing this many times and keeping track of the sample summary data, you can see how the summary measures vary from sample to sample. We will have much more to say about this variation later in the chapter.

Figure 7.2 Selecting a Simple Random Sample

	A	B	C	D	E	F
1	**Simple random sampling**					
2						
3	**Summary statistics**					
4		Mean	Median	Stdev		
5	Population	$39,985	$38,500	$7,377		
6	Sample	$41,490	$42,850	$5,323		
7						
8	**Population**			**Random sample**		
9	Family	Income		Family	Income	Random #
10	1	$43,300		1	$43,300	0.04545
11	2	$44,300		2	$44,300	0.1496768
12	3	$34,600		12	$51,500	0.23527
13	4	$38,000		7	$42,700	0.2746325
14	5	$44,700		13	$35,900	0.3003506
15	6	$45,600		15	$43,000	0.3197393
16	7	$42,700		6	$45,600	0.3610983
17	8	$36,900		3	$34,600	0.3852641
18	9	$38,400		9	$38,400	0.4427564
19	10	$33,700		14	$35,600	0.4447877
20	11	$44,100		5	$44,700	0.4505899
21	12	$51,500		40	$41,000	0.4597361
47	38	$46,900		39	$37,300	0.8644119
48	39	$37,300		8	$36,900	0.9059098
49	40	$41,000		10	$33,700	0.9637509

The procedure described in Example 7.1 can be used in Excel to select a simple random sample of any size from any population. All you need is a frame that lists the population values. Then it is just a matter of inserting random numbers, freezing them, and sorting on the random numbers.

Perhaps surprisingly, simple random samples are used infrequently in real applications. There are several reasons for this.

- Because each sampling unit has the same chance of being sampled, simple random sampling can result in samples that are spread over a large geographical region. This can make sampling extremely expensive, especially if personal interviews are used.
- Simple random sampling requires that all sampling units be identified prior to sampling. Sometimes this is infeasible.
- Simple random sampling can result in underrepresentation or overrepresentation of certain segments of the population. For example, if the primary—but not sole—interest is in the graduate student subpopulation of university students, a simple random sample of *all* university students might not provide enough information about the graduate students.

Despite this, most of the statistical analysis in this book assumes simple random samples. The analysis is considerably more complex for other types of random samples and is best left to more advanced books on sampling.

EXAMPLE

7.2 SAMPLING ACCOUNTS RECEIVABLE AT SPRING MILLS

The file **Accounts Receivable Finished.xlsx** contains 280 accounts receivable for Spring Mills Company. There is a single variable, the amount of the bill owed. The file contains the bill amounts for 25 random samples of size 15 each. (They were generated by the method in Example 7.1.) Calculate the average amount owed in each random sample, and create a histogram of these 25 averages.

Objective

To demonstrate how sample means are distributed.

Solution

In most real-world applications, you would generate only a *single* random sample from a population, so why have we generated 25 random samples in this example? The reason is that we want to introduce the concept of a sampling distribution, in this case the sampling distribution of the sample mean. This is the distribution of *all possible* sample means you could generate from all possible samples (of a given size) from a population. By generating a fairly large number of random samples from the population of accounts receivable, you can see what the approximate sampling distribution of the sample mean looks like.

The 25 random samples, one per row, are listed in Figure 7.3. We then used the AVERAGE function in column Q to calculate their sample means, and we created a histogram of these 15 sample means. As you can see, the 15 sample means vary quite a lot, from a low of $332.00 to a high of $799.33. You can check that the population mean, the average of all 280 bill amounts, is $464.29. So the 15 sample means vary around this population mean and are spread out roughly as a bell-shaped curve, as shown in the histogram.

Figure 7.3 Random Samples and Sample Means

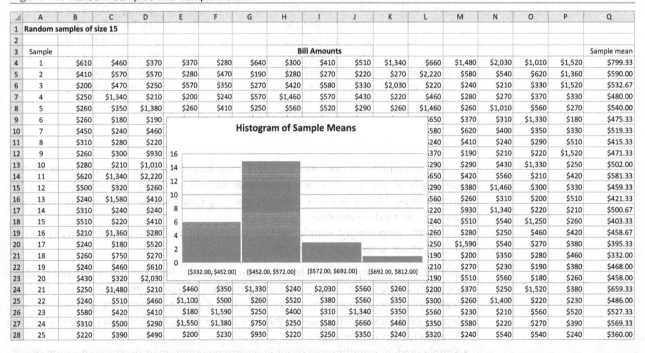

	A	B	C	D	E	F	G	H	I	J	K	L	M	N	O	P	Q
1	Random samples of size 15																
2																	
3	Sample						Bill Amounts										Sample mean
4	1	$610	$460	$370	$370	$280	$640	$300	$410	$510	$1,340	$660	$1,480	$2,030	$1,010	$1,520	$799.33
5	2	$410	$570	$570	$280	$470	$190	$280	$270	$220	$270	$2,220	$580	$540	$620	$1,360	$590.00
6	3	$200	$470	$250	$570	$350	$270	$420	$580	$330	$2,030	$220	$240	$210	$330	$1,520	$532.67
7	4	$250	$1,340	$210	$200	$240	$570	$1,460	$570	$430	$220	$460	$280	$270	$370	$330	$480.00
8	5	$260	$350	$1,380	$260	$410	$250	$560	$520	$290	$260	$1,460	$260	$1,010	$560	$270	$540.00
9	6	$260	$180	$190								$650	$370	$310	$1,330	$180	$475.33
10	7	$450	$240	$460								$580	$620	$400	$350	$330	$519.33
11	8	$310	$280	$220								$240	$410	$240	$290	$510	$415.33
12	9	$260	$300	$930								$370	$190	$210	$220	$1,520	$471.33
13	10	$280	$210	$1,010								$290	$290	$430	$1,330	$250	$502.00
14	11	$620	$1,340	$2,220								$650	$420	$560	$210	$420	$581.33
15	12	$500	$320	$260								$290	$380	$1,460	$300	$330	$459.33
16	13	$240	$1,580	$410								$560	$260	$310	$200	$510	$421.33
17	14	$310	$240	$240								$220	$930	$1,340	$220	$210	$500.67
18	15	$510	$220	$410								$240	$510	$540	$1,250	$260	$403.33
19	16	$210	$1,360	$280								$260	$280	$250	$460	$420	$458.67
20	17	$240	$180	$520								$250	$1,590	$540	$270	$380	$395.33
21	18	$260	$750	$270								$190	$200	$350	$280	$460	$332.00
22	19	$240	$460	$610								$210	$270	$230	$190	$380	$468.00
23	20	$430	$320	$2,030								$190	$510	$560	$180	$260	$458.00
24	21	$250	$1,480	$210	$460	$350	$1,330	$240	$2,030	$560	$260	$200	$370	$250	$1,520	$380	$659.33
25	22	$240	$510	$460	$1,100	$500	$260	$520	$380	$560	$350	$300	$260	$1,400	$220	$230	$486.00
26	23	$580	$420	$410	$180	$1,590	$250	$400	$310	$1,340	$350	$560	$230	$210	$560	$520	$527.33
27	24	$310	$500	$290	$1,550	$1,380	$750	$250	$580	$660	$460	$350	$580	$220	$270	$390	$569.33
28	25	$220	$390	$490	$200	$230	$930	$220	$250	$350	$240	$320	$240	$540	$540	$240	$360.00

This histogram approximates the sampling distribution of the sample mean. It is approximate because it is based on only 15 random samples out of all possible random samples of size 15. (The number of possible random samples of size 15 from a population of size 280 is an astronomically large number.) We will come back to this important idea when we discuss sampling distributions in Section 7-4.

In the next several subsections we describe sampling plans that are often used. These plans differ from simple random sampling both in the way the samples are chosen and in the way the data analysis is performed. However, we will barely touch on this latter issue. The details are quite complicated and are better left to a book devoted entirely to sampling.[1]

---

1 See, for example, the excellent book by Levy and Lemeshow (2008).

Fundamental Insight

Types of Random Samples

There are actually many methods for choosing random samples, some described only briefly in this book, and they all have their advantages and disadvantages from practical and statistical standpoints. Surprisingly, the simplest of these, where each subset of the population has the same chance of being chosen, is *not* the most frequently used method in real applications. This is basically because other more complex methods can make more efficient use of a given sample size. Nevertheless, the *concepts* you learn here remain essentially the same, regardless of the exact sampling method used.

7-3b Systematic Sampling

Suppose you are asked to select a random sample of 250 names from a large company's directory of employees. Let's also say that there are 55,000 names listed in alphabetical order in the directory. A **systematic sample** provides a convenient way to choose the sample. First, you divide the population size by the sample size: 55,000/250 = 220. Conceptually, you can think of dividing the directory into 250 "blocks" with 220 names per block. Next, you use a random mechanism to choose a number between 1 and 220. Suppose this number is 131. Then you choose the 131st name and every 220th name thereafter. So you would choose name 131, name 351, name 571, and so on. The result is a systematic sample of size $n = 250$.

In general, one of the first k members is selected randomly, and then every kth member after this one is selected. The value k is called the *sampling interval* and equals the ratio N/n, where N is the population size and n is the desired sample size.

Systematic sampling is quite different from simple random sampling because not every sample of size 250 has a chance of being chosen. In fact, there are only 220 different samples possible (depending on the first number chosen), and each of these is equally likely. Nevertheless, systematic sampling is generally similar to simple random sampling in its statistical properties. The key is the relationship between the ordering of the sampling units in the frame (the employee directory in this case) and the purpose of the study.

Systematic random samples are typically chosen because of their convenience.

If the purpose of the study is to analyze personal incomes, then there is probably no relationship between the alphabetical ordering of names in the directory and personal income. However, there are situations where the ordering of the sampling units is *not* random, which could make systematic sampling more or less appealing. For example, suppose that a company wants to sample randomly from its customers, and its customer list is in decreasing order of order volumes. That is, the largest customers are at the top of the list and the smallest are at the bottom. Then systematic sampling might be more representative than simple random sampling because it guarantees a wide range of customers in terms of order volumes.

However, some type of cyclical ordering in the list of sampling units can lead to very *unrepresentative* samples. As an extreme, suppose a company has a list of daily transactions (Monday through Saturday) and it decides to draw a systematic sample with the sampling interval equal to 6. Then if the first sampled day is Monday, all other days in the sample will be Mondays. This could clearly bias the sample. Except for obvious examples like this one, however, systematic sampling can be an attractive alternative to simple random sampling and is sometimes used because of its convenience.

7-3c Stratified Sampling

Suppose various subpopulations within the total population can be identified. These subpopulations are called *strata*. Then instead of taking a simple random sample from the entire population, it might make more sense to select a simple random sample from each stratum separately. This sampling method is called **stratified sampling**. It is a particularly useful approach when there is considerable variation *between* the various strata but relatively little variation *within* a given stratum.

> In stratified sampling, the population is divided into relatively homogeneous subsets called *strata*, and then random samples are taken from each stratum.

Stratified samples are typically chosen because they provide more accurate estimates of population parameters for a given sampling cost.

There are several advantages to stratified sampling. One obvious advantage is that separate estimates can be obtained within each stratum—which would not be obtained with a simple random sample from the entire population. Even if the samples from the individual strata are eventually pooled, it can be useful to have the total sample broken down into separate samples initially.

A more important advantage of stratified sampling is that the accuracy of the resulting population estimates can be increased by using appropriately defined strata. The trick is to define the strata so that there is less variability *within* the individual strata than in the population as a whole. You want strata such that there is relative homogeneity within the strata, but relative heterogeneity across the strata, with respect to the variable(s) being analyzed. By choosing the strata in this way, you can generally obtain more accuracy for a given sampling cost than you could obtain from a simple random sample at the same cost. Alternatively, you can achieve the same level of accuracy at a lower sampling cost.

The key to using stratified sampling effectively is selecting the appropriate strata. Suppose a company that advertises its product on television wants to estimate the reaction of viewers to the advertising. Here the population consists of all viewers who have seen the advertising. But what are the appropriate strata? The answer depends on the company's objectives and its product. The company could stratify the population by gender, by income, by age, by amount of television watched, by the amount of the product class consumed, and probably others. Without knowing more specific information about the company's objectives, it is impossible to say which of these stratification schemes is most appropriate.

Suppose that you have identified I nonoverlapping strata in a given population. Let N be the total population size, and let N_i be the population size of stratum i, so that

$$N = N_1 + N_2 + \ldots + N_I$$

To obtain a stratified random sample, you must first choose a total sample size n, and then choose a sample size n_i from each stratum i such that

$$n = n_1 + n_2 + \ldots + n_I$$

You can then select a simple random sample of the specified size from *each* stratum exactly as in Example 7.1.

However, how do you choose the individual sample sizes n_1 through n_I, given that the total sample size n has been chosen? For example, if you decide to sample 500 customers in total, how many should come from each stratum? There are many ways to choose sample sizes n_1 through n_I that sum to n, but probably the most popular method is to use **proportional sample sizes**. The idea is very simple. For example, if one stratum has 15% of the total population, you select 15% of the total sample from this stratum.

> With proportional sample sizes, the proportion of a stratum in the sample is the same as the proportion of that stratum in the population.

The advantage of proportional sample sizes is that they are very easy to determine. The disadvantage is that they ignore differences in variability among the strata. If such differences are large, more complex sample size calculations can be used, but they are not discussed here.

7-3d Cluster Sampling

Suppose that a company is interested in various characteristics of households in a particular city. The sampling units are households. You could select a random sample of households by one of the sampling methods already discussed. However, it might be more convenient to proceed somewhat differently. You could first divide the city into city blocks and consider the city blocks as sampling units. You could then select a simple random sample of city blocks and then sample all of the households in the chosen blocks. In this case the city blocks are called *clusters* and the sampling scheme is called **cluster sampling**.

> In cluster sampling, the population is separated into clusters, such as cities or city blocks, and then a random sample of the clusters is selected.

Cluster analysis is typically more convenient and less costly than other random sampling methods.

The primary advantage of cluster sampling is sampling convenience (and possibly lower cost). If an agency is sending interviewers to interview heads of household, it is much easier for them to concentrate on particular city blocks than to contact households throughout the city. The downside, however, is that the inferences drawn from a cluster sample can be less accurate for a given sample size than from other sampling plans.

Consider the following scenario. A nationwide company wants to survey its salespeople with regard to management practices. It decides to randomly select several sales districts (the clusters) and then interview all salespeople in the selected districts. It is likely that in any particular sales district the attitudes toward management are somewhat similar. This overlapping information means that the company is probably not getting the maximum amount of information per sampling dollar spent. Instead of sampling 20 salespeople from a given district, all of whom have similar attitudes, it might be better to sample 20 salespeople from different districts who have a wider variety of attitudes. Nevertheless, the relative convenience of cluster sampling sometimes outweighs these statistical considerations.

Selecting a cluster sample is straightforward. The key is to define the sampling units as the *clusters*—the city blocks, for example. Then a simple random sample of clusters can be chosen exactly as in Example 7.1. Once the clusters are selected, it is typical to sample all of the population members in each selected cluster, although it is also possible to randomly sample from the selected clusters.

7-3e Multistage Sampling

The cluster sampling scheme just described, where a sample of clusters is chosen and then all of the sampling units within each chosen cluster are taken, is called a **single-stage** sampling scheme. Real applications are often more complex than this, resulting in **multistage** sampling. For example, the Gallup organization uses multistage sampling in its nationwide surveys. A random sample of approximately 300 locations is chosen in the first stage of the sampling process. City blocks or other geographical areas are then randomly sampled from the first-stage locations in the second stage of the process. This is followed by a systematic sampling of households from each second-stage area. A total of about 1500 households comprise a typical Gallup poll.[2]

We will not pursue the topic of multistage sampling in this book. However, you should realize that real-world sampling procedures can be complex.

---

2 If you watch discussions of politics on the news, you are aware that the results of new polls are available on an almost daily basis from a variety of polling organizations. Surprisingly, the organization probably best known for polling, Gallup, announced in October 2015 that it was getting out of the political polling business. Its traditional polling method, evening calls to landline phones, evidently doesn't work in an environment dominated by cell phones and social media. Gallup will continue polling in other areas, just not political races.

Problems

Level A

1. The file **P02_07.xlsx** includes data on 204 employees at the (fictional) company Beta Technologies. For this problem, consider this data set as the population frame.
   a. Using the method in this section, generate 10 simple random samples of size 20 from this population.
   b. Calculate the population mean, median, and standard deviation of Annual Salary. Then calculate the sample mean, median, and standard deviation of Annual Salary for each of the samples in part **a**. Comment briefly on how they compare to each other and the population measures.

2. The file **P07_02.xlsx** contains data on the 1995 students who have gone through the MBA program at State University. You can consider this the population of State University's MBA students.
   a. Find the mean and standard deviation for each of the numerical variables in this population. Also, find the following proportions: the proportion of students who are male, the proportion of students who are international (not from the USA), the proportion of students under 30 years of age, and the proportion of students with an engineering undergrad major.
   b. Using the method in this section, generate a simple random sample of 100 students from this population, and find the mean and standard deviation of each numerical variable in the sample. Is there any way to know (without the information in part **a**) whether your summary measures for the sample are lower or higher than the (supposedly unknown) population summary measures?
   c. Use the method in this section to generate 10 simple random samples of size 100 of School Debt. For each, find the mean of School Debt and its deviation from the population mean in part **a** (negative if it is below the population mean, positive if it is above the population mean). What is the average of these 10 deviations? What would you expect it to be?
   d. We want random samples to be representative of the population in terms of various demographics. For each of the samples in part **c**, find each of the proportions requested in part **a**. Do these samples appear to be representative of the population in terms of age, gender, nationality, and undergrad major? Why or why not? If they are not representative, is it because there is something wrong with the sampling procedure?

3. The file **P02_35.xlsx** contains data from a survey of 500 randomly selected households.
   a. Suppose you decide to generate a systematic random sample of size 25 from this population of data. How many such samples are there? What is the mean of

Debt for each of the first three such samples, using the data in the order given?
   b. If you wanted to estimate the (supposedly unknown) population mean of Debt from a systematic random sample as in part **a**, why might it be a good idea to sort first on Debt? If you do so, what is the mean of Debt for each of the first three such samples?

4. Recall from Chapter 2 that the file **Supermarket Transactions.xlsx** contains over 14,000 transactions made by supermarket customers over a period of approximately two years. For this problem, consider this data set the population of transactions.
   a. If you were interested in estimating the mean of Revenue for the population, why *might* it make sense to use a stratified sample, stratified by product family, to estimate this mean?
   b. Suppose you want to generate a stratified random sample, stratified by product family, and have the total sample size be 250. If you use proportional sample sizes, how many transactions should you sample from each of the three product families?
   c. Using the sample sizes from part **b**, generate a corresponding stratified random sample. What are the individual sample means from the three product families? What are the sample standard deviations?

Level B

5. This problem illustrates an interesting variation of simple random sampling.
   a. Open a blank spreadsheet and use the RAND() function to create a column of 1000 random numbers. Don't freeze them. This is actually a simple random sample from the uniform distribution between 0 and 1. Use the COUNTIF function to count the number of values between 0 and 0.1, between 0.1 and 0.2, and so on. Each such interval should contain about 1/10 of all values. Do they? (Keep pressing the F9 key to see how the results change.)
   b. Repeat part **a**, generating a second column of random numbers, but now generate the first 100 as uniform between 0 and 0.1, the next 100 as uniform between 0.1 and 0.2, and so on, up to 0.9 to 1. (*Hint*: For example, to create a random number uniformly distributed between 0.5 and 0.6, use the formula =0.5+0.1*RAND(). Do you see why?) Again, use COUNTIF to find the number of the 1000 values in each of the intervals, although there shouldn't be any surprises this time. Why might this type of random sampling be preferable to the random sampling in part **a**? (*Note*: The sampling in part **a** is called Monte Carlo sampling, whereas the sampling in part **b** is basically Latin Hypercube sampling.)

6. Another type of random sample is called a *bootstrap sample*. (It comes from the expression "pulling yourself up by your own bootstraps.") Given a data set with *n* observations, a bootstrap sample, also of size *n*, is when you randomly sample from the data set *with replacement*. To do so, you keep choosing a random integer from 1 to *n* and include that item in the sample. The "with replacement" part means that you can sample the same item more than once. For example, if $n = 4$, the sampled items might be 1, 2, 2, and 4. Using the data in the file **Accounts Receivable.xlsx**, illustrate a simple method for choosing bootstrap samples with the RAND-BETWEEN and VLOOKUP functions. For each bootstrap sample, find the mean and standard deviation of Bill Amount. How do these compare to the similar measures for the original data set? (For more on bootstrap sampling, do a Web search. Wikipedia has a nice overview.)

7-4 Introduction to Estimation

The purpose of any random sample, simple or otherwise, is to estimate properties of a population from the data observed in the sample. The following is a good example to keep in mind. Suppose a government agency wants to know the average household income over the population of all households in Indiana. Then this unknown average is the population parameter of interest, and the government is likely to estimate it by sampling several representative households in Indiana and reporting the average of their incomes.

The mathematical procedures appropriate for performing this estimation depend on which properties of the population are of interest and which type of random sampling scheme is used. Because the details are considerably more complex for more complex sampling schemes such as multistage sampling, we will focus on *simple* random samples, where the mathematical details are relatively straightforward. Details for other sampling schemes such as stratified sampling can be found in Levy and Lemeshow (2008). However, even for more complex sampling schemes, the *concepts* are the same as those we discuss here; only the details change.

Throughout most of this section, we focus on the population mean of some variable such as household income. Our goal is to estimate this population mean by using the data in a randomly selected sample. We first discuss the types of errors that can occur.

7-4a Sources of Estimation Error

There are two basic sources of errors that can occur when sampling randomly from a population: *sampling error* and all other sources, usually lumped together as *nonsampling error*. **Sampling error** results from "unlucky" samples. As such, the term *error* is somewhat misleading. Suppose, for example, that the mean household income in Indiana is $58,225. (We can only assume that this is the true value. It wouldn't actually be known without taking a census.) A government agency wants to estimate this mean, so it randomly samples 500 Indiana households and finds that their average household income is $60,495. If the agency then infers that the mean of *all* Indiana household incomes is $60,495, the resulting sampling error is the difference between the reported value and the true value: $60,495 − $58,225 = $2270. In this case, the agency hasn't done anything wrong. This sampling error is essentially due to bad luck.

> Sampling error is the inevitable result of basing an inference on a random sample rather than on the entire population.

We will soon discuss how to measure the *potential* sampling error involved. The point here is that the resulting estimation error is not caused by anything the government agency is doing wrong—it might just get unlucky.

Nonsampling error is quite different and can occur for a variety of reasons. We discuss a few of them.

- Perhaps the most serious type of nonsampling error is **nonresponse bias**. This occurs when a portion of the sample fails to respond to the survey. Anyone who has ever conducted a questionnaire, whether by mail, by phone, or any other method, knows that the percentage of nonrespondents can be quite large. The question is whether this introduces estimation error. If the nonrespondents *would* have responded similarly to the respondents, not much is lost by not hearing from them. However, because the nonrespondents don't respond, there is typically no way of knowing whether they differ in some important respect from the respondents.

- Another source of nonsampling error is **nontruthful responses**. This is particularly a problem when there are sensitive questions in a questionnaire. For example, if the questions "Have you ever had an abortion?" or "Do you regularly use cocaine?" are asked, most people will answer "no," regardless of whether the true answer is "yes" or "no."

- Another type of nonsampling error is **measurement error**. This occurs when the responses to the questions do not reflect what the investigator had in mind. It might result from poorly worded questions, questions the respondents don't fully understand, questions that require the respondents to supply information they don't have, and so on. Undoubtedly, there have been times when you were filling out a questionnaire and said to yourself, "OK, I'll answer this as well as I can, but I know it's not what they want to know."

- One final type of nonsampling error is **voluntary response bias**. This occurs when the subset of people who respond to a survey differ in some important respect from all potential respondents. For example, suppose a population of students is surveyed to see how many hours they study per night. If the students who respond are predominantly those who get the best grades, the resulting sample mean number of hours could be biased on the high side.

From this discussion and your own experience with questionnaires, you should realize that the potential for nonsampling error is enormous. However, unlike sampling error, it cannot be measured with probability theory. It can be controlled only by using appropriate sampling procedures and designing good survey instruments. We will not pursue this topic any further here. If you are interested, however, you can learn about methods for controlling nonsampling error, such as proper questionnaire design, from books on survey sampling.

7-4b Key Terms in Sampling

We now set the stage for the rest of this chapter, as well as for the next two chapters. Suppose there is some numerical population parameter you want to know. This parameter could be a population mean, a population proportion, the difference between two population means, the difference between two population proportions, or others. Unless you measure each member of the population—that is, unless you take a census—you cannot learn the exact value of this population parameter. Therefore, you instead take a random sample of some type and *estimate* the population parameter from the data in the sample.

You typically begin by calculating a **point estimate** (or, simply, an *estimate*) from the sample data. This is a "best guess" of the population parameter. The difference between the point estimate and the true value of the population parameter is called the **sampling error** (or **estimation error**). You then use probability theory to estimate the magnitude of the sampling error. The key to this is the **sampling distribution** of the point estimate, which is defined as the distribution of the point estimates you would see from *all* possible samples (of a given sample size) from the population. Often you report the accuracy of the point estimate with an accompanying *confidence interval*. A **confidence interval** is an interval around the point estimate, calculated from the sample data, that is very likely to contain the true value of the population parameter. (We will say much more about confidence intervals in the next chapter.)

A point estimate is a single numeric value, a "best guess" of a population parameter, based on the data in a random sample.

The sampling error (or estimation error) is the difference between the point estimate and the true value of the population parameter being estimated.

The sampling distribution of any point estimate is the distribution of the point estimates from *all* possible samples (of a given sample size) from the population.

A confidence interval is an interval around the point estimate, calculated from the sample data, that is very likely to contain the true value of the population parameter.

Additionally, there are two other key terms you should know. First, consider the *mean* of the sampling distribution of a point estimate. It is the average value of the point estimates you would see from all possible samples. When this mean is equal to the true value of the population parameter, the point estimate is **unbiased**. Otherwise, it is *biased*. Naturally, unbiased estimates are preferred. Even if they sometimes miss on the low side and sometimes miss on the high side, they tend to be on target on average.

An unbiased **estimate** is a point estimate such that the mean of its sampling distribution is equal to the true value of the population parameter being estimated.

Unbiased estimates are desirable because they average out to the correct value. However, this isn't enough. Point estimates from different samples should vary as little as possible from sample to sample. If they vary wildly, a point estimate from a *single* random sample isn't very reliable. Therefore, it is common to measure the standard deviation of the sampling distribution of the estimate. This indicates how much point estimates from different samples vary. In the context of sampling, this standard deviation is called the **standard error** of the estimate. Ideally, estimates should have *small* standard errors.

The standard error of an estimate is the standard deviation of the sampling distribution of the estimate. It measures how much estimates vary from sample to sample.

The terms in this subsection are relevant for practically any population parameter you might want to estimate. In the following subsection we discuss them in the context of estimating a population mean.

7-4c Sampling Distribution of the Sample Mean

In this section we discuss the estimation of the population mean from some population. For example, you might be interested in the mean household income for all families in a particular city, the mean diameter of all parts from a manufacturing process, the mean amount of underreported taxes by all U.S. taxpayers, and so on. We label the unknown population mean by μ. (It is common to label population parameters with Greek letters.)

The point estimate of μ typically used, based on a sample from the population, is the sample mean $\overline{X}$, the average of the observations in the sample. There are other possible point estimates for a population mean besides the sample mean, such as the sample median, the **trimmed mean** (where all but the few most extreme observations are averaged), and others. However, it turns out that this "natural" estimate, the sample mean, has very good theoretical properties, so it is the point estimate used most often.

How accurate is $\overline{X}$ in estimating μ? That is, how large does the estimation error $\overline{X} - \mu$ tend to be? The sampling distribution of the sample mean $\overline{X}$ provides the key. Before describing this sampling distribution in some generality, we provide some insight into it by revisiting the population of 40 incomes in Example 7.1. There we showed how to generate a single random sample of size 10. For the particular sample we generated (see Figure 7.2), the sample mean was $41,490. Because the population mean of all 40 incomes is $39,985, the estimation error based on this particular sample is the difference $41,490 − $39,985, or $1505 on the high side.

However, this is only one of many possible samples. To see other possibilities, you could generate many random samples of size 10 from the population of 40 incomes. You could then calculate the sample mean for each random sample and create a histogram of these sample means. We did this, generating 100 random samples of size 10, with the result shown in Figure 7.4. Although this is not *exactly* the sampling distribution of the sample mean (because there are many more than 100 possible samples of size 10 from a population of size 40), it indicates approximately how the possible sample means are distributed. They are most likely to be near the population mean ($39,985), very unlikely to be more than about $3000 from the population mean, and have an approximately bell-shaped distribution.

Figure 7.4 Approximate Sampling Distribution of Sample Mean

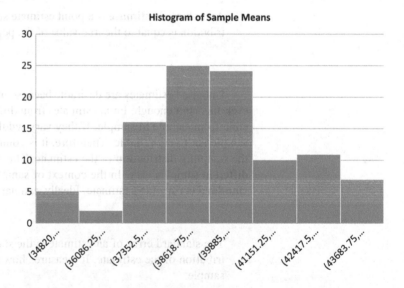

The insights in the previous paragraph can be generalized. It turns out that the sampling distribution of the sample mean has the following properties, regardless of the underlying population. First, it is an unbiased estimate of the population mean, as indicated in Equation (7.1). The sample means from some samples will be too low, and those from other samples will be too high, but on the average, they will be on target.

Unbiased Property of Sample Mean

$$E(\overline{X}) = \mu \qquad (7.1)$$

The second property involves the variability of the $\overline{X}$ estimate. Recall that the standard deviation of an estimate, called the standard error, indicates how much the estimate varies from sample to sample. The standard error of $\overline{X}$ is given in Equation (7.2). Here, $SE(\overline{X})$ is an abbreviation for the standard error of $\overline{X}$, σ is the standard deviation of the population, and n is the sample size. You can see that the standard error is large when the observations in the population are spread out (large σ), but that the standard error can be reduced by taking a larger sample.[3]

Standard Error of Sample Mean

$$SE(\overline{X}) = \sigma/\sqrt{n} \qquad\qquad (7.2)$$

There is one problem with the standard error in Equation (7.2). Its value depends on *another* unknown population parameter, σ. Therefore, it is customary to approximate the standard error by substituting the *sample* standard deviation, s, for σ. This leads to Equation (7.3).

Approximate Standard Error of Sample Mean

$$SE(\overline{X}) = s/\sqrt{n} \qquad\qquad (7.3)$$

As we discuss in the next subsection, the shape of the sampling distribution of $\overline{X}$ is approximately normal. Therefore, you can use the standard error exactly as you have used standard deviations in previous chapters to obtain confidence intervals for the population mean. Specifically, if you go out two standard errors on either side of the sample mean, as shown in Expression (7.4), you can be approximately 95% confident of capturing the population mean. Equivalently, you can be 95% confident that the estimation error will be no greater than two standard errors in magnitude.

(Approximate) Confidence Interval for Population Mean

$$\overline{X} \pm 2s/\sqrt{n} \qquad\qquad (7.4)$$

Fundamental Insight

Sampling Distributions and Standard Errors

Any point estimate, such as the sample mean, is random because it depends on the random sample that happens to be chosen. The sampling distribution of the point estimate is the probability distribution of point estimates from all possible random samples. This distribution describes how the sample means vary from one sample to another. The corresponding standard error is the standard deviation of the sampling distribution. These two concepts, sampling distribution and standard error, are the keys to statistical inference, as discussed here and in the next two chapters.

---

3 This formula for SE($\overline{X}$) assumes that the sample size n is small relative to the population size N. As a rule of thumb, we assume that n is no more than 5% of N. Later we provide a "correction" to this formula when n is a larger percentage of N.

The following example illustrates a typical use of sample information.

EXAMPLE

7.3 ESTIMATING THE MEAN OF ACCOUNTS RECEIVABLE

An internal auditor for a furniture retailer wants to estimate the average of all accounts receivable, where this average is taken over the population of all customer accounts. Because the company has approximately 10,000 accounts, an exhaustive enumeration of all accounts receivable is impractical. Therefore, the auditor randomly samples 100 of the accounts. The data from the sample appear in Figure 7.5, with several hidden rows. (See the file **Auditing Receivables.xlsx**.) What can the auditor conclude from this sample?

Figure 7.5 Sampling in Auditing
Example

	A	B	C	D	E
1	Random sample of accounts receivable				
2					
3	Population size	10000			
4	Sample size	100			
5					
6	Sample of receivables			Summary measures from sample	
7	Account	Amount		Sample mean	$278.92
8	1	$85		Sample stdev	$419.21
9	2	$1,061		Std Error of mean	$41.92
10	3	$0			
11	4	$1,260		With fpc	$41.71
12	5	$924			
13	6	$129			
105	98	$657			
106	99	$86			
107	100	$0			

Objective

To illustrate the meaning of standard error of the mean in a sample of accounts receivable.

Solution

The receivables for the 100 sampled accounts appear in column B. This is the only information available to the auditor, so he must base all conclusions on these sample data. Begin by calculating the sample mean and sample standard deviation in cells E7 and E8 with the AVERAGE and STDEV.S functions. Then use Equation (7.3) to calculate the (approximate) standard error of the mean in cell E9 with the formula

=E8/SQRT(B4)

The auditor should interpret these values as follows. First, the sample mean $279 is a point estimate of the unknown population mean. It provides a best guess for the average of the receivables from all 10,000 accounts. In fact, because the sample mean is an unbiased estimate of the population mean, there is no reason to suspect that $279 either underestimates or overestimates the population mean. Second, the standard error $42 provides a measure of accuracy of the $279 estimate. Specifically, there is about a 95% chance that the estimate differs by no more than two standard errors (about $84) from the true but unknown population mean. Therefore, the auditor can be approximately 95% confident that the mean from all 10,000 accounts is within the interval $279 ± $84, that is, between $195 and $363.

It is important to distinguish between the sample standard deviation s and the standard error of the mean, approximated by $s/\sqrt{n}$. The sample standard deviation in the auditing example, $419, measures the variability across *individual* receivables in the sample (or in the population). By scrolling down column B, you can see some very low amounts (many zeros) and some fairly large amounts. This variability is indicated by the rather large sample standard deviation s. However, this value does not measure the accuracy of the sample mean as an estimate of the population mean. To judge *its* accuracy, you need to divide s by the square root of the sample size n. The resulting standard error, about $42, is much smaller than the sample standard deviation. It indicates that you can be about 95% confident that the sampling error is no greater than $84. In short, sample means vary much less than individual observations from a given population.

The Finite Population Correction

We mentioned that Equation (7.2) [or Equation (7.3)] for the standard error of $\overline{X}$ is appropriate when the sample size n is small relative to the population size N. Generally, "small" means that n is no more than 5% of N. In most realistic samples this is certainly true. For example, political polls are typically based on samples of approximately 1000 people from the entire U.S. population.

There are situations, however, when the sample size is greater than 5% of the population. In this case the formula for the standard error of the mean should be modified with a **finite population correction**, or *fpc,* factor. The modified standard error of the mean appears in Equation (7.5), where the *fpc* is given by Equation (7.6). Note that this factor is always less than 1 (when $n > 1$) and it decreases as n increases. Therefore, the standard error of the mean decreases—and the accuracy increases—as n increases.

Standard Error of Mean with Finite Population Correction Factor

$$\text{SE}(\overline{X}) = fpc \times (s/\sqrt{n}) \tag{7.5}$$

Finite Population Correction Factor

$$fpc = \sqrt{\frac{N - n}{N - 1}} \tag{7.6}$$

To see how the *fpc* varies with n and N, consider the values in Table 7.1. Rather than listing n, we have listed the percentage of the population sampled, that is, $n/N \times 100\%$. It is clear that when 5% or less of the population is sampled, the *fpc* is very close to 1 and can safely be ignored. In this case you can use $s/\sqrt{n}$ as the standard error of the mean. Otherwise, you should use the modified formula in Equation (7.5).

Table 7.1 Finite Population Correction Factors

N	% Sampled	fpc
100	5	0.980
100	10	0.953
10,000	1	0.995
10,000	5	0.975
10,000	10	0.949
1,000,000	1	0.995
1,000,000	5	0.975
1,000,000	10	0.949

If less than 5% of the population is sampled, as is often the case, the fpc can safely be ignored.

In the auditing example, $n/N = 100/100{,}000 = 0.1\%$. This suggests that the *fpc* can safely be omitted. We illustrate this in cell E11 of Figure 7.5, which uses the formula from Equation (7.5):

=SQRT((B3-B4)/(B3-1))*E9

Clearly, it makes no practical difference in this example whether you use the *fpc* or not. The standard error, rounded to the nearest dollar, is $42 in either case.

Virtually all standard error formulas used in sampling include an *fpc* factor. However, because it is rarely necessary—the sample size is usually very small relative to the population size—we omit it from here on.

7-4d The Central Limit Theorem

Our discussion to this point has concentrated primarily on the mean and standard deviation of the sampling distribution of the sample mean. In this section we discuss this sampling distribution in more detail. Because of an important theoretical result called the **central limit theorem**, this sampling distribution is approximately *normal* with mean μ and standard deviation $\sigma/\sqrt{n}$. This theorem is the primary reason why the normal distribution appears in so many statistical results. The theorem can be stated as follows.

> For *any* population distribution with mean μ and standard deviation σ, the sampling distribution of the sample mean $\overline{X}$ is approximately normal with mean μ and standard deviation $\sigma/\sqrt{n}$, and the approximation improves as n increases.

The important part of this result is the *normality* of the sampling distribution. We know, without any conditions placed upon the sample size n, that the mean and standard deviation are μ and $\sigma/\sqrt{n}$. However, the central limit theorem also implies normality, provided that n is reasonably large.

Fundamental Insight

The Central Limit Theorem

This important result states that when you sum or average n randomly selected values from *any* distribution, normal or otherwise, the distribution of the sum or average is approximately *normal*, provided that n is sufficiently large. This is the primary reason why the normal distribution is relevant in so many real applications.

How large must n be for the approximation to be valid? Many textbooks suggest $n \geq 30$ as a rule of thumb. However, this depends heavily on the population distribution. If the population distribution is very *nonnormal*—extremely skewed or bimodal, for example—the normal approximation might not be accurate unless n is considerably greater than 30. On the other hand, if the population distribution is already approximately symmetric, the normal approximation is quite good for n considerably less than 30. In fact, in the special case where the population distribution itself is normal, the sampling distribution of $\overline{X}$ is *exactly* normal for *any* value of n.

The central limit theorem is not a simple concept to grasp. To help explain it, we use simulation in the following example.

EXAMPLE

7.4 AVERAGE WINNINGS FROM A WHEEL OF FORTUNE

Suppose you have the opportunity to play a game with a "wheel of fortune" (similar to the one in a popular television game show). When you spin a large wheel, it is equally likely to stop in any position. Depending on where it stops, you win anywhere from $0 to $1000. Let's suppose your winnings are actually based on not one spin, but on the average of n spins of the wheel. For example, if $n = 2$, your winnings are based on the average of two spins. If the first spin results in $580 and the second spin results in $320, you win the average, $450. How does the distribution of your winnings depend on n?

Objective

To illustrate the central limit theorem by a simulation of winnings in a game of chance.

Solution

First, what does this experiment have to do with random sampling? Here, the population is the set of all outcomes you could obtain from a *single* spin of the wheel—that is, all dollar values from $0 to $1000. Each spin results in one randomly sampled dollar value from this population. Furthermore, because we have assumed that the wheel is equally likely to land in any position, all possible values in the continuum from $0 to $1000 have the same chance of occurring. The resulting population distribution is called the *uniform distribution* on the interval from $0 to $1000. (See Figure 7.6, where the 1 on the horizontal axis corresponds to $1000.) It can be shown that the mean and standard deviation of this uniform distribution are $\mu = \$500$ and $\sigma = \$289$.[4]

Figure 7.6 Uniform Distribution

Uniform density function

Before we go any further, take a moment to test your own intuition. If you play this game once and your winnings are based on the average of n spins, how likely is that you will win at least $600 if $n = 1$? if $n = 3$? if $n = 10$? (The answers are 0.4, 0.27, and 0.14, respectively, where the last two answers are approximate and are based on the central limit theorem or the simulation. So you are much less likely to win big if your winnings are based on the average of many spins.)

Now we analyze the distribution of winnings based on the average of n spins. We do so by means of a sequence of simulations in Excel. (See the file **Wheel of Fortune Simulation.xlsx**, which is set up to work for any number of spins up to 10.) For each simulation, consider 1000 replications of an experiment. Each replication of the experiment simulates n spins of the wheel and calculates the average—that is, the winnings—from these n spins. Based on these 1000 replications, the average and standard deviation of winnings can be calculated, and a histogram of winnings can be formed, for any value of n. These will show clearly how the distribution of winnings depends on n.

The values in Figure 7.7 and the histogram in Figure 7.8 show the results for $n = 1$. Here there is no averaging—you spin the wheel once and win the amount shown. To replicate this experiment 1000 times and collect statistics, proceed as follows.

Calculating the Distribution of Winnings by Simulation

1. **Random outcomes.** To generate outcomes uniformly distributed between $0 and $1000, enter the formula

    =IF(B$9<=$B$6,$B$3+($B$4−$B$3)*RAND(), " ")

---

4 In general, if a distribution is uniform on the interval from a to b, its mean is the midpoint $(a + b)/2$ and its standard deviation is $(b - a)/\sqrt{12}$.

Figure 7.7 Simulation of Winnings from a Single Spin

	A	B	C	D	E	F	G	H	I	J	K	L
1	**Wheel of fortune simulation**											
2												
3	Minimum winnings	$0									**Summary measures of winnings**	
4	Maximum winnings	$1,000									Mean	$497
5											Stdev	$290
6	Number of spins	1									P(>600)	0.406
7												
8	**Simulation of spins**											
9	Spin	1	2	3	4	5	6	7	8	9	10	
10	Replication	Outcome	Outcome	Outcome	Outcome	Outcome	Outcome	Outcome	Outcome	Outcome	Outcome	Winnings
11	1	$404										$404
12	2	$893										$893
13	3	$111										$111
14	4	$764										$764
15	5	$960										$960
16	6	$363										$363
1007	997	$569										$569
1008	998	$869										$869
1009	999	$24										$24
1010	1000	$255										$255

Figure 7.8 Histogram of Simulated Winnings from a Single Spin

Histogram of Winnings

in cell B11 and copy it to the entire range B11:K1010. The effect of this formula, given the values in cells B3 and B4, is to generate a random number between 0 and 1 and multiply it by $1000. The effect of the IF part is to fill as many Outcome columns as there are spins in cell B6 and to leave the rest blank.

2. **Winnings.** Calculate the winnings in each row in column L as the average of the outcomes of the spins in that row. (Note that the AVERAGE function ignores blanks.)

3. **Summary measures.** Calculate the average and standard deviation of the 1000 winnings in column L with the AVERAGE and STDEV.S functions. These values appear in cells L4 and L5.

4. **Histogram.** Create a histogram of the values in column L.

Note the following from Figures 7.7 and 7.8:

• The sample mean of the winnings (cell L4) is very close to the population mean, $500.

• The standard deviation of the winnings (cell L5) is very close to the population standard deviation, $289.

• The histogram is nearly flat.

These properties should come as no surprise. When $n = 1$, the sample mean is a single observation—that is, no averaging takes place. Therefore, the sampling distribution of the sample mean is *equivalent* to the flat population distribution in Figure 7.6.

But what happens when $n > 1$? Figure 7.9 shows the results for $n = 2$. All you need to do is change the number of spins in cell B6, and everything updates automatically. The average winnings are again very close to $500, but the standard deviation of winnings is much lower. In fact, you should find that it is close to $\sigma/\sqrt{2} = 289/\sqrt{2} = \$204$, exactly as the theory predicts. In addition, the histogram of winnings is no longer flat. It is triangularly shaped—symmetric, but not really bell-shaped.

Figure 7.9 Histogram of Simulated Winnings from Two Spins

To develop similar simulations for $n = 3$, $n = 6$, $n = 10$, or any other n, simply change the number of spins in cell B6. The resulting histograms appear in Figures 7.10 through 7.12. They clearly show two effects of increasing n: (1) the histogram becomes more bell-shaped, and (2) there is less variability. However, the mean stays right at $500. This behavior is exactly what the central limit theorem predicts. In fact, because the population distribution is symmetric in this example—it is flat— you can see the effect of the central limit theorem for n much less than 30; it is already evident for n as low as 6.

Figure 7.10 Histogram of Simulated Winnings from Three Spins

Figure 7.11 Histogram of Simulated Winnings from Six Spins

Figure 7.12 Histogram of Simulated Winnings from Ten Spins

Finally, it is easy to answer the question we posed previously: How does the probability of winning at least $600 depend on *n*? For any specific value of *n*, you can find the fraction of the 1000 replications where the average of *n* spins is greater than $600 with a COUNTIF formula in cell L6. (The value shown in Figure 7.7, 0.406, is only a point estimate of the true probability, which turns out to be very close to 0.4.)

What are the main lessons from this example? For one, you can see that the sampling distribution of the sample mean (winnings) is bell-shaped when *n* is reasonably large. This is in spite of the fact that the population distribution is flat—far from bell-shaped. Actually, the population distribution could have *any* shape, not just uniform, and the bell-shaped property would still hold (although *n* might have to be larger than in the example). This bell-shaped normality property allows you to perform probability calculations with the NORM.DIST and NORM.INV functions, as discussed in Chapter 5.

Equally important, this example demonstrates the *decreased variability* in the sample means as *n* increases. Why should an increased sample size lead to decreased variability? This is due to averaging. Think about winning $750 based on the average of two spins. All you need is two lucky spins. In fact, one really lucky spin and an average spin will do. But think about winning $750 based on the average of 10 spins. Now you need a *lot* of really lucky spins—and virtually no unlucky ones. The point is that you are much less likely to obtain a really large (or really small) sample mean when *n* is large than when *n* is small. This is exactly what we mean when we say that the variability of the sample means decreases with larger sample sizes.

This decreasing variability is predicted by the formula for the standard error of the mean, $\sigma/\sqrt{n}$. As *n* increases, the standard error decreases. This is what drives the behavior in Figures 7.9 through 7.12. In fact, using $\sigma = \$289$, the (theoretical) standard errors for $n = 2, n = 3, n = 6$, and $n = 10$ are $204, $167, $118, and $91, respectively.

Finally, what does this decreasing variability have to do with estimating a population mean with a sample mean? Very simply, it means that the sample mean tends to be a more *accurate* estimate when the sample size is large. Because of the approximate normality from the central limit theorem, you know from Chapter 5 that there is about a 95% chance that the sample mean will be within two standard errors of the population mean. In other words, there is about a 95% chance that the sampling error will be no greater than two standard errors in magnitude. Therefore, because the standard error decreases as the sample size increases, the sampling error is likely to decrease as well.

> **Fundamental Insight**
>
> **The Averaging Effect**
>
> As you average more and more observations from a given distribution, the variance of the average decreases. This has a very intuitive explanation. For example, suppose you average only two observations. Then it is easy to get an abnormally large (or small) average. All it takes are two abnormally large (or small) observations. But if you average a much larger number of observations, you aren't likely to get an abnormally large (or small) average. The reason is that a few abnormally large observations will typically be cancelled by a few abnormally small observations. This cancellation produces the averaging effect. It also explains why a larger sample size tends to produce a more accurate estimate of a population mean.

7-4e Sample Size Selection

The problem of selecting the appropriate sample size in any sampling context is not an easy one (as illustrated in the chapter opener), but it must be faced in the planning stages, *before* any sampling is done. We focus here on the relationship between sampling error and sample size. As we discussed previously, the sampling error tends to decrease as the sample size increases, so the desire to minimize sampling error encourages us to select larger sample sizes. We should note, however, that several other factors encourage us to select *smaller* sample sizes. The ultimate sample size selection must achieve a trade-off between these opposing forces.

What are these other factors? First, there is the obvious cost of sampling. Larger samples cost more. Sometimes, a company or agency might have a budget for a given sampling project. If the sample size required to achieve an acceptable sampling error is 500, but the budget allows for a sample size of only 300, budget considerations will probably prevail.

Another problem caused by large sample sizes is timely collection of the data. Suppose a retailer wants to collect sample data from its customers to decide whether to run an advertising blitz in the coming week. Obviously, the retailer needs to collect the data quickly if they are to be of any use, and a large sample could require too much time to collect.

Finally, a more subtle problem caused by large sample sizes is the increased chance of *nonsampling* error, such as nonresponse bias. As we discussed previously in this chapter, there are many potential sources of nonsampling error, and they are usually very difficult to quantify. However, they are likely to *increase* as the sample size increases. Arguably, the potential increase in *sampling* error from a smaller sample could be more than offset by a decrease in nonsampling error, especially if the cost saved by the smaller sample size is used to reduce the sources of nonsampling error—conducting more follow-up of nonrespondents, for example.

Nevertheless, the determination of sample size is usually driven by sampling error considerations. If you want to estimate a population mean with a sample mean, then the key is the standard error of the mean, given by

$$\text{SE}(\overline{X}) = \sigma / \sqrt{n}$$

The central limit theorem says that if n is reasonably large, there is about a 95% chance that the magnitude of the sampling error will be no more than two standard errors. Because σ is fixed in the formula for $\text{SE}(\overline{X})$, n can be chosen to make $2\text{SE}(\overline{X})$ acceptably small.

Fundamental Insight

Effect of Larger Sample Sizes

Accurate estimates of population parameters require small standard errors, and small standard errors require large sample sizes. However, standard errors are typically inversely proportional to the *square root* of the sample size (or sample sizes). The implication is that if you want to decrease the standard error by a given factor, you must increase the sample size by a much larger factor. For example, to decrease the standard error by a factor of 2, you must increase the sample size by a factor of 4. Accurate estimates are not cheap.

We postpone further discussion of sample size selection until the next chapter, where we will discuss in detail how it can be used to control confidence interval length.

7-4f Summary of Key Ideas in Simple Random Sampling

To this point, we have covered some very important concepts. Because we build on these concepts in later chapters, we summarize them here.

- To estimate a population mean with a simple random sample, the sample mean is typically used as a "best guess." This estimate is called a *point estimate*. That is, $\overline{X}$ is a point estimate of μ.
- The accuracy of the point estimate is measured by its standard error. It is the standard deviation of the sampling distribution of the point estimate. The standard error of $\overline{X}$ is approximately $s/\sqrt{n}$, where s is the sample standard deviation.
- A *confidence interval* (with 95% confidence) for the population mean extends to approximately two standard errors on either side of the sample mean.
- From the *central limit theorem*, the sampling distribution of $\overline{X}$ is approximately normal when n is reasonably large.
- There is approximately a 95% chance that any particular $\overline{X}$ will be within two standard errors of the population mean μ.
- The sampling error can be reduced by increasing the sample size n. Appropriate sample size formulas for controlling confidence interval length are given in the next chapter.

Problems

Solutions for problems whose numbers appear within a colored box can be found in the Student Solution Files.

Level A

7. A manufacturing company's quality control personnel have recorded the proportion of defective items for each of 500 monthly shipments of one of the computer components that the company produces. The data are in the file **P07_07.xlsx**. The quality control department manager does not have sufficient time to review all of these data. Rather, she would like to examine the proportions of defective items for a sample of these shipments. For this problem, you can assume that the population is the data from the 500 shipments.

a. Generate a simple random sample of size 25 from the data.

b. Calculate a point estimate of the population mean from the sample selected in part **a**. What is the sampling error, that is, by how much does the sample mean differ from the population mean?

c. Calculate a good approximation for the standard error of the mean.

d. Repeat parts **b** and **c** after generating a simple random sample of size 50 from the population. Is this estimate bound to be more accurate than the one in part **b**? Is its standard error bound to be smaller than the one in part **c**?

8. The manager of a local fast-food restaurant is interested in improving the service provided to customers who use the restaurant's drive-up window. As a first step in this process, the manager asks his assistant to record the time it takes to serve a large number of customers at the final window in the facility's drive-up system. The results are in the file **P07_08.xlsx**, which consists of nearly 1200 service times. For this problem, you can assume that the population is the data in this file.
   a. Generate a simple random sample of size 30 from the data.
   b. Calculate a point estimate of the population mean from the sample selected in part **a**. What is the sampling error, that is, by how much does the sample mean differ from the population mean?
   c. Calculate a good approximation for the standard error of the mean.
   d. If you wanted to halve the standard error from part **c**, what approximate sample size would you need? Why is this only approximate?

9. The file **P02_16.xlsx** contains traffic data from 256 weekdays on four variables. Each variable lists the number of arrivals during a specific 5-minute period of the day. For this problem, consider this data set a simple random sample from all possible weekdays.
   a. For each of the four variables, find the sample mean. If each of these is used as an estimate from the corresponding (unknown) population mean, is there any reason to believe that they either underestimate or overestimate the population means? Why or why not?
   b. What are the (approximate) standard errors of the estimates in part **a**? How can you interpret these standard errors? Be as specific as possible.
   c. Is it likely that the estimates in part **a** are accurate to within 0.4 arrival? Why or why not? (Answer for each variable separately.)

10. The file **P02_35.xlsx** contains data from a survey of 500 randomly selected households. For this problem, consider this data set a simple random sample from all possible households, where the number of households in the population is well over 1,000,000.
   a. Create a new variable, Total Income, that is the sum of First Income and Second Income.
   b. For each of the four variables Total Income, Monthly Payment, Utilities, and Debt, find the sample mean. If each of these is used as an estimate from the corresponding (unknown) population mean, is there any reason to believe that they either underestimate or overestimate the corresponding population means? Why or why not?
   c. What are the (approximate) standard errors of the estimates in part **b**? How can you interpret these standard errors? Be as specific as possible. Is the finite population correction required? Why or why not?
   d. Is it likely that the estimate of Total Income in part **b** is accurate to within $1500? Why or why not?

11. The file **P02_10.xlsx** contains midterm and final exam scores for 96 students in a corporate finance course. For this problem, assume that these 96 students represent a sample of the 175 students taking the course, and that these 175 students represent the relevant population.
   a. Assuming the same instructor is teaching all four sections of this course and that the 96 students are the students in two of these sections, is it fair to say that the 96 students represent a *random* sample from the population? Does it matter?
   b. Find the sample mean and the standard error of the sample mean, based on the 96 students in the file. Should the finite population correction be used? What is the standard error without it? What is the standard error with it?

Level B

12. Create a simulation similar to the one in the **Wheel of Fortune Similation.xlsx** file. However, suppose that the outcome of each spin is no longer uniformly distributed between $0 and $1000. Instead, it is the number of 7's you get in 20 rolls of two dice. In other words, each spin results in a binomially distributed random number with parameters $n = 20$ and $p = 1/6$ (because the chance of rolling a 7 is 1 out of 6). The simulation should still allow you to vary the number of "spins" from 1 to 10, and the "winnings" is still the average of the outcomes of the spins. What is fundamentally different from the simulation in the text? Does the central limit theorem still work? Explain from the results you obtain.

13. Suppose you plan to take a simple random sample from a population with N members. Specifically, you plan to sample a percentage p of the population. If p is 1%, is the finite population correction really necessary? Does the answer depend on N? Explain. Then answer the same questions when p is 5%, 10%, 25%, and 50%, respectively. In general, explain what goes wrong if the finite population correction is really necessary but isn't used.

14. The file **P07_14.xlsx** contains a very small population of only five members. For each member, the height of the person is listed. The purpose of this problem is to let you see exactly what a sampling distribution is. Find the *exact* sampling distribution of the sample mean with sample size 3. Verify that Equation (7.1) holds, that is, the mean of this sampling distribution is equal to the population mean. Also, verify that Equation (7.2) holds, that is, the standard deviation of this sampling distribution is equal to the population standard deviation divided by the square root of 3. (*Hint*: You will have to do this by brute force. There are 125 different samples of size 3 that could be drawn from this population. These include samples with duplicate members, and order counts. For example, they include (1,1,2), (1,2,1), (2,1,1), and (1,1,1). You will need to find the sample mean of each and then find the mean and standard deviation of these sample means.)

7-5 Conclusion

This chapter has provided the fundamental concepts behind statistical inference. We discussed ways to obtain random samples from a population; how to calculate a point estimate of a particular population parameter, the population mean; and how to measure the accuracy of this point estimate. The key idea is the sampling distribution of the estimate and specifically its standard deviation, called the standard error of the estimate. Due to the central limit theorem, the sampling distribution of the sample mean is approximately normal, which implies that the sample mean will be within two standard errors of the population mean in approximately 95% of all random samples. In the next two chapters we build on these important concepts.

Summary of Key Terms

TERM	SYMBOL	EXPLANATION	PAGE	EQUATION
Population		Contains all members about which a study intends to make inferences	281	
Frame		A list of all members of the population	281	
Sampling units		Potential members of a sample from a population	281	
Probability sample		Any sample that is chosen by using a random mechanism	281	
Judgmental sample		Any sample that is chosen according to a sampler's judgment rather than a random mechanism	281	
Simple random sample		A sample where each member of the population has the same chance of being chosen	282	
Systematic sample		A sample where one of the first k members is selected randomly, and then every kth member after this one is selected	287	
Stratified sampling		Sampling in which the population is divided into relatively homogeneous subsets called *strata*, and then random samples are taken from each of the strata	288	
Proportional sample sizes (in stratified sampling)		The property of each stratum selected having the same proportion from stratum to stratum	289	
Cluster sampling		A sample where the population is separated into clusters, such as cities or city blocks, and then a random sample of the clusters is selected	289	
Sampling error		The inevitable result of basing an inference on a sample rather than on the entire population	292	
Nonsampling error		Any type of estimation error that is not sampling error, including nonresponse bias, nontruthful responses, measurement error, and voluntary response bias	293	
Point estimate		A single numeric value, a "best guess" of a population parameter, based on the data in a sample	294	
Sampling error (or estimation error)		Difference between the estimate of a population parameter and the true value of the parameter	294	
Sampling distribution		The distribution of the point estimates from *all* possible samples (of a given sample size) from the population	294	
Confidence interval		An interval around the point estimate, calculated from the sample data, where the true value of the population parameter is very likely to be	294	
Unbiased estimate		An estimate where the mean of its sampling distribution equals the value of the parameter being estimated	294	

Key Terms (continued)

TERM	SYMBOL	EXPLANATION	PAGE	EQUATION
Standard error of an estimate		The standard deviation of the sampling distribution of the estimate	294	
Mean of sample mean	$E(\overline{X})$	Indicates property of unbiasedness of sample mean	296	7.1
Standard error of sample mean	$SE(\overline{X})$	Indicates how sample means from different samples vary	296	7.2, 7.3
Confidence interval for population mean		An interval that is very likely to contain the population mean	296	7.4
Finite population correction	fpc	A correction for the standard error when the sample size is fairly large relative to the population size	298	7.5, 7.6
Central limit theorem		States that the distribution of the sample mean is approximately normal for sufficiently large sample sizes	299	

Problems

Note: Because the material in this chapter is more conceptual than calculation-based, we have included only conceptual questions here. You will get plenty of practice with calculations in the next two chapters, which build upon the concepts in this chapter.

Conceptual Questions

C.1. Suppose that you want to know the opinions of American secondary school teachers about establishing a national test for high school graduation. You obtain a list of the members of the National Education Association (the largest teachers' union) and mail a questionnaire to 3000 teachers chosen at random from this list. In all, 823 teachers return the questionnaire. Identify the relevant *population*. Do you believe there is a good possibility of nonsampling error? Why or why not?

C.2. A sportswriter wants to know how strongly the residents of Indianapolis, Indiana, support the local minor league baseball team, the Indianapolis Indians. He stands outside the stadium before a game and interviews the first 30 people who enter the stadium. Suppose that the newspaper asks you to comment on the approach taken by this sportswriter in performing the survey. How would you respond?

C.3. A large corporation has 4520 male and 567 female employees. The organization's equal employment opportunity officer wants to poll the opinions of a random sample of employees. To give adequate attention to the opinions of female employees, exactly how should the EEO officer sample from the given population? Be specific.

C.4. Suppose that you want to estimate the mean monthly gross income of all households in your local community. You decide to estimate this population parameter by calling 150 randomly selected residents and asking each individual to report the household's monthly income. Assume that you use the local phone directory as the frame in selecting the households to be included in your sample. What are some possible sources of error that might arise in your effort to estimate the population mean?

C.5. Provide an example of when you might want to take a stratified random sample instead of a simple random sample, and explain what the advantages of a stratified sample might be.

C.6. Provide an example of when you might want to take a cluster random sample instead of a simple random sample, and explain what the advantages of a cluster sample might be. Also, explain how you would choose the cluster sample.

C.7. Do you agree with the statement that nonresponse error can be overcome with larger samples? If you agree, explain why. If you disagree, provide an example that backs up your opinion.

C.8. When pollsters take a random sample of about 1000 people to estimate the mean of some quantity over a population of millions of people, how is it possible for them to estimate the accuracy of the sample mean?

C.9. Suppose you want to estimate the population mean of some quantity when the population consists of millions of members (such as the population of all U.S. households). How is it possible that you can obtain a fairly accurate estimate, using the sample mean of only about 1000 randomly selected members?

C.10. What is the difference between a *standard deviation* and a *standard error*? Be precise.

C.11. Explain as precisely as possible what it means that the sample mean is an *unbiased* estimate of the population mean [as indicated in Equation (7.1)].

C.12. Explain the difference between the standard error formulas in equations (7.2) and (7.3). Why is Equation (7.3) the one necessarily used in real situations?

C.13. Explain as precisely as possible what Equation (7.4) means, and the reason for the 2 in the formula.

C.14. Explain as precisely as possible the role of the finite population correction. In which types of situations is it necessary? Is it necessarily used in the typical polls you see in the news?

C.15. In the wheel of fortune simulation with, say, three spins, many people mistakenly believe that the distribution of the average is the flat graph in Figure 7.7, that is, they believe the average of three spins is *uniformly* distributed between $0 and $1000. Explain intuitively why they are wrong.

C.16. Explain the difference between a point estimate for the mean and a confidence interval for the mean. Which provides more information?

C.17. Explain as precisely as possible what the central limit theorem says about averages.

C.18. Many people seem to believe that the central limit theorem "kicks in" only when n is at least 30. Why is this not necessarily true? When is such a large n necessary?

C.19. Suppose you are a pollster and are planning to take a sample that is very small relative to the population. In terms of estimating a population mean, can you say that a sample of size $9n$ is about 3 times as accurate as a sample of size n? Why or why not? Does the answer depend on the population size? For example, would it matter if the population size were 50 million instead of 10 million?

C.20. You saw in Equation (7.1) that the sample mean is an unbiased estimate of the population mean. However, some estimates of population parameters are biased. In such cases, there are two sources of error in estimating the population parameter: the bias and the standard error. To understand these, imagine a rifleman shooting at a bull's-eye. The rifleman could be aiming wrong and/or his shots could vary wildly from shot to shot. If he is aiming wrong but his shots are very consistent, what can you say about his bias and standard error? Answer the same question if he is correctly aiming at the bull's-eye but is very inconsistent. Can you say which of these two situations is worse?

CHAPTER 8
Confidence Interval Estimation

nazarovsergey/Shutterstock.com

ESTIMATING A COMPANY'S TOTAL TAXABLE INCOME

In Example 7.3 in the previous chapter, we illustrated how sampling can be used in auditing. Another illustration of sampling in auditing appears in Example 8.5 of this chapter. In both examples, the point of the sampling is to discover some property (such as a mean or a proportion) from a large population of a company's accounts by examining a small fraction of these accounts and projecting the results to the population. An article by Press (1995) offers an interesting variation on this problem. He poses the question of how a government revenue agency should assess a business taxpayer's income for tax purposes on the basis of a sample audit of the company's business transactions. A sample of the company's transactions will indicate a taxable income for each sampled transaction. The methods of this chapter will be applied to the sample information to obtain a confidence interval for the total taxable income owed by the company.

Suppose for the sake of illustration that this confidence interval extends from $1,000,000 to $2,200,000 and is centered at $1,600,000. In other words, the government's best guess of the company's taxable income is $1,600,000, and the government is fairly confident that the true taxable income is between $1,000,000 and $2,200,000. How much tax should it assess the company? Press argues that the agency would like to maximize its revenue while minimizing the risk that the company will be assessed more than it really owes. This last assumption, that the government does not want to *overassess* the company, is crucial. By making several reasonable assumptions, he argues that the agency should base the tax on the *lower* limit of the confidence interval, in this case, $1,000,000.

On the other hand, if the agency were indifferent between overcharging and undercharging, then it would base the tax on the midpoint, $1,600,000, of the confidence interval. Using this strategy, the agency would overcharge in about half the cases and undercharge in the other half. This would certainly be upsetting to companies—it would appear that the agency is flipping a coin to decide whether to overcharge or undercharge.

If the government agency does indeed decide to base the tax on the *lower* limit of the confidence interval, Press argues that it can still increase its tax revenue—by increasing the sample size of the audit. When the sample size increases, the confidence interval shrinks in width, and the lower limit, which governs the agency's tax revenue, almost surely increases. But there is some point at which larger samples are not warranted, for the simple reason that larger samples cost more money to obtain. Therefore, there is an optimal size that will balance the cost of sampling with the desire to obtain more tax revenue.

8-1 Introduction

This chapter expands on the ideas from the previous chapter. Given an observed data set, the goal is to make inferences to some larger population. Two typical examples follow:

- A mail-order company has accounts with thousands of customers. The company would like to infer the average time its customers take to pay their bills, so it randomly samples a relatively small number of its customers, sees how long these customers take to pay their bills, and draws inferences about the entire population of customers.

• A manufacturing company is considering two compensation schemes to implement for its workers. It believes that these two different compensation schemes might provide different incentives and hence result in different worker productivity. To see whether this is true, the company randomly assigns groups of workers to the two different compensation schemes for a period of three months and observes their productivity. Then it attempts to infer whether any differences observed in the experiment can be generalized to the overall worker population.

In each of these examples, there is an unknown population parameter a company would like to estimate. In the mail-order example, the unknown parameter is the mean length of time customers take to pay their bills. Its true value could be discovered only by learning how long *every* customer in the entire population takes to pay its bills. This is not really possible, given the large number of customers. In the manufacturing example, the unknown parameter is a mean difference, the difference between the mean productivities with the two different compensation schemes. This mean difference could be discovered only by subjecting each worker to each compensation scheme and measuring their resulting productivities. This procedure would almost certainly be impossible from a practical standpoint. Therefore, the companies in these examples are likely to select random samples and base their estimates of the unknown population parameters on the sample data.

The inferences discussed in this chapter are always based on an underlying probability model, which means that some type of random mechanism must generate the data. Two random mechanisms are generally used. The first involves sampling randomly from a larger population, as we discussed in the previous chapter. This is the mechanism responsible for generating the sample of customers in the mail-order example. Regardless of whether the sample is a simple random sample or a more complex random sample, such as a stratified sample, the fact that it is *random* allows us to use the rules of probability to make inferences about the population as a whole.

The second commonly used random mechanism is called a *randomized experiment*. The compensation scheme example just described is a typical randomized experiment. Here the company selects a set of subjects (employees), randomly assigns them to two different *treatment groups* (compensation schemes), and then compares some quantitative measure (productivity) across the groups. The fact that the subjects are *randomly* assigned to the two treatment groups is useful for two reasons. First, it allows us to rule out a number of factors that might have led to differences across groups. For example, assuming that males and females are randomly spread across the two groups, we can rule out gender as the cause of any observed group differences. Second, the random selection allows us to use the rules of probability to infer whether observed differences can be generalized to all employees.

Generally, statistical inferences are of two types: *confidence interval estimation* and *hypothesis testing*. The first of these is the subject of the current chapter; hypothesis testing is discussed in the next chapter. They differ primarily in their point of view. For example, the mail-order company might sample 100 customers and find that they average 15.5 days before paying their bills. In confidence interval estimation, the data are used to obtain a point estimate and a **confidence interval** around this point estimate. In this example the point estimate is 15.5 days. It is a best guess for the mean bill-paying time in the entire customer population. Then, using the methods in this chapter, the company might find that a 95% confidence interval for the mean bill-paying time in the population is from 13.2 days to 17.8 days. The company is now 95% confident that the true mean bill-paying time in the population is within this interval.

Hypothesis testing takes a different point of view. There, the goal is to check whether the observed data provide support for a particular hypothesis. In the compensation scheme example, suppose the manager believes that workers will have higher productivity if they are paid by salary than by an hourly wage. He runs the three-month randomized

We actually introduced 95% confidence intervals for the mean in the previous chapter. We generalize this method in the current chapter.

experiment described previously and finds that the salaried workers produce on average eight more parts per day than the hourly workers. Now he must make one of two conclusions. Either salaried workers are in general no more productive than hourly workers and the ones in the experiment just got lucky, or salaried workers really *are* more productive. The next chapter explains how to decide which of these conclusions is more reasonable.

There are only a few key ideas in this chapter, and the most important of these, *sampling distributions*, was introduced in the previous chapter. It is important to concentrate on these key ideas and not get bogged down in formulas or numerical calculations. Software such as Excel is generally available to take care of these calculations. The job of a businessperson is much more dependent on knowing which methods to use in which situations and how to interpret computer outputs than on memorizing and plugging into formulas.

8-2 Sampling Distributions

Most confidence intervals are of the form in Equation (8.1). For example, when estimating a population mean, the point estimate is the sample mean, the standard error is the sample standard deviation divided by the square root of the sample size, and the multiple is approximately 2. To learn why it works this way, you must first understand sampling distributions. This knowledge will then be put to use in the next section.

Typical Form of Confidence Interval

$$\text{Point Estimate} \pm \text{Multiple} \times \text{Standard Error} \qquad (8.1)$$

In the previous chapter, we introduced the sampling distribution of the sample mean $\overline{X}$ and saw how it was related to the central limit theorem. In general, whenever you make inferences about one or more population parameters, such as a mean or the difference between two means, you always base this inference on the sampling distribution of a point estimate, such as the sample mean. Although the *concepts* of point estimates and sampling distributions are no different from those in the previous chapter, there are some new details to learn.

We again begin with the sample mean $\overline{X}$. The central limit theorem states that if the sample size n is reasonably large, then for *any* population distribution, the sampling distribution of $\overline{X}$ is approximately normal with mean μ and standard deviation $\sigma/\sqrt{n}$, where μ and σ are the population mean and standard deviation. An equivalent statement is that the standardized quantity Z defined in Equation (8.2) is approximately normal with mean 0 and standard deviation 1.

Standardized Z-Value

$$Z = \frac{\overline{X} - \mu}{\sigma/\sqrt{n}} \qquad (8.2)$$

Typically, this fact is used to make inferences about an unknown population mean μ. There is one problem, however—the population standard deviation σ is almost never known. This parameter, σ, is called a *nuisance parameter*. Although it is typically not the parameter of primary interest, its value is needed for making inferences about the mean μ. The solution appears to be straightforward: Replace the nuisance parameter σ by the *sample* standard deviation s in the formula for Z and proceed from there. However, when σ is replaced by s, this introduces a new source of variability, and the sampling distribution is no longer normal. It is instead called the **t distribution**, a close relative of the normal distribution that appears in a variety of statistical applications.

8-2a The t Distribution

We first set the stage for this new sampling distribution. We are interested in estimating a population mean μ with a sample of size n. We assume the population distribution is normal with unknown standard deviation σ. We intend to base inferences on the standardized value of $\overline{X}$ from Equation (8.2), where σ is replaced by the sample standard deviation s, as shown in Equation (8.3). Then the standardized value in Equation (8.3) has a t distribution with $n - 1$ degrees of freedom.

Standardized Value

$$t = \frac{\overline{X} - \mu}{s/\sqrt{n}}$$

(8.3)

The *degrees of freedom* is a numerical parameter of the t distribution that defines the precise shape of the distribution. Each time we encounter a t distribution, we will specify its degrees of freedom. In this particular sampling context, where we are basing inferences about μ on the sampling distribution of $\overline{X}$, the degrees of freedom turns out to be 1 less than the sample size n.

The t distribution and the standard normal distribution are practically the same when the degrees of freedom parameter is large.

The t distribution looks very much like the standard normal distribution. It is bell-shaped and centered at 0. The only difference is that it is slightly more spread out, and this increase in spread is greater for *small* degrees of freedom. In fact, when n is large, so that the degrees of freedom is large, the t distribution and the standard normal distribution are practically indistinguishable. This is illustrated in Figure 8.1. With 5 degrees of freedom, it is possible to see the increased spread in the t distribution. With 30 degrees of freedom, the t and standard normal curves are practically the same curve.

Figure 8.1 The t and Standard Normal Distributions

t with 30 df and standard normal

t with 5 df

The t-value in Equation (8.3) is very much like a typical Z-value such as in Equation (8.2). That is, the **t-value** represents the number of standard errors by which the sample mean differs from the population mean. For example, if a t-value is 2.5, the sample mean is 2.5 standard errors above the population mean. Or if a *t*-value is −2.5, the sample mean is 2.5 standard errors below the population mean. Also, *t*-values greater in magnitude than 3 are quite unusual because of the same property of the normal distribution: It is very unlikely for a random value to be more than three standard deviations from its mean.

> A *t*-value indicates the number of standard errors by which a sample mean differs from a population mean.

Because of this interpretation, *t*-values are perfect candidates for the *multiple* term in Equation (8.1), as you will soon see. First, however, we briefly examine some Excel® functions that are useful for working with the *t* distribution in Excel.

Chapter 5 explained how to use Excel's NORM.S.DIST and NORM.S.INV functions to calculate probabilities or percentiles from the standard normal distribution. There are similar Excel functions for the *t* distribution. Unfortunately, these functions are somewhat more difficult to master than their normal counterparts. The file **t Calculations.xlsx** spells out the possibilities (see Figure 8.2). The top three examples show how to find the probability to the left or right of a given value. The bottom three examples show how to find the value with a given probability beyond it in one or both tails. You can refer to this figure as often as necessary when you work with the *t* distribution.

Figure 8.2 Excel Functions for the *t* Distribution

	A	B	C	D	E	F	G
1	Calculations for the *t* distribution						
2							
3	Sample size	30					
4	Degrees of freedom	29					
5							
6	One-tailed probabilities			Formulas in Excel 2010 (or later)			
7	Value	−2					
8	Probability in left tail	0.9725		=T.DIST(−B7,B4,TRUE)			
9							
10	Value	2					
11	Probability in right tail	0.0275		=T.DIST.RT(B10,B4)			
12							
13	Two-tailed probability						
14	Value	2					
15	Probability in both tails	0.0549 ←		=T.DIST.2T(B14,B4)			
16				Half of this probability is in each tail			
17	Inverse calculations						
18	Probability in left tail	0.05					
19	Value	−1.699		=T.INV(B18,B4)			
20							
21	Probability in right tail	0.05					
22	Value	1.699		=T.INV(1−B21,B4)			
23							
24	Probability in both tails	0.05 ←		Half of this probability is in each tail			
25	Value	2.045		=T.INV.2T(B24,B4)			

8-2b Other Sampling Distributions

The *t* distribution, a close relative of the normal distribution, is used to make inferences about a population mean when the population standard deviation is unknown. Throughout this chapter (and later chapters) you will see other contexts where the *t* distribution appears. The theme is always the same—one or more means are of interest, and one or more standard deviations are unknown.

The t (and normal) distributions are not the only sampling distributions you will encounter. Two other close relatives of the normal distribution that appear in various contexts are the *chi-square* and F distributions. These are used primarily to make inferences about variances (or standard deviations), as opposed to means. We omit the details of these distributions for now, but you will see them in later sections.

Problems

Solutions for problems whose numbers appear within a colored box can be found in the Student Solution Files.

Level A

1. Calculate the following probabilities using Excel.
   a. $P(t_{10} \geq 1.75)$, where t_{10} has a t distribution with 10 degrees of freedom.
   b. $P(t_{100} \geq 1.75)$, where t_{100} has a t distribution with 100 degrees of freedom. How do you explain the difference between this result and the one obtained in part **a**?
   c. $P(Z \geq 1.75)$, where Z is a standard normal random variable. Compare this result to the results obtained in parts **a** and **b**. How do you explain the differences in these probabilities?
   d. $P(t_{20} \leq -0.80)$, where t_{20} has a t distribution with 20 degrees of freedom.
   e. $P(t_3 \leq -0.80)$, where t_3 has a t distribution with 3 degrees of freedom. How do you explain the difference between this result and the result obtained in part **d**?

2. Calculate the following quantities using Excel.
   a. $P(-2.00 \leq t_{10} \leq 1.00)$, where t_{10} has a t distribution with 10 degrees of freedom.
   b. $P(-2.00 \leq t_{100} \leq 1.00)$, where t_{100} has a t distribution with 100 degrees of freedom. How do you explain the difference between this result and the one obtained in part **a**?
   c. $P(-2.00 \leq Z \leq 1.00)$, where Z is a standard normal random variable. Compare this result to the results obtained in parts **a** and **b**. How do you explain the differences in these probabilities?
   d. Find the 68th percentile of the t distribution with 20 degrees of freedom.
   e. Find the 68th percentile of the t distribution with 3 degrees of freedom. How do you explain the difference between this result and the result obtained in part **d**?

3. Calculate the following quantities using Excel.
   a. Find the value of x such that $P(t_{10} > x) = 0.75$, where t_{10} has a t distribution with 10 degrees of freedom.
   b. Find the value of y such that $P(t_{100} > y) = 0.75$, where t_{100} has a t distribution with 100 degrees of freedom. How do you explain the difference between this result and the result obtained in part **a**?
   c. Find the value of z such that $P(Z > z) = 0.75$, where Z is a standard normal random variable. Compare this result to the results obtained in parts **a** and **b**. How do you explain the differences in the values of x, y, and z?

8-3 Confidence Interval for a Mean

We now come to the main topic of this chapter: using properties of sampling distributions to construct confidence intervals. We assume that data have been generated by some random mechanism, either by observing a random sample from some population or by performing a randomized experiment. The goal is to infer the values of one or more population parameters such as the mean, the standard deviation, or a proportion from sample data. For each such parameter, you use the data to calculate a point estimate, which can be considered a best guess for the unknown parameter. You then calculate a confidence interval around the point estimate to measure its accuracy.

We begin by deriving a confidence interval for a population mean μ, and we discuss its interpretation. Although the particular details pertain to a specific parameter, the mean, the same ideas carry over to other parameters as well, as will be described in later sections. As usual, the sample mean $\overline{X}$ is used as the point estimate of the unknown population mean μ.

To obtain a confidence interval for μ, you first specify a **confidence level**, usually 90%, 95%, or 99%. You then use the sampling distribution of the point estimate to determine the *multiple* of the standard error (SE) to go out on either side of the point estimate to achieve the given confidence level. If the confidence level is 95%, the value used most frequently in applications, the multiple is approximately 2. More precisely, it is a *t*-value. That is, a typical confidence interval for μ is of the form in Equation (8.4), where $SE(\overline{X}) = s/\sqrt{n}$.

Confidence Interval for Population Mean

$$\overline{X} \pm t\text{-multiple} \times SE\,(\overline{X}) \qquad \textbf{(8.4)}$$

To obtain the correct *t*-multiple, let α be one minus the confidence level (expressed as a decimal). For example, if the confidence level is 90%, then $\alpha = 0.10$. Then the appropriate *t*-multiple is the value that cuts off probability $\alpha/2$ in each tail of the *t* distribution with $n - 1$ degrees of freedom. For example, if $n = 30$ and the confidence level is 95%, cell B25 of Figure 8.2 indicates that the correct *t*-value is 2.045. Then the corresponding 95% confidence interval for μ is

$$\overline{X} \pm 2.045(s/\sqrt{n})$$

If the confidence level is instead 90%, the appropriate *t*-value is 1.699 (change the probability in cell B24 to 0.10 to see this), and the resulting 90% confidence interval is

$$\overline{X} \pm 1.699(s/\sqrt{n})$$

If the confidence level is 99%, the appropriate *t*-value is 2.756 (change the probability in cell B24 to 0.01 to see this), and the resulting 99% confidence interval is

$$\overline{X} \pm 2.756(s/\sqrt{n})$$

Confidence interval lengths increase when you ask for higher confidence levels, but they tend to decrease when you use larger sample sizes.

Note that as the confidence level increases, the length of the confidence interval also increases. Because narrow confidence intervals are desirable, this presents a trade-off. You can either have less confidence and a narrow interval, or you can have more confidence and a wide interval. However, you can also take a larger sample. As *n* increases, the standard error $s/\sqrt{n}$ tends to decrease, so the length of the confidence interval tends to decrease for *any* confidence level. (Why doesn't it decrease for sure? The larger sample *might* result in a larger value of *s* that could offset the increase in *n*.)

Example 8.1 illustrates confidence interval estimation for a population mean.

EXAMPLE

8.1 CUSTOMER RESPONSE TO A NEW SANDWICH

A fast-food restaurant recently added a new sandwich to its menu. To estimate the popularity of this sandwich, a random sample of 40 customers who ordered the sandwich were surveyed. Each of these customers was asked to rate the sandwich on a scale of 1 to 10, 10 being the best. (See the file **Satisfaction Ratings.xlsx**.) The manager wants to estimate the mean satisfaction rating over the entire population of customers by finding a 95% confidence interval. How should she proceed?

Objective

To obtain a 95% confidence interval for the mean satisfaction rating of the new sandwich.

Solution

The method is spelled out in Figure 8.3 by the formulas shown in column D. The calculations follow directly from Equation (8.4). As in Figure 8.2, the T.INV.2T function is used to find the correct multiple. Its arguments are one minus the confidence level and the degrees of freedom. The result is that the 95% confidence interval extends from 5.739 to 6.761.

Figure 8.3 Analysis of New Sandwich Data

	A	B	C	D	E	F
1	Confidence interval for population mean					
2	Confidence level	95%				
3						
4	Sample size	40		=COUNT(Data!B2:B41)		
5	Sample mean	6.250		=AVERAGE(Data!B2:B41)		
6	Sample standard deviation	1.597		=STDEV.S(Data!B2:B41)		
7	Standard error of mean	0.253		=B6/SQRT(B4)		
8	Degrees of freedom	39		=B4−1		
9	Multiple	2.02		=T.INV.2T(1−$B$2,B8)		
10	Lower limit	5.739		=B5−B9*B7		
11	Upper limit	6.761		=B5+B9*B7		

Because the Excel calculations for a confidence interval are always the same (for a mean or for other population parameters), we have created a template file, **Confidence Interval Template.xlsx**, you can use. It has a sheet for each of the population parameters discussed in this chapter. For example, the sheet CI Mean shown in Figure 8.4 explains how to use the template for a population mean. The best way to proceed is to copy the appropriate template sheet to your data file and then follow the directions in the text box. If you do this for the sandwich rating data, you get the results in Figure 8.3, where we have shaded the only cells you need to change in orange and the confidence interval in yellow. The template sheets not only provide a quick way to get the correct results, but they also provide formulas you can examine to see how the confidence intervals are calculated.

Figure 8.4 Template Sheet for a Confidence Interval for a Mean

	A	B	C	D	E	F	G	H	I	J	K	L
1	Confidence interval for population mean											
2	Confidence level	95%										
3												
4	Sample size	0										
5	Sample mean	#REF!										
6	Sample standard deviation	#REF!										
7	Standard error of mean	#REF!										
8	Degrees of freedom	−1										
9	Multiple	#NUM!										
10	Lower limit	#REF!										
11	Upper limit	#REF!										
12												
13												
14												
15												
16												

This template calculates a confidence interval for a population mean. Proceed as follows.

1. If you like, change the confidence level in cell B2.

2. Enter the sample size, sample mean, and sample standard deviation in cells B4 to B6. You can use the current formulas in these cells, replacing "Data" with the range of your numeric data variable, but feel free to fill these cells in any appropriate way.

3. Optionally, change the labels to fit the context of your problem.

The confidence interval will appear automatically in the yellow cells.

In any case, the principal results are that (1) the best guess for the population mean rating is 6.250, and (2) a 95% confidence interval for the population mean rating extends from 5.739 to 6.761. The manager can be 95% confident that the true mean rating over all customers who might try the sandwich is within this confidence interval.

We stated previously that as the confidence level increases, the length of the confidence interval increases. You can convince yourself of this by entering different confidence levels such as 90% or 99%. The lower and upper limits of the confidence interval will change automatically, getting closer together for the 90% level and farther apart for the 99% level. Just remember that you, the analyst, can choose the confidence level, but 95% is the level most commonly chosen.

Before leaving this example, we discuss the assumptions that lead to the confidence interval. First, you might question whether the sample is really a *random* sample—or whether it matters. Perhaps the manager used some random mechanism to select the customers to be surveyed. More likely, however, she simply surveyed 40 consecutive customers who tried the sandwich on a given day. This is called a *convenience sample* and is not really a *random* sample. However, unless there is some reason to believe that these 40 customers differ in some relevant aspect from the entire population of customers, it is probably safe to treat them as a random sample.

A second assumption is that the population distribution is *normal*. We made this assumption when we introduced the *t* distribution. Obviously, the population distribution *cannot* be exactly normal because it is concentrated on the 10 possible satisfaction ratings, and the normal distribution describes a continuum. However, this is probably not a problem for two reasons. First, confidence intervals based on the *t* distribution are *robust* to violations of normality. This means that the resulting confidence intervals are approximately valid for any populations that are *approximately* normal. Second, the normal population assumption is less crucial for larger sample sizes because of the central limit theorem. A sample size of 40 should be large enough.

Finally, it is important to recognize what this confidence interval implies and what it doesn't imply. In the entire population of customers who ordered this sandwich, there is a distribution of satisfaction ratings. Some fraction rate it as 1, some rate it as 2, and so on. All we are trying to determine here is the *average* of all these ratings. Based on the analysis, the manager can be 95% confident that this (still unknown) average is between 5.739 and 6.761. However, this confidence interval doesn't tell her other characteristics of the population of ratings that might be of interest, such as the proportion of customers who rate the sandwich 6 or higher. It only provides information about the *mean* rating. Later in this chapter, you will see how to find a confidence interval for a proportion, which allows you to analyze another important characteristic of a population distribution.

In the sandwich example, we said that the manager can be 95% confident that the true mean rating is between 5.739 and 6.761. What does this statement really mean? Contrary to what you might expect, it does *not* mean that the true mean lies between 5.739 and 6.761 with probability 0.95. Either the true mean is inside this interval or it is not. The true meaning of a 95% confidence interval is based on the *procedure* used to obtain it. Specifically, if you use this procedure on a large number of random samples, all from the same population, then approximately 95% of the resulting confidence intervals will be "good" ones that include the true mean, and the other 5% will be "bad" ones that do not include the true mean. Unfortunately, when you have only a single sample, as in the sandwich example, you have no way of knowing whether your confidence interval is one of the good ones or one of the bad ones, but you can be 95% confident that you obtained one of the good intervals.

This simulation is performed only to illustrate the true meaning of a "95% confidence interval."

Because this is such an important concept, we illustrate it in Figure 8.5 with simulation. (See the file **Confidence Interval Simulation Finished.xlsx**. There is no "unfinished" version of this file.) The data in column B are generated randomly from a normal distribution with the *known* values of μ and σ in cells B3 and B4. (Examine cell A7 to see how a random value from a normal distribution can be generated.) Then the confidence interval procedure is used to calculate a 95% confidence interval for the true value of μ, exactly as in the sandwich example. However, because the true value of μ is known, it is possible to record a 1 in cell H6 if the true mean is inside the interval and a 0 otherwise. The appropriate formula is

=IF(AND(B3>=D14,B3<=D15),1,0)

Figure 8.5 Simulation Demonstration of Confidence Intervals

	A	B	C	D	E	F	G	H
1	Interpretation of a "95% confidence interval"							
2								
3	Population mean	100		This simulation uses a *normal* population for illustration. But you could generate the random sample from another distribution (e.g., triangular) to see if the confidence intervals are still *valid*, i.e, if the % in cell H7 is about 95%.				
4	Population stdev	20						
5								
6	Random sample		Confidence interval for mean				Mean captured?	1
7	120.45		Confidence level	95%			% of CI's capturing mean	94.8%
8	102.64		Sample size	30				
9	90.53		Sample mean	102.25			Data table to replicate confidence interval	
10	96.62		Sample Std Dev	21.900			Replication	Mean captured?
11	79.30		Std Error of mean	3.998				1
12	104.31		Degrees of freedom	29			1	1
13	105.24		t multiple	2.045			2	1
14	113.68		Lower limit	94.071			3	1
15	91.96		Upper limit	110.426			4	1
16	77.90						5	1
17	102.31		Graphical representation				6	1
18	65.95		Limit	Height			7	1
19	146.16		94.07	1			8	1
20	137.09		110.43	1			9	1
21	85.01						10	1
22	60.69		Mean	Height			11	1
23	132.82		100	1			12	1
24	148.33						13	1
25	107.77						14	1
26	108.08						15	1
27	111.81						16	1
28	80.89				Confidence limits		17	1
29	107.94				Mean		18	1
30	120.05						19	1
31	72.57						20	0
32	100.84						21	1
33	115.28		80.00 90.00 100.00 110.00 120.00				22	1
34	106.82						23	1
35	84.95						24	1
36	89.48						25	1

Finally, a data table can be used to replicate the simulated results 1000 times.[1] Specifically, the formula in H11 is

$$=G6$$

Then to build the data table in the range G11:H1011, leave the row input cell box empty and specify any blank cell as the column input cell. Finally, the AVERAGE function can be used in cell H7 to find the fraction of 1's in the range H12:H1011.

You can see that 948 of the simulated confidence intervals (each based on a *different* random sample of size 30) contain the true mean 100. In theory, 950 of the 1000 intervals should cover the true mean, and this is almost exactly what occurred. Of course, in a particular application you might unluckily obtain the 20th sample (in row 31). However, without knowing that the true mean is 100, you would have no way of knowing that you obtained a "bad" interval.

Fundamental Insight

True Meaning of a 95% Confidence Interval

Given the data in a particular sample, a 95% confidence interval for the mean will either include the (unknown) population mean or it won't. The true meaning of a 95% confidence interval is that if the same *procedure* is used on many different random samples, about 95% of the resulting confidence intervals will include the population mean, and only about 5% won't. Therefore, you can be 95% confident that any particular confidence interval you happen to get is a "good" one.

We also show this graphically in the file. (See Figure 8.5.) The small square in this graph is positioned at the known mean and never changes. The blue line represents a particular confidence interval. Press the F9 key to force a recalculation. The position of the blue line will change. About 95% of the time, the blue line will straddle the small square—the confidence interval will include the true mean—but about 1 time out of 20, it will not. This also illustrates the meaning of a "95% confidence interval."

Problems

Solutions for problems whose numbers appear within a colored box can be found in the Student Solution Files.

Level A

4. A manufacturing company's quality control personnel have recorded the proportion of defective items for each of 500 monthly shipments of one of the computer components that the company produces. The data are in the file **P07_07.xlsx**. The quality control department manager does not have sufficient time to review all of these data. Rather, she would like to examine the proportions of defective items for a sample of these shipments.
   a. Generate a simple random sample of size 25.

   b. Using the sample generated in part **a**, calculate a 95% confidence interval for the mean proportion of defective items over all monthly shipments. Assume that the population consists of the proportion of defective items for each of the given 500 monthly shipments.
   c. Interpret the 95% confidence interval constructed in part **b**.
   d. Does the 95% confidence interval contain the actual population mean in this case? If not, explain why not. What proportion of many similarly constructed confidence intervals should include the true population mean?

5. The file **P08_05.xlsx** contains salary data on all NFL players in each of the years 2002 to 2009. Because this file contains all players for each of these years, you can calculate the *population mean* for each year if *population*

---

1 Depending on the speed of your computer, it can take a few seconds to simulate 1000 samples of size 30 in this data table. Therefore, it is a good idea to set the recalculation mode to "automatic except tables." (You can find this option under the Calculation Options dropdown menu on the Formulas ribbon.) That way, the data table recalculates only if you explicitly tell it to (by pressing the F9 key).

is defined as all NFL players that year. However, proceed as in the previous chapter to select a random sample of size 50 from the 2009 population. Based on this random sample, calculate a 95% confidence interval for the mean NFL total salary in 2009. Does it contain the population mean? Repeat this procedure several times until you find a random sample where the population mean is *not* included in the confidence interval.

6. The file **P08_06.xlsx** contains data on repetitive task times for each of two workers. John has been doing this task for months, whereas Fred has just started. Each time listed is the time (in seconds) to perform a routine task on an assembly line. The times shown are in chronological order.
   a. Calculate a 95% confidence interval for the mean time it takes John to perform the task. Do the same for Fred.
   b. Do you believe both of the confidence intervals in part **a** are valid and/or useful? Why or why not? Which of the two workers would you rather have, assuming that task time is the only issue?

7. The manager of a local fast-food restaurant is interested in improving the service provided to customers who use the restaurant's drive-up window. As a first step in this process, the manager asks an assistant to record the time (in seconds) it takes to serve a large number of customers at the final window in the facility's drive-up system. The file **P08_07.xlsx** contains a random sample of 200 service times during the busiest hour of the day.
   a. Identify the relevant population.
   b. Calculate and interpret a 95% confidence interval for the mean service time of all customers arriving during the busiest hour of the day at this fast-food operation.
   c. If the manager wants to improve service, at least during the busiest time of day, does this confidence interval provide useful information? What useful information does it *not* provide?

Level B

8. Continuing Problem 5, generate a random sample of 50 players for each of the eight years in the file **P08_05.xlsx**. For each of these samples, calculate a 95% confidence interval for the mean total salary for that year. What is the confidence level that any particular one of these confidence intervals includes the population mean for that year? Is this the same confidence level that *all eight* of these confidence intervals include the respective population means? Why or why not?

9. The file **Confidence Interval Simulation.xlsx** generates observations randomly from a *normal* population. Suppose instead that each observation in column A is exponentially distributed with mean 10. (Refer to Section 5-6 for a brief explanation of the exponential distribution.) Unlike a normal distribution, an exponential distribution is very skewed to the right. A value from this distribution can be generated with the formula =−10*LN(RAND()). Rerun the simulation, still with sample size 30, with this exponential distribution. Are 95% confidence intervals still *valid*? That is, is the percentage in cell H7 approximately equal to 95%, as it should be? Press the F9 key a few times to check this.

10. Answer the questions in the previous problem when the population is a *mixture* of two normal distributions. Specifically, suppose each observation has a 65% chance of coming from a normal distribution with mean 100 and standard deviation 20, and a 35% chance of coming from a normal distribution with mean 200 and standard deviation 40. What is the mean of this mixture distribution? (*Hint*: Use an IF function to generate each random value in column A.)

8-4 Confidence Interval for a Total[2]

There are situations where a population mean is not the population parameter of most interest. A good example is the auditing example discussed in the previous chapter (Example 7.3). Rather than estimating the mean amount of receivables *per account*, the auditor might be more interested in the *total* amount of all receivables, summed over all accounts. In this section we provide a point estimate and a confidence interval for a population total.

First, we introduce some notation. Let T be a population total we want to estimate, such as the total of all receivables, and let $\hat{T}$ be a point estimate of T based on a simple random sample of size n from a population of size N. We first need a point estimate of T. For the population total T, it is reasonable to sum all of the values in the sample, denoted T_s, and then "project" this total to the population with Equation (8.5), where the second equality follows because the sample total T_s divided by the sample size n is the sample mean $\bar{X}$.

---

2 This section can be omitted without any loss of continuity.

Point Estimate for Population Total

$$\hat{T} = \frac{N}{n}T_s = N\overline{X} \qquad (8.5)$$

Equation (8.5) is quite intuitive. For example, suppose there are 1000 accounts in the population, you sample 50 of them, and you observe a sample total of $5000. Then, because only 1/20 of the population was sampled, a natural estimate of the population total is $20 \times \$5000 = \$100,000$.

Like the sample mean $\overline{X}$, the estimate $\hat{T}$ has a sampling distribution. The mean and standard deviation of this sampling distribution are given in Equations (8.6) and (8.7), where σ is again the population standard deviation.

Mean and Standard Error of Point Estimate for Population Total

$$E(\hat{T}) = T \qquad (8.6)$$

$$SE(\hat{T}) = N\sigma/\sqrt{n} \qquad (8.7)$$

Because σ is usually unknown, s is used instead of σ to obtain the approximate standard error of $\hat{T}$ given in Equation (8.8). The second equality follows because $s/\sqrt{n}$ is the standard error of $\overline{X}$.

Approximate Standard Error of Point Estimate for Population Total

$$SE(\hat{T}) = Ns/\sqrt{n} = N \times SE(\overline{X}) \qquad (8.8)$$

Note from Equation (8.6) that $\hat{T}$ is an unbiased estimate of the population total T. Therefore, it has no tendency to either overestimate or underestimate T.

From Equations (8.5) and (8.8), the point estimate of T is the point estimate of the mean multiplied by N, and the standard error of this point estimate is the standard error of the sample mean multiplied by N. We illustrate this procedure in the following example.

EXAMPLE

8.2 ESTIMATING TOTAL TAX REFUNDS

The Internal Revenue Service would like to estimate the total net amount of refund due to a particular set of 1,000,000 taxpayers. Each taxpayer will either receive a refund, in which case the net refund is positive, or will have to pay an amount due, in which case the net refund is negative. Therefore the *total* net amount of refund is a natural quantity of interest; it is the net amount the IRS will have to pay out (or receive, if negative). Find a 95% confidence interval for this total using the refunds from a random sample of 500 taxpayers in the file **IRS Refunds.xlsx**.

Objective

To find a 95% confidence interval for the total (net) amount the IRS must pay out to these 1,000,000 taxpayers.

Solution

The confidence interval appears in Figure 8.6. We used the CI Total sheet from the template file to perform the calculations. Note in particular how the sample mean is multiplied by the population size in cell E8 and how the standard error of the mean is also multiplied by the population size in cell E9. The effect is to scale the usual confidence interval for the mean by the population size.

Figure 8.6 Analysis of IRS Refund Data

⊿	A	B	C	D	E	F
1	Confidence interval for population total					
2	Confidence level	95%				
3						
4	Population size	1,000,000				
5	Sample size	500		=COUNT(Data!B2:B501)		
6	Sample mean	294.980		=AVERAGE(Data!B2:B501)		
7	Sample standard deviation	581.312		=STDEV.S(Data!B2:B501)		
8	Estimate of total	$294,980,000		=B4*B6		
9	Standard error of total	$25,997,048		=B4*B7/SQRT(B5)		
10	Degrees of freedom	499		=B5–1		
11	Multiple	1.96		=T.INV.2T(1–$B$2,B10)		
12	Lower limit	$243,902,836		=B8–B11*B9		
13	Upper limit	$346,057,164		=B8+B11*B9		

Based on these calculations, the IRS can be 95% confident that it will need to pay out somewhere between about 244 and 346 million dollars to these 1,000,000 taxpayers.

Problems

Solutions for problems whose numbers appear within a colored box can be found in the Student Solution Files.

Level A

11. The file **P02_16.xlsx** contains the number of arrivals at a turnpike tollbooth for each of four 5-minute intervals for each of 256 days. For this problem, assume that each column, such as arrivals from 8:00 AM to 8:05 AM, is a random sample of all arrivals from the corresponding hour of the day, such as 8:00 AM to 9:00 AM. Calculate a 95% confidence interval for the mean number of arrivals during each corresponding hour of the day, that is, one for 8:00 AM to 9:00 AM, one for 9:00 AM to 10:00 AM, and so on.

12. A lightbulb manufacturer wants to estimate the total number of defective bulbs contained in all of the boxes shipped by the company during the past week. Production personnel at this company have recorded the number of defective bulbs found in each of 50 randomly selected boxes shipped during the past week. These data are provided in the file **P08_12.xlsx**. Calculate a 95% confidence interval for the total number of defective bulbs contained in the 1000 boxes shipped by this company during the past week.

13. Auditors of a particular bank are interested in comparing the reported value of all 2265 customer savings account balances with their own findings regarding the actual value of such assets. Rather than reviewing the records of each savings account at the bank, the auditors decide to examine a representative sample of savings account balances. The population from which they will sample is given in the file **P08_13.xlsx**.

a. Select 10 simple random samples, each consisting of 100 savings account balances from this population.

b. For each sample generated in part **a**, calculate a 95% confidence interval for the total value of all 2265 savings account balances within this bank. How many of them include the (known) population total?

Level B

14. Suppose you are gambling on a roulette wheel. Each time the wheel is spun, the result is one of the outcomes 0, 1, and so on through 36. Of these outcomes, 16 are red, 16 are black, and 1 is green. On each spin you bet $5 that a red outcome will occur and $1 that the green outcome will occur. If red occurs, you win a net $4. (You win $10 from red and nothing from green.) If green occurs, you win a net $24. (You win $30 from green and nothing from red.) If black occurs, you lose everything you bet for a loss of $6.

a. Use random numbers to generate 20 plays from this strategy. Each play should indicate the net amount won or lost. Then, based on these 20 outcomes, calculate a 95% confidence interval for the total net amount won or lost from 1000 plays of the game. Would you conclude that this strategy is a winning one for you?

b. Repeat part **a**, but with slightly changed rules. Now your betting strategy is the same, but if red occurs, your net gain is $5 (you win $11 from red, nothing from green). Comment on whether this slight change makes much of a difference in the mean total from 1000 bets.

8-5 Confidence Interval for a Proportion

How often have you heard on the evening news a survey finding such as, "52% of the public agree with the president's handling of the economy, with a sampling error of plus or minus 3%"? Surveys are often used to estimate proportions, such as the proportion of the public who agree with the president's handling of the economy. We now discuss how to form a confidence interval for any population proportion p.

The basic procedure is very similar to the procedure for a population mean. It requires a point estimate, the standard error of this point estimate, and a multiple that depends on the confidence level. Then the confidence level has the same form as in Equation (8.1):

$$\text{point estimate} \pm \text{multiple} \times \text{standard error}$$

In the news example the point estimate is 52% and the "multiple $\times$ standard error" is 3%. Therefore, the confidence interval extends from 49% to 55%. Although the news show doesn't state the confidence level explicitly, it is 95% by convention. In words, they are 95% confident that the percentage of the public who agree with the president's handling of the economy is somewhere between 49% and 55%.

The theory that leads to this result is fairly straightforward. Consider any property that each member of a population either has or does not have. As examples, the property might be that

- a person agrees with the president's handling of the economy
- a person has purchased a company's product at least once in the past three months
- the diameter of a part is within specification limits
- a customer's account is at least two months overdue
- a customer's rating of a new sandwich is at least 6 on a 10-point scale.

In each of these examples, let p be the proportion of the population with the property. From a random sample of size n, let $\hat{p}$ be the sample proportion of members with the property. For example, if 10 out of 50 sampled members have the property, then $\hat{p} = 10/50 = 0.2$. Then $\hat{p}$ is used as a point estimate of p.

It can be shown that for sufficiently large n, the sampling distribution of $\hat{p}$ is approximately *normal* with mean p and standard error $\sqrt{p(1-p)/n}$. Because p is the unknown parameter, $\hat{p}$ is substituted for p in this standard error to obtain the following approximate standard error of $\hat{p}$:

Standard Error of Sample Proportion

$$\text{SE}(\hat{p}) = \sqrt{\frac{\hat{p}(1-\hat{p})}{n}} \qquad (8.9)$$

Finally, the multiple used to obtain a confidence interval for p is a Z-value. (It is *not* a *t*-value.) It is the standard normal value that cuts off an appropriate probability in each tail. For example, the *z*-multiple for a 95% confidence interval is 1.96 because this value cuts off probability 0.025 in each tail of the standard normal distribution. In general, the confidence interval has the form in Equation (8.10):

Confidence Interval for a Proportion

$$\hat{p} \pm z\text{-multiple} \times \sqrt{\frac{\hat{p}(1-\hat{p})}{n}} \qquad (8.10)$$

This confidence interval is based on the assumption of a large sample size. A rule of thumb for checking the validity of this assumption is the following. Let p_L and p_U be the lower and upper limits of the confidence interval. Then the sample size is sufficiently large—and the confidence interval is valid—if $np_L > 5$, $n(1 - p_L) > 5$, $np_U > 5$, and $n(1 - p_U) > 5$. Essentially, these mean that n should be reasonably large and the two limiting values of p should not be too close to 0 or 1. We illustrate the procedure in the following example.

EXAMPLE

8.3 ESTIMATING THE RESPONSE TO A NEW SANDWICH

The fast-food manager from Example 8.1 has already sampled 40 customers to estimate the population mean rating of the restaurant's new sandwich. Recall that each rating is on a 1-to-10 scale, 10 being the best. The manager would now like to use the same sample to estimate the proportion of customers who rate the sandwich at least 6. Her thinking is that these are the customers who are likely to purchase the sandwich on subsequent visits.

Objective

To illustrate the procedure for finding a confidence interval for the proportion of customers who rate the new sandwich at least 6 on a 10-point scale.

Solution

The calculations appear in Figure 8.7. (See the file **Satisfaction Ratings Finished.xlsx**.) We used the CI Proportion sheet from the template file to perform the calculations. These calculations correspond exactly to Equation (8.10). Note in particular how the sample proportion is calculated directly from the sample data with a COUNTIF function. Also, note the formula for the z multiple in row 6. The argument for the NORM.S.INV function is $95\% + 5\%/2$, or 97.5%. The effect is to find the value that cuts off 2.5% in the right tail. You will see this type of calculation quite often.

Figure 8.7 Confidence Interval for Proportion

⊿	A	B	C	D	E	F
1	Confidence interval for proportion with rating at least 6					
2	Confidence level	95%				
3						
4	Sample size	40		=COUNT(Data!B2:B41)		
5	Number with property of interest	25		=COUNTIF(Data!B2:B41,">=6")		
6	Sample proportion	0.625		=B5/B4		
7	Standard error of proportion	0.077		=SQRT(B6*(1–B6)/B4)		
8	Multiple	1.960		=NORM.S.INV($B$2+(1–$B$2)/2)		
9	Lower limit	0.475		=B6–B8*B7		
10	Upper limit	0.775		=B6+B8*B7		

The output is fairly good news for the manager. Based on this sample of size 40, she can be 95% confident that the percentage of all customers who would rate the sandwich 6 or higher is somewhere between 47.5% and 77.5%. Of course, she realizes that this is a very wide interval, so there is still a lot of uncertainty about the *true* population proportion. To reduce the length of this interval, she would need to sample more customers—quite a few more customers. Typically, confidence intervals for proportions are fairly wide unless n is quite large.

The data for this example are in "long" form, where there is an observation for each customer. In this case, formulas are required in cells B4 and B5 for the counts. However, the required counts for proportions examples are often given in tables. In this case, you can enter the given counts directly into the template.

In news shows, you have probably noticed that they almost always quote a sampling error of plus or minus 3%. In words, the "plus or minus" part of their 95% confidence interval is 3%, or 0.03. How large a sample size must they use to achieve this? The "plus or minus" part of the confidence interval is 1.96 times the standard error of $\hat{p}$, so we must have

$$1.96 \times \sqrt{\hat{p}(1 - \hat{p})/n} = 0.03$$

Now, the quantity $\hat{p}(1 - \hat{p})$ is fairly constant for values of $\hat{p}$ between 0 and 1, provided that $\hat{p}$ isn't too close to 0 or 1. To get a reasonable estimate of the required n, we use $\hat{p} = 0.5$. Then we have

$$1.96 \times \sqrt{(0.5)(0.5)/n} = 0.03$$

Solving for n, we obtain $n = [(1.96)(0.5)/0.03]^2 \approx 1067$.

This is a rather remarkable result. To obtain a 95% confidence interval of this length for a population proportion, where the population consists of *millions* of people, only about 1000 people need to be sampled. The remarkable fact is that this small a sample can provide such accurate information about such a large population.

One of many business applications of confidence intervals for proportions is in auditing. Auditors typically use *attribute sampling* to check whether certain procedures are being followed correctly. The term "attribute" means that each item checked is done either correctly or incorrectly—there is no in-between. Examples of items not done correctly might include (1) an invoice copy that is not initialed by an accounting clerk, (2) an invoice quantity that does not agree with the quantity on the shipping document, (3) an invoice price that does not agree with the price on an authorized price list, and (4) an invoice with a clerical inaccuracy. Typically, an auditor focuses on one of these types of errors and then estimates the proportion of items with this type of error.

Fundamental Insight

Sample Size for Estimating a Proportion

To obtain an estimate of a proportion that is accurate to within 3 percentage points with 95% confidence, it is sufficient to sample approximately 1000 members of the population, *regardless of the population size*. This remarkable fact allows news broadcasters to make such statements about various proportions on a nightly basis. By sampling only about 1000 people from the entire country, they can estimate quite accurately what the entire population believes.

Because auditors are concerned primarily with how *large* the proportion of errors might be, they usually calculate *one-sided* confidence intervals for proportions. Instead of using sample data to find lower and upper limits p_L and p_U of a confidence interval, they automatically use $p_L = 0$ and then determine an upper limit p_U such that the 95% confidence interval is from 0 to p_U. A simple modification of the confidence interval in Equation (8.10) provides the result in Equation (8.11), where the z-multiple is chosen so that the entire probability (0.05 for a 95% interval) is in the right tail. For a 95% confidence level, the relevant z-multiple is 1.645.

Upper Limit of a One-Sided Confidence Interval for a Proportion

$$p_U = \hat{p} + z\text{-multiple} \times \sqrt{\hat{p}(1 - \hat{p})/n} \qquad \textbf{(8.11)}$$

One further complication occurs, however. This formula for p_U relies on the large-sample approximation of the normal distribution to the binomial distribution. Auditors typically use an *exact* procedure to find p_U that is based directly on the binomial distribution. We illustrate how this is done in the following example.

EXAMPLE

8.4 AUDITING FOR PRICE ERRORS

An auditor wants to check the proportion of invoices that contain price errors—that is, prices that do not agree with those on an authorized price list. He checks 93 randomly sampled invoices and finds that two of them include price errors. What can he conclude, in terms of a one-sided 95% confidence interval, about the proportion of all invoices with price errors?

Objective

To find the upper limit of a one-sided 95% confidence interval for the proportion of errors in the context of attribute sampling in auditing.

Solution

The results appear in Figure 8.8. (See the file **One-Sided Confidence Interval Finished.xlsx**. It is *not* based on the template file because the template file only calculates two-sided confidence intervals.) The sample proportion is $p = 2/93 = 0.0215$ and the upper confidence limit based on the large-sample approximation is 0.046. This latter value is calculated in cell B14 with the formula

=B7+B13*SQRT(B7*(1-B7)/B5)

However, note that $np_U = 93(0.046) = 4.278$, which is less than 5. This indicates that the large-sample approximation might not be valid.

Figure 8.8 Analysis of Auditing Example

	A	B	C	D	E	F	G	H	I	J
1	**An exact one-sided confidence interval in auditing**									
2										
3	Confidence level	95%								
4	Number of errors	2								
5	Sample size	93								
6										
7	Sample proportion	0.0215					Goal Seek	?	×	
8										
9	Exact upper confidence limit for p		Goal seek condition				Set cell:	$D$10		
10	Upper limit	0.066		0.050	=	0.05	To value:	0.05		
11							By changing cell:	$B$10		
12	Large-sample upper confidence limit for p									
13	z-multiple	1.645					OK	Cancel		
14	Upper limit	0.046								

A more valid procedure, based on the binomial distribution, appears in row 10. It turns out that if p_U is the appropriate upper confidence limit, then p_U satisfies the following equation.

Formula for Upper Confidence Limit

$$P(X \le k) = \alpha \qquad\qquad (8.12)$$

Here, X is binomially distributed with parameters n and p_U, k is the observed number of errors, and α is one minus the confidence level. There is no way to find p_U directly (by means of a formula) from Equation (8.12). However, you can use Excel's Goal Seek tool, as illustrated in the figure. First, enter *any* trial value of p_U in cell B10 and the binomial formula

=BINOM.DIST(B4,B5,B10,TRUE)

in cell D10. [This formula calculates $P(X \leq k)$ from the trial value in cell B10.] Then use Goal Seek from the What-If Analysis dropdown menu on the Data ribbon, with cell D10 as the Set cell, 0.05 as the target value, and cell B10 as the changing cell.

The resulting value of p_U is 0.066. This is considerably different (from the auditor's point of view) from the 0.046 value found from the large-sample approximation. It allows the auditor to state with 95% confidence that the percentage of invoices with price errors is no greater than 6.6%, based on the two errors out of 93 observed in the sample.

Problems

Level A

15. A drugstore manager needs to purchase adequate supplies of various brands of toothpaste to meet the ongoing demands of its customers. In particular, the company is interested in estimating the proportion of its customers who favor the country's leading brand of toothpaste, Crest. The Data sheet of the file **P08_15 .xlsx** contains the toothpaste brand preferences of 200 randomly selected customers, obtained recently through a customer survey. Calculate a 95% confidence interval for the proportion of all of the company's customers who prefer Crest toothpaste. How might the manager use this confidence interval for purchasing decisions?

16. The employee benefits manager of a large public university would like to estimate the proportion of full-time employees who prefer adopting the first (plan A) of three available health care plans in the next annual enrollment period. A random sample of the university's employees and their tentative health care preferences are given in the file **P08_16.xlsx**.

a. Calculate a 90% confidence interval for the proportion of all the university's employees who favor plan A.

b. The file also includes the classification of each employee (administrative staff, support staff, or faculty). Calculate a separate 90% confidence interval for each of these groups for the proportion who favor plan A. How do these confidence intervals compare to one another? How do their lengths compare to the confidence interval in part **a**? Is this what you would expect? Explain.

17. A market research consultant hired by a leading soft-drink company wants to determine the proportion of consumers who favor its low-calorie brand over the leading low-calorie competitor in a particular geographic region. A random sample of 250 consumers from the market under investigation is provided in the file **P08_17.xlsx**.

a. Calculate a 90% confidence interval for the proportion of all consumers in this market who prefer the company's brand.

b. The file contains the gender and age group for each customer in the sample. Calculate a separate 90% confidence for each gender for the proportion who prefer the company's brand. Then do the same for each age group. Explain briefly how these confidence intervals compare to each other and to the confidence interval in part **a**.

8-6 Confidence Interval for a Standard Deviation[3]

In Section 8-3 we focused primarily on estimation of a population *mean*. We had to deal with the population standard deviation σ in its role as a nuisance parameter. That is, we needed an estimate of σ to estimate the standard error of the sample mean. However, there are cases where the variability in the population, measured by σ, is of primary interest in its own right. We describe a procedure for obtaining a confidence interval for σ in this section.

The theory is somewhat more complex than for the case of the mean. As you might expect, the sample standard deviation s is used as a point estimate of σ. However, the sampling distribution of s is not symmetric—in particular, it is not the normal distribution or the t distribution. Rather, the appropriate sampling distribution is a right-skewed

---

3 This section can be omitted without any loss of continuity.

distribution called the **chi-square distribution**. Like the t distribution, the chi-square distribution has a degrees of freedom parameter, which (for this procedure) is again $n - 1$.

Tables of the chi-square distribution, for selected degrees of freedom, appear in many statistics books, but the necessary information can be obtained more easily with Excel's chi-square functions, as illustrated in Figure 8.9. (See the file **Chi-Square Calculations Finished.xlsx**.)

Figure 8.9 Excel Functions for the Chi-Square Distribution

	A	B	C	D	E	F
1	Calculations for the chi-square distribution					
2						
3	Degrees of freedom	15				
4						
5	One-tailed probabilities					
6	Value	10				
7	Probability in left tail	0.180		=CHISQ.DIST(B6,B3,TRUE)		
8						
9	Value	25				
10	Probability in right tail	0.050		=CHISQ.DIST.RT(B9,B3)		
11						
12	Inverse calculations					
13	Probability in left tail	0.05				
14	Value	7.261		=CHISQ.INV(B13,B3)		
15						
16	Probability in right tail	0.05				
17	Value	24.996		=CHISQ.INV.RT(B16,B3)		

Because of the skewness of the sampling distribution of s, a confidence interval for σ is *not* centered at s. That is, the confidence interval is *not* the point estimate plus or minus a multiple of a standard error. Instead, s is always closer to the left endpoint of the confidence interval than to the right endpoint. Specifically, the endpoints of a confidence for the population standard deviation extends from $s\sqrt{(n-1)/c_1}$ to $s\sqrt{(n-1)c_2}$. Here, c_1 is the value that cuts off probability $(1-\alpha)/2$ in the *right* tail of the chi-square distribution with $n-1$ degrees of freedom, and c_2 similarly cuts off probability $(1-\alpha)/2$ in the *left* tail. For example, if the confidence level is 95%, these values cut off probability 0.025 in each tail. Note that c_1 is *larger* than c_2, so the left endpoint of the confidence interval is indeed *lower* than the right endpoint. The procedure is illustrated in the following example.

EXAMPLE

8.5 ANALYZING VARIABILITY IN DIAMETERS OF MACHINE PARTS

A machine produces parts that are supposed to have diameter 10 centimeters. However, due to inherent variability, some diameters are greater than 10 and some are less. The production supervisor is concerned about two things. First, he is concerned that the mean diameter is not what it should be, 10 centimeters. Second, he is worried about the extent of variability in the diameters. Even if the mean is on target, excessive variability implies that many of the parts will fail to meet specifications. To analyze the process, he randomly samples 50 parts during the course of a day and measures the diameter of each part to the nearest millimeter. (See the file **Part Diameters.xlsx**.) Should the supervisor be concerned about the results from this sample?

Objective
To find a confidence interval for the standard deviation of part diameters, and to see how variability affects the proportion of unusable parts produced.

Solution

Because the manager is concerned about the mean *and* the standard deviation of diameters, it is useful to obtain 95% confidence intervals for both. We calculated each with the template file, using the CI Mean and CI Std Dev sheets. The confidence interval for the mean, not shown here, extends from 9.986 to 10.005. The confidence interval for the standard deviation, shown in Figure 8.10, extends from 0.043 to 0.131. Two chi-square values that cut off probability 0.025 in each tail are calculated first, and they are then used to calculate the endpoints of the confidence interval.

This interval extends from 0.029 cm to 0.043 cm. Is this good news or bad news? It depends. Let's say that a part is unusable if its diameter is more than 0.065 cm from the target. Let's also assume that the true mean is right on target and that the standard deviation is at the *upper* end of the confidence interval, that is, $\sigma = 0.043$ cm. Finally, assume that the population distribution of diameters is normal. Then the calculation in cell E23 shows that 13.1% of the parts will be unusable. It adds the normal probabilities of being below or above the usable range.

Figure 8.10 Analysis of Parts Data

	A	B	C	D	E	F	G	H	I	J
1	**Confidence interval for population standard deviation**									
2	Confidence level	95%								
3										
4	Sample size	50		=COUNT(Data!B2:B51)						
5	Sample standard deviation	0.034		=STDEV.S(Data!B2:B51)						
6	Degrees of freedom	49		=B4−1						
7	Lower chi-sq value	31.555		=CHISQ.INV((1−$B$2)/2,B6)						
8	Upper chi-sq value	70.222		=CHISQ.INV.RT((1−$B$2)/2,B6)						
9	Lower limit	0.029		=SQRT(B6)*B5/SQRT(B8)						
10	Upper limit	0.043		=SQRT(B6)*B5/SQRT(B7)						
11										
12	**Proportion of unusable parts**									
13	Maximum deviation for usability	0.065								
14	Assumed mean	10								
15	Assumed standard deviation	0.043								
16	Proportion unusable	0.131		=NORM.DIST(10−B13,B14,B15,TRUE)+(1−NORM.DIST(10+B13,B14,B15,TRUE))						
17										
18	**Twoway data table for finding proportion unusable as a function of mean and stdev**									
19		Assumed standard deviation								
20		0.131	0.029	0.034	0.043					
21	Assumed mean	9.986	0.041	0.080	0.149					
22		9.996	0.025	0.060	0.130					
23		10.005	0.026	0.061	0.131					

To pursue this analysis one step further, the two-way data table in Figure 8.10 is useful. The means used in column B are the lower confidence limit, the sample mean, and the upper confidence limit. Similarly, the assumed standard deviations used in row 20 are the lower confidence limit, the sample standard deviation, and the upper confidence limit. To form the table, enter the formula =B16 in cell B20, highlight the range B20:E23, and create a data table with cells B15 and B14 as the row and column input cells.

Each value in the body of the data table is the resulting proportion of unusable parts. Obviously, a mean close to the target and a small standard deviation are best, but even this best-case scenario results in 2.5% unusable parts (see cell C22). However, a mean off target and a large standard deviation can lead to as many as 14.9% unusable parts (see cell E21). In any case, the message for the supervisor is clear—he must work to reduce the underlying variability in the process. This variability is hurting him much more than an off-target mean.

Problems

Solutions for problems whose numbers appear within a colored box can be found in the Student Solution Files.

Level A

18. Senior management of a large consulting firm is concerned about a growing decline in the organization's weekly number of billable hours. Ideally, the organization expects each professional employee to spend *at* *least* 40 hours per week on work. The file **P08_18.xlsx** contains the work hours reported by a random sample of employees in a typical week.

a. Calculate a 95% confidence interval for the *mean* number of hours worked by the company's employees in a typical week.

b. Calculate a 95% confidence interval for the *standard deviation* of the number of hours worked by the company's employees in a typical week.

c. Given the target range of 40 to 60 hours of work per week, should senior management be concerned about the number of hours their employees are currently devoting to work? Explain how the answers to *both* parts **a** and **b** help to answer this question.

Level B

19. The file **P08_06.xlsx** contains data on repetitive task times for each of two workers. John has been doing this task for months, whereas Fred has just started. Each time listed is the time (in seconds) to perform a routine task on an assembly line. The times shown are in chronological order.

a. Calculate a 95% confidence interval for the standard deviation of times for John. Do the same for Fred. What do these indicate?

b. Given that these times are listed chronologically, how useful are the confidence intervals in part **a**? Specifically, is there any evidence that the variation in times is changing over time for either of the two workers?

8-7 Confidence Interval for the Difference Between Means

Statisticians call these general types of problems "comparison problems." They are among the most important types of problems tackled with statistical methods.

One of the most important applications of statistical inference is the comparison of two population means. There are many applications to business, including the following.

Applications of Comparisons of Means in Business

- Men and women shop at a retail clothing store. The manager would like to know how much more (or less), on average, a woman spends on a typical purchase occasion than a man.
- Two airline companies fly similar routes. A consumer organization would like to check how much the average delay differs between the two airlines, where delay is defined as the actual arrival time at the destination minus the scheduled arrival time.
- A supermarket chain mails coupons for various products to a randomly selected subset of its customers in a particular city. Its other customers in this city receive no such coupons. The chain would like to check how much the average amount spent on these products differs between the two sets of customers over the next couple of months.
- A computer company has a customer service center that responds to customers' questions and complaints. The center employs two types of people: those who have had a recent course in dealing with customers (but little actual experience) and those with a lot of experience dealing with customers (but no formal course). The company would like to know how these two types of employees differ with respect to the average number of customer complaints of poor service in the last six months.
- A consulting company hires business students directly out of undergraduate school. The new hires all take a problem-solving test. They then go through an intensive three-month training program, after which they take another similar problem-solving test. The company wants to know how much the average test score improves after the training program.
- A car dealership often deals with husband–wife pairs shopping for cars. To check whether husbands react differently than their wives to the sales presentation, husbands and wives are asked (separately) to rate the quality of the sales presentation. The dealership wants to know how much husbands differ from their wives in terms of average ratings.

Each of these examples deals with a difference between means from two populations. However, the first four examples differ in one important respect from the last two. In the last two examples, there is a natural *pairing* across the two samples. In the first of these, each employee takes a test before a course and then a test after the course, so that each employee is naturally paired with himself or herself. In the final example, husbands and wives are naturally paired with one another. There is no such pairing in the first four examples. Instead, we assume that the samples in these first four examples are chosen *independently* of one another. We need to distinguish these two cases, *independent samples* and *paired samples*, in the discussion that follows.

8-7a Independent Samples

The framework for this situation is the following. We are interested in some quantity, such as dollars spent or airplane delay, for each of two populations. The population means are μ_1 and μ_2, and the population standard deviations are σ_1 and σ_2. We take random samples of sizes n_1 and n_2 (not necessarily equal) from the populations to estimate the difference between means, $\mu_1 - \mu_2$. A point estimate of this difference is the natural one, the difference between sample means, $\overline{X}_1 - \overline{X}_2$. Starting with this estimate, we want to form a confidence interval for the unknown population mean difference, $\mu_1 - \mu_2$.

The appropriate sampling distribution of the difference between sample means is again the t distribution, now with $n_1 + n_2 - 2$ degrees of freedom.[4] Therefore, a confidence interval for $\mu_1 - \mu_2$ is given by Expression (8.13). The t-multiple is the value that cuts off the appropriate probability (depending on the confidence level) in each tail of the t distribution with $n_1 + n_2 - 2$ degrees of freedom. For example, if the confidence level is 95% and $n_1 = n_2 = 30$, the appropriate t-multiple is 2.002, which can be found in Excel with the function **T.INV(0.025,58)**.

Confidence Interval for Difference Between Means

$$\overline{X}_1 - \overline{X}_2 \pm t\text{-multiple} \times SE(\overline{X}_1 - \overline{X}_2) \qquad \textbf{(8.13)}$$

The standard error, $SE(\overline{X}_1 - \overline{X}_2)$, is more involved. We must first make the assumption that the population standard deviations are equal, that is, $\sigma_1 = \sigma_2$. (We shortly present an alternative procedure for the situation where the population standard deviations are *not* assumed to be equal.) Then an estimate of this common standard deviation is provided by the "pooled" estimate from both samples, labeled s_p.

Pooled Estimate of Common Standard Deviation

$$s_p = \sqrt{\frac{(n_1 - 1)s_1^2 + (n_2 - 1)s_2^2}{n_1 + n_2 - 2}} \qquad \textbf{(8.14)}$$

Here, s_1 and s_2 are the sample standard deviations from the two samples. This pooled estimate is somewhere between s_1 and s_2, with the relative sample sizes determining its exact value. Then the standard error of $\overline{X}_1 - \overline{X}_2$ is given by Equation (8.15):

Standard Error of Difference Between Sample Means

$$SE(\overline{X}_1 - \overline{X}_2) = s_p\sqrt{\frac{1}{n_1} + \frac{1}{n_2}} \qquad \textbf{(8.15)}$$

This procedure, usually referred to as "two-sample t," is illustrated in the following example.

---

4 This assumes that either the population distributions are normal or that the sample sizes are reasonably large, conditions that are at least approximately met in a wide variety of applications.

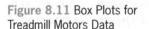

EXAMPLE

8.6 RELIABILITY OF TREADMILL MOTORS AT SURESTEP

SureStep Company manufactures high-quality treadmills for use in exercise clubs. SureStep currently purchases its motors for these treadmills from supplier A. However, it is considering a change to supplier B, which offers a slightly lower cost. The only question is whether supplier B's motors are as reliable as supplier A's. To check this, SureStep installs motors from supplier A on 30 of its treadmills and motors from supplier B on another 30 of its treadmills. It then runs these treadmills under typical conditions and, for each treadmill, records the number of hours until the motor fails. (See the file **Treadmill Motors.xlsx**. It has two data columns, one for the supplier and one for the lifetime.) What can SureStep conclude?

Objective

To find a confidence interval for the difference between mean lifetimes of motors, and to see how this confidence interval can help SureStep choose the better supplier.

Solution

In any comparison problem it is a good idea to look initially at side-by-side box plots of the two samples. These appear in Figure 8.11. These show that (1) the distributions of times until failure are skewed to the right for each supplier, (2) the mean for supplier A is somewhat greater than the mean for supplier B, and (3) there are several outliers. There seems to be little doubt that supplier A's motors will last longer on average than supplier B's—or is there? A confidence interval for the mean difference allows you to see whether the differences apparent in the box plots can be generalized to *all* motors from the two suppliers.

Figure 8.11 Box Plots for
Treadmill Motors Data

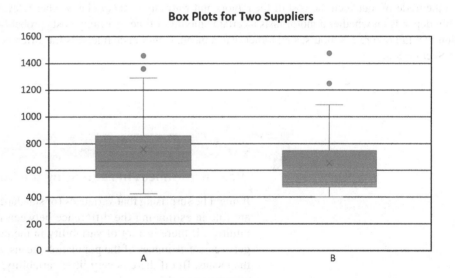

The calculations appear in Figure 8.12. They were performed by the CI Mean Diff sheet from the template file. As you can see, the sample means differ by approximately 93 hours, the sample standard deviations are of roughly the same magnitude, and the confidence interval for the difference between means extends from −47.549 to 233.815.

These calculations are fairly complex, but remember that you have to fill in only the orange cells; the template does the rest. Still, the following comments are useful:

1. The sample means are calculated with AVERAGEIF functions. The formula for sample mean 1 averages only over the A's, and the formula for sample mean 2 averages only over the B's.
2. There is no corresponding "STDEVIF" function, so the array formulas in cells B11 and B12 are necessary. The template only requires you to fill in the data ranges, but you have to complete the formulas by pressing Ctrl+Shift+Enter (all three keys at once), not just Enter. This creates the curly brackets; you don't type them.
3. We stated earlier that there is a version of the procedure that does *not* require the equal-standard deviation assumption. The template takes care of this automatically. It performs a test for equal variances (discussed in the next chapter) in

Figure 8.12 Analysis of
Treadmill Motors Data

	A	B	C	D	E	F	G	H	I	J	K
1	Confidence interval for difference between means										
2	Confidence level	95%									
3											
4	Category 1	A									
5	Category 2	B									
6	Sample size 1	30		=COUNTIF(Data!$A$2:$A$61,B4)							
7	Sample size 2	30		=COUNTIF(Data!$A$2:$A$61,B5)							
8	Sample mean 1	748.800		=AVERAGEIF(Data!$A$2:$A$61,B4,Data!$B$2:$B$61)							
9	Sample mean 2	655.667		=AVERAGEIF(Data!$A$2:$A$61,B5,Data!$B$2:$B$61)							
10	Sample mean difference (1 minus 2)	93.133		=B8−B9							
11	Sample std dev 1	283.881		{=STDEV.S(IF(Data!$A$2:$A$61=B4,Data!$B$2:$B$61))}							
12	Sample std dev 2	259.986		{=STDEV.S(IF(Data!$A$2:$A$61=B5,Data!$B$2:$B$61))}							
13	Pooled std dev	272.196		=SQRT(((B6−1)*B11^2+(B7−1)*B12^2)/B15)							
14	Standard error of diff	70.281		=IF(B22>0.1,B13*SQRT(1/B6+1/B7),SQRT(B11^2/B6+B12^2/B7))							
15	Degrees of freedom	58		=IF(B22>0.1,B6+B7−2,ROUND(B14^4/((B11^2/B6)^2/(B6−1)+(B12^2/B7)^2/(B7−1)),0))							
16	Multiple	2.00		=T.INV.2T(1−$B$2,B15)							
17	Lower limit	−47.549		=B10−B16*B14							
18	Upper limit	233.815		=B10+B16*B14							
19											
20	Test for equal variances										
21	Ratio of sample variances	1.192		=(B11/B12)^2							
22	p-value	0.639		=2*(0.5 − ABS(0.5 − F.DIST(B21,B6−1,B7−1,TRUE)))							

rows 20–22. A large (> 0.1) p-value for this test is evidence of unequal variances or equivalently of unequal standard deviations. The formulas in cells B14 and B15 check for this and enter the appropriate formulas in either case. For this example, the p-value is large, 0.639, so the equal-standard deviation assumption is warranted.

The confidence interval extends from a negative value to a positive value, but it's mostly positive. If SureStep had to make a guess, it would say that supplier A's motors last longer on average. Should SureStep continue with supplier A? This depends on the trade-off between the cost of the motors and warranty costs (and any other relevant costs). Because the warranty probably depends on whether a motor lasts a certain amount of time, warranty costs probably depend on a *proportion* (the proportion that fail before 500 hours, say) rather than a mean. Confidence intervals for differences between proportions are discussed in Section 8-8.

Fundamental Insight

Role of Variances in Estimating the Difference Between Means

It might be surprising that variances (or standard deviations) play such an important role in estimating the difference between means, but this is actually quite intuitive. If there is a lot of variability in the populations, it is more difficult to get accurate estimates of the population means, and hence the difference between the means. But if there is very little variability, it is much easier to estimate the means accurately.

8-7b Paired Samples

When the samples to be compared are paired in some natural way, such as a pre-test and post-test for each person, or husband–wife pairs, there is a more appropriate form of analysis than the two-sample procedure. Consider the example where each new employee takes a test, then receives a three-month training course, and afterward takes another similar test. There is likely to be a fairly strong correlation between the pre-test and post-test scores. Employees who score relatively low on the first test are likely to score relatively low on the second test, and employees who score relatively high on the first test are likely to score relatively high on the second test. The two-sample procedure in the previous section for *independent* samples does not take this correlation into account and therefore ignores important information. The paired procedure described in this section, on the other hand, uses this information to advantage.

The procedure itself is straightforward. It does not directly analyze two separate variables (pre-test scores and post-test scores, for example); it analyzes their *differences*. For each pair in the sample, the difference between the two scores for the pair is calculated. Then a *one*-sample analysis, as in Section 8-3, is performed on these differences. This is illustrated in the following example.

EXAMPLE

8.7 HUSBAND AND WIFE REACTIONS TO SALES PRESENTATIONS

Stevens Honda-Buick automobile dealership often sells to husband-wife pairs. The manager would like to check whether the sales presentation is viewed any more or less favorably by the husbands than by the wives. If it is, then some new training might be recommended for its salespeople. To check for differences, a random sample of husbands and wives are asked (separately) to rate the sales presentation on a scale of 1 to 10, 10 being the most favorable rating. (See the **Sales Presentation Ratings.xlsx** file, where there are two columns, one for husbands and one for their wives.) What can the manager conclude from these data?

Objective

To use a paired-sample procedure to find a confidence interval for the mean difference between husbands' and wives' ratings of sales presentations.

Solution

The procedure is straightforward, as illustrated in Figure 8.13. It uses the CI Paired Mean Diff sheet from the template file. You are first asked to calculate the differences in column A, where each difference is a husband rating minus a wife rating. Then the template uses the same one-sample mean formulas on the differences as in Example 8.1. The sample mean Husband minus Wife difference is 1.629 and a 95% confidence interval for this difference extends from 1.057 to 2.200.

Figure 8.13 Sales Presentation Analysis

	A	B	C	D	E	F	G	H
1	Difference		Confidence interval for difference (husbands - wives)					
2	3		Confidence level	95%				
3	−1							
4	3		Sample size	35		=COUNT(Difference)		
5	2		Sample mean diff	1.629		=AVERAGE(Difference)		
6	3		Sample std dev of diff	1.664256		=STDEV.S(Difference)		
7	1		Standard error	0.281		=D6/SQRT(D4)		
8	3		Degrees of freedom	34		=D4−1		
9	−1		Multiple	2.032		=T.INV.2T(1−D2,D8)		
10	−1		Lower limit	1.057		=D5−D9*D7		
11	2		Upper limit	2.200		=D5+D9*D7		
12	3							
13	1							
14	3							
15	−1							

Before leaving this example, we again note that the finished version of the file shows what would have happened if the two-sample procedure had been used on the Husband and Wife variables. The resulting confidence interval for the mean difference extends from 0.895 to 2.362, which is somewhat *longer* than the confidence interval from the paired-sample procedure. This is typical. When the two-sample procedure is used in a situation where the paired-sample procedure is more appropriate, the data are not used as efficiently. The effect is that the standard error of the difference tends to be larger, and the resulting confidence interval tends to be longer.

Why is the paired-sample procedure appropriate here? It is *not* just because husbands and wives naturally come in pairs. It is because they tend to react similarly to one another. You can check that the correlation between the husbands' scores and their wives' scores is 0.442. (This can be found with Excel's CORREL function on the Husband and Wife variables.) This is far from a perfect correlation, but it is large enough to warrant using the paired-sample procedure.

In general, the paired-sample procedure is appropriate when the samples are naturally paired in some way *and* there is a reasonably large positive correlation between the pairs. In this case the paired-sample procedure makes more efficient use of the data and generally results in narrower confidence intervals.

Problems

Solutions for problems whose numbers appear within a colored box can be found in the Student Solution Files.

Level A

20. The director of a university's career development center is interested in comparing the starting annual salaries of male and female students who recently graduated from the university and commenced full-time employment. The director has formed pairs of male and female graduates with the same major and similar grade-point averages. Specifically, she has collected a random sample of 50 such pairs and has recorded the starting annual salary of each person. These data are provided in the file **P08_20.xlsx**. Calculate a 95% confidence interval for the mean difference between similar male and female graduates of this university. Interpret your result.

21. A real estate agent has collected a random sample of 75 houses that were recently sold in a suburban community. She is particularly interested in comparing the appraised value and recent selling price of the houses in this particular market. The data are provided in the file **P08_21.xlsx**. Using this sample data, calculate a 95% confidence interval for the mean difference between the appraised values and selling prices of the houses sold in this suburban community. Interpret the confidence interval for the real estate agent.

22. *The Wall Street Journal CEO Compensation Study* analyzed CEO pay from many U.S. companies with fiscal year 2008 revenue of at least $5 billion that filed their proxy statements between October 2008 and March 2009. The data are in the file **P02_30.xlsx**.
    a. Create a new column, Total, that is the sum of columns D and E.
    b. After combining Telecommunications and Technology into a single company type, there are nine company types. For each of these, calculate a 95% confidence interval for the difference between the mean of Total for

that company type and mean of Total for all other company types. Comment on what these nine confidence intervals indicate about CEO pay in different industries.

Level B

23. The file **P02_35.xlsx** contains data from a survey of 500 randomly selected households.
    a. Separate the households in the sample by the location of their residence within the given community. For each of the four locations, use the sample information to calculate a 90% confidence interval for the mean annual income (sum of first income and second income) of all relevant households. Compare these four interval estimates. You might also consider generating box plots of the total income for households in each of the four locations.
    b. Calculate a 90% confidence interval for the difference between the mean annual income of all households in the first (i.e., SW) and second (i.e., NW) sectors of this community. Calculate similar 90% confidence intervals for the differences between the mean annual income levels of all households from all other pairs of locations (i.e., first and third, first and fourth, second and third, second and fourth, and third and fourth). Summarize your findings.

24. A company employs two shifts of workers. Each shift produces a type of gasket where the thickness is the critical dimension. The average thickness and the standard deviation of thickness for shift 1, based on a random sample of 30 gaskets, are 10.53 mm and 0.14 mm. The similar figures for shift 2, based on a random sample of 25 gaskets, are 10.55 mm and 0.17 mm. Let $\mu_1 - \mu_2$ be the mean difference in thickness between shifts 1 and 2.
    a. Calculate a 95% confidence interval for $\mu_1 - \mu_2$.
    b. Based on your answer to part **a**, are you convinced that the gaskets from shift 2 are, on average, wider than those from shift 1? Why or why not?
    c. How would your answers to parts **a** and **b** change if the sample sizes were instead 300 and 250?

8-8 Confidence Interval for the Difference Between Proportions

The final confidence interval we examine is a confidence interval for the difference between two population proportions. As in the previous section, this comparison procedure finds many real applications. Several potential business applications follow.

Applications of Comparisons of Proportions in Business

- When an appliance store is about to have a sale, it sometimes sends selected customers a mailing to notify them of the sale. On other occasions it includes a coupon for 5% off the sale price in these mailings. The store's manager would like to know whether the inclusion of coupons affects the proportion of customers who respond.
- A manufacturing company has two plants that produce identical products. The company wants to know how much the proportion of out-of-spec products differs across the two plants.
- A pharmaceutical company has developed a new over-the-counter sleeping pill. To judge its effectiveness, the company runs an experiment where one set of randomly chosen people takes the new pill and another set takes a placebo. (Neither set knows which type of pill they are taking.) The company judges the effectiveness of the new pill by comparing the proportions of people who fall asleep within a certain amount of time with the new pill and with the placebo.
- An advertising agency would like to check whether men are more likely than women to switch TV channels when a commercial comes on. The agency runs an experiment where the channel-switching behavior of randomly chosen men and women can be monitored, and it collects data on the proportion of viewers who switch channels on at least half of the commercial times. The agency then compares these proportions across gender.

The basic form of analysis in each of these examples is the same as in the two-sample analysis for differences between means. However, instead of comparing two means, we now compare two proportions.

Formally, let p_1 and p_2 represent the two unknown population proportions, and let $\hat{p}_1$ and $\hat{p}_2$ be the two sample proportions, based on samples of sizes n_1 and n_2. Then the point estimate of the difference between proportions, $p_1 - p_2$, is the difference between sample proportions, $\hat{p}_1 - \hat{p}_2$. If the sample sizes are reasonably large, the sampling distribution of $\hat{p}_1 - \hat{p}_2$ is approximately normal.[5]

Therefore, a confidence interval for $p_1 - p_2$ is given by Equation (8.16). Here, the z-multiple is the usual value from the standard normal distribution that cuts off the appropriate probability in each tail (1.96 for a 95% confidence interval, for example). Also, the standard error of $\hat{p}_1 - \hat{p}_2$ is given by Equation (8.17).

Confidence Interval for Difference Between Proportions

$$\hat{p}_1 - \hat{p}_2 \pm z\text{-multiple} \times \text{SE}(\hat{p}_1 - \hat{p}_2) \tag{8.16}$$

Standard Error of Difference Between Sample Proportions

$$\text{SE}(\hat{p}_1 - \hat{p}_2) = \sqrt{\frac{\hat{p}_1(1 - \hat{p}_1)}{n_1} + \frac{\hat{p}_2(1 - \hat{p}_2)}{n_2}} \tag{8.17}$$

The following example illustrates this procedure.

---

5 This large-sample assumption is valid as long as $n_i \hat{p}_i > 5$ and $n_i(1 - \hat{p}_i) > 5$ for $i = 1$ and $i = 2$.

EXAMPLE

8.8 SALES RESPONSE TO COUPONS FOR DISCOUNTS ON APPLIANCES

An appliance store is about to have a big sale. It selects 300 of its best customers and randomly divides them into two sets of 150 customers each. It then mails a notice of the sale to all 300 customers but includes a coupon for an extra 5% off the sale price to the second set of customers only. As the sale progresses, the store keeps track of which of these customers purchase appliances. Some of the resulting data appear in Figure 8.14. (See the file **Coupon Effectiveness.xlsx**.) What can the store's manager conclude about the effectiveness of the coupons?

Figure 8.14 Coupon Data

	A	B	C
1	Customer	Received coupon	Purchased
2	1	No	No
3	2	No	No
4	3	No	No
5	4	No	Yes
6	5	Yes	No
7	6	Yes	Yes
8	7	No	Yes
9	8	Yes	No
10	9	Yes	No
11	10	No	No

Objective

To find a confidence interval for the difference between proportions of customers purchasing appliances with and without 5% discount coupons.

Solution

The solution, using the CI Proportion Diff sheet from the template file, is shown in Figure 8.15. (See the file **Coupon Effectiveness Finished.xlsx**.) You can see that 36.67% of customers who received a coupon purchased something, as

Figure 8.15 Analysis of Coupon Data

	A	B	C	D	E	F	G	H	I
1	Confidence interval for difference between proportions purchased								
2	Confidence level	95%							
3									
4	Received coupon 1	Yes							
5	Received coupon 2	No							
6	Sample size 1	150		=COUNTIF(Data!$B$2:$B$301,B4)					
7	Sample size 2	150		=COUNTIF(Data!$B$2:$B$301,B5)					
8	Number 1 purchased	55		=COUNTIFS(Data!$B$2:$B$301,B4,Data!$C$2:$C$301,"Yes")					
9	Number 2 purchased	35		=COUNTIFS(Data!$B$2:$B$301,B5,Data!$C$2:$C$301,"Yes")					
10	Sample proportion 1	0.367		=B8/B6					
11	Sample proportion 2	0.233		=B9/B7					
12	Sample proportion diff	0.133		=B10–B11					
13	Standard error	0.052		=SQRT(B10*(1–B10)/B6+B11*(1–B11)/B7)					
14	Multiple	1.960		=NORM.S.INV($B$2+(1–$B$2)/2)					
15	Lower limit	0.031		=B12–B14*B13					
16	Upper limit	0.236		=B12+B14*B13					

opposed to only 23.33% of those who didn't receive a coupon. The difference, 36.67% − 23.33% = 13.33% (or 0.1333), is the quantity of interest. Specifically, the sample difference is 13.33%, and the objective is to find a confidence interval for this difference for the entire population. Using Equations (8.16) and (8.17), the relevant confidence interval formulas are spelled out in column D. They show that the confidence interval for the difference between proportions extends from 0.031 to 0.236 (all positive). So there is good reason to conclude that the proportion who purchase is *larger* for those who receive a coupon.

The data for this last example are in "long" form, where there is a Yes/No value for each customer. This means that formulas are required for the counts in cells B6 to B9. However, the data are often in tabular form, where the required counts are given. In this case, you can enter these counts directly into the template.

Problems

Solutions for problems whose numbers appear within a colored box can be found in the Student Solution Files.

Level A

25. A company that advertises on the Web wants to know which search engine its customers prefer as their primary search engine: Google or Bing. Specifically, the company wants to know whether the preference depends on the browser being used. The file **P08_25.xlsx** contains counts of 800 customers' favorite search engine, broken down by the browser used.
    a. Calculate a 95% confidence interval for the difference between two proportions: the proportion of Internet Explorer users whose favorite search engine is Google and the similar proportion of Firefox users.
    b. Repeat part **a**, replacing Google with Bing.
    c. Interpret the results in parts **a** and **b**. Do the search engine preferences seem to depend on the browser used?

26. A market research consultant hired by a leading soft-drink company is interested in estimating the difference between the proportions of female and male consumers who favor the company's low-calorie brand over the leading competitor's low-calorie brand in a particular geographical region. A random sample of 250 consumers from the market under investigation is provided in the file **P08_17.xlsx**. After separating the 250 randomly selected consumers by *gender*, calculate a 95% confidence interval for the difference between these two proportions. Of what value might this interval estimate be to marketing managers at the company?

Level B

27. The file **P02_35.xlsx** contains data from a survey of 500 randomly selected households. Researchers would like to use the available sample information to see whether home ownership rates vary by household *location*. For example, is there a nonzero difference between the proportions of individuals who own their homes (as opposed to those who rent their homes) in households located in the first (i.e., SW) and second (i.e., NW) sectors of this community? Use the given sample to calculate a 95% confidence interval that estimates this difference between proportions in home ownership rates for each pair of locations. Interpret and summarize your results. (The solution should include six confidence intervals.)

28. Continuing from problem 26, marketing managers at the soft-drink company have asked their market research consultant to explore further the difference between the proportions of women and men who prefer drinking their brand over the leading competitor. Specifically, the company's managers would like to know whether the difference between the proportions of female and male consumers who favor their brand varies by the *age* of the consumers. Use the same data as in problem 29 to assess whether estimates of this difference vary across the four given age categories: under 20, between 20 and 40, between 40 and 60, and over 60. Use a 95% confidence level for each of the *four* required confidence intervals. Summarize your findings. What recommendations would you make to the marketing managers in light of your findings?

8-9 Sample Size Selection

In this section we discuss the most widely used methods for achieving a confidence interval of a specified length. Confidence intervals are a function of three things: (1) the data in the sample, (2) the confidence level, and (3) the sample size(s). We briefly discuss the role of the first two in terms of their effect on confidence interval length and then discuss the effect of sample size in more depth.

The data in the sample directly affect the length of a confidence interval through their sample standard deviation(s). It might appear that because of *random* sampling, you have no control over the sample data, but this is not entirely true. In the case of surveys from a population, there are random sampling plans that can reduce the amount of variability in the sample and hence reduce confidence interval length. Indeed, this is the primary reason for using the stratified sampling procedure discussed in the previous chapter.

Variance reduction is also possible in randomized experiments. There is a whole area of statistics called *experimental design* that suggests how to perform experiments to obtain the most information from a given amount of sample data. Although this is often aimed at scientific and medical research, it is also appropriate in business contexts. For example, the automobile dealership in Example 8.7 was wise to use *paired* husband–wife data rather than two independent samples of men and women. The pairing leads to a potential reduction in variability and hence a narrower confidence interval.

The *confidence level* has a clear effect on confidence interval length. As the confidence level increases, the length of the confidence interval increases as well. For example, a 99% confidence interval is always longer than a 95% confidence interval, assuming that they are both based on the same data. However, the confidence level is rarely used to *control* the length of the confidence interval. Instead, the confidence level choice is usually based on convention, and 95% is by far the most commonly used value. In fact, it is the default level built into most software packages.

The most obvious way to control confidence interval length is to choose the sample size(s) appropriately. The rest of this section explains to do this. For each parameter we discuss, the goal is to make the length of a confidence interval sufficiently narrow. Because each confidence interval discussed so far (with the exception of the confidence interval for a standard deviation) is a point estimate plus or minus some quantity, we focus on the "plus or minus" part, called the *half-length* of the interval. The usual approach is to specify the half-length B you would like to obtain. Then you find the sample size(s) necessary to achieve this half-length.

Fundamental Insight

Confidence Interval Length

The length of any confidence interval is influenced by three things: the sample size, the confidence level, and the variability in the population. The confidence level is typically set at 95%, and you have no control over the variability in the population (except possibly by choosing an appropriate experimental design). Therefore, the best way to control confidence interval length is through the choice of the sample size.

We begin with a confidence interval for the mean. From Section 8-3, the relevant formula is

$$\overline{X} \pm t\text{-multiple} \times s/\sqrt{n}$$

The goal is to make the half-length of this interval equal to some prescribed value B. For example, if you want the confidence interval to be of the form $\overline{X} \pm 5$, you use $B = 5$. Actually, it is not possible to achieve this half-length B *exactly*, but you can come close.

By setting

$$t\text{-multiple} \times s/\sqrt{n} = B$$

and solving for n, the appropriate sample size is

$$n = \left(\frac{t\text{-multiple} \times s}{B}\right)^2$$

Unfortunately, sample size selection must be done *before* a sample is observed. Therefore, no value of s is yet available. Also, because the t-multiple depends on n (through the degrees of freedom parameter), it is not clear which t-multiple to use.

The usual solution is to replace s by some reasonable estimate σ_{est} of the population standard deviation σ, and to replace the t-multiple with the corresponding z -multiple from the standard normal distribution. The latter replacement is justified because z-values and t-values are practically equal unless n is very small. The resulting **sample size formula** is given in Equation (8.18). This formula generally results in a noninteger value of n, in which case the practice is to round n up to the next larger integer.

Sample Size Formula for Estimating a Mean

$$n = \left(\frac{z\text{-multiple} \times \sigma_{est}}{B} \right)^2 \qquad (8.18)$$

The following example, an extension of Example 8.1, shows how to implement Equation (8.18).

EXAMPLE

8.9 SAMPLE SIZE SELECTION FOR ESTIMATING REACTION TO A NEW SANDWICH

The fast-food manager in Example 8.1 surveyed 40 customers, each of whom rated a new sandwich on a scale of 1 to 10. Based on the data, a 95% confidence interval for the mean rating of all potential customers extended from 5.739 to 6.761, with a half-length of $(6.761 - 5.739)/2 = 0.511$. How large a sample would be needed to reduce this half-length to approximately 0.3?

Objective

To find the sample size of customers required to achieve a sufficiently narrow confidence interval for the mean rating of the new sandwich.

Solution

Equation (8.18) for n uses three inputs: the z-multiple, which is 1.96 for a 95% confidence level; the prescribed confidence interval half-length B, which is 0.3 for this example; and an estimate σ_{est} of the standard deviation. This final quantity must be guessed, but based on the given sample of size 40, the observed sample standard deviation, 1.597, from Example 8.1 can be used. Therefore, Equation (8.18) yields

$$n = \left(\frac{1.96(1.597)}{0.3} \right)^2 = 108.86$$

which is rounded up to $n = 109$. The claim, then, is that if the manager surveys 109 customers, a 95% confidence interval will have approximate half-length 0.3. Its *exact* half-length will differ slightly from 0.3 because the standard deviation from the sample will almost surely not be exactly 1.597.

Figure 8.16 shows how this formula can be implemented in Excel. It is part of the CI Sample Sizes sheet from the template file. Here, the CEILING function is used to round *up* to the nearest integer. You can see that a sample size of 109 is required.

Figure 8.16 Sample Size for Mean

▲	A	B	C	D	E	F
1	**Confidence interval for a mean**					
2	Confidence level	95%				
3	Half-length of interval	0.30				
4	Std dev (estimate)	1.597				
5	z multiple	1.960		=NORM.S.INV(B2+(1–B2)/2)		
6	Sample size	109		=CEILING((B5*B4/B3)^2,1)		

What if the manager is at the planning stage and doesn't have a "preliminary" sample of size 40? What standard deviation estimate should she use for σ_{est} (because the value 1.597 is no longer available)? This is not an easy question to answer, but because of the role of σ_{est} in Equation (8.18), it is crucial for the determination of n. The manager basically has three choices: (1) she can base her estimate of the standard deviation on historical data, assuming relevant historical data are available; (2) she can take a small preliminary sample to get an estimate of the standard deviation; or (3) she can simply guess a value for the standard deviation. We do not recommend the third option, but there are cases in which it is the only feasible option available.

We have demonstrated the use of Equation (8.18) for a sample mean. In the same way, it can also be used in the paired-sample procedure. In this case the resulting value of n refers to the number of *pairs* that should be included in the sample, and σ_{est} refers to an estimate of the standard deviation of the *differences* (Husband scores minus Wife scores, for example).

The sample-size analysis for the mean carries over with very few changes to other parameters. We discuss three other parameters in this section: a *proportion*, the *difference between two means*, and the *difference between two proportions*. In each case the required confidence interval can be obtained by setting the half-length equal to a prescribed value B and solving for n.

There are two points worth mentioning. First, the confidence interval for the difference between means uses a t-multiple. As was done for the mean, this can be replaced by a z-multiple, which is perfectly acceptable in most situations. Second, the confidence intervals for differences between means or proportions require *two* sample sizes, one for each sample. The formulas below assume that each sample uses the *same* sample size, denoted by n. Each of these formulas is implemented in the CI Sample Sizes sheet of the template file.

The sample size formula for a proportion p is given by Equation (8.19). Here, p_{est} is an estimate of the population proportion p. A *conservative* value of n can be obtained by using $p_{est} = 0.5$. It is conservative in the sense that the sample size obtained by using $p_{est} = 0.5$ guarantees a confidence interval half-length no greater than B, regardless of the true value of p.

Sample Size Formula for Estimating a Proportion

$$n = \left(\frac{z\text{-multiple}}{B}\right)^2 p_{est}(1 - p_{est}) \qquad (8.19)$$

The sample size formula for the difference between means is given by Equation (8.20). Here, σ_{est} is an estimate of the standard deviation of *each* population, where we assume (as in Section 8-7a) that the two populations have a *common* standard deviation σ.

Sample Size Formula for Estimating the Difference Between Means

$$n = 2\left(\frac{z\text{-multiple} \times \sigma_{est}}{B}\right)^2 \qquad \textbf{(8.20)}$$

Finally, the sample size formula for the difference between proportions is given by Equation (8.21). Here, p_{1est} and p_{2est} are estimates of the two unknown population proportions p_1 and p_2. As in the case of a single proportion, a conservative value of n is obtained by using the estimates $p_{1est} = p_{2est} = 0.5$.

Sample Size Formula for Estimating the Difference Between Proportions

$$n = \left(\frac{z\text{-multiple}}{B}\right)^2 [p_{1est}(1 - p_{1est}) + p_{2est}(1 - p_{2est})] \qquad \textbf{(8.21)}$$

EXAMPLE

8.10 SAMPLE SIZE SELECTION FOR ESTIMATING THE PROPORTION WHO HAVE TRIED A NEW SANDWICH

Suppose that the fast-food manager from the previous example wants to estimate the proportion of customers who have tried its new sandwich. She wants a 90% confidence interval for this proportion to have half-length 0.05. For example, if the sample proportion turns out to be 0.42, a 90% confidence interval should be (approximately) 0.42 ± 0.05. How many customers need to be surveyed?

Objective

To find the sample size of customers required to achieve a sufficiently narrow confidence interval for the proportion of customers who have tried the new sandwich.

Solution

If the manager has no idea what the proportion is, she can use $p_{est} = 0.5$ in Equation (8.19) to obtain a conservative value of n. The appropriate z-multiple is now 1.645 because this value cuts off probability 0.05 in each tail of the standard normal distribution. (Remember that we are asking for a 90% confidence level, not the usual 95% level.) Therefore, the required value of n is

$$n = \left(\frac{1.645}{0.05}\right)^2 (0.5)(1 - 0.5) \approx 271$$

On the other hand, if the manager is fairly sure that the proportion who have tried the new sandwich is around 0.3, she can use $p_{est} = 0.3$ instead. The resulting output is shown in Figure 8.17.

These calculations indicate that if you have more specific information about the unknown proportion, you can use a smaller sample size—in this case 228 rather than 271. Also, note

Again, remember that lower confidence levels result in narrower confidence intervals.

Figure 8.17 Sample Size for Proportion

▲	A	B	C	D	E	F	G
8	**Confidence interval for a proportion**						
9	Confidence level	90%					
10	Half-length of interval	0.05					
11	Proportion (estimate)	0.30					
12	z multiple	1.645		=NORM.S.INV(B9+(1–B9)/2)			
13	Sample size	228		=CEILING((B12/B10)^2*B11*(1–B11),1)			

that we selected a 90% confidence level rather than the usual 95% level. There is a trade-off here. Using 90% rather than 95% obviously provides less confidence in the result, but it requires a smaller sample size. You can check that the required sample sizes for a 95% confidence level increase from the current values, 271 and 228, to 385 and 323, respectively.

EXAMPLE

8.11 SAMPLE SIZE SELECTION FOR ANALYZING CUSTOMER COMPLAINTS

A computer company has a customer service center that responds to customers' questions and complaints. The center employs two types of people: those who have had a recent course in dealing with customers (but little actual experience) and those with a lot of experience dealing with customers (but no formal course). The company wants to estimate the difference between these two types of employees in terms of the average number of customer complaints regarding poor service in the last six months. The company plans to obtain information on a randomly selected sample of each type of employee, using equal sample sizes. How many employees should be in each sample to achieve a 95% confidence interval with approximate half-length 2?

Objective

To see how many employees in each experimental group must be sampled to achieve a sufficiently narrow confidence interval for the difference between the mean numbers of complaints.

Solution

Equation (8.20) should be used with z-multiple 1.96 and $B = 2$. However, this formula also requires a value for σ_{est}, an estimate of the (assumed) common standard deviation for each group of employees, and there is no obvious estimate available. The manager might use the following argument. Based on a brief look at complaint data, he believes that some employees receive as few as 6 complaints over a six-month period, whereas others receive as many as 36 (about six per month). Now he can estimate σ_{est} by arguing that all observations are likely to be within three standard deviations of the mean, so that the range of data—minimum to maximum—is about six standard deviations. Therefore, he sets

$$6\sigma_{est} = 36 - 6 = 30$$

and obtains $\sigma_{est} = 5$. Using this value in Equation (8.20), the required sample size is

$$n = 2\left(\frac{1.96(5)}{2}\right)^2 \approx 49$$

The output in Figure 18.18 confirms this value.

Some analysts prefer the estimate

$$4\sigma_{est} = 36 - 6 = 30$$

that is, $\sigma_{est} = 7.5$, arguing that the quoted range (6 to 36) might not include "extreme" values and hence might extend to only *two* standard deviations on either side of the mean. By using this estimate of the standard deviation, you can check that the required sample size increases from 49 to 109. The important point here is that the estimate of the standard deviation can have a dramatic effect on the required sample size. (And don't forget that this size sample must be taken from *each* group of employees.)

Figure 8.18 Sample Size for Difference Between Means

	A	B	C	D	E	F
15	**Confidence interval for the difference between two means**					
16	Confidence level	95%				
17	Half-length of interval	2.00				
18	Common std dev (estimate)	5.00				
19	z multiple	1.960		=NORM.S.INV(B16+(1–B16)/2)		
20	Sample size (each sample)	49		=CEILING(2*(B19*B18/B17)^2,1)		

The following example illustrates what can happen when you ask for extremely accurate confidence intervals.

EXAMPLE

8.12 SAMPLE SIZE SELECTION FOR ANALYZING PROPORTIONS OF OUT-OF-SPEC PRODUCTS

A manufacturing company has two plants that produce identical products. The production supervisor wants to know how much the proportion of out-of-spec products differs across the two plants. He suspects that the proportion of out-of-spec products in each plant is in the range of 3% to 5%, and he wants a 99% confidence interval to have approximate half-length 0.005 (or 0.5%). How many items should he sample from each plant?

Objective

To see how many products in each plant must be sampled to achieve a sufficiently narrow confidence interval for the difference between the proportions of out-of-spec products.

Solution

Equation (8.21) should be used with z-multiple 2.576 (the value that cuts off probability 0.005 in each tail of the standard normal distribution), $B = 0.005$, and $p_{1est} = p_{2est} = 0.05$. The reasoning for the latter is that the supervisor believes each proportion is around 3% to 5%, and the most conservative (largest) sample size corresponds to using the larger 5% value. Then the required sample size is

$$n = \left(\frac{2.576}{0.005}\right)^2 [0.05(0.95) + 0.05(0.95)] \simeq 25{,}213$$

This sample size (from *each* sample) is almost certainly prohibitive, so the supervisor realizes he must lower his goals. One way is to decrease the confidence level, say, from 99% to 95%. Another way is to increase the desired half-length from 0.005 to, say, 0.025. We implemented both of these changes in Figure 8.19. Even now each required sample size is 584. Obviously, narrow confidence intervals for differences between proportions can require large sample sizes.

Figure 8.19 Sample Size for Difference Between Proportions

	A	B	C	D	E	F	G	H
22	**Confidence interval for the difference between two proportions**							
23	Confidence level	95%						
24	Half-length of interval	0.025						
25	Proportion 1 (estimate)	0.050						
26	Proportion 2 (estimate)	0.050						
27	z multiple	1.960		=NORM.S.INV(B23+(1–B23)/2)				
28	Sample size (each sample)	584		=CEILING((B27/B24)^2*(B25*(1–B25)+B26*(1–B26)),1)				

Problems

Solutions for problems whose numbers appear within a colored box can be found in the Student Solution Files.

Level A

29. Elected officials in a California city are preparing the annual budget for their community. They would like to estimate how much their constituents living in this city are typically paying each year in real estate taxes. Given that there are over 100,000 homeowners in this city, the officials have decided to sample a representative subset of taxpayers and study their tax payments.

    a. What sample size is required to generate a 95% confidence interval for the mean annual real estate tax payment with a half-length of $100? Assume that the best estimate of the population standard deviation σ is $535.

    b. If a random sample of the size from part **a** is selected and a 95% confidence interval for the mean is calculated from this sample, will the half-length of the confidence interval be equal to $100? Explain why or why not.

    c. Now suppose that the officials want to construct a 95% confidence interval with a half-length of $75. What sample size is required to achieve this objective? Again, assume that the best estimate of the population standard deviation σ is $535. Explain the difference between this result and the result from part **a**.

30. You have been assigned to determine whether more people prefer Coke or Pepsi. Assume that roughly half the population prefers Coke and half prefers Pepsi. How large a sample do you need to take to ensure that you can estimate, with 95% confidence, the proportion of people preferring Coke within 2% of the actual value?

31. You are trying to estimate the average amount a family spends on food during a year. In the past the standard deviation of the amount a family has spent on food during a year has been approximately $1000. If you want to be 99% sure that you have estimated average family food expenditures within $50, how many families do you need to survey?

32. In past years, approximately 20% of all U.S. families purchased potato chips at least once a month. You are interested in determining the fraction of all U.S. families that currently purchase potato chips at least once a month. How many families must you survey if you want to be 99% sure that your estimate of the relevant proportion is accurate within 2%?

33. Continuing Problem 29, suppose that the officials in this city want to estimate the proportion of taxpayers whose annual real estate tax payments exceed $2000.

    a. What sample size is required to generate a 99% confidence interval for this proportion with a half-length of 0.10? Assume for now that the relevant population proportion p is close to 0.50.

    b. Assume now that officials discover another source that suggests that approximately 30% of all property owners in this community pay more than $2000 annually in real estate taxes. What sample size is now required to generate the 99% confidence interval requested in part **a**?

    c. Why is there a difference between your answers to parts **a** and **b**?

    d. If a random sample of the size from part **a** is selected and a 99% confidence for the proportion is calculated from this sample, will the half-length of the confidence interval be equal to 0.10? Explain why or why not.

Level B

34. Continuing the previous problem, suppose that the officials in this city want to estimate the difference between the proportions, labeled p_1 and p_2, of taxpayers living in neighborhood 1 whose annual real estate tax payments exceed $2000 and the similar proportion for taxpayers living in neighborhood 2.

    a. What sample size (randomly selected from all taxpayers residing in each of neighborhoods 1 and 2) is required to generate a 90% confidence interval for this difference between proportions with a half-length of 0.10? Assume for now that p_1 and p_2 are both close to 0.5.

    b. We assumed that the two population proportions in part **a** are both close to 0.5. Use a two-way data table to find the required (common) sample size when each of the population proportions is allowed to vary from 0.1 to 0.9 in increments of 0.1. Comment on the sensitivity of the required sample size to the magnitudes of the population proportions.

8-10 Conclusion

When you want to estimate a population parameter from sample data, one of the most useful ways to do so is to report a point estimate and a corresponding confidence interval. This confidence interval provides a quick sense of where the true parameter lies. It essentially quantifies the amount of uncertainty in the point estimate. Obviously, narrow confidence intervals are desired. You have seen that the length of a confidence interval is determined by the variability in the data, the confidence level, usually set at 95%, and the sample size(s). Finally, you have also seen how sample size formulas can be used at the planning stage to achieve confidence intervals that are sufficiently narrow.

Summary of Key Terms

TERM	EXPLANATION	EXCEL	PAGES	EQUATION
Confidence interval	An interval that, with a stated level of confidence, captures a population parameter		313	8.1
t distribution	The sampling distribution of the standardized sample mean when the sample standard deviation is used in place of the population standard deviation	T.DIST, T.INV, and other Excel T functions	314	8.2
Confidence level	Percentage (usually 90%, 95%, or 99%) that indicates how confident you are that the confidence interval captures the true population parameter		318	
Confidence interval for a mean	Interval that is likely to capture a population mean	Excel formulas in **Confidence Interval Template.xlsx** file	318	8.4
Confidence interval for a total	Interval that is likely to capture the total of all observations in a population	Excel formulas in **Confidence Interval Template.xlsx** file	324	
Confidence interval for a proportion	Interval that is likely to capture the proportion of all population members that satisfy a specified property	Excel formulas in **Confidence Interval Template.xlsx** file	327	8.10
Confidence interval for a standard deviation	Interval that is likely to capture a population standard deviation	Excel formulas in **Confidence Interval Template.xlsx** file	331	
Chi-square distribution	Skewed distribution useful for estimating standard deviations	CHI.DIST, CHI.INV, and other Excel CHI functions	332	
Confidence interval for difference between means with independent samples	Interval that is likely to capture the difference between two population means when the samples are independent	Excel formulas in **Confidence Interval Template.xlsx** file	335–336	8.13–8.15
Confidence interval for difference between means with paired samples	Interval that is likely to capture the difference between two population means when the samples are paired in a natural way	Excel formulas in **Confidence Interval Template.xlsx** file	339	
Confidence interval for difference between proportions	Interval that is likely to capture the difference between similarly defined proportions from two populations	Excel formulas in **Confidence Interval Template.xlsx** file	342	8.16, 8.17
Sample size formulas	Formulas that specify the sample size(s) required to obtain sufficiently narrow confidence intervals	Excel formulas in **Confidence Interval Template.xlsx** file	345–348	8.18–8.21

Problems

Solutions for problems whose numbers appear within a colored box can be found in the Student Solution Files.

Conceptual Questions

C.1. Under what conditions, if any, is it *not* correct to assume that the sampling distribution of the sample mean is approximately normally distributed?

C.2. When, if ever, is it appropriate to use the standard normal distribution as a substitute for the *t* distribution with $n - 1$ degrees of freedom in estimating a population mean?

C.3. "Assuming that all else remains constant, the length of a confidence interval for a population mean increases whenever the confidence level and sample size increase simultaneously." Is this statement true or false? Explain your choice.

C.4. Assuming all else remains constant, what happens to the length of a 95% confidence interval for a population parameter when the sample size is reduced by half? You can assume that the resulting sample size is still quite large. Justify your answer.

C.5. "The probability is 0.99 that a 99% confidence interval contains the true value of the relevant population parameter." Is this statement true or false? Explain your choice.

C.6. Suppose you have a list of salaries of *all* professional athletes in a given sport in a given year. For example, you might have the salaries of all Major League

Baseball players in 2018. Does it make sense to find a 95% confidence interval for the mean salary? If so, what is the relevant population?

C.7. Suppose that someone proposes a new way to calculate a 95% confidence interval for a mean. This could involve *any* arithmetic on the given data. For example, it *could* say to go out 1.75 interquartile ranges (IQRs) on either side of the median. What would it mean to say that this procedure produces *valid* 95% confidence intervals? How could you use simulation to check whether the procedure produces valid 95% confidence intervals?

C.8. The sample size formula for a confidence interval for the population mean requires an estimate of the population standard deviation. Intuitively, why is this the case? Specifically, why is the required sample size larger if the population standard deviation is larger?

C.9. Suppose a 95% confidence interval for a population mean has been calculated, and it extends from 123.7 to 155.2. Some people would then state, "The probability that the population mean is between 123.7 and 155.2 is 0.95." Why is this, strictly speaking, an invalid statement? How would you rephrase it to make it a valid statement?

C.10. Researchers often create multiple 95% confidence intervals based on a given data set. For example, if the variable of interest is home price and there are five neighborhoods in the population, they might create 10 confidence intervals, one for each difference between mean home prices for a given pair of neighborhoods. (There are 10 pairs.) Can they then conclude that there is 95% confidence that *all* 10 of their confidence intervals will include the corresponding population mean differences? Why or why not?

C.11. Based on a given random sample, suppose you calculate a 95% confidence interval for the following difference: the mean test score for students under 25 years old minus the mean test score for students at least 25 years old, and the confidence interval extends from −14.3 to 1.2. How would you interpret these results? Would you claim that older students, on average, score higher on this test? Would you claim that, on average, it is possible that the younger students score higher on this test?

Level A

35. A sample of 15 quality control managers with more than 20 years experience have an average salary of $68,000 and a sample standard deviation of $19,000.
   a. You can be 95% confident that the mean salary for all quality managers with at least 20 years of experience is between what two numbers? What assumption are you making about the distribution of salaries?
   b. What size sample is needed to ensure that you can estimate the population mean salary of all quality

managers with more than 20 years of experience and have only one chance in 100 of being off by more than $500?

36. Political polls typically sample randomly from the U.S. population to investigate the percentage of voters who favor some candidate or issue. The number of people polled is usually on the order of 1000. Suppose that one such poll asks voters how they feel about the President's handling of environmental issues. The results show that 575 out of the 1280 people polled say they either approve or strongly approve of the President's handling. Find a 95% confidence interval for the proportion of the entire voter population who approve or strongly approve of the President's handling. If the same sample proportion were found in a sample twice as large—that is 1150 out of 2560—how would this affect the confidence interval? How would the confidence interval change if the confidence level were 90% instead of 95%?

37. Referring to the previous problem, you often hear the results of such a poll in the news. In fact, the newscasters usually report something such as, "44.9% of the population approve or strongly approve of the President's handling of the environment. The margin of error in this result is plus or minus 3%." Where does this 3% comes from? If the pollsters want the margin of error to be plus or minus 3%, how does this lead to a sample size of approximately 1000?

38. The widths of 100 elevator rails have been measured. The sample mean and standard deviation of the elevator rails are 2.05 inches and 0.01 inch.
   a. Calculate a 95% confidence interval for the average width of an elevator rail. Do you need to assume that the widths of elevator rails are normally distributed?
   b. How large a sample of elevator rails would you have to measure to ensure that you could estimate, with 95% confidence, the average diameter of an elevator rail within 0.01 inch?

39. You want to determine the percentage of Fortune 500 CEOs who think Indiana University (IU) deserves its current *Business Week* rating. You mail a questionnaire to all 500 CEOs and 100 respond. Exactly half of the respondents believe IU does deserve its ranking.
   a. Calculate a 95% confidence interval for the fraction of Fortune 500 CEOs who believe IU deserves its ranking.
   b. Suppose again that you want to estimate the fraction of Fortune 500 CEOs who believe IU deserves its ranking. Your goal is to have only a 5% chance of having your estimate be in error by more than 0.02. What size sample would you need to take? Is it possible to implement this result?
   c. Is the finite population correct (*fpc*) from the previous chapter relevant here? Why or why not?

40. The SEC requires companies to file annual reports concerning their financial status. It is impossible to audit every account receivable. Suppose an auditor audits a random sample of 49 accounts receivable invoices and finds a sample average of $128 and a sample standard deviation of $53.

   a. Calculate a 99% confidence interval for the mean size of an accounts receivable invoice. Does your answer require the sizes of the accounts receivable invoices to be normally distributed?

   b. How large a sample is required for you to be 99% sure that the estimate of the mean invoice size is accurate within $5?

41. An opinion poll surveyed 900 people and reported that 36% believe a certain governor broke campaign financing laws in his election campaign.

   a. Calculate a 95% confidence interval for the population proportion of people who believe the governor broke campaign financing laws. Does the result of the poll convince you that fewer than 38% of all U.S. citizens favor that viewpoint?

   b. Suppose 10,000 (not 900) people are surveyed and 36% believe that the governor broke campaign financing laws. Would you now be convinced that fewer than 38% of all U.S. citizens favor that viewpoint? Why is your answer different than in part **a**?

   c. How many people would you have to survey to be 99% confident that you can estimate to within 1% the fraction of people who believe the governor broke campaign financing laws?

42. The file **P08_07.xlsx** contains a random sample of 200 service times during the busiest hour of the day at a particular fast-food restaurant. Calculate a 95% confidence interval for each of the following population parameters. Then explain how each result might be useful to the manager of the restaurant in terms of improving service.

   a. The mean service time

   b. The standard deviation of service times

   c. The proportion of service times longer than 90 seconds

   d. The proportion of service times shorter than 60 seconds

43. We know that IQs are normally distributed with a mean of 100 and standard deviation of 15. Suppose you want to verify this, so you take 100 random samples of size four each and, for each sample, calculate a 95% confidence interval for the mean IQ. You expect that approximately 95 of these intervals will contain the true mean IQ (100) and approximately five of these intervals will not contain the true mean. Use simulation in Excel to check whether this is the case.

44. In Section 8-9, we gave a sample size formula for confidence interval estimation of a mean. If the confidence level is 95%, then because the z-multiple is about 2, this formula is essentially

$$n = \frac{4\sigma^2}{B^2}$$

However, this formula is based on the assumption that the sample size n will be small relative to the population size N. If this is *not* the case, the appropriate formula turns out to be

$$n = \frac{N\sigma^2}{\sigma^2 + (N-1)B^2/4}$$

(This is based on the same idea as the finite population correction from the previous chapter.) Now suppose you want to find a 95% confidence interval for a population mean. Based on preliminary (or historical) data, you believe that the population standard deviation is approximately 15. You want the confidence interval to have length 4. That is, you want the confidence interval to be of the form $\overline{X} \pm 2$. What sample size is required if $N = 400$? if $N = 800$? if $N = 10,000$? if $N = 100,000,000$? How would you summarize these findings in words?

45. Ritter Manufacturing Company has kept track of machine hours and overhead costs at its main manufacturing plant for the past 52 weeks. The data appear in the file **P08_45.xlsx**. Ritter has studied these data to understand the relationship between machine hours and overhead costs. Although the relationship is far from perfect, Ritter believes a fairly accurate prediction of overhead costs can be obtained from machine hours through the equation

Estimated Overhead $= 746.5078 + 3.3175*$ Machine Hours

By substituting any observed value of Machine Hours into this equation, Ritter obtains an estimated value of Overhead, which is always somewhat different from the true value of Overhead. The difference is called the prediction error.

   a. Calculate a 95% confidence interval for the mean prediction error. Do the same for the *absolute* prediction error. (For example, the prediction error in week 1, actual overhead minus predicted overhead, is −94.5303. The absolute prediction error is the absolute value, 94.5303.)

   b. A close examination of the data suggests that week 45 is a possible outlier. Illustrate this by creating a box plot of the prediction errors. In what sense is week 45 an outlier? See whether week 45 has much effect on the confidence intervals from part **a** by recalculating these confidence intervals, this time with week 45 deleted. Discuss your findings briefly.

Problems 46 through 55 are related to the data in the file ***P08_46.xlsx***. *This file contains data on 400 customers' orders from ElecMart, a company that sells electronic appliances by mail order. (This same data set was used in Example 3.4 of Chapter 3.) You can consider the data as a random sample from all of ElecMart's orders.*

46. Calculate a 95% confidence interval for the mean total cost of all customer orders. Then do this separately for each of the four regions. Create side-by-side box plots of total cost for the four regions. Does the positive skewness in these box plots invalidate the confidence interval procedure used?

47. Calculate a 95% confidence interval for the proportion of all customers whose order is for more than $100. Then do this separately for each of the three times of day.

48. Calculate a 95% confidence interval for the proportion of all customers whose orders contain at least three items *and* cost at least $100 total.

49. Calculate a 95% confidence interval for the difference between the mean amount of the highest cost item purchased for the High customer category and the similar mean for the Medium customer category. Do the same for the difference between the Medium and Low customer categories. Because of the way these customer categories are defined, you would probably expect these mean differences to be positive. Is this what the data indicate?

50. Of the subpopulation of customers who order in the evening, consider the proportion who are female. Similarly, of the subpopulation of customers who order in the morning, consider the proportion who are female. Calculate a 95% confidence interval for the difference between these two proportions.

51. Calculate a 95% confidence interval for the difference between the following two proportions: the proportion of female customers who order during the evening and the proportion of male customers who order during the evening.

52. Calculate a 95% confidence interval for the difference between the following means: the mean total order cost for West customers and the mean total order cost for Northeast customers. Do the same for the other combinations: West versus Midwest, West versus South, Northeast versus South, Northeast versus Midwest, and South versus Midwest.

53. Calculate a 95% confidence interval for the difference between the mean cost per item for female orders and the similar mean for males.

Level B

54. Let $p_{E,F}$ be the proportion of female orders that are paid for with the ElecMart credit card, and let $p_{E,M}$ be the similar proportion for male orders.

a. Calculate a 95% confidence interval for $p_{E,F}$; for $p_{E,M}$; and for the difference $p_{E,F} - p_{E,M}$.

b. Let $p_{E,F,Wd}$ be the proportion of female orders on weekdays that are paid for with the ElecMart credit card, and let $p_{E,F,We}$ be the similar proportion for weekends. Define $p_{E,M,Wd}$ and $p_{E,M,We}$ similarly for males. Calculate a 95% confidence interval for the difference $(p_{E,F,Wd} - p_{E,M,Wd}) - (p_{E,F,We} - p_{E,M,We})$. Interpret this difference in words. Why might it be of interest to ElecMart?

55. Suppose these 400 orders are a sample of the 4295 orders made during this time period, and suppose 2531 of these orders were placed by females. Calculate a 95% confidence interval for the total paid for all 4295 orders. Do the same for all 2531 orders placed by females. Do the same for all 1764 orders placed by males.

Problems 56 through 61 are related to the data in the file P08_56.xlsx. This file contains data on 91 billings from Rebco, a company that sells plumbing supplies to retailers. You can consider the data as a random sample from all of Rebco's billings.

56. Calculate a 95% confidence interval for the mean amount of all Rebco's bills. Do the same for each customer size separately.

57. Calculate a 95% confidence interval for the mean number of days it takes Rebco's customers (as a combined group) to pay their bills. Do the same for each customer size separately. Create a box plot for the variable Days, based on all 91 billings. Also, create side-by-side box plots for Days for the three separate customer sizes. Do any of these suggest problems with the validity of the confidence intervals?

58. Calculate a 95% confidence interval for the proportion of all large customers who pay bills of at least $1000 at least 15 days after they are billed.

59. Calculate a 95% confidence interval for the proportion of all bills paid within 15 days. Calculate a 95% confidence interval for the difference between the proportion of large customers who pay within 15 days and the similar proportion of medium-size customers. Calculate a 95% confidence interval for the difference between the proportion of medium-size customers who pay within 15 days and the similar proportion of small customers.

60. Suppose a bill is considered late if it is paid after 20 days. In this case its "lateness" is the number of days over 20. For example, a bill paid 23 days after billing has a lateness of 3, whereas a bill paid 18 days after billing has a lateness of 0. Calculate a 95% confidence interval for the mean amount of lateness for all customers. Calculate similar confidence intervals for each customer size separately. Why is the distribution of lateness certainly not normal? Do you think this matters for the validity of the confidence interval?

61. Suppose Rebco can earn interest at the rate of 0.011% daily on excess cash. The company realizes that it could earn extra interest if its customers paid their bills more promptly.

a. Calculate a 95% confidence interval for the mean amount of interest it could gain if each of its customers paid exactly one day more promptly. Calculate similar confidence intervals for each customer class separately.

b. Suppose these 91 billings represent a random sample of the 2792 billings Rebco generates during the year. Calculate a 95% confidence interval for the total amount of extra interest it could gain by getting each of these 2792 billings to be paid two days more promptly.

62. The file **P08_62.xlsx** contains data on the first 100 customers who entered a two-teller bank on Friday. All variables in this file are times, measured in minutes.

   a. Calculate a 95% confidence interval for the mean amount of time a customer spends in service with a teller.

   b. The bank is most interested in mean waiting times because customers get upset when they have to spend a lot of time waiting in line. Use the usual procedure to calculate a 95% confidence interval for the mean waiting time per customer.

   c. Your answer in part **b** is not valid! (It is much too narrow. It makes you believe you have a much more accurate estimate of the mean waiting time than you really have.) We made two implicit assumptions when we stated the confidence interval procedure for a mean: (1) The individual observations come from the same distribution, and (2) the individual observations are probabilistically independent. Why are both of these, particularly (2), violated for the customer waiting times? [*Hint:* For (1), how do the first few customers differ from "typical" customers? For (2), if you are behind someone in line who has to wait a long time, what do you suspect about your own waiting time?]

   d. Following up on assumption (2) of part **c**, you might expect waiting times of successive customers to be *autocorrelated*, that is, correlated with each other. Large waiting times tend to be followed by large waiting times, and small by small. Check this with another template file we have provided for Chapter 12, **Autocorrelation Template.xlsx**. An autocorrelation of a certain lag, say, lag 2, is the correlation in waiting times between a customer and the second customer behind her. Do these successive waiting times appear to be autocorrelated? (A *valid* confidence interval for the mean waiting time takes autocorrelations into account—but it is considerably more difficult to calculate.)

Problems 63 through 65 are related to the data in the file **P08_63.xlsx**. *SoftBus Company sells PC equipment and customized software to small companies to help them manage their day-to-day business activities. Although SoftBus spends time with all customers to understand their needs, the customers are eventually on their own to use the equipment and software intelligently. To understand its customers better, SoftBus recently sent questionnaires to a large number of prospective customers. Key personnel—those who would be using the software—were asked to fill out the questionnaire. Soft-Bus received 82 usable responses, as shown in the file. You can assume that these employees represent a random sample of all of SoftBus's prospective customers.*

63. Create a histogram of the PC Knowledge variable. [Because there are only five possible responses (1–5), this histogram should have only five bars.] Repeat this separately for those who own a PC and those who do not. Then calculate a 95% confidence interval for the mean value of PC Knowledge for all of SoftBus's prospective customers; and of all its prospective customers who own PCs; and of all its prospective customers who do not own PCs. The PC Knowledge variable obviously can't be exactly normally distributed because it has only five possible values. Do you think this invalidates the confidence intervals? Explain your choice.

64. SoftBus believes it can afford to spend much less time with customers who own PCs and score at least 4 on PC Knowledge. Let's call these the "PC-savvy" customers. On the other hand, SoftBus believes it will have to spend a lot of time with customers who do not own a PC and score 2 or less on PC Knowledge. Let's call these the "PC-illiterate" customers.

   a. Calculate a 95% confidence interval for the proportion of all prospective customers who are PC-savvy. Calculate a similar confidence interval for the proportion who are PC-illiterate.

   b. Repeat part **a** twice, once for the subpopulation of customers who have at least 12 years of experience and once for the subpopulation who have less than 12 years of experience.

   c. Again repeat part **a** twice, once for the subpopulation of customers who have no more than a high school diploma and once for the subpopulation who have more than a high school diploma.

   d. Calculate a 95% confidence interval for the difference between two proportions: the proportion of all customers with some college education who are PC-savvy and the similar proportion of all customers with no college education. Repeat this, substituting "PC-savvy" with "PC-illiterate."

   e. Discuss any insights you gain from parts **a** through **d** that might be of interest to SoftBus.

65. Following up on the previous problem, SoftBus believes its profit from each prospective customer depends on the customer's level of PC knowledge. It divides the customers into three classes: PC-savvy, PC-illiterate, and all others (where the first two classes are as defined in the previous problem). As a rough guide, SoftBus figures it can gain profit P_1 from each PC-savvy customer, profit P_3 from each PC-illiterate customer, and profit P_2 from each of the others.

   a. What values of P_1, P_2, and P_3 seem reasonable? For example, would you expect $P_1 < P_2 < P_3$ or the opposite?

   b. Using any reasonable values for P_1, P_2, and P_3, calculate a 95% confidence interval for the mean profit per customer that SoftBus can expect to obtain.

Problems 66 through 69 are related to the data in the file **P08_66.xlsx**. *Comfy Company sells medium-priced* *patio furniture through a mail-order catalog. It has operated primarily in the East but is now expanding to the Southwest. To get off to a good start, it plans to send potential customers a catalog with a discount coupon. However, Comfy is not sure how large a discount is needed to entice customers to buy. It experiments by sending catalogs to selected residents in six cities. Tucson and San Diego receive coupons for 5% off any furniture within the next two months, Phoenix and Santa Fe receive coupons for 10% off, and Riverside and Albuquerque receive coupons for 15% off.*

66. Calculate a 95% confidence interval for the proportion of customers who will purchase at least one item if they receive a coupon for 5% off. Repeat for 10% off and for 15% off.

67. Calculate a 95% confidence interval for the proportion of customers who will purchase at least one item and pay at least $500 total if they receive a coupon for 5% off. Repeat for 10% off and for 15% off.

68. Comfy wonders whether the customers who receive larger discounts are buying more expensive items. Recalling that the value in the Total Paid column is *after* the discount, calculate a 95% confidence interval for the difference between the mean *original price per item* for customers who purchase something with the 5% coupon and the similar mean for customers who purchase something with the 10% coupon. Repeat with 5% and 10% replaced by 10% and 15%. What can you conclude?

69. Comfy wonders whether there are differences across pairs of cities that receive the *same* discount.
    a. Calculate a 95% confidence interval for the difference between the mean amount spent in Tucson and the similar mean in San Diego. (These means should include the "0 purchases.") Repeat this for the difference between Phoenix and Santa Fe and then between Riverside and Albuquerque. Does city appear to make a difference?
    b. Repeat part a, but instead of analyzing differences between means, analyze differences between proportions of customers who purchase something. Does city appear to make a difference?

*Problems 70 through 73 are related to the data in the file **P08_70.xlsx**. Niyaki Company sells Blu-ray disc players through a number of retail stores. On one popular model, there is a standard warranty that covers parts for the first six months and labor for the first year. Customers are always asked whether they wish to purchase an extended service plan for $50 that extends the original warranty two more months—that is, to 30 months on parts and 36 months on service. To get a better understanding of warranty costs, the company has gathered data on 70 Blu-ray units purchased. This data is listed in the Data1 sheet of the file **P08_70.xlsx**. The*

two costs in this sheet (columns D and E) are tracked only for repairs covered by warranty. [Otherwise, the customer bears the cost(s).]

70. Create a histogram of the time until first failure for this type of disc player. Then calculate a 95% confidence interval for the mean time until failure for this type of disc player. Does the shape of the histogram invalidate the confidence interval? Why or why not?

71. Calculate a 95% confidence interval for the proportion of customers who purchase the extended service plan. Calculate a 95% confidence interval for the proportion of all customers who would benefit by purchasing the extended service plan.

72. Calculate a 95% confidence interval for Niyaki's mean net warranty cost per unit sold (net of the $50 paid for the plan for those who purchase it). You can assume that this mean is for the *first* failure only; subsequent failures of the same units are ignored here.

73. This problem follows up on the previous two problems with the data in the Data2 sheet of the file. Here Niyaki did more investigation on the same 70 customers. It tracked subsequent failures and costs (if any) that occurred within the warranty period. (*Note*: Only two customers had three failures within the warranty period, and parts weren't covered for either on the third failure. Also, no one had more than three failures within the warranty period.)
    a. With these data, calculate the confidence intervals requested in the previous two problems.
    b. Suppose that Niyaki sold this Blu-ray model to 12,450 customers during the year. Calculate a 95% confidence interval for its total net cost due to warranties from all of these sales.

74. The file **P08_74.xlsx** contains data on 856 customers who have either tried or not tried a company's new frozen lasagna dinner. (This data set was used in Example 3.5 in Chapter 3.) The manager of the company would like to compare the proportion of customers who have tried the lasagna across various subpopulations. For each of the following, calculate a 95% confidence interval for the difference between the proportions who have tried the lasagna for the two specified subpopulations. Explain briefly how the results help the manager to understand his customers. (*Hint*: One approach is to use pivot tables to get the count data you need.)
    a. Those with weight under 190 versus those with weight at least 190
    b. Females versus males
    c. Those who live alone versus those who do not live alone
    d. Those who live in a home or condo versus those who live in an apartment
    e. Those who live in the South or West versus those who live in the East

f. Those who average five or more trips to the mall per month versus those who average fewer than five trips to the mall per month.

75. The formula for a 95% confidence interval for a mean (sample mean plus or minus approximately two standard errors) is so well-rooted in statistical theory and practice that you might not even consider other possibilities. However, many researchers and even practitioners favor a totally different method of calculating a 95% confidence interval for the mean. It is called the *bootstrap* method. Starting with a sample of size *n*, they generate many "bootstrap samples," calculate the sample mean of each, and report the 2.5 and 97.5 percentiles of these sample means as the endpoints of the confidence interval. Each bootstrap sample is a random sample of size *n*, *with replacement*, from the given data. That is, each member of a bootstrap sample is equally likely to be any of the original *n* data points. Implement this in Excel, starting with the sample of 50 salaries in the file **P08_75.xlsx**. Create at least 100 bootstrap samples. Compare the resulting bootstrap confidence interval with the traditional one. (*Hint*: The bootstrap samples can be generated quickly with a combination of the RANDBETWEEN and VLOOKUP functions.)

CASE 8.1 Harrigan University Admissions

Harrigan University is a liberal arts university in the Midwest that attempts to attract the highest-quality students, especially from its region of the country. It has gathered data on 178 applicants who were accepted by Harrigan (a random sample from all acceptable applicants over the past several years). The data are in the file **C08_01.xlsx**. The variables are as follows:

- Accepted: whether the applicant accepts Harrigan's offer to enroll
- MainRival: whether the applicant enrolls at Harrigan's main rival university
- HSClubs: number of high school clubs applicant served as an officer
- HSSports: number of varsity letters applicant earned
- HSGPA: applicant's high school GPA
- HSPctile: applicant's percentile (in terms of GPA) in his or her graduating class
- HSSize: number of students in applicant's graduating class
- SAT: applicant's combined SAT score
- Combined Score: a combined score for the applicant used by Harrigan to rank applicants

The derivation of the combined score is a closely kept secret by Harrigan, but it is basically a weighted average of the various components of high school performance and SAT. Harrigan is concerned that it is not getting enough of the best students, and worse yet, that many of these best students are going to Harrigan's main rival. Solve the following problems and then, based on your analysis, comment on whether Harrigan appears to have a legitimate concern.

1. Calculate a 95% confidence interval for the proportion of all acceptable applicants who accept Harrigan's invitation to enroll. Do the same for all acceptable applicants with a combined score less than 330, with a combined score between 330 and 375, and then with a combined score greater than 375. (Note that 330 and 375 are approximately the first and third quartiles of the Combined Score variable.)

2. Calculate a 95% confidence interval for the proportion of all acceptable students with a combined score less than the median (356) who choose Harrigan's rival over Harrigan. Do the same for those with a combined score greater than the median.

3. Calculate 95% confidence intervals for the mean combined score, the mean high school GPA, and the mean SAT score of all acceptable students who accept Harrigan's invitation to enroll. Do the same for all acceptable students who choose to enroll elsewhere. Then calculate 95% confidence intervals for the differences between these means, where each difference is a mean for students enrolling at Harrigan minus the similar mean for students enrolling elsewhere.

4. Harrigan is interested (as are most schools) in getting students who are involved in extracurricular activities (clubs and sports). Does it appear to be doing so? Calculate a 95% confidence interval for the proportion of all students who decide to enroll at Harrigan who have been officers of at least two clubs. Calculate a similar confidence interval for those who have earned at least four varsity letters in sports.

5. The combined score Harrigan calculates for each student gives some advantage to students who rank highly in a *large* high school relative to those who rank highly in a small high school. Therefore, Harrigan wonders whether it is relatively more successful in attracting students from large high schools than from small high schools. Calculate one or more confidence intervals for relevant parameters to shed some light on this issue.

CASE 8.2 Employee Retention at D&Y

Demand for systems analysts in the consulting industry is greater than ever. Graduates with a combination of business and computer knowledge—some even from liberal arts programs—are getting great offers from consulting companies. Once these people are hired, they frequently switch from one company to another as competing companies lure them away with even better offers. One consulting company, D&Y, has collected data on a sample of systems analysts with undergraduate degrees they hired several years ago. The data are in the file **C08_02.xlsx**. The variables are as follows:

- Starting Salary: employee's starting salary at D&Y
- On Road Pct: percentage of time employee has spent on the road with clients
- State Univ: whether the employee graduated from State University (D&Y's principal source of recruits)
- CIS Degree: whether the employee majored in Computer Information Systems (CIS) or a similar computer-related area
- Stayed 3 Years: whether the employee stayed at least three years with D&Y
- Tenure: tenure of employee at D&Y (months) if he or she moved before three years

D&Y is trying to learn everything it can about retention of these valuable employees. You can help by solving the following problems and then, based on your analysis, presenting a report to D&Y.

1. Although starting salaries are in a fairly narrow band, D&Y wonders whether they have anything to do with retention.

   a. Calculate a 95% confidence interval for the mean starting salary of all employees who stay at least three years with D&Y. Do the same for those who leave before three years. Then calculate a 95% confidence interval for the difference between these means.

   b. Among all employees whose starting salary is below the median ($37,750), calculate a 95% confidence interval for the proportion who stay with D&Y for at least three years. Do the same for the employees with starting salaries above the median. Then calculate a 95% confidence interval for the difference between these proportions.

2. D&Y wonders whether the percentage of time on the road might influence who stays and who leaves. Repeat the previous problem, but now do the analysis in terms of percentage of time on the road rather than starting salary. (The median percentage of time on the road is 54%.)

3. Find a 95% confidence interval for the mean tenure (in months) of all employees who leave D&Y within three years of being hired. Why is it not possible with the given data to calculate a confidence interval for the mean tenure at D&Y among *all* systems analysts hired by D&Y?

4. State University's students, particularly those in its nationally acclaimed CIS area, have traditionally been among the best of D&Y's recruits. But are they relatively hard to retain? Calculate one or more relevant confidence intervals to help you make an argument one way or the other.

CASE 8.3 Delivery Times at SnowPea Restaurant

The SnowPea Restaurant is a Chinese carryout/delivery restaurant. Most of SnowPea's deliveries are within a 10-mile radius, but it occasionally delivers to customers more than 10 miles away. SnowPea employs a number of delivery people, four of whom are relatively new hires. The restaurant has recently been receiving customer complaints about excessively long delivery times. Therefore, SnowPea has collected data on a random sample of deliveries by its four new delivery people during the peak dinner time. The data are in the file **C08_03.xlsx**. The variables are as follows:

- Deliverer: which person made the delivery
- Prep Time: time from when order was placed until delivery person started driving it to the customer
- Travel Time: time to drive from SnowPea to customer
- Distance: distance (miles) from SnowPea to customer

Solve the following problems and then, based on your analysis, write a report that makes reasonable recommendations to SnowPea management.

1. SnowPea is concerned that one or more of the new delivery people might be slower than others.

   a. Let μ_{Di} and μ_{Ti} be the mean delivery time and mean total time for delivery person i, where the total time is the sum of the delivery and prep times. Calculate 95% confidence intervals for each of these means for each delivery person. Although these might be interesting, give two reasons why they are not really fair measures for comparing the efficiency of the delivery people.

   b. Responding to the criticisms in part **a**, calculate a 95% confidence interval for the mean speed of delivery for each delivery person, where speed is measured as miles per hour during the trip from SnowPea to the customer. Then calculate 95% confidence intervals for the mean difference in speed between each pair of delivery people.

2. SnowPea would like to advertise that it can achieve a total delivery time of no more than M minutes for all customers within a 10-mile radius. On all orders that take more than M minutes, SnowPea will give the customers a $10 certificate on their next purchase.

   a. Assuming for now that the delivery people in the sample are representative of all of SnowPea's delivery people, calculate a 95% confidence interval for the proportion of deliveries (within the 10-mile limit) that will be on time if $M = 25$ minutes; if $M = 30$ minutes; if $M = 35$ minutes.

   b. Suppose SnowPea makes 1000 deliveries within the 10-mile limit. For each of the values of M in part **a**, calculate a 95% confidence interval for the total dollar amount of certificates it will have to pay for being late.

3. The policy in the previous problem is simple to state and simple to administer. However, it is somewhat unfair to customers who live close to SnowPea—they will never get $10 certificates. A fairer, but more complex, policy is the following. SnowPea first analyzes the data and finds that total delivery times can be predicted fairly well with the equation

Predicted Delivery Time $= 14.8 + 2.06*$Distance

(This is based on regression analysis, the topic of Chapters 10 and 11.) Also, most of these predictions are within 5 minutes of the actual delivery times. Therefore, whenever SnowPea receives an order over the phone, it looks up the customer's address in its computerized geographical database to find distance, calculates the predicted delivery time based on this equation, rounds this to the nearest minute, adds 5 minutes, and guarantees this delivery time or else a $10 certificate. It does this for *all* customers, even those beyond the 10-mile limit.

   a. Assuming again that the delivery people in the sample are representative of all of SnowPea's delivery people, calculate a 95% confidence interval for the proportion of all deliveries that will be within the guaranteed total delivery time.

   b. Suppose SnowPea makes 1000 deliveries. Calculate a 95% confidence interval for the total dollar amount of certificates it will have to pay for being late.

CHAPTER 9

Hypothesis Testing

Christophe Pallot/Agence Zoom/Getty Images

OFFICIAL SPONSORS OF THE OLYMPICS

Hypothesis testing is one of the most frequently used tools in academic research, including research in the area of business. Many studies pose interesting questions, stated as hypotheses, and then test these with appropriate statistical analysis of experimental data. One such study is reported in McDaniel and Kinney (1996). They investigate the effectiveness of "ambush marketing" in prominent sports events such as the Olympic Games. Many companies pay significant amounts of money, perhaps $10 million, to become official sponsors of the Olympics. Ambushers are their competitors, who pay no such fees but nevertheless advertise heavily during the Olympics, with the intention of linking their own brand image to the event in the minds of consumers. The question McDaniel and Kinney investigate is whether consumers are confused into thinking that the ambushers are the official sponsors.

At the time of the 1994 Winter Olympics in Lillehammer, Norway, the researchers ran a controlled experiment using 215 subjects ranging in age from 19 to 49 years old. Approximately half of the subjects—the "control group"—viewed a 20-minute tape of a women's skiing event in which several actual commercials for official sponsors in four product categories were interspersed. (The categories were fast food, automobile, credit card, and insurance; the official sponsors were McDonald's, Chrysler, VISA, and John Hancock.) The other half—the "treatment group"—watched the same tape but with commercials for competing ambushers. (The ambushers were Wendy's, Ford, American Express, and Northwestern Mutual, all of which advertised during the 1994 Olympics.) After watching the tape, each subject was asked to fill out a questionnaire. This questionnaire asked subjects to recall the official Olympics sponsors in each product category, to rate their attitudes toward the products, and to state their intentions to purchase the products.

McDaniel and Kinney tested several hypotheses. First, they tested the hypothesis that there would be *no* difference between the control and treatment groups in terms of which products they would recall as official Olympics sponsors. The experimental evidence allowed them to reject this hypothesis decisively. For example, the vast majority of the control group, who watched the McDonald's commercial, recalled McDonald's as being the official sponsor in the fast-food category. But a clear majority of the treatment group, who watched the Wendy's commercial, recalled Wendy's as being the official sponsor in this category. Evidently, Wendy's commercial was compelling.

Because the ultimate objective of commercials is to increase purchases of a company's brand, the researchers also tested the hypothesis that viewers of official sponsor commercials would rate their intent to purchase that brand *higher* than viewers of ambusher commercials would rate their intent to purchase the ambusher brand. After all, isn't this why the official sponsors were paying large fees? However, except for the credit card category, the data did *not* support this hypothesis. VISA viewers did indeed rate their intent to use VISA higher than American Express viewers rated their intent to use American Express. But in the other three product categories, the ambusher brand came out *ahead* of the official brand in terms of intent to purchase (although the differences were not statistically significant).

There are at least two important messages this research should convey to business. First, if a company is going to spend a lot of money to become an official sponsor of an event such as the Olympic Games, it must create a more vivid link in the mind of consumers between its product and the event. Otherwise, the company might be wasting its money. Second, ambush marketing is very possibly a wise strategy. By seeing enough of the ambushers' commercials during the event, consumers get confused into thinking that the ambusher is an official sponsor. In addition, previous research in the area suggests that consumers do not view ambushers negatively for using an ambush strategy.

9-1 Introduction

When you make inferences about a population on the basis of sample data, you can perform the analysis in either of two ways. You can proceed as in the previous chapter, where you calculate a point estimate of a population parameter and then form a confidence interval around this point estimate. In this way you bring no preconceived ideas to the analysis but instead let the data speak for themselves in estimating the parameter's true value.

Hypothesis testing is a form of decision making under uncertainty, where you decide which of two competing hypotheses to accept, based on sample data. However, it is performed in a very specific way, as described in this chapter.

In contrast, an analyst often has a particular theory, or hypothesis, that he or she would like to test. This hypothesis might be that a new packaging design will produce more sales than the current design, that a new drug will have a higher cure rate for a given disease than any drug currently on the market, that people who smoke cigarettes are more susceptible to heart disease than nonsmokers, and so on. In this case the analyst typically collects sample data and checks whether the data provide enough evidence to support the hypothesis.

The hypothesis that the analyst is attempting to prove is called the **alternative hypothesis**. It is also frequently called the **research hypothesis**. The opposite of the alternative hypothesis is called the **null hypothesis**. It usually represents the current thinking or status quo. That is, the null hypothesis is usually the accepted theory that the analyst is trying to *disprove*. In the previous examples the null hypotheses are:

- The new packaging design is no better than the current design.
- The new drug has a cure rate no higher than other drugs on the market.
- Smokers are no more susceptible to heart disease than nonsmokers.

The burden of proof is traditionally on the alternative hypothesis. It is up to the analyst to provide enough evidence in support of the alternative; otherwise, the null hypothesis will continue to be accepted. A slight amount of evidence in favor of the alternative is usually not enough. For example, if a slightly higher percentage of people are cured with a new drug in a sequence of clinical tests, this still might not be enough evidence to warrant introducing the new drug to the market. In general, we reject the null hypothesis—and accept the alternative—only if the results of the hypothesis test are *statistically significant*, a concept explained in this chapter.

> The null hypothesis is usually the current thinking, or status quo. The alternative, or research, hypothesis is usually the hypothesis a researcher wants to prove. The burden of proof is on the alternative hypothesis.

Confidence interval estimation and hypothesis testing use data in much the same way and they often report basically the same results, only from different points of view. There continues to be a debate (largely among academic researchers) over which of these two procedures is more useful. We believe that in a business context, confidence interval estimation is more useful and enlightening than hypothesis testing. However, hypothesis testing continues to be a key aspect of statistical analysis. Indeed, statistical software packages routinely include the elements of standard hypothesis tests in their outputs. You will see this, for example, when you study regression analysis in Chapters 10 and 11. Therefore, it is important to understand the fundamentals of hypothesis testing so that you can interpret this output correctly.

9-2 | Concepts in Hypothesis Testing

Before we plunge into the details of specific hypothesis tests, it is useful to discuss the *concepts* behind hypothesis testing. There are a number of concepts and statistical terms involved, all of which lead eventually to the key concept of statistical significance. The following example provides context for this discussion.

EXAMPLE

9.1 A NEW PIZZA STYLE AT PEPPERONI PIZZA RESTAURANT

The manager of Pepperoni Pizza Restaurant has recently begun experimenting with a new method of baking pepperoni pizzas. He personally believes that the new method produces a better-tasting pizza, but he would like to base the decision whether to switch from the old method to the new method on customer reactions. Therefore, he performs an experiment. For 100 randomly selected customers who order a pepperoni pizza for home delivery, he includes both an old-style and a free new-style pizza in the order. All he asks is that these customers rate the *difference* between pizzas on a −10 to +10 scale, where −10 means that they strongly favor the old style, +10 means they strongly favor the new style, and 0 means they are indifferent between the two styles. Once he gets the ratings from the customers, how should he proceed?

We begin by stating that Example 9.1 is used primarily to explain hypothesis-testing concepts. We do *not* mean to imply that the manager would necessarily use a hypothesis-testing procedure to decide whether to switch from the old method to the new method. First, hypothesis testing does not take costs into account. If the new method of making pizzas uses more expensive cheese, for example, then hypothesis testing would ignore this important aspect of the decision problem. Second, even if the costs of the two pizza-making methods are equivalent, the manager might base his decision on a simple point estimate and possibly a confidence interval. For example, if the sample mean rating is 1.8 and a 95% confidence interval for the mean rating extends from 0.3 to 3.3, this in itself should probably be enough evidence to make the manager switch to the new method.

We come back to these ideas—basically, that hypothesis testing is not necessarily the best procedure to use in a business decision-making context—throughout this chapter. However, with these caveats in mind, we discuss how the manager *might* proceed by using hypothesis testing.

9-2a Null and Alternative Hypotheses

Remember that the hypothesis the manager is trying to prove is called the alternative, or research, hypothesis, whereas the null hypothesis represents the status quo. In this example the manager would like to prove that the new method provides better-tasting pizza, so this becomes the alternative hypothesis. The opposite, that the old-style pizzas are at least as good as the new-style pizzas, becomes the null hypothesis. We assume he judges which of these is true on the basis of the mean rating over the entire customer population, labeled μ. If $\mu \leq 0$, the null hypothesis is true. Otherwise, if $\mu > 0$, the alternative hypothesis is true.

Hypotheses for Pizza Example

Null hypothesis: $\mu \le 0$
Alternative hypothesis: $\mu > 0$
where μ is the mean population rating

Usually, the null hypothesis is labeled H_0 and the alternative hypothesis is labeled H_a. Therefore, in our example they can be specified as $H_0{:}\mu \le 0$ and $H_a{:}\mu > 0$. This is typical. The null and alternative hypotheses divide all possibilities into two nonoverlapping sets, exactly one of which must be true. In our case the mean rating is either less than or equal to 0, or it is positive. Exactly one of these possibilities *must* be true, and the manager's goal is to use sample data to decide which is true.

Traditionally, hypothesis testing has been phrased as a decision-making problem, where an analyst decides either to accept the null hypothesis or reject it, based on the sample evidence. In our example, accepting the null hypothesis means deciding that the new-style pizza is not really better than the old-style pizza and presumably discontinuing the new style. In contrast, rejecting the null hypothesis means deciding that the new-style pizza is indeed better than the old-style pizza and presumably switching to the new style.

9-2b One-Tailed Versus Two-Tailed Tests

The form of the alternative hypothesis can be either *one-tailed* or *two-tailed*, depending on what the analyst is trying to prove. The pizza manager's alternative hypothesis is **one-tailed** because he is hoping to prove that the customers' ratings are, on average, greater than 0. The only sample results that will lead to rejection of the null hypothesis are those in a particular direction, namely, those where the sample mean rating is *positive*. On the other hand, if the manager sets up his rating scale in the reverse order, so that *negative* ratings favor the new-style pizza, the test is still one-tailed, but now only negative sample means lead to rejection of the null hypothesis.

In contrast, a **two-tailed test** is one where results in either of two directions can lead to rejection of the null hypothesis. A slight modification of the pizza example where a two-tailed alternative might be appropriate is the following. Suppose the manager currently uses two methods for producing pepperoni pizzas. He is thinking of discontinuing one of these methods if it appears that customers, on average, favor one method over the other. Therefore, he runs the same experiment as before, but now the hypotheses he tests are $H_0{:}\mu = 0$ versus $H_a{:}\mu \ne 0$, where μ is again the mean rating across the customer population. In this case either a large positive sample mean *or* a large negative sample mean will lead to rejection of the null hypothesis—and presumably to discontinuing one of the production methods.

A one-tailed alternative is one that is supported only by evidence in a single direction.
A two-tailed alternative is one that is supported by evidence in either of two directions.

Once the hypotheses are set up, it is easy to detect whether the test is one-tailed or two-tailed. One-tailed alternatives are phrased in terms of " $>$ " or "$<$" whereas two-tailed alternatives are phrased in terms of "$\ne$". The question is whether to set up hypotheses for a particular problem as one-tailed or two-tailed. There is no *statistical* answer to this question. It depends entirely on what an analyst is trying to prove. If the pizza manager is trying to prove that the new-style pizza is better than the old-style pizza—only results on one side will lead to a switch—a one-tailed alternative is appropriate. However, if he is trying to decide whether to discontinue either of two existing production methods—where results on *either* side will lead to a switch—then a two-tailed alternative is appropriate.

9-2c Types of Errors

Regardless of whether the manager decides to accept or reject the null hypothesis, it *might* be the wrong decision. He might incorrectly reject the null hypothesis when it is true ($\mu \leq 0$), and he might incorrectly accept the null hypothesis when it is false ($\mu > 0$). In the tradition of hypothesis testing, these two types of errors have acquired the names *type I* and *type II errors*. In general, you commit a **type I error** when you incorrectly *reject* a null hypothesis that is true. You commit a **type II error** when you incorrectly *accept* a null hypothesis that is false. These ideas appear graphically in Figure 9.1.

Figure 9.1 Types of Errors in Hypothesis Testing

		Truth	
		H_0 is true	H_a is true
Decision	Reject H_0	Type I error	No error
	Do not reject H_0	No error	Type II error

The pizza manager commits a type I error if he concludes, based on sample evidence, that the new-style pizza is better (and switches to it) when in fact the entire customer population would, on average, favor the old-style pizza. In contrast, he commits a type II error if he concludes, again based on sample evidence, that the new style is no better (and discontinues it) when in fact the entire customer population would, on average, favor the new style.

> Type I error: Switching to new style when it is no better than old style
>
> Type II error: Staying with old style when new style is better

The traditional hypothesis-testing procedure favors caution in terms of rejecting the null hypothesis. The thinking is that if you reject the null hypothesis and it is really true, then you commit a type I error—which is bad. Given this rather conservative way of thinking, you are inclined to accept the null hypothesis unless the sample evidence provides *strong* support for the alternative hypothesis. Unfortunately, you can't have it both ways. When you accept the null hypothesis, you risk committing a type II error.

This is exactly the dilemma the pizza manager faces. If he wants to avoid a type I error (where he switches to the new style but really shouldn't), then he will require fairly convincing evidence from the survey that he *should* switch. If he observes *some* evidence supporting the new style, such as a sample mean rating of $+1.5$, this evidence might not be strong enough to make him switch. However, if he decides not to switch, he risks committing a type II error.

9-2d Significance Level and Rejection Region

The question, then, is how strong the evidence in favor of the alternative hypothesis must be to reject the null hypothesis. Two approaches to this problem are commonly used. In the first, you prescribe the probability of a type I error that you are willing to tolerate. This type I error probability is usually denoted by α and is most commonly set equal to 0.05, although $\alpha = 0.01$ and $\alpha = 0.10$ are also frequently used. The value of α, expressed as a percentage like 5%, is called the **significance level** of the test. Then, given the value of α, you use statistical theory to determine a *rejection region*. If the sample evidence falls in the **rejection region**, you reject the null hypothesis; otherwise, you accept it. The rejection region is chosen precisely so that the probability of a type I error is at most α. Sample evidence that falls into the rejection region is called **statistically significant at the α level**. For example, if $\alpha = 0.05$, the evidence is statistically significant at the 5% level.

> The rejection region is the set of sample data that leads to the rejection of the null hypothesis.
>
> The significance level, α, determines the size of the rejection region. Sample results in the rejection region are called statistically significant at the α level.

It is important to understand the effect of varying α. If α is small, such as 0.01, the probability of a type I error is small. Therefore, a lot of sample evidence in favor of the alternative hypothesis is required before the null hypothesis can be rejected. Equivalently, the rejection region in this case is small. In contrast, when α is larger, such as 0.10, the rejection region is larger, and it is easier to reject the null hypothesis.

9-2e Significance from p-values

A second more popular approach is to avoid the use of a significance level α and instead simply report *how significant* the sample evidence is. This is done by means of a *p*-value. The idea is quite simple—and very important. Suppose in the pizza example that the true mean rating (if it could be observed) is $\mu = 0$. In other words, the customer population, on average, judges the two styles of pizza to be equal. Now suppose the sample mean rating is +2.5. The manager has two options at this point. (Remember that he doesn't know that μ equals 0; he observes only the sample.) He can conclude that (1) the null hypothesis is true—the new-style pizza is not preferred over the old style—and he just observed an unlucky sample, or (2) the null hypothesis is *not* true—customers do prefer the new-style pizza—and the sample he observed is a typical one for such customers.

The *p*-value of the sample quantifies this. The ***p*-value** is the probability of seeing a random sample *at least as extreme as the observed sample*, given that the null hypothesis is true. Here, "extreme" is relative to the null hypothesis. For example, a sample mean rating of +3.5 from the pizza customers is more extreme evidence than a sample mean rating of +2.5. Each provides some evidence against the null hypothesis, but the former provides stronger, more extreme evidence.

> The *p*-value of a sample is the probability of seeing a sample with at least as much evidence in favor of the alternative hypothesis as the sample actually observed. The smaller the *p*-value, the more evidence there is in favor of the alternative hypothesis.

Let's suppose that the pizza manager collects data from the 100 sampled customers and finds that the *p*-value for the sample is 0.03. This means that *if* the entire customer population, on average, judges the two types of pizza to be approximately equal, then only three random samples out of 100 would provide as much evidence in support of the new style as the observed sample. So should he conclude that the null hypothesis is true and he just happened to observe an unlucky sample, or should he conclude that the null hypothesis is *not* true? There is no clear *statistical* answer to this question; it depends on how convinced the manager must be before switching. But we can say in general that smaller *p*-values indicate more evidence in support of the alternative hypothesis. If a *p*-value is sufficiently small, then almost any analyst will conclude that rejecting the null hypothesis (and accepting the alternative) is the more reasonable decision.

How small is a "small" p-value? This is largely a matter of semantics, but Figure 9.2 indicates the attitude of many analysts. A p-value less than 0.01 is regarded as convincing evidence that the alternative hypothesis is true. After all, fewer than one sample out of 100 would provide this much support for the alternative hypothesis if it weren't true. If the p-value is between 0.01 and 0.05, there is strong evidence in favor of the alternative hypothesis. Unless the consequences of making a type I error are really serious, this is typically enough evidence to reject the null hypothesis.

Figure 9.2 Evidence in Favor of the Alternative Hypothesis

The interval between 0.05 and 0.10 is a grayer area. If a researcher is trying to prove a research hypothesis and observes a p-value between 0.05 and 0.10, she will probably be reluctant to publish her results as "proof" of the alternative hypothesis, but she will probably be encouraged to continue her research and collect more sample evidence. Finally, p-values larger than 0.10 are generally interpreted as weak evidence (or no evidence) in support of the alternative.

There is a strong connection between the α-level approach and the p-value approach. Specifically, the null hypothesis can be rejected at a specified significance level α only if the p-value from the sample is less than or equal to α. Equivalently, the sample evidence is statistically significant at a given α level only if its p-value is less than or equal to α. For example, if the p-value from a sample is 0.03, the null hypothesis can be rejected at the 10% and the 5% significance levels but not at the 1% level. The p-value essentially states *how* significant a given sample is.

> *A p-value measures how unlikely the observed sample results are, given that the null hypothesis is true. Therefore, a low p-value provides evidence for rejecting the null hypothesis and accepting the alternative.*

Sample evidence is statistically significant at the α level only if the p-value is less than α.

The advantage of the p-value approach is that you don't have to choose a significance level α ahead of time. Because it is far from obvious what value of α to choose in any particular situation, this is certainly an advantage. Another compelling advantage is that p-values for standard hypothesis tests are included in virtually all statistical software output. In addition, all p-values can be interpreted in basically the same way: A small p-value provides support for the alternative hypothesis.

Fundamental Insight

Key Role of p-values

The single most important thing to remember from this chapter is the role of p-values. This is especially important because p-values are listed in virtually all outputs from statistical software. If a p-value is small, the result is statistically significant, meaning that the null hypothesis can be rejected in favor of the alternative.

Analysts don't always agree on how "small" a p-value needs to be—some say less than 0.01, some say less than 0.05, and some say less than 0.10. But nearly all analysts agree that if a p-value is greater than 0.10, the result is *not* statistically significant, which means that there is not enough evidence to reject the null hypothesis.

9-2f Type II Errors and Power

A type II error occurs when the alternative hypothesis is true but there isn't enough evidence in the sample to reject the null hypothesis. This type of error is traditionally considered less important than a type I error, but it can lead to serious consequences in real situations. For example, in medical trials on a proposed new cancer drug, a type II error occurs if the new drug is really superior to existing drugs but experimental evidence is not sufficiently conclusive to warrant marketing the new drug. For patients suffering from cancer, this is a serious error.

As we stated previously, the alternative hypothesis is typically the hypothesis a researcher wants to prove. If it is in fact true, the researcher wants to be able to reject the null hypothesis and hence avoid a type II error. The probability that she is able to do so is called the **power** of the test—that is, the power is one minus the probability of a type II error. There are several ways to achieve high power, the most obvious of which is to increase sample size. By sampling more members of the population, you are better able to see whether the alternative is really true and hence avoid a type II error if the alternative is indeed true. As in the previous chapter, there are formulas that specify the sample size required to achieve a certain power for a given set of hypotheses. We will not pursue these in this book, but you should be aware that they exist.

> The power of a test is one minus the probability of a type II error. It is the probability of correctly rejecting the null hypothesis when the alternative hypothesis is true.

9-2g Hypothesis Tests and Confidence Intervals

The results of hypothesis tests are often accompanied by confidence intervals. This provides two complementary ways to interpret the data. However, there is a more formal connection between the two, at least for two-tailed tests. Let α be the stated significance level of the test. We will state the connection for the most commonly used level, $\alpha = 0.05$, although it extends to any α value. The connection is that the null hypothesis can be rejected at the 5% significance level if and only if a 95% confidence interval does *not* include the hypothesized value of the parameter.

> When using a confidence interval to perform a two-tailed hypothesis test, reject the null hypothesis if and only if the hypothesized value does *not* lie inside a confidence interval for the parameter.

As an example, consider the test of $H_0: \mu = 0$ versus $H_a: \mu \neq 0$. Suppose a 95% confidence interval for μ extends from 1.35 to 3.42, so that it does *not* include the hypothesized value 0. Then H_0 can be rejected at the 5% significance level, and the p-value from the sample must be less than 0.05. On the other hand, if a 95% confidence interval for μ extends from -1.25 to 2.31 (negative to positive), the null hypothesis cannot be rejected at the 5% significance level, and the p-value must be greater than 0.05.

There is also a correspondence between one-tailed hypothesis tests and *one-sided* confidence intervals, but we will not pursue it here.

9-2h Practical Versus Statistical Significance

We have stated that statistically significant results are those that produce sufficiently small p-values. In other words, **statistically significant results** are those that provide strong evidence in support of the alternative hypothesis. You frequently hear about studies, particularly in the medical sciences, that produce statistically significant results. For example, you might hear that mice injected with one kind of drug develop significantly more cancer cells than mice injected with a second kind of drug.

The point of this section is that such results are not necessarily significant in terms of *importance*. They might be significant only in the statistical sense. An example of what could happen is the following. An education researcher wants to see whether quantitative SAT scores differ, on average, across gender. He sets up the hypotheses $H_0:\mu_M = \mu_F$ versus $H_a:\mu_M \neq \mu_F$, where μ_M and μ_F are the mean quantitative SAT scores for males and females, respectively. He then randomly samples scores from 4000 males and 4000 females and finds the male and female sample averages to be 521 and 524. He also finds that the sample standard deviation for each group is about 50. Based on these numbers, the *p*-value for the sample data turns out to be approximately 0.007. (You will learn how to make this calculation later in the chapter.) Therefore, he claims that the results are significant proof that males do score differently (lower) than females.

If you read these results in a newspaper, your immediate reaction might be, "Who cares?" After all, the difference between 521 and 524 is not very large from a practical point of view. So why does the education researcher get to make his claim? The reasoning is as follows. In all likelihood, the means μ_M and μ_F are not *exactly* equal. There is bound to be some difference between genders over the entire population. If the researcher takes large enough samples—and 4000 is plenty large—he is almost certain to obtain enough evidence to "prove" that the means are not equal. That is, he will almost surely obtain *statistically* significant results. However, the difference he finds, as in the numbers we quoted, might be of little *practical* significance. No one really cares whether females score three points higher or lower than males. If the difference were on the order of 30 to 40 points, then the result would be more interesting.

As this example illustrates, there is always a possibility of statistical significance but not practical significance, especially with large sample sizes. To be fair, we should also mention the opposite case, which typically occurs with small sample sizes. Here the results are sometimes not *statistically* significant even though the truth about the population(s), if it were known, would be of *practical* significance. Let's assume that a medical researcher wants to test whether a new form of treatment produces a higher cure rate for a deadly disease than the best treatment currently on the market. Due to expenses, the researcher is able to run a controlled experiment on only a relatively small number of patients with the disease. Unfortunately, the results of the experiment are inconclusive. They show some evidence that the new treatment works better, but the *p*-value for the test is only 0.25.

In the scientific community these results would not be enough to warrant a switch to the new treatment. However, it is certainly possible that the new treatment, if it were used on a large number of patients, would provide a "significant" improvement in the cure rate—where "significant" now means *practical* significance. In this type of situation, the researcher could easily fail to discover practical significance because the sample sizes are not large enough to detect it statistically.

From here on, when we use the term "significant," we mean *statistically* significant. However, you should always keep the ideas in this section in mind. A statistically significant result is not necessarily of practical importance. Conversely, a result that fails to be statistically significant is not necessarily one that should be ignored.

Extremely large samples can easily lead to statistically significant results that are not practically significant. In contrast, small samples can fail to produce statistically significant results that might indeed be practically significant.

9-3 Hypothesis Tests for a Population Mean

Now that we have covered the general concepts behind hypothesis testing and the principal sampling distributions (in the previous two chapters), the mechanics of hypothesis testing are fairly straightforward. We discuss in some detail how the procedure works for a population mean. Then in later sections we illustrate similar hypothesis tests for other parameters.

As with confidence intervals, the key to the analysis is the sampling distribution of the sample mean. Recall that if you subtract the true mean μ from the sample mean and divide the difference by the standard error $s/\sqrt{n}$, the result has a t distribution with $n - 1$ degrees of freedom. In a hypothesis-testing context, the true mean to use is the null hypothesis value, that is, the borderline value between the null and alternative hypotheses. This value is usually labeled μ_0, where the subscript indicates that it is based on the *null* hypothesis.

To run the test, referred to as the *t test for a population mean*, you calculate the *test statistic* in Equation (9.1). This *t*-value indicates how many standard errors the sample mean is from the null value, μ_0. If the null hypothesis is true, or more specifically, if $\mu = \mu_0$, this test statistic has a t distribution with $n - 1$ degrees of freedom. The *p*-value for the test is the probability beyond the test statistic in both tails (for a two-tailed alternative) or in a single tail (for a one-tailed alternative) of the t distribution.

Test Statistic for Test of Mean

$$t\text{-value} = \frac{\overline{X} - \mu_0}{s/\sqrt{n}} \qquad (9.1)$$

We illustrate the procedure by continuing the pizza manager's problem in Example 9.1.

EXAMPLE

9.1 A NEW PIZZA STYLE AT PEPPERONI PIZZA RESTAURANT (CONTINUED)

Recall that the manager of Pepperoni Pizza Restaurant is running an experiment to test the hypotheses $H_0: \mu \leq 0$ versus $H_a: \mu > 0$, where μ is the mean rating in the entire customer population. Here, each customer rates the difference between an old-style pizza and a new-style pizza on a scale from -10 to $+10$, where negative ratings favor the old style and positive ratings favor the new style. The ratings for 40 randomly selected customers are listed in the file **Pizza Ratings.xlsx**. Is there sufficient evidence from these sample data for the manager to reject H_0?

Objective

To use a one-sample t test to see whether consumers prefer the new-style pizza to the old style.

Solution

As in the previous chapter, we include a template file, **Hypothesis Test Template.xlsx**, to calculate the details of most of the tests in this chapter. It is very similar to the template file for confidence intervals. The results for this example are based on the HT Mean template sheet and appear in Figure 9.3. (See the file **Pizza Ratings Finished.xlsx**.) Again, orange shading is used for the cells you need to fill. The template automatically calculates the formulas in the other cells. In this case, you need to specify the type of test from a dropdown list in cell B2, the hypothesized mean in cell B3, and the sample size, sample mean, and sample standard deviation, based on the data.

From the summary statistics, you can see that the sample mean is $\overline{X} = 2.10$ and the sample standard deviation is $s = 4.717$. This positive sample mean provides some evidence in favor of the alternative hypothesis, but given the rather large value of s, does it provide *enough* evidence to reject H_0?

To run the test, you calculate the test statistic in cell B9, using the borderline null hypothesis value $\mu_0 = 0$, and report how much probability is beyond it in the right tail of the appropriate t distribution. The *right* tail is appropriate because the alternative is one-tailed of the "greater than" variety.

Figure 9.3 Analysis of Pizza Data

	A	B	C	D	E	F	G	H	I
1	**Hypothesis test for population mean**								
2	Type of alternative hypothesis	One-tailed – greater than							
3	Hypothesized mean	0							
4									
5	Sample size	40		=COUNT(Data!B2:B41)					
6	Sample mean	2.100		=AVERAGE(Data!B2:B41)					
7	Sample standard deviation	4.717		=STDEV.S(Data!B2:B41)					
8	Standard error of mean	0.746		=B7/SQRT(B5)					
9	Test statistic (t distribution)	2.816		=(B6–B3)/B8					
10	Degrees of freedom	39		=B5–1					
11	p-value	0.004		=IF(B2="One-tailed – greater than", T.DIST.RT(B9,B10),					
12				IF(B2="One-tailed – less than", T.DIST(B9,B10,TRUE),					
13				T.DIST.2T(ABS(B9),B10)))					

The *t*-value indicates that the sample mean is slightly more than 2.8 standard errors to the right of the null value, 0. Intuitively, this provides a lot of evidence in favor of the alternative—it is quite unlikely to see a sample mean 2.8 standard errors to the right of a "true" mean. The probability beyond this value in the right tail of a *t* distribution with $n - 1 = 39$ degrees of freedom is approximately 0.004, as shown in cell B11. Note how the template uses a nested IF formula for the *p*-value. This covers all three possible types of alternative hypotheses: greater than, less than, or not equal to.

The *p*-value for the test indicates that these sample results would be *very* unlikely if the null hypothesis were true. The manager has two choices at this point. He can conclude that the null hypothesis is true and he obtained a very unlikely sample, or he can conclude that the alternative hypothesis is true—and presumably switch to the new-style pizza. This second conclusion certainly appears to be the more reasonable choice.

Another way of interpreting the results of the test is in terms of traditional significance levels. The null hypothesis can be rejected at the 1% significance level because the *p*-value is less than 0.01. It can also be rejected at the 5% level or the 10% level because the *p*-value is also less than 0.05 and 0.10. Just remember that the *p*-value is the preferred way to report the results because it indicates exactly *how* significant these sample results are.

> ## Fundamental Insight
>
> ### Test Statistics and ρ-values
>
> All hypothesis tests are implemented by calculating a test statistic from the data and seeing how far out this test statistic is in one or both tails of some well-known distribution. The details of this procedure might or might not be included in the output from statistical software, but the *p*-value is always included. The *p*-value specifies the probability in the tail (or tails) beyond the test statistic. In words, it measures how unlikely such an extreme value of the test statistic is if the null hypothesis is true.

Before leaving this example, we ask one last question. Should the manager switch to the new-style pizza on the basis of these sample results? We would probably recommend "yes." There is no indication that the new-style pizza costs any more to make than the old-style pizza, and the sample evidence is fairly convincing that customers, on average, prefer the new-style pizza. Therefore, unless there are reasons for not switching that we haven't mentioned here, we recommend the switch. However, if it costs more to make the new-style pizza (and its price is no higher), hypothesis testing is *not* the best way to perform the decision analysis.

To complete this example, we mention how the result would change if, for whatever reason, the manager wanted to run a two-tailed test. First, the "Two-tailed - not equal to" option would be selected in cell B2. Then the formula for the *p*-value would use the T.DIST.2T function, which would double the *p*-value. This is true in general. The *p*-value for a two-tailed test is always double the *p*-value for a corresponding one-tailed test.

Problems

Solutions for problems whose numbers appear within a colored box can be found in the Student Solution Files.

Level A

1. The file **P09_01.xlsx** contains a random sample of 100 lightbulb lifetimes. The company that produces these lightbulbs wants to know whether it can claim that its lightbulbs typically last more than 1000 burning hours.
a. Identify the null and alternative hypotheses.
b. Can this lightbulb manufacturer claim that its lightbulbs typically last more than 1000 hours at the 5% significance level? What about at the 1% significance level? Explain your answers.

2. A manufacturer is interested in determining whether it can claim that the boxes of detergent it sells contain, on average, more than 500 grams of detergent. The firm selects a random sample of 100 boxes and records the amount of detergent (in grams) in each box. The data are provided in the file **P09_02.xlsx**.
a. Identify the null and alternative hypotheses.
b. Is there statistical support for the manufacturer's claim? Explain.

3. A producer of steel cables wants to know whether the steel cables it produces have an average breaking strength of 5000 pounds. An average breaking strength of less than 5000 pounds would not be adequate, and to produce steel cables with an average breaking strength in excess of 5000 pounds would unnecessarily increase production costs. The producer collects a random sample of 64 steel cable pieces. The breaking strength for each of these cable pieces is recorded in the file **P09_03.xlsx**.
a. Identify the null and alternative hypotheses.
b. Using a 5% significance level, what statistical conclusion can the producer reach regarding the average breaking strength of its steel cables? Would the conclusion be any different at the 1% level? Explain your answers.

4. A U.S. Navy recruiting center knows from past experience that the heights of its recruits have traditionally been normally distributed with mean 69 inches. The recruiting center wants to test the claim that the average height of this year's recruits is greater than 69 inches. To do this, recruiting personnel take a random sample of 64 recruits from this year and record their heights. The data are provided in the file **P09_04.xlsx**.
a. Identify the null and alternative hypotheses.
b. On the basis of the available sample information, do the recruiters find support for the given claim at the 5% significance level? Explain.
c. Use the sample data to calculate a 95% confidence interval for the average height of this year's recruits.

Based on this confidence interval, what conclusion should recruiting personnel reach regarding the given claim?

5. Suppose you wish to test $H_0: \mu \leq 10$ versus $H_a: \mu > 10$ at the $\alpha = 0.05$ significance level. Furthermore, suppose that you observe values of the sample mean and sample standard deviation when $n = 40$ that do *not* lead to the rejection of H_0. Is it true that you might reject H_0 if you observed the same values of the sample mean and sample standard deviation from a sample with $n > 40$? Why or why not?

Level B

6. A study is performed in a large southern town to determine whether the average amount spent on food per four-person family in the town is significantly different from the national average. A random sample of the weekly grocery bills of two-person families in this town is given in the file **P09_06.xlsx**. Assume the national average amount spent on food for a four-person family is $150.
a. Identify the null and alternative hypotheses.
b. Is the sample evidence statistically significant? If so, at what significance levels can you reject the null hypothesis?
c. For which values of the sample mean (i.e., average weekly grocery bill) would you reject the null hypothesis at the 1% significance level? For which values of the sample mean would you reject the null hypothesis at the 10% level?

7. An aircraft manufacturer needs to buy aluminum sheets with an average thickness of 0.05 inch. The manufacturer knows that significantly thinner sheets would be unsafe and considerably thicker sheets would be too heavy. A random sample of 100 sheets from a potential supplier is collected. The thickness of each sheet in this sample is measured (in inches) and recorded in the file **P09_07.xlsx**.
a. Identify the null and alternative hypotheses.
b. Based on the results of an appropriate hypothesis test, should the aircraft manufacturer buy aluminum sheets from this supplier? Explain why or why not.
c. For which values of the sample mean (i.e., average thickness) would the aircraft manufacturer decide to buy sheets from this supplier? Assume a significance level of 5% in answering this question.

8. Suppose you observe a random sample of size n from a normally distributed population. If you are able to reject $H_0: \mu = \mu_0$ in favor of a two-tailed alternative hypothesis at the 10% significance level, is it true that you can definitely reject H_0 in favor of the appropriate one-tailed alternative at the 5% significance level? Why or why not?

9-4 Hypothesis Tests for Other Parameters

Just as we developed confidence intervals for a variety of parameters, we can develop hypothesis tests for other parameters. They are based on the same sampling distributions discussed in the previous chapter, and they are run and interpreted exactly as the tests for the mean in the previous section. In each case the sample data are used to calculate a test statistic that has a well-known sampling distribution. Then a corresponding p-value measures the support for the alternative hypothesis. Beyond this, only the details change, as we illustrate in this section. Fortunately, the relevant sheets from the template file take care of most of these details.

9-4a Hypothesis Test for a Population Proportion

To test a population proportion p, recall that the sample proportion $\hat{p}$ has a sampling distribution that is approximately normal when the sample size is reasonably large. Specifically, the distribution of the standardized value

$$\frac{\hat{p} - p}{\sqrt{p(1 - p)/n}}$$

is approximately normal with mean 0 and standard deviation 1. This leads to the following **z test for a population proportion**.

Let p_0 be the borderline value of p between the null and alternative hypotheses. Then p_0 is substituted for p to obtain the test statistic in Equation (9.2). The p-value of the test is found by seeing how much probability is beyond this test statistic in the tail (or tails) of the standard normal distribution.[1] A rule of thumb for checking the large-sample assumption of this test is to check whether $np_0 > 5$ and $n(1 - p_0) > 5$.

Test Statistic for Test of Proportion

$$z\text{-value} = \frac{\hat{p} - p_0}{\sqrt{p_0(1 - p_0)/n}} \qquad (9.2)$$

The following example illustrates this test of proportion.

EXAMPLE

9.2 CUSTOMER COMPLAINTS AT WALPOLE APPLIANCE COMPANY

Walpole Appliance Company has a customer service department that handles customer questions and complaints. This department's processes are set up to respond quickly and accurately to customers who phone in or email their concerns. However, there is a sizable minority of customers who prefer to write letters. Traditionally, the customer service department has not been very efficient in responding to these customers.

Letter writers first receive an email asking them to call customer service (which is exactly what letter writers wanted to avoid in the first place), and when they do call, the customer service representative who answers the phone typically has no knowledge of the customer's problem. As a result, the department manager estimates that 15% of letter writers have not obtained a satisfactory response within 30 days of the time their letters were first received. The manager's goal is to reduce this value by at least half, that is, to 7.5% or less.

---

1 Do not confuse the unknown proportion p with the p-value of the test. They are logically different concepts and just happen, by tradition, to share the same letter p.

To do so, she changes the process for responding to letter writers. Under the new process, these customers now receive a prompt and courteous form letter that responds to their problem. (This is possible because the vast majority of concerns can be addressed by one of several form letters.) Each form letter states that if the customer still has problems, he or she can call the department. The manager also files the original letters so that if customers do call back, the representative who answers will be able to find their letters quickly and respond intelligently. With this new process in place, the manager has tracked 400 letter writers and has found that only 23 of them are classified as "unsatisfied" after a 30-day period. Does it appear that the manager has achieved her goal?

Objective

To use a test for a proportion to see whether the new process of responding to complaint letters results in an acceptably low proportion of unsatisfied customers.

Solution

The manager's goal is to reduce the proportion of unsatisfied customers after 30 days from 0.15 to 0.075 or less. Because the burden of proof is on her to "prove" that she has accomplished this goal, we set up the hypotheses as $H_0:p \geq 0.075$ versus $H_a:p < 0.075$, where p is the proportion of all letter writers who are still unsatisfied after 30 days. The sample proportion she has observed is $\hat{p} = 23/400 = 0.0575$. This is obviously less than 0.075, but is it *enough* less to reject the null hypothesis?

The test can be performed with the HT Proportion sheet from the template file, as shown in Figure 9.4. See the file **Customer Complaints Finished.xlsx.** Note that the standard error and z-value test statistic are calculated according to Equation (9.2), and the p-value is the probability to the *left* of the test statistic, calculated with the NORM.S.DIST function.

Figure 9.4 Analysis of Customer Complaints

	A	B	C	D	E	F	G	H	I
1	**Hypothesis test for proportion**								
2	Type of alternative hypothesis	One-tailed – less than							
3	Hypothesized proportion	0.075							
4									
5	Sample size	400		=Data!B6					
6	Number with property of interest	23		=Data!B4					
7	Sample proportion	0.058		=B6/B5					
8	Standard error of proportion	0.013		=SQRT(B3*(1–B3)/B5)					
9	Test statistic (z value)	–1.329		=(B7–B3)/B8					
10	p-value	0.092		=IF(B2="One-tailed – greater than",1–NORM.S.DIST(B9,TRUE),					
11				IF(B2="One-tailed – less than",NORM.S.DIST(B9,TRUE),					
12				2*(1–NORM.S.DIST(ABS(B9),TRUE))))					

The p-value might not be as low as you expected—or as low as the manager would like. In spite of the fact that the sample proportion appears to be well below the target proportion of 0.075, the evidence in support of the alternative hypothesis is not overwhelming. In statistical terminology, the results are significant at the 10% level, but not at the 5% or 1% levels.

The last sheet of the finished file (not shown here) calculates a 95% confidence interval for the unknown proportion p. This confidence interval extends from 0.035 to 0.080. It includes the target value, 0.075, but just barely. In this sense it also provides some support for the argument that the manager has indeed achieved her goal.[2]

Analysts might disagree on whether a hypothesis test or a confidence interval is the more appropriate way to present these results. However, we see them as complementary and do not necessarily favor one over the other. The bottom line is that they both provide some, but not totally conclusive, evidence that the manager has achieved her goal.

---

2 If you are very observant, you will note that the standard error in cell E7 for the hypothesis test uses the target proportion 0.075. In contrast, the standard error for the confidence interval uses the sample proportion 0.0575. The sampling distribution for a hypothesis test always uses the borderline value between H_0 and H_a. But because confidence intervals are not connected to any hypotheses, their standard errors must rely on sample data. In most cases, however, the two standard errors are practically the same.

9-4b Hypothesis Tests for Difference Between Population Means

This comparison problem—comparing two population means—is one of the most important problems analyzed with statistical methods. It can be analyzed with confidence intervals, hypothesis tests, or both.

We now discuss the comparison problem, where the **difference between two population means** is tested. As in the previous chapter, the form of the analysis depends on whether the two samples are independent or paired. For variety, we begin with the paired case.

If the samples are paired, then the test, referred to as the *t* **test for difference between means from paired samples**, proceeds exactly as in Section 9-3, using the differences as the single variable of analysis. That is, if $\overline{D}$ is the sample mean difference between *n* pairs, D_0 is the hypothesized difference (the borderline value between H_0 and H_a), and s_D is the sample standard deviation of the differences, then the test is based on the test statistic in Equation (9.3). If D_0 is the true mean difference, this test statistic has a *t* distribution with $n - 1$ degrees of freedom. The validity of the test also requires that *n* be reasonably large and/or the population of *differences* be approximately normally distributed.

Test Statistic for Paired Samples Test of Difference Between Means

$$t\text{-value} = \frac{\overline{D} - D_0}{s_D / \sqrt{n}} \tag{9.3}$$

In contrast, if the samples are independent, the test is referred to as the *t* **test for difference between means from independent samples**. If the population standard deviations are equal, the two-sample theory discussed in Section 8-7 is relevant. It leads to the test statistic in Equation (9.5). Here, $\overline{X}_1$ and $\overline{X}_2$ are the two sample means, D_0 is the hypothesized difference, n_1 and n_2 are the sample sizes, and s_p is the same pooled estimate of the common population standard deviation as in the previous chapter:

Estimate of Common Standard Deviation

$$s_p = \sqrt{\frac{(n_1 - 1)s_1^2 + (n_2 - 1)s_2^2}{n_1 + n_2 - 2}} \tag{9.4}$$

If D_0 is the true mean difference, this test statistic has a *t* distribution with $n_1 + n_2 - 2$ degrees of freedom. The validity of this test again requires that the sample sizes be reasonably large and/or the populations be approximately normally distributed.

Test Statistic for Independent Samples Test of Difference Between Means

$$t\text{-value} = \frac{(\overline{X}_1 - \overline{X}_2) - D_0}{s_p \sqrt{1/n_1 + 1/n_2}} \tag{9.5}$$

The following example illustrates the paired-sample *t* test.

EXAMPLE

9.3 MEASURING THE EFFECTS OF TRADITIONAL AND NEW STYLES OF SOFT-DRINK CANS

Beer and soft-drink companies have become very concerned about the style of their cans. There are cans with fluted and embossed sides and cans with six-color graphics and holograms. Coca-Cola even introduced a contoured can, shaped like the old-fashioned Coke bottle minus the neck. Evidently, these companies believe the style of the can makes a difference to consumers, which presumably translates into higher sales.

Assume that a soft-drink company is considering a style change to its current can, which has been the company's trademark for many years. To determine whether this new style is popular with consumers, the company runs a number of focus group sessions around the country. At each of these sessions, randomly selected consumers are allowed to examine the new and traditional styles, exchange ideas, and offer their opinions. Eventually, they fill out a form where, among other questions, they are asked to respond to the following items, each on a scale of 1 to 7, 7 being the best:

• Rate the attractiveness of the traditional-style can (AO).
• Rate the attractiveness of the new-style can (AN).
• Rate the likelihood that you would buy the product with the traditional-style can (WBO).
• Rate the likelihood that you would buy the product with the new-style can (WBN).

(A and WB stand for "attractiveness" and "would buy," and O and N stand for "old" and "new.") The data are listed in the file **Soft-Drink Cans.xlsx**. What can the company conclude from these data? Are hypothesis tests appropriate?

Objective

To use paired-sample t tests for differences between means to see whether consumers rate the attractiveness, and their likelihood to purchase, higher for a new-style can than for the traditional-style can.

Solution

First, it is a good idea to examine summary statistics for the data. The averages from each survey item are shown at the bottom of Figure 9.5. They indicate some support for the new-style can. Also, you might expect the ratings for a given consumer to be correlated. This turns out to be the case, as shown by the relatively large positive correlations in Figure 9.5. These large positive correlations indicate that if you want to examine differences between survey items, a paired-sample procedure will make the most efficient use of the data. Of course, a paired-sample procedure also makes sense because each consumer answers each item on the form. If this is confusing, think about the following alternative setup, where there are four *separate* groups of consumers. The first group responds to item 1 only, the second group responds to item 2 only, and so on. Then the responses to the various items are in no way paired, and an *independent-sample* procedure would be used instead. However, this experimental design is not as efficient as the paired design in terms of making the best use of a given amount of data.

Figure 9.5 Data and Summary Measures for Soft-Drink Cans

	A	B	C	D	E
1	Consumer	AO	AN	WBO	WBN
2	1	5	7	4	1
3	2	7	7	6	6
4	3	6	7	7	6
5	4	1	3	1	1
6	5	3	4	1	1
179	178	5	4	4	3
180	179	3	4	1	3
181	180	3	5	6	7
182					
183	Averages	4.41	4.95	3.86	4.34
184					
185	Correlations	AO	AN	WBO	WBN
186	AO	1.000	0.740	0.746	0.594
187	AN	0.740	1.000	0.595	0.401
188	WBO	0.746	0.595	1.000	0.774
189	WBN	0.594	0.401	0.774	1.000

There are several differences of interest. The two most obvious are the difference between the attractiveness ratings of the two styles and the difference between the likelihoods of buying the two styles—that is, column B minus column C and column D minus column E. A third difference of interest is the difference between the attractiveness ratings of the new style and the likelihoods of buying the new can—that is, column C minus column E. This difference indicates whether *perceptions* of the new-style can are likely to translate into actual *sales*. Finally, a fourth difference that might be of interest is the difference between the third difference (column C minus column E) and the similar difference for the old style (column B minus column D). This checks whether the translation of perceptions into sales is any different for the two styles of cans.

All of these differences appear next to the original data in Figure 9.6.

Figure 9.6 Original and Difference Variables for Soft-Drink Can Data

	A	B	C	D	E	F	G	H	I	J
1	Consumer	AO	AN	WBO	WBN	AO–AN	WBO–WBN	AN–WBN	AO–WBO	(AN–WBN)–(AO–WBO)
2	1	5	7	4	1	–2	3	6	1	5
3	2	7	7	6	6	0	0	1	1	0
4	3	6	7	7	6	–1	1	1	–1	2
5	4	1	3	1	1	–2	0	2	0	2
6	5	3	4	1	1	–1	0	3	2	1
179	178	5	4	4	3	1	1	1	1	0
180	179	3	4	1	3	–1	–2	1	2	–1
181	180	3	5	6	7	–2	–1	–2	–3	1

For each of the differences, you can test the mean difference over all potential consumers with a paired-sample analysis. (You actually run the one-sample procedure on the difference variables.) Exactly as in the previous chapter, each difference variable is treated as a *single* sample and the same t test as in Section 9-3 is run on this sample. In each case the hypothesized difference, D_0, is 0. The only question is whether to run one-tailed or two-tailed tests. This depends on the prior beliefs of the company. We have run them all as two-tailed tests. In any case, you can change two-tailed p-values to one-tailed p-values by dividing by 2.

The results for all five differences appear in Figure 9.7. The calculations were made with the HT Paired Mean Diff sheet from the template file and were then rearranged to all be on the same sheet. Here are some comments on the results.

Figure 9.7 Analysis of Differences

	A	B	C	D	E	F
1	**Hypothesis test for difference**	AO–AN	WBO–WBN	AN–WBN	AO–WBO	(AN–WBN)–(AO–WBO)
2	Type of alternative hypothesis	Two-tailed – not equal to	Two-tailed – not equal to	Two-tailed – not equal to	Two-tailed – not equal to	Two-tailed – not equal to
3	Hypothesized difference	0	0	0	0	0
4						
5	Sample size	180	180	180	180	180
6	Sample mean diff	–0.539	–0.478	0.611	0.550	0.061
7	Sample std dev of diff	1.351	1.347	2.213	1.309	2.045
8	Standard error	0.101	0.100	0.165	0.098	0.152
9	Test statistic (t-value)	–5.351	–4.758	3.705	5.639	0.401
10	Degrees of freedom	179	179	179	179	179
11	p-value	0.000	0.000	0.000	0.000	0.689

- From the output for AO − AN, there is overwhelming evidence that consumers, on average, rate the attractiveness of the new design higher than the attractiveness of the current design. The t-distributed test statistic is −5.351, calculated as

$$\frac{-0.539 - 0}{0.101} = -5.351$$

The corresponding p-value for a two-tailed test of the mean difference is (to four decimal places) 0.0000. A 99% confidence interval (not shown) for the mean difference extends from −0.801 to −0.277. Note that this 99% confidence interval does *not* include the hypothesized value 0. This is consistent with the fact that the two-tailed p-value is less than 0.01. (Recall the relationship between confidence intervals and two-tailed hypothesis tests from Section 9-2g.)

- The results are basically the same for the difference between consumers' likelihoods of buying the product with the two styles, WBO − WBN. Again, consumers are definitely more likely, on average, to buy the product with the new-style can. A 99% confidence interval for the mean difference (not shown) extends from −0.739 to −0.216, which is again all negative.

- The company's hypothesis that consumers' ratings of attractiveness of the new-style can are greater, on average, than their likelihoods of buying the product with this style can is confirmed. In this case, the relevant difference is AN − WBN. Although the results are shown for a two-tailed test, the results for a one-tailed "greater than" test are easy to infer. You simply divide the *p*-value in cell D11 by 2.
- There is no evidence that the difference between attractiveness ratings and the likelihood of buying is any different for the new-style can than for the current-style can. Here the relevant difference is (AN − WBN) − (AO − WBO). The test statistic for a two-tailed test of this difference is 0.401 and the corresponding *p*-value, 0.689, isn't even close to any of this traditional significance levels. Furthermore, a 99% confidence interval for this mean difference (not shown) extends from a negative value, −0.336, to a positive value, 0.458.

These results are further supported by histograms of the difference variables, such as those shown in Figures 9.8 and 9.9. (Box plots could be used instead.) The histogram in Figure 9.8 shows many more negative differences than positive differences. This leads to the large negative test statistic and the all-negative confidence interval. In contrast, the histogram in Figure 9.9 is almost perfectly symmetric around 0 and hence provides no evidence that this mean difference is *not* zero.

Figure 9.8 Histogram of the AO-AN Variable

Figure 9.9 Histogram of the (AN-WBN)- (AO-WBO) Variable

This example illustrates once again how hypothesis tests and confidence intervals provide complementary information, although the confidence intervals are arguably more useful here. The hypothesis test for the first difference, for example, shows that the average rating for the new style is undoubtedly larger than for the current style. This is useful information, but it is even more useful to know *how much* larger the average for the new style is. A confidence interval provides this information.

We conclude this example by recalling the distinction between practical significance and statistical significance. Due to the extremely low *p*-values, the results in columns B to E of Figure 9.7, leave no doubt as to statistical significance. But this could be due to the large sample size. That is, if the true mean differences are even slightly different from 0, large samples will almost surely discover this and report small *p*-values. The soft-drink company, on the other hand, is more interested in knowing whether the observed differences are of any practical importance. This is not a statistical question. It is a question of what differences are important for the *business*. We suspect that the company would indeed be quite impressed with the observed differences in the sample—and might very well switch to the new-style can.

> ### Fundamental Insight
>
> #### Significance and Sample Size in Tests of Differences
>
> The contrast between statistical and practical significance is especially evident in tests of differences between means. If the sample sizes are relatively small, it is likely that no *statistical* significance will be found, even though the real difference between means, if they could be estimated more accurately with more data, might be *practically* significant. On the other hand, if the sample sizes are very large, then just about any difference between sample means is likely to be *statistically* significant, even though the real difference between means might be of no *practical* importance.

The following example illustrates the *independent* two-sample *t* test. You can tell that a paired-sample procedure is not appropriate because there is no attempt to match the observations in the two samples in any way. Indeed, this is obvious because the sample sizes are not equal.

EXAMPLE

9.4 PRODUCTIVITY DUE TO EXERCISE AT INFORMATRIX SOFTWARE COMPANY

Many companies have installed exercise facilities at their plants. The goal is not only to provide a bonus (free use of exercise equipment) for their employees, but to make the employees more productive by getting them in better shape. One such (fictional) company, Informatrix Software Company, installed exercise equipment on site a year ago. To check whether it has had a beneficial effect on employee productivity, the company gathered data on a sample of 80 randomly chosen employees, all between the ages of 30 and 40 and all with similar job titles and duties. The company observed which of these employees use the exercise facility regularly (at least three times per week on average). This group included 23 of the 80 employees in the sample. The other 57 employees were asked whether they exercise regularly elsewhere, and 6 of them replied that they do. The remaining 51, who admitted to being nonexercisers, were then compared to the combined group of 29 exercisers.

The comparison was based on the employees' productivity over the year, as rated by their supervisors. Each rating was on a scale of 1 to 25, 25 being the best. To increase the validity of the study, neither the employees nor the supervisors were told that a study was in progress. In particular, the supervisors did not know which employees were involved in the study or which were exercisers. The data from the study are listed in the file **Exercise & Productivity.xlsx**. It includes a Yes/No column on whether the person is an exerciser and a column of ratings. Do these data support the company's (alternative) hypothesis that exercisers outperform nonexercisers on average? Can the company infer that any difference between the two groups is due to exercise?

Objective

To use a two-sample *t* test for the difference between means to see whether regular exercise increases worker productivity.

Solution

To see whether there is any indication of a difference between the two groups, a good first step is to create side-by-side plots of the Rating variable. These appear in Figure 9.10.

Side-by-side box plots are typically a good way to begin the analysis when comparing two populations.

Figure 9.10 Box Plots for
Exercise Data

Box Plot of Ratings by Exerciser

Although there is a great deal of overlap between the two distributions, the distribution for the exercisers is somewhat higher than that for the nonexercisers. Also, the variances of the two distributions appear to be roughly the same, although there is slightly more variation in the nonexerciser distribution.

A formal test of the mean difference uses the hypotheses $H_0: \mu_1 - \mu_2 \leq 0$ versus $H_a: \mu_1 - \mu_2 > 0$, where μ_1 and μ_2 are the mean ratings for the exerciser and nonexerciser populations. It makes sense to use a one-tailed test, with the alternative of the "greater than" variety, because the company expects higher ratings, on average, for the exercisers. The output for this test appears in Figure 9.10. The calculations were performed by the HT Mean Diff sheet from the template file. If you compare these formulas to the two-sample confidence interval formulas in the previous chapter, you will see that they are very similar. Again, array formulas are used for the sample standard deviations (because Excel has no STDEVIF function), a test for equality of the two variances is shown in the bottom section, and the standard error of the difference and the degrees of freedom depend on the p-value of this test for equal variances.

The output shows that the observed sample mean difference, 2.725, is indeed positive. That is, the exercisers in the sample outperformed the nonexercisers by 2.725 rating points on average. The output also shows that (1) the standard error of the sample mean difference is 1.142, (2) the test statistic is 2.387, and (3) the p-value for a one-tailed test is slightly less than 0.01. In words, the data provide enough evidence to reject the null hypothesis at the 1% significance level, as well as at the 5% and 10% levels. It is clear that exercisers perform better, in terms of mean ratings, than nonexercisers. A 95% confidence interval for this mean difference (not shown) is all negative; it extends from −4.988 to −0.452.

This answers the first question we posed, but it doesn't answer the second. There is no way to be sure that the higher ratings for the exercisers are a direct result of exercise. It is possible that employees who exercise are naturally more ambitious and hard-working people, and that this extra drive is responsible for *both* their exercising and their higher ratings. This study is an *observational study*. The company observes two randomly selected groups of employees and analyzes the results. It does not explicitly control for other factors, such as personality, that might be responsible for differences in ratings. Therefore, the company can never be sure that there is a causal relationship between exercise and performance ratings. All the company can state is that exercisers appear, on average, to be more productive than nonexercisers—for whatever reason.

The test reported at the bottom of Figure 9.11 is a formal test of the hypothesis $H_0: \sigma_1^2/\sigma_2^2 = 1$ versus $H_a: \sigma_1^2/\sigma_2^2 \neq 1$, where the parameter being tested is the *ratio* of the two population variances. (The details behind this test are explained in the following subsection.) If this null hypothesis can be rejected on the basis of a low p-value in cell B22, then the equal-variance assumption is almost certainly *not* valid, and the procedure that does not assume equal variances is used. The p-value in cell B11, 0.145, suggests that the evidence *against* equal population variances is far from overwhelming, so it is safe to use equal-variance procedure for this example.

Figure 9.11 Analysis of Exercise Data

	A	B	C	D	E	F	G	H	I	J	K
1	Hypothesis test for difference between means										
2	Type of alternative hypothesis	One-tailed – greater than									
3	Hypothesized difference	0.00									
4											
5	Category 1	Yes		Yes							
6	Category 2	No		No							
7	Sample size 1	29		=COUNTIF(Data!$B$2:$B$81,B5)							
8	Sample size 2	51		=COUNTIF(Data!$B$2:$B$81,B6)							
9	Sample mean 1	16.862		=AVERAGEIF(Data!$B$2:$B$81,B5,Data!$C$2:$C$81)							
10	Sample mean 2	14.137		=AVERAGEIF(Data!$B$2:$B$81,B6,Data!$C$2:$C$81)							
11	Sample mean difference (1 minus 2)	2.725		=B9 – B10							
12	Sample std dev 1	4.103		=STDEV.S(IF(Data!$B$2:$B$81=B5,Data!$C$2:$C$81))							
13	Sample std dev 2	5.307		=STDEV.S(IF(Data!$B$2:$B$81=B6,Data!$C$2:$C$81))							
14	Pooled std dev	4.909		=SQRT(((B7 – 1)*B12^2+(B8 – 1)*B13^2)/B17)							
15	Standard error of diff	1.142		=IF(B22>0.1,B14*SQRT(1/B7+1/B8),SQRT(B12^2/B7+B13^2/B8))							
16	Test statistic (t-value)	2.387		=(B11 – B3)/B15							
17	Degrees of freedom	78		=IF(B22>0.1,B7+B8 – 2,ROUND(B15^4/((B12^2/B7)^2/(B7 – 1)+(B13^2/B8)^2/(B8 – 1)),0))							
18	p-value	0.010		=IF($B$2="One-tailed – greater than", T.DIST.RT(B16,B17),							
19				IF($B$2="One-tailed – less than", T.DIST(B16,B17,TRUE),T.DIST.2T(ABS(B16),B17)))							
20	Test for equal variances										
21	Ratio of sample variances	0.598		=(B12/B13)^2							
22	p-value	0.145		=2*(0.5 – ABS(0.5 – F.DIST(B21,B7 – 1,B8 – 1,TRUE)))							

9-4c Hypothesis Test for Equal Population Variances

As we just explained, the two-sample procedure for a difference between population means depends on whether population variances are equal. Therefore, it is natural to test first for equal variances. This test, referred to as the **F test for equality of two variances**, is phrased in terms of the *ratio* of population variances, σ_1^2/σ_2^2. The null hypothesis is that this ratio is 1 (equal variances), whereas the alternative is that it is not 1 (unequal variances). The test statistic for this test is the ratio of sample variances:

$$F\text{-value} = s_1^2/s_2^2$$

Assuming that the population variances are equal, this test statistic has an F distribution with $n_1 - 1$ and $n_2 - 1$ degrees of freedom.

The F distribution is a distribution of positive values and is always skewed to the right. It typically appears in tests of equal variances.

The **F distribution**, named after the famous statistician R. A. Fisher, is another sampling distribution that arises frequently in statistical studies. (It will appear again in the next two chapters on regression.) Because it always describes a ratio, there are two degrees of freedom parameters, one for the numerator and one for the denominator, and the numerator degrees of freedom is always quoted first.

To run the test, you first calculate the ratio of variances. (See cell B21 in Figure 9.11.) It then implements the F test to calculate the corresponding p-value (in cell B22). For our purposes, the most important thing is the p-value from the test. A small p-value provides strong evidence that the population variances are *not* equal. Otherwise, an equal-variance assumption is reasonable. The p-value for the exercise data, 0.145, provides *some* evidence of unequal variances, but the evidence is certainly not overwhelming.

As Figure 9.11 indicates, this F test for equal variances is automatically run in the HT Mean Diff sheet from the template file because it is a natural part of the two-sample test for a mean difference. However, this F test can also be important in its own right, aside from any interest in mean differences. Therefore, it is implemented in a separate HT Ratio of Variances sheet in the template file.

9-4d Hypothesis Test for Difference Between Population Proportions

One of the most common uses of hypothesis testing is to test whether two population proportions are equal. The following z **test for difference between proportions** can then be used. Let p_1 and p_2 be the two population proportions, and let $\hat{p}_1$ and $\hat{p}_2$ be the corresponding sample proportions, based on sample sizes n_1 and n_2. The goal is to test whether the sample proportions differ enough to conclude that the *population* proportions are not equal. As usual, a test on the difference $\hat{p}_1 - \hat{p}_2$, requires a standard error. If the null hypothesis is true, so that $p_1 = p_2$, then it can be shown that the standard error of $\hat{p}_1 - \hat{p}_2$ is given by Equation (9.6), where $\hat{p}_c$ is the pooled proportion from the two samples combined. For example, if $\hat{p}_1 = 20/85$ and $\hat{p}_2 = 34/115$, then $\hat{p}_c = (20 + 34)/(85 + 115) = 54/200$. The reason for using this pooled estimate is that if the null hypothesis is true and the two population proportions are equal, it makes sense to base an estimate of this common proportion on the *combined* sample of data.

Standard Error for Difference between Sample Proportions

$$\mathrm{SE}(\hat{p}_1 - \hat{p}_2) = \sqrt{\hat{p}_c(1 - \hat{p}_c)(1/n_1 + 1/n_2)} \qquad \textbf{(9.6)}$$

Given this standard error, the rest is straightforward. Assuming that the sample sizes are reasonably large, the test statistic in Equation (9.7) has (approximately) a standard normal distribution. The test can be run as illustrated in the following example.

Test Statistic for Difference between Proportions

$$z\text{-value} = \frac{\hat{p}_1 - \hat{p}_2}{\mathrm{SE}(\hat{p}_1 - \hat{p}_2)} \qquad \textbf{(9.7)}$$

EXAMPLE

9.5 EMPLOYEE EMPOWERMENT AT ARMCO COMPANY

ArmCo Company, a large manufacturer of automobile parts, has several plants in the United States. For years, ArmCo employees have complained that their suggestions for improvements in the manufacturing processes have been ignored by upper management. In the spirit of employee empowerment, ArmCo management at the Midwest plant decided to initiate a number of policies to respond to employee suggestions. For example, a mailbox was placed in a central location, and employees were encouraged to drop suggestions into this box. No such initiatives were taken at the other ArmCo plants. As expected, there was a great deal of employee enthusiasm at the Midwest plant shortly after the new policies were implemented, but the question was whether life would revert to normal and the enthusiasm would dampen with time.

To check this, 100 randomly selected employees at the Midwest plant and 300 employees from other plants were asked to fill out a questionnaire six months after the implementation of the new policies at the Midwest plant. Employees were instructed to respond to each item on the questionnaire by checking either a "yes" box or a "no" box. Two specific items on the questionnaire were the following:

• Management at this plant is generally responsive to employee suggestions for improvements in the manufacturing processes.
• Management at this plant is more responsive to employee suggestions now than it used to be.

The results of the questionnaire for these two items appear in Figure 9.12. (See the file **Empowerment.xlsx**.) Note that the given data for this example are *counts*, not long Yes/No columns of individual observations. Does it appear that the policies at the Midwest plant are appreciated? Should ArmCo implement these policies in its other plants?

Figure 9.12 Data for Employee Empowerment Example

	A	B	C
1	**Employee empowerment results**		
2			
3	**Item 1: Management responds**		
4	Category	Midwest	Other
5	Yes	39	93
6	No	61	207
7	Totals	100	300
8			
9	**Item 2: Things have improved**		
10	Category	Midwest	Other
11	Yes	68	159
12	No	32	141
13	Totals	100	300

Objective

To use a test for the difference between proportions to see whether a program of accepting employee suggestions is appreciated by employees.

Solution

For either questionnaire item, let p_1 be the proportion of "yes" responses that would be obtained at the Midwest plant if the questionnaire were given to all of its employees, and define p_2 similarly for the other plants. Management certainly hopes to find a larger proportion of "yes" responses (to either item) at the Midwest plant than at the other plants, so the appropriate test is one-tailed, with the hypotheses set up as $H_0: p_1 - p_2 \leq 0$ versus $H_a: p_1 - p_2 > 0$. (These could also be written as $H_0: p_1 \leq p_2$ versus $H_0: p_1 > p_2$, but this has no effect on the test.)

Using the counts in Figure 9.12, the test for either difference follows directly from Equations (9.5) and (9.6). The results are shown in Figure 9.13, with calculations made by the HT Proportion Diff sheet from the template file. (See the file **Empowerment Finished.xlsx**.)

Figure 9.13 Analysis of Empowerment Data

	A	B	C	D	E	F	G	H	I	J
1	**Hypothesis test for difference between proportions**									
2	Type of alternative hypothesis	One-tailed – greater than	One-tailed – greater than							
3										
4		Management responds	Things have improved							
5	Category 1	Midwest	Midwest							
6	Category 2	Other	Other							
7	Sample size 1	100	100		=Data!B13					
8	Sample size 2	300	300		=Data!C13					
9	Number 1 with property of interest	39	68		=Data!B11					
10	Number 2 with property of interest	93	159		=Data!C11					
11	Sample proportion 1	0.390	0.680		=C9/C7					
12	Sample proportion 2	0.310	0.530		=C10/C8					
13	Sample proportion diff	0.080	0.150		=C11 – C12					
14	Pooled sample proportion	0.330	0.568		=(C9+C10)/(C7+C8)					
15	Standard error of difference	0.054	0.057		=SQRT(C14*(1 – C14)*(1/C7+1/C8))					
16	Test statistic (z distribution)	1.473	2.622		=C13/C15					
17	p-value	0.070	0.004		=IF(C2="One-tailed – greater than", 1 – NORM.S.DIST(C16,TRUE),					
18					IF(C2="One-tailed – less than", NORM.S.DIST(C16,TRUE),					
19					2*(1 – NORM.S.DIST(ABS(C16),TRUE))))					

The p-values for the two tests (row 17) are 0.070 and 0.004. These results should be fairly good news for management. There is moderate, but not overwhelming, support for the hypothesis that management at the Midwest plant is more responsive than at the other plants, at least as perceived by employees. There is convincing support for the hypothesis that things have improved more at the Midwest plant than at the other plants. Corresponding 95% confidence intervals for the differences between proportions (not shown here) are included in the finished version of the file. Because they are almost completely positive, they support the hypothesis-test findings. Moreover, they provide a range of plausible values for the differences between the population proportions.

The only real downside to these findings, from Midwest management's point of view, is the sample proportion $\hat{p}_1$ for the first item. Only 39% of the sampled employees at the Midwest plant believe that management generally responds to their suggestions, even though 68% believe things are better than they used to be. A reasonable conclusion by ArmCo management is that they are on the right track at the Midwest plant, and the policies initiated there ought to be initiated at other plants, but more must be done at *all* plants.

Problems

Solutions for problems whose numbers appear within a colored box can be found in the Student Solution Files.

Level A

9. In the past, 60% of all undergraduate students enrolled at State University earned their degrees within four years of matriculation. A random sample of 95 students from the class that matriculated in the fall of 2012 was recently selected to test whether there has been a change in the proportion of students who graduate within four years. Administrators found that 40 of these 95 students graduated in the spring of 2016 (i.e., four academic years after matriculation).
   a. Given the sample outcome, calculate a 95% confidence interval for the relevant population proportion. Does this interval estimate suggest that there has been a change in the proportion of students who graduate within four years? Why or why not?
   b. Suppose now that State University administrators want to test the claim made by faculty that the proportion of students who graduate within four years at State University has fallen *below* the historical value of 60% this year. Use this sample proportion to test their claim. Report a *p*-value and interpret it.

10. Suppose a well-known baseball player states that, at this stage of his career, he is a "300 hitter" or better. That is, he claims that he gets a hit in at least 30% of his at-bats. Over the next month of the baseball season, this player has 105 at-bats and gets 33 hits.
   a. Identify the null and alternative hypotheses from the player's point of view.
   b. Is there enough evidence from this month's data to reject the null hypothesis at the 5% significance level?
   c. We might raise two issues with this test. First, does the data come from a *random* sample from some population? Second, what is the relevant population? Discuss these issues. Do you think the test in part **b** is valid? Is it meaningful?

11. The director of admissions of a distinguished (i.e., top-20) MBA program is interested in studying the proportion of entering students in similar graduate business programs who have achieved a composite score on the Graduate Management Admissions Test (GMAT) in excess of 630. In particular, the admissions director believes that the proportion of students entering top-rated programs with such composite GMAT scores is now 50%. To test this hypothesis, he has collected a random sample of MBA candidates entering his program in the fall of 2019. He believes that these students' GMAT scores are indicative of the scores earned by their peers in his program and in competitors' programs. The GMAT scores for these 125 individuals are given in the Data 2019 sheet of the file **P09_11.xlsx**. (You can ignore the data in the Data

2009 sheet for now.) Test the admission director's claim at the 5% significance level and report your findings. Does your conclusion change when the significance level is increased to 10%?

12. A market research consultant hired by a leading soft-drink company wants to determine the proportion of consumers who favor its low-calorie drink over the leading competitor's low-calorie drink in a particular urban location. A random sample of 250 consumers from the market under investigation is provided in the file **P08_17.xlsx**.
   a. Calculate a 95% confidence interval for the proportion of all consumers in this market who prefer this company's drink over the competitor's. What does this confidence interval tell us?
   b. Does the confidence interval in part **a** support the claim made by one of the company's marketing managers that more than half of the consumers in this urban location favor its drink over the competitor's? Explain your answer.
   c. Comment on the sample size used in this study. Specifically, is the sample unnecessarily large? Is it too small? Explain your reasoning.

13. The CEO of a medical supply company is committed to expanding the proportion of highly qualified women in the organization's staff of salespersons. He claims that the proportion of women in similar sales positions across the country in 2019 is less than 50%. Hoping to find support for his claim, he directs his assistant to collect a random sample of salespersons employed by his company, which is thought to be representative of sales staffs of competing organizations in the industry. These data are listed in the Data 2019 sheet of the file **P09_13.xlsx**. (You can ignore the data in the Data 2014 sheet for now.) Test this manager's claim using the given sample data and report a *p*-value. Is there statistical support for his hypothesis that the proportion of women in similar sales positions across the country is less than 50%?

14. Management of a software development firm would like to establish a wellness program during the lunch hour to enhance the physical and mental health of its employees. Before introducing the wellness program, management must first be convinced that a sufficiently large majority of its employees are not already exercising at lunchtime. Specifically, it plans to initiate the program only if less than 40% of its personnel take time to exercise prior to eating lunch. To make this decision, management has surveyed a random sample of 100 employees regarding their midday exercise activities. The results of the survey are given in the Before sheet of the file **P09_14.xlsx**. Is there sufficient evidence at the 10% significance level for managers of this organization to initiate a corporate wellness program? Why or why not? What about at the 1% significance level?

15. The managing partner of a major consulting firm is trying to assess the effectiveness of expensive computer skills training given to all new entry-level professionals. In an effort to make such an assessment, she administers a computer skills test immediately before and after the training program to each of 40 randomly chosen employees. The pretraining and posttraining scores of these 40 individuals are recorded in the file **P09_15.xlsx**. Do the given sample data support the claim at the 10% significance level that the organization's training program is increasing the new employee's working knowledge of computing? What about at the 1% significance level?

16. A large buyer of household batteries wants to decide which of two equally priced brands to purchase. To do this, he takes a random sample of 100 batteries of each brand. The lifetimes, measured in hours, of the randomly chosen batteries are recorded in the file **P09_16.xlsx**.
   a. Using the given sample data, calculate a 95% confidence interval for the difference between the mean lifetimes of brand 1 and brand 2 batteries. Based on this confidence interval, which brand would you advise the buyer to purchase? Would you even need a confidence interval to make this recommendation? Explain.
   b. Repeat part **a** with a 99% confidence interval.
   c. How are your results in parts **a** and **b** related to hypothesis testing? Be specific.

17. The managers of a chemical manufacturing plant want to determine whether recent safety training workshops have reduced the weekly number of reported safety violations at the facility. The management team has randomly selected weekly safety violation reports for each of 25 weeks prior to the safety training and 25 weeks after the safety workshops. These data are provided in the file **P09_17.xlsx**. Given this evidence, is it possible to conclude that the safety workshops have been effective in reducing the number of safety violations reported per week? Report a *p*-value and interpret your findings for the management team.

18. A real estate agent has collected a random sample of 75 houses that were recently sold in a suburban community. She is particularly interested in comparing the appraised value and recent selling price of the houses in this particular market. The values of these two variables for each of the 75 randomly chosen houses are provided in the file **P08_21.xlsx**. Using these sample data, test whether there is a statistically significant mean difference between the appraised values and selling prices of the houses sold in this suburban community. Report a *p*-value. For which levels of significance is it appropriate to conclude that *no* difference exists between these two values? Which is more appropriate, a one-tailed test or a two-tailed test? Explain your reasoning.

19. The owner of two submarine sandwich shops located in a particular city would like to know how the mean daily sales of the first shop (located in the downtown area) compares to that of the second shop (located on the southwest side of town). In particular, he would like to determine whether the mean daily sales levels of these two restaurants are essentially equal. He records the sales (in dollars) made at each location for 30 randomly chosen days. These sales levels are given in the file **P09_19.xlsx**. Calculate a 95% confidence level for the mean difference between the daily sales of restaurant 1 and restaurant 2. Based on this confidence interval, is it possible to conclude that there is a statistically significant mean difference at the 5% level of significance? Explain why or why not. Can you infer from this confidence interval whether there is a statistically significant mean difference at the 10% level? What about at the 1% level? Again, explain why or why not.

20. Suppose that an investor wants to compare the risks associated with two different stocks. One way to measure the risk of a given stock is to measure the variation in the stock's daily price changes. The investor obtains a random sample of 25 daily price changes for stock 1 and 25 daily price changes for stock 2. These data are provided in the file **P09_20.xlsx**. Explain why this investor can compare the risks associated with the two stocks by testing the null hypothesis that the variances of the stocks' price changes are equal. Perform this test, using a 10% significance level, and interpret the results.

21. A manufacturing company wants to determine whether there is a difference between the variance of the number of units produced per day by one machine operator and the similar variance for another machine operator. The file **P09_21.xlsx** contain the number of units produced by operator 1 and operator 2, respectively, on each of 25 days. Note that these two sets of days are not necessarily the same, so you can assume that the two samples are *independent* of one another.
   a. Identify the null and alternative hypotheses in this situation.
   b. Do these sample data indicate a statistically significant difference at the 10% level? Explain your answer. With your conclusion, which possible error could you be making, a type I or type II error?
   c. At which significance levels could you *not* reject the null hypothesis?

22. A large buyer of household batteries wants to decide which of two equally priced brands to purchase. To do this, he takes a random sample of 100 batteries of each brand. The lifetimes, measured in hours, of the batteries are recorded in the file **P09_16.xlsx**. Before testing for the difference between the mean lifetimes of these two batteries, he must first determine whether the underlying population variances are equal.
   a. Perform a test for equal population variances. Report a *p*-value and interpret its meaning.
   b. Based on your conclusion in part **a**, which test statistic should be used in performing a test for the difference between population *means*? Perform this test and interpret the results.

23. Do undergraduate business students who major in finance earn, on average, higher annual starting salaries than their peers who major in marketing? Before addressing this question through a statistical hypothesis

test, you should determine whether the variances of annual starting salaries of the two types of majors are equal. The file **P09_23.xlsx** contains (hypothetical) starting salaries of 50 randomly selected finance majors and 50 randomly chosen marketing majors.
   a. Perform a test for equal population variances. Report a *p*-value and interpret its meaning.
   b. Based on your conclusion in part **a**, which test statistic should you use in performing a test for the existence of a difference between population means? Perform this test and interpret the results.
24. The CEO of a medical supply company is committed to expanding the proportion of highly qualified women in the organization's large staff of salespersons. Given the recent hiring practices of his human resources director, he claims that the company has increased the proportion of women in sales positions throughout the organization between 2014 and 2019. Hoping to find support for his claim, he directs his assistant to collect random samples of the salespersons employed by the company in 2014 and 2019. These data are listed in the file **P09_13.xlsx**. Test the CEO's claim using the sample data and report a *p*-value. Is there statistical support for the claim that his strategy is effective?
25. The director of admissions of a top-20 MBA program is interested in studying the proportion of entering students in similar graduate business programs who have achieved a composite score on the Graduate Management Admissions Test (GMAT) in excess of 630. In particular, the admissions director believes that the proportion of students entering top-rated programs with such composite GMAT scores is higher in 2019 than it was in 2009. To test this hypothesis, he has collected random samples of MBA candidates entering his program in the fall of 2019 and in the fall of 2009. He believes that these students' GMAT scores are indicative of the scores earned by their peers in his program and in competitors' programs. The GMAT scores for the randomly selected students entering in each year are listed in the file **P09_11.xlsx**. Test the admission director's claim at the 5% significance level and report your findings. Does your conclusion change when the significance level is increased to 10%?
26. Managers of a software development firm have established a wellness program during the lunch hour to enhance the physical and mental health of their employees. Now, they would like to see whether the wellness program has increased the proportion of employees who exercise regularly during the lunch hour. To make this assessment, the managers surveyed a random sample of 100 employees about their noontime exercise habits *before* the wellness program was initiated. Later, *after* the program was initiated, *another* 100 employees were independently chosen and surveyed about their lunchtime exercise habits. The results of these two surveys are given in the file **P09_14.xlsx**.

   a. Calculate a 95% confidence interval for the difference in the proportions of employees who exercise regularly during their lunch hour before and after the implementation of the corporate wellness program.
   b. Does the confidence interval found in part **a** support the claim that the wellness program has increased the proportion of employees who exercise regularly during the lunch hour? If so, at which levels of significance is this claim supported?
   c. Would your results in parts **a** and **b** differ if the *same* 100 employees surveyed before the program were also surveyed after the program? Explain.
27. An Environmental Protection Agency official asserts that more than 80% of the plants in the northeast region of the United States meet air pollution standards. An antipollution advocate is not convinced by the EPA's claim. She takes a random sample of 64 plants in the northeast region and finds that 56 meet the federal government's pollution standards.
   a. Does the sample information support the EPA's claim at the 5% level of significance?
   b. For which values of the sample proportion (based on a sample size of 64) would the sample data support the EPA's claim, using a 5% significance level?
   c. Would the conclusion found in part **a** change if the sample proportion remained constant but the sample size increased to 124? Explain why or why not.

Level B

28. A television network decides to cancel one of its shows if it is convinced that less than 14% of the viewing public are watching this show.
   a. If a random sample of 1500 households with televisions is selected, what sample proportion values will lead to this show's cancellation, assuming a 5% significance level?
   b. What is the probability that this show will be cancelled if 13.4% of all viewing households are watching it? That is, what is the probability that a sample will lead to rejection of the null hypothesis? You can assume that 13.4% is the *population* proportion (even though it wouldn't be known to the network).
29. An economic researcher wants to know whether he can reject the null hypothesis, at the 10% significance level, that no more than 20% of the households in Pennsylvania make more than $70,000 per year.
   a. If 200 Pennsylvania households are chosen at random, how many of them would have to be earning more than $70,000 per year to allow the researcher to reject the null hypothesis?
   b. Assuming that the true proportion of *all* Pennsylvania households with annual incomes of at least $70,000 is 0.217, find the probability of *not* rejecting a *false* null hypothesis when the sample size is 200.

30. Senior partners of an accounting firm are concerned about recent complaints by some female managers that they are paid less than their male counterparts. In response to these charges, the partners ask their human resources director to record the salaries of female and male managers with equivalent education, work experience, and job performance. A random sample of these pairs of managers is provided in the file **P09_30.xlsx**. That is, each male-female pair is matched in terms of education, work experience, and job performance.
   a. Do these data support the claim made by the female managers? Report and interpret a p-value.
   b. Assuming a 5% significance level, which values of the sample mean difference between the female and male salaries would support the claim of discrimination against female managers?

31. Do undergraduate business students who major in finance earn, on average, higher annual starting salaries than their peers who major in marketing? Address this question through a statistical hypothesis test. The file **P09_23.xlsx** contains the (hypothetical) starting salaries of 50 randomly selected finance majors and 50 randomly selected marketing majors.
   a. Is it appropriate to perform a paired-comparison t test with these data? Explain why or why not.
   b. Perform an appropriate hypothesis test with a 5% significance level. Summarize your findings.
   c. How large would the difference between the mean starting salaries of finance and marketing majors have to be before you could conclude that finance majors earn more on average? Employ a 5% significance level in answering this question.

32. The file **P02_35.xlsx** contains data from a survey of 500 randomly selected households. Test for the existence of a significant difference between the mean debt levels of the households in the first (i.e., SW) and second (i.e., NW) sectors of this community. Perform similar hypothesis tests for the differences between the mean debt levels of households from all other pairs of locations (i.e., first and third, first and fourth, second and third, second and fourth, and third and fourth). Summarize your findings.

33. Elected officials in a Florida city are preparing the annual budget for their community. They want to determine whether their constituents living across town are typically paying the same amount in real estate taxes each year. Given that there are over 20,000 homeowners in this city, they have decided to sample a representative subset of taxpayers and thoroughly study their tax payments. A randomly selected set of 170 homeowners is given in the file **P09_33.xlsx**. Specifically, the officials want to test whether there is a difference between the mean real estate tax bill paid by residents of the *first* neighborhood of this town and each of the remaining five neighborhoods. That is, each *pair* referenced below is from neighborhood 1 and one of the other neighborhoods.

a. Before conducting any hypothesis tests on the difference between various pairs of mean real estate tax payments, perform a test for equal population variances for each pair of neighborhoods. For each pair, report a p-value and interpret its meaning.
b. Based on your conclusions in part **a**, which test statistic should be used in performing a test for a difference between population means in each pair?
c. Given your conclusions in part **b**, perform an appropriate test for the difference between mean real estate tax payments in each pair of neighborhoods. For each pair, report a p-value and interpret its meaning.

34. Suppose that you sample two normal populations independently. The variances of these two populations are σ_1^2 and σ_2^2. You take random samples of sizes n_1 and n_2 and observe sample variances of s_1^2 and s_2^2.
   a. If $n_1 = n_2 = 21$, how large must the fraction s_1/s_2 be before you can reject the null hypothesis that σ_1^2 is no greater than σ_2^2 at the 5% significance level?
   b. Answer part **a** when $n_1 = n_2 = 41$.
   c. If s_1 is 25% greater than s_2, approximately how large must n_1 and n_2 be if you are able to reject the null hypothesis in part **a** at the 5% significance level? Assume that n_1 and n_2 are equal.

35. Two teams of workers assemble automobile engines at a manufacturing plant in Michigan. Quality control personnel inspect a random sample of the teams' assemblies and judge each assembly to be acceptable or unacceptable. A random sample of 127 assemblies from team 1 shows 12 unacceptable assemblies. A similar random sample of 98 assemblies from team 2 shows 5 unacceptable assemblies.
   a. Calculate a 95% confidence interval for the difference between the proportions of unacceptable assemblies from the two teams.
   b. Based on the confidence interval found in part **a**, is there sufficient evidence to conclude, at the 5% significance level, that the two teams differ with respect to their proportions of unacceptable assemblies?
   c. For which values of the difference between these two sample proportions could you conclude that a statistically significant difference exists at the 5% level?

36. A market research consultant hired by a leading soft-drink company is interested in determining whether there is a difference between the proportions of female and male consumers who favor the company's low-calorie brand over the leading competitor's low-calorie brand in a particular urban location. A random sample of 250 consumers from the market under investigation is provided in the file **P08_17.xlsx**.
   a. After separating the 250 randomly selected consumers by gender, perform the statistical test and report a p-value. At which levels of α will the market research consultant conclude that there is essentially no difference between the proportions of female and male consumers who prefer this company's brand to the competitor's brand in this urban area?

b. Marketing managers at this company have asked their market research consultant to explore further the potential differences in the proportions of women and men who prefer drinking the company's brand to the competitor's brand. Specifically, the company's managers wants to know whether the potential difference between the proportions of female and male consumers who favor the company's brand varies by the age of the consumers. Using the same random sample of consumers as in part **a**, assess whether this difference varies across the four given age categories: under 20, between 20 and 40, between 40 and 60, and over 60. Specifically, run the test in part **a** four times, one for each age group. Are the results the same for each age group?

37. The employee benefits manager of a large public university wants to determine whether differences exist in the proportions of various groups of full-time employees who prefer adopting the second (i.e., plan B) of three available health care plans in the coming annual enrollment period. A random sample of the university's employees and their tentative health care preferences is given in the file **P08_16.xlsx**.

a. Perform tests for differences in the proportions of employees within respective classifications who favor plan B in the coming year. For instance, the first such test should examine the difference between the proportion of administrative employees who favor plan B and the proportion of the support staff who prefer plan B.

b. Report a *p*-value for each of your hypothesis tests and interpret your results. How might the benefits manager use the information you have derived from these tests?

38. The file **P02_35.xlsx** contains data from a survey of 500 randomly selected households. Researchers would like to use the available sample information to test whether home ownership rates vary by household location. For example, is there a nonzero difference between the proportions of individuals who own their homes (as opposed to those who rent their homes) in households located in the first (i.e., SW) and second (i.e., NW) sectors of this community? Use the sample data to test for a difference in home ownership rates in these two sectors as well as for those of other pairs of household locations. In each test, use a 5% significance level. Interpret and summarize your results. (You should perform and interpret a total of six hypothesis tests.)

39. For testing the difference between two proportions, $\sqrt{\hat{p}_c(1 - \hat{p}_c)(1/n_1 + 1/n_2)}$ is used as the approximate standard error of $\hat{p}_1 - \hat{p}_2$, where $\hat{p}_c$ is the pooled sample proportion. Explain why this is reasonable when the null-hypothesized value of $p_1 - p_2$ is zero. Why would this not be a good approximation when the null-hypothesized value of $p_1 - p_2$ is a nonzero number? What would you recommend using for the standard error of $\hat{p}_1 - \hat{p}_2$ in that case?

9-5 Tests for Normality

In this section we discuss several **tests for normality**.[3] As you have already seen, many statistical procedures are based on the assumption that population data are normally distributed. The tests in this section allow you to test this assumption. The null hypothesis is that the population is normally distributed, whereas the alternative is that the population distribution is not normal. Therefore, the burden of proof is on showing that the population distribution is *not* normal. Unless there is sufficient evidence to this effect, the normal assumption will continue to be accepted.

The first test we discuss is called a **chi-square goodness-of-fit test**. It is quite intuitive. A histogram of the sample data is compared to the *expected* bell-shaped histogram that would be observed if the data were normally distributed with the *same* mean and standard deviation as in the sample. If the two histograms are sufficiently similar, the null hypothesis of normality is accepted. Otherwise, it can be rejected.

The chi-square test for normality makes a comparison between the observed histogram and a histogram based on normality.

The test is based on a numerical measure of the difference between the two histograms. Let C be the number of categories in the histogram, and let O_i be the observed number of observations in category i. Also, let E_i be the expected number of observations in category i if the population were normal with the same mean and standard deviation as in the sample. Then the goodness-of-fit measure in Equation (9.8) is used as a test statistic. If the null hypothesis of normality is true, this test statistic has (approximately) a chi-square distribution with $C - 3$ degrees of freedom. Because *large* values of the test statistic indicate a poor fit—the O_i's do not match up well with the E_i's—the *p*-value for the test is the probability to the right of the test statistic in the chi-square distribution with $C - 3$ degrees of freedom.

---

3 The tests in this section could (with a lot of work) be implemented with Excel-only formulas. However, it is much easier to implement them with StatTools, as we will do here.

Test Statistic for Chi-Square Test of Normality

$$\chi^2\text{-value} = \sum_{i=1}^{C}(O_i - E_i)^2/E_i \qquad (9.8)$$

(Here, χ is the Greek letter chi.)

Although it is possible to perform this test with Excel-only formulas, it is certainly preferable to use StatTools, as illustrated in Example 9.6.

EXAMPLE

9.6 DISTRIBUTION OF METAL STRIP WIDTHS IN MANUFACTURING

A company manufactures strips of metal that are supposed to have width of 10 centimeters. For purposes of quality control, the manager plans to run some statistical tests on these strips. However, realizing that these statistical procedures assume normally distributed widths, he first tests this normality assumption on 90 randomly sampled strips. How should he proceed?

Objective

To use the chi-square goodness-of-fit test to see whether a normal distribution of the metal strip widths is reasonable.

Solution

The sample data appear in Figure 9.14, where each width is measured to three decimal places. (See the file **Testing Normality Finished.xlsx**.) A histogram of the widths is also shown.

Figure 9.14 Data for Testing Normality

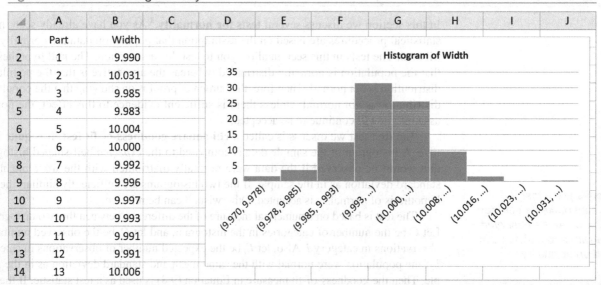

To run the test, select Chi-Square Test from the StatTools Normality Tests dropdown list, which leads to a dialog box where you can either specify the bins for a histogram or you can accept StatTools's default bins. For now, do the latter.[4] The resulting histograms in Figure 9.15 provide visual evidence of the goodness of fit. The left bars represent the observed frequencies (the O_is), and the right bars represent the expected frequencies for a normal distribution (the E_is). The normal fit to the data appears to be quite good.

---

4 You might try defining the bins differently and rerunning the test. The category definitions *can* make a difference in the results. This is a minor disadvantage of the chi-square test.

Figure 9.15 Observed and
Normal Histograms`

The StatTools output in Figure 9.16 confirms this statistically. Each value in column E is an E_i, calculated as the total number of observations multiplied by the normal probability of being in the corresponding category. Column F contains the individual $(O_i - E_i)^2/E_i$ terms, and cell B11 contains their sum, the chi-square test statistic. The corresponding p-value in cell B12 is 0.5206.

Figure 9.16 Chi-Square Test of Normality

	A	B	C	D	E	F
7		Width				
8	*Chi-Square Test*	**Width Data**				
9	Mean	9.999256				
10	Std Dev	0.009728				
11	Chi-Square Stat.	4.2027				
12	p-Value	0.5206				
13						
14						
15	*Chi-Squared Bins*	**Bin Min**	**Bin Max**	**Actual**	**Normal**	**Distance**
16	Bin #1	−Inf	9.983000	5	4.2630	0.1274
17	Bin #2	9.983000	9.988167	6	7.1827	0.1948
18	Bin #3	9.988167	9.993333	14	12.9751	0.0810
19	Bin #4	9.993333	9.998500	20	17.7934	0.2736
20	Bin #5	9.998500	10.003667	13	18.5249	1.6477
21	Bin #6	10.003667	10.008833	19	14.6421	1.2970
22	Bin #7	10.008833	10.014000	9	8.7859	0.0052
23	Bin #8	10.014000	+Inf	4	5.8328	0.5759

Remember that the burden of proof is on showing that the distribution is *not* normal. The high p-value here indicates that there is not enough evidence to reject the null hypothesis of normality, and this finding is confirmed on the next two sheets.

This large p-value provides no evidence whatsoever of non-normality. It implies that if this procedure were repeated on many random samples, each taken from a population known to be normal, a fit at least this poor would occur in over 50% of the samples. Stated differently, fewer than 50% of the fits would be *better* than the one observed here. Therefore, the manager can feel comfortable in making a normal assumption for this population.

We make several comments about this chi-square procedure. First, the test *does* depend on which (and how many) bins you use for the histogram. Reasonable choices are likely to lead to the same conclusion, but this is not guaranteed. Second, the test is not very effective unless the sample size is large: at least 80 or 100, say. Only then can you begin to see the true shape of the histogram and judge accurately whether it is normal. Finally, the test tends to be *too* sensitive if the sample size is really large. In this case any little "bump" on the observed histogram is likely to lead to a conclusion of non-normality. This is one more example of practical versus statistical significance. With a large sample size you might be able to reject normality with a high degree of certainty, but the practical difference between the observed and normal histograms could very well be unimportant.

The Lilliefors test is based on a comparison of the cdf from the data and a normal cdf.

The chi-square test of normality is an intuitive one because it is based on histograms. However, it suffers from the first two points discussed in the previous paragraph. In particular, it is not as *powerful* as other available tests. This means that it is often unable to distinguish between normal and non-normal distributions, and hence it often fails to reject the null hypothesis of normality when it should be rejected. A more powerful test is called the *Lilliefors test*.[5] This test is based on the *cumulative distribution function* (cdf), which shows the probability of being less than or equal to any particular value. Specifically, the **Lilliefors test** compares two cdfs: the cdf from a normal distribution and the cdf corresponding to the given data. This latter cdf, called the *empirical cdf*, shows the fraction of observations less than or equal to any particular value. If the data come from a normal distribution, the normal and empirical cdfs should be quite close. Therefore, the Lilliefors test compares the *maximum vertical distance* between the two cdfs and compares it to specially tabulated values. If this maximum vertical distance is sufficiently large, the null hypothesis of normality can be rejected.

To run the Lilliefors test for the Width variable in Example 9.6, select Lilliefors Test from the StatTools Normality Tests dropdown list. StatTools then shows the numerical outputs in Figure 9.17 and the corresponding graph in Figure 9.18 of the normal and empirical cdfs. The numeric output indicates that the maximum vertical distance between the two curves is 0.0513. It also provides a number of "CVal" values for comparison. If the test statistic is larger than any of these, the null hypothesis of normality can be rejected at the corresponding significance level. In this case, however, the test statistic is relatively small—not nearly large enough to reject the normal hypothesis at any of the usual significance levels. This conclusion agrees with the one based on the chi-square goodness-of-fit test (as well as the closeness of the two curves in Figure 9.18). Nevertheless, you should be aware that the two tests do not agree on *all* data sets.

Figure 9.17 Lilliefors Test Results

	A	B
7		Width
8	*Lilliefors Test Results*	Width Data
9	Sample Size	90
10	Sample Mean	9.999256
11	Sample Std Dev	0.009728
12	Test Statistic	0.0513
13	CVal (15% Sig. Level)	0.0810
14	CVal (10% Sig. Level)	0.0856
15	CVal (5% Sig. Level)	0.0936
16	CVal (2.5% Sig. Level)	0.0998
17	CVal (1% Sig. Level)	0.1367

---

5 This is actually a special case of the more general and widely known *Kolmogorov-Smirnoff* (or K-S) test.

Figure 9.18 Normal and Empirical Cumulative Distribution Functions

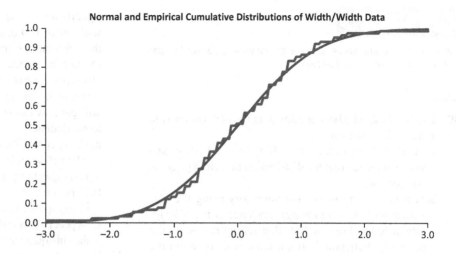

If data are normally distributed, the points on the corresponding Q-Q plot should be close to a 45° line.

We conclude this section with a popular, but informal, test of normality. This is based on a plot called a **quantile-quantile** (or **Q-Q**) **plot**. Although the technical details for forming this plot are somewhat complex, it is basically a scatterplot of the standardized values from the data set versus the values that would be expected if the data were perfectly normally distributed (with the same mean and standard deviation as in the data set). If the data are, in fact, normally distributed, the points in this plot tend to cluster around a 45° line. Any large deviation from a 45° line signals some type of non-normality. Again, however, this is not a *formal* test of normality. A Q-Q plot is usually used only to obtain a general idea of whether the data are normally distributed and, if they are not, what type of non-normality exists. For example, if points on the right of the plot are well *above* a 45° line, this is an indication that the largest observations in the data set are larger than would be expected from a normal distribution. Therefore, these points might be high-end outliers and/or a signal of positive skewness.

To obtain a Q-Q plot for the Width variable in Example 9.6, select Q-Q Normal Plot from the StatTools Normality Tests dropdown list and check each option at the bottom of the dialog box. The Q-Q plot for the Width data in Example 9.6 appears in Figure 9.19. Although the points in this Q-Q plot do not all lie *exactly* on a 45° line, they are about as close to doing so as can be expected from real data. Therefore, there is no reason to question the normal hypothesis for these data—the same conclusion as from the chi-square and Lilliefors tests. (Note that in the StatTools Q-Q plot dialog box, you can elect to plot *standardized Q*-values. This option was used in Figure 9.19. The plot with *unstandardized Q*-values, not shown here, provides virtually the same information. The only difference is in the scale of the vertical axis.)

Figure 9.19 Q-Q Plot with Standardized Q-Values

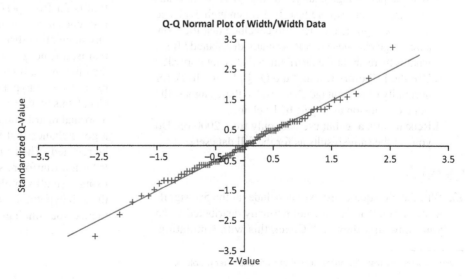

Problems

Solutions for problems whose numbers appear within a colored box can be found in the Student Solution Files.

Level A

40. The file **P02_11.xlsx** contains data on 148 houses sold in a certain suburban region.
  a. Create a histogram of the selling prices. Is there any visual evidence that the distribution of selling prices is *not* normal?
  b. Test the selling prices for normality using the chi-square test. Is there enough evidence at the 5% significance level to conclude that selling prices are *not* normally distributed? If so, what is there about the distribution that is not normal?
  c. Use the Lilliefors test and the Q-Q plot to check for normality of selling prices. Do these suggest the same conclusion as in part **b**? Explain.

41. The file **P09_33.xlsx** contains real estate taxes paid by a sample of 170 homeowners in a Florida city.
  a. Create a histogram of the taxes paid. Is there any visual evidence that the distribution of taxes paid is *not* normal?
  b. Test the taxes paid for normality using the chi-square test. Is there enough evidence at the 5% significance level to conclude that taxes paid are *not* normally distributed? If so, what is there about the distribution that is not normal?
  c. Use the Lilliefors test and the Q-Q plot to check for normality of taxes paid. Do these suggest the same conclusion as in part **b**? Explain.

42. The file **P09_42.xlsx** contains many years of monthly percentage changes in the Dow Jones Industrial Average (DJIA). (This is the same data set that was used for Example 2.6 in Chapter 2.)
  a. Create a histogram of the percentage changes in the DJIA. Is there any visual evidence that the distribution of the Dow percentage changes is *not* normal?
  b. Test the percentage changes of the DJIA for normality using the chi-square test. Is there enough evidence at the 5% significance level to conclude that the Dow percentage changes are *not* normally distributed? If so, what is there about the distribution that is not normal?
  c. Use the Lilliefors test and the Q-Q plot to check for normality of percentage changes. Do these suggest the same conclusion as in part **b**? Explain.
  d. Repeat parts **a–c**, but use data only from 2000 on. Do you get the same results as for the full data set?

Level B

43. Will the chi-square test ever conclude, at the 5% significance level, that data are not normally distributed when you know that they are? Check this with simulation.

Specifically, generate n normally distributed numbers with mean 100 and standard deviation 15. You can do this with the formula **=NORM.INV(RAND(),100,12)**. Do *not* freeze them; keep them random. Then run the chi-square normality test on the random numbers. Because the chi-square results are linked to the data, you will get new chi-square results every time you press F9 to recalculate.
  a. Using $n = 150$, do you ever get a p-value less than 0.05? If so, what does such a p-value mean? Would you *expect* to get a few such p-values? Explain.
  b. Repeat part **a** using $n = 1000$. Do the results change in any qualitative way?
  c. Repeat parts **a** and **b**, but use the Lilliefors test instead of the chi-square test. Do you get the same basic results?

44. Repeat the previous problem but with a *non*-normal population. Specifically, generate n random numbers from a fifty-fifty mixture of two normal distributions with respective means 90 and 110 and common standard deviation 10. You can do this with the formula **=IF(RAND()<0.5,NORM.INV(RAND(),90,10),NORM.INV(RAND(),110,10))** This is *not* a normal distribution because it has two peaks.)

45. The file **P09_45.xlsx** contains measurements of ounces in randomly selected cans from a soft-drink filling machine. These cans reportedly contain 12 ounces, but because of natural variation, the actual amounts differ slightly from 12 ounces.
  a. Can the company legitimately state that the amounts in cans are *normally* distributed?
  b. *Assuming* that the distribution is normal with the mean and standard deviation found in this sample, calculate the probability that at least half of the *next* 100 cans filled will contain less than 12 ounces.
  c. If the test in part **a** indicated that the data are *not* normally distributed, how might you calculate the probability requested in part **b**?

46. The chi-square test for normality discussed in this section is far from perfect. If the sample is too small, the test tends to accept the null hypothesis of normality for any population distribution even remotely bell-shaped; that is, it is not *powerful* in detecting non-normality. On the other hand, if the sample is very large, it will tend to reject the null hypothesis of normality for *any* data set.[6] Check this by using simulation. First, simulate data from a normal distribution using a large sample size. Is there a good chance that the null hypothesis will (wrongly) be rejected? Then simulate data from a non-normal distribution (uniform, say, or the mixture in Problem 44) using a small sample size. Is there a good chance that the null hypothesis will (wrongly) not be rejected? Summarize your findings in a short report.

---

6 Actually, all of the tests for normality suffer from this latter problem.

9-6 Chi-Square Test for Independence

The test we discuss in this section, like one of the tests for normality from the previous section, uses the name "chi-square." However, this test, called the **chi-square test for independence**, has an entirely different objective. It is used in situations where a population is categorized in two different ways. For example, people might be characterized by their smoking habits and their drinking habits. The question then is whether these two attributes are independent in a probabilistic sense. They are *independent* if information on a person's drinking habits is of no use in predicting the person's smoking habits (and vice versa). In this particular example, however, you might suspect that the two attributes are *dependent*. In particular, you might suspect that heavy drinkers are more likely (than non-heavy drinkers) to be heavy smokers, and you might suspect that nondrinkers are more likely (than drinkers) to be nonsmokers. The chi-square test for independence enables you to test this empirically.

Rejecting independence does not indicate the form of dependence. To see this, you must look more closely at the data.

The null hypothesis for this test is that the two attributes are independent. Therefore, statistically significant results are those that indicate some sort of dependence. As always, this puts the burden of proof on the alternative hypothesis. In the smoking–drinking example, we will continue to believe that smoking and drinking habits are unrelated—that is, independent—unless there is sufficient evidence from the data that they are dependent. Furthermore, even if we are able to conclude that they are dependent, the test itself does not indicate the *form* of dependence. It could be that heavy drinkers tend to be nonsmokers, and nondrinkers tend to be heavy smokers. Although this is unlikely, it is definitely a form of dependence. The only way we can decide which form of dependence exists is to look closely at the data.

The data for this test consist of *counts* in various combinations of categories. These are usually arranged in a rectangular *contingency table*, also called a *cross-tabs*, or, using Excel terminology, a pivot table. For example, if there are three smoking categories and three drinking categories, the table will have three rows and three columns, for a total of nine cells. The count in a cell is the number of observations in that particular combination of categories. The following example illustrates this data setup and the resulting analysis.

> The chi-square test for independence is based on the counts in a contingency (or cross-tabs) table. It tests whether the row variable is probabilistically independent of the column variable.

EXAMPLE

9.7 RELATIONSHIP BETWEEN DEMANDS FOR DESKTOPS AND LAPTOPS AT BIG OFFICE

Big Office, a chain of large office supply stores, sells a variety of Windows and Mac laptops. Company executives want to know whether the demands for these two types of computers are related in any way. They might act as complementary products, where high demand for Windows laptops accompanies high demand for Mac laptops (computers in general are hot), they might act as substitute products (demand for one takes away demand for the other), or their demands might be unrelated. Because of limitations in its information system, Big Office does not have the exact demands for these products. However, it does have daily information on categories of demand, listed in aggregate (that is, over all stores). These data appear in Figure 9.20. (See the file **Laptop Demand.xlsx**.) Each day's demand for each type of computer is categorized as Low, Medium Low, Medium High, or High. The table is based on 250 days, so that the counts add to 250. The individual counts show, for example, that demand was high for both Windows *and* Mac laptops on 11 of the 250 days. For convenience, the row and column totals are provided in the margins. Based on these data, can Big Office conclude that demands for these two products are independent?

Figure 9.20 Laptop Demand
Data

	A	B	C	D	E	F	G
1	Demands at Big Office						
2							
3			Windows laptops				
4			Low	Medium Low	Medium High	High	
5	Mac laptops	Low	4	17	17	5	43
6		Medium Low	8	23	22	27	80
7		Medium High	16	20	14	20	70
8		High	10	17	19	11	57
9			38	77	72	63	250

Objective

To use the chi-square test of independence to test whether demand for Windows laptops is independent of demand for Mac laptops.

Solution

The idea of the test is to compare the actual counts in the table with what would be *expected* under independence. If the actual counts are sufficiently far from the expected counts, the null hypothesis of independence can be rejected. The *distance* measure used to check how far apart they are, shown in Equation (9.9), is essentially the same chi-square statistic used in the chi-square test for normality. Here, O_{ij} is the actual count in cell i,j (row i, column j), E_{ij} is the expected count for this cell assuming independence, and the sum is over all cells in the table. If this test statistic is sufficiently large, the independence hypothesis can be rejected. (We provide more details of the test shortly.)

Test Statistic for Chi-Square Test for Independence

$$\text{chi-square test statistic} = \sum_{ij}(O_{ij} - E_{ij})^2/E_{ij} \qquad (9.9)$$

What is expected under independence? The totals in row 9 indicate that demand for Windows laptops was low on 38 of the 250 days. Therefore, if you had to estimate the probability of low demand for Windows laptops, your estimate would be $38/250 = 0.152$. Now, if demands for the two products were independent, you should arrive at this *same* estimate from the data in any of rows 5 through 8. That is, a probability estimate for Windows laptops should be the same regardless of the demand for Mac laptops. The probability estimate of low Windows demand from row 5, for example, is $4/43 = 0.093$. Similarly, for rows 6, 7, and 8 it is $8/80 = 0.100$, $16/70 = 0.229$, and $10/57 = 0.175$, respectively. These calculations provide some evidence that Windows and Mac laptops act as *substitute* products—the probability of low Windows demand is larger when Mac demand is medium high or high than when it is low or medium low.

This reasoning is the basis for calculating the E_{ij}s. Specifically, it can be shown that the relevant formula for E_{ij} is given by Equation (9.10), where R_i is the row total in row i, C_j is the total in column j, and N is the number of observations. For example, E_{11} for these data is $43(38)/250 = 6.536$, which is slightly larger than the corresponding observed count, $O_{11} = 4$.

Expected Counts Assuming Row and Column Independence

$$E_{ij} = R_i C_j / N \qquad (9.10)$$

The results appear in Figure 9.21. (Neither a template nor StatTools is required.) The formulas shown in the figure follow directly from Equations (9.9) and (9.10). The *p*-value of the test, 0.045, can be interpreted in the usual way. Specifically, the null hypothesis of independence can be rejected at the 5% or 10% significance levels, but not at the 1% level. There is a fairly strong evidence that the demands for the two products are *not* independent.

Figure 9.21 Output for Chi-Square Test

⊿	I	J	K	L	M	N	O	P	Q
1	**Test of independence**								
2									
3	Expected counts assuming independence							Formula in cell C15	
4			Low	Medium Low	Medium High	High		(copied to table)	
5		Low	6.54	13.24	12.38	10.84		=$G5*C$9/$G$9	
6		Medium Low	12.16	24.64	23.04	20.16			
7		Medium High	10.64	21.56	20.16	17.64			
8		High	8.66	17.56	16.42	14.36			
9									
10	Table of (O−E)^2/E values							Formula in cell C22	
11			Low	Medium Low	Medium High	High		(copied to table)	
12		Low	0.98	1.07	1.72	3.14		=(C15−C5)^2/C15	
13		Medium Low	1.42	0.11	0.05	2.32			
14		Medium High	2.70	0.11	1.88	0.32			
15		High	0.21	0.02	0.41	0.79			
16									
17	Test statistic	17.242		=SUM(C22:F25)					
18	Degrees of freedom	9		=(4−1)*(4−1)					
19	p-value	0.045		=CHISQ.DIST.RT(B27,B28)					

If the alternative hypothesis of dependence is accepted, the output in Figure 9.22 can be used to examine its form. These two tables show the counts as percentages of row totals and as percentages of column totals. If the demands *were* independent, the rows of this first table should be identical, and the columns of the second table should be identical. This is because each row in the first table shows the distribution of Windows demand for a given category of Mac demand, whereas each column in the second table shows the distribution of Mac demand for a given category of Windows demand. A close study of these percentages again provides some evidence that the two products act as substitutes, but the evidence is not overwhelming.

Tables of counts expressed as percentages of rows or of columns are useful for judging the form (and extent) of any possible dependence.

Figure 9.22 Counts Shown as Percentages

⊿	B	C	D	E	F
11	Counts as % of rows				
12		Low	Medium Low	Medium High	High
13	Low	9.3%	39.5%	39.5%	11.6%
14	Medium Low	10.0%	28.8%	27.5%	33.8%
15	Medium High	22.9%	28.6%	20.0%	28.6%
16	High	17.5%	29.8%	33.3%	19.3%
17					
18	Counts as % of columns				
19		Low	Medium Low	Medium High	High
20	Low	10.5%	22.1%	23.6%	7.9%
21	High	26.3%	22.1%	26.4%	17.5%

Finally, it is worth noting that the table of counts necessary for the chi-square test of independence can be a pivot table. For example, the pivot table in Figure 9.23 shows counts of the Married and Own Home attributes. (For Married, 1 means married, 0 means unmarried, and for Own Home, 1 means a home owner, 0 means not a home owner. This pivot table is based on the data in the **Catalog Marketing.xlsx** file from Chapter 2.) To see whether these two attributes are independent, the chi-square test would be performed on the table of counts. You might want to check that the *p*-value for the test is 0.000 (to three decimals), so that Married and Own Home are definitely *not* independent.

Figure 9.23 Using a Pivot
Table for a Chi-Square Test

Count	Own Home ▼		
Married ▼	0	1	Grand Total
0	307	191	498
1	177	325	502
Grand Total	484	516	1000

Problems

Solutions for problems whose numbers appear within a colored box can be found in the Student Solution Files.

Level A

47. The file **P08_46.xlsx** contains data on 400 orders placed to ElecMart company over a period of several months. For each order, the file lists the time of day, the type of credit card used, the region of the country where the customer resides, and others. (This is the same data set used in Example 3.4 of Chapter 3.) Use a chi-square test for independence to see whether the following variables are independent. If the variables appear to be related, discuss the form of dependence you see.
   a. Time and Region
   b. Region and Buy Category
   c. Gender and Card Type

48. The file **P08_17.xlsx** categorizes 250 randomly selected consumers on the basis of their gender, their age, and their preference for our brand or a competitor's brand of a low-calorie soft drink. Use a chi-square test for independence to see whether the drink preference is independent of gender, and then whether it is independent of age. If you find any dependence, discuss its nature.

49. The file **P02_11.xlsx** contains data on 148 houses that were recently sold. Two variables in this data set are the selling price of the house and the number of bedrooms in the house. We want to use a chi-square test for independence to see whether these two variables are independent. However, this test requires *categorical* variables, and Selling Price is essentially continuous. Therefore, to run the test, first divide the prices into several categories: less than 120, 120 to 130, 130 to 140, and greater than 140. Then run the test and report your results.

Level B

50. The file **P03_50.xlsx** contains annual salaries for all NBA basketball players in each of five seasons.

a. Using only the data for the most recent season (2008–2009), check whether there is independence between position and salary. To do this, first change any hyphenated position such as C-F to the first listed, in this case C. (Presumably, this is the player's primary position.) Then make Salary categorical with four categories: the first is all salaries below the first quartile, the second is all salaries from the first quartile to the median, and so on. Explain your findings.
b. Repeat part **a** but with a Yes/No playoff team categorization instead of position. The playoff teams in that season were Atlanta, Boston, Chicago, Cleveland, Dallas, Denver, Detroit, Houston, Los Angeles Lakers, Miami, New Orleans, Orlando, Philadelphia, Portland, San Antonio, and Utah.

51. The file **P09_51.xlsx** contains data on 1000 randomly selected Walmart customers. The data set includes demographic variables for each customer as well as their salaries and the amounts they have spent at Walmart during the past year.
a. A lookup table in the file suggests a way to categorize the salaries. Use this categorization and chi-square tests of independence to see whether Salary is independent of (1) Age, (2) Gender, (3) Home, or (4) Married. Discuss any types of dependence you find.
b. Repeat part **a**, replacing Salary with Amount Spent. First you must categorize Amount Spent. Create four categories for Amount Spent based on the four quartiles. The first category is all values of Amount Spent below the first quartile of Amount Spent, the second category is between the first quartile and the median, and so on.

52. The file **P09_52.xlsx** contains data on close to 10,000 customers from several large cities in the United States. The variables include the customers' gender and their first choice among several types of movies. Perform chi-square tests of independence to test whether the following variables are related. If they are, discuss the form of dependence you see.
a. State and First Choice
b. City and First Choice
c. Gender and First Choice

9-7 Conclusion

The concepts and procedures in this chapter form a cornerstone in both applied and theoretical statistics. Of particular importance is the interpretation of a *p*-value, especially because *p*-values are reported in virtually all statistical software packages. A *p*-value summarizes the evidence in support of an alternative hypothesis, which is usually the hypothesis an analyst is trying to prove. Small *p*-values provide support for the alternative hypothesis, whereas large *p*-values provide little or no support for it.

Although hypothesis testing continues to be an important tool for analysts, it is important to note its limitations, particularly in business applications. First, given a choice between a confidence interval for some population parameter and a test of this parameter, we generally favor the confidence interval. For example, a confidence interval not only indicates whether a mean difference is 0, but it also provides a plausible range for this difference. Second, many business *decision* problems cannot be handled adequately with hypothesis-testing procedures. Either they ignore important cost information or they treat the consequences of incorrect decisions (type I and type II errors) in an inappropriate way. Finally, the *statistical* significance at the core of hypothesis testing is sometimes quite different from the *practical* significance that is of most interest to business managers.

Summary of Key Terms

TERM	EXPLANATION	EXCEL	PAGES	EQUATION
Null hypothesis	Hypothesis that represents the current thinking or status quo		365	
Alternative hypothesis	Typically, the hypothesis the analyst is trying to prove or research hypothesis		365	
One-tailed test	Test where values in only one direction will lead to rejection of the null hypothesis		367	
Two-tailed test	Test where values in both directions will lead to rejection of the null hypothesis		367	
Type I error	Error committed when null hypothesis is true but is rejected		367	
Type II error	Error committed when null hypothesis is false but is not rejected		367	
Significance level	The probability of a type I error an analyst chooses		368	
Rejection region	Sample results that lead to rejection of null hypothesis		368	
Statistically significant results	Sample results that lead to rejection of null hypothesis		368	
p-value	Probability of observing a sample result at least as extreme as the one actually observed		369	
Power	Probability of correctly rejecting the null when it is false		371	
t test for a population mean	Test for a mean from a single population	Excel formulas in **Hypothesis Test Template.xlsx** file	372	9.1
z test for a population proportion	Test for a proportion from a single population	Excel formulas in **Hypothesis Test Template.xlsx** file	377	9.2
t test for difference between means from paired samples	Test for the difference between two population means when samples are paired in a natural way	Excel formulas in **Hypothesis Test Template.xlsx** file	379	9.3
t test for difference between means from independent samples	Test for the difference between two population means when samples are independent	Excel formulas in **Hypothesis Test Template.xlsx** file	379	9.4, 9.5
F test for equality of two variances	Test for equality of two population variances, used to check an assumption of two-sample *t* test for difference between means	Excel formulas in **Hypothesis Test Template.xlsx** file	387	
F distribution	Skewed distribution useful for testing equality of variances	F.DIST, F.INV, and other F functions	387	
z test for difference between proportions	Test for difference between similarly defined proportions from two populations	Excel formulas in **Hypothesis Test Template.xlsx** file	388	9.6, 9.7
Tests for normality	Tests to check whether a population is normally distributed; possibilities include chi-square test, Lilliefors test, and Q-Q plot	StatTools/Normality Tests	395	9.8
Chi-square test for independence	Test to check whether two attributes are probabilistically independent	Excel formulas	402	9.9, 9.10

Problems

Solutions for problems whose numbers appear within a colored box can be found in the Student Solution Files.

Conceptual Questions

C.1. Suppose you are testing the null hypothesis that a mean equals 75 versus a two-tailed alternative. If the true (but unknown) mean is 80, what kind of error *might* you make? When will you *not* make this error?

C.2. Suppose you hear the claim that a given test, such as the chi-square test for normality, is not very *powerful*. What exactly does this mean? If another test, such as the Lilliefors test, is claimed to be more powerful, how is it better than the less powerful test?

C.3. Explain exactly what it means for a test statistic to fall in the rejection region.

C.4. Give an example of when a one-sided test on a population mean would make more sense than a two-tailed test. Give an example of the opposite. In general, why do we say that there is no *statistical* way to decide whether a test should be run as a one-tailed test or a two-tailed test?

C.5. For any given hypothesis test, that is, for any specification of the null and alternative hypotheses, explain why you could make only a type I error or a type II error, but not both. When would you make a type I error? When would you make a type II error? Answer as generally as possible.

C.6. What are the null and alternative hypotheses in the chi-square or Lilliefors test for normality? Where is the burden of proof? Might you argue that it should go in the other direction? Explain.

C.7. We didn't discuss the role of sample size in this chapter as thoroughly as we did for confidence intervals in the previous chapter, but more advanced books do include sample size formulas for hypothesis testing. Consider the situation where you are testing the null hypothesis that a population mean is less than or equal to 100 versus a one-tailed alternative. A sample size formula might indicate the sample size needed to make the power at least 0.90 when the true mean is 103. What are the trade-offs here? Essentially, what is the advantage of a larger sample size?

C.8. Suppose that you wish to test a researcher's claim that the mean height in meters of a normally distributed population of rosebushes at a nursery has increased from its commonly accepted value of 1.60. To carry out this test, you obtain a random sample of size 150 from this population. This sample yields a mean of 1.80 and a standard deviation of 1.30. What are the appropriate null and alternative hypotheses? Is this a one-tailed or two-tailed test?

C.9. Suppose that you wish to test a manager's claim that the proportion of defective items generated by a particular production process has decreased from its long-run historical value of 0.30. To carry out this test, you

obtain a random sample of 300 items produced through this process. The test indicates a p-value of 0.01. What exactly is this p-value telling you? At what levels of significance can you reject the null hypothesis?

C.10. Suppose that a 99% confidence interval for the proportion p of all Lakeside residents whose annual income exceeds 80,000 extends from 0.10 to 0.18. The confidence interval is based on a random sample of 150 Lakeside residents. Using this information and a 1% significance level, you wish to test H_0: $p = 0.08$ versus H_a: $p \neq 0.08$. Based on the given information, are you able to reject the null hypothesis? Why or why not?

C.11. Suppose that you are performing a one-tailed hypothesis test. "Assuming that everything else remains constant, a decrease in the test's level of significance (α) leads to a higher probability of rejecting the null hypothesis." Is this statement true or false? Explain your reasoning.

C.12. Can pleasant aromas help people work more efficiently? Researchers conducted an investigation to answer this question. Fifty students worked a paper-and-pencil maze ten times. On five attempts, the students wore a mask with floral scents. On the other five attempts, they wore a mask with no scent. The 10 trials were performed in random order and each used a different maze. The researchers found that the subjects took less time to complete the maze when wearing the scented mask. Is this an example of an *observational study* or a *controlled experiment?* Explain.

Level A

53. The file **P09_53.xlsx** contains the number of days 44 mothers spent in the hospital after giving birth (in the year 2005). Before health insurance rules were changed (the change was effective January 1, 2005), the average number of days spent in a hospital by a new mother was two days. For a 5% level of significance, do the data in the file indicate (the research hypothesis) that women are now spending less time in the hospital after giving birth than they were prior to 2005? Explain your answer in terms of the p-value for the test.

54. Eighteen readers took a speed-reading course. The file **P09_54.xlsx** contains the number of words that they could read before and after the course. Test the alternative hypothesis at the 5% significance level that reading speeds have increased, on average, as a result of the course. Explain your answer in terms of the p-value. Do you need to assume that reading speeds (before and after) are normally distributed? Why or why not?

55. Statistics have shown that a child 0 to 4 years of age has a 0.0002 probability of getting cancer in any given year. Assume that during each of the last seven years there have been 100 children ages 0 to 4 years whose parents work in a university's business school. Four of these children have gotten cancer. Use this evidence to test whether the incidence of childhood cancer among children ages 0 to 4 years whose parents work at this business school exceeds the national average. State your hypotheses and determine the appropriate *p*-value.

56. African Americans in a St. Louis suburb sued the city claiming they were discriminated against in school-teacher hiring. Of the city's population, 5.7% were African American; of 405 teachers in the school system, 15 were African American. Set up appropriate hypotheses and determine whether African Americans are underrepresented. Does your answer depend on whether you use a one-tailed or two-tailed test? In discrimination cases, the Supreme Court always uses a two-tailed test at the 5% significance level. (Source: U.S. Supreme Court Case, *Hazlewood v. City of St. Louis*)

57. We hear that teenagers in today's world spend too much time playing video games. Does this have a significant effect on the grades they earn at school? You could test by this dividing students into two groups, those whose current high school grade-point average (GPA) is 3.0 or above and those whose GPA is below 3.0. Then you could sample students from each of these groups, discover the numbers of hours per week spent playing video games, and run a test to see whether high-GPA students average less time playing video games than low-GPA students. Run such a test on the (fictional) data in the file **P09_57.xlsx** and report the results. If the results are significant, does this prove that too many hours spent playing video games *causes* lower GPAs? Explain.

58. Sixty people have rated a new beer on a taste scale of 0 to 100. Their ratings are in the file **P09_58.xlsx**. Marketing has determined that the beer will be a success if the average taste rating exceeds 75. Using a 5% significance level, is there sufficient evidence to conclude that the beer will be a success? Discuss your result in terms of a *p*-value. Assume ratings are at least approximately normally distributed.

59. Fifty people were asked to rate a competitive beer on a taste scale of 0 to 100. Another 50 people were asked to rate our beer on the same taste scale. The file **P09_59.xlsx** contains the results. Do these data provide sufficient evidence to conclude, at the 1% significance level, that people believe our beer tastes better than the competitor's? Assume ratings are at least approximately normally distributed. Would you reach the same conclusion if only the data from the first 10 people in each group were used?.

60. Callaway is thinking about entering the golf ball market. The company will make a profit if its market share is more than 20%. A market survey indicates that 140 of 624 golf ball purchasers will buy a Callaway golf ball.
    a. Is this enough evidence to persuade Callaway to enter the golf ball market?
    b. How would you make the decision if you were Callaway management? Would you use hypothesis testing?

61. Sales of a new product will be profitable if the average of sales per store exceeds 100 per week. The product was test-marketed for one week at 10 stores, with the results listed in the file **P09_61.xlsx**. Assume that sales at each store are at least approximately normally distributed.
    a. Is this enough evidence to persuade the company to market the new product?
    b. How would you make the decision if you were deciding whether to market the new product? Would you use hypothesis testing?

62. A recent study concluded that children born to mothers who take Prozac tend to have more birth defects than children born to mothers who do not take Prozac.
    a. What do you think the null and alternative hypotheses were for this study?
    b. If you were a spokesperson for Eli Lilly (the company that produces Prozac), how might you rebut the conclusions of this study?

Level B

63. Suppose that you are the state superintendent of a state's public schools. You want to know whether decreasing the class size in grades 1 through 3 will improve student performance. Explain how you would set up a test to determine whether decreased class size improves student performance. What hypotheses would you use in this experiment? (This was actually done and smaller class size did help, particularly with minority students.)

64. The file **P02_35.xlsx** contains data from a survey of 500 randomly selected households. Economic researchers would like to test for a significant difference between the mean annual income levels of the first household wage earners in the first (i.e., SW) and second (i.e., NW) sectors of this community. In fact, they intend to perform similar hypothesis tests for the differences between the mean annual income levels of the first household wage earners from all other pairs of locations (i.e., first and third, first and fourth, second and third, second and fourth, and third and fourth).
    a. Before conducting any hypothesis tests on the difference between various pairs of mean income levels, perform a test for equal population variances in each pair of locations. For each pair, report a *p*-value and interpret its meaning.
    b. Based on your conclusions in part a, which test statistic should be used in performing a test for the existence of a difference between population means?
    c. Given your conclusions in part b, perform a test for the existence of a difference in mean annual income levels in each pair of locations. For each pair, report a *p*-value and interpret its meaning.

65. A group of 25 husbands and wives were chosen randomly. Each person was asked to indicate the most he or she would be willing to pay for a new car (assuming each had decided to buy a new car). The results are

shown in the file **P09_65.xlsx**. Can you accept the alternative hypothesis that the husbands are willing to spend more, on average, than the wives at the 5% significance level? What is the associated *p*-value? Is it appropriate to use a paired-sample or independent-sample test? Does it make a difference? Explain your reasoning.

66. A company is concerned with the high cholesterol levels of many of its employees. To help combat the problem, it opens an exercise facility and encourages its employees to use this facility. After a year, it chooses a random 100 employees who claim they use the facility regularly, and another 200 who claim they don't use it at all. The cholesterol levels of these 300 employees are checked, with the results shown in the file **P09_66.xlsx**.

   a. Is this sample evidence "proof" that the exercise facility, when used, tends to lower the mean cholesterol level? Phrase this as a hypothesis-testing problem and do the appropriate analysis. Do you feel comfortable that your analysis answers the question definitively (one way or the other)? Why or why not?

   b. Repeat part **a**, but replace "mean cholesterol level" with "percentage with level over 215." (The company believes that any level over 215 is dangerous.)

   c. What can you say about causality? Could you ever conclude from such a study that the exercise *causes* low cholesterol? Why or why not?

67. Suppose that you are trying to compare two populations on some variable (GMAT scores of men versus women, for example). Specifically, you are testing the null hypothesis that the means of the two populations are equal versus a two-tailed hypothesis. Are the following statements correct? Why or why not?

   a. A given difference (such as five points) between sample means from these populations will probably not be considered statistically significant if the sample sizes are small, but it will probably be considered statistically significant if the sample sizes are large.

   b. Virtually any difference between the population means will lead to statistically significant sample results if the sample sizes are sufficiently large.

68. Continuing the previous problem, analyze part **b** in Excel as follows. Start with hypothetical population mean GMAT scores for men and women, along with population standard deviations. Enter these at the top of a worksheet. You can make the two means as close as you like, but not identical. Simulate a sample of men's GMAT scores with your mean and standard deviation in column A. Do the same for women in column B. The sample sizes do not have to be the same, but you can make them the same. Then run the test for the difference between two means. (The point of this problem is that if the population means are fairly close and you pick relatively small sample sizes, the sample mean differences probably won't be significant. If you find this, generate new samples of a larger sample size and redo the test. Now they might be significant. If not, try again with a

still larger sample size. Eventually, you should get statistically significant differences.)

69. This problem concerns course scores (on a $0-100$ scale) for a large undergraduate computer programming course. The class is composed of both underclassmen (freshmen and sophomores) and upperclassmen (juniors and seniors). Also, the students can be categorized according to their previous mathematical background from previous courses as "low" or "high" mathematical background. The data for these students are in the file **P09_69.xlsx**. The variables are:

   - Score: score on a $0-100$ scale

   - Upper Class: 1 for an upperclassman, 0 otherwise

   - High Math: 1 for a high mathematical background, 0 otherwise

   For the following questions, assume that the students in this course represent a random sample from all college students who might take the course. This latter group is the population.

   a. Calculate a 90% confidence interval for the population mean score for the course. Do the same for the mean of all upperclassmen. Do the same for the mean of all upperclassmen with a high mathematical background.

   b. The professor believes he has enough evidence to "prove" the research hypothesis that upperclassmen score at least five points better, on average, than lowerclassmen. Do you agree? Answer by running the appropriate test.

   c. If a "good" grade is one that is at least 80, is there enough evidence to reject the null hypothesis that the fraction of good grades is the same for students with low math backgrounds as those with high math backgrounds? Which do you think is more appropriate, a one-tailed or two-tailed test? Explain your reasoning.

70. A cereal company wants to see which of two promotional strategies, supplying coupons in a local newspaper or including coupons in the cereal package itself, is more effective. (In the latter case, there is a label on the package indicating the presence of the coupon inside.) The company randomly chooses 80 Kroger's stores around the country—all of approximately the same size and overall sales volume—and promotes its cereal one way at 40 of these sites, and the other way at the other 40 sites. (All are at different geographical locations, so local newspaper ads for one of the sites should not affect sales at any other site.) Unfortunately, as in many business experiments, there is a factor beyond the company's control, namely, whether its main competitor at any particular site happens to be running a promotion of its own. The file **P09_70.xlsx** has 80 observations on three variables:

   - Sales: number of boxes sold during the first week of the company's promotion

   - Promotion Type: 1 if coupons are in local paper, 0 if coupons are inside box

   - Competitor Promotion: 1 if main competitor is running a promotion, 0 otherwise

a. Based on all 80 observations, calculate (1) the difference in sample mean sales between stores running the two different promotional types (and indicate which sample mean is larger), (2) the standard error of this difference, and (3) a 90% confidence interval for the population mean difference.

b. Test whether the population mean difference is zero (the null hypothesis) versus a two-tailed alternative. State whether you should accept or reject the null hypothesis, and why.

c. Repeat part **b**, but now restrict the population to stores where the competitor is not running a promotion of its own.

d. Based on data from all 80 observations, can you accept the (alternative) hypothesis, at the 5% level, that the mean company sales drop by at least 30 boxes when the competitor runs its own promotion (as opposed to not running its own promotion)?

e. We often use the term *population* without really thinking what it means. For this problem, explain in words exactly what the population mean refers to. What is the relevant population?

71. There is a lot of concern about "salary compression" in universities. This is the effect of paying huge salaries to attract newly-minted Ph.D. graduates to university tenure-track positions and not having enough left in the budget to compensate tenured faculty as fully as they might deserve. In short, it is very possible for a new hire to make a larger salary than a person with many years of valuable experience. The file **P09_71.xlsx** contains (fictional but realistic) salaries for a sample of business school professors, some already tenured and some not yet through the tenure process. Formulate reasonable null and alternative hypotheses and then test them with this data set. Write a short report of your findings.

CASE 9.1 Regression Toward the Mean

In Chapters 10 and 11, you will study regression, a method for relating one variable to other explanatory variables. However, the term *regression* has sometimes been used in a slightly different way, meaning "regression toward the mean." The example often cited is of male heights. If a father is unusually tall, for example, his son will typically be taller than average but not as tall as the father. Similarly, if a father is unusually short, the son will typically be shorter than average but not as short as the father. We say that the son's height tends to regress toward the mean. This case illustrates how regression toward the mean can occur.

Suppose a company administers an aptitude test to all of its job applicants. If an applicant scores below some value, he or she cannot be hired immediately but is allowed to retake a similar exam at a later time. In the interim the applicant can presumably study to prepare for the second exam. If we focus on the applicants who fail the exam the first time and then take it a second time, we would probably expect them to score better on the second exam. One plausible reason is that they are more familiar with the exam the second time. However, we will rule this out by assuming that the two exams are sufficiently different from one another. A second plausible reason is that the applicants have studied between exams, which has a beneficial effect. However, we will argue that even if studying has *no beneficial effect whatsoever*, these applicants will tend to do better the second time around. The reason is regression toward the mean. All of these applicants scored unusually low on the first exam, so they will tend to regress toward the mean on the second exam—that is, they will tend to score higher.

You can employ simulation to demonstrate this phenomenon, using the following model. Assume that the scores of *all* potential applicants are normally distributed with mean μ and standard deviation σ. Because we are assuming that any studying between exams has no beneficial effect, this distribution of scores is the *same* on the second exam as on the first. An

applicant fails the first exam if his or her score is below some cutoff value L. Now, we would certainly expect scores on the two exams to be positively correlated, with some correlation ρ. (This is the Greek letter "rho," often used for a population correlation.) That is, if everyone took both exams, applicants who scored high on the first would tend to score high on the second, and those who scored low on the first would tend to score low on the second. (This isn't regression to the mean, but simply that some applicants are better than others.)

Given this model, you can proceed by simulating many pairs of scores, one pair for each applicant. The scores for each exam should be normally distributed with parameters μ and σ, but the trick is to make them correlated. You can use our Binormal function to do this. (Binormal is short for *bivariate normal*.) This function is supplied in the file **C09_01.xlsm**. (Binormal is *not* a built-in Excel function.) It takes a pair of means (both equal to μ), a pair of standard deviations (both equal to σ), and a correlation ρ as arguments, with the syntax = **BINORMAL** (*means, stdevs, correlation*). To enter the formula, highlight two adjacent cells such as B5 and C5, type the formula, and press Ctrl+Shift+Enter. (This is because Binormal is an *array* function.) Then copy and paste to generate similar values for other applicants.

Once you have generated pairs of scores for many applicants, you should ignore all pairs except for those where the score on the first exam is less than L. (Sorting is suggested here, but freeze the random numbers first.) For these pairs, test whether the mean score on the second exam is *higher* than on the first, using a paired-samples test. If it is, you have demonstrated regression toward the mean. As you will probably discover, however, the results will depend on the values of the parameters you choose for μ, σ, ρ, and L. You should experiment with these. Assuming that you are able to demonstrate regression toward the mean, can you explain intuitively why it occurs?

CASE   9.2 Friday Effect in the Stock Market

Many people believe that there is a "Friday effect" in the stock market. They don't necessarily spell out exactly what they mean by this, but there is a sense that stock prices tend to be lower on Fridays than on other days. Because stock prices are readily available on the Web, it should be fairly easy to test this (alternative) hypothesis empirically. Before

collecting data and running a test, however, you must decide *exactly* which hypotheses you want to test because there are several possibilities. Formulate at least two sets of null/alternative hypotheses. Then gather some stock price data and test your hypotheses. Can you conclude that there is a statistically significant Friday effect in the stock market?

CASE   9.3 Removing Vioxx from the Market

For years, the drug Vioxx, developed and marketed by Merck, was one of the blockbuster drugs on the market. One of a number of so-called Cox-2 anti-inflammatory drugs, Vioxx was considered by many people a miracle drug for alleviating the pain from arthritis and other painful afflictions. Vioxx was marketed heavily on television, prescribed by most physicians, and used by an estimated two million Americans.

All of that changed in October 2004, when the results of a large study were released. The study, which followed approximately 2600 subjects over a period of about 18 months, concluded that Vioxx use over a long period of time caused a significant increase in the risk of developing serious heart problems. Merck almost immediately pulled Vioxx from the American market and doctors stopped prescribing it. On the basis of the study, Merck faced not only public embarrassment but the prospect of huge financial losses.

More specifically, the study had 1287 patients use Vioxx for an 18-month period, and it had another 1299 patients use a placebo over the same period. After 18 months, 45 of

the Vioxx patients had developed serious heart problems, whereas only 25 patients on the placebo developed such problems.

Given these results, would you agree with the conclusion that Vioxx caused a *significant* increase in the risk of developing serious heart problems? First, answer this from a purely statistical point of view, where *significant* means statistically significant. What hypothesis should you test, and how should you run the test? When you run the test, what is the corresponding *p*-value? Next, look at it from the point of view of patients. If you were a Vioxx user, would these results cause you significant worry? After all, some of the subjects who took placebos also developed heart problems, and 45 might not be considered that much larger than 25. Finally, look at it from Merck's point of view. Are the results practically significant to the company? What does it stand to lose? Develop an estimate, no matter how wild it might be, of the financial losses Merck might incur. Just think of all of those American Vioxx users and what they might do.

PART 4
REGRESSION ANALYSIS AND TIME SERIES FORECASTING

CHAPTER 10

Regression Analysis: Estimating Relationships

Nemanja Zotovic/Shutterstock.com

HEWLETT PACKARD DELIVERING PROFITABLE GROWTH FOR HPDIRECT.COM

Hewlett Packard (HP) is one of the world's largest providers of information technology infrastructure, software, services, and solutions. The company has traditionally marketed its products and services through third parties which comprised its sales networks and retail partnerships. However, as the Internet became popular in the 1990s, HP revisited its marketing strategy, and in 1998 it launched HPDirect.com, an online sales channel where customers could order products online and have them delivered to their homes. This posed a challenge for HP because it had to be careful not to alienate retail partners such as Best Buy and Walmart. It also faced fierce competition in the online market from Dell which, by the early 2000s, had become the leader in Internet-based sales.

As discussed in Tandon et al. (2013), HPDirect.com management was tasked in 2008 with growing its online sales by 150% over a three-year period, a particularly difficult challenge given its limited marketing budget. HPDirect.com marketing teams had to increase the number of visits to its online portal and attract customers who were most likely to make a purchase. To do this, they had to estimate visitors' potential to buy from their browsing behavior and, for visitors who had previously bought at HP, they had to estimate future demand for products based on past purchasing patterns. Furthermore, on the supply side, HP required highly accurate forecasts of product demand to ensure that their supply chain could match that demand. Inaccurate forecasts could lead to understaffing, with the resulting order cancellations and unhappy customers, or overstaffing, with increased costs at suppliers. Finally, the teams had to determine which marketing channels to use to reach different customers for different products. In short, the HPDirect.com had to find ways to better understand its customer base: their purchase preferences and their expected future purchase behavior.

The problem was attacked by data scientists in a group at HP called Global Analytics (GA). They used various method discussed in this book, including mathematical programming (optimization), Bayesian modeling, regression, time series forecasting, and simulation. They divided their solution process into three parts.

The goals of the first solution set were:

- To multiple regression to identify the key drivers of online traffic and their relative impacts. For example, the regression with weekly traffic to notebook Web pages had an R-square of 0.7, and its statistically significant explanatory variables were: marketing spend on search and display ads; use of coupons on the websites; holiday events; and the presence of desktop- or supplies-related promotions in the email message and the number of such email campaigns during the forecast period. The first three of these had a positive effect on notebook traffic; the last had a negative effect.

- To time series forecasting methods to predict the number of online visitors to each product category Web page. Although the forecasting methods used are somewhat more complex than those discussed in Chapter 12, their goals are the same: to identify the main components of Web traffic, trend and seasonality.
- To use linear programming to help the marketing teams optimize their budget allocations to the various marketing channels.

The goal of their second solution set was to use data-driven methods (similar to the data mining methods discussed in Chapter 17) to determine which customers are most likely to purchase which products, and when. This allowed them to direct marketing messages to the right customers for the right products at the right times. Essentially, customers are scored on whether they intend to purchase in the next three months, which product they are likely to purchase, and whether they are likely to respond to a marketing message such as an email. Then the customers with the largest scores on various combinations are targeted in an appropriate way. This prevents an unfocussed campaign where, for example, customers who are unlikely to purchase a product are bombarded by emails for that product.

Their third and final set of solutions was aimed at improving downstream warehouse operations by providing more accurate demand forecasts to their supply chain members. These forecasts had to consider current trends and the increased demand from the two earlier sets of solutions. As in the first solution set, this solution used a combination of multiple regression and time series forecasting methods, where the regression used lagged values of demand and marketing variables.

The results of the three-pronged solution process have been impressive. The improvements in customer targeting, budget allocation, and order forecasting resulted in additional revenue of $117 million over three years. This included (1) an increase of 2.6% in annual traffic, resulting in $44 million in incremental sales; (2) a 60% conversion rate increase from marketing and a 15% increase in average order size, resulting in $63 million in additional revenues; and (3) a cost reduction of $2 million through better inventory management, equivalent (assuming a 5 to 1 sales margin ratio) to $10 million in incremental sales.

10-1 Introduction

Regression analysis is the study of relationships between variables. It is one of the most useful tools for a business analyst because it applies to so many situations. Some potential uses of regression analysis in business include the following:

- How do wages of employees depend on years of experience, years of education, and gender?
- How does the current price of a stock depend on its own past values, as well as the current and past values of a market index?
- How does a company's current sales level depend on its current and past advertising levels, the advertising levels of its competitors, the company's own past sales levels, and the general level of the market?
- How does the total cost of producing a batch of items depend on the total quantity of items that have been produced?
- How does the selling price of a house depend on such factors as the appraised value of the house, the square footage of the house, the number of bedrooms in the house, and perhaps others?

Each of these questions asks how a single variable, such as selling price or employee wages, depends on other relevant variables. If you can estimate this relationship, you can not only better understand how the world operates, but you can also do a better job of predicting the variable in question. For example, you can not only understand how a company's sales are affected by its advertising, but you can also use the company's records of current and past advertising levels to predict future sales.

The branch of statistics that studies such relationships is called **regression analysis**, and it is the subject of this chapter and the next. Because of its generality and applicability, regression analysis is one of the most pervasive of all statistical methods in the business world. There are several ways to categorize regression analysis. One categorization is based on the overall purpose of the analysis. As suggested previously, there are two potential objectives of regression analysis: to understand how the world operates and to make predictions. Either of these objectives could be paramount in any particular application. If the variable in question is employee salary and you are using variables such as years of experience, level of education, and gender to explain salary levels, the purpose of the analysis is probably to understand how the world operates—that is, to explain how the variables combine in any given company to determine salaries. More specifically, the purpose of the analysis might be to discover whether there is any gender discrimination in salaries, after allowing for differences in work experience and education level.

The primary objective of the analysis can also be prediction. A good example of this is when the variable in question is company sales, and variables such as advertising and past sales levels are used as explanatory variables. In this case it is certainly important for the company to know how the relevant variables impact its sales. But the company's primary objective is probably to predict *future* sales levels, given current and past values of the explanatory variables. A company could even use a regression model for a what-if analysis, where it predicts future sales for many conceivable patterns of advertising and then selects its advertising level on the basis of these predictions.

Fortunately, the same regression analysis enables you to solve both problems simultaneously. That is, it indicates how the world operates and it enables us to make predictions. So although the objectives of regression studies might differ, the same basic analysis always applies.

A second categorization of regression analysis is based on the type of data being analyzed. There are two basic types: cross-sectional data and time series data. *Cross-sectional data* are usually data gathered from approximately the same period of time from a population. The housing and wage examples mentioned previously are typical cross-sectional studies. The first concerns a sample of houses, presumably sold during a short period of time, such as houses sold in Florida during the first couple of months of 2019. The second concerns a sample of employees observed at a particular point in time, such as a sample of automobile workers observed at the beginning of 2020.

In contrast, *time series data* involve one or more variables that are observed at several, usually equally spaced, points in time. The stock price example mentioned previously fits this description. You observe the price of a particular stock and possibly the price of a market index at the beginning of every week, say, and then try to explain the movement of the stock's price through time.

Regression analysis can be applied equally well to cross-sectional and time series data. However, there are technical reasons for treating time series data somewhat differently. The primary reason is that time series variables are usually related to their own past values. This property of many time series variables is called *autocorrelation*, and it adds complications to the analysis that we will discuss only briefly.

A third categorization of regression analysis involves the number of explanatory variables in the analysis. First, we need to introduce some terms. In every regression study there is a single variable that we are trying to explain or predict, called the **dependent variable** (also called the **response** variable or the **target** variable). To help explain or predict the dependent variable, we use one or more **explanatory variables** (also called **independent** variables or **predictor** variables).[1] If there is a single explanatory variable, the analysis is called **simple regression**. If there are several explanatory variables, it is called **multiple regression**.

Regression can be used to understand how the world operates, and it can be used for prediction.

Regression can be used to analyze cross-sectional data or time series data.

---

1 The traditional terms used in regression are *dependent* and *independent* variables. However, because these terms can cause confusion with probabilistic independence, a completely different concept, there has been an increasing use of the terms *response* and *explanatory* (or *predictor*) variables. We tend to prefer the terms *dependent* and *explanatory*, but this is largely a matter of taste.

> The dependent (or response or target) variable is the single variable being explained by the regression. The explanatory (or independent or predictor) variables are used to explain the dependent variable.

There are important differences between simple and multiple regression. The primary difference, as the name implies, is that simple regression is simpler. The calculations are simpler, the interpretation of output is somewhat simpler, and fewer complications can occur. We will begin with a simple regression example to introduce the ideas of regression. But simple regression is really just a special case of multiple regression, and there is little need to single it out for separate discussion—especially when computer software is available to perform the calculations in either case.

> A simple regression analysis includes a single explanatory variable, whereas multiple regression can include any number of explanatory variables.

"Linear" regression allows you to estimate linear relationships as well as some nonlinear relationships.

A final categorization of regression analysis is of linear versus nonlinear models. The only type of regression analysis we study here is *linear* regression. Generally, this means that the relationships between variables are *straight-line* relationships, whereas the term *nonlinear* implies curved relationships. By focusing on linear regression, it might appear that we are ignoring the many nonlinear relationships that exist in the business world. However, linear regression can often be used to estimate nonlinear relationships. As you will see, the term *linear regression* is more general than it appears. Admittedly, many of the relationships we study can be explained adequately by straight lines. But it is also true that many nonlinear relationships can be *linearized* by suitable mathematical transformations. Therefore, the only relationships we are ignoring in this book are those—and there are some—that cannot be transformed to linear. Such relationships can be studied, but only by advanced methods beyond the level of this book.

In this chapter we focus on line-fitting and curve-fitting; that is, on estimating equations that describe relationships between variables. We also discuss the interpretation of these equations, and we provide numeric measures that indicate the goodness of fit of the estimated equations. In the next chapter we extend the analysis to statistical inference of regression output.

10-2 Scatterplots: Graphing Relationships

A good way to begin any regression analysis is to draw one or more scatterplots. As discussed in Chapter 3, a scatterplot is a graphical plot of two variables, an *X* and a *Y*. If there is any relationship between the two variables, it is usually apparent from the scatterplot.

Example 10.1, which we will continue through the chapter, illustrates the usefulness of scatterplots. It is a typical example of cross-sectional data.

EXAMPLE

10.1 SALES VERSUS PROMOTIONS AT PHARMEX

Pharmex is a chain of drugstores that operates around the country. To see how effective its advertising and other promotional activities are, the company has collected data from 50 randomly selected metropolitan regions. In each region it has compared its own promotional expenditures and sales to those of the leading competitor in the region over the past year. There are two variables:

• Promote: Pharmex's promotional expenditures as a percentage of those of the leading competitor
• Sales: Pharmex's sales as a percentage of those of the leading competitor

Note that each of these variables is an *index*, not a dollar amount. For example, if Promote equals 95 for some region, this indicates that Pharmex's promotional expenditures in that region are 95% as large as those for the leading competitor in that region. The company expects that there is a positive relationship between these two variables, so that regions with relatively larger expenditures have relatively larger sales. However, it is not clear what the nature of this relationship is. The data are listed in the file **Drugstore Sales.xlsx**. (See Figure 10.1 for a listing of the data, with several rows hidden.) What type of relationship, if any, is apparent from a scatterplot?

Figure 10.1 Data for Drugstore Example

◢	A	B	C	D	E	F	G
1	Region	Promote	Sales				
2	1	77	85				
3	2	110	103				
4	3	110	102		Each value is a percentage of		
5	4	93	109		what the leading competitor did.		
6	5	90	85				
7	6	95	103				
49	48	100	98				
50	49	95	108				
51	50	96	87				

Objective

To use a scatterplot to examine the relationship between promotional expenses and sales at Pharmex.

Solution

It is customary to put the explanatory variable on the horizontal axis and the dependent variable on the vertical axis. In this example the store believes large promotional expenditures tend to "cause" larger values of sales, so Sales is on the vertical axis and Promote is on the horizontal axis. The resulting scatterplot appears in Figure 10.2.

Figure 10.2 Scatterplot of Sales Versus Promote

Sales Versus Promote

This scatterplot indicates that there is indeed a positive relationship between Promote and Sales—the points tend to rise from bottom left to top right—but the relationship is not perfect. If it were perfect, a given value of Promote would predict the value of Sales exactly. Clearly, this is not the case. For example, there are five regions with promotional values of 96 but all of them have different sales values. So the scatterplot indicates that while the variable Promote is helpful for predicting Sales, it does not lead to perfect predictions.

Finally, we briefly discuss causation. There is a tendency for an analyst (such as a drugstore manager) to say that larger promotional expenses *cause* larger sales values. However, unless the data are obtained in a carefully controlled experiment—which is certainly not the case here—you can never be absolutely sure about causation. One reason is that you can't always be sure which direction the causation goes. Does X cause Y, or does Y cause X? Another reason is that you can almost never rule out the possibility that some other variable is causing the variation in *both* of the observed variables. Although this is unlikely in this drugstore example, it is still a possibility.

Fundamental Insight

Regression and Causation

A successful regression analysis does not necessarily imply that the X variables *cause* Y to vary in a certain way. This is one possibility, but there are two others. First, even if a regression of Y versus X is promising, it could very easily be that Y is causing X; that is, the causality could go in the opposite direction. Second and more common, there could be other variables (not included in the regression) that are causing *both* Y and the X variables to vary.

Example 10.2 uses time series data to illustrate several other features of scatterplots. We will follow this example throughout the chapter as well.

EXAMPLE

10.2 EXPLAINING OVERHEAD COSTS AT BENDRIX

Bendrix Company manufactures various types of parts for automobiles. The manager of the factory wants to get a better understanding of overhead costs. These overhead costs include supervision, indirect labor, supplies, payroll taxes, overtime premiums, depreciation, and a number of miscellaneous items such as insurance, utilities, and janitorial and maintenance expenses. Some of these overhead costs are *fixed* in the sense that they do not vary appreciably with the volume of work being done, whereas others are *variable* and do vary directly with the volume of work. The fixed overhead costs tend to come from the supervision, depreciation, and miscellaneous categories, whereas the variable overhead costs tend to come from the indirect labor, supplies, payroll taxes, and overtime categories. However, it is not easy to draw a clear line between the fixed and variable overhead components.

The Bendrix manager has tracked total overhead costs for the past 36 months. To help explain these, he has also collected data on two variables that are related to the amount of work done at the factory. These variables are:

• Machine Hours: number of machine hours used during the month
• Production Runs: the number of separate production runs during the month

The first of these is a direct measure of the amount of work being done. To understand the second, we note that Bendrix manufactures parts in large batches. Each batch corresponds to a production run. Once a production run is completed, the factory must set up for the next production run. During this setup there is typically some downtime while the machinery is reconfigured for the part type scheduled for production in the next batch. Therefore, the manager believes that both of these variables could be responsible (in different ways) for variations in overhead costs. Do scatterplots support this belief?

Objective

To use scatterplots to examine the relationships among overhead, machine hours, and production runs at Bendrix.

Solution

The data appear in Figure 10.3 (with several hidden rows). (See the **Overhead Costs.xlsx** file.) Each observation (row) corresponds to a single month. The goal is to find possible relationships between the Overhead variable and the Machine Hours and Production Runs variables, but because these are time series variables, you should also be on the lookout for any relationships between these variables and the Month variable. That is, you should also investigate any time series behavior in these variables.

Figure 10.3 Data for Bendrix Overhead Example

	A	B	C	D
1	Month	Machine Hours	Production Runs	Overhead
2	1	1539	31	99798
3	2	1284	29	87804
4	3	1490	27	93681
5	4	1355	22	82262
6	5	1500	35	106968
35	34	1723	35	107828
36	35	1413	30	88032
37	36	1390	54	117943

This data set illustrates, even with a modest number of variables, how the number of potentially useful scatterplots can grow quickly. At the very least, you should examine the scatterplot between each potential explanatory variable (Machine Hours and Production Runs) and the dependent variable (Overhead). These appear in Figures 10.4 and 10.5. You can see that Overhead tends to increase as either Machine Hours increases or Production Runs increases. However, both relationships are far from perfect.

Figure 10.4 Scatterplot of Overhead Versus Machine Hours

Figure 10.5 Scatterplot of Overhead Versus Production Runs

To check for possible time series patterns, you can also create a time series graph for any of the variables. One of these, the time series graph for Overhead, is shown in Figure 10.6. It indicates a fairly random pattern through time, with no apparent upward trend or other obvious time series pattern. You can check that time series graphs of the Machine Hours and Production Runs variables also indicate no obvious time series patterns.

Finally, when there are multiple explanatory variables, you should check for relationships among them. The scatterplot of Machine Hours versus Production Runs appears in Figure 10.7. (Either variable could be chosen for the vertical axis.) This "cloud" of points indicates no relationship worth pursuing.

This is precisely the role of scatterplots: to provide a visual representation of relationships or the lack of relationships between variables.

Figure 10.6 Time Series Graph of Overhead Versus Month

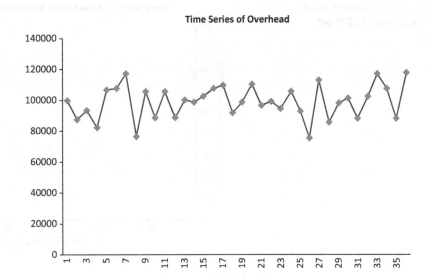

Figure 10.7 Scatterplot of Machine Hours Versus Production Runs

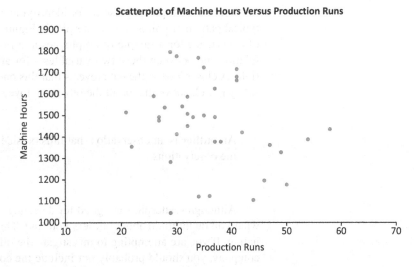

In summary, the Bendrix manager should continue to explore the positive relationship between Overhead and each of the Machine Hours and Production Runs variables. However, none of the variables appears to have any time series behavior, and the two potential explanatory variables do not appear to be related to each other.

Linear Versus Nonlinear Relationships

Scatterplots are extremely useful for detecting behavior that might not be obvious otherwise. We illustrate some of these in the next few subsections. First, the typical relationship you hope to see is a straight-line, or *linear*, relationship. This doesn't mean that all points lie on a straight line—this is too much to expect in real-world data—but that the points tend to cluster around a straight line. The scatterplots in Figures 10.2, 10.4, and 10.5 all exhibit linear relationships. At least, there is no obvious curvature.

The scatterplot in Figure 10.8, on the other hand, illustrates a relationship that is clearly nonlinear. The data in this scatterplot are 1990 data on more than 100 countries. The variables listed are life expectancy (of newborns, based on current mortality conditions) and GNP per capita. The obvious curvature in the scatterplot can be explained as follows. For poor countries, a slight increase in GNP per capita has a large effect on life expectancy. However, this effect decreases for wealthier countries. A straight-line relationship is definitely not appropriate for these data. However, as discussed previously, "linear" regression—after an appropriate transformation of the data—might still be applicable.

Figure 10.8 Scatterplot of Life Expectancy Versus GNP per Capita

Outliers

Scatterplots are especially useful for identifying **outliers**, observations that lie outside the typical pattern of points. The scatterplot in Figure 10.9 shows annual salaries versus years of experience for a sample of employees at a fictional company. There is a clear linear relationship between these two variables—for all employees except the point at the top right. A closer look at the data reveals that this one employee is the company CEO, whose salary is well above that of all the other employees.

> An **outlier** is an observation that falls outside of the general pattern of the rest of the observations.

Although scatterplots are good for detecting outliers, they do not necessarily indicate what you ought to do about outliers you find. This depends entirely on the particular situation. If you are attempting to investigate the salary structure for typical employees at a company, you should probably not include the company CEO. First, the CEO's salary is not determined in the same way as the salaries for typical employees. Second, if you do include the CEO in the analysis, it can greatly distort the results for the mass of typical employees. In other situations, however, it might *not* be appropriate to eliminate outliers just to make the analysis come out more nicely.

It is difficult to generalize about the treatment of outliers, but the following points are worth noting.

- If an outlier is clearly not a member of the population of interest, it is probably best to delete it from the analysis. This is the case for the company CEO in Figure 10.9.
- If it isn't clear whether outliers are members of the relevant population, you can run the regression analysis with them and again without them. If the results are practically the same in both cases, it is probably best to report the results with the outliers included. Otherwise, you can report both sets of results with a verbal explanation of the outliers.

Figure 10.9 Scatterplot
of Salary Versus Years of
Experience

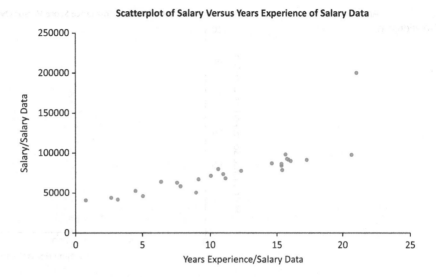

Unequal Variance

Occasionally, there is a clear relationship between two variables, but the variance of the dependent variable depends on the value of the explanatory variable. Figure 10.10 illustrates a common example of this. It shows the amount spent at an online store versus salary for the customers in the data set. There is a clear upward relationship, but the variability of amount spent increases as salary increases. This is evident from the *fan* shape. As you will see in the next chapter, this unequal variance violates one of the assumptions of linear regression analysis, and there are techniques to deal with it.

Figure 10.10 Unequal Variance
of Dependent Variable in a
Scatterplot

No Relationship

A scatterplot can provide one other useful piece of information: It can indicate that there is *no* relationship between a pair of variables, at least none worth pursuing. This is usually the case when the scatterplot appears as a shapeless swarm of points, as illustrated in Figure 10.11. Here the variables are an employee performance score and the number of overtime hours worked in the previous month for a sample of employees. There is virtually no hint of a relationship between these two variables in this plot, and if these are

Figure 10.11 An Example of No Relationship

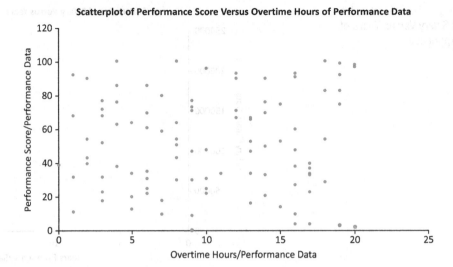

Scatterplot of Performance Score Versus Overtime Hours of Performance Data

the only two variables in the data set, the analysis can stop right here. Some people who use statistics evidently believe that a computer can perform magic on a set of numbers and find relationships that were completely hidden. Occasionally this is true, but when a scatterplot appears as in Figure 10.11, the variables are not related in any useful way, and that's all there is to it.

10-3 Correlations: Indicators of Linear Relationships

Scatterplots provide graphical indications of relationships, whether they are linear, non-linear, or essentially nonexistent. **Correlations** are numerical summary measures that indicate the strength of linear relationships between pairs of variables.[2] A correlation between a pair of variables is a single number that summarizes the information in a scatterplot. A correlation can be very useful, but it has an important limitation: It measures the strength of *linear* relationships only. If there is a nonlinear relationship, as suggested by a scatterplot, the correlation can be completely misleading. With this important limitation in mind, let's look a bit more closely at correlations.

The usual notation for a correlation between two variables X and Y is r_{XY}. (The subscripts can be omitted if the variables are clear from the context.) The formula for r_{XY} is given by Equation (10.1). Note that it is a sum of products in the numerator, divided by the product $s_X s_Y$ of the sample standard deviations of X and Y. This requires a considerable amount of computation, so correlations are almost always computed by software packages.

Formula for Correlation

$$r_{XY} = \frac{\Sigma\,(X_i - \overline{X})(Y_i - \overline{Y})/(n-1)}{s_X s_Y} \qquad (10.1)$$

The numerator of Equation (10.1) is also a measure of association between two variables X and Y, called the **covariance** between X and Y. Like a correlation, a covariance is a single

2 This section includes some material from Chapter 3 that we repeat here because of its importance in regression analysis.

number that measures the strength of the linear relationship between two variables. By looking at the sign of the covariance or correlation—plus or minus—you can tell whether the two variables are positively or negatively related. The drawback to a covariance, however, is that its magnitude depends on the units in which the variables are measured.

The magnitude of a covariance is difficult to interpret because it depends on the units of measurement.

To illustrate, the covariance between Overhead and Machine Hours in the Bendrix manufacturing data set is 1,333,138. (It can be found with Excel's COVAR function.) However, if each overhead value is divided by 1000, so that overhead costs are expressed in thousands of dollars, and each value of Machine Hours is divided by 100, so that machine hours are expressed in hundreds of hours, the covariance decreases by a factor of 100,000 to 13.33138. This is in spite of the fact that the basic relationship between these variables has not changed and the revised scatterplot has exactly the same shape. For this reason it is difficult to interpret the magnitude of a covariance, and we concentrate instead on correlations.

Unlike covariances, correlations have the attractive property that they are unaffected by the units of measurement. The rescaling described in the previous paragraph has no effect on the correlation between Overhead and Machine Hours. In either case the correlation is 0.632. All correlations are between -1 and $+1$, inclusive. The sign of a correlation, plus or minus, determines whether the linear relationship between two variables is positive or negative. In this respect, a correlation is like a covariance. However, the strength of the linear relationship between the variables is measured by the absolute value, or magnitude, of the correlation. The closer this magnitude is to 1, the stronger the linear relationship is.

A correlation close to -1 or $+1$ indicates a strong linear relationship. A correlation close to 0 indicates virtually no linear relationship.

A correlation equal to 0 or near 0 indicates practically no linear relationship. A correlation with magnitude close to 1, on the other hand, indicates a strong linear relationship. At the extreme, a correlation equal to -1 or $+1$ occurs only when the linear relationship is perfect—that is, when all points in the scatterplot lie on a straight line. Although such extremes virtually never occur in business applications, large correlations greater in magnitude than 0.9, for example, are not at all uncommon.

Looking back at the scatterplots for the Pharmex drugstore data in Figure 10.2, you can see that the correlation between Sales and Promote is positive—as the upward-sloping scatter of points suggests. It turns out to be 0.673. This is a moderately large correlation. It confirms the pattern in the scatterplot, namely, that the points increase linearly from left to right but with considerable variation around any particular straight line.

Similarly, the scatterplots for the Bendrix manufacturing data in Figures 10.4 and 10.5 indicate moderately large positive correlations, 0.632 and 0.521, between Overhead and Machine Hours and between Overhead and Production Runs. However, the correlation indicated in Figure 10.7 between Machine Hours and Production Runs, -0.229, is quite small and indicates almost no relationship between these two variables.

Correlations can be misleading when variables are related nonlinearly.

You must be careful when interpreting the correlations in Figures 10.8 and 10.9. The scatterplot between life expectancy and GNP per capita in Figure 10.8 is obviously nonlinear, and correlations are relevant descriptors only for *linear* relationships. If anything, the correlation in this example, 0.616, tends to underestimate the true strength of the relationship—the nonlinear one—between life expectancy and GNP per capita. In contrast, the correlation between salary and years of experience in Figure 10.9 is large, 0.894, but it is not nearly as large as it would be if the outlier were omitted. (It is then 0.992.) This example illustrates the considerable effect a single outlier can have on a correlation.

An obvious question is whether a given correlation is "large." This is a difficult question to answer directly. Clearly, a correlation such as 0.992 is quite large—the points tend to cluster very tightly around a straight line. Similarly, a correlation of 0.034 is quite small—the points tend to be a shapeless swarm. But there is a continuum of in-between values, as exhibited in Figures 10.2, 10.4, and 10.5. We give a more definite answer to this question when we examine the *square* of the correlation later in this chapter.

You can calculate a single correlation in Excel with the CORREL function. If you need to create a table of correlations for several variables, you can use the INDIRECT function method described in Chapter 3 (see the finished version of the Golf Stats file) or you can use an add-in such as StatTools.

Finally, we reiterate the important limitation of correlations (and covariances), namely, that they apply only to *linear* relationships. If a correlation is close to zero, you cannot automatically conclude that there is no relationship between the two variables. You should look at a scatterplot first. The chances are that the points are a shapeless swarm and that no relationship exists. But it is also possible that the points cluster around some curve. In this case the correlation is a misleading measure of the relationship.

10-4 Simple Linear Regression

Scatterplots and correlations are very useful for indicating linear relationships and the strengths of these relationships. But they do not *quantify* the relationships. For example, it is clear from the scatterplot of the Pharmex drugstore data that sales are related to promotional expenditures. But the scatterplot does not specify exactly what this relationship is. If the expenditure index for a given region is 95, what would you predict this region's sales index to be? Or if one region's expenditure index is 5 points larger than another's, how much larger would you predict the sales index of the former to be? To answer these questions, the relationship between the dependent variable Sales and the explanatory variable Promote must be quantified.

In this section we answer these types of questions for *simple* linear regression, where there is a *single* explanatory variable. We do so by fitting a straight line through the scatterplot of the dependent variable Y versus the explanatory variable X and then basing the answers to the questions on the fitted straight line. But which straight line? We address this issue next.

Remember that "simple" linear regression does not mean "easy"; it means only that there is a single explanatory variable.

10-4a Least Squares Estimation

The scatterplot between Sales and Promote, repeated in Figure 10.12, hints at a linear relationship between these two variables. It would not be difficult to draw a straight line through these points to produce a reasonably good fit. In fact, a possible linear fit is indicated in the graph. But we proceed more systematically than simply drawing lines freehand. Specifically, we choose the line that makes the vertical distances from the points to the line as small as possible, as explained next.

Figure 10.12 Scatterplot with Trend Line Superimposed

Consider the magnified graph in Figure 10.13. Several points in the scatterplot are shown, along with a line drawn through them. Note that the vertical distance from the horizontal axis to any point, which is just the value of Sales for that point, can be decomposed into two parts: the vertical distance from the horizontal axis to the line, and the vertical distance from the line to the point. The first of these is called the **fitted value**, and the second is called the **residual**. The idea is very simple. By using a straight line to reflect the relationship between Sales and Promote, you predict a given Sales to be at the height of the line above any particular value of Promote. That is, you predict Sales to equal the fitted value.

> A **fitted value** is the predicted value of the dependent variable. Graphically, it is the height of the line above a given explanatory value. The corresponding **residual** is the difference between the actual and fitted values of the dependent variable.

Figure 10.13 Fitted Values and Residuals

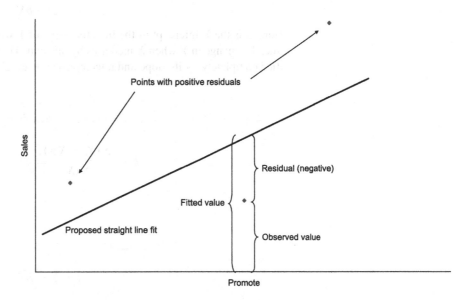

However, the relationship is not perfect. Not all (perhaps not any) of the points lie exactly on the line. The differences are the residuals. They show how much the observed values differ from the fitted values. If a particular residual is positive, the corresponding point is above the line; if it is negative, the point is below the line. The only time a residual is zero is when the point lies directly on the line. The relationship between observed values, fitted values, and residuals is very general and is stated in Equation (10.2).

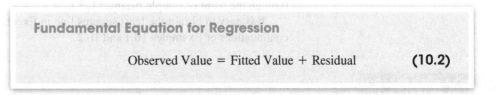

Fundamental Equation for Regression

$$\text{Observed Value} = \text{Fitted Value} + \text{Residual} \qquad \textbf{(10.2)}$$

We can now explain how to choose the best-fitting line through the points in the scatterplot. It is the line with the *smallest sum of squared residuals*. The resulting line is called the **least squares line**. Why do we use the sum of *squared* residuals? Why not minimize some other measure of the residuals? First, it is not appropriate to simply minimize the sum of the residuals. This is because the positive residuals would cancel the negative residuals. In fact, the least squares line has the property that the sum of the residuals is always exactly zero. Alternatively, we could minimize the sum of the *absolute values* of the residuals, and this is a perfectly reasonable procedure. However, for technical and historical reasons, it is not the procedure usually chosen. The minimization of the sum of squared residuals is deeply rooted in statistical tradition, and it works well.

> The **least squares line** is the line that minimizes the sum of the squared residuals. It is the line quoted in regression outputs.

The minimization problem itself is a calculus problem and is not discussed here. Virtually all statistical software packages perform this minimization automatically, so you do not need to be concerned with the technical details. However, we do provide the formulas for the least squares line.

Recall from basic algebra that the equation for any straight line can be written as

$$Y = a + bX$$

Here, a is the Y-intercept of the line, the value of Y when $X = 0$, and b is the slope of the line, the change in Y when X increases by one unit. Therefore, the least squares line is specified completely by its slope and intercept. These are given by Equations (10.3) and (10.4).

Equation for Slope in Simple Linear Regression

$$b = \frac{\Sigma (X_i - \overline{X})(Y_i - \overline{Y})}{\Sigma (X_i - \overline{X})^2} = r_{XY} \frac{s_Y}{s_X} \qquad \textbf{(10.3)}$$

Equation for Intercept in Simple Linear Regression

$$a = \overline{Y} - b\overline{X} \qquad \textbf{(10.4)}$$

We have presented these formulas primarily for conceptual purposes, not for hand calculations—the software takes care of the calculations. From the formula on the right for b, you can see that it is closely related to the correlation between X and Y. Specifically, if the standard deviations, s_X and s_Y, of X and Y are kept constant, the slope b of the least squares line varies directly with the correlation between the two variables. The effect of the formula for a is not quite as interesting. It simply forces the least squares line to go through the point of sample means, $(\overline{X}, \overline{Y})$.

It is easy to obtain the least squares line in Excel. We illustrate this in the following continuations of Examples 10.1 and 10.2.

EXAMPLE

10.1 SALES VERSUS PROMOTIONS AT PHARMEX (CONTINUED)

Find the least squares line for the Pharmex drugstore data, using Sales as the dependent variable and Promote as the explanatory variable.

Objective

To find the least squares line for sales as a function of promotional expenses at Pharmex.

Solution

To find the least squares line in Excel, there are several ways you can proceed. First, when you superimpose a trend line on a scatterplot of Y versus X, you can request the equation of the line. We did this in Figure 10.12. It shows that the intercept is 25.126 and the slope is 0.7623.

A second method is to use Excel's built-in INTERCEPT and SLOPE functions. Each of these takes two arguments: the range of the Y-values and the range of the X-values. These (along with other Excel functions to be discussed shortly) appear in Figure 10.14. However, these functions apply only to *simple* regression, where there is a single X variable. They can't be used when there are multiple X variables.

Figure 10.14 Excel's Built-in Regression Functions

◢	E	F	G	H	I	J	K	L	M
1	Excel regression functions (one X variable only)								
2	25.126		=INTERCEPT(C2:C51,B2:B51)						
3	0.762		=SLOPE(C2:C51,B2:B51)						
4	0.453		=RSQ(C2:C51,B2:B51)						
5	7.395		=STEYX(C2:C51,B2:B51)						
6									
7	0.762	25.126		=LINEST(C2:C51,B2:B51,TRUE,TRUE)					
8	0.121	11.883		(entered as an array function with Ctrl+Shift+Enter)					
9	0.453	7.395							
10	39.737	48							
11	2172.88	2624.74							

> The functions used in rows 2-5 are limited in that they apply only when there is a *single* independent variable.

A third method is to use Excel's LINEST function, also illustrated in Figure 10.14. This is a truly strange function, and we don't really recommend it, but it is available for simple *or* multiple regression. As explained in the finished version of the Pharmex file, LINEST is an array function, so you must first select the range for the output, then type the function, and then press Ctrl+Shift+Enter. As you can see in Figure 10.14, the first row (of five rows) of the LINEST output contains the same slope and intercept as before.

A fourth option is to use the Regression tool in Excel's built-in Analysis ToolPak add-in. We discussed this add-in briefly in Chapter 1, and a description of it is available at the first author's website: http://kelley.iu.edu/albrightbooks/Free_downloads .htm. Regression is arguably the best use for Analysis ToolPak, but it still has serious drawbacks, especially when you want to experiment with a number of regression equations. In short, it works, but it can be tedious to use. This is because it requires all the X variables for the regression to be in contiguous columns. (The same is true for the LINEST function.) This can involve a lot of rearrangement of the data.

Unfortunately, if you want to perform serious regression with Excel, its built-in tools do not really suffice. For this reason, we will instead rely heavily on StatTools in this chapter and the next chapter. StatTools is easy to use, it is powerful, and it provides the same types of regression output found in virtually all statistical software packages.

To perform the analysis, select Regression from the StatTools Regression and Classification dropdown list. Then fill in the resulting dialog box as shown in Figure 10.15. Specifically, select Multiple as the Regression Type (this type is used for both single and multiple regression in StatTools), and select Promote as the single I variable and Sales as the single D variable. (Here, I and D stand for independent and dependent. Remember that there is always a *single* D variable, but in multiple regression there can be several I variables.)

We will not use the Wizard at the top of this dialog box, but you should be aware of the three extra Regression tabs, shown in Figures 10.16, 10.17, and 10.18. These three tabs provide a number of options. Specifically, the options in Figure 10.17 allow you to request several diagnostic graphs. We typically request the graph of fitted values versus residuals, but you can request as many as you like.

Figure 10.15 StatTools
Regression Dialog Box

Figure 10.16 StatTools
Regression Parameters Tab

Figure 10.17 StatTools
Regression Graphs Tab

Figure 10.18 StatTools
Regression Options Tab

The regression output includes three parts. The first is the main regression output shown in Figure 10.19. The last two are a scatterplot of residuals and fitted values requested in the regression dialog box and a list of fitted values and residuals, a few of which are shown in Figure 10.20. (The list of fitted values and residuals is part of the output only if you select at least one of the optional graphs in Figure 10.17.)

Figure 10.19 StatTools Regression Output for Drugstore Example

	A	B	C	D	E	F	G
8	Multiple Regression for Sales	Multiple	R-Square	Adjusted	Std. Err. of	Rows	
9	Summary	R		R-square	Estimate	Ignored	
10		0.6730	0.4529	0.4415	7.394732934	0	
11							
12		Degrees of	Sum of	Mean of	F	p-Value	
13	ANOVA Table	Freedom	Squares	Squares			
14	Explained	1	2172.880392	2172.880392	39.73661179	< 0.0001	
15	Unexplained	48	2624.739608	54.68207516			
16							
17		Coefficient	Standard	t-Value	p-Value	Confidence Interval 95%	
18	Regression Table		Error			Lower	Upper
19	Constant	25.12642006	11.8825852	2.114558377	0.0397	1.234881256	49.01795886
20	Promote	0.762296485	0.120928454	6.303698263	< 0.0001	0.519153532	1.005439438

Figure 10.20 StatTools Scatterplot and Partial List of Residuals Versus Fitted Values

Graph Data	Sales	Fit	Residuals
1	85	83.8232494	1.176750604
2	103	108.9790334	−5.979033397
3	102	108.9790334	−6.979033397

We will eventually interpret all of the output in Figure 10.19, but for now, we focus on only a small part of it. Specifically, the intercept and slope of the least squares line appear under the Coefficient label in cells B19 and B20. They imply that the equation for the least squares line is[3]

$$\text{Predicted Sales} = 25.1264 + 0.7623\,\text{Promote}$$

In many applications, it makes no sense to have the explanatory variable(s) equal to zero. Then the intercept term has no practical or economic meaning.

The regression equation for this example can be interpreted as follows. The slope, 0.7623, indicates that the sales index tends to increase by about 0.76 for each one-unit increase in the promotional expenses index. Alternatively, if two regions are compared, where the second region spends one unit more than the first region, the predicted sales index for the second region is 0.76 larger than the predicted sales index for the first region. The interpretation of the intercept is less important. It is literally the predicted sales index for a region that does zero promotions. However, no region in the sample has anywhere near a zero promotion value. Therefore, in a situation like this, where the range of observed values for the explanatory variable does not include zero, it is best to think of the intercept term as simply an "anchor" for the least squares line that enables predictions of Y values for the range of observed X values.

A shapeless swarm of points in a scatterplot of residuals versus fitted values is typically good news. It means that no regression assumptions are violated.

A useful graph in almost any regression analysis is a scatterplot of residuals (on the vertical axis) versus fitted values. This scatterplot for the Pharmex data appears in Figure 10.20 (along with a few of the residuals and fitted values used to create the chart). You typically examine such a scatterplot for any obvious patterns. A good fit not only has small residuals, but it has residuals scattered *randomly* around zero with no apparent pattern. This appears to be the case for the Pharmex data.

---

3 We always report the left side of the estimated regression equation as the *predicted* value of the dependent variable. It is not the *actual* value of the dependent variable because the observations do not all lie on the estimated regression line.

> **StatTools Tip**
>
> **Educational Comments**
>
> StatTools provides optional cell comments to help you learn its outputs (regression or otherwise). To enable these comments, open the Applications Settings dialog box from the StatTools Utilities dropdown list and switch the Educational Comments setting from False (the default) to True.

EXAMPLE

10.2 EXPLAINING OVERHEAD COSTS AT BENDRIX (CONTINUED)

The Bendrix manufacturing data set has two potential explanatory variables, Machine Hours and Production Runs. Eventually, we will estimate a regression equation with *both* variables included. However, if we include only one at a time, what do they tell us about overhead costs?

Objective

To regress overhead expenses at Bendrix against machine hours and then against production runs.

Solution

The regression output for Overhead with Machine Hours as the single explanatory variable appears in Figure 10.21. The output when Production Runs is the only explanatory variable appears in Figure 10.22. The two least squares lines are therefore

$$\text{Predicted Overhead} = 48621 + 34.7\text{Machine Hours} \tag{10.5}$$

and

$$\text{Predicted Overhead} = 75606 + 655.1\text{Production Runs} \tag{10.6}$$

Figure 10.21 StatTools Regression Output for Overhead Versus Machine Hours

	A	B	C	D	E	F	G
8	*Multiple Regression for Overhead*	**Multiple R**	**R-Square**	**Adjusted R-square**	**Std. Err. of Estimate**	**Rows Ignored**	
9	*Summary*						
10		0.6319	0.3993	0.3816	8584.739353	0	
11							
12		**Degrees of Freedom**	**Sum of Squares**	**Mean of Squares**	**F**	**p-Value**	
13	*ANOVA Table*						
14	Explained	1	1665463368	1665463368	22.59856473	< 0.0001	
15	Unexplained	34	2505723492	73697749.75			
16							
17		**Coefficient**	**Standard Error**	**t-Value**	**p-Value**	**Confidence Interval 95%**	
18	*Regression Table*					Lower	Upper
19	Constant	48621.35463	10725.3327	4.533319013	< 0.0001	26824.85615	70417.85312
20	Machine Hours	34.70223642	7.299902097	4.753794772	< 0.0001	19.86705047	49.53742238

Figure 10.22 StatTools Regression Output for Overhead Versus Production Runs

	A	B	C	D	E	F	G
8	*Multiple Regression for Overhead*	**Multiple R**	**R-Square**	**Adjusted R-square**	**Std. Err. of Estimate**	**Rows Ignored**	
9	*Summary*						
10		0.5205	0.2710	0.2495	9457.239463	0	
11							
12		**Degrees of Freedom**	**Sum of Squares**	**Mean of Squares**	**F**	**p-Value**	
13	*ANOVA Table*						
14	Explained	1	1130247999	1130247999	12.6370288	0.0011	
15	Unexplained	34	3040938861	89439378.26			
16							
17		**Coefficient**	**Standard Error**	**t-Value**	**p-Value**	**Confidence Interval 95%**	
18	*Regression Table*					Lower	Upper
19	Constant	75605.51571	6808.610629	11.10439704	< 0.0001	61768.75415	89442.27728
20	Production Runs	655.0706602	184.2746779	3.554859885	0.0011	280.5794579	1029.561862

Clearly, these two equations are quite different, although each effectively breaks Overhead into a fixed component and a variable component. Equation (10.5) implies that the fixed component of overhead is about $48,621. Bendrix can expect to incur this amount even if zero machine hours are used. The variable component is the 34.7Machine Hours term. It implies that the expected overhead increases by about $35 for each extra machine hour. Equation (10.6), on the other hand, breaks overhead down into a fixed component of $75,606 and a variable component of about $655 per each production run.

The difference between these two equations can be attributed to the fact that neither tells the whole story. If the manager's goal is to split overhead into a fixed component and a variable component, the variable component should include *both* of the measures of work activity (and maybe others) to give a more complete explanation of overhead. We will explain how to do this when this example is revisited with *multiple* regression.

10-4b Standard Error of Estimate

We now examine fitted values and residuals to see how they lead to a useful summary measure for a regression equation. In a typical simple regression model, the expression $a + bX$ is the fitted value of Y. Graphically, it is the height of the estimated line above the value X. The fitted value is often denoted as $\hat{Y}$ (pronounced Y-hat):[4]

$$\hat{Y} = a + bX$$

Then a typical residual, denoted by e, is the difference between the observed value Y and the fitted value $\hat{Y}$. The following is a restatement of Equation (10.2):

$$e = Y - \hat{Y}$$

A few of the fitted values and associated residuals for the Pharmex drugstore example are shown in Figure 10.23. (These columns are inserted automatically by StatTools's Regression procedure when you request the optional scatterplot of residuals versus fitted values.)

Figure 10.23 Fitted Values and Residuals for Pharmex Example

	A	B	C	D
43	Graph Data	Sales	Fit	Residuals
44	1	85	83.8232494	1.176750604
45	2	103	108.9790334	−5.979033397
46	3	102	108.9790334	−6.979033397
47	4	109	96.01999315	12.98000685
48	5	85	93.7331037	−8.733103699
49	6	103	97.54458612	5.455413876
50	7	110	101.3560685	8.643931452
51	8	86	89.92162127	−3.921621275
52	9	92	98.30688261	−6.306882608
53	10	87	88.3970283	−1.397028305

The magnitudes of the residuals provide a good indication of how useful the regression line is for predicting Y values from X values. However, because there are numerous residuals, it is useful to summarize them with a single numerical measure. This measure, called the **standard error of estimate** and denoted s_e, is essentially the standard deviation of the residuals. It is given by Equation (10.7).

Formula for Standard Error of Estimate

$$s_e = \sqrt{\frac{\sum e_i^2}{n - 2}}$$

(10.7)

4 We could also write Predicted Y instead of $\hat{Y}$, but the latter notation is common in the statistics literature.

About two-thirds of the fitted Ŷ values are typically within one standard error of the actual Y values. About 95% are within two standard errors.

Because the average of the residuals from a least squares fit is always zero, this is identical to the standard deviation of the residuals except for the denominator $n - 2$, not the usual $n - 1$. As you will see in more generality later on, the rule is to subtract the number of parameters being estimated from the sample size n to obtain the denominator. Here there are two parameters being estimated: the intercept a and the slope b.

The usual empirical rules for standard deviations can be applied to the standard error of estimate. For example, about two-thirds of the residuals are typically within one standard error of their mean (which is zero). Stated another way, about two-thirds of the observed Y values are typically within one standard error of the corresponding fitted $\hat{Y}$ values. Similarly, about 95% of the observed Y values are typically within two standard errors of the corresponding fitted $\hat{Y}$ values.[5]

The standard error of estimate s_e is included in all regression outputs. Alternatively, it can be calculated directly with Excel's STEYX function (when there is only one X variable) in the form

In general, the standard error of estimate indicates the level of accuracy of predictions made from the regression equation. The smaller it is, the more accurate predictions tend to be.

$$= \text{STEYX } (Y\text{-range},X\text{-range})$$

The standard error for the Pharmex data appears in cell E10 of Figure 10.19. (It also appears in cells E5 and F9 of Figure 10.14 from built-in Excel functions.) Its value, approximately 7.39, indicates the typical magnitude of error when using promotional expenses, via the regression equation, to predict sales. More specifically, if the regression equation is used to predict sales for many regions, about two-thirds of the predictions will be within 7.39 of the actual sales values, and about 95% of the predictions will be within two standard errors, or 14.78, of the actual sales values.

Is this level of accuracy good? One measure of comparison is the standard deviation of the sales variable, namely, 9.90. (This is obtained by the usual STDEV.S function applied to the observed sales values.) It can be interpreted as the standard deviation of the residuals around a *horizontal* line positioned at the mean value of Sales. This is the relevant regression line if there are no explanatory variables—that is, if Promote is ignored. In other words, it is a measure of the prediction error if the sample mean of Sales is used as the prediction for *every* region and Promote is ignored. Unfortunately, the standard error of estimate, 7.39, is not much less than 9.90. This means that the Promote variable adds a relatively small amount to prediction accuracy. Predictions with it are not much better than predictions without it. A standard error of estimate *well* below 9.90 would certainly be preferred.

The standard error of estimate can often be used to judge which of several potential regression equations is the most useful. In the Bendrix manufacturing example we estimated two regression lines, one using Machine Hours and one using Production Runs. From Figures 10.21 and 10.22, their standard errors are approximately $8585 and $9457. These imply that Machine Hours is a slightly better predictor of overhead. The predictions based on Machine Hours will tend to be slightly more accurate than those based on Production Runs. Of course, the predictions based on *both* predictors should yield even more accurate predictions, as you will see when we discuss multiple regression for this example.

10-4c R-Square

We now discuss another important measure of the goodness of fit of the least squares line: R^2 (pronounced "R-square"). Along with the standard error of estimate s_e, it is the most frequently quoted measure in regression analyses. With a value always between 0 and 1, R^2 always has exactly the same interpretation: It is the *fraction of variation of the dependent variable explained by the regression line*. (It is often expressed as a percentage, so you hear about the *percentage* of variation explained by the regression line.)

> R^2 is the percentage of variation of the dependent variable explained by the regression.

---

[5] This requires that the residuals be at least approximately normally distributed, a requirement discussed in the next chapter.

To see more precisely what this means, we look briefly into the derivation of R^2. In the previous section we suggested that one way to measure the regression equation's ability to predict is to compare the standard error of estimate, s_e, to the standard deviation of the dependent variable, s_Y. The idea is that s_e is (essentially) the standard deviation of the residuals, whereas s_Y is the standard deviation of the residuals from a horizontal regression line at height $\overline{Y}$, the sample mean of the dependent variable. Therefore, if s_e is small compared to s_Y (that is, if s_e/s_Y is small), the regression line is evidently doing a good job of explaining the variation of the dependent variable.

The R^2 measure is based on this idea. It is defined by Equation (10.8). (This value can be calculated with Excel's RSQ function when there is a single X variable, but it is always reported by regression software packages.) Equation (10.8) indicates that when the residuals are small, R^2 will be close to 1, but when they are large, R^2 will be close to 0.

Formula for R^2

$$R^2 = 1 - \frac{\Sigma\, e_i^2}{\Sigma\, (Y_i - \overline{Y})^2} \qquad \textbf{(10.8)}$$

R^2 measures the goodness of a linear fit. The better the linear fit is, the closer R^2 is to 1.

You can see from cell C10 of Figure 10.19 that the R^2 measure for the Pharmex drugstore data is 0.453. (This value also appears in cells E4 and E9 of Figure 10.14 from built-in Excel functions, and it is available as a trend-line option, as illustrated in Figure 10.12.) In words, the single explanatory variable Promote is able to explain only 45.3% of the variation in the Sales variable. This is not particularly good—the same conclusion we made when we based goodness of fit on s_e. There is still 54.7% of the variation left unexplained. Of course, we would like R^2 to be as close to 1 as possible. Usually, the only way to increase it is to use better and/or more explanatory variables.

Analysts often compare equations on the basis of their R^2 values. You can see from Figures 10.21 and 10.22 that the R^2 values using Machine Hours and Production Runs as single explanatory variables for the Bendrix overhead data are 39.9% and 27.1%, respectively. These provide one more piece of evidence that Machine Hours is a slightly better predictor of Overhead than Production Runs. They also suggest that the percentage of variation of Overhead explained could be increased by including *both* variables in a single equation. This is true, as you will see shortly.

In simple linear regression, R^2 is the square of the correlation between the dependent variable and the explanatory variable.

There is a good reason for the notation R^2. It turns out that R^2 is the square of the correlation between the observed Y values and the fitted $\hat{Y}$ values. This correlation appears in all regression outputs as the *multiple R*. For the Pharmex data it is 0.673, as seen in cell B10 of Figure 10.19. Aside from rounding, the square of 0.673 is 0.453, which is the R^2 value next to it. In the case of simple linear regression, when there is only a single explanatory variable in the equation, the correlation between the Y variable and the fitted $\hat{Y}$ values is the same as the absolute value of the correlation between the Y variable and the explanatory X variable. For the Pharmex data you already saw that the correlation between Sales and Promote is indeed 0.673.

This interpretation of R^2 as the square of a correlation helps to clarify the issue of when a correlation is "large." For example, if the correlation between two variables Y and X is ±0.8, the regression of Y on X will have an R^2 of 0.64; that is, the regression with X as the only explanatory variable will explain 64% of the variation in Y, this percentage drops to 49%; if the correlation increases to ±0.9, the percentage increases to 81%. The point is that before a single variable X can explain a large percentage of the variation in some other variable Y, the two variables must be highly correlated—in *either* a positive or negative direction.

Problems

Solutions for problems whose numbers appear within a colored box can be found in the Student Solution Files.

Level A

1. Explore the relationship between the selling prices (Y) and the appraised values (X) of the 148 homes in the file **P02_11.xlsx** by estimating a simple linear regression model. Interpret the standard error of estimate s_e and R^2 and the least squares line for these data.
   a. Is there evidence of a *linear* relationship between the selling price and appraised value? If so, characterize the relationship. Is it positive or negative? Is it weak or strong?
   b. For which of the three remaining variables, the size of the home, the number of bedrooms, and the number of bathrooms, is the relationship with the home's selling price *stronger*? Justify your choice with additional simple linear regression models.

2. The file **P02_10.xlsx** contains midterm and final exam scores for 96 students in a corporate finance course. Each row contains the two exam scores for a given student, so you might expect them to be positively correlated.
   a. Create a scatterplot of the final exam score (Y) versus the midterm score (X). Based on the visual evidence, would you say that the scores for the two exams are strongly related? Is the relationship a linear one?
   b. Superimpose a trend line on the scatterplot, and use the option to display the equation and the R^2 value. What does this equation indicate in terms of predicting a student's final exam score from his or her midterm score? Be specific.
   c. Run a regression to confirm the trend-line equation from part **b**. What does the standard error of estimate say about the accuracy of the prediction requested in part **b**?

3. A company produces electric motors for use in home appliances. One of the company's production managers is interested in examining the relationship between inspection costs in a month (X) and the number of motors produced that month that were returned by dissatisfied customers (Y). He has collected the data in the file **P10_03.xlsx** for the past 36 months. Estimate a simple linear regression equation using the given data and interpret it for this production manager. Also, interpret s_e and R^2 for these data.

4. The owner of Original Italian Pizza restaurant chain wants to understand which variable most strongly influences the sales of his specialty deep-dish pizza. He has gathered data on the monthly sales of deep-dish pizzas at his restaurants and observations on other potentially relevant variables for each of several outlets in central Indiana. These data are provided in the file **P10_04.xlsx**. Estimate a simple linear regression equation between the quantity sold (Y) and each of the following candidates for the best explanatory variable: average price of deep-dish pizzas, monthly advertising expenditures, and disposable income per household in the areas surrounding the outlets. Which variable is *most* strongly associated with the number of pizzas sold? Explain your choice.

5. The human resources manager of DataCom, Inc., wants to examine the relationship between annual salaries (Y) and the number of years employees have worked at DataCom (X). These data have been collected for a sample of employees and are given in columns B and C of the file **P10_05.xlsx.**
   a. Estimate the relationship between Y and X. Interpret the least squares line.
   b. How well does the estimated simple linear regression equation fit the given data? Provide evidence for your answer.

6. The file **P10_06.xlsx** contains information on over 200 movies that were released during 2006 and 2007.
   a. Create two scatterplots and corresponding correlations, one of Total US Gross (Y) versus 7-day Gross (X) and one of Total US Gross (Y) versus 14-day Gross (X). Based on the visual evidence, is it possible to predict the total U.S. gross of a movie from its first week's gross or its first two weeks' gross?
   b. Run two simple regressions corresponding to the two scatterplots in part **a**. Explain exactly what they tell you about the movie business. How accurate would the two predictions requested in part **a** tend to be? Be as specific as possible.

7. Examine the relationship between the average utility bills for homes of a particular size (Y) and the average monthly temperature (X). The data in the file **P10_07.xlsx** include the average monthly bill and temperature for each month of the past year.
   a. Use the given data to estimate a simple linear regression equation. Interpret the least squares line.
   b. How well does the estimated regression equation fit the given data? How might you do a better job of explaining the variation of the average utility bills for homes of a certain size?

8. The file **P10_08.xlsx** contains data on the top 200 professional golfers in 2017. (The same data set, covering multiple years, was used in Example 3.4 in Chapter 3.)
   a. Create a new variable, Earnings per Round, and the ratio of Earnings to Rounds. Then create five scatterplots and corresponding correlations, each with Earnings per Round on the Y axis. The X-axis variables are those that most golf enthusiasts probably think are related to Earnings per Round: Yards/Drive, Driving Accuracy, Greens in Regulation, Putting Average, and Sand Save Pct. Comment on the results. Are any of these highly related to Earnings per Round? Do the correlations have the signs you would expect (positive or negative)?

b. For the two most highly correlated variables with Earnings per Round (positive or negative), run the regressions corresponding to the scatterplots. Explain exactly what they tell you about predicting Earnings per Round. How accurate do you think these predictions would be?

9. Management of a home appliance store wants to understand the growth pattern of the monthly sales of Blu-ray disc players over the past two years. The managers have recorded the relevant data in the file **P10_09.xlsx**. Have the sales of this product been growing linearly over these months? Using simple linear regression, explain why or why not.

10. Do the selling prices of houses in a given community vary systematically with their sizes (as measured in square feet)? Answer this question by estimating a simple regression equation where the selling price of the house is the dependent variable and the size of the house is the explanatory variable. Use the sample data given in the file **P10_10.xlsx**. Interpret your estimated equation and the associated R^2.

11. The file **P10_11.xlsx** contains annual observations of the American minimum wage. Has the minimum wage been growing at roughly a *constant* rate over this period? Use simple linear regression analysis to address this question. Explain the results you obtain. (You can ignore the data in column C for now.)

12. Based on the data in the file **P02_23.xlsx** from the U.S. Department of Agriculture, explore the relationship between the number of farms (X) and the average size of a farm (Y) in the United States. Specifically, estimate a simple linear regression equation and interpret it.

13. Estimate the relationship between monthly electrical power usage (Y) and home size (X) using the data in the file **P10_13.xlsx**. Interpret your results. How well does a

simple linear regression equation explain the variation in monthly electrical power usage?

14. The file **P02_12.xlsx** includes data on the 50 top graduate programs in the United States, according to a recent *U.S. News & World Report* survey. Columns B, C, and D contain ratings: an overall rating, a rating by peer schools, and a rating by recruiters. The other columns contain data that might be related to these ratings.
   a. Find a table of correlations between all of the numerical variables. From these correlations, which variables in columns E–L are most highly correlated with the various ratings?
   b. For the Overall rating, run a regression using it as the dependent variable and the variable (from columns E–L) most highly correlated with it. Interpret this equation. Could you have guessed the value of R^2 before running the regression? Explain. What does the standard error of estimate indicate?
   c. Repeat part **b** with the Peers rating as the dependent variable. Repeat again with the Recruiters rating as the dependent variable. Discuss any differences among the three regressions in parts **b** and **c**.

Level B

15. If you haven't already done Problem 6 on 2006–2007 movies, do it now. The scatterplots of Total US Gross versus 7-day Gross or 14-day Gross indicate some possible outliers at the right—the movies that did great during their first week or two. Identify these outliers (you can decide how many qualify) and move them out of the data set. Then redo Problem 6 without the outliers. Comment on whether you get very different results. Specifically, do these outliers affect the slope of either regression line? Do they affect the standard error of estimate or R^2?

10-5 Multiple Regression

In general, there are two possible approaches to obtaining improved fits in regression. The first is to examine a scatterplot of residuals for nonlinear patterns and then make appropriate modifications to the regression equation. We will discuss this approach later in the chapter. The second approach is more straightforward: Add more explanatory variables to the regression equation. In the Bendrix manufacturing example, we deliberately included only a single explanatory variable in the equation at a time to keep the equations simple. But because scatterplots indicate that both explanatory variables are also related to Overhead, it makes sense to try including both in the regression equation. With any luck, the linear fit should improve.

When you include several explanatory variables in the regression equation, you move into the realm of *multiple* regression. Some of the concepts from simple regression carry over naturally to multiple regression, but some change considerably. The following list provides a starting point that we expand on throughout this section.

Characteristics of Multiple Regression

- Graphically, you are no longer fitting a *line* to a set of points. If there are exactly two explanatory variables, you are fitting a *plane* to the data in three-dimensional space. There is one dimension for the dependent variable and one for each of the two explanatory variables. Although you can imagine a flat plane passing through a swarm of points, it is difficult to graph this on a two-dimensional screen. And if there are more than two explanatory variables, you can only imagine the regression plane; drawing in four or more dimensions is impossible.
- The regression equation is still estimated by the least squares method—that is, by minimizing the sum of squared residuals. However, it is definitely not practical to implement this method by hand. A statistical add-in such as Analysis ToolPak or StatTools is required.
- Simple regression is actually a special case of multiple regression—that is, an equation with a single explanatory variable can be considered a "multiple" regression equation.
- There is a slope term for each explanatory variable in the equation. The interpretation of these slope terms is somewhat different than in simple regression, as will be explained shortly.
- The standard error of estimate and R^2 summary measures are almost exactly the same as in simple regression, as explained in Section 10-5b.
- Many *types* of explanatory variables can be included in the regression equation, as will be explained in Section 10-6. To a large part, these are responsible for the wide applicability of multiple regression in the business world. However, the burden is on you to choose the *best* set of explanatory variables. This generally presents a challenge.

10-5a Interpretation of Regression Coefficients

A typical slope term measures the expected change in Y when the corresponding X increases by one unit.

If Y is the dependent variable and X_1 through X_k are the explanatory variables, then a typical multiple regression equation has the form shown in Equation (10.9), where a is again the Y-intercept and b_1 through b_k are the slopes. Collectively, a and the b's in Equation (10.9) are called the **regression coefficients**. The intercept a is the expected value of Y when all the X's equal zero. (This makes sense only if it is practical for all the X's to equal zero, which is seldom the case.) Each slope coefficient is the expected change in Y when this particular X increases by one unit *and the other X's in the equation remain constant*. For example, b_1 is the expected change in Y when X_1 increases by one unit and the other X's in the equation, X_2 through X_k, remain constant.

General Multiple Regression Equation

$$\text{Predicted } Y = a + b_1X_1 + b_2X_2 + \cdots + b_kX_k \qquad \textbf{(10.9)}$$

This extra proviso, "when the other X's in the equation remain constant," is crucial for the interpretation of the regression coefficients. In particular, it means that the estimates of the b's depend on which other X's are included in the regression equation. We illustrate these ideas in the following continuation of Example 10.2.

EXAMPLE

10.2 EXPLAINING OVERHEAD COSTS AT BENDRIX (CONTINUED)

Estimate and interpret the equation for Overhead when both explanatory variables, Machine Hours and Production Runs, are included in the regression equation.

Objective

To estimate the equation for overhead costs at Bendrix as a function of machine hours and production runs.

Solution

To obtain the regression output with StatTools, select Regression from the StatTools Regression and Classification dropdown list and fill out the resulting dialog box as shown in Figure 10.24.[6] As before, choose the Multiple option, specify the single *D* variable and the two *I* variables, and check any optional graphs you want to see. (We selected the first and third graph options. Refer to Figure 10.17.)

Figure 10.24 StatTools Multiple Regression Dialog Box

The main regression output appears in Figure 10.25. The coefficients in the range B19:B21 indicate that the estimated regression equation is

$$\text{Predicted Overhead} = 3997 + 43.54\text{Machine Hours} + 883.62\text{Production Runs} \qquad \textbf{(10.10)}$$

The interpretation of Equation (10.10) is that if the number of production runs is held constant, the overhead cost is expected to increase by $43.54 for each extra machine hour, and if the number of machine hours is held constant, the overhead cost is expected to increase by $883.62 for each extra production run. The Bendrix manager can interpret the intercept, $3997, as the fixed component of overhead. The slope terms involving Machine Hours and Production Runs are the variable components of overhead.

---

6 Alternatively, you could use Analysis ToolPak to get essentially the same regression output.

Figure 10.25 Multiple Regression Output for Bendrix Example

	A	B	C	D	E	F	G
8	*Multiple Regression for Overhead*	Multiple	R-Square	Adjusted	Std. Err. of	Rows	
9	*Summary*	R		R-square	Estimate	Ignored	
10		0.9308	0.8664	0.8583	4108.99309	0	
11							
12		Degrees of	Sum of	Mean of	F	p-Value	
13	*ANOVA Table*	Freedom	Squares	Squares			
14	Explained	2	3614020661	1807010330	107.0261279	< 0.0001	
15	Unexplained	33	557166199.1	16883824.22			
16							
17		Coefficient	Standard	t-Value	p-Value	Confidence Interval 95%	
18	*Regression Table*		Error			Lower	Upper
19	Constant	3996.678209	6603.650932	0.605222512	0.5492	−9438.550632	17431.90705
20	Machine Hours	43.53639812	3.5894837	12.12887472	< 0.0001	36.23353862	50.83925761
21	Production Runs	883.6179252	82.25140753	10.74289124	< 0.0001	716.2761784	1050.959672

It is interesting to compare Equation (10.10) with the separate equations for Overhead involving only a single variable each. From the previous section these are

$$\text{Predicted Overhead} = 48621 + 34.7 \text{Machine Hours}$$

and

$$\text{Predicted Overhead} = 75606 + 655.1 \text{Production Runs}$$

The coefficient of Machine Hours has increased from 34.7 to 43.5 and the coefficient of Production Runs has increased from 655.1 to 883.6. Also, the intercept is now lower than either intercept in the single-variable equations. In general, it is difficult to guess the changes that will occur when more explanatory variables are added to the equation, but it is likely that changes *will* occur.

The estimated coefficient of any explanatory variable typically depends on which other explanatory variables are included in the equation.

The reasoning is that when Machine Hours is the only variable in the equation, Production Runs is *not* being held constant—it is being ignored—so in effect the coefficient 34.7 of Machine Hours indicates the effect of Machine Hours *and* the omitted Production Runs on Overhead. But when both variables are included, the coefficient 43.5 of Machine Hours indicates the effect of Machine Hours only, holding Production Runs constant. Because the coefficients of Machine Hours in the two equations have different *meanings*, it is not surprising that they have different numeric estimates.

Fundamental Insight

Multiple Regression, Correlations, and Scatterplots

When there are multiple potential X's for a regression on Y, it is useful to calculate correlations and scatterplots of Y versus each X. But remember that correlations and scatterplots are for *two variables only*; they do not necessarily tell the whole story. Sometimes, as in this overhead example, a multiple regression can be quite different than might be expected from correlations and scatterplots alone. Specifically, the R^2 value for the multiple regression can be considerably smaller *or* larger than might be expected.

10-5b Interpretation of Standard Error of Estimate and R-Square

The multiple regression output in Figure 10.25 is very similar to simple regression output. In particular, cells C10 and E10 again show R^2 and the standard error of estimate s_e. Also, the square root of R^2 appears in cell B10. The interpretation of these quantities is almost exactly the same as in simple regression. The standard error of estimate is essentially the standard deviation of residuals, but it is now given by Equation (10.11), where n is the number of observations and k is the number of explanatory variables in the equation.

Formula for Standard Error of Estimate in Multiple Regression

$$s_e = \sqrt{\frac{\Sigma e_i^2}{n - k - 1}}$$

(10.11)

Fortunately, you can interpret s_e exactly as before. It is a measure of the typical prediction error when the multiple regression equation is used to predict the dependent variable. In this example, about two-thirds of the predictions should be within one standard error, or $4109, of the actual overhead cost. By comparing this with the standard errors from the single-variable equations for Overhead, $8585 and $9457, you can see that the multiple regression equation will tend to provide predictions that are more than twice as accurate as the single-variable equations—a big improvement.

The R^2 value is again the percentage of variation of the dependent variable explained by the combined set of explanatory variables. In fact, it even has the same formula as before [see Equation (10.8)]. For the Bendrix data, Machine Hours and Production Runs combine to explain 86.6% of the variation in Overhead. This is a big improvement over the single-variable equations that were able to explain only 39.9% and 27.1% of the variation in Overhead. Remarkably, the combination of the two explanatory variables explains a larger percentage than the *sum* of their individual effects. This is not common, but this example shows that it is possible.

The square root of R^2 shown in cell B10 of Figure 10.25 (the multiple R) is again the correlation between the fitted values and the observed values of the dependent variable. For the Bendrix data the correlation between them is 0.931, quite high. A graphical indication of this high correlation can be seen in one of the requested scatterplots, the plot of fitted versus observed values of Overhead. This scatterplot appears in Figure 10.26. If the

R^2 is always the square of the correlation between the actual and fitted Y values— in both simple and multiple regression.

Figure 10.26 StatTools Scatterplot of Fitted Values Versus Observed Values of Overhead

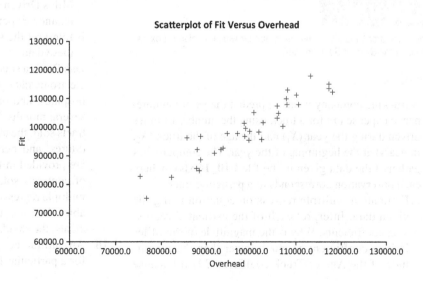

regression equation gave *perfect* predictions, all of the points in this plot would lie on a 45° line—each fitted value would *equal* the corresponding observed value. Although a perfect fit virtually never occurs, the closer the points are to a 45° line, the better the fit is, as indicated by R^2 or its square root.

Although the R^2 value is one of the most frequently quoted values from a regression analysis, it does have one serious drawback: R^2 can only *increase* when extra explanatory variables are added to an equation. This can lead to "fishing expeditions," where you keep adding variables to an equation, some of which have no conceptual relationship to the dependent variable, just to inflate the R^2 value. To avoid adding extra variables that do not really belong, an **adjusted R^2** value is typically listed in regression outputs. This adjusted value appears in cell D10 of Figure 10.25. Although it has no direct interpretation as "percentage of variation explained," it *can* decrease when unnecessary explanatory variables are added to an equation. Therefore, it serves as an index that you can monitor. If you add variables and the adjusted R^2 *decreases*, the extra variables are essentially not pulling their weight and should probably be omitted. We will say much more about this issue in the next chapter.

> **Adjusted R^2** is a measure that adjusts R^2 for the number of explanatory variables in the equation. It is used primarily to monitor whether extra explanatory variables really belong in the equation.

Fundamental Insight

R^2, Adjusted R^2, and Standard Error of Estimate

Sometimes a regression equation is "built" by successively adding explanatory variables to an equation. As more variables are added, it is a mathematical fact that R^2 *must* increase; it cannot decrease. However, the standard error of estimate *can* increase, and the adjusted R^2 *can* decrease, each signaling that the extra variables are not useful and should probably be omitted from the equation. In fact, the purpose of adjusted R^2 is to monitor whether the equation is getting better or worse as more variables are added.

Problems

Solutions for problems whose numbers appear within a colored box can be found in the Student Solution Files.

Level A

16. A trucking company wants to predict the yearly maintenance expense (Y) for a truck using the number of miles driven during the year (X_1) and the age of the truck (X_2, in years) at the beginning of the year. The company has gathered the data given in the file **P10_16.xlsx**, where each observation corresponds to a particular truck.
    a. Estimate a multiple regression equation using the given data. Interpret each of the estimated regression coefficients. Why is the magnitude of the Miles Driven coefficient so much lower than the magnitude of the Age of Truck coefficient? Is it because

Miles Driven is not as important in predicting Maintenance Expense?
    b. Interpret the standard error of estimate s_e and R^2 for these data.

17. DataPro is a small but rapidly growing firm that provides electronic data-processing services to commercial firms, hospitals, and other organizations. For each of the past several months, DataPro has tracked the number of contracts sold, the average contract price, advertising expenditures, and personal selling expenditures. These data are provided in the file **P10_17.xlsx**. Using the number of contracts sold as the dependent variable, estimate a multiple regression equation with three explanatory variables. Interpret each of the estimated regression coefficients, the standard error of estimate, and R^2.

18. An antique collector believes that the price received for a particular item increases with its age and with the

number of bidders. The file **P10_18.xlsx** contains data on these three variables for several recently auctioned comparable items.

   a. Estimate a multiple regression equation using the given data. Interpret each of the estimated regression coefficients. Is the antique collector correct in believing that the price received for the item increases with its age and with the number of bidders?

   b. Interpret the standard error of estimate s_e and R^2. Does it appear that predictions of price from this equation will be very accurate?

19. Stock market analysts are continually looking for reliable predictors of stock prices. Consider the problem of modeling the price per share of electric utility stocks (Y). Two variables thought to influence this stock price are return on average equity (X_1) and annual dividend rate (X_2). The stock price, returns on equity, and dividend rates on a randomly selected day for several electric utility stocks are provided in the file **P10_19.xlsx.**

   a. Estimate a multiple regression equation using the given data. Interpret each of the estimated regression coefficients.

   b. Interpret the standard error of estimate s_e, R^2, and the adjusted R^2. Does it appear that predictions of price from this equation will be very accurate?

20. The manager of a commuter rail transportation system was recently asked by her governing board to determine which factors have a significant impact on the demand for rides in the large city served by the transportation network. The system manager collected data on variables thought to be possibly related to the number of weekly riders on the city's rail system. The file **P10_20.xlsx** contain these data.

   a. What do you expect the signs of the coefficients of the explanatory variables in this multiple regression equation to be? Why? (Answer this *before* running the regression.)

   b. Estimate a multiple regression equation using the given data. Interpret each of the estimated regression coefficients. Are the signs of the estimated coefficients consistent with your expectations in part **a**?

   c. What proportion of the total variation in the number of weekly riders is *not* explained by this estimated multiple regression equation?

21. Consider the enrollment data for *Business Week*'s top U.S. graduate business programs in the file **P10_21.xlsx.** Use the data in the MBA Data sheet to estimate a multiple regression equation to assess whether there is a relationship between the total number of full-time students (Enrollment) and the following explanatory variables: (a) the proportion of female students, (b) the proportion of minority students, and (c) the proportion of international students enrolled at these business schools.

   a. Interpret the coefficients of the estimated regression equation. Do any of these results surprise you? Explain.

   b. How well does the estimated regression equation fit the given data?

22. A regional express delivery service company recently conducted a study to investigate the relationship between the cost of shipping a package (Y), the package weight (X_1), and the distance shipped (X_2). Several packages were randomly selected from among the large number received for shipment, and a detailed analysis of the shipping cost was conducted for each package. These sample observations are given in the file **P10_22.xlsx.**

   a. Estimate a simple linear regression equation involving shipping cost and package weight. Interpret the slope coefficient of the least squares line and the R^2 value.

   b. Add another explanatory variable, distance shipped, to the regression model in part **a**. Estimate and interpret this expanded equation. How does the R^2 value for this multiple regression equation compare to that of the simple regression equation in part **a**? Explain any difference between the two R^2 values. Interpret the *adjusted* R^2 value for the revised equation.

Level B

23. The owner of a restaurant in Bloomington, Indiana, has recorded sales data for the past several years. He has also recorded data on potentially relevant variables. The data are listed in the file **P10_23.xlsx.**

   a. Estimate a simple linear regression equation involving annual sales (the dependent variable) and the size of the population residing within 10 miles of the restaurant (the explanatory variable). Interpret the R^2 value.

   b. Add another explanatory variable—annual advertising expenditures—to the regression equation in part **a**. Estimate and interpret this expanded equation. How does the R^2 value for this equation compare to the equation in part **a**? Explain any difference between the two R^2 values. What, if anything, does the *adjusted* R^2 value for the revised equation indicate?

   c. Add one more explanatory variable to the multiple regression equation estimated in part **b**. In particular, estimate and interpret the coefficients of a multiple regression equation that includes the *previous* year's advertising expenditure. How does the inclusion of this third explanatory variable affect the R^2 and adjusted R^2 values, in comparison to the corresponding values for the equation of part **b**? Explain any changes in these values.

24. Continuing Problem 8 on the 2017 golfer data in the file **P10_08.xlsx**, the simple linear regressions for Earnings per Round were perhaps not as good as you expected. Create a new variable, Birdies per Round, in column R. Then explore several multiple regressions for Earnings per Round, using the variables in columns K–O and R. Proceed as follows.

   a. Create a table of correlations for these variables.

   b. Run a regression of Earnings per Round versus the most highly correlated variable (positive or negative) with Earnings per Round. Then run a second regression with the two most highly correlated variables with Earnings per Round. Then run a third with the three most highly correlated, and so on until all six explanatory variables are in the equation.

c. Comment on the changes you see from one equation to the next. Does the coefficient of a variable entered earlier change as you enter more variables? How much better do the equations get, in terms of standard error of estimate and R^2, as you enter more variables? Does adjusted R^2 ever indicate that an equation is *worse* than the one before it?

d. The bottom line is whether these variables, as a whole, do a very good job of predicting Earnings per Round. Would you say they do? Why or why not?

25. Using the sample data given in the file **P10_10.xlsx**, use multiple regression to predict the selling price of houses in a given community. Proceed as follows.

a. Add one explanatory variable at a time and estimate each regression equation along the way. Report and explain changes in the standard error of estimate s_e, R^2, and adjusted R^2 as each explanatory variable is added to the model. Does it matter in which order you add the variables? Try at least two different orderings to answer this question.

b. Interpret each of the estimated regression coefficients in the full equation, that is, the equation with all explanatory variables included.

c. What proportion of the total variation in the selling price is explained by the multiple regression equation that includes all four explanatory variables?

10-6 Modeling Possibilities

Once you move from simple to multiple regression, the floodgates open. Many types of explanatory variables are potential candidates for inclusion in the regression equation. In this section we examine several new types of explanatory variables. These include dummy variables, interaction variables, and nonlinear transformations. The techniques in this section provide you with many alternative approaches to modeling the relationship between a dependent variable and potential explanatory variables. In many applications these techniques produce much better fits than you could obtain without them.

Fundamental Insight

Modeling Possibilities

As the title of this section suggests, these techniques are modeling *possibilities*. They provide a wide variety of explanatory variables to choose from. However, this does not mean that it is wise to include all or even many of these new types of explanatory variables in any particular regression equation. The chances are that only a few, if any, will significantly improve the fit. Knowing which explanatory variables to include requires a great deal of practical experience with regression, as well as a thorough understanding of the data in its context. The material in this section should *not* be an excuse for a mindless fishing expedition.

10-6a Dummy Variables

Some potential explanatory variables are categorical and cannot be measured on a quantitative scale. However, these categorical variables are often related to the dependent variable, so you need a way to include them in a regression equation. The trick is to use **dummy variables**, also called **indicator** or **0–1** variables. Dummy variables are variables that indicate which category a given observation is in. If a dummy variable for a given category equals 1, the observation is in that category; if it equals 0, the observation is not in that category.

> A **dummy variable** is a variable with possible values 0 and 1. It equals 1 if the observation is in a particular category and 0 if it is not.

Categorical variables are used in two situations. The first and perhaps most common situation is when a categorical variable has only two categories. A good example of this is a gender variable that has the two categories "male" and "female." In this case only a *single* dummy variable is required, and you have the choice of assigning the 1's to either category. If the dummy variable is called Gender, you can code Gender as 1 for males and 0 for females, or you can code Gender as 1 for females and 0 for males. You just need to be consistent and specify explicitly which coding scheme you are using.

The other situation is when there are more than two categories. A good example of this is when you have quarterly time series data and you want to treat the quarter of the year as a categorical variable with four categories, 1 through 4. Then you can create four dummy variables, Q1 through Q4. For example, Q2 equals 1 for all second-quarter observations and 0 for all other observations. Although you can create four dummy variables, only three of them—*any* three—should be used in a regression equation, as we will explain shortly.

Example 10.3 illustrates how to create, use, and interpret dummy variables in regression analysis.

EXAMPLE

10.3 POSSIBLE GENDER DISCRIMINATION IN BANK SALARIES

Fifth National Bank of Springfield is facing a gender discrimination suit.[7] The charge is that its female employees receive substantially smaller salaries than its male employees. The bank's employee data are listed in the file **Bank Salaries.xlsx**. For each of its 208 employees, the data set includes the following variables:

- Education: education level, a categorical variable with categories 1 (finished high school), 2 (finished some college courses), 3 (obtained a bachelor's degree), 4 (took some graduate courses), 5 (obtained a graduate degree)
- Grade: a categorical variable indicating the current job level, the possible levels being 1 through 6 (6 is highest)
- Years1: years of experience with this bank
- Years2: number of years of work experience at another bank prior to working at Fifth National
- Age: employee's current age
- Gender: a categorical variable with values "Female" and "Male"
- PC Job: a categorical yes/no variable depending on whether the employee's current job is computer-related
- Salary: current annual salary

Figure 10.27 lists a few of the observations. Do these data provide evidence that there is discrimination against females in terms of salary?

Objective
To analyze whether the bank discriminates against females in terms of salary.

---

[7] This example and the accompanying data set are based on a real case from 1995. Only the bank's name has been changed.

Figure 10.27 Selected Data for Bank Example

	A	B	C	D	E	F	G	H	I
1	Employee	Education	Grade	Years1	Years2	Age	Gender	PC Job	Salary
2	1	3	1	3	1	26	Male	No	$32,000
3	2	1	1	14	1	38	Female	No	$39,100
4	3	1	1	12	0	35	Female	No	$33,200
5	4	2	1	8	7	40	Female	No	$30,600
6	5	3	1	3	0	28	Male	No	$29,000
7	6	3	1	3	0	24	Female	No	$30,500
8	7	3	1	4	0	27	Female	No	$30,000
9	8	3	1	8	2	33	Male	No	$27,000
10	9	1	1	4	0	62	Female	No	$34,000
11	10	3	1	9	0	31	Female	No	$29,500

Solution

A naive approach to this problem is to compare the average female salary to the average male salary. This can be done with a pivot table, as in Chapter 3, or with a more formal hypothesis test, as in Chapter 9. Using these methods, you can check that the average of all salaries is $39,922, the female average is $37,210, the male average is $45,505, and the difference between the male and female averages is statistically significant at any reasonable level of significance. In short, the females definitely earn less. But perhaps there is a reason for this. They might have lower education levels, they might have been hired more recently, and so on. The question is whether the difference between female and male salaries is still evident after taking these other attributes into account. This is a perfect task for regression.

The first task is to create dummy variables for the various categorical variables. You can do this manually with IF functions. (You can also use the StatTools Dummy procedure.) To do it manually, create a dummy variable Female based on Gender in any blank column by entering the formula **=IF(F2="Female",1,0)** and copying it down. Note that females are coded as 1's and males as 0's. (Remember that the quotes are necessary when a text value is used in an IF function.)

It is also possible to add dummies to effectively collapse categories.

Sometimes you might want to collapse several categories. For example, you might want to collapse the five education categories into three categories: 1, (2,3), and (4,5). The new second category includes employees who have taken undergraduate courses or have completed a bachelor's degree, and the new third category includes employees who have taken graduate courses or have completed a graduate degree. It is easy to do this. You can again use IF functions, or you can simply add the Educ2 and Educ3 columns to get the dummy for the new second category. Similarly, you add the Educ4 and Educ5 columns for the new third category. (Do you see why this works?)

Once the dummies have been created, you can run a regression analysis with Salary as the dependent variable, using any combination of numeric and dummy explanatory variables. Indeed, this is the procedure that must be used with most statistical software packages: create dummy variables and then run regressions that include the dummies. However, Stat-Tools now lets you avoid the first step of creating *explicit* dummies in new columns. It lets you run regressions with *implicit* dummies. This keeps the original data set intact (no need for a lot of extra columns), and it is much quicker and less tedious.

First, however, there are two general rules you should always follow, regardless of the statistical software being used:

1. You shouldn't use any of the *original* categorical variables, such as Education, that the dummies are based on.
2. You should always use *one fewer dummy* than the number of categories for any categorical variable.

Always include one fewer dummy than the number of categories. The omitted dummy corresponds to the reference category.

This second rule is a technical one. If you violate it, the statistical software (StatTools or other packages) will display an error message. For example, if you want to use education level as an explanatory variable, you should enter only four of the five dummies Educ1 through Educ5. *Any* four of these can be used. The omitted dummy then corresponds to the *reference* category. The interpretation of any dummy variable coefficient is relative to this reference category. When there are only two categories, as with the gender variable, the common procedure is to name the variable with the category, such as Female, that corresponds to the 1's. If you create the dummy variables manually, you probably will not even bother to create a dummy for males. In this case "Male" automatically becomes the reference category.

To explain dummy variables in regression, it is useful to proceed in several steps in this example. (After you get used to the procedure, you can combine all of these steps into a single step. Alternatively, you can use a stepwise procedure, as explained in the next chapter.) Each step will have a dummy for Female and one or more additional explanatory variables.

The first regression will include a dummy for Female and the experience variables, Years1 and Years2. If you want to run this regression with StatTools, you should fill out the StatTools Regression dialog box as shown in Figure 10.28. Note that each variable has a Data Type: Numeric or Category. StatTools chooses this type automatically, based on whether the column is totally numeric. If you check a Category variable such as Gender, StatTools implicitly creates a dummy variable for all but one of its categories and then uses these in the regression. (StatTools chooses the reference category as the last one in alphabetical order, in this case, Male.)

Figure 10.28 StatTools Regression Dialog Box for Including Gender

The resulting output appears in Figure 10.29. As usual, the Coefficient column lists the coefficients of the regression equation. To help with interpretation, StatTools provides the option of listing the regression equations for the various categories. (Refer to the Display Regression Equation option in Figure 10.18.) Specifically, the Female and Male equations appear in rows 26 and 27. They are identical except that the intercept of the Male equation is about $8080 larger than the intercept of the Female equation, and this difference is precisely the coefficient of the Gender dummy in row 22.

You can interpret the coefficient -8080 of the Female dummy variable as the average salary disadvantage for females relative to males *after controlling for job experience*. Therefore, gender discrimination still appears to be a very plausible conclusion. However, note that the R^2 value is only 49.2%. Perhaps there is still more to the story.

The next step is to add education level to the equation by including four of the five education level dummies. If you want to do this with StatTools, you should fill out the StatTools Regression dialog box as shown in Figure 10.30. Note that the Data Type for Education is originally Numeric, but it is more appropriate to change this to Category, as shown. After all, the values for Education are codes, not really numbers. Then when you check Education, dummies for the first four education levels are created implicitly and included in the regression equation. (The reference category, education level 5, is again the last in alphabetical order.)

Figure 10.29 Regression Output with Experience and Gender Variables Included

	A	B	C	D	E	F	G
8	*Multiple Regression for Salary*	**Multiple R**	**R-Square**	**Adjusted R-square**	**Std. Err. of Estimate**	**Rows Ignored**	
9	*Summary*						
10		0.7016	0.4923	0.4848	8079.397428	0	
11							
12		**Degrees of Freedom**	**Sum of Squares**	**Mean of Squares**	**F**	**p-Value**	
13	*ANOVA Table*						
14	**Explained**	3	12910668018	4303556006	65.92794149	< 0.0001	
15	**Unexplained**	204	13316439212	65276662.81			
16							
17		**Coefficient**	**Standard Error**	**t-Value**	**p-Value**	**Confidence Interval 95%**	
18	*Regression Table*					**Lower**	**Upper**
19	**Constant**	35491.66097	1341.021528	26.4661381	< 0.0001	32847.62127	38135.70067
20	**Years1**	987.9936807	80.92814461	12.20828286	< 0.0001	828.4308231	1147.556538
21	**Years2**	131.3379165	180.9229477	0.72593288	0.4687	−225.3807836	488.0566166
22	**Gender (Female)**	−8080.212123	1198.170124	−6.74379369	< 0.0001	−10442.5973	−5717.82695
23							
24							
25	*Regression Equation*	**Gender**					
26		Female	Salary = 27411.44884291 + 987.99368068 Years1 + 131.33791653 Years2				
27		Male	Salary = 35491.66096617 + 987.99368068 Years1 + 131.33791653 Years2				

Figure 10.30 StatTools
Regression Dialog box with
Education Included

The resulting output, with the equations again spelled out at the bottom, appears in Figure 10.31. There is an equation for each combination of Gender and Education categories, or 10 equations in all. As before, only the intercepts differ. In particular, you can check that the difference between the Female and Male intercepts, for any specific education level, is always the Gender coefficient in row 26. This means that after controlling for experience and education, there is a $4501 "penalty" for being a female.

Figure 10.31 Regression Output with Education Dummies Included

	A	B	C	D	E	F	G
8	Multiple Regression for Salary	Multiple	R-Square	Adjusted	Std. Err. of	Rows	
9	Summary	R		R-square	Estimate	Ignored	
10		0.8030	0.6449	0.6324	6824.373646	0	
11							
12		Degrees of	Sum of	Mean of	F	p-Value	
13	ANOVA Table	Freedom	Squares	Squares			
14	Explained	7	16912692100	2416098871	51.87870279	< 0.0001	
15	Unexplained	200	9314415131	46572075.65			
16							
17		Coefficient	Standard	t-Value	p-Value	Confidence Interval 95%	
18	Regression Table		Error			Lower	Upper
19	Constant	38383.56442	1256.726747	30.54249025	< 0.0001	35905.42969	40861.69914
20	Education (1)	−11770.20898	1510.213706	−7.793737359	< 0.0001	−14748.19368	−8792.224276
21	Education (2)	−11609.96717	1526.771671	−7.604258965	< 0.0001	−14620.60246	−8599.331876
22	Education (3)	−7005.652529	1232.284246	−5.685094615	< 0.0001	−9435.589179	−4575.715878
23	Education (4)	−4450.367963	2561.737956	−1.737245589	0.0839	−9501.849364	601.1134383
24	Years1	1032.930137	69.60252669	14.84041148	< 0.0001	895.681177	1170.179096
25	Years2	362.2341784	158.1233928	2.290832317	0.0230	50.43125717	674.0370996
26	Gender (Female)	−4501.322074	1085.767439	−4.145751578	< 0.0001	−6642.342787	−2360.301361
27							
28							
29	Regression Equation	Education	Gender				
30		1	Female	Salary = 22112.03336304 + 1032.93013654 Years1 + 362.23417837 Years2			
31		1	Male	Salary = 26613.35543724 + 1032.93013654 Years1 + 362.23417837 Years2			
32		2	Female	Salary = 22272.27517399 + 1032.93013654 Years1 + 362.23417837 Years2			
33		2	Male	Salary = 26773.59724819 + 1032.93013654 Years1 + 362.23417837 Years2			
34		3	Female	Salary = 26876.58981424 + 1032.93013654 Years1 + 362.23417837 Years2			
35		3	Male	Salary = 31377.91188844 + 1032.93013654 Years1 + 362.23417837 Years2			
36		4	Female	Salary = 29431.87437998 + 1032.93013654 Years1 + 362.23417837 Years2			
37		4	Male	Salary = 33933.19645418 + 1032.93013654 Years1 + 362.23417837 Years2			
38		5	Female	Salary = 33882.24234286 + 1032.93013654 Years1 + 362.23417837 Years2			
39		5	Male	Salary = 38383.56441706 + 1032.93013654 Years1 + 362.23417837 Years2			

The coefficients of the Education dummies in rows 20–23 are all relative to the reference category, education level 5. Because these coefficients are all negative, they indicate how much less the average salary for that education level is, relative to level 5, after controlling for experience and gender. For example, a person with education level 4 tends to be paid about $4450 less than a similar person with education level 5.

Note that the R^2 value is now 64.5%, quite a bit larger than when the education dummies were not included. We appear to be getting closer to the truth. In particular, you can see that there appears to be gender discrimination in salaries, even after accounting for job experience and education level.

One further explanation for gender differences in salary might be job grade. Perhaps females tend to be in lower job grades, which would help explain why they get lower salaries on average. One way to check this is with a pivot table, as in Figure 10.32, with job grade in the Rows area, gender in the Columns area, and counts, displayed as percentages of columns in the Values area. Clearly, females tend to be concentrated at the lower job grades. For example, 28.85% of all employees are at the lowest job grade, but 34.29% of all females are at this grade and only 17.65% of males are at this grade. The opposite is true at the higher job grades. This certainly helps to explain why females get lower salaries on average.

It is possible to go one step further to see the effect of job grade on salary. As with the education dummies, dummies for job grade could be entered in the regression. The regression output, not shown here, is available in the Regression 3 sheet of the finished version of the file. It indicates that there is still a penalty for being a female, but this penalty has been reduced to about $2563 due to controlling for job grade.

Figure 10.32 Pivot Table of
Job Grade Counts for Bank Data

	A	B	C	D
13	Count of Employee Gender			
14	Grade	Female	Male	Grand Total
15	1	34.29%	17.65%	28.85%
16	2	20.71%	19.12%	20.19%
17	3	25.71%	10.29%	20.67%
18	4	12.14%	16.18%	13.46%
19	5	6.43%	17.65%	10.10%
20	6	0.71%	19.12%	6.73%
21	Grand Total	100.00%	100.00%	100.00%

The regression indicates that being in lower job grades implies lower salaries, but it doesn't explain why females are in the lower job grades in the first place.

However, using job grade to "explain" gender discrimination is not really appropriate. The real question is why females are predominantly in the low job grades in the first place. Perhaps this is the real source of gender discrimination. Perhaps management is not advancing the females as quickly as it should, which naturally results in lower salaries for females. In a sense, job grade is not really an explanatory variable; it is a dependent variable.

We conclude this example for now, but we will say more about it in the next two subsections.

10-6b Interaction Variables

Consider the following regression equation for a dependent variable Y versus a numerical variable X and a dummy variable D. If the estimated equation is of the form

Generic Equation with No Interaction

$$\hat{Y} = a + b_1X + b_2D \qquad (10.12)$$

then this equation can be written as two separate equations:

$$\hat{Y} = (a + b_2) + b_1X$$

and

$$\hat{Y} = a + b_1X$$

The first corresponds to $D = 1$, and the second corresponds to $D = 0$. The only difference between these two equations is the intercept term; the slope for each is b_1. Geometrically, they correspond to two *parallel* lines that are a vertical distance b_2 apart. For example, if D corresponds to gender, there is a female line and a parallel male line. The effect of X on Y is the same for females and males. When X increases by one unit, Y is expected to change by b_1 units for males or females.

In effect, when you include *only* a dummy variable in a regression equation, as in Equation (10.12), you are allowing the intercepts of the two lines to differ (by an amount b_2), but you are *forcing* the lines to be parallel. To be more realistic, you might want to allow them to have different slopes, in addition to possibly different intercepts. You can do this by including an **interaction variable**. Algebraically, an interaction variable is the *product* of two variables. Its inclusion allows the effect of one of the variables on Y to depend on the value of the other variable.

> An **interaction variable** is the product of two explanatory variables. You can include such a variable in a regression equation if you believe the effect of one explanatory variable on Y depends on the value of another explanatory variable.

Suppose you create the interaction variable XD (the product of X and D) and then estimate the equation

$$\hat{Y} = a + b_1 X + b_2 D + b_3 XD$$

As usual, this equation can be rewritten as two separate equations, depending on whether $D = 0$ or $D = 1$. If $D = 1$, terms can be combined to write

$$\hat{Y} = (a + b_2) + (b_1 + b_3)X$$

If $D = 0$, the dummy and interaction variables drop out and the equation becomes

$$\hat{Y} = a + b_1 X$$

The notation is not important. The important part is that the interaction term, $b_3 XD$, allows the slope of the regression line to differ between the two categories.

The following continuation of Example 10.3 illustrates one possible use of interaction variables.

EXAMPLE

10.3 POSSIBLE GENDER DISCRIMINATION IN BANK SALARIES (CONTINUED)

Earlier we estimated an equation for Salary using the numeric explanatory variables Years1 and Years2 and the dummy variable for Female. If we drop the Years2 variable from this equation (for simplicity) and rerun the regression, we obtain the equation

Predicted Salary with No Interactions

$$\text{Predicted Salary} = 35824 + 981\text{Years1} - 8012\text{Female} \tag{10.13}$$

The R^2 value for this equation is 49.1%. If an interaction variable between Years1 and Female is added to this equation, what is its effect?

Objective

To use multiple regression with an interaction variable to see whether the effect of years of experience on salary is different across the two genders.

Solution

As with dummy variables, most statistical software packages require you to create explicit interaction variables before including them in a regression. This can be done with Excel product formulas or with the StatTools Data Utilities tools. However, with the current version of StatTools, explicit interaction variables are not necessary. StatTools will again create them implicitly.[8]

---

[8] We continue to use StatTools because it is quicker. However, if you create the dummy and interaction with Excel formulas, you will get the same regression with Analysis ToolPak.

To do this with StatTools, you should first check the Include Derived Variables box at the bottom of the Regression dialog box and then click the resulting Add button. This opens the dialog box shown in Figure 10.33, where several types of derived variables can be specified. In this case, we checked the Years1 and Gender variables and selected the Interaction with Category Variable option. This creates the product of Years1 and the Female dummy, which appears in the regression dialog box in Figure 10.34. Now you can check the derived variable (as an independent variable), along with the other usual variables.

Figure 10.33 StatTools Add
Derived Variable Dialog Box

Figure 10.34 StatTools
Regression Dialog Box with
Derived Variable

The multiple regression output appears in Figure 10.35. The coefficients of the Female dummy and the interaction appear in cells B21 and B22, and the Female and Male equations are spelled out in rows 26 and 27. Note that the intercepts are different, and because of the interaction term, the slopes are also different.

Figure 10.35 StatTools Regression Output with an Interaction Variable

	A	B	C	D	E	F	G
8	**Multiple Regression for Salary**	**Multiple R**	**R-Square**	**Adjusted R-square**	**Std. Err. of Estimate**	**Rows Ignored**	
9	**Summary**						
10		0.7991	0.6386	0.6333	6816.298288	0	
11							
12		**Degrees of Freedom**	**Sum of Squares**	**Mean of Squares**	**F**	**p-Value**	
13	**ANOVA Table**						
14	Explained	3	16748875071	5582958357	120.1620182	< 0.0001	
15	Unexplained	204	9478232160	46461922.35			
16							
17		**Coefficient**	**Standard Error**	**t-Value**	**p-Value**	**Confidence Interval 95%**	
18	**Regression Table**					**Lower**	**Upper**
19	Constant	30430.02774	1216.574332	25.01287998	< 0.0001	28031.35571	32828.69977
20	Years1	1527.761719	90.46033769	16.88874659	< 0.0001	1349.40461	1706.118829
21	Gender (Female)	4098.251879	1665.842019	2.46016839	0.0147	813.7763213	7382.727436
22	Gender (Female) * Years1	−1247.798369	136.6757036	−9.129628276	< 0.0001	−1517.276508	−978.3202292
23							
24							
25	**Regression Equation**	**Gender**					
26		Female	Salary = 34528.27961831 + 279.96335081 Years1				
27		Male	Salary = 30430.02773957 + 1527.76171939 Years1				

Figure 10.36 Nonparallel Female and Male Salary Lines

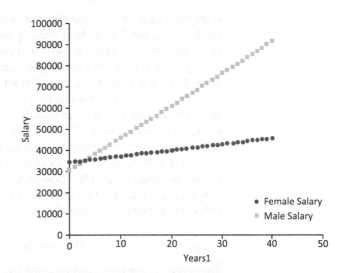

Graphically, these equations appear as in Figure 10.36. The Y-intercept for the female line is slightly higher—females with no experience with Fifth National tend to start out slightly higher than males—but the slope of the female line is much smaller. That is, males tend to move up the salary ladder more quickly than females. Again, this provides another confirmation, although a somewhat different one, of gender discrimination against females. In addition, the R^2 value with the interaction variable has increased from 49.1% to 63.9%. The interaction variable has definitely added to the explanatory power of the equation.

There are clearly pros and cons to adding interaction variables. On the plus side, they allow for more complex and interesting models, and they can lead to significantly better fits. On the minus side, they can become difficult to interpret correctly. Therefore, we recommend that you add them only when there is good economic and statistical justification for doing so.

> **Fundamental Insight**
>
> ### Interaction Variables
>
> Interaction variables can make a regression more difficult to interpret, and they are certainly not always necessary. However, without them, the effect of each X on Y is *independent* of the values of the other X's in the equation. If you believe, for example, that the effect of years of experience on salary is different for males than it is for females, the *only* way to capture this behavior is to include an interaction variable between years of experience and gender.

Postscript to Example 10.3

When regression analysis is used in a legal case, as it was in the bank gender discrimination example, it can uncover multiple versions of the "truth." That is, by including or omitting variables, the resulting equations can imply quite different things about the issue in question, in this case, gender discrimination. If one side claims, for example, that the equation

$$\text{Predicted Salary} = 35492 + 988\,\text{Years1} + 131\,\text{Years2} - 8080\,\text{Female}$$

is the true equation for explaining how salaries are determined at the bank, it is ludicrous for them to claim that the bank literally does it this way. No one believes that bank executives sit down and say: "We will start everyone at \$35,492. Then we will add \$988 for every year of experience with our bank and \$131 for every year of prior work experience at another bank. Finally, we will subtract \$8080 from this total if the person is female." All the analysts can claim is that the given regression equation is consistent, to a greater or lesser extent, with the observed data. If a number of regression equations, such as the ones estimated in this example, all point to lower salaries for females after controlling for other factors, then it doesn't matter whether management is deliberately discriminating against females according to some preconceived formula; the regression analysis indicates that females *are* compensated less than males with the same qualifications. Without a smoking gun, it is very difficult for either side to *prove* anything, but regression analysis permits either side to present evidence that is most consistent with the data.

10-6c Nonlinear Transformations

The general linear regression equation has the form

$$\text{Predicted } Y = a + b_1 X_1 + b_2 X_2 + \cdots + b_k X_k$$

You typically include nonlinear transformations in a regression equation because of economic considerations or curvature detected in scatterplots.

It is *linear* in the sense that the right side of the equation is a constant plus a sum of products of constants and variables. However, there is no requirement that the dependent variable Y or the explanatory variables X_1 through X_k be the *original* variables in the data set. Most often they are, but they can also be transformations of original variables. You already saw one example of this in the previous section with interaction variables. They are not original variables but are instead products of original (or even transformed) variables. The software treats them in the same way as original variables; only the interpretation differs. In this section we look at several possible **nonlinear transformations** of variables. These are often used because of curvature detected in scatterplots. They can also arise because of economic considerations. That is, economic theory often leads to particular nonlinear transformations.

You can transform the dependent variable Y or any of the explanatory variables, the X's. You can also do both. In either case there are a few nonlinear transformations that are typically used. These include the natural logarithm, the square root, the reciprocal, and the square. The purpose of each of these is usually to "straighten out" the points in a scatterplot. If several different transformations straighten out the data equally well, the one that is easiest to interpret is preferred.

We begin with Example 10.4, where only the X variable needs to be transformed.

EXAMPLE

10.4 DEMAND VERSUS COST FOR ELECTRICITY

Public Service Electric Company produces different quantities of electricity each month, depending on the demand. The file **Cost of Power.xlsx** lists the number of units of electricity produced (Units) and the total cost of producing these (Cost) for a 36-month period. The data appear in Figure 10.37 (with several hidden rows). How can regression be used to analyze the relationship between Cost and Units?

Figure 10.37 Data for Electric Power Example

	A	B	C
1	Month	Cost	Units
2	1	45623	601
3	2	46507	738
4	3	43343	686
5	4	46495	736
6	5	47317	756
35	34	46295	667
36	35	45218	705
37	36	45357	637

Objective

To see whether the cost of supplying electricity is a nonlinear function of demand, and, if it is, what form the nonlinearity takes.

Solution

A good place to start is with a scatterplot of Cost versus Units. This appears in Figure 10.38. It indicates a definite positive relationship and one that is nearly linear. However, there is also some evidence of curvature in the plot. The points increase slightly less rapidly as Units increases from left to right. In economic terms, there might be economies of scale, so that the marginal cost of electricity decreases as more units of electricity are produced.

Figure 10.38 Scatterplot of Cost Versus Units for Electricity Example

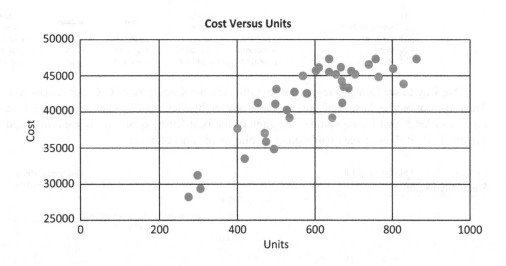

Nevertheless, you can first use regression to estimate a *linear* relationship between Cost and Units. The resulting regression equation is

$$\text{Predicted Cost} = 23651 + 30.53\text{Units}$$

A scatterplot of residuals versus fitted values often indicates the need for a nonlinear transformation.

The corresponding R^2 and s_e are 73.6% and $2734. It is always a good idea to request a scatterplot of the residuals versus the fitted values. This scatterplot is shown in Figure 10.39. Note that the residuals to the far left and the far right are all negative, whereas the majority of the residuals in the middle are positive. Admittedly, the pattern is far from perfect—there are several negative residuals in the middle—but this plot certainly suggests nonlinear behavior.

Figure 10.39 Residuals from a
Straight-Line Fit

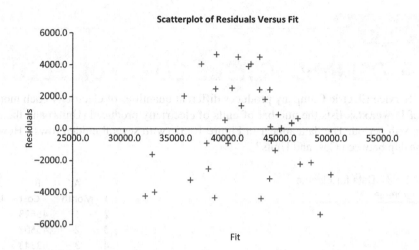

This negative–positive–negative behavior of residuals suggests a *parabola*—that is, a **quadratic** relationship with the *square* of Units included in the equation. The next step is to create a new variable (Units)^2 in the data set. You can do this manually with the formula **=C4^2** in cell D4, copied down. Alternatively, you can create the squared variable implicitly as a StatTools derived variable in the Regression dialog box. Then you can use multiple regression to estimate the equation for Cost with *both* explanatory variables, Units and (Units)^2, included. The resulting equation is shown in Figure 10.40. Note that R^2 has increased to 82.2% and s_e has decreased to $2281.

Figure 10.40 Regression Output with Squared Term Included

	A	B	C	D	E	F	G
8	*Multiple Regression for Cost*	Multiple		Adjusted	Std. Err. of	Rows	
9	*Summary*	R	R-Square	R-square	Estimate	Ignored	
10		0.9064	0.8216	0.8108	2280.799771	0	
11							
12		Degrees of	Sum of	Mean of	F	p-Value	
13	*ANOVA Table*	Freedom	Squares	Squares			
14	Explained	2	790511518.3	395255759.1	75.98080405	< 0.0001	
15	Unexplained	33	171667570.7	5202047.597			
16							
17			Standard			Confidence Interval 95%	
18	*Regression Table*	Coefficient	Error	t-Value	p-Value	Lower	Upper
19	Constant	5792.798287	4763.058499	1.216192975	0.2325	–3897.717092	15483.31367
20	Units	98.35039079	17.23690011	5.705804997	< 0.0001	63.28165383	133.4191277
21	Units^2	–0.059972929	0.015066406	–3.980573026	0.0004	–0.090625763	–0.029320096

One way to see how this regression equation fits the scatterplot of Cost versus Units (in Figure 10.38) is to use Excel's Trendline option. To do so, activate the scatterplot, right-click on any point, select Add Trendline, and select the Polynomial type or order 2, that is, a quadratic. A graph of the best-fitting quadratic is superimposed on the scatterplot, as shown in Figure 10.41. It shows a reasonably good fit, plus an obvious curvature.

Figure 10.41 Quadratic Fit in
Electricity Example

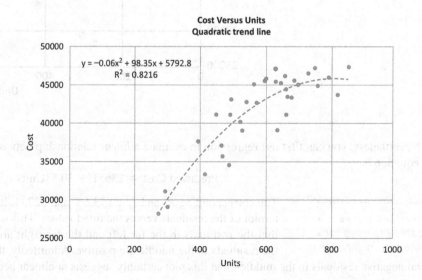

The main downside to a quadratic regression equation is that there is no easy way to interpret the coefficients of Units and (Units)^2. For example, you can't conclude from the 98.35 coefficient of Units that Cost increases by 98.35 dollars when Units increases by one. The reason is that when Units increases by one, (Units)^2 doesn't stay constant; it *also* increases. All you can say is that the terms in the quadratic combine to explain the nonlinear relationship between units produced and total cost.

Excel's Trendline option allows you to superimpose a number of different curves on a scatterplot. Note that the coefficient of (Units)^2, about −0.06, is a small negative value. First, the fact that it is negative makes the parabola bend downward. This produces the decreasing marginal cost behavior, where every extra unit of electricity incurs a smaller cost. Actually, the curve in Figure 10.41 eventually goes *downhill* for large values of Units, but this part of the curve is irrelevant because the company evidently never produces such large quantities. Second, you should not be fooled by the small magnitude of this coefficient. Remember that it is the coefficient of Units *squared*, which is a large quantity. Therefore, the effect of the product −0.0600 (Units)^2 is sizable.

There is at least one other possibility you can examine. Rather than a quadratic fit, you can try a logarithmic fit. In this case you need to create a new variable, Log(Units), the natural logarithm of Units, and then regress Cost against the *single* variable Log(Units). To create the new variable, you can use a formula with Excel's LN function or you can create a derived "log" variable in the StatTools Regression dialog box. Also, you can superimpose a logarithmic curve on the scatterplot of Cost versus Units by using Excel's Trendline feature with the logarithm option. This curve appears in Figure 10.42. To the naked eye, it appears to be similar, and about as good a fit, as the quadratic curve in Figure 10.41.

Figure 10.42 Logarithmic Fit to Electricity Data

The resulting regression equation is listed in Figure 10.42. Its R^2 and s_e values (the latter not shown) are 79.8% and 2393. These latter values indicate that the logarithmic fit is not quite as good as the quadratic fit. However, the advantage of the logarithmic equation is that it is easier to interpret. In fact, one reason **logarithmic transformations** of variables are used so widely in regression analysis is that they have a meaningful interpretation.

In general, if b is the coefficient of the log of X, the expected change in Y when X increases by 1% is approximately 0.01 times b. In the present case, where the log of an *explanatory* variable is used, you can interpret its coefficient as follows. Suppose that Units increases by 1%, for example, from 600 to 606. Then the equation in Figure 10.42 implies that the expected Cost will increase by approximately 0.01(16654) = 166.54 dollars. In words, every 1% increase in Units is accompanied by an expected $166.54 increase in Cost. Note that for larger values of Units, a 1% increase represents a larger absolute increase (from 700 to 707 instead of from 600 to 606, for example). But each such 1% increase entails the *same* increase in Cost. This is another way of describing the decreasing marginal cost property.

The electricity example has shown two possible nonlinear transformations of the *explanatory* variable (or variables) that you can use. All you need to do is create the transformed X's and run the regression. The interpretation of statistics such as R^2 and s_e is exactly the same as before; only the interpretation of the coefficients of the transformed X's changes. It is also possible to transform the dependent variable Y, as discussed next.

Constant Elasticity Relationships

A particular type of nonlinear relationship that has firm grounding in economic theory is called a **constant elasticity relationship**. It is also called a **multiplicative relationship**. It has the form shown in Equation (10.14).

Formula for Multiplicative Relationship

$$\text{Predicted } Y = aX_1^{b_1}X_2^{b_2}\cdots X_k^{b_k} \qquad (10.14)$$

One property of this type of relationship is that the effect of a one-unit change in any X on Y depends on the levels of the other X's in the equation. This is not true for the *additive* relationships of the form

$$\text{Predicted } Y = a + b_1X_1 + b_2X_2 + \cdots + b_kX_k$$

that we have been discussing. For additive relationships, when any X increases by one unit, the predicted value of Y changes by the corresponding b units, regardless of the levels of the other X's. However, multiplicative relationships have the following nice property.

In a **multiplicative** (or **constant elasticity**) **relationship**, the dependent variable is expressed as a *product* of explanatory variables raised to powers. When any explanatory variable X changes by 1%, the predicted value of the dependent variable changes by a constant *percentage*, regardless of the value of this X or the values of the other Xs.

The term *constant elasticity* comes from economics. Economists define the elasticity of Y with respect to X as the percentage change in Y that accompanies a 1% increase in X. Often this is in reference to a demand–price relationship. Then the *price elasticity* is the percentage decrease in demand when price increases by 1%. Usually, the elasticity depends on the current value of X. For example, the price elasticity when the price is \$35 might be different than when the price is \$50. However, if the relationship is of the form

$$\text{Predicted } Y = aX^b$$

then the elasticity is *constant*, the same for any value of X. In fact, it is approximately equal to the exponent b. For example, if Predicted $Y = 2X^{-1.5}$, the constant elasticity is approximately -1.5, so that when X increases by 1%, the predicted value of Y decreases by approximately 1.5%.

The constant elasticity for any X is approximately equal to the exponent of that X.

The constant elasticity property carries over to the multiple-X relationship in Equation (10.14). Then each exponent is the approximate elasticity for its X. For example, if Predicted $Y = 2X_1^{-1.5}X_2^{0.7}$, you can make the following statements:

- When X_1 increases by 1%, the predicted value of Y decreases by approximately 1.5%, regardless of the current values of X_1 and X_2.
- When X_2 increases by 1%, the predicted value of Y increases by approximately 0.7%, regardless of the current values of X_1 and X_2.

You can use linear regression to estimate the nonlinear relationship in Equation (10.14) by taking natural logarithms of *all* variables. Here two properties of logarithms are used: (1) the log of a product is the sum of the logs, and (2) the log of X^b is b times the log of X. Therefore, taking logs of both sides of Equation (10.14) gives

$$\text{Predicted } \text{Log}(Y) = \text{Log}(a) + b_1\text{Log}(X_1) + \cdots + b_k\text{Log}(X_k)$$

This equation is *linear* in the log variables $\text{Log}(X_1)$ through $\text{Log}(X_k)$, so you can estimate it in the usual way with multiple regression. You can then interpret the coefficients of the explanatory variables directly as elasticities.

> ### Fundamental Insight
>
> #### Using Logarithmic Transformations in Regression
>
> If scatterplots suggest nonlinear relationships, there are an unlimited number of nonlinear transformations of Y and/or the X's that could be tried in a regression analysis. The reason that logarithmic transformations are arguably the most frequently used nonlinear transformations, besides the fact that they often produce good fits, is that they can be interpreted naturally in terms of percentage changes. This interpretability is an important advantage over other potential nonlinear transformations.

One example of a multiplicative relationship is the *learning curve* model. A **learning curve** relates the unit production time (or cost) to the cumulative volume of output since that production process first began. Empirical studies indicate that production times tend to decrease by a relatively constant *percentage* every time cumulative output doubles. To model this phenomenon, let Y be the time required to produce a unit of output, and let X be the *cumulative* amount of output that has been produced so far. If we assume that the relationship between Y and X is of the constant elasticity form

$$\text{Predicted } Y = aX^b$$

then it can be shown that whenever X doubles, the predicted value of Y decreases to a *constant* percentage of its previous value. This constant is often called the *learning rate*. For example, if the learning rate is 80%, then each doubling of cumulative production yields a 20% reduction in unit production time. It can be shown that the learning rate satisfies the following equation.

> ### Equation for Learning Rate
>
> $$b = \text{LN(learning rate)}/\text{LN}(2) \qquad \textbf{(10.15)}$$

(where LN refers to the natural logarithm). So once you estimate b, you can use Equation (10.15) to estimate the learning rate.

The following example illustrates a typical application of the learning curve model.

EXAMPLE

10.5 THE LEARNING CURVE FOR PRODUCTION OF A NEW PRODUCT

Presario Company produces a variety of small industrial products. It has just finished producing 22 batches of a new product (new to Presario) for a customer. The file **Learning Curve.xlsx** contains the times (in hours) to produce each batch. These data are listed in Figure 10.43 (with several hidden rows). Clearly, the times have tended to decrease as Presario has gained more experience in making the product. Does the multiplicative learning model apply to these data, and what does it imply about the learning rate?

Figure 10.43 Data for Learning Curve Example

▲	A	B	C	D
1	Batch	Time	Log(Batch)	Log(Time)
2	1	125.00	0	4.828313737
3	2	110.87	0.693147181	4.708358344
4	3	105.35	1.098612289	4.65728814
5	4	103.34	1.386294361	4.638024523
6	5	98.98	1.609437912	4.59491781
7	6	99.90	1.791759469	4.604169686
20	19	82.06	2.944438979	4.407450687
21	20	82.81	2.995732274	4.416548827
22	21	76.52	3.044522438	4.337552145
23	22	78.45	3.091042453	4.362461479

Objective

To use a multiplicative regression equation to estimate the learning rate for production time.

Solution

One way to check whether the multiplicative learning model is reasonable is to create the log variables Log(Time) and Log(Batch) in the usual way (with Excel's LN function) and then see whether a scatterplot of Log(Time) versus Log(Batch) is approximately *linear*. The multiplicative model implies that it should be. Such a scatterplot appears in Figure 10.44, along with a superimposed linear trend line and the corresponding equation. The fit appears to be quite good.

Figure 10.44 Scatterplot of Log Variables with Linear Trend Superimposed

Log(Time) Versus Log(Batch)

$y = -0.155x + 4.834$

There are two ways to interpret this equation. First, because it is a constant elasticity relationship, the coefficient −0.155 can be interpreted as an elasticity. That is, when Batch increases by 1%, Time tends to decrease by approximately 0.155%.

Although this interpretation is correct, it is not as useful as the "doubling" interpretation discussed previously. Equation (10.15) states that the estimated learning rate satisfies

$$-0.155 = \text{LN(learning rate)}/\text{LN(2)}$$

Solving for the learning rate [multiply through by LN(2) and then take antilogs], you can see that it is 0.898, or approximately 90%. In words, whenever cumulative production doubles, the time to produce a batch decreases by about 10%.

Presario could use this regression equation to predict future production times. For example, suppose the customer places an order for 15 more batches of the same product. Note that Presario is already partway up the learning curve, that is, these batches are numbers 23 through 37, and the company already has experience producing the product. You can use the equation shown in Figure 10.44 to predict the log of production time for each batch. Then you can take their antilogs and sum them to obtain the total production time. The calculations are shown in rows 24 through 39 of Figure 10.45. You enter the batch numbers and calculate their logs in columns A and C. Then you substitute the values of Log(Batch) in column C into the regression equation to obtain the predicted values of Log(Time) in column E. Finally, you use Excel's EXP function to calculate the antilogs of these predictions in column B, and you calculate their sum in cell B39. The total predicted time to finish the order is about 1115 hours.

Figure 10.45 Using the
Learning Curve Model for
Predictions

	A	B	C	D	E	F
22	21	76.52	3.044522438	4.337552145		
23	22	78.45	3.091042453	4.362461479		
24	23	77.324	3.135494216	4.348009995		
25	24	76.816	3.17805383	4.341413654		
26	25	76.332	3.218875825	4.335086627		
27	26	75.869	3.258096538	4.329007785		
28	27	75.426	3.295836866	4.323158388		
29	28	75.003	3.33220451	4.317521744		
30	29	74.596	3.36729583	4.312082919		
31	30	74.205	3.401197382	4.306828497		
32	31	73.829	3.433987204	4.301746382		
33	32	73.466	3.465735903	4.296825631		
34	33	73.117	3.496507561	4.292056313		
35	34	72.779	3.526360525	4.287429384		
36	35	72.453	3.555348061	4.282936587		
37	36	72.137	3.583518938	4.278570366		
38	37	71.832	3.610917913	4.274323782		
39		1115.183	⟵	Predicted time for next 15 batches		

Problems

Solutions for problems whose numbers appear within a colored box can be found in the Student Solution Files.

Level A

26. In a study of housing demand, a county assessor is interested in developing a regression model to estimate the selling price of residential properties within her jurisdiction. She randomly selects several houses and records the selling price in addition to the following values: the size of the house (in square feet), the total number of rooms in the house, the age of the house, and an indication of whether the house has an attached garage. These data are stored in the file **P10_26.xlsx**.

    a. Estimate and interpret a multiple regression equation that includes the four potential explanatory variables. How do you interpret the coefficient of the Attached Garage variable?

    b. Evaluate the estimated regression equation's goodness of fit.

    c. Use the estimated equation to predict the sales price of a 3000-square-foot, 20-year-old home that has seven rooms but no attached garage. How accurate is your prediction?

27. A manager of boiler drums wants to use regression analysis to predict the number of worker-hours needed to erect the drums in future projects. Data for several randomly selected boilers have been collected. In addition to worker-hours (Y), the variables measured include boiler capacity, boiler design pressure, boiler type, and drum type. All of these measurements are listed in the file **P10_27.xlsx**.

    a. Estimate an appropriate multiple regression equation to predict the number of worker-hours needed to erect boiler drums.

    b. Interpret the estimated regression coefficients.

    c. According to the estimated regression equation, what is the difference between the mean number of worker-hours required for erecting industrial and utility field boilers?

    d. According to the estimated regression equation, what is the difference between the mean number of worker-hours required for erecting boilers with steam drums and those with mud drums?

    e. Given the estimated regression equation, predict the number of worker-hours needed to erect a utility-field, steam-drum boiler with a capacity of 550,000 pounds per hour and a design pressure of 1400 pounds per square inch. How accurate is your prediction?

    f. Given the estimated regression equation, predict the number of worker-hours needed to erect an industrial-field, mud-drum boiler with a capacity of 100,000 pounds per hour and a design pressure of 1000 pounds per square inch. How accurate is your prediction?

28. Suppose that a regional express delivery service company wants to estimate the cost of shipping a package (Y) as a function of cargo type, where cargo type includes the following possibilities: fragile, semifragile, and durable. Costs for several randomly chosen packages of approximately the same weight and same

distance shipped, but of different cargo types, are provided in the file **P10_28.xlsx.**
  a. Estimate an appropriate multiple regression equation to predict the cost of shipping a given package.
  b. Interpret the estimated regression coefficients. You should find that the estimated intercept and slope of the equation are sample means. Which sample means are they?
  c. According to the estimated regression equation, which cargo type is the *most* costly to ship? Which cargo type is the *least* costly to ship?
  d. How well does the estimated equation fit the given sample data? How do you think the model's goodness of fit could be improved?
  e. Given the estimated regression equation, predict the cost of shipping a package with semifragile cargo.

29. The file **P10_11.xlsx** contains annual observations (in column B) of the American minimum wage. The basic question here is whether the minimum wage has been growing at roughly a *constant* rate over this period.
  a. Create a time series graph for these data. Comment on the observed behavior of the minimum wage over time.
  b. Estimate a linear regression equation of the minimum wage versus time (the Year variable). What does the estimated slope indicate?
  c. Analyze the residuals from the equation in part **b**. Are they essentially random? If not, return to part **b** and revise your equation appropriately. Then interpret the revised equation.

30. Estimate a regression equation that *adequately* estimates the relationship between monthly electrical power usage (Y) and home size (X) using the data in the file **P10_13.xlsx**. Interpret your results. How well does your model explain the variation in monthly electrical power usage?

31. An insurance company wants to determine how its annual operating costs depend on the number of home insurance (X_1) and automobile insurance (X_2) policies that have been written. The file **P10_31.xlsx** contains relevant information for several branches of the insurance company. The company believes that a multiplicative model might be appropriate because operating costs typically increase by a constant percentage as the number of either type of policy increases by a given percentage. Use the given data to estimate a multiplicative model for this insurance company. Interpret your results. Does a multiplicative model provide a good fit with these data? Answer by calculating the appropriate standard error of estimate and R^2 value, based on *original* units of the dependent variable.

32. Suppose that an operations manager is trying to determine the number of labor hours required to produce the *i*th unit of a certain product. Consider the data provided in the file **P10_32.xlsx**. For example, the second unit produced required 517 labor hours, and the 600th unit required 34 labor hours.
  a. Use the given data to estimate a relationship between the total number of units produced and the labor hours

required to produce the last unit in the total set. Interpret your findings.
  b. Use your estimated relationship to predict the number of labor hours that will be needed to produce the 800th unit.

Level B

33. The human resources manager of DataCom, Inc., wants to predict the annual salaries of given employees using the potential explanatory variables in the file **P10_05.xlsx.**
  a. Estimate an appropriate multiple regression equation to predict the annual salary of a given DataCom employee using all of the data in columns C–H.
  b. Interpret the estimated regression coefficients.
  c. According to the estimated regression model, is there a difference between the mean salaries earned by male and female employees at DataCom? If so, how large is the difference? According to your equation, does this difference depend on the values of the other explanatory variables? Explain.
  d. According to the estimated regression model, is there a difference between the mean salaries earned by employees in the sales department and those in the advertising department at DataCom? If so, how large is the difference? According to your equation, does this difference depend on the values of the other explanatory variables? Explain.
  e. According to the estimated regression model, in which department are DataCom employees paid the *highest* mean salary (after controlling for other explanatory variables)? In which department are DataCom employees paid the *lowest* mean salary?
  f. Given the estimated regression model, predict the annual salary of a female employee who served in a similar department at another company for 10 years prior to coming to work at DataCom. This woman, a graduate of a four-year collegiate business program, has been supervising 12 subordinates in the purchasing department since joining the organization five years ago.

34. Does the rate of violent crime acts vary across different regions of the United States? Answer this with the data in the file **P10_34.xlsx** as requested below.
  a. Estimate an appropriate regression model to explain the variation in violent crime rate across the four given regions of the United States. Interpret the estimated equation. Rank the four regions from highest to lowest according to their mean violent crime rate. Could you have done this without regression? Explain.
  b. How would you modify the regression model in part **a** to account for possible differences in the violent crime rate across the various subdivisions of the given regions? Estimate your revised regression equation and interpret your findings. Rank the nine subdivisions from highest to lowest according to their mean violent crime rate.

35. Continuing Problems 6 and 15 on the 2006–2007 movie data in the file **P02_02.xlsx**, create a new variable Total Revenue that is the sum of Total US Gross, International Gross, and US DVD Sales. How well can this new variable be predicted from the data in columns C–F? For Distributor, relabel the categories so that there are only two: Large Distributor and Small Distributor. The former is any distributor that had at least 12 movies in this period, and the latter is all the rest. For Genre, relabel the categories to be Comedy, Drama, Adventure, Action, Thriller/Suspense, and Other. (Other includes Black Comedy, Documentary, Horror, Musical, and Romantic Comedy.) Interpret the coefficients of the estimated regression equation. How would you explain the results to someone in the movie business? Do you think that predictions of total revenue from this regression equation will be very accurate? Why?

36. Continuing Problem 18, suppose that the antique collector believes that the *rate of increase* of the auction price with the age of the item will be driven upward by a large number of bidders. How would you revise the multiple regression equation developed previously to model this feature of the problem?
  a. Estimate your revised equation using the data in the file **P10_18.xlsx**.
  b. Interpret each of the estimated coefficients in your revised model.
  c. Does this revised model fit the given data better than the original multiple regression model? Explain why or why not.

37. Continuing Problem 19, revise the previous multiple regression equation to include an interaction term between the return on average equity (X_1) and annual dividend rate (X_2).
  a. Estimate your revised equation using the data provided in the file **P10_19.xlsx**.
  b. Interpret each of the estimated coefficients in your revised equation. In particular, how do you interpret the coefficient for the interaction term in the revised equation?
  c. Does this revised equation fit the given data better than the original multiple regression equation? Explain why or why not.

38. Continuing Problem 22, suppose that one of the managers of this regional express delivery service company is trying to decide whether to add an interaction term involving the package weight (X_1) and the distance shipped (X_2) in the previous multiple regression equation.
  a. Why would the manager want to add such a term to the regression equation?
  b. Estimate the revised equation using the data given in the file **P10_22.xlsx**.
  c. Interpret each of the estimated coefficients in your revised equation. In particular, how do you interpret the coefficient for the interaction term in the revised equation?
  d. Does this revised equation fit the data better than the original multiple regression equation? Explain why or why not.

10-7 Validation of the Fit

The fit from a regression analysis is often overly optimistic. When you use the least squares procedure on a given set of data, all the idiosyncrasies of that data set are exploited to obtain the best possible fit. However, there is no guarantee that the fit will be as good when the estimated regression equation is applied to *new* data. In fact, it usually isn't. This is particularly important when the goal is to use the regression equation to predict new values of the dependent variable. The usual situation is that you use a given data set to estimate a regression equation. Then you gather new data on the *explanatory* variables and use these, along with the already-estimated regression equation, to predict the new (but unknown) values of the dependent variable.

One way to see whether this procedure will be successful is to split the original data set into two subsets: one subset for estimation and one subset for validation. A regression equation is estimated from the first subset. Then the values of explanatory variables from the second subset are substituted into this equation to obtain predicted values for the dependent variable. Finally, these predicted values are compared to the *known* values of the dependent variable in the second subset. If the agreement is good, there is reason to believe that the regression equation will predict well for new data. This procedure is called **validating the fit**.

This validation procedure is fairly simple to perform in Excel. We illustrate it for the Bendrix manufacturing data in Example 10.2. (See the file **Overhead Costs Validation.xlsx**.) There we used 36 monthly observations to regress Overhead on Machine Hours and Production Runs. The regression output is repeated in Figure 10.46. In particular, it shows an R^2 value of 86.6% and an s_e value of $4109.

Figure 10.46 StatTools Regression Output for Bendrix Example

	A	B	C	D	E	F	G
8	**Multiple Regression for Overhead**	**Multiple R**	**R-Square**	**Adjusted R-square**	**Std. Err. of Estimate**	**Rows Ignored**	
9	**Summary**						
10		0.9308	0.8664	0.8583	4108.99309	0	
11							
12		**Degrees of Freedom**	**Sum of Squares**	**Mean of Squares**	**F**	**p-Value**	
13	**ANOVA Table**						
14	Explained	2	3614020661	1807010330	107.0261279	< 0.0001	
15	Unexplained	33	557166199.1	16883824.22			
16							
17		**Coefficient**	**Standard Error**	**t-Value**	**p-Value**	**Confidence Interval 95%**	
18	**Regression Table**					Lower	Upper
19	Constant	3996.678209	6603.650932	0.605222512	0.5492	−9438.550632	17431.90705
20	Machine Hours	43.53639812	3.5894837	12.12887472	< 0.0001	36.23353862	50.83925761
21	Production Runs	883.6179252	82.25140753	10.74289124	< 0.0001	716.2761784	1050.959672

Now suppose that this data set is from one of Bendrix's two plants. The company would like to predict overhead costs for the other plant by using data on machine hours and production runs at the other plant. The first step is to see how well the regression from Figure 10.46 fits data from the other plant. This validation on the 36 months of data is shown in Figure 10.47.

Figure 10.47 Validation of Bendrix Regression Results

	A	B	C	D	E	F
1	**Validation data**					
2						
3	Coefficients from regression equation (based on original data)					
4	Constant	Machine Hours	Production Runs			
5	3996.6782	43.5364	883.6179			
6						
7	Comparison of summary measures					
8		Original	Validation			
9	R-square	0.8664	0.7733			
10	StErr of Est	4108.99	5256.50			
11						
12	Month	Machine Hours	Production Runs	Overhead	Fitted	Residual
13	1	1374	24	92414	85023	7391
14	2	1510	35	92433	100663	−8230
15	3	1213	21	81907	75362	6545
16	4	1629	27	93451	98775	−5324
17	5	1858	28	112203	109629	2574
46	34	1529	29	94325	96189	−1864
47	35	1389	47	98474	105999	−7525
48	36	1350	34	90857	92814	−1957

Fundamental Insight

Training and Validation Sets

This practice of *partitioning* a data set into a set for estimation and a set for validation is becoming much more common as larger data sets become available. It allows you to see how a given procedure such as regression works on a data set where you *know* the Y's. If it works well, you have more confidence that it will work well on a new data set where you do *not* know the Y's. This partitioning is a routine part of data mining, which is covered in Chapter 17. In data mining, the first data set is usually called the *training* set, and the second data set is called the *validation* or *testing* set.

To obtain the results in this figure, proceed as follows.

Procedure for Validating Regression Results

1. **Copy old results.** Copy the results from the original regression to the ranges A5:C5 and B9:B10.
2. **Calculate fitted values and residuals.** The fitted values are now the predicted values of overhead for the other plant, based on the original regression equation. Find these by substituting the new values of Machine Hours and Production Runs into the original equation. Specifically, enter the formula

   =$A$5+SUMPRODUCT($B$5:$C$5,B13:C13)

   in cell E13 and copy it down. Then calculate the residuals (prediction errors for the other plant) by entering the formula

   =D13-E13

   in cell F13 and copying it down.
3. **Calculate summary measures.** You can see how well the original equation fits the new data by calculating R^2 and s_e values. Recall that R^2 in general is the square of the correlation between observed and fitted values. Therefore, enter the formula

   =CORREL(E13:E48,D13:D48)^2

   in cell C9. The s_e value is essentially the average of the squared residuals, but it uses the denominator $n - 3$ (when there are two explanatory variables) rather than $n - 1$. Therefore, enter the formula

   =SQRT(SUMSQ((F13:F48)/33)

   in cell C10.

Excel's SUMSQ function is often handy. It sums the squares of values in a range.

The results in Figure 10.47 are typical. The validation results are usually not as good as the original results. The value of R^2 has decreased from 86.6% to 77.3%, and the value of s_e has increased from $4109 to $5257. Nevertheless, Bendrix might conclude that the original regression equation is adequate for making future predictions at either plant.

10-8 Conclusion

In this chapter we have illustrated how to fit an equation to a set of points and how to interpret the resulting equation. We have also discussed two measures, R^2 and s_e, that indicate the goodness of fit of the regression equation. Although the general technique is called *linear* regression, it can be used to estimate nonlinear relationships through suitable transformations of variables. We are not finished with our study of regression, however. In the next chapter we make some statistical assumptions about the regression model and then discuss the types of inferences that can be made from regression output. In particular, we discuss the accuracy of the estimated regression coefficients, the accuracy of predictions made from the regression equation, and the choice of explanatory variables to include in the regression equation.

Summary of Key Terms

TERM	SYMBOL	EXPLANATION	EXCEL	PAGE	EQUATION
Regression analysis		A general method for estimating the relationship between a dependent variable and one or more explanatory variables		419	
Dependent (or response) variable	Y	The variable being estimated or predicted in a regression analysis		420	
Explanatory (or independent) variables	X's	The variables used to explain or predict the dependent variable		420	
Simple regression		A regression model with a single explanatory variable	Excel's INTERCEPT and SLOPE functions, Stat-Tools, or Analysis ToolPak	420	
Multiple regression		A regression model with any number of explanatory variables	StatTools or Analysis ToolPak	420	
Correlation	r_{XY}	A measure of the strength of the linear relationship between two variables X and Y	Excel's CORREL function or StatTools	428	10.1
Fitted value		The predicted value of the dependent variable, found by substituting explanatory values into the regression equation		431	10.2
Residual		The difference between the actual and fitted values of the dependent variable		431	10.2
Least squares line		The regression equation that minimizes the sum of squared residuals	StatTools or Analysis ToolPak	432	10.3, 10.4
Standard error of estimate	s_e	Essentially, the standard deviation of the residuals; indicates the magnitude of the prediction errors	Excel's STEYX function (for a single X), StatTools, or Analysis ToolPak	438	10.7, 10.11
R-square	R^2	The percentage of variation in the response variable explained by the regression model	Excel's RSQ function (for a single X), StatTools, or Analysis ToolPak	440	10.8
Adjusted R^2		A measure similar to R^2, but adjusted for the number of explanatory variables in the equation		447	
Regression coefficients	a, b's	The constant and the coefficients of the explanatory variables in a regression equation	StatTools or Analysis ToolPak	443	10.9
Dummy (or indicator) variables		Variables coded as 0 or 1, used to capture categorical variables in a regression analysis		450	
Interaction variables		Products of explanatory variables, used when the effect of one on the dependent variable depends on the value of the other		457	
Nonlinear transformations		Variables created to capture nonlinear relationships in a regression model		460	
Quadratic relationship		A regression model with linear and squared explanatory variables	StatTools or Analysis ToolPak	462	
Model with logarithmic transformations		A regression model using logarithms of Y and/or Xs	StatTools or Analysis ToolPak	464	
Constant elasticity (or multiplicative) relationship		A relationship where predicted Y changes by a constant percentage when any X changes by 1%; requires logarithmic transformations	StatTools or Analysis ToolPak	464	10.14
Learning curve		A particular multiplicative relationship used to indicate how cost or time in production decreases over time	StatTools or Analysis ToolPak	465	10.15
Validation of fit		Checks how well a regression model based on one sample predicts a related sample		471	

Problems

Solutions for problems whose numbers appear within a colored box can be found in the Student Solution Files.

Conceptual Questions

C.1. Consider the relationship between yearly wine consumption (liters of alcohol from drinking wine, per person) and yearly deaths from heart disease (deaths per 100,000 people) in 19 developed countries. Suppose that you read a newspaper article in which the reporter states the following:

Researchers find that the correlation between yearly wine consumption and yearly deaths from heart disease is −0.84. Thus, it is reasonable to conclude that increased consumption of alcohol from wine causes fewer deaths from heart disease in industrialized societies.

Comment on the reporter's interpretation of the correlation in this situation.

C.2. "It is generally appropriate to delete all outliers in a data set that are apparent in a scatterplot." Do you agree with this statement? Explain.

C.3. How would you interpret the relationship between two numeric variables when the estimated least squares regression line for them is essentially *horizontal* (slope 0)?

C.4. Suppose that you generate a scatterplot of residuals versus fitted values of the dependent variable for an estimated regression equation. Furthermore, you find the correlation between the residuals and fitted values to be 0.829. Does this provide a good indication that the estimated regression equation is satisfactory? Explain why or why not.

C.5. Suppose that you have generated three alternative multiple regression equations to explain the variation in a particular dependent variable. The regression output for each equation can be summarized as follows:

	Equation 1	Equation 2	Equation 3
No. of X's	4	6	9
R^2	0.76	0.77	0.79
Adjusted R^2	0.75	0.74	0.73

Which of these equations would you select as "best"? Explain your choice.

C.6. Suppose you want to investigate the relationship between a dependent variable Y and two potential explanatory variables X_1 and X_2. Is the R^2 value for the equation with both X variables included necessarily at least as large as the R^2 value from each equation with only a single X? Explain why or why not. Could the R^2 value for the equation with both X variables included be *larger* than the sum of the R^2 values from the separate equations, each with only a single X included? Is there any intuitive explanation for this?

C.7. Suppose you believe that two variables X and Y are related, but you have no idea which way the causality goes. Does X cause Y or vice versa (or maybe even neither)? Can you tell by regressing Y on X and then regressing X on Y? Explain. Also, provide at least one real example where the direction of causality would be ambiguous.

C.8. Suppose you have two columns of monthly data, one on advertising expenditures and one on sales. If you use this data set, as is, to regress sales on advertising, will it adequately capture the behavior that advertising in one month doesn't really affect sales in *that* month but only in *future* months? What should you do, in terms of regression, to capture this timing effect?

C.9. Suppose you want to predict reading speed using, among other variables, the device the person is reading from. This device could be a regular book, an iPad, a Kindle, or others. Therefore, you create dummy variables for device. How, exactly, would you do it? If you use regular book as the reference category and another analyst uses, say, Kindle as the reference category, will you get the same regression results? Explain.

C.10. Explain the benefits of using natural logarithms of variables, either of Y or of the X's, as opposed to other possible nonlinear functions, when scatterplots (or possibly economic considerations) indicate that nonlinearities should be taken into account. Explain exactly how you interpret regression coefficients if logs are taken only of Y, only of the X's, or of both Y and the X's.

C.11. The number of cars per 1000 people is known for virtually every country in the world. For many countries, however, per capita income is not known. How might you estimate per capita income for countries where it is unknown?

Level A

39. Many companies manufacture products that are at least partially produced using chemicals (e.g., paint, gasoline, and steel). In many cases, the quality of the finished product is a function of the temperature and pressure at which the chemical reactions take place. Suppose that a particular manufacturer wants to model the quality (Y) of a product as a function of the temperature (X_1) and the pressure (X_2) at which it is produced. The file **P10_39.xlsx** contains data obtained from a carefully designed experiment involving these variables. Note that the assigned quality score can range from a minimum of 0 to a maximum of 100 for each manufactured product.

a. Estimate a multiple regression equation that includes the two given explanatory variables. Does the estimated equation fit the data well?

b. Add an interaction term between temperature and pressure and run the regression again. Does the inclusion of the interaction term improve the model's goodness of fit?

c. Interpret each of the estimated coefficients in the two equations. How are they different? How do you interpret the coefficient for the interaction term in the second equation?

40. A power company located in southern Alabama wants to predict the peak power load (i.e., the maximum amount of power that must be generated each day to meet demand) as a function of the daily high temperature (X). A random sample of summer days is chosen, and the peak power load and the high temperature are recorded each day. The file **P10_40.xlsx** contains these observations.

a. Create a scatterplot for these data. Comment on the observed relationship between Y and X.

b. Estimate an appropriate regression equation to predict the peak power load for this power company. Interpret the estimated regression coefficients.

c. Analyze the estimated equation's residuals. Do they suggest that the regression equation is adequate? If not, return to part **b** and revise your equation. Continue to revise the equation until the results are satisfactory.

d. Use your final equation to predict the peak power load on a summer day with a high temperature of 100 degrees.

41. Management of a home appliance store would like to understand the growth pattern of the monthly sales of Blu-ray disc players over the past two years. Managers have recorded the relevant data in the file **P10_09.xlsx**.

a. Create a scatterplot for these data. Comment on the observed behavior of monthly sales at this store over time.

b. Estimate an appropriate regression equation to explain the variation of monthly sales over the given time period. Interpret the estimated regression coefficients.

c. Analyze the estimated equation's residuals. Do they suggest that the regression equation is adequate? If not, return to part **b** and revise your equation. Continue to revise the equation until the results are satisfactory.

42. A small computer chip manufacturer wants to forecast monthly operating costs as a function of the number of units produced during a month. The company has collected several months of data in the file **P10_42.xlsx**.

a. Determine an equation that can be used to predict monthly production costs from units produced. Are there any outliers?

b. How could the regression line obtained in part **a** be used to determine whether the company was efficient or inefficient during any particular month?

43. The file **P02_07.xlsx** includes data on 204 employees at the (fictional) company Beta Technologies.

a. Create a recoded version of Education, where 0 or 2 is recoded as 1, 4 is recoded as 2, and 6 or 8 is recoded as 3. Then create dummy variables for these three categories.

b. Use pivot tables to explore whether average salary depends on gender, and whether it depends on the recoded Education. Then use scatterplots to explore whether salary is related to age, prior experience, and Beta experience. Briefly state your results.

c. Run a regression of salary versus gender, age, prior experience, Beta experience, and any two of the education dummies, and interpret the results.

d. If any of the potential explanatory variables seems to be unrelated to salary, based on the results from part **b**, run one or more regressions without such a variable. Comment on whether it makes much of a difference in the regression outputs.

44. The file **P10_44.xlsx** contains data that relate the unit cost of producing a fuel pressure regulator to the cumulative number of fuel pressure regulators produced at an automobile production plant. For example, the 4000th unit cost $13.70 to produce.

a. Fit a learning curve to these data.

b. You would predict that doubling cumulative production reduces the cost of producing a regulator by what amount?

45. The *beta* of a stock is found by running a regression with the monthly return on a market index as the explanatory variable and the monthly return on the stock as the dependent variable. The beta of the stock is then the slope of this regression line.

a. Explain why most stocks have a positive beta.

b. Explain why a stock with a beta with absolute value greater than one is more volatile than the market index and a stock with a beta less than one (in absolute value) is less volatile than the market index.

c. Use the data in the file **P10_45.xlsx** to estimate the beta for each of the four companies listed: Caterpillar, Goodyear, McDonalds, and Ford. Use the S&P 500 as the market index.

d. For each of these companies, what percentage of the variation in its returns is explained by the variation in the market index? What percentage is unexplained by variation in the market index?

e. Verify (using Excel's COVAR and VARP functions) that the beta for each company is given by

$$\frac{\text{Covariance between Company and Market}}{\text{Variance of Market}}$$

Also, verify that the correlation between each company's returns and the market's returns is the square root of R^2.

46. Continuing the previous problem, explore whether the beta for these companies changes through time. For example, are the betas based on 1990s data different from those based on 2000s data? Or are data based on only five years of data different from those based on longer time periods?

47. The file **Catalog Marketing.xlsx** contains recent data on 1000 HyTex customers. (This is the same data set used in Example 2.7 in Chapter 2.)

a. Create a pivot table of average amount spent versus the number of catalogs sent. Is there any evidence that these two variables are related? Would it make sense to enter Catalogs, as is, in a regression equation for Amount Spent, or should dummies be used? Explain.

b. Create a pivot table of average amount spent versus History. Is there any evidence that these two variables are related? Would it make sense to enter History, as is, in a regression equation for Amount Spent, or should dummies be used? Explain.

c. Answer part **b** with History replaced by Age.

d. Base on your results from parts **a** through **c**, estimate an appropriate regression equation for Amount Spent, using the appropriate forms for Catalogs, History, and Age, plus the variables Gender, Own Home, Married, and Close. Interpret this equation and comment on its usefulness in predicting Amount Spent.

48. A common complaint of university students is that tenure-track instructors care a lot more about their research than their teaching and general availability to students. The file **P10_48.xlsx** contains hypothetical data on 75 tenure-track instructors where you can check whether these complaints are justified. The explanatory variables are (1) whether the instructor holds regular office hours, (2) average teaching evaluation on a 1–6 scale, and (3) number of published articles. The dependent variable is the instructor's current annual salary. Use regression on this data set and comment on the results. In particular, can Salary be explained almost as well by the number of articles as by all three explanatory variables combined?

49. The file **P10_49.xlsx** contains the amount of money spent advertising a product and the number of units sold for several months.

a. Assume that the only factor influencing monthly sales is advertising. Fit the following three curves to these data: linear ($Y = a + bX$), exponential ($Y = ab^X$), and multiplicative ($Y = aX^b$). Which equation fits the data best?

b. Interpret the best-fitting equation.

c. Using the best-fitting equation, predict sales during a month in which $60,000 is spent on advertising.

50. A golf club manufacturer is trying to determine how the price of a set of clubs affects the demand for clubs. The file **P10_50.xlsx** contains the price of a set of clubs and the monthly sales.

a. Assume the only factor influencing monthly sales is price. Fit the following three curves to these data: linear ($Y = a + bX$), exponential ($Y = ab^X$), and multiplicative ($Y = aX^b$). Which equation fits the data best?

b. Interpret your best-fitting equation.

c. Using the best-fitting equation, predict sales during a month in which the price is $470.

51. The file **P03_55.xlsx** lists the average salary for each Major League Baseball (MLB) team from 2004 to 2011, along with the number of team wins in each of these years.

a. Rearrange the data so that there are four long columns: Team, Year, Salary, and Wins. There should be 8*30 values for each.

b. Create a scatterplot of Wins (Y) versus Salary (X). Is there any indication of a relationship between these two variables? Is it a linear relationship?

c. Run a regression of Wins versus Salary. What does it say, if anything, about teams buying their way to success?

52. Repeat the previous problem with the basketball data in the file **P03_56.xlsx**. (Now there will be 6*30 rows in the rearranged data set.)

53. Repeat Problem 51 with the football data in the file **P03_57.xlsx**. (Now there will be 8*32 rows in the rearranged data set.)

54. Baker Company wants to develop a budget to predict how overhead costs vary with activity levels. Management is trying to decide whether direct labor hours (DLH) or units produced is the better measure of activity for the firm. Monthly data for the preceding 24 months appear in the file **P10_54.xlsx**. Use regression analysis to determine which measure, DLH or Units (or both), should be used for the budget. How would the regression equation be used to obtain the budget for the firm's overhead costs?

55. The auditor of Kiely Manufacturing is concerned about the number and magnitude of year-end adjustments that are made annually when the financial statements of Kiely Manufacturing are prepared. Specifically, the auditor suspects that the management of Kiely Manufacturing is using discretionary write-offs to manipulate the reported net income. To check this, the auditor has collected data from 25 companies that are similar to Kiely Manufacturing in terms of manufacturing facilities and product lines. The cumulative reported third-quarter income and the final net income reported are listed in the file **P10_55.xlsx** for each of these 25 companies. If Kiely Manufacturing reports a cumulative third-quarter income of $2,500,000 and a preliminary net income of $4,900,000, should the auditor conclude that the relationship between cumulative third-quarter income and the annual income for Kiely Manufacturing differs from that of the 25 companies in this sample? Explain why or why not.

56. The file **P10_56.xlsx** contains some interesting data on the U.S. presidential elections from 1880 through 2008. The variable definitions are on the Source sheet. The question is whether the Vote variable can be predicted very well from the other variables.

a. Create pivot tables and/or scatterplots to check whether Vote appears to be related to the other variables. Comment on the results.

b. Run a regression of Vote versus the other variables (not including Year). Do the coefficients go in the direction (positive or negative) you would expect? If you were going to use the regression equation to predict Vote for the next election and you had the relevant data for the explanatory variables for that year, how accurate do you think your prediction would be?

Level B

57. We stated in the beginning of the chapter that regression can be used to understand the way the world works. That is, you can look at the regression coefficients (their signs and magnitudes) to see the effects of the explanatory variables on the dependent variable. However, is it possible that apparently small changes in the data can lead to very different-looking equations? The file **P10_57.**

xlsx lets you explore this question. Columns K–R contain data on over 100 (fictional) homes that were recently sold. The regression equation for this original data set is given in the range T15:U21. (It was found with StatTools in the usual way.) Columns C–I contain slight changes to the original data, with the amount of change determined by the adjustable parameters in row 2. (Look at the formulas in columns C–I to see how the original data have been changed randomly.) The regression equation for the changed data appears in the range T6:U12. It has been calculated through special matrix functions (not Stat-Tools), so that it changes automatically when the random data change. (These require the 1's in column B.) Experiment by pressing the F9 key or changing the adjustable parameters to see how much the two regression equations can differ. After experimenting, briefly explain how you think housing pricing works—or can you tell?

58. The file **P02_35.xlsx** contains data from a survey of 500 randomly selected households. For this problem, use Monthly Payment as the dependent variable in several regressions, as explained below.

   a. Beginning with Family Size, iteratively add one explanatory variable and estimate the resulting regression equation to explain the variation in Monthly Payment. If adding any explanatory variable causes the *adjusted* R^2 measure to fall, do not include that variable in subsequent versions of the regression model. Otherwise, include the variable and consider adding the next variable in the set. Which variables are included in the final version of your regression model? (Add dummies for Location in a single step, and use Total Income rather than First Income and Second Income separately.)

   b. Interpret the final estimated regression equation you obtained through the process outlined in part **a**. Also, interpret the standard error of estimate s_e, R^2, and the adjusted R^2 for the final estimated model.

59. (This problem is based on an actual court case in Philadelphia.) In the 1994 congressional election, the Republican candidate outpolled the Democratic candidate by 400 votes (excluding absentee ballots). The Democratic candidate outpolled the Republican candidate by 500 absentee votes. The Republican candidate sued (and won), claiming that vote fraud must have played a role in the absentee ballot count. The Republican's lawyer ran a regression to predict (based on past elections) how the absentee ballot margin could be predicted from the votes tabulated on voting machines. Selected results are given in the file **P10_59.xlsx**. Show how this regression could be used by the Republican to "prove" his claim of vote fraud.

60. In the world of computer science, Moore's law is famous. Although there are various versions of this law, they all say something to the effect that computing power *doubles* every two years. Several researchers estimated this law with regression using real data in 2006. Their paper can be found online at http://download.

intel.com/pressroom/pdf/computertrendsrelease.pdf. For example, one interesting chart appears on page S1, backed up with regression results on another page. What exactly do these results say about doubling every two years (or do they contradict Moore's law)?

61. (The data for this problem are fictitious, but they are not far off.) For each of the top 25 business schools, the file **P10_61.xlsx** contains the average salary of a professor. Thus, for Indiana University (number 15 in the rankings), the average salary is $46,000. Use this information and regression to show that IU is doing a great job with its available resources.

62. Suppose the correlation between the average height of parents and the height of their firstborn male child is 0.5. You are also told that:

   - The average height of all parents is 66 inches.
   - The standard deviation of the average height of parents is 4 inches.
   - The average height of all male children is 70 inches.
   - The standard deviation of the height of all male children is 4 inches.

   If a mother and father are 73 and 80 inches tall, respectively, how tall do you predict their son to be? Explain why this is called "regression toward the mean."

63. As indicated by the opening vignette to this chapter, a motel chain could use regression to determine good locations for new motels from data on existing motels. The data in the file **P10_63.xlsx** provide one possibility. The Existing Sites sheet contains data on 90 motels in the chain. The cell comments in row 1 explain the variables, and the last variable, Operating Margin, is used as the dependent variable. The Potential Sites sheet contains data on five potential sites, but the dependent variable for these sites is unknown. Run a regression on the first sheet and discuss the results. Then use the regression equation to predict Operating Margin for the potential sites. Where would you suggest the company should locate one or more new motels? Note that the data on Indoor Pool have been omitted for the potential sites. After all, the company gets to decide whether to build an indoor pool. How should you handle this variable in the predictions?

64. For each of the four data sets in the file **P10_64.xlsx**, calculate the least squares line. For which of these data sets would you feel comfortable in using the least squares line to predict Y?

65. Suppose you run a regression on a data set of X and Y values and obtain a least squares line of $Y = 12 - 3X$.

   a. If you double each value of X, what is the new least squares line?

   b. If you triple each value of Y, what is the new least squares line?

   c. If you add 6 to each value of X, what is the new least squares line?

   d. If you subtract 4 from each value of Y, what is the new least squares line?

66. The file **P10_66.xlsx** contains monthly cost accounting data on overhead costs, machine hours, and direct material costs. This problem will help you explore the meaning of R^2 and the relationship between R^2 and correlations.

   a. Create a table of correlations between the individual variables.

   b. If you ignore the two explanatory variables Machine Hours and Direct Material Cost and predict each Overhead Cost as the *mean* of Overhead Cost, then a typical "error" is Overhead Cost minus the mean of Overhead Cost. Find the sum of squared errors using this form of prediction, where the sum is over all observations.

   c. Now run three regressions: (1) Overhead Cost (OHCost) versus Machine Hours, (2) OHCost versus Direct Material Cost, and (3) OHCost versus both Machine Hours and Direct Material Cost. (The first two are simple regressions, the third is a multiple regression.) For each, find the sum of squared residuals, and divide this by the sum of squared errors from part **b**. What is the relationship between this ratio and the associated R^2 for that equation? (Now do you see why R^2 is referred to as the percentage of variation explained?)

   d. For the first two regressions in part **c**, what is the relationship between R^2 and the corresponding correlation between the dependent and explanatory variable? For the third regression it turns out that the R^2 can be expressed as a complicated function of all three correlations in part **a**. That is, the function involves not just the correlations between the dependent variable and each explanatory variable, but also the correlation between the explanatory variables. Note that this R^2 is not just the sum of the R^2 values from the first two regressions in part **c**. Why do you think this is true, intuitively? However, R^2 for the multiple regression is still the square of a correlation—namely, the correlation between the observed and predicted values of OHCost. Verify that this is the case for these data.

67. The file **P10_67.xlsx** contains hypothetical starting salaries for MBA students directly after graduation. The file also lists their years of experience prior to the MBA program and their class rank in the MBA program (on a $0-100$ scale).

   a. Estimate the regression equation with Salary as the dependent variable and Experience and Class Rank as the explanatory variables. What does this equation imply? What does the standard error of estimate s_e tell you? What about R^2?

   b. Repeat part **a**, but now include the interaction term Experience*Class Rank (the product) in the equation as well as Experience and Class Rank individually. Answer the same questions as in part **a**. What evidence is there that this extra variable (the interaction variable) is worth including? How do you interpret

this regression equation? Why might you expect the interaction to be present in real data of this type?

68. In a simple regression of Y versus X, what is the relationship between the estimated slope, labeled b, and the correlation between Y and X, labeled r? Are they the same? Do they always have the same sign? Is it possible for r to be close to 1 and for b to be close to 0? Is it possible for r to be close to 0 and for b to be large? Explore this with simulation in the following way. Choose any values a and b for the intercept and slope of a linear relationship between X and Y and choose any value s for the standard error of estimate. Then generate a set of X values randomly. It doesn't really matter how you do this, but for this problem, generate them from a normal distribution with mean 100 and standard deviation 10. Then generate each Y value from the equation $Y = a + bX + e$, where the error e is normally distributed with mean 0 and standard deviation s. Given your generated data, calculate the *estimated* slope of the regression line with Excel's SLOPE function and calculate the correlation between Y and X with Excel's CORREL function. Once you have this setup, you can press the F9 key to get new results, or you can change your values of a, b, and s. Based on the simulated results, can you answer the original questions? [*Hint*: Remember Equation (10.3).]

69. Wilhoit Company has observed that there is a linear relationship between indirect labor expense and direct labor hours. Data for direct labor hours and indirect labor expense for 18 months are given in the file **P10_69.xlsx**. At the start of month 7, all cost categories in the Wilhoit Company increased by 10%, and they stayed at this level for months 7 through 12. Then at the start of month 13, another 10% across-the-board increase in all costs occurred, and the company operated at this price level for months 13 through 18.

   a. Plot the data. Verify that the relationship between indirect labor expense and direct labor hours is approximately linear within each six-month period. Use regression (three times) to estimate the slope and intercept during months 1 through 6, during months 7 through 12, and during months 13 through 18.

   b. Use regression to fit a straight line to all 18 data points simultaneously. What values of the slope and intercept do you obtain?

   c. Perform a price level adjustment to the data and re-estimate the slope and intercept using all 18 data points. Assuming no cost increases for month 19, what is your prediction for indirect labor expense if there are 35,000 direct labor hours in month 19?

   d. Interpret your results. What causes the difference in the linear relationship estimated in parts **b** and **c**?

70. Bohring Company manufactures a sophisticated radar unit that is used in a fighter aircraft built by Seaways Aircraft. The first 50 units of the radar unit have been completed, and Bohring is preparing to submit a proposal to Seaways Aircraft to manufacture the next 50 units. Bohring wants to submit a competitive bid, but at the same time, it wants to ensure that all the costs of manufacturing the radar unit are fully covered. As part of this process, Bohring is attempting to develop a standard for the number of labor hours required to manufacture each radar unit. Developing a labor standard has been a continuing problem in the past. The file **P10_70.xlsx** lists the number of labor hours required for each of the first 50 units of production. Bohring accountants want to see whether regression analysis, together with the concept of learning curves, can help solve the company's problem.

71. Sometimes it is instructive to generate random data that have a given relationship and then use regression on the generated data to see if the estimated regression is basically the same as that used to generate the data in the first place.

    a. Let X be normally distributed with mean 100 and standard deviation 10, and let Y equal $100 + 5X$ plus a normally distributed random residual with mean 0 and standard deviation 40. Generate 50 observations.

    b. Copy the random data and paste as values in another range of the worksheet. Then run the regression on the copy (the frozen values).

    c. Repeat part **b** several times to see if you get basically the same regression results each time. That is, each run should be on a *different* set of frozen data.

    d. Write a short report of your method and your findings.

CASE 10.1 Quantity Discounts at Firm Chair Company

Firm Chair Company manufactures customized wood furniture and sells the furniture in large quantities to major furniture retailers. Jim Bolling has recently been assigned to analyze the company's pricing policy. He has been told that quantity discounts were usually given. For example, for one type of chair, the pricing changed at quantities of 200 and 400—that is, these were the price breaks, where the marginal cost of the next chair changed. For this type of chair, the file **C10_01.xlsx** contains the quantity and total price to the customer for 81 orders. Use regression to help Jim discover the pricing structure that Firm Chair evidently used. (*Note*: A linear regression of Total Price versus Quantity will give you a "decent" fit, but you can do much better by introducing appropriate variables into the regression.)

CASE 10.2 Housing Price Structure in Mid City

Sales of single-family houses have been brisk in Mid City this year. This has especially been true in older, more established neighborhoods, where housing is relatively inexpensive compared to the new homes being built in the newer neighborhoods. Nevertheless, there are also many families who are willing to pay a higher price for the prestige of living in one of the newer neighborhoods. The file **C10_02.xlsx** contains data on 128 recent sales in Mid City. For each sale, the file shows the neighborhood (1, 2, or 3) in which the house is located, the number of offers made on the house, the square footage, whether the house is made primarily of brick, the number of bathrooms, the number of bedrooms, and the selling price. Neighborhoods 1 and 2 are more traditional neighborhoods, whereas neighborhood 3 is a newer, more prestigious neighborhood.

Use regression to estimate and interpret the pricing structure of houses in Mid City. Here are some considerations.

1. Do buyers pay a premium for a brick house, all else being equal?

2. Is there a premium for a house in neighborhood 3, all else being equal?

3. Is there an *extra* premium for a brick house in neighborhood 3, in addition to the usual premium for a brick house?

4. For purposes of estimation and prediction, could neighborhoods 1 and 2 be collapsed into a single "older" neighborhood?

CASE 10.3 Demand for French Bread at Howie's Bakery

Howie's Bakery is one of the most popular bakeries in town, and the favorite at Howie's is French bread. Each day of the week, Howie's bakes a number of loaves of French bread, more or less according to a daily schedule. To maintain its fine reputation, Howie's gives away to charity any loaves not sold on the day they are baked. Although this occurs frequently, it is also common for Howie's to run out of French bread on any given day—more demand than supply. In this case, no extra loaves are baked that day; the customers have to go elsewhere (or come back to Howie's the next day) for their French bread. Although French bread at Howie's is always popular, Howie's stimulates demand by running occasional 10% off sales.

Howie's has collected data for 20 consecutive weeks, 140 days in all. These data are listed in the file **C10_03.xlsx**.

The variables are Day (Monday–Sunday), Supply (number of loaves baked that day), On Sale (whether French bread is on sale that day), and Demand (loaves actually sold that day). Howie's would like you to see whether regression can be used successfully to estimate Demand from the other data in the file. Howie reasons that if these other variables can be used to predict Demand, then he might be able to determine his daily supply (number of loaves to bake) in a more cost-effective way.

How successful is regression with these data? Is Howie correct that regression can help him determine his daily supply? Is any information missing that would be useful? How would you obtain it? How would you use it? Is this extra information *really* necessary?

CASE 10.4 Investing for Retirement

Financial advisors offer many types of advice to customers, but they generally agree that one of the best things people can do is invest as much as possible in tax-deferred retirement plans. Not only are the earnings from these investments exempt from income tax (until retirement), but the investment itself is tax-exempt. This means that if a person invests, say, $10,000 of his $100,000 income in a tax-deferred retirement plan, he pays income tax that year on only $90,000 of his income. This is probably the best method available to most people for avoiding tax payments. However, which group takes advantage of this attractive investment opportunity: everyone, people with low salaries, people with high salaries, or who?

The file **C10_04.xlsx** lets you investigate this question. It contains data on 194 (hypothetical) couples: number of dependent children, combined annual salary of husband and wife, current mortgage on home, average amount of other (nonmortgage) debt, and percentage of combined income invested in tax-deferred retirement plans (assumed to be limited to 15%, which is realistic). Using correlations, scatterplots, and regression analysis, what can you conclude about the tendency of this group of people to invest in tax-deferred retirement plans?

CHAPTER 11

Regression Analysis: Statistical Inference

Syda Productions/Shutterstock.com

FORECASTING IN THE TIRE INDUSTRY

Improving long-term forecast accuracy is crucial to management in most supply chain areas. There is heavy reliance on forecasts from experts. However, experts are often known to be biased, and they are usually unable to properly weight large numbers of external indicators. With data on so many external indicators available, it seems like they should be helpful in providing more accurate forecasts. Indeed, most industry experts believe these indicators have potential, but the difficulty lies in using them appropriately in analytical forecasting models.

Sagaert et al. (2018) report on a study in the tire industry where such an analytical forecasting model was developed for a client company, a supplier in the tire industry. The goal was to improve forecast accuracy for time horizons up to 12 months. As the authors explain, the tire industry is highly sensitive to external factors. If there is an economic upswing, this causes an increase in road hauls, which requires more trucks. This causes truck tires to wear out faster, and replacement-tire demand increases. Also, when there is sustained economic growth, companies tend to add extra capacity, including investing in new trucks and corresponding tires. The combined effect of purchases of replacement tires and new truck tires impacts the timing of tire sales. The new truck tires are replaced when the original tires wear out, so their replacement lags behind the increase in economic activity. This argument suggests that economic activity, measured in an appropriate way, *could* be a leading indicator of tire-replacement sales.

One way of measuring economic activity is GDP, but it is too aggregated to provide details on changes in the economic system that are pertinent to tire sales. Fortunately, data are readily available on many potential leading indicators of tire sales, perhaps *too* many. This was the problem faced by the team of analysts. They realized that the extrapolation methods discussed in the next chapter, such as exponential smoothing, have limited usefulness because they ignore external factors that are related to tire sales. Therefore, they turned to regression models with lagged versions of potential leading indicators as explanatory variables. For example, to provide a 12-month ahead forecast of tire sales for January 2020, that is, a forecast made in January 2019, only data on the leading indicators from January 2019 and before could be used; more recent data wouldn't yet be available. The question is which leading indicators and which lags of them to use in a regression. The authors refer to this as the "short-fat" data problem, where the number of potential explanatory variables is very large relative to the number of useful observations on each of them (many columns, not very many rows).

In their study for the client company, they had 66 months of historical data on tire sales, and they were able to collect data on nearly 68,000 macroeconomic indicators from the FRED database of the Federal Reserve Bank of St. Louis. It would be nearly impossible to sift through all these potential explanatory variables (in addition to lagged versions of them) with the methods and software in this book. However, they were able to use a more advanced tool called least absolute shrinkage selection operator (LASSO) regression. LASSO uses the basic ideas of least squares regression, but its algorithms can automatically select the most useful variables from a large number of variables. LASSO minimizes a "cost" function that balances two objectives: the usual mean squared fitting error and the sum of the absolute values of the regression coefficients (suitably scaled). The effect is that coefficients of the variables that don't contribute much to the fit are forced to zero, leaving only the few most important variables.

The analysts tested their method against two benchmarks. The first used the method currently used by the company, the Winters' exponential smoothing method discussed in the next chapter. The second used multiple regression with a trend variable, seasonal index variables, and one leading indicator, the one that correlated most highly with tire sales. As an example of the results, the mean absolute percentage error (MAPE) for 12-month ahead forecasts using benchmarks 1 and 2 and the LASSO method were 24.0%, 30.3%, and 18.2%, respectively. For all forecasting horizons (1 to 12 months ahead) combined, the percentages were 18.6%, 20.3%, and 15.6%, respectively. These latter percentages indicate a 16.1% improvement over the company benchmark. In addition, the LASSO method made fewer really large forecast errors than the benchmarks, particularly for long-range forecasts.

One important advantage of the LASSO method (and of regression in general) is that the forecasts are transparent. Industry experts can see which leading indicators are selected and thus gain a better understanding of how their markets work. It also gives their sales reps a tool for better managing and reacting to market changes. Finally, because LASSO is a regression model-based method, prediction intervals, not simply single-number forecasts, are available. This provides forecasters with a measure of the uncertainty of their forecasts.

11-1 Introduction

The previous chapter discussed how to fit a regression equation to a set of points by using the least squares method. The purpose of this regression equation is to provide a good fit to the points in the sample so that you can understand the relationship between a dependent variable and one or more explanatory variables. The entire emphasis of the discussion in the previous chapter was on finding a regression model that fits the observations in the sample. In this chapter we take a slightly different point of view. We assume that the observations in the sample are taken from some larger population. For example, the sample of 50 regions from the Pharmex drugstore example could represent a sample of all the regions where Pharmex does business. In this case, we might be interested in the relationship between variables in the entire population, not just in the sample.

There are two basic problems we discuss in this chapter. The first has to do with a *population regression model*. We want to infer its characteristics—that is, its intercept and slope term(s)—from the corresponding terms estimated by least squares. We also want to know which explanatory variables belong in the equation. There are typically a large number of *potential* explanatory variables, and it is often not clear which of these do the best job of explaining variation in the dependent variable. In addition, we would like to infer whether there is any population regression equation worth pursuing. It is possible that the potential explanatory variables provide very little explanation of the dependent variable.

The second problem we discuss in this chapter is *prediction*. We touched on the prediction problem in the previous chapter, primarily in the context of predicting the dependent variable for part of the sample held out for validation purposes. In reality, we had the values of the dependent variable for that part of the sample, so prediction was not really necessary. Now we go beyond the sample and predict values of the dependent variable for *new* observations. There is no way to check the accuracy of these predictions, at least not right away, because the values of the dependent variable are not yet known. However, it is possible to calculate prediction intervals to measure the accuracy of the predictions.

11-2 The Statistical Model

To perform statistical inference in a regression context, a **statistical model** is required; that is, we must first make several assumptions about the population. Throughout the analysis these assumptions remain exactly that—they are only assumptions, not facts. These assumptions represent an idealization of reality, and as such, they are never likely to be entirely satisfied for the population in any real study. From a practical point of view, all we can ask is that they represent a close approximation to reality. If this is the case, then the analysis in this chapter is valid. But if the assumptions are grossly violated, statistical inferences that are based on these assumptions should be viewed with suspicion. Although we can never be entirely certain of the validity of the assumptions, there are ways to check for gross violations, and we discuss some of these.

Regression Assumptions

- There is a population regression line. It joins the *means* of the dependent variable for all values of the explanatory variables. For any fixed values of the explanatory variables, the mean of the errors is zero.
- For any values of the explanatory variables, the variance (or standard deviation) of the dependent variable is a constant, the same for all such values.
- For any values of the explanatory variables, the dependent variable is normally distributed.
- The errors are probabilistically independent.

Because these assumptions are so crucial to the regression analysis that follows, it is important to understand exactly what they mean. Assumption 1 is probably the most important. It implies that for some set of explanatory variables, there is an exact linear relationship in the population between the *means* of the dependent variable and the values of the explanatory variables.

More precisely, let Y be the dependent variable, and assume that there are k explanatory variables, X_1 through X_k. Let $\mu_{Y|X_1,\ldots,X_k}$ be the mean of all Y's for any fixed values of the X's. Then assumption 1 implies that there is an exact linear relationship between the mean $\mu_{Y|X_1,\ldots,X_k}$ and the X's. That is, it implies that there are coefficients α and β_1 through β_k such that the following equation holds for all values of the X's:

These explanatory variables could be original variables or variables you create, such as dummies, interactions, or nonlinear transformations.

Population Regression Line Joining Means

$$\mu_{Y|X_1,\ldots,X_k} = \alpha + \beta_1 X_1 + \cdots + \beta_k X_k \qquad (11.1)$$

It is common to use Greek letters to denote population parameters and regular letters for their sample estimates.

In the terminology of the previous chapter, α is the intercept term, and β_1 through β_k are the slope terms. We use Greek letters for these coefficients to denote that they are *unobservable* population parameters. Assumption 1 implies the existence of a population regression equation and the corresponding α and β's. However, it tells us nothing about the *values* of these parameters. They still need to be estimated from sample data, using the least squares method to do so.

Equation (11.1) says that the *means* of the Y's lie on the population regression line. However, it is clear from a scatterplot that most *individual* Y's do not lie on this line. The vertical distance from any point to the line is called an **error**. The error for any point, labeled ε, is the difference between Y and $\mu_{Y|X_1,\ldots,X_k}$, that is,

$$Y = \mu_{Y|X_1,\ldots,X_k} + \varepsilon$$

By substituting the assumed linear form for $\mu_{Y|X_1,\ldots,X_k}$, we obtain Equation (11.2). This equation states that each value of Y is equal to a fitted part plus an error. The fitted part is the linear expression $\alpha + \beta_1 X_1 + \cdots + \beta_k X_k$. The error ε is sometimes positive, in which case the point is above the regression line, and sometimes negative, in which case the point is below the regression line. The last part of assumption 1 states that these errors average to zero in the population, so that the positive errors exactly cancel the negative errors.

> **Population Regression Line with Error**
>
> $$Y = \alpha + \beta_1 X_1 + \cdots + \beta_k X_k + \varepsilon \qquad (11.2)$$

Note that an error ε is not quite the same as a residual e. An error is the vertical distance from a point to the (unobservable) population regression line. A residual is the vertical distance from a point to the *estimated* regression line. Residuals can be calculated from observed data; errors cannot.

Assumption 2 concerns variation around the population regression line. It states that the variation of the Y's about the regression line is the *same*, regardless of the values of the X's. A technical term for this property is **homoscedasticity**. A simpler term is **constant error variance**. In the Pharmex example (Example 10.1), constant error variance implies that the variation in Sales values is the same regardless of the value of Promote. As another example, recall the Bendrix manufacturing example (Example 10.2). There we related overhead costs (Overhead) to the number of machine hours (Machine Hours) and the number of production runs (Production Runs). Constant error variance implies that overhead costs vary just as much for small values of Machine Hours and Production Runs as for large values—or any values in between.

There are many situations where assumption 2 is questionable. The variation in Y often increases as X increases—a violation of assumption 2. We presented an example of this in Figure 10.10 (repeated here in Figure 11.1), which is based on customer spending at an online store. This scatterplot shows the amount spent versus salary for a sample of the company's customers. Clearly, the variation in the amount spent increases as salary increases, which makes intuitive sense. Customers with small salaries have little disposable income, so they tend to spend small amounts at online stores. Customers with large salaries have more disposable income. Some of them spend a lot of it at online stores and some spend only a little of it—hence, a larger variation. Scatterplots with this "fan" shape are not uncommon in real studies, and they exhibit a clear violation of assumption 2.[1] We say that the data in this graph exhibit **heteroscedasticity**, or more simply, **nonconstant error variance**. These terms are summarized in the following box.

> **Homoscedasticity** means that the variability of Y values is the same for all X values.
> **Heteroscedasticity** means that the variability of Y values is larger for some X values than for others.

The easiest way to detect nonconstant error variance is through a visual inspection of a scatterplot. You create a scatterplot of the dependent variable versus an explanatory variable X and see whether the points vary more for some values of X than for others. You can also examine the residuals with a residual plot, where residual values are on the vertical axis and some other variable (Y or one of the X's) is on the horizontal axis. If the

1 The fan shape in Figure 11.1 is probably the most common form of nonconstant error variance, but it is not the only possible form.

Figure 11.1 Illustration of
Nonconstant Error Variance

residual plot exhibits a fan shape or other evidence of nonconstant error variance, this also indicates a violation of assumption 2.

Assumption 3 is equivalent to stating that the errors are normally distributed. You can check this by forming a histogram (or a Q-Q plot, discussed in Chapter 9) of the residuals. If assumption 3 holds, the histogram should be approximately symmetric and bell-shaped, and the points in the Q-Q plot should be close to a 45° line. But if there is an obvious skewness, too many residuals more than, say, two standard deviations from the mean, or some other nonnormal property, this indicates a violation of assumption 3.

Finally, assumption 4 requires probabilistic independence of the errors. Intuitively, this assumption means that information on some of the errors provides no information on the values of other errors. For example, if you are told that the overhead costs for months 1 through 4 are all above the regression line (positive residuals), you cannot infer anything about the residual for month 5 if assumption 4 holds.

Assumption 4 (independence of residuals) is usually in doubt only for time series data.

For cross-sectional data, there is generally little reason to doubt the validity of assumption 4 unless the observations are ordered in some particular way. For cross-sectional data assumption 4 is usually taken for granted. However, for time series data, assumption 4 is often violated. This is because of a property called *autocorrelation*. For now, we simply mention that one output given automatically in many regression packages is the *Durbin–Watson statistic*. The Durbin–Watson statistic is one measure of autocorrelation, so it is one measure of the extent to which assumption 4 is violated. We briefly discuss this Durbin–Watson statistic toward the end of this chapter and in the next chapter.

There is one other important assumption. No explanatory variable can be an *exact* linear combination of any other explanatory variables. Another way of stating this is that there should be no exact linear relationship between any set of explanatory variables. This would be violated, for example, if one variable were an exact multiple of another, or if one variable were equal to the sum of several other variables. More generally, the violation occurs if one of the explanatory variables can be written as a weighted sum of several of the others. This is called *exact multicollinearity*.

Exact multicollinearity means that at least one of the explanatory variables is redundant and is not needed in the regression equation.

If exact multicollinearity exists, it means that there is *redundancy* in the data. One of the X's could then be eliminated without any loss of information. For example, suppose Machine Hours1 is machine hours measured in hours, and Machine Hours2 is machine hours measured in *hundreds* of hours. Then it is clear that these two variables contain exactly the same information, and one of them could (and should) be eliminated.

As another example, suppose that Ad1, Ad2, and Ad3 are the amounts spent on radio ads, television ads, and newspaper ads. Also, suppose that Total Ad is the amount spent on radio, television, and newspaper ads combined. Then there is an exact linear relationship among these variables:

$$\text{Total Ad} = \text{Ad1} + \text{Ad2} + \text{Ad3}$$

In this case there is no need to include Total Ad in the analysis because it contains no information that is not already contained in the variables Ad1, Ad2, and Ad3.

Generally, it is fairly simple to spot an exact linear relationship such as these and then exclude the redundant variable from the analysis. However, if you do *not* spot the relationship and try to run the regression analysis with the redundant variable included, regression packages will typically respond with an error message. If the package interrupts the analysis with an error message containing the words "exact multicollinearity" or "linear dependence," you should look for a redundant explanatory variable.

Although this problem can be a nuisance, it is usually caused by an oversight and can be fixed easily by eliminating a redundant variable. A more common problem is *multicollinearity*, where explanatory variables are highly, but not *exactly*, correlated. A typical example is an employee's years of experience and age. Although these two variables are not equal for all employees, they are likely to be highly correlated. If they are both included as explanatory variables in a regression analysis, the software will not issue any error messages, but the estimates it produces can be unreliable and difficult to interpret. We will discuss multicollinearity in more detail later in this chapter.

11-3 Inferences About the Regression Coefficients

In this section we explain how to make inferences about the population regression coefficients from sample data. We begin by making the assumptions discussed in the previous section. In particular, the first assumption states that there is a population regression line. Equation (11.2) for this line is repeated here:

$$Y = \alpha + \beta_1 X_1 + \cdots + \beta_k X_k + \varepsilon$$

We refer to α and the β's collectively as the *regression coefficients*. Again, Greek letters are used to indicate that these quantities are unknown and unobservable. There is one other unknown constant in the model: the variance of the errors. Regression assumption 2 states that the errors have a constant variance, the same for all values of the X's. We label this constant variance σ^2. Equivalently, the common standard deviation of the errors is σ.

This is how it looks in theory. There is a fixed set of explanatory variables, and given these variables, the problem is to estimate α, the β's, and σ. In practice, however, it is not usually this straightforward. In real regression applications, the choice of relevant explanatory variables is almost never obvious. There are at least two guiding principles: relevance and data availability. You certainly want variables that are related to the dependent variable. The best situation is when there is an established economic or physical theory to guide you. For example, economic theory suggests that the demand for a product (dependent variable) is related to its price (possible explanatory variable). But there are not enough established theories to cover every situation. You often have to use the available data, plus some trial and error, to determine a *useful* set of explanatory variables. In this sense, it is usually pointless to search for one single "true" population regression equation. Instead, you typically estimate several competing models, each with a different set of explanatory variables, and ultimately select one of them as being the most useful.

Typically, the most challenging part of a regression analysis is deciding which explanatory variables to include in the regression equation.

Deciding which explanatory variables to include in a regression equation is probably the most difficult part of any applied regression analysis. Available data sets frequently offer an overabundance of potential explanatory variables. In addition, it is possible and often useful to create new variables from original variables, such as their logarithms. So where do you stop? Is it best to include every conceivable explanatory variable that might be related to the dependent variable? One overriding principle is **parsimony**—explaining the most with the least. For example, if a dependent variable can be explained just as well (or nearly as well) with two explanatory variables as with five explanatory variables, the principle of parsimony says to use only two. Models with fewer explanatory variables are generally easier to interpret, so they are preferred whenever possible.

> The principle of **parsimony** is to explain the most with the least. It favors a model with fewer explanatory variables, assuming that this model explains the dependent variable almost as well as a model with additional explanatory variables.

Before you can determine which equation has the best set of explanatory variables, however, you must be able to estimate the unknown parameters for a given equation. That is, for a given set of explanatory variables X_1 through X_k, you must be able to estimate α, the β's, and σ. Fortunately, you learned how to do this in the previous chapter. The estimates of α and the β's are the least squares estimates of the intercept and slope terms. For example, the 36 months of overhead data in the Bendrix example were used to estimate the equation

Predicted Overhead $= 3997 + 43.54$Machine Hours $+ 883.62$Production Runs

This implies that the least squares estimates of α, β_1, and β_2 are 3997, 43.54, and 883.62. Furthermore, because the residuals are really estimates of the errors, the standard error of estimate s_e is an estimate of σ. For the same overhead equation, this estimate is $s_e = \$4109$.

However, as you learned in Chapter 8, there is more to statistical estimation than finding point estimates of population parameters. Each potential sample from the population typically leads to *different* point estimates. For example, if Bendrix estimates the equation for overhead from a different 36-month period (or possibly from another of its plants), the results will almost certainly be different. Therefore, we now discuss how these point estimates vary from sample to sample.

11-3a Sampling Distribution of the Regression Coefficients

The key idea is again sampling distributions. Recall that the sampling distribution of any estimate derived from sample data is the distribution of this estimate over all possible samples. This idea can be applied to the least squares estimate of a regression coefficient. For example, the sampling distribution of b_1, the least squares estimate of β_1, is the distribution of b_1's you would see if you observed many samples and ran a least squares regression on each of them.

Fortunately, mathematicians have derived the required sampling distributions. We state the main result as follows. Let β be any of the β's, and let b be the least squares estimate of β. If the regression assumptions hold, the standardized value $(b - \beta)/s_b$ has a t distribution with $n - k - 1$ degrees of freedom. Here, k is the number of explanatory variables included in the equation, and s_b is the estimated standard deviation of the sampling distribution of b.

> **Sampling Distribution of a Regression Coefficient**
>
> Assuming that the regression assumptions are valid, the standardized value
> $$t = \frac{b - \beta}{s_b}$$
> has a t distribution with $n - k - 1$ degrees of freedom.

This result has three important implications. First, the estimate b is *unbiased* in the sense that its mean is β, the true but unknown value of the slope. If the b's were estimated from repeated samples, some would underestimate β and others would overestimate β, but on average they would be on target.

Second, the estimated standard deviation of b is labeled s_b. It is usually called the **standard error of the regression coefficient**, or more simply, the standard error of b. This standard error is related to the standard error of estimate s_e, but it is not the same. Generally, the formula for s_b is quite complicated, and it is not shown here, but its value is printed in all standard regression outputs. It measures how much the b's would vary from sample to sample. A small value of s_b is preferred—it means that b is a more accurate estimate of the true coefficient β.

Finally, the shape of the distribution of b is symmetric and bell-shaped. The relevant distribution is the t distribution with $n - k - 1$ degrees of freedom.

Fundamental Insight

Standard Errors in Regression

There are two quite different standard errors in regression outputs. The standard error of estimate, usually shown at the top of the output, is a measure of the error you are likely to make when you use the regression equation to predict a value of Y. In contrast, the standard errors of the regression coefficients measure the accuracy of the individual coefficients.

We have stated this result for a typical coefficient of one of the X's. These are usually the coefficients of most interest. However, exactly the same result holds for the intercept term α. Now we illustrate how this sampling distribution is used.

EXAMPLE

11.1 EXPLAINING OVERHEAD COSTS AT BENDRIX

This example is a continuation of the Bendrix manufacturing example from the previous chapter. As before, the dependent variable is Overhead and the explanatory variables are Machine Hours and Production Runs. What inferences can be made about the regression coefficients?

Objective

To use standard regression output to make inferences about the regression coefficients of machine hours and production runs in the equation for overhead costs.

Solution

The regression output is shown in Figure 11.2. (See the file **Overhead Costs Finished.xlsx**.) This output, from StatTools, is practically identical to regression outputs from all statistical software packages. The estimates of the regression coefficients appear under the label Coefficient in the range B19:B21. These values estimate the true, but unobservable, population coefficients. The next column, labeled Standard Error, shows the s_b values. Specifically, 3.589 is the standard error of the coefficient of Machine Hours, and 82.251 is the standard error of the coefficient of Production Runs.

Each b represents a point estimate of the corresponding β, based on this particular sample. The corresponding s_b indicates the accuracy of this point estimate. For example, the point estimate of β_1, the effect on Overhead of a one-unit increase in Machine Hours (when Production Runs is held constant), is 43.536, and its standard error is 3.589. You can be about 95% confident that the true β_1 is within two standard errors of this point estimate. Similar statements can be made for the coefficient of Production Runs and the intercept (Constant) term.

Figure 11.2 Regression Output for Bendrix Example

	A	B	C	D	E	F	G
8	*Multiple Regression for Overhead*	Multiple	R-Square	Adjusted	Std. Err. of	Rows	
9	*Summary*	R		R-square	Estimate	Ignored	
10		0.9308	0.8664	0.8583	4108.99309	0	
11							
12		Degrees of	Sum of	Mean of	F	p-Value	
13	*ANOVA Table*	Freedom	Squares	Squares			
14	Explained	2	3614020661	1807010330	107.0261279	<0.0001	
15	Unexplained	33	557166199.1	16883824.22			
16							
17		Coefficient	Standard	t-Value	p-Value	Confidence Interval 95%	
18	*Regression Table*		Error			Lower	Upper
19	Constant	3996.678209	6603.650932	0.605222512	0.5492	–9438.550632	17431.90705
20	Machine Hours	43.53639812	3.5894837	12.12887472	<0.0001	36.23353862	50.83925761
21	Production Runs	883.6179252	82.25140753	10.74289124	<0.0001	716.2761784	1050.959672

As with any population parameter, the sample data can be used to obtain a **confidence interval for a regression coefficient**. For example, Figure 11.2 shows that a 95% confidence interval for the coefficient of Machine Hours extends from 36.233 to 50.839. In general, a confidence interval for any β is of the form

$$b \pm t\text{-multiple} \times s_b$$

where the t-multiple depends on the confidence level and the degrees of freedom (here $n - k - 1$). Most statistical packages, including StatTools, provide these 95% confidence intervals for the regression coefficients automatically.

11-3b Hypothesis Tests for the Regression Coefficients and p-Values

There is another important piece of information in regression outputs: the t-values for the individual regression coefficients. These are shown in the "t-Value" column of the regression output in Figure 11.2. Each t-value is the ratio of the estimated coefficient to its standard error, as shown in Equation (11.3). Therefore, it indicates how many standard errors the regression coefficient is from zero. For example, the t-value for Machine Hours is about 12.13, so the regression coefficient of Machine Hours, 43.536, is more than 12 of its standard errors to the right of zero. Similarly, the coefficient of Production Runs is more than 10 of its standard errors to the right of zero.

t-value for Test of Regression Coefficient

$$t\text{-value} = b/s_b \qquad (11.3)$$

A t-value can be used in an important **hypothesis test for a regression coefficient**. To motivate this test, suppose you want to decide whether a particular explanatory variable belongs in the regression equation. A sensible criterion for making this decision is to check whether the corresponding regression coefficient is zero. After all, if a variable's coefficient is zero, there is no point in including this variable in the equation because the zero coefficient will cancel its effect on the dependent variable.

Therefore, it is reasonable to test whether a variable's coefficient is zero. This is usually tested versus a *two-tailed* alternative. The null and alternative hypotheses are of the form $H_0:\beta = 0$ versus $H_a:\beta \neq 0$. If you can reject the null hypothesis and conclude that this coefficient is *not* zero, you then have an argument for including the variable in the regression equation. Conversely, if you cannot reject the null hypothesis, you might decide to eliminate this variable from the equation.

Most statistical packages, including StatTools, make this test easy to run by reporting the corresponding *p*-value for the test. The *p*-value is interpreted exactly as in Chapter 9. It is the probability (in both tails) of the relevant t distribution beyond the listed t-value. For example, referring again to Figure 11.2, the t-value for Machine Hours is 12.13, and the associated *p*-value is less than 0.0001. This means that there is virtually no probability beyond the observed t-value. In words, you are still not exactly sure of the true coefficient of Machine Hours, but you are virtually sure it is not zero. The same can be said for the coefficient of Production Runs.

In practice, you typically run a multiple regression with several explanatory variables and scan their *p*-values. If the *p*-value of a variable is low, then this variable should be kept in the equation; if *p*-value is high, you might consider eliminating this variable from the equation. In Section 11-5, we will discuss this *include/exclude decision* in greater depth.

The test for whether a regression coefficient is zero can be run by looking at the corresponding p-value: Reject the "equals zero" hypothesis if the p-value is small, say, less than 0.05.

11-3c A Test for the Overall Fit: The ANOVA Table

The t-values for the regression coefficients allow you to see which of the potential explanatory variables are useful in explaining the dependent variable. But it is conceivable that *none* of these variables does a very good job. That is, it is conceivable that the entire group of explanatory variables explains only an insignificant portion of the variability of the dependent variable. Although this is the exception rather than the rule in most applications, it can happen. An indication of this is that you obtain a very small R^2 value. In this section we state a formal procedure for testing the overall fit, or explanatory power, of a regression equation.

Suppose the dependent variable is Y and the explanatory variables are X_1 through X_k. Then the proposed population regression equation is

$$Y = \alpha + \beta_1 X_1 + \cdots + \beta_k X_k + \varepsilon$$

To say that this equation has absolutely no explanatory power means that the same value of Y will be predicted regardless of the values of the X's. In this case it makes no difference which values of the X's are used, because they all lead to the same predicted value of Y. But the only way this can occur is if all the β's are 0. So the formal hypothesis test in this section is $H_0:\beta_1 = \cdots = \beta_k = 0$ versus the alternative that at least one of the β's is not zero. If the null hypothesis can be rejected, as it can in the majority of applications, this means that the explanatory variables *as a group* provide at least some explanatory power. These hypotheses are summarized as follows.

> The null hypothesis is that coefficients of all explanatory variables are zero. The alternative is that at least one of these coefficients is not zero.

At first glance, it might appear that this null hypothesis can be tested by looking at the individual t-values. If they are all small (statistically insignificant), then the null hypothesis of no fit cannot be rejected; otherwise, it can be rejected. However, as you will see in the next section, it is possible, because of multicollinearity, to have all small t-values even though the variables as a whole have *significant* explanatory power.

The correct approach is to use an F test. This is sometimes referred to as the ANOVA (analysis of variance) test because the elements for calculating the required F-value are shown in an **ANOVA table for regression**. In general, an ANOVA table analyzes different sources of variation. In the case of regression, the variation of interest is the variation of the dependent variable Y. The *total variation* of this variable is the sum of squared deviations about the mean and is labeled *SST* (sum of squares total).

$$SST = \sum (Y_i - \overline{Y})^2$$

The ANOVA table splits this total variation into two parts, the part *explained* by the regression equation, and the part left *unexplained*. The unexplained part is the sum of squared residuals, usually labeled *SSE* (sum of squared errors):

$$SSE = \sum e_i^2 = \sum (Y_i - \hat{Y}_i)^2$$

The explained part is then the difference between the total and unexplained variation. It is usually labeled *SSR* (sum of squares due to regression):

$$SSR = SST - SSE$$

The F test is a formal procedure for testing whether the explained variation is large compared to the unexplained variation. Specifically, each of these sources of variation has an associated degrees of freedom (df). For the explained variation, $df = k$, the number of explanatory variables. For the unexplained variation, $df = n - k - 1$, the sample size minus the total number of coefficients (including the intercept term). The ratio of either sum of squares to its degrees of freedom is called a mean square, or MS. The two mean squares in this case are MSR and MSE, given by

$$MSR = \frac{SSR}{k}$$

and

$$MSE = \frac{SSE}{n - k - 1}$$

Note that MSE is the square of the standard error of estimate, that is,

$$MSE = s_e^2$$

The MSE shown in the ANOVA table of regression output is always the square of the standard error of estimate.

Finally, the ratio of these mean squares is the required F-ratio for the test:

$$F\text{-ratio} = \frac{MSR}{MSE}$$

When the null hypothesis of no explanatory power is true, this F-ratio has an F distribution with k and $n - k - 1$ degrees of freedom. If the F-ratio is small, the explained variation is small relative to the unexplained variation, and there is evidence that the regression equation provides little explanatory power. But if the F-ratio is large, the explained variation is large relative to the unexplained variation, and you can conclude that the equation does have at least *some* explanatory power.

As usual, the F-ratio has an associated p-value that allows you to run the test easily. In this case the p-value is the probability to the *right* of the observed F-ratio in the appropriate F distribution. This p-value is reported in most regression outputs, along with the elements that lead up to it. If it is sufficiently small, less than 0.05, say, you can conclude that the explanatory variables as a whole have at least some explanatory power.

The regression output for the Bendrix example is repeated in Figure 11.3. The ANOVA table is in rows 13 through 15. The degrees of freedom are in column B, the sums of squares are in column C, the mean squares are in column D, the F-ratio is in cell E14, and its associated p-value is in cell F14. As predicted, this F-ratio is "off the charts," and the p-value is practically zero.

This information wouldn't be much comfort for the Bendrix manager who is trying to understand the causes of variation in overhead costs. This manager already *knows* that machine hours and production runs are related positively to overhead costs—everyone in the company knows that. What he really wants is a set of explanatory variables that yields a high R^2 and a low s_e. The low p-value in the ANOVA tables does not guarantee these. All it guarantees is that Machine Hours and Production Runs are of *some* help in explaining variations in Overhead.

The ANOVA table can be used as a screening device. If the explanatory variables do not explain a significant percentage of the variation in the dependent variable, you can either discontinue the analysis or search for an entirely new set of explanatory variables. But even if the F-ratio in the ANOVA table is extremely significant (as it usually is), there is still no guarantee that the regression equation provides a good enough fit for practical uses. This depends on other measures such as s_e and R^2.

Figure 11.3 StatTools Regression Output for Bendrix Example

	A	B	C	D	E	F	G
1	Multiple Regression for Overhead	Multiple	R-Square	Adjusted	Std. Err. of	Rows	Outliers
2	Summary	R		R-square	Estimate	Ignored	
3		0.9308	0.8664	0.8583	4108.993	0	0
4							
5		Degrees of	Sum of	Mean of	F	p-Value	
6	ANOVA Table	Freedom	Squares	Squares			
7	Explained	2	3614020661	1807010330	107.026	<0.0001	
8	Unexplained	33	557166199.1	16883824.22			
9							
10		Coefficient	Standard	t-Value	p-Value	Confidence Interval 95%	
11	Regression Table		Error			Lower	Upper
12	Constant	3996.678	6603.651	0.605	0.5492	−9438.551	17431.907
13	Machine Hours	43.536	3.589	12.129	<0.0001	36.234	50.839
14	Production Runs	883.618	82.251	10.743	<0.0001	716.276	1050.960

Problems

Solutions for problems whose numbers appear within a colored box can be found in the Student Solution Files.

Level A

1. Explore the relationship between the selling prices (Y) and the appraised values (X) of the 148 homes in the file **P02_11.xlsx** by estimating a simple linear regression equation. Find a 95% confidence interval for the model's slope parameter (β_1). What does this confidence interval tell you about the relationship between Y and X for these data?

2. The owner of the Original Italian Pizza restaurant chain would like to predict the sales of his specialty, deep-dish pizza. He has gathered data on the monthly sales of deep-dish pizzas at his restaurants and observations on other potentially relevant variables for each of his 15 outlets in central Indiana. These data are provided in the file **P10_04.xlsx**.
  a. Estimate a multiple regression model between the quantity sold (Y) and the explanatory variables in columns C–E.
  b. Is there evidence of any violations of the key assumptions of regression analysis?

c. Which of the variables in this equation have regression coefficients that are statistically different from zero at the 5% significance level?
d. Given your findings in part **c**, which variables, if any, would you choose to remove from the equation estimated in part **a**? Why?

3. The file **P02_10.xlsx** contains midterm and final exam scores for 96 students in a corporate finance course. Based on a regression equation for the final exam score as a function of the midterm exam score, find a 95% confidence interval for the slope of the population regression line. State exactly what this confidence interval indicates.

4. A trucking company wants to predict the yearly maintenance expense (Y) for a truck using the number of miles driven during the year (X_1) and the age of the truck (X_2, in years) at the beginning of the year. The company has gathered the information given in the file **P10_16.xlsx**. Each observation corresponds to a particular truck.
  a. Estimate a multiple regression equation using the given data.
  b. Find 95% confidence intervals for the regression coefficients of X_1 and X_2. Based on these interval estimates, which variable, if any, would you choose to remove from the equation estimated in part **a**? Why?

5. Based on the data in the file **P02_23.xlsx** from the U.S. Department of Agriculture, explore the relationship between the number of farms (X) and the average size of a farm (Y) in the United States.
   a. Use the given data to estimate a simple linear regression model.
   b. Test whether there is sufficient evidence to conclude that the slope parameter (β_1) is *less than* zero. Use a 5% significance level.
   c. Based on your finding in part **b**, is it possible to conclude that a linear relationship exists between the number of farms and the average farm size during the given time period? Explain.

6. An antique collector believes that the price received for a particular item increases with its age and the number of bidders. The file **P10_18.xlsx** contains data on these three variables for 32 recently auctioned comparable items.
   a. Estimate an appropriate multiple regression model using the given data.
   b. Interpret the ANOVA table for this model. In particular, does this set of explanatory variables provide at least *some* power in explaining the variation in price? Report a p-value for this hypothesis test.

7. The file **P10_06.xlsx** contains information on over 200 movies that were released during 2006–2007. Run a regression of Total US Gross versus 7-day Gross, and then run a multiple regression of Total US Gross versus 7-day Gross and 14-day Gross. Report the 95% confidence interval for the coefficient of 7-day Gross in each equation. What exactly do these confidence intervals tell you about the effect of 7-day Gross on Total US Gross? Why are they not at all the same? What is the relevant population that this data set is a sample from?

8. The file **P10_10.xlsx** contains data on 150 homes that were sold recently in a particular community.
   a. Find a table of correlations between all of the variables. Do the correlations between Price and each of the other variables have the sign (positive or negative) you would expect? Explain briefly.
   b. Run a regression of Price versus Rooms. What does the 95% confidence interval for the coefficient of Rooms tell you about the effect of Rooms on Price for the entire population of such homes?
   c. Run a multiple regression of Price versus Home Size, Lot Size, Rooms, and Bathrooms. What is the 95% confidence interval for the coefficient of Rooms now? Why do you think it can be so different from the one in part **b**? Based on this regression, can you reject the null hypothesis that the population regression coefficient of Rooms is zero versus a two-tailed alternative? What does this mean?

9. Suppose that a regional express delivery service company wants to estimate the cost of shipping a package (Y) as a function of cargo type, where cargo type includes the following possibilities: fragile, semifragile, and durable. Costs for several randomly chosen packages of approximately the same weight and same distance shipped, but of different cargo types, are provided in the file **P10_28.xlsx**.
   a. Estimate an appropriate multiple regression equation to predict the cost of shipping a given package.
   b. Interpret the ANOVA table for this model. In particular, do the explanatory variables included in your equation in part **a** provide at least *some* power in explaining the variation in shipping costs? Interpret the p-value for this hypothesis test.

10. The file **P10_05.xlsx** contains salaries for a sample of DataCom employees, along with several variables that might be related to salary. Run a multiple regression of Salary versus Years Employed, Years Education, Gender, and Number Supervised. For each of these variables, explain exactly what the results in the Coefficient, Standard Error, t-value, and p-value columns mean. Based on the results, can you reject the null hypothesis that the population coefficient of any of these variables is zero versus a two-tailed alternative at the 5% significance level? If you can, what would you probably do next in the analysis?

Level B

11. A multiple regression with 36 observations and three explanatory variables yields the ANOVA table in Table 11.1.

Table 11.1   ANOVA Table

	Degrees of Freedom	Sum of Squares
Explained		1211
Unexplained		
Total		2567

   a. Complete this ANOVA table.
   b. Can you conclude at the 1% significance level that these three explanatory variables have *some* power in explaining variation in the dependent variable?

12. Suppose you find the ANOVA table shown in Table 11.2 for a simple linear regression.

Table 11.2   ANOVA Table

	Degrees of Freedom	Sum of Squares
Explained		52
Unexplained	87	
Total		1598

   a. Find the correlation between X and Y, assuming that the slope of the least squares line is negative.
   b. Find the p-value for the test of the hypothesis of no explanatory power at all. What does it tell you in this particular case?

11-4 Multicollinearity

Recall that the coefficient of any variable in a regression equation indicates the effect of this variable on the dependent variable, provided that the other variables in the equation remain constant. Another way of stating this is that the coefficient represents the effect of this variable on the dependent variable *in addition to* the effects of the other variables in the equation. In the Bendrix example, if Machine Hours and Production Runs are included in the equation for Overhead, the coefficient of Machine Hours indicates the *extra* amount Machine Hours explains about variation in Overhead, in addition to the amount already explained by Production Runs. Similarly, the coefficient of Production Runs indicates the extra amount Production Runs explains about variation in Overhead, in addition to the amount already explained by Machine Hours. Therefore, the relationship between an explanatory variable X and the dependent variable Y is not always accurately reflected in the coefficient of X; it depends on which *other* X's are included or not included in the equation.

This is especially true when *multicollinearity* exists. **Multicollinearity** is the presence of a fairly strong linear relationship between two or more explanatory variables. Unfortunately, multicollinearity is quite common, and it can make regression output difficult to interpret.

> **Multicollinearity** occurs when there is a fairly strong linear relationship among a set of explanatory variables.

Consider Example 11.2. It is a contrived example, but it is useful for illustrating the potential effects of multicollinearity.

EXAMPLE

11.2 HEIGHT VERSUS FOOT LENGTH

We want to explain a person's height by means of foot length. The dependent variable is Height, and the explanatory variables are Right and Left, the length of the right foot and the length of the left foot, respectively. What can occur when Height is regressed on *both* Right and Left?

Objective

To illustrate the problem of multicollinearity when both foot length variables are used in a regression for height.

Solution

Clearly, there is no need to include both Right and Left in an equation for Height—either one of them suffices—but we include them both to make a point. It is likely that there is a large correlation between height and foot size, so you would expect this regression equation to do a good job. For example, the R^2 value will probably be large. But what about the coefficients of Right and Left? Here there is a problem. The coefficient of Right indicates the right foot's effect on Height *in addition to* the effect of the left foot. This additional effect is probably minimal. That is, after the effect of Left on Height has been taken into account, the extra information provided by Right is probably minimal. But it goes the other way also. The extra effect of Left, in addition to that provided by Right, is probably also minimal.

To show what can happen numerically, we used simulation to generate a hypothetical data set of heights and left and right foot lengths. We did this so that, except for random error, height is approximately 31.8 plus 3.2 times foot length (all expressed in inches). (See Figure 11.4 and the file **Heights Simulation Finished.xlsx**. You can check the formulas in columns A–D (and read the explanation in the file) to see how we generated the data with the desired properties. The correlation between Height and either Right or Left is quite large, and the correlation between Right and Left is very close to 1 (see cells G7 to G9).

Figure 11.4   Simulated
Height Data

	A	B	C	D	E	F	G	H
1	Parameters of foot size distribution				Parameters of regression, given generic foot size			
2	Mean	12.95			Intercept	31.8		
3	Stdev1	3.1			Slope	3.2		
4	Stdev2	0.2			StErr of Est	3.0		
5								
6	Generic foot size	Left	Right	Height			Correlation	
7	13.561	13.853	13.247	72.534		Left vs Right	0.996	
8	10.992	11.241	10.81	68.622		Left vs Height	0.958	
9	8.268	8.109	8.007	54.934		Right vs Height	0.959	
10	15.425	15.934	15.242	86.149				
11	14.753	14.736	14.813	82.331				
12	13.546	13.719	13.718	80.071				
13	12.067	12.188	11.883	68.589				
14	16.467	16.528	16.497	86.128				

We copied the data to three separate sheets, each time pasting as values, and we ran a regression of Height versus Right and Left on each of these sheets. (The pasted data on each sheet are different because of random numbers.) The outputs tell a somewhat confusing story. The multiple R and the corresponding R^2 are about as expected, given the correlations between Height and either Right or Left. In particular, the multiple R is close to the correlation between Height and either Right or Left. Also, the s_e value is quite small, about 3.0. It implies that predictions of height from this regression equation will typically be off by only about three inches.

Multicollinearity often causes regression coefficients to have the "wrong" sign, t-values to be too small, and p-values to be too large.

However, the coefficients of Right and Left are not at all what you might expect, given that the heights were generated as approximately 31.8 plus 3.2 times foot length. On the first regression they are 2.898 and 0.455; on the second (shown in Figure 11.5) they are −0.873 and 4.102; and on the third they are 1.018 and 2.189. This is what can happen when multicollinearity is present. The coefficients can vary wildly from one sample to the next, and a coefficient can even have the "wrong" sign. (All correlations are positive, so no coefficients should be negative.) Also, it is impossible to predict which, if any, of the coefficients will be statistically significant.

Figure 11.5 An Example of Height versus Foot Length

	A	B	C	D	E	F	G
1	**Multiple Regression for Height**	**Multiple R**	**R-Square**	**Adjusted R-Square**	**Std. Err. of Estimate**	**Rows Ignored**	**Outliers**
2	**Summary**						
3		0.9447	0.8924	0.8902	3.057	0	0
4							
5		**Degrees of Freedom**	**Sum of Squares**	**Mean of Squares**	**F**	**p-Value**	
6	**ANOVA Table**						
7	**Explained**	2	7519.7074	3759.8537	402.347	< 0.0001	
8	**Unexplained**	97	906.4449746	9.344793553			
9							
10		**Coefficient**	**Standard Error**	**t-Value**	**p-Value**	**Confidence Interval 95%**	
11	**Regression Table**					**Lower**	**Upper**
12	**Constant**	31.734	1.524	20.820	< 0.0001	28.709	34.759
13	**Left**	−0.873	1.115	−0.783	0.4357	−3.086	1.340
14	**Right**	4.102	1.108	3.702	0.0004	1.903	6.301

The problem is that although both Right and Left are clearly related to Height, it is impossible for the least squares method to distinguish their *separate* effects. However, note that the sum of the coefficients in each of the regression equations is approximately 3.2, the value that was used to generate the data. This means that each estimated equation will work well for *predicting* heights, in spite of not producing reliable estimates of the individual coefficients of Right and Left.

Multicollinearity typically causes unreliable estimates of regression coefficients, but it does not generally cause poor predictions.

This example illustrates an extreme form of multicollinearity, where two explanatory variables are very highly correlated. In general, there are various degrees of multicollinearity. In each of them, there is a linear relationship between two or more explanatory variables, and this relationship makes it difficult to estimate the individual effects of the X's on the dependent variable. The symptoms of multicollinearity can be "wrong" signs of the coefficients, smaller-than-expected t-values, and larger-than-expected (insignificant) p-values. In other words, variables that are really related to the dependent variable can look like they aren't related, based on their p-values. The reason is that their effects on Y are already explained by other X's in the equation.

Moderate to extreme multicollinearity poses a problem in many regression applications. Unfortunately, there are usually no easy remedies.

Sometimes multicollinearity is easy to spot and treat. For example, it would be silly to include both Right and Left foot length in the equation for Height. They are obviously very highly correlated and either one suffices in the equation for Height. One of them— either one—should be excluded from the equation. However, multicollinearity is not usually this easy to treat or even diagnose.

Fundamental Insight

Effect of Multicollinearity

Multicollinearity occurs when X's are highly correlated with one another, and it is a problem in many regression applications. It prevents you from separating the individual influences of the X's on Y. In short, it prevents you from seeing clearly how the world works. However, multicollinearity is *not* a problem if you simply want to use a regression equation as a "black box" for predictions.

StatTools includes optional regression output for detecting multicollinearity. (This type of output is available in many other statistical software packages as well.) These options appear on the Options tab of the Regression dialog box, as shown in Figure 11.6. If you check the Check Multicollinearity box, you will get two extra columns in the Regression Table section of the regression output: VIF and R-Square. (You can also check the Display Correlation Matrix box to get the usual matrix of correlations for all variables in the regression.) The R-Square for any X variable is the usual R-square value from a regression with that X as the *dependent* variable and the other X's as the explanatory variables. It indicates how related that X is to the other X's. The VIF (variance inflation factor) is then defined as 1/(1–R-square).

These measures are illustrated in Figure 11.7. (See the file **Salary Multicollinearity Finished.xlsx**.) This data set has salaries for 300 employees. The explanatory variables are Gender, Age, Experience (years of work experience in the industry), and Seniority (years with this company). The R-Square column (as well as the matrix of correlations at the bottom) indicates that Age, Experience, and Seniority are a definite source of multicollinearity. They are highly correlated, and any one of them can be explained by the other two. The VIF is basically the same as the R-Square in the sense that if one of them is large, the other is also large. The educational comment next to VIF states the following: "A VIF of 1 means that there is no correlation among the k-th predictor and the remaining predictor variables, and hence the variance of k-th regression coefficient is not inflated at all. The general rule of thumb is that VIFs exceeding 4 warrant further investigation, while VIFs exceeding 10 are signs of serious multicollinearity requiring correction."

Figure 11.6 StatTools
Multicollinearity Options

Figure 11.7   Regression Output with Multicollinearity Diagnostics

	A	B	C	D	E	F	G	H	I
1	*Multiple Regression for Salary*	Multiple R	R-Square	Adjusted R-square	Std. Err. of Estimate	Rows Ignored	Outliers		
2	*Summary*								
3		0.9755	0.9516	0.9509	4964.209	0	1		
4									
5		Degrees of Freedom	Sum of Squares	Mean of Squares	F	p-Value			
6	*ANOVA Table*								
7	Explained	4	1.42789E+11	35697211405	1448.552	< 0.0001			
8	Unexplained	295	7269795846	24643375.75					
9									
10		Coefficient	Standard Error	t-Value	p-Value	Confidence Interval 95%		Multicollinearity Checking	
11	*Regression Table*					Lower	Upper	VIF	R-Square
12	Constant	49714.255	3815.818	13.028	<0.0001	42204.580	57223.930		
13	Gender (Female)	−2967.637	616.555	−4.813	<0.0001	−4181.041	−1754.232	1.001	0.001
14	Age	−309.744	148.123	−2.091	0.0374	−601.255	−18.233	31.504	0.968
15	Experience	388.641	190.562	2.039	0.0423	13.608	763.675	38.153	0.974
16	Seniority	2997.964	94.860	31.604	<0.0001	2811.276	3184.652	5.595	0.821
17									
18									
19	*Correlation Matrix*	Salary	Gender (Female)	Age	Experience	Seniority			
20	Salary	1.000	−0.093	0.857	0.882	0.973			
21	Gender (Female)	−0.093	1.000	−0.028	−0.026	−0.033			
22	Age	0.857	−0.028	1.000	0.984	0.884			
23	Experience	0.882	−0.026	0.984	1.000	0.905			
24	Seniority	0.973	−0.033	0.884	0.905	1.000			

According to these rules of thumb, this data set has a serious multicollinearity issue that requires correction. The most obvious correction would be to eliminate Age and/or Experience and rerun the regression. Unfortunately, it is not always this obvious how to deal with multicollinearity. The outputs discussed here allow you to detect multicollinearity, but they don't provide a foolproof method for correcting it.

Problems

Level A

13. Using the data given in the file **P10_10.xlsx**, estimate a multiple regression equation to predict the price of houses in a given community. Employ all available explanatory variables. Is there evidence of multicollinearity in this model? Explain why or why not.

14. Consider the data for *Business Week*'s top U.S. MBA programs in the MBA Data sheet of the file **P10_21.xlsx**. Use these data to estimate a multiple regression model to assess whether there is a relationship between the enrollment and the following explanatory variables: (a) the percentage of international students, (b) the percentage of female students, (c) the percentage of Asian American students, (d) the percentage of minority students, and (e) the resident tuition and fees at these business schools.
    a. Determine whether each of the regression coefficients for the explanatory variables in this model is statistically different from zero at the 5% significance level. Summarize your findings.
    b. Is there evidence of multicollinearity in this model? Explain why or why not.

15. The manager of a commuter rail transportation system was recently asked by her governing board to determine the factors that have a significant impact on the demand for rides in the large city served by the transportation network. The system manager has collected data on variables that might be related to the number of weekly riders on the city's rail system. The file **P10_20.xlsx** contains these data.
    a. Estimate a multiple regression model using all of the available explanatory variables. Perform a test of significance for each of the model's regression coefficients. Are the signs of the estimated coefficients consistent with your expectations?
    b. Is there evidence of multicollinearity in this model? Explain why or why not. If multicollinearity is present, explain what you would do to remedy this problem.

Level B

16. The file **P10_05.xlsx** contains salaries for a sample of DataCom employees, along with several variables that might be related to salary.
    a. Estimate the relationship between Y (Salary) and X (Years Employed) using simple linear regression. (For this problem, ignore the other potential explanatory variables.) Is there evidence to support the hypothesis that the coefficient for the number of years employed is statistically different from zero at the 5% significance level?
    b. Estimate a multiple regression model to explain annual salaries of DataCom employees with X and X^2 as explanatory variables. Perform relevant hypothesis tests to determine the significance of the regression coefficients of these two variables. Summarize your findings.
    c. How do you explain your findings in part **b** in light of the results found in part **a**?

17. The owner of a restaurant in Bloomington, Indiana, has recorded sales data for the past several years. He has also recorded data on potentially relevant variables. The data appear in the file **P10_23.xlsx**.
    a. Estimate a multiple regression equation that includes annual sales as the dependent variable and the following explanatory variables: year, size of the population residing within 10 miles of the restaurant, annual advertising expenditures, and advertising expenditures in the *previous* year.
    b. Which of the explanatory variables have significant effects on sales at the 10% significance level? Do any of these results surprise you? Explain why or why not.
    c. Exclude all insignificant explanatory variables from the equation in part **a** and estimate the equation with the remaining variables. Comment on the significance of each remaining variable.
    d. Based on your analysis of this problem, does multicollinearity appear to be present in the original or revised versions of the model? Explain.

11-5 Include/Exclude Decisions

In this section we make further use of the *t*-values of regression coefficients. In particular, we explain how they can be used to make **include/exclude decisions** for explanatory variables in a regression equation. Section 11-3 explained how a *t*-value can be used to test whether a population regression coefficient is zero. But does this mean that you should automatically include a variable if its *t*-value is significant and automatically exclude it if its *t*-value is insignificant? The decision is not always this simple.

> **Fundamental Insight**
>
> ### Searching for the "True" Regression Equation
>
> Finding the best X's (or the best form of the X's) to include in a regression equation is often the most difficult part of a regression analysis. There are two important things to keep in mind. First, it is rather pointless to search for the "true" regression equation. There are often several equations that, for all practical purposes, are equally *useful* for describing how the world works or making predictions. Second, the guidelines provided here for including and excluding variables are not ironclad rules. They typically involve choices at the margin, that is, between equations that are very similar and equally useful. In short, there is often no single "correct answer."

The goal is always to get the best fit possible, and the principle of parsimony suggests using the fewest number of variables. This presents a trade-off, where there are not always easy answers. On the one hand, more variables certainly increase R^2, and they usually reduce the standard error of estimate s_e. On the other hand, fewer variables are better for parsimony. To help with the decision, we present several guidelines. These guidelines are not hard and fast rules, and they are sometimes contradictory. In real applications there are often several equations that are equally good for all practical purposes, and it is rather pointless to search for a single "true" equation.

Guidelines for Including/Excluding Variables in a Regression Equation

1. Look at a variable's t-value and its associated p-value. If the p-value is above some accepted significance level, such as 0.05, this variable is a candidate for exclusion.
2. Check whether a variable's t-value is less than 1 or greater than 1 in magnitude. If it is less than 1, then it is a mathematical fact that s_e will decrease (and adjusted R^2 will increase) if this variable is excluded from the equation. If it is greater than 1, the opposite is true. Because of this, some analysts advocate excluding variables with t-values less than 1 and including variables with t-values greater than 1.
3. Look at t-values and p-values, rather than correlations, when making include/exclude decisions. An explanatory variable can have a fairly high correlation with the dependent variable, but because of *other* variables included in the equation, it might not be needed. This would be reflected in a low t-value and a high p-value, and this variable could possibly be excluded for reasons of parsimony. This often occurs in the presence of multicollinearity.
4. When there is a group of variables that are in some sense logically related, it is sometimes a good idea to include all of them or exclude all of them. In this case, their individual t-values are less relevant. Instead, a "partial F test" (not discussed in this book) can be used to make the include/exclude decision.
5. Use economic and/or physical theory to decide whether to include or exclude variables, and put less reliance on t-values and/or p-values. Some variables might really *belong* in an equation because of their theoretical relationship with the dependent variable, and their low t-values, possibly the result of an unlucky sample, should not necessarily disqualify them from being in the equation. Similarly, a variable that has no economic or physical relationship with the dependent variable might have a significant t-value just by chance. This does not necessarily mean that it should be

included in the equation. You should not use statistical software blindly to hunt for "good" explanatory variables. You should have some idea, before running the software, of which variables belong and which do not belong.

Again, these guidelines can give contradictory signals. Specifically, guideline 2 bases the include/exclude decision on whether the magnitude of the t-value is greater or less than 1. However, analysts who base the decision on statistical significance at the usual 5% level, as in guideline 1, typically exclude a variable from the equation unless its t-value is at least 2 (approximately). This latter approach is more stringent—fewer variables will be retained—but it is probably the more popular approach. However, either approach is likely to result in similar equations for all practical purposes.

In our experience, you should not agonize too much about whether to include or exclude a variable "at the margin." If you decide to exclude a variable that doesn't add much explanatory power, you get a somewhat cleaner equation, and you probably won't see any dramatic shifts in R^2 or s_e. On the other hand, if you decide to keep such a variable in the equation, the equation is less parsimonious and you have one more variable to interpret, but otherwise, there is no real penalty for including it.

We illustrate how these guidelines can be used in the following example.

EXAMPLE

11.3 EXPLAINING SPENDING AMOUNTS AT HYTEX

The file **Catalog Marketing.xlsx** contains data on 1000 customers who purchased products from HyTex Company in the current year. (This is a slightly different version of the file that was used in Chapter 2.) HyTex is a direct marketer of stereo equipment, personal computers, and other electronic products. HyTex advertises entirely by mailing catalogs to its customers. The company spends a great deal of money on its catalog mailings, and it wants to be sure that this is paying off in sales. For each customer there are data on the following variables:

• Age: age of the customer at the end of the current year
• Gender: coded as 1 for males, 0 for females
• Own Home: coded as 1 if customer owns a home, 0 otherwise
• Married: coded as 1 if customer is currently married, 0 otherwise
• Close: coded as 1 if customer lives reasonably close to a shopping area that sells similar merchandise, 0 otherwise
• Salary: combined annual salary of customer and spouse (if any)
• Children: number of children living with customer
• Previous Customer: coded as 1 if customer purchased from HyTex during the previous year, 0 otherwise
• Previous Spent: total amount of purchases made from HyTex during the previous year
• Catalogs: number of catalogs sent to the customer this year
• Amount Spent: total amount of purchases made from HyTex this year

Estimate and interpret a regression equation for Amount Spent based on all of these variables.

Objective
To see which potential explanatory variables are useful for explaining current year spending amounts at HyTex with multiple regression.

Solution
With this much data, 1000 observations, it is possible to set aside part of the data set for validation, as discussed in Section 10-7. Although any split can be used, we decided to base the regression on the first 750 observations and use the other 250 for validation. Therefore, if you use StatTools, you should select only the range through row 751 when defining the StatTools data set.

You can begin by entering all of the potential explanatory variables. The goal is then to exclude variables that aren't necessary, based on their t-values and p-values. The multiple regression output with all explanatory variables appears in Figure 11.8. It indicates a fairly good fit. The R^2 value is 74.7% and s_e is about $491. Given that the actual amounts spent in the current year vary from a low of under $50 to a high of over $5500, with a median of about $950, a typical prediction error of around $491 is decent but not great.

Figure 11.8 Regression Output with All Explanatory Variables Included

	A	B	C	D	E	F	G
1	*Multiple Regression for Amount Spent*	Multiple R	R-Square	Adjusted R-square	Std. Err. of Estimate	Rows Ignored	Outliers
1	*Summary*						
3		0.8643	0.7470	0.7435	491.451	0	8
4							
5		Degrees of Freedom	Sum of Squares	Mean of Squares	F	p-Value	
6	*ANOVA Table*						
7	Explained	10	526916948.1	52691694.81	218.163	<0.0001	
8	Unexplained	739	178486506.7	241524.3663			
9							
10		Coefficient	Standard Error	t-Value	p-Value	Confidence Interval 95%	
11	*Regression Table*					Lower	Upper
12	Constant	197.392	85.864	2.299	0.0218	28.826	365.957
13	Age	0.601	1.260	0.477	0.6332	−1.871	3.074
14	Gender	−57.492	37.902	−1.517	0.1297	−131.901	16.916
15	Own home	23.307	40.356	0.578	0.5638	−55.919	102.533
16	Married	8.688	48.543	0.179	0.8580	−86.612	103.987
17	Close	−418.734	45.236	−9.257	< 0.0001	−507.540	−329.928
18	Salary	0.018	0.001	15.519	< 0.0001	0.016	0.020
19	Children	−161.487	21.003	−7.689	< 0.0001	−202.720	−120.254
20	Previous Customer	−546.008	63.479	−8.601	< 0.0001	−670.629	−421.387
21	Previous Spent	0.268	0.053	5.088	< 0.0001	0.165	0.372
22	Catalogs	43.946	2.862	15.356	< 0.0001	38.328	49.565

From the p-value column, you can see that there are four variables, Age, Gender, Own Home, and Married, that have p-values well above 0.05. These are the obvious candidates for exclusion from the equation. You could rerun the equation with all four of these variables excluded, but it is a better practice to exclude one variable at a time. It is possible that when one of these variables is excluded, another one of them will become significant (the Right–Left foot phenomenon).

Actually, this did not happen. We first excluded the variable with the largest p-value, Married, and reran the regression. At this point, Age, Gender, and Own Home still had large p-values, so we excluded Age, the variable with the largest remaining p-value, and reran the regression. Next, we excluded Own Home, the variable with the largest remaining p-value, and finally, we excluded Gender because its p-value was still large. The resulting output appears in Figure 11.9. The R^2 and s_e values of 74.6% and $491 are almost the same as they were with all variables included, and all of the p-values are very small.

Figure 11.9 Regression Output with Insignificant Variables Excluded

	A	B	C	D	E	F	G
1	*Multiple Regression for Amount Spent*	Multiple R	R-Square	Adjusted R-square	Std. Err. of Estimate	Rows Ignored	Outliers
1	*Summary*						
3		0.8636	0.7458	0.7438	491.228	0	8
4							
5		Degrees of Freedom	Sum of Squares	Mean of Squares	F	p-Value	
6	*ANOVA Table*						
7	Explained	6	526113683.9	87685613.98	363.381	<0.0001	
8	Unexplained	743	179289770.9	241305.2099			
9							
10		Coefficient	Standard Error	t-Value	p-Value	Confidence Interval 95%	
11	*Regression Table*					Lower	Upper
12	Constant	205.094	70.315	2.917	0.0036	67.053	343.134
13	Close	−416.246	45.085	−9.233	< 0.0001	−504.755	−327.738
14	Salary	0.018	0.001	19.877	< 0.0001	0.016	0.020
15	Children	−161.158	20.483	−7.868	< 0.0001	−201.369	−120.947
16	Previous Customer	−543.595	63.299	−8.588	< 0.0001	−667.861	−419.329
17	Previous Spent	0.272	0.053	5.184	< 0.0001	0.169	0.376
18	Catalogs	43.807	2.854	15.348	< 0.0001	38.203	49.410

Interpretation of Regression Equation

This final regression equation can be interpreted as follows:

- The coefficient of Close implies that an average customer living close to stores with this type of merchandise spent about $416 less than an average customer living far from such stores.
- The coefficient of Salary implies that, on average, about 1.8 cents of every extra salary dollar was spent on HyTex merchandise.
- The coefficient of Children implies that about $161 *less* was spent for every extra child living at home.
- The Previous Customer and Previous Spent terms are more difficult to interpret. Both of these terms are zero for customers who didn't purchase from HyTex in the previous year. For those who did, the terms become $-544 + 0.27$Previous Spent. The coefficient 0.27 implies that each extra dollar spent the previous year can be expected to contribute an extra 27 cents in the current year. The -544 literally means that if you compare a customer who didn't purchase from HyTex last year to another customer who purchased only a tiny amount, the latter is expected to spend about $544 less than the former this year. However, none of the latter customers were in the data set. A look at the data shows that of all customers who purchased from HyTex last year, almost all spent at least $100 and most spent considerably more. In fact, the median amount spent by these customers last year was about $900 (the median of all positive values for the Previous Spent variable). If you substitute this median value into the expression $-544 + 0.27$Previous Spent, you obtain -298. Therefore, this "median" spender from last year can be expected to spend about $298 less this year than the previous year nonspender.
- The coefficient of Catalogs implies that each extra catalog can be expected to generate about $44 in extra spending.

We conclude this example with two cautionary notes. First, if you validate this final regression equation on the other 250 customers, using the procedure from Section 10-7, you will find R^2 and s_e values of 73.2% and $490. (This analysis is included in the finished version of the file.) These are very promising. They are very close to the values based on the original 750 customers. Second, we haven't tried all possibilities yet. We haven't tried nonlinear or interaction variables, nor have we looked at different coding schemes (such as treating Catalogs as a categorical variable and using dummy variables to represent it). Also, we haven't checked for nonconstant error variance (Figure 11.1 is based on this data set) or looked at the potential effects of outliers.

Problems

Level A

18. The Undergraduate Data sheet of the file **P10_21.xlsx** contains information on undergraduate business programs in the United States, including various rankings by *Business Week*. Use multiple regression to explore the relationship between the median starting salary and the following set of potential explanatory variables: annual cost, full-time enrollment, faculty–student ratio, average SAT score, and average ACT score. Which explanatory variables should be included in a final version of this regression equation? Justify your choices. Is multicollinearity a problem? Why or why not?

19. A manager of boiler drums wants to use regression analysis to predict the number of worker-hours needed to erect the drums in future projects. Consequently, data for several randomly selected boilers were collected. In addition to worker-hours (Y), the variables measured include boiler capacity, boiler design pressure, boiler type, and drum type. All of these measurements are listed in the file **P10_27.xlsx**. Estimate an appropriate multiple regression model to predict the number of worker-hours needed to erect given boiler drums using

all available explanatory variables. Which explanatory variables should be included in a final version of this regression model? Justify your choices.

20. The file **P02_35.xlsx** contains data from a survey of 500 randomly selected households.
   a. In an effort to explain the variation in the size of the monthly home mortgage or rent payment, estimate a multiple regression equation that includes all of the potential household explanatory variables.
   b. Using the regression output, determine which of the explanatory variables should be excluded from the regression equation. Justify your choices.
   c. Do you obtain substantially different results if you combine First Income and Second Income into a Total Income variable and then use the latter as the only income explanatory variable?

21. The file **P02_07.xlsx** includes data on 204 employees at the (fictional) company Beta Technologies.
   a. Estimate a multiple regression equation to explain the variation in employee salaries at Beta Technologies using all of the potential explanatory variables.
   b. Using the regression output, determine which of the explanatory variables, if any, should be excluded from the regression equation. Justify your choices.
   c. Regardless of your answer to part **b**, exclude the *least* significant variable (not counting the constant) and

estimate the resulting equation. Would you conclude that this equation and the one from part **a** are equally good? Explain.

22. Stock market analysts are continually looking for reliable predictors of stock prices. Consider the problem of modeling the price per share of electric utility stocks (Y). Two variables thought to influence such a stock price are return on average equity (X_1) and annual dividend rate (X_2). The stock price, returns on equity, and dividend rates on a randomly selected day

for several electric utility stocks are provided in the file **P10_19.xlsx**.

a. Estimate a multiple regression model using the given data. Include linear terms as well as an interaction term involving the return on average equity (X_1) and annual dividend rate (X_2).

b. Which of the three explanatory variables (X_1, X_2, and X_1X_2) should be included in a final version of this regression model? Explain. Does your conclusion make sense in light of your knowledge of corporate finance?

11-6 Stepwise Regression

Multiple regression represents an improvement over simple regression because it allows any number of explanatory variables to be included in the analysis. Sometimes, however, the large number of potential explanatory variables makes it difficult to know which variables to include. Many statistical packages provide some assistance by including automatic equation-building options. These options estimate a series of regression equations by successively adding (or deleting) variables according to prescribed rules. Generically, the methods are referred to as **stepwise regression**.

Before discussing how stepwise procedures work, consider a naive approach to the problem. You have already looked at correlation tables for indications of linear relationships. Why not simply include all explanatory variables that have large correlations with the dependent variable? There are two reasons for not doing this. First, although a variable is highly correlated with the dependent variable, it might also be highly correlated with other explanatory variables. Therefore, this variable might not be needed in the equation once the other explanatory variables have been included. This happens quite often.

Second, even if a variable's correlation with the dependent variable is small, its contribution when it is included with a number of other explanatory variables can be greater than anticipated. Essentially, this variable can have something unique to say about the dependent variable that none of the other variables provides, and this fact might not be apparent from the correlation table. This behavior doesn't happen as often, but it is possible.

For these reasons it is sometimes useful to let the software discover the best combination of variables by means of a stepwise procedure. There are a number of procedures for building equations in a stepwise manner, but they all share a basic idea. Suppose there is an existing regression equation and you want to add another variable to this equation from a set of variables not yet included. At this point, the variables already in the equation have explained a certain percentage of the variation of the dependent variable. The residuals represent the part still unexplained. Therefore, in choosing the next variable to enter the equation, you should choose the one that is most highly correlated with the current residuals. If none of the remaining variables is highly correlated with the residuals, you can quit. This is the essence of stepwise regression. However, besides adding variables to the equation, a stepwise procedure might also delete a variable. This is sometimes reasonable because a variable entered early in the procedure might no longer be needed, given the presence of other variables that have entered subsequently.

Many statistical packages have three types of equation-building procedures: forward, backward, and stepwise. A *forward* procedure begins with no explanatory variables in the equation and successively adds one at a time until no remaining variables make a significant contribution. A *backward* procedure begins with *all* potential explanatory variables in the equation and deletes them one at a time until further deletion would do more harm than good. Finally, a true *stepwise* procedure is much like a forward procedure, except that it also considers possible deletions along the way. All of these procedures have the same basic objective—to find an equation with a small s_e and a large R^2 (or adjusted R^2). There is no guarantee that they will all produce exactly the same final equation, but in most cases their final results are very similar. The important thing to realize is that the equations estimated along the way, including the final equation, are estimated exactly as before—by least squares. Therefore, none of these procedures produces any new results. They merely take the burden off the user of having to decide ahead of time which variables to include in the equation.

StatTools implements each of the forward, backward, and stepwise procedures. To use them, select the dependent variable and a set of *potential* explanatory variables. Then specify the criterion for adding and/or deleting variables from the equation. This can be done in two ways, with an *F*-value or a *p*-value. (You make this choice in the Parameters tab of the StatTools Regression dialog box.) We suggest using *p*-values because they are easier to understand, but either method is easy to use. In the *p*-value method, you select a *p*-value such as the default value of 0.05. If the regression coefficient for a potential entering variable would have a *p*-value less than 0.05 (if it were entered), then it is a candidate for entering (if the forward or stepwise procedure is used). The procedure selects the variable with the *smallest p*-value as the next entering variable. Similarly, if any currently included variable has a *p*-value greater than some value such as the default value of 0.10, then (with the stepwise and backward procedures) it is a candidate for leaving the equation. The methods stop when there are no candidates (according to their *p*-values) for entering or leaving the current equation.

The following is a continuation of the HyTex example and illustrates these stepwise procedures.

Fundamental Insight

Stepwise Regression

The option to let the statistical software build the regression equation automatically makes the various versions of stepwise regression very popular with many users. However, keep in mind that it does nothing that can't be done with multiple regression, where the choice of *X*'s is specified manually. And sometimes a careful manual selection of the *X*'s to include is better than letting the software make the selection mindlessly. Stepwise regression has its place, but it shouldn't be a substitute for thoughtful analysis.

EXAMPLE

11.3 EXPLAINING SPENDING AMOUNTS AT HYTEX (CONTINUED)

The analysis of the HyTex data (for the first 750 customers in the data set) resulted in a regression equation that included all potential explanatory variables except for Age, Gender, Own Home, and Married. These were excluded because their *t*-values are large and their *p*-values are small (less than 0.05). Do forward, backward, and stepwise procedures produce the same regression equation for the amount spent in the current year?

Objective

To use stepwise regression procedures to analyze the HyTex data.

Solution

Each of these options is found in the StatTools Regression dialog box.[2] It is just a matter of choosing the appropriate option from the Regression Type dropdown list, as shown in Figure 11.10. In each, specify Amount Spent as the dependent variable

---

2 Excel's Analysis ToolPak add-in doesn't have any stepwise regression options.

Figure 11.10 StatTools Dialog Box for Stepwise Regression

Figure 11.11 Request for Detailed Step Information

and select all of the other variables (besides Customer) as *potential* explanatory variables. Optionally, you can also check the Include Detailed Step Information box in the Options tab, as shown in Figure 11.11. This provides a summary of the steps in the regression output.

It turns out that each stepwise procedure (stepwise, forward, and backward) produces the same *final* equation that we obtained previously, with all variables except Age, Gender, Own Home, and Married included. This often happens, but not always. As Figure 11.12 indicates, the stepwise procedure adds the variables in the order Salary, Catalogs, Close, Children, Previous Customer, and Previous Spent. The forward procedure (not shown) does exactly the same. The backward procedure (also not shown) starts with *all* variables in the equation and then eliminates variables in the order Age, Married, Own Home, and Gender. The final equation appears in the regression output. Again, however, this final equation's output is *exactly* the same as when multiple regression is used with these particular variables.

Figure 11.12 Regression Output from Stepwise Procedure

	A	B	C	D	E	F	G
1	*Stepwise Regression for Amount Spent*	Multiple R	R-Square	Adjusted R-square	Std. Err. of Estimate	Rows Ignored	Outliers
2	*Summary*						
3		0.8636	0.7458	0.7438	491.228	0	8
4							
5		Degrees of Freedom	Sum of Squares	Mean of Squares	F	p-Value	
6	*ANOVA Table*						
7	Explained	6	526113683.9	87685613.98	363.381	<0.0001	
8	Unexplained	743	179289770.9	241305.2099			
9							
10		Coefficient	Standard Error	t-Value	p-Value	Confidence Interval 95%	
11	*Regression Table*					Lower	Upper
12	Constant	205.094	70.315	2.917	0.0036	67.053	343.134
13	Salary	0.018	0.001	19.877	<0.0001	0.016	0.020
14	Catalogs	43.807	2.854	15.348	<0.0001	38.203	49.410
15	Close	−416.246	45.085	−9.233	<0.0001	−504.755	−327.738
16	Children	−161.158	20.483	−7.868	<0.0001	−201.369	−120.947
17	Previous Customer	−543.595	63.299	−8.588	<0.0001	−667.861	−419.329
18	Previous Spent	0.272	0.053	5.184	<0.0001	0.169	0.376
19							
20		Multiple R	R-Square	Adjusted R-square	Std. Err. of Estimate	Enter or Exit	
21	*Step Information*						
22	Salary	0.6837	0.4674	0.4667	708.682	Enter	
23	Catalogs	0.7841	0.6148	0.6138	603.085	Enter	
24	Close	0.8192	0.6710	0.6697	557.726	Enter	
25	Children	0.8477	0.7187	0.7171	516.136	Enter	
26	Previous Customer	0.8583	0.7366	0.7349	499.698	Enter	
27	Previous Spent	0.8636	0.7458	0.7438	491.228	Enter	

Stepwise regression or any of its variations can be very useful for narrowing down the set of all possible explanatory variables to a set that is useful for explaining a dependent variable. However, these procedures should not be used as a substitute for thoughtful analysis. With the availability of such procedures in statistical software, there is sometimes a tendency to turn the analysis over to the computer and accept its output. A good analyst does not just collect as much data as possible, throw it into a software package, and blindly report the results. There should always be some rationale, whether it is based on economic theory, business experience, or common sense, for the variables that are used to explain a given dependent variable. A thoughtless use of stepwise regression can sometimes capitalize on chance to obtain an equation with a reasonably large R^2 but no useful or practical interpretation. It is very possible that such an equation will not generalize well to new data.

Finally, keep in mind that if one stepwise procedure produces slightly different outputs than another (for example, one might include a variable, the other might exclude it), the differences are typically very small and are not worth agonizing about. The two equations typically have very similar R^2 values and standard errors of estimate, and they typically produce very similar predictions. If anything, most analysts prefer the smaller equation because of parsimony, but they realize that the differences are "at the margin."

Problems

Level A

23. The Undergraduate Data sheet of the file **P10_21.xlsx** contains information on undergraduate business programs in the United States, including various rankings by *Business Week*. Use forward, backward, and stepwise regression analysis to explore the relationship between the median starting salary and the following set of potential explanatory variables: annual cost, full-time enrollment, faculty–student ratio, average SAT score, and average ACT score. Do these three methods all lead to the same regression equation? If not, do you think any of the final equations are substantially better than any of the others?

24. The file **P11_24.xlsx** contains data on the top 200 professional golfers in each of the years 2003–2017. (The same data set was used in Example 3.3 in Chapter 3.)

    a. Create one large data set in a new sheet called All Years that has the data for all years stacked on top of one other. (This is possible because the variables are the same in each year.) In this combined data set, create a new column called Earnings per Round, the ratio of Earnings to Rounds. Similarly, create three other new variables, Eagles per Round, Birdies per Round, and Bogies per Round.

    b. Using the data set from part **a**, run a forward regression of Earnings per Round versus the following potential explanatory variables: Age, Yards/Drive, Driving Accuracy, Greens in Regulation, Putting Average, Sand Save Pct, Eagles per Round, Birdies per Round, and Bogies per Round. Given the results, comment on what seems to be important on the professional tour in terms of earnings per round. For any variable that does *not* end up in the equation, is it omitted because it is not related to Earnings per Round or because its effect is explained by other variables in the equation?

    c. Repeat part **b** with backward regression. Do you get the same, or basically the same, results?

25. In a study of housing demand, a county assessor is interested in developing a regression model to estimate the selling price of residential properties within her jurisdiction. She randomly selects several houses and records the selling price in addition to the following values: the size of the house (in hundreds of square feet), the total number of rooms in the house, the age of the house, and an indication of whether the house has an attached garage. These data are listed in the file **P10_26.xlsx**.

    a. Use stepwise regression to decide which explanatory variables should be included in the assessor's statistical model. Use the p-value method with a cutoff value of 0.05 for entering and leaving. Summarize your findings.

    b. How do the results in part **a** change when the critical p-value for entering and leaving is increased to 0.10? Explain any differences between the regression equation obtained here and the one found in part **a**.

26. Continuing Problem 2 with the data in the file **P10_04 .xlsx**, employ stepwise regression to evaluate your conclusions regarding the specification of a regression model to predict the sales of deep-dish pizza by the Original Italian Pizza restaurant chain. Use the p-value method with a cutoff value of 0.05 for entering and leaving. Compare your conclusions in Problem 2 with those derived from a stepwise regression.

Level B

27. How sensitive are stepwise regression results to small changes in the data? This problem allows you to explore this. The file **P11_27.xlsm** can be used to generate 100 randomly chosen observations from a given population. It contains macros that help you do this. Specifically, the means, standard deviations, and correlations for the population of 10 X's and Y are given in rows 2–14. The macro has already been used to generate a "generic" row of data in row 16. It is done so that the X's and Y are normally distributed with the given means, standard deviations, and correlations. Press the F9 key a few times to see how the data in row 16 change. There is also a button you can click. When you do so, the generic row 16 is copied to rows 20–119 to generate new random data, and the new random data are frozen. Click the button a few times to see how this works. Designate a StatTools data set in the range A19:L119 and run stepwise regression on the data. Then generate new data by clicking the button and run stepwise regression again. Repeat this a few times. Then explain the results. Do all of the stepwise regressions produce about the same results? Are they consistent with the parameters in the top section, particularly the correlations involving Y in row 14?

28. Repeat the previous problem at least once, using means, standard deviations, and correlations of your choice. The interesting thing you will discover is that you can't arbitrarily enter just any correlations between -1 and $+1$. For many choices, the generic row will exhibit #VALUE! errors. This means that no population could possibly have the correlations you entered. Try to find correlations that do *not* produce the #VALUE! errors.

11-7 Outliers

In all of the regression examples so far, we have ignored the possibility of outliers. Unfortunately, outliers cannot be ignored in many real applications. They are often present, and they can often have a substantial effect on the results. In this section we briefly discuss outliers in the context of regression—how to detect them and what to do about them.

You probably tend to think of an **outlier** as an observation that has an extreme value for at least one variable. For example, if salaries in a data set are mostly in the $40,000 to $80,000 range, but one salary is $350,000, this observation is clearly an outlier with respect to salary. However, outliers are not always this obvious in a regression context. An observation can be considered an outlier for one or more of the following reasons.

Potential Characteristics of an Outlier

Outliers can come in several forms, as indicated in this list.

- It has an extreme value for at least one variable.
- Its value of the dependent variable is much larger or smaller than predicted by the regression line, and its residual is abnormally large in magnitude. An example appears in Figure 11.13. The line in this scatterplot fits most of the points, but it misses badly on the one obvious outlier. This outlier has a large positive residual, but its Y value is not abnormally large. Its Y value is only large relative to points with the same X value that it has.

Figure 11.13 Outlier with a Large Residual

- Its residual is not only large in magnitude, but this point "tilts" the regression line toward it. An example appears in Figure 11.14. The two lines shown are the regression lines with the outlier and without it. The outlier makes a big difference in the slope and intercept of the regression line. This type of outlier is called an **influential point**, for the obvious reason.
- Its values of individual explanatory variables are not extreme, but they fall outside the general pattern of the other observations. An example appears in Figure 11.15. Here, we assume that the two variables shown, Years (years of experience) and Rating (an employee's performance rating) are both explanatory variables for some other dependent variable (Salary) that isn't shown in the plot. The obvious outlier does not have an abnormal value of either Years or Rating, but it falls well outside the pattern of most employees.

Figure 11.14 Outlier That Tilts the Regression Line

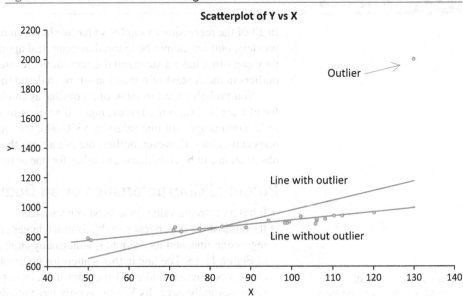

Figure 11.15 Outlier Outside the Pattern of Explanatory Variables

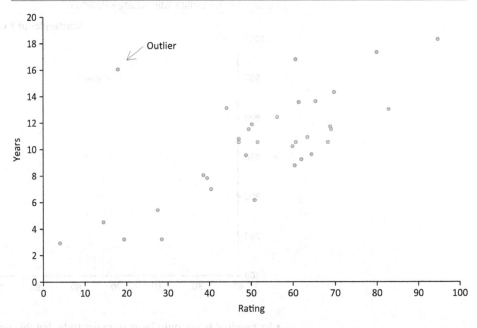

Once outliers have been identified, there is still the dilemma of what to do with them. In most cases the regression output will look "nicer" if you delete outliers, but this is not necessarily appropriate. If you can argue that the outlier isn't really a member of the relevant population, then it is appropriate and probably best to delete it. But if no such argument can be made, then it is not really appropriate to delete the outlier just to make the analysis come out nicer. Perhaps the best advice in this case is the advice we gave in the previous chapter: Run the analysis with the outliers and run it again without them. If the key outputs do not change much, then it does not really matter whether the outliers are included or not. If the key outputs change substantially, then report the results both with and without the outliers, along with a verbal explanation.

The following, a continuation of the bank discrimination example, illustrates this procedure.

EXAMPLE

11.4 POSSIBLE GENDER DISCRIMINATION IN BANK SALARIES

Recall from Example 10.3 of the previous chapter that Fifth National Bank has 208 employees. The data for these employees are listed in the file **Bank Salaries.xlsx**. Are there any obvious outliers? In what sense are they outliers? Does it matter to the regression results, particularly those concerning gender discrimination, whether the outliers are removed?

Objective

To locate possible outliers in the bank salary data, and to see to what extent they affect the regression model.

Solution

There are several places to look for outliers. An obvious place is the Salary variable. The box plot in Figure 11.16 shows that there are several employees making substantially more in salary than most of the employees. You could consider these outliers and remove them, arguing perhaps that these are senior managers who shouldn't be included in the analysis. We leave it to you to check whether the regression results are any different with these high-salary employees than without them.

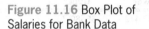
Figure 11.16 Box Plot of Salaries for Bank Data

Another place to look is at a scatterplot of the residuals versus the fitted values. This type of plot shows points with abnormally large residuals. For example, we ran the regression with Female, Years1, the interaction between Female and Years1, and four education dummies, and we obtained the output and scatterplot in Figures 11.17 and 11.18. This scatterplot has several points that could be considered outliers, but we focus on the point identified in the figure. The residual for this point is approximately $-23,000$. Given that s_e for this regression is approximately 5900, this residual is about four standard errors below zero—quite extreme. If you examine this point more closely, you will see that it corresponds to employee 208, a 62-year-old female employee in the highest job grade. She has 33 years of experience with Fifth National, she has a graduate degree, and she earns only $30,000. She is clearly an unusual employee, and there are probably special circumstances that can explain her small salary, although we can only guess at what they are.[3]

In any case, if you delete this employee and rerun the regression with the same variables, you will obtain the output in Figure 11.19.[4] Now, recalling that gender discrimination is the key issue in this example, you can compare the coefficients of Female and the interaction term in the two outputs. The coefficient of Female has dropped from 4899 to 3774. In words, the

---

3 StatTools recently added an outlier detection feature. To use it, check the Identify Outliers in Graphs option on the Graphs tab and the Identify Outliers in Data Set option in the the Options tab. For the bank data, it lists employee 208 as an outlier.
4 As you can see in cell G3, StatTools identified two *new* outliers in the reduced data set. This can happen.

Y-intercept for the female regression line used to be about $4900 higher than for the male line; now it is only about $3800 higher. More importantly, the coefficient of the interaction term has changed from −1030 to −858. This coefficient indicates how much less steep the female line for Salary versus Years1 is than the male line. So a change from −1030 to −858 indicates *less* discrimination against females now than before. In other words, this unusual female employee accounts for a good bit of the discrimination argument—although a strong argument still exists even without her.

Figure 11.17 Regression Output with Outlier Included

	A	B	C	D	E	F	G
1	*Multiple Regression for Salary*	Multiple R	R-Square	Adjusted R-square	Std. Err. of Estimate	Rows Ignored	Outliers
2	*Summary*						
3		0.8552	0.7314	0.7220	5935.254	0	1
4							
5		Degrees of Freedom	Sum of Squares	Mean of Squares	F	p-Value	
6	*ANOVA Table*						
7	Explained	7	19181659773	2740237110	77.787	<0.0001	
8	Unexplained	200	7045447458	35227237.29			
9							
10		Coefficient	Standard Error	t-Value	p-Value	Confidence Interval 95%	
11	*Regression Table*					Lower	Upper
12	Constant	34209.087	1202.708	28.443	<0.0001	31837.472	36580.702
13	Education (1)	−9428.090	1337.292	−7.050	<0.0001	−12065.092	−6791.089
14	Education (2)	−8881.541	1309.717	−6.781	<0.0001	−11464.167	−6298.916
15	Education (3)	−5840.749	1079.353	−5.411	<0.0001	−7969.121	−3712.377
16	Education (4)	−3565.196	2230.635	−1.598	0.1116	−7963.776	833.384
17	Years1	1456.388	79.761	18.259	<0.0001	1299.107	1613.669
18	Gender (Female)	4898.656	1454.087	3.369	0.0009	2031.347	7765.965
19	Gender (Female) * Years1	−1029.858	121.924	−8.447	<0.0001	−1270.279	−789.437

Figure 11.18 Scatterplot of Residuals versus Fitted Values with Outlier Identified

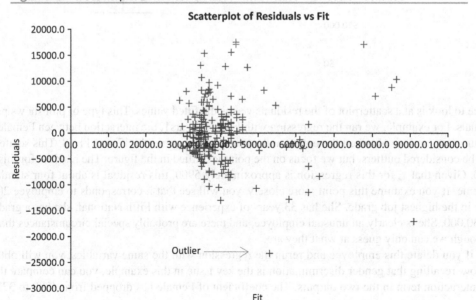

Figure 11.19 Regression Output with Outlier Excluded

	A	B	C	D	E	F	G
1	*Multiple Regression for Salary*	Multiple R	R-Square	Adjusted R-square	Std. Err. of Estimate	Rows Ignored	Outliers
2	*Summary*						
3		0.8690	0.7551	0.7465	5670.503	0	2
4							
5		Degrees of Freedom	Sum of Squares	Mean of Squares	F	p-Value	
6	*ANOVA Table*						
7	Explained	7	19729421790	2818488827	87.654	<0.0001	
8	Unexplained	199	6398765306	32154599.53			
9							
10		Coefficient	Standard Error	t-Value	p-Value	Confidence Interval 95%	
11	*Regression Table*					Lower	Upper
12	Constant	34604.091	1152.430	30.027	<0.0001	32331.549	36876.633
13	Education (1)	−10547.475	1301.794	−8.102	<0.0001	−13114.556	−7980.393
14	Education (2)	−9769.933	1266.879	−7.712	<0.0001	−12268.162	−7271.703
15	Education (3)	−6429.143	1039.520	−6.185	<0.0001	−8479.031	−4379.255
16	Education (4)	−4180.842	2135.551	−1.958	0.0517	−8392.055	30.371
17	Years1	1449.596	76.218	19.019	<0.0001	1299.297	1599.896
18	Gender (Female)	3774.315	1411.667	2.674	0.0081	990.569	6558.060
19	Gender (Female) * Years1	−858.202	122.613	−6.999	<0.0001	−1099.989	−616.415

Problems

Level A

29. The file **P11.29.xlsx** contains data on the top 40 golfers in 2008. (It is a subset of the data examined in earlier chapters.) This was the year when Tiger Woods won the U.S. Open in June and then had year-ending surgery directly afterward. Using all golfers, run a forward stepwise regression of Earnings per Round versus the potential explanatory variables in columns B–G. (Don't use Earnings in column H.) Then create a second data set that omits Tiger Woods and repeat the regression on this smaller data set. Are the results about the same? Explain the effect, if any, of the Tiger Woods outlier on the regression.

30. The file **P02_07.xlsx** includes data on 204 employees at the (fictional) company Beta Technologies.
   a. Run a forward stepwise regression of Annual Salary versus Gender, Age, Prior Experience, Beta Experience, and Education. Would you say this equation does a good job of explaining the variation in salaries?
   b. Add a new employee to the end of the data set, a top-level executive. The values of Gender through Annual Salary for this person are, respectively, 0, 56, 10, 15, 6, and $500,000. Run the regression in part **a** again, including this executive. Are the results much

different? Is it "fair" to exclude this executive when analyzing the salary structure at this company?

Level B

31. Statistician Frank J. Anscombe created a data set to illustrate the importance of doing more than just examining the standard regression output. These data are provided in the file **P10_64.xlsx**.
   a. Regress Y_1 on X. How well does the estimated equation fit the data? Is there evidence of a linear relationship between Y_1 and X at the 5% significance level?
   b. Regress Y_2 on X. How well does the estimated equation fit the data? Is there evidence of a linear relationship between Y_2 and X at the 5% significance level?
   c. Regress Y_3 on X. How well does the estimated equation fit the data? Is there evidence of a linear relationship between Y_3 and X at the 5% significance level?
   d. Regress Y_4 on X_4. How well does the estimated equation fit the data? Is there evidence of a linear relationship between Y_4 and X_4 at the 5% significance level?
   e. Compare these four simple linear regression equations (1) in terms of goodness of fit and (2) in terms of overall statistical significance.
   f. How do you explain these findings, considering that each of the regression equations is based on a *different* set of variables?
   g. What role, if any, do outliers have on each of these estimated regression equations?

11-8 Violations of Regression Assumptions

Much of the theoretical research in the area of regression has dealt with violations of the regression assumptions discussed in Section 11-2. There are three issues: how to detect violations of the assumptions, what goes wrong if the violations are ignored, and what to do about them if they are detected. Detection is usually relatively easy. You can look at scatterplots, histograms, and time series graphs for visual signs of violations, and there are a number of numeric measures (many not covered here) that have been developed for diagnostic purposes. The second issue, what goes wrong if the violations are ignored, depends on the type of violation and its severity. The third issue is the most difficult to resolve. There are some relatively easy fixes and some that are well beyond the level of this book. In this section we briefly discuss some of the most common violations and a few possible remedies for them.

11-8a Nonconstant Error Variance

The second regression assumption states that the variance of the errors should be *constant* for all values of the explanatory variables. This is a lot to ask, and it is almost always violated to some extent. Fortunately, mild violations do not have much effect on the validity of the regression output, so you can usually ignore them.

However, one particular form of nonconstant error variance occurs fairly often and should be dealt with. This is the fan shape shown earlier in the scatterplot of Amount Spent versus Salary in Figure 11.1. As salaries increase, the variability of amounts spent also increases. Although this fan shape appears in the scatterplot of the dependent variable Amount Spent versus the explanatory variable Salary, it also appears in the scatterplot of residuals versus fitted values if you regress Amount Spent versus Salary. If you ignore this nonconstant error variance, the standard error of the regression coefficient of Salary is inaccurate, and a confidence interval for this coefficient or a hypothesis test concerning it can be misleading.

A fan shape can cause an incorrect value for the standard error of estimate, so that confidence intervals and hypothesis tests for the regression coefficients are not valid.

There are at least two ways to deal with this fan-shape phenomenon. The first is to use a different estimation method than least squares. It is called *weighted least squares*, and it is an option available in some statistical software packages. However, it is fairly advanced, so we will not discuss it here.

The second method is simpler. When you see a fan shape, where the variability increases from left to right in a scatterplot, you can try a logarithmic transformation of the dependent variable. The reason this often works is that the logarithmic transformation squeezes the large values closer together and pulls the small values farther apart. The scatterplot of the log of Amount Spent versus Salary is in Figure 11.20. Clearly, the fan shape evident in Figure 11.1 is gone.

A logarithmic transformation of Y can sometimes cure the fan-shape problem.

This logarithmic transformation is not a magical cure for all instances of nonconstant error variance. For example, it appears to have introduced some curvature into the plot in Figure 11.20. However, when the distribution of the dependent variable is heavily skewed to the right, as it often is, the logarithmic transformation is worth exploring.

11-8b Nonnormality of Residuals

The third regression assumption states that the error terms are normally distributed. You can check this assumption fairly easily by forming a histogram of the residuals. You can even perform a formal test of normality of the residuals by using the procedures discussed in Section 9-5 of Chapter 9. However, unless the distribution of the residuals is severely nonnormal, the inferences made from the regression output are still approximately valid. In addition, one common form of nonnormality is skewness to the right, and this can often be remedied by the same logarithmic transformation of the dependent variable that remedies nonconstant error variance.

Figure 11.20 Scatterplot without Fan Shape

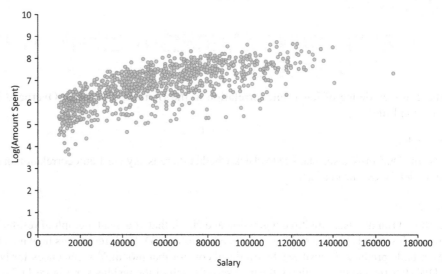

Scatterplot of Log(Amount Spent) vs Salary

11-8c Autocorrelated Residuals

The fourth regression assumption states that the error terms are probabilistically independent. This assumption is usually valid for cross-sectional data, but it is often violated for time series data. The problem with time series data is that the residuals are often correlated with nearby residuals, a property called **autocorrelation of residuals**. The most frequent type of autocorrelation is positive autocorrelation. For example, if residuals separated by one month are correlated—called *lag 1 autocorrelation*—in a positive direction, then an overprediction in January, for example, will likely lead to an overprediction in February, and an underprediction in January will likely lead to an underprediction in February. If this autocorrelation is large, serious prediction errors can occur if it is not dealt with appropriately.

A numeric measure has been developed to check for lag 1 autocorrelation. It is called the **Durbin–Watson statistic** (after the two statisticians who developed it), and it is quoted automatically in the regression output of many statistical software packages. The Durbin–Watson (DW) statistic is scaled to be between 0 and 4. Values close to 2 indicate very little lag 1 autocorrelation, values below 2 indicate positive autocorrelation, and values above 2 indicate negative autocorrelation.

A Durbin–Watson statistic below 2 signals that nearby residuals are positively correlated with one another.

Because *positive* autocorrelation is the usual culprit, the question becomes how much below 2 the DW statistic must be before you should react. There is a formal hypothesis test for answering this question, and a set of tables appears in some statistics texts. Without going into the details, we simply state that when the number of time series observations, n, is about 30 and the number of explanatory variables is fairly small, say, 1 to 5, then any DW statistic less than 1.2 should get your attention. If n increases to around 100, then you shouldn't be concerned unless the DW statistic is below 1.5.

If e_i is the ith residual, the formula for the DW statistic is

$$DW = \frac{\sum_{i=2}^{n}(e_i - e_{i-1})^2}{\sum_{i=1}^{n}e_i^2}$$

This is obviously not very attractive for hand calculation, so the StatDurbinWatson function is included in StatTools. To use it, run any regression and check the option to create a graph of residuals versus fitted values. This automatically creates columns of fitted values and residuals. Then enter the formula

=StatDurbinWatson(*ResidRange*)

in any cell, substituting the actual range of residuals for "ResidRange."

The following continuation of Example 11.1 with the Bendrix manufacturing data— the only time series data set we have analyzed with regression—checks for possible lag 1 autocorrelation.

EXAMPLE

11.1 EXPLAINING OVERHEAD COSTS AT BENDRIX (CONTINUED)

Is there any evidence of lag 1 autocorrelation in the Bendrix data when Overhead is regressed on Machine Hours and Production Runs?

Objective

To use the Durbin–Watson statistic to check whether there is any lag 1 autocorrelation in the residuals from the Bendrix regression model for overhead costs.

Solution

You should run the usual multiple regression and check that you want a graph of residuals versus fitted values. The results are shown in Figure 11.21. The residuals are listed in column D. Each represents how much the regression overpredicts (if negative) or underpredicts (if positive) the overhead cost for that month. You can check for lag 1 autocorrelation in two ways, with the DW statistic and by examining the time series graph of the residuals in Figure 11.22.

The DW statistic is calculated in cell F39 of Figure 11.21 with the formula

=StatDurbinWatson(D39:D76)

Figure 11.21 StatTools Regression Output with Residuals and DW Statistic

	A	B	C	D	E	F	G
38	*Graph Data*	Overhead	Fit	Residuals	Durbin-Watson for residuals		
39	1	99798	98391.35059	1406.649409		1.313	
40	2	87804	85522.33322	2281.666779			
41	3	93681	92723.59538	957.4046174			
42	4	82262	82428.09201	−166.0920107			
43	5	106968	100227.9028	6740.097234			
44	6	107925	107869.3954	55.60458248			
45	7	117287	114933.4723	2353.52769			

Figure 11.22 Time Series Graph of Residuals

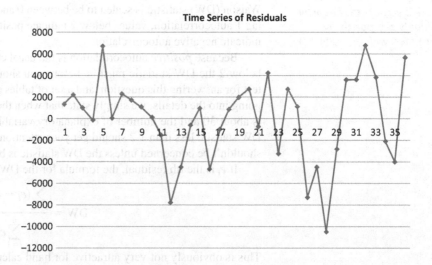

Time Series of Residuals

(Remember that StatDurbinWatson is *not* a built-in Excel® function. It is available only if StatTools is loaded.) Based on our guidelines for DW values, 1.313 suggests positive autocorrelation—it is less than 2—but not enough to cause concern.[5] This general conclusion is supported by the time series graph. Serious autocorrelation of lag 1 would tend to show longer runs of residuals alternating above and below the horizontal axis—positives would tend to follow positives, and negatives would tend to follow negatives. There is some indication of this behavior in the graph but not an excessive amount.

---

5 A more formal test, using Durbin–Watson tables, supports this conclusion.

What should you do if the DW statistic signals significant autocorrelation? Unfortunately, the answer to this question would take us much more deeply into time series analysis than we can go in this book. Suffice it to say that time series analysis in the context of regression can become very complex, and there are no easy fixes for the autocorrelation that often occurs.

Problems

Level A

32. A company produces electric motors for use in home appliances. One of the company's production managers is interested in examining the relationship between the dollars spent per month in inspecting finished motor products (X) and the number of motors produced during that month that were returned by dissatisfied customers (Y). He has collected the data in the file **P10_03.xlsx** to explore this relationship for the past 36 months.
   a. Estimate a simple linear regression equation using the given data and interpret it. What does the ANOVA table indicate for this model?
   b. Examine the residuals of the regression equation. Do you see evidence of any violations of the regression assumptions?
   c. Conduct a Durbin–Watson test on the model's residuals. Interpret the result of this test.
   d. In light of your result in part **c**, do you recommend modifying the original regression model? If so, how would you revise it?

33. Examine the relationship between the average utility bills for homes of a particular size (Y) and the average monthly temperature (X). The data in the file **P10_07.xlsx** include the average monthly bill and temperature for each month of the past year.
   a. Use the given data to estimate a simple linear regression equation. How well does the estimated regression model fit the given data? What does the ANOVA table indicate for this model?
   b. Examine the residuals of the regression equation. Do you see evidence of any violations of the regression assumptions?
   c. Conduct a Durbin–Watson test on the model's residuals. Interpret the result of this test.
   d. In light of your result in part **c**, do you recommend modifying the original regression model? If so, how would you revise it?

34. The manager of a commuter rail transportation system was recently asked by her governing board to predict the demand for rides in the large city served by the transportation network. The system manager has collected data on variables thought to be related to the number of weekly riders on the city's rail system. The file **P10_20.xlsx** contains these data.
   a. Estimate a multiple regression equation using all of the available explanatory variables. What does the ANOVA table indicate for this model?
   b. Is there evidence of auto correlated residuals in this model? Explain why or why not.

11-9 Prediction

Once you have estimated a regression equation from a set of data, you might want to use this equation to predict the value of the dependent variable for *new* observations. As an example, suppose that a retail chain is considering opening a new store in one of several proposed locations. It naturally wants to choose the location that will result in the largest revenues. The problem is that the revenues for the new locations are not yet known. They can be observed only after stores are opened in these locations, and the chain cannot afford to open more than one store at the current time. An alternative is to use regression analysis. Using data from *existing* stores, the chain can run a regression of the dependent variable revenue on several explanatory variables such as population density, level of wealth in the vicinity, number of competitors nearby, ease of access given the existing roads, and so on.

Assuming that the regression equation has a reasonably large R^2 and, even more important, a reasonably small s_e, the chain can then use this equation to predict revenues for the proposed locations. It will gather values of the explanatory variables for each of the proposed locations, substitute these into the regression equation, and look at the predicted revenue for each proposed location. All else being equal, the chain will probably choose the location with the highest predicted revenue.

As another example, suppose that you are trying to explain the starting salaries for undergraduate college students. You want to predict the *mean* salary of all graduates with certain characteristics, such as all male marketing majors from state-supported universities. To do this, you first gather salary data from a sample of graduates from various universities. Included in this data set are relevant explanatory variables for each graduate in the sample, such as the type of university, the student's major, GPA, years of work experience, and so on. You then use these data to estimate a regression equation for starting salary and substitute the relevant values of the explanatory variables into the regression equation to obtain the required prediction.

Regression can be used to predict Y for a single observation, or it can be used to predict the mean Y for many observations, all with the same X values.

These two examples illustrate two types of prediction problems in regression. The first problem, illustrated by the retail chain example, is the more common of the two. Here the objective is to predict the value of the dependent variable for one or more *individual* members of the population. In this specific example you are trying to predict the future revenue for several potential locations of the new store. In the second problem, illustrated by the salary example, the objective is to predict the *mean* of the dependent variable for all members of the population with certain values of the explanatory variables. In the first problem you are predicting an individual value; in the second problem you are predicting a mean.

The second problem is inherently easier than the first in the sense that the resulting prediction is bound to be more accurate. The reason is intuitive. Recall that the mean of the dependent variable for any fixed values of the explanatory variables lies on the population regression line. Therefore, if you can accurately estimate this line—that is, if you can accurately estimate the regression coefficients—you can accurately predict the required mean. In contrast, most individual points do *not* lie on the population regression line. Therefore, even if your estimate of the population regression line is perfectly accurate, you still cannot predict exactly where an individual point will fall.

Stated another way, when you predict a mean, there is a single source of error: the possibly inaccurate estimates of the regression coefficients. But when you predict an individual value, there are two sources of error: the inaccurate estimates of the regression coefficients and the inherent variation of individual points around the regression line. This second source of error often dominates the first.

We illustrate these comments in Figure 11.23. For the sake of illustration, the dependent variable is salary and the single explanatory variable is years of experience with the company. Let's suppose that you want to predict either the salary for a particular employee with 10 years of experience or the mean salary of all employees with 10 years of experience. The two lines in this graph represent the population regression line (which in reality is unobservable) and the estimated regression line. For each prediction problem the point prediction—the best guess—is the value above 10 on the estimated regression line. The error in predicting the mean occurs because the two lines in the graph are not the same—that is, the estimated line is not quite correct. The error in predicting the individual value (the point shown in the graph) occurs because the two lines are not the same and also because this point does not lie on the population regression line.

Figure 11.23 Prediction Errors for an Individual Value and a Mean

Observed point

Prediction error for individual value

Prediction error for mean

Salary

Estimated regression line

Population regression line

YrsExper

10

One general aspect of prediction becomes apparent by looking at this graph. If we let X's denote the explanatory variables, predictions for values of the X's close to their means are likely to be more accurate than predictions for X's far from their means. In the graph, the mean of YrsExper is about 7. (This is approximately where the two lines cross.) Because the slopes of the two lines are different, they get farther apart as YrsExper gets farther from 7 (on either side). As a result, predictions tend to become less accurate.

This phenomenon shows up as higher standard errors of prediction as the X's get farther from their means. However, for extreme values of the X's, there is another problem. Suppose, for example, that all values of YrsExper in the data set are between 1 and 15, and you attempt to predict the salary for an employee with 25 years of experience. This is called *extrapolation*; you are attempting to predict beyond the limits of the sample.

The problem here is that there is no guarantee, and sometimes no reason to believe, that the relationship within the range of the sample is valid outside of this range. It is perfectly possible that the effect of years of experience on salary is considerably different in the 25-year range than in the range of the sample. If it is, then extrapolation is bound to yield inaccurate predictions. In general, you should avoid extrapolation whenever possible. If you really want to predict the salaries of employees with 25-plus years of experience, you should include some employees of this type in the original sample.

We now discuss how to make predictions and how to estimate their accuracy, both for individual values and for means. To keep it simple, we first assume that there is a single explanatory variable X. We choose a fixed "trial" value of X, labeled X_0, and predict the value of a single Y or the mean of all Y's when X equals X_0. For both prediction problems the **point prediction**, or best guess, is found by substituting into the right side of the estimated regression equation. Graphically, this is the height of the estimated regression line above X_0.

It is more difficult to predict for extreme X's than for X's close to the mean. Trying to predict for X's beyond the range of the data set (extrapolation) is quite risky.

To calculate a **point prediction**, substitute the given values of the X's into the estimated regression equation.

The standard error of prediction for a single Y is approximately equal to the standard error of estimate.

To measure the accuracy of these point predictions, you calculate a standard error for each prediction. These **standard errors of prediction** can be interpreted in the usual way. For example, you are about 68% certain that the actual values will be within one standard error of the point predictions, and you are about 95% certain that the actual values will be within two standard errors of the point predictions. For the individual prediction problem, the standard error is labeled s_{ind} and is given by Equation (11.4). As indicated by the approximate equality on the right, when the sample size n is large and X_0 is fairly close to $\overline{X}$, the last two terms inside the square root are relatively small, and this standard error of prediction can be approximated by s_e, the standard error of estimate.

Standard Error of Prediction for an Individual Y

$$s_{\text{ind}} = s_e \sqrt{1 + \frac{1}{n} + \frac{(X_0 - \overline{X})^2}{\sum_{i=1}^{n}(X_i - \overline{X})^2}} \simeq s_e \qquad (11.4)$$

The standard error of prediction for a mean of Y's is approximately equal to the standard error of estimate divided by the square root of the sample size.

For the prediction of the mean, the standard error is labeled s_{mean} and is given by Equation (11.5). Here, if X_0 is fairly close to $\overline{X}$, the last term inside the square root is relatively small, and this standard error of prediction is approximately equal to the expression on the right.

Standard Error of Prediction for the Mean Y

$$s_{\text{mean}} = s_e \sqrt{\frac{1}{n} + \frac{(X_0 - \overline{X})^2}{\sum\limits_{i=1}^{n}(X_i - \overline{X})^2}} \simeq s_e/\sqrt{n} \qquad (11.5)$$

These standard errors can be used to calculate a 95% prediction interval for an individual value and a 95% confidence interval for a mean value. Exactly as in Chapter 8, you go out a t-multiple of the relevant standard error on either side of the point prediction. The t-multiple is the value that cuts off 0.025 probability in the right-hand tail of a t distribution with $n - 2$ degrees of freedom.

The term *prediction interval* (rather than confidence interval) is used for an individual value because an individual value of Y is not a population *parameter*; it is an individual data point. However, the interpretation is basically the same. If you calculate a 95% prediction interval for many members of the population, you can expect their actual Y values to fall within the corresponding prediction intervals about 95% of the time.

To see how this can be implemented in Excel, we revisit the Bendrix example of predicting overhead expenses.

EXAMPLE

11.1 PREDICTING OVERHEAD AT BENDRIX (CONTINUED)

We have already used regression to analyze overhead expenses at Bendrix, based on 36 months of data. Suppose Bendrix expects the values of Machine Hours and Production Runs for the next three months to be 1430, 1560, 1520, and 35, 45, 40, respectively. What are their point predictions and 95% prediction intervals for Overhead for these three months?

Objective
To predict Overhead at Bendrix for the next three months, given anticipated values of Machine Hours and Production Runs.

Solution
StatTools has the capability to provide predictions, 95% prediction intervals (for individual values), and 95% confidence intervals (for the means), but you must set up a second data set to capture the results. This second data set can be placed next to (or below) the original data set. It should have the same variable name headings, and it should include values of the explanatory variable to be used for prediction. For this example we called the original data set Original Data and the new data set Data for Prediction. The regression dialog box and results in Data for Prediction appear in Figures 11.24 and 11.25. In Figure 11.24, note that the Prediction option is checked in the Options tab, and the second data set is specified in the corresponding drop-down list.

Referring to Figure 11.25, the second data set should initially contain the data in columns F to H and blanks below the Overhead label in column I. Then when the regression is run (with the Prediction option checked), the values in the Overhead column and the columns to its right are filled in.

The Overhead values in column I are the point predictions for the next three months, and the LowerLimit95 and UpperLimit95 values in column J and K indicate the 95% prediction intervals for these individual months. (The confidence intervals in columns L and M are not really relevant for this data set. For example, the confidence interval in row 2 would be for the mean Overhead of *all* months with the given values of Machine Hours and Production Runs in row 2.) You can see from the wide prediction intervals how much uncertainty remains. The reason is the relatively large standard error of estimate, s_e. If you could halve the value of s_e, the length of the prediction interval would be only half as large. Contrary to what you might expect, this is not a sample size problem. That is, a larger sample size would probably *not* produce a smaller value of s_e. The problem is that Machine Hours and Production Runs are not perfectly correlated with Overhead. The only way to decrease s_e and get more accurate predictions is to find other explanatory variables that are more closely related to Overhead.

Figure 11.24 StatTools
Regression Dialog Box for
Including Predictions

Figure 11.25 Prediction of Overhead

	F	G	H	I	J	K	L	M
1	Month	Machine Hours	Production Runs	Overhead	PredictionLowerLimit95	PredictionUpperLimit95	ConfidenceLowerLimit95	ConfidenceUpperLimit95
2	37	1430	35	97180.35	88700.80	105659.91	95760.34	98600.37
3	38	1560	45	111676.27	103002.95	120349.58	109365.42	113987.11
4	39	1520	40	105516.72	96993.16	114040.28	103854.00	107179.44

Problems

Level A

35. The file **P10_05.xlsx** contains salaries for a sample of DataCom employees, along with several variables that might be related to salary.

   a. Estimate an appropriate multiple regression equation to predict the annual salary of a given DataCom employee.

   b. Given the estimated regression model, predict the annual salary of a male employee who served in a similar department at another company for five years prior to coming to work at DataCom. This man, a graduate of a four-year collegiate business program, has been supervising six subordinates in the sales department since joining the organization seven years ago.

   c. Find a 95% prediction interval for the salary earned by the employee in part **b**.

   d. Find a 95% confidence interval for the mean salary earned by all DataCom employees sharing the characteristics provided in part **b**.

   e. How can you explain the difference between the widths of the intervals in parts **c** and **d**?

36. The owner of a restaurant has recorded sales data for the past 19 years. He has also recorded data on potentially relevant variables. The data appear in the file **P10_23.xlsx**.

   a. Estimate a regression equation for sales as a function of population, advertising in the current year, and advertising in the previous year. Can you expect predictions of sales in *future* years to be very accurate if they are based on this regression equation? Explain.

   b. The company would like to predict sales in the next year (year 20). It doesn't know what the population will be in year 20, so it assumes no change from year 19. Its planned advertising level for year 20 is $30,000. Find a prediction and a 95% prediction interval for sales in year 20.

37. A power company located in southern Alabama wants to predict the peak power load (i.e., Y, the maximum amount of power that must be generated each day to meet demand) as a function of the daily high temperature (X). A random sample of summer days is chosen, and the peak power load and the high temperature are recorded on each day. The file **P10_40.xlsx** contain these observations.

   a. Use the given data to estimate a simple linear regression equation. How well does the regression equation fit the given data?

   b. Examine the residuals of the estimated regression equation. Do you see evidence of any violations of the assumptions regarding the errors of the regression model?

   c. Calculate the Durbin–Watson statistic on the model's residuals. What does it indicate?

   d. Given your result in part d, do you recommend modifying the original regression model in this case? If so, how would you revise it?

   e. Use the final version of your regression equation to predict the peak power load on a summer day with a high temperature of 90 degrees.

   f. Find a 95% prediction interval for the peak power load on a summer day with a high temperature of 90 degrees.

   g. Find a 95% confidence interval for the *average* peak power load on all summer days with a high temperature of 90 degrees.

11-10 Conclusion

In these two chapters on regression, you have seen how useful regression analysis can be for a variety of business applications and how statistical software such as StatTools enables you to obtain relevant output—both graphical and numerical—with very little effort. However, you have also seen that there are many concepts that you must understand well before you can use regression analysis appropriately. Given that user-friendly software is available, it is all too easy to generate enormous amounts of regression output and then misinterpret or misuse much of it.

At the very least, you should (1) be able to interpret the standard regression output, including statistics on the regression coefficients, summary measures such as R^2 and s_e, and the ANOVA table; (2) know what to look for in the many scatterplots available; (3) know how to use dummy variables, interaction terms, and nonlinear transformations to improve a fit; and (4) be able to spot clear violations of the regression assumptions. However, we haven't covered everything. Indeed, many entire books are devoted exclusively to regression analysis. Therefore, you should recognize when you *don't* know enough to handle a regression problem such as nonconstant error variance or autocorrelation appropriately. In this case, you should consult a statistical expert.

Summary of Key Terms

TERM	SYMBOL	EXPLANATION	EXCEL	PAGES	EQUATION
Statistical model		A theoretical model including several assumptions that must be satisfied, at least approximately, for inferences from regression output to be valid		484	11.1
Error	ε	The difference between the actual Y value and the predicted value from the population regression line		485	
Homoscedasticity (and heteroscedasticity)		Equal (and unequal) variance of the dependent variable for different values of the explanatory variables		485, 486	
Parsimony		The concept of explaining the most with the least		489	
Standard error of a regression coefficient	s_b	Measures how much the estimates of a regression coefficient vary from sample to sample	StatTools	489	
Confidence interval for a regression coefficient		An interval likely to contain the population regression coefficient	StatTools	491	
t-value for test of regression coefficient	t	The ratio of the estimate of a regression coefficient to its standard error, used to test whether the coefficient is 0	StatTools	491	11.3

Key Terms (continued)

TERM	SYMBOL	EXPLANATION	EXCEL	PAGES	EQUATION
Hypothesis test for a regression coefficient		Typically a two-tailed test, where the null hypothesis is that the regression coefficient is 0	StatTools	491	
ANOVA table for regression		Used to test whether the explanatory variables, as a whole, have any significant explanatory power	StatTools	493	
Multicollinearity		Occurs when there is a fairly strong linear relationship between explanatory variables		496	
Include/exclude decisions		Guidelines for deciding whether to include or exclude potential explanatory variables		502	
Stepwise regression		A class of automatic equation-building methods, where variables are added (or deleted) in order of their importance	StatTools	507	
Outliers		Observations that lie outside the general pattern of points and can have a substantial effect on the regression model		512	
Influential point		A point that can "tilt" the regression line		513	
Autocorrelation of residuals		Lack of independence in the series of residuals, especially relevant for time series data		519	
Durbin–Watson statistic		A measure of the autocorrelation between residuals, useful for time series data	StatDurbin-Watson, a StatTools function	519	
Point prediction		The predicted value of Y from the regression equation		523	
Standard errors of prediction	s_{ind}, s_{mean}	Measures of the accuracy of prediction when predicting Y for an individual observation, or predicting the mean of all Y's, for fixed values of the explanatory variables	StatTools	524	11.4, 11.5

Problems

Conceptual Questions

C.1. Suppose a regression output produces the following 99% confidence interval for one of the regression coefficients: $[-32.47, -16.88]$. Given this information, should an analyst reject the null hypothesis that this population regression coefficient is equal to zero? Explain your answer.

C.2. Explain why it is not possible to estimate a linear regression model that contains *all* dummy variables associated with a particular categorical explanatory variable.

C.3. Suppose you have a data set that includes *all* of the professional athletes in a given sport over a given period of time, such as *all* NFL football players during the 2017–2019 seasons, and you use regression to estimate a variable of interest. Are the inferences discussed in this chapter relevant? Recall that we have been assuming that the data represent a random sample of some larger population. In this sports example, what is the larger population—or is there one?

C.4. Distinguish between the test of significance of an individual regression coefficient and the ANOVA test. When, if ever, are these two statistical tests essentially equivalent?

C.5. Which of these intervals based on the same estimated regression equation with fixed values of the explanatory variables would be *wider*: (1) a 95% prediction interval for an individual value of Y or (2) a 95% confidence interval for the mean value of Y? Explain your answer. How do you interpret the wider of these two intervals in words?

C.6. Regression outputs from virtually all statistical packages look the same. In particular, the section on coefficients lists the coefficients, their standard errors, their t-values, their p-values, and (possibly) 95% confidence intervals for them. Explain how all of these are related.

C.7. If you are building a regression equation in a forward stepwise manner, that is, by adding one variable at a time, explain why it is useful to monitor the adjusted R^2 and the standard error of estimate. Why is it not as useful to monitor R^2?

C.8. You run a regression with two explanatory variables and notice that the p-value in the ANOVA table is extremely small but the p-values of both explanatory variables are larger than 0.10. What is the probable reason? Can you conclude that neither explanatory variable does a good job in predicting the dependent variable?

C.9. Why are outliers sometimes called *influential* observations? What *could* happen to the slope of a regression of Y versus a single X when an outlier is included versus when it is not included? Will this necessarily happen when a point is an outlier? Answer by giving a couple of examples.

C.10. The Durbin–Watson test is for detecting lag 1 autocorrelation in the residuals. Which values of DW signal *positive* autocorrelation? If you observe such a DW value but ignore it, what might go wrong with predictions based on the regression equation? Specifically, if the data are time series data, and your goal is to predict the next six months, what might go wrong with the predictions?

Level A

38. For several consecutive weeks you have observed the sales (in number of cases) of canned tomatoes at Mr. D's supermarket. Each week you kept track of the following:

- Was a promotional notice placed in all shopping carts for canned tomatoes?
- Was a coupon given for canned tomatoes?
- Was a price reduction (none, 1, or 2 cents off) given?

The file **P11_38.xlsx** contains these data.

a. Use multiple regression to determine how these factors influence sales.

b. Discuss how you can tell whether autocorrelation, heteroscedasticity, or multicollinearity might be a problem.

c. Predict sales of canned tomatoes during a week in which Mr. D's uses a shopping cart notice, a coupon, and a one-cent price reduction.

39. The file **P11_39.xlsx** contains quarterly data on pork sales. Price is in dollars per hundred pounds, quantity sold is in billions of pounds, per capita income is in dollars, U.S. population is in millions, and GDP is in billions of dollars.

a. Use the data to develop a regression equation that could be used to predict the quantity of pork sold during future periods. Discuss how you can tell whether heteroscedasticity, autocorrelation, or multicollinearity might be a problem.

b. Suppose that during each of the next two quarters, price is 45, U.S. population is 240, GDP is 2620, and per capita income is 10,000. (These are in the units described previously.) Predict the quantity of pork sold during each of the next two quarters.

40. The file **P11_40.xlsx** contains monthly sales for a photography studio and the price charged per portrait during each month. Use regression to estimate an equation for predicting the current month's sales from last month's sales and the current month's price.

a. If the price of a portrait during month 21 is $30, predict month 21 sales.

b. Discuss how you can tell whether autocorrelation, multicollinearity, or heteroscedasticity might be a problem.

41. The file **P11_41.xlsx** contains data on a motel chain's revenue and advertising. Note that column C is simply column B "pushed down" a row.

a. If the goal is to get the best-fitting regression equation for Revenue, which of the Advertising variables should be used? Or is it better to use both?

b. Using the best-fitting equation from part **a**, make predictions for the motel chain's revenues during the next four quarters. Assume that advertising during each of the next four quarters is $50,000.

c. Does autocorrelation of the residuals from the best-fitting equation appear to be a problem?

42. The file **P11_42.xlsx** contains the quarterly revenues (in millions of dollars) of a utility company for several years. The goal is to use these data to build a multiple regression model that can be used to forecast future revenues.

a. Which variables should be included in the regression? Explain your rationale for including or excluding variables. (Look at a time series graph for clues.)

b. Interpret the coefficients of your final equation.

c. Make a forecast for revenues during the next quarter. Also, estimate the probability that revenue in the next quarter will be at least $150 million. (*Hint*: Use the standard error of prediction and the fact that the errors are approximately normally distributed.)

43. The belief that larger majorities for a president in a presidential election help the president's party increase its representation in the House and Senate is called the *coattail* effect. The file **P11_43.xlsx** lists the percentage by which each president since 1948 won the election and the number of seats in the House and Senate gained (or lost) during each election by the elected president's party. Are these data consistent with the idea of presidential coattails?

44. When potential workers apply for a job that requires extensive manual assembly of small intricate parts, they are initially given three different tests to measure their manual dexterity. The ones who are hired are then periodically given a performance rating on a 0 to 100 scale that combines their speed and accuracy in performing the required assembly operations. The file **P11_44.xlsx** lists the test scores and performance ratings for a randomly selected group of employees. It also lists their seniority (months with the company) at the time of the performance rating.

a. Look at a matrix of correlations. Can you say with certainty (based only on these correlations) that the R^2 value for the regression will be at least 35%? Why or why not?

b. Is there any evidence (from the correlation matrix) that multicollinearity will be a problem? Why or why not?

c. Run the regression of Performance Rating versus all four explanatory variables. List the equation, the value of R^2, and the value of s_e. Do all of the coefficients have the signs (negative or positive) you would expect? Briefly explain.

d. Referring to the equation in part c, if a worker (outside of the 80 in the sample) has 15 months of seniority and test scores of 57, 71, and 63, find a prediction and an approximate 95% prediction interval for this worker's Performance Rating score.

e. One of the t-values for the coefficients in part c is less than 1. Explain briefly why this occurred. Does it mean that this variable is not related to Performance Rating?

f. Arguably, the three test measures provide overlapping (or redundant) information. For the sake of parsimony (explaining "the most with the least"), it might be sensible to regress Performance Rating versus only two explanatory variables, Seniority and Average Test, where Average Test is the average of the three test scores—that is, Average Test = (Test1 + Test2 + Test3)/3. Run this regression and report the same measures as in part c: the equation itself, R^2, and s_e. Can you argue that this equation is just as good as the equation in part c? Explain briefly.

45. Nicklaus Electronics manufactures electronic components used in the computer and space industries. The annual rate of return on the market portfolio and the annual rate of return on Nicklaus Electronics stock for the last 36 months are listed in the file **P11_45.xlsx**. The company wants to calculate the *systematic risk* of its common stock. (It is systematic in the sense that it represents the part of the risk that Nicklaus shares with the market as a whole.) The rate of return Y_t in period t on a security is hypothesized to be related to the rate of return m_t on a market portfolio by the equation

$$Y_t = \alpha + \beta m_t + \varepsilon_t$$

Here, α is the risk-free rate of return, β is the security's systematic risk, and ε_t is an error term. Estimate the systematic risk of the common stock of Nicklaus Electronics. Would you say that Nicklaus stock is a risky investment? Why or why not?

46. The auditor of Kaefer Manufacturing uses regression analysis during the analytical review stage of the firm's annual audit. The regression analysis attempts to uncover relationships that exist between various account balances. Any such relationship is subsequently used as a preliminary test of the reasonableness of the reported account balances. The auditor wants to determine whether a relationship exists between the balance of accounts receivable at the end of the month and that month's sales. The file **P11_46.xlsx** contains data on these two accounts for the last 36 months. It also shows the sales levels two months before month 1.

a. Is there any statistical evidence to suggest a relationship between the monthly sales level and accounts receivable?

b. Referring to part a, would the relationship be described any better by including this month's sales and the previous month's sales (called *lagged sales*) in the equation for accounts receivable? What about adding the sales from more than a month ago to the equation? For this problem, why might it make accounting sense to include lagged sales variables in the equation? How do you interpret their coefficients?

c. During month 37, which is a fiscal year-end month, the sales were $1,800,000. The reported accounts receivable balance was $3,000,000. Does this reported amount seem consistent with past experience? Explain.

47. A company gives prospective managers four separate tests for judging their potential. For a sample of 30 managers, the test scores and the subsequent job effectiveness ratings (Rating) given one year later are listed in the file **P11_47.xlsx**.

a. Look at scatterplots and the table of correlations for these five variables. Does it appear that a multiple regression equation for Rating, with the test scores as explanatory variables, will be successful? Can you foresee any problems in obtaining accurate estimates of the individual regression coefficients?

b. Estimate the regression equation that includes all four test scores, and find 95% confidence intervals for the coefficients of the explanatory variables. How can you explain the negative coefficient of Test3, given that the correlation between Rating and Test3 is positive?

c. Can you reject the null hypothesis that these test scores, as a whole, have no predictive ability for job effectiveness at the 1% level? Why or why not?

d. If a new prospective manager has test scores of 83, 74, 65, and 77, what do you predict his job effectiveness rating will be in one year? What is the standard error of this prediction?

48. Confederate Express is attempting to determine how its monthly shipping costs depend on the number of units shipped during a month. The file **P11_48.xlsx** contains the number of units shipped and total shipping costs for the last 15 months.

a. Use regression to determine a relationship between units shipped and monthly shipping costs.

b. Plot the errors for the predictions in order of time sequence. Is there any unusual pattern?

c. You have now been told that there was a trucking strike during months 11 through 15, and you believe that this might have influenced shipping costs. How can the analysis in part **a** be modified to account for the effects of the strike? After accounting for the effects of the strike, does the unusual pattern in part **b** disappear?

49. The file **P11_49.xlsx** contains monthly data on fatal automobile crashes in the United States in each of eight three-hour intervals. Suppose you didn't have the data on the midnight to 3AM time interval. How well could multiple regression be used to predict the data for this interval? Which time intervals are most useful in this prediction? Is multicollinearity a problem?

Level B

50. You want to determine the variables that influence bus usage in major American cities. For several cities, the following data are listed in the file **P11_50.xlsx**:
- Bus travel (annual, in thousands of hours)
- Income (average per capita income)
- Population (in thousands)
- Land area (in square miles)

a. Use these data to fit the multiplicative equation

$$\text{BusTravel} = \alpha \text{Income}^{\beta_1} \text{Population}^{\beta_2} \text{LandArea}^{\beta_3}$$

b. Are all variables significant at the 5% level?
c. Interpret the estimated values of β_1, β_2, and β_3.

51. The file **P11_51.xlsx** contains data on managers at a large (fictional) corporation. The variables are Salary (current annual salary), Years Experience (years of experience in the industry), Years Here (years of experience with this company), and Mgt Level (current level in the company, coded 1 to 4). You want to regress Salary on the potential explanatory variables. What is the best way to do so? Specifically, how should you handle Mgt Level? Should you include both Years Experience and Years Here or only one of them, and if only one, which one? Present your results, and explain them and your reasoning behind them.

52. A toy company has assigned you to analyze the factors influencing the sales of its most popular doll. The number of these dolls sold during the last 23 years is given in the file **P11_52.xlsx**. The following factors are thought to influence sales of these dolls:
- Was there a recession?
- Were the dolls on sale at Christmas?
- Was there an upward trend over time?

a. Determine an equation that can be used to predict annual sales of these dolls. Make sure that all variables in your equation are significant at the 10% level.
b. Interpret the coefficients in your equation.
c. Are there any outliers?
d. Is heteroscedasticity or autocorrelation of residuals a problem?

e. During the current year (year 24), a recession is predicted and the dolls will be put on sale at Christmas. There is a 1% chance that sales of the dolls will exceed what value? You can assume here that heteroscedasticity and autocorrelation are *not* a problem. (*Hint*: Use the standard error of prediction and the fact that the errors are approximately normally distributed.)

53. The file **P11_53.xlsx** shows the "yield curve" (at monthly intervals). For example, in January 1985 the annual rate on a three-month T-bill was 7.76% and the annual rate on a 30-year government bond was 11.45%. Use regression to determine which interest rates tend to move together most closely.

54. The file **P03_63.xlsx** contains 2009 data on R&D expenses and many financial variables for 85 U.S. publicly traded companies in the computer and electronic product manufacturing industry. The question is whether R&D expenses can be predicted from any combination of the potential variables. Use scatterplots, correlations (possibly on nonlinear transformations of variables) to search for promising relationships. Eventually, find a regression that seems to provide the best explanatory power for R&D expenses. Interpret this best equation and indicate how good a fit it provides.

55. The June 1997 issue of *Management Accounting* gave the following rule for predicting your current salary if you are a managerial accountant. Take $31,865. Next, add $20,811 if you are top management, add $3604 if you are senior management, or subtract $11,419 if you are entry management. Then add $1105 for every year you have been a managerial accountant. Add $7600 if you have a master's degree or subtract $12,467 if you have no college degree. Add 11,257 if you have a professional certification. Finally, add $8667 if you are male.

a. How do you think the journal derived this method of predicting an accountant's current salary? Be specific.
b. How could a managerial accountant use this information to determine whether he or she is significantly underpaid?

56. A business school committee was charged with studying admissions criteria to the school. Until that time, only juniors were admitted. Part of the committee's task was to see whether freshman courses would be equally good predictors of success as freshman and sophomore courses combined. Here, we take "success" to mean doing well in I-core (the integrated core, a combination of the junior level finance, marketing, and operations courses, F301, M301, and P301). The file **P11_56.xlsx** contains data on 250 students who had just completed I-core. For each student, the file lists their grades in the following courses:
- M118 (freshman)—finite math
- M119 (freshman)—calculus
- K201 (freshman)—computers
- W131 (freshman)—writing

- E201, E202 (sophomore)—micro- and macroeconomics
- L201 (sophomore)—business law
- A201, A202 (sophomore)—accounting
- E270 (sophomore)—statistics
- Core (junior)—finance, marketing, and operations

Except for Core, each value is a grade point for a specific course (such as 3.7 for an A−). For Core, each value is the average grade point for the three courses comprising Core.

a. The Core grade point is the eventual dependent variable in a regression analysis. Look at the correlations between all variables. Is multicollinearity likely to be a problem? Why or why not?

b. Run a multiple regression using all of the potential explanatory variables. Now, eliminate the variables as follows. (This is a reasonable variation of the procedures discussed in the chapter.) Look at 95% confidence intervals for their coefficients (as usual, not counting the intercept term). Any variable whose confidence interval contains the value zero is a candidate for exclusion. For all such candidates, eliminate the variable with the t-value lowest in magnitude. Then rerun the regression, and use the same procedure to possibly exclude another variable. Keep doing this until 95% confidence intervals of the coefficients of all remaining variables do *not* include zero. Report this final equation, its R^2 value, and its standard error of estimate s_e.

c. Give a quick summary of the properties of the final equation in part **b**. Specifically, (1) do the variables have the "correct" signs, (2) which courses tend to be the best predictors, (3) are the predictions from this equation likely to be much good, and (4) are there any obvious violations of the regression assumptions?

d. Redo part **b**, but now use as your potential explanatory variables only courses taken in the freshman year. As in part **b**, report the final equation, its R^2, and its standard error of estimate s_e.

e. Briefly, do you think there is enough predictive power in the freshman courses, relative to the freshman and sophomore courses combined, to change to a sophomore admit policy? (Answer only on the basis of the regression results; don't get into other merits of the argument.)

57. The file **P11_57.xlsx** has (somewhat old) data on several countries. The variables are listed here.

- Country: name of country
- GNP per Capita: GNP per capita
- Population Growth: average annual percentage change in population, 1980–1990
- Calories: daily per capita calorie content of food used for domestic consumption
- Life Expectancy: average life expectancy of newborns given current mortality conditions
- Fertility: births per woman given current fertility rates

With data such as these, cause and effect are difficult to determine. For example, does low Life Expectancy cause GNP per Capita to be low, or vice versa? Therefore, the purpose of this problem is to experiment with the following sets of dependent and explanatory variables. In each case, look at scatterplots (and use economic reasoning) to find and estimate the best form of the equation, using only linear and logarithmic variables. Then interpret precisely what each equation is saying.

a. Dependent: Life Expectancy; Explanatories: Calories, Fertility

b. Dependent: Life Expectancy; Explanatories: GNP per Capita, Population Growth

c. Dependent: GNP per Capita; Explanatories: Population Growth, Calories, Fertility

58. Suppose an economist has been able to gather data on the relationship between demand and price for a particular product. After analyzing scatterplots and using economic theory, the economist decides to estimate an equation of the form $Q = aP^b$, where Q is quantity demanded and P is price. An appropriate regression analysis is then performed, and the estimated parameters turn out to be $a = 1000$ and $b = -1.3$. Now consider two scenarios: (1) the price increases from $10 to $12.50; (2) the price increases from $20 to $25.

a. Do you predict the percentage decrease in demand to be the same in scenario 1 as in scenario 2? Why or why not?

b. What is the predicted percentage decrease in demand in scenario 1? What about scenario 2? Be as exact as possible. (*Hint:* Remember from economics that an elasticity shows directly what happens for a "small" percentage change in price. These changes aren't that small, so you'll have to do some calculating.)

59. A human resources analyst believes that in a particular industry, the wage rate ($/hr) is related to seniority by an equation of the form $W = ae^{bS}$, where W equals wage rate and S equals seniority (in years). However, the analyst suspects that both parameters, a and b, might depend on whether the workers belong to a union. Therefore, the analyst gathers data on a number of workers, both union and nonunion, and estimates the following equation with regression:

$$\ln(W) = 2.14 + 0.027S + 0.12U + 0.006SU$$

Here $\ln(W)$ is the natural log of W, U is 1 for union workers and 0 for nonunion workers, and SU is the product of S and U.

a. According to this model, what is the predicted wage rate for a nonunion worker with 0 years of seniority? What is it for a union worker with 0 years of seniority?

b. Explain exactly what this equation implies about the predicted effect of seniority on wage rate for a nonunion worker and for a union worker.

60. A company has recorded its overhead costs, machine hours, and labor hours for the past 60 months. The data

are in the file **P11_60.xlsx**. The company decides to use regression to explain its overhead hours linearly as a function of machine hours and labor hours. However, recognizing good statistical practice, it decides to estimate a regression equation for the first 36 months and then validate this regression with the data from the last 24 months. That is, it will substitute the values of machine and labor hours from the last 24 months into the regression equation that is based on the first 36 months and see how well it does.

a. Run the regression for the first 36 months. Explain briefly why the coefficient of labor hours is not significant.

b. For this part, use the regression equation from part **a** with both variables still in the equation (even though one was insignificant). Fill in the fitted and residual columns for months 37 through 60. Then do relevant calculations to see whether the R^2 (or multiple R) and the standard error of estimate s_e are as good for these 24 months as they are for the first 36 months. Explain your results briefly. (*Hint*: Remember the meaning of the multiple R and the standard error of estimate.)

61. Pernavik Dairy produces and sells a wide range of dairy products. Because most of the dairy's costs and prices are set by a government regulatory board, most of the competition between the dairy and its competitors takes place through advertising. The controller of Pernavik has developed the sales and advertising levels for the last 52 weeks. These appear in the file **P11_61.xlsx**. Note that the advertising levels for the three weeks prior to week 1 are also listed. The controller wonders whether Pernavik is spending too much money on advertising. He argues that the company's contribution-margin ratio is about 10%. That is, 10% of each sales dollar goes toward covering fixed costs. This means that each advertising dollar has to generate at least $10 of sales or the advertising is not cost-effective. Use regression to determine whether advertising dollars are generating this type of sales response. (*Hint*: It is very possible that the sales value in any week is affected not only by advertising this week, but also by advertising levels in the past one, two, or three weeks. These are called *lagged* values of advertising. Try regression models with lagged values of advertising included, and see whether you get better results.)

62. Pierce Company manufactures drill bits. The production of the drill bits occurs in lots of 1000 units. Due to the intense competition in the industry and the correspondingly low prices, Pierce has undertaken a study of the manufacturing costs of each of the products it manufactures. One part of this study concerns the overhead costs associated with producing the drill bits. Senior production personnel have determined that the number of lots produced, the direct labor hours used,

and the number of production runs per month might help to explain the behavior of overhead costs. The file **P11_62.xlsx** contains the data on these variables for the past 36 months.

a. How well can you can predict overhead costs on the basis of these variables with a linear regression equation? Why might you be disappointed with the results?

b. A production supervisor believes that labor hours and the number of production run setups affect overhead because Pierce uses a lot of supplies when it is working on the machines and because the machine setup time for each run is charged to overhead. As he says, "When the rate of production increases, we use overtime until we can train the additional people that we require for the machines. When the rate of production falls, we incur idle time until the surplus workers are transferred to other parts of the plant. So it would seem to me that there will be an additional overhead cost whenever the level of production changes. I would also say that because of the nature of this rescheduling process, the bigger the change in production, the greater the effect of the change in production on the increase in overhead." How might you use this information to find a better regression equation than in part **a**? (*Hint*: Develop a new explanatory variable, and assume that the number of lots produced in the month preceding month 1 was 5964.)

63. Danielson Electronics manufactures color television sets for sale in a highly competitive marketplace. Recently Ron Thomas, the marketing manager of Danielson Electronics, has been complaining that the company is losing market share because of a poor-quality image, and he has asked that the company's major product, the 25-inch console model, be redesigned to incorporate a higher quality level. The company general manager, Steve Hatting, is considering the request to improve the product quality but is not convinced that consumers will be willing to pay the additional expense for improved quality. As the company controller, you are in charge of determining the cost-effectiveness of improving the quality of the television sets. With the help of the marketing staff, you have obtained a summary of the average retail price of the company's television set and the prices of 29 competitive sets. In addition, you have obtained from *The Shoppers' Guide*, a magazine that evaluates and reports on various consumer products, a quality rating of the television sets produced by Danielson Electronics and its competitors. The file **P11_63 .xlsx** summarizes these data. According to *The Shoppers' Guide*, the quality rating, which varies from 0 to 10 (10 being the highest level of quality), considers such factors as the quality of the picture, the frequency of repair, and the cost of repairs. Discussions with the product design group suggest that the cost of

manufacturing this type of television set is $125 + Q^2$, where Q is the quality rating.

a. Regress Average Price versus Quality Rating. Does the regression equation imply that customers are willing to pay a premium for quality? Explain.

b. Given the results from part **a**, is there a preferred level of quality for this product? Assume that the quality level will affect only the price charged and not the level of sales of the product.

c. How might you answer part b if the level of sales is also affected by the quality level (or alternatively, if the level of sales is affected by price)?

64. The file **P11_64.xlsx** contains data on gasoline consumption and several economic variables. The variables are gasoline consumption for passenger cars (Gas Used), service station price excluding taxes (Station Price), retail price of gasoline including state and federal taxes (Retail Price), Consumer Price Index for all items (CPI), Consumer Price Index for public transportation (CPIT), number of registered passenger cars (Cars), average miles traveled per gallon (MPG), and real per capita disposable income (Income).

a. Regress Gas Used linearly versus CPIT, Cars, MPG, Income, and Deflated Price, where Deflated Price is the deflated retail price of gasoline (Retail Price divided by CPI). What signs would you expect the coefficients to have? Do they have these signs? Which of the coefficients are statistically significant at the 5% significance level?

b. Suppose the government makes the claim that for every one cent of tax on gasoline, there will be a $1 billion increase in tax revenue. Use the estimated equation in part **a** to support or refute the government's claim.

65. On October 30, 1995, the citizens of Quebec went to the polls to decide the future of their province. They were asked to vote "Yes" or "No" on whether Quebec, a predominantly French-speaking province, should secede from Canada and become a sovereign country. The "No" side was declared the winner, but only by a thin margin. Immediately following the vote, however, allegations began to surface that the result was closer than it should have been. [Source: Cawley and Sommers (1996)]. In particular, the ruling separatist Parti Québécois, whose job was to decide which ballots were rejected, was accused by the "No" voters of systematic electoral fraud by voiding thousands of "No" votes in the predominantly allophone and anglophone electoral divisions of Montreal. (An *allophone* refers to someone whose first language is neither English nor French. An *anglophone* refers to someone whose first language is English.) Cawley and Sommers examined whether electoral fraud had been committed by running a regression, using data from the 125 electoral divisions in the October 1995 referendum. The dependent variable was REJECT, the percentage of rejected ballots in the electoral division. The explanatory variables were as follows:

- ALLOPHONE: percentage of allophones in the electoral division
- ANGLOPHONE: percentage of anglophones in the electoral division
- REJECT94: percentage of rejected votes from that electoral division during a similar referendum in 1994
- LAVAL: dummy variable equal to 1 for electoral divisions in the Laval region, 0 otherwise
- LAV_ALL: interaction (i.e., product) of LAVAL and ALLOPHONE

The estimated regression equation (with t-values in parentheses) is

$$\text{Prediced REJECT} = \underset{(5.68)}{1.112} + \underset{(4.34)}{0.020}\,\text{ALLOPHONE}$$

$$+ \underset{(0.12)}{0.001}\,\text{ANGLOPHONE} + \underset{(2.64)}{0.223}\,\text{REJECT94}$$

$$- \underset{(-8.61)}{3.773}\,\text{LAVAL} + \underset{(15.62)}{0.387}\,\text{LAV\_ALL}$$

The R^2 value was 0.759. Based on this analysis, Cawley and Sommers state that, "The evidence presented here suggests that there were voting irregularities in the October 1995 Quebec referendum, especially in Laval." Discuss how they came to this conclusion.

66. Suppose you are trying to explain variations in salaries for technicians in a particular field of work. The file **P11_66.xlsx** contains annual salaries for 200 technicians. It also shows how many years of experience each technician has, as well as his or her education level. There are four education levels, as explained in the comment in cell D1. Three suggestions are put forth for the relationship between Salary and these two explanatory variables:

- You should regress Salary linearly versus the two given variables, Experience and Education.
- All that really matters in terms of education is whether the person got a college degree or not. Therefore, you should regress Salary linearly versus Experience and a dummy variable indicating whether he or she got a college degree.
- Each level of education might result in different jumps in salary. Therefore, you should regress Salary linearly versus Experience and dummy variables for the different education levels.

a. Run the indicated regressions for each of these three suggestions. Then (1) explain what each equation is saying and how the three are different (focus here on the coefficients), (2) which you prefer, and (3) whether (or how) the regression results in your preferred equation contradict the average salary results shown in the Pivot Table sheet of the file.

b. Consider the four workers shown on the Prediction sheet of the file. (These are four new workers, not among the original 200.) Using your preferred equation, calculate a predicted salary and a 95% prediction interval for each of these four workers.

c. It turns out (you don't have to check this) that the interaction between years of experience and education level is *not* significant for this data set. In general, however, argue why you might expect an interaction between them for salary data of technical workers. What form of interaction would you suspect? (There is not necessarily one right answer, but argue convincingly one way or the other for a positive or a negative interaction.)

67. The file **P03_55.xlsx** contains baseball data on all MLB teams from during the years 2004–2011. For each year and team, the total salary and the number of (regular-season) wins are listed.

a. Rearrange the data so that there are six columns: Team, Year, Salary Last Year, Salary This Year, Wins Last Year, and Wins This Year. You don't need rows for 2004 rows, because the data for 2003 isn't available for Salary Last Year and Wins Last Year. Your ending data set should have 7*30 rows of data.

b. Run a multiple regression for Wins This Year versus the other variables (besides Team). Then run a forward stepwise regression with these same variables. Compare the two equations, and explain exactly what the coefficients of the equation from the forward method imply about wins.

c. The Year variable *should* be insignificant. Is it? Why would it be contradictory for the "true" coefficient of Year to be anything other than zero?

d. Statistical inference from regression equations is all about inferring from the given data to a larger population. Does it make sense to talk about a larger population in this situation? If so, what is the larger population?

68. Do the previous problem, but use the basketball data on all NBA teams in the file **P03_56.xlsx**.

69. Do the previous problem, but use the football data on all NFL teams in the file **P03_57.xlsx**.

70. The file **P03_65.xlsx** contains basketball data on all NBA teams for five seasons. The SRS (simple rating system) variable is a measure of how good a team is in any given year. (It is explained in more detail in the comment in cell F3.)

a. Given the explanation of SRS, it makes sense to use multiple regression, with PTS and O_PTS as the explanatory variables, to predict SRS. Do you get a good fit?

b. Suppose instead that the goal is to predict Wins. Try multiple regression, using the variables in columns G–AH or variables calculated from them. For example, instead of FG and FGA, you could try FG/FGA, the fraction of attempted field goals made. You will have to guard against exact multicollinearity. For example, PTS can be calculated exactly from FG, 3P, and FT. This is a good time to use some form of stepwise regression. How well is your best equation able to predict Wins?

71. Do the preceding problem, but now use the football data in the file **P03_66.xlsx**. (This file contains offensive and defensive ratings in the OSRS and DSRS variables, but you can ignore them for this problem. Focus only on the SRS rating in part **a**.)

CASE 11.1 Heating Oil at Dupree Fuels[6]

Dupree Fuels is facing a difficult problem. Dupree sells heating oil to residential customers. Given the amount of competition in the industry, both from other home heating oil suppliers and from electric and natural gas utilities, the price of the oil supplied and the level of service are critical in determining a company's success. Unlike electric and natural gas customers, oil customers are exposed to the risk of running out of fuel. Home heating oil suppliers therefore have to guarantee that the customer's oil tank will not be allowed to run dry. In fact, Dupree's service pledge is, "50 free gallons on us if we let you run dry." Beyond the cost of the oil, however, Dupree is concerned about the perceived reliability of his service if a customer is allowed to run out of oil.

To estimate customer oil use, the home heating oil industry uses the concept of a *degree-day*, equal to the difference between the average daily temperature and 68 degrees Fahrenheit. So if the average temperature on a given day is 50, the degree-days for that day will be 18. (If the degree-day calculation results in a negative number, the degree-day number is recorded as 0.) By keeping track of the number of degree-days since the customer's last oil fill, knowing the size of the customer's oil tank, and estimating the customer's oil consumption as a function of the number of degree-days, the oil supplier can estimate when the customer is getting low on fuel and then resupply the customer.

Dupree has used this scheme in the past but is disappointed with the results and the computational burdens it places on the company. First, the system requires that a consumption-per-degree-day figure be estimated for each customer to reflect that customer's consumption habits, size of home, quality of home insulation, and family size.

6 Cases 11.1 through 11.3 are based on problems from *Advanced Management Accounting*, 2nd edition, by Robert S. Kaplan and Anthony A. Atkinson, 1989, Upper Saddle River, NJ: Prentice Hall. We thank them for allowing us to adapt their problems.

Because Dupree has more than 1500 customers, the computational burden of keeping track of all of these customers is enormous. Second, the system is crude and unreliable. The consumption per degree-day for each customer is computed by dividing the oil consumption during the preceding year by the degree-days during the preceding year. Customers have tended to use less fuel than estimated during the colder months and more fuel than estimated during the warmer months. This means that Dupree is making more deliveries than necessary during the colder months and customers are running out of oil during the warmer months.

Dupree wants to develop a consumption estimation model that is practical and more reliable. The following data are available in the file **C11_01.xlsx**:

- The number of degree-days since the last oil fill and the consumption amounts for 40 customers.
- The number of people residing in the homes of each of the 40 customers. Dupree thinks that this might be important

in predicting the oil consumption of customers using oil-fired water heaters because it provides an estimate of the hot-water requirements of each customer. Each of the customers in this sample uses an oil-fired water heater.

- An assessment, provided by Dupree sales staff, of the home type of each of these 40 customers. The home type classification, which is a number between 1 and 5, is a composite index of the home size, age, exposure to wind, level of insulation, and furnace type. A low index implies a lower oil consumption per degree-day, and a high index implies a higher consumption of oil per degree-day. Dupree thinks that the use of such an index will allow them to estimate a consumption model based on a sample data set and then to apply the same model to predict the oil demand of each of his customers.

Use regression to see whether a statistically reliable oil consumption model can be estimated from the data.

CASE 11.2 Developing a Flexible Budget at the Gunderson Plant

The Gunderson Plant manufactures the industrial product line of FGT Industries. Plant management wants to be able to get a good, yet quick, estimate of the manufacturing overhead costs that can be expected each month. The easiest and simplest method to accomplish this task is to develop a flexible budget formula for the manufacturing overhead costs. The plant's accounting staff has suggested that simple linear regression be used to determine the behavior pattern of the overhead costs. The regression data can provide the basis for the flexible budget formula. Sufficient evidence is available to conclude that manufacturing overhead costs vary with direct labor hours. The actual direct labor hours and the corresponding manufacturing overhead costs for each month of the last three years have been used in the linear regression analysis.

The three-year period contained various occurrences not uncommon to many businesses. During the first year, production was severely curtailed during two months due to wildcat strikes. In the second year, production was reduced in one month because of material shortages, and increased significantly (scheduled overtime) during two months to meet the units required for a one-time sales order. At the end of the second year, employee benefits were raised significantly as the result of a labor agreement. Production during the third year was not affected by any special circumstances. Various members of Gunderson's accounting staff raised some issues regarding the historical data collected for the regression analysis. These issues were as follows.

- Some members of the accounting staff believed that the use of data from all 36 months would provide a more accurate portrayal of the cost behavior. While they recognized that any of the monthly data could include

efficiencies and inefficiencies, they believed these efficiencies and inefficiencies would tend to balance out over a longer period of time.
- Other members of the accounting staff suggested that only those months that were considered normal should be used so that the regression would not be distorted.
- Still other members felt that only the most recent 12 months should be used because they were the most current.
- Some members questioned whether historical data should be used at all to form the basis for a flexible budget formula.

The accounting department ran two regression analyses of the data—one using the data from all 36 months and the other using only the data from the last 12 months. The information derived from the two linear regressions is shown below (t-values shown in parentheses). The 36-month regression is

$$OH_t = 123,810 + 1.60 \, DLH_t, \qquad R^2 = 0.32$$
$$(1.64)$$

The 12-month regression is

$$OH_t = 109,020 + 3.00 \, DLH_t, \qquad R^2 = 0.48$$
$$(3.01)$$

Questions

1. Which of the two results (12 months versus 36 months) would you use as a basis for the flexible budget formula?
2. How would the four specific issues raised by the members of Gunderson's accounting staff influence your willingness to use the results of the statistical analyses as the basis for the flexible budget formula? Explain your answer.

CASE 11.3 Forecasting Overhead at Wagner Printers

Wagner Printers performs all types of printing, including custom work, such as advertising displays, and standard work, such as business cards. Market prices exist for standard work, and Wagner Printers must match or better these prices to get the business. The key issue is whether the existing market price covers the cost associated with doing the work. On the other hand, most of the custom work must be priced individually. Because all custom work is done on a job-order basis, Wagner routinely keeps track of all the direct labor and direct materials costs associated with each job. However, the overhead for each job must be estimated. The overhead is applied to each job using a predetermined (normalized) rate based on estimated overhead and labor hours. Once the cost of the prospective job is determined, the sales manager develops a bid that reflects both the existing market conditions and the estimated price of completing the job.

In the past, the normalized rate for overhead has been computed by using the historical average of overhead per direct labor hour. Wagner has become increasingly concerned about this practice for two reasons. First, it hasn't produced accurate forecasts of overhead in the past. Second, technology has changed the printing process, so that the labor

content of jobs has been decreasing, and the normalized rate of overhead per direct labor hour has steadily been increasing. The file **C11_03.xlsx** shows the overhead data that Wagner has collected for its shop for the past 52 weeks. The average weekly overhead for the last 52 weeks is $54,208, and the average weekly number of labor hours worked is 716. Therefore, the normalized rate for overhead that will be used in the upcoming week is about $76 (=54208/716) per direct labor hour.

Questions

1. Determine whether you can develop a more accurate estimate of overhead costs.
2. Wagner is now preparing a bid for an important order that may involve a considerable amount of repeat business. The estimated requirements for this project are 15 labor hours, 8 machine hours, $150 direct labor cost, and $750 direct material cost. Using the existing approach to cost estimation, Wagner has estimated the cost for this job as $2040(= 150 + 750 + (76 × 15)). Given the existing data, what cost would you estimate for this job?

CHAPTER 12
Time Series Analysis and Forecasting

Monkey Business Images/Shutterstock.com

REVENUE MANAGEMENT AT HARRAH'S CHEROKEE CASINO & HOTEL

Real applications of forecasting are almost never done in isolation. They are typically one part—a crucial part—of an overall quantitative solution to a business problem. This is certainly the case at Harrah's Cherokee Casino & Hotel in North Carolina, as explained in an article by Metters et al. (2008). This casino uses revenue management (RM) on a daily basis to increase its revenue from its gambling customers. As customers call to request reservations at the casino's hotel, the essential problem is to decide which reservations to accept and which to deny. The idea is that there is an opportunity cost from accepting early requests from lower-valued customers because higher-valued customers might request the same rooms later on.

As the article explains, there are several unique features about casinos, and this casino in particular, that make a quantitative approach to RM successful. First, the detailed behaviors of customers can be tracked, via electronic cards they use while placing bets in the electronic gambling machines, so that the casino can create a large database of individual customers' gambling patterns. This allows the casino to segment the customers into different groups, based on how much they typically bet in a given night. For example, one segment might contain all customers who bet between $500 and $600 per night. When a customer calls for a room reservation and provides his card number, the casino can immediately look up his information in the database and see which segment he is in.

A second reason for the successful use of RM is that customers differ substantially in the price they are willing to pay for the same commodity, in this case a stay at the casino's hotel. Actually, many don't pay anything for the room or the food—these are frequently complimentary from the casino—but they pay by losing money at gambling. Some customers typically gamble thousands of dollars per night while others gamble much less. (This is quite different from the disparities in other hotels or in air travel, where a business traveler might pay twice as much as a vacationer, but not much more.) Because some customers are much more valuable than others, there are significant opportunity costs from treating all customers alike.

A third reason for the success of RM at this casino is that the casino can afford to hold out for the best-paying customers until the last minute. The reason is that a significant percentage of the customers from all segments wait until the last minute to make their reservations. In fact, they often make them while driving, say, from Atlanta to the casino. Therefore, the casino can afford to deny requests for reservations to lower-valued customers made a day or two in advance, knowing that last-minute reservations, very possibly from higher-valued customers, will fill up the casino's rooms. Indeed, the occupancy rate is virtually always 98% or above.

The overall RM solution includes (1) data collection and customer segmentation, as explained above, (2) forecasting demand for reservations from each customer segment, (3) a linear programming (LP) optimization model that is run frequently to decide which reservations to accept, and (4) a customer relationship management model to entice loyal customers to book rooms on nights with lower demand. The forecasting model is very similar to the Winters' exponential smoothing model discussed in this chapter. Specifically, the model uses the large volume of historical data to forecast customer demand by each customer segment for any particular night in the future. These forecasts include information about time-related or seasonal patterns (weekends are busier, for example) and any special events that are scheduled. Also, the forecasts are updated daily as the night in question approaches. These forecasts are then used in an LP optimization model to determine which requests to approve. For example, the LP model might indicate that, given the current status of bookings and three nights to go, requests for rooms on the specified night should be accepted only for the four most valuable customer segments. As the given night approaches and the number of booked rooms changes, the LP model is rerun many times and provides staff with the necessary information for real-time decisions. (By the way, a customer who is refused a room at the casino is often given a free room at another nearby hotel. This customer can still be valuable enough to offset the price of the room at the other hotel.)

It is difficult to measure the effect of this entire RM system because it has always been in place since the casino opened. But there is no doubt that it is effective. Despite the fact that it serves no alcohol and has only electronic games, not the traditional gaming tables, the casino has nearly full occupancy and returns a 60% profit margin on gross revenue—double the industry norm.

12-1 Introduction

Many decision-making applications depend on a forecast of some quantity. Here are several examples.

- When a service organization, such as a fast-food restaurant, plans its staffing over some time period, it must forecast the customer demand as a function of time. This might be done at a very detailed level, such as the demand in successive 15-minute periods, or at a more aggregate level, such as the demand in successive weeks.
- When a company plans its ordering or production schedule for a product it sells to the public, it must forecast the customer demand for this product so that it can stock appropriate quantities—neither too many nor too few.
- When an organization plans to invest in stocks, bonds, or other financial instruments, it typically attempts to forecast movements in stock prices and interest rates.
- When government officials plan policy, they attempt to forecast movements in macroeconomic variables such as inflation, interest rates, and unemployment.

Forecasting is a very difficult task, both in the short run and in the long run. Typically, forecasts are based on historical data. Analysts search for patterns or relationships in the historical data, and then make forecasts. There are two problems with this approach. The first is that it is not always easy to uncover historical patterns or relationships. In particular, it is often difficult to separate the noise, or random behavior, from the underlying patterns. Some forecasts can even overdo it, by attributing importance to patterns that are in fact random variations and are unlikely to repeat themselves.

The second problem is that there are no guarantees that past patterns will continue in the future. A new war could break out somewhere in the world, a company's competitor could introduce a new product into the market, the bottom could fall out of the stock market, and so on. Each of these shocks to the system being studied could drastically alter the future in a highly unpredictable way. This partly explains why forecasts are almost always wrong. Unless they have inside information to the contrary, analysts will typically assume that history will repeat itself. But we all know that history does *not* always repeat itself. Therefore, there are many famous forecasts that turned out to be way off the mark, even though the analysts made reasonable assumptions and used standard forecasting techniques. Nevertheless, forecasts are required throughout the business world, so the methods discussed in this chapter find frequent use.

12-2 Forecasting Methods: An Overview

There are many forecasting methods available, and all practitioners have their favorites. To say the least, there is little agreement among practitioners or academics as to the best forecasting method. The methods can generally be divided into three groups: (1) *judgmental* methods, (2) *extrapolation* (or *time series*) methods, and (3) *econometric* (or *causal*) methods. The first of these is basically nonquantitative and will not be discussed here; the last two are quantitative. In this section we describe extrapolation and econometric methods in some generality. In the rest of the chapter, we go into more detail, particularly about the extrapolation methods.

12-2a Extrapolation Models

Extrapolation models are quantitative models that use past data of a time series variable—and nothing else, except possibly time itself—to forecast future values of the variable. The idea is that past movements of a variable, such as a company's sales or U.S. exports to Japan, can be used to forecast future values of the variable. Many extrapolation models are available, including trend-based regression, autoregression, moving averages, and exponential smoothing. Some of these models are relatively simple, both conceptually and in terms of the calculations required, whereas others are quite complex. Also, as the names imply, some of these models use the same regression methods from the previous two chapters, whereas others do not.

All of these extrapolation models search for *patterns* in the historical series and then extrapolate these patterns into the future. Some try to track long-term upward or downward trends and then project these. Some try to track the seasonal patterns (such as sales up in November and December, down in other months) and then project these. Basically, the more complex the model, the more closely it tries to track historical patterns. Researchers have long believed that good forecasting models should be able to track the ups and downs—the zigzags on a graph—of a time series. This has led to voluminous research and increasingly complex methods. But is complexity always better?

Surprisingly, empirical evidence shows that complexity is *not* always better. This is documented in a quarter-century review article by Armstrong (1986) and an article by Schnarrs and Bavuso (1986). (Admittedly, these reviews are old, but similar reviews done today would probably find similar results.) They document a number of empirical studies on literally thousands of time series forecasts where complex models fared no better, and sometimes even worse, than simple models. In fact, the Schnarrs and Bavuso article presents evidence that a naive forecast from a "random walk" model sometimes outperforms all of the more sophisticated extrapolation models. This naive model forecasts that next period's value will be the same as this period's value. So if today's closing stock price is 51.375, it forecasts that tomorrow's closing stock price will be 51.375. This model is certainly simple, and it sometimes works quite well. We discuss random walks in more detail in Section 12-5.

The evidence in favor of simpler models is not accepted by everyone, particularly not those who have spent years investigating complex models, and complex models continue to be studied and used. However, there is a very plausible reason why simple models can provide reasonably good forecasts. The whole goal of extrapolation models is to extrapolate historical patterns into the future. But it is often difficult to determine which patterns are real and which represent noise—random ups and downs that are not likely to repeat themselves. Also, if something important changes (a competitor introduces a new product or there is an oil embargo, for example), it is certainly possible that historical patterns will change. A potential problem with complex models is that they can track a historical series *too* closely. That is, they sometimes track patterns that are really noise. Simpler models, on the other hand, track only the most basic underlying patterns and therefore can be more flexible and accurate in forecasting the future.

12-2b Econometric Models

Econometric models, also called causal or regression-based models, use regression to forecast a time series variable by using other explanatory time series variables. For example, a company might use a causal model to regress future sales on its advertising level, the population income level, the interest rate, and possibly others. In one sense, regression analysis involving time series variables is similar to the regression analysis discussed in the previous two chapters. The same least squares approach and the same multiple regression software can be used in many time series regression models.

However, causal regression models for time series data present mathematical challenges that go well beyond the level of this book. To get a glimpse of the potential difficulties, suppose a company wants to use a regression model to forecast its monthly sales for some product, using two other time series variables as predictors: its monthly advertising levels for the product and its main competitor's monthly advertising levels for a competing product. The resulting regression equation has the form

Prediction from Regression Equation

$$\text{Predicted } Y_t = a + b_1 X_{1t} + b_2 X_{2t} \qquad (12.1)$$

Here, Y_t is the company's sales in month t, and X_{1t} and X_{2t} are, respectively, the company's and the competitor's advertising levels in month t. This regression model might provide some useful results, but there are some issues that must be faced.

One issue is that the appropriate "lags" for the regression equation must be determined. Do sales this month depend only on advertising levels *this* month, as specified in Equation (12.1), or also on advertising levels in the previous month, the previous two months, and so on? A second issue is whether to include lags of the *sales* variable in the regression equation as explanatory variables. Presumably, sales in one month might depend on the level of sales in previous months (as well as on advertising levels). A third issue is that the two advertising variables can be autocorrelated and cross-correlated. *Auto-correlation* means correlated with itself. For example, the company's advertising level in one month might depend on its advertising levels in previous months. *Cross-correlation* means being correlated with a lagged version of another variable. For example, the company's advertising level in one month might be related to the competitor's advertising levels in previous months, or the competitor's advertising in one month might be related to the company's advertising levels in previous months.

These are difficult issues, and the way in which they are addressed can make a big difference in the usefulness of the regression model. We will examine several regression-based models in this chapter, but we won't discuss situations such as the one just described, where one time series variable Y is regressed on one or more time series of X's.

12-2c Combining Forecasts

There is one other general forecasting method that is worth mentioning. In fact, it has attracted a lot of attention in recent years, and many researchers believe that it has potential for increasing forecast accuracy. The method is simple—it combines two or more forecasts to obtain the final forecast. The reasoning behind this method is also simple: The forecast errors from different forecasting methods might cancel one another. The forecasts that are combined can be of the same general type—extrapolation forecasts, for example—or they can be of different types, such as judgmental and extrapolation.

The *number* of forecasts to combine and the *weights* to use in combining them have been the subject of several research studies. Although the findings are not entirely consistent, it appears that the marginal benefit from each individual forecast after the first two or three is minor. Also, there is not much evidence to suggest that the simplest weighting scheme—weighting each forecast equally, that is, averaging them—is any less accurate than more complex weighting schemes.

12-2d Components of Time Series Data

In Chapter 2 we discussed time series graphs, a useful graphical way of displaying time series data. We now use these time series graphs to help explain and identify four important components of a time series. These components are called the *trend* component, the *seasonal* component, the *cyclic* component, and the *random* (or *noise*) component.

We start by looking at a very simple time series. This is a time series where every observation has the same value. Such a series is shown in Figure 12.1. The graph in this figure shows time (t) on the horizontal axis and the observed values (Y) on the vertical axis. We assume that Y is measured at regularly spaced intervals, usually days, weeks, months, quarters, or years, with Y_t being the value of the observation at time period t. As indicated in Figure 12.1, the individual observation points are usually joined by straight lines to make any patterns in the time series more apparent. Because all observations in this time series are equal, the resulting time series graph is a horizontal line. We refer to this time series as the *base* series. We will now illustrate more interesting time series built from this base series.

Figure 12.1 Base Series

If the observations increase or decrease regularly through time, we say that the time series has a **trend**. The graphs in Figure 12.2 illustrate several possible trends. The *linear* trend in Figure 12.2a occurs if a company's sales increase by the same amount from period to period. This constant per period change is then the slope of the linear trend line. The curve in Figure 12.2b is an *exponential* trend. It occurs in a business such as the personal computer business, where sales increased at a tremendous rate (at least during the 1990s, the boom years). For this type of curve, the *percentage* increase in Y_t from period to period remains constant. The curve in Figure 12.2c is an *S-shaped* trend. This type of trend is appropriate for a new product that takes a while to catch on, then exhibits a rapid increase in sales as the public becomes aware of it, and finally tapers off to a fairly constant level because of market saturation. The series in Figure 12.2 all represent *upward* trends. Of course, there are *downward* trends of the same types.

Figure 12.2 Series with Trends

(a) Linear trend (b) Exponential trend (c) S-shaped trend

Many time series have a seasonal component, that is, they exhibit **seasonality**. For example, a company's sales of swimming pool equipment increase every spring, then stay relatively high during the summer, and then drop off until next spring, at which time the yearly pattern repeats itself. An important aspect of the seasonal component is that the *same* seasonal pattern tends to repeat itself every year.

Figure 12.3 illustrates two possible seasonal patterns. In Figure 12.3a there is nothing but the seasonal component. That is, if there were no seasonal variation, the series would be the base series in Figure 12.1. Figure 12.3b illustrates a seasonal pattern superimposed on a linear trend line.

Figure 12.3 Series with Seasonality

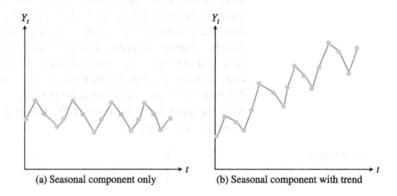

(a) Seasonal component only   (b) Seasonal component with trend

The third component of a time series is the **cyclic component**. By studying past movements of many business and economic variables, it becomes apparent that there are business cycles that affect many variables in similar ways. For example, during a recession housing sales generally go down, unemployment goes up, stock prices go down, and so on. But when the recession is over, these variables tend to move in the opposite direction. Unfortunately, the cyclic component is more difficult to predict than the seasonal component. The reason is that seasonal variation is much more regular, whereas cyclic variation tends to be irregular. For example, swimming pool supplies sales *always* start to increase during the spring. Cyclic variation, on the other hand, depends on the irregular length of the business cycle. A further distinction is that the length of a seasonal cycle is generally one year; the length of a business cycle is generally longer than one year and its actual length is difficult to predict.

The graphs in Figure 12.4 illustrate the cyclic component of a time series. In Figure 12.4a cyclic variation is superimposed on the base series in Figure 12.1. In Figure 12.4b this same cyclic variation is superimposed on the series in Figure 12.3b. The resulting graph has trend, seasonal variation, and cyclic variation.

Figure 12.4 Series with Cyclic Component

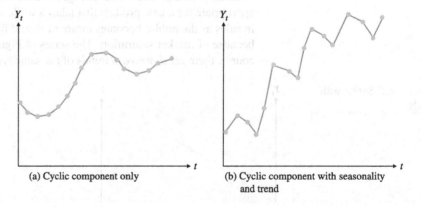

(a) Cyclic component only   (b) Cyclic component with seasonality and trend

The final component in a time series is called **random variation**, or simply **noise**. This unpredictable component gives most time series graphs their irregular, zigzag appearance.

Figure 12.5 Series with Noise

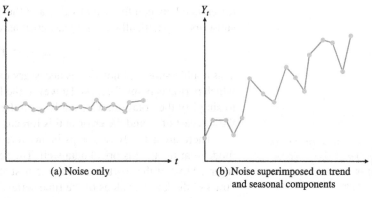

(a) Noise only

(b) Noise superimposed on trend and seasonal components

Figure 12.6 Series with More Noise

(a) Noise only

(b) Noise superimposed on trend and seasonal components

Usually, a time series can be determined only to a certain extent by its trend, seasonal, and cyclic components. Then other factors determine the rest. These other factors can be inherent randomness, unpredictable "shocks" to the system, the unpredictable behavior of human beings who interact with the system, and so on. These factors combine to create unpredictability in almost all time series.

Figures 12.5 and 12.6 show the effect that noise can have on a time series graph. The graph on the left of each figure shows the random component only, superimposed on the base series. Then on the right of each figure, the random component is superimposed on the trend-with-seasonal-component graph from Figure 12.3b. The difference between Figures 12.5 and 12.6 is the relative magnitude of the noise. When it is small, as in Figure 12.5, the other components emerge fairly clearly; they are not disguised by the noise. But if the noise is large in magnitude, as in Figure 12.6, the noise makes it very difficult to distinguish the other components.

12-2e Measures of Accuracy

We now introduce some notation and discuss aspects common to most forecasting methods. In general, Y denotes the variable of interest. Then Y_t denotes the observed value of Y at time t. Typically, the first observation (the most distant one) corresponds to period $t = 1$, and the last observation (the most recent one) corresponds to period $t = T$, where T denotes the number of historical observations of Y. The periods themselves might be days, weeks, months, quarters, years, or any other common unit of time.

Suppose that Y_{t-k} has just been observed and you want to make a "k-period-ahead" forecast; that is, you want to use the information through time $t - k$ to forecast Y_t. The resulting forecast is denoted by $F_{t-k,t}$. The first subscript indicates the period in which the forecast is made, and the second subscript indicates the period being forecast. As an example, if the data are monthly and September 2019 corresponds to $t = 67$, then a forecast of Y_{69}, the value in November 2019, would be labeled $F_{67,69}$. The **forecast error** is the difference between the actual value and the forecast. It is denoted by E with appropriate subscripts. Specifically, the forecast error associated with $F_{t-k,t}$ is

$$E_{t-k,t} = Y_t - F_{t-k,t}$$

This double-subscript notation is necessary to specify when the forecast is being made and which period is being forecast. However, the former is often clear from context. Therefore, to simplify the notation, we usually drop the first subscript and write F_t and E_t to denote the forecast of Y_t and the error in this forecast.

You first develop a model to fit the historical data. Then you use this model to forecast the future.

There are actually two steps in any forecasting procedure. The first step is to build a model that fits the historical data well. The second step is to use this model to forecast the future. Most of the work goes into the first step. For any trial model, you see how well it "tracks" the known values of the time series. Specifically, the one-period-ahead forecasts, F_t (or more precisely, $F_{t-1,t}$) are calculated from the model, and these are compared to the known values, Y_t, for each t in the historical time period. The goal is to find a model that produces small forecast errors, E_t. Presumably, if the model tracks the *historical* data well, it will also forecast *future* data well. Of course, there is no guarantee that this is true, but it is often a reasonable assumption.

A model that makes any one of these error measures small tends to make the other two small as well.

Forecasting software packages typically report several summary measures of the forecast errors. The most important of these are **MAE (mean absolute error)**, **RMSE (root mean square error)**, and **MAPE (mean absolute percentage error)**. These are defined in Equations (12.2), (12.3), and (12.4). Typically, models that make any one of these measures small tend to make the others small, so you can choose whichever measure you want to minimize. In the following formulas, N denotes the number of terms in each sum. This value is typically slightly less than T, the number of historical observations, because it is usually not possible to provide a forecast for each historical period.

Mean Absolute Error

$$MAE = \left(\sum_{t=1}^{N} |E_t| \right) \Big/ N \qquad (12.2)$$

Root Mean Square Error

$$RMSE = \sqrt{\left(\sum_{t=1}^{N} E_t^2 \right) \Big/ N} \qquad (12.3)$$

Mean Absolute Percentage Error

$$MAPE = 100\% \times \left(\sum_{t=1}^{N} |E_t/Y_t| \right) \Big/ N \qquad (12.4)$$

RMSE is similar to a standard deviation in that the errors are squared. Because of the square root, it is in the same units as those of the forecast variable. The MAE is similar to the RMSE, except that absolute values of errors are used instead of squared errors. The MAPE is probably the most easily understood measure because it does not depend on the units of the forecast variable; it is always stated as a percentage. For example, the statement that the forecasts are off on average by 2% has a clear meaning, even if you do not know the units of the variable being forecast.

Some forecasting software packages choose the best model from a given class (such as the best exponential smoothing model) by minimizing MAE, RMSE, or MAPE. However, small values of these measures guarantee only that the model tracks the *historical* observations well. There is still no guarantee that the model will forecast *future* values accurately.

One other measure of forecast errors is the *average* of the errors. Recall from the regression chapters that the residuals from any regression equation, which are analogous to forecast errors, always average to zero. This is a mathematical property of the least-squares method. However, there is no such guarantee for forecasting errors based on non-regression methods. For example, it is very possible that most of the forecast errors, and the corresponding average, are *negative*. This would imply a *bias*, where the forecasts tend to be too high. Or the average of the forecast errors could be *positive*, in which case the forecasts tend to be too low. If you choose an "appropriate" forecasting method, based on the evidence from a time series graph, this type of bias is not likely to be a problem, but it is easy to check. Furthermore, if a company realizes that its forecasting method produces forecasts that are consistently, say, 5% below the actual values, it could simply multiply its forecasts by 1/0.95 to remove the bias.

> **Fundamental Insight**
>
> ### Extrapolation and Noise
>
> There are two important things to remember about extrapolation methods. First, by definition, all such methods try to extrapolate historical patterns into the future. If history doesn't essentially repeat itself, for whatever reason, these methods are doomed to failure. In fact, if you *know* that something has changed fundamentally, you probably should not use an extrapolation method. Second, it does no good to track noise and then forecast it into the future. For this reason, most extrapolation methods try to smooth out the noise, so that the underlying patterns are more apparent.

We now examine a number of useful forecasting models. You should be aware that more than one of these models can be appropriate for any particular time series data. For example, a random walk model and an autoregression model could be equally effective for forecasting stock price data. (Remember also that forecasts from more than one model can be combined to obtain a possibly better forecast.) We try to provide some insights into choosing the best type of model for various types of time series data, but ultimately the choice depends on the type of time series and the experience of the analyst.

12-3 Testing for Randomness

All forecasting models have the general form shown in Equation (12.5). The fitted value in this equation is the part calculated from past data and any other available information (such as the season of the year), and it is used as a forecast for Y. The residual is the forecast error, the difference between the observed value of Y and the forecast:

Typical Forecasting Equation

$$Y_t = \text{Fitted Value} + \text{Residual} \qquad (12.5)$$

In a time series context the terms residual and forecast error are used interchangeably.

For time series data, there is a residual for each historical period, that is, for each value of *t*. We want this time series of residuals to be random noise, as discussed in Section 12-2d. The reason is that if this series of residuals is not noise, it can be modeled further. For example, if the residuals trend upwardly, the forecasting model can be modified to include this trend component in the *fitted* value. The point is that the fitted value should include all components of the original series that can possibly be forecast, and the leftover residuals should be unpredictable noise.

We first discuss ways to determine whether a time series of residuals is random noise (which we usually abbreviate to "random"). The simplest method, but not always a reliable one, is to examine time series graphs of residuals visually. Nonrandom patterns are sometimes easy to detect. For example, the time series graphs in Figures 12.7 through 12.11 illustrate some common nonrandom patterns. In Figure 12.7, there is an upward trend. In Figure 12.8, the variance increases through time (larger zigzags to the right). Figure 12.9 exhibits seasonality, where observations in certain months are consistently larger than those in other months. There is a meandering pattern in Figure 12.10, where large observations tend to be followed by other large observations, and small observations tend to be followed by other small observations. Finally, Figure 12.11 illustrates the opposite behavior, where there are *too many* zigzags—large observations tend to follow small observations and vice versa. None of the time series in these figures is random.

Figure 12.7 A Series with Trend

Figure 12.8 A Series with Increasing Variance Through Time

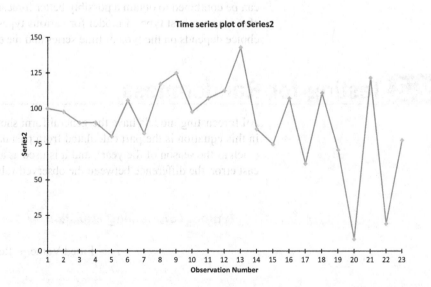

Figure 12.9 A Series with
Seasonality

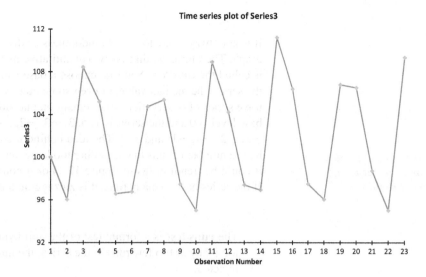

Figure 12.10 A Series That
Meanders

Figure 12.11 A Series That
Oscillates Frequently

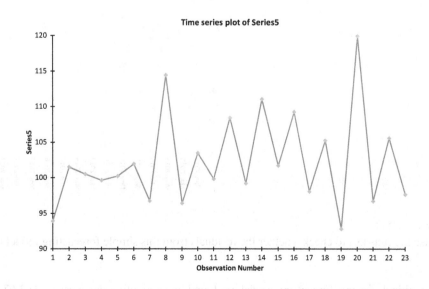

12-3a The Runs Test

It is not always easy to detect randomness or the lack of it from the visual inspection of a graph. Therefore, we discuss two quantitative methods that test for randomness. The first is called the *runs test*. You first choose a base value, which could be the average value of the series, the median value, or even some other value. Then a **run** is defined as a consecutive series of observations that remain on one side of this base level. For example, if the base level is 0 and the series is 1, 5, 3, −3, −2, −4, −1, 3, 2, there are three runs: 1, 5, 3; −3, −2, −4, −1; and 3, 2. The idea behind the runs test is that a random series should have a number of runs that is neither too large nor too small. If the series has too few runs, it could be trending (as in Figure 12.7) or it could be meandering (as in Figure 12.10). If the series has too many runs, it is zigzagging too often (as in Figure 12.11).

This runs test can be used on any time series, not just a series of residuals.

> The **runs test** is a formal test of the null hypothesis of randomness. If there are too many or too few runs in the series, the null hypothesis of randomness can be rejected.

We do not provide the mathematical details of the runs test, but the following example illustrates its use.

EXAMPLE

12.1 FORECASTING MONTHLY STEREO SALES

Monthly sales for a chain of stereo retailers are listed in the file **Stereo Sales.xlsx**. They cover a four-year period during which there was no upward or downward trend in sales and no clear seasonality. This behavior is apparent in the time series graph of sales in Figure 12.12. Therefore, a simple forecast model of sales is to use the *average* of the series, 182.67, as a forecast of sales for each month. Do the resulting residuals represent random noise?

Figure 12.12 Time Series Graph of Stereo Sales

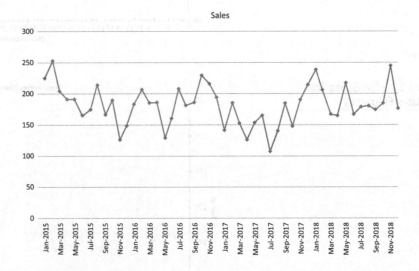

Objective

To use the runs test to check whether the residuals from this simple forecasting model represent random noise.

Solution

The residuals for this forecasting model are found by subtracting the average, 182.67, from each observation. Therefore, the plot of the residuals (not shown here) has exactly the same shape as the plot of sales. The only difference is that it is shifted down by 182.67 and has mean 0. The runs test can now be used to check whether there are too many or too few runs around the base value of 0 in this residual plot. To implement this in Excel, we have created a template file, **Runs Test Template.xlsx**. The instructions in this file indicate how it should be used. Basically, you copy your data, in this case the residuals, to column A and copy a formula in cell B2 down to keep track of runs. The results for this example appear in Figure 12.13.

Figure 12.13 Runs Test for Randomness

	A	B	C	D	E
1	Residual	Start Run		Runs test	
2	43.333	1		Cutoff value for defining runs	0.00
3	71.333	0			
4	21.333	0		# of observations	48
5	10.333	0		# below (or equal to) cutoff	22
6	8.333	0		# above cutoff	26
7	−16.667	1		# of runs (R)	20
8	−7.667	0			
9	34.333	1		Exp(R)	24.8333
10	−15.667	1		StDev(R)	3.4027
11	9.333	1		z-value	−1.4204
12	−55.667	1		p-value for two-tailed test	0.1555
13	−34.667	0			
14	1.333	1			

The important elements of this output are the following:

- The number of observed runs is 20, in cell E7. These are runs above or below the cutoff value of 0 in cell E2, which is the average of the residuals.
- The number of runs *expected* under an assumption of randomness is 24.833, in cell E9. (This follows from a probability argument not shown here.) Therefore, the series of residuals has too *few* runs. Positive values tend to follow positive values, and negative values tend to follow negative values.
- The z-value in cell E11, −1.42, indicates how many standard errors the observed number of runs is below the expected number of runs. The corresponding p-value indicates how extreme this z-value is. It can be interpreted like other p-values for hypothesis tests. If it is small, say, less than 0.05, the null hypothesis of randomness can be rejected. However, the p-value for this example is only 0.1555. Therefore, there is not convincing evidence of nonrandomness in the residuals. In other words, it is reasonable to conclude that the residuals represent noise.

A small p-value in the runs test provides evidence of nonrandomness.

12-3b Autocorrelation

Like the runs test, autocorrelations can be calculated for any time series, not just a series of residuals.

In this section we discuss another way to check for randomness of a time series of residuals—we examine the **autocorrelations** of the residuals. The "auto" means that successive observations are correlated with one another. For example, in the most common form of autocorrelation, *positive* autocorrelation, large observations tend to follow large observations, and small observations tend to follow small observations. In this case, the runs test is likely to pick it up because there will be fewer runs than expected. Another way to check for the same nonrandomness is to calculate the autocorrelations of the time series.

> An **autocorrelation** is a type of correlation used to measure whether values of a time series are related to their own past values.

To understand autocorrelations, it is first necessary to understand what it means to *lag* a time series. This concept is easy to illustrate in Excel. We again use the monthly stereo sales data in the **Stereo Sales.xlsx** file. To lag by one month, you simply "push down" the series by one row. See column D of Figure 12.14. Note that there is a blank cell at the top of the lagged series (in cell D2). This is due to the lack of a December 2014 observation. You can continue to push the series down one row at a time to obtain other lags. For example, the lag 3 version of the series appears in column F. Now there are three missing observations at the top. Note that in December 2015, say, the first, second, and third lags correspond to the observations in November 2015, October 2015, and September 2015, respectively. That is, lags are previous observations, removed by a certain number of periods from the present time. These lagged columns can be obtained by copying and pasting the original series.

Figure 12.14 Lags for Stereo Sales

▲	A	B	C	D	E	F
1	Month	Sales	Residual	Lag1 Residual	Lag2 Residual	Lag3 Residual
2	Jan-2015	226	43.333			
3	Feb-2015	254	71.333	43.333		
4	Mar-2015	204	21.333	71.333	43.333	
5	Apr-2015	193	10.333	21.333	71.333	43.333
6	May-2015	191	8.333	10.333	21.333	71.333
7	Jun-2015	166	−16.667	8.333	10.333	21.333
8	Jul-2015	175	−7.667	−16.667	8.333	10.333
9	Aug-2015	217	34.333	−7.667	−16.667	8.333
10	Sep-2015	167	−15.667	34.333	−7.667	−16.667

Fundamental Insight

Role of Autocorrelation in Time Series Analysis

Due to the mathematical level of this book, we do not discuss autocorrelation in much detail. However, it is the key to many forecasting methods, especially more complex methods. This is not surprising. Autocorrelations essentially specify how observations in nearby time periods are related, so this information is often useful in forecasting. However, it is not at all obvious how this information should be used—hence the complexity of some forecasting methods.

Then the autocorrelation of lag k, for any integer k, is essentially the correlation between the original series and the lag k version of the series. For example, in Figure 12.14 the lag 1 autocorrelation is the correlation between the observations in columns C and D. Similarly, the lag 2 autocorrelation is the correlation between the observations in columns C and E.[1]

We have shown the lagged versions of Sales in Figure 12.14, and we have explained autocorrelations in terms of these lagged variables, to help motivate the concept of autocorrelation. However, we have created another template file, **Autocorrelation Template. xlsx**, much like the runs test template, to take care of the calculations. This is illustrated in the following continuation of Example 12.1.

---

1 You can ignore the exact details of the calculations here. Just be aware that the formula for autocorrelations differs slightly from the correlation formula in Chapter 3, although the difference is very slight and of no practical importance.

EXAMPLE

12.1 FORECASTING MONTHLY STEREO SALES (CONTINUED)

The runs test on the stereo sales data suggests that the pattern of sales is not completely random. There is some tendency for large values to follow large values, and for small values to follow small values. Do autocorrelations support this evidence?

Objective

To examine the autocorrelations of the residuals from the forecasting model for evidence of nonrandomness.

Solution

The results from the template are shown in Figure 12.15. We asked for autocorrelations up to lag 12. Besides these 12 auto-correlations, the template calculates the Durbin–Watson statistic discussed in the previous chapter, and it creates a chart called a **correlogram** of the autocorrelations. A typical autocorrelation of lag k indicates the relationship between observations k periods apart. For example, the autocorrelation of lag 3, 0.0814, indicates that there is very little relationship between residuals separated by three months.

Figure 12.15 Correlogram and Autocorrelations of Residuals

	A	B	C	D	E	F	G
1	Residual	Centered Series		Lag	Autocorrelation		D-W statistic
2	43.333	43.333		1	0.3492		1.262
3	71.333	71.333		2	0.0772		
4	21.333	21.333		3	0.0814		
5	10.333	10.333		4	−0.0095		
6	8.333	8.333		5	−0.1353		
7	−16.667	−16.667		6	0.0206		
8	−7.667	−7.667		7	−0.1494		
9	34.333	34.333		8	−0.1492		
10	−15.667	−15.667		9	−0.2626		
11	9.333	9.333		10	−0.1792		
12	−55.667	−55.667		11	0.0121		
13	−34.667	−34.667		12	−0.0516		
14	1.333	1.333					
15	26.333	26.333					
16	3.333	3.333					
17	5.333	5.333					

How large is a "large" autocorrelation? Under the assumption of randomness, it can be shown that the standard error of any autocorrelation is approximately $1/\sqrt{T}$, in this case $1/\sqrt{48} = 0.1443$. (Recall that T denotes the number of observations in the series.) If the series is random, then only an occasional autocorrelation will be larger than two standard errors in magnitude. Therefore, any autocorrelation that *is* larger than two standard errors in magnitude is worth your attention. For this example, the only "large" autocorrelation for the residuals is the first, or lag 1, autocorrelation of 0.3492. The fact that it is *positive* indicates once again that there is some tendency for large residuals to follow large residuals and for small to follow small. The autocorrelations for other lags are less than two standard errors in magnitude and can safely be ignored.

Typically, you can ask for autocorrelations up to as many lags as you like. However, there are several practical considerations to keep in mind. First, it is common practice to ask for no more lags than 25% of the number of observations. For example, if there are 48 observations, you should ask for no more than 12 autocorrelations (lags 1 to 12).

Second, the first few lags are typically the most important. Intuitively, if there is any relationship between successive observations, it is likely to be between nearby observations. The June 2018 observation is more likely to be related to the May 2018 observation than to the October 2017 observation. Sometimes there is a fairly large spike in the correlogram at some large lag, such as lag 9. However, this can often be dismissed as a random blip unless there is some obvious reason for its occurrence. A similarly large autocorrelation at lag 1 or 2 is usually taken more seriously. The one exception to this is a *seasonal* lag. For example, an autocorrelation at lag 12 for monthly data corresponds to a relationship between observations a year apart, such as May 2018 and May 2017. If this autocorrelation is significantly large, it probably should not be ignored.

As discussed briefly in the previous chapter, one measure of the lag 1 autocorrelation, often the most important autocorrelation, is provided by the Durbin–Watson (DW) statistic. This statistic is automatically calculated in the template. Its value for the residuals in this example is 1.262, as shown in Figure 12.15. The DW statistic is always between 0 and 4. A DW value of 2 indicates *no* lag 1 autocorrelation, a DW value less than 2 indicates *positive* autocorrelation, and a DW value greater than 2 indicates *negative* autocorrelation. The current DW value, 1.262, is considerably less than 2, another indication that the lag 1 autocorrelation of the residuals is positive and possibly significant. There are tables of significance levels for DW statistics (how much less than 2 must DW be to be significant?), but they are not presented here.

Autocorrelation analysis is somewhat advanced. However, it is the basis for many useful forecasting methods.

We will not examine autocorrelations much further in this book. However, many advanced forecasting techniques are based largely on the examination of the autocorrelation structure of time series. This autocorrelation structure indicates how a series is related to its own past values through time, which can be very valuable information for forecasting *future* values.

Problems

Solutions for problems whose numbers appear within a colored box can be found in the Student Solution Files.

Level A

1. The file **P12_01.xlsx** contains the monthly number of airline tickets sold by a travel agency. Is this time series *random*? Perform a runs test and find a few autocorrelations to support your answer.

2. The file **P12_02.xlsx** contains the weekly sales at a local bookstore for each of the past 25 weeks. Is this time series *random*? Perform a runs test and find a few autocorrelations to support your answer.

3. The number of employees on the payroll at a food-processing plant is recorded at the start of each month. These data are provided in the file **P12_03.xlsx**. Perform a runs test and find a few autocorrelations to determine whether this time series is random.

4. The quarterly numbers of applications for home mortgage loans at a branch office of Northern Central Bank are recorded in the file **P12_04.xlsx**. Perform a runs test and find a few autocorrelations to determine whether this time series is random.

5. The number of reported accidents at a manufacturing plant was recorded at the start of each month. These data are provided in the file **P12_05.xlsx**. Is this time series *random*? Perform a runs test and find a few autocorrelations to support your answer.

6. The file **P12_06.xlsx** contains the weekly sales at an electronics store for each of the past 36 weeks. Perform a runs test and find a few autocorrelations to determine whether this time series is random.

Level B

7. Determine whether the RAND() function in Excel actually generates a random stream of numbers. Generate at least 100 random numbers to test their randomness with a runs test and with autocorrelations. Summarize your findings.

8. Use a runs test and calculate autorrelations to decide whether the random series explained in each part of this problem (**a–c**) are random. For each part, generate at least 100 random numbers in the series.

a. A series of independent normally distributed values, each with mean 70 and standard deviation 5.

b. A series where the first value is normally distributed with mean 70 and standard deviation 5, and each succeeding value is normally distributed with mean equal to the *previous* value and standard deviation 5. (For example, if the fourth value is 67.32, then the fifth value will be normally distributed with mean 67.32.)

c. A series where the first value, Y_1, is normally distributed with mean 70 and standard deviation 5, and each succeeding value, Y_t, is normally distributed with mean $(1 + a_t)Y_{t-1}$ and standard deviation $5(1 + a_t)$, where the a_t values are independent and normally distributed with mean 0 and standard deviation 0.2. (For example, if $Y_{t-1} = 67.32$ and $a_t = -0.2$, then Y_t will be normally distributed with mean $0.8(67.32) = 53.856$ and standard deviation $0.8(5) = 4$.)

12-4 Regression-Based Trend Models

Many time series follow a long-term trend except for random variation. This trend can be upward or downward. A straightforward way to model this trend is to estimate a regression equation for Y_t, using time t as the *single* explanatory variable. In this section we discuss the two most frequently used trend models, *linear* trend and *exponential* trend.

12-4a Linear Trend

A linear trend means that the time series variable changes by a constant *amount* each time period. The relevant equation is Equation (12.6), where, as in previous regression equations, a is the intercept, b is the slope, and e_t is an error term.[2]

> **Linear Trend Model**
>
> $$Y_t = a + bt + e_t \qquad\qquad (12.6)$$

The interpretation of b is that it represents the expected change in the series from one period to the next. If b is positive, the trend is upward; if b is negative, the trend is downward. The intercept term a is less important. It literally represents the expected value of the series at time $t = 0$. If time t is coded so that the first observation corresponds to $t = 1$, then a is where the series was one period before the observations began. However, it is possible that time is coded in another way. For example, if the data are annual, starting in 1997, the first value of t might be entered as 1997, which means that the intercept a then corresponds to a period 1997 years earlier. Clearly, its value should not be taken literally in this case.

As always, a graph of the time series is a good place to start. It indicates whether a **linear trend** is likely to provide a good fit. Generally, the graph should rise or fall at approximately a constant rate through time, without too much random variation. But even if there is a lot of random variation—a lot of zigzags—a linear trend to the data might still be a good starting point. Then the *residuals* from this trend line, which should have no remaining trend, could be tested for randomness.

EXAMPLE

12.2 MONTHLY U.S. POPULATION

The file **US Population.xlsx** contains monthly population data for the United States from January 1952 to December 2017 (in thousands). During this period, the population has increased steadily from about 156 million to about 327 million. The time series graph of these data appears in Figure 12.16. How well does a linear trend fit these data? Are the residuals from this fit random?

Objective

To fit a linear trend line to monthly population and examine its residuals for randomness.

Solution

The graph in Figure 12.16 indicates a clear upward trend with little or no curvature. Therefore, a linear trend is certainly plausible. In fact, the best-fitting linear trend line is shown in the figure, using the same Excel Trendline tool we have used before.

---

2 It is traditional in the regression literature to use Greek letters for population parameters and Roman letters for estimates of them. However, we decided to use only Roman letters in the regression sections of this chapter.

Figure 12.16 Time Series
Graph of U.S. Population

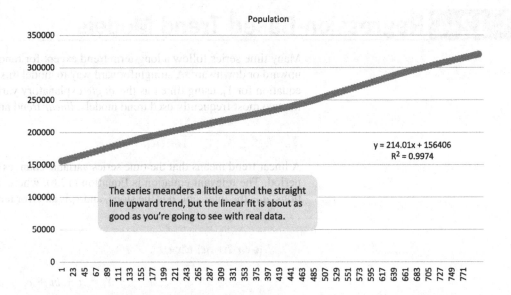

The series meanders a little around the straight line upward trend, but the linear fit is about as good as you're going to see with real data.

To estimate this linear trend with regression, a variable with consecutive integers is required. This time variable appears in column C of the data set, using the consecutive values 1 through 756. You can then run a simple regression of Population versus Time, with the results shown in Figure 12.17. (We used Excel's built-in functions to estimate the regression equation. This is possible because there is a *single* explanatory variable, the Time variable in column C.) The estimated linear trend line (which also appears in Figure 12.16) is

$$\text{Forecast Population} = 156406.2 + 214.01\,\text{Time}$$

Figure 12.17 Regression for
Linear Trend

	A	B	C	D	E	F	G	H
1	Month	Population	Time	Forecast	Error		Intercept	156406.2
2	Jan-1952	156309	1	156620.2	−311.2		Slope	214.0077
3	Feb-1952	156527	2	156834.2	−307.2		StErr	2511.1
4	Mar-1952	156731	3	157048.2	−317.2		R-Square	0.997
5	Apr-1952	156943	4	157262.2	−319.2			
6	May-1952	157140	5	157476.2	−336.2			
7	Jun-1952	157343	6	157690.2	−347.2			
8	Jul-1952	157553	7	157904.3	−351.3			

This equation implies that the population tends to increase by 214.01 thousand per month. (The 156406.2 value in this equation is the predicted population at time 0; that is, December 1951.) To use this equation to forecast future population values, you can substitute later values of Time into the regression equation, so that each future forecast is 214.01 larger than the previous forecast. For example, the forecast for January 2015 is

$$\text{Forecast Population Jan-2018} = 156406.2 + 214.01(793) = 326114$$

The linear fit is not perfect, as the plot of the residuals in Figure 12.18 indicates. These residuals tend to meander, staying negative for a while, then positive, then negative, and then positive. You can check that the runs test for these residuals produces a very small *p*-value, and that many of its autocorrelations are significantly positive. In short, these residuals are definitely *not* random noise, and they could possibly be modeled further. However, we will not pursue this analysis here. In fact, it is not at all obvious how the autocorrelations of the residuals *could* be exploited to get a better forecast model than the linear trend.

Figure 12.18 Time Series
Graph of Forecast Errors

12-4b Exponential Trend

In contrast to a linear trend, an exponential trend is appropriate when the time series changes by a constant *percentage* (as opposed to a constant dollar amount) each period. Then the appropriate regression equation is Equation (12.7), where c and b are constants, and u_t represents a *multiplicative* error term.

Exponential Trend Model

$$Y_t = ce^{bt}u_t \qquad (12.7)$$

Equation (12.7) is useful for understanding how an exponential trend works, as we will discuss, but it is not useful for estimation. For that, a *linear* equation is required. Fortunately, linearity can be achieved by taking natural logarithms of both sides of Equation (12.7). (The key is that the logarithm of a product is the sum of the logarithms.) The result appears in Equation (12.8), where $a = \ln(c)$ and $e_t = \ln(u_t)$. This equation represents a *linear* trend, but the dependent variable is now the logarithm of the original Y_t. This implies the following important fact: If a time series exhibits an exponential trend, then a plot of its logarithm versus time should be approximately linear.

Equivalent Linear Trend for Logarithm of Y

$$\ln(Y_t) = a + bt + e_t \qquad (12.8)$$

An exponential trend for Y is equivalent to a linear trend for the logarithm of Y.

Because the software performs the calculations, your main responsibility is to interpret the final result. This is fairly easy. It can be shown that the coefficient b (expressed as a percentage) is approximately the percentage change per period. For example, if $b = 0.05$, the series is increasing by approximately 5% per period.[3] Conversely, if $b = -0.05$, the series is decreasing by approximately 5% per period.

An exponential trend can be estimated with regression, but only after the log transformation has been made on Y_t. We illustrate this in the following example.

EXAMPLE

12.3 QUARTERLY PC DEVICE SALES

The file **PC Device Sales.xlsx** contains quarterly sales data (in millions of dollars) for a large PC device manufacturer during a 15-year period. Are the company's sales growing exponentially through this entire period?

Objective

To estimate the company's exponential growth and to see whether it has been maintained during the entire 15-year period.

Solution

We first estimate and interpret an exponential trend for the first 10 years. Then we see how well the projection of this trend into the future fits the data in the most recent five years. The time series graph for the first 10 years appears in Figure 12.19. You can use Excel's Trendline tool, with the Exponential option, to superimpose an exponential trend line and the corresponding equation on this plot. The fit is evidently quite good. Equivalently, Figure 12.20 illustrates the time series of log sales for this same period, with a *linear* trend line superimposed. Its fit is equally good.

Figure 12.19 Time Series Graph of Sales with Exponential Trend Superimposed

Sales (first 10 years)

$y = 62.188e^{0.0654x}$

You can also use regression to estimate this exponential trend, as shown in Figure 12.21. (We again use Excel functions to perform the regression.) To produce this output, you must first add a time variable in column C (with values 1 through 40) and create a logarithmic transformation of Sales in column D. Then you can regress Log(Sales) on Time (using the data for the first 10 years only) to obtain the regression output. Note that its two coefficients in cells L2 and L3 are the same as those shown for the linear trend in Figure 12.20. If you take the antilog of the constant 4.130 (with the formula **=EXP(L2)**), you will obtain the constant *multiple* shown in Figure 12.19. It corresponds to the constant c in Equation (12.7).

What does it all mean? The estimated Equation (12.7) is

$$\text{Forecast Sales} = 62.188e^{0.0654t}$$

---

3 More precisely, this percentage change is $e^b - 1$. For example, when $b = 0.05$, this is $e^b - 1 = 5.13\%$.

Figure 12.20 Time Series Graph of Log Sales with Linear Trend Superimposed

Figure 12.21 Regression for Estimating Exponential Trend

	A	B	C	D	E	F	G	H	I	J	K	L	M	N	O
1	Quarter	Sales	Time	Log Sales	Forecast	Error	SqError	AbsError	AbsPctError		Regression coefficients (first 10 years only)				
2	Q1-2002	61.14	1	4.113166316	66.39	−5.25	27.599	5.254	0.086		Intercept	4.130			
3	Q2-2002	64.07	2	4.159976236	70.88	−6.81	46.423	6.813	0.106		Slope	0.0654			
4	Q3-2002	66.18	3	4.192378302	75.68	−9.50	90.193	9.497	0.144						
5	Q4-2002	72.76	4	4.287166354	80.79	−8.03	64.557	8.035	0.110		Measures of forecast error (first 10 years only)				
6	Q1-2003	84.70	5	4.439115602	86.26	−1.56	2.429	1.559	0.018		RMSE	33.69			
7	Q2-2003	90.05	6	4.500365072	92.09	−2.04	4.169	2.042	0.023		MAE	23.08			
8	Q3-2003	106.06	7	4.664004972	98.32	7.74	59.913	7.740	0.073		MAPE	8.30%			
9	Q4-2003	118.21	8	4.772462704	104.97	13.24	175.335	13.241	0.112						

The most important constant in this equation is the coefficient of Time, 0.0654. Expressed as a percentage, this coefficient implies that the company's sales increased by approximately 6.54% per quarter throughout this 10-year period. (The constant multiple, 62.188, is the forecast of sales at time 0; that is, quarter 4 of 2001.) To calculate the forecasts in column E, we first used the regression equation to forecast the log of sales and then used the EXP to find the antilog. Specifically, the formula in cell E2 is = **EXP($L$2 + $L$3*C2)**, which can then be copied down. (It is important to realize that without the EXP function, you would be calculating forecasts of log sales, which are of little interest.)

Has this exponential growth continued in the most recent five years? It has *not,* due possibly to slumping sales in the computer industry or increased competition from other manufacturers. This is apparent from the time series graph of the two series Sales and Forecast, for all years, shown in Figure 12.22. It is clear that sales in the later years did not exhibit nearly the 6.54% growth observed in the early years. As the company should realize, nothing this good lasts forever.

Figure 12.22 Time Series Graph of Forecasts Superimposed on Sales for the Entire Period

Before leaving this example, we comment briefly that any of the three forecast error measures discussed previously are easy to find, as shown in Figure 12.21. (You can check the formulas in the finished version of the file.) For example, forecasts for the 10-year estimation period were off, on average, by 8.30%, but as you can check, forecasts for the quarters *after* 2011 were off by much more.

Problems

Level A

9. The file **P12_01.xlsx** contains the monthly number of airline tickets sold by a travel agency.
   a. Does a linear trend appear to fit these data well? If so, estimate and interpret the linear trend model for this time series. Also, interpret the R^2 and s_e values.
   b. Provide an indication of the typical forecast error generated by the estimated model in part **a**.
   c. Is there evidence of some seasonal pattern in these sales data? If so, characterize the seasonal pattern.

10. The file **P12_10.xlsx** contains the annual revenues for a convenience store. (The store opened at the beginning of this period in what turned out to be a popular location.) Does a linear or exponential trend fit these data well? If so, estimate and interpret the best trend model for this time series. Also, interpret the R^2 and s_e values.

11. The file **P12_11.xlsx** contains annual U.S. federal debt from 1960 through 2011. Fit an exponential growth curve to these data. Write a short report to summarize your findings. If the U.S. federal debt continues to rise at the exponential rate you find, approximately what will its value be at the end of 2020?

12. The file **P12_12.xlsx** contains five years of monthly data on a company's sales (number of units sold). The company suspects that except for random noise, its sales are growing by a constant *percentage* each month and will continue to do so for at least the near future.
   a. Explain briefly whether the plot of the series visually supports the company's suspicion.
   b. Fit the appropriate regression model to the data. Report the resulting equation and state explicitly what it says about the percentage growth per month.
   c. What are the RMSE and MAPE for the forecast model in part **b**? In words, what do they measure? Considering their magnitudes, does the model seem to be doing a good job?

   d. In words, how does the model make forecasts for future months? Specifically, given the forecast value for the last month in the data set, what simple arithmetic could you use to obtain forecasts for the next few months?

13. The file **P12_13.xlsx** contains quarterly data on GDP. (The data are expressed in billions of chained 2005 dollars, and they are seasonally adjusted.)
   a. Look at a time series plot of GDP. Does it suggest a linear relationship; an exponential relationship?
   b. Use regression to estimate an exponential relationship between GDP and Time (starting with 1 for Q1-1966). Interpret this equation. Would you say that the fit is good?
   c. How would the exponential fit differ if you included only the data through the end of year 2007?

Level B

14. The file **P03_30.xlsx** gives monthly exchange rates (units of local currency per U.S. dollar) for nine currencies. Technical analysts believe that by charting past changes in exchange rates, it is possible to predict future changes of exchange rates. After analyzing the autocorrelations for these data, do you believe that technical analysis has potential?

15. The unit sales of a new drug for the first 25 months after its introduction to the marketplace are recorded in the file **P12_15.xlsx**.
   a. Estimate a linear trend equation using the given data. How well does the linear trend fit these data? Are the residuals from this linear trend model *random*?
   b. If the residuals from this linear trend model are *not* random, propose another regression-based trend model that more adequately explains the long-term trend in this time series. Estimate the alternative model(s) using the given data. Check the residuals from the model(s) for randomness. Summarize your findings.
   c. Given the best estimated model of the trend in this time series, interpret R^2 and s_e.

12-5 The Random Walk Model

Random series are sometimes building blocks for other time series models. The model we now discuss, the **random walk model**, is an example of this. In a random walk model, the series itself is not random. However, its *differences*—that is, the changes from one period to the next—are random. This type of behavior is typical of stock price data, as well as various other time series data. For example, the graph in Figure 12.23 shows monthly closing prices for a manufacturer's stock from January 2012 through April 2018. (See the file **Stock Prices.xlsx**.) This series is not random, as can be seen from its gradual upward trend at the beginning and the general meandering behavior throughout. The runs test and autocorrelations (not shown) for the series itself confirm that the series is not random. (There are significantly *fewer* runs than expected, and the autocorrelations are significantly *positive* for many lags.)

Figure 12.23 Time Series Graph of Stock Prices

If it were April 2018, and you were asked to forecast the company's prices for the next few months, it is intuitive that you would not use the average of the historical values as your forecast. This forecast would tend to be too low because of the overall upward trend. Instead, you might base your forecast on the most recent observation. This is exactly what the random walk model does.

Equation (12.9) for the random walk model is given as follows, where m (for mean difference) is a constant and e_t is a random series (noise) with mean 0 and a standard deviation that remains *constant* through time.

Random Walk Model

$$Y_t = Y_{t-1} + m + e_t \qquad (12.9)$$

If we let $DY_t = Y_t - Y_{t-1}$, the change in the series from time $t - 1$ to time t (where D stands for difference), then the random walk model can be rewritten as in Equation (12.10). This implies that the differences form a random series with mean m and a constant standard deviation. An estimate of m is the average of the differences, labeled $\bar{Y}_D$, and an estimate of the standard deviation is the sample standard deviation of the differences, labeled s_D.

Difference Form of Random Walk Model

$$DY_t = m + e_t \qquad (12.10)$$

In words, a series that behaves according to this random walk model has random differences, and the series tends to trend upward (if $m > 0$) or downward (if $m < 0$) by an amount m each period. If you are standing in period t and want to forecast Y_{t+1}, then a reasonable forecast is given by Equation (12.11). That is, you add the estimated trend to the current observation to forecast the next observation.

One-Step-Ahead Forecast for Random Walk Model

$$F_{t+1} = Y_t + \overline{Y}_D \qquad \qquad (12.11)$$

For the stock price data, this random walk model is easy to implement. (See the finished version of the file.) First, a column of differences is created. The time series of these differences is shown in Figure 12.24, and their mean is slightly positive, 0.418. (The runs test and the autocorrelations for this difference series, not shown, indicate that the differences are random.) Then each future forecast adds a multiple of 0.418 to the last observed stock price. For example, the forecast for July 2018 adds 3(0.418) to the April 2018 stock price.

Figure 12.24 Time Series Graph of Stock Price Differences

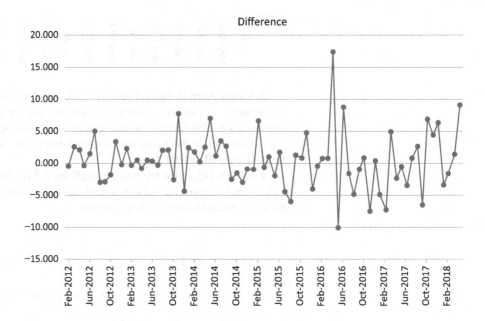

If the mean difference is (practically) zero, this random walk model is sometimes called the naive forecasting model, and forecasting is particularly simple. For example, after observing the April value, the forecast for May is the April value. Then after observing the May value, the forecast for June is the May value. And so on.

Problems

Level A

16. The file **P12_16.xlsx** contains the daily closing prices of American Express stock for a one-year period.
    a. Use the random walk model to forecast the closing price of this stock on the next trading day.
    b. You can be about 95% certain that the forecast made in part **a** will be off by no more than how many dollars?

17. The closing value of the AMEX Airline Index for each trading day for a one-year period is given in the file **P12_17.xlsx**.

    a. Use the random walk model to forecast the closing price of this stock on the next trading day.
    b. You can be about 68% certain that the forecast made in part **a** will be off by no more than how many dollars?

18. The file **P12_18.xlsx** contains the daily closing prices of Chevron stock for a one-year period.
    a. Use the random walk model to forecast the closing price of this stock on the next trading day.
    b. You can be about 99.7% certain that the forecast made in part **a** will be off by no more than how many dollars?

19. The closing value of the Dow Jones Industrial Average for each trading day for a two-year period is provided in the file **P12_19.xlsx**.
   a. Use the random walk model to forecast the closing price of this index on the next trading day. Is a random walk model justified with these data?
   b. Would it be wise to use the random walk model to forecast the closing price of this index for a trading day approximately *one month* after the next trading day? Explain why or why not.

20. Continuing the previous problem, the *weekly* closing values of the Dow Jones Industrial Average are listed in the file **P12_20.xlsx**. Answer the same questions as in the previous problem, but now for weeks instead of days.

21. The closing price of a share of JP Morgan Chase stock for each trading day for a one-year period is recorded in the file **P12_21.xlsx**.
   a. Use the random walk model to forecast the closing price of this stock on each of the next 10 trading days.
   b. You can be about 68% certain that the last forecast made in part **a** will be off by no more than how many dollars?

22. The purpose of this problem is to get you used to the concept of autocorrelation in a time series. You could do this with any time series, but here you should use the series of convenience store revenues in the file **P12_10.xlsx**.
   a. First, do it the quick way. Use the Autocorrelation procedure in StatTools to get a list of autocorrelations and a corresponding correlogram of the revenues. You can choose the number of lags.
   b. Now do it the more time-consuming way. Create columns of lagged versions of Revenue—3 lags will suffice. Next, look at scatterplots of Revenue versus its first few lags. If the autocorrelations are large, you should see fairly tight scatters—that's what autocorrelation is all about. Also, generate a correlation

matrix to see the correlations between Revenue and its first few lags. These should be approximately the same as the autocorrelations from part **a**. (Autocorrelations are calculated slightly differently than regular correlations, which accounts for any slight discrepancies you might notice—but these discrepancies should be minor.)
   c. Create the first differences of Revenue in a new column. (You can do this manually with formulas, or you can use StatTools's Difference procedure on the Data Utilities menu.) Now repeat parts **a** and **b** with the differences instead of the original closing prices—that is, examine the autocorrelations of the differences. They should be small, and the scatterplots of the differences versus lags of the differences should be shapeless swarms. This illustrates what happens when the differences of a time series variable have insignificant autocorrelations.
   d. Write a short report of your findings.

Level B

23. Consider a random walk model with the following equation: $Y_t = Y_{t-1} + 500 + e_t$, where e_t is a normally distributed random series with mean 0 and standard deviation 10.
   a. Use Excel to simulate a time series that behaves according to this random walk model.
   b. Use the time series you constructed in part **a** to forecast the next observation.

24. The file **P12_24.xlsx** contains the daily closing prices of Procter & Gamble stock from April 2017 to April 2018. Use only the 2017 data to estimate the trend component of the random walk model. Next, use the estimated random walk model to forecast the behavior of the time series for the 2018 dates in the series. Comment on the accuracy of the generated forecasts over this period. How could you improve the forecasts as you progress through the 2018 trading days?

12-6 Moving Averages Forecasts

Perhaps the simplest and one of the most frequently used extrapolation models is the **moving averages model**. To implement this model, you first choose a **span**, the number of terms in each average. Let's say the data are monthly and you choose a span of six months. Then the forecast of next month's value is the average of the values of the last six months. For example, you average January to June to forecast July, you average February to July to forecast August, and so on. This procedure is the reason for the term *moving* averages.

The role of the span is important. If the span is large—say, 12 months—then many observations go into each average, and extreme values have relatively little effect on the forecasts. The resulting series of forecasts will be much smoother than the original series. (For this reason, the moving averages method is called a *smoothing* method.) In contrast, if the span is small—say, three months—then extreme observations have a larger effect on the forecasts, and the forecast series will be less smooth. In the extreme, if the span is 1, there is no smoothing at all. The method simply forecasts next month's value to be the same as the current month's value. This is the *naive* forecasting model mentioned in the previous section. It is a special case of the random walk model with the mean difference equal to 0.

What span should you use? This requires some judgment. If you believe the ups and downs in the series are random noise, then you don't want future forecasts to react too quickly to these ups and downs, and you should use a relatively large span. But if you want to track every little zigzag—under the belief that each up or down is predictable—then you should use a smaller span. You shouldn't be fooled, however, by a plot of the (smoothed) forecast series superimposed on the original series. This graph will almost always look better when a small span is used, because the forecast series will appear to track the original series better. Does this mean it will always provide better future forecasts? Not necessarily. There is little point in tracking random ups and downs closely if they represent unpredictable noise.

The following example illustrates the use of moving averages.

EXAMPLE

12.4 HOUSES SOLD IN THE UNITED STATES

The file **House Sales.xlsx** contains monthly data on the number of new one-family houses sold in the United States (in thousands) from January 2010 through February 2018. (These data, available from the U.S. Census Bureau website, are listed as seasonally adjusted at an annual rate.)[4] A time series graph of the data appears in Figure 12.25. Housing sales have been trending steadily upward during this period. Does a moving averages model fit this series well? What span should be used?

Figure 12.25 Time Series Graph of Monthly House Sales

Objective

To see whether a moving averages model with an appropriate span fits the housing sales data.

Solution

Although the moving averages method is quite easy to implement in Excel—you just form an average of the appropriate span and copy it down—it can be tedious. It is much easier to implement with StatTools. The StatTools forecasting procedure is fairly general in that it allows you to forecast with several methods, either with or without taking seasonality into account. Because this is your first exposure to this procedure, we will go through it in some detail in this example.

To use the StatTools Forecasting procedure, select Forecast from the StatTools Time Series and Forecasting dropdown list. This brings up a dialog box with three tabs in its bottom section. The Time Scale tab, shown in Figure 12.26, allows you to select the time period. The Forecast Settings tab, shown in Figure 12.27, allows you to select a forecasting method. Finally, the Graphs to Display tab, not shown here, allows you to select several optional time series graphs. For now, fill out the dialog box sections as shown and select the Forecast Overlay option in the Graphs to Display tab. Note from Figure 12.27 that the moving averages method is being used with a span of 3, and it will generate forecasts for the next 12 months.

---

4 Government data are often reported in seasonally adjusted form, with the seasonality removed, to make any trends more apparent.

Figure 12.26 StatTools Forecast Dialog Box, Time Scale Tab

Figure 12.27 StatTools Forecast Dialog Box, Forecast Settings Tab

Another option in Figure 12.27 (not used here) is that you can elect to "hold out" a subset of the series for validation purposes. If you hold out several periods at the end of the series for validation, any model that is built is estimated only for the non-holdout observations, and summary measures are reported for the non-holdout and holdout subsets separately.

The output consists of several parts, as shown in Figures 12.28, 12.29, and 12.30. We actually ran the analysis twice, once for a span of 3 and once for a span of 12. These figures show the comparison. (We also obtained output for a span of 6, with results fairly similar to those for a span of 3.) First, the summary measures MAE, RMSE, and MAPE of the forecast errors are shown in Figure 12.28. As you can see, the forecasts using a span of 3 are slightly more accurate. For example, they are off by about 5.81% on average, whereas the similar measure with a span of 12 is 6.89%.

The essence of the forecasting method is captured in column C of Figure 12.29 for a span of 3 (with many hidden rows). Each value in the historical period in this column is an average of the three preceding values in column B. The forecast errors are then just the differences between columns B and C. For the future periods, the forecast formulas in column C use observations when they are available. If they are not available, previous forecasts are used. For example, the forecast for April 2018 is the average of the *observed* values in January and February 2018 and the *forecast* value in March 2018.

Figure 12.28 Moving Averages Summary Output

	A	B	C	D	E	F	G
1	*Moving Averages Forecasts for Houses Sold*					*Moving Averages Forecasts for Houses Sold*	
2	*Forecasting Constant*					*Forecasting Constant*	
3	Span	3				Span	12
4							
5							
6	*Moving Averages*					*Moving Averages*	
7	Mean Abs Err	25.53				Mean Abs Err	32.25
8	Root Mean Sq Err	33.16				Root Mean Sq Err	39.55
9	Mean Abs Per% Err	5.81%				Mean Abs Per% Err	6.89%

Figure 12.29 Moving Averages Detailed Output

	A	B	C	D	E	F	G	H	I
34	*Forecasting Data*	Houses Sold	Forecast	Error		*Forecasting Data*	Houses Sold	Forecast	Error
35	Jan-2010	345.00				Jan-2010	345.00		
36	Feb-2010	336.00				Feb-2010	336.00		
37	Mar-2010	381.00				Mar-2010	381.00		
38	Apr-2010	422.00	354.00	68.00		Apr-2010	422.00		
39	May-2010	280.00	379.67	−99.67		May-2010	280.00		
127	Sep-2017	639.00	580.67	58.33		Sep-2017	639.00	588.67	50.33
128	Oct-2017	616.00	587.33	28.67		Oct-2017	616.00	594.42	21.58
129	Nov-2017	711.00	604.67	106.33		Nov-2017	711.00	597.67	113.33
130	Dec-2017	653.00	655.33	−2.33		Dec-2017	653.00	608.67	44.33
131	Jan-2018	622.00	660.00	−38.00		Jan-2018	622.00	617.42	4.58
132	Feb-2018	618.00	662.00	−44.00		Feb-2018	618.00	619.33	−1.33
133	Mar-2018		631.00			Mar-2018		619.58	
134	Apr-2018		623.67			Apr-2018		618.05	
135	May-2018		624.22			May-2018		620.39	
136	Jun-2018		626.30			Jun-2018		621.58	
137	Jul-2018		624.73			Jul-2018		621.80	
138	Aug-2018		625.08			Aug-2018		626.62	
139	Sep-2018		625.37			Sep-2018		632.25	
140	Oct-2018		625.06			Oct-2018		631.69	
141	Nov-2018		625.17			Nov-2018		633.00	
142	Dec-2018		625.20			Dec-2018		626.50	
143	Jan-2019		625.14			Jan-2019		624.29	
144	Feb-2019		625.17			Feb-2019		624.48	

The graphs in Figure 12.30 show the behavior of the forecasts. The forecast series with span 3 (the graph on the left) follows the ups and downs of the actual series fairly closely. In contrast, the 12-month moving average series is much smoother.

Figure 12.30 Moving Averages Forecasts with Span 3 (Left) and Span 12 (Right)

One interesting feature of the moving average method is that *future* forecasts tend to be quite flat. This is apparent in Figure 12.30. This is a basic property of moving average forecasts: *future* forecasts tend to be close to the last few values of the series.

The moving averages method we have presented is the simplest of a group of moving average methods used by professional forecasters. We *smoothed* exactly once; that is, we took moving averages of several observations at a time and used these as forecasts. More complex methods smooth more than once, basically to get rid of random noise. They take moving averages, then moving averages of these moving averages, and so on for several stages. This can become quite complex, but the objective is simple—to smooth the data so that underlying patterns are easier to see.

Problems

Level A

25. The file **P12_16.xlsx** contains the daily closing prices of American Express stock for a one-year period.
    a. Using a span of 3, forecast the price of this stock for the next trading day with the moving average method. How well does this method with span 3 forecast the known observations in this series?
    b. Repeat part **a** with a span of 10.
    c. Which of these two spans appears to be more appropriate? Justify your choice.
26. The closing value of the AMEX Airline Index for each trading day for a one-year period is given in the file **P12_17.xlsx**.
    a. How well does the moving average method track this series when the span is 4; when the span is 12?
    b. Using the more appropriate span, forecast the closing value of this index on the next trading day with the moving average method.
27. The closing value of the Dow Jones Industrial Average for each trading day for a two-year period is provided in the file **P12_19.xlsx**.
    a. Using a span of 2, forecast the price of this index on the next trading day with the moving average method. How well does the moving average method with span 2 forecast the known observations in this series?

    b. Repeat part **a** with a span of 5; with a span of 15.
    c. Which of these three spans appears to be most appropriate? Justify your choice.
28. The file **P12_10.xlsx** contains annual revenues for a convenience store. If you want to forecast revenue for the next few years with the moving averages method, what span should you use? Will any span work well?.
29. The file **P12_29.xlsx** contains monthly revenues for a company over a four-year period. Use the moving average method to forecast this company's revenues for the 12 months. What span seems to work best?.
30. The file **P02_28.xlsx** contains total monthly U.S. retail sales data. Use the method of moving averages with one or more spans of your choice to forecast U.S. retail sales for the next 12 months. Comment on the performance of your model. What makes this time series more challenging to forecast?

Level B

31. Consider a random walk model with the following equation: $Y_t = Y_{t-1} + e_t$, where e_t is a random series with mean 0 and standard deviation 1. Specify a moving average model that is equivalent to this random walk model. In particular, what is the appropriate span in the equivalent moving average model? What is the smoothing effect of this span?

12-7 Exponential Smoothing Forecasts

There are two possible criticisms of the moving averages method. First, it puts equal weight on each value in a typical moving average. Many analysts would argue that if next month's forecast is to be based on the previous 12 months' observations, more weight should be placed on the more recent observations. The second criticism is that the moving averages method requires a lot of data storage. This is particularly true for companies that routinely make forecasts of hundreds or even thousands of items. If 12-month moving averages are used for 1000 items, then 12,000 values are needed for next month's forecasts. This may or may not be a concern, given today's inexpensive computer storage.

Exponential smoothing is a method that addresses both of these criticisms. It bases its forecasts on a weighted average of past observations, with more weight on the more recent observations, and it requires very little data storage. In addition, it is not difficult for most business people to understand, at least conceptually. Therefore, this method is used widely in the business world, particularly when frequent and automatic forecasts of many items are required.

There are many variations of exponential smoothing. The simplest is appropriately called *simple* exponential smoothing. It is relevant when there is no pronounced trend or seasonality in the series. If there is a trend but no seasonality, *Holt's* method is applicable. If, in addition, there is seasonality, *Winters'* method can be used. (These last two methods are often collectively called the *Holt-Winters* model.) This does not exhaust the types of exponential smoothing models—researchers have invented other variations—but these three models will suffice for us.

> **Simple exponential smoothing** is appropriate for a series with no pronounced trend or seasonality. **Holt's method** is appropriate for a series with trend but no seasonality. **Winters' method** is appropriate for a series with seasonality (and possibly trend).

12-7a Simple Exponential Smoothing

The level is an estimate of where the series would be if it were not for random noise.

We now examine simple exponential smoothing in some detail. We first introduce two new terms. Every exponential model has at least one **smoothing constant**, a number between 0 and 1. Simple exponential smoothing has a single smoothing constant denoted by α. (Its role is discussed shortly.) The second new term is L_t, called the *level* of the series at time t. This value is not observable but can only be estimated. Essentially, it is an estimate of where the series would be at time t if there were no random noise. Then the simple exponential smoothing method is defined by the following two equations, where F_{t+k} is the forecast of Y_{t+k} made at time t:

> **Simple Exponential Smoothing Formulas**
>
> $$L_t = \alpha Y_t + (1 - \alpha)L_{t-1} \qquad \textbf{(12.12)}$$
>
> $$F_{t+k} = L_t \qquad \textbf{(12.13)}$$

Even though you usually don't have to substitute into these equations manually, you should understand what they say. Equation (12.12) shows how to update the estimate of the level. It is a weighted average of the current observation, Y_t, and the previous level, L_{t-1}, with respective weights α and $1 - \alpha$. Equation (12.13) shows how forecasts are made. It says that the k-period-ahead forecast, F_{t+k}, made of Y_{t+k} in period t is the most recently estimated level, L_t. This is the *same* for any positive value of k. The idea is that in simple exponential smoothing, you believe that the series is not really going anywhere. So as soon as you estimate where the series ought to be in period t (if it weren't for random noise), you use this as the forecast for any future period.

The smoothing constant α is analogous to the span in moving averages. There are two ways to see this. The first way is to rewrite Equation (12.12), using the fact that the forecast error, E_t, made in forecasting Y_t at time $t - 1$ is $Y_t - F_t = Y_t - L_{t-1}$. Using algebra, Equation (12.12) can be rewritten as Equation (12.14).

Equivalent Formula for Simple Exponential Smoothing

$$L_t = L_{t-1} + \alpha E_t \qquad \textbf{(12.14)}$$

This equation says that the next estimate of the level is adjusted from the previous estimate by adding a multiple of the most recent forecast error. This makes sense. If the previous forecast was too high, then E_t is negative, and the estimate of the level is adjusted downward. The opposite is true if the previous forecast was too low. However, Equation (12.14) says that the method does not adjust by the entire magnitude of E_t, but only by a fraction of it. If α is small, say, $\alpha = 0.1$, the adjustment is minor; if α is close to 1, the adjustment is large. So if you want the method to react quickly to movements in the series, you should choose a large α; otherwise, you should choose a small α.

Another way to see the effect of α is to substitute recursively into the equation for L_t. By performing some algebra, you can verify that L_t satisfies Equation (12.15), where the sum extends back to the first observation at time $t = 1$.

Another Equivalent Formula for Simple Exponential Smoothing

$$L_t = \alpha Y_t + \alpha(1 - \alpha)Y_{t-1} + \alpha(1 - \alpha)^2 Y_{t-2} + \alpha(1 - \alpha)^3 Y_{t-3} + \cdots \qquad \textbf{(12.15)}$$

Equation (12.15) shows how the exponentially smoothed forecast is a weighted average of previous observations. Furthermore, because $1 - \alpha$ is less than 1, the weights on the Y's decrease from time t backward. If α is close to 0, then $1 - \alpha$ is close to 1 and the weights decrease very slowly. In other words, observations from the distant past continue to have a large influence on the next forecast. This means that the graph of the forecasts will be relatively smooth, just as with a large span in the moving averages method. But if α is close to 1, the weights decrease rapidly, and only very recent observations have much influence on the next forecast. In this case forecasts react quickly to sudden changes in the series. This is equivalent to a small span in moving averages.

Small smoothing constants provide forecasts that respond slowly to changes in the series. Large smoothing constants do the opposite.

What value of α should you use? There is no universally accepted answer to this question. Some practitioners recommend always using a value around 0.1 or 0.2. Others recommend experimenting with different values of α until a measure such as RMSE or MAPE is minimized. Some packages even have an optimization feature to find this optimal value of α. (This is the case with StatTools.) But just as we discussed in the moving averages section, the value of α that tracks the historical series most closely does not necessarily guarantee the most accurate *future* forecasts.

> **Fundamental Insight**
>
> ### Smoothing Constants in Exponential Smoothing
>
> All versions of exponential smoothing use one or more smoothing constants between 0 and 1. To make any of these methods produce smoother forecasts, and hence react less quickly to noise, you should use smaller smoothing constants, such as 0.1 or 0.2. When larger smoothing constants are used, the historical forecasts might appear to track the actual series fairly closely, but they might just be tracking random noise.

EXAMPLE

12.4 HOUSES SOLD IN THE UNITED STATES (CONTINUED)

Previously, we used the moving averages method to forecast monthly housing sales in the United States. (See the **House Sales. xlsx** file.) How well does simple exponential smoothing work with this data set? Which smoothing constant should be used?

Objective

To see how well a simple exponential smoothing model, with an appropriate smoothing constant, fits the housing sales data.

Solution

You can use StatTools to implement the simple exponential smoothing model, specifically equations (12.12) and (12.13). You do this again by selecting Forecast from the StatTools Time Series and Forecasting dropdown list. Specifically, you fill in the forecast dialog box essentially as with moving averages, except that you select the simple exponential smoothing option in the Forecast Settings tab (see Figure 12.31). You should also choose a smoothing constant (0.2 was chosen here, but any other value could be chosen) or you can elect to find an optimal smoothing constant.

Figure 12.31 StatTools Forecast Settings for Exponential Smoothing

The results appear in Figures 12.32, 12.33 (with many hidden rows), and 12.34. The heart of the method takes place in columns C, D, and E of Figure 12.33. Column C calculates the smoothed levels (L_t) from Equation (12.12), column D calculates the forecasts (F_t) from Equation (12.13), and column E calculates the forecast errors (E_t) as the observed values minus the forecasts. Although the Excel formulas do not appear in the figure, you can examine them in the StatTools output.

Figure 12.32 Simple Exponential Smoothing Summary Output

	A	B
1	*Simple Exponential Smoothing Forecasts for Houses Sold*	
2	*Forecasting Constant*	
3	Level (Alpha)	0.200
4		
5		
6	*Simple Exponential*	
7	Mean Abs Err	28.82
8	Root Mean Sq Err	35.86
9	Mean Abs Per% Err	6.59%

Figure 12.33 Simple Exponential Smoothing Detailed Output

	A	B	C	D	E
34	*Forecasting Data*	Houses Sold	Level	Forecast	Error
35	Jan-2010	345.00	345.00		
36	Feb-2010	336.00	343.20	345.00	−9.00
37	Mar-2010	381.00	350.76	343.20	37.80
38	Apr-2010	422.00	365.01	350.76	71.24
39	May-2010	280.00	348.01	365.01	−85.01
129	Nov-2017	711.00	622.19	599.99	111.01
130	Dec-2017	653.00	628.35	622.19	30.81
131	Jan-2018	622.00	627.08	628.35	−6.35
132	Feb-2018	618.00	625.27	627.08	−9.08
133	Mar-2018			625.27	
134	Apr-2018			625.27	
135	May-2018			625.27	
136	Jun-2018			625.27	
137	Jul-2018			625.27	
138	Aug-2018			625.27	
139	Sep-2018			625.27	
140	Oct-2018			625.27	
141	Nov-2018			625.27	
142	Dec-2018			625.27	
143	Jan-2019			625.27	
144	Feb-2019			625.27	

Figure 12.34 Simple Exponential Smoothing Forecasts

Forecast and Original Observations

Every exponential smoothing method requires *initial* values, in this case the initial smoothed level in cell C35. There is no way to calculate this value, L_1, from Equation (12.12) because the *previous* value, L_0, is unknown. Different implementations of exponential smoothing initialize in different ways. StatTools initializes by setting L_1 equal to Y_1 (in cell B35). The effect of initializing in different ways is usually minimal because any effect of early data is usually washed out as forecasts are made into the future.

Note that the 12 future forecasts (rows 133 down) are all equal to the last calculated smoothed level, the one for February 2018 in cell C132. The fact that these remain constant is a consequence of the assumption behind *simple* exponential smoothing, namely, that the series is not really going anywhere. Therefore, the last smoothed level is the best available indication of future values of the series.

Figure 12.34 shows the forecast series superimposed on the original series. You can see the obvious smoothing effect of a relatively small α level. If the various zigzags in the original series are really random noise, then perhaps the forecasts shouldn't try to track these random ups and downs too closely. That is, perhaps a forecast series that emphasizes the basic underlying pattern is preferred.

In the next subsection, Holt's method is used on this series to see whether it captures the trend better than simple exponential smoothing.

You can see several summary measures of the forecast errors in Figure 12.32. The MAE and RMSE indicate that the forecasts from this model are typically off by a magnitude of about 29 to 36 thousand, and the MAPE indicates that they are off by about 6.6%. These are fairly sizable errors. One way to reduce the errors is to use a different smoothing method. We will try this in the next subsection with Holt's method. Another way to reduce the errors is to use a different smoothing constant. There are two methods you can use. First, you can simply enter different values in the smoothing constant cell in the Forecast sheet. All formulas, including those for MAE, RMSE, and MAPE, will update automatically.

Second, you can check the Optimize Parameters option in the Forecast dialog box shown in Figure 12.31. This automatically runs an optimization algorithm to find the smoothing constant that minimizes RMSE. (StatTools is programmed to minimize RMSE. However, you could try minimizing MAPE, say, by using Excel's Solver add-in.) When this optimization option is used for the housing data, the results (not shown here but available in the finished version of the file) indicate an optimal smoothing constant of 0.542 and slightly lower values of MAE, RMSE, and MAPE than before. This larger smoothing constant produces a less smooth forecast curve and slightly better error measures. However, there is no guarantee that *future* forecasts made with this optimal smoothing constant will be any better than with a smoothing constant of 0.2.

12-7b Holt's Model for Trend

The trend term in Holt's method estimates the change from one period to the next.

The simple exponential smoothing model generally works well if there is no obvious trend in the series. But if there is a trend, this method consistently lags behind it. For example, if the series is constantly increasing, simple exponential smoothing forecasts will be consistently low. Holt's method rectifies this by dealing with trend explicitly. In addition to the level of the series, L_t, Holt's method includes a trend term, T_t, and a corresponding smoothing constant β. The interpretation of L_t is exactly as before. The interpretation of T_t is that it represents an estimate of the *change* in the series from one period to the next. The equations for Holt's model are as follows.

Formulas for Holt's Exponential Smoothing Method

$$L_t = \alpha Y_t + (1 - \alpha)(L_{t-1} + T_{t-1}) \qquad \textbf{(12.16)}$$

$$T_t = \beta(L_t - L_{t-1}) + (1 - \beta)T_{t-1} \qquad \textbf{(12.17)}$$

$$F_{t+k} = L_t + kT_t \qquad \textbf{(12.18)}$$

Equation (12.16) says that the updated level is a weighted average of the current observation and the previous level plus the estimated change. Equation (12.17) says that the updated trend is a weighted average of the difference between two consecutive levels and the previous trend. Finally, Equation (12.18) says that the k-period-ahead forecast made in period t is the estimated level plus k times the estimated change per period. Of course, these equations are typically implemented with software.

Everything we said about α for simple exponential smoothing applies to both α and β in Holt's model. The new smoothing constant β controls how quickly the method reacts to observed changes in the trend. If β is small, the method reacts slowly. If it is large, the method reacts more quickly. There are now two smoothing constants to select. Some practitioners suggest using a small value of α (0.1 to 0.2, say) and setting β equal to α. Others suggest using an optimization option (available in StatTools) to select the optimal smoothing constants. We illustrate Holt's method in the following continuation of the housing sales example.

EXAMPLE

12.4 HOUSES SOLD IN THE UNITED STATES (CONTINUED)

We again examine the monthly data on housing sales in the United States. In the previous subsection, you saw that simple exponential smoothing, even with an optimal smoothing constant, does only a fair job of forecasting housing sales. Given that there are trends in housing sales over this period, Holt's method might be expected to perform better. Does it?

Objective

To see whether Holt's method, with appropriate smoothing constants, captures the trends in the housing sales data better than simple exponential smoothing (or moving averages).

Solution

You implement Holt's method in StatTools almost exactly as for simple exponential smoothing. The only difference is that you can now choose *two* smoothing constants, as shown in Figure 12.35. They can have different values, but they have both been chosen to be 0.2 for this example.

Figure 12.35 StatTools Dialog Box for Holt's Method

The StatTools outputs in Figures 12.36, 12.37, and 12.38 are also very similar to the simple exponential smoothing outputs. The only difference is that there is now a trend column, column D, in the numerical output. You can check that the formulas in columns C, D, and E implement equations (12.16), (12.17), and (12.18). As before, an initialization is required in row 42. These require values of L_1 and T_1 to get the method started. Different implementations of Holt's method obtain these initial values in slightly different ways, but the effect is fairly minimal in most cases. (You can check cells C36 and D36 to see how StatTools does it.)

The error measures in Figure 12.36 for Holt's method are slightly better than for simple exponential smoothing with smoothing constant 0.2, but these measures can be sensitive to the smoothing constants. Therefore, a second run of Holt's method was performed, using the Optimize Parameters option. This resulted in somewhat better results (not shown here but available in the finished version of the file). The optimal smoothing constants are $\alpha = 0.458$ and $\beta = 0.000$, and the MAE, RMSE, and MAPE values are very similar to those from simple exponential smoothing with an optimal smoothing constant. The zero smoothing constant for trend doesn't mean that there is no trend. It just means that the *initial* estimate of trend, the average change from the first time period to the last, is kept throughout. These "optimal" results are due, at least in part, to the way StatTools determines the initial trend term. In any case, the results using 0.2 for the two smoothing constants appear to be quite good and "believable." As Figure 12.38 indicates, the *future* forecasts now increase. This is what you would expect, given that the series itself has trended upward.

Figure 12.36 Holt's Method Summary Output

	A	B
1	*Holt's Exponential Smoothing Forecasts for Houses Sold*	
2	*Forecasting Constants*	
3	Level (Alpha)	0.200
4	Trend (Beta)	0.200
5		
6		
7	*Holt's Exponential*	
8	Mean Abs Err	26.31
9	Root Mean Sq Err	34.36
10	Mean Abs Per% Err	6.28%

Figure 12.37 Holt's Method Detailed Output

	A	B	C	D	E	F
35	*Forecasting Data*	Houses Sold	Level	Trend	Forecast	Error
36	Jan-2010	345.00	345.00	2.79		
37	Feb-2010	336.00	345.43	2.31	347.79	−11.79
38	Mar-2010	381.00	354.39	3.64	347.74	33.26
39	Apr-2010	422.00	370.83	6.20	358.04	63.96
40	May-2010	280.00	357.63	2.32	377.03	−97.03
129	Oct-2017	616.00	613.26	1.58	612.58	3.42
130	Nov-2017	711.00	634.07	5.43	614.84	96.16
131	Dec-2017	653.00	642.20	5.97	639.50	13.50
132	Jan-2018	622.00	642.93	4.92	648.17	−26.17
133	Feb-2018	618.00	641.88	3.73	647.85	−29.85
134	Mar-2018				645.61	
135	Apr-2018				649.33	
136	May-2018				653.06	
137	Jun-2018				656.78	
138	Jul-2018				660.51	
139	Aug-2018				664.24	
140	Sep-2018				667.96	
141	Oct-2018				671.69	
142	Nov-2018				675.41	
143	Dec-2018				679.14	
144	Jan-2019				682.86	
145	Feb-2019				686.59	

Figure 12.38 Holt's Method Forecasts

Forecast and Original Observations

Problems

Level A

32. Consider the airline ticket data in the file **P12_01.xlsx**.
    a. Create a time series chart of the data. Based on what you see, which of the exponential smoothing models do you think should be used for forecasting? Why?
    b. Use simple exponential smoothing to forecast these data, using no holdout period and requesting 12 months of future forecasts. Use the default smoothing constant of 0.1.
    c. Repeat part **b**, optimizing the smoothing constant. Does it make much of an improvement?
    d. Write a short report to summarize your results.

33. Consider the applications for home mortgages data in the file **P12_04.xlsx**.
    a. Create a time series chart of the data. Based on what you see, which of the exponential smoothing models do you think should be used for forecasting? Why?
    b. Use simple exponential smoothing to forecast these data, using no holdout period and requesting four quarters of future forecasts. Use the default smoothing constant of 0.1.
    c. Repeat part **b**, optimizing the smoothing constant. Does it make much of an improvement?
    d. Write a short report to summarize your results.

34. Consider the American Express closing price data in the file **P12_16.xlsx**.
    a. Create a time series chart of the data. Based on what you see, which of the exponential smoothing models do you think should be used for forecasting? Why?
    b. Use Holt's exponential smoothing to forecast these data, using no holdout period and requesting 20 days of future forecasts. Use the default smoothing constants of 0.1.
    c. Repeat part **b**, optimizing the smoothing constants. Does it make much of an improvement?
    d. Repeat parts **a** and **b**, this time using a holdout period of 50 days.
    e. Write a short report to summarize your results.

35. Consider the poverty level data in the file **P02_44.xlsx**.
    a. Create a time series chart of the data. Based on what you see, which of the exponential smoothing models do you think should be used for forecasting? Why?
    b. Use simple exponential smoothing to forecast these data, using no holdout period and requesting three years of future forecasts. Use the default smoothing constant of 0.1.
    c. Repeat part **b**, optimizing the smoothing constant. Make sure you request a chart of the series with the forecasts superimposed. Does the Optimize Parameters option make much of an improvement?
    d. Write a short report to summarize your results. Considering the chart in part **c**, would you say the forecasts are adequate?

Problems 36 through 38 ask you to apply the exponential smoothing formulas. These do not require StatTools. In fact, they do not even require Excel. You can do them with a calculator (or with Excel).

36. An automobile dealer is using Holt's method to forecast weekly car sales. Currently, the level is estimated to be 50 cars per week, and the trend is estimated to be six cars per week. During the current week, 30 cars are sold. After observing the current week's sales, forecast the number of cars three weeks from now. Use $\alpha = \beta = 0.3$.

37. You have been assigned to forecast the number of aircraft engines ordered each month from an engine manufacturing company. At the end of February, the forecast is that 100 engines will be ordered during April. Then during March, 120 engines are actually ordered.
    a. Using $\alpha = 0.3$, determine a forecast (at the end of March) for the number of orders placed during April and during May. Use simple exponential smoothing.
    b. Suppose that MAE = 16 at the end of March. At the end of March, the company can be 68% sure that April orders will be between what two values, assuming normally distributed forecast errors? (*Hint*: It can be shown that the standard deviation of forecast errors is approximately 1.25 times MAE.)

38. Simple exponential smoothing with $\alpha = 0.3$ is being used to forecast sales of SLR (single lens reflex) cameras at an appliance store. Forecasts are made on a monthly basis. After August camera sales are observed, the forecast for September is 100 cameras.
    a. During September, 120 cameras are sold. After observing September sales, what is the forecast for October camera sales? What is the forecast for November camera sales?
    b. It turns out that June sales were recorded as 10 cameras. Actually, however, 100 cameras were sold in June. After correcting for this error, what is the forecast for October camera sales?

Level B

39. Holt's method assumes an *additive* trend. For example, a trend of five means that the level will increase by five units per period. Suppose that there is actually a *multiplicative* trend. For example, if the current estimate of the level is 50 and the current estimate of the trend is 1.2, the forecast of demand increases by 20% per period. So the forecast demand for next period is 50(1.2) and forecast demand for two periods in the future is $50(1.2)^2$. If you want to use a multiplicative trend in Holt's method, you should use equations of the form:

$$L_t = \alpha Y_t + (1 - \alpha)(I)$$

$$T_t = \beta(II) + (1 - \beta)T_{t-1}$$

    a. What should (*I*) and (*II*) be?
    b. Suppose you are working with monthly data and month 12 is December, month 13 is January, and so on.

Also suppose that $L_{12} = 100$ and $T_{12} = 1.2$, and you observe $Y_{13} = 200$. At the end of month 13, what is the forecast for Y_{15}? Assume $\alpha = \beta = 0.5$ and a multiplicative trend.

40. A version of simple exponential smoothing can be used to predict the outcome of sporting events. To illustrate, consider pro football. Assume for simplicity that all games are played on a neutral field. Before each day of play, assume that each team has a rating. For example, if the rating for the Bears is +10 and the rating for the Bengals is +6, the Bears are predicted to beat the Bengals by $10 - 6 = 4$ points. Suppose that the Bears play the Bengals and win by 20 points. For this game, the model underpredicted the Bears' performance by $20 - 4 = 16$ points. Assuming that the best α for pro football is 0.10, the Bears' rating will increase by $16(0.1) = 1.6$ points and the Bengals' rating will decrease by 1.6 points. In a rematch, the Bears will then be favored by $(10 + 1.6) - (6 - 1.6) = 7.2$ points.

a. How does this approach relate to the equation $L_t = L_{t-1} + \alpha E_t$?
b. Suppose that the home field advantage in pro football is three points; that is, home teams tend to outscore equally rated visiting teams by an average of three points a game. How could the home field advantage be incorporated into this system?
c. How might you determine the *best* α for pro football?
d. How could the ratings for each team at the beginning of the season be chosen?
e. Suppose this method is used to predict pro football (16-game schedule), college football (11-game schedule), college basketball (30-game schedule), and pro basketball (82-game schedule). Which sport do you think will have the smallest optimal α? Which will have the largest optimal α? Why?
f. Why might this approach yield poor forecasts for major league baseball?

12-8 Seasonal Models

So far we have said practically nothing about seasonality. Seasonality is the consistent month-to-month (or quarter-to-quarter) differences that occur each year. (It could also be the day-to-day differences that occur each week.) For example, there is seasonality in beer sales—high in the summer months, lower in other months. Toy sales are also seasonal, with a huge peak in the months preceding Christmas. In fact, if you start thinking about time series variables that you are familiar with, the majority of them probably have some degree of seasonality.

How can you tell whether there is seasonality in a time series? The easiest way is to check whether a graph of the time series has a *regular* pattern of ups and/or downs in particular months or quarters. Although random noise can sometimes mask such a pattern, the seasonal pattern is usually fairly obvious. (We have also included the file **Check for Seasonality Finished.xlsx** in the finished examples folder. It indicates one possible way to check for seasonality.)

Government agencies often perform part of the second method for us—that is, they deseasonalize the data.

There are basically three methods for dealing with seasonality. First, you can use Winters' exponential smoothing model. It is similar to simple exponential smoothing and Holt's method, except that it includes another component, and corresponding smoothing constant, to capture seasonality. Second, you can *deseasonalize* the data, then use any forecasting method to model the deseasonalized data, and finally "reseasonalize" these forecasts. Finally, you can use multiple regression with dummy variables for the seasons. We discuss all these methods in this section.

Seasonal models are usually classified as *additive* or *multiplicative*. Suppose that the series contains monthly data, and that the average of the 12 monthly values for a typical year is 150. An **additive** model finds seasonal indexes, one for each month, that are *added* to the monthly average, 150, to get any month's value. For example, if the index for March is 22, then a typical March value is $150 + 22 = 172$. If the seasonal index for September is -12, then a typical September value is $150 - 12 = 138$. A **multiplicative** model also finds seasonal indexes, but they are *multiplied* by the monthly average to get any month's value. Now if the index for March is 1.3, a typical March value is $150(1.3) = 195$. If the index for September is 0.9, then a typical September value is $150(0.9) = 135$.

> In an **additive seasonal model**, an appropriate seasonal index is added to a base forecast. These indexes, one for each season, typically average to 0.

> In a **multiplicative seasonal model**, a base forecast is multiplied by an appropriate seasonal index. These indexes, one for each season, typically average to 1.

Either an additive or a multiplicative model can be used to forecast seasonal data. However, because multiplicative models are somewhat easier to interpret and have worked well in applications, we focus on them. Note that the seasonal index in a multiplicative model can be interpreted as a percentage. Using the figures in the previous paragraph as an example, March tends to be 30% above the monthly average, whereas September tends to be 10% below it. Software packages usually ensure that the seasonal indexes in a multiplicative model average to 1.

12-8a Winters' Exponential Smoothing Model

We now turn to Winters' exponential smoothing model. It is very similar to Holt's model—it again has level and trend terms and corresponding smoothing constants α and β—but it also has seasonal indexes and a corresponding smoothing constant γ (gamma). This new smoothing constant controls how quickly the method reacts to observed changes in the seasonal pattern. If γ is small, the method reacts slowly. If it is large, the method reacts more quickly. As with Holt's model, there are equations for updating the level and trend terms, and there is one extra equation for updating the seasonal indexes. For completeness, we list these equations, but they are best left to the software. In Equation (12.21), S_t refers to the multiplicative seasonal index for period t. In equations (12.19), (12.21), and (12.22), M refers to the number of seasons ($M = 4$ for quarterly data, $M = 12$ for monthly data).

Formulas for Winters' Exponential Smoothing Model

$$L_t = \alpha \frac{Y_t}{S_{t-M}} + (1 - \alpha)(L_{t-1} + T_{t-1}) \qquad (12.19)$$

$$T_t = \beta(L_t - L_{t-1}) + (1 - \beta)T_{t-1} \qquad (12.20)$$

$$S_t = \gamma \frac{Y_t}{L_t} + (1 - \gamma)S_{t-M} \qquad (12.21)$$

$$F_{t+k} = (L_t + kT_t)S_{t+k-M} \qquad (12.22)$$

To see how the forecasting in Equation (12.22) works, suppose you have observed data through June and you want a forecast for the coming September, that is, a three-month-ahead forecast. (In this case t refers to June and $t + k = t + 3$ refers to September.) The method first adds 3 times the current trend term to the current level. This gives a forecast for September that would be appropriate if there were no seasonality. Next, it multiplies this forecast by the most recent estimate of September's seasonal index (the one from the previous September) to get the forecast for September. We illustrate the method in the following example.

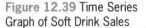

12.5 QUARTERLY SOFT DRINK SALES

The data in the **Soft Drink Sales.xlsx** file represent quarterly sales (in millions of dollars) for a soft drink company from quarter 1 of 2003 through quarter 4 of 2018. There has been an upward trend in sales during this period, and there is also a fairly regular seasonal pattern, as shown in Figure 12.39. Sales in the warmer quarters, 2 and 3, are consistently higher than in the colder quarters, 1 and 4. How well can Winters' method track this upward trend and seasonal pattern?

Figure 12.39 Time Series Graph of Soft Drink Sales

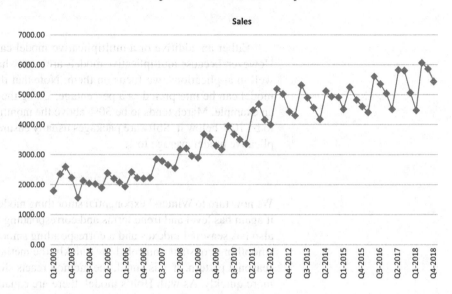

Objective

To see how well Winters' method, with appropriate smoothing constants, can forecast the company's seasonal soft drink sales.

Solution

To use Winters' method with StatTools, you proceed exactly as with any of the other exponential smoothing methods. Specifically, fill in the Forecast dialog box as shown in Figure 12.38, selecting Winters' method and forecasting four quarters into the future (all of 2019). Note that we chose 0.2 for the first two smoothing constants and a larger smoothing constant, 0.4, for seasonality. This is often recommended, but you can experiment with other smoothing constants or check the Optimize option.

Figure 12.40 StatTools Forecast Settings for Soft Drink Sales

The results from Winters' method are shown in Figures 12.41, 12.42, and 12.43. The output in Figure 12.42 is very similar to output from Holt's method, except there is now a column, column E, for the estimated seasonal indexes. These change slightly over time, due to Equation (12.21), but you can see how they consistently pick up the pattern of lower sales in quarters 1 and 4 and higher sales in quarters 2 and 3.

The graph of the forecasts superimposed on the original series, shown in Figure 12.43, indicates that Winters' method clearly picks up the seasonal pattern and the upward trend and projects both of these into the future.

Figure 12.41 Winters' Method Summary Output

	A	B
1	*Winters' Exponential Smoothing Forecasts for Sales*	
2	*Forecasting Constants*	
3	**Level (Alpha)**	0.200
4	**Trend (Beta)**	0.200
5	**Season (Gamma)**	0.400
6		
7		
8	*Winters' Exponential*	
9	**Mean Abs Err**	186.18
10	**Root Mean Sq Err**	232.51
11	**Mean Abs Per% Err**	5.49%

Figure 12.42 Winters' Method Detailed Output

	A	B	C	D	E	F	G
	Forecasting Data	**Sales**	**Level**	**Trend**	**Season**	**Forecast**	**Error**
36							
37	**Q1-2003**	1807.37	2052.06	55.99	0.88		
38	**Q2-2003**	2355.32	2113.77	57.13	1.11	2323.84	31.48
39	**Q3-2003**	2591.83	2229.02	68.76	1.10	2285.83	306.00
40	**Q4-2003**	2236.39	2302.23	69.65	0.97	2214.92	21.47
97	**Q1-2018**	4497.47	5357.78	34.54	0.87	4805.87	−308.40
98	**Q2-2018**	6075.52	5417.52	39.58	1.11	5936.78	138.74
99	**Q3-2018**	5868.67	5482.69	44.70	1.06	5734.27	134.40
100	**Q4-2018**	5432.24	5560.06	51.23	0.96	5276.32	155.92
101	**Q1-2019**					4865.31	
102	**Q2-2019**					6280.67	
103	**Q3-2019**					6048.77	
104	**Q4-2019**					5554.86	

Figure 12.43 Winters' Method Forecasts

Forecast and Original Observations

The finished version of the file also shows that the optimal smoothing constants for Winters' method are 0.928, 0, and 0, not exactly what you would expect. As with Holt's method, these results are due to the way StatTools initializes the method. Because of this, we recommend using "good" smoothing constants, like those in Figure 12.41, but not necessarily optimizing.

The three exponential smoothing methods we have examined are not the only ones available. For example, there are linear and quadratic models available in some software packages. These are somewhat similar to Holt's model except that they use only a single smoothing constant. There are also adaptive exponential smoothing models, where the smoothing constants themselves are allowed to change over time. Although these more complex models have been studied thoroughly in the academic literature and are used by some practitioners, they typically offer only marginal gains in forecast accuracy over the models we have examined.

12-8b Deseasonalizing: The Ratio-to-Moving-Averages Method

You have probably seen references to time series data that have been **deseasonalized**. (Websites often use the abbreviations SA and NSA for seasonally adjusted and non-seasonally adjusted.) The reason why data are often published in deseasonalized form is that readers can then spot trends more easily. For example, if you see a time series of sales that has not been deseasonalized, and it shows a large increase from November to December, you might not be sure whether this represents a real increase in sales or a seasonal phenomenon (Christmas sales). However, if this increase is really just a seasonal effect, the deseasonalized version of the series will show no such increase in sales.

Economists and statisticians have a variety of sophisticated methods for deseasonalizing time series data, but they are typically variations of the **ratio-to-moving-averages method** described here. This method is applicable when seasonality is multiplicative, as described in the previous section. The goal is to find the seasonal indexes, which can then be used to deseasonalize the data. For example, if the estimated index for June is 1.3, this means that June's values are typically about 30% larger than the average for all months. Therefore, June's value is *divided* by 1.3 to obtain the (smaller) deseasonalized value. Similarly, if February's index is 0.85, then February's values are 15% below the average for all months, so February's value is divided by 0.85 to obtain the (larger) deseasonalized value.

> To **deseasonalize** an observation when using a multiplicative model of seasonality, *divide* it by the appropriate seasonal index.

To find the seasonal index for June 2019 (or any other month) in the first place, you essentially divide June's observation by the average of the 12 observations surrounding June. (This is the reason for the term *ratio* in the name of the method.) There is one minor problem with this approach. June 2019 is not exactly in the middle of any 12-month sequence. If you use the 12 months from January 2019 to December 2019, June 2019 is in the *first* half of the sequence; if you use the 12 months from December 2018 to November 2019, June 2019 is in the *last* half of the sequence. Therefore, you can compromise by averaging the January-to-December and December-to-November averages. This is called a *centered* average. Then the seasonal index for June is June's observation divided by this centered average. The following equation shows more specifically how it works.

$$\text{Jun2019 index} = \frac{\text{Jun2019}}{\left(\dfrac{\text{Dec2018} + \ldots + \text{Nov2019}}{12} + \dfrac{\text{Jan2019} + \ldots + \text{Dec2019}}{12}\right)\Big/ 2}$$

If the series covers several years, the procedure produces several June indexes, one for each year. The usual way to combine them is to average them. This single average index for June is then used to deseasonalize *all* June observations.

Once the seasonal indexes are obtained, each observation is divided by its seasonal index to deseasonalize the data. The deseasonalized data can then be forecast by *any* of the methods we have described (other than Winters' method, which wouldn't make much sense). For example, Holt's method or the moving averages method could be used to forecast the deseasonalized data. Finally, the forecasts are "reseasonalized" by *multiplying* them by the seasonal indexes.

As this description suggests, the method is not meant for hand calculations. However, it is straightforward to implement in StatTools, as we illustrate in the finished version of the soft drink sales file. All you need to do is check a Deseasonalize box and then choose a forecasting method, such as Holt's, for the deseasonalized series. As you can see in the file, the results are very similar to the results from Winters' method.

12-8c Estimating Seasonality with Regression

We now examine a regression approach to forecasting seasonal data that uses **dummy variables** for the seasons. Depending on how you write the regression equation, you can create either an additive or a multiplicative seasonal model.

As an example, suppose that the data are quarterly data with a possible linear trend. Then you can create dummy variables Q_1, Q_2, and Q_3 for the first three quarters (using quarter 4 as the reference quarter) and estimate the additive equation

$$\text{Forecast } Y_t = a + bt + b_1 Q_1 + b_2 Q_2 + b_3 Q_3$$

The coefficients of the dummy variables, b_1, b_2 and b_3, indicate how much each quarter differs from the reference quarter, quarter 4, and the coefficient b represents the trend.

For example, suppose the estimated equation is

$$\text{Forecast } Y_t = 130 + 25t + 15Q_1 + 5Q_2 - 20Q_3$$

Then the average increase from one quarter to the next is 25 (the coefficient of t). This is the trend effect. However, quarter 1 averages 15 units higher than quarter 4, quarter 2 averages 5 units higher than quarter 4, and quarter 3 averages 20 units lower than quarter 4. These coefficients indicate the seasonal effects.

As discussed in Chapter 10, it is also possible to estimate a *multiplicative* model using dummy variables for seasonality (and possibly time for trend). Then you would estimate the equation

$$\text{Forecast } Y_t = ae^{bt}e^{b_1 Q_1}e^{b_2 Q_2}e^{b_3 Q_3}$$

or, after taking logs,

$$\text{Forecast Log } Y_t = \text{Log} a + bt + b_1 Q_1 + b_2 Q_2 + b_3 Q_3$$

Either of these approaches is reasonable, but because of its simplicity, we illustrate only the additive model in the following continuation of the soft drink sales example.

EXAMPLE

12.5 QUARTERLY SOFT DRINK SALES (CONTINUED)

Returning to the soft drink sales data (see the file **Soft Drink Sales.xlsx**), does a regression approach provide forecasts that are as accurate as those provided by the other seasonal methods in this chapter?

Objective

To use an additive regression equation, with dummy variables for seasons and a time variable for trend, to forecast soft drink sales.

Solution

Figure 12.44 illustrates the data setup. Besides the Sales and Time variables, you need to create dummy variables for three of the four quarters. You can then use multiple regression, with Sales as the dependent variable, and Time, Q1, Q2, and Q3 as the explanatory variables.

Figure 12.44 Data Setup for Regression Model with Dummies

◢	A	B	C	D	E	F
1	Quarter	Sales	Time	Q1	Q2	Q3
2	Q1-2003	1807.37	1	1	0	0
3	Q2-2003	2355.32	2	0	1	0
4	Q3-2003	2591.83	3	0	0	1
5	Q4-2003	2236.39	4	0	0	0
6	Q1-2004	1549.14	5	1	0	0
7	Q2-2004	2105.79	6	0	1	0
8	Q3-2004	2041.32	7	0	0	1
9	Q4-2004	2021.01	8	0	0	0

The regression output appears in Figure 12.45. Of particular interest are the coefficients of the explanatory variables. The coefficient of Time means that deseasonalized sales increase by about 65.2 per quarter. Also, the coefficients of Q1, Q2, and Q3 mean that sales in quarters 1, 2, and 3 are, respectively, about 260 below, 547 above, and 354 above sales in the reference quarter, quarter 4. This pattern is quite comparable to the pattern of seasonal indexes you saw in previous models for these data.

Figure 12.45 Regression Output for Additive Model

◢	A	B	C	D	E	F	G
1	Multiple Regression for Sales	Multiple	R-Square	Adjusted	Std. Err. of	Rows	Outliers
2	Summary	R		R-square	Estimate	Ignored	
3		0.9721	0.9450	0.9413	313.357	0	0
4							
5		Degrees of	Sum of	Mean of	F	p-Value	
6	ANOVA Table	Freedom	Squares	Squares			
7	Explained	4	99629528.07	24907382.02	253.658	<0.0001	
8	Unexplained	59	5793372.719	98192.75796			
9							
10		Coefficient	Standard	t-Value	p-Value	Confidence Interval 95%	
11	Regression Table		Error			Lower	Upper
12	Constant	1480.231	106.553	13.892	<0.0001	1267.019	1693.443
13	Time	65.184	2.124	30.685	<0.0001	60.934	69.435
14	Q1	−259.794	110.972	−2.341	0.0226	−481.847	−37.740
15	Q2	546.560	110.870	4.930	<0.0001	324.710	768.411
16	Q3	353.661	110.809	3.192	0.0023	131.933	575.389

To compare the forecast accuracy of this method to earlier models, you must perform several steps manually. (See Figure 12.46 for reference.) First, calculate the forecasts in column G by entering the formula

$$\text{=Regression!\$B\$12+MMULT(Data!C2:F2,Regression!\$B\$13:\$B\$16)}$$

in cell G2 and copying it down. (This formula assumes the regression output is in a sheet named Regression. It uses Excel's MMULT function to sum the products of explanatory values and regression coefficients. Because it is an array formula, you must press Ctrl+Shift+Enter when you enter it. Next, calculate the errors, squared errors, absolute errors, and absolute percentage errors in columns H, I, J, and K, and summarize them in the usual way in column N.

Note that these summary measures are somewhat larger for this regression model than those from Winters' method. Still, the corresponding graph in Figure 12.46 shows that the regression method has successfully picked up the trend and the seasonal pattern.

Figure 12.46 Forecasts, Forecast Errors, and Summary Measures from Regression

	G	H	I	J	K	L	M	N
1	Forecast	Error	Sq Error	Abs Error	Pct Abs Error		Error measures	
2	1285.62	521.75	272221.87	521.75	28.87%		MAE	232.12
3	2157.16	198.16	39267.68	198.16	8.41%		RMSE	300.87
4	2029.44	562.39	316277.72	562.39	21.70%		MAPE	7.10%
5	1740.97	495.42	245443.56	495.42	22.15%			
6	1546.36	2.78	7.74	2.78	0.18%			
7	2417.90	−312.11	97410.17	312.11	14.82%			
8	2290.18	−248.86	61931.81	248.86	12.19%			
9	2001.70	19.31	372.72	19.31	0.96%			
10	1807.09	63.37	4015.17	63.37	3.39%			
11	2678.63	−288.07	82985.93	288.07	12.05%			
12	2550.92	−352.89	124529.80	352.89	16.05%			
13	2262.44	−215.61	46488.07	215.61	10.53%			
14	2067.83	−133.64	17860.03	133.64	6.91%			
15	2939.37	−532.96	284045.89	532.96	22.15%			
16	2811.65	−562.59	316512.64	562.59	25.01%			
17	2523.18	−311.62	97105.58	311.62	14.09%			
18	2328.57	−91.52	8375.58	91.52	4.09%			
19	3200.11	−343.68	118113.42	343.68	12.03%			
20	3072.39	−272.82	74431.47	272.82	9.75%			

This method of detecting seasonality by using dummy variables in a regression equation is always an option. The other variables included in the regression equation could be time t, lagged versions of Y_t, and/or current or lagged versions of other explanatory variables. These variables would capture any time series behavior other than seasonality. Just remember that there should always be one less dummy variable than the number of seasons. If the data are quarterly, three dummies are needed; if the data are monthly, 11 dummies are needed. If the coefficients of any of these dummies turn out to be statistically insignificant, they can be omitted from the equation. Then the omitted terms are effectively combined with the reference season. For example, if the Q_1 term were omitted, then quarters 1 and 4 would essentially be combined and treated as the reference season, and the other two seasons would be compared to them through their dummy variable coefficients.

Problems

Level A

41. University Credit Union is open Monday through Saturday. Winters' method is being used (with $\alpha = \beta = \gamma = 0.5$) to predict the number of customers entering the bank each day. After incorporating the arrivals on Monday, October 16, the seasonal indexes are: Monday, 0.90; Tuesday, 0.70; Wednesday, 0.80; Thursday, 1.1; Friday, 1.2; Saturday, 1.3.

Also, the current estimates of level and trend are 200 and 1. On Tuesday, October 17, 182 customers enter the bank. At the close of business on October 17, forecast the number of customers who will enter the bank on each of the next six business days.

42. A local bank is using Winters' method with $\alpha = 0.2$, $\beta = 0.1$, and $\gamma = 0.5$ to forecast the number of customers served each day. The bank is open Monday through Friday. At the end of the previous week, the following seasonal indexes have been estimated: Monday, 0.80;

Tuesday, 0.90; Wednesday, 0.95; Thursday, 1.10; Friday, 1.25. Also, the current estimates of level and trend are 20 and 1. After observing that 30 customers are served by the bank on this Monday, forecast the number of customers who will be served on each of the next five business days.

43. Suppose Winters' method is used to forecast quarterly U.S. retail sales (in billions of dollars). At the end of the first quarter of 2018, the seasonal indexes are: quarter 1, 0.94; quarter 2, 1.02; quarter 3, 1.0; quarter 4, 1.05. Also, the current estimates of level and trend are 1,168 and 7. During the second quarter of 2018, retail sales are $1,188 billion. Assume $\alpha = 0.2$, $\beta = 0.4$, and $\gamma = 0.5$.
   a. At the end of the second quarter of 2018, develop a forecast for retail sales during the third and fourth quarters of 2018.
   b. At the end of the second quarter of 2018, develop a forecast for the first and second quarter of 2019.

44. The file **P02_55.xlsx** contains monthly retail sales of beer, wine, and liquor at U.S. liquor stores.
   a. Is seasonality present in these data?
   b. Use the StatTools Deseasonalize option and then forecast the deseasonalized data for each month of the next year using the moving average method with an appropriate span.
   c. Does Holt's exponential smoothing method, with optimal smoothing constants, outperform the moving average method used in part **b**? Demonstrate why or why not.

45. Continuing the previous problem, how do your responses to the questions change if you employ Winters' method to handle seasonality in this time series? Explain. Which forecasting method do you prefer, Winters' method or one of the methods used in the previous problem? Defend your choice.

46. The file **P12_46.xlsx** contains monthly time series data for total U.S. retail sales of building materials, garden equipment, and supplies dealers.
   a. Is seasonality present in these data? If so, characterize the seasonality pattern.
   b. Use the Deseasonalize option in StatTools to forecast the deseasonalized data for each month of the next year using the moving average method with an appropriate span.
   c. Does Holt's exponential smoothing method, with optimal smoothing constants, outperform the moving average method employed in part **b**? Demonstrate why or why not.

47. The file **P12_47.xlsx** consists of the monthly retail sales levels of U.S. gasoline service stations.
   a. Is there a seasonal pattern in these data? If so, how do you explain this seasonal pattern?
   b. Forecast this time series for the first four months of the next year using the most appropriate method for these data. Defend your choice of forecasting method.

48. The number of employees on the payroll at a food processing plant is recorded at the start of each month. These data are provided in the file **P12_03.xlsx**.
   a. Is there a seasonal pattern in these data? If so, how do you explain this seasonal pattern?
   b. Forecast this time series for the first four months of the next year using the most appropriate method. Defend your choice of forecasting method.

49. The file **P12_49.xlsx** contains total monthly U.S. retail sales data. Compare the effectiveness of Winters' method with that of the ratio-to-moving-average method in deseasonalizing this time series. Using the deseasonalized time series generated by each of these two methods, forecast U.S. retail sales with the most appropriate method. Defend your choice of forecasting method.

50. Suppose that a time series consisting of six years (2014–2019) of quarterly data exhibits obvious seasonality. Assume that the seasonal indexes turn out to be 0.75, 1.45, 1.25, and 0.55.
   a. If the last four observations of the series (the four quarters of 2019) are 2502, 4872, 4269, and 1924, calculate the deseasonalized values for the four quarters of 2019.
   b. Suppose that a plot of the deseasonalized series shows an upward linear trend, except for some random noise. Therefore, you estimate a linear regression equation for this series versus time and obtain the following equation:

   Predicted deseasonalized value $= 2250 + 51$Quarter

   Here the time variable Quarter is coded so that Quarter $= 1$ corresponds to first quarter 2014, Quarter $= 24$ corresponds to fourth quarter 2019, and the others fall in between. Forecast the actual (not deseasonalized) values for the four quarters of 2020.

51. The file **P12_51.xlsx** contains monthly data on the nonfarm hire rate in the United States from 2005 until mid-2015.
   a. What evidence is there that seasonality is important in this series? Find seasonal indexes (by any method you like) and state briefly what they mean.
   b. Forecast the next 12 months by using a linear trend on the seasonally adjusted data. State briefly the steps you use to obtain this type of forecast.

52. Quarterly sales for a department store over a six-year period are given in the file **P12_52.xlsx**.
   a. Use multiple regression to develop an equation that can be used to predict future quarterly sales. (*Hint*: Use dummy variables for the quarters and a time variable for the quarter number, 1 to 24.)
   b. Letting Y_t be the sales during quarter t, discuss how to estimate the following equation for this series.

   $$Y_t = ab_1^t b_2^{X_1} b_3^{X_2} b_4^{X_3}$$

   Here X_1 is a dummy for first quarters, X_2 is a dummy for second quarters, and X_3 is a dummy for third quarters.
   c. Interpret the results from part **b**.
   d. Which model appears to yield better predictions for sales, the one in part **a** or the one in part **b**?

53. A shipping company is attempting to determine how its shipping costs for a month depend on the number of units shipped during a month. The number of units shipped and total shipping cost for the last 15 months are given in the file **P12_53.xlsx**.
  a. Determine a relationship between units shipped and monthly shipping cost.
  b. Plot the errors for the predictions in order of time sequence. Is there any unusual pattern?
  c. It turns out that there was a trucking strike during months 11 through 15, and you believe that this might have influenced shipping costs. How can the answer to part **a** be modified to account for the effect of the strike? After accounting for this effect, does the unusual pattern in part **b** disappear?

Level B

54. Consider a monthly series of air conditioner (AC) sales. In the discussion of Winters' method, a monthly seasonality of 0.80 for January, for example, means that during January, AC sales are expected to be 80% of the sales during an average month. An alternative approach to modeling seasonality, called an *additive model*, is to let the seasonality factor for each month represent how far above average AC sales are during the current month. For instance, if $S_{Jan} = -50$, then AC sales during January are expected to be 50 fewer than AC sales during an average month. (This is 50 ACs, not 50%.) Similarly, if $S_{July} = 90$, then AC sales during July are expected to be 90 more than AC sales during an average month. Let
S_t = Seasonality for month t after observing month t demand
L_t = Estimate of level after observing month t demand
T_t = Estimate of trend after observing month t demand
Then the Winters' method equations given in the text should be modified as follows:

$$L_t = \alpha(I) + (1 - \alpha)(L_{t-1} + T_{t-1})$$

$$T_t = \beta(L_t - L_{t-1}) + (1 - \beta)T_{t-1}$$

$$S_t = \gamma(II) + (1 - \gamma)S_{t-12}$$

  a. What should (*I*) and (*II*) be?
  b. Suppose that month 13 is January, $L_{12} = 30$, $T_{12} = -3$, $S_1 = -50$, and $S_2 = -20$. Let $\alpha = \gamma = \beta = 0.5$. Suppose 12 ACs are sold during month 13. At the end

of month 13, what is the forecast for AC sales during month 14 using this additive model?

55. Winters' method assumes a multiplicative seasonality but an additive trend. For example, a trend of 5 means that the level will increase by five units per period. Suppose that there is actually a *multiplicative* trend. Then (ignoring seasonality) if the current estimate of the level is 50 and the current estimate of the trend is 1.2, the forecast of demand increases by 20% per period. So the forecast demand for the next period is 50(1.2) and forecast demand for two periods in the future is $50(1.2)^2$. If you want to use a multiplicative trend in Winters' method, you should use the following equations (assuming a period is a month):

$$L_t = \alpha\left(\frac{Y_t}{S_{t-12}}\right) + (1 - \alpha)(I)$$

$$T_t = \beta(II) + (I - \beta)T_{t-1}$$

$$S_t = \gamma\left(\frac{Y_t}{L_t}\right) + (1 - \gamma)S_{t-12}$$

  a. What should (*I*) and (*II*) be?
  b. Suppose that you are working with monthly data and month 12 is December, month 13 is January, and so on. Also, suppose that $L_{12} = 100$, $T_{12} = 1.2$, $S_1 = 0.90$, $S_2 = 0.70$, and $S_3 = 0.95$. If you have just observed $Y_{13} = 200$, what is the forecast for Y_{15} using $\alpha = \beta = \gamma = 0.5$ and a multiplicative trend?

56. Consider the file **P12_49.xlsx**, which contains total monthly U.S. retail sales data. Does a regression approach for estimating seasonality provide forecasts that are as accurate as those provided by Winters' method? Compare the summary measures of forecast errors associated with each method for deseasonalizing this time series. Summarize the results of these comparisons.

57. The file **P12_46.xlsx** contains monthly time series data for total U.S. retail sales of building materials, garden equipment, and supplies dealers. Does a regression approach for estimating seasonality provide forecasts that are as accurate as those provided by Winters' method? Compare the summary measures of forecast errors associated with each method for deseasonalizing the given time series. Summarize the results of these comparisons.

12-9 Conclusion

We have covered a lot of ground in this chapter. Because forecasting is such an important activity in business, it has received a tremendous amount of attention by both academics and practitioners. All the methods discussed in this chapter—and more—are actually used, often on a day-to-day basis. There is no point in arguing which of these methods is best. They all have their strengths and weaknesses. The most important point is that when they are applied properly, they have been found to be useful in real business situations.

Summary of Key Terms

TERM	EXPLANATION	EXCEL	PAGE	EQUATION
Extrapolation models	Forecasting models where only past values of a variable (and possibly time itself) are used to forecast future values		541	
Econometric models	Forecasting models based on regression, where other time series variables are used as explanatory variables (also called causal or regression-based models)		542	
Trend	A systematic increase or decrease of a time series variable through time		544	
Seasonality	A regular pattern of ups and downs based on the season of the year, typically months or quarters		544	
Cyclic component	An irregular pattern of ups and downs caused by business cycles		544	
Noise (or random variation)	The unpredictable ups and downs of a time series variable		545	
Forecast error	The difference between the actual value and the forecast		546	
Mean absolute error (MAE)	The average of the absolute forecast errors		547	12.2
Root mean square error (RMSE)	The square root of the average of the squared forecast errors		547	12.3
Mean absolute percentage error (MAPE)	The average of the absolute percentage forecast errors		547	12.4
Runs test	A test of whether the forecast errors are random noise	Runs test template file	551	
Autocorrelations	Correlations of a time series variable with lagged versions of itself	Autocorrelation template file	552	
Correlogram	A bar chart of autocorrelations at different lags	Autocorrelation template file	554	
Linear trend model	A regression model where a time series variable changes by a constant amount each time period	Excel functions or StatTools	557	12.6
Exponential trend model	A regression model where a time series variable changes by a constant percentage each time period	Excel functions or StatTools	559	12.7
Random walk model	A model indicating that the differences between adjacent observations of a time series variable are constant except for random noise		562	12.9–12.11
Moving averages model	A forecasting model where the average of several past observations is used to forecast the next observation	StatTools	565	
Span	The number of observations in each average of a moving averages model		565	
Exponential smoothing models	A class of forecasting models where forecasts are based on weighted averages of previous observations, giving more weight to more recent observations	StatTools	570	
Smoothing constants	Constants between 0 and 1 that prescribe the weight attached to previous observations and hence the smoothness of the series of forecasts		571	

Key Terms (continued)

TERM	EXPLANATION	EXCEL	PAGE	EQUATION
Simple exponential smoothing	An exponential smoothing model useful for time series with no prominent trend or seasonality	StatTools	571	12.12–12.15
Holt's method	An exponential smoothing model useful for time series with trend but no seasonality	StatTools	571	12.16–12.18
Winters' method	An exponential smoothing model useful for time series with seasonality (and possibly trend)	StatTools	571	12.19–12.22
Additive seasonal model	A model where a seasonal index is added to a base forecast (indexes typically average to 0)		580	
Multiplicative seasonal model	A model where a seasonal index is multiplied by a base forecast (indexes typically average to 1)		580	
Deseasonalizing	A method for removing the seasonal component from a time series	StatTools	584	
Ratio-to-moving-averages method	A method for deseasonalizing a time series, so that some other method can then be used to forecast the deseasonalized series		584	
Dummy variables for seasonality	A regression-based method for forecasting seasonality, where dummy variables are used for the seasons	StatTools	585	

Problems

Conceptual Questions

C.1 "A truly random series will likely have a very small number of runs." Is this statement true or false? Explain your choice.

C.2 Distinguish between a *correlation* and an *autocorrelation*. How are these measures similar? How are they different?

C.3 Under what conditions would you prefer a simple exponential smoothing model to the moving averages method for forecasting a time series?

C.4 Is it more appropriate to use an *additive* or a *multiplicative* model to forecast seasonal data? Summarize the difference(s) between these two types of seasonal models.

C.5 Suppose that monthly data on some time series variable exhibit a clear upward trend but no seasonality. You decide to use moving averages, with any appropriate span. Will there tend to be a systematic bias in your forecasts? Explain why or why not.

C.6 Suppose that monthly data on some time series variable exhibit obvious seasonality. Can you use moving averages, with any appropriate span, to track the seasonality well? Explain why or why not.

C.7 Suppose that quarterly data on some time series variable exhibit obvious seasonality, although the seasonal pattern varies somewhat from year to year. Which method will work best: Winters' method or regression with dummy variables for quarters (and possibly a time variable for trend)? Why?

C.8 Most companies that use (any version of) exponential smoothing use fairly small smoothing constants such as 0.1 or 0.2. Why don't they tend to use larger values.

Level A

58. The file **P12_58.xlsx** contains monthly data on consumer revolving credit (in millions of dollars) through credit unions.

   a. Use these data to forecast consumer revolving credit through credit unions for the next 12 months. Do it in two ways. First, fit an exponential trend to the series. Second, use Holt's method with optimized smoothing constants.

   b. Which of these two methods appears to provide the best forecasts? Answer by comparing their MAPE values.

59. The file **P12_59.xlsx** contains revenue (in millions of dollars) for Procter & Gamble. Create a time series graph of these data. Then superimpose a trend line with Excel's Trendline option. Which of the possible Trendline options seems to provide the best fit? Using this option, what are your forecasts for the next two years?

60. The file **P12_60.xlsx** lists annual revenues (in millions of dollars) for Nike. Create a time series graph of these data. Then superimpose a trend line with Excel's Trendline option. Which of the possible Trendline options seems to provide the best fit? Using this option, what are your forecasts for the next two years?

61. The file **P12_61.xlsx** contains annual data on carbon dioxide (CO_2) levels since 1959, measured at the Mauna Loa Observatory in Hawaii. Fit linear, exponential, and quadratic (polynomial of order 2) trends to these data. In terms of MAD, which fit is best? Using the best fit, forecast CO_2 levels for the next 10 years.

62. The file **P12_62.xlsx** contains data on a motel chain's revenue and advertising.
    a. Use these data and multiple regression to make predictions of the motel chain's revenues during the next four quarters. Assume that advertising during each of the next four quarters is $50,000. (*Hint*: Try using advertising, lagged by one quarter, as an explanatory variable.)
    b. Use simple exponential smoothing to make predictions for the motel chain's revenues during the next four quarters.
    c. Use Holt's method to make forecasts for the motel chain's revenues during the next four quarters.
    d. Use Winters' method to determine predictions for the motel chain's revenues during the next four quarters.
    e. Which of these forecasting methods would you expect to be the most accurate for these data?

63. The file **P12_63.xlsx** contains data on monthly U.S. permits for new housing units (in thousands of houses).
    a. Using Winters' method, find values of α, β, and γ that yield an RMSE as small as possible. Does this method track the housing crash in recent years?
    b. Although we have not discussed autocorrelation for smoothing methods, good forecasts derived from smoothing methods should exhibit no substantial autocorrelation in their forecast errors. Is this true for the forecasts in part **a**?
    c. At the end of the observed period, what is the forecast of housing sales during the next few months?

64. Let Y_t be the sales during month t (in thousands of dollars) for a photography studio, and let P_t be the price charged for portraits during month t. The data are in the file **P11_45.xlsx**. Use regression to fit the following model to these data:

$$Y_t = a + b_1 Y_{t-1} + b_2 P_t + e_t$$

    This equation indicates that last month's sales and the current month's price are explanatory variables. The last term, e_t, is an error term.
    a. If the price of a portrait during month 21 is $10, what would you predict for sales in month 21?
    b. Does there appear to be a problem with autocorrelation of the residuals?

Level B

65. The file **P12_65.xlsx** contains five years of monthly data for a company. The first variable is Time (1 to 60). The second variable, Sales1, contains data on sales of a product. Note that Sales1 increases linearly throughout the period, with only a minor amount of noise. (The third variable, Sales2, is discussed and used in the next problem.) For this problem use the Sales1 variable to see how the following forecasting methods are able to track a linear trend.
    a. Forecast this series with the moving average method with various spans such as 3, 6, and 12. What can you conclude?
    b. Forecast this series with simple exponential smoothing with various smoothing constants such as 0.1, 0.3, 0.5, and 0.7. What can you conclude?
    c. Now repeat part **b** with Holt's exponential smoothing method, again for various smoothing constants. Can you do significantly better than in parts **a** and **b**?
    d. What can you conclude from your findings in parts **a**, **b**, and **c** about forecasting this type of series?

66. The Sales2 variable in the file from the previous problem was created from the Sales1 variable by multiplying by monthly seasonal factors. Basically, the summer months are high and the winter months are low. This might represent the sales of a product that has a linear trend and seasonality.
    a. Repeat parts **a**, **b**, and **c** from the previous problem to see how well these forecasting methods can deal with trend *and* seasonality.
    b. Now use Winters' method, with various values of the three smoothing constants, to forecast the series. Can you do much better? Which smoothing constants work well?
    c. Use the ratio-to-moving-average method, where you first deseasonalize the series and then forecast (by any appropriate method) the deseasonalized series. Does this perform as well as, or better than, Winters' method?
    d. What can you conclude from your findings in parts **a**, **b**, and **c** about forecasting this type of series?

67. The file **P12_67.xlsx** contains monthly time series data on corporate bond yields. These are averages of daily figures, and each is expressed as an annual rate. The variables are:
    • Yield AAA: average yield on AAA bonds
    • Yield BAA: average yield on BAA bonds

    If you examine either Yield variable, you will notice that the autocorrelations of the series are not only large for many lags, but that the lag 1 autocorrelation of the *differences* is significant. This is very common. It means that the series is not a random walk and that it is probably possible to provide a better forecast than the naive forecast from the random walk model. Here is the idea. The large lag 1 autocorrelation of the differences means that the differences are related to the first lag of the differences. This relationship can be estimated by creating the difference variable and a lag of it, then regressing the former on the latter, and finally using this information to forecast the original Yield variable.

a. Verify that the autocorrelations are as described, and form the difference variable and the first lag of it. Call these DYield and L1DYield (where D means difference and L1 means first lag).

b. Run a regression with DYield as the dependent variable and L1DYield as the single explanatory variable. In terms of the original variable Yield, this equation can be written as

$$\text{Yield}_t - \text{Yield}_{t-1} = a + b(\text{Yield}_{t-1} - \text{Yield}_{t-2})$$

Solving for Yield_t is equivalent to the following equation that can be used for forecasting:

$$\text{Yield}_t = a + (1 + b)\text{Yield}_{t-1} - b\text{Yield}_{t-2}$$

Try it—that is, try forecasting the next month from the known last two months' values. How might you forecast values two or three months from the last observed month? (*Hint*: If you do not have an *observed* value to use in the right side of the equation, use a forecast value.)

c. The autocorrelation structure led us to the equation in part **b**. That is, the autocorrelations of the original series took a long time to die down, so we looked at the autocorrelations of the differences, and the large spike at lag 1 led to regressing DYield on L1DYield. In turn, this ultimately led to an equation for Yield_t in terms of its first two lags. Now see what you would have obtained if you had tried regressing Yield_t on its first two lags in the first place—that is, if you had used regression to estimate the equation

$$\text{Yield}_t = a + b_1\text{Yield}_{t-1} + b_2\text{Yield}_{t-2}$$

When you use multiple regression to estimate this equation, do you get the same equation as in part **b**?

68. The file **P12_68.xlsx** lists monthly and annual values of the average surface air temperature of the earth (in degrees Celsius). (Actually, the data are indexes, relative to the period 1951–1980 where the average temperature was about 14 degrees Celsius. So if you want the actual temperatures, you can add 14 to all values.) A look at the time series shows a gradual upward trend, starting with negative values and ending with (mostly) positive values. This might be used to support the claim of global warming. For this problem, use only the annual averages in column N.

a. Is this series a random walk? Explain.

b. Regardless of your answer in part **a**, use a random walk model to forecast the next value (2010) of the series. What is your forecast, and what is an approximate 95% forecast interval, assuming normally distributed forecast errors?

c. Forecast the series in three ways: (i) simple exponential smoothing ($\alpha = 0.35$), (ii) Holt's method ($\alpha = 0.5$, $\beta = 0.1$), and (iii) simple exponential smoothing ($\alpha = 0.3$) on trend-adjusted data, that is, the residuals from regressing linearly versus time. (These smoothing constants are close to optimal.) For each of these, list the MAPE, the RMSE, and the forecast for next year. Also, comment on any "problems" with forecast errors from any of these three approaches. Finally, compare the qualitative features of the three forecasting methods. For example, how do their short-run or longer-run forecasts differ? Is any one of the methods clearly superior to the others?

d. Does your analysis predict convincingly that global warming has been occurring? Explain.

69. The file **P12_69.xlsx** contains data on mass layoff events in all industries in the United States. (See the file for an explanation of how mass layoff events are counted.) There are two versions of the data: nonseasonally adjusted and seasonally adjusted. Presumably, seasonal factors can be found by dividing the non-seasonally adjusted values by the seasonally adjusted values. For example, the seasonal factor for April 1995 is 1431/1492=0.959. How well can you replicate these seasonal factors with appropriate StatTools analyses?

CASE 12.1 Arrivals at the Credit Union

The Eastland Plaza Branch of the Indiana University Credit Union was having trouble getting the correct staffing levels to match customer arrival patterns. On some days, the number of tellers was too high relative to the customer traffic, so that tellers were often idle. On other days, the opposite occurred. Long customer waiting lines formed because the relatively few tellers could not keep up with the number of customers. The credit union manager, James Chilton, knew that there was a problem, but he had little of the quantitative training he believed would be necessary to find a better staffing solution. James figured that the problem could be broken down into three parts. First, he needed a reliable forecast of each day's number of customer arrivals. Second, he needed to translate these forecasts into staffing levels that would make an adequate trade-off between teller idleness and customer waiting. Third, he needed to translate these staffing levels into individual teller work assignments—who should come to work when.

The last two parts of the problem require analysis tools (queueing and scheduling) that we have not covered. However, you can help James with the first part—forecasting. The file **C12_01.xlsx** lists the number of customers entering this credit union branch each day of the past year. It also lists other information: the day of the week, whether the day was a staff or faculty payday, and whether the day was the day before or after a holiday. Use this data set to develop one or more forecasting models that James could use to help solve his problem. Based on your model(s), make any recommendations about staffing that appear reasonable.

CASE | 12.2 Forecasting Weekly Sales at Amanta

Amanta Appliances sells two styles of refrigerators at more than 50 locations in the Midwest. The first style is a relatively expensive model, whereas the second is a standard, less expensive model. Although weekly demand for these two products is fairly stable from week to week, there is enough variation to concern management at Amanta. There have been relatively unsophisticated attempts to forecast weekly demand, but they haven't been very successful. Sometimes demand (and the corresponding sales) are lower than forecast, so that inventory costs are high. Other times the forecasts are too low. When this happens and on-hand inventory is not sufficient to meet customer demand, Amanta requires expedited shipments to keep customers happy—and this nearly wipes out Amanta's profit margin on the expedited units.[5] Profits at Amanta would almost certainly increase if demand could be forecast more accurately.

Data on weekly sales of both products appear in the file **C12_02.xlsx**. A time series chart of the two sales variables indicates what Amanta management expected—namely, there is no evidence of any upward or downward trends or of any seasonality. In fact, it might appear that each series is an unpredictable sequence of random ups and downs. But is this really true? Is it possible to forecast either series, with some degree of accuracy, with an extrapolation method (where only past values of *that* series are used to forecast current and future values)? Which method appears to be best? How accurate is it? Also, is it possible, when trying to forecast sales of one product, to somehow incorporate current or past sales of the *other* product in the forecast model? After all, these products might be "substitute" products, where high sales of one go with low sales of the other, or they might be complementary products, where sales of the two products tend to move in the *same* direction.

APPENDIX | Alternative Forecasting Software

We have illustrated Palisade's StatTools add-in for implementing forecasting methods. There are two alternatives you might want to try. First, Microsoft introduced a forecasting tool in Excel 2016. You can find it as the Forecast Sheet button on the Data ribbon. (As of mid-2018, this tool hadn't yet been included in Excel for Mac.) This forecasting tool implements a version of exponential smoothing, as explained on Microsoft's websites. However, it is difficult to tell exactly how their algorithm works; you see only the forecasts, no formulas, and almost no tweaking is possible. This is why we didn't cover this tool in the chapter.

The second alternative is to use the Time Series Analysis component of the DADM_Tools add-in, freely available at the author's website: https://kelley.iu.edu/albrightbooks/free_downloads.htm. This implements moving averages and the three exponential smoothing methods discussed in the chapter. Although its outputs are similar to those of StatTools, it has several possible advantages:

- It uses a different method of initializing the exponential smoothing parameters, the same method used by the professional Stata statistical software. Unlike StatTools, this initialization is based only on an early subset of the historical data, not on *all* the historical data. Admittedly, this might not make much difference in future forecasts, but it is more in line with the underlying goal of exponential smoothing to learn through time.
- It automatically reports that the values of the smoothing constants that minimize each of the error measures. For example, for Holt's method, it evaluates RMSE for each combination of alpha and beta from 0.05 to 0.95 in increments of 0.05 and reports the best combination.
- If you request them, it performs a runs test and lists autocorrelations of the forecast errors.
- It works with Windows and the Mac.

When relevant, we have provided StatTools and DADM_Tools versions of the examples and problem solutions.

---

5 Because Amanta uses expediting when necessary, its sales each week are equal to its customer demands. Therefore, the terms "demand" and "sales" are used interchangeably.

PART 5
OPTIMIZATION AND SIMULATION MODELING

CHAPTER 13
Introduction to Optimization Modeling

INVENTORY OPTIMIZATION AT GM

Nestor Rizhniak/Shutterstock.com

The key to selling automobiles in the United States is the relationship between manufacturers, dealers, and customers. When customers want to make a purchase, they almost always visit a dealer and purchase a vehicle from the lot. If their vehicle of choice is not on the lot, that dealer can make a request from a nearby dealer who might have the requested vehicle. The manufacturer keeps track of purchases at dealers and supplies them with new automobiles as necessary.

The article by Inman et al. (2017) describes how General Motors (GM) developed two optimization models to determine new-vehicle inventory at its dealers. The first model finds the optimal number of vehicles to build for each dealer. The second model finds the optimal vehicle configurations each dealer should stock. These models differ from the traditional way GM had determined the number of vehicles to stock and their configurations. In the past, the standard approach of finding the level of inventory necessary to achieve a given fill rate, such as meeting 98% of customer demand with on-hand inventory, was used to determine the stock level. The configurations to stock were determined by ranking configurations by demand and stocking those with the highest rankings. Inman and his team used a different approach. For the number of vehicles to stock, they maximized variable profit (revenue minus variable cost) minus carrying costs. For the configurations, they used a "set-covering" approach to find a set of configurations that would cover the observed variety of customer demands.

In the first model, determining the optimal number to stock on dealers' lots helps GM make better production decisions (overtime, assembly line rate, and number of shifts) and marketing decisions (rebates and advertising). To optimize this number, Inman's team rejected the argument that carrying costs are incurred only by the dealers and therefore should not be a concern of GM management. Instead, they took a total supply chain viewpoint, with GM and its dealers considered a single entity. This led them to optimizing variable profit minus carrying costs. Besides, they argue that carrying costs go beyond the traditional costs of inventory such as floor space, insurance, and cost of capital. Customers typically want the newest model vehicle, so the longer vehicles remain on the dealers' lots, the more heavily the dealers must discount their prices to sell them. This type of "carrying cost" hurts both GM and the dealers, and it provides an incentive to hold less inventory. Their model also considers diversions, where if a customer's first choice is not in stock, the customer might divert to their second choice and hence still purchase a GM vehicle.

The second model, determining the optimal set of configurations to stock, is possibly even more challenging. A "full" configuration specifies every option possible: color, body style, powertrain, and a host of others. Determining which full configurations to stock would not only be virtually impossible (because of the vast number of configurations) but also pointless. Most customers are looking for a few key features, such as color, and they don't really care about others. Therefore, Inman's team concentrated on "partial" configurations, the sets of features that appear to be in highest demand at any given dealer. This greatly limits the number of decision variables in the optimization model. In addition, they rejected the standard procedure of stocking only the partial configurations in highest demand. To them, it made more sense to "cover" the range of configurations customers wanted. As a simple example, even if data indicate that black and white vehicles are most popular, it still doesn't make sense to stock all black and white vehicles. At least a few customers will want blue, red, or green vehicles, so at least a few of these should be on dealers' lots.

The result of the team's models is an inventory-balancing report tool. For each model vehicle the dealer stocks, the report shows a column for each partial configuration. These partial configurations account for all the dealer's sales. The report provides details familiar to dealers, who can then use their judgment to fine-tune their ordering decisions. After developing the tool, more than 800 dealers piloted it for six months. These dealers averaged a three to five percent increase in sales and revenue compared to a control group of about 7000 dealers not using the tool.

Inman's team's models have also helped GM to reduce overall retail inventory. Traditionally, GM held more retail inventory than its competitors, but with the help of the optimization models, GM's 2015 year-end inventory was 61 days-supply (the number of days to deplete supply at typical customer demand rates), down 14% from 2014 and substantially lower than Ford's 79 days-supply and Fiat Chrysler's 81 days-supply.

13-1 Introduction

In this chapter, we introduce spreadsheet optimization, one of the most powerful and flexible methods of quantitative analysis. The specific type of optimization we will discuss here is **linear programming** (LP). LP is used in all types of organizations, often on a daily basis, to solve a wide variety of problems. These include problems in labor scheduling, inventory management, selection of advertising media, bond trading, management of cash balances, operation of an electrical utility's hydroelectric system, routing of delivery vehicles, blending in oil refineries, hospital staffing, and many others. The goal of this chapter is to introduce the basic elements of LP: the types of problems it can solve, how LP problems can be modeled in Excel®, and how Excel's Solver add-in can be used to find optimal solutions. Then in the next chapter we will examine a variety of LP applications, and we will also look at applications of integer and nonlinear programming, two important extensions of LP.

13-2 Introduction to Optimization

We first discuss optimization in general. All optimization problems have several common elements. They all have *decision variables*, the variables whose values the decision maker is allowed to choose. Either directly or indirectly, the values of these variables determine such outputs as total cost, revenue, and profit. Essentially, they are the variables a company or organization must know to function properly; they determine everything else. All optimization problems have an *objective function* (**objective**, for short) to be optimized—maximized or minimized. Finally, most optimization problems have **constraints** that must be satisfied. These are usually physical, logical, or economic restrictions, depending on the nature of the problem. In searching for the values of the decision variables that optimize the objective, only those values that satisfy all the constraints are allowed.

Excel uses its own terminology for optimization, and we will use it as well. Excel refers to the decision variables as the **decision variable cells**.[1] These cells must contain numbers that are allowed to change freely; they are *not* allowed to contain formulas.

---

[1] In Excel 2007 and previous versions, Excel's Solver add-in referred to these as "changing cells." Starting with Excel 2010, it refers to them as "decision variable cells" (or simply "variable cells"), so we will use the newer terminology.

Excel refers to the objective as the **objective cell**. There can be only one objective cell, which could contain profit, total cost, total distance traveled, or others, and it must be related through formulas to the decision variable cells. When the decision variable cells change, the objective cell should change accordingly.

> The **decision variable cells** contain the values that can be changed to optimize the objective.
>
> The **objective cell** contains the quantity to be minimized or maximized.
>
> The **constraints** impose restrictions on the values in the decision variable cells.

Finally, there must be appropriate cell formulas that operationalize the constraints. For example, one constraint might indicate that the amount of labor used can be no more than the amount of labor available. In this case, there must be cells for each of these two quantities, and typically at least one of them (probably the amount of labor used) will be related through formulas to the decision variable cells. Constraints can come in a variety of forms. One very common form is **nonnegativity**. This type of constraint states that decision variable cells must have nonnegative (zero or positive) values. Nonnegativity constraints are usually included for physical reasons. For example, it is impossible to produce a negative number of automobiles.

> **Nonnegativity constraints** imply that decision variable cells must contain nonnegative values.

Typically, most of your effort goes into the development of the model.

There are basically two steps in solving an optimization problem. The first step is to develop the model. Here you decide what the decision variables are, what the objective is, which constraints are required, and how everything is related. If you are developing an algebraic model, you must derive the correct algebraic expressions. If you are developing a spreadsheet model, the focus of this book, you must relate all variables with appropriate cell formulas. In particular, you must ensure that your model contains formulas that relate the decision variable cells to the objective cell and formulas that operationalize the constraints. This model development step is where most of your effort goes.

The second step in any optimization model is to optimize. This means that you must systematically choose the values of the decision variables that make the objective as large (for maximization) or small (for minimization) as possible and satisfy all the constraints. Some terminology is useful here. Any set of values of the decision variables that satisfies all of the constraints is called a **feasible solution**. The set of all feasible solutions is called the **feasible region**. In contrast, an **infeasible solution** is a solution that violates at least one constraint. Infeasible solutions are not allowed. The desired feasible solution is the one that provides the best value—minimum for a minimization problem, maximum for a maximization problem—of the objective. This solution is called the **optimal solution**.

> A **feasible solution** is a solution that satisfies all the constraints.
>
> The **feasible region** is the set of all feasible solutions.
>
> An **infeasible solution** violates at least one of the constraints and is not allowed.
>
> The **optimal solution** is the feasible solution that optimizes the objective.

Although most of the effort typically goes into the model development step, much of the published research in optimization has been about the optimization step. Algorithms have been devised for searching through the feasible region to find the optimal solution.

An algorithm is a prescription for carrying out the steps required to achieve some goal, such as finding an optimal solution. An algorithm is typically translated into a computer program that performs the work.

One such algorithm is called the **simplex method**. It is used for *linear* models. There are other more complex algorithms used for other types of models (those with integer decision variables and/or nonlinearities).

We will not discuss the details of these algorithms. They have been programmed into Excel's **Solver** add-in. All you need to do is develop the model and then tell Solver what the objective cell is, what the decision variable cells are, what the constraints are, and what type of model (linear, integer, or nonlinear) you have. Solver then finds the best feasible solution with the appropriate algorithm. You should appreciate that if you used a trial-and-error procedure, even a clever and fast one, it could take hours, weeks, or even years to complete. However, by using the appropriate algorithm, Solver typically finds the optimal solution in a matter of seconds.

There is really a *third* step in the optimization process: **sensitivity analysis**. You typically choose values of input variables, such as unit costs, forecasted demands, and resource availabilities, and then find the optimal solution for these particular input values. This provides a single "answer." However, in any realistic situation, it is wishful thinking to believe that all the input values you use are exactly correct. Therefore, it is useful—indeed, mandatory in most applied studies—to follow up the optimization step with what-if questions. What if the unit costs increased by 5%? What if forecasted demands were 10% lower? What if resource availabilities could be increased by 20%? What effects would such changes have on the optimal solution? This type of sensitivity analysis can be done in an informal manner or it can be highly structured. Fortunately, as with the optimization step itself, good software allows you to obtain answers to various what-if questions quickly and easily.

13-3 A Two-Variable Product Mix Model

We begin with a very simple two-variable example of a *product mix* problem. This is a type of problem frequently encountered in business where a company must decide its product mix—how much of each of its potential products to produce—to maximize its net profit. You will see how to model this problem algebraically and then how to model it in Excel. You will also see how to find its optimal solution with Solver. Next, because it contains only two decision variables, you will see how it can be solved graphically. Although this graphical solution is not practical for most problems, it provides useful insights into general LP models. The final step is then to ask a number of what-if questions about the completed model.

EXAMPLE

13.1 ASSEMBLING AND TESTING COMPUTERS AT PC TECH

The PC Tech company assembles and then tests two models of computers, Basic and XP. For the coming month, the company wants to decide how many of each model to assemble and then test. No computers are in inventory from the previous month, and because these models are going to be changed after this month, the company doesn't want to hold any inventory after this month. It believes the most it can sell this month are 600 Basics and 1200 XPs. Each Basic sells for $300 and each XP sells for $450. The cost of component parts for a Basic is $150; for an XP it is $225. Labor is required for assembly and testing. There are at most 10,000 assembly hours and 3000 testing hours available. Each labor hour for assembling costs $11 and each labor hour for testing costs $15. Each Basic requires five hours for assembling and one hour for testing, and each XP requires six hours for assembling and two hours for testing. PC Tech wants to know how many of each model it should produce (assemble and test) to maximize its net profit, but it cannot use more labor hours than are available, and it does not want to produce more than it can sell.

Objective

To use LP to find the best mix of computer models that stays within the company's labor availability and maximum sales constraints.

Solution

The essence of spreadsheet modeling is transforming a "story problem" into an Excel model. Based on our teaching experience, a "bridge" between the two is often needed, especially for complex models. Therefore, in the next few chapters, most examples in the book will start with a "big picture" diagram to help you understand the model—what the key elements are and how they are related—and get you ready for the eventual spreadsheet model.[2] Each diagram is in its own Excel file, such as **Product Mix 1 Big Picture.xlsx** for this example. (These big picture files are available, just like the example files.) A screenshot of this big picture appears in Figure 13.1.

Pictures such as this one bridge the gap between the problem statement and the ultimate spreadsheet (or algebraic) model.

BigPicture Tip

Playing a slide show

If you load the BigPicture add-in (from the Palisade group of programs) and then open the big picture file, you can see more than this static diagram. First, each of the shapes in the diagram can have a "note," much like an Excel cell comment. When you move the cursor over the shape, the note appears. Second, the software allows you to create slide shows. We have done this for all of the big pictures in the book. This lets you see how the model "evolves," and each slide is accompanied by a "pop-up" text box explanation to help you understand the model even better. To run the slide show, click the Play button on the BigPicture ribbon and then the Next Slide button for each new slide. When you are finished, click the Stop button.

Figure 13.1 Big Picture for Product Mix Model

We have adopted a color-coding/shape convention for these big pictures.

Our Big Picture Conventions

- Blue rectangles indicate given inputs.
- Red ovals indicate decision variables.
- Green rectangles with rounded tops indicate uncertain quantities (relevant for Chapters 15 and 16).
- Yellow rounded rectangles indicate calculated quantities.
- Shapes with thin gray borders indicate bottom line outputs or quantities to optimize.
- Arrows indicate that one quantity helps determine another. However, if an arrow includes an inequality or equality sign, as you will often see in the optimization chapters, the arrow indicates a constraint.

The decision variables in this product mix model are straightforward. The company must decide how many Basics to produce and how many XPs to produce. Once these are known, they can be used with the problem inputs to calculate the number of computers sold, the labor used, and the revenue and cost. However, as you will see with other models in this chapter and the next chapter, determining the decision variables is not always this obvious.

---

2 We have created these diagrams with Palisade's BigPicture add-in, part of the DecisionTools Suite.

Algebraic Model

In the traditional *algebraic* solution method, you first identify the decision variables.[3] In this small problem they are the numbers of computers to produce. We label these x_1 and x_2, although any other labels would do. The next step is to write expressions for the total net profit and the constraints in terms of the x's. Finally, because only nonnegative amounts can be produced, explicit constraints are added to ensure that the x's are nonnegative. The resulting **algebraic model** is

$$\text{Maximize } 80x_1 + 129x_2$$

subject to:

$$5x_1 + 6x_2 \leq 10000$$
$$x_1 + 2x_2 \leq 3000$$
$$x_1 \leq 600$$
$$x_2 \leq 1200$$
$$x_1, x_2 \geq 0$$

To understand this model, consider the objective first. Each Basic produced sells for $300, and the total cost of producing it, including component parts and labor, is $150 + 5(11) + 1(15) = \$220$, so the profit margin is $80. Similarly, the profit margin for an XP is $129. Each profit margin is multiplied by the number of computers produced, and these products are then summed over the two computer models to obtain the total net profit.

The first two constraints are similar. For example, each Basic requires five hours for assembling and each XP requires six hours for assembling, so the first constraint says that the total hours required for assembling is no more than the number available, 10,000. The third and fourth constraints are the maximum sales constraints for Basics and XPs. Finally, negative amounts cannot be produced, so nonnegativity constraints on x_1 and x_2 are included.

For many years, all LP problems were modeled this way in textbooks. In fact, many commercial LP computer packages are still written to accept LP problems in essentially this format. Since around 1990, however, a more intuitive method of expressing LP problems has become popular. This method takes advantage of the power and flexibility of spreadsheets. Actually, LP problems could always be *modeled* in spreadsheets, but now with the addition of Excel's Solver add-in, spreadsheets have the ability to *solve*—that is, optimize—LP problems as well. We use Excel's Solver for all examples in this book.[4]

Many commercial optimization packages require, as input, an algebraic model of a problem. If you ever use one of these packages, you will have to think algebraically.

Graphical Solution

When there are only two decision variables in an LP model, as there are in this product mix model, you can solve the problem graphically. Although this **graphical solution** approach is not practical in most realistic optimization models—where there are many more than two decision variables—the graphical procedure illustrated here still yields important insights for general LP models.

In general, if the two decision variables are labeled x_1 and x_2, then the steps of the method are to express the constraints and the objective in terms of x_1 and x_2, graph the constraints to find the feasible region [the set of all pairs (x_1, x_2) satisfying the constraints, where x_1 is on the horizontal axis and x_2 is on the vertical axis], and then move the objective through the feasible region until it is optimized.

This graphical approach works only for problems with two decision variables. Recall from algebra that any line of the form $ax_1 + bx_2 = c$ has slope $-a/b$. This is because it can be put into the slope – intercept form $x_2 = c/b - (a/b)x_1$.

To do this for the product mix problem, note that the constraint on assembling labor hours can be expressed as $5x_1 + 6x_2 \leq 10000$. To graph this, consider the associated equality (replacing $\leq$ with $=$) and find where the associated line crosses the axes. Specifically, when $x_1 = 0$, then $x_2 = 10000/6 = 1666.7$; and when $x_2 = 0$, then $x_1 = 10000/5 = 2000$. This produces the line labeled "assembling hour constraint" in Figure 13.2. It has slope $-5/6 = -0.83$. The set of all points that satisfy the assembling hour constraint includes the points on this line plus the points *below* it, as indicated by the arrow drawn from the line. [The feasible points are below the line because the point $(0, 0)$ is obviously below the line, and $(0, 0)$ clearly satisfies the assembly hour constraint.] Similarly, the testing hour and maximum sales constraints are shown in the figure. The points that satisfy all three of these constraints and are nonnegative comprise the feasible region, which is below the heavier lines in the figure.

---

3 This is not a book about algebraic models; the main focus is on *spreadsheet* modeling. However, we present algebraic models of the examples in this chapter for comparison with the corresponding spreadsheet models.

4 The Solver add-in built into Excel was developed by a third-party software company, Frontline Systems. This company develops much more powerful versions of Solver for commercial sales, but its standard version built into Microsoft Excel suffices for us. More information about Solver software offered by Frontline can be found at www.solver.com.

Figure 13.2 Graphical Solution to Two-Variable Product Mix Problem

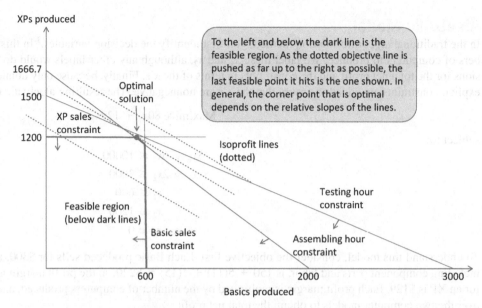

To see which feasible point maximizes the objective, it is useful to draw a sequence of lines where, for each, the objective is constant. A typical line is of the form $80x_1 + 129x_2 = c$, where c is a constant. Any such line has slope $-80/129 = -0.620$, regardless of the value of c. This line is steeper than the testing hour constraint line (slope -0.5), but not as steep as the assembling hour constraint line (slope -0.83). Then the idea is to move a line with this slope up and to the right, making c larger, until it just barely touches the feasible region. The last feasible point it touches is the optimal point.

Several lines with slope -0.620 are shown in Figure 13.2. The middle dotted line is the one with the largest net profit that still touches the feasible region. The associated optimal point is clearly the point where the assembling hour and XP maximum sales lines intersect. You will eventually find (from Solver) that this point is (560,1200), but even if you didn't have the Solver add-in, you could find the coordinates of this point by solving two equations (the ones for assembling hours and XP maximum sales) in two unknowns.

Again, the graphical procedure illustrated here can be used only for the simplest of LP models, those with two decision variables. However, the type of behavior pictured in Figure 13.2 generalizes to *all* LP problems. In general, all feasible regions are (the multidimensional versions of) polygons. That is, they are bounded by straight lines (actually *hyperplanes*) that intersect at several *corner points*. There are five corner points in Figure 13.2, three of which are on the axes. [One of them is (0,0).] When the dotted objective line is moved as far as possible toward better values, the last feasible point it touches is one of the corner points. The actual corner point it last touches is determined by the slopes of the objective and constraint lines. Because there are only a finite number of corner points, it suffices to search among this finite set, not the infinite number of points in the entire feasible region.[5] This insight is largely responsible for the efficiency of the simplex method for solving LP problems.

Although limited in use, the graphical approach yields the important insight that the optimal solution to any LP model is a corner point of a polygon. This limits the search for the optimal solution and makes the simplex method possible.

Fundamental Insight

Geometry of LP Models and the Simplex Method

The feasible region in any LP model is always a multidimensional version of a polygon, and the objective is always a hyperplane, the multidimensional version of a straight line. The objective should always be moved as far as possible in the maximizing or minimizing direction until it just touches the edge of the feasible region. Because of this geometry, the optimal solution is always a corner point of the polygon. The simplex method for LP works so well because it can search through the finite number of corner points extremely efficiently and recognize when it has found the best corner point. This rather simple insight, plus its clever implementation in software packages, has saved companies many, many millions of dollars in the past 50 years.

---

5 This is not entirely true. If the objective line is exactly parallel to one of the constraint lines, there can be *multiple optimal solutions*—a whole line segment of optimal solutions. Even in this case, however, at least one of the optimal solutions is a corner point.

Spreadsheet Model

We now turn our focus to *spreadsheet* modeling. There are many ways to develop an LP **spreadsheet model**. Everyone has his or her own preferences for arranging the data in the various cells. We do not provide exact prescriptions, but we do present enough examples to help you develop good habits. The common elements in all LP spreadsheet models are the inputs, decision variable cells, objective cell, and constraints.

- **Inputs.** All numeric inputs—that is, all numeric data given in the statement of the problem—should appear somewhere in the spreadsheet. Our convention is to color all of the input cells blue. We also try to put most of the inputs in the upper left section of the spreadsheet. However, we sometimes violate this convention when certain inputs fit more naturally somewhere else.
- **Decision variable cells.** Instead of using variable names, such as x, spreadsheet models use a set of designated cells for the decision variables. The values in these cells can be changed to optimize the objective. The values in these cells must be allowed to vary freely, so there should *not* be any formulas in the decision variable cells. To designate them clearly, our convention is to color them red.
- **Objective cell.** One cell, called the objective cell, contains the value of the objective. Solver systematically varies the values in the decision variable cells to optimize the value in the objective cell. This cell must be linked, either directly or indirectly, to the decision variable cells by formulas. Our convention is to color the objective cell gray.

Our coloring conventions

Color all input cells blue.
Color all of the decision variable cells red.
Color the objective cell gray.

- **Constraints.** Excel does not show the constraints directly on the spreadsheet. Instead, they are specified in a Solver dialog box, to be discussed shortly. For example, a set of related constraints might be specified by

B16:C16 < = B18:C18

This implies two separate constraints. The value in B16 must be less than or equal to the value in B18, and the value in C16 must be less than or equal to the value in C18. We will always assign range names to the ranges that appear in the constraints. Then a typical constraint might be specified as

Number_to_produce < = Maximum_sales

This is much easier to read and understand. (If you don't want to use range names, you don't have to. Solver models work fine with cell addresses only.)
- **Nonnegativity.** Normally, the decision variables—that is, the values in the decision variable cells—must be nonnegative. These constraints do not need to be written explicitly; you simply check an option in the Solver dialog box to indicate that the decision variable cells should be nonnegative. Note, however, that if you want to constrain any *other* cells to be nonnegative, you must specify their constraints explicitly.

Overview of the Solution Process

As mentioned previously, the complete solution of a problem involves three stages. In the model development stage you enter all of the inputs, trial values for the decision variable cells, and formulas relating these in a spreadsheet. This stage is the most crucial because it is here that all of the ingredients of the model are included and related appropriately. In particular, the spreadsheet *must* relate the objective to the decision variable cells, either directly or indirectly, so that if the values in the decision variable cells vary, the objective value varies accordingly. Similarly, the spreadsheet must include formulas for the various constraints (usually their left sides) that are related directly or indirectly to the decision variable cells.

After the model is developed, you can proceed to the second stage—invoking Solver. At this point, you formally designate the objective cell, the decision variable cells, the constraints, and selected options, and you tell Solver to find the *optimal* solution. If the first stage has been done correctly, the second stage is usually very quick and straightforward.

The third stage is sensitivity analysis. Here you see how the optimal solution changes (if at all) as selected inputs are varied. This often provides important insights about the behavior of the model.

We now illustrate this procedure for the product mix problem in Example 13.1.

Where Do the Numbers Come From?

There are a variety of inputs in PC Tech's problem, some easy to find and others more difficult. Here are some ideas on how they might be obtained.

• The unit costs in rows 3, 4, and 10 should be easy to obtain. (See Figure 13.3.) These are the going rates for labor and the component parts. Note, however, that the labor costs are probably regular-time rates. If the company wants to consider overtime hours, then the overtime rate (and labor hours availability during overtime) would be necessary, and the model would need to be modified.

Figure 13.3 Two-Variable Product Mix Model with an Infeasible Solution

▲	A	B	C	D	E	F	G
1	Assembling and testing computers				Range names used:		
2					Hours_available	=Model!$D$21:$D$22	
3	Cost per labor hour assembling	$11			Hours_used	=Model!$B$21:$B$22	
4	Cost per labor hour testing	$15			Maximum_sales	=Model!$B$18:$C$18	
5					Number_to_produce	=Model!$B$16:$C$16	
6	Inputs for assembling and testing a computer				Total_profit	=Model!$D$25	
7		Basic	XP				
8	Labor hours for assembly	5	6				
9	Labor hours for testing	1	2				
10	Cost of component parts	$150	$225				
11	Selling price	$300	$450				
12	Unit margin	$80	$129				
13							
14	Assembling, testing plan (# of computers)						
15		Basic	XP				
16	Number to produce	600	1200				
17		<=	<=				
18	Maximum sales	600	1200				
19							
20	Constraints (hours per month)	Hours used		Hours available			
21	Labor availability for assembling	10200	<=	10000			
22	Labor availability for testing	3000	<=	3000			
23							
24	Net profit ($ this month)	Basic	XP	Total			
25		$48,000	$154,800	$202,800			

• The resource usages in rows 8 and 9, often called *technological coefficients*, should be available from the production department. These people know how much labor it takes to assemble and test these computer models.

• The unit selling prices in row 11 have actually been *chosen* by PC Tech's management, probably in response to market pressures and the company's own costs.

• The maximum sales values in row 18 are probably forecasts from the marketing and sales department. These people have some sense of how much they can sell, based on current outstanding orders, historical data, and the prices they plan to charge.

• The labor hour availabilities in rows 21 and 22 are probably based on the current workforce size and possibly on new workers who could be hired in the short run. Again, if these are regular-time hours and overtime is possible, the model would have to be modified to include overtime.

Developing the Spreadsheet Model

The spreadsheet model appears in Figure 13.3. (See the file **Product Mix 1 Finished.xlsx**.) To develop this model, use the following steps.

Developing the Product Mix 1 Model

1. **Inputs.** Enter all of the inputs from the statement of the problem in the blue cells as shown.
2. **Range names.** Create the range names shown in columns E and F. Our convention is to enter enough range names, but not to go overboard. Specifically, we enter enough range names so that the setup in the Solver dialog box, to be explained

shortly, is entirely in terms of range names. Of course, you can add more range names if you like (or you can omit them altogether). The following tip indicates a quick way to create range names.

Excel Tip

Shortcut for Creating Range Names

Select a range such as A16:C16 that includes nice labels in column A and the range you want to name in columns B and C. Then, from the Formulas ribbon, select Create from Selection and accept the default. You automatically get the labels in cells A16 as the range name for the range B16:C16. (Note that if the label contains spaces or other "illegal" characters, they are replaced by underscores in the range name.) This shortcut illustrates the usefulness of adding concise but informative labels next to ranges you want to name.

---

3. **Unit margins.** Enter the formula

$$=B11-B8*\$B\$3-B9*\$B\$4-B10$$

in cell B12 and copy it to cell C12 to calculate the unit profit margins for the two models. (Enter relative/absolute addresses that allow you to copy whenever possible.)

4. **Decision variable cells.** Enter any two values for the decision variable cells in the Number_to_produce range. Any trial values can be used initially; Solver will eventually find the optimal values. Note that the two values shown in Figure 13.3 cannot be optimal because they use more assembling hours than are available. However, you do not need to worry about satisfying constraints at this point; Solver will take care of this later on.

At this stage, it is pointless to try to outguess the optimal solution. Any values in the decision variable cells will suffice.

5. **Labor hours used.** To operationalize the labor availability constraints, you must calculate the amounts used by the production plan. To do this, enter the formula

$$=SUMPRODUCT(B8:C8,Number\_to\_produce)$$

in cell B21 for assembling and copy it to cell B22 for testing. This formula is a shortcut for the following fully written out formula:

$$=B8*B16+C8*C16$$

The SUMPRODUCT function is very useful in spreadsheet models, especially LP models, and you will see it often. Here, it multiplies the number of hours per computer by the number of computers for each model and then sums these products over the two models. When there are only two products in the sum, as in this example, the SUMPRODUCT formula is not really any simpler than the written-out formula. However, imagine that there are 50 models. Then the SUMPRODUCT formula is *much* simpler to enter (and read). For this reason, you should use it whenever possible. Note that each range in this function, B8:C8 and Number_to_produce, is a one-row, two-column range. It is important in the SUMPRODUCT function that the two ranges be exactly the same size and shape.

The "linear" in linear programming is all about sums of products. Therefore, the SUMPRODUCT function is natural and should be used whenever possible.

6. **Net profits.** Enter the formula

$$=B12*B16$$

in cell B25, copy it to cell C25, and sum these to get the total net profit in cell D25. This latter cell is the objective to maximize. Note that if you didn't care about the net profits for the two *individual* models, you could calculate the total net profit with the formula

$$=SUMPRODUCT(B12:C12,Number\_to\_produce)$$

As you see, the SUMPRODUCT function appears once again. It and the **SUM** function are the most used functions in LP models.

Experimenting with Possible Solutions

The next step is to specify the decision variable cells, the objective cell, and the constraints in a Solver dialog box and then instruct Solver to find the optimal solution. However, before you do this, it is instructive to try a few guesses in the decision variable cells. There are two reasons for doing so. First, by entering different sets of values in the decision variable cells, you can confirm that the formulas in the other cells are working correctly. Second, this experimentation can help you to develop a better understanding of the model.

For example, the profit margin for XPs is much larger than for Basics, so you might suspect that the company should produce only XPs. The most it can produce is 1200 (maximum sales), and this uses fewer labor hours than are available. This solution appears in Figure 13.4. However, you can probably guess that it is far from optimal. There are still many labor hours available, so the company could use them to produce some Basics and make more profit.

You can continue to try different values in the decision variable cells, attempting to get as large a total net profit as possible while staying within the constraints. Even for this small model with only two decision variable cells, the optimal solution is not totally obvious. You can only imagine how much more difficult it is when there are hundreds or even thousands of decision variable cells and many constraints. This is why software such as Excel's Solver is required. Solver uses a quick and efficient algorithm to search through all feasible solutions (or more specifically, all corner points) and eventually find the optimal solution. Fortunately, it is quite easy to use, as we now explain.

Figure 13.4 Two-Variable Product Mix Model with a Suboptimal Solution

	A	B	C	D	E	F	G
1	Assembling and testing computers				Range names used:		
2					Hours_available	=Model!$D$21:$D$22	
3	Cost per labor hour assembling	$11			Hours_used	=Model!$B$21:$B$22	
4	Cost per labor hour testing	$15			Maximum_sales	=Model!$B$18:$C$18	
5					Number_to_produce	=Model!$B$16:$C$16	
6	Inputs for assembling and testing a computer				Total_profit	=Model!$D$25	
7		Basic	XP				
8	Labor hours for assembly	5	6				
9	Labor hours for testing	1	2				
10	Cost of component parts	$150	$225				
11	Selling price	$300	$450				
12	Unit margin	$80	$129				
13							
14	Assembling, testing plan (# of computers)						
15		Basic	XP				
16	Number to produce	0	1200				
17		<=	<=				
18	Maximum sales	600	1200				
19							
20	Constraints (hours per month)	Hours used		Hours available			
21	Labor availability for assembling	7200	<=	10000			
22	Labor availability for testing	2400	<=	3000			
23							
24	Net profit ($ this month)	Basic	XP	Total			
25		$0	$154,800	$154,800			

Using Solver

To invoke Excel's Solver, select Solver from the Data ribbon. (If there is no such item on your PC, you need to *load* Solver. To do so, click the File button, then Options, then Add-Ins, and then Go at the bottom of the dialog box. This displays the list of available add-ins. If there is a Solver Add-in item in the list, check it to load Solver. If there is no *The Solver item is under the Tools menu on the Mac.* such item, you need to rerun the Microsoft Office installer and elect to install Solver. It should be included in a typical install, but some people elect not to install it the first time around.) The dialog box in Figure 13.5 appears.[6] It has three important sections that you must fill in: the objective cell, the decision variable cells, and the constraints. For the product mix problem, you can fill these in by typing cell references or you can point, click, and drag the appropriate ranges in the usual way. Better yet, if there are any named ranges, these range names appear instead of cell addresses when you drag the ranges. In fact, for reasons of readability, our convention is to use only range names, not cell addresses, in this dialog box.

Figure 13.5 Solver Dialog Box
(since Excel 2010)

Figure 13.5 Solver Dialog Box
(since Excel 2010)

Excel Tip

Range Names in Solver Dialog Box

Our usual procedure is to use the mouse to select the relevant ranges for the Solver dialog box. Fortunately, if these ranges have already been named, the range names will automatically replace the cell addresses.

1. **Objective.** Select the Total_profit cell as the objective cell, and click the Max option. (Actually, the default option is Max.)
2. **Decision variable cells.** Select the Number_to_produce range as the decision variable cells.
3. **Constraints.** Click the Add button to bring up the dialog box in Figure 13.6. Here you specify a typical constraint by entering a cell reference or range name on the left, the type of constraint from the dropdown list in the middle, and a cell reference, range name, or numeric value on the right. Use this dialog box to enter the constraint

Number_to_produce < =Maximum_sales

(*Note:* You can type these range names into the dialog box, or you can drag them in the usual way. If you drag them, the cell addresses shown in the figure eventually change into range names if range names exist.) Then click the Add button and enter the constraint

Hours_used < =Hours_available

Figure 13.6 Add Constraint
Dialog Box

Excel Tip

Inequality and Equality Labels in Spreadsheet Models

The $\leq$ signs in cells B17:C17 and C21:C22 (see Figure 13.3 or Figure 13.4) are not a necessary part of the Excel model. They are entered simply as labels in the spreadsheet and do not substitute for entering the constraints in the Add Constraint dialog box. However, they help to document the model, so we include them in all the examples. In fact, you should try to plan your spreadsheet models so that the two sides of a constraint are in nearby cells, with "gutter" cells in between where you can attach labels like $\leq$, $\geq$, or $=$. This convention tends to make the resulting spreadsheet models more readable.

Solver Tip

Entering Constraints in Groups

Constraints typically come in groups. Beginners often enter these one at a time, such as B16 $\leq$ B18 and C16 $\leq$ C18, in the Solver dialog box. This can lead to a long list of constraints, and it is time-consuming. It is better to enter them as a group, as in B16:C16 $\leq$ B18:C18. This is not only quicker, but it also takes advantage of range names you have created. For example, this group ends up as Number_to_produce$\leq$Maximum_Sales.

Then click OK to get back to the Solver dialog box. The first constraint says to produce no more than can be sold. The second constraint says to use no more labor hours than are available.

4. **Nonnegativity.** Because negative production quantities make no sense, you must tell Solver *explicitly* to make the decision variable cells nonnegative. To do this, check the Make Unconstrained Variables Non-Negative option shown in Figure 13.5. This automatically ensures that all decision variable cells are nonnegative.

Checking the Non-Negative option ensures only that the decision variable cells will be nonnegative.

5. **Linear model.** There is one last step before clicking the Solve button. As stated previously, Solver uses one of several numerical algorithms to solve various types of models. The models discussed in this chapter are all *linear* models. (We will discuss the properties that distinguish linear models shortly.) Linear models can be solved most efficiently with the simplex method. To instruct Solver to use this method, make sure Simplex LP is selected in the Select a Solving Method dropdown list in Figure 13.5.

6. **Optimize.** Click the Solve button in the dialog box in Figure 13.5. At this point, Solver does its work. It searches through a number of possible solutions until it finds the optimal solution. (You can watch the progress on the lower left of the screen, although for small models the process is virtually instantaneous.) When it finishes, it displays the message shown in Figure 13.7. You can then instruct it to return the values in the decision variable cells to their original (probably nonoptimal) values or retain the optimal values found by Solver. In most cases you should choose the latter. For now, click OK to keep the Solver solution. You should see the solution shown in Figure 13.8.

Figure 13.7 Solver Results Message

Figure 13.8   Two-Variable Product Mix Model with the Optimal Solution

▲	A	B	C	D	E	F	G
1	**Assembling and testing computers**				**Range names used:**		
2					Hours_available	=Model!$D$21:$D$22	
3	Cost per labor hour assembling	$11			Hours_used	=Model!$B$21:$B$22	
4	Cost per labor hour testing	$15			Maximum_sales	=Model!$B$18:$C$18	
5					Number_to_produce	=Model!$B$16:$C$16	
6	Inputs for assembling and testing a computer				Total_profit	=Model!$D$25	
7		Basic	XP				
8	Labor hours for assembly	5	6				
9	Labor hours for testing	1	2				
10	Cost of component parts	$150	$225				
11	Selling price	$300	$450				
12	Unit margin	$80	$129				
13							
14	Assembling, testing plan (# of computers)						
15		Basic	XP				
16	Number to produce	560	1200				
17		<=	<=				
18	Maximum sales	600	1200				
19							
20	Constraints (hours per month)	Hours used		Hours available			
21	Labor availability for assembling	10000	<=	10000			
22	Labor availability for testing	2960	<=	3000			
23							
24	Net profit ($ this month)	Basic	XP	Total			
25		$44,800	$154,800	$199,600			

Discussion of the Solution

This solution indicates that PC Tech should produce 560 Basics and 1200 XPs. This plan uses all available labor hours for assembling, has a few leftover labor hours for testing, produces as many XPs as can be sold, and produces a few less Basics than could be sold. No plan can provide a net profit larger than this one—that is, without violating at least one of the constraints.

The solution in Figure 13.8 is typical of solutions to optimization models in the following sense. Of all the inequality constraints, some are satisfied exactly and others are not. In this solution the XP maximum sales and assembling labor constraints are met exactly. Each of these is called a **binding constraint**. However, the Basic maximum sales and testing labor constraints do *not* hold as equalities. Each of these is called a **nonbinding constraint**. You can think of the binding constraints as bottlenecks. They are the constraints that prevent the objective from being improved. If it were not for the binding constraints on maximum sales and labor, PC Tech could obtain an even larger net profit.

An inequality constraint is **binding** if the solution makes it an equality. Otherwise, it is **nonbinding**.

In a typical optimal solution, you should pay particular attention to two aspects of the solution. First, you should check which of the decision variables are *positive* (as opposed to 0). Generically, these are the "activities" that are done at a positive level. In a product mix model, they are the products included in the optimal mix. Second, you should check which of the constraints are binding. Again, these represent the bottlenecks that keep the objective from improving.

> **Fundamental Insight**
>
> ### Binding and Nonbinding Constraints
>
> Most optimization models contain constraints expressed as inequalities. In an optimal solution, each such constraint is either binding (holds as an equality) or nonbinding. It is important to identify the binding constraints because they are the constraints that prevent the objective from improving. A typical constraint is on the availability of a resource. If such a constraint is binding, the objective could typically improve by having more of that resource. But if such a resource constraint is nonbinding, more of that resource would not improve the objective at all.

13-4 Sensitivity Analysis

Many analysts view the "finished" model as a starting point for many what-if questions. We agree.

Sensitivity for the Product Mix 1 Model

Having found the optimal solution, it might appear that the analysis is complete. But in real LP applications the solution to a *single* model is hardly ever the end of the analysis. It is almost always useful to perform a sensitivity analysis to see how (or if) the optimal solution changes as one or more inputs vary. We illustrate systematic ways of doing so in this section. Actually, we discuss two approaches. The first uses an optional sensitivity report that Solver offers. The second uses an add-in called SolverTable that Albright developed.

13-4a Solver's Sensitivity Report

When you run Solver, the dialog box in Figure 13.7 offers you the option to obtain a sensitivity report.[7] This report is based on a well-established theory of sensitivity analysis in optimization models, especially LP models. This theory was developed around algebraic models that are arranged in a "standardized" format. Essentially, all such algebraic models look alike, so the same type of sensitivity report applies to all of them. Specifically, they have an objective function of the form $c_1x_1 + \cdots + c_nx_n$, where n is the number of decision variables, the c's are constants, and the x's are the decision variables, and each constraint can be expressed as $a_1x_1 + \cdots + a_nx_n \leq b$, $a_1x_1 + \cdots + a_nx_n \geq b$, or $a_1x_1 + \cdots + a_nx_n = b$, where the a's and b's are constants. **Solver's sensitivity report** performs two types of sensitivity analysis: (1) on the coefficients of the objective, the c's, and (2) on the right sides of the constraints, the b's.

We illustrate the typical analysis by looking at the sensitivity report for PC Tech's product mix model in Example 13.1. For convenience, the algebraic model is repeated here.

$$\text{Maximize } 80x_1 + 129x_2$$

subject to:

$$5x_1 + 6x_2 \leq 10000$$
$$x_1 + 2x_2 \leq 3000$$
$$x_1 \leq 600$$
$$x_2 \leq 1200$$
$$x_1, x_2 \geq 0$$

On this Solver run, a sensitivity report is requested in Solver's final dialog box. (See Figure 13.7.) The sensitivity report appears on a new worksheet, as shown in Figure 13.9.[8]

---

7 It also offers Answer and Limits reports. We don't find these particularly useful, so we will not discuss them here.

8 If your table looks different from ours, make sure you chose the simplex method. Otherwise, Solver uses a nonlinear algorithm and produces a different type of sensitivity report.

Figure 13.9 Solver Sensitivity Results

A	B	C	D	E	F	G	H
6	Variable Cells						
7			Final	Reduced	Objective	Allowable	Allowable
8	Cell	Name	Value	Cost	Coefficient	Increase	Decrease
9	$B$16	Number to produce Basic	560	0	80	27.5	80
10	$C$16	Number to produce XP	1200	33	129	1E+30	33
11							
12	Constraints						
13			Final	Shadow	Constraint	Allowable	Allowable
14	Cell	Name	Value	Price	R.H. Side	Increase	Decrease
15	$B$21	Labor availability for assembling Hours used	10000	16	10000	200	2800
16	$B$22	Labor availability for testing Hours used	2960	0	3000	1E+30	40

It contains two sections. The top section is for sensitivity to changes in the two coefficients, 80 and 129, of the decision variables in the objective. Each row in this section indicates how the optimal solution changes if one of these coefficients changes. The bottom section is for the sensitivity to changes in the right sides, 10000 and 3000, of the labor constraints. Each row of this section indicates how the optimal solution changes if one of these availabilities changes. (The maximum sales constraints represent a special kind of constraint—*upper bounds* on the decision variable cells. Upper bound constraints are handled in a special way in the Solver sensitivity report, as described shortly.)

In the first row of the top section, the *allowable increase* and *allowable decrease* indicate how much the coefficient of profit margin for Basics in the objective, currently 80, could change before the optimal product mix would change. If the coefficient of Basics stays within this allowable range, from 0 (decrease of 80) to 107.5 (increase of 27.5), the optimal product mix—the set of values in the decision variable cells—does not change at all. However, outside of these limits, the optimal mix between Basics and XPs *might* change.

To see what this implies, change the selling price in cell B11 from 300 to 299, so that the profit margin for Basics decreases to $79. This change is well within the allowable decrease of 80. If you rerun Solver, you will obtain the *same* values in the decision variable cells, although the objective value will decrease. Next, change the value in cell B11 to 330. This time, the profit margin for Basics increases by 30 from its original value of $300. This change is outside the allowable increase, so the solution might change. If you rerun Solver, you will indeed see a change—the company now produces 600 Basics and fewer than 1200 XPs.

The **reduced costs** in the second column indicate, in general, how much the objective coefficient of a decision variable that is currently 0 or at its upper bound must change before that variable changes (becomes positive or decreases from its upper bound). The interesting variable in this case is the number of XPs, currently at its upper bound of 1200. The reduced cost for this variable is 33, meaning that the number of XPs will stay at 1200 unless the profit margin for XPs decreases by at least $33. Try it. Starting with the original inputs, change the selling price for XPs to $420, a change of less than $33. If you rerun Solver, you will find that the optimal plan still calls for 1200 XPs. Then change the selling price to $410, a change of more than $33 from the original value. After rerunning Solver, you will find that *fewer* than 1200 XPs are in the optimal mix.

> The **reduced cost** for any decision variable with value 0 in the optimal solution indicates how much better that coefficient must be before that variable enters at a positive level. The reduced cost for any decision variable at its upper bound in the optimal solution indicates how much worse its coefficient must be before it will decrease from its upper bound. The reduced cost for any variable between 0 and its upper bound in the optimal solution is irrelevant.

Now turn to the bottom section of the report in Figure 13.9. Each row in this section corresponds to a constraint, although upper bound constraints on decision variable cells are omitted in this section. To have this part of the report make economic sense, the model should be developed as has been done here, where the right side of each constraint is a numeric constant (not a formula). Then the report indicates how much these right-side constants can change before the optimal solution changes. To understand this more fully, the concept of a shadow price is required. A **shadow price** indicates the change in the objective when a right-side constant changes.

> The term **shadow price** is an economic term. It indicates the change in the optimal value of the objective when the right side of some constraint changes by one unit.

A shadow price is reported for each constraint. For example, the shadow price for the assembling labor constraint is 16. This means that if the right side of this constraint increases by one hour, from 10000 to 10001, the optimal value of the objective will increase by $16. It works in the other direction as well. If the right side of this constraint *decreases* by one hour, from 10000 to 9999, the optimal value of the objective will decrease by $16. However, as the right side continues to increase or decrease, this $16 change in the objective might not continue. This is where the reported allowable increase and allowable decrease are relevant. As long as the right side increases or decreases within its allowable limits, the same shadow price of 16 still applies. Beyond these limits, however, a different shadow price might apply.

You can prove this for yourself. First, increase the right side of the assembling labor constraint by 200 (exactly the allowable increase), from 10000 to 10200, and rerun Solver. (Don't forget to reset other inputs to their original values if you have made changes.) You will see that the objective indeed increases by 16(200)=$3200, from $199,600 to $202,800. Now increase this right side by one more hour, from 10200 to 10201 and rerun Solver. You will observe that the objective doesn't increase at all. This means that the shadow price beyond 10200 is *less than* 16; in fact, it is zero. This is typical. When a right side increases beyond its allowable increase, the new shadow price is typically less than the original shadow price (although it doesn't always fall to zero, as in this example).

Fundamental Insight

Resource Availability and Shadow Prices

If a resource constraint is binding in the optimal solution, the company is willing to pay up to some amount, the shadow price, to obtain more of the resource. This is because the objective improves by having more of the resource. However, there is typically a *decreasing marginal effect*: As the company owns more and more of the resource, the shadow price tends to decrease. This is usually because *other* constraints become binding, which causes extra units of this resource to be less useful (or not useful at all).

The idea is that a constraint "costs" the company by keeping the objective from being better than it would be. A shadow price indicates how much the company would be willing to pay (in units of the objective) to "relax" a constraint. In this example, the company would be willing to pay $16 for each extra assembling hour. This is because such a change would increase the net profit by $16. But beyond a certain point—200 hours in this example—further relaxation of the constraint does no good, and the company is not willing to pay for any further increases.

The constraint on testing hours is slightly different. It has a shadow price of zero. In fact, the shadow price for a nonbinding constraint is *always* zero, which makes sense. If the right side of this constraint is changed from 3000 to 3001, nothing at all happens to the optimal product mix or the objective value; there is just one more unused testing hour. However, the allowable decrease of 40 indicates that something *does* change when the right side reaches 2960. At this point, the constraint becomes binding—the number of testing hours used equals the number of testing hours available—and beyond this, the optimal product mix starts to change. By the way, the allowable increase for this constraint, shown as 1+E30, means that it is essentially infinite. The right side of this constraint can be increased above 3000 indefinitely, and nothing will change in the optimal solution.

Fundamental Insight

The Effect of Constraints on the Objective

If a constraint is added or an existing constraint becomes more constraining (for example, less of some resource is available), the objective can only get worse; it can never improve. The easiest way to understand this is to think of the feasible region. When a constraint is added or an existing constraint becomes more constraining, the feasible region shrinks, so some solutions that were feasible before, maybe even the optimal solution, are no longer feasible. The opposite is true if a constraint is deleted or an existing constraint becomes less constraining. In this case, the objective can only improve; it can never get worse. Again, the idea is that when a constraint is deleted or an existing constraint becomes less constraining, the feasible region expands. In this case, all solutions that were feasible before are still feasible, and there are some additional feasible solutions available.

13-4b SolverTable Add-In

Solver's sensitivity report is almost impossible to unravel for some models. In these cases SolverTable is preferable because of its easily interpreted results.

The reason Solver's sensitivity report makes sense for the product mix model is that the spreadsheet model is virtually a direct translation of a standard algebraic model. However, given the flexibility of spreadsheets, this is not always the case. We have seen many perfectly good spreadsheet models—and have developed many ourselves—that are structured quite differently from their standard algebraic-model counterparts. In these cases, we have found Solver's sensitivity report to be more confusing than useful. Therefore, Albright developed an Excel add-in called SolverTable. **SolverTable** allows you to ask sensitivity questions about any of the input variables, not just coefficients of the objective and right sides of constraints, and it provides straightforward answers.

We haven't been able to program a version of Solver Table for the Mac.

The SolverTable add-in is on this textbook's website.[9] To install it, simply copy the SolverTable files to a folder on your hard drive. These files include the add-in itself (the .xlam file) and the online help file. To load SolverTable, you can proceed in either of two ways:

1. Open the **SolverTable.xlam** file just as you open any other Excel file.
2. Go to the add-ins list in Excel (click the File button, then Options, then Add-Ins, then Go) and check the SolverTable item. If it isn't in the list, Browse for the **SolverTable.xlam** file.

---

9 It is also available from the Free Downloads link on the authors' website at www.kelley.iu.edu/albrightbooks.

The advantage of the second option is that if SolverTable is checked in the add-ins list, it will open automatically every time you open Excel (and you can always uncheck it if you don't want it to open automatically).

The SolverTable add-in was developed to mimic Excel's built-in data table tool. Recall that data tables allow you to vary one or two inputs in a spreadsheet model and see instantaneously how selected outputs change. SolverTable is similar except that it runs Solver for every new input (or pair of inputs), and the current version also provides automatic charts of the results. There are two ways it can be used.

- **One-way table.** A one-way table means that there is a *single* input cell and *any number* of output cells. That is, there can be a single output cell or multiple output cells.
- **Two-way table.** A two-way table means that there are *two* input cells and one or more output cells. (You might recall that an Excel two-way data table allows only *one* output. SolverTable allows more than one. It creates a separate table for each selected output as a function of the two inputs.)

We illustrate some of the possibilities for the product mix example. Specifically, we check how sensitive the optimal production plan and net profit are to (1) changes in the selling price of XPs, (2) the number of labor hours of both types available, and (3) the maximum sales of the two models.

We chose the input range from 350 to 550 in increments of 25, but you can choose any desired range of input values.

We assume that the model has been formulated and optimized, as shown in Figure 13.8, and that the SolverTable add-in has been loaded. To run SolverTable, click the Run SolverTable button on the SolverTable ribbon. You will be asked whether there is a Solver model on the active sheet. (Note that the *active* sheet at this point should be the sheet containing the model. If it isn't, click Cancel and then activate this sheet.) You are then given the choice between a one-way or a two-way table. For the first sensitivity question, choose the one-way option. You will see the dialog box in Figure 13.10. For the sensitivity analysis on the XP selling price, fill it in as shown. Note that ranges can be entered as cell addresses or range names. Also, multiple ranges in the Outputs box must be separated by commas.

On the Mac, keep your finger on the command key.

Excel Tip

Selecting Multiple Ranges

If you need to select multiple output ranges, the trick is to keep your finger on the Ctrl key as you drag the ranges. This automatically enters the separating comma(s) for you. Actually, the same trick works for selecting multiple decision variable cell ranges in Solver's dialog box. It even works for entering multiple range arguments in any Excel function.

When you click OK, Solver solves a separate optimization problem for each of the nine rows of the table and then reports the requested outputs (number produced and net profit) in the table, as shown in Figure 13.11. It can take a while, depending on the speed of your computer and the complexity of the model, but everything is automatic. However, if you want to update this table—by using different XP selling prices in column A, for example—you must repeat the procedure. Note that if the requested outputs are included in named ranges, the range names are used in the SolverTable headings. For example, the label Number_to_produce_1 indicates that this output is the first cell in the Number_to_produce range. The label Total_profit indicates that this output is the *only* cell in the Total_profit range. If a requested output is not part of a named range, its cell address is used as the label in the SolverTable results.

Figure 13.10 SolverTable
One-Way Dialog Box

Figure 13.11 SolverTable
Results for Varying XP Price

▲	A	B	C	D	E	F	G
1	Oneway analysis for Solver model in Model worksheet						
2							
3	Selling Price XP (cell $C$11) values along side, output cell(s) along top						
4		Number_to_produce_1	Number_to_produce_2	Total_profit			
5	$350	600	1166.667	$81,833			
6	$375	600	1166.667	$111,000			
7	$400	600	1166.667	$140,167			
8	$425	560	1200	$169,600			
9	$450	560	1200	$199,600			
10	$475	560	1200	$229,600			
11	$500	560	1200	$259,600			
12	$525	560	1200	$289,600			
13	$550	560	1200	$319,600			

The outputs in this table show that when the selling price of XPs is relatively low, the company should make as many Basics as it can sell and a few less XPs, but when the selling price is relatively high, the company should do the opposite. Also, the net profit increases steadily through this range. You can calculate these changes (which are not part of the SolverTable output) in column E. The increase in net profit per every extra $25 in XP selling price is close to, but not always exactly equal to, $30,000.

SolverTable also produces the chart in Figure 13.12. There is a dropdown list in cell K4 where you can choose any of the SolverTable outputs. (We selected the total profit, cell D25.) The chart then shows the data for that column from the table in Figure 13.11. Here there is a steady increase (slope about $30,000) in net profit as the XP selling price increases.

Figure 13.12 Associated
SolverTable Chart for Total
Profit

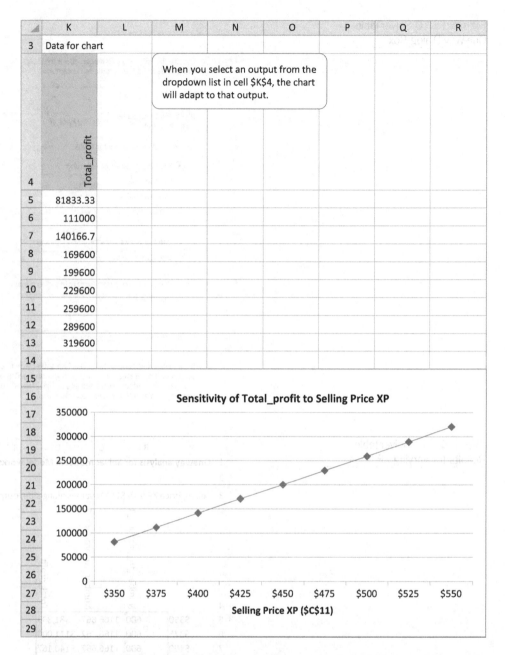

The second sensitivity question asks you to vary two inputs, the two labor avail-abilities, simultaneously. This requires a two-way SolverTable, so you should fill in the SolverTable dialog box as shown in Figure 13.13. Here two inputs and two input ranges are specified, and multiple output cells are again allowed. An output table is generated for *each* of the output cells, as shown in Figure 13.14. For example, the top table shows how the optimal number of Basics varies as the two labor availabilities vary. Comparing the columns of this top table, it is apparent that the optimal number of Basics becomes increasingly sensitive to the available assembling hours as the number of available testing hours increases. The SolverTable output also includes two charts (not shown here) that let you graph any row or any column of any of these tables.

The third sensitivity question, involving maximum sales of the two models, reveals the flexibility of SolverTable. Instead of letting these two inputs vary independently in a two-way SolverTable, it is possible to let both of them vary according to a *single* percentage change. For example, if this percentage change is 10%, both maximum sales increase by 10%. The trick is to modify the model so that one percentage-change cell drives changes in both maximum sales. The modified model appears in Figure 13.15. Starting with the origi-nal model, enter the original values, 600 and 1200, in new cells, E18 and F18. (Do *not* copy the range B18:C18 to E18:F18. This would make the right side of the constraint E18:F18,

Figure 13.13 SolverTable Two-Way Dialog Box

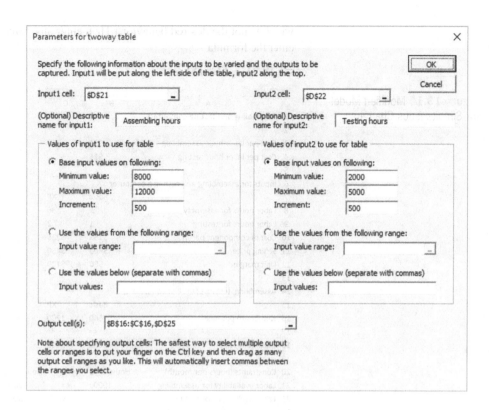

Figure 13.14 Two-Way SolverTable Results

	A	B	C	D	E	F	G	H	I	J
3	Assembling hours (cell $D$21) values along side, Testing hours (cell $D$22) values along top, output cell in corner									
4	Number_to_produce_1	2000	2500	3000	3500	4000	4500	5000		
5	8000	600	250	160	160	160	160	160		
6	8500	600	500	260	260	260	260	260		
7	9000	600	600	360	360	360	360	360		
8	9500	600	600	460	460	460	460	460		
9	10000	600	600	560	560	560	560	560		
10	10500	600	600	600	600	600	600	600		
11	11000	600	600	600	600	600	600	600		
12	11500	600	600	600	600	600	600	600		
13	12000	600	600	600	600	600	600	600		
14										
15	Number_to_produce_2	2000	2500	3000	3500	4000	4500	5000		
16	8000	700	1125	1200	1200	1200	1200	1200		
17	8500	700	1000	1200	1200	1200	1200	1200		
18	9000	700	950	1200	1200	1200	1200	1200		
19	9500	700	950	1200	1200	1200	1200	1200		
20	10000	700	950	1200	1200	1200	1200	1200		
21	10500	700	950	1200	1200	1200	1200	1200		
22	11000	700	950	1200	1200	1200	1200	1200		
23	11500	700	950	1200	1200	1200	1200	1200		
24	12000	700	950	1200	1200	1200	1200	1200		
25										
26	Total_profit	2000	2500	3000	3500	4000	4500	5000		
27	8000	$138,300	$165,125	$167,600	$167,600	$167,600	$167,600	$167,600		
28	8500	$138,300	$169,000	$175,600	$175,600	$175,600	$175,600	$175,600		
29	9000	$138,300	$170,550	$183,600	$183,600	$183,600	$183,600	$183,600		
30	9500	$138,300	$170,550	$191,600	$191,600	$191,600	$191,600	$191,600		
31	10000	$138,300	$170,550	$199,600	$199,600	$199,600	$199,600	$199,600		
32	10500	$138,300	$170,550	$202,800	$202,800	$202,800	$202,800	$202,800		
33	11000	$138,300	$170,550	$202,800	$202,800	$202,800	$202,800	$202,800		
34	11500	$138,300	$170,550	$202,800	$202,800	$202,800	$202,800	$202,800		
35	12000	$138,300	$170,550	$202,800	$202,800	$202,800	$202,800	$202,800		

which is not the desired behavior.) Then enter any percentage change in cell G18. Finally, enter the formula

$$=E18*(1 + \$G\$18)$$

Figure 13.15 Modified Model for Simultaneous Changes

	A	B	C	D	E	F	G	H
1	**Assembling and testing computers**							
2								
3	Cost per labor hour assembling	$11						
4	Cost per labor hour testing	$15						
5								
6	Inputs for assembling and testing a computer							
7		Basic	XP					
8	Labor hours for assembly	5	6					
9	Labor hours for testing	1	2					
10	Cost of component parts	$150	$225					
11	Selling price	$300	$450		The trick here is to let the			
12	Unit margin	$80	$129		*single* value in cell G18 drive			
13					both values in cells B18 and			
14	Assembling, testing plan (# of computers)				C18 from their original values.			
15		Basic	XP					
16	Number to produce	560	1200					
17		<=	<=		Original values		% change in both	
18	Maximum sales	600	1200		600	1200	0%	
19								
20	Constraints (hours per month)	Hours used		Hours available				
21	Labor availability for assembling	10000	<=	10000				
22	Labor availability for testing	2960	<=	3000				
23								
24	Net profit ($ this month)	Basic	XP	Total				
25		$44,800	$154,800	$199,600				

in cell B18 and copy it to cell C18. Now a one-way SolverTable can be used with the percentage change in cell G18 to drive two different inputs simultaneously. The SolverTable dialog box should be set up as in Figure 13.16, with the corresponding results in Figure 13.17.

Figure 13.16 SolverTable One-Way Dialog Box

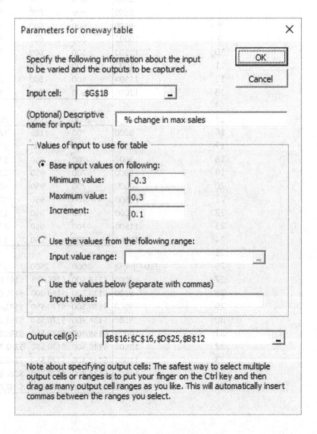

Figure 13.17 Sensitivity to Percentage Change in Maximum Sales

	A	B	C	D	E	F	G
1	Oneway analysis for Solver model in Modified Model worksheet						
2							
3	% change in max sales (cell $G$18) values along side, output cell(s) along top						
4		Number_to_produce_1	Number_to_produce_2	Total_profit	$B$12		
5	−30%	420	840	$141,960	$80		
6	−20%	480	960	$162,240	$80		
7	−10%	540	1080	$182,520	$80		
8	0%	560	1200	$199,600	$80		
9	10%	500	1250	$201,250	$80		
10	20%	500	1250	$201,250	$80		
11	30%	500	1250	$201,250	$80		

You should always scan these sensitivity results to see if they make sense. For example, if the company can sell 20% or 30% more of both models, it makes no more profit than if it can sell only 10% more. The reason is labor availability. By this point, there isn't enough labor to produce the increased demand.

It is always possible to run a sensitivity analysis by changing inputs manually in the spreadsheet model and rerunning Solver. The advantages of SolverTable are that it enables you to perform a *systematic* sensitivity analysis for any selected inputs and outputs, and it keeps track of the results in a table and associated chart(s). You will see other applications of this useful add-in later in this chapter and in the next chapter.

13-4c A Comparison of Solver's Sensitivity Report and SolverTable

Sensitivity analysis in optimization models is extremely important, so it is important that you understand the pros and cons of the two tools in this section. Here are some points to keep in mind.

- Solver's sensitivity report focuses only on the coefficients of the objective and the right sides of the constraints. SolverTable allows you to vary *any* of the inputs.
- Solver's sensitivity report provides useful information through its reduced costs, shadow prices, and allowable increases and decreases. This same information can be obtained with SolverTable, but it requires a little more work and some experimentation with the appropriate input ranges.
- Solver's sensitivity report is based on changing only one objective coefficient or one right side at a time. This one-at-a-time restriction prevents you from answering some questions directly. SolverTable is more flexible in this respect.
- Solver's sensitivity report is based on a well-established mathematical theory of sensitivity analysis in linear programming. If you lack this mathematical background— as many users do—the outputs can be difficult to understand, especially for somewhat "nonstandard" spreadsheet formulations. In contrast, SolverTable's outputs are straightforward. You can vary one or two inputs and see directly how the optimal solution changes.
- Solver's sensitivity report is not even available for integer-constrained models, and its interpretation for nonlinear models is more difficult than for linear models. SolverTable's results have the same interpretation for any type of optimization model.
- Solver's sensitivity report comes with Excel. SolverTable is a separate add-in that is not included with Excel—but it is included with this book and is freely available from the Free Downloads link at the authors' website, www.kelley.iu.edu/albrightbooks.

In summary, each of these tools can be used to answer certain questions. We tend to favor SolverTable because of its flexibility, but in the optimization examples in this chapter and the next chapter, we will illustrate both tools.

13-5 Properties of Linear Models

Linear programming is an important subset of a larger class of models called **mathematical programming models**.[10] All such models select the levels of various activities that can be performed, subject to a set of constraints, to maximize or minimize an objective such as total profit or total cost. In PC Tech's product mix example, the activities are the numbers of PCs to produce, and the purpose of the model is to find the levels of these activities that maximize the total net profit subject to specified constraints.

In terms of this general setup—selecting the optimal levels of activities—there are three important properties that LP models possess that distinguish them from general mathematical programming models: *proportionality*, *additivity*, and *divisibility*.

Proportionality means that if the level of any activity is multiplied by a constant factor, the contribution of this activity to the objective, or to any of the constraints in which the activity is involved, is multiplied by the same factor. For example, suppose the production of Basics is cut from its optimal value of 560 to 280—that is, it is multiplied by 0.5. Then the amounts of labor hours from assembling and from testing Basics are both cut in half, and the net profit contributed by Basics is also cut in half.

Proportionality is a perfectly valid assumption in the product mix model, but it is often violated in certain types of models. For example, in various *blending* models used by petroleum companies, chemical outputs vary in a nonlinear manner as chemical inputs are varied. For example, if a chemical input is doubled, the resulting chemical output is not necessarily doubled. This type of behavior violates the proportionality property, and it requires *nonlinear* optimization, which we discuss in the next chapter.

The **additivity** property implies that the sum of the contributions from the various activities to any constraint equals the total contribution to that constraint. For example, if the two PC models use, respectively, 560 and 2400 testing hours (as in Figure 13.8), then the total number used in the plan is the *sum* of these amounts, 2960 hours. Similarly, the additivity property applies to the objective. That is, the value of the objective is the *sum* of the contributions from the various activities. In the product mix model, the net profits from the two PC models sum to the total net profit. The additivity property implies that the contribution of any decision variable to the objective or to any constraint is *independent* of the levels of the other decision variables.

The **divisibility** property simply means that both integer and noninteger levels of the activities are allowed. In the product mix model, we got integer values in the optimal solution, 560 and 1200, just by luck. For slightly different inputs, they could easily have been fractional values. In general, if you want the levels of some activities to be integer values, there are two possible approaches: (1) You can solve the LP model without integer constraints, and if the solution turns out to have fractional values, you can attempt to round them to integer values; or (2) you can explicitly constrain certain decision variables to have integer values. However, the latter approach requires *integer programming*, which we discuss in the next chapter. At this point, we simply state that in general, integer-constrained problems are *much* more difficult to solve than problems without integer constraints.

So far, the discussion of these three properties, especially proportionality and additivity, is fairly abstract. How can you recognize whether a model satisfies proportionality and

---

10 The word *programming* in linear programming or mathematical programming has nothing to do with computer programming. It originated with the British term *programme*, which is essentially a plan or a schedule of operations.

additivity? This is easy if the model is described algebraically. In this case the objective must be of the form

$$a_1x_1 + a_2x_2 + \cdots + a_nx_n$$

where n is the number of decision variables, the a's are constants, and the x's are decision variables. This expression is called a *linear combination* of the x's. Also, each constraint must be equivalent to a form where the left side is a linear combination of the x's and the right side is a constant. For example, the following is a typical linear constraint:

$$3x_1 + 7x_2 - 2x_3 \leq 50$$

It is not quite so easy to recognize proportionality and additivity—or the lack of them—in a spreadsheet model, because the logic of the model is typically embedded in a series of cell formulas. However, the ideas are the same. First, the objective cell must ultimately (possibly through a series of formulas in intervening cells) be a sum of products of constants and decision variable cells, where a "constant" means that it does not depend on decision variable cells. Second, each side of each constraint must ultimately be either a constant or a sum of products of constants and decision variable cells. This explains why linear models contain so many SUM and SUMPRODUCT functions.

It is usually easier to recognize when a model is *not* linear. Two particular situations that lead to nonlinear models are when (1) there are products or quotients of expressions involving decision variable cells or (2) there are nonlinear functions, such as squares, square roots, or logarithms, that involve decision variable cells. These are typically easy to spot, and they guarantee that the model is nonlinear.

Real-life problems are almost never exactly linear. However, linear approximations often yield very useful results.

Whenever you model a real problem, you usually make some simplifying assumptions. This is certainly the case with LP models. The world is frequently *not* linear, which means that an entirely realistic model typically violates some or all of the three properties in this section. However, numerous successful applications of LP have demonstrated the usefulness of linear models, even if they are only *approximations* of reality. If you suspect that the violations are serious enough to invalidate a linear model, you should use an integer or nonlinear model, as we illustrate in the next chapter.

In terms of Excel's Solver, if the model is linear—that is, if it satisfies the proportionality, additivity, and divisibility properties—you should check the Simplex LP option. Then Solver uses the simplex method, a very efficient method for a linear model, to solve the problem. Actually, you can check the Simplex LP option even if the divisibility property is violated—that is, for linear models with integer-constrained variables—but Solver then embeds the simplex method in a more complex algorithm in its solution procedure.

Linear Models and Scaling[11]

In some cases you might be sure that a model is linear, but when you check the Simplex LP option and then solve, you get a Solver message to the effect that the conditions for linearity are not satisfied. This can indicate a logical error in your formulation, so that the proportionality and additivity conditions are indeed not satisfied. However, it can also indicate that Solver erroneously *thinks* the linearity conditions are not satisfied, which is typically due to roundoff error in its calculations—not any error on your part. If the latter occurs and you are convinced that the model is correct, you can try *not* using the simplex method to see whether that works. If it does not, you should consult your instructor. It is possible that the non-simplex algorithm employed by Solver simply cannot find the solution to your problem.

In any case, it always helps to have a *well-scaled* model. In a well-scaled model, all numbers are roughly the same magnitude. If the model contains some very large numbers—100,000 or more, say—and some very small numbers—0.001 or less, say—it is *poorly scaled* for the methods used by Solver, and roundoff error is more likely to be an issue, not only in Solver's test for linearity conditions but in all its algorithms.

---

11 This section might seem overly technical. However, when you develop a model that you are sure is linear and Solver then tells you it doesn't satisfy the linear conditions, you will appreciate this section.

You can decrease the chance of getting an incorrect "Conditions for Assume Linear Model are not satisfied" message by changing Solver's Precision setting.

If you believe your model is poorly scaled, there are three possible remedies. The first is to check the Use Automatic Scaling option in Solver. (It is found by clicking on the Options button in the main Solver dialog box.) This might help and it might not; we have had mixed success. (Frontline Systems, the company that develops Solver, has told us that the only drawback to checking this box is that the solution procedure can be slower.) The second option is to redefine the units in which the various quantities are defined. Finally, you can change the Precision setting in Solver's Options dialog box to a larger number, such 0.00001 or 0.0001. (The default has five zeros.)

Excel Tip

Rescaling a Model

Suppose you have a range of input values expressed, say, in dollars, and you would like to reexpress them in thousands of dollars, that is, you would like to divide each value by 1000. There is a simple copy/paste way to do this. Enter the value 1000 in some unused cell and copy it. Then select the range you want to rescale, and from the Paste dropdown menu, select Paste Special and then the Divide option. No formulas are required; your original values are automatically rescaled (and you can then delete the 1000 cell). You can use this same method to add, subtract, or multiply by a constant.

13-6 Infeasibility and Unboundedness

Infeasibility and Unboundedness

A perfectly reasonable model can have no feasible solutions because of too many constraints.

In this section we discuss two things that can go wrong when you invoke Solver. Both of these might indicate that there is a mistake in the model. Therefore, because mistakes are common in LP models, you should be aware of the error messages you might encounter.

The first problem is **infeasibility**. Recall that a solution is *feasible* if it satisfies all the constraints. Among all the feasible solutions, you are looking for the one that optimizes the objective. However, it is possible that there are no feasible solutions to the model. There are generally two reasons for this: (1) there is a mistake in the model (an input was entered incorrectly, such as a $\leq$ symbol instead of $\geq$) or (2) the problem has been so constrained that there are no solutions left. In the former case, a careful check of the model should find the error. In the latter case, you might need to change, or even eliminate, some of the constraints.

To show how an infeasible problem could occur, suppose in PC Tech's product mix problem you change the maximum sales constraints to *minimum* sales constraints (and leave everything else unchanged). That is, you change these constraints from $\leq$ to $\geq$. If Solver is then used, the message in Figure 13.18 appears, indicating that Solver cannot find a feasible solution. The reason is clear: There is no way, given the constraints on labor hours, that the company can produce these minimum sales values. The company's only choice is to set at least one of the minimum sales values lower. In general, there is no foolproof way to remedy the problem when a "no feasible solution" message appears. Careful checking and rethinking are required.

A second problem is **unboundedness**. In this case, the model has been formulated in such a way that the objective is unbounded—that is, it can be made as large (or as small, for minimization problems) as you like. If this occurs, you have probably entered a wrong input or forgotten some constraints. To see how this could occur in the product mix problem, suppose that you change *all* constraints to be $\leq$ instead of $\geq$. Now there is no upper bound on available labor hours or the number of PCs the company can sell. If you make these changes in the model and then use Solver, the message in Figure 13.19 appears, stating that the objective cell does not converge. In other words, the total net profit can grow without bound.

Figure 13.18 No Feasible
Solution Message

Figure 13.19 Unbounded
Solution Message

Except in very rare situations, if Solver informs you that your model is unbounded, you have made an error.

Infeasibility and unboundedness are quite different in a practical sense. It is quite possible for a reasonable model to have no feasible solutions. For example, the marketing department might impose several constraints, the production department might add some more, the engineering department might add even more, and so on. Together, they might constrain the problem so much that there are no feasible solutions left. The only way out is to change or eliminate some of the constraints. An unboundedness problem is quite different. There is no way a realistic model can have an unbounded solution. If you get the message shown in Figure 13.19, then you must have made a mistake: You entered an input incorrectly, you omitted one or more constraints, or there is a logical error in your model.

Problems

Solutions for problems whose numbers appear within a colored box can be found in the Student Solution Files.

Level A

1. Other sensitivity analyses besides those discussed could be performed on the PC Tech product mix model. Use SolverTable to perform each of the following. In each case keep track of the values in the decision variable cells and the objective cell, and discuss your findings.

a. Let the selling price for Basics vary from $220 to $350 in increments of $10.

b. Let the labor cost per hour for assembling vary from $5 to $20 in increments of $1.

c. Let the labor hours for testing a Basic vary from 0.5 to 3.0 in increments of 0.5.

d. Let the labor hours for assembling and testing an XP vary independently, the first from 4.5 to 8.0 and the second from 1.5 to 3.0, both in increments of 0.5.

2. In PC Tech's product mix model, assume there is another PC model, the VXP, that the company can produce in addition to Basics and XPs. Each VXP requires eight hours for assembling, three hours for testing, $275 for component parts, and sells for $560. At most 50 VXPs can be sold.

a. Modify the spreadsheet model to include this new product, and use Solver to find the optimal product mix.

b. You should find that the optimal solution is *not* integer-valued. If you round the values in the decision variable cells to the nearest integers, is the resulting solution still feasible? If not, how might you obtain a feasible solution that is at least close to optimal?

3. Continuing the previous problem, perform a sensitivity analysis on the selling price of VXPs. Let this price vary from $500 to $650 in increments of $10, and keep track of the values in the decision variable cells and the objective cell. Discuss your findings.

4. Again continuing problem 2, suppose that you want to force the optimal solution to be integers. Do this in Solver by adding a new constraint. Select the decision variable cells for the left side of the constraint, and in the middle dropdown list, select the "int" option (for "integer"). How does the optimal integer solution compare to the optimal noninteger solution in problem 2? Are the decision variable cell values rounded versions of those in problem 2? Is the objective value more or less than in problem 2?

5. If all inputs in PC Tech's product mix model are nonnegative (as they should be for any realistic version of the problem), are there any input values such that the resulting model has no feasible solutions? (Refer to the graphical solution.)

6. There are five corner points in the feasible region for the PC Tech product mix model. We identified the coordinates of one of them: (560, 1200). Identify the coordinates of the others.

a. Only one of these other corner points has positive values for both decision variable cells. Discuss the changes in the selling prices of either or both models that would be necessary to make this corner point optimal.

b. Two of the other corner points have one decision variable cell value positive and the other zero. Discuss the changes in the selling prices of either or both models that would be necessary to make either of these corner points optimal.

Level B

7. Using the graphical solution of the PC Tech product mix model as a guide, suppose there are only 2800 testing hours available. How do the answers to the previous problem change? (Is the previous solution still optimal? Is it still feasible?)

8. Again continuing problem 2, perform a sensitivity analysis where the selling prices of Basics and XPs simultaneously change by the same percentage, but the selling price of VXPs remains at its original value. Let the percentage change vary from −25% to 50% in increments of 5%, and keep track of the values in the decision variable cells and the total profit. Discuss your findings.

9. Consider the graphical solution to the PC Tech product mix model. Now imagine that another constraint—*any* constraint—is added. Which of the following three things are possible: (1) the feasible region shrinks; (2) the feasible region stays the same; (3) the feasible region expands? Which of the following three things are possible: (1) the optimal value in objective cell decreases; (2) the optimal value in objective cell stays the same; (3) the optimal value in objective cell increases? Explain your answers. Do they hold just for this particular model, or do they hold in general?

13-7 A Larger Product Mix Model

The problem we examine in this section is a direct extension of the product mix model in the previous section. There are two modifications. First, the company makes eight computer models, not just two. Second, testing can be done on either of two lines, and these two lines have different characteristics.

13.2 PRODUCING COMPUTERS AT PC TECH WITH TWO TESTING LINES

As in the previous example, PC Tech must decide how many of each of its computer models to assemble and test, but there are now eight available models, not just two. Each computer must be assembled and then tested, but there are now two lines for testing. The first line tends to test faster, but its labor costs are slightly higher, and each line has a certain number of hours available for testing. Any computer can be tested on either line. The inputs for the model are same as before: (1) the hourly labor costs for assembling and testing, (2) the required labor hours for assembling and testing any computer model, (3) the cost of component parts for each model, (4) the selling prices for each model, (5) the maximum sales for each model, and (6) labor availabilities. These input values are listed in the file **Product Mix 2.xlsx**. As before, the company wants to determine the product mix that maximizes its total net profit.

Objective

To use LP to find the mix of computer models that maximizes total net profit and stays within the labor hour availability and maximum sales constraints.

Where Do the Numbers Come From?

The same comments as in Example 13.1 apply here.

Solution

The diagram shown in Figure 13.20 (see the file **Product Mix 2 Big Picture.xlsx**) is similar to the one for the smaller product mix model, but it is not the same. You must choose the number of computers of each model to produce on each line, the sum of which cannot be larger than the maximum that can be sold. This choice determines the labor hours of each type used and all revenues and costs. No more labor hours can be used than are available.

Figure 13.20 Big Picture for Larger Product Mix Model

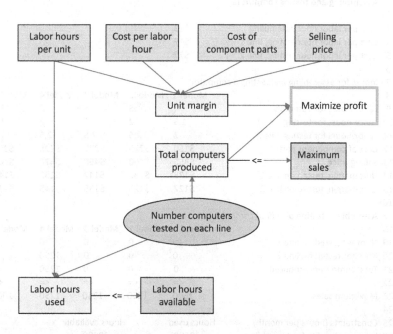

It might not be immediately obvious what the decision variable cells are for this model (at least not before you look at Figure 13.20). You might think that the company simply needs to decide how many computers of each model to produce. However, because of the two testing lines, this is not enough information. The company must also decide how many of each model to test *on each line*. For example, suppose they decide to test 100 model 4's on line 1 and 300 model 4's on line 2. This means they will need to assemble (and ultimately sell) 400 model 4's. In other words, given the detailed plan of how many to test on each line, everything else is determined. But without the detailed plan, there is not enough information to complete the model. This is the type of reasoning you must use to determine the appropriate decision variables for any LP model.

Algebraic Model

We will not spell out the algebraic model for this expanded version of the product mix model because it is so similar to the two-variable product mix model. However, we will say that it is larger, and hence probably more intimidating. Now we need decision variables of the form x_{ij}, the number of model j computers to test on line i, and the total net profit and each labor availability constraint will include a long SUMPRODUCT formula involving these variables. Instead of focusing on these algebraic expressions, we turn directly to the spreadsheet model.

Developing the Spreadsheet Model

The spreadsheet in Figure 13.21 illustrates the solution procedure for PC Tech's product mix problem. (See the file **Product Mix 2 Finished.xlsx.**) The first stage is to develop the spreadsheet model step by step.

Developing the Product
Mix 2 Model

1. **Inputs.** Enter the various inputs in the blue ranges. Again, remember that our convention is to color all input cells blue. Enter only *numbers*, not formulas, in input cells. They should always be numbers directly from the problem statement. (In this case, we supplied them in the spreadsheet template.)

2. **Range names.** Name the ranges indicated. According to our convention, there are enough named ranges so that the Solver dialog box contains only range names, no cell addresses. Of course, you can name additional ranges if you like. (You can again use the range-naming shortcut explained in the Excel tip for the previous example. That is, you can take advantage of labels in adjacent cells, except for the Profit cell.)

3. **Unit margins.** Note that two rows of these are required, one for each testing line, because the costs of testing on the two lines are not equal. To calculate them, enter the formula

=B$13-$B$3*B$9-$B4*B10-B$12

in cell B14 and copy it to the range B14:I15.

Figure 13.21 Larger Product Mix Model with Infeasible Solution

	A	B	C	D	E	F	G	H	I	J
1	Assembling and testing computers									
2										
3	Cost per labor hour assembling	$11								
4	Cost per labor hour testing, line 1	$19								
5	Cost per labor hour testing, line 2	$17								
6										
7	Inputs for assembling and testing a computer									
8		Model 1	Model 2	Model 3	Model 4	Model 5	Model 6	Model 7	Model 8	
9	Labor hours for assembly	4	5	5	5	5.5	5.5	5.5	6	
10	Labor hours for testing, line 1	1.5	2	2	2	2.5	2.5	2.5	3	
11	Labor hours for testing, line 2	2	2.5	2.5	2.5	3	3	3.5	3.5	
12	Cost of component parts	$150	$225	$225	$225	$250	$250	$250	$300	
13	Selling price	$350	$450	$460	$470	$500	$525	$530	$600	
14	Unit margin, tested on line 1	$128	$132	$142	$152	$142	$167	$172	$177	
15	Unit margin, tested on line 2	$122	$128	$138	$148	$139	$164	$160	$175	
16										
17	Assembling, testing plan (# of computers)									
18		Model 1	Model 2	Model 3	Model 4	Model 5	Model 6	Model 7	Model 8	
19	Number tested on line 1	0	0	0	0	0	500	1000	800	
20	Number tested on line 2	0	0	0	1250	0	0	0	0	
21	Total computers produced	0	0	0	1250	0	500	1000	800	
22		<=	<=	<=	<=	<=	<=	<=	<=	
23	Maximum sales	1500	1250	1250	1250	1000	1000	1000	800	
24										
25	Constraints (hours per month)	Hours used		Hours available						
26	Labor availability for assembling	19300	<=	20000						
27	Labor availability for testing, line 1	6150	<=	5000						
28	Labor availability for testing, line 2	3125	<=	6000						
29										
30	Net profit ($ per month)	Model 1	Model 2	Model 3	Model 4	Model 5	Model 6	Model 7	Model 8	Totals
31	Tested on line 1	$0	$0	$0	$0	$0	$83,500	$172,000	$141,600	$397,100
32	Tested on line 2	$0	$0	$0	$184,375	$0	$0	$0	$0	$184,375
33										$581,475

4. **Decision variable cells.** As discussed above, the decision variable cells are the red cells in rows 19 and 20. You do *not* have to enter the values shown in Figure 13.21. You can use any trial values initially; Solver will eventually find the *optimal* values. Note that the four values shown in Figure 13.21 cannot be optimal because they do not satisfy all the constraints. Specifically, this plan uses more labor hours for assembling than are available. However, you do not need to worry about satisfying constraints at this point; Solver will take care of this later.

5. **Labor used.** Enter the formula

    =SUMPRODUCT(B9:E9,Total_computers_produced)

    in cell B26 to calculate the number of assembling hours used. Similarly, enter the formulas

    =SUMPRODUCT(B10:I10,Number_tested_on_line_1)

    and

    =SUMPRODUCT(B11:I11,Number_tested_on_line_2)

    in cells B27 and B28 for the labor hours used on each testing line.

> **Excel Tip**
>
> **Copying Formulas with Range Names**
>
> When you enter a range name in an Excel formula and then copy the formula, the range name reference acts like an absolute reference. Therefore, it wouldn't work to copy the formula in cell B27 to cell B28. However, this would work if range names hadn't been used. This is one potential disadvantage of range names that you should be aware of.

6. **Revenues, costs, and profits.** The area from row 30 down shows the summary of monetary values. Actually, only the total profit in cell J33 is needed, but it is also useful to calculate the net profit from each computer model on each testing line. To obtain these, enter the formula

    =B14*B19

    in cell B31 and copy it to the range B31:I32. Then sum these to obtain the totals in column J. The total in cell J33 is the objective to maximize.

Experimenting with Other Solutions

Before going any further, you might want to experiment with other values in the decision variable cells. However, it is a real challenge to guess the optimal solution. It is tempting to fill up the decision variable cells corresponding to the largest unit margins. However, this totally ignores their use of the scarce labor hours. If you can guess the optimal solution to this model, you are better than we are!

Using Solver

The Solver dialog box should be filled out as shown in Figure 13.22. (Again, note that there are enough named ranges so that only range names appear in this dialog box.) Except that this model has two rows of decision variable cells, the Solver setup is identical to the one in Example 13.1.

Discussion of the Solution

When you click Solve, you obtain the optimal solution shown in Figure 13.23. The optimal plan is to produce computer models 1, 4, 6, and 7 only, some on testing line 1 and others on testing line 2. This plan uses all the available labor hours for assembling and testing on line 1, but about 1800 of the testing line 2 hours are not used. Also, maximum sales are achieved only for computer models 1, 6, and 7. This is typical of an LP solution. Some of the constraints are met exactly— they are binding—whereas others contain a certain amount of "slack." The binding constraints prevent PC Tech from earning an even higher profit.

You typically gain insights into a solution by checking which constraints are binding.

Figure 13.22 Solver Dialog Box

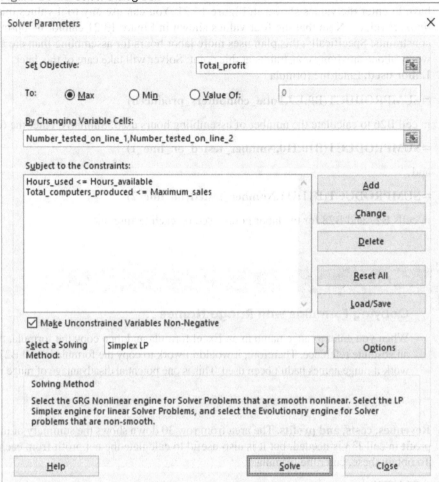

Roundoff Error

Because of the way numbers are stored and calculated on a computer, the optimal values in the decision variable cells and elsewhere can contain small roundoff errors. For example, the value that really appears in cell E20 on one of our PCs is 475.000002015897, not exactly 475. For all practical purposes, this number can be treated as 475, and we have formatted it as such in the spreadsheet. (It appears that roundoff in Solver results are less of a problem in recent versions of Excel.)

Sensitivity Analysis

If you want to experiment with different inputs to this problem, you can simply change the inputs and then rerun Solver. The second time you use Solver, you do not have to specify the objective and decision variable cells or the constraints. Excel remembers these settings and saves them when you save the file.

You can also use SolverTable to perform a more systematic sensitivity analysis on one or more input variables. One possibility appears in Figure 13.24, where the number of available assembling labor hours is allowed to vary from 18,000 to 25,000 in increments of 1000, and the numbers of computers produced and profit are designated as outputs. There are several ways to interpret the output from this sensitivity analysis. First, you can look at columns B through I to see how the product mix changes as more assembling labor

Figure 13.23 Optimal Solution to Larger Product Mix Model

	A	B	C	D	E	F	G	H	I	J
1	**Assembling and testing computers**									
2										
3	Cost per labor hour assembling	$11								
4	Cost per labor hour testing, line 1	$19								
5	Cost per labor hour testing, line 2	$17								
6										
7	Inputs for assembling and testing a computer									
8		Model 1	Model 2	Model 3	Model 4	Model 5	Model 6	Model 7	Model 8	
9	Labor hours for assembly	4	5	5	5	5.5	5.5	5.5	6	
10	Labor hours for testing, line 1	1.5	2	2	2	2.5	2.5	2.5	3	
11	Labor hours for testing, line 2	2	2.5	2.5	2.5	3	3	3.5	3.5	
12	Cost of component parts	$150	$225	$225	$225	$250	$250	$250	$300	
13	Selling price	$350	$450	$460	$470	$500	$525	$530	$600	
14	Unit margin, tested on line 1	$128	$132	$142	$152	$142	$167	$172	$177	
15	Unit margin, tested on line 2	$122	$128	$138	$148	$139	$164	$160	$175	
16										
17	Assembling, testing plan (# of computers)									
18		Model 1	Model 2	Model 3	Model 4	Model 5	Model 6	Model 7	Model 8	
19	Number tested on line 1	1500	0	0	125	0	0	1000	0	
20	Number tested on line 2	0	0	0	475	0	1000	0	0	
21	Total computers produced	1500	0	0	600	0	1000	1000	0	
22		<=	<=	<=	<=	<=	<=	<=	<=	
23	Maximum sales	1500	1250	1250	1250	1000	1000	1000	800	
24										
25	Constraints (hours per month)	Hours used		Hours available						
26	Labor availability for assembling	20000	<=	20000						
27	Labor availability for testing, line 1	5000	<=	5000						
28	Labor availability for testing, line 2	4187.5	<=	6000						
29										
30	Net profit ($ per month)	Model 1	Model 2	Model 3	Model 4	Model 5	Model 6	Model 7	Model 8	Totals
31	Tested on line 1	$191,250	$0	$0	$19,000	$0	$0	$172,000	$0	$382,250
32	Tested on line 2	$0	$0	$0	$70,063	$0	$163,500	$0	$0	$233,563
33										$615,813

hours become available. For assembling labor hours from 18,000 to 23,000, the only thing that changes is that more model 4's are produced. Beyond 23,000, however, the company starts to produce model 3's and produces fewer model 7's. Second, you can see how extra labor hours add to the total profit. Note exactly what this increased profit means. For example, when labor hours increase from 20,000 to 21,000, the model requires that the company must *pay* $11 apiece for these extra hours (if it uses them). But the *net* effect is that profit increases by $29,500, or $29.50 per extra hour. In other words, the labor cost increases by $11,000 [=$11(1000)], but this is more than offset by the increase in revenue that comes from having the extra labor hours.

As column J illustrates, it is worthwhile for the company to obtain extra assembling labor hours, even though it has to pay for them, because its profit increases. However, the increase in profit per extra labor hour—the *shadow price* of assembling labor hours—is not constant. In the top part of the table, it is $29.50 (per extra hour), but it then decreases to $20.44 and then $2.42. The accompanying SolverTable chart of column J illustrates this decreasing shadow price through its decreasing slope.

SolverTable Technical Tip

Charts and Roundoff

As SolverTable performs its Solver runs, it reports and then charts the values found by Solver. These can include small roundoff errors and slightly misleading charts. For example, the chart in Figure 13.25 shows one possibility, where we varied the cost of testing on line 2 and charted the assembling hours used. Throughout the range, this output value was 20,000, but because of slight roundoff in two of the cells (19999.9999999292 and 20000.0000003259 on our PC), the chart doesn't appear to be flat. If you see this behavior, you can change the chart manually by modifying its vertical scale.

Figure 13.24 Sensitivity to Assembling Labor Hours

	A	B	C	D	E	F	G	H	I	J
1	Oneway analysis for Solver model in Model worksheet									
2										
3	Assembling labor (cell $D$26) values along side, output cell(s) along top									
4		Total_computers_produced_1	Total_computers_produced_2	Total_computers_produced_3	Total_computers_produced_4	Total_computers_produced_5	Total_computers_produced_6	Total_computers_produced_7	Total_computers_produced_8	Total_profit
5	18000	1500	0	0	200	0	1000	1000	0	$556,813
6	19000	1500	0	0	400	0	1000	1000	0	$586,313
7	20000	1500	0	0	600	0	1000	1000	0	$615,813
8	21000	1500	0	0	800	0	1000	1000	0	$645,313
9	22000	1500	0	0	1000	0	1000	1000	0	$674,813
10	23000	1500	0	0	1200	0	1000	1000	0	$704,313
11	24000	1500	0	700	1250	0	1000	500	0	$724,750
12	25000	1500	0	1250	1250	0	1000	60	0	$727,170
13										

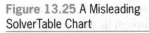

Sensitivity of Total_profit to Assembling labor chart (x-axis: Assembling labor ($D$26) from 18000 to 25000; y-axis: 0 to 800000)

Figure 13.25 A Misleading SolverTable Chart

Sensitivity of Hours_used_1 to Testing cost 2 chart (x-axis: Testing cost 2 ($B$5) from $10 to $25)

Figure 13.26 Solver's Sensitivity Report

	A	B	C	D	E	F	G	H
6		Variable Cells						
7				Final	Reduced	Objective	Allowable	Allowable
8		Cell	Name	Value	Cost	Coefficient	Increase	Decrease
9		$B$19	Number tested on line 1 Model 1	1500	0	127.5	1E+30	2.125
10		$C$19	Number tested on line 1 Model 2	0	−20	132	20	1E+30
11		$D$19	Number tested on line 1 Model 3	0	−10	142	10	1E+30
12		$E$19	Number tested on line 1 Model 4	125	0	152	2.833333333	1.7
13		$F$19	Number tested on line 1 Model 5	0	−25.875	142	25.875	1E+30
14		$G$19	Number tested on line 1 Model 6	0	−2.125	167	2.125	1E+30
15		$H$19	Number tested on line 1 Model 7	1000	0	172	1E+30	4.125
16		$I$19	Number tested on line 1 Model 8	0	−6.75	177	6.75	1E+30
17		$B$20	Number tested on line 2 Model 1	0	−2.125	122	2.125	1E+30
18		$C$20	Number tested on line 2 Model 2	0	−20	127.5	20	1E+30
19		$D$20	Number tested on line 2 Model 3	0	−10	137.5	10	1E+30
20		$E$20	Number tested on line 2 Model 4	475	0	147.5	1.136363636	2.083333333
21		$F$20	Number tested on line 2 Model 5	0	−23.75	138.5	23.75	1E+30
22		$G$20	Number tested on line 2 Model 6	1000	0	163.5	1E+30	1.25
23		$H$20	Number tested on line 2 Model 7	0	−6.375	160	6.375	1E+30
24		$I$20	Number tested on line 2 Model 8	0	−2.5	174.5	2.5	1E+30
25								
26		Constraints						
27				Final	Shadow	Constraint	Allowable	Allowable
28		Cell	Name	Value	Price	R.H. Side	Increase	Decrease
29		$B$26	Labor availability for assembling Hours used	20000	29.5	20000	3250	2375
30		$B$27	Labor availability for testing, line 1 Hours used	5000	2.25	5000	950	250
31		$B$28	Labor availability for testing, line 2 Hours used	4187.5	0	6000	1E+30	1812.5
32		$B$21	Total computers produced Model 1	1500	6.125	1500	166.6666667	812.5
33		$C$21	Total computers produced Model 2	0	0	1250	1E+30	1250
34		$D$21	Total computers produced Model 3	0	0	1250	1E+30	1250
35		$E$21	Total computers produced Model 4	600	0	1250	1E+30	650
36		$F$21	Total computers produced Model 5	0	0	1000	1E+30	1000
37		$G$21	Total computers produced Model 6	1000	1.25	1000	431.8181818	590.9090909
38		$H$21	Total computers produced Model 7	1000	4.125	1000	100	590.9090909
39		$I$21	Total computers produced Model 8	0	0	800	1E+30	800

Finally, you can gain additional insight from Solver's sensitivity report, shown in Figure 13.26. However, you have to be careful in interpreting this report. Unlike Example 13.1, there are no upper bound (maximum sales) constraints on the *decision variable cells*. The maximum sales constraints are on the total computers produced (row 21 of the model), not the decision variable cells. Therefore, the only nonzero reduced costs in the top part of the table are for decision variable cells currently at zero (not those at their upper bounds as in the previous example). Each nonzero reduced cost indicates how much the profit margin for this activity would have to change before this activity would be profitable. Also, there is a row in the bottom part of the table for each constraint, *including* the maximum sales constraints. The interesting values are again the shadow prices. The first two indicate the amount the company would pay for an extra assembling or line 1 testing labor hour. (Does the 29.5 value look familiar? Compare it to the SolverTable results above.) The shadow prices for all *binding* maximum sales constraints indicate how much more profit the company could make if it could increase its demand by one computer of that model.

The information in this sensitivity report is all relevant and definitely provides some insights if studied carefully. However, this really requires you to know the rules Solver uses to create this report. That is, it requires a fairly in-depth knowledge of the theory behind LP sensitivity analysis, more than we have provided here. Fortunately, we believe the same basic information—and more—can be obtained in a more intuitive way by creating appropriate SolverTable reports.

Problems

Level A

Solutions for problems whose numbers appear within a colored box can be found in the Student Solution Files.

10. Modify PC Tech's two-line product mix model so that there is no maximum sales constraint. (This is easy to do in the Solver dialog box. Just highlight the constraint and click on the Delete button.) Does this make the problem unbounded? Does it change the optimal solution at all? Explain its effect.

11. In PC Tech's two-line product mix model it makes sense to change the maximum sales constraint to a "minimum sales" constraint, simply by changing the direction of the inequality. Then the input values in row 23 can be considered customer demands that must be met. Make this

change and rerun Solver. What do you find? What do you find if you run Solver again, this time making the values in row 23 one-quarter of their current values?

12. In PC Tech's two-line product mix model, use SolverTable to run a sensitivity analysis on the cost per assembling labor hour, letting it vary from $5 to $20 in increments of $1. Keep track of the computers produced in row 21, the hours used in the range B26:B28, and the total profit. Discuss your findings. Are they intuitively what you expected?

13. Create a two-way SolverTable for PC Tech's two-line product mix model, where total profit is the only output and the two inputs are the testing line 1 hours and testing line 2 hours available. Let the former vary from 4000 to 6000 in increments of 500, and let the latter vary from 3000 to 5000 in increments of 500. Discuss the changes in profit you see as you look across the various rows of the table. Discuss the changes in profit you see as you look down the various columns of the table.

14. In PC Tech's two-line product mix model, model 8 has fairly high profit margins, but it isn't included at all in the optimal mix. Use SolverTable, along with some experimentation on the correct range, to find the (approximate) selling price required for model 8 before it enters the optimal product mix.

Level B

15. Suppose you want to increase *all three* resource availabilities in PC Tech's two-line product mix model simultaneously by the same percentage. You want this percentage to vary from −25% to 50% in increments of 5%. Modify the spreadsheet model slightly so that this sensitivity analysis can be performed with a *one-way* SolverTable, using the percentage change as the single input. Keep track of the computers produced in row 21, the hours used in the range B26:B28, and the total profit. Discuss the results.

16. Some analysts complain that spreadsheet models are difficult to resize. You can be the judge of this. Suppose the current PC Tech two-line product mix problem is changed so that there is an extra resource, packaging labor hours, and two additional PC models, 9 and 10. What additional input data are required? What modifications are necessary in the spreadsheet model (including range name changes)? Make up values for any extra required input data and incorporate these into a modified spreadsheet model. Then optimize with Solver. Do you conclude that it is easy to resize a spreadsheet model? (By the way, algebraic models are typically *much* easier to resize.)

17. In Solver's sensitivity report for PC Tech's two-line product mix model, the allowable decrease for available assembling hours is 2375. This means that something happens when assembling hours fall to $20,000 - 2375 = 17,625$. See what this means by first running Solver with 17,626 available hours and then again with 17,624 available hours. Explain how the two solutions compare to the original solution and to each other.

13-8 A Multiperiod Production Model

The product mix examples illustrate a very important type of LP model. However, LP models come in many forms. For variety, we now present a different type of model that can also be solved with LP. (In the next chapter we provide other examples, linear and otherwise.) The distinguishing feature of the following model is that it relates decisions made during several time periods. This type of problem occurs when a company must make a decision now that will have ramifications in the future. The company does not want to focus completely on the short run and ignore the long run.

EXAMPLE

13.3 PRODUCING FOOTBALLS IN MULTIPLE TIME PERIODS

Pigskin Company produces footballs. Pigskin must decide how many footballs to produce each month. The company has decided to use a six-month planning horizon. The forecasted monthly demands for the next six months are 10,000, 15,000, 30,000, 35,000, 25,000, and 10,000. Pigskin wants to meet these demands on time, knowing that it currently has 5000 footballs in inventory and that it can use a given month's production to help meet the demand for that month. (For simplicity, we assume that production occurs during the month, and demand occurs at the end of the month.) During each month there is enough production capacity to produce up to 30,000 footballs, and there is enough storage capacity to store up to 10,000 footballs at the end of the month, after demand has occurred. The forecasted production costs per football for the next six months are $12.50, $12.55, $12.70, $12.80, $12.85, and $12.95, respectively. The holding cost per football held in inventory at the end of any month is figured at 5% of the production cost for that month. (This cost includes the cost of storage and also the cost of money tied up in inventory.) The selling price for footballs is not considered relevant to the production decision because Pigskin will satisfy all customer demand exactly when it occurs—at whatever the selling price is. In other words, total revenue for the planning horizon is *fixed*, regardless of production decisions. Therefore, Pigskin wants to determine the production schedule that minimizes the total production and holding costs.

Objective

To use LP to find the production schedule that meets demand on time and minimizes total production and inventory holding costs.

Where Do the Numbers Come From?

The input values for this problem are not all easy to find. Here are some thoughts on where they might be obtained.

- The initial inventory should be available from the company's database system or from a physical count.
- The unit production costs would probably be estimated in two steps. First, the company might ask its cost accountants to estimate the current unit production cost. Then it could examine historical trends in costs to estimate inflation factors for future months.
- The holding cost percentage is typically difficult to determine. Depending on the type of inventory being held, this cost can include storage and handling, rent, property taxes, insurance, spoilage, and obsolescence. It can also include capital costs—the cost of money that could be used for other purposes.
- The demands are probably forecasts made by the marketing and sales department. They might be "seat-of-the-pants" forecasts, or they might be the result of a formal quantitative forecasting procedure as discussed in Chapter 12. Of course, if there are already some orders on the books for future months, these are included in the demand figures.
- The production and storage capacities are probably supplied by the production department. They are based on the size of the workforce, the available machinery, availability of raw materials, and physical space.

Solution

The variables for this model appear in Figure 13.27. There are two keys to relating these variables. First, the months cannot be treated independently. This is because the ending inventory in one month is the beginning inventory for the next month. Second, to ensure that demand is satisfied on time, the amount on hand after production in each month must be at least as large as the demand for that month. This constraint must be included explicitly in the model.

Figure 13.27 Big Picture for Production Planning Model

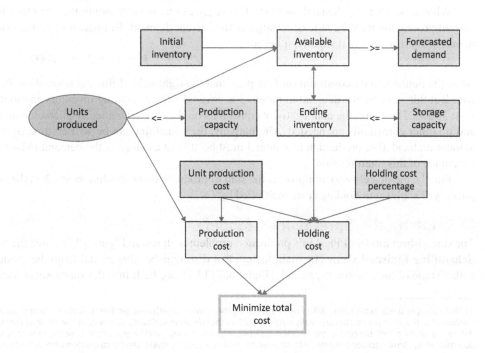

When you model this type of problem, you must be very specific about the *timing* of events. Depending on the assumptions you make, there can be a variety of potential models. For example, when does the demand for footballs in a given month occur: at the beginning of the month, at the end of the month, or continually throughout the month? The same question can be asked about production in a given month. The answers to these two questions indicate how much of the production in a given month can be used to help satisfy the demand in that month. Also, are the maximum storage constraint and the holding cost based on the *ending* inventory in a month, the *average* amount of inventory in a month, or the *maximum* inventory in a month? Each of these possibilities is reasonable and could be implemented.

By modifying the timing assumptions in this type of model, alternative—and equally realistic—models with very different solutions can be obtained.

To simplify the model, we assume that (1) all production occurs at the beginning of the month, (2) all demand occurs *after* production, so that all units produced in a month can be used to satisfy that month's demand, and (3) the storage constraint and the holding cost are based on *ending* inventory in any month. (You are asked to modify these assumptions in the problems.)

Algebraic Model

In the traditional algebraic model, the decision variables are the *production quantities* for the six months, labeled P_1 through P_6. It is also convenient to let I_1 through I_6 be the corresponding *end-of-month inventories* (after demand has occurred).[12] For example, I_3 is the number of footballs left over at the end of month 3. Therefore, the obvious constraints are on production and inventory storage capacities: $P_j \leq 30000$ and $I_j \leq 10000$ for $1 \leq j \leq 6$.

In addition to these constraints, *balance* constraints that relate the P's and I's are necessary. In any month the inventory from the previous month plus the current production equals the current demand plus leftover inventory. If D_j is the forecasted demand for month j, the balance equation for month j is

$$I_{j-1} + P_j = D_j + I_j$$

The balance equation for month 1 uses the known beginning inventory, 5000, for the previous inventory (the I_{j-1} term). By putting all variables (P's and I's) on the left and all known values on the right (a standard LP convention), these balance constraints can be written as

$$P_1 - I_1 = 1000 - 5000$$
$$I_1 + P_2 - I_2 = 15000$$
$$I_2 + P_3 - I_3 = 30000$$
$$I_3 + P_4 - I_4 = 35000$$
$$I_4 + P_5 - I_5 = 25000$$
$$I_5 + P_6 - I_6 = 10000$$

(13.1)

As usual, there are nonnegativity constraints: all P's and I's must be nonnegative.

What about meeting demand on time? This requires that in each month the inventory from the preceding month plus the current production must be at least as large as the current demand. But take a look, for example, at the balance equation for month 3. By rearranging it slightly, it becomes

$$I_3 = I_2 + P_3 - 30000$$

Now, the nonnegativity constraint on I_3 implies that the right side of this equation, $I_2 + P_3 - 30000$, must also be nonnegative. But this implies that demand in month 3 is covered—the beginning inventory in month 3 plus month 3 production is at least 30000. Therefore, the nonnegativity constraints on the I's *automatically* guarantee that all demands will be met on time, and no other constraints are needed. Alternatively, the constraint can be written directly as $I_2 + P_3 \geq 30000$. In words, the amount on hand after production in month 3 must be at least as large as the demand in month 3. The spreadsheet model takes advantage of this interpretation.

Finally, the objective to minimize is the sum of production and holding costs. It is the sum of unit production costs multiplied by P's, plus unit holding costs multiplied by I's.

Developing the Spreadsheet Model

The spreadsheet model of Pigskin's production problem is shown in Figure 13.28. (See the file **Production Scheduling Finished.xlsx**.) The main feature that distinguishes this model from the product mix model is that some of the constraints, namely, Equations (13.1), are built into the spreadsheet itself by means of

Developing the Production Planning Model

---

12 This example illustrates a subtle difference between algebraic and spreadsheet models. It is often convenient in algebraic models to define "decision variables," in this case the I's, that are really determined by other decision variables, in this case the P's. In spreadsheet models, however, we typically define the decision variable cells as the smallest set of variables that must be chosen—in this case the production quantities. Then values that are determined by these decision variable cells, such as the ending inventory levels, can be calculated with spreadsheet formulas.

Figure 13.28 Production Planning Model with a Suboptimal Solution

	A	B	C	D	E	F	G	H	I	J	K
1	Multiperiod production model								Range names used		
2									Demand	=Model!$B$18:$G$18	
3	Input data								Ending_inventory	=Model!$B$20:$G$20	
4	Initial inventory	5000							On_hand_after_production	=Model!$B$16:$G$16	
5	Holding cost as % of prod cost	5%							Production_capacity	=Model!$B$14:$G$14	
6									Storage_capacity	=Model!$B$22:$G$22	
7	Month	Month 1	Month 2	Month 3	Month 4	Month 5	Month 6		Total_Cost	=Model!$H$28	
8	Production cost/unit	$12.50	$12.55	$12.70	$12.80	$12.85	$12.95		Units_produced	=Model!$B$12:$G$12	
9											
10	Production plan										
11	Month	1	2	3	4	5	6				
12	Units produced	15000	15000	30000	30000	25000	10000				
13		<=	<=	<=	<=	<=	<=				
14	Production capacity	30000	30000	30000	30000	30000	30000				
15											
16	On hand after production	20000	25000	40000	40000	30000	15000				
17		>=	>=	>=	>=	>=	>=				
18	Demand	10000	15000	30000	35000	25000	10000				
19											
20	Ending inventory	10000	10000	10000	5000	5000	5000				
21		<=	<=	<=	<=	<=	<=				
22	Storage capacity	10000	10000	10000	10000	10000	10000				
23											
24	Summary of costs										
25	Month	Month 1	Month 2	Month 3	Month 4	Month 5	Month 6	Totals			
26	Production costs	$187,500	$188,250	$381,000	$384,000	$321,250	$129,500	$1,591,500			
27	Holding costs	$6,250	$6,275	$6,350	$3,200	$3,213	$3,238	$28,525			
28	Totals	$193,750	$194,525	$387,350	$387,200	$324,463	$132,738	$1,620,025			

formulas. This means that the only decision variable cells are the production quantities. The ending inventories shown in row 20 are *determined* by the production quantities and Equations (13.1). As you see, the decision variables in an algebraic model (the P's and I's) are not *necessarily* the same as the decision variable cells in an equivalent spreadsheet model. (The only decision variable cells in the spreadsheet model correspond to the P's.)

To develop the spreadsheet model in Figure 13.28, proceed as follows.

1. **Inputs.** Enter the inputs in the blue cells. Again, these are all entered as *numbers* directly from the problem statement. (Unlike some spreadsheet modelers who prefer to put all inputs in the upper left corner of the spreadsheet, we enter the inputs wherever they fit most naturally. Of course, this takes some planning before diving in.)

2. **Name ranges.** Name the ranges indicated. Note that all but one of these (Total_cost) can be named easily with the range-naming shortcut, using the labels in column A.

3. **Production quantities.** Enter *any* values in the range Units_produced as production quantities. As always, you can enter values that you believe are good, maybe even optimal. This is not crucial, however, because Solver eventually finds the *optimal* production quantities.

4. **On-hand inventory.** Enter the formula

   =B4+B12

   in cell B16. This calculates the first month's on-hand inventory after production (but before demand). Then enter the typical formula

   =B20+C12

   for on-hand inventory after production in month 2 in cell C16 and copy it across row 16.

5. **Ending inventories.** Enter the formula

   =B16-B18

   for ending inventory in cell B20 and copy it across row 20. This formula calculates ending inventory in the current month as on-hand inventory before demand minus the demand in that month.

6. **Production and holding costs.** Enter the formula

   =B8*B12

   in cell B26 and copy it across to cell G26 to calculate the monthly production costs. Then enter the formula

   =$B$5*B8*B20

   in cell B27 and copy it across to cell G27 to calculate the monthly holding costs. Note that these are based on monthly ending inventories. Finally, calculate the cost totals in column H with the SUM function.

In multiperiod problems, there is often one formula for the first period and a slightly different (copyable) formula for all other periods.

Using Solver

To use Solver, fill out the main dialog box as shown in Figure 13.29. The logic behind the constraints is straightforward. The constraints are that (1) the production quantities cannot exceed the production capacities, (2) the on-hand inventories after production must be at least as large as the demands, and (3) the ending inventories cannot exceed the storage capacities. Check the Non-Negative option and select the Simplex LP method, and then click Solve.

Figure 13.29 Solver Dialog Box for Production Planning Model

Discussion of the Solution

The optimal solution from Solver appears in Figure 13.30. The solution can be interpreted best by comparing production quantities to demands. In month 1, Pigskin should produce just enough to meet month 1 demand (taking into account the initial inventory of 5000). In month 2, it should produce 5000 more footballs than month 2 demand, and then in month 3 it should produce just enough to meet month 3 demand, while still carrying the extra 5000 footballs in inventory from month 2 production. In month 4, Pigskin should finally use these 5000 footballs, along with the maximum production amount, 30,000, to meet

Figure 13.30 Optimal Solution for Production Planning Model

	A	B	C	D	E	F	G	H	I	J	K
1	**Multiperiod production model**								**Range names used**		
2									Demand	=Model!$B$18:$G$18	
3	**Input data**								Ending_inventory	=Model!$B$20:$G$20	
4	Initial inventory	5000							On_hand_after_production	=Model!$B$16:$G$16	
5	Holding cost as % of prod cost	5%							Production_capacity	=Model!$B$14:$G$14	
6									Storage_capacity	=Model!$B$22:$G$22	
7	Month	Month 1	Month 2	Month 3	Month 4	Month 5	Month 6		Total_Cost	=Model!$H$28	
8	Production cost/unit	$12.50	$12.55	$12.70	$12.80	$12.85	$12.95		Units_produced	=Model!$B$12:$G$12	
9											
10	**Production plan**										
11	Month	1	2	3	4	5	6				
12	Units produced	5000	20000	30000	30000	25000	10000				
13		<=	<=	<=	<=	<=	<=				
14	Production capacity	30000	30000	30000	30000	30000	30000				
15											
16	On hand after production	10000	20000	35000	35000	25000	10000				
17		>=	>=	>=	>=	>=	>=				
18	Demand	10000	15000	30000	35000	25000	10000				
19											
20	Ending inventory	0	5000	5000	0	0	0				
21		<=	<=	<=	<=	<=	<=				
22	Storage capacity	10000	10000	10000	10000	10000	10000				
23											
24	**Summary of costs**										
25	Month	Month 1	Month 2	Month 3	Month 4	Month 5	Month 6	Totals			
26	Production costs	$62,500	$251,000	$381,000	$384,000	$321,250	$129,500	$1,529,250			
27	Holding costs	$0	$3,138	$3,175	$0	$0	$0	$6,313			
28	Totals	$62,500	$254,138	$384,175	$384,000	$321,250	$129,500	$1,535,563			

month 4 demand. Then in months 5 and 6 it should produce exactly enough to meet these months' demands. The total cost is $1,535,563, most of which is production cost.

Could you have guessed this optimal solution? Upon reflection, it makes perfect sense. Because the monthly holding costs are large relative to the differences in monthly production costs, there is little incentive to produce footballs before they are needed to take advantage of a "cheap" production month. Therefore, Pigskin Company produces foot balls in the month when they are needed—when possible. The only exception to this rule is the 20,000 footballs produced during month 2 when only 15,000 are needed. The extra 5000 footballs produced in month 2 are needed, however, to meet the month 4 demand of 35,000, because month 3 production capacity is used entirely to meet the month 3 demand. Thus month 3 capacity is not available to meet the month 4 demand, and 5000 units of month 2 capacity are used to meet the month 4 demand.

You can often improve your intuition by trying to reason why Solver's solution is indeed optimal.

Fundamental Insight

Multiperiod Optimization Problems and Myopic Solutions

Many optimization problems are of a multiperiod nature, where a sequence of decisions must be made over time. When making the *first* of these decisions, the one for this week or this month, say, it is usually best to include future decisions in the model, as has been done here. If you ignore future periods and make the initial decision based only on the first period, the resulting decision is called *myopic* (short-sighted). Myopic decisions are occasionally optimal, but not very often. The idea is that if you act now in a way that looks best in the short run, it might lead you down a strategically unattractive path for the long run.

Sensitivity Analysis

SolverTable can now be used to perform a number of interesting sensitivity analyses. We illustrate two possibilities. First, note that the most inventory ever carried at the end of a month is 5000, although the storage capacity each month is 10,000. Perhaps this is because the holding cost percentage, 5%, is fairly large. Would more ending inventory be carried if this holding cost percentage were lower? Or would even less be carried if it were higher? You can check this with the SolverTable output shown in Figure 13.31. Now the single input cell is cell B5, and the *single* output is the maximum ending inventory ever held, which you can calculate in cell B31 with the formula

If you want Solver Table to keep track of a quantity that is not in your model, you need to create it with an appropriate formula in a new cell.

= MAX(Ending_inventory)

As the SolverTable results indicate, the storage capacity limit is reached only when the holding cost percentage falls to 1%. (This output doesn't indicate which month or how many months the ending inventory is at the upper limit.) On the other hand, even when the holding cost percentage reaches 10%, the company still continues to hold a maximum ending inventory of 5000.

Figure 13.31 Sensitivity of Maximum Inventory to Holding Cost

▲	A	B	C	D	E	F	G
1	Oneway analysis for Solver model in Model worksheet						
2							
3	Holding cost pct (cell $B$5) values along side, output cell(s) along top						
4		$B$31					
5	1%	10000	Sometimes you'd like to use SolverTable				
6	2%	5000	on an output that isn't explicitly part of				
7	3%	5000	the model. In that case, just calculate it				
8	4%	5000	in a new cell (as in cell B31 in the Model				
9	5%	5000	sheet) and then use SolverTable.				
10	6%	5000					
11	7%	5000					
12	8%	5000					
13	9%	5000					
14	10%	5000					

A second possible sensitivity analysis is suggested by the way the optimal production schedule would probably be implemented. The optimal solution to Pigskin's model specifies the production level for each of the next six months. In reality, however, the company would probably implement the model's recommendation only for the *first* month. Then at the beginning of the second month, it would gather new forecasts for the *next* six months, months 2 through 7, solve a new six-month model, and again implement the model's recommendation for the first of these months, month 2. If the company continues in this manner, we say that it is following a six-month **rolling planning horizon**.

The question, then, is whether the assumed demands (really, forecasts) toward the end of the planning horizon have much effect on the optimal production quantity in month 1. We would hope not, because these forecasts could be quite inaccurate. The two-way Solver table in Figure 13.32 shows how the optimal month 1 production quantity varies with the forecasted demands in months 5 and 6. As you can see, if the errors in the forecasted demands for months 5 and 6 remain fairly small, the optimal month 1 production quantity remains at 5000. This is good news. It means that the optimal production quantity in month 1 is fairly insensitive to the possibly inaccurate forecasts for months 5 and 6.

Figure 13.32 Sensitivity of Month 1 Production to Demand in Months 5 and 6

◢	A	B	C	D	E	F	G	H	I	J
1	**Twoway analysis for Solver model in Model worksheet**									
2										
3	Month 5 demand (cell $F$18) values along side, Month 6 demand (cell $G$18) values along top, output cell in corner									
4	Units_produced_1	10000	20000	30000						
5	10000	5000	5000	5000						
6	20000	5000	5000	5000						
7	30000	5000	5000	5000						

Solver's sensitivity report for this model appears in Figure 13.33. The bottom part of this report is fairly straightforward to interpret. The first six rows are for sensitivity to changes in the demand, whereas the last six are for sensitivity to changes in the storage capacity. (There are no rows for the production capacity constraints because these are simple upper-bound

Figure 13.33 Solver Sensitivity Report for Production Planning Model

◢	A	B	C	D	E	F	G	H
6		Variable Cells						
7				Final	Reduced	Objective	Allowable	Allowable
8		Cells	Name	Value	Cost	Coefficient	Increase	Decrease
9		$B$12	Units produced Month 1	5000	0	16.31750006	1E+30	0.575000009
10		$C$12	Units produced Month 2	20000	0	15.74250005	0.575000009	0.477500009
11		$D$12	Units produced Month 3	30000	−0.477500009	15.26500004	0.477500009	1E+30
12		$E$12	Units produced Month 4	30000	−1.012500019	14.73000003	1.012500019	1E+30
13		$F$12	Units produced Month 5	25000	0	14.14000002	1.602500028	0.54250001
14		$G$12	Units produced Month 6	10000	0	13.59750001	0.54250001	13.59750001
15								
16		Constraints						
17				Final	Shadow	Constraint	Allowable	Allowable
18		Cells	Name	Value	Price	R.H. Side	Increase	Decrease
19		$B$16	On hand after production <=	10000	0.575000009	10000	10000	5000
20		$C$16	On hand after production <=	20000	0	15000	5000	1E+30
21		$D$16	On hand after production <=	35000	0	30000	5000	1E+30
22		$E$16	On hand after production <=	35000	1.602500028	35000	5000	5000
23		$F$16	On hand after production <=	25000	0.54250001	25000	5000	20000
24		$G$16	On hand after production <=	10000	13.59750001	10000	10000	10000
25		$B$20	Ending inventory >=	0	0	10000	1E+30	10000
26		$C$20	Ending inventory >=	5000	0	10000	1E+30	5000
27		$D$20	Ending inventory >=	5000	0	10000	1E+30	5000
28		$E$20	Ending inventory >=	0	0	10000	1E+30	10000
29		$F$20	Ending inventory >=	0	0	10000	1E+30	10000
30		$G$20	Ending inventory >=	0	0	10000	1E+30	10000

constraints on the decision variables. Recall that Solver's sensitivity report handles this type of constraint differently from "normal" constraints.) In contrast, the top part of the report is virtually impossible to unravel. This is because the objective coefficients of the decision variables are each based on *multiple* inputs. (Each is a combination of unit production costs and the holding cost percentage.) Therefore, if you want to know how the solution will change if you change a single unit production cost or the holding cost percentage, this report does not answer your question. This is one case where a sensitivity analysis with SolverTable is much more straightforward and intuitive. It allows you to change *any* of the model's inputs and directly see the effects on the solution.

Modeling Issues

We assume that Pigskin uses a six-month planning horizon. Why six months? In multiperiod models such as this, the company has to make forecasts about the future, such as the level of customer demand. Therefore, the length of the planning horizon is usually the length of time for which the company can make reasonably accurate forecasts. Here, Pigskin evidently believes that it can forecast up to six months from now, so it uses a six-month planning horizon.

Problems

Level A

18. Can you guess the results of a sensitivity analysis on the initial inventory in the Pigskin model? See if your guess is correct by using SolverTable and allowing the initial inventory to vary from 0 to 10,000 in increments of 1000. Keep track of the values in the decision variable cells and the objective cell.

19. Modify the Pigskin model so that there are eight months in the planning horizon. You can make up reasonable values for any extra required data. Don't forget to modify range names. Then modify the model again so that there are only four months in the planning horizon. Do either of these modifications change the optimal production quantity in month 1?

20. As indicated by the algebraic formulation of the Pigskin model, there is no real need to calculate inventory on hand after production and constrain it to be greater than or equal to demand. An alternative is to calculate ending inventory directly and constrain it to be nonnegative. Modify the current spreadsheet model to do this. (Delete rows 16 and 17, and calculate ending inventory appropriately. Then add an *explicit* nonnegativity constraint on ending inventory.)

21. In one modification of the Pigskin model, the maximum storage constraint and the holding cost are based on the *average* inventory (not ending inventory) for a given month, where the average inventory is defined as the sum of beginning inventory and ending inventory, divided by 2, and beginning inventory is *before* production or demand.

Modify the Pigskin model with this new assumption, and use Solver to find the optimal solution. How does this change the optimal production schedule? How does it change the optimal total cost?

Level B

22. Modify the Pigskin spreadsheet model so that except for month 6, demand does not have to be met on time. The only requirement is that all demand must be met eventually by the end of month 6. How does this change the optimal production schedule? How does it change the optimal total cost?

23. Modify the Pigskin spreadsheet model so that demand in any of the first five months must be met no later than a month late, whereas demand in month 6 must be met on time. For example, the demand in month 3 can be met partly in month 3 and partly in month 4. How does this change the optimal production schedule? How does it change the optimal total cost?

24. Modify the Pigskin spreadsheet model in the following way. Assume that the timing of demand and production are such that only 70% of the production in a given month can be used to satisfy the demand in that month. The other 30% occurs too late in that month and must be carried as inventory to help satisfy demand in later months. How does this change the optimal production schedule? How does it change the optimal total cost? Then use SolverTable to see how the optimal production schedule and optimal cost vary as the percentage of production usable for this month's demand (now 70%) is allowed to vary from 20% to 100% in increments of 10%.

13-9 A Comparison of Algebraic and Spreadsheet Models

To this point you have seen algebraic optimization models and corresponding spreadsheet models. How do they differ? If you review the two product mix examples in this chapter, we believe you will agree that (1) the algebraic models are quite straightforward and (2) the spreadsheet models are almost direct translations into Excel of the algebraic models.

In particular, each algebraic model has a set of x's that corresponds to the decision variable cell range in the spreadsheet model. In addition, each objective and each left side of each constraint in the spreadsheet model corresponds to a linear expression involving x's in the algebraic model.

However, the Pigskin production planning model is quite different. The spreadsheet model includes one set of decision variable cells, the production quantities, and everything else is related to these through spreadsheet formulas. In contrast, the algebraic model has *two* sets of variables, the P's for the production quantities and the I's for the ending inventories, and together these constitute the *decision variables*. These two sets of variables must then be related algebraically, which is done through a series of *balance equations*.

This is a typical situation in algebraic models, where one set of variables (the production quantities) corresponds to the *real* decision variables, and other sets of variables, along with extra equations or inequalities, are introduced to capture the logic. We believe—and this belief is reinforced by years of teaching experience—this extra level of abstraction makes algebraic models much more difficult for typical users to develop and comprehend. It is the primary reason we have decided to focus almost exclusively on spreadsheet models in this book.

13-10 A Decision Support System

If your job is to develop an LP spreadsheet model to solve a problem such as Pigskin's production problem, you will be considered the "expert" in LP. Many people who need to use such models, however, are *not* experts. They might understand the basic ideas behind LP and the types of problems it is intended to solve, but they will not know the details. In this case it is useful to provide these users with a **decision support system** (DSS) that can help them solve problems without having to know technical details.

We will not teach you in this book how to build a full-scale DSS, but we will show you what a typical DSS looks like and what it can do.[13] (We consider only DSSs built around spreadsheets. There are many other platforms for developing DSSs that we will not consider.) Basically, a spreadsheet-based DSS contains a spreadsheet model of a problem, such as the one in Figure 13.26. However, as a user, you will probably never even see this model. Instead, you will see a front end and a back end. The front end allows you to select input values for your particular problem. The user interface for this front end can include several features, such as buttons, dialog boxes, toolbars, and menus—the things you are used to seeing in Windows applications. The back end will then produce a report that explains the solution in nontechnical terms.

Developing a Decision Support System

We illustrate a DSS for a slight variation of the Pigskin problem in the file **Decision Support.xlsm**. This file has three worksheets. When you open the file, you see the Explanation sheet shown in Figure 13.34. It contains two buttons, one for setting up the problem (getting the user's inputs) and one for solving the problem (running Solver). When you click the Set Up Problem button, you are asked for the inputs: the initial inventory, the forecasted demands for each month, and others. An example appears in Figure 13.35. These input boxes should be self-explanatory, so that all you need to do is enter the values you want to try. (To speed up the process, the inputs from the previous run are shown by default.) After you have entered these inputs, you can view the Model sheet. This sheet contains a spreadsheet model similar to the one in Figure 13.30 but with the inputs you just entered.

---

13 For readers interested in learning more about this DSS, this textbook's essential resource website includes notes about its development in the file **Developing the Decision Support Application.docx**, under Chapter 13 Example Files, and the accompanying videos provide details for developing a slightly less complex DSS for a product mix model. If you are interested in learning more about spreadsheet DSSs in general, Albright has written the book *VBA for Modelers*, now in its fifth edition. It contains a primer on the VBA language and presents many applications and instructions for creating DSSs with VBA.

Figure 13.34 Explanation
Sheet for DSS

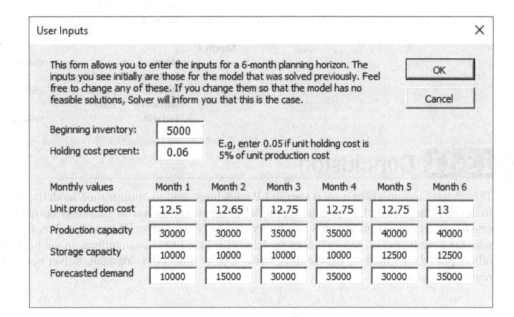

Figure 13.35 Dialog Box for
Obtaining User Inputs

Now go back to the Explanation sheet and click the Find Optimal Solution button. This automatically sets up the Solver dialog box and runs Solver. There are two possibilities. First, it is possible that there is no feasible solution to the problem with the inputs you entered. In this case you see a message to this effect, as in Figure 13.36. In most cases, however, the problem has a feasible solution. In this case you see the Report sheet, which summarizes the optimal solution in nontechnical terms. Part of one sample output appears in Figure 13.37.

Figure 13.36 Indication of No
Feasible Solutions

After studying this report, you can then click the Solve Another Problem button, which takes you back to the Explanation sheet so that you can solve a new problem. All this is done automatically with Excel macros. These macros use Microsoft's Visual Basic for Applications (VBA) programming language to automate various tasks. In most professional applications, nontechnical people can just enter inputs and view reports. Therefore, the Model sheet and VBA code will most likely be hidden and protected from users.

Figure 13.37 Optimal Solution
Report

Monthly schedule

Month 1

Units		Dollars	
Start with	5000		
Produce	5000	Production cost	$62,500
Demand is	10000		
End with	0	Holding cost	$0

Month 2

Units		Dollars	
Start with	0		
Produce	15000	Production cost	$189,750
Demand is	15000		
End with	0	Holding cost	$0

Month 3

Units		Dollars	
Start with	0		
Produce	30000	Production cost	$382,500
Demand is	30000		
End with	0	Holding cost	$0

13-11 Conclusion

This chapter has provided a good start to LP modeling—and to optimization modeling in general. You have learned how to develop three basic LP spreadsheet models, how to use Solver to find their optimal solutions, and how to perform sensitivity analyses with Solver's sensitivity reports or the SolverTable add-in. You have also learned how to recognize whether a mathematical programming model satisfies the linear assumptions. In the next chapter you will see a variety of other optimization models, but the three basic steps of model development, Solver optimization, and sensitivity analysis remain the same.

Summary of Key Terms

TERM	EXPLANATION	EXCEL	PAGES
Linear programming	Refers to optimization models with a linear objective and linear constraints, often abbreviated as LP		600
Objective	The value, such as profit, to be optimized in an optimization model		601
Constraints	Conditions that must be satisfied in an optimization model		601
Decision variable cells	Cells that contain the values of the decision variables	Specify in Solver dialog box	601
Objective cell	Cell that contains the value of the objective	Specify in Solver dialog box	601
Nonnegativity constraints	Constraints that require the decision variables to be nonnegative, usually for physical reasons		601
Feasible solution	A solution that satisfies all constraints		602
Feasible region	The set of all feasible solutions		602
Infeasible solution	A solution that doesn't satisfy all constraints		602
Optimal solution	The feasible solution that has the best value of the objective		602

TERM	EXPLANATION	EXCEL	PAGES
Solver	Add-in that ships with Excel for performing optimization, developed by Frontline Systems	Solver on Data ribbon	602
Simplex method	An efficient algorithm for finding the optimal solution in a linear programming model		602
Sensitivity analysis	Seeing how the optimal solution changes as selected input values change		602
Algebraic model	A model that expresses the constraints and the objective algebraically		604
Graphical solution	Shows the constraints and objective graphically so that the optimal solution can be identified; useful only when there are two decision variables		605
Spreadsheet model	A model that uses spreadsheet formulas to express the logic of the model		607
Binding constraint	A constraint that holds as an equality		615
Nonbinding constraint	An inequality constraint where there is a difference between the two sides of the inequality		615
Solver's sensitivity report	Report available from Solver that shows sensitivity to objective coefficients and right sides of constraints	Available in Solver dialog box after Solver runs	616
Reduced cost	Amount the objective coefficient of a variable currently equal to zero must change before it is optimal for that variable to be positive, or the amount the objective of a variable currently at its upper bound must change before that variable decreases from its upper bound		617
Shadow price	The change in the objective for a change in the right side of a constraint; indicates amount a company would pay for more of a scarce resource		617
SolverTable	Add-in developed by Albright that performs sensitivity analysis to any inputs and reports results in tabular and graphical form	SolverTable tab	619
Selecting multiple ranges	Useful when decision variable cells, e.g., are in noncontiguous ranges	Pressing Ctrl key, drag ranges, one after the other	620
Mathematical programming model	Any optimization model, whether linear, integer, or nonlinear		626
Proportionality, additivity, divisibility	Properties of optimization model that result in a linear programming model		627
Infeasibility	Condition where a model has no feasible solutions		629
Unboundedness	Condition where there is no limit to the objective; almost always a sign of an error in the model		629
Rolling planning horizon	Multiperiod model where only the decision in the first period is implemented, and then a new multiperiod model is solved in succeeding periods		647
Decision support system	System where a user can enter inputs to a model and see outputs, but need not be concerned with technical details		650

Problems

Conceptual Questions

C.1. Suppose you use Solver to find the optimal solution to a maximization model. Then you remember that you omitted an important constraint. After adding the constraint and running Solver again, is the optimal value of the objective guaranteed to decrease? Why or why not?

C.2. Consider an optimization model with a number of resource constraints. Each indicates that the amount of the resource used cannot exceed the amount available. Why is the shadow price of such a resource constraint always zero when the amount used in the optimal solution is *less than* the amount available?

C.3. If you add a constraint to an optimization model, and the previously optimal solution satisfies the new constraint, will this solution still be optimal with the new constraint added? Why or why not?

C.4. Why is it generally necessary to add nonnegativity constraints to an optimization model? Wouldn't Solver automatically choose nonnegative values for the decision variable cells?

C.5. Suppose you have a *linear* optimization model where you are trying to decide which products to produce to maximize profit. What does the additive assumption imply about the profit objective? What does the proportionality assumption imply about the profit objective? Be as specific as possible. Can you think of any *reasonable* profit functions that would *not* be linear in the amounts of the products produced?

C.6. In a typical product mix model, where a company must decide how much of each product to produce to maximize profit, discuss possible situations where there might not be any feasible solutions. Could these be realistic? If you had such a situation in your company, how might you proceed?

C.7. In a typical product mix model, where a company must decide how much of each product to produce to maximize profit, there are sometimes customer demands for the products. We used upper-bound constraints for these: Don't produce more than you can sell. Would it be realistic to have lower-bound constraints instead: Produce at least as much as is demanded? Would it be realistic to have both (where the upper bounds are greater than the lower bounds)? Would it be realistic to have equality constraints: Produce exactly what is demanded?

C.8. In a typical production scheduling model like Pigskin's, if there are no production capacity constraints—the company can produce as much as it needs in any time period—but there are storage capacity constraints and demand must be met on time, is it possible that there will be no feasible solutions? Why or why not?

C.9. In a production scheduling problem like Pigskin's, suppose the company must produce *several* products to meet customer demands. Would it suffice to solve a separate model for each product, as we did for Pigskin, or would one big model for all products be necessary? If the latter, discuss what this big model might look like.

C.10. In any optimization model such as those in this chapter, we say that the model is unbounded (and Solver will indicate as such) if there is no limit to the value of the objective. For example, if the objective is profit, then for any dollar value, no matter how large, there is a feasible solution with profit at least this large. In the real world, why are there never any unbounded models? If you run Solver on a model and get an "unbounded" message, what should you do?

Level A

25. A chemical company manufactures three chemicals: A, B, and C. These chemicals are produced via two production processes: 1 and 2. Running process 1 for an hour costs $400 and yields 300 units of A, 100 units of B, and 100 units of C. Running process 2 for an hour costs $100 and yields 100 units of A and 100 units of B. To meet customer demands, at least 1000 units of A, 500 units of B, and 300 units of C must be produced daily.
   a. Use Solver to determine a daily production plan that minimizes the cost of meeting the company's daily demands.
   b. Confirm graphically that the daily production plan from part **a** minimizes the cost of meeting the company's daily demands.
   c. Use SolverTable to see what happens to the decision variables and the total cost when the hourly processing cost for process 2 increases in increments of $0.50. How large must this cost increase be before the decision variables change? What happens when it continues to increase beyond this point?

26. A furniture company manufactures desks and chairs. Each desk uses four units of wood, and each chair uses three units of wood. A desk contributes $400 to profit, and a chair contributes $250. Marketing restrictions require that the number of chairs produced be at least twice the number of desks produced. There are 2000 units of wood available.
   a. Use Solver to maximize the company's profit.
   b. Confirm graphically that the solution in part **a** maximizes the company's profit.
   c. Use SolverTable to see what happens to the decision variables and the total profit when the availability of wood varies from 1000 to 3000 in 100-unit increments. Based on your findings, how much would the company be willing to pay for each extra unit of wood over its current 2000 units? How much profit would the company lose if it lost any of its current 2000 units?

27. A farmer in Iowa owns 450 acres of land. He is going to plant each acre with wheat or corn. Each acre planted with wheat yields $2000 profit, requires three workers, and requires two tons of fertilizer. Each acre planted with corn yields $3000 profit, requires two workers, and requires four tons of fertilizer. There are currently 1000 workers and 1200 tons of fertilizer available.

  a. Use Solver to help the farmer maximize the profit from his land.

  b. Confirm graphically that the solution from part **a** maximizes the farmer's profit from his land.

  c. Use SolverTable to see what happens to the decision variables and the total profit when the availability of fertilizer varies from 200 tons to 2200 tons in 100-ton increments. When does the farmer discontinue producing wheat? When does he discontinue producing corn? How does the profit change for each 10-ton increment?

28. During the next four months, a customer requires, respectively, 500, 650, 1000, and 700 units of a commodity, and no backlogging is allowed (that is, the customer's requirements must be met on time). Production costs are $50, $80, $40, and $70 per unit during these months. The storage cost from one month to the next is $20 per unit (assessed on ending inventory). It is estimated that each unit on hand at the end of month 4 can be sold for $60. Assume there is no beginning inventory.

  a. Determine how to minimize the net cost incurred in meeting the demands for the next four months.

  b. Use SolverTable to see what happens to the decision variables and the total cost when the initial inventory varies from 0 to 1000 in 100-unit increments. How much lower would the total cost be if the company started with 100 units in inventory, rather than none? Would this same cost decrease occur for every 100-unit increase in initial inventory?

29. A company faces the following demands during the next three weeks: week 1, 2000 units; week 2, 1000 units; week 3, 1500 units. The unit production costs during each week are as follows: week 1, $130; week 2, $140; week 3, $150. A holding cost of $20 per unit is assessed against each week's ending inventory. At the beginning of week 1, the company has 500 units on hand. In reality, not all goods produced during a month can be used to meet the current month's demand. To model this fact, assume that only half of the goods produced during a week can be used to meet the current week's demands.

  a. Determine how to minimize the cost of meeting the demand for the next three weeks.

  b. Revise the model so that the demands are of the form $D_t + kC_t$, where D_t is the original demand (from above) in month t, k is a given factor, and C_t is an amount of change in month t demand. Develop the model in such a way that you can use SolverTable to analyze changes in the amounts produced and the total cost when k varies from 0 to 10 in 1-unit increments,

for any fixed values of the Cs. For example, try this when $C_1 = 200$, $C_2 = 500$, and $C_3 = 300$. Describe the behavior you observe in the table. Can you find any reasonable C's that induce *positive* production levels in week 3?

30. Maggie Stewart loves desserts, but due to weight and cholesterol concerns, she has decided that she must plan her desserts carefully. There are two possible desserts she is considering: snack bars and ice cream. After reading the nutrition labels on the snack bar and ice cream packages, she learns that each serving of a snack bar weighs 37 grams and contains 120 calories and 5 grams of fat. Each serving of ice cream weighs 65 grams and contains 160 calories and 10 grams of fat. Maggie will allow herself no more than 450 calories and 25 grams of fat in her daily desserts, but because she loves desserts so much, she requires at least 120 grams of dessert per day. Also, she assigns a "taste index" to each gram of each dessert, where 0 is the lowest and 100 is the highest. She assigns a taste index of 95 to ice cream and 85 to snack bars (because she prefers ice cream to snack bars).

  a. Use Solver to find the daily dessert plan that stays within her constraints and maximizes the total taste index of her dessert.

  b. Confirm graphically that the solution from part **a** maximizes Maggie's total taste index.

  c. Use a two-way Solver table to see how the optimal dessert plan varies when the calories per snack bar and per ice cream vary. Let the former vary from 80 to 200 in increments of 10, and let the latter vary from 120 to 300 in increments of 10.

31. For a telephone survey, a marketing research group needs to contact at least 600 wives, 480 husbands, 400 single adult males, and 440 single adult females. It costs $3 to make a daytime call and (because of higher labor costs) $5 to make an evening call. The file **P13_31.xlsx** lists the results that can be expected. For example, 30% of all daytime calls are answered by a wife, 15% of all evening calls are answered by a single male, and 40% of all daytime calls are not answered at all. Due to limited staff, at most 40% of all phone calls can be evening calls.

  a. Determine how to minimize the cost of completing the survey.

  b. Use SolverTable to investigate changes in the unit cost of either type of call. Specifically, investigate changes in the cost of a daytime call, with the cost of an evening call fixed, to see when (if ever) *only* daytime calls or *only* evening calls will be made. Then repeat the analysis by changing the cost of an evening call and keeping the cost of a daytime call fixed.

32. A furniture company manufactures tables and chairs. Each table and chair must be made entirely out of oak or entirely out of pine. A total of 15,000 board feet of oak and 21,000 board feet of pine are available. A table requires either 17 board feet of oak or 30 board feet of pine, and a chair requires either 5 board feet of oak or 13 board feet of pine. Each table can be sold for $800, and each chair for $300.

a. Determine how the company can maximize its revenue.

b. Use SolverTable to investigate the effects of simultaneous changes in the selling prices of the products. Specifically, see what happens to the total revenue when the selling prices of oak products and the selling prices of pine products are allowed to vary (independently) by as much as plus or minus 30%, in increments of 10%, from their original values. Revise your model from the previous problem so that you can use SolverTable to investigate these changes. Can you conclude that total revenue changes *linearly* within this range?

33. A manufacturing company makes two products. Each product can be made on either of two machines. The time (in hours) required to make each product on each machine is listed in the file **P13_33.xlsx**. Each month, 500 hours of time are available on each machine. Each month, customers are willing to buy up to the quantities of each product at the prices also given in the same file. The company's goal is to maximize the revenue obtained from selling units during the next two months.

a. Determine how the company can meet this goal. Assume that it will not produce any units in a month that it cannot sell in that month.

b. Use SolverTable to see what happens if customer demands for each product in each month simultaneously change by as much as plus or minus 30%, in increments of 10%, from their current values. Revise the model so that you can use SolverTable to investigate the effect of these changes on total revenue. Does revenue change in a linear manner over this range? Can you explain intuitively why it changes in the way it does?

34. There are three factories on the Momiss River. Each emits two types of pollutants, labeled P_1 and P_2, into the river. If the waste from each factory is processed, the pollution in the river can be reduced. It costs $1500 to process a ton of factory 1 waste, and each ton processed reduces the amount of P_1 by 0.10 ton and the amount of P_2 by 0.45 ton. It costs $1000 to process a ton of factory 2 waste, and each ton processed reduces the amount of P_1 by 0.20 ton and the amount of P_2 by 0.25 ton. It costs $2000 to process a ton of factory 3 waste, and each ton processed reduces the amount of P_1 by 0.40 ton and the amount of P_2 by 0.30 ton. The state wants to reduce the amount of P_1 in the river by at least 30 tons and the amount of P_2 by at least 40 tons.

a. Use Solver to determine how to minimize the cost of reducing pollution by the desired amounts. Are the LP proportionality and additivity assumptions reasonable in this problem?

b. Use SolverTable to investigate the effects of increases in the minimal reductions required by the state. Specifically, see what happens to the amounts of waste processed at the three factories and the total cost if both requirements (currently 30 and 40 tons, respectively) are increased by the *same* percentage. Revise your model so that you can use SolverTable to investigate these changes when the percentage increase varies from 10% to 100% in increments of 10%. Do the amounts processed at the three factories and the total cost change in a linear manner?

Level B

35. A company manufactures two types of trucks. Each truck must go through the painting shop and the assembly shop. If the painting shop were completely devoted to painting type 1 trucks, 800 per day could be painted, whereas if the painting shop were completely devoted to painting type 2 trucks, 700 per day could be painted. If the assembly shop were completely devoted to assembling truck 1 engines, 1500 per day could be assembled, whereas if the assembly shop were completely devoted to assembling truck 2 engines, 1200 per day could be assembled. It is possible, however, to paint *both* types of trucks in the painting shop. Similarly, it is possible to assemble both types in the assembly shop. Each type 1 truck contributes $1000 to profit; each type 2 truck contributes $1500. Use Solver to maximize the company's profit. (*Hint*: One approach, but not the only approach, is to try a graphical procedure first and then deduce the constraints from the graph.)

36. A company manufactures mechanical heart valves from the heart valves of pigs. Different heart operations require valves of different sizes. The company purchases pig valves from three different suppliers. The cost and size mix of the valves purchased from each supplier are given in the file **P13_36.xlsx**. Each month, the company places an order with each supplier. At least 500 large, 300 medium, and 300 small valves must be purchased each month. Because of the limited availability of pig valves, at most 500 valves per month can be purchased from each supplier.

a. Use Solver to determine how the company can minimize the cost of acquiring the needed valves.

b. Use SolverTable to investigate the effect on total cost of increasing its minimal purchase requirements each month. Specifically, see how the total cost changes as the minimal purchase requirements of large, medium, and small valves all increase from their original values by the *same* percentage. Revise your model so that SolverTable can be used to investigate these changes when the percentage increase varies from 2% to 20% in increments of 2%. Explain intuitively what happens when this percentage is at least 16%.

37. A company that builds sailboats wants to determine how many sailboats to build during each of the next four quarters. The demand during each of the next four quarters is as follows: first quarter, 160 sailboats; second quarter, 240 sailboats; third quarter, 300 sailboats; fourth quarter, 100 sailboats. The company must meet demands on time. At the beginning of the first quarter, the company has an inventory of 40 sailboats. At the beginning of each quarter, the company must decide how many sailboats to build during that quarter. For simplicity, assume that sailboats built during a quarter can be used to meet demand for that quarter. During each quarter, the company can build up to 160 sailboats with regular-time labor at a total cost of $1600 per sailboat. By having employees work overtime during a quarter, the company can build additional sailboats with overtime labor at a total cost of $1800 per sailboat. At the end of each quarter (after production has occurred and the current quarter's demand has been satisfied), a holding cost of $80 per sailboat is incurred.

a. Determine a production schedule to minimize the sum of production and inventory holding costs during the next four quarters.

b. Use SolverTable to see whether any changes in the $80 holding cost per sailboat could induce the company to carry more or less inventory. Revise your model so that SolverTable can be used to investigate the effects on ending inventory during the four-quarter period of systematic changes in the unit holding cost. (Assume that even though the unit holding cost changes, it is still constant over the four-quarter period.) Are there any (nonnegative) unit holding costs that would induce the company to hold *more* inventory than it holds when the holding cost is $80? Are there any unit holding costs that would induce the company to hold *less* inventory than it holds when the holding cost is $80?

38. During the next two months an automobile manufacturer must meet (on time) the following demands for trucks and cars: month 1, 400 trucks and 800 cars; month 2, 300 trucks and 300 cars. During each month at most 1000 vehicles can be produced. Each truck uses two tons of steel, and each car uses one ton of steel. During month 1, steel costs $700 per ton; during month 2, steel is projected to cost $800 per ton. At most 2500 tons of steel can be purchased each month. (Steel can be used only during the month in which it is purchased.) At the beginning of month 1, 100 trucks and 200 cars are in the inventory. At the end of each month, a holding cost of $200 per vehicle is assessed. Each car gets 20 miles per gallon (mpg), and each truck gets 10 mpg. During each month, the vehicles produced by the company must average at least 16 mpg.

a. Determine how to meet the demand and mileage requirements at minimum total cost.

b. Use SolverTable to see how sensitive the total cost is to the 16 mpg requirement. Specifically, let this requirement vary from 14 mpg to 18 mpg in increments of 0.25 mpg. Explain intuitively what happens when the requirement is greater than 17 mpg.

39. A textile company produces shirts and pants. Each shirt requires two square yards of cloth, and each pair of pants requires three square yards of cloth. During the next two months the following demands for shirts and pants must be met (on time): month 1, 1000 shirts and 1500 pairs of pants; month 2, 1200 shirts and 1400 pairs of pants. During each month the following resources are available: month 1, 9000 square yards of cloth; month 2, 6000 square yards of cloth. In addition, cloth that is available during month 1 and is not used can be used during month 2. During each month it costs $8 to produce an article of clothing with regular-time labor and $16 with overtime labor. During each month a total of at most 2500 articles of clothing can be produced with regular-time labor, and an unlimited number of articles of clothing can be produced with overtime labor. At the end of each month, a holding cost of $3 per article of clothing is incurred.

a. Determine how to meet demands for the next two months (on time) at minimum cost. Assume that 100 shirts and 200 pairs of pants are already in inventory at the beginning of month 1.

b. Use a two-way SolverTable to investigate the effect on total cost of two *simultaneous* changes. The first change is to allow the ratio of overtime to regular-time production cost (currently $16/$8 = 2) to decrease from 20% to 80% in increments of 20%, while keeping the regular time cost at $8. The second change is to allow the production capacity *each* month (currently 2500) to decrease by 10% to 50% in increments of 10%. The idea here is that less regular-time capacity is available, but overtime becomes relatively cheaper. Is the net effect on total cost positive or negative?

40. Each year, a shoe manufacturing company faces demands (which must be met on time) for pairs of shoes as shown in the file **P13_40.xlsx**. Employees work three consecutive quarters and then receive one quarter off. For example, a worker might work during quarters 3 and 4 of one year and quarter 1 of the next year. During a quarter in which an employee works, he or she can produce up to 500 pairs of shoes. Each worker is paid $5000 per quarter. At the end of each quarter, a holding cost of $10 per pair of shoes is incurred.

a. Determine how to minimize the cost per year (labor plus holding) of meeting the demands for shoes. To simplify the model, assume that at the end of each year, the ending inventory is 0. (You can assume that a given worker gets the *same* quarter off during each year.)

b. Suppose the company can pay a flat fee for a training program that increases the productivity of all of its workers. Use SolverTable to see how much the company would be willing to pay for a training program that increases worker productivity from 500 pairs of shoes per quarter to P pairs of shoes per quarter, where P varies from 525 to 700 in increments of 25.

41. A small appliance manufacturer must meet (on time) the following demands: quarter 1, 3000 units; quarter 2, 2000 units; quarter 3, 4000 units. Each quarter, up to 2700 units can be produced with regular-time labor, at a cost of $40 per unit. During each quarter, an unlimited number of units can be produced with overtime labor, at a cost of $60 per unit. Of all units produced, 20% are unsuitable and cannot be used to meet demand. Also, at the end of each quarter, 10% of all units on hand spoil and cannot be used to meet any future demands. After each quarter's demand is satisfied and spoilage is accounted for, a cost of $15 per unit in ending inventory is incurred.
   a. Determine how to minimize the total cost of meeting the demands of the next three quarters. Assume that 1000 usable units are available at the beginning of quarter 1.
   b. The company wants to know how much money it would be worth to decrease the percentage of unsuitable items and/or the percentage of items that spoil. Write a short report that provides relevant information. Base your report on three uses of SolverTable: (1) where the percentage of unsuitable items decreases and the percentage of items that spoil stays at 10%, (2) where the percentage of unsuitable items stays at 20% and the percentage of items that spoil decreases, and (3) where both percentages decrease. Does the sum of the separate effects on total cost from the first two tables equal the combined effect from the third table? Include an answer to this question in your report.

42. A pharmaceutical company manufactures two drugs at Los Angeles and Indianapolis. The cost of manufacturing a pound of each drug depends on the location, as indicated in the file **P13_42.xlsx**. The machine time (in hours) required to produce a pound of each drug at each city is also shown in this table. The company must produce at least 1000 pounds per week of drug 1 and at least 2000 pounds per week of drug 2. It has 500 hours per week of machine time at Indianapolis and 400 hours per week at Los Angeles.
   a. Determine how the company can minimize the cost of producing the required drugs.
   b. Use SolverTable to determine how much the company would be willing to pay to purchase a combination of A extra hours of machine time at Indianapolis and B extra hours of machine time at Los Angeles, where A and B can be any positive multiples of 10 up to 50.

43. A company manufactures two products on two machines. The number of hours of machine time and labor depends on the machine and product as shown in the file **P13_43.xlsx**. The cost of producing a unit of each product depends on which machine produces it. These unit costs also appear in the same file. There are 200 hours available on each of the two machines, and there are 400 labor hours available total. This month at least 200 units of product 1 and at least 240 units of product 2 must be produced. Also, at least half of the product 1 requirement must be produced on machine 1, and at least half of the product 2 requirement must be produced on machine 2.
   a. Determine how the company can minimize the cost of meeting this month's requirements.
   b. Use SolverTable to see how much the "at least half" requirements are costing the company. Do this by changing *both* of these requirements from "at least half" to "at least x percent," where x can be any multiple of 5% from 0% to 50%.

CASE 13.1 Shelby Shelving

Shelby Shelving is a small company that manufactures two types of shelves for grocery stores. Model S is the standard model; model LX is a heavy-duty version. Shelves are manufactured in three major steps: stamping, forming, and assembly. In the stamping stage, a large machine is used to stamp (i.e., cut) standard sheets of metal into appropriate sizes. In the forming stage, another machine bends the metal into shape. Assembly involves joining the parts with a combination of soldering and riveting. Shelby's stamping and forming machines work on both models of shelves. Separate assembly departments are used for the final stage of production.

The file **C13_01.xlsx** contains relevant data for Shelby. (See Figure 13.38.) The hours required on each machine for

each unit of product are shown in the range B5:C6 of the Accounting Data sheet. For example, the production of one model S shelf requires 0.25 hour on the forming machine. Both the stamping and forming machines can operate for 800 hours each month. The model S assembly department has a monthly capacity of 1900 units. The model LX assembly department has a monthly capacity of only 1400 units. Currently Shelby is producing and selling 400 units of model S and 1400 units of model LX per month.

Model S shelves are sold for $1800, and model LX shelves are sold for $2100. Shelby's operation is fairly small in the industry, and management at Shelby believes it cannot raise prices beyond these levels because of the competition. However, the marketing department believes that Shelby can

Figure 13.38 Data for Shelby Case

	A	B	C	D	E	F	G	H	I
1	**Shelby Shelving Data for Current Production Schedule**								
2									
3	Machine requirements (hours per unit)					Given monthly overhead cost data			
4		Model S	Model LX	Available			Fixed	Variable S	Variable LX
5	Stamping	0.3	0.3	800		Stamping	$125,000	$80	$90
6	Forming	0.25	0.5	800		Forming	$95,000	$120	$170
7						Model S Assembly	$80,000	$165	$0
8		Model S	Model LX			Model LX Assembly	$85,000	$0	$185
9	Current monthly production	400	1400						
10						Standard costs of the shelves -- *based on the current production levels*			
11	Hours spent in departments						Model S	Model LX	
12		Model S	Model LX	Totals		Direct materials	$1,000	$1,200	
13	Stamping	120	420	540		Direct labor:			
14	Forming	100	700	800		Stamping	$35	$35	
15						Forming	$60	$90	
16	Percentages of time spent in departments					Assembly	$80	$85	
17		Model S	Model LX			Total direct labor	$175	$210	
18	Stamping	22.2%	77.8%			Overhead allocation			
19	Forming	12.5%	87.5%			Stamping	$149	$159	
20						Forming	$150	$229	
21	Unit selling price	$1,800	$2,100			Assembly	$365	$246	
22						Total overhead	$664	$635	
23	Assembly capacity	1900	1400			Total cost	$1,839	$2,045	

sell as much as it can produce at these prices. The costs of production are summarized in the Accounting Data sheet. As usual, values in blue cells are given, whereas other values are calculated from these.

Management at Shelby just met to discuss next month's operating plan. Although the shelves are selling well, the overall profitability of the company is a concern. The plant's engineer suggested that the current production of model S shelves be cut back. According to him, "Model S shelves are sold for $1800 per unit, but our costs are $1839. Even though we're selling only 400 units a month, we're losing money on each one. We should decrease production of model S." The controller disagreed. He said that the problem was the model S assembly department trying to absorb a large overhead with a small production volume. "The model S units are making a contribution to overhead. Even though production doesn't cover all of the fixed costs, we'd be worse off with lower production."

Your job is to develop an LP model of Shelby's problem, then run Solver, and finally make a recommendation to Shelby management, with a short verbal argument supporting the engineer or the controller.

Notes on Accounting Data Calculations

The fixed overhead is distributed using activity-based costing principles. For example, at current production levels, the forming machine spends 100 hours on model S shelves and 700 hours on model LX shelves. The forming machine is used 800 hours of the month, of which 12.5% of the time is spent on model S shelves and 87.5% is spent on model LX shelves. The $95,000 of fixed overhead in the forming department is distributed as $11,875(= 95,000 \times 0.125)$ to model S shelves and $83,125(= 95,000 \times 0.875)$ to model LX shelves. The fixed overhead per unit of output is allocated as $29.69(= 11,875/400)$ for model S and $59.38(= 83,125/1400)$ for model LX. In the calculation of the standard overhead cost, the fixed and variable costs are added together, so that the overhead cost for the forming department allocated to a model S shelf is $149.69(= 29.69 + 120$, shown in cell G20 rounded up to $150). Similarly, the overhead cost for the forming department allocated to a model LX shelf is $229.38(= 59.38 + 170$, shown in cell H20 rounded down to $229).

CHAPTER 14

Optimization Models

OPTIMIZATION OF WORK CENTER LOCATIONS AT VERIZON

Verizon, the telecommunications giant, must continually install, maintain, and expand its infrastructure. This requires many technicians and vehicles located at garage work centers (GWCs). Each GWC serves as a home base for technicians, it provides parts, supplies, and tools, and it provides parking for vehicles. The article by Allen et al. (2017) describes how a team at Verizon used optimization to determine where to locate GWCs and how to assign technicians to GWCs to provide appropriate service levels at minimum cost.

The analysis involved approximately 500 GWCs and 23,000 technicians at Verizon. Each technician is assigned to a GWC and is then dispatched from the GWC to a service region called a wire center (WC) as the need arises. Therefore, the decisions on the number and locations of GWCs, which WCs are served by which GWCs, and which technicians are assigned to which GWCs, have a direct impact on productivity and operating costs. Verizon's problem is a classical optimization problem in management science. If there are two few, or poorly placed, GWCs, travel costs will be large and the level of service will suffer. In addition, technicians will spend too much time traveling, time that could be used for actual work. If there are too many GWCs, overhead costs such as leasing costs will be large. Therefore, an appropriate trade-off had to be found.

The optimization model the analysts developed is a mixed-integer programming model, where some decision variables are continuous and others are integer-valued, often binary (0-1). For example, for each potential GWC site has an associated binary variable: 1 if the site is used and 0 otherwise. If a potential GWC was an existing site, a binary value of 0 would mean closing it and reassigning its technicians to another GWC. If a potential GWC was a new site, a binary value of 1 would mean building a new GWC. In addition, each GWC-WC combination has an associated binary variable: 1 if the WC is assigned to the GWC and 0 otherwise. Because of Verizon policy, the model assumed that that at most two GWCs can serve a single WC.

A significant part of the effort involved the collection and verification of the many required data inputs. These include: distances between potential GWCs and WCs; the capacity of each potential GWC to support technicians; the operating cost of each potential GWC; and the demand at each WC, expressed as the number of technician hours required per day. The data came from multiple systems and databases, so they had to be checked for consistency and accuracy. It was important to develop a standardized data process so that the model could be run in the future to adapt to changes in demand and operations.

The Verizon analysts fortunately discovered a simplification for their large mixed-integer optimization model. The study involved 12 states where Verizon operates. However, due to union rules or public utility commission restrictions, no interactions normally occur across state lines. In fact, two large states, Pennsylvania and New York, could each be divided into two parts that had little interaction. This allowed the analysts to decompose one large model into 14 smaller models. Even so, some states' models were still quite large, with hundreds of thousands of decision variables and hundreds of thousands of constraints. This is much too large to be solved in Excel, the focus in this book, but the optimization software package used in the study, CPLEX, was able to solve each model in a few minutes.

Naturally, once the model was up and running, the stakeholders asked a number of "what if" questions. To help answer these, the analysts made several runs, each time fixing the number of GWCs closed at a value ranging from zero to the point where no feasible solutions were possible. They found that when no GWCs were closed, significant savings in labor and vehicle costs were achieved by optimally reassigning WCs to current GWCs. These savings continued to increase when only a few GWCs were closed. However, beyond some number of GWC closures, the total of all costs started to increase. The optimal number of closures is where the total cost stops decreasing and begins to increase.

Verizon estimates that this model has resulted in savings of $18 million annually, and the company plans to continue using the model, on even a larger scale, in the future.

14-1 Introduction

In a survey of Fortune 500 firms, 85% of those responding said that they use optimization. In this chapter, we discuss some of the optimization models that are most often applied to real-world applications. Some typical examples include:

• scheduling bank clerks for check encoding
• optimizing the operation of an oil refinery
• planning dairy production at a creamery
• scheduling production of products at a fiberglass manufacturer
• optimizing a Wall Street firm's bond portfolio.

There are two basic goals in this chapter. The first is to illustrate some of the many real applications that can take advantage of optimization. You will see that these applications cover a wide range, from oil production to worker scheduling to cash management. The second goal is to increase your facility in modeling optimization problems on a spreadsheet. We present a few principles that will help you model a wide variety of problems. The best way to learn, however, is to see many examples and work through numerous problems. In short, mastering the art of spreadsheet optimization modeling takes hard work and practice. You will have plenty of opportunity to do both with the material in this chapter.

Although a wide variety of problems can be formulated as *linear* programming models, there are some that cannot. Either they require *integer* variables or they are *nonlinear* in the decision variables. We include examples of integer programming and nonlinear programming models in this chapter, just to give you a taste of what is involved.[1] You will see that the modeling process for these types of problems is not much different than for linear optimization problems. Once the models are developed, Excel's Solver can be used to solve them. Then SolverTable can be used to perform sensitivity analysis. However, these integer and nonlinear models are inherently more difficult to solve. Solver must use more complex algorithms and is not always guaranteed to find an optimal solution. Nevertheless, you will see that Solver provides the power to solve a great variety of realistic business problems.

Although there is a tremendous amount of theory behind the *algorithms* that solve these problems, the modeling process itself is fairly straightforward, and you can learn it best by seeing a variety of examples. Therefore, we proceed in this chapter by modeling (and then solving) a diverse class of problems that arise in business. The exercises

---

1 Besides the nonlinear models discussed in this chapter, which can be solved with Solver's GRG nonlinear algorithm, there is an even more difficult class of nonlinear models called *nonsmooth* models. Although we will not discuss nonsmooth models, we can recommend Solver's Evolutionary algorithm for these difficult models. These nonsmooth problems can also be solved with the Evolver add-in, part of Palisade's DecisionTools® Suite, but we won't discuss Evolver in this book.

throughout the chapter provide even more examples of how optimization models can be applied.

All these models can benefit from sensitivity analysis, done formally with the SolverTable add-in or informally by changing one or more inputs and rerunning Solver. For reasons of space, we present only a few of the many possible sensitivity analyses. However, we stress that in real applications, model development is just the beginning of the overall analysis. It is then usually followed by extensive sensitivity analysis.

14-2 Employee Scheduling Models

Many organizations must determine how to schedule employees to provide adequate service. The following example illustrates how to use linear programming (with integer constraints) to schedule employees on a daily basis.

EXAMPLE

14.1 SCHEDULING EMPLOYEES AT BRIGGS

Briggs, a small business company, requires different numbers of full-time employees on different days of the week. The number of full-time employees required each day is given in Table 14.1. Union rules state that each full-time employee must work five consecutive days and then receive two days off. For example, an employee who works Monday to Friday must be off on Saturday and Sunday. Briggs wants to meet its daily requirements using only full-time employees. Its objective is to minimize the number of full-time employees on its payroll.

Table 14.1 Employee Requirements

Day of Week	Minimum Number of Employees Required
Monday	17
Tuesday	13
Wednesday	15
Thursday	19
Friday	14
Saturday	16
Sunday	11

Objective

To develop an optimization model that relates five-day shift schedules to daily numbers of employees available, and to use Solver to find a schedule that uses the fewest number of employees and meets all daily workforce requirements.

Where Do the Numbers Come From?

The only inputs needed for this problem are the minimum employee requirements in Table 14.1, but these are not easy to obtain. They would probably be obtained through a combination of two quantitative techniques: forecasting (Chapter 12) and queueing analysis (not covered in this book). The company would first use historical data to forecast customer arrival patterns throughout a typical week. It would then use queueing analysis to translate these arrival patterns into employee requirements on a daily basis. Actually, we have kept the problem relatively simple by considering only *daily* requirements. In a realistic setting, the organization might forecast employee requirements on an hourly or even a 15-minute basis.

Solution

A diagram of this model appears in Figure 14.1. (See the file **Employee Scheduling Big Picture.xlsx**.) The trickiest part is identifying the appropriate decision variables. You might think that the decision variables are the numbers of employees working on the various days of the week. Clearly, these values must eventually be

In real employee-scheduling problems, much of the work involves forecasting and queueing analysis to obtain employee requirements. This must be done before an optimal schedule can be found.

determined. However, it is not enough to specify, for example, that 18 employees are working on Monday. The problem is that this doesn't indicate when these 18 employees start their five-day shifts. Without this knowledge, it is impossible to implement the five-consecutive-day, two-day-off requirement. (If you don't believe this, try developing your own model with the wrong decision variables. You will eventually reach a dead end.)

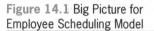
Figure 14.1 Big Picture for Employee Scheduling Model

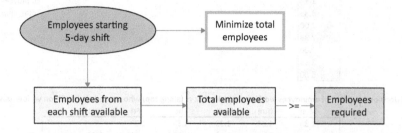

The trick is to define the decision variables as the numbers of employees working each of the seven possible five-day shifts. By knowing these values, the other output variables can be calculated. For example, the number working on Thursday is the sum of those who begin their five-day shifts on Sunday, Monday, Tuesday, Wednesday, and Thursday.

The key to this model is choosing the correct decision variables.

Fundamental Insight

Choosing the Decision Variables

The decision variables should always be chosen so that their values determine all required outputs in the model. In other words, their values should tell the company exactly how to run its business. Sometimes the choice of decision variables is obvious, but in many cases (as in this employee scheduling model), the proper choice of decision variables takes some deeper thinking about the problem. An improper choice of decision variables typically leads to a dead end, where their values do not supply enough information to calculate required outputs or implement certain constraints.

Note that this is a "wraparound" problem. We assume that the daily requirements in Table 14.1 and the employee schedules continue week after week. So, for example, the employees assigned to the Thursday through Monday shift always wrap around from one week to the next on their five-day shift.

Developing the Spreadsheet Model

The spreadsheet model for this problem is shown in Figure 14.2. (See the file **Employee Scheduling Finished. xlsx**.) To develop this model, proceed as follows.

Developing the Employee Scheduling Model

1. **Inputs and range names.** Enter the number of employees needed on each day of the week (from Table 14.1) in the blue cells, and create the range names shown.
2. **Employees beginning each day.** Enter *any* trial values for the number of employees beginning work on each day of the week in the Employees_starting range. These beginning days determine the possible five-day shifts. For example, the employees in cell B4 work Monday through Friday.
3. **Employees on hand each day.** The key to this solution is to realize that the numbers in the Employees_starting range— the decision variable cells—do not represent the number of employees who will show up each day. As an example, the number in cell B4 represent those who start on Monday work Monday through Friday. Therefore, enter the formula

= $B$4

in cell B14 and copy it across to cell F14. Proceed similarly for rows 15–20, being careful to take "wraparounds" into account. For example, the workers starting on Thursday work Thursday through Sunday, plus Monday. Then calculate the total number who are available on each day by entering the formula

= SUM(B14:B20)

in cell B23 and copying it across row 23.

Figure 14.2 Employee Scheduling Model with Optimal (Non-Integer) Solution

	A	B	C	D	E	F	G	H		I	J	K
1	Employee scheduling model									Range names used		
2										Employees_available	=Model!$B$23:$H$23	
3	Decision variables: number of employees starting their five-day shift on various days									Employees_required	=Model!$B$25:$H$25	
4	Mon	1.33								Employees_Starting	=Model!$B$4:$B$10	
5	Tue	3.33								Total_employees	=Model!$B$28	
6	Wed	2.00										
7	Thu	7.33										
8	Fri	0.00										
9	Sat	3.33										
10	Sun	5.00										
11												
12	Result of decisions: number of employees working on various days (along top) who started their shift on various days (along side)											
13		Mon	Tue	Wed	Thu	Fri	Sat	Sun				
14	Mon	1.33	1.33	1.33	1.33	1.33						
15	Tue		3.33	3.33	3.33	3.33	3.33					
16	Wed			2.00	2.00	2.00	2.00	2.00				
17	Thu	7.33			7.33	7.33	7.33	7.33				
18	Fri	0.00	0.00			0.00	0.00	0.00				
19	Sat	3.33	3.33	3.33			3.33	3.33				
20	Sun	5.00	5.00	5.00	5.00			5.00				
21												
22	Constraint on employee availabilities											
23	Employees available	17.00	13.00	15.00	19.00	14.00	16.00	17.67				
24		>=	>=	>=	>=	>=	>=	>=				
25	Employees required	17	13	15	19	14	16	11				
26												
27	Objective to maximize											
28	Total employees	22.33										

Excel Tip

The shortcut on the Mac is command+return.

Ctrl + Enter Shortcut

You often enter a typical formula in a cell and then copy it. One way to do this efficiently is to select the entire range, here B23:H23. Then enter the typical formula, here **=SUM(B14:B20)**, and press Ctrl+Enter. This has the same effect as copying, but it is slightly quicker.

4. **Total employees.** Calculate the total number of employees in cell B28 with the formula

=SUM(Employees_starting)

Note that there is no double-counting in this sum. For example, the employees in cells B4 and B5 are *not* the same people.

At this point, you might want to experiment with the numbers in the decision variable cell range to see whether you can guess an optimal solution (without looking at Figure 14.2). It is not that easy. Each employee who starts on a given day works the next four days as well, so when you find a solution that meets the minimal requirements for the various days, you usually have a few more employees available on some days than are needed.

Using Solver

Invoke Solver and fill out its main dialog box as shown in Figure 14.3. (You don't need to include the integer constraint yet. This will be discussed shortly.) Make sure you check the Non-Negative option and select the Simplex LP method.

Discussion of the Solution

The optimal solution shown in Figure 14.2 has one drawback: It requires the number of employees starting work on some days to be a fraction. Because part-time employees are not allowed (an assumption of the model), this solution is unrealistic. However, it is simple to add an integer constraint on the decision variable cells. This integer constraint appears in Figure 14.3. (To create this integer constraint in Solver's Add Constraint dialog box, select the Employees_starting for the left side, and select "int" in the middle dropdown list. The word "integer" will automatically appear in the right side of the constraint.) With this integer constraint, the optimal solution appears in Figure 14.4.

Figure 14.3 Solver Dialog Box for Employee Scheduling Model

Figure 14.4 Optimal Integer Solution to Employee Scheduling Model

	A	B	C	D	E	F	G	H	I	J	K
1	Employee scheduling model								Range names used		
2									Employees_available	=Model!$B$23:$H$23	
3	Decision variables: number of employees starting their five-day shift on various days								Employees_required	=Model!$B$25:$H$25	
4	Mon	2							Employees_Starting	=Model!$B$4:$B$10	
5	Tue	3							Total_employees	=Model!$B$28	
6	Wed	3									
7	Thu	7									
8	Fri	0									
9	Sat	4									
10	Sun	4									
11											
12	Result of decisions: number of employees working on various days (along top) who started their shift on various days (along side)										
13		Mon	Tue	Wed	Thu	Fri	Sat	Sun			
14	Mon	2	2	2	2	2					
15	Tue		3	3	3	3	3				
16	Wed			3	3	3	3	3			
17	Thu	7			7	7	7	7			
18	Fri	0	0			0	0	0			
19	Sat	4	4	4			4	4			
20	Sun	4	4	4	4			4			
21											
22	Constraint on employee availabilities										
23	Employees available	17	13	16	19	15	17	18			
24		>=	>=	>=	>=	>=	>=	>=			
25	Employees required	17	13	15	19	14	16	11			
26											
27	Objective to maximize										
28	Total employees	23									

> **Technical Tip**
>
> **Solver Integer Optimality Setting**
>
> *Set Solver's Integer Optimality to zero to ensure that you get the optimal integer solution. Be aware, however, that this can incur significant extra computing time for larger models.*
>
> When working with integer constraints, you should be aware of Solver's Integer Optimality setting. The idea is as follows. As Solver searches for the best integer solution, it is often able to find a "good" integer solution fairly quickly, but it often has to spend a lot of time finding slightly better solutions. A nonzero setting allows it to quit early. The default setting is 1 (percent). (It used to be 5, which you still might see, depending on your version of Excel.) This means that if Solver finds a feasible integer solution that is guaranteed to have an objective value no more than 1% from the optimal value, it will quit and report this good solution (which might even be the optimal solution). Therefore, if you keep this default setting, your integer solutions will sometimes not be optimal, but they will be close. If you want to ensure that you get an optimal solution, you can change the Solver setting to zero. (Click the Options button, and then under the All Methods tab, uncheck Ignore Integer Constraints and enter a value in the Integer Optimality (%) box.)

The decision variable cells in the optimal solution indicate the numbers of workers who start their five-day shifts on the various days. You can then look at the *columns* of the B14:H20 range to see which employees are working on any given day. This optimal solution is typical in scheduling problems. Due to a labor constraint—each employee must work five consecutive days and then have two days off—it is typically impossible to meet the minimum employee requirements exactly. To ensure that there are enough employees available on busy days, it is necessary to have more than enough on hand on light days.

Multiple optimal solutions have different values in the decision variable cells, but they all have the same objective value.

Another interesting aspect of this problem is that when you solve it, you might get a *different* schedule that is still optimal—that is, a solution that still uses a total of 23 employees and meets all constraints. This is a case of **multiple optimal solutions**, not at all uncommon in linear optimization problems. In fact, it is typically good news for a manager, who can then choose among the optimal solutions using other, possibly nonquantitative criteria.

Sensitivity Analysis

The most obvious type of sensitivity analysis in this example is to analyze the effect of employee requirements on the optimal solution. Specifically, let's suppose the number of employees needed on each day of the week increases by two, four, or six. How does this change the total number of employees needed? You can answer this with SolverTable, but you must first modify the model slightly, as shown in Figure 14.5. The problem is that we want to increase *each* of the daily minimal required values by the same amount. The trick is to enter the original requirements in row 12, enter a trial value for the extra number required per day in cell K12, enter the formula =B12+$K$12 in cell B27, and then copy this formula across to cell H27. Then you can use the one-way SolverTable option, using the Extra cell as the single input, letting it vary from 0 to 6 in increments of 2, and specifying the Total_employees cell as the single output cell.

To run some sensitivity analyses with SolverTable, you need to modify the original model slightly to incorporate the effect of the input being varied.

The results appear in Figure 14.6. When the requirement increases by two each day, only two extra employees are necessary (scheduled appropriately). However, when the requirement increases by four each day, *more* than four extra employees are necessary. The same is true when the requirement increases by six each day. This might surprise you at first, but there is an intuitive reason: Each extra worker works only five days of the week.

We did not use Solver's sensitivity report here for two reasons. First, Solver does not offer a sensitivity report for models with integer constraints. Second, even if the integer constraints are deleted, Solver's sensitivity report does not answer questions about *multiple* input changes, as we have asked here. It is used for questions about one-at-a-time changes to inputs, such as a change to Thursday's worker requirement. In this sense, SolverTable is a more flexible tool.

Modeling Issues

- The employee scheduling example is called a *static* scheduling model because we assume that the company faces the same situation each week. In reality, demands change over time, employees take vacations in the summer, and so on, so the company does not face the same situation each week. A *dynamic* scheduling model (not covered here) is necessary for such problems.

Figure 14.5 Modified Employee Scheduling Model

	A	B	C	D	E	F	G	H	I	J	K
1	Employee scheduling model								Range names used		
2									Employees_available	=Model!$B$23:$H$23	
3	Decision variables: number of employees starting their five-day shift on various days								Employees_required	=Model!$B$25:$H$25	
4	Mon	2							Employees_Starting	=Model!$B$4:$B$10	
5	Tue	3							Total_employees	=Model!$B$28	
6	Wed	3									
7	Thu	7									
8	Fri	0									
9	Sat	4									
10	Sun	4									
11											
12	Employees required (original values)	17	13	15	19	14	16	11		Extra required each day	0
13											
14	Result of decisions: number of employees working on various days (along top) who started their shift on various days (along side)										
15		Mon	Tue	Wed	Thu	Fri	Sat	Sun			
16	Mon	2	2	2	2	2					
17	Tue		3	3	3	3	3				
18	Wed			3	3	3	3	3			
19	Thu	7			7	7	7	7			
20	Fri	0	0			0	0	0			
21	Sat	4	4	4			4	4			
22	Sun	4	4	4	4			4			
23											
24	Constraint on employee availabilities										
25	Employees available	17	13	16	19	15	17	18			
26		>=	>=	>=	>=	>=	>=	>=			
27	Employees required	17	13	15	19	14	16	11			
28											
29	Objective to maximize										
30	Total employees	23									

> Note how the original model has been modified so that the extra value in cell K12 drives all of the requirements in row 27.

Figure 14.6 Sensitivity to Number of Extra Employees Required per Day

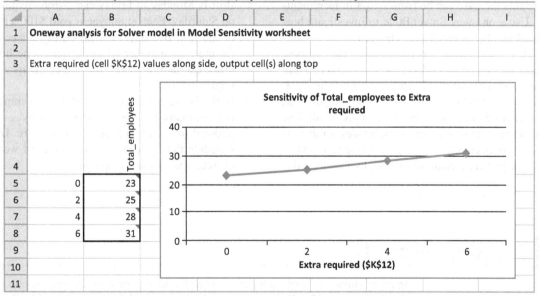

	A	B	C
1	Oneway analysis for Solver model in Model Sensitivity worksheet		
3	Extra required (cell $K$12) values along side, output cell(s) along top		
5		0	23
6		2	25
7		4	28
8		6	31

- In a weekly scheduling model for a supermarket or a fast-food restaurant, the number of decision variables can grow quickly and optimization software such as Solver will have difficulty finding an optimal solution. In such cases, heuristic methods (essentially clever trial-and-error algorithms) have been used to find good solutions to the problem. For example, Love and Hoey (1990) indicate how this was done for a particular staff scheduling problem.

Heuristic solutions are often close to optimal, but they are never guaranteed to be optimal.

- Our model can easily be expanded to handle part-time employees, the use of overtime, and alternative objectives such as maximizing the number of weekend days off received by employees. You are asked to explore such extensions in the problems.

Problems

Solutions for problems whose numbers appear within a colored box can be found in the Student Solution Files.

Level A

1. Modify the Briggs employee scheduling model so that employees are paid $10 per hour on weekdays and $15 per hour on weekends. Change the objective so that you now minimize the weekly payroll. (You can assume that each employee works eight hours per day.) Is the previous optimal solution still optimal?

2. How much influence can the employee requirements for one, two, or three days have on the weekly schedule in the Briggs employee scheduling example? You are asked to explore this in the following questions.
   a. Let Monday's requirements change from 17 to 25 in increments of 1. Use SolverTable to see how the total number of employees changes.
   b. Suppose the Monday and Tuesday requirements can each, independently of one another, increase from 1 to 8 in increments of 1. Use a two-way SolverTable to see how the total number of employees changes.
   c. Suppose the Monday, Tuesday, and Wednesday requirements each increase by the *same* amount, where this increase can be from 1 to 8 in increments of 1. Use a one-way SolverTable to investigate how the total number of employees changes.

3. In the Briggs employee scheduling example, suppose each full-time employee works eight hours per day. Thus, Monday's requirement of 17 workers can be viewed as a requirement of 8(17) = 136 hours. The company can meet its daily labor requirements by using both full-time and part-time employees. During each week a full-time employee works eight hours a day for five consecutive days, and a part-time employee works four hours a day

for five consecutive days. A full-time employee costs the company $15 per hour, whereas a part-time employee (with reduced fringe benefits) costs the company only $10 per hour. Union requirements limit part-time labor to 25% of weekly labor requirements.
   a. Modify the model as necessary, and then use Solver to minimize the post office's weekly labor costs.
   b. Use SolverTable to determine how a change in the part-time labor limitation (currently 25%) influences the optimal solution.

Level B

4. In the Briggs employee scheduling example, suppose the employees want more flexibility in their schedules. They want to be allowed to work five consecutive days followed by two days off *or* to work three consecutive days followed by a day off followed by two consecutive days followed by another day off. Modify the original model (with integer constraints) to allow this flexibility. Might this be a good deal for management as well as labor? Explain.

5. In the Briggs employee scheduling example, suppose the company can force employees to work one day of overtime each week on the day immediately following this five-day shift. For example, an employee whose regular shift is Monday to Friday can also be required to work on Saturday. Each employee is paid $100 a day for each of the first five days worked during a week and $135 for the overtime day (if any). Determine how the post office can minimize the cost of meeting its weekly work requirements.

6. In the Briggs employee scheduling example, suppose the company has 28 full-time employees and is not allowed to fire any of them or hire more. Determine a schedule that maximizes the number of weekend days off received by these employees.

14-3 Blending Models

In many situations, various inputs must be blended to produce desired outputs. In many of these situations, **blending models** can be used to find the optimal combination of outputs as well as the mix of inputs that are used to produce the desired outputs. The following are some typical examples of blending problems.

Inputs	Outputs
Meat, filler, water	Different types of sausage
Various types of oil	Heating oil, gasolines, aviation fuels
Carbon, iron, molybdenum	Different types of steels
Different types of pulp	Different kinds of recycled paper

Example 14.2 illustrates how to model a typical blending problem in Excel. Although this example is small relative to blending problems in real applications, it is still probably too complex for you to guess the optimal solution.

EXAMPLE

14.2 BLENDING AT CHANDLER OIL

Chandler Oil has 5000 barrels of crude oil 1 and 10,000 barrels of crude oil 2 available. Chandler sells gasoline and heating oil. These products are produced by blending the two crude oils together. Each barrel of crude oil 1 has a "quality level" of 10 and each barrel of crude oil 2 has a quality level of 5.[2] Gasoline must have an average quality level of at least 8, whereas heating oil must have an average quality level of at least 6. Gasoline sells for $75 per barrel, and heating oil sells for $60 per barrel. In addition, if any barrels of the crude oils are left over, they can be sold for $65 and $50 per barrel, respectively. We assume that demand for heating oil and gasoline is unlimited, so that all of Chandler's production can be sold. Chandler wants to maximize its revenue from selling gasoline, heating oil, and any leftover crude oils.

Objective

To develop an optimization model for finding the revenue-maximizing plan that meets quality constraints and stays within limits on crude oil availabilities.

Where Do the Numbers Come From?

Most of the inputs for this problem should be easy to obtain.

• The selling prices for outputs are dictated by market pressures.

• The availabilities of inputs are based on crude supplies from the suppliers.

• The quality levels of crude oils are known from chemical analysis, whereas the required quality levels for outputs are specified by Chandler, probably in response to competitive or regulatory pressures.

Solution

The variables and constraints required for this blending model are shown in Figure 14.7. (See the file **Blending Oil Big Picture.xlsx**.) The key is the selection of the appropriate decision variables. You might think it is sufficient to specify the amounts of the two crude oils used and the amounts of the two products produced. However, this is not enough. The problem is that this information doesn't tell Chandler how to *make* the outputs from the inputs. The company instead needs to have a blending plan: how much of each input to use in the production of a barrel of each output. Once you understand that this blending plan is the basic decision, all other output variables follow in a straightforward manner.

In typical blending problems, the correct decision variables are the amounts of each input blended into each output.

Figure 14.7 Big Picture for Oil Blending Model

A secondary, but very important, issue in typical blending models is how to implement the quality constraints. (The constraints here are in terms of a generic "quality." In other blending problems they are often expressed in terms of percentages of some ingredient(s). For example, a typical quality constraint is that some output can contain no more than 2% sulfur.) When we explain how to develop the spreadsheet model, we will discuss the preferred way of implementing the quality constraints.

---

2 To avoid being overly technical, we use the generic term *quality level*. In real oil blending, qualities of interest might be octane rating, viscosity, and others.

Developing the Spreadsheet Model

The spreadsheet model for this problem appears in Figure 14.8. (See the file **Blending Oil Finished.xlsx**.) To develop it, proceed as follows.

Developing the Blending Model

1. **Inputs and range names.** Enter the unit selling prices, quality levels for inputs, required quality levels for outputs, and availabilities of inputs in the blue cells. Then name the ranges as indicated.
2. **Inputs blended into each output.** The quantities Chandler must specify are the barrels of each input used to produce each output. Enter *any* trial values for these quantities in the Blending_plan range. For example, the value in cell B13 is the amount of crude oil 1 used to make gasoline and the value in cell C13 is the amount of crude oil 1 used to make heating oil. The Blending_plan range contains the decision variable cells.
3. **Inputs used and outputs sold.** Calculate the row sums (in column D) and column sums (in row 15) of the Blending_plan range. There is a quick way to do this. Select both the row and column where the sums will go (select one, then hold down the Ctrl key and select the other), and click the AutoSum (Σ) button on the Home ribbon. This creates SUM formulas in the selected cells. Then calculate the leftover barrels of each crude oil in column G by subtracting the amount used from the amount available.
4. **Quality achieved.** Keep track of the quality level of gasoline and heating oil in the Quality_ obtained range as follows. Begin by calculating for each output the average quality (AQ) in the inputs used to produce this output:

Hold down the command key on the Mac.

From here on, the solutions shown are optimal. However, remember that you can start with any solution. It doesn't even have to be feasible.

$$AQ \text{ in gasoline} = 10 * \text{Oil 1 in gasoline} + 5 * \text{Oil 2 in gasoline}$$
$$AQ \text{ in heating oil} = 10 * \text{Oil 1 in heating oil} + 5 * \text{Oil 2 in heating oil}$$

Figure 14.8 Oil Blending Model

	A	B	C	D	E	F	G	H
1	Oil blending model					Range names used		
2						Available	=Model!$F$13:$F$14	
3	Properties of crude oil inputs	Value per barrel	Quality level			Barrels_sold	=Model!$B$15:$C$15	
4	Crude oil 1	$65	10			Blending_plan	=Model!$B$13:$C$14	
5	Crude oil 2	$50	5			Leftover	=Model!$G$13:$G$14	
6						Quality_obtained	=Model!$B$19:$C$19	
7	Properties of outputs	Gasoline	Heating oil			Quality_required	=Model!$B$21:$C$21	
8	Selling price per barrel	$75	$60			Total_revenue	=Model!$B$24	
9	Required quality level	8	6			Used	=Model!$D$13:$D$14	
10								
11	Blending plan (barrels of crude in each output)							
12		Gasoline	Heating oil	Used		Available	Leftover	
13	Crude oil 1	3000	2000	5000	<=	5000	0	
14	Crude oil 2	2000	8000	10000	<=	10000	0	
15	Barrels sold	5000	10000					
16								
17	Quality constraints with cleared denominators					Quality constraints in "intuitive" form		
18		Gasoline	Heating oil			Gasoline	Heating oil	
19	Quality obtained	40000	60000			8	6	
20		>=	>=			>=	>=	
21	Quality required	40000	60000			8	6	
22								
23	Objective to maximize							
24	Total revenue	$975,000						

The gasoline quality constraint is then

$$AQ \text{ in gasoline} \geq 8 * \text{Gasoline sold} \qquad (14.1)$$

Similarly, the heating oil quality constraint is

$$AQ \text{ in heating oil} \geq 6 * \text{Heating oil sold} \qquad (14.2)$$

To implement Inequalities (14.1) and (14.2), calculate the AQ for gasoline in cell B19 with the formula

=SUMPRODUCT(B13:B14,$C$4:$C$5)

and copy this formula to cell C19 to generate the AQ for heating oil.

5. **Quality required.** Calculate the required average quality for gasoline and heating oil in cells B21 and C21. Specifically, determine the required average quality for gasoline in cell B21 with the formula

=B9*B15

and copy this formula to cell C21 for heating oil.

6. **Revenue.** Calculate the total revenue in cell B24 with the formula

=SUMPRODUCT(B15:C15,B8:C8) + SUMPRODUCT(G13:G14,B4:B5)

Using Solver

Fill out the main Solver dialog box as shown in Figure 14.9. As usual, check the Non-Negative option and select the Simplex LP method before optimizing. You should obtain the optimal solution shown in Figure 14.8.

Figure 14.9 Solver Dialog Box for Blending Model

Discussion of the Solution

The optimal solution implies that Chandler should make 5000 barrels of gasoline with 3000 barrels of crude oil 1 and 2000 barrels of crude oil 2. The company should also make 10,000 barrels of heating oil with 2000 barrels of crude oil 1 and 8000 barrels of crude oil 2. With this blend, Chandler will obtain a revenue of $975,000, all from selling gasoline and heating oil.

As stated previously, this problem is sufficiently complex to defy intuition. Clearly, gasoline is more profitable per barrel than heating oil, but given the crude availability and the quality constraints, it turns out that Chandler should sell twice as much heating oil as gasoline. This would have been very difficult to guess ahead of time.

This solution uses all of the inputs to produce outputs; no crude oils are left over to sell. However, if you change the value of crude oil 2 to $55 and rerun Solver, you will see a much different solution, where no heating oil is produced and a lot of crude oil 2 is left over for sale. (Try it to convince yourself.) Why would the cheaper crude oil 2 be sold rather than the more expensive crude oil 1? The reason is quality. Gasoline requires a higher quality, and crude oil 1 is able to deliver it.

Sensitivity Analysis

We perform two typical sensitivity analyses on this blending model. In each, we see how revenue and the amounts of the inputs and outputs sold vary. In the first analysis, we use the unit selling price of gasoline as the input and let it vary from $50 to $90 in increments of $5. The SolverTable results appear in Figure 14.10. Two things are of interest. First, as the price of gasoline increases from $55 to $65, Chandler starts producing gasoline and less heating oil, exactly as you would expect. Second, when the price of gasoline gets to $80 or more, no heating oil is produced, and leftover crude oil 2 is sold instead. Third, the revenue can only increase or stay the same, as the changes in column G (calculated manually) indicate.

Figure 14.10 Sensitivity to the Selling Price of Gasoline

	A	B	C	D	E	F	G
1	Oneway analysis for Solver model in Model worksheet						
2							
3	Selling price gasoline (cell $B$8) values along side, output cell(s) along top						
4		Barrels_sold_1	Barrels_sold_2	Leftover_1	Leftover_2	Total_revenue	Increase
5	$50	0	12500	2500	0	$912,500	
6	$55	0	12500	2500	0	$912,500	$0
7	$60	0	12500	2500	0	$912,500	$0
8	$65	5000	10000	0	0	$925,000	$12,500
9	$70	5000	10000	0	0	$950,000	$25,000
10	$75	5000	10000	0	0	$975,000	$25,000
11	$80	8333.333	0	0	6666.667	$1,000,000	$25,000
12	$85	8333.333	0	0	6666.667	$1,041,667	$41,667
13	$90	8333.333	0	0	6666.667	$1,083,333	$41,667

In the second sensitivity analysis, we vary the availability of crude 1 from 2000 barrels to 20,000 barrels in increments of 1000 barrels. The resulting SolverTable output appears in Figure 14.11. These results make sense if you analyze them carefully. First, the revenue increases, but at a decreasing rate, as more crude 1 is available. This is a common occurrence in LP models. As more of a resource is made available, revenue can only increase or remain the same, but each extra unit of the resource produces less (or at least no more) revenue than the previous unit. Second, the amount of gasoline produced increases, whereas the amount of heating oil produced decreases. Here's why: Crude 1 has a higher quality than crude 2, and gasoline requires higher quality. Gasoline also sells for a higher price. Therefore, as more crude 1 is available, Chandler can produce more gasoline, receive more revenue, and still meet quality standards. However, that there is one exception to this, when only 2000 barrels of crude oil 1 are available. In this case, no gasoline is sold and leftover crude oil 2 is sold instead.

A Caution about Blending Constraints

Before concluding this example, we discuss why the model is linear. The key is the implementation of the quality constraints, shown in Inequalities (14.1) and (14.2). To keep a model linear, each side of an inequality constraint must be a constant, the product of a constant and a variable, or a sum of such products. If the quality constraints are implemented as in Inequalities (14.1) and (14.2), the constraints are indeed linear. However, it is arguably more natural to rewrite this type of constraint by dividing through by the amount sold. For example, the modified gasoline constraint becomes

$$\frac{AQ \text{ in gasoline}}{Gasoline \text{ sold}} \geq 8 \qquad\qquad (14.3)$$

Figure 14.11 Sensitivity to the Availability of Crude 1

	A	B	C	D	E	F	G
1	Oneway analysis for Solver model in Model worksheet						
2							
3	Crude oil 1 available (cell $F$13) values along side, output cell(s) along top						
4		Barrels_sold_1	Barrels_sold_2	Leftover_1	Leftover_2	Total_revenue	Increase
5	2000	0	10000	0	2000	$700,000	
6	3000	1000	12000	0	0	$795,000	$95,000
7	4000	3000	11000	0	0	$885,000	$90,000
8	5000	5000	10000	0	0	$975,000	$90,000
9	6000	7000	9000	0	0	$1,065,000	$90,000
10	7000	9000	8000	0	0	$1,155,000	$90,000
11	8000	11000	7000	0	0	$1,245,000	$90,000
12	9000	13000	6000	0	0	$1,335,000	$90,000
13	10000	15000	5000	0	0	$1,425,000	$90,000
14	11000	17000	4000	0	0	$1,515,000	$90,000
15	12000	19000	3000	0	0	$1,605,000	$90,000
16	13000	21000	2000	0	0	$1,695,000	$90,000
17	14000	23000	1000	0	0	$1,785,000	$90,000
18	15000	25000	0	0	0	$1,875,000	$90,000
19	16000	26000	0	0	0	$1,950,000	$75,000
20	17000	27000	0	0	0	$2,025,000	$75,000
21	18000	28000	0	0	0	$2,100,000	$75,000
22	19000	29000	0	0	0	$2,175,000	$75,000
23	20000	30000	0	0	0	$2,250,000	$75,000

Although this form of the constraint is perfectly valid—and is possibly more natural to many people—it has two drawbacks. First, it makes the model nonlinear. This is because the left side is no longer a sum of products; it involves a quotient. We prefer linear models whenever possible. Second, suppose it turns out that Chandler's optimal solution calls for *no* gasoline to be sold. Then Inequality (14.3) involves division by zero, and this causes an error in Excel. Because of these two drawbacks, it is best to "clear denominators" in all such blending constraints.

Fundamental Insight

Clearing Denominators

Some constraints, particularly those that arise in blending models, are most naturally expressed in terms of ratios. For example, the percentage of sulfur in a product is a ratio: (amount of sulfur in product)/(total amount of product). This ratio could then be constrained to be less than or equal to 6%, for example. This is a perfectly valid way to express the constraint, but it has the undesirable effect of making the model nonlinear. The fix is simple: multiply through by the denominator of the ratio. This has the added benefit of ensuring that division by zero will not occur.

Modeling Issues

In reality, a company using a blending model would run the model periodically and set production on the basis of the current inventory of inputs and the current forecasts of demands and prices. Then the forecasts and the input levels would be updated, and the model would be run again to determine the next period's production.

Problems

Level A

7. Use SolverTable in the Chandler blending model to see whether, by increasing the selling price of gasoline, you can get an optimal solution that produces only gasoline, no heating oil. Then use SolverTable again to see whether, by increasing the selling price of heating oil, you can get an optimal solution that produces only heating oil, no gasoline.

8. Use SolverTable in the Chandler blending model to find the shadow price of crude oil 1—that is, the amount Chandler would be willing to spend to acquire more crude oil 1. Does this shadow price change as Chandler keeps getting more of crude oil 1? Answer the same questions for crude oil 2.

9. How sensitive is the Chandler optimal blending solution (barrels of each output sold and profit) to the required quality levels? Answer this by running a two-way SolverTable with these three outputs. You can choose the values of the two inputs to vary.

10. In the Chandler blending model, suppose there is a chemical ingredient called C1 that both gasoline and heating oil need. At least 3% of every barrel of gasoline must be C1, and at least 5% of every barrel of heating oil must be C1. Suppose that 4%

of all crude oil 1 is C1 and 6% of all crude oil 2 is C1. Modify the blending model to incorporate the constraints on C1, and then optimize. Don't forget to clear denominators.

11. In the current version of the Chandler blending model, a barrel of any input results in a barrel of output. However, in a real blending problem there can be losses. Suppose a barrel of input results in only a fraction of a barrel of output. Specifically, each barrel of either crude oil used for gasoline results in only 0.95 barrel of gasoline, and each barrel of either crude used for heating oil results in only 0.97 barrel of heating oil. Modify the model to incorporate these losses and then find the optimal solution.

Level B

12. We warned you about clearing denominators in the quality constraints. This problem indicates what happens if you don't do so.
   a. Implement the quality constraints in the Chandler blending model as indicated in Inequality (14.3). Then run Solver with the simplex method. What happens? What if you run Solver with the GRG nonlinear method?
   b. Repeat part **a**, but increase the selling price of heating oil to $120 per barrel. What happens now?

14-4 Logistics Models

In many situations a company produces products at locations called *origins* and ships these products to customer locations called *destinations*. Typically, each origin has a limited capacity that it can ship, and each destination must receive a required quantity of the product. **Logistics models** can be used to determine the minimum-cost shipping method for satisfying customer demands.

14-4a Transportation Models

We begin by assuming that the only possible shipments are those directly from an origin to a destination. That is, no shipments between origins or between destinations are allowed. Such a problem has traditionally been called a *transportation problem*.

EXAMPLE

14.3 SHIPPING CARS AT GRAND PRIX AUTOMOBILE

The Grand Prix Automobile Company manufactures automobiles in three plants and then ships them to four regions of the country. The plants can supply the amounts listed in the right column of Table 14.2. The customer demands by region are listed in the bottom row of this table, and the unit costs of shipping an automobile from each plant to each region are listed in the middle of the table. Grand Prix wants to find the lowest-cost shipping plan for meeting the demands of the four regions without exceeding the capacities of the plants.

Table 14.2 Input Data for Grand Prix Example	Region 1	Region 2	Region 3	Region 4	Capacity
Plant 1	131	218	266	120	450
Plant 2	250	116	263	278	600
Plant 3	178	132	122	180	500
Demand	450	200	300	300	

Objective

To develop an optimization model for finding the least-cost way of shipping the automobiles from plants to regions, staying within plant capacities and meeting regional demands.

Where Do the Numbers Come From?

A typical transportation problem requires three sets of numbers: capacities (or supplies), demands (or requirements), and unit shipping (and possibly production) costs.

• The *capacities* indicate the most each plant can supply in a given amount of time—a month, say—under current operating conditions. In some cases it might be possible to increase the "base" capacities, by using overtime, for example. In such cases the model could be modified to determine the amounts of additional capacity to use (and pay for).

• The customer *demands* are typically estimated from some type of forecasting model (as discussed in Chapter 12). The forecasts are often based on historical customer demand data.

• The *unit shipping costs* come from a transportation cost analysis—what does it really cost to send a single automobile from any plant to any region? This is not an easy question to answer, and it requires an analysis of the best mode of transportation (such as railroad, ship, or truck). However, companies typically have the required data. Actually, the unit "shipping" cost can also include the unit production cost at each plant. However, if this cost is the same across all plants, as we are tacitly assuming here, it can be omitted from the model.

Solution

The variables and constraints required for this model are shown in Figure 14.12. (See the file **Transportation Big Picture. xlsx.**) The company must choose the number of autos to send from each plant to each region—a shipping plan. Then it can calculate the total number of autos sent out of each plant and the total number received by each region.

Figure 14.12 Big Picture for Transportation Model

Representing Transportation in a Network Model

A network diagram of this model appears in Figure 14.13. This diagram is typical of network models. It consists of nodes and arcs. A *node*, indicated by an oval, generally represents a geographical location. In this case the nodes on the left correspond to plants, and the nodes on the right correspond to regions. An *arc*, indicated by an arrow, generally represents a route for getting a product from one node to another. Here, the arcs all go from a plant node to a region node—from left to right.

In a transportation problem, all flows go from left to right— from origins to destinations. You will see more complex network structures in the next subsection.

The problem data fit nicely on such a diagram. The capacities are placed next to the plant nodes, the demands are placed next to the region nodes, and the unit shipping costs are placed on the arcs. The decision variables are usually called *flows*. They represent the amounts shipped on the various arcs. Sometimes (although not in this problem), there are upper limits on the flows on some or all of the arcs. These upper limits, called *arc capacities*, can also be shown on the diagram.[3]

---

3 There can even be lower limits, other than zero, on certain flows, but we don't consider any such constraints here.

Figure 14.13 Network
Representation of
Transportation Model

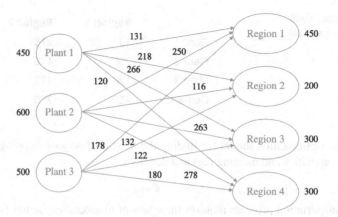

Developing the Spreadsheet Model

The spreadsheet model appears in Figure 14.14. (See the file **Transportation Finished.xlsx.**) To develop this model, perform the following steps.

Developing the Transportation Model

1. **Inputs.**[4] Enter the unit shipping costs, plant capacities, and region demands in the blue cells.
2. **Shipping plan.** Enter any trial values for the shipments from plants to regions in the Shipping_plan range. These are the decision variable cells. Note that this rectangular range is exactly the same shape as the range where the unit shipping costs are entered. This is a natural model design, and it simplifies the formulas in the following steps.
3. **Numbers shipped from plants.** To calculate the amount shipped out of each plant in the range G13:G15, select this range and click the AutoSum (Σ) button.

Figure 14.14 Transportation Model

▲	A	B	C	D	E	F	G	H	I	J	K
1	Grand Prix transportation model								Range names used:		
2									Capacity	=Model!$I$13:$I$15	
3	Unit shipping costs								Demand	=Model!$C$18:$F$18	
4			To						Shipping_Plan	=Model!$C$13:$F$15	
5			Region 1	Region 2	Region 3	Region 4			Total_cost	=Model!$B$21	
6	From	Plant 1	$131	$218	$266	$120			Total_received	=Model!$C$16:$F$16	
7		Plant 2	$250	$116	$263	$278			Total_shipped	=Model!$G$13:$G$15	
8		Plant 3	$178	$132	$122	$180					
9											
10	Shipping plan, and constraints on supply and demand										
11			To								
12			Region 1	Region 2	Region 3	Region 4	Total shipped		Capacity		
13	From	Plant 1	150	0	0	300	450	<=	450		
14		Plant 2	100	200	0	0	300	<=	600		
15		Plant 3	200	0	300	0	500	<=	500		
16		Total received	450	200	300	300					
17			>=	>=	>=	>=					
18		Demand	450	200	300	300					
19											
20	Objective to minimize										
21	Total cost	$176,050									

4. **Amounts received by regions.** Similarly, calculate the amount shipped to each region in the range C16:F16 by selecting the range and clicking the AutoSum button.
5. **Total shipping cost.** Calculate the total cost of shipping power from the plants to the regions in the Total_cost cell with the formula

   =SUMPRODUCT(C6:F8,Shipping_plan)

   This formula sums all products of unit shipping costs and amounts shipped. You now see the benefit of placing unit shipping costs and amounts shipped in similar-size rectangular ranges—you can then use the SUMPRODUCT function.

---

4 From here on, we might not remind you about creating range names, but we will continue to list our suggested range names on the spreadsheets.

Using Solver

Invoke Solver with the settings shown in Figure 14.15. As usual, check the Non-Negative option and select the Simplex LP method before optimizing.

Figure 14.15 Solver Dialog Box for Transportation Model

Discussion of the Solution

The Solver solution appears in Figure 14.14 and is illustrated graphically in Figure 14.16. The company incurs a total shipping cost of $176,050 by using the shipments listed in Figure 14.16. Except for the six routes shown, no other routes are used. Most of the shipments occur on the low-cost routes, but this is not always the case. For example, the route

It is typical in transportation models, especially large models, that only a small number of the possible routes are used.

Figure 14.16 Graphical Representation of Optimal Solution

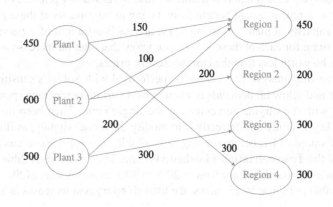

from plant 2 to region 1 is relatively expensive, and it is used. On the other hand, the route from plant 3 to region 2 is relatively cheap, but it is not used. A good shipping plan tries to use cheap routes, but it is constrained by capacities and demands.

Note that the available capacity is not all used. The reason is that total capacity is 1550, whereas total demand is only 1250. Even though the demand constraints are of the "≥" type, there is clearly no reason to send the regions more than they request because it only increases shipping costs. Therefore, the optimal plan sends them the minimal amounts they request and no more. In fact, the demand constraints could have been modeled as "=" constraints, and Solver would have found exactly the same solution.

Sensitivity Analysis

There are many sensitivity analyses you could perform on the basic transportation model. For example, you could vary any one of the unit shipping costs, capacities, or demands. The effect of any such change in a single input is captured nicely in Solver's sensitivity report, shown in Figure 14.17. The top part indicates the effects of changes in the unit shipping costs. The results here are typical. For all routes with positive flows, the corresponding reduced cost is zero, whereas for all routes not currently being used, the reduced cost indicates how much *less* the unit shipping cost would have to be before the company would start shipping along that route. For example, if the unit shipping cost from plant 2 to region 3 decreased by more than $69, this route would become attractive.

Figure 14.17 Solver's Sensitivity Report for Transportation Model

Cell	Name	Final Value	Reduced Cost	Objective Coefficient	Allowable Increase	Allowable Decrease
Variable Cells						
$C$13	Plant 1 Region 1	150	0	131	119	13
$D$13	Plant 1 Region 2	0	221	218	1E+30	221
$E$13	Plant 1 Region 3	0	191	266	1E+30	191
$F$13	Plant 1 Region 4	300	0	120	13	239
$C$14	Plant 2 Region 1	100	0	250	39	72
$D$14	Plant 2 Region 2	200	0	116	88	116
$E$14	Plant 2 Region 3	0	69	263	1E+30	69
$F$14	Plant 2 Region 4	0	39	278	1E+30	39
$C$15	Plant 3 Region 1	200	0	178	13	69
$D$15	Plant 3 Region 2	0	88	132	1E+30	88
$E$15	Plant 3 Region 3	300	0	122	69	194
$F$15	Plant 3 Region 4	0	13	180	1E+30	13

Cell	Name	Final Value	Shadow Price	Constraint R.H. Side	Allowable Increase	Allowable Decrease
Constraints						
$G$13	Plant 1 Total shipped	450	−119	450	100	150
$G$14	Plant 2 Total shipped	300	0	600	1E+30	300
$G$15	Plant 3 Total shipped	500	−72	500	100	200
$C$16	Total received Region 1	450	250	450	300	100
$D$16	Total received Region 2	200	116	200	300	200
$E$16	Total received Region 3	300	194	300	200	100
$F$16	Total received Region 4	300	239	300	150	100

The bottom part of this report is useful because of its shadow prices. For example, plants 1 and 3 are currently shipping at capacity, so the company would benefit from having more capacity at these plants. In particular, the report indicates that each extra unit of capacity at plant 1 is worth $119, and each extra unit of capacity at plant 3 is worth $72. However, because the allowable increase for each of these is 100, you know that after an increase in capacity of 100 at either plant, further increases will probably be worth less than the current shadow prices.

One interesting analysis that cannot be performed with Solver's sensitivity report is to keep shipping costs and capacities constant and allow all demands to change by a certain percentage (positive or negative). To perform this analysis, use SolverTable, with the varying percentage as the single input. Then keep track of the total cost and any amounts shipped of interest. The key to doing this correctly is to modify the model slightly, as illustrated in the previous chapter and Example 14.1, before running SolverTable. The appropriate modifications appear in the third sheet of the **Transportation Finished.xlsx** file. Then run SolverTable, allowing the percentage change in all demands to vary from −20% to 30% in increments of 5%, and keep track of total cost. As the table in Figure 14.18 shows, the total shipping cost increases at an increasing rate as the

The key to this sensitivity analysis is to modify the model slightly before running SolverTable.

demands increase. However, at some point the problem has no feasible solutions. As soon as the total demand is greater than the total capacity, it is impossible to meet all demand.

Figure 14.18 Sensitivity Analysis to Percentage Changes in All Demands

	A	B	C	D	E	F	G	H
1	Oneway analysis for Solver model in Modified Model for Sensitivity worksheet							
2								
3	Change in demands (cell $I$10) values along side, output cell(s) along top							
4		Total_cost						
5	−20%	$130,850						
6	−15%	$140,350						
7	−10%	$149,850						
8	−5%	$162,770						
9	0%	$176,050						
10	5%	$189,330						
11	10%	$202,610						
12	15%	$215,890						
13	20%	$229,170						
14	25%	Not feasible						
15	30%	Not feasible						

An Alternative Model

The transportation model in Figure 14.14 is a very natural one. In the graphical representation in Figure 14.13, all arcs go from left to right, that is, from plants to regions. Therefore, the rectangular range of shipments allows you to calculate shipments out of plants as row sums and shipments into regions as column sums. In anticipation of later models in this chapter, however, where the graphical network can be more complex, we present an alternative model of the transportation problem. (See the file **Transportation Alternative Finished.xlsx**.)

First, it is useful to introduce some additional network terminology. Recall that flows are the amounts shipped on the various arcs. The direction of the arcs indicates which way the flows are allowed to travel. An arc pointed into a node is called an *inflow*, whereas an arrow pointed out of a node is called an *outflow*. In the basic transportation model, all outflows originate from suppliers, and all inflows go toward demanders. However, general networks can have both inflows and outflows for any given node.

With this general structure in mind, the typical network model has one decision variable cell per arc. It indicates how much (if any) to send along that arc in the direction of the arrow. Therefore, it is often useful to model network problems by listing all arcs and their corresponding flows in one long list. Then constraints can be indicated in a separate section of the spreadsheet. Specifically, for each node in the network, there is a **flow balance constraint**. These flow balance constraints for the basic transportation model are the supply and demand constraints already discussed, but they can be more general for other network models, as will be discussed in the next subsection.

Although this model is possibly less natural than the original model, it generalizes better to other logistics models.

The alternative model of the Grand Prix problem appears in Figure 14.19. The plant and region indexes and the associated unit shipping costs are entered manually in the range A5:C16. Each row in this range corresponds to an arc in the network. For example, row 12 corresponds to the arc from plant 2 to region 4, with unit shipping cost $278. Then the decision variable cells for the flows are in column D. (If there were arc capacities, they could be placed to the right of the flows.)

The flow balance constraints are conceptually straightforward. Each cell in the Outflow and Inflow ranges in column G contains the appropriate sum of flows. For example, cell G6, the outflow from plant 1, represents the sum of cells D5 through D8, whereas cell G12, the inflow to plant 1, represents the sum of cells D5, D9, and D13. Fortunately, there is an easy way to enter these summation formulas.[5] The trick is to use Excel's built-in SUMIF function (see explanation below). For example, the formula in cell G6 is

=SUMIF(Origin,F6,Flow)

This formula compares the plant number in cell F6 to the Origin range in column A and sums all flows where they are equal— that is, it sums all flows out of plant 1. This formula can be copied down to cell G8 to obtain the flows out of the other plants. For flows into regions, the similar formula in cell G12 for the flow into region 1 is

=SUMIF(Destination,F12,Flow)

---

5 Try entering these formulas as simple sums even for a 3 × 4 transportation model, and you will see why the SUMIF function is so handy.

Figure 14.19 Alternative Form of Transportation Model

	A	B	C	D	E	F	G	H	I	J	K	L	M
1	Grand Prix transportation model: a more general network formulation										Range names used:		
2											Capacity	=Model!$I$6:$I$8	
3	Network structure and flows					Flow balance constraints					Demand	=Model!$I$12:$I$15	
4	Origin	Destination	Unit cost	Flow		Capacity constraints					Destination	=Model!$B$5:$B$16	
5	1	1	131	150		Plant	Outflow		Capacity		Flow	=Model!$D$5:$D$16	
6	1	2	218	0		1	450	<=	450		Inflow	=Model!$G$12:$G$15	
7	1	3	266	0		2	300	<=	600		Origin	=Model!$A$5:$A$16	
8	1	4	120	300		3	500	<=	500		Outflow	=Model!$G$6:$G$8	
9	2	1	250	100							Total_Cost	=Model!$B$19	
10	2	2	116	200		Demand constraints							
11	2	3	263	0		Region	Inflow		Demand				
12	2	4	278	0		1	450	>=	450				
13	3	1	178	200		2	200	>=	200				
14	3	2	132	0		3	300	>=	300				
15	3	3	122	300		4	300	>=	300				
16	3	4	180	0									
17													
18	Objective to minimize												
19	Total Cost	$176,050											

and this can be copied down to cell G15 for flows into the other regions. In general, the SUMIF function finds all cells in the first argument that satisfy the criterion in the second argument and then sums the corresponding cells in the third argument. It is a very handy function—and not just for network modeling.

Excel Function

SUMIF

The SUMIF function is useful for summing values in a certain range if cells in a related range satisfy a given condition. It has the syntax **=SUMIF(compareRange,criterion,sumRange)**, where compareRange and sumRange are similar-size ranges. This formula checks each cell in compareRange to see whether it satisfies the criterion. If it does, it adds the corresponding value in sumRange to the overall sum. For example, **=SUMIF(A12:A13,1,D12:D23)** sums all values in the range D12:D23 where the corresponding cell in the range A12:A23 has the value 1.

This use of the SUMIF function, along with the list of origins, destinations, unit costs, and flows in columns A through D, is the key to the model. The rest is straightforward. The total cost is a SUMPRODUCT of unit costs and flows, and the Solver dialog box is set up as shown in Figure 14.20.

This alternative model generalizes nicely to other network problems. Essentially, it shows that all network models look alike. There is an additional benefit from this alternative model. Suppose that flows from certain plants to certain regions are not allowed. (Maybe no roads exist.) It is not easy to disallow such routes in the original model. One option is to allow the "disallowed" routes but to impose extremely large unit shipping costs on them. This works, but it is wasteful because it adds decision variable cells that do not really belong in the model. However, the alternative network model simply omits arcs that are not allowed. For example, if the route from plant 2 to region 4 is not allowed, you simply omit the data in the range A12:D12. This creates a model with exactly as many decision variable cells as allowable arcs. This additional benefit can be very valuable when the number of potential arcs in the network is huge—even though the vast majority of them are disallowed—which is the situation in many large network models.

The alternative network model not only accommodates more general networks, but it is more efficient because it has fewer decision variable cells.

We do not necessarily recommend this more general network model for simple transportation problems. In fact, it is probably less natural than the original model in Figure 14.14. However, it paves the way for the more complex network problems discussed next.

Modeling Issues

• The customer demands in typical transportation problems can be handled in one of two ways. First, you can think of these forecasted demands as minimal requirements that must be sent to the customers. This is how regional demands were treated here. Alternatively, you could consider the demands as maximal sales quantities, the most each region can sell. Then you would constrain the amounts sent to the regions to be less than or equal to the forecasted demands. Whether the demand

Figure 14.20 Solver Dialog Box for Alternative Transportation Model

constraints are expressed as "≥" or "≤" (or even "=") constraints depends on the context of the problem—do the dealers need at least this many, do they need exactly this many, or can they sell only this many?

Depending on how you treat the demand constraints, you can get several variations of the basic transportation model.

- If all the supplies and demands for a transportation problem are integers, the optimal Solver solution automatically has integer-valued shipments. Explicit integer constraints are not required. (This might not be obvious, but it has been proved mathematically.) This is a very important benefit. It means that the "fast" simplex method can be used rather than much slower integer algorithms.

- Shipping costs are often nonlinear (and "nonsmooth") due to quantity discounts. For example, if it costs $3 per item to ship up to 100 items between locations and $2 per item for each additional item, the proportionality assumption of LP is violated and the resulting transportation model is nonlinear. Shipping problems that involve quantity discounts are generally more difficult to solve.

- Excel's Solver uses the simplex method to solve transportation problems. There is a streamlined version of the simplex method, called the *transportation simplex method*, that is much more efficient than the ordinary simplex method for transportation problems. Large transportation problems are usually solved with the transportation simplex method. See Winston (2003) for a discussion of the transportation simplex method.

14-4b More General Logistics Models

The objective of many real-world network models is to ship goods from one set of locations to another at minimum cost, subject to various constraints. There are many variations of these models. The simplest models include a single product that must be shipped via one mode of transportation (truck, for example) in a particular period of time. More complex models—and much larger ones—can include multiple products, multiple modes of transportation, and/or multiple time periods. We discuss one such problem in this section.

Basically, the general logistics problem is like the transportation problem except for two possible differences. First, arc capacities are often imposed on some or all of the arcs. These become simple upper-bound constraints in the model. Second and more significant, there can be inflows *and* outflows associated with any node. Nodes are generally categorized as origins, destinations, and transshipment points. An *origin* is a location that starts with a certain supply (or a capacity for supplying). A *destination* is the opposite; it requires a certain amount to end up there. A *transshipment point* is a location where goods simply pass through.

> ### Fundamental Insight
>
> #### Flow Balance Constraints
>
> All network optimization models have some form of flow balance constraints at the various nodes of the network. This flow balance relates the amount that enters the node to the amount that leaves the node. In many network models, the simple structure of these flow balance constraints guarantees that the optimal solutions have integer values. It also enables specialized network versions of the simplex method to solve the huge network models typically encountered in real logistics applications.

The best way to think of these categories is in terms of net inflow and net outflow. The *net inflow* for any node is defined as total inflow minus total outflow for that node. The *net outflow* is the negative of this, total outflow minus total inflow. Then an origin is a node with positive net outflow, a destination is a node with positive net inflow, and a transshipment point is a node with net outflow (and net inflow) equal to 0. It is important to realize that inflows are sometimes allowed to origins, but their *net* outflows are positive. Similarly, outflows from destinations are sometimes allowed, but their *net* inflows are positive. For example, if Cincinnati and Memphis are manufacturers (origins) and Dallas and Phoenix are retail locations (destinations), it is possible that flow could go from Cincinnati to Memphis to Dallas to Phoenix.

There are typically two types of constraints in logistics models (besides nonnegativity of flows). The first type represents the arc capacity constraints, which are simple upper bounds on the arc flows. The second type represents the **flow balance constraints**, one for each node. For an origin, this constraint is typically of the form **Net Outflow = Capacity** or possibly **Net Outflow ≤ Capacity**. For a destination, it is typically of the form **Net Inflow ≥ Demand** or possibly **Net Inflow = Demand**. For a transshipment point, it is of the form **Net Inflow = 0** (which is equivalent to **Net Outflow = 0**).

It is easy to visualize these constraints in a graphical representation of the network by simply examining the flows on the arrows leading into and out of the various nodes. We illustrate a typical logistics model in Example 14.4.

EXAMPLE

14.4 PRODUCING AND SHIPPING TOMATO PRODUCTS AT REDBRAND

RedBrand Company produces a tomato product at three plants. This product can be shipped directly to the company's two customers or it can first be shipped to the company's two warehouses and then to the customers. Figure 14.21 is a network representation of RedBrand's problem. Nodes 1, 2, and 3 represent the plants (these are the origins, denoted by S for supplier), nodes 4 and 5 represent the warehouses (these are the transshipment points, denoted by T), and nodes 6 and 7 represent the customers (these are the destinations, denoted by D). Note that some shipments are allowed among plants, among warehouses, and among customers. Also, some arcs have arrows on both ends. This means that flow is allowed in either direction.

Figure 14.21 Graphical Representation of Logistics Model

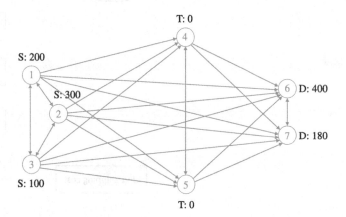

The cost of producing the product is the same at each plant, so RedBrand is concerned with minimizing the total shipping cost incurred in meeting customer demands. The production capacity of each plant (in tons per year) and the demand of each customer are shown in Figure 14.21. For example, plant 1 (node 1) has a capacity of 200, and customer 1 (node 6) has a demand of 400. In addition, the cost (in thousands of dollars) of shipping a ton of the product between each pair of locations is listed in Table 14.3, where a blank indicates that RedBrand cannot ship along that arc. We also assume that at most 200 tons of the product can be shipped along any arc. This is the common arc capacity. RedBrand wants to determine a minimum-cost shipping schedule.

Table 14.3 Shipping Costs for RedBrand Example (in $1000s)

To node							
From node	1	2	3	4	5	6	7
1	5.0	3.0	5.0	5.0	20.0	20.0	
2	9.0		9.0	1.0	1.0	8.0	15.0
3	0.4	8.0		1.0	0.5	10.0	12.0
4					1.2	2.0	12.0
5				0.8		2.0	12.0
6							1.0
7						7.0	

Objective

To develop an optimization model for finding the minimum-cost way to ship the tomato product from suppliers to customers, possibly through warehouses, so that customer demands are met and supplier capacities are not exceeded.

Where Do the Numbers Come From?

The network configuration itself would come from geographical considerations—which routes are physically possible (or sensible) and which are not. The numbers would be derived as in the Grand Prix automobile example. (See Example 14.3 for further discussion.)

Solution

The variables and constraints for this logistics model are shown in Figure 14.22. (See the file **RedBrand Logistics Big Picture. xlsx.**) The key to the model is handling the flow balance constraints. You will see exactly how to implement these when we give step-by-step instructions for developing the spreadsheet model. However, it is not enough, for example, to specify that the flow out of plant 2 is less than or equal to the capacity of plant 2. The reason is that there might also be flow *into* plant 2 (from another plant). Therefore, the correct flow balance constraint for plant 2 is that its outflow must be less than or equal to its capacity plus its inflow. Equivalently, the *net* outflow from plant 2 must be less than or equal to its capacity.

Other than arc capacity constraints, the only constraints are flow balance constraints.

Figure 14.22 Big Picture for
Logistics Model

Developing the Spreadsheet Model

To set up the spreadsheet model, proceed as follows. (See Figure 14.23 and the file **RedBrand Logistics Finished.xlsx**. Also, refer to the network in Figure 14.21.)

1. **Origins and destinations.** Enter the node numbers (1 to 7) for the origins and destinations of the various arcs in the range A8:B33. Note that the disallowed arcs are not entered in this list.

2. **Input data.** Enter the unit shipping costs (in thousands of dollars), the common arc capacity, the plant capacities, and the customer demands in the blue cells. Again, only the nonblank entries in Table 14.3 are used to fill the column of unit shipping costs.

Developing the Logistics Model

3. **Flows on arcs.** Enter *any* initial values for the flows in the range D8:D33. These are the decision variable cells.

4. **Arc capacities.** To indicate a common arc capacity for all arcs, enter the formula

   $= \$B\$4$

   in cell F8 and copy it down column F.

Figure 14.23 Logistics Model

	A	B	C	D	E	F	G	H	I	J	K
1	RedBrand shipping model										
2											
3	Inputs										
4	Common arc capacity	200									
5											
6	Network structure, flows, and arc capacity constraints							Node balance constraints			
7		Origin	Destination	Unit Cost	Flow		Arc Capacity	Plant constraints			
8		1	2	5	0	<=	200		Node	Plant net outflow		Plant capacity
9		1	3	3	180	<=	200		1	180	<=	200
10		1	4	5	0	<=	200		2	300	<=	300
11		1	5	5	0	<=	200		3	100	<=	100
12		1	6	20	0	<=	200					
13		1	7	20	0	<=	200		Warehouse constraints			
14		2	1	9	0	<=	200		Node	Warehouse net outflow		Required
15		2	3	9	0	<=	200		4	0	=	0
16		2	4	1	120	<=	200		5	0	=	0
17		2	5	1	0	<=	200					
18		2	6	8	180	<=	200		Customer constraints			
19		2	7	15	0	<=	200		Node	Customer net inflow		Customer demand
20		3	1	0.4	0	<=	200		6	400	>=	400
21		3	2	8	0	<=	200		7	180	>=	180
22		3	4	1	80	<=	200					
23		3	5	0.5	200	<=	200		Range names used			
24		3	6	10	0	<=	200		Arc_Capacity	=Model!$F$8:$F$33		
25		3	7	12	0	<=	200		Customer_demand	=Model!$K$20:$K$21		
26		4	5	1.2	0	<=	200		Customer_net_inflow	=Model!$I$20:$I$21		
27		4	6	2	200	<=	200		Destination	=Model!$B$8:$B$33		
28		4	7	12	0	<=	200		Flow	=Model!$D$8:$D$33		
29		5	4	0.8	0	<=	200		Origin	=Model!$A$8:$A$33		
30		5	6	2	200	<=	200		Plant_capacity	=Model!$K$9:$K$11		
31		5	7	12	0	<=	200		Plant_net_outflow	=Model!$I$9:$I$11		
32		6	7	1	180	<=	200		Total_cost	=Model!$B$36		
33		7	6	7	0	<=	200		Unit_Cost	=Model!$C$8:$C$33		
34									Warehouse_net_outflow	=Model!$I$15:$I$16		
35	Objective to minimize										
36	Total cost	$3,260									

5. **Flow balance constraints.** Nodes 1, 2, and 3 are supply nodes, nodes 4 and 5 are transshipment points, and nodes 6 and 7 are demand nodes. Therefore, set up the left sides of the flow balance constraints appropriately for these three cases. Specifically, enter the net *outflow* for node 1 in cell I9 with the formula

=**SUMIF(Origin,H9,Flow)-SUMIF(Destination,H9,Flow)**

and copy it down to cell I11. This formula subtracts flows into node 1 from flows out of node 1 to obtain net outflow for node 1. Next, copy this *same* formula to cells I15 and I16 for the warehouses. (Remember that, for transshipment nodes, the left side of the constraint can be net outflow *or* net inflow, whichever you prefer. The reason is that if net outflow is zero, net inflow must also be zero.) Finally, enter the net *inflow* for node 6 in cell I20 with the formula

=**SUMIF(Destination,H20,Flow)-SUMIF(Origin,H20,Flow)**

and copy it to cell I21. This formula subtracts flows out of node 6 from flows into node 6 to obtain the net inflow for node 6.

We generally prefer positive numbers on the right sides of constraints. This is why we calculate net outflows for origins and net inflows for destinations.

6. **Total shipping cost.** Calculate the total shipping cost (in thousands of dollars) in cell B36 with the formula

=**SUMPRODUCT(Unit_cost,Flow)**

Using Solver

The Solver dialog box should be set up as in Figure 14.24. The objective is to minimize total shipping costs, subject to the three types of flow balance constraints and the arc capacity constraints.

Figure 14.24 Solver Dialog Box for Logistics Model

Discussion of the Solution

The optimal solution in Figure 14.23 indicates that RedBrand's customer demand can be satisfied with a shipping cost of $3,260,000. This solution appears graphically in Figure 14.25. Note in particular that plant 1 produces 180 tons (under capacity) and ships it all to plant 3, not directly to warehouses or customers. Also, note that all shipments from the warehouses go directly to customer 1. Then customer 1 ships 180 tons to customer 2. We purposely chose unit shipping costs (probably unrealistic ones) to produce this type of behavior, just to show that it *can* occur. As you can see, the costs of shipping from plant 1 directly to warehouses or customers are relatively large compared to the cost of shipping directly to plant 3. Similarly, the costs of shipping from plants or warehouses directly to customer 2 are prohibitive. Therefore, RedBrand ships to customer 1 and lets customer 1 forward some of its shipment to customer 2.

Figure 14.25 Optimal Flows for Logistics Model

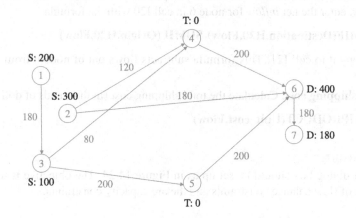

Sensitivity Analysis

How much effect does the arc capacity have on the optimal solution? Currently, three of the arcs with positive flow are at the arc capacity of 200. You can use SolverTable to see how sensitive this number and the total cost are to the arc capacity.[6] In this case the single input cell for SolverTable is cell B4, which is varied from 150 to 300 in increments of 25. Two quantities are designated as outputs: total cost and the number of arcs at arc capacity. As before, if you want to keep track of an output that does not already exist, you can create it with an appropriate formula in a new cell before running SolverTable. Specifically, you can enter the formula =COUNTIF(Flow,B4) in an unused cell. This formula counts the arcs with flow equal to arc capacity. (See the finished version of the file for a note about this formula.)

The SolverTable output in Figure 14.26 is what you would expect. As the arc capacity decreases, more flows bump up against it, and the total cost increases. But even when the arc capacity is increased to 300, two flows are constrained by it. In this sense, even a large arc capacity can cost RedBrand money.

Excel Function

COUNTIF

The COUNTIF function counts the number of values in a given range that satisfy some criterion. The syntax is =COUNTIF(range, criterion). For example, the formula =COUNTIF(D8:D33,150) counts the number of cells in the range D8:D33 that contain the value 150. This formula could also be entered as =COUNTIF(D8:D33,"=150"). Similarly, the formula =COUNTIF(D8:D33,">=100") counts the number of cells in this range with values greater than or equal to 100.[7]

---

6 Solver's sensitivity report would not answer our question. This report is useful only for one-at-a-time changes in inputs, and here we are simultaneously changing the upper limit for *each* flow. However, this report (its bottom section) can be used to assess the effects of changes in plant capacities or customer demands.

7 The COUNTIF and SUMIF functions are limited in that they allow only one condition, such as ">=10". For this reason, Microsoft added two new functions in Excel 2007, COUNTIFS and SUMIFS, that allow multiple conditions. You can learn about them in online help.

Figure 14.26 Sensitivity to Arc Capacity

	A	B	C	D	E	F	G
1	Oneway analysis for Solver model in Model worksheet						
2							
3	Common arc capacity (cell $B$4) values along side, output cell(s) along top						
4		Total_cost	Arcs_at_capacity				
5	150	$4,120	5				
6	175	$3,643	6				
7	200	$3,260	3				
8	225	$2,998	3				
9	250	$2,735	3				
10	275	$2,473	3				
11	300	$2,320	2				

Modeling Issues

• There are many variations of this basic logistics model. Two variations are illustrated in the files **RedBrand Logistics Multiple Products Finished.xlsx** and **RedBrand Logistics Shrinkage Finished.xlsx**. In the first variation, two products compete for the same arc capacity. In the second, there is shrinkage at the warehouses due to spoilage.

• Excel's Solver uses the simplex method to solve logistics models. However, the simplex method can be simplified dramatically for these types of models. The simplified version of the simplex method, called the *network simplex method*, is much more efficient than the ordinary simplex method. Specialized computer codes have been written to implement the network simplex method, and all large logistics problems are solved by using the network simplex method. This is fortunate because real logistics models tend to be extremely large. See Winston (2003) for a discussion of this method.

• If the given supplies and demands for the nodes are integers and all arc capacities are integers, the logistics model always has an optimal solution with all integer flows. Again, this is very fortunate for large problems—you get integer solutions "for free" without having to use an integer programming algorithm. However, this "integers for free" benefit is guaranteed only for the basic logistics model, as in the original RedBrand model. When the model is modified in certain ways, such as by adding a shrinkage factor, the optimal solution is no longer guaranteed to be integer-valued.

Problems

Level A

13. In the original Grand Prix example, the total capacity of the three plants is 1550, well above the total customer demand. Would it help to have 100 more units of capacity at plant 1? What is the most Grand Prix would be willing to pay for this extra capacity? Answer the same questions for plant 2 and for plant 3. Explain why extra capacity can be valuable even though the company already has more total capacity than it requires.

14. The optimal solution to the original Grand Prix problem indicates that with a unit shipping cost of $132, the route from plant 3 to region 2 is evidently too expensive—no autos are shipped along this route. Use SolverTable to see how much this unit shipping cost would have to be reduced before some autos would be shipped along this route.

15. In the RedBrand example, suppose the plants cannot ship to each other and the customers cannot ship to each other. Modify the model appropriately, and rerun Solver. How much does the total cost increase because of these disallowed routes?

16. Modify the RedBrand example so that all flows must be from plants to warehouses and from warehouses to customers. Disallow all other arcs. How much does this restriction cost RedBrand, relative to the original optimal shipping cost?

17. In the RedBrand example, the costs for shipping from plants or warehouses to customer 2 were purposely made high so that it would be optimal to ship to customer 1 and then let customer 1 ship to customer 2. Use SolverTable appropriately to do the following. Decrease the unit shipping costs from plants and warehouses to customer 1, all by the same amount, until it is no longer optimal for customer 1 to ship to customer 2. Describe what happens to the optimal shipping plan at this point.

18. In the RedBrand example, the arc capacity is the same for all allowable arcs. Modify the model so that each arc has its own arc capacity. You can make up the arc capacities.

19. Continuing the previous problem, make the problem even more general by allowing upper bounds (arc capacities) *and* lower bounds for the flows on the allowable arcs. Some of the upper bounds can be very large numbers, effectively indicating that there is no arc capacity for these arcs, and the lower bounds can be zero or positive. If they are positive, they indicate that some positive flow must occur on these arcs. Modify the model appropriately to handle these upper and lower bounds. You can make up the upper and lower bounds.

20. Suppose in the original Grand Prix example that the routes from plant 2 to region 1 and from plant 3 to region 3 are not allowed. (Perhaps there are no railroad lines for these routes.) How would you modify the original model (Figure 14.14) to rule out these routes? How would you modify the alternative model (Figure 14.19) to do so? Discuss the pros and cons of these two approaches.

21. The RedBrand model in the file **RedBrand Logistics Multiple Product Finished.xlsx** assumes that the unit shipping costs are the same for both products. Modify the model so that each product has its own unit shipping costs. You can assume that the original unit shipping costs apply to product 1, and you can make up new unit shipping costs for product 2.

Level B

22. Here is a problem to challenge your intuition. In the original Grand Prix example, reduce the capacity of plant 2 to 300. Then the total capacity is equal to the total demand. Rerun Solver on the modified model. You should find that the optimal solution uses all capacity and exactly meets all demands with a total cost of $176,050. Now increase the capacity of plant 1 and the demand at region 2 by one automobile each, and optimize again. What happens to the optimal total cost? How can you explain this "more for less" paradox?

23. Continuing the previous problem (with capacity 300 at plant 2), suppose you want to see how much extra capacity and extra demand you can add to plant 1 and region 2 (the same amount to each) before the total shipping cost stops decreasing and starts increasing. Use SolverTable appropriately to find out. (You will probably need to use some trial and error on the range of input values.) Can you explain intuitively what causes the total cost to stop decreasing and start increasing?

24. Modify the original Grand Prix example by increasing the demand at each region by 200, so that total demand is well above total plant capacity. However, now interpret these "demands" as "maximum sales," the most each region can accommodate, and change the "demand" constraints to become "≤" constraints, not "≥" constraints. How does the optimal solution change? Does it make realistic sense? If not, how might you change the model to obtain a realistic solution?

25. Modify the original Grand Prix example by increasing the demand at each region by 200, so that total demand is well above total plant capacity. This means that some demands cannot be supplied. Suppose there is a unit "penalty" cost at each region for not supplying an automobile. Let these unit penalty costs be $600, $750, $625, and $550 for the four regions. Develop a model to minimize the sum of shipping costs and penalty costs for unsatisfied demands. (*Hint*: Introduce a fourth plant with plenty of capacity, and set its unit shipping costs to the regions equal to the unit penalty costs. Then interpret an auto shipped from this fictional plant to a region as a unit of demand not satisfied.)

26. How difficult is it to expand the RedBrand model? Answer this by adding a new plant, two new warehouses, and three new customers, and modify the spreadsheet model appropriately. You can make up the required input data. Would you conclude that these types of spreadsheet models scale easily?

27. In the RedBrand model in the file **RedBrand Logistics Shrinkage Finished.xlsx**, change the assumptions. Now instead of assuming that there is some shrinkage at the warehouses, assume that there is shrinkage in delivery along each *route*. Specifically, assume that a certain percentage of the units sent along each arc perish in transit—from faulty refrigeration, for example—and this percentage can differ from one arc to another. Modify the model appropriately to take this type of behavior into account. You can make up the shrinkage factors, and you can assume that arc capacities apply to the amounts originally shipped, not to the amounts after shrinkage. (Make sure your input data permit a *feasible* solution. After all, if there is too much shrinkage, it will be impossible to meet demands with available plant capacity. Increase the plant capacities if necessary.)

28. Consider a modification of the RedBrand model where there are N plants, M warehouses, and L customers. Assume that the only allowable arcs are from plants to warehouses and from warehouses to customers. If *all* such arcs are allowable—all plants can ship to all warehouses and all warehouses can ship to all customers—how many decision variable cells are in the spreadsheet model? Keeping in mind that Excel's Solver can handle at most 200 decision variable cells, provide some combinations of N, M, and L that barely stay within Solver's limit.

29. Continuing the previous problem, develop a sample model with your own choices of N, M, and L that barely stay within Solver's limit. You can make up any input data. The important point here is the layout and formulas of the spreadsheet model.

14-5 Aggregate Planning Models

In this section, we extend the production planning model discussed in Example 13.3 of the previous chapter to include a situation where the number of workers available influences the possible production levels. We allow the workforce level to be modified each period through the hiring and firing of workers. Such models, where we determine workforce levels and production schedules for a multiperiod time horizon, are called **aggregate planning models**. There are many variations of aggregate planning models, depending on the detailed assumptions made. We consider a fairly simple version and then ask you to modify it in the problems.

EXAMPLE

14.5 AGGREGATE PLANNING AT SURESTEP

During the next four months SureStep Company must meet (on time) the following demands for pairs of shoes: 3000 in month 1; 5000 in month 2; 2000 in month 3; and 1000 in month 4. At the beginning of month 1, 500 pairs of shoes are on hand, and SureStep has 100 workers. A worker is paid $1500 per month. Each worker can work up to 160 hours a month before he or she receives overtime. A worker can work up to 20 hours of overtime per month and is paid $13 per hour for overtime labor. It takes four hours of labor and $15 of raw material to produce a pair of shoes. At the beginning of each month, workers can be hired or fired. Each hired worker costs $1600, and each fired worker costs $2000. At the end of each month, a holding cost of $3 per pair of shoes left in inventory is incurred. All production in a given month can be used to meet that month's demand. SureStep wants to determine its optimal production schedule and labor policy.

Objective

To develop an optimization model that relates workforce and production decisions to monthly costs, and to find the minimum-cost solution that meets forecasted demands on time and stays within limits on overtime hours and production capacity.

Where Do the Numbers Come From?

There are a number of required inputs for this type of problem. Some, including initial inventory, holding costs, and demands, are similar to requirements for Example 13.3 in the previous chapter, so we won't discuss them again here. Others might be obtained as follows.

- The data on the current number of workers, the regular hours per worker per month, the regular hourly wage rates, and the overtime hourly rate, should be well known. The maximum number of overtime hours per worker per month is probably either the result of a policy decision by management or a clause in the workers' contracts.

- The costs for hiring and firing a worker are not trivial. The hiring cost includes training costs and the cost of decreased productivity due to the fact that a new worker must learn the job. The firing cost includes severance costs and costs due to loss of morale. Neither the hiring nor the firing cost would be simple to estimate accurately, but the human resources department should be able to estimate their values.

- The unit production cost is a combination of two inputs: the raw material cost per pair of shoes and the labor hours per pair of shoes. The raw material cost is the going rate from the supplier(s). The labor per pair of shoes represents the "production function"—the average labor required to produce a unit of the product. The operations managers should be able to supply this number.

Solution

A diagram for this model appears in Figure 14.27. (See the file **Aggregate Planning Big Picture. xlsx.**) It is divided into three parts: a section for workers, a section for shoes, and a section relating workers to shoe production. As you see, there are many variables to keep track of. In fact, the most difficult aspect of modeling this problem is knowing which variables the company gets to choose—the decision variables—and which variables are *determined* by these decisions. It should be clear that the company gets to choose the number of workers to hire and fire and the number of shoes to produce. Also, because management sets only an upper limit on overtime hours, it gets to decide how many overtime hours to use within this limit. But once

The key to this model is choosing the decision variables that determine the required outputs.

Figure 14.27 Big Picture for Aggregate Planning Model

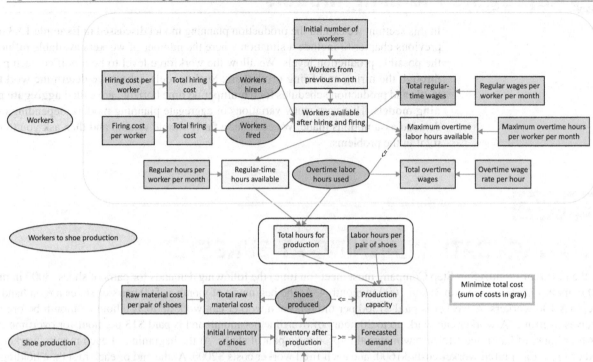

it decides the values of these variables, everything else is determined. We will show how these are determined through detailed cell formulas, but you should mentally go through the yellow calculated values (those in rounded rectangles) and deduce how they are determined by the decision variables. Also, you should convince yourself that the three constraints listed are the ones, and the only ones, that are required.

Developing the Spreadsheet Model

The spreadsheet model appears in Figure 14.28. (See the file **Aggregate Planning 1 Finished.xlsx**.) It can be developed as follows.

Developing the Basic Aggregate Planning Model

1. **Inputs and range names.** Enter the input data and create the range names listed.
2. **Production, hiring, and firing plan.** Enter *any* trial values for the number of pairs of shoes produced each month, the overtime hours used each month, the workers hired each month, and the workers fired each month. These four ranges, in rows 18, 19, 23, and 30, comprise the decision variable cells.
3. **Workers available each month.** In cell B17 enter the initial number of workers available with the formula

   =B5

   Because the number of workers available at the beginning of any other month (before hiring and firing) is equal to the number of workers from the previous month, enter the formula

   =B20

   in cell C17 and copy it to the range D17:E17. Then calculate the number of workers available in month 1 (after hiring and firing) in cell B20 with the formula

   =B17+B18-B19

   and copy this formula to the range C20:E20 for the other months.

   This is common in multiperiod problems. You usually have to relate a beginning value in one period to an ending value from the previous period.

4. **Overtime capacity.** Because each available worker can work up to 20 hours of overtime in a month, enter the formula

   =$B$7*B20

   in cell B25 and copy it to the range C25:E25.

Figure 14.28 Aggregate Planning Model

	A	B	C	D	E	F	G	H	I
1	SureStep aggregate planning model								
2									
3	Input data						Range names used:		
4	Initial inventory of shoes	500					Forecasted_demand	=Model!$B$36:$E$36	
5	Initial number of workers	100					Inventory_after_production	=Model!$B$34:$E$34	
6	Regular hours/worker/month	160					Maximum_overtime_labor_hours_available	=Model!$B$25:$E$25	
7	Maximum overtime hours/worker/month	20					Overtime_labor_hours_used	=Model!$B$23:$E$23	
8	Hiring cost/worker	$1,600					Production_capacity	=Model!$B$32:$E$32	
9	Firing cost/worker	$2,000					Shoes_produced	=Model!$B$30:$E$30	
10	Regular wages/worker/month	$1,500					Total_cost	=Model!$F$46	
11	Overtime wage rate/hour	$13					Workers_fired	=Model!$B$19:$E$19	
12	Labor hours/pair of shoes	4					Workers_hired	=Model!$B$18:$E$18	
13	Raw material cost/pair of shoes	$15							
14	Holding cost/pair of shoes in inventory/month	$3							
15									
16	Worker plan	Month 1	Month 2	Month 3	Month 4				
17	Workers from previous month	100	94	93	50				
18	Workers hired	0	0	0	0				
19	Workers fired	6	1	43	0				
20	Workers available after hiring and firing	94	93	50	50				
21									
22	Regular-time hours available	15040	14880	8000	8000				
23	Overtime labor hours used	0	80	0	0				
24		<=	<=	<=	<=				
25	Maximum overtime labor hours available	1880	1860	1000	1000				
26									
27	Total hours for production	15040	14960	8000	8000				
28									
29	Production plan	Month 1	Month 2	Month 3	Month 4				
30	Shoes Produced	3760	3740	2000	1000				
31		<=	<=	<=	<=				
32	Production capacity	3760	3740	2000	2000				
33									
34	Inventory after production	4260	5000	2000	1000				
35		>=	>=	>=	>=				
36	Forecasted demand	3000	5000	2000	1000				
37	Ending inventory	1260	0	0	0				
38									
39	Monetary outputs	Month 1	Month 2	Month 3	Month 4	Totals			
40	Hiring cost	$0	$0	$0	$0	$0			
41	Firing cost	$12,000	$2,000	$86,000	$0	$100,000			
42	Regular-time wages	$141,000	$139,500	$75,000	$75,000	$430,500			
43	Overtime wages	$0	$1,040	$0	$0	$1,040			
44	Raw material cost	$56,400	$56,100	$30,000	$15,000	$157,500			
45	Holding cost	$3,780	$0	$0	$0	$3,780			
46	Totals	$213,180	$198,640	$191,000	$90,000	$692,820	⟵ Objective to minimize		

5. **Production capacity.** Because each worker can work 160 regular-time hours per month, calculate the regular-time hours available in month 1 in cell B22 with the formula

=$B$6*B20

and copy it to the range C22:E22 for the other months. Then calculate the total hours available for production in cell B27 with the formula

=SUM(B22:B23)

and copy it to the range C27:E27 for the other months. Finally, because it takes four hours of labor to make a pair of shoes, calculate the production capacity in month 1 with the formula

=B27/$B$12

in cell B32 and copy it to the range C32:E32.

6. **Inventory each month.** Calculate the inventory after production in month 1 (which is available to meet month 1 demand) with the formula

=B4+B30

in cell B34. For any other month, the inventory after production is the previous month's ending inventory plus that month's production, so enter the formula

=B37+C30

in cell C34 and copy it to the range D34:E34. Then calculate the month 1 ending inventory in cell B37 with the formula

=B34-B36

and copy it to the range C37:E37.

In Example 13.3 from the previous chapter, production capacities were given inputs. Now they are based on the size of the workforce, which itself is a decision variable.

7. **Monthly costs.** Calculate the various costs shown in rows 40 through 45 for month 1 by entering the formulas

=$B$8*B18

=$B$9*B19

=$B$10*B20

=$B$11*B23

=$B$13*B30

=$B$14*B37

in cells B40 through B45. Then copy the range B40:B45 to the range C40:E45 to calculate these costs for the other months.

8. **Totals.** In row 46 and column F, use the SUM function to calculate cost totals, with the value in F46 being the overall total cost to minimize.

Excel Tip

Press the command key on the Mac.

Calculating Row and Column Sums with AutoSum

A common operation in spreadsheet models is to calculate row and column sums for a rectangular range, as we did for costs in step 8. There is a very quick way to do this. Select the row and column where the sums will go (remember to press the Ctrl key to select nonadjacent ranges) and click the AutoSum (Σ) button. This enters all of the sums automatically. It even calculates the "grand sum" in the corner (cell F46 in the example) if this cell is part of the selection.

Using Solver

The Solver dialog box should be filled in as shown in Figure 14.29. Note that the decision variable cells include four separate named ranges. To enter these in the dialog box, drag the four ranges, keeping your finger on the Ctrl key. (Alternatively, you can drag a range, type a comma, drag a second range, type another comma, and so on.) As usual, you should also check the Non-Negative option and select the Simplex LP method before optimizing. *Press the command key on the Mac.*

Note that there are integer constraints on the numbers hired and fired. You could also constrain the numbers of shoes produced to be integers. However, integer constraints typically require longer solution times. Therefore, it is often best to omit such constraints, especially when the optimal values are fairly large, such as the production quantities in this model. If the solution then has noninteger values, you can usually round them to integers for a solution that is at least close to the optimal integer solution.

Discussion of the Solution

The optimal solution is given in Figure 14.28. Observe that SureStep should never hire any workers, and it should fire six workers in month 1, one worker in month 2, and 43 workers in month 3. Eighty hours of overtime are used, but only in month 2. The company produces over 3700 pairs of shoes during each of the first 2 months, 2000 pairs in month 3, and 1000 pairs in month 4. A total cost of $692,820 is incurred. The Solver solution will recommend overtime hours only when regular-time production capacity is exhausted. This is because overtime labor is more expensive.

Again, you would probably not force the number of pairs of shoes produced each month to be an integer. It makes little difference whether the company produces 3760 or 3761 pairs of shoes during a month, and forcing each month's shoe production to be an integer can greatly increase the time Solver needs to find an optimal solution. On the other hand, it is somewhat more important to ensure that the numbers of workers hired and fired each month are integers, given the relatively small numbers of workers involved.

Because integer constraints make a model more difficult to solve, use them sparingly—only when they are really needed.

Finally, if you want to ensure that Solver finds the optimal solution in a problem where some or all of the decision variable cells must be integers, you should go into Options (in the Solver dialog box) and make sure the Integer Optimality is set to zero. Otherwise, Solver might stop when it finds a solution that is only *close* to optimal.

Figure 14.29 Solver Dialog Box for Aggregate Planning Model

Sensitivity Analysis

There are many possible sensitivity analyses for this SureStep model. We illustrate one of them with SolverTable, where we see how the overtime hours used and the total cost vary with the overtime wage rate.[8] The results appear in Figure 14.30. When the wage rate is really low, the company uses considerably more overtime hours, whereas when it is sufficiently large, the company uses no overtime hours. It is not surprising that the company uses much more overtime when the overtime rate is $7 or $9 per hour. The *regular*-time wage rate is $9.375 per hour (= 1500/160). Of course, the company would never pay *less* per hour for overtime than for regular time.

The Rolling Planning Horizon Approach

In reality, an aggregate planning model is usually implemented via a rolling planning horizon. To illustrate, we assume that SureStep works with a four-month planning horizon. To implement the SureStep model in the rolling planning horizon context, we view the demands as forecasts and solve a four-month model with these forecasts. However, the company would implement only the month 1 production and work scheduling recommendation. Thus (assuming that the numbers of workers hired and fired in a month must be integers) the company would hire no workers, fire six workers, and produce 3760 pairs of shoes with regular-time labor in month 1. Next, the company would observe month 1's actual demand. Suppose it is 2950. Then SureStep would begin month 2 with 1310 (= 4260 − 2950) pairs of shoes and 94 workers. It would now enter 1310 in cell B4 and 94 in cell B5 (referring to Figure 14.28). Then it would replace the demands in the Demand range with the updated forecasts for the *next* four months. Finally, SureStep would rerun Solver and use the production levels and hiring and firing recommendations in column B as the production level and workforce policy for month 2.

The term "backlogging" means that the customer's demand is met at a later date. The term "back-ordering" means the same thing.

---

8 Solver's sensitivity report isn't even available here because of the integer constraints.

Figure 14.30 Sensitivity to Overtime Wage Rate

	A	B	C	D	E	F	G
1	Oneway analysis for Solver model in Model worksheet						
2							
3	Overtime rate (cell $B$11) values along side, output cell(s) along top						
4		Overtime_labor_hours_used_1	Overtime_labor_hours_used_2	Overtime_labor_hours_used_3	Overtime_labor_hours_used_4	Total_cost	
5	$7	1620	1660	0	0	$684,755	
6	$9	80	1760	0	0	$691,180	
7	$11	0	80	0	0	$692,660	
8	$13	0	80	0	0	$692,820	
9	$15	0	80	0	0	$692,980	
10	$17	0	80	0	0	$693,140	
11	$19	0	0	0	0	$693,220	
12	$21	0	0	0	0	$693,220	

Model with Backlogging Allowed

In many situations, backlogging of demand is allowed—that is, customer demand can be met at a later date. We now show how to modify the SureStep model to include the option of backlogging demand. We assume that at the end of each month a cost of $20 is incurred for each unit of demand that remains unsatisfied at the end of the month. This is easily modeled by allowing a month's ending inventory to be negative. For example, if month 1's ending inventory is −10, a shortage cost of $200 (and no inventory holding cost) is incurred. To ensure that SureStep produces any shoes at all, we constrain the ending inventory in month 4 to be nonnegative. This implies that all demand is *eventually* satisfied by the end of the four-month planning horizon. We now need to modify the monthly cost calculations to incorporate costs due to backlogging.

Developing the Aggregate Planning Backlogging Model

There are actually several modeling approaches to this backlogging problem. We show the most natural approach in Figure 14.31. (See the file **Aggregate Planning 2 Finished.xlsx**.) To begin, enter the per-unit monthly shortage cost in cell B15. (A new row was inserted for this cost input.) Note in row 38 how the ending inventory in months 1 through 3 can be positive (leftovers) or negative (shortages). You can account correctly for the resulting costs with IF functions in rows 46 and 47. For holding costs, enter the formula

$$=IF(B38>0,\$B\$14*B38,0)$$

in cell B46 and copy it across. For shortage costs, enter the formula

$$=IF(B38<0,-\$B\$15*B38,0)$$

in cell B47 and copy it across. (The minus sign makes this a *positive* cost.)

Figure 14.31 Nonlinear Aggregate Planning Model Using IF Functions

	A	B	C	D	E	F
37	Forecasted demand	3000	5000	2000	1000	
38	Ending inventory	1260	−20	−500	0	
39						
40	**Monetary outputs**	Month 1	Month 2	Month 3	Month 4	Totals
41	Hiring cost	$0	$0	$0	$0	$0
42	Firing cost	$12,000	$2,000	$110,000	$0	$124,000
43	Regular-time wages	$141,000	$139,500	$57,000	$57,000	$394,500
44	Overtime wages	$0	$0	$0	$0	$0
45	Raw material cost	$56,400	$55,800	$22,800	$22,500	$157,500
46	Holding cost	$3,780	$0	$0	$0	$3,780
47	Shortage cost	=IF(B38<0,−$B$15*B38,0)			$0	$10,400
48	Totals	IF(logical_test,[value_if_true], [value_if_false])			9,500	$690,180

Although these formulas calculate holding and shortage costs accurately, the IF functions make the objective cell a *nonlinear* function of the decision variable cells, and Solver's GRG nonlinear algorithm must be used, as indicated in Figure 14.32.[9] (How do you know the model is nonlinear? Although there is a mathematical reason, it is easier to try running Solver with the simplex algorithm. Solver will then *inform* you that the model is nonlinear.)

Figure 14.32 Solver Dialog Box for the GRG Nonlinear Algorithm

We ran Solver with this setup from a variety of initial solutions in the decision variable cells, and it always found the optimal solution. But we were lucky. When certain functions, including IF, MIN, MAX, and ABS, are used to relate the objective cell to the decision variable cells, the resulting model becomes not only nonlinear but *nonsmooth*. Essentially, nonsmooth functions can have sharp edges or discontinuities. Solver's GRG nonlinear algorithm can handle "smooth" nonlinearities, but it has trouble with nonsmooth functions. Sometimes it gets lucky, as it did here, and other times it finds a nonoptimal solution that is not even close to the optimal solution. For example, we changed the unit shortage cost from $20 to $40 and reran Solver. Starting from a solution where all decision variable cells contain zero, Solver stopped at a solution with total cost $726,360, even though the optimal solution has total cost $692,820. So we weren't so lucky this time.

The moral is that you should avoid these nonsmooth functions in optimization models if at all possible. If you *do* use them, as we have done here, you should run Solver several times, starting from different initial solutions. There is still no guarantee that you will get the optimal solution, but you will see more evidence of how Solver is progressing. (Alternatively, you can use the Evolutionary Solver, which became a part of Excel's Solver in Excel 2010. You can also use the Evolver add-in, part of Palisade's DecisionTools® Suite.)

9 GRG stands for generalized reduced gradient. This is a technical term for the mathematical algorithm used. The other algorithm available in Solver (starting with Excel 2010) is the Evolutionary algorithm. It can handle IF functions, but we will not discuss this algorithm here.

> **Solver Tip**
>
> **Nonsmooth Functions**
>
> There is nothing inherently wrong with using IF, MIN, MAX, ABS, and other nonsmooth functions in spreadsheet optimization models. The problem is that Solver's GRG nonlinear algorithm cannot handle these functions in a predictable manner.

There are sometimes alternatives to using IF, MIN, MAX, and ABS functions that make a model linear. Unfortunately, these alternatives are often far from intuitive, and we will not cover them here. (If you are interested, we have included the "linearized" version of the backlogging model in the file **Aggregate Planning 3 Finished.xlsx**.)

> **Fundamental Insight**
>
> **Nonsmooth Functions and Solver**
>
> Excel's Solver, as well as most other commercial optimization software packages, has trouble with nonsmooth nonlinear functions. These nonsmooth functions typically have sharp edges or discontinuities that make them difficult to handle in optimization models, and (in Excel) they typically contain functions such as IF, MAX, MIN, ABS, and a few others. There is nothing *wrong* with using such functions to implement complex logic in Excel optimization models. The problem is that Solver cannot handle models with these functions predictably. This is not really the fault of Solver. Such problems are inherently difficult.

Problems

Level A

30. Extend SureStep's original (no backlogging) aggregate planning model from four to six months. Try several different values for demands in months 5 and 6, and run Solver for each. Is your optimal solution for the *first* four months the same as the one in the example?

31. The current solution to SureStep's no-backlogging aggregate planning model does quite a lot of firing. Run a one-way SolverTable with the firing cost as the input variable and the numbers fired as the outputs. Let the firing cost increase from its current value to double that value in increments of $400. Do high firing costs eventually induce the company to fire fewer workers?

32. SureStep is currently getting 160 regular-time hours from each worker per month. This is actually calculated from 8 hours per day times 20 days per month. For this, they are paid $9.375 per hour (= 1500/160). Suppose workers can change their contract so that they have to work only 7.5 hours per day regular time—everything above this becomes overtime—and their regular-time wage rate increases to $10 per hour. They will still work 20 days per month. Does this change the optimal no-backlogging solution?

33. Suppose SureStep could begin a machinery upgrade and training program to increase its worker productivity. This program would result in the following values of labor hours per pair of shoes over the next four months: 4, 3.9, 3.8, and 3.8. How much would this new program be worth to SureStep, at least for this four-month planning horizon with no backlogging? How might you evaluate the program's worth *beyond* the next four months?

Level B

34. In the current no-backlogging problem, SureStep doesn't hire any workers, and it uses almost no overtime. This is evidently because of low demand. Change the demands to 6000, 8000, 5000, and 3000, and rerun Solver. Is there now any hiring and/or overtime? With this new demand pattern, explore the trade-off between hiring and overtime by running a two-way SolverTable. As inputs, use the hiring cost per worker and the maximum overtime hours allowed per worker per month, varied over reasonable ranges. As outputs, use the total number of workers hired over the four months and the total number of overtime hours used over the four months. Discuss the results.

35. In the SureStep no-backlogging problem, change the demands so that they become 6000, 8000, 5000, and 3000. Also, change the problem slightly so that newly hired workers take six hours to produce a pair of shoes during their first month of employment. After that, they take only four hours per pair of shoes. Modify the model appropriately, and use Solver to find the optimal solution.

36. You saw that the "natural" way to model SureStep's backlogging problem, with IF functions, leads to a non-smooth model that Solver has difficulty handling. There is another version of the problem that is also difficult for Solver. Suppose SureStep wants to meet all demands on time (no backlogging), but it wants to keep its employment level as constant over time as possible. To induce this, it charges a cost of $1000 each month on the absolute difference between the beginning number of workers and the number after hiring and firing—that is, the absolute difference between the values in rows 17 and 20 of the original spreadsheet model. Implement this extra cost in the model in the "natural" way, using the ABS function. Using demands of 6000, 8000, 5000, and 3000, see how well Solver does in solving this non-smooth model. Try several initial solutions, and see whether Solver gets the same optimal solution from each of them.

14-6 Financial Models

The majority of optimization examples described in management science textbooks are in the area of operations: scheduling, blending, logistics, aggregate planning, and others. This is probably warranted, because many of the most successful management science applications in the business world have been in these areas. However, optimization and other management science methods have also been applied successfully in a number of financial areas, and they deserve recognition. In this section, we begin the discussion with two typical applications of optimization in finance. The first involves investment strategy. The second involves pension fund management.

EXAMPLE

14.6 FINDING AN OPTIMAL INVESTMENT STRATEGY AT BARNEY-JONES

At the present time, the beginning of year 1, Barney-Jones Investment Corporation has $100,000 to invest for the next four years. There are five possible investments, labeled A through E. The timing of cash outflows and cash inflows for these investments is somewhat irregular. For example, to take part in investment A, cash must be invested at the beginning of year 1, and for every dollar invested, there are returns of $0.50 and $1.00 at the beginnings of years 2 and 3. Information for the other investments follows, where all returns are per dollar invested:[10]

- Investment B: Invest at the beginning of year 2, receive returns of $0.50 and $1.00 at the beginnings of years 3 and 4
- Investment C: Invest at the beginning of year 1, receive return of $1.20 at the beginning of year 2
- Investment D: Invest at the beginning of year 4, receive return of $1.90 at the beginning of year 5
- Investment E: Invest at the beginning of year 3, receive return of $1.50 at the beginning of year 4

We assume that any amounts can be invested in these strategies and that the returns are the same for each dollar invested. However, to create a diversified portfolio, Barney-Jones wants to limit the amount put into any investment to $75,000. The company wants an investment strategy that maximizes the amount of cash on hand at the beginning of year 5. At the beginning of any year, it can invest only cash on hand, which includes returns from previous investments. Any cash not invested in any year can be put in a short-term money market account that earns 3% annually.

---

10 You might criticize this model for assuming *known* returns in future years. If the returns are actually uncertain with given probability distributions, the RISKOptimizer tool in @RISK (part of Palisade's DecisionTools Suite) can be used to find the investment strategy that maximizes the *expected* return. However, we won't discuss this possibility here.

Objective

To develop an optimization model that relates investment decisions to total ending cash, and to use Solver to find the strategy that maximizes ending cash and invests no more than a given amount in any one investment.

Where Do the Numbers Come From?

There is no mystery here. We assume that the terms of each investment are spelled out, so that Barney-Jones knows exactly when money must be invested and what the amounts and timing of returns will be. Of course, this would not be the case for many real-world investments, such as money put into the stock market, where considerable uncertainty is involved. We consider one such example of investing with uncertainty when we study portfolio optimization in Section 14-8.

Solution

The variables and constraints for this investment model are shown in Figure 14.33. (See the file **Investing Big Picture.xlsx**.) On the surface, this problem appears to be very straightforward. You must decide how much to invest in the available invest-ments at the beginning of each year, using only the cash available. If you try modeling this problem without our help, however, we suspect that you will have some difficulty. It took us a few tries to get a model that is easy to read and generalizes to other similar investment problems. Note that the second constraint in the table can be expressed in two ways. It can be expressed as shown, where the cash on hand *after* investing is nonnegative, or it can be expressed as "cash invested in any year must be less than or equal to cash on hand at the beginning of that year." These are equivalent. The one you choose is a matter of taste.

There are often multiple equivalent ways to state a constraint. You can choose the one that is most natural for you.

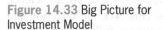
Figure 14.33 Big Picture for Investment Model

Developing the Spreadsheet Model

The spreadsheet model for this investment problem appears in Figure 14.34. (See the file **Investing Finished.xlsx**.) To set up this spreadsheet, proceed as follows.

Developing the Investment Model

1. **Inputs and range names.** As usual, enter the given inputs in the blue cells and name the ranges indicated. Pay particular attention to the two shaded tables. This is probably the first model you have encountered where model development is affected significantly by the way you enter the inputs, specifically, the information about the investments. We suggest separating cash outflows from cash inflows, as shown in the two ranges B11:F14 and B19:F23. The top table indicates when investments can be made, where a blank (equivalent to a 0) indicates no possible investment, and $1.00 indicates a dollar of investment. The bottom table then indicates the amounts and timing of returns per dollar invested.

The two input tables allow you to create copyable SUMPRODUCT formulas for cash outflows and inflows. Careful spreadsheet planning can often greatly simplify the necessary formulas.

Figure 14.34 Investment Model

	A	B	C	D	E	F	G	H	I	J
1	Investments with irregular timing of returns							Range names used		
2								Cash_after_investing	=Model!$E$32:$E$35	
3	Inputs							Dollars_invested	=Model!$B$26:$F$26	
4	Initial amount to invest	$100,000						Final_cash	=Model!$B$38	
5	Maximum per investment	$75,000						Maximum_per_investment	=Model!$B$28:$F$28	
6	Interest rate on cash	3%								
7										
8	Cash outlays on investments (all incurred at beginning of year)									
9		Investment								
10	Year	A	B	C	D	E				
11	1	$1.00		$1.00						
12	2		$1.00							
13	3					$1.00				
14	4				$1.00					
15										
16	Cash returns from investments (all incurred at beginning of year)									
17		Investment								
18	Year	A	B	C	D	E				
19	1									
20	2	$0.50		$1.20						
21	3	$1.00	$0.50							
22	4		$1.00			$1.50				
23	5				$1.90					
24										
25	Investment decisions									
26	Dollars invested	$64,286	$75,000	$35,714	$75,000	$75,000				
27		<=	<=	<=	<=	<=				
28	Maximum per investment	$75,000	$75,000	$75,000	$75,000	$75,000				
29										
30	Constraints on cash balance									
31	Year	Beginning cash	Returns from investments	Cash invested	Cash after investing					
32	1	$100,000	$0	$100,000	$0	>=	0			
33	2	$0	$75,000	$75,000	–$0	>=	0			
34	3	–$0	$101,786	$75,000	$26,786	>=	0			
35	4	$27,589	$187,500	$75,000	$140,089	>=	0			
36	5	$144,292	$142,500							
37										
38	Final cash	$286,792	←———	Objective to maximize: final cash at beginning of year 5						

2. **Investment amounts.** Enter *any* trial values in the Dollars_invested range. This range contains the decision variable cells. Also put a link to the maximum investment amount per investment by entering the formula

= $B$5

in cell B28 and copying it across.

3. **Cash balances and flows.** The key to the model is the section in rows 32 through 36. For each year, you need to calculate the beginning cash held from the previous year, the returns from investments that are due in that year, the investments made in that year, and cash balance after investments. Begin by entering the initial cash in cell B32 with the formula

= B4

Moving across, calculate the return due in year 1 in cell C32 with the formula

= SUMPRODUCT(B19:F19,Dollars_invested)

Admittedly, no returns come due in year 1, but this formula can be copied down column C for other years. Next, calculate the total amount invested in year 1 in cell D32 with the formula

= SUMPRODUCT(B11:F11,Dollars_invested)

Now find the cash balance after investing in year 1 in cell E32 with the formula

= B32 + C32-D32

The only other required formula is the formula for the cash available at the beginning of year 2. Because any cash not invested earns 3% interest, enter the formula

= E32*(1 + $B$6)

in cell B33. This formula, along with those in cells C32, D32, and E32, can now be copied down. (The zeros in column G are entered manually as a reminder of the nonnegativity constraint on cash after investing.)

4. Ending cash. The ending cash at the beginning of year 5 is the sum of the amount in the money market and any returns that come due in year 5. Calculate this sum with the formula

=SUM(B36:C36)

in cell B38. (*Note*: Here is the type of error to watch out for. We originally failed to calculate the return in cell C36 and mistakenly used the beginning cash in cell B36 as the objective cell. We realized our error when the optimal solution called for no money in investment D, which is clearly an attractive investment. The moral is that you can often catch errors by looking at the *plausibility* of the results.)

Always look at the Solver solution for signs of implausibility. This can often help you spot an error in your model.

Review of the Model

Take a careful look at this model and how it has been set up. There are undoubtedly alternative ways to model this problem, but the attractive feature of this model is the way the tables of inflows and outflows in rows 11 through 14 and 19 through 23 create *copyable* formulas for returns and investment amounts in columns C and D of rows 32 through 35. This same model setup, with only minor modifications, will work for *any* set of investments, regardless of the timing of investments and their returns. This is a quality you should strive for in your spreadsheet models: generalizability.

Using Solver

To find the optimal investment strategy, fill in the main Solver dialog box as shown in Figure 14.35. Note that the explicit nonnegativity constraint is necessary, even though the Non-Negative option is checked. Again, this is because the Non-Negative option covers only the decision variable cells. If you want other output cells to be nonnegative, you must constrain them explicitly.

Figure 14.35 Solver Dialog Box for Investment Model

Discussion of the Results

The optimal solution appears in Figure 14.34. Let's follow the cash. The company spends all its cash in year 1 on the two available investments, A and C ($64,286 in A, $35,714 in C). A total of $75,000 in returns from these investments is available in year 2, and it is all invested in investment B. At the beginning of year 3, a total of $101,786 is available from investment A and B returns, and $75,000 of this is invested in investment E. This leaves $26,786 for the money market, which grows to $27,589 at the beginning of year 4. In addition, returns totaling $187,500 from investments B and E come due in year 4. Of this total cash of $215,089, $75,000 is invested in investment D, and the rest, $140,089, is put in the money market. The return from investment D, $142,500, plus the money available from the money market, $144,292, equals the final cash in the objective cell, $286,792.

Sensitivity Analysis

A close look at the optimal solution in Figure 14.34 indicates that Barney-Jones is penalizing itself by imposing a maximum of $75,000 per investment. This upper limit is forcing the company to put cash into the money market fund, despite this fund's low rate of return. Therefore, a natural sensitivity analysis is to see how the optimal solution changes as this maximum value changes. You can perform this sensitivity analysis with a one-way SolverTable, shown in Figure 14.36.[11] The maximum in cell B5 is the input cell, varied from $75,000 to $225,000 in increments of $25,000, and the optimal decision variable cells and objective cell are outputs. As you can see, the final cash (column G) grows steadily as the maximum allowable investment amount increases. This is because the company can take greater advantage of the attractive investments and put less in the money market account.

Figure 14.36 Sensitivity of Optimal Solution to Maximum Investment Amount

	A	B	C	D	E	F	G
1	Oneway analysis for Solver model in Model worksheet						
3	Max per investment (cell $B$5) values along side, output cell(s) along top						
4		Dollars_invested_1	Dollars_invested_2	Dollars_invested_3	Dollars_invested_4	Dollars_invested_5	Final_cash
5	$75,000	$64,286	$75,000	$35,714	$75,000	$75,000	$286,792
6	$100,000	$61,538	$76,923	$38,462	$100,000	$100,000	$320,731
7	$125,000	$100,000	$50,000	$0	$125,000	$125,000	$353,375
8	$150,000	$100,000	$50,000	$0	$150,000	$125,000	$375,125
9	$175,000	$100,000	$50,000	$0	$175,000	$125,000	$396,875
10	$200,000	$100,000	$50,000	$0	$200,000	$125,000	$418,625
11	$225,000	$100,000	$50,000	$0	$225,000	$125,000	$440,375

You can go one step further with the two-way SolverTable in Figure 14.37. Now both the maximum investment amount and the money market rate are inputs, and the maximum amount ever put in the money market fund is the single output. Because this latter amount is not calculated in the spreadsheet model, you need to calculate it with the formula =MAX(Cash_after_investing) in an unused cell before using it as the output cell for SolverTable. In every case, even with a large maximum investment amount and a low money market rate, the company puts *some* money into the money market account. The reason is simple. Even when the maximum investment amount is $225,000, the company

To perform sensitivity on an output variable not calculated explicitly in your spreadsheet model, calculate it in some unused portion of the spreadsheet before running SolverTable.

11 Because Solver's sensitivity reports do not help answer our specific sensitivity questions in this example or the next example, we discuss only SolverTable results.

evidently has more cash than this to invest at some point (probably at the beginning of year 4). Therefore, it will have to put some of it in the money market.

Figure 14.37 Sensitivity of Maximum in Money Market to Two Inputs

◢	A	B	C	D	E	F	G	H	I
1	Twoway analysis for Solver model in Model worksheet								
2									
3	Interest on cash (cell $B$6) values along side, Max per investment (cell $B$5) values along top, output cell in corner								
4	Maximum_in_money_market	$75,000	$100,000	$125,000	$150,000	$175,000	$200,000	$225,000	
5	0.5%	$139,420	$126,923	$112,500	$87,500	$62,500	$37,500	$12,500	
6	1.0%	$139,554	$126,923	$112,500	$87,500	$62,500	$37,500	$12,500	
7	1.5%	$139,688	$126,923	$112,500	$87,500	$62,500	$37,500	$12,500	
8	2.0%	$139,821	$126,923	$112,500	$87,500	$62,500	$37,500	$12,500	
9	2.5%	$139,955	$126,923	$112,500	$87,500	$62,500	$37,500	$12,500	
10	3.0%	$140,089	$126,923	$112,500	$87,500	$62,500	$37,500	$12,500	
11	3.5%	$140,223	$126,923	$112,500	$87,500	$62,500	$37,500	$12,500	
12	4.0%	$140,357	$126,923	$112,500	$87,500	$62,500	$37,500	$12,500	
13	4.5%	$140,491	$126,923	$112,500	$87,500	$62,500	$37,500	$12,500	

The following example illustrates a common situation where fixed payments are due in the future and current funds must be allocated and invested so that their returns are sufficient to make the payments. We place this in a pension fund context.

EXAMPLE

14.7 MANAGING A PENSION FUND AT ARMCO

James Judson is the financial manager in charge of the company pension fund at Armco Incorporated. James knows that the fund must be sufficient to make the payments listed in Table 14.4. Each payment must be made on the first day of each year. James is going to finance these payments by purchasing bonds. It is currently the beginning of year 1, and three bonds are available for immediate purchase. The prices and coupons for the bonds are as follows. (All coupon payments arrive in time to meet the pension payments for the year in which they arrive.)

• Bond 1 costs $980 and yields a $60 coupon in years 2 through 5 and a $1060 payment on maturity in year 6.
• Bond 2 costs $970 and yields a $65 coupon in years 2 through 11 and a $1065 payment on maturity in year 12.
• Bond 3 costs $1050 and yields a $75 coupon in years 2 through 14 and a $1075 payment on maturity in year 15.

Table 14.4 Payments for Pension Example

Year	Payment	Year	Payment	Year	Payment
1	$11,000	6	$18,000	11	$25,000
2	$12,000	7	$20,000	12	$30,000
3	$14,000	8	$21,000	13	$31,000
4	$15,000	9	$22,000	14	$31,000
5	$16,000	10	$24,000	15	$31,000

James must decide how much cash to allocate (from company coffers) to meet the initial $11,000 payment and buy enough bonds to make future payments. He knows that any excess cash on hand can earn an annual rate of 4% in a fixed-rate account. How should he proceed?

Objective

To develop an optimization model that relates initial allocation of money and bond purchases to future cash availabilities, and to minimize the initialize allocation of money required to meet all future pension fund payments.

Where Do the Numbers Come From?

As in the previous financial example, the inputs are fairly easy to obtain. A pension fund has known liabilities that must be met in future years, and information on bonds and fixed-rate accounts is widely available.

Solution

The variables and constraints required for this pension fund model are shown in Figure 14.38. (See the file **Pension Fund Management Big Picture.xlsx**.) When modeling this problem, there is a new twist that involves the money James must allocate now for his funding problem. It is clear that he must decide how many bonds of each type to purchase now (note that no bonds are purchased in the *future*), but he must also decide how much money to allocate from company coffers. This allocated money has to cover the initial pension payment this year *and* the bond purchases. In addition, James wants to find the *minimum* allocation that will suffice. Therefore, this initial allocation serves two roles in the model. It is a decision variable *and* it is the objective to minimize. In terms of spreadsheet modeling, it is perfectly acceptable to make the objective cell one of the decision variable cells, and this is done here. You will not see this in many models—because the objective typically involves a linear combination of several decision variables—but it is occasionally the most natural way to proceed.

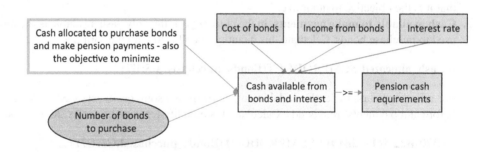

Figure 14.38 Big Picture for Pension Fund Management Model

Fundamental Insight

The Objective as a Decision Variable Cell

In all optimization models, the objective cell has to be a function of the decision variable cells, that is, the objective value should change as values in the decision variable cells change. It is perfectly consistent with this requirement to have the objective cell *be* one of the decision variable cells. This doesn't occur in very many optimization models, but it is sometimes useful, even necessary.

Developing the Spreadsheet Model

The completed spreadsheet model is shown in Figure 14.39. (See the file **Pension Fund Management Finished.xlsx**.) You can create it with the following steps.

1. **Inputs and range names.** Enter the given data and name the ranges as indicated. Note that the bond costs in the range B5:B7 have been entered as *positive* quantities. Some financial analysts might prefer that they be entered as negative numbers, indicating outflows. It doesn't really matter, however, as long as you are careful with the Excel formulas later on.
2. **Cash allocated and bonds purchased.** As discussed previously, the cash allocated in year 1 and the numbers of bonds purchased are both decision variables, so enter *any* values for these in the

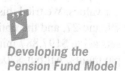

Developing the Pension Fund Model

Always document your spreadsheet conventions as clearly as possible.

Figure 14.39 Pension Fund Management Model

	A	B	C	D	E	F	G	H	I	J	K	L	M	N	O	P
1	Pension fund management															
2																
3	Costs (year 1) and income (in other years) from bonds															
4		Year 1	Year 2	Year 3	Year 4	Year 5	Year 6	Year 7	Year 8	Year 9	Year 10	Year 11	Year 12	Year 13	Year 14	Year 15
5	Bond 1	$980	$60	$60	$60	$60	$1,060									
6	Bond 2	$970	$65	$65	$65	$65	$65	$65	$65	$65	$65	$65	$1,065			
7	Bond 3	$1,050	$75	$75	$75	$75	$75	$75	$75	$75	$75	$75	$75	$75	$75	$1,075
8																
9	Interest rate	4.00%														
10																
11	Number of bonds (allowing fractional values) to purchase now															
12	Bond 1	73.69														
13	Bond 2	77.21														
14	Bond 3	28.84														
15																
16	Cash allocated	$197,768	←	Objective to minimize, also a decision variable cell												
17																
18	Constraints to meet payments															
19		Year 1	Year 2	Year 3	Year 4	Year 5	Year 6	Year 7	Year 8	Year 9	Year 10	Year 11	Year 12	Year 13	Year 14	Year 15
20	Cash available	$20,376	$21,354	$21,332	$19,228	$16,000	$85,298	$77,171	$66,639	$54,646	$41,133	$25,000	$84,390	$58,728	$31,000	$31,000
21		>=	>=	>=	>=	>=	>=	>=	>=	>=	>=	>=	>=	>=	>=	>=
22	Cash required	$11,000	$12,000	$14,000	$15,000	$16,000	$18,000	$20,000	$21,000	$22,000	$24,000	$25,000	$30,000	$31,000	$31,000	$31,000
23																
24	Range names used:															
25	Bonds_purchased	=Model!$B$12:$B$14														
26	Cash_allocated	=Model!$B$16														
27	Cash_available	=Model!$B$20:$P$20														
28	Cash_required	=Model!$B$22:$P$22														

The value in cell B16 is the money allocated to make the current payment and buy bonds now. It is both a decision variable cell and the objective cell to minimize.

Cash_allocated and Bonds_purchased ranges. Note that the color-coding convention for the Cash_allocated cell has to be modified. Because it is both a decision variable cell and the objective cell, we colored it red but added a note to emphasize that it is the objective to minimize.

3. **Cash available to make payments.** In the current year, the only cash available is the money initially allocated minus cash used to purchase bonds. Calculate this quantity in cell B20 with the formula

$$= \text{Cash\_allocated-SUMPRODUCT(Bonds\_purchased,B5:B7)}$$

For all other years, the cash available comes from two sources: excess cash invested at the fixed interest rate the year before and payments from bonds. Calculate this quantity for year 1 in cell C20 with the formula

$$= \text{(B20-B22)*(1 + \$B\$9) + SUMPRODUCT(Bonds\_purchased,C5:C7)}$$

and copy it across row 20 for the other years.

As you can see, this model is fairly straightforward to develop once you understand the role of the amount allocated in cell B16. However, we have often given this problem as an assignment to our students, and many fail to deal correctly with the amount allocated. (They usually forget to make it a decision variable cell.) So make sure you understand what we have done, and why we have done it this way.

Using Solver

The main Solver dialog box should be filled out as shown in Figure 14.40. Once again, notice that the Cash_allocated cell is both the objective cell and one of the decision variable cells.

Discussion of the Solution

The optimal solution appears in Figure 14.39. You might argue that the numbers of bonds purchased should be constrained to integer values. We tried this and the optimal solution changed very little: The optimal numbers of bonds to purchase changed to 74, 79, and 27, and the optimal money to allocate increased to $197,887. With this integer solution, shown in Figure 14.41, James sets aside $197,887 initially. Any less than this would not work—he couldn't make enough from bonds to meet future pension payments. All but $20,387 of this (see cell B20) is spent on bonds, and of the $20,387, $11,000 is used to make the current pension payment. After this, the amounts in row 20, which are always sufficient to make the payments in row 22, are composed of returns from bonds and cash, with interest, from the previous year. Even more so than in previous examples, there is no way to guess this optimal solution. The timing of bond returns and the irregular pension payments make a spreadsheet optimization model absolutely necessary.

Figure 14.40 Solver Dialog
Box for Pension Fund Model

Figure 14.41 Optimal Integer Solution for Pension Fund Model

	A	B	C	D	E	F	G	H	I	J	K	L	M	N	O	P
1	Pension fund management															
2																
3	Costs (year 1) and income (in other years) from bonds															
4	Year	Year 1	Year 2	Year 3	Year 4	Year 5	Year 6	Year 7	Year 8	Year 9	Year 10	Year 11	Year 12	Year 13	Year 14	Year 15
5	Bond 1	$980	$60	$60	$60	$60	$1,060									
6	Bond 2	$970	$65	$65	$65	$65	$65	$65	$65	$65	$65	$65	$1,065			
7	Bond 3	$1,050	$75	$75	$75	$75	$75	$75	$75	$75	$75	$75	$75	$75	$75	$1,075
8																
9	Interest rate	4.00%														
10																
11	Number of bonds (allowing fractional values) to purchase now															
12	Bond 1	74.00														
13	Bond 2	79.00														
14	Bond 3	27.00														
15																
16	Cash allocated	$197,887	←	Objective to minimize, also a decision variable cell												
17																
18	Constraints to meet payments															
19	Year	Year 1	Year 2	Year 3	Year 4	Year 5	Year 6	Year 7	Year 8	Year 9	Year 10	Year 11	Year 12	Year 13	Year 14	Year 15
20	Cash available	$20,387	$21,363	$21,337	$19,231	$16,000	$85,600	$77,464	$66,923	$54,919	$41,396	$25,252	$86,422	$60,704	$32,917	$31,019
21		>=	>=	>=	>=	>=	>=	>=	>=	>=	>=	>=	>=	>=	>=	>=
22	Cash required	$11,000	$12,000	$14,000	$15,000	$16,000	$18,000	$20,000	$21,000	$22,000	$24,000	$25,000	$30,000	$31,000	$31,000	$31,000

Sensitivity Analysis

Because the bond information and pension payments are fixed, there is only one obvious direction for sensitivity analysis: on the fixed interest rate in cell B9. We tried this, allowing this rate to vary from 2% to 6% in increments of 0.5% and keeping track of the optimal decision variable cells, including the objective cell. The results appear in Figure 14.42 (without the integer constraints). They indicate that as the interest rate increases, James can get by with fewer bonds of types 1 and 2, and he can allocate less money for the problem. The reason is that he is making more interest on excess cash.

Figure 14.42 Sensitivity to
Fixed Interest Rate

	A	B	C	D	E	F	G
1	Oneway analysis for Solver model in Model with Integers worksheet						
2							
3	Interest rate (cell $B$9) values along side, output cell(s) along top						
4		Bonds_purchased_1	Bonds_purchased_2	Bonds_purchased_3	Cash_allocated		
5	2.00%	77.00	80.00	28.00	$202,219		
6	2.40%	77.00	80.00	27.00	$201,372		
7	2.80%	76.00	80.00	27.00	$200,469		
8	3.20%	75.00	80.00	27.00	$199,605		
9	3.60%	75.00	79.00	27.00	$198,769		
10	4.00%	74.00	79.00	27.00	$197,887		
11	4.40%	73.00	79.00	27.00	$197,060		
12	4.80%	73.00	77.00	28.00	$196,208		
13	5.20%	72.00	77.00	28.00	$195,369		
14	5.60%	71.00	78.00	27.00	$194,574		
15	6.00%	71.00	76.00	28.00	$193,787		

Problems

Level A

37. Modify the Barney-Jones investment model so that there is a minimum amount that must be put into any investment, although this minimum can vary by investment. For example, the minimum amount for investment A might be $0, whereas the minimum amount for investment D might be $50,000. These minimum amounts should be inputs; you can make up any values you like. Run Solver on your modified model.

38. In the Barney-Jones investment model, increase the maximum amount allowed in any investment to $150,000. Then run a one-way sensitivity analysis to the money market rate on cash. Capture one output variable: the maximum amount of cash ever put in the money market account. You can choose any reasonable range for varying the money market rate.

39. We claimed that our model for Barney-Jones is generalizable. Try generalizing it to the case where there are two more potential investments, F and G. Investment F requires a cash outlay in year 2 and returns $0.50 in *each* of the next four years. Investment G requires a cash outlay in year 3 and returns $0.75 in each of years 5, 6, and 7. Modify the model as necessary, making the objective the final cash after year 7.

40. In our version of the Barney-Jones model, we ran investments across columns and years down rows. Some financial analysts prefer the opposite. Modify the spreadsheet model so that years go across columns and investments

go down rows. Run Solver to ensure that your modified model is correct. (We suggest two possible ways to do this, and you can experiment to see which you prefer. First, you could start over on a blank worksheet. Second, you could use Copy and then Paste Special with the Transpose option.)

41. In the Armco pension fund model, suppose there is a fourth bond, bond 4. Its unit cost in year 1 is $1020, it returns coupons of $70 in years 2 through 7 and a payment of $1070 in year 8. Modify the model to incorporate this extra bond, and reoptimize. Does the solution change—that is, should James purchase any of bond 4?

42. In the Armco pension fund model, suppose there is an upper limit of 60 on the number of bonds of any particular type that can be purchased. Modify the model to incorporate this extra constraint and then optimize. How much more money does James need to allocate initially?

43. In the Armco pension fund model, suppose James has been asked to see how the optimal solution will change if the required payments in years 8 through 15 all increase by the same percentage, where this percentage could be anywhere from 5% to 25%. Use an appropriate one-way SolverTable to help him out, and write a memo describing the results.

44. Our version of the Armco pension fund model is streamlined, perhaps too much. It does all of the calculations concerning cash flows in row 20. James decides he would like to break these out into several rows of calculations: Beginning cash (for year 1, this is the amount allocated; for other years, it is the unused cash, plus interest, from the previous year), Amount spent on bonds (positive in year 1 only),

Amount received from bonds (positive for years 2 through 15 only), Cash available for making pension fund payments, and, below the Pension payment row, Cash left over (amount invested in the fixed interest rate). Modify the model by inserting these rows, enter the appropriate formulas, and run Solver. You should obtain the same result, but you get more detailed information.

Level B

45. Suppose the investments in the Barney-Jones model sometimes require cash outlays in more than one year. For example, a $1 investment in investment B might require $0.25 to be spent in year 1 and $0.75 to be spent in year 2. Does the current model easily accommodate such investments? Try it with some cash outlay data you can make up, run Solver, and interpret your results.

46. In the Armco pension fund model, you know that if the amount of money allocated initially is *less* than

the amount found by Solver, James will not be able to meet all of the pension fund payments. Use the current model to demonstrate that this is true. To do so, enter a value less than the optimal value in cell B16. Then run Solver, but remove the Cash_allocated cell as a decision variable cell and as the objective cell. (If there is no objective cell, Solver simply tries to find a solution that satisfies all of the constraints.) What do you find?

47. Continuing the previous problem in a slightly different direction, continue to use the Cash_allocated cell as a decision variable cell, but add a constraint that it must be less than or equal to any value, such as $195,000, that is *less* than its current optimal value. With this constraint, James will again not be able to meet all of the pension fund payments. Create a new objective cell to minimize the total amount of payments not met. The easiest way to do this is with IF functions. Unfortunately, this makes the model nonsmooth, and Solver might have trouble finding the optimal solution. Try it and see.

14-7 Integer Optimization Models

In this section you will learn how to model some problems by using 0–1 variables (and possibly other integer variables) as decision variables. A **0–1 variable**, or **binary variable**, is a variable that must equal 0 or 1. Usually a 0–1 variable corresponds to an activity that is or is not undertaken. If the 0–1 variable corresponding to the activity equals 0, the activity is not undertaken; if it equals 1, the activity is undertaken.

Optimization models in which some or all of the variables must be integers are known as **integer programming (IP) models**. You have already seen examples of integer constraints in the discussion of scheduling employees, aggregate planning, and pension fund management. This section illustrates methods that are needed to formulate IP models of complex situations. You should be aware that Solver typically has a much harder time solving an IP problem than an LP problem. In fact, Solver is unable to solve some IP problems, even when they have an optimal solution. The reason is that these problems are inherently difficult, no matter which software package is used. However, as you will see in this section, your ability to model complex problems increases tremendously when you are able to use IP, particularly with 0–1 variables.

Fundamental Insight

Difficulty of Integer Programming Models

You might suspect that IP models would be *easier* to solve than LP models. After all, there are only a finite number of feasible integer solutions in an IP model, whereas there are infinitely many feasible (integer and noninteger) solutions in an LP model. However, exactly the opposite is true. IP models are *much* more difficult than LP models. All IP algorithms try to perform an efficient search through the typically huge number of feasible integer solutions. General-purpose algorithms such as branch and bound can be very effective for modest-size problems, but they can fail (or require extremely long computing times) on the large problems often faced in real applications. In such cases, analysts must develop special-purpose optimization algorithms, or perhaps even heuristics, to find "good," but not necessarily optimal, solutions.

14-7a Capital Budgeting Models

Perhaps the simplest types of IP models are **capital budgeting models**. Example 14.8 perfectly illustrates the go/no-go decisions inherent in many IP models.

EXAMPLE

14.8 CAPITAL BUDGETING AT TATHAM

The Tatham Company is considering seven investments. The cash required for each investment and the net present value (NPV) each investment adds to the firm are listed in Table 14.5. Each NPV is based on a stream of future revenues, and it includes the cash requirement, which is incurred right away. The table also lists the return of investment (ROI) for each investment, defined as the ratio of NPV to cash required, minus 1. The budget for investment is $15 million. Tatham wants to find the investment policy that maximizes its total NPV. The crucial assumption here is that if Tatham wants to take part in any of these investments, it must go all the way. It cannot, for example, go halfway in investment 1 by investing $2.5 million and realizing an NPV of $2.8 million. In fact, if partial investments were allowed, you wouldn't need IP; you could use LP.

Table 14.5 Data for the Capital Budgeting Example ($ millions)

Investment	Cash Required	NPV	ROI
1	$5.0	$5.6	12.0%
2	$2.4	$2.7	12.5%
3	$3.5	$3.9	11.4%
4	$5.9	$6.8	15.3%
5	$6.9	$7.7	11.6%
6	$4.5	$5.1	13.3%
7	$3.0	$3.3	10.0%

Objective

To use binary IP to find the set of investments that stays within budget and maximizes total NPV.

Where Do the Numbers Come From?

The initial required cash and the available budget are easy to obtain. Obtaining the NPV for each investment is more difficult. A time sequence of anticipated revenues from the investments and a discount factor are required. In any case, financial analysts should be able to estimate the required NPVs.

Solution

The variables and constraints required for this model appear in Figure 14.43. (See the file **Capital Budgeting Big Picture. xlsx**.) The most important part is that the decision variables must be binary, where a 1 means that an investment is chosen and a 0 means that it isn't. These variables cannot have fractional values such as 0.5, because partial investments are not allowed. When you set up the Solver dialog box, you must add explicit binary constraints in the Constraints section.

Figure 14.43 Big Picture for Capital Budgeting Model

Developing the Spreadsheet Model

To form the spreadsheet model, which is shown in Figure 14.44, proceed as follows. (See the file **Capital Budgeting Finished.xlsx**.)

Developing the Capital Budgeting Model

1. **Inputs.** Enter the initial cash requirements, the NPVs, and the budget in the blue ranges. The ROIs aren't absolutely required, but you can calculate them in row 7.
2. **0–1 values for investments.** Enter *any* trial 0–1 values for the investments in row 10. Actually, you can even enter fractional values such as 0.5 in these cells. Solver's binary constraints will eventually force them to be 0 or 1.
3. **Cash invested.** Calculate the total cash invested in cell B14 with the formula

A SUMPRODUCT formula, where one of the ranges has 0–1 values, just sums the values in the other range that correspond to the I's.

   =SUMPRODUCT(B5:H5,Decisions)

Figure 14.44 Capital Budgeting Model

▲	A	B	C	D	E	F	G	H	I	J	K	L
1	Capital budgeting model									Range names used		
2										Budget	=Model!$D$14	
3	Input data on potential investments ($ millions)									Decisions	=Model!$B$10:$H$10	
4	Investment	1	2	3	4	5	6	7		Total_cost	=Model!$B$14	
5	Cost	$5.0	$2.4	$3.5	$5.9	$6.9	$4.5	$3.0		Total_NPV	=Model!$B$17	
6	NPV	$5.6	$2.7	$3.9	$6.8	$7.7	$5.1	$3.3				
7	ROI	12.0%	12.5%	11.4%	15.3%	11.6%	13.3%	10.0%				
8												
9	Decisions: whether to invest											
10	1 if yes, 0 if no	0	0	1	0	1	1	0				
11												
12	Budget constraint											
13		Total cost		Budget								
14		$14.9	<=	$15								
15												
16	Objective to maximize											
17	Total NPV	$16.7										

Note that this formula sums the costs *only* for those investments with 0–1 variables equal to 1. To see this, think how the SUMPRODUCT function works when one of its ranges is a 0–1 range. It effectively sums the cells in the other range corresponding to the 1's.

4. **NPV contribution.** Calculate the NPV contributed by the investments in cell B17 with the formula

   =SUMPRODUCT(B6:H6,Decisions)

Again, this sums only the NPVs of the investments with 0–1 variables equal to 1.

Using Solver

The Solver dialog box appears in Figure 14.45. The objective is to maximize the total NPV while staying within the budget. However, the decision variable cells must be *constrained* to be 0–1. Solver makes this simple, as shown in Figure 14.46. You add a constraint with the decision variable cells in the left box and choose the *bin* option in the middle box. The word "binary" in the right box is then added automatically. Note that if *all* decision variable cells are binary, the Non-Negative option is optional (because 0 and 1 are certainly nonnegative), but you should still choose the Simplex LP method if the model is linear, as it is here.[12] Finally, in the Solver Options dialog box, you should make sure the Ignore Integer Constraints option is *not* checked.

Solver makes it easy to specify binary constraints, by choosing the bin option.

Discussion of the Solution

The optimal solution in Figure 14.44 indicates that Tatham can obtain a maximum NPV of $16.7 million by selecting investments 3, 5, and 6. These three investments consume only $14.9 million of the available budget, with $100,000 left over. However, this $100,000 is not nearly enough—because of the "investing all the way" requirement—to invest in any of the remaining investments.

---

12 All the models in this section satisfy two of the three properties of linear models in Chapter 13: proportionality and additivity. Even though they clearly violate the third assumption, divisibility, which precludes integer constraints, they are still considered linear by Solver. Therefore, you should still choose the Simplex LP method.

Figure 14.45 Solver Dialog
Box for Capital Budgeting Model

Figure 14.46 Specifying a
Binary Constraint

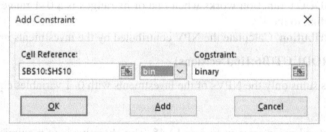

If Tatham's investments are ranked on the basis of ROI (see row 7 of Figure 14.44), the ranking from best to worst is 4, 6, 2, 5, 1, 3, 7. Using your economic intuition, you might expect the investments to be chosen in this order—until the budget runs out. However, the optimal solution does not do this. It selects the second-, fourth-, and sixth-best investments, and it ignores the best. To understand why it does this, imagine investing in the order from best to worst, according to row 7, until the budget allows no more. By the time you have chosen investments 4, 6, and 2, you will have consumed $12.8 million of the budget, and the remainder, $2.2 million, is not sufficient to invest in any of the rest. This strategy provides an NPV of only $14.6 million. A smarter strategy, the optimal solution from Solver, gains you an extra $2.1 million in NPV.

Sensitivity Analysis

SolverTable can be used on models with binary variables exactly as you have used it in previous models.[13] Here you can use it to see how the total NPV varies as the budget increases. Select the Budget cell as the single input cell, allow it to vary from $15 million to $25 million in increments of $1 million, and keep track of the total investment cost, the total NPV, and the binary variables. The results are shown in Figure 14.47. Clearly, Tatham can achieve a larger NPV with a larger budget, but as the

---

Figure 14.47 Sensitivity to Budget

	A	B	C	D	E	F	G	H	I	J	K
1	Oneway analysis for Solver model in Model worksheet										
2											
3	Budget (cell $D$14) values along side, output cell(s) along top										
4		Decisions_1	Decisions_2	Decisions_3	Decisions_4	Decisions_5	Decisions_6	Decisions_7	Total_cost	Total_NPV	Increase in NPV
5	$15	0	0	1	0	1	1	0	$14.9	$16.7	
6	$16	1	0	1	0	0	1	1	$16.0	$17.9	$1.2
7	$17	0	0	1	1	0	1	1	$16.9	$19.1	$1.2
8	$18	1	1	0	1	0	1	0	$17.8	$20.2	$1.1
9	$19	1	0	1	1	0	1	0	$18.9	$21.4	$1.2
10	$20	1	1	1	1	0	0	1	$19.8	$22.3	$0.9
11	$21	1	1	0	1	0	1	1	$20.8	$23.5	$1.2
12	$22	1	0	1	1	0	1	1	$21.9	$24.7	$1.2
13	$23	1	0	1	0	1	1	1	$22.9	$25.6	$0.9
14	$24	0	0	1	1	1	1	1	$23.8	$26.8	$1.2
15	$25	1	1	0	1	1	1	0	$24.7	$27.9	$1.1

increases in column K indicate, each extra $1 million of budget does *not* have the same effect on total NPV. Note also how the selected investments vary as the budget increases. This somewhat strange behavior is due to the "lumpiness" of the inputs and the all-or-nothing nature of the problem.

Effect of Solver Integer Optimality Setting

To illustrate the effect of the Solver Integer Optimality setting, compare the SolverTable results in Figure 14.48 with those in Figure 14.47. Each is for the Tatham capital budgeting model, but Figure 14.48 uses Solver's (old) default setting of 5%, whereas Figure 14.47 uses a setting of 0%. The four shaded cells in Figure 14.48 indicate *lower* total NPVs than the corresponding cells in Figure 14.47. In these three cases, Solver stopped short of finding the true optimal solutions because it found solutions within the 5% of the optimal objective value and then quit.

When the Integer Optimality setting is 5% instead of 0%, Solver's solution might not be optimal, but it will be close.

Figure 14.48 Results with Integer Optimality at 5%

	A	B	C	D	E	F	G	H	I	J
1	Oneway analysis for Solver model in Model worksheet									
2										
3	Budget (cell $D$14) values along side, output cell(s) along top									
4		Decisions_1	Decisions_2	Decisions_3	Decisions_4	Decisions_5	Decisions_6	Decisions_7	Total_cost	Total_NPV
5	$15	0	0	1	0	1	1	0	$14.9	$16.7
6	$16	0	1	0	1	0	1	1	$15.8	$17.9
7	$17	0	1	1	1	0	1	0	$16.3	$18.5
8	$18	1	1	0	1	0	1	0	$17.8	$20.2
9	$19	1	0	1	1	0	1	0	$18.9	$21.4
10	$20	0	1	1	1	0	1	1	$19.3	$21.8
11	$21	1	1	0	1	0	1	1	$20.8	$23.5
12	$22	1	1	1	1	0	1	0	$21.3	$24.1
13	$23	0	1	0	1	1	1	1	$22.7	$25.6
14	$24	0	1	1	1	1	1	0	$23.2	$26.2
15	$25	1	1	0	1	1	1	0	$24.7	$27.9

Modeling Issues

- Capital budgeting models with cash requirements in multiple time periods can also be handled. Figure 14.49 shows one possibility. (See the **Capital Budgeting Multiple Period Finished.xlsx** file.) The costs in rows 5 and 6 are *both* incurred if any given investment is selected. Now there are two budget constraints, one in each year, but otherwise the model is exactly as before. Note that some investments can have a zero cost in year 1 and a positive cost in year 2. This effectively means that these investments are undertaken in year 2 rather than year 1. Also, it is easy to modify the model to incorporate costs in years 3, 4, and so on.

Figure 14.49 Two-Period Capital Budgeting Model

	A	B	C	D	E	F	G	H
1	Capital budgeting model with costs in multiple periods							
2								
3	Input data on potential investments ($ millions)							
4	Investment	1	2	3	4	5	6	7
5	Year 1 cost	$4.0	$2.0	$1.0	$3.0	$3.9	$1.5	$0.0
6	Year 2 cost	$1.0	$0.4	$2.5	$2.9	$3.0	$3.0	$3.0
7	NPV	$5.6	$2.7	$3.9	$6.8	$7.7	$5.1	$3.3
8	ROI	12.0%	12.5%	11.4%	15.3%	11.6%	13.3%	10.0%
9								
10	Decisions: whether to invest							
11	1 if yes, 0 if no	1	1	0	1	0	0	0
12								
13	Budget constraint							
14		Total cost		Budget				
15	Year 1	$9.0	<=	$9				
16	Year 2	$4.3	<=	$6				
17								
18	Objective to maximize							
19	Total NPV	$15.1						

- If Tatham could choose a *fractional* amount of an investment, you could maximize its NPV by deleting the binary constraint. The optimal solution to the resulting LP model has a total NPV of $17.064 million. All of investments 2, 4, and 6, and 44% of investment 1 are chosen.[14] However, there is no way to round the decision variable cell values from this LP solution to obtain the optimal IP solution. Sometimes the solution to an IP model *without* the integer constraints bears little resemblance to the optimal IP solution.
- Any IP model involving 0–1 variables with only one constraint is called a **knapsack problem.** Think of the problem faced by a hiker going on an overnight hike. For example, suppose that the hiker's knapsack can hold only 35 pounds, and she must choose which of several available items to take on the hike. The benefit derived from each item is analogous to the NPV of each project, and the weight of each item is analogous to the cash required by each investment. The single constraint is analogous to the budget constraint—that is, only 35 pounds can fit in the knapsack. In a knapsack problem, the goal is to get the most value in the knapsack without overloading it.

14-7b Fixed-Cost Models

Fixed-cost models are used when a fixed cost is incurred if an activity is undertaken at *any positive* level. This cost is independent of the level of the activity and is known as a **fixed cost** (or fixed charge). Here are three examples of fixed costs:

- Construction of a warehouse incurs a fixed cost that is the same whether the warehouse is used at partial or full capacity.
- A cash withdrawal from a bank incurs a fixed cost, independent of the size of the withdrawal.
- A machine that is used to make several products must be set up for the production of each product. Regardless of the number of units of a product the company produces, the same fixed cost (lost production due to the setup time) is incurred.

In these examples a fixed cost is incurred if an activity is undertaken at any positive level, and zero fixed cost is incurred if the activity is not undertaken at all. Although it might

14 If you try this with the **Capital Budgeting.xlsx** file, delete the binary constraint, but don't forget to constrain the decision variables to be nonnegative and less than or equal to 1.

not be obvious, this feature makes the problem inherently *nonlinear,* which means that a straightforward application of LP is not possible. However, Example 14.9 illustrates how a clever use of binary variables results in a *linear* model.

> ## Fundamental Insight
>
> ### Binary Variables for Modeling
>
> Binary variables are often used to transform a non-linear model into a linear (integer) model. For example, a fixed cost is not a linear function of the level of some activity; it is either incurred or it isn't incurred. This type of all-or-nothing behavior is difficult for nonlinear algorithms to handle. However, this behavior can often be handled easily by using binary variables to make the model linear. Still, large models with many binary variables can be difficult to solve. One approach is to solve the model without integer constraints and then round fractional values to the nearest integer (0 or 1). Unfortunately, this approach is typically not very good because the rounded solution is often infeasible. Even if it is feasible, its objective value can be considerably worse than the *optimal* objective value.

EXAMPLE

14.9 TEXTILE MANUFACTURING AT GREAT THREADS

Great Threads Company is capable of manufacturing shirts, shorts, pants, skirts, and jackets. Each type of clothing requires Great Threads to acquire the appropriate type of machinery. The machinery needed to manufacture each type of clothing must be rented at the weekly rates shown in Table 14.6. This table also lists the amounts of cloth and labor required per unit of clothing, as well as the selling price and the unit variable cost for each type of clothing. There are 4000 labor hours and 4500 square yards (sq yd) of cloth available in a given week. The company wants to find a solution that maximizes its weekly profit.

Table 14.6 Data for Great Threads Example

	Rental Cost	Labor Hours	Cloth (sq yd)	Selling Price	Unit Variable Cost
Shirts	$1500	2.0	3.0	$35	$20
Shorts	$1200	1.0	2.5	$40	$10
Pants	$1600	6.0	4.0	$65	$25
Skirts	$1500	4.0	4.5	$70	$30
Jackets	$1600	8.0	5.5	$110	$35

Objective

To develop a linear model with binary variables that can be used to maximize the company's profit, correctly accounting for fixed costs and staying within resource availabilities.

Where Do the Numbers Come From?

Except for the fixed costs, this is the same basic problem as the product mix problem (Examples 13.1 and 13.2) in the previous chapter. Therefore, the same discussion there about input variables applies here. As for the fixed costs, they are the given rental rates for the machinery.

Solution

The variables and constraints required for this model are shown in Figure 14.50. (See the file **Fixed Cost Manufacturing Big Picture.xlsx**.) Note that the cost of producing x shirts during a week is 0 if $x = 0$, but it is $1500 + 20x$ if $x > 0$. This cost structure violates the proportionality assumption (discussed in the previous chapter) that is needed for a linear model.

If proportionality were satisfied, the cost of making, say, 10 shirts would be double the cost of making five shirts. However, because of the fixed cost, the total cost of making five shirts is $1600, and the cost of making 10 shirts is only $1700. This violation of proportionality requires you to use binary variables to obtain a *linear* model.

Figure 14.50 Big Picture for Fixed-Cost Manufacturing Model

Developing the Spreadsheet Model

The spreadsheet model, shown in Figure 14.51, can now be developed as follows. (See the file **Fixed Cost Manufacturing Finished.xlsx**.)

Developing the Fixed-Cost Manufacturing Model

Figure 14.51 Fixed-Cost Manufacturing Model

	A	B	C	D	E	F	G	H	I	J	K
1	**Great Threads fixed cost clothing model**								**Range names used:**		
2									Effective_capacity	=Model!$B$18:$F$18	
3	**Input data on products**								Rent_equipment	=Model!$B$14:$F$14	
4		Shirts	Shorts	Pants	Skirts	Jackets			Profit	=Model!$B$29	
5	Labor hours/unit	2	1	6	4	8			Resource_available	=Model!$D$22:$D$23	
6	Cloth (sq. yd.)/unit	3	2.5	4	4.5	5.5			Resource_used	=Model!$B$22:$B$23	
7									Units_produced	=Model!$B$16:$F$16	
8	Selling price/unit	$35	$40	$65	$70	$110					
9	Variable cost/unit	$20	$10	$25	$30	$35					
10	Fixed cost for equipment	$1,500	$1,200	$1,600	$1,500	$1,600					
11											
12	**Production plan, constraints on capacity**										
13		Shirts	Shorts	Pants	Skirts	Jackets					
14	Rent equipment	0	1	0	0	1					
15											
16	Units produced	0	965.52	0	0	379.31					
17		<=	<=	<=	<=	<=					
18	Effective capacity	0.00	1800.00	0.00	0.00	500.00					
19											
20	**Constraints on resources**										
21		Resource used		Available							
22	Labor hours	4000.00	<=	4000							
23	Cloth	4500.00	<=	4500							
24											
25	**Monetary outputs**										
26	Revenue	$80,345									
27	Variable cost	$22,931									
28	Fixed cost for equipment	$2,800									
29	Profit	$54,614	←	**Objective to maximize**							

1. **Inputs.** Enter the given inputs.
2. **Binary values for clothing types.** Enter *any* trial values for the binary variables for the various clothing types in the Rent_equipment range. For example, a 1 in cell C14 implies that the machinery for making shorts is rented and its fixed cost is incurred.
3. **Production quantities.** Enter *any* trial values for the numbers of the various clothing types produced in the Units_produced range. At this point you could enter "illegal" values, such as 0 in cell B14 and a positive value in cell B16. This is illegal because it implies that the company produces some shirts but doesn't incur the fixed cost of the machinery for shirts. However, Solver will eventually disallow such illegal combinations.
4. **Labor and cloth used.** In cell B22 enter the formula

   =SUMPRODUCT(B5:F5,Units_produced)

   to calculate total labor hours, and copy this to cell B23 for cloth.
5. **Effective capacities.** Here is the tricky part of the model. You need to ensure that if any of a given type of clothing is produced, then its binary variable equals 1. This ensures that the model incurs the fixed cost of renting the machine for this type of clothing. You could easily implement these constraints with IF statements. For example, to implement the constraint for shirts, you could enter the following formula in cell B14:

   =IF(B16>0,1,0)

   However, Solver is unable to deal with IF functions predictably. Therefore, the fixed-cost constraints are modeled in a different way, as follows:

$$\text{Shirts produced} \le \text{Maximum capacity} \times (\text{0–1 variable for shirts}) \qquad \textbf{(14.4)}$$

   There are similar inequalities for the other types of clothing.

   Here is the logic behind Inequality (14.4). If the 0–1 variable for shirts is 0, the right side of the inequality is 0, which means that the left side must be 0—no shirts can be produced. That is, if the binary variable for shirts is 0, so that no fixed cost for shirts is incurred, then Inequality (14.4) does not allow Great Threads to "cheat" and produce a positive number of shirts. On the other hand, if the binary variable for shirts is 1, the inequality is certainly true and is essentially redundant. It simply states that the number of shirts produced must be no greater than the *maximum* number that could be produced. Inequality (14.4) rules out the one case that needs to be ruled out—namely, that Great Threads produces shirts but avoids the fixed cost.

   To implement Inequality (14.4), a maximum capacity is required. To obtain this, suppose the company puts all of its resources into producing shirts. Then the number of shirts that can be produced is limited by the smaller of

$$\frac{\text{Available labor hours}}{\text{Labor hours per shirt}}$$

   and

$$\frac{\text{Available square yards of cloth}}{\text{Square yards of cloth per shirt}}$$

   Therefore, the smaller of these—the most limiting—can be used as the maximum needed in Inequality (14.4). To implement this logic, calculate the effective capacity for shirts in cell B18 with the formula

   =B14*MIN($D$22/B5,$D$23/B6)

   Then copy this formula to the range C16:F16 for the other types of clothing.[15] By the way, this MIN formula causes no problems for Solver because it does not involve *decision variable* cells, only input cells.
6. **Monetary values.** Calculate the total sales revenue and the total variable cost by entering the formula

   =SUMPRODUCT(B8:F8, Units_produced)

   in cell B26 and copying it to cell B27. Then calculate the total fixed cost in cell B28 with the formula

   =SUMPRODUCT(B10:F10, Rent_equipment)

   This formula sums the fixed costs only for those products with binary variables equal to 1. Finally, calculate the total profit in cell B29 with the formula

   =B26-B27-B28

---

15 Why not set the upper limit on shirts equal to a huge number like 1,000,000? The reason is that Solver works most efficiently when the upper limit is as tight—that is, as low—as possible. A tighter upper limit means fewer potential feasible solutions for Solver to search through.

Using Solver

The Solver dialog box is shown in Figure 14.52. The goal is to maximize profit, subject to using no more labor hours or cloth than are available, and ensure that production is less than or equal to *effective* capacity. The key is that this effective capacity is zero if none of a given type of clothing is produced. As usual, check the Non-Negative option, and set the Integer Optimality to zero (under the Options button). By the clever use of binary decision variables, the resulting model is *linear*, which means that the simplex algorithm can be used.

Figure 14.52 Solver Dialog Box for Fixed-Cost Model

Although Solver finds the optimal solution automatically, you should understand the effect of the logical upper-bound constraint on production. It rules out a solution such as the one shown in Figure 14.53. This solution calls for a positive production level of pants but does not incur the fixed cost of the pants equipment. The logical upper-bound constraint rules this out because it prevents a positive value in row 16 if the corresponding binary value in row 14 is 0. In other words, if the company wants to produce some pants, the constraint in Inequality (14.4) forces the associated binary variable to be 1, thus incurring the fixed cost for pants.

Inequality (14.4) does *not* rule out the situation you see for skirts, where the binary value is 1 and the production level is 0. However, Solver will never choose this type of solution as optimal. Solver recognizes that the binary value in this case can be changed to 0, so that the fixed cost for skirt equipment is not incurred.

Discussion of the Solution

The optimal solution appears in Figure 14.51. It indicates that Great Threads should produce about 966 shorts and 379 jackets, but no shirts, pants, or skirts. The total profit is $54,614. The binary variables for shirts, pants, and skirts are all 0, which forces production of these products to be 0. However, the binary variables for shorts and jackets, the products that are produced, are 1. This ensures that the fixed cost of producing shorts and jackets is included in the total cost.

Figure 14.53 An Illegal (and Nonoptimal) Solution

	A	B	C	D	E	F
1	Great Threads fixed cost clothing model					
2						
3	Input data on products					
4		Shirts	Shorts	Pants	Skirts	Jackets
5	Labor hours/unit	2	1	6	4	8
6	Cloth (sq. yd.)/unit	3	2.5	4	4.5	5.5
7						
8	Selling price/unit	$35	$40	$65	$70	$110
9	Variable cost/unit	$20	$10	$25	$30	$35
10	Fixed cost for equipment	$1,500	$1,200	$1,600	$1,500	$1,600
11						
12	Production plan, constraints on capacity					
13		Shirts	Shorts	Pants	Skirts	Jackets
14	Rent equipment	0	1	0	1	1
15						
16	Units produced	0	500.00	450.00	0	100.00
17		<=	<=	<=	<=	<=
18	Effective capacity	0.00	1800.00	0.00	1000.00	500.00
19						
20	Constraints on resources					
21		Resource used		Available		
22	Labor hours	4000.00	<=	4000		
23	Cloth	3600.00	<=	4500		
24						
25	Monetary outputs					
26	Revenue	$60,250				
27	Variable cost	$19,750				
28	Fixed cost for equipment	$4,300				
29	Profit	$36,200	←	Objective to maximize		

It might be helpful to think of this solution as occurring in two stages. In the first stage Solver determines which products to produce—in this case, shorts and jackets only. Then in the second stage, Solver decides how *many* shorts and jackets to produce. If you knew that the company plans to produce shorts and jackets only, you could then ignore the fixed costs and determine the best production quantities with the same types of product mix models discussed in the previous chapter. However, these two stages—deciding which products to produce and how many of each to produce—are interrelated, and Solver considers both of them in its solution process.

The Great Threads management might not be very excited about producing shorts and jackets only. Suppose the company wants to ensure that at least three types of clothing are produced at positive levels. One approach is to add another constraint—namely, that the sum of the binary values in row 14 is greater than or equal to 3. You can check, however, that when this constraint is added and Solver is rerun, the binary variable for skirts becomes 1,
As always, adding constraints can only make the objective worse. In this case, it means decreased profit.

but no skirts are produced. Shorts and jackets are more profitable than skirts, so only shorts and jackets are produced. (See Figure 14.54.) The new constraint forces Great Threads to rent an extra piece of machinery (for skirts), but it doesn't force the company to use it. To force the company to produce some skirts, you would also need to add a constraint on the value in E16, such as E16 > = 100. Any of these additional constraints will cost Great Threads money, but if, as a matter of policy, the company wants to produce more than two types of clothing, this is its only option.

Sensitivity Analysis
Because the optimal solution currently calls for only shorts and jackets to be produced, an interesting sensitivity analysis is to see how much incentive is required for other products to be produced. One way to model this is to increase the selling price for a non-produced product such as skirts in a one-way SolverTable. The results of this, keeping track of all binary variables and profit, are shown in Figure 14.55. When the selling price for skirts is $85 or less, the company continues to produce only shorts and jackets. However, when the selling price is $90 or greater, the company stops producing shorts and jackets and produces *only* skirts. You can check that the optimal production quantity of skirts is 1000 when the selling price of skirts is any value $90 or above. The only reason that the profits in Figure 14.55 increase from row 9 down is that the revenues from these 1000 skirts increase.

A Model with IF Functions
In case you are still not convinced that the binary variable approach is required, and you think IF functions could be used instead, take a look at the last sheet in the finished version of the file. The resulting model *looks* the same as in Figure 14.51, but it incorporates the following changes:

- The binary range is no longer part of the decision variable cells range. Instead, the formula =IF(B16>0,1,0) is entered in cell B14 and copied across to cell F14. Logically, this probably appears more natural. If a production quantity is positive, a 1 is entered in row 14, which means that the fixed cost is incurred.

Figure 14.54 Fixed-Cost Model with Extra Constraint

	A	B	C	D	E	F	G	H	I
1	Great Threads fixed cost clothing model								
2									
3	Input data on products								
4		Shirts	Shorts	Pants	Skirts	Jackets			
5	Labor hours/unit	2	1	6	4	8			
6	Cloth (sq. yd.)/unit	3	2.5	4	4.5	5.5			
7									
8	Selling price/unit	$35	$40	$65	$70	$110			
9	Variable cost/unit	$20	$10	$25	$30	$35			
10	Fixed cost for equipment	$1,500	$1,200	$1,600	$1,500	$1,600			
11									
12	Production plan, constraints on capacity								
13		Shirts	Shorts	Pants	Skirts	Jackets	Sum		Required
14	Rent equipment	0	1	0	1	1	3	>=	3
15									
16	Units produced	0	965.52	0	0	379.31			
17		<=	<=	<=	<=	<=			
18	Effective capacity	0.00	1800.00	0.00	1000.00	500.00			
19									
20	Constraints on resources								
21		Resource used		Available					
22	Labor hours	4000.00	<=	4000					
23	Cloth	4500.00	<=	4500					
24									
25	Monetary outputs								
26	Revenue	$80,345							
27	Variable cost	$22,931							
28	Fixed cost for equipment	$4,300							
29	Profit	$53,114	←	Objective to maximize					

Figure 14.55 Sensitivity of Binary Variables to Selling Price of Skirts

	A	B	C	D	E	F	G
1	Oneway analysis for Solver model in Model worksheet						
2							
3	Selling price skirts (cell $E$8) values along side, output cell(s) along top						
4		Rent_equipment_1	Rent_equipment_2	Rent_equipment_3	Rent_equipment_4	Rent_equipment_5	Profit
5	$70	0	1	0	0	1	$54,614
6	$75	0	1	0	0	1	$54,614
7	$80	0	1	0	0	1	$54,614
8	$85	0	1	0	0	1	$54,614
9	$90	0	0	0	1	0	$58,500
10	$95	0	0	0	1	0	$63,500
11	$100	0	0	0	1	0	$68,500

- The effective capacities are calculated in row 18 with IF functions. Specifically, the formula =IF(B16>0,MIN($D$22/B5,$D$23/B6),0) is entered in cell B18 and copied across to cell F18.
- The Solver dialog box is modified as shown in Figure 14.56. The Rent_equipment range is not part of the decision variable cells range, and there is no binary constraint. However, the simplex method cannot be used because the IF functions make the model nonlinear.

When we ran Solver on this modified model, we found inconsistent results, depending on the initial production quantities entered in row 16. For example, when we entered initial values all equal to 0, the Solver solution was exactly that—all 0's. Of course, this solution is *terrible* because it leads to a profit of $0. However, when we entered initial production quantities all equal to 100, Solver found the correct optimal solution, the same as in Figure 14.51. Was this just lucky? To check, we tried another initial solution, where the production quantities for shorts and jackets were 0, and the production quantities for shirts, pants, and skirts were all 500. In this case Solver found a solution where only skirts are produced. Of course, we know this is not optimal.

Figure 14.56 Solver Dialog
Box When IF Functions Are Used

Figure 14.56 Solver Dialog
Box When IF Functions Are Used

Actually, the problem with using the GRG Nonlinear method indicated in Figure 14.56 is that this model is "nonsmooth," and the GRG Nonlinear method doesn't work well on nonsmooth models. Starting in Excel 2010, there is another option—the Evolutionary method. This method works well on nonsmooth models, but it guarantees only an approximately optimal solution, and it is relatively slow. It is not discussed further in this book.

In any case, the IF-function approach is not the way to go. Its success depends on the initial values in the decision variable cells, and this requires good (or lucky) guesses. The binary approach ensures that Solver finds the correct solution.

14-7c Set-Covering Models

In a **set-covering model**, each member of a given set (set 1) must be "covered" by an acceptable member of another set (set 2). The objective in a set-covering problem is to minimize the number of members in set 2 necessary to cover all the members in set 1. For example, set 1 might consist of all the cities in a county and set 2 might consist of the cities in which a fire station is located. A member of set 2 covers, or handles the needs of, a city in set 1 if the fire station is located within, say, 10 minutes of the city. The goal is to minimize the number of fire stations needed to cover all cities. Set-covering models have been applied to areas as diverse as airline crew scheduling, truck dispatching, political redistricting, and capital investment. The following example illustrates a typical set-covering model.

EXAMPLE

14.10 HUB LOCATION AT WESTERN AIRLINES

Western Airlines has decided that it wants to design a hub system in the United States. Each hub is used for connecting flights to and from cities within 1000 miles of the hub. Western runs flights among the following cities: Atlanta, Boston, Chicago, Denver, Houston, Los Angeles, New Orleans, New York, Pittsburgh, Salt Lake City, San Francisco, and Seattle. The company wants to determine the smallest number of hubs it will need to cover all of these cities, where a city is "covered" if it is within 1000 miles of at least one hub. Table 14.7 lists the cities that are within 1000 miles of other cities.

Table 14.7 Data for Western Airlines Set-Covering Example

	Cities Within 1000 Miles
Atlanta (AT)	AT, CH, HO, NO, NY, PI
Boston (BO)	BO, NY, PI
Chicago (CH)	AT, CH, NY, NO, PI
Denver (DE)	DE, SL
Houston (HO)	AT, HO, NO
Los Angeles (LA)	LA, SL, SF
New Orleans (NO)	AT, CH, HO, NO
New York (NY)	AT, BO, CH, NY, PI
Pittsburgh (PI)	AT, BO, CH, NY, PI
Salt Lake City (SL)	DE, LA, SL, SF, SE
San Francisco (SF)	LA, SL, SF, SE
Seattle (SE)	SL, SF, SE

Objective

To develop a binary model to find the minimum number of hub locations that can cover all cities.

Where Do the Numbers Come From?

Western has evidently made a policy decision that its hubs will cover cities within a 1000-mile radius. Then the cities covered by any hub location can be found from a map. In a later sensitivity analysis, we explore how the solution changes when the allowable coverage distance varies.

Solution

The variables and constraints for this set-covering model appear in Figure 14.57. (See the file **Locating Hubs Big Picture. xlsx**.) The model is straightforward. There is a binary variable for each city to indicate whether a hub is located there. Then the number of hubs that cover each city is constrained to be at least one. There are no monetary costs in this version of the problem. The goal is to minimize the number of hubs.

Figure 14.57 Big Picture for Hub Location Model

Developing the Spreadsheet Model

The spreadsheet model for Western is shown in Figure 14.58. (See the file **Locating Hubs Finished.xlsx**.) It can be developed as follows.

Developing the Hub Location Model

Figure 14.58 Hub Location Model

▲	A	B	C	D	E	F	G	H	I	J	K	L	M	N	O	P	Q
1	Western Airlines hub location model																
2																	
3	Input data: which cities are covered by which potential hubs														Range names used:		
4		Potential hub													Hubs_covered_by	=Model!$B$25:$B$36	
5	City		AT	BO	CH	DE	HO	LA	NO	NY	PI	SL	SF	SE	Total_hubs	=Model!$B$39	
6	AT		1	0	1	0	1	0	1	1	1	0	0	0	Used_as_hub	=Model!$B$21:$M$21	
7	BO		0	1	0	0	0	0	0	1	1	0	0	0			
8	CH		1	0	1	0	0	0	1	1	1	0	0	0			
9	DE		0	0	0	1	0	0	0	0	0	1	0	0			
10	HO		1	0	0	0	1	0	1	0	0	0	0	0			
11	LA		0	0	0	0	0	1	0	0	0	1	1	0			
12	NO		1	0	1	0	1	0	1	0	0	0	0	0			
13	NY		1	1	1	0	0	0	0	1	1	0	0	0			
14	PI		1	1	1	0	0	0	0	1	1	0	0	0			
15	SL		0	0	0	1	0	1	0	0	0	1	1	1			
16	SF		0	0	0	0	0	1	0	0	0	1	1	1			
17	SE		0	0	0	0	0	0	0	0	0	1	1	1			
18																	
19	Decisions: which cities to use as hubs																
20			AT	BO	CH	DE	HO	LA	NO	NY	PI	SL	SF	SE			
21	Used as hub		0	0	0	0	1	0	0	1	0	1	0	0			
22																	
23	Constraints that each city must be covered by at least one hub																
24	City	Hubs covered by		Required													
25	AT	2	>=	1													
26	BO	1	>=	1													
27	CH	1	>=	1													
28	DE	1	>=	1													
29	HO	1	>=	1													
30	LA	1	>=	1													
31	NO	1	>=	1													
32	NY	1	>=	1													
33	PI	1	>=	1													
34	SL	1	>=	1													
35	SF	1	>=	1													
36	SE	1	>=	1													
37																	
38	Objective to minimize																
39	Total hubs	3															

1. **Inputs.** Enter the information from Table 14.7 in the input cells. A 1 in a cell indicates that the column city covers the row city, whereas a 0 indicates that the column city does not cover the row city. For example, the three 1's in row 7 indicate that Boston, New York, and Pittsburgh are the only cities within 1000 miles of Boston.
2. **Binary values for hub locations.** Enter *any* trial values of 0's or 1's in the Use_as_hub range to indicate which cities are used as hubs. These are the decision variable cells.
3. **Cities covered by hubs.** Calculate the total number of hubs within 1000 miles of Atlanta in cell B25 with the formula

   =SUMPRODUCT(B6:M6,Use_as_hub)

   For any binary values in the decision variable cells range, this formula sums the number of hubs that cover Atlanta. Then copy this to the rest of the Hubs_covered_by range. Note that a value in the Hubs_covered_by range can be 2 or greater. This indicates that a city is within 1000 miles of multiple hubs.
4. **Number of hubs.** Calculate the total number of hubs used in cell B39 with the formula

   =SUM(Use_as_hub)

Using Solver

The completed Solver dialog box is shown in Figure 14.59. The goal is to minimize the total number of hubs, subject to covering each city by at least one hub and ensuring that the decision variable cells are binary.

Figure 14.59 Solver Dialog
Box for Hub Location Model

Solver Parameters   ×

Se_t Objective: | Total_hubs |

To: ○ _M_ax   ● Mi_n_   ○ _V_alue Of: | 0 |

_B_y Changing Variable Cells:
| Used_as_hub |

_S_ubject to the Constraints:
| Hubs_covered_by >= 1
Used_as_hub = binary |

[_A_dd]
[_C_hange]
[_D_elete]
[_R_eset All]
[_L_oad/Save]

☑ Ma_k_e Unconstrained Variables Non-Negative

_S_elect a Solving
Method: | Simplex LP | [O_p_tions]

Solving Method

Select the GRG Nonlinear engine for Solver Problems that are smooth nonlinear. Select the LP Simplex engine for linear Solver Problems, and select the Evolutionary engine for Solver problems that are non-smooth.

[_H_elp]   [_S_olve]   [C_l_ose]

Discussion of the Solution

Figure 14.60 is a graphical representation of the optimal solution, where the double ovals indicate hub locations and the large circles indicate ranges covered by the hubs. (These large circles are not drawn to scale. In reality, they should be circles of

Figure 14.60 Graphical
Solution to Hub Location Model

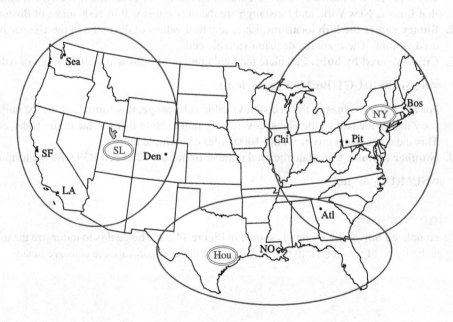

radius 1000 miles centered at the hubs.) Three hubs—in Houston, New York, and Salt Lake City—are needed.[16] The Houston hub covers Houston, Atlanta, and New Orleans. The New York hub covers Atlanta, Pittsburgh, Boston, New York, and Chicago. The Salt Lake City hub covers Denver, Los Angeles, Salt Lake City, San Francisco, and Seattle. Atlanta is the only city covered by two hubs; it can be serviced by New York or Houston.

Sensitivity Analysis

An interesting sensitivity analysis for Western's problem is to see how the solution is affected by the mile limit. Currently, a hub can service all cities within 1000 miles. What if the limit were 800 or 1200 miles, say? To answer this question, you must first collect data on actual distances among all of the cities. Once you have a table of these distances, you can build the binary table, corresponding to the range B6:M17 in Figure 14.58, with IF functions. The modified model appears in the file **Locating Hubs with Distances Finished.xlsx** (not shown here). You can check that the typical formula in B24 is $=IF(B8<=\$B\$4,1,0)$, which is then copied to the rest of the B24:M35 range.[17] You can then run SolverTable, selecting cell B4 as the single input cell, letting it vary from 800 to 1200 in increments of 100, and designating the hub locations and the number of hubs as outputs. The SolverTable results in Figure 14.61 show the effect of the mile limit. When this limit is lowered to 800 miles, four hubs are required, but when it is increased to 1100 or 1200, only two hubs are required. Note that the solution shown for the 1000-mile limit is different from the previous solution in Figure 14.58, but it still requires three hubs. (This is a case of multiple optimal solutions.)

Figure 14.61 Sensitivity to Mile Limit

	A	B	C	D	E	F	G	H	I	J	K	L	M	N
1	Oneway analysis for Solver model in Model worksheet													
2														
3	Mile limit (cell $B$4) values along side, output cell(s) along top													
4		Used_as_hub_1	Used_as_hub_2	Used_as_hub_3	Used_as_hub_4	Used_as_hub_5	Used_as_hub_6	Used_as_hub_7	Used_as_hub_8	Used_as_hub_9	Used_as_hub_10	Used_as_hub_11	Used_as_hub_12	Total_hubs
5	800	1	1	0	0	0	0	0	0	0	1	0	1	4
6	900	1	1	0	0	0	0	0	0	0	1	0	0	3
7	1000	1	1	0	0	0	0	0	0	0	1	0	0	3
8	1100	0	0	1	0	0	0	0	0	0	1	0	0	2
9	1200	0	0	1	0	0	1	0	0	0	0	0	0	2

Problems

Level A

48. Solve the following modifications of the Tatham capital budgeting model. (Solve each part independently of the others.)

   a. Suppose that at most two of projects 1 through 5 can be selected.

   b. Suppose that if investment 3 is selected, then investment 1 must also be selected.

   c. Suppose that at least one of investments 1 and 2 *must* be selected.

   d. Suppose that investment 5 can be selected only if *both* investments 2 and 3 are selected.

49. In the Tatham capital budgeting model we supplied the NPV for each investment. Suppose instead that you are given only the streams of cash inflows from each investment

shown in the file **P14_49.xlsx**. This file also shows the cash requirements and the budget. You can assume that (1) all cash outflows occur at the beginning of year 1; (2) all cash inflows occur at the ends of their respective years; and (3) the company uses a 8% discount rate for calculating its NPVs. Which investments should the company make?

50. Solve the previous problem using the input data in the file **P14_50.xlsx**.

51. Solve Problem 49 with the extra assumption that the investments can be grouped naturally as follows: 1–4, 5–8, 9–12, 13–16, and 17–20.

   a. Find the optimal investments when at most one investment from each group can be selected.

   b. Find the optimal investments when at least one investment from each group must be selected. (If the budget isn't large enough to permit this, increase the budget to a larger value.)

---

16 There are multiple optimal solutions for this model, all requiring three hubs, so you might obtain a different solution from ours.

17 We have warned you about using IF functions in Solver models. However, the current use affects only the *inputs* to the problem, not quantities that depend on the decision variable cells. Therefore, it causes no problems.

52. In the Tatham capital budgeting model, investment 4 has the largest ROI, but it is not selected in the optimal solution. How much NPV is lost if Tatham is *forced* to select investment 4? Answer by solving a suitably modified model.

53. As it currently stands, investment 7 in the Tatham capital budgeting model has the lowest ROI, 10%. Keeping this same ROI, can you change the cash requirement and NPV for investment 7 in such a way that it *is* selected in the optimal solution? Does this lead to any general insights? Explain.

54. Expand the Tatham capital budgeting model so that there are now 20 possible investments. You can make up the data on cash requirements, NPVs, and the budget. However, use the following guidelines:
- The cash requirements and NPVs for the various investments can vary widely, but the ratio of NPV to cost should be between 1.05 and 1.25 for each investment.
- The budget should allow somewhere between 5 and 10 of the investments to be selected.

55. Suppose in the Tatham capital budgeting model that each investment requires $100,000 during year 2 and only $300,000 is available for investment during year 2.
  a. Assuming that available money uninvested at the end of year 1 cannot be used during year 2, what combination of investments maximizes NPV?
  b. Suppose that any uninvested money at the end of year 1 *can* be used for investment in year 2. Does your answer to part **a** change?

56. How difficult is it to expand the Great Threads fixed-cost model to accommodate another type of clothing? Answer by assuming that the company can also produce sweatshirts. The rental cost for sweatshirt equipment is $1100, the variable cost per unit and the selling price are $15 and $45, respectively, and each sweatshirt requires one labor hour and 3.5 square yards of cloth.

57. Referring to the previous problem, if it is optimal for the company to produce sweatshirts, use SolverTable to see how much larger the fixed cost of sweatshirt machinery would have to be before the company would *not* produce any sweatshirts. However, if the solution to the previous problem calls for no sweatshirts to be produced, use SolverTable to see how much lower the fixed cost of sweatshirt machinery would have to be before the company *would* start producing sweatshirts.

58. In the Great Threads fixed-cost model, the production quantities in row 16 were not constrained to be integers. Presumably, any fractional values could be safely rounded to integers. See whether this is true. Constrain these quantities to be integers and then run Solver. Are the optimal integer values the same as the rounded fractional values in Figure 14.51?

59. In the optimal solution to the Great Threads fixed-cost model, the labor hour and cloth constraints are both binding—the company is using all it has.
  a. Use SolverTable to see what happens to the optimal solution when the amount of available cloth increases from its current value. (You can choose the range of input values to use.) Capture all of the decision variable cells, the labor hours and cloth used, and the profit as outputs. The real issue here is whether the company can profitably use more cloth when it is already constrained by labor hours.
  b. Repeat part **a**, but reverse the roles of labor hours and cloth. That is, use the available labor hours as the input for SolverTable.

60. In the optimal solution to the Great Threads fixed-cost model, no pants are produced. Suppose Great Threads has an order for 300 pairs of pants that *must* be produced. Modify the model appropriately and use Solver to find the new optimal solution. (Is it enough to put a lower bound of 300 on the production quantity in cell D16? Will this automatically force the binary value in cell D14 to be 1? Explain.) How much profit does the company lose because of having to produce pants?

61. In the original Western Airlines set-covering model, we assumed that each city must be covered by at least one hub. Suppose that for added flexibility in flight routing, Western requires that each city must be covered by at least two hubs. How do the model and optimal solution change?

62. In the original Western Airlines set-covering model, we used the number of hubs as the objective to minimize. Suppose instead that there is a fixed cost of locating a hub in any city, where these fixed costs can vary across cities. Make up some reasonable fixed costs, modify the model appropriately, and use Solver to find the solution that minimizes the sum of fixed costs.

63. Set-covering models such as the original Western Airlines model often have multiple optimal solutions. See how many alternative optimal solutions you can find. Of course, each must use three hubs because we know this is optimal. (*Hint:* Use various initial values in the decision variable cells and then run Solver repeatedly.)[18]

64. How hard is it to expand a set-covering model to accommodate new cities? Answer this by modifying the second set-covering model. (See the file **Locating Hubs with Distances Finished.xlsx**.) Add several cities that must be served: Memphis, Dallas, Tucson, Philadelphia, Cleveland, and Buffalo. You can look up the distances from these cities to each other and to the other cities on the Web, or you can make up approximate distances.
  a. Modify the model appropriately, assuming that these new cities must be covered *and* are candidates for hub locations.

---

18 One of our colleagues at Indiana University, Vic Cabot, now deceased, worked for years trying to develop a general algorithm (not just trial and error) for finding *all* alternative optimal solutions to optimization models. It turns out that this is a very difficult problem—and one that Vic never completely solved.

b. Modify the model appropriately, assuming that these new cities must be covered but are *not* candidates for hub locations.

Level B

65. The models in this section are often called *combinatorial* models because each solution is a combination of the various 0's and 1's, and there are only a finite number of such combinations. For the Tatham capital budgeting model, there are seven investments, so there are $2^7 = 128$ possible solutions (some of which are infeasible). This is a fairly large number, but not *too* large. Solve the model *without* Solver by listing all 128 solutions. For each, calculate the total cash requirement and total NPV for the model. Then manually choose the one that stays within the budget and has the largest NPV.

66. Make up an example, as described in Problem 54, with 20 possible investments. However, do it so that the ratios of NPV to cash requirement are in a very tight range, such as from 1.0 to 1.1. Then use Solver to find the optimal solution when the Solver Integer Optimality is set to its default value of 5%, and record the solution. Next, solve again with the Integer Optimality set to zero. Do you get the same solution? Try this on a few more instances of the model, where you keep tinkering with the inputs. The question is whether the Integer Optimality setting matters in these types of narrow-range problems.

67. In the Great Threads fixed-cost model, we found an upper bound on production of any clothing type by calculating the amount that could be produced if *all* of the resources were devoted to this clothing type.
a. What if you instead use a very large value such as 1,000,000 for this upper bound? Try it and see whether you get the same optimal solution.
b. Explain why *any* such upper bound is required. Exactly what role does it play in the model?

68. In the last sheet of the finished version of the Great Threads file, we illustrated one way to model the Great Threads problem with IF functions, but saw that this approach doesn't work. Try a slightly different approach here. Eliminate the binary variables in row 14 altogether, and eliminate the upper bounds in row 18 and the corresponding upper bound constraints in the Solver dialog box. (The only constraints are now on resource availability.) However, use IF functions to calculate the total fixed cost of renting equipment, so that if the amount of any clothing type is positive, then its fixed cost is added to the total fixed cost. Is Solver able to handle this model? Does it depend on the initial values in the decision variable cells? (You will have to use Solver's nonlinear algorithm, not the simplex method.)

14-8 Nonlinear Optimization Models

In many optimization models the objective and/or the constraints are nonlinear functions of the decision variables. Such an optimization model is called a **nonlinear programming (NLP) model**. In this section we discuss how to use Excel's Solver to find optimal solutions to NLP models. We then discuss two interesting applications, including the important portfolio optimization model.

14-8a Difficult Issues in Nonlinear Optimization

When you solve an LP model with Solver, you are guaranteed that the solution obtained is an optimal solution. When you solve an NLP model, however, it is very possible that Solver will obtain a suboptimal solution. This is because a nonlinear function can have *local* optimal solutions that are not the *global* optimal solution. A **local optimal solution** is one that is better than all nearby points, whereas the **global optimum** is the one that beats all points in the entire feasible region. If there are one or more local optimal solutions that are not globally optimal, then it is entirely possible that Solver will stop at one of them. Unfortunately, this is not what you want; you want the global optimum.

There are mathematical conditions that guarantee the Solver solution is indeed the global optimum. However, these conditions are often difficult to check, and they aren't always satisfied. A much simpler approach is to run Solver several times, each time with different starting values in the decision variable cells. In general, if Solver obtains the same optimal solution in all cases, you can be fairly confident—but still not absolutely sure—that Solver has found the global optimal solution. On the other hand, if you try different starting values for the decision variable cells and obtain several different solutions, you should keep the best solution found so far. That is, you should keep the solution with the lowest objective value (for a minimization problem) or the highest objective value (for a maximization problem).

Fundamental Insight

Local Optimal Solution Versus Global Optimal Solution

Nonlinear objective functions can behave in many ways that make them difficult to optimize. In particular, they can have local optimal solutions that are not globally optimal, and nonlinear optimization algorithms can stop at such local optimal solutions. The important property of linear objectives that makes the simplex method so successful—namely, that the optimal solution is a corner point—doesn't hold for nonlinear objectives. Now any point in the feasible region can conceivably be optimal. This not only makes the search for the optimal solution more difficult, but it also makes it much more difficult to recognize whether a promising solution (a local optimum) is indeed the global optimum. This is why researchers have spent so much effort trying to obtain conditions that, when true, guarantee that a local optimum must be a global optimum. Unfortunately, these conditions are often difficult to check, and they aren't always satisfied.

14-8b Managerial Economics Models

Many problems in economics are nonlinear but can be solved with Solver. The following example illustrates a nonlinear pricing model.

EXAMPLE

14.11 ELECTRICITY PRICING AT FLORIDA POWER AND LIGHT

Florida Power and Light (FPL) faces demands during both on-peak and off-peak times. FPL must determine the price per megawatt hour (mWh) to charge during both on-peak and off-peak periods. The monthly demand for power during each period (in millions of mWh) is related to price as follows:

$$D_p = 2.253 - 0.013P_p + 0.003P_o \tag{14.5}$$

$$D_o = 1.142 - 0.015P_o + 0.005P_p \tag{14.6}$$

Here, D_p and P_p are demand and price during on-peak times, whereas D_o and P_o are demand and price during off-peak times. Note from the signs of the coefficients that an increase in the on-peak price decreases the demand for power during the on-peak period but *increases* the demand for power during the off-peak period. Similarly, an increase in the price for the off-peak period decreases the demand for the off-peak period but *increases* the demand for the on-peak period. In economic terms, this implies that on-peak power and off-peak power are *substitutes* for one another. In addition, it costs FPL $75 per month to maintain one mWh of capacity. The company wants to determine a pricing strategy and a capacity level that maximize its monthly profit.

The positive coefficients of prices in these demand equations indicate substitute behavior. A larger price for one product tends to induce customers to demand more of the other.

Objective

To use a nonlinear model to determine prices and capacity when there are two different daily usage patterns: on-peak and off-peak.

Where Do the Numbers Come From?

As usual, a cost accountant should be able to estimate the unit cost of capacity. The real difficulty here is estimating the demand functions in Equations (14.5) and (14.6). This requires either sufficient historical data on prices and demands (for both on-peak and off-peak periods) or educated guesses from management.

Solution

The variables and constraints for this model are shown in Figure 14.62. (See the file **Electricity Pricing Big Picture.xlsx**.) The company must decide on two prices and the amount of capacity to maintain. Because this capacity level, once determined, is relevant for on-peak and off-peak periods, it must be large enough to meet demands for both periods. This is the reasoning behind the constraints.

The capacity must be at least as large as the on-peak and off-peak demands. There is no incentive for the capacity to be larger than the maximum of these two demands.

Due to the relationships between the demand and price variables, it is not obvious what FPL should do. The pricing decisions determine demand, and larger demand requires larger capacity, which costs money. In addition, revenue is price multiplied by demand, so it is not clear whether price should be low or high to increase revenue.

Figure 14.62 Big Picture for Electricity Pricing Model

Developing the Spreadsheet Model

The spreadsheet model appears in Figure 14.63. (See the file **Electricity Pricing Finished.xlsx**.) It can be developed as follows:

1. **Inputs.** Enter the parameters of the demand functions and the cost of capacity in the light blue ranges.
2. **Prices and capacity level.** Enter *any* trial prices (per mWh) for on-peak and off-peak power in the Prices range, and enter *any* trial value for the capacity level in the Capacity cell. These are the three values FPL has control over, so they become the decision variable cells.
3. **Demands.** Calculate the demand for the on-peak period by substituting into Equation (14.5). That is, enter the formula

Developing the Electricity Pricing Model

$$=B6+SUMPRODUCT(Prices,C6:D6)$$

in cell B19. Similarly, enter the formula

$$=B7+SUMPRODUCT(Prices,C7:D7)$$

in cell C19 for the off-peak demand.

Figure 14.63 Electricity Pricing Model

	A	B	C	D	E	F	G	H
1	Electricity pricing model							
2								
3	Input data					Range names used:		
4	Coefficients of demand functions					Capacity	=Model!$B$15	
5		Constant	On-peak price	Off-peak price		Common_Capacity	=Model!$B$21:$C$21	
6	On-peak demand	2.253	−0.013	0.003		Demands	=Model!$B$19:$C$19	
7	Off-peak demand	1.142	0.005	−0.015		Prices	=Model!$B$13:$C$13	
8						Profit	=Model!$B$26	
9	Cost of capacity/mWh	$75						
10								
11	Decisions							
12		On-peak	Off-peak					
13	Price per mWh	$137.57	$75.85					
14								
15	Capacity (millions of mWh)	0.692						
16								
17	Constraints on demand (in million of mWh)							
18		On-peak	Off-peak					
19	Demand	0.692	0.692					
20		<=	<=					
21	Capacity	0.692	0.692					
22								
23	Monetary summary ($ millions)							
24	Revenue	147.712						
25	Cost of capacity	51.908						
26	Profit	95.804						

4. **Copy capacity.** To indicate the capacity constraints, enter the formula

=Capacity

in cells B21 and C21. The reason for creating these links is that the two demand cells in row 19 need to be paired with two capacity cells in row 21 so that the Solver constraints can be specified appropriately. (Solver doesn't allow a "two versus one" constraint such as B19:C19 <= B15.)

5. **Monetary values.** Calculate the daily revenue, cost of capacity, and profit in the corresponding cells with the formulas

=SUMPRODUCT(Demands,Prices)

=Capacity*B9

and

=B24-B25

Using Solver

The Solver dialog box should be filled in as shown in Figure 14.64. The goal is to maximize profit by setting appropriate prices and capacity and ensuring that demand never exceeds capacity. You should also check the Non-Negative option (prices and capacity cannot be negative), and you should select the GRG Nonlinear method. Again, this is because prices are multiplied by demands, which are functions of prices, so that profit is a nonlinear function of the prices.

Discussion of the Solution

The Solver solution in Figure 14.63 indicates that FPL should charge $137.57 per mWh during the on-peak period and $75.85 during the off-peak-load period.[19] These prices generate demands of 0.692 million mWh in both periods, which is therefore the capacity required. The cost of this capacity is $51.908 million. When this is subtracted from the revenue of $147.712 million, the monthly profit becomes $95.804 million.

19 With these prices, if a typical customer uses 1.5 mWh in a month, two-thirds of which is on-peak usage, the bill for the month will be $137.57 + $75.85/2=$175.50. This seems reasonable.

Figure 14.64 Solver Dialog Box for the Electricity Pricing Model

To gain some insight into this solution, consider what happens if FPL changes the peak-load price slightly from its optimal value of $137.57. If FPL decreases the price to $137, say, you can check that the on-peak demand increases to 0.700 and the off-peak demand decreases to 0.689. The net effect is that revenue increases slightly, to $148.118. However, the on-peak demand is now greater than capacity, so FPL must increase its capacity from 0.692 to 0.700. This increases the cost of capacity to $52.500, which more than offsets the increase in revenue. A similar chain of effects occurs if FPL increases the on-peak price to $138. In this case, on-peak demand decreases, off-peak demand increases, and total revenue decreases. Although FPL can get by with lower capacity, the net effect is slightly less profit. Fortunately, Solver evaluates these trade-offs for you when it finds the optimal solution.

Varying the values of the decision variables slightly from their optimal values sometimes provides insight into the optimal solution.

Is the Solver Solution Optimal?

It is not difficult to show that the constraints for this model are linear and the objective is a *concave* function. This is enough to guarantee that there are no local maxima that are not globally optimal. In short, this guarantees that the Solver solution is optimal.

Sensitivity Analysis

To gain even more insight, you can use SolverTable to see the effects of changing the unit cost of capacity, allowing it to vary from $60 to $80 in increments of $2. The results appear in Figure 14.65. They indicate that as the cost of capacity increases, the on-peak and off-peak prices both increase, the capacity decreases, and profit decreases. The latter two effects are probably intuitive, but we challenge you to explain the effects on price.

Figure 14.65 Sensitivity to Cost of Capacity

	A	B	C	D	E	F	G
1	Oneway analysis for Solver model in Model worksheet						
2							
3	Cost of capacity (cell $B$9) values along side, output cell(s) along top						
4		Prices_1	Prices_2	Capacity	Profit		
5	$60	$133.82	$72.10	0.730	106.466		
6	$62	$134.32	$72.60	0.725	105.012		
7	$64	$134.82	$73.10	0.720	103.568		
8	$66	$135.32	$73.60	0.715	102.134		
9	$68	$135.82	$74.10	0.710	100.710		
10	$70	$136.32	$74.60	0.705	99.295		
11	$72	$136.82	$75.10	0.700	97.891		
12	$74	$137.32	$75.60	0.695	96.497		
13	$76	$137.82	$76.10	0.690	95.113		
14	$78	$138.32	$76.60	0.685	93.738		
15	$80	$138.82	$77.10	0.680	92.374		

14-8c Portfolio Optimization Models

Given a set of investments, how do financial analysts determine the portfolio that has the lowest risk and yields a high expected return? This question was answered by Harry Markowitz in the 1950s. For his work on this and other investment topics, he received the Nobel Prize in economics in 1991. The ideas discussed in this section are the basis for most methods of *asset allocation* used by Wall Street firms. For example, **portfolio optimization models** are used to determine the percentage of assets to invest in stocks, gold, and Treasury bills. Before proceeding, however, you need to learn about some important formulas involving the expected value and variance of sums of random variables.

Weighted Sums of Random Variables

Let R_i be the (random) return earned during a year on a dollar invested in investment i. For example, if $R_i = 0.10$, a dollar invested at the beginning of the year grows to $1.10 by the end of the year, whereas if $R_i = -0.20$, a dollar invested at the beginning of the year decreases in value to $0.80 by the end of the year. We assume that n investments are available. Let x_i be the fraction of our money invested in investment i. We assume that $x_1 + x_2 + \cdots + x_n = 1$, so that all of our money is invested. (To prevent shorting a stock—that is, selling shares we don't own—we assume that $x_i \geq 0$.) Then the annual return on our investments is given by the random variable R_p, where

$$R_p = R_1 x_1 + R_2 x_2 + \cdots + R_n x_n$$

(The subscript p on R_p stands for "portfolio.")

Let μ_i be the expected value (also called the mean) of R_i, let σ_i^2 be the variance of R_i (so that σ_i is the standard deviation of R_i), and let ρ_{ij} be the correlation between R_i and R_j. To do any work with investments, you must understand how to use the following formulas, which relate the data for the individual investments to the expected return and the variance of return for a *portfolio* of investments.

$$\text{Expected value of } R_p = \mu_1 x_1 + \mu_2 x_2 + \cdots + \mu_n x_n \quad \textbf{(14.7)}$$

$$\text{Variance of } R_p = \sigma_1^2 x_1^2 + \sigma_2^2 x_2^2 + \cdots + \sigma_n^2 x_n^2 + \Sigma_{ij} \rho_{ij} \sigma_i \sigma_j x_i x_j \quad \textbf{(14.8)}$$

The latter summation in Equation (14.8) is over all pairs of investments. The quantities in Equations (14.7) and (14.8) are important in portfolio selection because of the risk–return trade-off investors need to make. Investors want to choose portfolios with high return, measured by the expected value in Equation (14.7), but they also want portfolios with low risk, usually measured by the variance in Equation (14.8).

Equation (14.8) can be rewritten slightly by using *covariances* instead of correlations. The covariance between two stock returns is another measure of the relationship between the two returns, but unlike a correlation, it is *not* scaled to be between -1 and $+1$. This is because covariances are affected by the units in which the returns are measured. Although a covariance is a somewhat less intuitive measure than a correlation, it is used so frequently by financial analysts that we use it here as well. If c_{ij} is the estimated covariance between stocks i and j, then $c_{ij} = r_{ij}s_is_j$. (Here, r is an estimated correlation, and s is an estimated standard deviation.) Using this equation and the fact that the correlation between any stock and itself is 1, we can also write $c_{ii} = s_i^2$ for each stock i. Therefore, an equivalent form of Equation (14.8) is the following.

$$\text{Estimated variance of } R_p = \Sigma_{i,j}c_{ij}x_ix_j \qquad \textbf{(14.9)}$$

This allows you to calculate the portfolio variance with Excel's matrix functions, as explained next.

Matrix Functions in Excel

Matrix Multiplication in Excel

Equation (14.9) for the variance of portfolio return looks intimidating, particularly if there are many potential investments. Fortunately, two built-in Excel matrix functions, MMULT and TRANSPOSE, simplify the calculation. In this subsection we illustrate how to use these two functions. Then in the next subsection we use them in the portfolio selection model.

A *matrix* is a rectangular array of numbers. The matrix is an $i \times j$ matrix if it consists of i rows and j columns. For example,

$$A = \begin{pmatrix} 1 & 2 & 3 \\ 4 & 5 & 6 \end{pmatrix}$$

is a 2×3 matrix, and

$$B = \begin{pmatrix} 1 & 2 \\ 3 & 4 \\ 5 & 6 \end{pmatrix}$$

is a 3×2 matrix. If the matrix has only a single row, it is called a *row vector*. Similarly, if it has only a single column, it is called a *column vector*.

If matrix A has the same number of columns as matrix B has rows, it is possible to calculate the *matrix product* of A and B, denoted AB. The entry in row i, column j of the product AB is obtained by summing the products of the values in row i of A with the corresponding values in column j of B. If A is an $i \times k$ matrix and B is a $k \times j$ matrix, the product AB is an $i \times j$ matrix.

For example, if

$$A = \begin{pmatrix} 1 & 2 & 3 \\ 2 & 4 & 5 \end{pmatrix}$$

and

$$B = \begin{pmatrix} 1 & 2 \\ 3 & 4 \\ 5 & 6 \end{pmatrix}$$

then AB is the following 2×2 matrix:

$$AB = \begin{pmatrix} 1(1) + 2(3) + 3(5) & 1(2) + 2(4) + 3(6) \\ 2(1) + 4(3) + 5(5) & 2(2) + 4(4) + 5(6) \end{pmatrix} = \begin{pmatrix} 22 & 28 \\ 39 & 50 \end{pmatrix}$$

The Excel MMULT function performs matrix multiplication in a single step. The spreadsheet in Figure 14.66 indicates how to multiply matrices of different sizes. (See the file **Matrix Multiplication Finished.xlsx**.) For example, to multiply matrix 1 by matrix 2 (which is possible because matrix 1 has three columns and matrix 2 has three rows), select the two-row, two-column range B13:C14, type the formula

=MMULT(B4:D5,B7:C9)

and press Ctrl+Shift+Enter (all three keys at once). You should select a range with two rows and two columns because matrix 1 has two rows and matrix 2 has two columns.

The matrix multiplication in cell B24 indicates that (1) it is possible to multiply three matrices together by using MMULT twice, and (2) the TRANSPOSE function can be used to convert a column vector to a row vector (or vice versa), if necessary. Here, you want to multiply Column 1 by the product of Matrix 3 and Column 1. However, Column 1 is 3×1, and Matrix 3 is 3×3, so Column 1 multiplied by Matrix 3 doesn't work. Instead, you must transpose Column 1 to make it 1×3. Then the result of multiplying all three together is a 1×1 matrix (a number). It can be calculated by selecting cell B24, typing the formula

=MMULT(TRANSPOSE(I4:I6),MMULT(B17:D19,I4:I6))

and pressing Ctrl+Shift+Enter. This formula uses MMULT twice because MMULT can multiply only *two* matrices at a time.

Figure 14.66 Examples of Matrix Multiplication in Excel

	A	B	C	D	E	F	G	H	I	J	K	L	M	N
1	Matrix multiplication in Excel													
2														
3	Typical multiplication of two matrices							Multiplication of a matrix and a column						
4	Matrix 1	1	2	3				Column 1	2					
5		2	4	5					3					
6									4					
7	Matrix 2	1	2											
8		3	4					Matrix 1 times Column 1, with formula =MMULT(B4:D5,I4:I6)						
9		5	6					Select range with 2 rows, 1 column, enter formula, press Ctrl+Shift+Enter						
10									20					
11	Matrix 1 times Matrix 2, with formula =MMULT(B4:D5,B7:C9)								36					
12	Select range with 2 rows, 2 columns, enter formula, press Ctrl+Shift+Enter.													
13		22	28					Multiplication of a row and a matrix						
14		39	50					Row 1	4	5				
15														
16	Multiplication of a quadratic form (row times matrix times column)							Row 1 times Matrix 1, with formula =MMULT(I14:J14,B4:D5)						
17	Matrix 3	2	1	3				Select range with 1 row, 3 columns, enter formula, press Ctrl+Shift+Enter						
18		1	−1	0					14	28	37			
19		3	0	4										
20								Multiplication of a row and a column						
21	Quadratic form							Row 2	1	6	3			
22	Transpose of Column 1 times Matrix 3 times Column 1													
23	Formula is =MMULT(TRANSPOSE(I4:I6),MMULT(B17:D19,I4:I6))							Row 2 times Column 1, with formula =MMULT(I22:K22,I4:I6)						
24	Select range with 1 row, 1 column, enter formula, press Ctrl+Shift+Enter							Select range with 1 row, 1 column, enter formula, press Ctrl+Shift+Enter						
25		123							32					

Press control + shift + return on a Mac.

Excel Function

MMULT

The MMULT and TRANSPOSE functions are useful for matrix operations. They are called array functions because they operate on an entire range, not just a single cell. The MMULT function multiplies two matrices and has the syntax **=*MMULT*(range1,range2)**, where range1 must have as many columns as range2 has rows. To use this function, select a range that has as many rows as range1 and as many columns as range2, type the formula, and press Ctrl+Shift+Enter. The resulting formula will have curly brackets around it in the Excel formula bar. You should not type these curly brackets. Excel enters them automatically to remind you that this is an array formula.

The Portfolio Selection Model

Most investors have two objectives in forming portfolios: to obtain a large expected return and to obtain a small variance (to minimize risk). The problem is inherently nonlinear because the portfolio variance is nonlinear in the investment amounts. The most common way of handling this two-objective problem is to specify a minimal required expected return and then minimize the variance subject to the constraint on the expected return. The following example illustrates how to do this.

EXAMPLE

14.12 PORTFOLIO OPTIMIZATION AT PERLMAN & BROTHERS

The investment company Perlman & Brothers intends to invest a given amount of money in three stocks. From past data, the means and standard deviations of annual returns have been estimated as shown in Table 14.8. The correlations between the annual returns on the stocks are listed in Table 14.9. The company wants to find a minimum-variance portfolio that yields an expected annual return of at least 0.12 (that is, 12%).

Table 14.8 Estimated Means and Standard Deviations of Stock Returns	Stock	Mean	Standard Deviation
	1	0.14	0.20
	2	0.11	0.15
	3	0.10	0.08

Table 14.9 Estimated Correlations between Stock Returns	Combination	Correlation
	Stocks 1 and 2	0.6
	Stocks 1 and 3	0.4
	Stocks 2 and 3	0.7

Objective

To use NLP to find the portfolio that minimizes the risk, measured by portfolio variance, subject to achieving an expected return of at least 12%.

Where Do the Numbers Come From?

Financial analysts typically estimate the required means, standard deviations, and correlations for stock returns from historical data. However, you should be aware that there is no guarantee that these estimates, based on *historical* return data, are relevant for *future* returns. If analysts have new information about the stocks, they should incorporate this new information into their estimates.

Solution

The variables and constraints for this model appear in Figure 14.67. (See the file **Portfolio Selection Big Picture.xlsx**.) One interesting aspect of this model is that it is *not* necessary to specify the amount of money invested—it could be $100, $1000, $1,000,000, or any other amount. The model determines the *fractions* of this amount to invest in the various stocks, and these fractions are relevant for any investment amount. The only requirement is that the fractions should sum to 1, so that all of the money is invested. Besides this, the fractions are constrained to be *nonnegative* to prevent shorting stocks.[20] Finally, the expected portfolio return is constrained to be at least as large as a specified expected return, such as 12%.

Developing the Spreadsheet Model

The individual steps are now listed. (See Figure 14.68 and the file **Portfolio Selection Finished.xlsx**.)

1. **Inputs.** Enter the inputs in the input cells. These include the estimates of means, standard deviations, and correlations, as well as the required expected return.

Developing the Portfolio Selection Model

_____
20 If you want to allow shorting, do not check the Non-Negative option in the Solver dialog box.

Figure 14.67 Big Picture for Portfolio Selection Model

2. **Fractions invested.** Enter *any* trial values in the Investment_weights range for the fractions of Perlman's money placed in the three investments. Then sum these with the SUM function in cell B19.

3. **Expected annual return.** Use Equation (14.7) to calculate the expected annual return in cell B23 with the formula

   =SUMPRODUCT(B5:D5,Investment_weights)

4. **Covariance matrix.** Equation (14.9) is used to calculate the portfolio variance. To do this, you must first calculate a matrix of covariances. Using the general formula for covariance, $c_{ij} = r_{ij}s_is_j$ (which holds even when $i = j$, because $r_{ii} = 1$), these can be calculated from the inputs by using lookups. Specifically, enter the formula

   =HLOOKUP($F9,$B$4:$D$6,3)*B9*HLOOKUP(G$8,$B$4:$D$6,3)

Figure 14.68 Portfolio Selection Model

	A	B	C	D	E	F	G	H	I
1	Portfolio selection model								
2									
3	**Stock input data**								
4		Stock 1	Stock 2	Stock 3					
5	Mean return	0.14	0.11	0.1					
6	StDev of return	0.2	0.15	0.08					
7									
8	Correlations	Stock 1	Stock 2	Stock 3		Covariances	Stock 1	Stock 2	Stock 3
9	Stock 1	1	0.6	0.4		Stock 1	0.04	0.018	0.0064
10	Stock 2	0.6	1	0.7		Stock 2	0.018	0.0225	0.0084
11	Stock 3	0.4	0.7	1		Stock 3	0.0064	0.0084	0.0064
12									
13	**Investment decisions**								
14		Stock 1	Stock 2	Stock 3					
15	Investment weights	0.500	0.000	0.500					
16									
17	**Constraint on investing everything**								
18		Total weights		Required value					
19		1.00	=	1					
20									
21	**Constraint on expected portfolio return**								
22		Mean portfolio return		Required mean return					
23		0.120	>=	0.120					
24									
25	**Portfolio variance**	0.0148							
26	Portfolio stdev	0.1217							
27									
28	**Range names used:**								
29	Investment_weights	=Model!$B$15:$D$15							
30	Mean_portfolio_return	=Model!$B$23							
31	Portfolio_stdev	=Model!$B$26							
32	Portfolio_variance	=Model!$B$25							
33	Required_mean_return	=Model!$D$23							
34	Total_weights	=Model!$B$19							

in cell G9, and copy it to the range G9:I11. (B9 captures the relevant correlation. The two HLOOKUP terms capture the appropriate standard deviations.)

5. **Portfolio variance.** Although the mathematical details are not presented here, it can be shown that the summation in Equation (14.9) is the product of three matrices: a row of fractions invested multiplied by the covariance matrix multiplied by a column of fractions invested. To calculate it, enter the formula

=MMULT(Investment_weights,MMULT(G9:I11,TRANSPOSE(Investment_weights)))

in cell B25 and press Ctrl+Shift+Enter. (Remember that Excel puts curly brackets around this formula. You should *not* type these curly brackets.) This formula uses two MMULT functions. Again, this is because MMULT can multiply only two matrices at a time. The formula first multiplies the last two matrices and then multiplies this product by the first matrix.

6. **Portfolio standard deviation.** Most financial analysts talk in terms of portfolio *variance*. However, it is probably more intuitive to talk about portfolio *standard deviation* because it is in the same units as the returns. Calculate the standard deviation in cell B26 with the formula

=SQRT(Portfolio_variance)

Actually, either cell B25 or B26 can be used as the objective cell to minimize. Minimizing the square root of a function is equivalent to minimizing the function itself.

Using Solver

The completed Solver dialog box is shown in Figure 14.69. The constraints specify that the expected return must be at least as large as the minimal required expected return, and all the company's money must be invested. The decision variable cells are constrained to be nonnegative (to avoid short selling), and because of the squared terms in the variance formula, you must select the GRG Nonlinear method.

Figure 14.69 Solver Dialog Box for Portfolio Selection Model

Discussion of the Solution

The solution in Figure 14.68 indicates that the company should put half of its money in each of stocks 1 and 3, and it should not invest in stock 2 at all. This might be somewhat surprising, given that the ranking of riskiness of the stocks is 1, 2, 3, with stock 1 being the most risky but also having the highest expected return. However, the correlations play an important role in portfolio selection, so you can usually not guess the optimal portfolio on the basis of the means and standard deviations alone.

The portfolio standard deviation of 0.1217 can be interpreted in a probabilistic sense. If stock returns are approximately *normally* distributed, the actual portfolio return will be within one standard deviation of the expected return with probability about 0.68, and the actual portfolio return will be within two standard deviations of the expected return with probability about 0.95. Given that the expected return is 12%, this implies a lot of risk—two standard deviations below this mean is a *negative* return (or loss) of slightly more than 12%.

Is the Solver Solution Optimal?

The constraints for this model are linear, and it can be shown that the portfolio variance is a *convex* function of the investment fractions. This is sufficient to guarantee that the Solver solution is indeed optimal.

Sensitivity Analysis

This model begs for a sensitivity analysis on the minimum required return. When the company requires a larger expected return, it must assume a larger risk. This behavior is illustrated in Figure 14.70, where SolverTable has been used with cell D23

Figure 14.70
The Efficient Frontier

	A	B	C	D	E	F	G	H	I
1	Oneway analysis for Solver model in Model worksheet								
2									
3	Required return (cell $D$23) values along side, output cell(s) along top								
4		Investment_weights_1	Investment_weights_2	Investment_weights_3	Mean_portfolio_return	Portfolio_stdev			
5	0.100	0.000	0.000	1.000	0.100	0.0800			
6	0.105	0.125	0.000	0.875	0.105	0.0832			
7	0.110	0.250	0.000	0.750	0.110	0.0922			
8	0.115	0.375	0.000	0.625	0.115	0.1055			
9	0.120	0.500	0.000	0.500	0.120	0.1217			
10	0.125	0.625	0.000	0.375	0.125	0.1397			
11	0.130	0.750	0.000	0.250	0.130	0.1591			
12	0.135	0.875	0.000	0.125	0.135	0.1792			
13	0.140	1.000	0.000	0.000	0.140	0.2000			
14									

as the single input cell, varied from 0.10 to 0.14 in increments of 0.005. Note that values outside this range are of little interest. Stock 3 has the minimum expected return, 0.10, and stock 1 has the highest expected return, 0.14, so no portfolio can have an expected return outside of this range.

The results indicate that the company should put more and more into risky stock 1 as the required return increases—and stock 2 continues to be unused. The accompanying scatter chart (with the option to "connect the dots") shows the risk–return trade-off. As the company assumes more risk, as measured by portfolio standard deviation, the expected return increases, but at a decreasing rate.

The curve in this chart is called the *efficient frontier*. Points on the efficient frontier can be achieved by appropriate portfolios. Points below the efficient frontier can be achieved, but they are not as good as points on the efficient frontier because they have a lower expected return for a given level of risk. In contrast, points above the efficient frontier are unachievable—the company cannot achieve this high an expected return for a given level of risk.

Modeling Issues

• Typical real-world portfolio selection problems involve a large number of potential investments, certainly many more than three. This admittedly requires more input data, particularly for the correlation matrix, but the basic model does not change at all. In particular, the matrix formula for portfolio variance is exactly the same. This shows the power of using Excel's matrix functions. Without them, the formula for portfolio variance would be a long, involved sum.

• If Perlman is allowed to short a stock, the fraction invested in that stock is allowed to be negative. To implement this, you can eliminate the nonnegativity constraints on the decision variable cells.

• An alternative objective might be to minimize the probability that the portfolio loses money. This possibility is illustrated in one of the problems.

Problems

Level A

69. In the FPL electricity pricing model, the demand functions have positive and negative coefficients of prices. The negative coefficients indicate that as the price of a product increases, demand for *that* product decreases. The positive coefficients indicate that as the price of a product increases, demand for the *other* product increases.

  a. Increase the magnitudes of the negative coefficients from −0.013 and −0.015 to −0.018 and −0.023, and rerun Solver. Are the changes in the optimal solution intuitive? Explain.

  b. Increase the magnitudes of the positive coefficients from 0.005 and 0.003 to 0.007 and 0.005, and rerun Solver. Are the changes in the optimal solution intuitive? Explain.

  c. Make the changes in parts **a** and **b** simultaneously and rerun Solver. What happens now?

70. In the FPL electricity pricing model, we assumed that the capacity level is a decision variable. Assume now that capacity has already been set at 0.65 million of mWh. (Note that the cost of capacity is now a sunk cost, so it is irrelevant to the decision problem.) Change the model appropriately and run Solver. Then use SolverTable to see how sensitive the optimal solution is to the capacity level, letting it vary over some relevant range. Does it appear that the optimal prices will be set so that

demand is always equal to capacity for at least one of the two periods of the day?

71. For each of the following, answer whether it makes sense to multiply the matrices of the given sizes. In each case where it makes sense, demonstrate an example in Excel, where you can make up the numbers.

  a. AB, where A is 3×4 and B is 4×1

  b. AB, where A is 1×4 and B is 4×1

  c. AB, where A is 4×1 and B is 1×4

  d. AB, where A is 1×4 and B is 1×4

  e. ABC, where A is 1×4, B is 4×4, and C is 4×1

  f. ABC, where A is 3×3, B is 3×3, and C is 3×1

  g. $A^{T}B$, where A is 4×3 and B is 4×3, and A^{T} denotes the transpose of A

72. Add a new stock, stock 4, to the Perlman portfolio optimization model. Assume that the estimated mean and standard deviation of return for stock 4 are 0.125 and 0.175, respectively. Also, assume the correlations between stock 4 and the original three stocks are 0.3, 0.5, and 0.8. Run Solver on the modified model, where the required expected portfolio return is again 0.12. Is stock 4 in the optimal portfolio? Then run SolverTable as in the example. Is stock 4 in any of the optimal portfolios on the efficient frontier?

73. In the Perlman portfolio optimization model, stock 2 is not in the optimal portfolio. Use SolverTable to see whether it ever enters the optimal portfolio as its correlations with stocks 1 and 3 vary. Specifically, use a two-way SolverTable with two inputs, the correlations between stock 2 and stocks 1 and 3, each allowed to vary from 0.1 to 0.9. Capture as outputs the three decision variable cells. Discuss the results. (*Note*: You will have to change the model slightly. For example, if you use cells B10 and C11 as the two SolverTable input cells, you will have to ensure that cells C9 and D10 change accordingly. This is easy. Just enter formulas in these latter two cells.)

74. The stocks in the Perlman portfolio optimization model are all *positively* correlated. What happens when they are *negatively* correlated? Answer for each of the following scenarios. In each case, two of the three correlations are the negatives of their original values. Discuss the differences between the optimal portfolios in these three scenarios.

   a. Change the signs of the correlations between stocks 1 and 2 and between stocks 1 and 3. (Here, stock 1 tends to go in a different direction from stocks 2 and 3.)

   b. Change the signs of the correlations between stocks 1 and 2 and between stocks 2 and 3. (Here, stock 2 tends to go in a different direction from stocks 1 and 3.)

   c. Change the signs of the correlations between stocks 1 and 3 and between stocks 2 and 3. (Here, stock 3 tends to go in a different direction from stocks 1 and 2.)

75. The file **P14_75.xlsx** contains historical monthly returns for 28 companies. For each company, calculate the estimated mean return and the estimated variance of return. Then calculate the estimated correlations between the companies' returns. Note that "return" here means *monthly* return.

76. The file **P14_76.xlsx** includes contains the data from the previous problem. It also contains fractions in row 3 for creating a portfolio. These fractions are currently all equal to 1/28, but they can be changed to any values you like, so long as they continue to sum to 1. For any such fractions, find the estimated mean, variance, and standard deviation of the resulting portfolio return.

Level B

77. Continuing the previous problem, find the portfolio that achieves an expected monthly return of at least 0.01(1%) and minimizes portfolio variance. Then use SolverTable to sweep out the efficient frontier. Create a chart of this efficient frontier from your SolverTable results. What are the relevant lower and upper limits on the required expected monthly return?

78. In many cases you can assume that the portfolio return is at least approximately *normally* distributed. Then you can use Excel's NORM.DIST function as in Chapter 5 to calculate the probability that the portfolio return is negative. The relevant formula is **=NORM.DIST(0,*mean*,*stdev*,TRUE)**, where *mean* and *stdev* are the expected portfolio return and standard deviation of portfolio return, respectively.

   a. Modify the Perlman portfolio optimization model slightly, and then run Solver to find the portfolio that achieves at least a 12% expected return and minimizes the probability of a negative return. Do you get the same optimal portfolio as before? What is the probability that the return from this portfolio will be negative?

   b. Using the model in part **a**, create a chart of the efficient frontier. However, this time put the probability of a negative return on the horizontal axis.

14-9 Conclusion

This chapter has led you through spreadsheet optimization models of many diverse problems. No standard procedure can be used to model all problems. However, there are several keys to most models.

• First, determine the decision variables. For example, in blending problems it is important to realize that the decision variables are the amounts of inputs used to produce outputs, and in employee scheduling problems, it is important to realize that the decision variables are the number of employees who start their five-day shift each day of the week.

• Set up the model so that you can easily calculate what you want to maximize or minimize (usually profit or cost). For example, in the aggregate planning model it is a good idea to calculate total cost by calculating the monthly cost of the various activities in separate rows and then summing the subtotals.

• Set up the model so that the relationships between the cells in the spreadsheet and the constraints of the problem are readily apparent. For example, in the employee scheduling model it is convenient to calculate the number of people working each day of the week adjacent to the minimum required number of people for each day of the week.

• Optimization models do not always fall into ready-made categories. A model might involve a combination of the ideas discussed in the production scheduling, blending, and aggregate planning examples. In fact, many real applications are not strictly analogous to any of the models we have discussed. However, exposure to the models in this chapter should give you the insights you need to solve a wide variety of interesting problems.

Summary of Key Terms

TERM	EXPLANATION	PAGES
Employee scheduling models	Models for choosing the staffing levels to meet workload requirements	663
Multiple optimal solutions	Situation where several solutions obtain the same optimal objective value	668
Blending models	Models where inputs must be mixed in the right proportions to produce outputs	670
Logistics models	Models where goods must be shipped from one set of locations to another at minimal cost	676
Flow balance constraint	Constraint that relates the flow into a node and the flow out of the node	682
Aggregate planning models	Models where workforce levels and production levels must be set to meet customer demand	693
Integer programming (IP) models	Models where at least some of the decision variables must be integers	714
Binary variable	Integer variable that must be 0 or 1; used to indicate whether an activity takes place	714
Capital budgeting models	Models where a subset of investment activities is chosen from a set of possible activities	714
Fixed-cost models	Models where fixed costs are incurred for various activities if they are done at any positive level	720
Set-covering models	Models where members of one set must be selected to cover services to members of another set	729
Nonlinear programming (NLP) models	Models where either the objective function or the constraints (or both) are nonlinear functions of the decision variables	735
Global optimum	Solution that is the best in the entire feasible region	735
Local optimal solution	Solution that is better than all nearby solutions (but might not be optimal globally)	735
Portfolio optimization models	Models that attempt to find the portfolio of securities that achieves the best balance between risk and return	740

Problems

Conceptual Exercises

C.1. The employee scheduling model in this chapter was purposely made small (only seven decision variable cells). What would make a similar problem for a company like McDonald's much harder? What types of constraints would be required? How many decision variable cells (approximately) might there be?

C.2. Explain why it is problematic to include a constraint such as the following in an LP model for a blending problem:

$$\frac{\text{Total octane in gasoline 1 blend}}{\text{Barrels of gasoline 1 blended daily}} \geq 10$$

C.3. "It is essential to constrain all shipments in a transportation problem to have integer values to ensure that the optimal LP solution consists entirely of integer-valued shipments." Is this statement true or false? Why?

C.4. What is the relationship between transportation models and more general logistics models? Explain how these two types of linear optimization models are similar and how they are different.

C.5. Unlike the small logistics models presented here, real-world logistics problems can be huge. Imagine the global problem a company like FedEx faces each day. Describe as well as you can the types of decisions and constraints it has. How large (number of decision variables, number of constraints) might such a problem be?

C.6. Suppose you develop and solve an integer programming model with a cost-minimization objective. Assume the optimal solution yields an objective cell value of $500,000. Now, consider the same linear optimization model without the integer restrictions. That is, suppose you drop the requirement that the decision variable cells be integer-valued and reoptimize with Solver. How does the optimal objective cell value for this modified model (called the *LP relaxation* of the IP model) compare to the original total cost value of $500,000? Explain your answer.

C.7. The portfolio optimization model presented here is the standard model: minimize the variance (or standard deviation) of the portfolio, as a measure of risk, for a given required level of expected return. In general, the goal is to keep risk low and expected return high. Can you think of other ways to model the problem to achieve these basic goals? Is high variability all *bad* risk?

Level A

79. A bus company believes that it will need the following numbers of bus drivers during each of the next five years: 60 drivers in year 1; 70 drivers in year 2; 50 drivers in year 3; 65 drivers in year 4; 75 drivers in year 5. At the beginning of each year, the bus company must decide how many drivers to hire or fire. It costs $4000 to hire a driver and $2000 to fire a driver. A driver's salary is $45,000 per year. At the beginning of year 1 the company has 50 drivers. A driver hired at the beginning of a year can be used to meet the current year's requirements and is paid full salary for the current year.
  a. Determine how to minimize the bus company's salary, hiring, and firing costs over the next five years.
  b. Use SolverTable to determine how the total number hired, total number fired, and total cost change as the unit hiring and firing costs *each* increase by the same percentage.

80. A pharmaceutical company produces the drug NasaMist from four chemicals. Today, the company must produce 1000 pounds of the drug. The three active ingredients in NasaMist are A, B, and C. By weight, at least 8% of NasaMist must consist of A, at least 4% of B, and at least 2% of C. The cost per pound of each chemical and the amount of each active ingredient in one pound of each chemical are given in the file **P14_80.xlsx**. It is necessary that at least 100 pounds of chemical 2 and at least 450 pounds of chemical 3 be used.
  a. Determine the cheapest way of producing today's batch of NasaMist.
  b. Use SolverTable to see how much the percentage of requirement of A is really costing the company. Let the percentage required vary from 6% to 12%.

81. A bank is attempting to determine where to invest its assets during the current year. At present, $500,000 is available for investment in bonds, home loans, auto loans, and personal loans. The annual rates of return on each type of investment are known to be the following: bonds, 6%; home loans, 8%; auto loans, 5%; personal loans, 10%. To ensure that the bank's portfolio is not too risky, the bank's investment manager has placed the following three restrictions on the bank's portfolio:
  • The amount invested in personal loans cannot exceed the amount invested in bonds.
  • The amount invested in home loans cannot exceed the amount invested in auto loans.
  • No more than 25% of the total amount invested can be in personal loans.

  Help the bank maximize the annual return on its investment portfolio.

82. A fertilizer company blends silicon and nitrogen to produce two types of fertilizers. Fertilizer 1 must be at least 40% nitrogen and sells for $70 per pound. Fertilizer 2 must be at least 70% silicon and sells for $40 per pound. The company can purchase up to 8000 pounds of nitrogen at $15 per pound and up to 10,000 pounds of silicon at $10 per pound.
  a. Assuming that all fertilizer produced can be sold, determine how the company can maximize its profit.
  b. Use SolverTable to explore the effect on profit of changing the minimum percentage of nitrogen required in fertilizer 1.
  c. Suppose the availabilities of nitrogen and silicon both increase by the same percentage from their current values. Use SolverTable to explore the effect of this change on profit.

83. Optimization models are used by many Wall Street firms to select a desirable bond portfolio. The following is a simplified version of such a model. A company is considering investing in four bonds; $1 million is available for investment. The expected annual return, the worst-case annual return on each bond, and the *duration* of each bond are given in the file **P14_83.xlsx**. (The duration of a bond is a measure of the bond's sensitivity to interest rates.) The company wants to maximize the expected return from its bond investments, subject to three constraints:
  • The worst-case return of the bond portfolio must be at least 8%.
  • The average duration of the portfolio must be at most 6. For example, a portfolio that invests $600,000 in bond 1 and $400,000 in bond 4 has an average duration of $[600,000(3) + 400,000(9)]/1,000,000 = 5.4$.
  • Because of diversification requirements, at most 40% of the total amount invested can be invested in a single bond.

  Determine how the company can maximize the expected return on its investment.

84. At the beginning of year 1, you have $10,000. Investments A and B are available; their cash flows are shown in the file **P14_84.xlsx**. Assume that any money not invested in A or B earns interest at an annual rate of 2%.
  a. Determine how to maximize your cash on hand at the beginning of year 4.
  b. Use SolverTable to determine how a change in the year 2 return for investment A changes the optimal solution to the problem.
  c. Use SolverTable to determine how a change in the year 3 return of investment B changes the optimal solution to the problem.

85. An oil company produces two types of gasoline, G1 and G2, from two types of crude oil, C1 and C2. G1 is allowed to contain up to 4% impurities, and G2 is allowed to contain up to 3% impurities. G1 sells for $48 per barrel, whereas G2 sells for $72 per barrel. Up to 4200 barrels of G1 and up to 4300 barrels of G2 can be sold. The cost per barrel of each crude, their availability, and the level of impurities in each crude are listed in the file **P14_85.xlsx**. Before blending the crude oil into gas, any amount of each crude can be "purified" for a cost of $3.00 per barrel. Purification eliminates half of the impurities in the crude oil.
  a. Determine how to maximize profit.
  b. Use SolverTable to determine how an increase in the availability of C1 affects the optimal profit.
  c. Use SolverTable to determine how an increase in the availability of C2 affects the optimal profit.
  d. Use SolverTable to determine how a change in the profitability of G2 changes profitability and the types of gas produced.

86. The government is auctioning off oil leases at two sites: 1 and 2. At each site 10,000 acres of land are to be auctioned. Cliff Ewing, Blake Barnes, and Alexis Pickens are bidding for the oil. Government rules state that no bidder can receive more than 40% of the land being auctioned. Cliff has bid $10,000 per acre for site 1 land and $20,000 per acre for site 2 land. Blake has bid $9000 per acre for site 1 land and $22,000 per acre for site 2 land. Alexis has bid $11,000 per acre for site 1 land and $19,000 per acre for site 2 land.
  a. Determine how to maximize the government's revenue.
  b. Use SolverTable to see how changes in the government's rule on 40% of all land being auctioned affect the optimal revenue. Why can the optimal revenue not decrease if this percentage required increases? Why can the optimal revenue not increase if this percentage required decreases?

87. An automobile company produces cars in Los Angeles and Detroit and has a warehouse in Atlanta. The company supplies cars to customers in Houston and Tampa. The costs of shipping a car between various points are listed in the file **P14_87.xlsx**, where a blank means that a shipment is not allowed. Los Angeles can produce up to 1100 cars, and Detroit can produce up to 2900 cars. Houston must receive 2400 cars, and Tampa must receive 1500 cars.
  a. Determine how to minimize the cost of meeting demands in Houston and Tampa.
  b. Modify the answer to part **a** if shipments between Los Angeles and Detroit are not allowed.
  c. Modify the answer to part **a** if shipments between Houston and Tampa are allowed at a cost of $5 per car.

88. An oil company produces oil from two wells. Well 1 can produce up to 150,000 barrels per day, and well 2 can produce up to 200,000 barrels per day. It is possible to ship oil directly from the wells to the company's customers in Los Angeles and New York. Alternatively, the company could transport oil to the ports of Mobile and Galveston and then ship it by tanker to New York or Los Angeles, respectively. Los Angeles requires 160,000 barrels per day, and New York requires 140,000 barrels per day. The costs of shipping 1000 barrels between various locations are shown in the file **P14_88.xlsx**, where a blank indicates shipments that are not allowed. Determine how to minimize the transport costs in meeting the oil demands of Los Angeles and New York.

89. Based on Bean et al. (1987). Boris Milkem's firm owns six assets. The expected selling price (in millions of dollars) for each asset is given in the file **P14_89.xlsx**. For example, if asset 1 is sold in year 2, the firm receives $20 million. To maintain a regular cash flow, Milkem must sell at least $20 million of assets during year 1, at least $30 million worth during year 2, and at least $35 million worth during year 3. Determine how Milkem can maximize his total revenue from assets sold during the next three years.

90. Based on Sonderman and Abrahamson (1985). In treating a brain tumor with radiation, physicians want the maximum amount of radiation possible to bombard the tissue containing the tumors. The constraint is, however, that there is a maximum amount of radiation that normal tissue can handle without suffering tissue damage. Physicians must therefore decide how to aim the radiation so as to maximize the radiation that hits the tumor tissue subject to the constraint of not damaging the normal tissue. As a simple example, suppose there are six types of radiation beams (beams differ in where they are aimed and their intensity) that can be aimed at a tumor. The region containing the tumor has been divided into six regions: three regions contain tumors and three contain normal tissue. The amount of radiation delivered to each region by each type of beam is shown in the file **P14_90.xlsx**. If each region of normal tissue can handle at most 60 units of radiation, which beams should be used to maximize the total amount of radiation received by the tumors?

91. A leading hardware company produces three types of computers: Pear computers, Apricot computers, and Orange computers. The relevant data are given in the file **P14_91.xlsx**. The equipment cost is a fixed cost; it is incurred if any of this type of computer is produced. A total of 30,000 chips and 12,000 hours of labor are available. The company wants to produce at least two types of computers.

a. Determine how the company can maximize its profit.

b. For any computer type *not* in the optimal product mix, use SolverTable to find how much larger its unit margin would have to be before it would enter the optimal product mix.

92. A food company produces tomato sauce at five different plants. The tomato sauce is then shipped to one of three warehouses, where it is stored until it is shipped to one of the company's four customers. All of the inputs for the problem are given in the file **P14_92.xlsx**, as follows:

- The plant capacities (in tons)

- The cost per ton of producing tomato sauce at each plant and shipping it to each warehouse

- The cost of shipping a ton of sauce from each warehouse to each customer

- The customer requirements (in tons) of sauce

- The fixed annual cost of operating each plant and warehouse.

The company must decide which plants and warehouses to open, and which routes from plants to warehouses and from warehouses to customers to use. All customer demand must be met. A given customer's demand can be met from more than one warehouse, and a given plant can ship to more than one warehouse.

a. Determine the minimum-cost method for meeting customer demands.

b. Use SolverTable to see how a change in the capacity of plant 1 affects the total cost.

c. Use SolverTable to see how a change in the customer 2 demand affects the total cost.

93. You are given the following means, standard deviations, and correlations for the annual return on three potential investments. The means are 0.12, 0.15, and 0.20. The standard deviations are 0.20, 0.30, and 0.40. The correlation between stocks 1 and 2 is 0.65, between stocks 1 and 3 is 0.75, and between stocks 2 and 3 is 0.41. You have $100,000 to invest and can invest no more than half of your money in any single investment. Determine the minimum-variance portfolio that yields an expected annual return of at least 0.14.

94. You have $50,000 to invest in three stocks. Let R_i be the random variable representing the annual return on $1 invested in stock i. For example, if $R_i = 0.12$, then $1 invested in stock i at the beginning of a year is worth $1.12 at the end of the year. The means are $E(R_1) = 0.14$, $E(R_2) = 0.11$, and $E(R_3) = 0.10$. The variances are $Var\ R_1 = 0.20$, $Var\ R_2 = 0.08$, and $Var\ R_3 = 0.18$. The correlations are $r_{12} = 0.8$, $r_{13} = 0.7$, and $r_{23} = 0.9$.

Determine the minimum-variance portfolio that attains an expected annual return of at least 0.12.

Level B

95. The risk index of an investment can be obtained by taking the absolute values of percentage changes in the value of the investment for each year and averaging them. Suppose you are trying to determine the percentages of your money to invest in stocks, 3-month Treasury bills, and 10-year Treasury bonds. The file **P14_95.xlsx** lists the annual returns (percentage changes in value) for these investments since 1970. Let the risk index of a portfolio be the weighted average of the risk indices of these investments, where the weights are the fractions of the portfolio assigned to the investments. Suppose the amount of each investment must be between 20% and 50% of the total invested. You would like the risk index of your portfolio to equal 0.12, and your goal is to maximize the expected return on your portfolio. Determine the maximum expected return on your portfolio, subject to the stated constraints. Use the average return earned by each investment during these years as your estimate of expected return.

96. Broker Sonya Wong is currently trying to maximize her profit in the bond market. Four bonds are available for purchase and sale at the bid and ask prices shown in the file **P14_96.xlsx**. Sonya can buy up to 1000 units of each bond at the ask price or sell up to 1000 units of each bond at the bid price. During each of the next three years, the person who sells a bond will pay the owner of the bond the cash payments listed in the same file. Sonya's goal is to maximize her revenue from selling bonds minus her payment for buying bonds, subject to the constraint that after each year's payments are received, her current cash position (due only to cash payments from bonds and not purchases or sales of bonds) is nonnegative. Note that her current cash position can depend on past coupons and that cash accumulated at the end of each year earns 2.5% annual interest. Determine how to maximize net profit from buying and selling bonds, subject to the constraints previously described. Why do you think we limit the number of units of each bond she can buy or sell?

97. A financial company is considering investing in three projects. If it fully invests in a project, the realized cash flows (in millions of dollars) will be as listed in the file **P14_97.xlsx**. For example, project 1 requires a cash outflow of $3 million today and returns $5.5 million three years from now. The company currently has $2 million in cash. At each time point (0, 6, 12, 18, 24, and 30 months from now), the company can, if desired, borrow up to $2 million at 3.5% interest (per six months). Leftover cash earns 3% interest (per six months). For example, if after borrowing and investing at the current time, the company has $1 million, it will receive $30,000 in

interest six months from now. The company's goal is to maximize cash on hand after cash flows three years from now are accounted for. What investment and borrowing strategy should it use? Assume that the company can invest in a fraction of a project. For example, if it invests in one-half of project 3, it has cash outflows of −$1 million now and six months from now.

98. You are a CFA (chartered financial analyst). An overextended client has come to you because she needs help paying off her credit card bills. She owes the amounts on her credit cards listed in the file **P14_98 .xlsx**. The client is willing to allocate up to $5000 per month to pay off these credit cards. All cards must be paid off within 36 months. The client's goal is to minimize the total of all her payments. To solve this problem, you must understand how interest on a loan works. To illustrate, suppose the client pays $5000 on Saks during month 1. Then her Saks balance at the beginning of month 2 is $20,000 − [5000 − 0.005(20,000)]$. This follows because she incurs $0.005(20,000)$ in interest charges on her Saks card during month 1. Help the client solve her problem. Once you have solved this problem, give an intuitive explanation of the solution found by Solver.

99. A food company produces two types of turkey cutlets for sale to fast-food restaurants. Each type of cutlet consists of white meat and dark meat. Cutlet 1 sells for $4 per pound and must consist of at least 70% white meat. Cutlet 2 sells for $3 per pound and must consist of at least 60% white meat. At most 6000 pounds of cutlet 1 and 2000 pounds of cutlet 2 can be sold. The two types of turkey used to manufacture the cutlets are purchased from a turkey farm. Each type 1 turkey costs $10 and yields five pounds of white meat and two pounds of dark meat. Each type 2 turkey costs $8 and yields three pounds of white meat and three pounds of dark meat. Determine how the company can maximize its profit.

100. Each hour from 10 A.M. to 7 P.M., a bank receives checks and must process them. Its goal is to process all checks the same day they are received. The bank has 13 check processing machines, each of which can process up to 500 checks per hour. It takes one worker to operate each machine. The bank hires both full-time and part-time workers. Full-time workers work 10 A.M. to 6 P.M., 11 A.M. to 7 P.M., or noon to 8 P.M. and are paid $160 per day. Part-time workers work either 2 P.M. to 7 P.M. or 3 P.M. to 8 P.M. and are paid $75 per day. The numbers of checks received each hour are listed in the file **P14_100. xlsx**. In the interest of maintaining continuity, the bank believes that it must have at least three full-time workers under contract. Develop a work schedule that processes all checks by 8 P.M. and minimizes daily labor costs.

101. An oil company has oil fields in San Diego and Los Angeles. The San Diego field can produce up to 500,000 barrels per day, and the Los Angeles field can produce up to 400,000 barrels per day. Oil is sent from the fields to a refinery, either in Dallas or in Houston. (Assume that each refinery has unlimited capacity.) To refine 100,000 barrels costs $700 at Dallas and $900 at Houston. Refined oil is shipped to customers in Chicago and New York. Chicago customers require 400,000 barrels per day, and New York customers require 300,000 barrels per day. The costs of shipping 100,000 barrels of oil (refined or unrefined) between cities are listed in the file **P14_101.xlsx**.
   a. Determine how to minimize the total cost of meeting all demands.
   b. If each refinery had a capacity of 380,000 barrels per day, how would you modify the model in part **a**?

102. An electrical components company produces capacitors at three locations: Los Angeles, Chicago, and New York. Capacitors are shipped from these locations to public utilities in five regions of the country: northeast (NE), northwest (NW), midwest (MW), southeast (SE), and southwest (SW). The cost of producing and shipping a capacitor from each plant to each region of the country is given in the file **P14_102.xlsx**. Each plant has an annual production capacity of 100,000 capacitors. Each year, each region of the country must receive the following number of capacitors: NE, 55,000; NW, 50,000; MW, 60,000; SE, 60,000; SW, 45,000. The company believes that shipping costs are too high, and it is therefore considering building one or two more production plants. Possible sites are Atlanta and Houston. The costs of producing a capacitor and shipping it to each region of the country are given in the same file. It costs $3 million (in current dollars) to build a new plant, and operating each plant incurs a fixed cost (in addition to variable shipping and production costs) of $50,000 per year. A plant at Atlanta or Houston will have the capacity to produce 100,000 capacitors per year. Assume that future demand patterns and production costs will remain unchanged. If costs are discounted at a rate of 12% per year, how can the company minimize the net present value (NPV) of all costs associated with meeting current and future demands?

103. Based on Bean et al. (1988). The owner of a shopping mall has 10,000 square feet of space to rent and wants to determine the types of stores that should occupy the mall. The minimum number and maximum number of each type of store and the square footage of each type are given in the file **P14_103 .xlsx**. The annual profit made by each type of store depends on the number of stores of that type in the mall. This dependence is given in the same file, where all profits are in units of $10,000. For example, if there are two department stores in the mall, each department store will earn $210,000 profit per year. Each store pays 5% of its annual profit as rent to the owner of the mall. Determine how the owner of the mall can maximize its rental income.

104. A city (labeled C for convenience) is trying to sell municipal bonds to support improvements in recreational facilities and highways. The face values (in thousands of dollars) of the bonds and the due dates (years from now) at which principal comes due are listed in the file **P14_104.xlsx**. An underwriting company (U) wants to underwrite C's bonds. A proposal to C for underwriting this issue consists of the following: (1) an interest rate, 3%, 4%, 5%, 6%, or 7%, for each bond, where coupons are paid annually, and (2) an up-front premium paid by U to C. U has determined the set of fair prices (in thousands of dollars) for the bonds listed in the same file. For example, if U underwrites bond 2 maturing two years from now at 5%, it will charge C $444,000 for that bond. U is constrained to use at most three different interest rates. U wants to make a profit of at least $46,000, where its profit is equal to the sale price of the bonds minus the face value of the bonds minus the premium U pays to C. To maximize the chance that U will get C's business, U wants to minimize the total cost of the bond issue to C, which is equal to the total interest on the bonds minus the premium paid by U. For example, if bond 1 is issued at a 4% rate, then C must pay two years of coupon interest: 2(0.04)($700,000) = $56,000. What assignment of interest rates to each bond and up-front premiums ensure that U will make the desired profit (assuming it gets the contract) and maximize the chance of U getting C's business? To maximize this chance, you can assume that U minimizes the net cost to C, that is, the cost of its coupon payments minus the premium from U to C.

CASE 14.1 Giant Motor Company

This problem deals with strategic planning issues for a large company.[21] The main issue is planning the company's production capacity for the coming year. At issue is the overall level of capacity and the type of capacity—for example, the degree of *flexibility* in the manufacturing system. The main tool used to aid the company's planning process is a mixed integer programming model. A *mixed* integer program has both integer and continuous variables.

Problem Statement

Giant Motor Company (GMC) produces three lines of cars for the domestic (U.S.) market: Lyras, Libras, and Hydras. The Lyra is a relatively inexpensive subcompact car that appeals mainly to first-time car owners and to households using it as a second car for commuting. The Libra is a sporty compact car that is sleeker, faster, and roomier than the Lyra. Without any options, the Libra costs slightly more than the Lyra; additional options increase the price further. The Hydra is the luxury car of the GMC line. It is significantly more expensive than the Lyra and Libra, and it has the highest profit margin of the three cars.

Retooling Options for Capacity Expansion

Currently GMC has three manufacturing plants in the United States. Each plant is dedicated to producing a single line of cars. In its planning for the coming year, GMC is considering the retooling of its Lyra and/or Libra plants. Retooling either plant would represent a major expense for the company. The retooled plants would have significantly increased production capacities. Although having greater *fixed* costs, the retooled plants would be more efficient and have lower *marginal* production costs—that is, higher *marginal* profit contributions. In addition, the retooled plants would be

flexible: They would have the capability of producing more than one line of cars.

The characteristics of the current plants and the retooled plants are given in Table 14.10. The retooled Lyra and Libra plants are prefaced by the word *new*. The fixed costs and capacities in Table 14.10 are given on an annual basis. A dash in the profit margin section indicates that the plant cannot manufacture that line of car. For example, the new Lyra plant would be capable of producing both Lyras and Libras but not Hydras. The new Libra plant would be capable of producing any of the three lines of cars. Note, however, that the new Libra plant has a slightly lower profit margin for producing Hydras than the Hydra plant does. The flexible new Libra plant is capable of producing the luxury Hydra model but is not quite as efficient as the current Hydra plant that is dedicated to Hydra production.

The fixed costs are annual costs that are incurred by GMC independent of the number of cars that are produced by the plant. For the current plant configurations, the fixed costs include property taxes, insurance, payments on the loan that was taken out to construct the plant, and so on. If a plant is retooled, the fixed costs will include the previous fixed costs plus the additional cost of the renovation. The additional renovation cost will be an annual cost representing the cost of the renovation amortized over a long period.

Demand for GMC Cars

Short-term demand forecasts have been very reliable in the past and are expected to be reliable in the future. (Longer-term forecasts are not so accurate.) The demand for GMC cars for the coming year is given in Table 14.11.

A quick comparison of plant capacities and demands in Tables 14.10 and 14.11 indicates that GMC is faced with

Table 14.10 Plant Characteristics	Lyra	Libra	Hydra	New Lyra	New Libra
Capacity (in 1000s)	1000	800	900	1600	1800
Fixed cost (in $millions)	2000	2000	2600	3400	3700
Profit Margin by Car Line (in $1000s)					
Lyra	2	—	—	2.5	2.3
Libra	—	3	—	3.0	3.5
Hydra	—	—	5	—	4.8

Table 14.11 Demand for GMC Cars

	Demand (in 1000s)
Lyra	1400
Libra	1100
Hydra	800

insufficient capacity. Partially offsetting the lack of capacity is the phenomenon of *demand diversion*. If a potential car buyer walks into a GMC dealer showroom wanting to buy a Lyra but the dealer is out of stock, frequently the salesperson can convince the customer to purchase the better Libra car, which is in stock. Unsatisfied demand for the Lyra is said to be *diverted* to the Libra. Only rarely in this situation can the salesperson convince the customer to switch to the luxury Hydra model.

From past experience GMC estimates that 30% of unsatisfied demand for Lyras is diverted to demand for Libras and 5% to demand for Hydras. Similarly, 10% of unsatisfied demand for Libras is diverted to demand for Hydras. For example, if the demand for Lyras is 1,400,000 cars, then the unsatisfied demand will be 400,000 if no capacity is added. Out of this unsatisfied demand, 120,000 (= 400,000 × 0.3) will materialize as demand for Libras, and 20,000 (= 400,000 × 0.05) will materialize as demand for Hydras. Similarly, if the demand for Libras is

1,220,000 cars (1,100,000 original demand plus 120,000 demand diverted from Lyras), then the unsatisfied demand for Lyras would be 420,000 if no capacity is added. Out of this unsatisfied demand, 42,000 (= 420,000 × 0.1) will materialize as demand for Hydras. All other unsatisfied demand is lost to competitors. The pattern of demand diversion is summarized in Table 14.12.

Table 14.12 Demand Diversion Matrix

	Lyra	Libra	Hydra
Lyra	NA	0.3	0.05
Libra	0	NA	0.10
Hydra	0	0.0	NA

Questions

GMC wants to decide whether to retool the Lyra and Libra plants. In addition, GMC wants to determine its production plan at each plant in the coming year. Based on the previous data, develop a mixed integer programming model (some variables integer-constrained, some not) for solving GMC's production planning–capacity expansion problem for the coming year. According to the optimal solution, what should GMC do? How sensitive is the optimal solution to key inputs? The file **C14_01.xlsx** gets you started.

CASE 14.2 GMS Stock Hedging

Kate Torelli, a security analyst for LionFund, has identified a gold-mining stock (ticker symbol GMS) as a particularly attractive investment. Torelli believes that the company has invested wisely in new mining equipment. Furthermore, the company has recently purchased mining rights on land that has high potential for successful gold extraction. Torelli notes that gold has underperformed in the stock market for the last decade and believes that the time is ripe for a large increase in gold prices. In addition, she reasons that conditions in the global monetary system make it likely that investors may once again turn to gold as a safe haven in which

to park assets. Finally, supply and demand conditions have improved to the point where there could be significant upward pressure on gold prices.

GMS is a highly leveraged company, so it is quite a risky investment by itself. Torelli is mindful of a passage from the annual report of a competitor, Baupost, which has an extraordinarily successful investment record: "Baupost has managed a decade of consistently profitable results despite, and perhaps in some respect due to, consistent emphasis on the avoidance of downside risk. We have frequently carried both high cash balances and costly market hedges. Our results are

Table 14.13 Scenarios and Probabilities for GMS Stock in 1 Month

	Scenario 1	Scenario 2	Scenario 3	Scenario 4	Scenario 5	Scenario 6	Scenario 7
Probability	0.05	0.10	0.20	0.30	0.20	0.10	0.05
GMS stock price($)	150	130	110	100	90	80	70

particularly satisfying when considered in the light of this sustained risk aversion." She would therefore like to *hedge* the stock purchase—that is, reduce the risk of an investment in GMS stock.

Currently GMS is trading at $100 per share. Torelli has constructed seven scenarios for the price of GMS stock one month from now. These scenarios and corresponding probabilities are shown in Table 14.13.

To hedge an investment in GMS stock, Torelli can invest in other securities whose prices tend to move in the direction opposite to that of GMS stock. In particular, she is considering over-the-counter put options on GMS stock as potential hedging instruments. The value of a put option increases as the price of the underlying stock decreases. For example, consider a put option with a strike price of $100 and a time to expiration of one month. This means that the owner of the put has the right to sell GMS stock at $100 per share one month in the future. Suppose that the price of GMS falls to $80 at that time. Then the holder of the put option can exercise the option and receive $20 (= 100 − 80). If the price of GMS falls to $70, the option would be worth $30 (= 100 − 70). However, if the price of GMS rises to $100 or more, the option expires worthless.

Torelli called an options trader at a large investment bank for quotes. The prices for three European-style put options are shown in Table 14.14. (A European put can be exercised only at the expiration date, not before.) Torelli wishes to invest $10 million in GMS stock and put options.

Questions

1. Based on Torelli's scenarios, what is the expected return of GMS stock? What is the standard deviation of the return of GMS stock?

2. After a cursory examination of the put option prices, Torelli suspects that a good strategy is to buy one put option A for each share of GMS stock purchased. What are the mean and standard deviation of return for this strategy?

3. Assuming that Torelli's goal is to minimize the standard deviation of the portfolio return, what is the optimal portfolio that invests all $10 million? (For simplicity, assume that fractional numbers of stock shares and put options can be purchased. Assume that the amounts invested in each security must be nonnegative. However, the number of options purchased need *not* equal the number of shares of stock purchased.) What are the expected return and standard deviation of return of this portfolio? How many shares of GMS stock and how many of each put option does this portfolio correspond to?

4. Suppose that short selling is permitted—that is, the nonnegativity restrictions on the portfolio weights are removed. Now what portfolio minimizes the standard deviation of return?

(*Hint*: A good way to attack this problem is to create a table of security returns, as indicated in Table 14.15, where only a few of the table entries are shown. To correctly calculate the standard deviation of portfolio return, you will need to incorporate the scenario probabilities. If r_i is the portfolio return in scenario i, and p_i is the probability of scenario i, then the standard deviation of portfolio return is

$$\sqrt{\sum_{i=1}^{7} P_i(r_i - \mu)^2}$$

where $\mu = \sum_{i=1}^{7} p_i r_i$ is the expected portfolio return.)

Table 14.14 Put Option Prices (Today) for GMS Case Study

	Put Option A	Put Option B	Put Option C
Strike Price ($)	90	100	110
Option Price ($)	2.20	6.40	12.50

Table 14.15 Table of Security Returns

	GMS Stock	Put Option A	Put Option B	Put Option C
Scenario 1			−100%	
2	30%			
⋮				
7				220%

CHAPTER 15
Introduction to Simulation Modeling

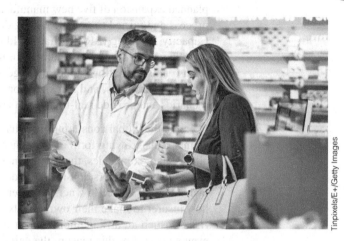

Tinpixels/E+/Getty Images

REAL APPLICATIONS OF SIMULATION WITH @RISK

This chapter introduces Palisade's @RISK add-in for simulation modeling in Excel. @ RISK is not only for academic use. Palisade has trained numerous well-known companies in the use of @RISK, and its website chronicles how many of these companies have used @RISK in their businesses. Here are a few of these applications.

- Merck, the multinational pharmaceutical company, recognizes the importance of value-at-risk in its risk management programs. (Value-at-risk, defined in the next chapter, is nearly the worst that can happen.) Merck is also aware that exchange rate volatility is one of the largest components of its value-at-risk. @RISK provides the flexibility to fit and evaluate alternative distributions of currency rates. The company must manage currency exposures in both the balance sheet and in future revenues. Evidently, simulating currency risks on the balance sheet is relatively straightforward. However, simulating hedged cash flow currency risk presents challenges because of accounting standards for derivative investments. It requires a model that can project economic and accounting hedge performance through time. This involves many uncertain variables, including option time decay and the volatility of option price components. @RISK has the power to handle this complexity, and for this reason, @RISK is Merck's analytic tool of choice.

- Benjamin Waisbren uses @RISK in all his negotiations. Waisbren is president of LSC Film Corporation, a company that provides the funding for major film productions, such as V for Vendetta, Blood Diamond, and 300. He recently used @RISK to complete a $200 million deal with Sony, giving his team, LStar Capital, a stake in nearly all movies produced by Sony. He estimates that because of @RISK modeling, closing costs on this deal were about $20 million lower than on similar deals. Since then, he has used @RISK to perform statistical analysis on risks in the motion picture business. This has led to surprisingly accurate predictions of how much a film will make on its opening day or weekend, as well as the amount film production will cost in any given number of months. Trained as a lawyer, Waisbren urges other law firms to train their employees in @RISK, arguing that this can save them huge amounts in complex negotiations.

- Amway, the global direct sales giant with annual sales over $10 billion and manufacturer of more than 450 different products in 18 plants in the U.S. and Southeast Asia, must make many detailed capacity planning decisions on a regular basis. In the past, a team from the IE (industrial engineering) team would gather data and use traditional modeling tools to evaluate various scenarios. This was time-consuming, and the results were often less than accurate by the time they were available. In 2014, faced with a planned expansion of five new manufacturing sites, the IE team sought a better solution process and turned to @RISK. They developed a simulation tool called Long Range Capacity Planning (LRCP) that could quickly evaluate thousands of what-if scenarios, accounting for the vast number of uncertainties faced by Amway's manufacturing teams. This tool allows plant managers to change variables such as demand, output rates, new products, and run sizes for a selected plant. Then it can simulate up to 20 scenarios and provide real-time results on which configurations work best.

- Deloitte, the global consulting firm, has used @RISK to help its cell captive insurance clients. This growing form of insurance occurs when a host insurer, the "cell captive," allows other companies, the "cell owners," to piggyback on the host's insurer's license, so that the cell owners don't have to deal with the costs and regulations of buying their own licenses. The cell owners can then perform some of the functions on behalf of the host insurer to make their own profits. However, the host insurer takes on significant risks in such an arrangement, and it is exposed to huge financial risks if disastrous events occur. For this reason, the cell owners are required to capitalize the cell at the outset, providing funds for the host insurer in case of a disaster. The big question is how much capital is required, and this is where @RISK enters the picture. It can be used to simulate many possible scenarios over a future time period such as a year, and its results can predict how bad things could be. In this case, Deloitte uses the 99.5th percentile as the relevant value, the amount of exposure faced by the host insurer in a "one-in-200-event."

15-1 Introduction

A **simulation model** is a computer model that imitates a real-life situation. It is like other mathematical models, but it explicitly incorporates uncertainty in one or more input variables. When you run a simulation, you allow these random input variables to take on various values, and you keep track of any resulting output variables of interest. In this way, you are able to see how the outputs vary as a function of the varying inputs.

The fundamental advantage of a simulation model is that it provides an entire distribution of results, not simply a single bottom-line result. As an example, suppose an automobile manufacturer is planning to develop and market a new model car. The company is ultimately interested in the net present value (NPV) of the cash flows from this car over the next 10 years. However, there are many uncertainties surrounding this car, including the yearly customer demands for it, the cost of developing it, and others. The company could develop a spreadsheet model for the 10-year NPV, using its *best guesses* for these uncertain quantities. It could then report the NPV based on these best guesses. However, this analysis would be incomplete and probably misleading because there is no guarantee that the NPV based on best-guess inputs is representative of the NPV that will actually occur. It is much better to treat the uncertainty explicitly with a simulation model. This involves entering probability distributions for the uncertain quantities and seeing how the NPV varies as the uncertain quantities vary.

Each different set of values for the uncertain quantities is a scenario. Simulation allows the company to generate many scenarios, each leading to a particular NPV. In the end, it sees a whole distribution of NPVs, not a single best guess. The company can see what the NPV will be on average, and it can also see worst-case and best-case results.

These approaches are summarized in Figures 15.1 and 15.2. Figure 15.1 indicates that the deterministic (nonsimulation) approach, using best guesses for the uncertain inputs, is generally *not* the appropriate method. It leads to the "flaw of averages," as we will discuss later in the chapter. The problem is that the outputs from the deterministic model are often not representative of the true outputs. The appropriate method is shown in Figure 15.2. Here the uncertainty is modeled explicitly with random inputs, and the end result is a probability distribution for each of the important outputs.

Figure 15.1 Inappropriate Deterministic Model

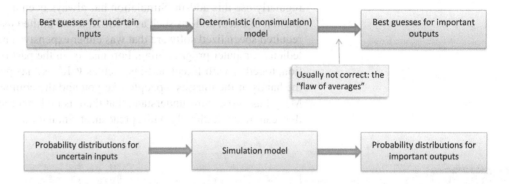

Figure 15.2 Appropriate Simulation Model

Simulation models are also useful for determining how sensitive a system is to changes in operating conditions. For example, the operations of a supermarket could be simulated. Once the simulation model has been developed, it could then be run (with suitable modifications) to ask a number of what-if questions. For example, if the supermarket experiences a 20% increase in business, what will happen to the average time customers must wait for service?

A huge benefit of computer simulation is that it enables managers to answer these types of what-if questions without actually changing (or building) a physical system. For example, the supermarket might want to experiment with the number of open registers to see the effect on customer waiting times. The only way it can *physically* experiment with more registers than it currently owns is to purchase more equipment. Then if it determines that this equipment is not a good investment—customer waiting times do not decrease appreciably—the company is stuck with expensive equipment it doesn't need. Computer simulation is a much less expensive alternative. It provides the company with an electronic replica of what would happen *if* the new equipment were purchased. Then, if the simulation indicates that the new equipment is worth the cost, the company can be confident that purchasing it is the right decision. Otherwise, it can abandon the idea of the new equipment *before* the equipment has been purchased.

Spreadsheet simulation modeling is similar to the other modeling applications in this book. You begin with input variables and then relate these with appropriate Excel® formulas to produce output variables of interest. The main difference is that simulation uses *random* numbers to drive the process. These random numbers are generated with special functions that we will discuss in detail. Each time the spreadsheet recalculates, all the random numbers change. This provides the ability to model the logical process once and then use Excel's recalculation to generate many different scenarios. By collecting the data from these scenarios, you can see the most likely values of the outputs and the best-case and worst-case values of the outputs.

In this chapter we begin by illustrating spreadsheet models that can be developed with built-in Excel functionality. However, because simulation is such an important tool for analyzing real problems, add-ins to Excel have been developed to streamline the process of developing and analyzing simulation models. Therefore, we then introduce @RISK, one of the most popular simulation add-ins. This add-in not only augments the simulation capabilities of Excel, but it also enables you to analyze models much more quickly and easily.

Like the other Palisade add-ins, @RISK works only with Excel for Windows, not with Excel for Mac.

The purpose of this chapter is to introduce basic simulation concepts, show how simulation models can be developed in Excel, and demonstrate the capabilities of @RISK. Then in the next chapter, armed with the necessary simulation tools, we will explore a variety of simulation models.

Before proceeding, you might ask whether simulation is really used in the business world. The answer is a resounding "yes." The chapter opener described an airline example, and many other examples can be found online. For example, if you visit www.palisade .com, you will see descriptions of interesting @RISK applications from companies that regularly use this add-in. Simulation has always been a powerful tool, but until the introduction of Excel add-ins such as @RISK, it had limited use for several reasons. It typically required specialized software that was either expensive and difficult to learn, or it required tedious computer programming. Fortunately, in the past two decades, spreadsheet simulation, together with Excel add-ins such as @RISK, has put this powerful methodology in the hands of the masses—people like you and the companies you are likely to work for. Many businesses now understand that there is no longer any reason to ignore uncertainty; they can model it directly with spreadsheet simulation.

15-2 Probability Distributions for Input Variables

In spreadsheet simulation models, input cells can contain random numbers. Any output cells then vary as these random inputs change.

In this section we discuss the building blocks of spreadsheet simulation models: **probability distributions for input variables** that capture uncertainty. All spreadsheet simulation models are similar to the spreadsheet models from previous chapters. They have a number of cells that contain values of input variables. The other cells then contain formulas that embed the logic of the model and eventually lead to the output variable(s) of interest. The primary difference between the spreadsheet models you have developed so far and simulation models is that at least one of the input variable cells in a simulation model contains *random* numbers. Each time the spreadsheet recalculates, the random numbers change, and the new random values of the inputs produce new values of the outputs. This is the essence of simulation—it enables you to see how outputs vary as random inputs change.

> **Excel Tip**
>
> **Recalculation Key**
>
> The easiest way to make a spreadsheet recalculate is to press the **F9 key**. This is often called the "recalc" key.

Technically speaking, input cells do not contain random numbers; they contain *probability distributions*. In general, a probability distribution indicates the possible values of a variable and the probabilities of these values. As a very simple example, you might indicate by an appropriate formula (to be described later) that you want a probability distribution with possible values 50 and 100, and corresponding probabilities 0.7 and 0.3. If you force the sheet to recalculate repeatedly and watch this input cell, you will see the value 50 about 70% of the time and the value 100 about 30% of the time. No other values besides 50 and 100 will appear.

When you enter a given probability distribution in a random input cell, you are describing the possible values and the probabilities of these values that you believe mirror reality. There are many probability distributions to choose from, and you should always attempt to choose an *appropriate* distribution for each specific problem. This is not necessarily easy. Therefore, we address it in this section by answering several key questions:

- What types of probability distributions are available, and why do you choose one probability distribution rather than another in any particular simulation model?
- Which probability distributions can you use in simulation models, and how do you invoke them with Excel formulas?

In later sections we address one additional question: Does the choice of input probability distribution really matter—that is, are the *outputs* from the simulation sensitive to this choice?

Fundamental Insight

Basic Elements of Spreadsheet Simulation

A spreadsheet simulation model requires three elements: (1) a method for entering random quantities from specified probability distributions in input cells, (2) the usual types of Excel formulas for relating outputs to inputs, and (3) the ability to make the spreadsheet recalculate many times and capture the resulting outputs for statistical analysis. Excel has some capabilities for performing these steps, but Excel add-ins such as @RISK provide excellent tools for automating the process.

15-2a Types of Probability Distributions

Imagine a toolbox that contains the probability distributions you know and understand. As you obtain more experience in simulation modeling, you will naturally add probability distributions to your toolbox that you can then use in future simulation models. We begin by adding a few useful probability distributions to this toolbox. However, before adding any specific distributions, it is useful to provide a brief review of some important general characteristics of probability distributions.[1] These include the following distinctions:

- Discrete versus continuous
- Symmetric versus skewed
- Bounded versus unbounded
- Nonnegative versus unrestricted

Fundamental Insight

Choosing Probability Distributions for Uncertain Inputs

In simulation models, it is important to choose *appropriate* probability distributions for uncertain inputs. These choices can strongly affect the results. However, there are no "right answers." You need to choose the probability distributions that best describe the uncertainty, and this is usually not easy. However, the properties discussed in this section provide useful guidelines for making reasonable choices.

---

1 Much of this material was covered in Chapters 2 and 5, but it is reviewed here.

Discrete Versus Continuous

A probability distribution is *discrete* if it has a finite number of possible values.[2] For example, if you throw two dice and look at the sum of the faces showing, there are only 11 discrete possibilities: the integers 2 through 12. In contrast, a probability distribution is *continuous* if its possible values are essentially a continuum. An example is the amount of rain that falls during a month in Indiana. It could be any decimal value from 0 to, say, 15 inches.

The graph of a discrete distribution is a series of spikes, as shown in Figure 15.3.[3] The height of each spike is the probability of the corresponding value.

Figure 15.3 Typical Discrete Probability Distribution

The heights above a density function are not probabilities, but they still indicate relative likelihoods of the possible values.

In contrast, a continuous distribution is characterized by a *density function*, a smooth curve as shown in Figure 15.4. Recall from Chapter 5 that the height of the density function above any value indicates the relative likelihood of that value, and probabilities can be calculated as areas under the curve.

Sometimes it is convenient to treat a discrete probability distribution as continuous, and vice versa. For example, consider a student's random score on an exam that has 1000 possible points. If the grader scores each exam to the nearest integer, then even though the score is discrete with many possible integer values, it is probably more convenient to model its distribution as a continuum. Continuous probability distributions are typically more intuitive and easier to work with than discrete distributions when there are many possible values. In contrast, continuous distributions are sometimes *discretized* for simplicity. In this case, the continuum of possible values is replaced by a few typical values.

Symmetric Versus Skewed

A probability distribution can be symmetric or skewed to the left or right. Figures 15.4, 15.5, and 15.6 provide examples of these. You typically choose between a symmetric and skewed distribution on the basis of realism. For example, if you want to model a student's score on a 100-point exam, you will probably choose a left-skewed distribution. This is because a few poorly prepared students typically "pull down the curve." On the other hand, if you want to model the time it takes to serve a customer at a bank, you will probably choose a right-skewed distribution. This is because most customers take only a minute or two, but a few customers take a long time. Finally, if you want to model the monthly return on a stock, you might choose a distribution symmetric around zero, reasoning that

---

2 It is possible for a discrete variable to have a *countably infinite* number of possible values, such as all the nonnegative integers. However, this is not an important distinction for practical applications.

3 This figure and several later figures are from Palisade's @RISK add-in.

Figure 15.4 Typical Continuous
Probability Distribution

Figure 15.5 Positively Skewed
Probability Distribution

Figure 15.6 Negatively
Skewed Probability Distribution

the stock return is just as likely to be positive as negative and there is no obvious reason
for skewness in either direction.

Bounded Versus Unbounded

A probability distribution is *bounded* if there are values *A* and *B* such that no possible
value can be less than *A* or greater than *B*. The value *A* is then the *minimum* possible value,

and the value *B* is the *maximum* possible value. The distribution is *unbounded* if there are no such bounds. Of course, it is possible for a distribution to be bounded in one direction but not the other. As an example, the distribution of scores on a 100-point exam is bounded between 0 and 100. In contrast, the distribution of the amount of damages Mr. Jones submits to his insurance company in a year is bounded on the left by 0, but there is no natural upper bound. Therefore, you might model this amount with a distribution that is bounded by 0 on the left but is unbounded on the right. Alternatively, if you believe that no damage amount larger than $20,000 can occur, you could model this amount with a distribution that is bounded in both directions.

Nonnegative Versus Unrestricted

One important special case of bounded distributions is when the only possible values are *nonnegative*. For example, if you want to model the random cost of manufacturing a new product, you know that this cost must be nonnegative. There are many other such examples. In these cases, you should model the randomness with a probability distribution that is bounded below by 0. This prevents negative values that make no practical sense.

15-2b Common Probability Distributions

Think of the Probability Distributions.xlsx file as a "dictionary" of the most commonly used distributions. Keep it handy for reference.

Now that you know the *types* of probability distributions available, you can add some common probability distributions to your toolbox. The file **Probability Distributions.xlsx** was developed to help you learn and explore the distributions discussed in this section, plus others. Each sheet in this file illustrates a particular probability distribution. It describes the general characteristics of the distribution, indicates how you can generate random numbers from the distribution with Excel's built-in functions, with @RISK functions, or with Albright's RandGen add-in (freely available at https://kelley.iu.edu/albrightbooks/free_downloads.htm) and it includes histograms of these distributions from simulated data to illustrate their shapes.[4]

A family of distributions has a common name, such as "normal." Each member of the family is specified by one or more numerical parameters.

Each of the following distributions is really a *family* of distributions. Each member of the family is specified by one or more parameters. For example, there is a normal distribution for each possible mean and standard deviation you specify. Therefore, when you try to find an appropriate input probability distribution for a simulation model, you first have to choose an appropriate family, and then you have to select the appropriate parameters for that family.

Uniform Distribution

The **uniform distribution** is the "flat" distribution illustrated in Figure 15.7. It is bounded by a minimum and a maximum, and all values between these two extremes are equally likely. You can think of this as the "I have no idea" distribution. For example, a manager might realize that a building cost is uncertain. If she can state only that, "I know the cost will be between $20,000 and $30,000, but other than this, I have no idea what the cost will be," then a uniform distribution from $20,000 to $30,000 is a natural choice. However, even though some people do sometimes use the uniform distribution in such situations, this choice is usually not very realistic. If the manager really thinks about it, she can probably provide more information about the uncertain cost, such as, "The cost is more

---

4 Later sections of this chapter and all the next chapter discuss much of @RISK's functionality. For this section, the only functionality used is @RISK's collection of functions, such as RISKNORMAL and RISKTRIANG, for generating random numbers from various probability distributions. You can skim the details of these functions for now and refer back to them as necessary in later sections.

Figure 15.7 Uniform
Distribution

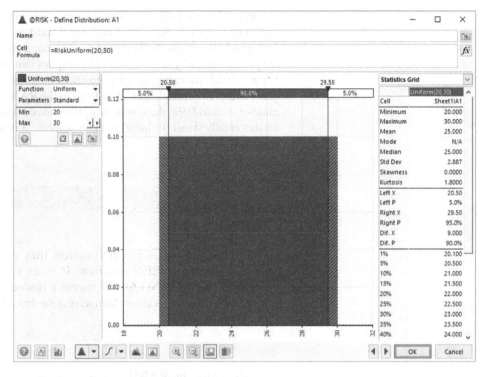

likely to be close to $25,000 than to either of the extremes." Then some distribution other
than the uniform is more appropriate.

Nevertheless, the uniform distribution is important for another reason. All simulation
software packages, including Excel, are capable of generating random numbers uniformly
distributed between 0 and 1. These are the building blocks of most simulated random
numbers, in that random numbers from other probability distributions are generated
from them.

In Excel, you can generate a uniformly distributed random number between 0 and 1
by entering the formula

=RAND()

in any cell. (The parentheses to the right of RAND indicate that this is an Excel function
with no arguments. These parentheses must be included.)

*The RAND function is Excel's
"building block" function
for generating random
numbers.*

*RAND and RANDBETWEEN
Functions*

Excel Function

RAND

To generate a random number equally likely to be anywhere between 0 and 1,
enter the formula **=RAND()** into any cell. Press the F9 key, or recalculate in
any other way, to make it change randomly.

In addition to being between 0 and 1, the numbers created by this function have two
important properties.

- **Uniform property.** Each time you enter the RAND function in a cell, all numbers
between 0 and 1 have the same chance of occurring. This means that approximately
10% of the numbers generated by the RAND function will be between 0.0 and 0.1;
10% of the numbers will be between 0.65 and 0.75; 60% of the numbers will be

between 0.20 and 0.80; and so on. This property explains why the random numbers are said to be *uniformly distributed* between 0 and 1.

- **Independence property.** Different random numbers generated by RAND functions are *probabilistically independent*. This implies that when you generate a random number in cell A5, for example, it has no effect on the values of any other random numbers generated in the spreadsheet. If one call to the RAND function yields a large random number such as 0.98, there is no reason to suspect that the next call to RAND will yield an abnormally small (or large) random number; it is unaffected by the value of the first random number.

Excel Function

RANDBETWEEN

There is one other Excel function that generates random numbers, the RANDBETWEEN function. It takes two integer arguments, as in **=RANDBETWEEN(1,6),** and returns a random integer between these values (including the two values themselves) so that all integers in this interval are equally likely.

To illustrate the RAND function, open a new workbook, enter the formula **=RAND()** in cell A4, and copy it to the range A4:A503. This generates 500 random numbers. Figure 15.8 displays a few of them. However, when you try this on your PC, you will undoubtedly obtain *different* random numbers. This is an inherent characteristic of simulation—no two answers are ever exactly alike. Now press the F9 recalc key. All the random numbers will change. In fact, each time you press the F9 key or do anything to make your spreadsheet recalculate, all cells containing the RAND function will change.

Figure 15.8 Uniformly Distributed Random Numbers Generated by the RAND Function

	A	B	C
1	**500 random numbers from RAND function**		
2			
3	Random number		
4	0.4023		
5	0.0978		
6	0.1494		
7	0.7144		
8	0.1751		
9	0.2523		
10	0.3183		
11	0.8947		

A histogram of the 500 random numbers appears in Figure 15.9. (Again, if you try this on your PC, the shape of your histogram will not be identical to the one shown in Figure 15.9, because it will be based on *different* random numbers.) From property 1, you would expect *equal* numbers of observations in the 10 categories. Obviously, the heights of the bars are *not* exactly equal, but the differences are due to chance—not to a faulty random number generator.

Figure 15.9 Histogram of the 500 Random Numbers Generated by the RAND Function

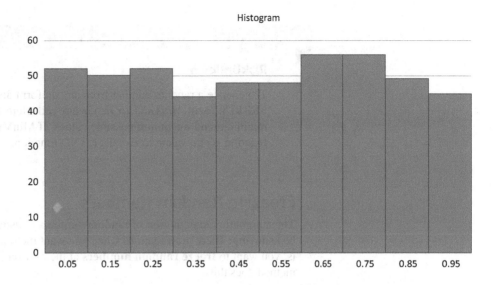

Technical Note

Pseudo-random Numbers

The "random" numbers generated by the *RAND* function (or by the random number generator in any simulation software package) are not really random. They are sometimes called pseudo-random numbers. Each successive random number follows the previous random number by a complex arithmetic operation. If you happen to know the details of this arithmetic operation, you can predict ahead of time exactly which random numbers will be generated by the *RAND* function. This is quite different from using a "true" random mechanism, such as spinning a wheel, to get the next random number—a mechanism that would be impractical to implement on a computer. Mathematicians and computer scientists have studied many ways to produce random numbers that have the two properties we just discussed, and they have developed many competing random number generators such as the *RAND* function in Excel. The technical details are not important here. The important point is that these random number generators produce numbers that appear to be random and are useful for simulation modeling.

It is simple to generate a uniformly distributed random number with a minimum and maximum other than 0 and 1. For example, the formula

=200+100*RAND()

generates a number uniformly distributed between 200 and 300. (Make sure you see why.) Alternatively, you can use the @RISK formula[5]

=RiskUniform(200,300)

You can take a look at this and other properties of the uniform distribution on the Uniform sheet in the **Probability Distributions.xlsx** file.

---

5 As with built-in Excel functions, case is irrelevant with @RISK functions. This function could be spelled as RISKUNIFORM, RiskUniform, riskuniform, or any other variation.

> **@RISK Function**
>
> ### RiskUniform
>
> To generate a random number from any uniform distribution, enter the formula **=RiskUniform(*MinVal,MaxVal*)** in any cell. Here, MinVal and MaxVal are the minimum and maximum possible values. If MinVal is 0 and MaxVal is 1, this function is equivalent to Excel's RAND function.

Freezing Random Numbers

The automatic recalculation of random numbers is usually useful, but sometimes it can be annoying. There are situations when you want the random numbers to stay fixed—that is, you want to **freeze random numbers** at their current values. The following three-step method does this.

Random numbers that have been frozen do not change when you press the F9 key.

1. Select the range that you want to freeze, such as A4:A503 in Figure 15.8.
2. Press Ctrl+c to copy this range.
3. With the same range still selected, select the Paste Values option from the Paste drop-down menu on the Home ribbon. This procedure pastes a copy of the range onto itself, except that the entries are now numbers, not formulas. Therefore, whenever the spreadsheet recalculates, these numbers do not change.

Exploring Distributions with @RISK

15-2c Using @RISK to Explore Probability Distributions

The **Probability Distributions.xlsx** file illustrates a few frequently used probability distributions, and it shows the formulas required to generate random numbers from these distributions. Another option is to use Palisade's @RISK add-in, which allows you to experiment with probability distributions with its **distribution functions**. Essentially, it allows you to see the shapes of various distributions and calculate probabilities for them, all in a user-friendly graphical interface.

To run @RISK, click the Windows Start button, go to the Programs tab, locate the Palisades DecisionTools® Suite, and select @RISK. After a few seconds, you will see the welcome screen, which you can close. At this point, you should have an @RISK tab and corresponding ribbon. (The Project button in the Tools group will be present only if you have Microsoft Project installed on your computer.) Select a blank cell in your worksheet and click the Define Distributions button on the @RISK ribbon (see Figure 15.10). You will see one of several galleries of distributions, depending on the tab you select. For example, Figure 15.11 shows the gallery of common distributions. Highlight one of the distributions and click Select Distribution. For example, choose the uniform distribution and enter 75 and 150 as the Min and Max parameters. You will see the shape of the distribution and a list of summary measures to the right, as shown in Figure 15.12. For example, it indicates that the mean and standard deviation of this uniform distribution are 112.5 and 21.65.

Everything in this window is interactive. Suppose you want to find the probability that a value from this distribution is less than 95. You can drag the left-hand "slider" in the diagram (the vertical line with the triangle at the top) to the position 95, as shown in

Figure 15.10 @RISK Ribbon

Figure 15.11 @RISK Gallery of Common Distributions

Figure 15.11 @RISK Gallery of Common Distributions

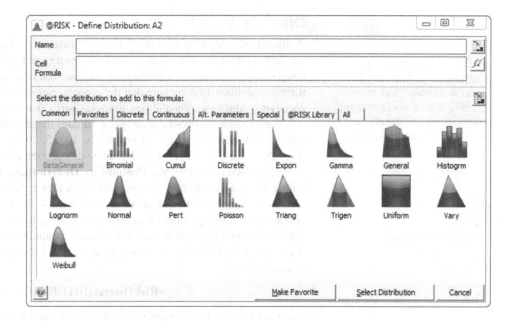

The interactive capabilities of @RISK's Define Distribution window, with its sliders, make it perfect for finding probabilities or percentiles for any given distribution.

Figure 15.12. You see immediately that the left-hand probability is 0.267. Similarly, if you want the probability that a value from this distribution is greater than 125, you can drag the right-hand slider to the position 125 to see that the required probability is 0.3333. (Rather than sliding, you can enter the numbers, such as 95 and 125, directly in the areas above the sliders.)

You can also enter probabilities instead of values. For example, if you want the value such that there is probability 0.10 to the left of it—the 10th percentile—you can enter 10% in the left space above the chart. You will see that the corresponding value is 82.5. Similarly, if you want the value such that there is probability 0.10 to the right of it, you can enter 10% in the right space above the chart, and you will see that the corresponding value is 142.5.

Figure 15.12 Uniform Distribution (from @RISK)

The Define Distribution window in @RISK is quick and easy. We urge you to use it and experiment with some of its options. By the way, you can click the second button from the left at the bottom of the window to copy the chart into an Excel worksheet. However, you then lose the interactive capabilities, such as moving the sliders.

Discrete Distribution

@RISK's way of generating a discrete random number is much simpler and more intuitive than Excel's method, which requires cumulative probabilities and a lookup function.

Generating Random Numbers with Excel Functions

A **discrete distribution** is useful for many situations, either when the uncertain quantity is not really continuous (the number of televisions demanded, for example) or when you want a discrete approximation to a continuous variable. You need to specify the possible values and their probabilities, making sure that the probabilities sum to 1. Because of this flexibility in specifying values and probabilities, discrete distributions can have practically any shape.

For example, suppose a manager estimates that the demand for a particular brand of television during the coming month will be 10, 15, 20, or 25, with respective probabilities 0.1, 0.3, 0.4, and 0.2. This typical discrete distribution is illustrated in Figure 15.13.

The Discrete sheet of the **Probability Distributions.xlsx** file indicates how to work with a discrete distribution. As you will see, a lookup table is required if you aren't using an add-in. We discuss this in detail in Section 15-4. For now, we simply mention that this is one case (of many) where it is much easier to generate random numbers with @RISK functions than with built-in Excel functions. Assuming that @RISK is loaded, you enter the function RiskDiscrete with two arguments: a list of possible values and a list of their probabilities, as in

$$=\textbf{RiskDiscrete(B11:B14,C11:C14)}$$

The Excel way, which requires cumulative probabilities and a lookup table, takes more work and is harder to remember.

Figure 15.13 Discrete Distribution (from @RISK)

@RISK Function

RiskDiscrete

To generate a random number from any discrete probability distribution, enter the formula =**RiskDiscrete(*vals,probs*)** into any cell. Here, *vals* is a list of possible values and *probs* is a list of their probabilities. You can list the values and probabilities inside curly brackets, as in the top of Figure 15.13, or you can reference ranges with these values and probabilities.

You might ask why a manager would choose this particular discrete distribution. First, it is clearly an approximation. After all, if it is possible to have demands of 20 and 25, it should also be possible to have demands between these values. Here, the manager approximates a discrete distribution with *many* possible values—all integers from 0 to 50, say—with a discrete distribution with a few typical values. This is fairly common in simulation modeling. Second, where do the probabilities come from? They are probably a blend of historical data (perhaps demand was near 15 in 30% of previous months) and the manager's subjective feelings about demand *next* month.

Normal Distribution

The *normal distribution* is the familiar bell-shaped curve that was discussed in detail in Chapter 5. (See Figure 15.14.) It is useful in simulation modeling as a continuous input distribution. However, it is *not* always the most appropriate distribution. It is symmetric, which can be a drawback when a skewed distribution is more realistic. Also, it allows negative values, which are not appropriate in many situations.

Figure 15.14 Normal Distribution (from @RISK)

A tip-off that a normal distribution might be an appropriate candidate for an input variable is a statement such as, "We believe the most likely value of demand is 100, and the chances are about 95% that demand will be no more than 40 units on either of side of this most likely value." Because a normally distributed value is within two standard deviations of its with probability 0.95, this statement translates easily to a mean of 100 and a standard deviation of 20. This does not imply that a normal distribution is the *only* candidate for the distribution of demand, but the statement suggests that the normal distribution is a good candidate.

The Normal sheet in the **Probability Distributions.xlsx** file indicates how you can generate normally distributed random numbers in Excel. This is one case where an add-in is not really necessary. The formula

=NORM.INV(RAND(),*Mean*,*Stdev*)

always works. Still, this is not as easy to remember as @RISK's formula

=RiskNormal(*Mean*,*Stdev*)

Triangular Distribution

The **triangular distribution** is somewhat similar to the normal distribution in that its density function rises to some point and then falls, but it is more flexible and intuitive than the normal distribution. Therefore, it is an excellent candidate for many continuous input variables. The shape of a triangular density function is literally a triangle, as shown in Figure 15.15. It is specified by three easy-to-understand parameters: the minimum possible value, the most likely value, and the maximum possible value. The high point of the triangle is above the most likely value. Therefore, if a manager states, "We believe the most likely development cost is $1.5 million, and we don't believe the development cost could possibly be less than $1.2 million or greater than $2.1 million," the triangular distribution with these three parameters is a natural choice. As in this numerical example, the triangular distribution can be skewed if the mostly likely value is closer to one extreme than another. Of course, it can also be symmetric if the most likely value is right in the middle.

A triangular distribution is a good choice in many simulation models because it can have a variety of shapes and its parameters are easy to understand.

Figure 15.15 Triangular Distribution (from @RISK)

The Triangular sheet of the **Probability Distributions.xlsx** file indicates how to generate random values from this distribution. As it indicates, there is no easy way to do it with Excel functions only. However, it is easy with @RISK, using the RiskTriang function, as in

=RiskTriang(B10,B11,B12)

This function takes three arguments: the minimum value, the most likely value, and the maximum value—in this order and separated by commas. You will see this function in many of our examples. Just remember that it has an abbreviated spelling: RiskTriang, not RiskTriangular.

> ### @RISK Function
>
> #### RiskTriang
>
> To generate a random number from a triangular distribution, enter the formula **=RiskTriang(*MinVal,MLVal,MaxVal*)** in any cell. Here, *MinVal* is the minimum possible value, *MLVal* is the most likely value, and *MaxVal* is the maximum value.

Binomial Distribution

The *binomial distribution* is a discrete distribution that was discussed extensively in Chapter 5. Recall that the binomial distribution applies to a very specific situation: when a number of independent and identical trials occur, and each trial results in a *success* or *failure*. Then the binomial random number is the number of successes in these trials. The two parameters of this distribution, *n* and *p*, are the number of trials and the probability of success on each trial.

A random number from a binomial distribution indicates the number of successes in a certain number of identical trials.

As an example, suppose an airline company sells 170 tickets for a flight and estimates that 80% of the people with tickets will actually show up for the flight. How many people will actually show up? It is tempting to state that *exactly* 80% of 170, or 136 people, will show up, but this neglects the inherent randomness. A more realistic way to model this situation is to say that each of the 170 people, independently of one another, will show up with probability 0.8. Then the number of people who actually show up is then binomially distributed with *n* = 170 and *p* = 0.8. (This assumes independent behavior across passengers, which might not be the case, for example, if whole families either show up or don't.) This distribution is illustrated in Figure 15.16.

Figure 15.16 Binomial Distribution (from @RISK)

The Binomial sheet of the **Probability Distributions.xlsx** file indicates how to generate random numbers from this distribution. Although it is possible to do this with Excel using the built-in BINOM.INV function and the RAND function, it is not very intuitive or easy to remember. The @RISK way is easier. In the airline example, you would generate the number who show up with the formula

$$=\text{RiskBinomial}(170, 0.8)$$

Note that the histogram in this figure is approximately bell-shaped. This is no accident. When the number of trials n is reasonably large and p isn't too close to 0 or 1, the binomial distribution can be approximated well by the normal distribution.

@RISK Function

RiskBinomial

To generate a random number from a binomial distribution, enter the formula $=\text{RiskBinomial}(n, p)$ in any cell. Here, n is the number of trials, and p is the probability of a success on each trial.

It is natural to ask which distribution to use for a given uncertain quantity such as the price of oil, the demand for laptops, and so on. Admittedly, the choices we make in later examples are sometimes fairly arbitrary. However, in real business situations the choice is not always clear-cut, and it can make a difference in the results. Stanford professor Sam Savage and two of his colleagues discuss this choice in a series of two articles on "Probability Management." They argue that with the increasing importance of simulation models in today's business world, input distributions should not only be chosen carefully, but they should be kept and maintained as important corporate assets. They shouldn't just be chosen in some ad hoc fashion every time they are needed. For example, if the price of oil is an important input in many of a company's decisions, then experts within the company should assess an appropriate distribution for the price of oil and modify it as necessary when new information arises. The authors even suggest a new company position, Chief Probability Officer, to control access to the company's probability distributions.

As you are reading these final two chapters, keep Savage's ideas in mind. The choice of probability distributions for inputs is not easy, but it is also not arbitrary. The choice *can* make a difference in the results. This is the reason why you want as many families of probability distributions in your toolbox as possible. You then have more flexibility in choosing a distribution that is appropriate for your situation.

Problems

Solutions for problems whose numbers appear within a colored box can be found in the Student Solution Files.

Level A

1. Use the RAND function and the Copy command to generate a set of 100 random numbers.
  a. What fraction of the random numbers are smaller than 0.5?
  b. What fraction of the time is a random number less than 0.5 followed by a random number greater than 0.5?
  c. What fraction of the random numbers are larger than 0.8?
  d. Freeze these random numbers. However, instead of pasting them over the original random numbers, paste them onto a new range. Then press the F9 recalculate key. The original random numbers should change, but the pasted copy should remain the same.

2. Use Excel's functions (not @RISK) to generate 1000 random numbers from a normal distribution with mean 100 and standard deviation 10.
  a. Calculate the mean and standard deviation of these random numbers. Are they approximately what you would expect?
  b. What fraction of these random numbers are within k standard deviations of the mean? Answer for $k = 1$; for $k = 2$; for $k = 3$. Are the answers close to what they should be (according to the empirical rules you learned in Chapters 2 and 5)?
  c. Create a histogram of the random numbers. Does this histogram have approximately the shape you would expect?

3. Use @RISK's Define Distributions tool to show a uniform distribution from 400 to 750. Then answer the following questions.
  a. What are the mean and standard deviation of this distribution?
  b. What are the 5th and 95th percentiles of this distribution?

c. What is the probability that a random number from this distribution is less than 450?

d. What is the probability that a random number from this distribution is greater than 650?

e. What is the probability that a random number from this distribution is between 500 and 700?

4. Use @RISK's Define Distributions tool to draw a normal distribution with mean 500 and standard deviation 100. Then answer the following questions.

a. What is the probability that a random number from this distribution is less than 450?

b. What is the probability that a random number from this distribution is greater than 650?

c. What is the probability that a random number from this distribution is between 500 and 700?

5. Use @RISK's Define Distributions tool to show a triangular distribution with parameters 300, 500, and 900. Then answer the following questions.

a. What are the mean and standard deviation of this distribution?

b. What are the 5th and 95th percentiles of this distribution?

c. What is the probability that a random number from this distribution is less than 450?

d. What is the probability that a random number from this distribution is greater than 650?

e. What is the probability that a random number from this distribution is between 500 and 700?

6. Use @RISK's Define Distributions tool to show a binomial distribution that results from 50 trials with probability of success 0.3 on each trial, and use it to answer the following questions.

a. What are the mean and standard deviation of this distribution?

b. You have to be more careful in interpreting @RISK probabilities with a discrete distribution such as this binomial. For example, if you move the left slider to 11, you find a probability of 0.139 to the left of it. But is this the probability of "less than 11" or "less than or equal to 11"? One way to check is to use Excel's BINOM.DIST function. Use this function to interpret the 0.139 value from @RISK.

c. Using part b to guide you, use @RISK to find the probability that a random number from this distribution will be greater than 17. Check your answer by using the BINOM.DIST function appropriately in Excel.

7. Use @RISK's Define Distributions tool to draw a triangular distribution with parameters 200, 300, and 600. Then superimpose a normal distribution on this drawing, choosing the mean and standard deviation to match those from the triangular distribution. (Click the Add Overlay button at the bottom of the window and then choose the distribution to superimpose.)

a. What are the 5th and 95th percentiles for these two distributions?

b. What is the probability that a random number from the triangular distribution is less than 400? What is this probability for the normal distribution?

c. Experiment with the sliders to answer questions similar to those in part **b**. Would you conclude that these two distributions differ most in the extremes (right or left) or in the middle? Explain.

8. We all hate to keep track of small change. By using random numbers, it is possible to eliminate the need for change and give the store and the customer a fair deal. This problem indicates how it could be done.

a. Suppose that you buy something for $0.20. How could you use random numbers (built into the cash register system) to decide whether you should pay $1.00 or nothing?

b. If you bought something for $9.60, how would you use random numbers to eliminate the need for change?

c. In the long run, why is this method fair to both the store and the customers? Would you personally (as a customer) be willing to abide by such a system?

Level B

9. A company is about to develop and then market a new product. It wants to build a simulation model for the entire process, and one key uncertain input is the development cost. For each of the following scenarios, choose an appropriate distribution together with its parameters, justify your choice in words, and use @RISK's Define Distributions tool to show your chosen distribution.

a. Company experts have no idea what the distribution of the development cost is. All they can state is "we are 95% sure it will be at least $450,000, and we are 95% sure it will be no more than $650,000."

b. Company experts can still make the same statement as in part **a**, but now they can also state: "We believe the distribution is symmetric, reasonably bell-shaped, and its most likely value is about $550,000."

c. Company experts can still make the same statement as in part **a**, but now they can also state: "We believe the distribution is skewed to the right, and its most likely value is about $500,000."

10. Continuing the preceding problem, suppose that another key uncertain input is the development time, which is measured in an *integer* number of months. For each of the following scenarios, choose an appropriate distribution together with its parameters, justify your choice in words, and use @RISK's Define Distributions tool to show your chosen distribution.

a. Company experts believe the development time will be from 6 to 10 months, but they have absolutely no idea which of these will result.

b. Company experts believe the development time will be from 6 to 10 months. They believe the probabilities of these five possible values will increase linearly to a most likely value at 8 months and will then decrease linearly.

c. Company experts believe the development time will be from 6 to 10 months. They believe that 8 months is twice as likely as either 7 months or 9 months and that either of these latter possibilities is three times as likely as either 6 months or 10 months.

15-3 Simulation and the Flaw of Averages

To help motivate simulation modeling in general, we present a simple example in this section. It will clearly show the distinction between Figure 15.1 (a deterministic model with best-guess inputs) and Figure 15.2 (an appropriate simulation model). In doing so, it illustrates a pitfall called the "flaw of averages."[6]

EXAMPLE

15.1 ORDERING CALENDARS AT WALTON BOOKSTORE

The Flaw of Averages

In August, Walton Bookstore must decide how many of next year's nature calendars to order. Each calendar costs the bookstore $7.50 and sells for $10. After January 1, all unsold calendars will be returned to the publisher for a refund of $2.50 per calendar. Walton believes that the number of calendars it can sell by January 1 follows some probability distribution with mean 200. Walton believes that ordering to the average demand, that is, ordering 200 calendars, is a good decision. Is it?

Objective

To illustrate the difference between a deterministic model with a best guess for uncertain inputs and a simulation model that incorporates uncertainty explicitly.

Where Do the Numbers Come From?

The monetary values are straightforward. The mean demand is probably an estimate based on historical demands for similar calendars.

Solution

The variables for this model are shown in Figure 15.17. (See the file **Ordering Calendars Big Picture.xlsx**.) Note that in addition to the "Big Picture" conventions illustrated in the two previous chapters, we use a green rectangle with a rounded top for uncertain quantities. An order quantity is chosen and demand is then observed. The ordering cost is based on the order quantity, the revenue is based on the smaller of the order quantity and demand, and there is a refund if demand is less than the order quantity.

Figure 15.17 Big Picture for Ordering Model

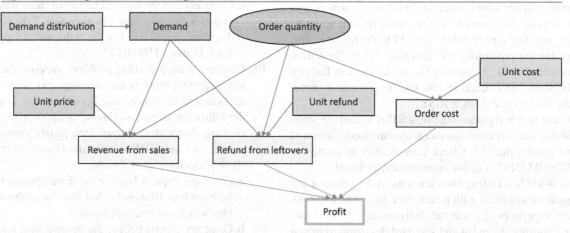

A deterministic model appears in Figure 15.18. (See the file **Ordering Calendars - Flaw of Averages Finished.xlsx**.) Assuming the best guess for demand, Walton orders to this average value, and it appears that the company's best guess for profit is $500.

---

6 As far as we know, the term "flaw of averages" was coined by Sam Savage, the same Stanford professor quoted earlier.

(The formulas in cells B16:F16 are straightforward and are listed in row 18. Before reading further, do you believe the *average* profit will be $500 when uncertainty in demand is introduced explicitly (and the company still orders 200 calendars)? Think what happens to profit when demand is less than 200 and when it is greater than 200. Are these two cases symmetric?

Figure 15.18 Deterministic Model

▲	A	B	C	D	E	F
1	Walton's bookstore - deterministic model					
2						
3	**Cost data**					
4	Unit cost	$7.50				
5	Unit price	$10.00				
6	Unit refund	$2.50				
7						
8	**Uncertain quantity**					
9	Demand (average shown)	200				
10						
11	**Decision variable**					
12	Order quantity	200				
13						
14	**Profit model**					
15		Demand	Revenue	Cost	Refund	Profit
16		200	$2,000.00	$1,500.00	$0.00	$500.00
17						
18	Formulas	=B11	=B7*MIN(B11,B14)	=B6*B14	=B8*MAX(B14-B11,0)	=C18-D18+E18

> This deterministic model gives no hint of what will happen when demand is treated explicitly as random. From the simulation model on the next sheet, we see that the average profit is nowhere near the $500 value in this sheet.

We now contrast this with a simulation model where the demand in cell B9 is replaced by a random number. For this example, we assume that demand is *normally* distributed with mean 200 and standard deviation 40, although these specific assumptions are not crucial for the qualitative aspects of the example. Specifically, cell B9 should contain the formula **=ROUND(RiskNormal(200,40),0)** where the ROUND function has been used to round to the nearest integer. (We assume that @RISK has been loaded.) Now the model appears as in Figure 15.19.

The random demand in cell B9 is now live, as are its dependents in row 16, so each time you press the F9 key, you get a new demand and associated profit. (This assumes that the @RISK "dice" button is toggled to colored, its "random" setting. More will be said about this setting later in the chapter.) Do you get about $500 in profit on average? Absolutely not! The situation isn't symmetric. The *largest* profit you can get is $500, which occurs about half the time, whenever demand is greater than 200. A typical example appears in the figure, where the excess demand of 54 is simply lost. However, when demand is *less* than 200, the profit is less than $500, and it keeps decreasing as demand decreases.

Figure 15.19 Simulation Model

▲	A	B	C	D	E	F
1	Walton's bookstore - simulation model					
2						
3	**Cost data**					
4	Unit cost	$7.50				
5	Unit price	$10.00				
6	Unit refund	$2.50				
7						
8	**Uncertain quantity (assumed normal with mean 200, stdev 40)**					
9	Demand (random)	254				
10						
11	**Decision variable**					
12	Order quantity	200				
13						
14	**Profit model**					
15		Demand	Revenue	Cost	Refund	Profit
16		254	$2,000.00	$1,500.00	$0.00	$500.00

We ran @RISK with 1000 iterations (which will be explained in detail in Section 15-5) and found the resulting histogram of 1000 simulated profits shown in Figure 15.20. The large spike on the right is due to the cases where demand is 200 or more and profit is $500. All the little spikes to the left are where demand is less than 200 and profit is less than $500, sometimes considerably less. You can see on the right that the *mean* profit, the average of the 1000 simulated profits, is only about $380, well less than the $500 suggested by the deterministic model.

Figure 15.20 Histogram of Simulated Profits (from @RISK)

The point of this simple example is that a deterministic model can be very misleading. In particular, the output from a deterministic model that uses best guesses for uncertain inputs is *not* necessarily equal to, or even close to, the average of the outputs from a simulation. This is exactly what "the flaw of averages" means.

Fundamental Insight

The Flaw of Averages

If a model contains uncertain inputs, it can be misleading to build a deterministic model by using the *means* of the inputs to predict an output. The resulting output value can be considerably different—lower or higher—than the mean of the output values obtained from running a simulation with uncertainty incorporated explicitly.

15-4 Simulation with Built-in Excel Tools

In this section, we show how spreadsheet simulation models can be developed and analyzed with Excel's built-in tools without using add-ins. As you will see, this is certainly possible, but it presents two problems. First, the @RISK functions illustrated in the **Probability Distributions.xlsx** file are not available. You are able to use only Excel's RAND function and transformations of it to generate random numbers from various probability distributions. (You can also use the RANDBETWEEN function, but except for special cases, this doesn't help much.) Second, there is a bookkeeping problem. Once you build an Excel model with output cells linked to appropriate random input cells, you can press the F9 key as often as you like to see how the outputs vary. However, there is no quick way to keep track of these output values and summarize them. This bookkeeping feature is the real strength of a simulation add-in such as @RISK. It can be done with Excel, usually with data tables, but summarizing the resulting data is completely up to the user—you. Therefore, we strongly recommend that you use the "Excel-only" method described in this section only if you don't have an add-in such as @RISK.

To illustrate the Excel-only procedure, we continue to analyze the calendar ordering problem from Example 15.1. This general problem occurs when a company (such as a news vendor) must make a one-time purchase of a product (such as a newspaper) to meet customer demands for a certain period of time. If the company orders too few newspapers, it will lose potential profit by not having enough on hand to satisfy its customers. If it orders too many, it will have newspapers left over at the end of the day that, at best, can be sold at a loss. More generally, the problem is to match supply to an uncertain demand, a very common problem in business. In much of the rest of this chapter, we will discuss variations of this problem, generally referred to as the *newsvendor* problem.

EXAMPLE

15.2 SIMULATING WITH EXCEL ONLY AT WALTON BOOKSTORE

Recall that Walton Bookstore must decide how many of next year's nature calendars to order. Each calendar costs the bookstore $7.50 and sells for $10. After January 1, all unsold calendars will be returned to the publisher for a refund of $2.50 per calendar. In this version, we assume that demand for calendars (at the full price) is given by the probability distribution shown in Table 15.1. Walton wants to develop a simulation model to help it decide how many calendars to order.

Table 15.1 Probability Distribution of Demand for Walton Example

Demand	Probability
100	0.30
150	0.20
200	0.30
250	0.15
300	0.05

Objective

To use built-in Excel tools—including the RAND function and data tables, but no add-ins—to simulate profit for several order quantities and ultimately choose the "best" order quantity.

Where Do the Numbers Come From?

The numbers in Table 15.1 are the key to the simulation model. They are discussed in more detail next.

Solution

We first discuss the probability distribution in Table 15.1. It is a discrete distribution with only five possible values: 100, 150, 200, 250, and 300. In reality, it is clear that other values of demand are possible. For example, there could be demand for exactly 187 calendars. In spite of its apparent lack of realism, we use this discrete distribution for two reasons. First, its simplicity is a nice feature to get you started with simulation modeling. Second, discrete distributions are often used in real business simulation models. Even though the discrete distribution is only an *approximation* to reality, it can still provide important insights.

As for the probabilities listed in Table 15.1, they are typically drawn from historical data or (if historical data are lacking) educated guesses. In this case, the manager of Walton Bookstore has presumably looked at demands for calendars in previous years, and he has used any information he has about the market for next year's calendars to estimate, for example, that the probability of a demand for 200 calendars is 0.30. The five probabilities in this table must sum to 1. Beyond this requirement, they should be as reasonable and consistent with reality as possible.

It is important to realize that this is really a decision problem under uncertainty. Walton must choose an order quantity *before* knowing the demand for calendars. Unfortunately, Solver cannot be used because of the uncertainty.[7] Therefore, we develop a simulation model for any *fixed* order quantity. Then we run this simulation model with various order quantities to see which one appears to be best.

Developing the Simulation Model

Now we discuss the ordering model. For any fixed order quantity, we show how Excel can be used to simulate 1000 replications (or any other number of replications). Each replication is an independent replay of the events that occur. To illustrate, suppose you want to simulate profit if Walton orders 200 calendars. Figure 15.21 illustrates the results obtained by simulating 1000 independent replications for this order quantity. (See the file **Ordering Calendars - Excel Only 1 Finished.xlsx**.) Note that there are many hidden rows in Figure 15.21. To develop this model, use the following steps.

Developing the Walton Model with Excel Tools Only

Figure 15.21 Walton Bookstore Simulation Model

	A	B	C	D	E	F	G	H	I	J	K
1	Simulation of Walton's bookstore							Range names used:			
2								LookupTable	=Model!$D$5:$F$9		
3	Cost data			Demand distribution				Order_quantity	=Model!$B$9		
4	Unit cost	$7.50		Cum Prob	Demand	Probability		Profit	=Model!$G$19:$G$1018		
5	Unit price	$10.00		0.00	100	0.30		Unit_cost	=Model!$B$4		
6	Unit refund	$2.50		0.30	150	0.20		Unit_price	=Model!$B$5		
7				0.50	200	0.30		Unit_refund	=Model!$B$6		
8	Decision variable			0.80	250	0.15					
9	Order quantity	200		0.95	300	0.05					
10											
11	Summary measures for simulation below										
12	Average profit	$204.13									
13	Stdev of profit	$328.04									
14	Minimum profit	−$250.00									
15	Maximum profit	$500.00									
16											
17	Simulation								Distribution of profit		
18	Replication	Random #	Demand	Revenue	Cost	Refund	Profit		Value	Frequency	Rel. Freq.
19	1	0.4695	150	$1,500	$1,500	$125	$125		−250	299	0.299
20	2	0.0022	100	$1,000	$1,500	$250	−$250		125	191	0.191
21	3	0.2614	100	$1,000	$1,500	$250	−$250		500	510	0.51
22	4	0.6220	200	$2,000	$1,500	$0	$500				
23	5	0.1417	100	$1,000	$1,500	$250	−$250				
1016	998	0.1005	100	$1,000	$1,500	$250	−$250				
1017	999	0.3798	150	$1,500	$1,500	$125	$125				
1018	1000	0.4530	150	$1,500	$1,500	$125	$125				
1019											

1. **Inputs.** Enter the cost data in the range B4:B6, the probability distribution of demand in the range E5:F9, and the proposed order quantity, 200, in cell B9. Pay particular attention to the way the probability distribution is entered (and compare to the Discrete sheet in the **Probability Distributions.xlsx** file). Columns E and F contain the possible demand values and the probabilities from Table 15.1. It is also necessary (see step 2 for the reasoning) to have the cumulative probabilities in column D. To calculate these, first enter the value 0 in cell D5. Then enter the formula

   =F5+D5

   in cell D6 and copy it to the range D7:D9.

2. **Generate random demands.** The key to the simulation is the generation of a customer demand in column C from a random number generated by the RAND function in column B and the probability distribution of demand. Here is how it works. The interval from 0 to 1 is split into five segments: 0.0 to 0.3 (length 0.3), 0.3 to 0.5 (length 0.2), 0.5 to 0.8 (length 0.3), 0.8 to 0.95 (length 0.15), and 0.95 to 1.0 (length 0.05). These lengths are the probabilities of the various demands. Then a demand is associated with each random number, depending on which interval the random number falls in. For example, if a random number is 0.5279, this falls in the third interval, so it is associated with the third possible demand value, 200.

---

7 @RISK contains a tool called RISKOptimizer that can be used for optimization in a simulation model, but we will not discuss it here.

To implement this procedure, you use a VLOOKUP function based on the range D5:F9 *This rather cumbersome* (range-named LookupTable). This table has the cumulative probabilities in column D and *procedure for generating a* the possible demand values in column E. In fact, the whole purpose of the cumulative *discrete random number is* probabilities in column D is to allow the use of the VLOOKUP function. To generate the *not necessary when you use* simulated demands, enter the formula *@RISK.*

=VLOOKUP(RAND(),LookupTable,2)

in cell C19. This formula compares any RAND value to the values in D5:D9 and returns the appropriate demand from E5:E9. (In the file, you will note that random cells are colored green. This coloring convention is not required, but we use it consistently to identify the random cells.)

This step is the key to the simulation, so make sure you understand exactly what it entails. The rest is bookkeeping, as indicated in the following steps.

3. **Revenue.** Once the demand is known, the number of calendars sold is the smaller of the demand and the order quantity. For example, if 150 calendars are demanded, 150 will be sold. But if 250 are demanded, only 200 can be sold (because Walton orders only 200). Therefore, to calculate the revenue in cell D19, enter the formula

=Unit_price*MIN(C19,Order_quantity)

4. **Ordering cost.** The cost of ordering the calendars does not depend on the demand; it is the unit cost multiplied by the number ordered. Calculate this cost in cell E19 with the formula

=Unit_cost*Order_quantity

5. **Refund.** If the order quantity is greater than the demand, there is a refund of $2.50 for each calendar left over; otherwise, there is no refund. Therefore, calculate the refund in cell F19 with the formula

=Unit_refund*MAX(Order_quantity-C19,0)

For example, if demand is 150, then 50 calendars are left over, and this MAX is 50, the larger of 50 and 0. However, if demand is 250, then no calendars are left over, and this MAX is 0, the larger of -50 and 0. (This calculation could also be accomplished with an IF function instead of a MAX function.)

6. **Profit.** Calculate the profit in cell G19 with the formula

=D19+F19-E19

7. **Copy to other rows.** This is a "one-line" simulation, where all of the logic is captured in a single row, row 19. For one-line simulations, which are fairly rare, you can replicate the logic with new random numbers very easily by copying down. Copy row 19 down to row 1018 to generate 1000 replications.

8. **Summary measures.** Each profit value in column G corresponds to one randomly generated demand. You usually want to see how these vary from one replication to another. First, calculate the average and standard deviation of the 1000 profits in cells B12 and B13 with the formulas

=AVERAGE(G19:G1018)

and

=STDEV.S(G19:G1018)

Similarly, calculate the smallest and largest of the 1000 profits in cells B14 and B15 with the MIN and MAX functions.

9. **Distribution of simulated profits.** There are only three possible profits, $-$250$, 125, or 500 (depending on whether demand is 100, 150, or at least 200—see the following discussion). You can use the COUNTIF function to count the number of times each of these possible profits is obtained. To do so, enter the formula

=COUNTIF($G$19:$G$1018,I19)

in cell J19 and copy it down to cell J21.

Checking Logic with Deterministic Inputs

It can be difficult to check whether the logic in your model is correct, because of the random numbers. The reason is that you usually get different output values, depending on the particular random numbers generated. Therefore, it is sometimes useful to enter well-chosen *fixed* values for the random inputs, just to see whether your logic is correct. We call these *deterministic checks.* In the present example, you might try several fixed demands, at least one of which is *less than* the order quantity and at least one of which is *greater than* the order quantity. For example, if you enter a fixed demand of 150, the revenue, cost, refund, and profit should be $1500, $1500, $125, and $125, respectively. Or if you enter a fixed demand of 250, these outputs are $2000, $1500, $0, and $500. There is no randomness in these values; every correct model should get these same values. If your model doesn't get these values, there must be a logic error in your model that has nothing to do with random numbers or simulation. Of course, you should fix any such logical errors before reentering the *random* demand and running the simulation.

You can make a similar check by keeping the random demand, repeatedly pressing the F9 key, and watching the outputs for the different random demands. For example, if the refund is not $0 every time demand exceeds the order quantity, you know you have a logical error in at least one formula. The advantage of deterministic checks is that you can compare your results with those of other users, using *agreed-upon test values* of the random quantities. You should all get exactly the same outputs.

Discussion of the Simulation Results

At this point, it is a good idea to stand back and see what you have accomplished. First, in the body of the simulation, rows 19 through 1018, you randomly generated 1000 possible demands and the corresponding profits. Because there are only five possible demand values (100, 150, 200, 250, and 300), there are only five possible profit values: $-$250$, $125, $500, $500, and $500. Also, for the order quantity 200, the profit is $500 regardless of whether demand is 200, 250, or 300. (Make sure you understand why.) A tally of the profit values in these rows, including the hidden rows, indicates that there are 299 rows with profit equal to $-$250$ (demand 100), 191 rows with profit equal to $125 (demand 150), and 510 rows with profit equal to $500 (demand 200, 250, or 300). The average of these 1000 profits is $204.13, and their standard deviation is $328.04. (Again, however, remember that your answers will probably differ from these because of different random numbers.)

Typically, a simulation model should capture one or more output variables, such as profit. These output variables depend on random inputs, such as demand. The goal is to estimate the probability distributions of the outputs. In the Walton simulation the estimated probability distribution of profit is

> *For this model, the output distribution is also discrete: There are only three possible profits for an order quantity of 200.*

$$P(\text{Profit} = -\$250) = 299/1000 = 0.299$$

$$P(\text{Profit} = \$125) = 191/1000 = 0.191$$

$$P(\text{Profit} = \$500) = 510/1000 = 0.510$$

The estimated mean of this distribution is $204.13 and the estimated standard deviation is $328.04. It is important to realize that if the entire simulation is run again with *different* random numbers, such as the ones you might have generated on your PC, the answers will probably be slightly different. For illustration, we pressed the F9 key five times and got the following average profits: $213.88, $206.00, $212.75, $219.50, and $189.50. This is truly a case of "answers will vary."

Notes about Confidence Intervals

It is common in computer simulations to estimate the mean of some distribution by the average of the simulated observations. The usual practice is then to accompany this estimate with a **confidence interval,** which indicates the accuracy of the estimate. You should recall from Chapter 8 that to obtain a confidence interval for the mean, you start with the estimated mean and then add and subtract a multiple of the *standard error* of the estimated mean. If the estimated mean (that is, the average) is $\overline{X}$, the confidence interval is given in the following formula.

> *The confidence interval provides a measure of accuracy of the mean profit, as estimated from the simulation.*

Confidence Interval for the Mean

$$\overline{X} \pm \text{Multiple} \times \text{Standard Error of } \overline{X}$$

The standard error of $\overline{X}$ is the standard deviation of the observations divided by the square root of n, the number of observations:

> *We repeat these basic facts about confidence intervals from Chapter 8 here for your convenience.*

Standard Error of $\overline{X}$

$$s/\sqrt{n}$$

Here, s is the standard deviation of the observations. You can obtain it with the STDEV.S function in Excel.

The *multiple* in the confidence interval formula depends on the confidence level and the number of observations. If the confidence level is 95%, for example, the multiple is very close to 2, so a good guideline is to go out two standard errors on either side of the average to obtain an approximate 95% confidence interval for the mean.

Approximate 95% Confidence Interval for the Mean

$$\overline{X} \pm 2s/\sqrt{n}$$

Analysts often plan a simulation so that the confidence interval for the mean of some important output will be sufficiently narrow. The reasoning is that narrow confidence intervals imply more precision about the estimated mean of the output variable. If the confidence level is fixed at some value such as 95%, the only way to narrow the confidence interval is to simulate more replications. Assuming that the confidence level is 95%, the following value of n is required to ensure that the resulting confidence interval will have a half-length approximately equal to some specified value B:

The idea is to choose the number of iterations large enough so that the resulting confidence interval will be sufficiently narrow.

Sample Size Determination

$$n = \frac{4 \times (\text{Estimated standard deviation})^2}{B^2}$$

This formula requires an estimate of the standard deviation of the output variable. For example, in the Walton simulation you can check (from the values in Figure 15.21) that the 95% confidence interval for mean profit with $n = 1000$ has half-length ($224.46 - $183.79)/2 = $20.33. Suppose that you want to reduce this half-length to $12.50—that is, you want $B = $12.50. You do not know the exact standard deviation of the profit distribution, but you can estimate it from the simulation as $328.04. Therefore, to obtain the required confidence interval half-length B, you need to simulate n replications, where

$$n = \frac{4(328.04)^2}{12.50^2} \approx 2755$$

(When this formula produces a noninteger, it is common to round upward.) The claim, then, is that if you rerun the simulation with 2755 replications rather than 1000 replications, the half-length of the 95% confidence interval for the mean profit will be close to $12.50.

Finding the Best Order Quantity

We are not yet finished with the Walton example. So far, the simulation has been run for only a single order quantity, 200. Walton's ultimate goal is to find the *best* order quantity. Even this statement must be clarified. What does "best" mean? As in Chapter 6, one possibility is to use the *expected* profit—that is, EMV—as the optimality criterion, but other characteristics of the profit distribution could influence the decision. You can obtain the required outputs with a data table. Specifically, you can use a data table to rerun the simulation for other order quantities. This data table and a corresponding chart are shown in Figure 15.22. (This is still part of the finished version of the **Ordering Calendars - Excel Only 1 Finished.xlsx** file.)

To create this table, enter the trial order quantities shown in the range M20:M28, enter the link =**B12** to the average profit in cell N19, and select the data table range M19:N28. Then select Data Table from the What-If Analysis dropdown list on the Data ribbon, specifying that the column input cell is B9 (see Figure 15.21). Finally, create a column chart of the average profits in the data table. An order quantity of 150 appears to maximize the average profit. Its average profit of $258.00 is slightly larger than the average profits from nearby order quantities and much larger than the profit gained from an order of 200 or more calendars. However, again keep in mind that this is a simulation, so that all these average profits depend on the particular random numbers generated. If you rerun the simulation with different random numbers, it is conceivable that some other order quantity could be best.

Figure 15.22 Data Table for
Walton Bookstore Simulation

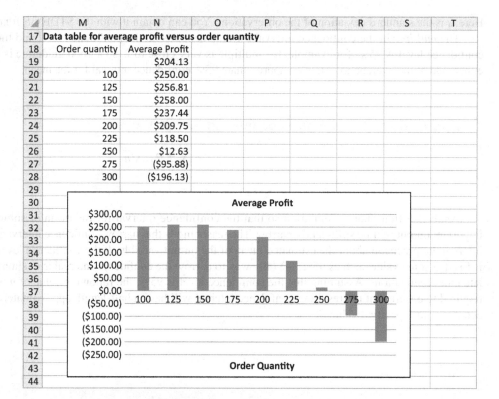

	Order quantity	Average Profit
17	**Data table for average profit versus order quantity**	
18	Order quantity	Average Profit
19		$204.13
20	100	$250.00
21	125	$256.81
22	150	$258.00
23	175	$237.44
24	200	$209.75
25	225	$118.50
26	250	$12.63
27	275	($95.88)
28	300	($196.13)

*To optimize in simulation
models, try various values of
the decision variable(s) and
run the simulation for each
of them.*

Using a Data Table to Repeat Simulations

The Walton simulation is a particularly simple one-line simulation model. All the logic—generating a demand and calculating the corresponding profit—can be captured in a single row. Then to replicate the simulation, you can simply copy
this row down as far as you like. Many simulation models are significantly more complex and require more than one row
to capture the logic. Nevertheless, they still result in one or more output quantities (such as profit) that you want to replicate. We now illustrate another method of replicating with Excel tools only that is more general (still using the Walton
example). It uses a data table to generate the replications. Refer to Figure 15.23 and the file **Ordering Calendars - Excel
Only 2 Finished.xlsx**.

Through row 19, the only difference between this model and the previous model is that the RAND function is embedded in the VLOOKUP function for demand in cell B19. This makes the model slightly more compact. As before, it uses the
given data at the top of the spreadsheet to construct a typical "prototype" of the simulation in row 19. This time, however,
you do not copy row 19 down. Instead, you create a data table in the range A23:B1023 to replicate the simulation 1000 times.

Figure 15.23 Using a Data Table to Simulate Replications

▲	A	B	C	D	E	F
17	Simulation					
18		Demand	Revenue	Cost	Refund	Profit
19		200	$2,000	$1,500	$0	$500
20						
21	Data table for replications, each shows profit from that replication					
22	Replication	Profit				
23		$500				
24	1	$125				
25	2	−$250				
26	3	$500				
27	4	−$250				
28	5	$125				
1021	998	$125				
1022	999	$500				
1023	1000	$500				

The key to simulating many replications in Excel (without an add-in) is to use a data table with any blank cell as the column input cell.

In column A, you list the replication numbers, 1 to 1000. Next, you enter the formula **=F19** in cell B23. This forms a link to the profit from the prototype row for use in the data table. Then you create a data table and enter *any blank cell* (such as C23) as the column input cell. (No row input cell is necessary, so its box should be left empty.) This tricks Excel into repeating the row 19 calculations 1000 times, each time with a new random number, and reporting the profits in column B of the data table. (If you wanted to see other simulated quantities, such as revenue, for each replication, you could add extra output columns to the data table.)

Excel Tip

How Data Tables Work

To understand this procedure, you must understand exactly how data tables work. When you create a data table, Excel takes each value in the left column of the data table (here, column A), substitutes it into the cell designated as the column input cell, recalculates the spreadsheet, and returns the output value (or values) you have requested in the top row of the data table (such as profit). It might seem silly to substitute each replication number from column A into a blank cell such as cell C23, but this part is really irrelevant. The important part is the recalculation. Each recalculation leads to a new random demand and corresponding profit, and these profits are the quantities you want to keep track of. Of course, this means that you should not freeze the quantity in cell B19 before forming the data table. The whole point of the data table is to use a different random number for each replication, and this will occur only if the random demand in row 19 is "live."

Using a Two-Way Data Table

You can carry this method one step further to see how the profit depends on the order quantity. Here you use a two-way data table with the replication number along the side and possible order quantities along the top. See Figure 15.24 and the file **Ordering Calendars - Excel Only 3 Finished.xlsx**. Now the data table range is A23:J1023, and the driving formula in cell A23 is again the link **=F19**. The column input cell should again be *any blank cell*, and the row input cell should be B9 (the order quantity). Each cell in the body of the data table shows a simulated profit for a particular replication and a particular order quantity, and each is based on a *different* random demand.

By averaging the numbers in each column of the data table (see row 14 in the file), you can see which is the best order quantity. It is also helpful to construct a column chart of these averages, as in Figure 15.25. Now, however, assuming you have not frozen anything, the data table and the corresponding chart will change each time you press the F9 key. To see whether 150 is always the best order quantity, you can press the F9 key and see whether the bar above 150 continues to be the highest. (It usually is, but not always.)

Figure 15.24 Using a Two-Way Data Table for the Simulation Model

	A	B	C	D	E	F	G	H	I	J
17	**Simulation**									
18		Demand	Revenue	Cost	Refund	Profit				
19		100	$1,000	$1,500	$250	−$250				
20										
21	**Data table showing profit for replications with various order quantities**									
22	Replication			Order quantity						
23	($250.00)	100	125	150	175	200	225	250	275	300
24	1	$250	$313	$375	−$125	$500	−375	625	125	−375
25	2	$250	$125	$375	$250	−$250	−375	−500	125	−375
26	3	$250	$313	$0	$438	$500	375	625	−250	−750
27	4	$250	$125	$375	$438	$500	0	250	−625	−750
28	5	$250	$125	$0	−$125	−$250	375	250	−625	−750
1021	998	$250	$125	$375	$438	−$250	0	−500	−625	−375
1022	999	$250	$313	$375	−$125	$125	375	−125	125	−750
1023	1000	$250	$125	$375	$438	$500	0	625	−625	−750

Figure 15.25 Column Chart of Average Profits for Different Order Quantities

By now you should appreciate the usefulness of data tables in spreadsheet simulations. They allow you to take a simulation model and replicate its key results as often as you like. This method makes summary statistics (over the entire group of replications) and corresponding charts fairly easy to obtain. Nevertheless, it takes some work to create the data tables, summary measures, and charts. In the next section you will see how the @RISK add-in does much of this work for you.

Fundamental Insight

Decisions Based on Simulation Results

Given the emphasis in Chapter 6 on the EMV criterion for decision making under uncertainty, you might believe that the mean of an output from a simulation is the only summary measure of the output relevant for decision making. However, this is not necessarily true. When you run a simulation, you approximate the entire distribution of an output, including its mean, its standard deviation, its percentiles, and more. As a decision maker, you could base your decision on any of these summary measures, not just the mean. For example, you could focus on making the standard deviation small, making the 5th percentile large, or others. The point is that the results from a simulation provide a lot more information about an output than simply its mean, and this information can be used for decision making.

Problems

Level A

11. Suppose you own an expensive car and purchase auto insurance. This insurance has a $1000 deductible, so that if you have an accident and the damage is less than $1000, you pay for it out of your pocket. However, if the damage is greater than $1000, you pay the first $1000 and the insurance pays the rest. In the current year there is probability 0.025 that you will have an accident. If you have an accident, the damage amount is normally distributed with mean $3000 and standard deviation $750.

   a. Use Excel to simulate the amount you have to pay for damages to your car. This should be a one-line simulation, so run 5000 iterations by copying it down. Then find the average amount you pay, the standard deviation of the amounts you pay, and a 95% confidence interval for the average amount you pay. (Note that many of the amounts you pay will be 0 because you have no accidents.)

   b. Continue the simulation in part **a** by creating a two-way data table, where the row input is the deductible amount, varied from $500 to $2000 in multiples of $500. Now find the average amount you pay, the standard deviation of the amounts you pay, and a 95% confidence interval for the average amount you pay for each deductible amount.

   c. Do you think it is reasonable to assume that damage amounts are *normally* distributed? What would you criticize about this assumption? What might you suggest instead?

12. In August of the current year, a car dealer is trying to determine how many cars of the next model year to order. Each car ordered in August costs $20,000. The demand for the dealer's next year models has the probability distribution shown in the file **P15_12.xlsx**. Each car sells for $25,000. If demand for next year's cars exceeds the number of cars ordered in August, the dealer must reorder at a cost of $22,000 per car. Excess cars can be disposed of at $17,000 per car. Use simulation to determine how many cars to order in August. For your optimal order quantity, find a 95% confidence interval for the expected profit.

13. In the Walton Bookstore model, suppose that Walton receives no money for the first 50 excess calendars returned but receives $2.50 for every calendar after the first 50 returned. Does this change the optimal order quantity?

14. A sweatshirt supplier is trying to decide how many sweatshirts to print for the upcoming NCAA basketball championships. The final four teams have emerged from the quarterfinal round, and there is now a week left until the semifinals, which are then followed in a couple of days by the finals. Each sweatshirt costs $10 to produce and sells for $25. However, in three weeks, any leftover sweatshirts will be put on sale for half price, $12.50. The supplier assumes that the demand for his sweatshirts during the next three weeks (when interest in the tournament is at its highest) has the distribution shown in the file **P15_14.xlsx**. The residual demand, after the sweatshirts have been put on sale, has the distribution also shown in this file. The supplier, being a profit maximizer, realizes that every sweatshirt sold, even at the sale price, yields a profit. However, he also realizes that any sweatshirts produced but not sold (even at the sale price) must be thrown away, resulting in a $10 loss per sweatshirt. Analyze the supplier's problem with a simulation model.

Level B

15. In the Walton Bookstore model with a discrete demand distribution, explain why an order quantity other than one of the possible demands cannot maximize the expected profit. (*Hint*: Consider an order of 190 calendars, for example. If this maximizes expected profit, then it must yield a higher expected profit than an order of 150 or 100. But then an order of 200 calendars must also yield a larger expected profit than 190 calendars. Why?)

15-5 Simulation with @RISK

Spreadsheet simulation modeling has become extremely popular in the past few decades, both in the academic and corporate communities. Much of the reason for this popularity is due to simulation add-ins such as **@RISK**. There are two primary advantages to using such an add-in. First, an add-in gives you easy access to many probability distributions you might want to use in your simulation models. You already saw in Section 15-2 how the RiskDiscrete, RiskNormal, and RiskTriang functions, among others, are easy to use and remember. Second, an add-in allows you to perform simulations much more easily than is possible with Excel alone. To replicate a simulation in Excel, you typically need to build a data table. Then you have to calculate summary statistics, such as averages, standard deviations, and percentiles, with built-in Excel functions. If you want graphs to enhance

@RISK provides a number of functions for simulating from various distributions, and it takes care of all the bookkeeping in spreadsheet simulations. Excel simulations without @RISK require much more work for the user.

the analysis, you have to create them. In short, you have to perform a number of time-consuming steps for each simulation. Simulation add-ins such as @RISK perform much of this work automatically.

Although we focus only on @RISK in this book, it is not the only simulation add-in available for Excel. Two worthy competitors are Crystal Ball, available from Oracle, and Risk Solver Platform, available from Frontline Systems, the developer of Solver. Both Crystal Ball and Risk Solver Platform have much of the same functionality as @RISK. However, the authors have a natural bias for @RISK—we have been permitted by its developer, Palisade Corporation, to provide the academic version with this book. (Instructions for accessing the academic version of this software can be found in the preface and on the cengage.com website.) If it were not included, you would have to purchase it from Palisade at a fairly steep price. Indeed, Microsoft Office does not include @RISK, Crystal Ball, Risk Solver Platform, or any other simulation add-in—you must purchase them separately.

15-5a @RISK Features

Here is an overview of some of @RISK's features. We will discuss these in more detail in this section.

- @RISK contains a number of functions such as RiskNormal and RiskDiscrete that make it easy to generate observations from a wide variety of probability distributions. You saw some of these in Section 15-2.
- You can designate any cell or range of cells in your simulation model as *output cells*. When you run the simulation, @RISK automatically keeps summary measures (averages, standard deviations, percentiles, and others) from the values generated in these output cells across the replications. It also creates graphs such as histograms of these values. In other words, @RISK takes care of tedious bookkeeping operations for you.
- @RISK has a special function, **RiskSimtable**, that allows you to run the same simulation several times, using a different value of some key input variable each time. This input variable is often a decision variable. For example, suppose that you want to simulate an inventory ordering policy as in the Walton Bookstore example. Your ultimate purpose is to compare simulation outputs across a number of possible order quantities such as 100, 150, 200, 250, and 300. If you use an appropriate formula involving the RiskSimtable function, the entire simulation is performed for each of these order quantities separately—with one click of a button. You can then compare the outputs to choose the best order quantity.

15-5b Loading @RISK

To build simulation models with @RISK, you must have Excel open with @RISK loaded. The first step, if you have not already done so, is to install the Palisade DecisionTools suite with its Setup program. Then you can load @RISK by clicking the Windows Start button, selecting the Programs group, selecting the Palisade DecisionTools group, and selecting @RISK. If Excel is already open, this loads @RISK inside Excel. If Excel is not yet open, this launches Excel and @RISK simultaneously. After @RISK is loaded, you see an @RISK tab and the corresponding @RISK ribbon in Figure 15.26.

Figure 15.26 @RISK Ribbon

15-5c @RISK Models with a Single Random Input

The majority of the work (and thinking) goes into developing the model. Setting up @RISK and then running it are relatively easy.

In the remainder of this section we will illustrate some of @RISK's functionality by revisiting the Walton Bookstore example. The next chapter demonstrates the use of @RISK in a number of interesting simulation models. Throughout this discussion, you should keep one very important idea in mind. The development of a simulation model is basically a two-step procedure. The first step is to build the model itself. This step requires you to enter the logic that transforms inputs (including @RISK functions such as RiskDiscrete) into outputs such as profit. This is where most of the work and thinking go, exactly as in models from previous chapters, and @RISK cannot do this for you. It is *your* job to enter the formulas that link inputs to outputs appropriately. However, once this logic has been incorporated, @RISK takes over in the second step. It automatically replicates your model, with different random numbers on each replication, and it reports any summary measures that you request in tabular or graphical form. Therefore, @RISK greatly decreases the amount of busy work you need to do, but it is not a magic bullet.

We begin by analyzing an example with a single random input variable.

EXAMPLE

15.3 USING @RISK AT WALTON BOOKSTORE

Recall that Walton Bookstore buys calendars for $7.50, sells them at the regular price of $10, and gets a refund of $2.50 for all calendars that cannot be sold. In contrast to Example 15.2, we assume now that Walton estimates a triangular probability distribution for demand, where the minimum, most likely, and maximum values of demand are 100, 175, and 300, respectively. The company wants to use this probability distribution, together with @RISK, to simulate the profit for any particular order quantity, with the ultimate goal of finding the best order quantity.

This is the same Walton Bookstore model as before, except that a triangular distribution for demand is used.

Objective

To learn @RISK's basic functionality by revisiting the Walton Bookstore problem.

Where Do the Numbers Come From?

The monetary values are the same as before. The parameters of the triangular distribution of demand are probably Walton's best subjective estimates, possibly guided by its experience with previous calendars. As in many simulation examples, the triangular distribution is chosen for simplicity. In this case, the manager would need to estimate only three quantities: the minimum possible demand, the maximum possible demand, and the most likely demand.

Solution

We use this example to illustrate important features of @RISK. We first show how it helps you to implement an appropriate input probability distribution for demand. Then we show how it can be used to build a simulation model for a specific order quantity and generate outputs from this model. Finally, we show how the RiskSimtable function can be used to simultaneously generate outputs from several order quantities so that you can choose the optimal order quantity.

Developing the Simulation Model

The spreadsheet model for profit is essentially the same model developed previously *without* @RISK, as shown in Figure 15.27. (See the file **Ordering Calendars - Basic Model Finished. xlsx.**) There are only a few new things to be aware of.

Developing the Walton Model with @RISK

@RISK Tip

Settings When Opening a Workbook

When you open a workbook with an @RISK model, such as those that accompany this chapter, you might be asked whether you want to change the current @RISK settings to match those stored in the workbook. You should generally click Yes. This changes settings, such as the number of iterations, to those you stored previously with the workbook instead of using @RISK default settings.

Figure 15.27 Simulation Model with a Fixed Order Quantity

	A	B	C	D	E	F	G	H	I	J
1	Simulation of Walton's Bookstore using @RISK							Range names used:		
2								Order_quantity	=Model!$B$9	
3	Cost data			Demand distribution - triangular				Profit	=Model!$F$13	
4	Unit cost	$7.50		Minimum	100			Unit_cost	=Model!$B$4	
5	Unit price	$10.00		Most likely	175			Unit_price	=Model!$B$5	
6	Unit refund	$2.50		Maximum	300			Unit_refund	=Model!$B$6	
7										
8	Decision variable									
9	Order quantity	200								
10										
11	Simulation									
12		Demand	Revenue	Cost	Refund	Profit				
13		255	$2,000	$1,500	$0	$500				
14										
15	Summary measures of profit from @RISK - based on 1000 iterations									
16	Minimum	−$242.50								
17	Maximum	$500.00								
18	Average	$337.51								
19	Standard deviation	$189.06								
20	5th percentile	−$47.50								
21	95th percentile	$500.00								
22	P(profit <= 300)	0.360								
23	P(profit > 400)	0.515								

1. **Input distribution.** To generate a random demand, enter the formula

   =ROUND(RiskTriang(E4,E5,E6),0)

   in cell B13 for the random demand. This uses the RiskTriang function to generate a demand from the triangular distribution. (As before, our convention is to color random input cells green.) Excel's ROUND function is used to round demand to the nearest integer. Recall from the discussion in Section 15-3 that Excel has no built-in functions to generate random numbers from a triangular distribution, but this is easy with @RISK.

2. **Output cell.** When the simulation runs, you want @RISK to keep track of profit. In @RISK's terminology, you need to designate the Profit cell, F13, as an *output cell*. To do this, select cell F13 and then click the Add Output button on the @RISK ribbon. (See Figure 15.26.) This adds **RiskOutput("*label*")**+ to the cell's formula. (Here, "label" is a label that @RISK uses for its reports. In this case it makes sense to use "Profit" as the label.) The formula in cell F13 changes from

   =C13+E13-D13

   to

   =RiskOutput("Profit")+C13+E13-D13

The plus sign following RiskOutput is simply @RISK's way of indicating that you want to keep track of the value in this cell (for reporting reasons) as the simulation progresses. Any number of cells can be designated in this way as output cells. They are typically the "bottom line" values of primary interest. Our convention is to color such cells gray.

The RiskOutput function indicates that a cell is an output cell, so that @RISK will keep track of its values throughout the simulation.

3. **Summary functions (optional).** There are several places where you can store @RISK results. One of these is to use @RISK statistical functions to place results in your model worksheet. @RISK provides several functions for summarizing output values. Some of these are illustrated in the range B16:B23 of Figure 15.27. They contain the formulas

=RiskMin(F13)

=RiskMax(F13)

These @RISK summary functions allow you to show simulation results on the same sheet as the model. However, they are totally optional.

=RiskMean(F13)

=RiskStddev(F13)

=RiskPercentile(F13,0.05)

=RiskPercentile(F13,0.95)

=RiskTarget(F13,300)

and

=1-RiskTarget(F13,400)

The values in these cells are not meaningful until you run the simulation (so do not be alarmed if they contain errors when you open the file). However, once the simulation runs, these formulas capture summary statistics of profit. For example, RiskMean calculates the average of the 1000 simulated profits, RiskPercentile finds the value such that the specified percentage of simulated profits are less than or equal to this value, and RiskTarget finds the percentage of simulated profits less than or equal to the specified value. Although these same summary statistics also appear in other @RISK reports, you might like to have them in the same worksheet as the model. (You can find a list of all @RISK statistical functions from the Simulation Result group in the Insert Function dropdown list on the @RISK ribbon.)

@RISK Feature

Color Coding

@RISK has an optional color coding feature. This option is in the Utilities group of the @RISK ribbon. It is a toggle. If it is toggled off, you see our blue/red/gray/green coloring. If it is toggled on, you see @RISK's color coding: blue for random input cells, red for output cells, green for statistical functions, and yellow for decision cells (for RISKOptimizer models). @RISK even allows you to change the coloring scheme if you prefer.

Running the Simulation

After you develop the model, the rest is straightforward. The procedure is always the same: (1) specify simulation settings, (2) run the simulation, and (3) examine the results.

1. **Simulation settings.** You must first choose some simulation settings. To do so, the buttons on the left in the Simulation group (see Figure 15.28) are useful. We typically do the following:

   • Set Iterations to a number such as 1000. (@RISK calls replications "iterations.") Any number can be used, but because the academic version of @RISK allows only 1000 uninterrupted iterations, we typically choose 1000.
   • Set Simulations to 1. In a later section, we will explain when you would request multiple simulations.

- The "dice" button is a toggle for what appears in your worksheet. If it is colored (Random), all random cells appear random (they change when you press the F9 key). If it is white (Static), only the *means* appear in random input cells and the F9 key has no effect. We tend to prefer the Random setting, but this setting is irrelevant when you run the simulation.

Simulation and Application Settings in @RISK

- Many more settings are available by clicking the Simulation Settings button to the left of the "dice" button, but the ones we mentioned should suffice. In addition, more permanent settings can be chosen from Application Settings in the Utilities dropdown list on the @RISK ribbon. You can experiment with these, but the only one we like to change is the Place Reports In setting in the Reports group. The default is to place reports in a new workbook. If you like the reports to be in the same workbook as your model, you can change this setting to Active Workbook.

Figure 15.28 Simulation Group on @RISK Ribbon

Leave Latin Hyper-cube sampling on. It produces more accurate results.

@RISK Technical Issues

Latin Hypercube Sampling and Mersenne Twister Generator

Two settings you shouldn't change are the Sampling Type and Generator settings (available from the Simulation Settings button and then the Sampling tab). They should remain at the default Latin Hypercube and Mersenne Twister settings. The Mersenne Twister is one of many algorithms for generating random numbers, and it has been shown to have very good statistical properties. (Not all random number generators do.) **Latin Hypercube sampling** is a more efficient way of sampling than the other option (Monte Carlo) because it produces a more accurate estimate of the output distribution. In fact, we were surprised how accurate it is. In repeated runs of this model, always using different random numbers, we virtually always got a mean profit within a few pennies of *$337.50*. It turns out that this is the true mean profit for this input distribution of demand. Amazingly, simulation estimates it correctly—almost exactly—on virtually every run. However, this means that a confidence interval for the mean, based on @RISK's outputs and the usual confidence interval formula (which assumes Monte Carlo sampling), is much wider (more pessimistic) than it should be. Therefore, we do not even calculate such confidence intervals from here on. However, it is not impossible. The accompanying video explains a method called Batch Means for calculating confidence intervals when Latin Hypercube sampling is used.

2. **Run the simulation.** To run the simulation, click the Start Simulation button on the @RISK ribbon. When you do so, @RISK repeatedly generates a random number for each random input cell, recalculates the worksheet, and keeps track of all output cell values. You can watch the progress at the bottom left of the screen. Also, if the Automatically Show Output Graph button (to the right of the dice button) is toggled to colored, you will see a histogram of the currently selected input or output cell being built as the simulation runs. If you find this annoying, you can toggle this button to white.

Latin Hypercube vs Monte Carlo Sampling

3. **Examine the results.** You must decide which results you want and where you want them. @RISK provides a lot of possibilities, and we mention the most frequently used.

- You can ask for summary measures in your model worksheet by using the @RISK statistical functions, such as RiskMean, discussed earlier.
- The quickest way to get results is to select an input or output cell (we chose the profit cell, F13) and then click the Browse Results button in the Results group of the @RISK ribbon. (See Figure 15.29.) This provides an interactive graph of the selected value, as shown in Figure 15.30. You can move the "sliders" (the two vertical bars) on this graph to see probabilities of various outcomes. The window you see from Browse Results is temporary—it goes away when you click Close. You can make a permanent copy of the chart by clicking the second button from the left (see the bottom of Figure 15.30) and choosing one of the copy options.

For a quick graph of the distribution of an output or input, select the output or input cell and click @RISK's Browse Results button.

Figure 15.29 Results Group on
@RISK Ribbon

Figure 15.30 Interactive Graph
of Profit Distribution

@RISK Tip

Graph Type

Once you get an @RISK graph such as the one in Figure 15.30, you can display it in several ways by clicking the fourth button's dropdown arrow at the bottom of the graph window. In particular, if your graph doesn't look quite like the ones shown here, try changing from Discrete Probability to Probability Density.

@RISK Tip

Percentiles Displayed on Graphs

The graph in Figure 15.35 has the right slider on 500 and shows 5% to the right of it. By default, @RISK puts the sliders at the 5th and 95th percentiles, so that 5% is on either side of them. For this example, 500 is indeed the 95th percentile (why?), but the picture is a bit misleading because there is no chance of a profit greater than 500. If you manually move the right slider away from 500 and back again, it will correctly indicate that there is no probability to the right of 500.

@RISK Tip

Saving Graphs and Tables

When you run a simulation with @RISK and then save your file, it asks whether you want to save your graphs and tables. We suggest that you save them. This makes your file slightly larger, but when you reopen it, the temporary graphs and tables, such as the histogram in Figure 15.30, are still available. Otherwise, you will have to rerun the simulation.

- You can click the Summary button (see Figure 15.29) to see the window in Figure 15.31 with the summary measures for Profit. In general, this report shows the summary for *all* designated inputs and outputs. By default, this Results Summary window shows a mini graph for each output and a number of numerical summary measures. It is also easy to customize. If you right-click anywhere on this table and choose Columns for Table, you can check or uncheck various options. For most of the later screenshots in this book, we elected *not* to show the Error column, but instead to show the standard deviation column.

For a quick (and customizable) report of the results, click @RISK's Summary button.

Figure 15.31 Summary Table of Profit Output

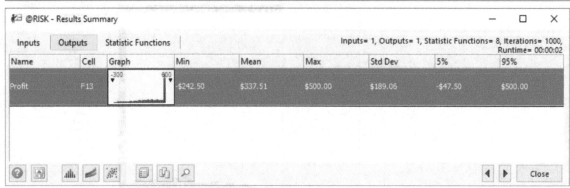

Name	Cell	Graph	Min	Mean	Max	Std Dev	5%	95%
Profit	F13		-$242.50	$337.51	$500.00	$189.06	-$47.50	$500.00

Inputs= 1, Outputs= 1, Statistic Functions= 8, Iterations= 1000, Runtime= 00:00:02

- You can click the Excel Reports button (see Figure 15.29) to choose from a number of reports that are placed on new worksheets. This is a good option if you want permanent (but non-interactive) copies of reports in your workbook. As an example, Figure 15.32 shows part of the Quick Reports option you can request. It has the same information as the summary report in Figure 15.31, plus more.

If you want permanent copies of the simulation results, click on @RISK's Excel Reports buttons and check the reports you want. They will be placed in new worksheets.

Figure 15.32 @RISK Quick Report

Simulation Summary Information	
Workbook Name	Ordering Calendars - Basi
Number of Simulations	1
Number of Iterations	1000
Number of Inputs	1
Number of Outputs	1
Sampling Type	Latin Hypercube
Simulation Start Time	7/24/2018 10:58
Simulation Duration	00:00:04
Random # Generator	Mersenne Twister
Random Seed	123

Summary Statistics for Profit			
Statistics		Percentile	
Minimum	-$243	5%	-$48
Maximum	$500	10%	$43
Mean	$338	15%	$103
Std Dev	$189	20%	$163
Variance	35744.95743	25%	$208
Skewness	-0.948717482	30%	$253
Kurtosis	2.797215761	35%	$290
Median	$410	40%	$328
Mode	$500	45%	$373
Left X	-$48	50%	$410
Left P	5%	55%	$455
Right X	$500	60%	$500
Right P	95%	65%	$500
Diff X	$548	70%	$500
Diff P	90%	75%	$500
#Errors	0	80%	$500
Filter Min	Off	85%	$500
Filter Max	Off	90%	$500
#Filtered	0	95%	$500

Discussion of the Simulation Results

The strength of @RISK is that it keeps track of any outputs you designate and then allows you to show the corresponding results as graphs or tables, in temporary windows or in permanent worksheets. As you have seen, @RISK provides several options for displaying results, and we encourage you to explore the possibilities. However, don't lose sight of the overall goal: to see how outputs vary as random inputs vary, and to generate reports that tell the story most effectively. For this particular example, the results in Figures 15.27, 15.30, 15.31, and 15.32 allow you to conclude the following:

- The smallest simulated profit (out of 1000) was −$242.50, the largest was $500, the average was $337.51, and the standard deviation of the 1000 profits was $189.06. Of all simulated profits, 5% were −$47.50 or below, 95% were $500 or above, 36% were less than or equal to $300, and 51.5% were larger than $400. (See Figure 15.27. These results are also available from the summary table in Figure 15.31 or the quick report in Figure 15.32.)
- The profit distribution for this order quantity is extremely skewed to the left, with a large bar at $500. (See Figure 15.30.) Do you see why? It is because profit is exactly $500 if demand is greater than or equal to the order quantity, 200. In other words, the probability that profit is $500 equals the probability that demand is at least 200. (This probability is 0.4.) Lower demands result in decreasing profits, which explains the gradual decline in the histogram from right to left.

Using RiskSimtable

Walton's ultimate goal is to choose an order quantity that provides a large average profit. You could rerun the simulation model several times, each time with a different order quantity in the order quantity cell, and compare the results. However, this has two drawbacks. First, it takes a lot of time and work. The second drawback is more subtle. Each time you run the simulation, you get a *different* set of random demands. Therefore, one of the order quantities could win the contest just by luck. For a fairer comparison, it is better to test each order quantity on the *same* set of random demands.

The RiskSimtable function in @RISK enables you to obtain a fair comparison quickly and easily. This function is illustrated in Figure 15.33. (See the file Ordering **Calendars - RiskSimtable Finished.xlsx**.) There are two modifications to the previous model. First, the order quantities to test are listed in row 9. (We chose these as representative order quantities. You could change, or add to, this list.) Second, instead of entering a *number* in cell B9, you enter the *formula*

The RiskSimtable function allows you to run several simulations at once—one for each value of some variable (often a decision variable).

=RiskSimtable(D9:H9)

Note that the list does not need to be entered in the spreadsheet (although it is a good idea to do so). You could instead enter the formula

=RiskSimtable({150,175,200,225,250})

where the list of numbers must be enclosed in curly brackets. In either case, the worksheet displays the first member of the list, 150, and the corresponding calculations for this first order quantity. However, the model is now set up to run the simulation for *all* order quantities in the list.

Figure 15.33 Model with a RiskSimtable Function

	A	B	C	D	E	F	G	H	I	J	K
1	Simulation of Walton's Bookstore using @RISK								Range names used:		
2									Order_quantity	=Model!$B$9	
3	Cost data			Demand distribution - triangular					Profit	=Model!$F$13	
4	Unit cost	$7.50		Minimum	100				Unit_cost	=Model!$B$4	
5	Unit price	$10.00		Most likely	175				Unit_price	=Model!$B$5	
6	Unit refund	$2.50		Maximum	300				Unit_refund	=Model!$B$6	
7											
8	Decision variable			Order quantities to try							
9	Order quantity	150		150	175	200	225	250			
10											
11	Simulated quantities										
12		Demand	Revenue	Cost	Refund	Profit					
13		187	$1,500	$1,125	$0	$375					
14											
15	Summary measures of profit from @RISK - based on 1000 iterations for each simulation										
16	Simulation	1	2	3	4	5					
17	Order quantity	150	175	200	225	250					
18	Minimum	$7.50	−$117.50	−$242.50	−$367.50	−$492.50					
19	Maximum	$375.00	$437.50	$500.00	$562.50	$625.00					
20	Average	$354.14	$367.17	$337.48	$270.29	$174.96					
21	Standard deviation	$59.04	$121.93	$189.12	$247.10	$287.01					
22	5th percentile	$202.50	$77.50	−$47.50	−$172.50	−$297.50					
23	95th percentile	$375.00	$437.50	$500.00	$562.50	$625.00					

To implement this, only one setting needs to be changed. As before, enter 1000 for the number of iterations, but also enter 5 for the number of simulations. @RISK then runs five simulations of 1000 iterations each, one simulation for each order quantity in the list, and it uses the *same* 1000 random demands for each simulation. This provides a fair comparison.

@RISK Function

RiskSimtable

To run several simulations all at once, enter the formula **=RiskSimtable(*Inputs*)** in any cell. Here, *Inputs* refers to a list of the values to be simulated, such as various order quantities. This can be a range reference or a list of values in curly brackets. Before running the simulation, make sure the number of simulations is set to the number of values in the *Inputs* list.

You can again get results from the simulation in various ways. Here are some possibilities.

- You can enter the same @RISK statistical functions in cells in the model work sheet, as shown in rows 18–23 of Figure 15.33. The trick is to realize that each such function has an optional last argument that specifies the simulation number. For example, the formulas in cells C20 and C22 are

=RiskMean($F$13,C16)

and

=RiskPercentile($F$13,0.05,C16)

Remember that the results in these cells are meaningless (or show up as errors) until you run the simulation.

- You can select the profit cell and click the Browse Results button to see a histogram of profits, as shown in Figure 15.34. By default, the histogram shown is for the *first* simulation, where the order quantity is 150. However, if you click the red histogram button with the pound sign, you can select any of the simulations. As an example, Figure 15.35 shows the histogram of profits for simulation 5, where the order quantity is 250. (Do you see why these two histograms are so different? When the order quantity is 150, there is a high probability of selling out, so the spike on the right is large. But the probability of selling out with an order quantity of 250 is much lower, so its spike at the right is much less dominant.)

- You can click the Summary button to get the results from all simulations shown in Figure 15.36. (These results match those in Figure 15.33.)

Figure 15.34 Histogram of Profit with Order Quantity 150

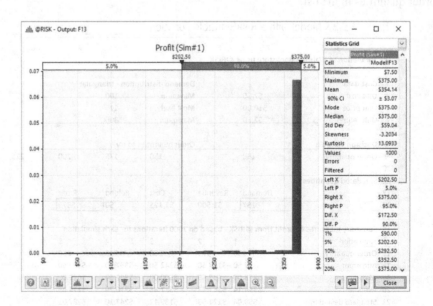

Statistics Grid	
	Profit (Sim#1)
Cell	ModelF13
Minimum	$7.50
Maximum	$375.00
Mean	$354.14
90% CI	± $3.07
Mode	$375.00
Median	$375.00
Std Dev	$59.04
Skewness	-3.2034
Kurtosis	13.0933
Values	1000
Errors	0
Filtered	0
Left X	$202.50
Left P	5.0%
Right X	$375.00
Right P	95.0%
Dif. X	$172.50
Dif. P	90.0%
1%	$90.00
5%	$202.50
10%	$292.50
15%	$352.50
20%	$375.00

• You can click the Excel Reports button to get any of several reports on permanent worksheets. Again, Quick Reports is a good choice. This produces several graphs and summary measures for each simulation, each on a different worksheet. This provides a lot of information with almost no work.

Figure 15.35 Histogram of
Profit with Order Quantity 250

Figure 15.36 Summary Report for All Five Simulations

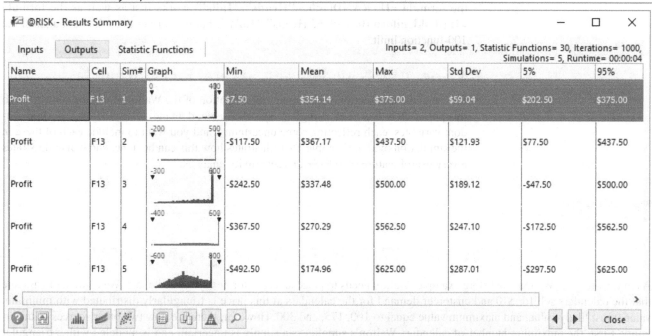

For this example, the results in Figures 15.33–15.36 are illuminating. You can see that an order quantity of 175 provides the largest *mean* profit. However, is this necessarily the "best" order quantity? This depends on the company's attitude toward risk. Larger order quantities incur more risk (their histograms are more spread out, their 5th and 95th percentiles are more extreme), but they also have more upside potential. On the other hand, a smaller order quantity, while having a somewhat smaller mean, might be preferable because of less variability. It is *not* an easy choice, but at least the simulation results provide plenty of information for making the decision.

15-5d Some Limitations of @RISK

The academic version of @RISK included has some limitations you should be aware of. (The commercial version of @RISK doesn't have these limitations. Also, the exact limitations could change as newer academic versions become available.)

- The simulation model must be contained in a single workbook with at most four worksheets, and each worksheet is limited to 300 rows and 100 columns.
- The number of @RISK input probability distribution functions, such as RiskNormal, is limited to 100.
- The number of unattended iterations is limited to 1000. You can request more than 1000, but you have to click a button after each 1000 iterations.
- All @RISK graphs contain a watermark.
- The Distribution Fitting tool can handle only 250 observations.

To avoid potential problems, close all other workbooks when running an @RISK model.

The first limitation shouldn't cause problems, at least not for the fairly small models discussed in this book. However, we recommend that you close all other workbooks when you are running an @RISK simulation model, *especially* if they also contain @ RISK functions. @RISK does a lot of recalculation, both in your active worksheet and in all other worksheets or workbooks that are open. So if you are experiencing slow simulations, this is probably the reason.

The second limitation can be a problem, especially in multiperiod problems. For example, if you are simulating 52 weeks of a year, and each week requires two random inputs, you are already over the 100-function limit. One way to get around this is to use built-in Excel functions for random inputs rather than @RISK functions whenever possible. For example, if you want to simulate the flip of a fair coin, the formula **=IF(RAND()<0.5,"Heads","Tails")** works just as well as the formula **=IF(RiskUniform(0, 1)<0.5,"Heads","Tails")**, but the former doesn't count against the 100-function limit.

15-5e @RISK Models with Several Random Inputs

We conclude this section with another modification of the Walton Bookstore example. To this point, there has been a single random variable, demand. Often there are several random variables, each reflecting some uncertainty, and you want to include each of these in the simulation model. Example 15.4 illustrates how this can be done, and it also illustrates a very useful feature of @RISK, its sensitivity analysis.

EXAMPLE

15.4 ADDITIONAL UNCERTAINTY AT WALTON BOOKSTORE

As in the previous Walton Bookstore example, Walton needs to place an order for next year's calendar. We continue to assume that the calendars sell for $10 and customer demand for the calendars at this price is triangularly distributed with minimum value, most likely value, and maximum value equal to 100, 175, and 300. However, there are now two other sources of uncertainty. First, the maximum number of calendars Walton's supplier can supply is uncertain and is modeled with a triangular distribution. Its parameters are 125 (minimum), 200 (most likely), and 250 (maximum). Once Walton places an order, the supplier will charge $7.50 per calendar *if* it can supply the entire Walton order. Otherwise, it will charge only $7.25 per calendar. Second, unsold calendars can no longer be returned to the supplier for a refund. Instead, Walton will put them on sale for $5 apiece after January 1. At that price, Walton believes the demand for leftover calendars is triangularly distributed with parameters 0, 50, and 75. Any calendars *still* left over, say, after March 1, will be thrown away. Walton again wants to use simulation to analyze the resulting profit for various order quantities.

Objective

To develop and analyze a simulation model with multiple sources of uncertainty using @RISK, and to introduce @RISK's sensitivity analysis features.

Where Do the Numbers Come From?

As in Example 15.3, the monetary values are straightforward, and the parameters of the triangular distributions are probably educated guesses, possibly based on experience with previous calendars.

Solution

The variables for this model, including the three sources of uncertainty, are shown in Figure 15.37. (See the file **Ordering Calendars - More Uncertainty Big Picture.xlsx**.) Using this as a guide, the first step, as always, is to develop the model. Then you can run the simulation with @RISK and examine the results.

Figure 15.37 Big Picture for Ordering Model with More Uncertainty

Developing the Simulation Model

The completed model is shown in Figure 15.38. (See the file **Ordering Calendars - More Uncertainty Finished.xlsx**.) The model itself requires a bit more logic than the previous Walton model. It can be developed with the following steps.

The Walton Model with Multiple Uncertain Inputs

1. **Random inputs.** There are three random inputs in this model: the maximum supply the supplier can provide Walton, the customer demand when the selling price is $10, and the customer demand for sale-price calendars. Generate these in cells B14, E14, and H14 (using the ROUND function to obtain integers) with the formulas

   =ROUND(RiskTriang(I5,I6,I7),0)

   =ROUND(RiskTriang (E5,E6,E7),0)

   and

   =ROUND(RiskTriang (F5,F6,F7),0)

   The formula in cell H14 generates the random *potential* demand for calendars at the sale price, even though there might not be any calendars left to put on sale.

2. **Actual supply.** The number of calendars supplied to Walton is the smaller of the number ordered and the maximum the supplier is able to supply. Calculate this value in cell C14 with the formula

   =MIN(B14,Order_quantity)

3. **Order cost.** Walton gets the reduced price, $7.25, if the supplier cannot supply the entire order. Otherwise, Walton must pay $7.50 per calendar. Therefore, calculate the total order cost in cell D14 with the formula (using the obvious range names)

   =IF(B14>=Order_quantity,Unit_cost_1,Unit_cost_2)*C14

Figure 15.38 @RISK Simulation Model with Three Random Inputs

	A	B	C	D	E	F	G	H	I	J
1	Simulation of Walton's Bookstore with more uncertainty									
2										
3	Cost data			Demand distribution: triangular						
4	Unit cost 1	$7.50			Regular price	Sale price		Supply distribution: triangular		
5	Unit cost 2	$7.25		Minimum	100	0		Minimum	125	
6	Regular price	$10.00		Most likely	175	50		Most likely	200	
7	Sale price	$5.00		Maximum	300	75		Maximum	250	
8										
9	Decision variable			Order quantities to try						
10	Order quantity	150		150	175	200	225	250		
11										
12	Simulated quantities					At regular price		At sale price		
13		Maximum supply	Actual supply	Cost	Demand	Revenue	Left over	Demand	Revenue	Profit
14		203	150	$1,125	208	$1,500	0	56	$0	$375
15										
16	Summary measures of profit from @RISK - based on 1000 iterations for each simulation							Range names used:		
17	Simulation	1	2	3	4	5		Order_quantity	=Model!$B$10	
18	Order quantity	150	175	200	225	250		Regular_price	=Model!$B$6	
19	Minimum	$55.00	−$102.50	−$290.00	−$347.50	−$371.00		Sale_price	=Model!$B$7	
20	Maximum	$409.75	$478.50	$547.25	$616.00	$676.50		Unit_cost_1	=Model!$B$4	
21	Average	$361.40	$389.50	$393.48	$395.10	$397.71		Unit_cost_2	=Model!$B$5	
22	Standard deviation	$44.00	$95.87	$149.25	$175.02	$178.30				
23	5th percentile	$265.00	$167.50	$49.00	$1.75	$11.75				
24	95th percentile	$375.00	$459.25	$525.25	$577.50	$593.50				

4. **Other quantities.** The rest of the model is straightforward. Calculate the revenue from regular-price sales in cell F14 with the formula

=Regular_price*MIN(C14,E14)

Calculate the number left over after regular-price sales in cell G14 with the formula

=MAX(C14-E14,0)

Calculate the revenue from sale-price sales in cell I14 with the formula

=Sale_price*MIN(G14,H14)

Finally, calculate profit in cell J14 with the formula

=F14+I14-D14

Then designate this cell as an @RISK output cell. If you like, you can also designate other cells (the revenue cells, for example) as output cells.

5. **Order quantities.** As before, enter the following RiskSimtable formula in cell B10 so that Walton can try different order quantities:

=RiskSimtable(D10:H10)

Running the Simulation

As usual, the next steps are to specify the simulation settings (we chose 1000 iterations and 5 simulations), and run the simulation. It is important to realize what @RISK does when it runs a simulation when there are several random input cells. In each iteration, @RISK generates a random value for each input variable *independently*. In this example, it generates a maximum supply in cell B14 from one triangular distribution, it generates a regular-price demand in cell E14 from another triangular distribution, and it generates a sale-price demand in cell H14 from a third triangular distribution. With these input values, it then calculates profit. For each order quantity, it then iterates this procedure 1000 times and keeps track of the corresponding profits.[8]

On each iteration, @RISK generates a new set of random inputs and calculates the corresponding output(s).

---

8 It is also possible to *correlate* the inputs, as we demonstrate in the next section.

Discussion of the Simulation Results

Selected results are listed in Figure 15.38 (at the bottom), and the profit histogram for an order quantity of 200 is shown in Figure 15.39. (The histograms for the other order quantities are similar to what you have seen before, with more skewness to the left and a larger spike to the right as the order quantity decreases.) For this order quantity, the results indicate an average profit of $393.48, a 5th percentile of $49.00, a 95th percentile of $525, and a distribution of profits that is again skewed to the left.

Figure 15.39 Histogram of Simulated Profits for Order Quantity 200

Sensitivity Analysis

We now demonstrate a useful feature of @RISK when there are several random input cells. This feature lets you see which of these inputs has the most effect on an output cell. To perform this analysis, select the profit cell, J14, and click the Browse Results button. You will see a histogram of profit, as we have already discussed, with a number of buttons at the bottom of the window. Click the red button with the pound sign to select a simulation. We chose #3, where the order quantity is 200. Then click the "tornado" button (the fifth button from the left) and choose Change in Output Mean from its dropdown list. This produces the graph in Figure 15.40. (The Regression and Correlation options produce similar results.)

Figure 15.40 Tornado Graph for Sensitivity Analysis

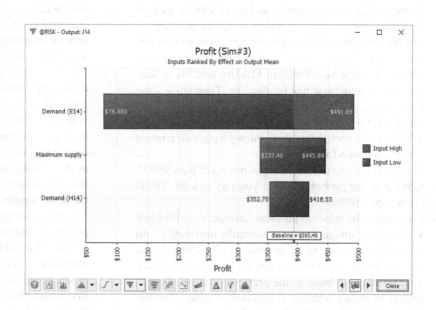

This figure shows graphically and numerically how each of the random inputs affects *A tornado graph indicates* profit: the longer the bar, the stronger the relationship between that input and profit. Specifi- *which of the random inputs* cally, each bar shows how the mean profit varies as each input varies over its range (and the *have large effects on an* other inputs are held constant). In this sense, you can see that the regular-price demand has by *output.* far the largest effect on profit. The other two inputs, maximum supply and sale-price demand, have much smaller effects. Identifying important input variables is important for real applications. If a random input has a large effect on an important output, then it is probably worth the time and money to learn more about this input and possibly reduce the amount of uncertainty involving it.

Problems

Level A

16. If you add several normally distributed random numbers, the result is normally distributed, where the mean of the sum is the sum of the individual means, and the variance of the sum is the sum of the individual variances. (Remember that variance is the square of standard deviation.) This is a difficult result to prove mathematically, but it is easy to demonstrate with simulation. To do so, run a simulation where you add three normally distributed random numbers, each with mean 100 and standard deviation 10. Your single output variable should be the sum of these three numbers. Verify with @RISK that the distribution of this output is approximately normal with mean 300 and variance 300 (hence, standard deviation $\sqrt{300} = 17.32$).

17. In Problem 11 from the previous section, we stated that the damage amount is normally distributed. Suppose instead that the damage amount is triangularly distributed with parameters 500, 1500, and 7000. That is, the damage in an accident can be as low as $500 or as high as $7000, the most likely value is $1500, and there is definite skewness to the right. (It turns out, as you can verify in @RISK, that the mean of this distribution is $3000, the same as in Problem 11.) Use @RISK to simulate the amount you pay for damage. Then answer the following questions. In each case, explain how the indicated event would occur.
   a. What is the probability that you pay a positive amount but less than $750?
   b. What is the probability that you pay more than $600?
   c. What is the probability that you pay exactly $1000 (the deductible)?

18. Continuing the previous problem, assume, as in Problem 11, that the damage amount is *normally* distributed with mean $3000 and standard deviation $750. Use @RISK to simulate the amount you pay for damage. Compare your results with those in the previous problem. Does it appear to matter whether you assume a triangular distribution or a normal distribution for damage amounts? Why isn't this a totally fair comparison? (*Hint:* Use

@RISK's Define Distributions tool to find the standard deviation for the triangular distribution.)

19. In Problem 12 of the previous section, suppose that the demand for cars is normally distributed with mean 100 and standard deviation 15. Use @RISK to determine the "best" order quantity—in this case, the one with the largest mean profit. Using the statistics and/or graphs from @RISK, discuss whether this order quantity would be considered best by the car dealer. (The point is that a decision maker can use more than just *mean* profit in making a decision.)

20. Use @RISK to analyze the sweatshirt situation in Problem 14 of the previous section. Do this for the discrete distributions given in the problem. Then do it for normal distributions. For the normal case, assume that the regular demand is normally distributed with mean 9800 and standard deviation 1300 and that the demand at the reduced price is normally distributed with mean 3800 and standard deviation 1400.

Level B

21. Although the normal distribution is a reasonable input distribution in many situations, it does have two potential drawbacks: (1) it allows negative values, even though they may be extremely improbable, and (2) it is a symmetric distribution. Many situations are modeled better with a distribution that allows only positive values and is skewed to the right. Two of these that have been used in many real applications are the gamma and lognormal distributions. @RISK enables you to generate observations from each of these distributions. The @RISK function for the gamma distribution is RiskGamma, and it takes two arguments, as in **=RiskGamma(3,10)**. The first argument, which must be positive, determines the shape. The smaller it is, the more skewed the distribution is to the right; the larger it is, the more symmetric the distribution is. The second argument determines the scale, in the sense that the product of it and the first argument equals the mean of the distribution. (The mean in this example is 30.) Also, the product of the second argument and the square root of the first argument is the standard deviation of the distribution. (In this example, it is $\sqrt{3}(10) = 17.32$.) The @RISK function for the lognormal distribution is RiskLognorm.

It has two arguments, as in **=RiskLognorm(40,10)**. These arguments are the mean and standard deviation of the distribution. Rework Example 15.2 for the following demand distributions. Do the simulated outputs have any different qualitative properties with these skewed distributions than with the triangular distribution used in the example?

a. Gamma distribution with parameters 2 and 85
b. Gamma distribution with parameters 5 and 35
c. Lognormal distribution with mean 170 and standard deviation 60

15-6 The Effects of Input Distributions on Results

In Section 15-2, we discussed input distributions. The randomness in input variables causes the variability in the output variables. We now briefly explore whether the choice of input distribution(s) makes much difference in the distribution of an output variable such as profit. This is an important question. If the choice of input distributions doesn't matter much, then you do not need to agonize over this choice. However, if it *does* make a difference, then you have to be more careful about choosing an appropriate input distribution. Unfortunately, it is impossible to answer the question definitively. The best we can say in general is, "It depends." Some models are more sensitive to changes in the shape or parameters of input distributions than others. Still, the issue is worth exploring.

We discuss two types of sensitivity analysis in this section. First, we check whether the shape of the input distribution matters. In the Walton Bookstore example, we assumed a triangularly distributed demand with some skewness. Are the results basically the same if a symmetric distribution such as the normal distribution is used instead? Second, we check whether the *independence* of input variables that has been assumed implicitly to this point is crucial to the output results. Many random quantities in real situations are *not* independent; they are positively or negatively correlated. Fortunately, @RISK enables you to build correlation into a model. We analyze the effect of this correlation.

15-6a Effect of the Shape of the Input Distribution(s)

We first explore the effect of the shape of the input distribution(s). As Example 15.5 indicates, if parameters that allow for a fair comparison are used, the shape can have a relatively minor effect.

EXAMPLE

15.5 EFFECT OF DEMAND DISTRIBUTION AT WALTON BOOKSTORE

We continue to explore the demand for calendars at Walton Bookstore. We keep the same unit cost, unit price, and unit refund for leftovers as in Example 15.3. However, in that example we assumed a triangular distribution for demand with parameters 100, 175, and 300. Assuming that Walton orders 200 calendars, is the distribution of profit affected if a *normal* distribution of demand is used instead?

Objective

To see whether a triangular distribution with some skewness gives the same profit distribution as a normal distribution for demand.

Where Do the Numbers Come From?

The numbers here are the same as in Example 15.3. However, as discussed next, the parameters of the normal distribution are chosen to provide a fair comparison with the triangular distribution used earlier.

Solution

It is important in this type of analysis to make a fair comparison. When you select a normal distribution for demand, you must choose a mean and standard deviation for this distribution. Which values should you choose? It seems only fair to choose the *same* mean and standard deviation that the triangular distribution has. To find the mean and standard deviation for a triangular distribution with given minimum, most likely, and maximum values, you can take advantage of @RISK's Define Distributions tool. Select any blank cell, click the Define Distributions button, select the triangular distribution, and enter the parameters 100, 175, and 300. You will see that the mean and standard deviation are 191.67 and 41.248, respectively. Therefore, for a fair comparison you should use a normal distribution with mean 191.67 and standard deviation 41.248. @RISK allows you to see a comparison of these two distributions, as in Figure 15.41. To get this chart, click the Add Overlay button, select the normal distribution from the gallery, and enter 191.67 and 41.248 as its mean and standard deviation.

For a fair comparison of alternative input distributions, the distributions should have (at least approximately) equal means and standard deviations.

Figure 15.41 Triangular and Normal Distributions for Demand

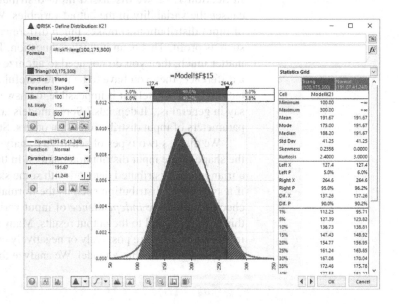

Developing the Simulation Model

The logic in this model is almost exactly the same as before. (See Figure 15.42 and the file **Ordering Calendars - Different Demand Distributions Finished.xlsx**.) However, a clever use of the RiskSimtable function allows you to run two simulations at once, one for the triangular distribution and one for the corresponding normal distribution. The following two steps are required.

The Walton Model with Alternative Input Distributions

Figure 15.42 @RISK Model for Comparing Two Input Distributions

	A	B	C	D	E	F	G	H	I
1	Simulation of Walton's Bookstore using @RISK - two possible demand distributions								
2									
3	Cost data			Demand distribution 1 - triangular			Demand distribution 2 - normal		
4	Unit cost	$7.50		Minimum	100		Mean	191.67	
5	Unit price	$10.00		Most likely	175		Stdev	41.248	
6	Unit refund	$2.50		Maximum	300				
7									
8	Decision variable								
9	Order quantity	200							
10									
11	Demand distribution to use	1	◄──	Formula is = RiskSimtable({1,2})					
12									
13	Simulated quantities								
14		Demand	Revenue	Cost	Refund	Profit			
15		149	$1,490	$1,500	$128	$118			
16									
17	Summary measures of profit from @RISK - based on 1000 iterations for each simulation								
18	Simulation	1	2						
19	Distribution	Triangular	Normal				Range names used:		
20	Minimum	−$242.50	−$730.00				Order_quantity	=Model!$B$9	
21	Maximum	$500.00	$500.00				Profit	=Model!$F$15	
22	Average	$337.47	$342.64				Unit_cost	=Model!$B$4	
23	Standard deviation	$189.13	$202.41				Unit_price	=Model!$B$5	
24	5th percentile	−$47.50	−$77.50				Unit_refund	=Model!$B$6	
25	95th percentile	$500.00	$500.00						

1. **RiskSimtable function.** It is useful to index the two distributions as 1 and 2. To indicate that you want to run the simulation with both of them, enter the formula

    =RiskSimtable({1,2})

    in cell B11. Remember that when you enter actual numbers in this function, rather than cell references, you must put curly brackets around the list.

2. **Demand.** When the value in cell B11 is 1, the demand distribution is triangular. When it is 2, the distribution is normal. Therefore, enter the formula

    =ROUND(IF(B11=1,RiskTriang(E4,E5,E6),RiskNormal(H4,H5)),0)

    in cell B15. The effect is that the first simulation will use the triangular distribution, and the second will use the normal distribution.

Look for ways to use the RiskSimtable function. It can really improve efficiency because it runs several simulations at once.

Running the Simulation

The only @RISK setting to change is the number of simulations. It should now be set to 2, the number of values in the RiskSimtable formula. Other than this, you run the simulation exactly as before.

Discussion of the Simulation Results

The comparison is shown numerically in Figure 15.43 and graphically in Figure 15.44. As you can see, there is more chance of really low profits when the demand distribution is normal, but each simulation results in the same maximum profit. Both of these statements make sense. The normal distribution, being unbounded on the left, allows for very low demands, and these occasional low demands result in very low profits. On the other side, Walton's maximum profit is $500 regardless of the input distribution (provided that it allows demands greater than the order quantity). This occurs when Walton's sells all it orders, in which case excess demand has no effect on profit. Note that the mean profits for the two distributions differ by only about $5.

Figure 15.43 Summary Results for Comparison Model

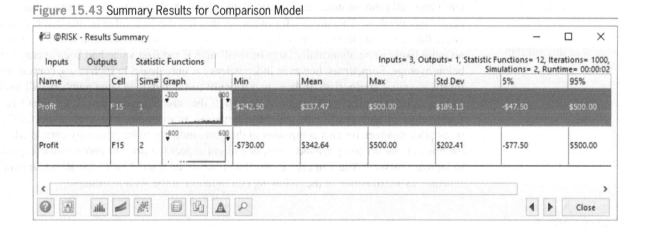

Figure 15.44 Graphical Results for Comparison Model

It is probably safe to conclude that the profit distribution in this model is not greatly affected by the choice of demand distribution, at least not when (1) the candidate input distributions have the same mean and standard deviation, and (2) their shapes are not *too* dissimilar. We would venture to guess that this general conclusion about insensitivity of output distributions to shapes of input distributions can be made in many simulation models. However, it is always worth checking, as we have done here, especially if there is a lot of money at stake.

Fundamental Insight

Shape of the Output Distribution

Predicting the shape of the output distribution from the shape(s) of the input distribution(s) is difficult. For example, normally distributed inputs don't necessarily produce normally distributed outputs. It is also difficult to predict how sensitive the shape of the output distribution is to the shape(s) of the input distribution(s). For example, normally and triangularly distributed inputs (with the same means and standard deviations) are likely to lead to similar output distributions, but there could be differences in the tails of the output distributions. In any case, you should examine the entire output distribution carefully, not just a few of its summary measures.

15-6b Effect of Correlated Inputs

Input variables in real-world problems are often correlated, which makes the material in this section important.

Until now, all random numbers generated with @RISK functions have been probabilistically independent. This means, for example, that if a random value in one cell is much larger than its mean, the random values in other cells are completely unaffected. They are no more likely to be abnormally large or small than if the first value had been average or below average. Sometimes, however, independence is unrealistic. In such cases, **correlated inputs** are more appropriate. If they are positively correlated, then large numbers will tend to go with large numbers, and small with small. If they are negatively correlated, then large will tend to go with small and small with large. As an example, you might expect daily stock price changes for two companies in the same industry to be positively correlated. If the price of one oil company increases, you might expect the price of another oil company to increase as well. You can create correlated inputs in @RISK with the **RiskCorrmat** function, as we illustrate in the following continuation of the Walton example.

EXAMPLE

15.6 CORRELATED DEMANDS AT WALTON BOOKSTORE

Suppose Walton Bookstore must order two different calendars. To simplify the example, we assume the calendars each have the same unit cost, unit selling price, and unit refund value as in previous examples. Also, we assume that each has a triangularly distributed demand with parameters 100, 175, and 300. However, we now assume they are "substitute" products, so that their demands are negatively correlated. This means that if a customer buys one, she is not likely to buy the other. Specifically, we assume a correlation of −0.9 between the two demands. How do these correlated inputs affect the distribution of profit, as compared to the situation where the demands are uncorrelated (correlation 0) or highly *positively* correlated (correlation 0.9)?

Objective

To see how @RISK enables us to simulate correlated demands, and to see the effect of correlated demands on profit.

Where Do the Numbers Come From?

The only new input here is the correlation. It is probably negative because the calendars are substitute products, but it is a difficult number to estimate accurately. This is a good candidate for a sensitivity analysis.

Solution

The key to building in correlation is @RISK's RiskCorrmat (correlation matrix) function. To use this function, you must include a correlation matrix in the model, as shown in the range J5:K6 of Figure 15.45. (See the file **Ordering Calendars - Correlated Demands Finished.xlsx**.) A correlation matrix must always have 1's along its diagonal (because a variable is always perfectly correlated with itself) and the correlations between variables elsewhere. Also, the matrix must be symmetric, so that the correlations above the diagonal are a mirror image of those below it. (You can enforce this by entering the formula =J6 in cell K5. Alternatively, @RISK allows you to enter the correlations only below the diagonal, or only above the diagonal, and it then infers the mirror images.)

Figure 15.45 Simulation Model with Correlated Demands

	A	B	C	D	E	F	G	H	I	J	K
1	Simulation of Walton's Bookstore using @RISK - correlated demands										
2											
3	Cost data - same for each product			Demand distribution for each product - triangular					Correlation matrix between demands		
4	Unit cost	$7.50		Minimum	100					Product 1	Product 2
5	Unit price	$10.00		Most likely	175				Product 1	1	−0.9
6	Unit refund	$2.50		Maximum	300				Product 2	−0.9	1
7							Note RiskSimtable function in cell J6.				
8	Decision variables								Possible correlations to try		
9	Order quantity 1	200								−0.9	0	0.9
10	Order quantity 2	200									
11									Range names used:		
12	Simulated quantities								Order_quantity_1	=Model!$B$9	
13		Demand	Revenue	Cost	Refund	Profit			Order_quantity_2	=Model!$B$10	
14	Product 1	178	$1,780	$1,500	$55	$335			Profit	=Model!$F$16	
15	Product 2	148	$1,480	$1,500	$130	$110			Unit_cost	=Model!$B$4	
16	Totals	326	$3,260	$3,000	$185	$445			Unit_price	=Model!$B$5	
17									Unit_refund	=Model!$B$6	
18	Summary measures of profit from @RISK - based on 1000 iterations										
19	Simulation	1	2	3							
20	Correlation	−0.9	0	0.9							
21	Minimum	$265.00	−$267.50	−$440.00							
22	Maximum	$1,000.00	$1,000.00	$1,000.00							
23	Average	$675.06	$675.06	$675.06							
24	Standard deviation	$158.73	$267.83	$365.64							
25	5th percentile	$392.50	$182.50	−$72.50							
26	95th percentile	$932.50	$1,000.00	$1,000.00							

To enter random values in any cells that are correlated, you start with a typical @RISK formula, such as

The RiskCorrmat function is "tacked on" as an extra argument to a typical random @RISK function.

=RiskTriang(E4,E5,E6)

Then you add an extra argument, the RiskCorrmat function, as follows:

=RiskTriang(E4,E5,E6,RiskCorrmat(J5:K6,1))

The first argument of the RiskCorrmat function is the correlation matrix range. The second is an index of the variable. In this example, the first calendar demand has index 1 and the second has index 2.

@RISK Function

RiskCorrmat

This function enables you to correlate two or more input variables. The function has the form **RiskCorrmat(*CorrMat,Index*)**, where *CorrMat* is a matrix of correlations and *Index* is an index of the variable being correlated to others. For example, if there are three correlated variables, *Index* is 1 for the first variable, 2 is for the second, and 3 is for the third. The RiskCorrmat function is not entered by itself. Rather, it is entered as the last argument of a random @RISK function, such as **=RiskTriang(10,15,30,RiskCorrmat(CorrMat,2))**.

Developing the Simulation Model

Armed with this knowledge, the simulation model in Figure 15.45 is straightforward and can be developed as follows.

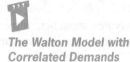

The Walton Model with Correlated Demands

1. **Inputs.** Enter the inputs in the blue ranges in columns B and E.
2. **Correlation matrix.** For the correlation matrix in the range J5:H6, enter 1's on the diagonal, and enter the formula

   =J6

   in cell K5 (or leave cell K5 blank). Then enter the formula

   =RiskSimtable(I9:K9)

   in cell J6. This allows you to simultaneously simulate negatively correlated demands, uncorrelated demands, and positively correlated demands.
3. **Order quantities.** Assume for now that the company orders the *same* number of each calendar, 200, so enter this value in cells B9 and B10. However, the simulation is set up so that you can experiment with any order quantities in these cells, including unequal values.
4. **Correlated demands.** Generate correlated demands by entering the formula

   =ROUND(RiskTriang(E4,E5,E6,RiskCorrmat(J5:K6,1)),0)

   in cell B14 for demand 1 and the formula

   =ROUND(RiskTriang(E4,E5,E6,RiskCorrmat(J5:K6,2)),0)

Correlations in @RISK Models

   in cell B15 for demand 2. The only difference between these is the index of the variable being generated. The first has index 1; the second has index 2.
5. **Other formulas.** The other formulas in rows 14 and 15 are identical to ones developed in previous examples, so they aren't presented again here. The quantities in row 16 are sums of rows 14 and 15. Also, the only @RISK output we designated is the total profit in cell F16, but you can designate others as output cells if you like.

Running the Simulation

You should set up and run @RISK exactly as before. For this example, set the number of iterations to 1000 and the number of simulations to 3 (because three different correlations are being tested).

Discussion of the Simulation Results

Selected numerical and graphical results are shown in Figures 15.46 and 15.47. You will probably be surprised to see that the *mean* total profit is the same, regardless of the correlation. This is no coincidence. In each of the three simulations, @RISK uses the *same* random numbers but "shuffles" them in different orders to get the correct correlations. This means that averages are unaffected. (The idea is that the average of the numbers 30, 26, and 48 is the same as the average of the numbers 48, 30, and 26.)

Figure 15.46 Summary Results for Correlated Model

Name	Cell	Sim#	Graph	Min	Mean	Max	Std Dev	5%	95%
Profit	F16	1		$265.00	$675.06	$1,000.00	$158.73	$392.50	$932.50
Profit	F16	2		-$267.50	$675.06	$1,000.00	$267.83	$182.50	$1,000.00
Profit	F16	3		-$440.00	$675.06	$1,000.00	$365.64	-$72.50	$1,000.00

@RISK - Results Summary

Inputs Outputs Statistic Functions

Inputs= 3, Outputs= 1, Statistic Functions= 18, Iterations= 1000, Simulations= 3, Runtime= 00:00:02

Figure 15.47 Graphical Results for Correlated Model

However, the correlation has a definite effect on the *distribution* of total profit. You can see this in Figure 15.46, for example, where the standard deviation of total profit increases as the correlation goes from negative to zero to positive. This same increase in variability is apparent in the histograms in Figure 15.47. Do you see intuitively why this increase in variability occurs? It is basically the "Don't put all of your eggs in one basket" effect. When the correlation is negative, high demands for one product tend to cancel low demands for the other product, so extremes in profit are rare. However, when the correlation is positive, high demands for the two products tend to go together, as do low demands. These make extreme profits on either end much more likely.

This same phenomenon would occur if you simulated an investment portfolio containing two stocks. When the stocks are positively correlated, the portfolio is much riskier (more variability) than when they are negatively correlated. Of course, this is the reason for diversifying a portfolio.

Modeling Issues

We illustrated the RiskCorrmat function for triangularly distributed values. However, it can be used with any of @RISK's distributions by tacking on RiskCorrmat as a last argument. You can even mix them. For example, assuming CMat is the range name for a 2 × 2 correlation matrix, you could enter the formulas

With the RiskCorrmat function, you can correlate random numbers from any distributions.

=**RiskNormal(10,2,RiskCorrmat(CMat,1))**

and

=**RiskUniform(100,200,RiskCorrmat(CMat,2))**

into any two cells. When you run the simulation, @RISK generates a sequence of normally distributed random numbers based on the first formula and another sequence of uniformly distributed random numbers based on the second formula. Then it shuffles them in some complex way until their correlation is approximately equal to the specified correlation in the correlation matrix.

> ### Fundamental Insight
>
> #### Correlated Inputs
>
> When you enter random inputs in an @RISK simulation model and then run the simulation, each iteration generates *independent* values for the random inputs. If you know or suspect that some of the inputs are positively or negatively correlated, you should build this correlation structure into the model explicitly with the RiskCorrmat function. This function might not change the mean of an output, but it can definitely affect the variability and shape of the output distribution.

Problems

Level A

22. Fizzy Company produces six-packs of soda cans. Each can is supposed to contain at least 12 ounces of soda. If the total weight in a six-pack is less than 72 ounces, Fizzy is fined $100 and receives no sales revenue for the six-pack. Each six-pack sells for $3.00. It costs Fizzy $0.02 per ounce of soda put in the cans. Fizzy can control the mean fill rate of its soda-filling machines. The amount put in each can by a machine is normally distributed with standard deviation 0.10 ounce.

    a. Assume that the weight of each can in a six-pack has a 0.8 correlation with the weight of the other cans in the six-pack. What mean fill quantity maximizes expected profit per six-pack? Try mean fill rates from 12.00 to 12.35 in increments of 0.05.

    b. If the weights of the cans in the six-pack are probabilistically independent, what mean fill quantity maximizes expected profit per six-pack? Try the same mean fill rates as in part a.

    c. How can you explain the difference in the answers to parts a and b?

23. When you use @RISK's correlation feature to generate correlated random numbers, how can you verify that they are correlated? Try the following. Use the RiskCorrmat function to generate two normally distributed random numbers, each with mean 100 and standard deviation 10, and with correlation 0.7. To run a simulation, you need an output variable, so sum these two numbers and designate the sum as an output variable. Now run @RISK. Click @RISK's Excel Reports button and check the Simulation Data option to see the actual simulated data.

    a. Use Excel's CORREL function to calculate the correlation between the two input variables. It should be close to 0.7. Then create a scatterplot of these two input variables. The plot should indicate a definite positive relationship.

    b. Are the two input variables correlated with the output? Use Excel's CORREL function to find out. Interpret your results intuitively.

24. Work the previous problem, but make the correlation between the two inputs equal to −0.7. Explain how the results change.

25. Work Problem 23, but now make the second input variable triangularly distributed with parameters 50, 100, and 500. This time, verify not only that the correlation between the two inputs is approximately 0.7, but also that the shapes of the two input distributions are approximately what they should be: normal for the first and triangular for the second. Do this by creating histograms in Excel. The point is that you can use @RISK's RiskCorrmat function to correlate random numbers from *different* distributions.

26. Suppose you are going to invest equal amounts in three stocks. The annual return from each stock is normally distributed with mean 0.01 (1%) and standard deviation 0.06. The annual return on your portfolio, the output variable of interest, is the average of the three stock returns. Run @RISK, using 1000 iterations, on each of the following scenarios.

    a. The three stock returns are highly correlated. The correlation between each pair is 0.9.

    b. The three stock returns are practically independent. The correlation between each pair is 0.1.

    c. The first two stocks are moderately correlated. The correlation between their returns is 0.4. The third stock's return is negatively correlated with the other two. The correlation between its return and each of the first two is −0.8.

    d. Compare the portfolio distributions from @RISK for these three scenarios. What do you conclude?

    e. You might think of a fourth scenario, where the correlation between each *pair* of returns is a large negative number such as −0.8. But explain intuitively why this makes no sense. Try to run the simulation with these negative correlations and see what happens.

27. The effect of the shapes of input distributions on the distribution of an output can depend on the output function. For this problem, assume there are 10 input variables. The goal is to compare the case where these 10 inputs each have a normal distribution with mean 1000 and standard deviation 250 to the case where they each have a triangular distribution with parameters 600, and 1700. (You can check with @RISK's Define Distributions window that even though this triangular distribution is very skewed, it has the same mean and approximately the same standard deviation as the normal distribution.) For each of the following outputs, run two @RISK simulations, one with the normally distributed inputs and one with the triangularly distributed inputs, and comment on the differences between the resulting output distributions. For each simulation run 1000 iterations.

    a. Let the output be the *average* of the inputs.

    b. Let the output be the *maximum* of the inputs.

    c. Calculate the average of the inputs. Then the output is the minimum of the inputs if this average is less than 1000; otherwise, the output is the maximum of the inputs.

Level B

28. The Business School at State University currently has three parking lots, each containing 155 spaces. Two hundred faculty members have been assigned to each lot. On a peak day, an average of 70% of all lot 1 parking sticker holders show up, an average of 72% of all

lot 2 parking sticker holders show up, and an average of 74% of all lot 3 parking sticker holders show up.

a. Given the current situation, estimate the probability that on a peak day, at least one faculty member with a sticker will be unable to find a spot. Assume that the number who show up at each lot is independent of the number who show up at the other two lots. Compare two situations: (1) each person can park only in the lot assigned to him or her, and (2) each person can park in any of the lots (pooling). (*Hint*: Use the RiskBinomial function.)

b. Now suppose the numbers of people who show up at the three lots are highly correlated (correlation 0.9). How are the results different from those in part **a**?

15-7 Conclusion

For years, simulation did not receive the attention it deserved in management science courses (or in business). The primary reason for this was the lack of easy-to-use simulation software. Now, with Excel's built-in simulation capabilities, plus powerful and affordable add-ins such as @RISK, simulation is receiving its rightful emphasis. The world is full of uncertainty, which is what makes simulation so valuable. Simulation models provide important insights that are missing in models that do not incorporate uncertainty explicitly. In addition, simulation models are relatively easy to understand and develop. In this chapter we have illustrated the basic ideas of simulation, how to perform simulation with Excel built-in tools, and how @RISK greatly enhances Excel's basic capabilities. In the next chapter we will build on this knowledge to develop and analyze simulation models in a variety of business areas.

Summary of Key Terms

TERM	EXPLANATION	EXCEL	PAGE
Simulation model	Model with random inputs that affect one or more outputs, where the randomness is modeled explicitly		760
F9 key	The "recalc" key, used to make a spreadsheet recalculate		762
Probability distributions for input variables	Specification of the possible values and their probabilities for random input variables; these distributions must be specified in any simulation model		762
Uniform distribution	The flat distribution, where all values in a bounded continuum are equally likely		766
RAND function	Excel's built-in random number generator; generates uniformly distributed random numbers between 0 and 1	=RAND()	767
RANDBETWEEN function	Excel's built-in function for generating equally likely random integers over an indicated range	=RANDBETWEEN (*min,max*)	768
Freeze random numbers	Change "volatile" random numbers into "fixed" numbers	Copy range, paste it onto itself with the Paste Values option	770
@RISK random functions	A set of functions, including RiskNormal and RiskTriang, for generating random numbers from various distributions		771
Discrete distribution	A general distribution where a discrete number of possible values and their probabilities are specified		772
Triangular distribution	Literally a triangle-shaped distribution, specified by a minimum value, a most likely value, and a maximum value		775
@RISK	A simulation add-in developed by Palisade	@RISK ribbon	794
RiskSimtable function	Used to run an @RISK simulation model for several values of some variable, often a decision variable		795

Key Terms (continued)

TERM	EXPLANATION	EXCEL	PAGE
RiskOutput function	Used to indicate that a cell contains an output that will be tracked by @RISK		798
Latin Hypercube sampling	An efficient way of simulating random numbers for a simulation model, where the results are more accurate than with other sampling methods		799
RiskCorrmat function	Used to correlate two or more random input variables		815
Correlated inputs	Random quantities, such as returns from stocks in the same industry, that tend to go together (or possibly go in opposite directions from one another)		815

Problems

Conceptual Questions

C.1. You are making several runs of a simulation model, each with a different value of some decision variable (such as the order quantity in the Walton calendar model), to see which decision value achieves the largest mean profit. Is it possible that one value beats another simply by random luck? What can you do to minimize the chance of a "better" value losing out to a "poorer" value?

C.2. If you want to replicate the results of a simulation model with Excel functions only, not @RISK, you can build a data table and let the column input cell be any blank cell. Explain why this works.

C.3. Suppose you simulate a gambling situation where you place many bets. On each bet, the distribution of your net winnings (loss if negative) is highly skewed to the left because there are some possibilities of really large losses but not much upside potential. Your only simulation output is the *average* of the results of all the bets. If you run @RISK with many iterations and look at the resulting histogram of this output, what will it look like? Why?

C.4. You plan to simulate a portfolio of investments over a multiyear period, so for each investment (which could be a particular stock or bond, for example), you need to simulate the change in its value for each of the years. How would you simulate these changes in a realistic way? Would you base it on historical data? What about correlations? Do you think the changes for different investments in a particular year would be correlated? Do you think changes for a particular investment in different years would be correlated? Do you think correlations would play a significant role in your simulation in terms of realism?

C.5. Big Hit Video must determine how many copies of a new video to purchase. Assume that the company's goal is to purchase a number of copies that maximizes its expected profit from the video during the next year. Describe how you would use simulation to shed light on this problem. Assume that each time a video is rented, it is rented for one day.

C.6. Many people who are involved in a small auto accident do not file a claim because they are afraid their insurance premiums will be raised. Suppose your insurance company has three rates. If you file a claim, you are moved to the next higher rate. How might you use simulation to determine whether you should file a claim?

C.7. A building contains 1000 lightbulbs. Each bulb lasts at most five months. The company maintaining the building is trying to decide whether it is worthwhile to practice a "group replacement" policy. Under a group replacement policy, all bulbs are replaced every T months (where T is to be determined). Also, bulbs are replaced when they burn out. Assume that it costs \$0.05 to replace each bulb during a group replacement and \$0.20 to replace each burned-out bulb if it is replaced individually. How would you use simulation to determine whether a group replacement policy is worthwhile?

C.8. Why is the RiskCorrmat function necessary? How does @RISK generate random inputs by default, that is, when RiskCorrmat is not used?

C.9. Consider the claim that normally distributed inputs in a simulation model are bound to lead to normally distributed outputs. Do you agree or disagree with this claim? Defend your answer.

C.10. It is very possible that when you use a correlation matrix as input to the RiskCorrmat function in an @RISK model, the program will inform you that this is an invalid correlation matrix. Provide an example of an obviously invalid correlation matrix involving at least three variables, and explain why it is invalid.

C.11. When you use a RiskSimtable function for a decision variable, such as the order quantity in the Walton model, explain how this provides a "fair" comparison across the different values tested.

C.12. Consider a situation where there is a cost that is either incurred or not. It is incurred only if the value of some random input is less than a specified cutoff value. Why might a simulation of this situation give a very different average value of the cost incurred than a deterministic model that treats the random input as *fixed* at its mean? What does this have to do with the "flaw of averages"?

Level A

29. Six months before its annual convention, the American Medical Association must determine how many rooms to reserve. At this time, the AMA can reserve rooms at a cost of $150 per room. The AMA believes the number of doctors attending the convention will be normally distributed with a mean of 5000 and a standard deviation of 1000. If the number of people attending the convention exceeds the number of rooms reserved, extra rooms must be reserved at a cost of $250 per room.
  a. Use simulation with @RISK to determine the number of rooms that should be reserved to minimize the expected cost to the AMA. Try possible values from 4100 to 4900 in increments of 100.
  b. Redo part **a** for the case where the number attending has a triangular distribution with minimum value 2000, maximum value 7000, and most likely value 5000. Does this change the substantive results from part a?

30. You have made it to the final round of the show *Let's Make a Deal*. You know that there is a $1 million prize behind either door 1, door 2, or door 3. It is equally likely that the prize is behind any of the three doors. The two doors without a prize have nothing behind them. You randomly choose door 2. Before you see whether the prize is behind door 2, host Monty Hall opens a door that has no prize behind it. Specifically, suppose that before door 2 is opened, Monty reveals that there is no prize behind door 3. You now have the opportunity to switch and choose door 1. Should you switch? Simulate this situation 1000 times. For each replication use an @RISK function to generate the door that leads to the prize. Then use another @RISK function to generate the door that Monty will open. Assume that Monty plays as follows: Monty knows where the prize is and will open an empty door, but he cannot open door 2. If the prize is really behind door 2, Monty is equally likely to open door 1 or door 3. If the prize is really behind door 1, Monty must open door 3. If the prize is really behind door 3, Monty must open door 1.

31. A new edition of a very popular textbook will be published a year from now. The publisher currently has 2000 copies on hand and is deciding whether to do another printing before the new edition comes out. The publisher estimates that demand for the book during the next year is governed by the probability distribution in the file **P15_31.xlsx**. A production run incurs a fixed cost of $10,000 plus a variable cost of $15 per book printed. Books are sold for $130 per book. Any demand that cannot be met incurs a penalty cost of $20 per book, due to loss of goodwill. Up to 500 of any leftover books can be sold to Barnes & Noble for $35 per book. The publisher is interested in maximizing expected profit. The following print-run sizes are under consideration: 0 (no production run) to 16,000 in increments of 2000. What decision would you recommend? Use simulation with 1000 replications. For your optimal decision, the publisher can be 90% certain that the actual profit associated with remaining sales of the current edition will be between what two values?

32. A hardware company sells a lot of low-cost, high-volume products. For one such product, it is equally likely that annual unit sales will be low or high. If sales are low (60,000), the company can sell the product for $10 per unit. If sales are high (100,000), a competitor will enter and the company will be able to sell the product for only $8 per unit. The variable cost per unit has a 25% chance of being $6, a 50% chance of being $7.50, and a 25% chance of being $9. Annual fixed costs are $30,000.
  a. Use simulation to estimate the company's expected annual profit.
  b. Find a 95% interval for the company's annual profit, that is, an interval such that about 95% of the actual profits are inside it.
  c. Now suppose that annual unit sales, variable cost, and unit price are equal to their respective *expected* values—that is, there is no uncertainty. Determine the company's annual profit for this scenario.
  d. Can you conclude from the results in parts **a** and **c** that the expected profit from a simulation is equal to the profit from the scenario where each input assumes its expected value? Explain.

33. A direct marketer of women's clothing, must determine how many telephone operators to schedule during each part of the day. The company estimates that the number of phone calls received each hour of a typical eight-hour shift can be described by the probability distribution in the file **P15_33.xlsx**. Each operator can handle 15 calls per hour and costs the company $20 per hour. Each phone call that is not handled is assumed to cost the company $6 in lost profit. Considering the options of employing 6, 8, 10, 12, 14, or 16 operators, use simulation to determine the number of operators that minimizes the expected hourly cost (labor costs plus lost profits).

34. Assume that all of a company's job applicants must take a test, and that the scores on this test are normally distributed. The *selection ratio* is the cutoff point used by the company in its hiring process. For example, a selection ratio of 20% means that the company will accept applicants for jobs who rank in the top 20% of all applicants. If the company chooses a selection ratio of 20%, the average test score of those selected will be 1.40 standard deviations above average. Use simulation to verify this fact, proceeding as follows.

a. Show that if the company wants to accept only the top 20% of all applicants, it should accept applicants whose test scores are at least 0.842 standard deviation above average. (No simulation is required here. Just use the appropriate Excel normal function.)

b. Now generate 1000 test scores from a normal distribution with mean 0 and standard deviation 1. The average test score of those selected is the average of the scores that are at least 0.842. Calculate this with an AVERAGEIF function. Then press the F9 key several times to see how this average changes with new random numbers. Is it much larger than the average of *all* applicants?

35. Lemington's is trying to determine how many Jean Hudson dresses to order for the spring season. Demand for the dresses is assumed to follow a normal distribution with mean 400 and standard deviation 100. The contract between Jean Hudson and Lemington's works as follows. At the beginning of the season, Lemington's reserves x units of capacity. Lemington's must take delivery for at least $0.8x$ dresses and can, if desired, take delivery on up to x dresses. Each dress sells for $160 and Hudson charges $50 per dress. If Lemington's does not take delivery on all x dresses, it owes Hudson a $5 penalty for each unit of reserved capacity that is unused. For example, if Lemington's orders 450 dresses and demand is for 400 dresses, Lemington's will receive 400 dresses and owe Jean 400($50) + 50($5). How many units of capacity should Lemington's reserve to maximize its expected profit?

36. A department store is trying to determine how many Hanson T-shirts to order. Currently the shirts are sold for $21, but at later dates the shirts will be offered at a 10% discount, then a 20% discount, then a 40% discount, then a 50% discount, and finally a 60% discount. Demand at the full price of $21 is believed to be normally distributed with mean 1800 and standard deviation 360. Demand at various discounts is assumed to be a multiple of full-price demand. These multiples, for discounts of 10%, 20%, 40%, 50%, and 60% are, respectively, 0.4, 0.7, 1.1, 2, and 50. For example, if full-price demand is 2500, then at a 10% discount customers would be willing to buy 1000 T-shirts. The unit cost of purchasing T-shirts depends on the number of T-shirts ordered, as shown in the file **P15_36.xlsx**. Use simulation to determine how many T-shirts the store should order. Model the problem so that the store first orders some quantity of T-shirts, then discounts deeper and deeper, as necessary, to sell all of the shirts.

Level B

37. The annual return on each of four stocks for each of the next five years is assumed to follow a normal distribution, with the mean and standard deviation for each stock, as well as the correlations between stocks, listed in the file **P15_37.xlsx**. You believe that the stock returns for these stocks in a given year are correlated, according to the correlation matrix given, but you believe the returns in different years are uncorrelated. For example, the returns for stocks 1 and 2 in year 1 have correlation 0.55, but the correlation between the return of stock 1 in year 1 and the return of stock 1 in year 2 is 0, and the correlation between the return of stock 1 in year 1 and the return of stock 2 in year 2 is also 0. The file has the formulas you might expect for this situation in the range C20:G23. You can check how the RiskCorrmat function has been used in these formulas. Just so that there is an @RISK output cell, calculate the average of all returns in cell B25 and designate it as an @RISK output. (This cell is not really important for the problem, but it is included because @RISK requires at least one output cell.)

a. Using the model exactly as it stands, run @RISK with 1000 iterations. The question is whether the correlations in the simulated data are close to what they should be. To check this, go to @RISK's Report Settings and check the Input Data option before you run the simulation. This gives you all of the simulated returns on a new sheet. Then calculate correlations for all pairs of columns in the resulting Inputs Data Report sheet. (StatTools can be used to create a matrix of all correlations for the simulated data.) Comment on whether the correlations are different from what they should be.

b. Recognizing that this is a common situation (correlation within years, no correlation across years), @RISK allows you to model it by adding a *third* argument to the RiskCorrmat function: the year index in row 19 of the **P15_37.xlsx** file. For example, the RiskCorrmat part of the formula in cell C20 becomes **=RiskNormal($B5,$C5, RiskCorrmat ($B$12:$E$15,$B20,C$19))**. Make this change to the formulas in the range C20:G23, rerun the simulation, and redo the correlation analysis in part **a**. Verify that the correlations between inputs are now more in line with what they should be.

38. It is surprising (but true) that if 23 people are in the same room, there is about a 50% chance that at least two people will have the same birthday. Suppose you want to estimate the probability that if 30 people are in the same room, at least two of them will have the same birthday. You can proceed as follows.

a. Generate random birthdays for 30 different people. Ignoring the possibility of a leap year, each person has a 1/365 chance of having a given birthday (label the days of the year 1 to 365). You can use the RANDBE-TWEEN function to generate birthdays.

b. Once you have generated 30 people's birthdays, how can you tell whether at least two people have the same birthday? One way is to use Excel's RANK function. (You can learn how to use this function in Excel's online help.) This function returns the rank of a number relative to a given group of numbers. In the case of a tie, two numbers are given the same rank. For example, if the set of numbers is 4, 3, 2, 5, the RANK function returns 2, 3, 4, 1. (By default, RANK gives 1 to the *largest* number.) If the set of numbers is 4, 3, 2, 4, the RANK function returns 1, 3, 4, 1.

c. After using the RANK function, you should be able to determine whether at least two of the 30 people have the same birthday. What is the (estimated) probability that this occurs?

39. United Electric (UE) sells refrigerators for $400 with a one-year warranty. The warranty works as follows. If any part of the refrigerator fails during the first year after purchase, UE replaces the refrigerator for an average cost of $100. As soon as a replacement is made, another one-year warranty period begins for the customer. If a refrigerator fails outside the warranty period, we assume that the customer immediately purchases another UE refrigerator. Suppose that the amount of time a refrigerator lasts follows a normal distribution with a mean of 1.8 years and a standard deviation of 0.3 year.

a. Estimate the average profit per year UE earns from a customer.

b. How could the approach of this problem be used to determine the optimal warranty period?

40. A Flexible Savings Account (FSA) plan allows you to put money into an account at the beginning of the calendar year that can be used for medical expenses. This amount is not subject to federal tax. As you pay medical expenses during the year, you are reimbursed by the administrator of the FSA until the money is exhausted. From that point on, you must pay your medical expenses out of your own pocket. On the other hand, if you put more money into your FSA than the medical expenses you incur, this extra money is lost to you. Your annual salary is $80,000 and your federal income tax rate is 30%.

a. Assume that your medical expenses in a year are normally distributed with mean $2000 and standard deviation $500. Build an @RISK model in which the output is the amount of money left to you after paying taxes, putting money in an FSA, and paying any extra medical expenses. Experiment with the amount of money put in the FSA, using a RiskSimtable function.

b. Rework part **a**, but this time assume a gamma distribution for your annual medical expenses. Use 16 and 125 as the two parameters of this distribution. These

imply the same mean and standard deviation as in part **a**, but the distribution of medical expenses is now skewed to the right, which is probably more realistic. Using simulation, see whether you should now put more or less money in an FSA than in the symmetric case in part **a**.

41. At the beginning of each week, a machine is in one of four conditions: 1 = excellent; 2 = good; 3 = average; 4 = bad. The weekly revenue earned by a machine in state 1, 2, 3, or 4 is $100, $90, $50, or $10, respectively. After observing the condition of the machine at the beginning of the week, the company has the option, for a cost of $200, of instantaneously replacing the machine with an excellent machine. The quality of the machine deteriorates over time, as shown in the file **P15_41.xlsx**. Four maintenance policies are under consideration:

- Policy 1: Never replace a machine.
- Policy 2: Immediately replace a bad machine.
- Policy 3: Immediately replace a bad or average machine.
- Policy 4: Immediately replace a bad, average, or good machine.

Simulate each of these policies for 50 weeks (using at least 250 iterations each) to determine the policy that maximizes expected weekly profit. Assume that the machine at the beginning of week 1 is excellent.

42. Simulation can be used to illustrate a number of results from statistics that are difficult to understand with nonsimulation arguments. One is the famous *central limit theorem*, which says that if you sample enough values from *any* population distribution and then average these values, the resulting average will be approximately normally distributed. Confirm this by using @RISK with the following population distributions (run a separate simulation for each): (a) discrete with possible values 1 and 2 and probabilities 0.2 and 0.8; (b) exponential with mean 1 (use the RiskExpon function with the single argument 1); (c) triangular with minimum, most likely, and maximum values equal to 1, 9, and 10. (Note that each of these distributions is very skewed.) Run each simulation with 10 values in each average, and run 1000 iterations to simulate 1000 averages. Create a histogram of the averages to see whether it is indeed bell-shaped. Then repeat, using 30 values in each average. Are the histograms based on 10 values qualitatively different from those based on 30?

43. In statistics we often use observed data to test a hypothesis about a population or populations. The basic method uses the observed data to calculate a test statistic (a single number), as discussed in Chapter 9. If the magnitude of this test statistic is sufficiently large, the null hypothesis is rejected in favor of the research hypothesis. As an example, consider a researcher who believes teenage girls sleep longer than teenage boys on average.

She collects observations on $n = 40$ randomly selected girls and $n = 40$ randomly selected boys. (Each observation is the average sleep time over several nights for a given person.) The averages are $\overline{X}_1 = 7.9$ hours for the girls and $\overline{X}_2 = 7.6$ hours for the boys. The standard deviation of the 40 observations for girls is $s_1 = 0.5$ hour; for the boys it is $s_2 = 0.7$ hour. The researcher, consulting Chapter 9, then calculates the test statistic

$$\frac{\overline{X}_1 - \overline{X}_2}{\sqrt{s_1^2/40 + s_2^2/40}} = \frac{7.9 - 7.6}{\sqrt{0.25/40 + 0.49/40}} = 2.206$$

Based on the fact that 2.206 is "large," she claims that her research hypothesis is confirmed—girls do sleep longer than boys.

You are skeptical of this claim, so you check it out by running a simulation. In your simulation you assume that girls and boys have the *same* mean and standard deviation of sleep times in the entire population, say, 7.7 and 0.6. You also assume that the distribution of sleep times is normal. Then you repeatedly simulate observations of 40 girls and 40 boys from this distribution and calculate the test statistic. The question is whether the observed test statistic, 2.206, is "extreme." If it is larger than most or all of the test statistics you simulate, then the researcher is justified in her claim; otherwise, this large a statistic could have happened easily by chance, even if the girls and boys have identical population means. Use @RISK to see which of these possibilities occurs.

44. A technical note in the discussion of @RISK indicated that Latin Hypercube sampling is more efficient than Monte Carlo sampling. This problem allows you to see what this means. The file **P15_44. xlsx** gets you started. There is a single output cell, B5. You can enter any random value in this cell, such as **RISKNORMAL(500,100)**. There are already @RISK statistical formulas in rows 9–12 to calculate summary measures of the output for each of 10 simulations. On the @RISK ribbon, click on the button to the left of the "dice" button to bring up the Simulation Settings dialog box, click on the Sampling tab, and make sure the Sampling Type is Latin Hypercube. Run 10 simulations with at least 1000 iterations each, and then paste the results in rows 9–12 as *values* in rows 17–20. Next, get back in Simulations Settings and change the Sampling Type to Monte Carlo, run the 10 simulations again, and paste the results in rows 9–12 as values into rows 23–26. For each row, 17–20 and 23–26, summarize the 10 numbers in that row with AVERAGE and STDEV. What do you find? Why do we say that Latin Hypercube sampling is more efficient? (Thanks

to Harvey Wagner at University of North Carolina for suggesting this problem.)

45. We are continually hearing reports on the nightly news about natural disasters—droughts in Texas, hurricanes in Florida, floods in California, and so on. We often hear that one of these was the "worst in over 30 years," or some such statement. Are natural disasters getting worse these days, or does it just appear so? How might you use simulation to answer this question? Here is one possible approach. Imagine that there are N areas of the country (or the world) that tend to have, to some extent, various types of weather phenomena each year. For example, hurricanes are always a potential problem for Florida, and fires are always a potential problem in southern California. You might model the severity of the problem for any area in any year by a normally distributed random number with mean 0 and standard deviation 1, where negative values are interpreted as good years and positive values are interpreted as bad years. (We suggest the normal distribution, but there is no reason other distributions couldn't be used instead.) Then you could simulate such values for all areas over a period of several years and keep track, say, of whether any of the areas have worse conditions in the current year than they have had in the past several years, where "several" could be 10, 20, 30, or any other number of years you want to test. What might you keep track of? How might you interpret your results?

46. The Weibull distribution is often used in engineering studies to model the random lifetime of a device. It is a right-skewed distribution and can be generated with the RiskWeibull function. This function takes two positive parameters, alpha and beta, that determine the shape and location of the distribution. Consider a piece of equipment that contains a battery with a Weibull-distributed lifetime (in days) with parameters alpha = 2 and beta = 80. (It can be shown that the mean and standard deviation of this distribution are about 70 and 37.) NASA is about to send this piece of equipment into space, where its mission is to last at least 600 days. The equipment will be accompanied by one battery and $n-1$ standby spare batteries, that is, n batteries total. When a battery fails, it will automatically be replaced by a spare, at least as long as there are any spares left.

a. Use simulation to estimate the probability that the equipment will accomplish its mission if $n = 10$ batteries are supplied.

b. Although the probability from part a is reasonably large, NASA wants it to be even higher. Use simulation to find the value of n so that the equipment will accomplish its mission with probability at least 0.99.

CASE 15.1 Ski Jacket Production

Egress, Inc., is a small company that designs, produces, and sells ski jackets and other coats. The creative design team has labored for weeks over its new design for the coming winter season. It is now time to decide how many ski jackets to produce in this production run. Because of the lead times involved, no other production runs will be possible during the season. Predicting ski jacket sales months in advance of the selling season can be quite tricky. Egress has been in operation for only three years, and its ski jacket designs were quite successful in two of those years. Based on realized sales from the last three years, current economic conditions, and professional judgment, 12 Egress employees have independently estimated demand for their new design for the upcoming season. Their estimates are listed in Table 15.2.

Table 15.2   Estimated Demands

14,000	16,000
13,000	8000
14,000	5000
14,000	11,000
15,500	8000
10,500	15,000

To assist in the decision on the number of units for the production run, management has gathered the data in Table 15.3. Note that S is the price Egress charges retailers. Any ski jackets that do not sell during the season can be sold by Egress to discounters for V per jacket. The fixed cost of plant and equipment is F. This cost is incurred regardless of the size of the production run.

Table 15.3   Monetary Values

Variable production cost per unit (C):	$80
Selling price per unit (S):	$100
Salvage value per unit (V):	$30
Fixed production cost (F):	$100,000

Questions

1. Egress management believes that a normal distribution is a reasonable model for the unknown demand in the coming year. What mean and standard deviation should Egress use for the demand distribution?
2. Use a spreadsheet model to simulate 1000 possible outcomes for demand in the coming year. Based on these scenarios, what is the expected profit if Egress produces $Q = 7800$ ski jackets? What is the expected profit if Egress produces $Q = 12,000$ ski jackets? What is the standard deviation of profit in these two cases?
3. Based on the same 1000 scenarios, how many ski jackets should Egress produce to maximize expected profit? Call this quantity Q.
4. Should Q equal mean demand or not? Explain.
5. Create a histogram of profit at the production level Q. Create a histogram of profit when the production level Q equals mean demand. What is the probability of a loss greater than $100,000 in each case?

CASE 15.2 Ebony Bath Soap

Management of Ebony, a leading manufacturer of bath soap, is trying to control its inventory costs. The weekly cost of holding one unit of soap in inventory is $30 (one unit is 1000 cases of soap). The marketing department estimates that weekly demand averages 120 units, with a standard deviation of 15 units, and is reasonably well modeled by a normal distribution. If demand exceeds the amount of soap on hand, those sales are *lost*—that is, there is no backlogging of demand. The production department can produce at one of three levels: 110, 120, or 130 units per week. The cost of changing the production level from one week to the next is $3000.

Management would like to evaluate the following production policy. If the current inventory is less than $L = 30$ units, they will produce 130 units in the next week. If the current inventory is greater than $U = 80$ units, they will produce 110 units in the next week. Otherwise, Ebony will continue at the previous week's production level.

Ebony currently has 60 units of inventory on hand. Last week's production level was 120.

Questions

1. Develop a simulation model for 52 weeks of operation at Ebony. Graph the inventory of soap over time. What is the total cost (inventory cost plus production change cost) for the 52 weeks?
2. Run the simulation for 500 iterations to estimate the average 52-week cost with values of U ranging from 30 to 80 in increments of 10. Keep $L = 30$ throughout.
3. Report the sample mean and standard deviation of the 52-week cost under each policy. Using the simulated results, is it possible to construct *valid* 90% confidence intervals for the average 52-week cost for each value of U? In any case, graph the average 52-week cost versus U. What is the best value of U for $L = 30$?
4. What other production policies might be useful to investigate?

APPENDIX   Simulation with DADM_Tools

This chapter has illustrated two ways to run simulations in Excel: by using Excel-only tools and by using @RISK. The former takes a lot of time for creating data tables and summarizing, and the latter uses an add-in that is almost *too* powerful with its large number of options. Albright has written a simulation program in his DADM_Tools add-in that you might want to try as an alternative. (It is freely available at https://kelley.iu.edu/albrightbooks/free_downloads.htm.) This program does much of what @RISK does, but it is much more straightforward, allowing many fewer options than @RISK. You build a simulation model in the same way as illustrated in this chapter, you fill out one dialog box to indicate the number of replications, the outputs, and optionally a decision variable (the counterpart to RiskSimtable), and you get the results in a new nicely formatted worksheet. For illustration, we have included versions of many of the examples and problem solutions that use this simulation program.

If you decide to use the DADM_Tools add-in for simulation, you should also install Albright's RandGen add-in (freely available at the same website). This add-in provides functions such as Normal_ and Triangular_ for generating random numbers. These functions are recognized by the simulation program.

CHAPTER 16
Simulation Models

Ron Buskirk/Alamy Stock Photo

EFFECTS OF MERIT PAY ON PAYROLL GROWTH AT DOD

The National Security Personnel System (NSPS), a Department of Defense (DoD) civilian personal-management system, was designed to provide more merit-based pay raises than the existing civil service system. However, a U.S. Army organization was concerned that increased merit raises would eventually result in an unaffordable total payroll. As reported by Huntsinger et al. (2012), he and a team of analysts were asked by the Army to develop a quantitative model that could determine the effect of merit pay increases on total payroll growth.

The team quickly realized that forecasting eventual payroll growth was a complex problem. Payroll growth depends on many uncertainties, including the number and salary of employees in each pay pool, annual employee ratings, employees leaving and being hired, cost-of-living raises, funds designated for merit raises, and the split between bonuses and pay raises. Nevertheless, they believed a simulation model could be developed to determine the most important factors affecting payroll growth. If a simulation using current policies showed an unacceptable level of payroll growth, the model could then be used to see whether policy changes could be made to bring payroll increases to more acceptable levels.

The current NSPS policy grouped employees into pay pools of 35 to over 300 members, usually within one organization. Employees in a given pay pool can belong to different pay bands. The base salaries move within a pay band in three ways: annual across-the-board raises, in-band pay raises for increased responsibilities, and merit raises based on performance ratings. The merit raises can be raises in base pay or one-time bonuses. Each organization can determine the split between the two, and this split can depend on the performance rating. For example, lower performers might receive a 50-50 split, whereas higher performers might receive a 75-25 split. The latter split benefits the employee because the level of his or her base pay has increased for future years, but it has an adverse effect on the long-term total payroll.

Another important effect that had to be captured in a simulation model is attrition. If employees who receive lower performance ratings become discouraged and leave the organization, while those who receive higher ratings stay, the organization could become top-heavy with higher paid employees. In addition, who should be hired to replace those who leave? It was traditional to replace employees at given salary levels with others at approximately the same salary levels, but there was no rule that it had to be done this way.

The team was eventually able to develop a simulation model that: (1) captured the important drivers of payroll increases; (2) was sufficiently flexible to allow policy changes; (3) was straightforward enough to be understood by those who requested the study; and (4) had a graphical user interface for exploring policy changes. The simulation model starts by generating random initial base salaries for the employees, based on current data. Then each year, it uses probabilities, again based on historical data, to generate performance ratings and hence merit raises and bonuses, depending on the merit raise-bonus split. It also randomly chooses which employees will leave and hires new people at randomly generated salaries to replace them.

Once the simulation model was completed, the analysts made 1000 simulation runs and judged policies based on the average percent that base salaries increased above the assumed 3% cost-of-living increases over 20 years. Using a base case from using current policies, the simulation showed an average increase in base salaries of approximately 30% over the cost of living percentage. This was deemed unacceptable. Then running various sensitivity analyses, they discovered two factors that could lower this increase. First, in the base case, the fraction of merit pay given as a raise (as opposed to a bonus) ranged from 45% for the lowest performers to 70% for the highest performers. By decreasing these percentages to 25% and 50%, the 30% overrun was reduced to 21%. Second, the base case hired replacements at approximately the same base salaries as those they replaced. By instead replacing them with employees earning about 20% less, the 30% overrun was reduced to 12%. Finally, by implementing both of these policy changes simultaneously, the 30% overrun was reduced to zero. Of course, the results of a simulation vary from run to run because of randomness. However, a statistical analysis of the results showed that with the implementation of these two policy changes, the actual 20-year pay increases were within 3% of the cost-of-living increases in about 750 of the 1000 replications.

In summary, the simulation model provided the Army with the information it needed. It showed that the current policy would indeed result in unacceptable totally payroll increases in the long run, and it discovered several policy changes the Army could make to bring these payroll increases down to acceptable levels.

16-1 Introduction

The previous chapter introduced most of the important concepts for developing and analyzing spreadsheet simulation models. It also discussed many of the features available in the powerful simulation add-in, @RISK, that accompanies this book. Now we apply the tools to a wide variety of problems that can be analyzed with simulation. We group the applications into four general areas: (1) operations models, (2) financial models, (3) marketing models, and (4) games of chance. The overriding theme in this chapter is that simulation models can yield important insights in all these areas. You do not need to cover all the models in this chapter or cover them in any particular order. You can cover the ones of most interest to you in practically any order.

16-2 Operations Models

Whether we are discussing the operations of a manufacturing or a service company, there is likely to be uncertainty that can be modeled with simulation. In this section, we look at examples of bidding for a government contract (uncertainty in the bids by competitors), warranty costs (uncertainty in the time until failure of an appliance), and drug production (uncertainty in the yield and timing).

16-2a Bidding for Contracts

In situations where a company must bid against competitors, simulation can often be used to determine the company's optimal bid. Usually the company does not know what its competitors will bid, but it might have an idea about the range of the bids its competitors will choose. In this section, we show how to use simulation to determine a bid that maximizes the company's expected profit.

EXAMPLE

16.1 BIDDING FOR A GOVERNMENT CONTRACT AT MILLER CONSTRUCTION

Miller Construction Company must decide whether to make a bid on a construction project. Miller believes it will cost the company $10,000 to complete the project (if it wins the contract), and it will cost $350 to prepare a bid. However, there is uncertainty about each of these. Upon further reflection, Miller assesses that the cost to complete the project has a triangular distribution with minimum, most likely, and maximum values $9000, $10,000, and $15,000. Similarly, Miller assesses that the cost to prepare a bid has a triangular distribution with parameters $300, $350, and $500. (Note the skewness in these distributions. Miller recognizes that cost overruns are much more likely than cost underruns.) Four potential competitors are going to bid against Miller. The lowest bid wins the contract, and the winner is then given the winning bid amount to complete the project. Based on past history, Miller believes that each potential competitor will bid, independently of the others, with probability 0.5. Miller also believes that each competitor's bid will be a multiple of its (Miller's) most likely cost to complete the project, where this multiple has a triangular distribution with minimum, most likely, and maximum values 0.9, 1.3, and 1.8, respectively. If Miller decides to prepare a bid, its bid amount will be a multiple of $500 in the range $10,500 to $15,000. The company wants to use simulation to determine which strategy to use to maximize its expected profit.

Objective

To simulate the profit to Miller from any particular bid, and to see which bid amount is best.

Where Do the Numbers Come From?

The data required here are the parameters of the distributions of Miller's costs, those of the competitors' bids, and the probability that a given competitor will place a bid. Triangular distributions are chosen for simplicity, although Miller could try other types of distributions. The parameters of these distributions are probably educated guesses, possibly based on previous contracts and bidding experience against these same competitors. The probability that a given competitor will place a bid can be estimated from these same competitors' bidding history.

Solution

The logic is shown in Figure 16.1. (See the file **Contract Bidding Big Picture.xlsx**.) You first simulate the number of competitors who will bid and then simulate their bids. Then for any bid Miller makes, you see whether Miller wins the contract, and if so, what its profit is.

Figure 16.1 Big Picture for Bidding Simulation Model

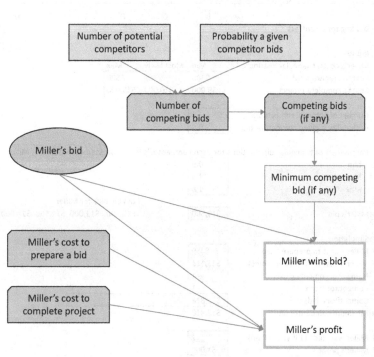

Developing the Simulation Model

The simulation model appears in Figure 16.2. (See the file **Contract Bidding Finished.xlsx.**) It can be developed with the following steps. (Note that this model does not check the possibility of Miller not bidding at all. But this case is easy. If Miller opts not to bid, the profit is a certain $0.)

Contract Bidding Model

1. **Inputs.** Enter the inputs in the blue cells.
2. **Miller's bid.** You can test all of Miller's possible bids simultaneously with the RiskSimtable function. To set up for this, enter the formula

Recall that the RiskSimtable function allows you to run a separate simulation for each value in its list.

=**RiskSimtable(D16:M16)**

in cell B16. As with all uses of this function, the spreadsheet shows the simulated values for the *first* bid, $10,500. However, when you run the simulation, you see outputs for all of the bids.
3. **Miller's costs.** Generate Miller's cost to prepare a bid in cell B19 with the formula

=**RiskTriang(B5,C5,D5)**

Then copy this to cell B20 to generate Miller's cost to complete the project.
4. **Competitors and their bids.** First, generate the random number of competitors who bid. This has a binomial distribution with four trials and probability of "success" equal to 0.5 for each trial, so enter the formula

=**RiskBinomial(B8,B9)**

in cell B21. Then generate random bids for the competitors who bid in row 23 by entering the formula

=**IF(B22<=$B$21,RiskTriang($B$12,$B$13,$B$14)*$C$6,"")**

in cell B23 and copying across. This generates a random bid for all competitors who bid, and it enters a blank for those who don't. (Remember that the random value is the *multiple* of Miller's most likely cost to complete the project.) Calculate the smallest of these (if there are any) in cell B24 with the formula

=**IF(B21>=1,MIN(B23:E23),"")**

Of course, Miller will not see these other bids until it has submitted its own bid.
5. **Win contract?** See whether Miller wins the bid by entering the formula

=**IF(OR(B16<B24,B21=0),1,0)**

in cell B26. Here, 1 means that Miller wins the bid, and 0 means a competitor wins the bid. If there are no competing bids, Miller wins for sure. Then designate this cell as an @RISK output cell. Recall that to designate a cell as an @RISK output

Figure 16.2 Bidding Simulation Model

▲	A	B	C	D	E	F	G	H	I	J	K	L	M
1	**Bidding for a contract**												
2													
3	**Inputs**												
4	Miller's costs, triangular distributed	Min	Most likely	Max									
5	Cost to prepare a bid	$300	$350	$500									
6	Cost to complete project	$9,000	$10,000	$15,000									
7													
8	Number of potential competitors	4											
9	Probability a given competitor bids	0.5											
10													
11	Parameters of triangular distributions for each competitor's bid (expressed as multiple of Miller's most likely cost to complete project)												
12	Min	0.9											
13	Most likely	1.3											
14	Max	1.8											
15				Possible bids for Miller									
16	Miller's bid	$10,500		$10,500	$11,000	$11,500	$12,000	$12,500	$13,000	$13,500	$14,000	$14,500	$15,000
17													
18	**Simulation**												
19	Miller's cost to prepare a bid	$459											
20	Miller's cost to complete project	$11,111											
21	Number of competing bids	1											
22	Competitor index	1	2	3	4								
23	Competitors' bids	$12,818											
24	Minimum competitor bid	$12,818											
25													
26	Miller wins bid? (1 if yes, 0 if no)	1											
27	Miller's profit	−$1,069											

cell, you select the cell and then click the Add Output button on @RISK's ribbon. You can then label this output appropriately. We used the label Wins Bid.

6. **Miller's profit.** If Miller submits a bid, the bid cost is lost for sure. Beyond that, the profit to Miller is the bid amount minus the cost of completing the project if the bid is won. Otherwise, Miller makes nothing. So enter the formula

$$=IF(B26=1,B16\text{-}B20,0)-B19$$

in cell B27. Then designate this cell as an additional @RISK output cell. (We named it Profit.)

Running the Simulation

Set the number of iterations to 1000, and set the number of simulations to 10 because there are 10 bid amounts Miller wants to test.

Discussion of the Simulation Results

The summary results appear in Figure 16.3. For each simulation—that is, each bid amount—there are two outputs: 1 or 0 to indicate whether Miller wins the contract and Miller's profit. The only interesting results for the 0–1 output are in the Mean column, which shows the fraction of iterations that resulted in 1's. So you can see, for example, that if Miller bids $12,000 (simulation #4), the probability of winning the bid is estimated to be about 0.57. This probability clearly decreases as Miller's bid increases.

Figure 16.3 Summary Results for Bidding Simulation

Name	Cell	Sim#	Min	Mean	Max	Std Dev	5%	95%
Wins Bid	B26	1	0	0.893	1	0.3092679	0	1
Wins Bid	B26	2	0	0.804	1	0.3971671	0	1
Wins Bid	B26	3	0	0.701	1	0.4580489	0	1
Wins Bid	B26	4	0	0.565	1	0.4960051	0	1
Wins Bid	B26	5	0	0.461	1	0.4987261	0	1
Wins Bid	B26	6	0	0.353	1	0.4781418	0	1
Wins Bid	B26	7	0	0.273	1	0.4457238	0	1
Wins Bid	B26	8	0	0.197	1	0.3979313	0	1
Wins Bid	B26	9	0	0.156	1	0.3630369	0	1
Wins Bid	B26	10	0	0.13	1	0.3364717	0	1
Profit	B27	1	-$4,672.64	-$1,130.98	$1,120.35	$1,266.51	-$3,595.30	$515.30
Profit	B27	2	-$4,172.64	-$656.26	$1,620.35	$1,174.58	-$3,043.94	$993.27
Profit	B27	3	-$3,672.64	-$256.69	$2,120.35	$1,088.08	-$2,414.08	$1,459.08
Profit	B27	4	-$3,172.64	$33.02	$2,620.35	$1,031.29	-$1,529.96	$1,935.97
Profit	B27	5	-$2,672.64	$169.65	$3,120.35	$1,072.15	-$964.13	$2,325.94
Profit	B27	6	-$2,172.64	$210.45	$3,620.35	$1,122.43	-$474.54	$2,693.47
Profit	B27	7	-$1,672.64	$214.82	$4,120.35	$1,193.63	-$463.95	$3,089.36
Profit	B27	8	-$1,172.64	$142.26	$4,620.35	$1,210.77	-$458.71	$3,252.75
Profit	B27	9	-$672.64	$109.91	$5,023.24	$1,254.27	-$457.14	$3,473.14
Profit	B27	10	-$496.52	$92.90	$5,523.24	$1,315.50	-$455.67	$3,856.25

@RISK - Results Summary — Inputs | Outputs | Statistic Functions — Inputs= 8, Outputs= 2, Statistic Functions= 0, Iterations= 1000, Simulations= 10, Runtime= 00:00:05

In terms of net profit, if you concentrate only on the Mean column, a bid amount of $13,500 (simulation #7) is the best. But as the other numbers in this figure indicate, the mean doesn't tell the whole story. For example, if Miller bids $13,500, it could win the bid but still lose a considerable amount of money because of cost overruns. The histogram of profit in Figure 16.4 indicates this more clearly. It shows that in spite of the positive mean, many of the outcomes are negative.

So what should Miller do? If it doesn't bid at all, its profit is a certain $0. If Miller is an *expected* profit maximizer, then the fact that several of the means in Figure 16.3 are positive indicates that bidding is better than not bidding, with a bid of $13,500 being the best bid. However, potential cost overruns and the corresponding losses are certainly a concern. Depending on Miller's degree of risk aversion, the company might decide to (1) not bid at all, or (2) bid higher than $13,500 to minimize

Figure 16.4 Histogram of Profit with $13,500 Bid

its worse loss. Still, we would caution Miller not to be *too* conservative. Rather than focusing on the Min (worst case) column in Figure 16.3, we would suggest focusing on the 5% column. This shows *nearly* how bad things could get (5% of the time it would be worse than this), and this 5th percentile remains fairly constant for higher bids.

16-2b Warranty Costs

When you buy a new product, it usually carries a warranty. A typical warranty might state that if the product fails within a certain period such as one year, you will receive a new product at no cost, and it will carry the *same* warranty. However, if the product fails after the warranty period, you have to bear the cost of replacing the product. Due to random life-times of products, we need a way to estimate the warranty costs (to the manufacturer) of a product. The following example illustrates how this can be accomplished with simulation.

EXAMPLE

16.2 WARRANTY COSTS AT YAKKON

Yakkon Company sells a popular camera for $400. This camera carries a warranty such that if the camera fails within 1.5 years, the company gives the customer a new camera for free. If the camera fails after 1.5 years, the warranty is no longer in effect. Every replacement camera carries exactly the same warranty as the original camera, and the cost to the company of sup-plying a new camera is always $225. Use simulation to estimate, for a given sale, the number of replacements under warranty and the NPV of profit from the sale, using a discount rate of 8%.

Objective

To use simulation to estimate the number of replacements under warranty and the total NPV of profit from a given sale.

Where Do the Numbers Come From?

The warranty information is a policy decision made by the company. The hardest input to estimate is the probability distribution of the lifetime of the product. We discuss this next.

Solution

The only randomness in this problem concerns the time until failure of a new camera. Yakkon could estimate the distribution of time until failure from historical data. This would probably indicate a right-skewed distribution, as shown in Figure 16.5. If you look through the list of distributions available in @RISK under Define Distributions, you will see several with this same basic shape. The one shown in Figure 16.5 is a commonly used distribution called the *gamma distribution*. We will use a gamma distribution in this example, although other choices such as the triangular are certainly possible.

The gamma distribution is a popular distribution when you want a right-skewed distribution of a positive quantity.

Figure 16.5 Right-Skewed Gamma Distribution

Selecting a Gamma Distribution

The **gamma distribution** is characterized by two parameters, α and β. These determine its shape and location. It can be shown that the mean and standard deviation are $\mu = \alpha\beta$ and $\sigma = \sqrt{\alpha}\beta$. Alternatively, for any desired values of the mean and standard deviation, these equations can be solved for α and β, which leads to $\alpha = \mu^2/\sigma^2$ and $\beta = \sigma^2/\mu$. So, for example, if you want a gamma distribution with mean 2.5 and standard deviation 1 (which in this example would be based on camera lifetime data from the past), you should choose $\alpha = 2.5^2/1^2 = 6.25$ and $\beta = 1^2/2.5 = 0.4$. These are the values shown in Figure 16.5 and the ones used for this example. The values in the figure (from @RISK) imply that the probability of failure before 1.5 years is about 0.15, so that the probability of failure out of warranty is about 0.85.

You can learn about distributions from @RISK's Define Distribution window.

Developing the Simulation Model

The variables for the model are shown in Figure 16.6, and the simulation model itself appears in Figure 16.7. (See the files **Warranty Costs Big Picture.xlsx** and **Warranty Costs Finished.xlsx**.) The particular random numbers in Figure 16.7 indicate an example (a rather unusual one) where there are two failures within warranty. However, because the lifetime of the second replacement (cell D17) is greater than 1.5, the company incurs only two replacement costs, as shown in cells B19 and C19. The model can be developed with the following steps.

1. **Inputs.** Enter the inputs in the blue cells.
2. **Parameters of gamma distribution.** As discussed previously, if you enter a desired mean and standard deviation (in cells B5 and B6), you have to calculate the parameters of the gamma distribution. Do this by entering the formulas

$$=B5^2/B6^2$$

and

$$=B6^2/B5$$

in cells B7 and B8.

3. **Lifetimes and times of failures.** Generate at most five lifetimes and corresponding times of failures. (Why only five? You could generate more, but it is extremely unlikely that this same customer would experience more than five failures within warranty, so five suffices.) As soon as a lifetime is greater than 1.5, the warranty period, no further lifetimes are required, in which case blanks can be recorded in row 17. With this in mind, enter the formulas

$$=RiskGamma(B7,B8)$$

$$=IF(B17<B10,RiskGamma(B7,B8),"")$$

and

$$=IF(C17="","",IF(C17<\$B\$10,RiskGamma(\$B\$7,\$B\$8),""))$$

in cells B17, C17, and C17, and copy the latter formula to cells E17 and F17. These formulas guarantee that once a blank is recorded in a cell, all cells to its right will also contain blanks. To get the actual times of failures, relative to time 0 when the customer originally purchases the camera, enter the formulas

$$=B17$$

and

$$=IF(C17="","",B18+C17)$$

in cells B18 and C18, and copy the latter across row 18. These values will be used for the NPV calculation because this requires the exact timing of cash flows.

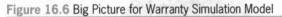

Figure 16.6 Big Picture for Warranty Simulation Model

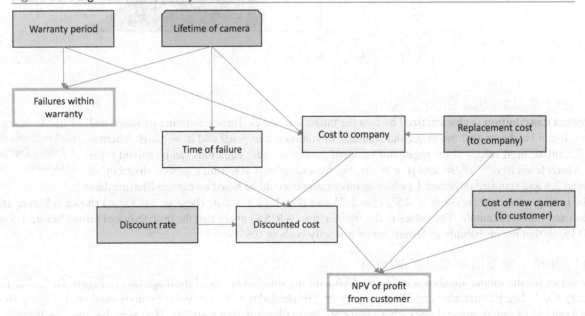

Figure 16.7 Warranty
Simulation Model

▲	A	B	C	D	E	F
1	**Warranty costs for camera**					
2						
3	**Inputs**					
4	Parameters of time to failure distribution of any new camera (Gamma)					
5	Desired mean	2.5				
6	Desired stdev	1				
7	Implied alpha	6.250				
8	Implied beta	0.400				
9						
10	Warranty period	1.5				
11	Cost of new camera (to customer)	$400				
12	Replacement cost (to company)	$225				
13	Discount rate	8%				
14						
15	**Simulation of new camera and its replacements (if any)**					
16	Camera	1	2	3	4	5
17	Lifetime	1.288	1.426	4.333		
18	Time of failure	1.288	2.714	7.047		
19	Cost to company	225	225	0	0	0
20	Discounted cost	203.77	182.59	0.00	0.00	0.00
21						
22	Failures within warranty	2.000				
23	NPV of profit from customer	($211.36)				

@RISK Function

RiskGamma

To generate a random number from the gamma distribution, use the RiskGamma function in the form
=RiskGamma(*alpha,beta*). The mean and standard deviation of this distribution are $\mu = \alpha\beta$ and $\sigma = \sqrt{\alpha}\beta$.
Equivalently, $\alpha = \mu^2/\sigma^2$ and $\beta = \sigma^2/\mu$.

4. **Costs and discounted costs.** In row 19, enter the replacement cost of $225 or 0, depending on whether a failure occurs within warranty, and in row 20 discount these costs back to time 0, using the failure times in row 18. To do this, enter the formulas

Excel's NPV function can be used only for cash flows that occur at the ends of the respective years. Otherwise, you have to discount cash flows manually.

=IF(B17<B10,B12,0)

and

=IF(C17="",0,IF(C17<$B$10,$B$12,0))

in cells B19 and C19, and copy this latter formula across row 19. Then enter the formula

=IF(B19>0,B19/(1+$B$13)^B18,0)

in cell B20, and copy it across row 20. This formula uses the well-known fact that the present value of a cash flow at time t is the cash flow multiplied by $1/(1 + r)^t$, where r is the discount rate.

5. **Outputs.** Calculate two outputs, the number of failures within warranty and the NPV of profit, with the formulas

=COUNTIF(B17:F17,"<"&$B$10)

and

=B11−B12−SUM(B20:F20)

in cells B22 and B23. Then designate these two cells as @RISK output cells. Note that the NPV is the margin from the sale (undiscounted) minus the sum of the discounted costs from replacements under warranty.

Running the Simulation
The @RISK setup is typical. Run 1000 iterations of a *single* simulation (because there is no RiskSimtable function).

Discussion of the Simulation Results
The @RISK summary statistics and histograms for the two outputs appear in Figures 16.8 and 16.9. They show a fairly clear picture. About 85% of the time, there are no failures under warranty and the company makes a profit of $175, the margin from the camera sale. However, there is about a 12% chance of exactly one failure under warranty, in which case the company's NPV of profit will be an approximate $50 loss (before discounting). Additionally, there is about a 3% chance that there will be even more failures under warranty, in which case the loss will be even greater. Note that in our 1000 iterations, the maximum number of failures under warranty was 4, and the maximum net loss was $515.94. On average, the NPV of profit was $139.75.

Figure 16.8 Histogram of
Number of Failures

Figure 16.9 Histogram of NPV
of Profit

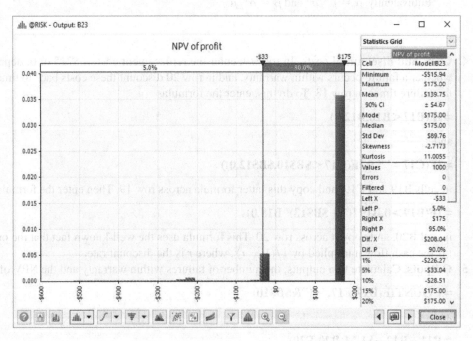

These results indicate that Yakkon is not suffering terribly from warranty costs. However, there are several ways the company could decrease the effects of warranty costs. First, it could increase the price of the camera. Second, it could decrease the warranty period, say, from 1.5 years to 1 year. Third, it could change the terms of the warranty. For example, it could stipulate that if the camera fails within a year, the customer gets a new camera for free, whereas if the time to failure is between 1 and 1.5 years, the customer pays some pro rata share of the replacement cost. Finally, it could try to sell the customer an extended warranty—at a hefty price. We ask you to explore these possibilities in the problems.

16-2c Drug Production with Uncertain Yield

In many manufacturing settings, products are produced in batches, and the usable *yields* from these batches are uncertain. This is particularly true in the drug industry. The following example illustrates how a drug manufacturer can take this uncertainty into account when planning production.

EXAMPLE

16.3 TRYING TO MEET AN ORDER DUE DATE AT WOZAC

Wozac Company is a drug manufacturer. Wozac has recently accepted an order from its best customer for 8000 ounces of a new miracle drug, and Wozac wants to plan its production schedule to meet the customer's promised delivery date of December 1. There are three sources of uncertainty that make planning difficult. First, the drug must be produced in batches, and there is uncertainty in the time required to produce a batch, which could be anywhere from 5 to 11 days. This uncertainty is described by the discrete distribution in Table 16.1. Second, the yield (usable quantity) from any batch is uncertain. Based on historical data, Wozac believes the yield can be modeled by a triangular distribution with minimum, most likely, and maximum values equal to 600, 1000, and 1100 ounces, respectively. Third, all batches must go through a rigorous inspection once they are completed. The probability that a typical batch passes inspection is only 0.8. With probability 0.2, the batch fails inspection, and *none* of it can be used to help fill the order. Wozac wants to use simulation to help decide how many days prior to the due date it should begin production.

Table 16.1 Distribution of Days to Complete a Batch

Days	Probability
5	0.05
6	0.10
7	0.20
8	0.30
9	0.20
10	0.10
11	0.05

Objective
To use simulation to determine when Wozac should begin production for this order so that there is a high probability of completing it by the due date.

Where Do the Numbers Come From?
The important inputs here are the probability distributions of the time to produce a batch, the yield from a batch, and the inspection result. The probabilities we have assumed would undoubtedly be based on previous production data. For example, the company might have observed that about 80% of all batches in the past passed inspection. Of course, a *discrete* distribution is natural for the number of days to produce a batch, and a *continuous* distribution is appropriate for the yield from a batch.

Solution
The variables for this model are shown in Figure 16.10. (See the file **Drug Production Big Picture.xlsx**.) The idea is to simulate successive batches—their days to complete, their yields, and whether they pass inspection—and keep a running total of the usable ounces obtained so far. IF functions can then be used to check whether the order is complete or another batch is required. You need to simulate only as many as batches as are required to meet the order, and you should keep track of the days

required to produce all of these batches. In this way, you can "back up" to see when production must begin to meet the due date. For example, if the simulation indicates that the order takes 96 days to complete, then production must begin on August 27, 96 days before the due date. (For simplicity, the model assumes that production occurs seven days a week.)

Figure 16.10 Big Picture for Drug Production Model

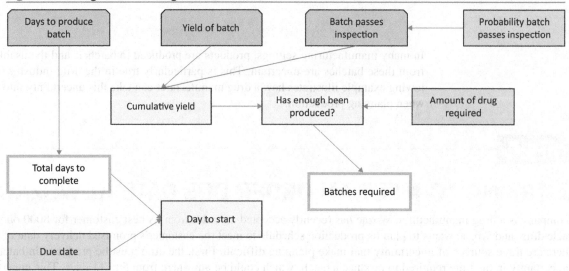

Developing the Simulation Model

The completed model appears in Figure 16.11. (See the file **Drug Production Finished.xlsx**.) It can be developed as follows.

Drug Production Model

1. **Inputs.** Enter the inputs in the blue cells.
2. **Batch indexes.** We don't know ahead of time how many batches will be required to fill the order. There should be enough rows in the simulation to cover the worst case that is likely to occur. After some experimentation, it is apparent that 25 batches are almost surely enough. Therefore, enter the batch indexes 1 through 25 in column A of the simulation section. (If 25 were not enough, you could always add more rows.) The idea, then, is to fill the *entire* range B16:F40 with formulas. However, you can use appropriate IF functions in these formulas so that if enough has already been produced to fill the order, blanks are inserted in the remaining rows. For example, the scenario shown in Figure 16.11 is one where 13 batches were required, so blanks appear below row 28.
3. **Days for batches.** Simulate the days required for batches in column B. To do this, enter the formulas

   = **RiskDiscrete(G6:G12,H6:H12)**

   and

   = **IF(F16<>"No","",RiskDiscrete($G$6:$G$12,$H$6:$H$12))**

   in cell B16 and B17, and copy the latter formula down to cell B40. The IF function enters a blank in this cell if there is not a No in column F for the previous batch, that is, if the order was just completed in the previous batch or it has been completed for some time. Similar logic appears in later formulas.
4. **Batch yields.** Simulate the batch yields in column C. To do this, enter the formulas

   = **RiskTriang(B9,C9,D9)**

   and

   = **IF(F16<>"No","",RiskTriang($B$9,$C$9,$D$9))**

   in cells C16 and C17, and copy the latter formula down to cell C40.
5. **Pass inspection?** Check whether each batch passes inspection with the formulas

   = **IF(RAND()<Probability_pass,"Yes","No")**

   and

   = **IF(F16<>"No","",IF(RAND()<Probability_pass,"Yes","No"))**

You can use Excel's RAND function inside an IF function to simulate whether some event occurs.

Figure 16.11 Drug Production Simulation Model

	A	B	C	D	E	F	G	H	I	J	K	L	M
1	**Planning production of a drug**												
2													
3	**Input section**												
4	Ounces required	8000					Distribution of days needed to produce a batch (discrete)						
5	Due date	1-Dec					Days	Probability					
6							5	0.05					
7	Distribution of yield (ounces) from each batch (triangular)						6	0.10					
8			Min	Most likely	Max		7	0.20					
9			600	1000	1100		8	0.30					
10							9	0.20					
11	Prob of passing inspection	0.8					10	0.10					
12							11	0.05					
13													
14	**Simulation model**							**Outputs**					
15	Batch		Days	Yield	Pass?	CumYield	Enough?	Batches required	13				
16	1		10	821.5	No	0.0	No	Days to complete	111				
17	2		6	786.3	Yes	786.3	No	Day to start	12-Aug				
18	3		9	1012.2	No	786.3	No						
19	4		8	843.7	Yes	1630.1	No	**Statistical summary measures**					
20	5		9	754.6	No	1630.1	No	Max batches reqd	20		Probability of meeting due date		
21	6		9	1060.4	Yes	2690.4	No				Start date		Probability
22	7		9	920.3	Yes	3610.8	No	Avg days reqd	93	30-Aug	15-Jul		0.990
23	8		10	713.7	Yes	4324.5	No	Min days reqd	62	30-Sep	1-Aug		0.955
24	9		8	958.0	Yes	5282.4	No	Max days reqd	161	23-Jun	15-Aug		0.836
25	10		9	1033.5	Yes	6315.9	No	5th perc days reqd	71	21-Sep	1-Sep		0.503
26	11		9	977.4	Yes	7293.3	No	95th perc days reqd	121	2-Aug	15-Sep		0.127
27	12		8	843.5	No	7293.3	No						
28	13		7	822.2	Yes	8115.5	Yes	**Range names used**					
29	14							Batches_required	=Model!$I$15				
30	15							Days_to_complete	=Model!$I$16				
31	16							Due_date	=Model!$B$5				
32	17							Probability_pass	=Model!$B$11				
33	18							Ounces_required	=Model!$B$4				

in cells D16 and D17, and copy the latter formula down to cell D40. Note that you could use @RISK's RiskUniform(0,1) function instead of RAND(), but there is no real advantage to doing so. They are essentially equivalent. (Besides, the academic version of @RISK imposes an upper limit of 100 @RISK input functions per model, so it is often a good idea to substitute built-in Excel® functions when possible.)

6. **Order filled?** To keep track of the cumulative usable production and whether the order has been filled in columns E and F, first enter the formulas

=IF(D16="Yes",C16,0)

and

=IF(E16>=Ounces_required,"Yes","Not yet")

in cells E16 and F16 for batch 1. Then enter the general formulas

=IF(F16<>"No","",IF(D17="Yes",C17+E16,E16))

and

=IF(F16<>"No","",IF(E17>=Ounces_required,"Yes","Not yet"))

in cells E17 and F17, and copy them down to row 40. Note that the entry in column F is "Not yet" if the order is not yet complete. In the row that completes the order, it changes to "Yes," and then it is blank in succeeding rows.

7. **Summary measures.** Calculate the batches and days required in cells I15 and I16 with the formulas

=INDEX(A16:A40,MATCH("Yes",F16:F40,0))

and

=SUM(B16:B40)

These are the two cells used as output cells for @RISK, so designate them as such. Also, calculate the day the order should be started to just meet the due date in cell I17 with the formula

=Due_date−I16

Date subtraction in Excel allows you to calculate the number of days between two given dates.

This formula uses date subtraction to find an elapsed time. (Again, the assumption is that production occurs every day of the week.)

This completes the simulation model development. The other entries in columns H through J will be explained shortly.

Fundamental Insight

Dealing with Uncertain Timing

Many simulations that model a process over multiple time periods must deal with uncertain timing of events, such as when the manufacturing of an order will finish, which year sales of a new product will begin, and many others. Essentially, the spreadsheet model must generate random numbers that determine the timing and then play out the events. This can require tricky IF functions and possibly other functions. However, the hard work often involves getting the logic correct for only the first period or two. Then this logic can be copied down for the other periods. In other words, some time spent on developing the first row or two can result in a powerful model.

Running the Simulation

Set the number of iterations to 1000 and the number of simulations to 1, and then run the simulation as usual.

Discussion of the Simulation Results

After running the simulation, you can obtain the distributions of the number of batches required and the number of days required in Figures 16.12 and 16.13.

Figure 16.12 Distribution of Batches Required

How should Wozac use this information? The key questions are how many batches will be required and (2) when production should start. To answer these questions, it is helpful to use several of @RISK's statistical functions. Recall that these functions can be entered directly into the Excel model worksheet. (Also, recall that they provide useful information only *after* the simulation has been run.) These functions provide no new information you don't already have from other @RISK windows, but they allow you to see (and manipulate) this information directly in the spreadsheet.

For the first question, enter the formula

=RiskMax(Batches_required)

in cell I20. (Refer to Figure 16.11.) It shows that the worst case from the 1000 iterations, in terms of batches required, is 20 batches. (If this maximum were 25, you would add more rows to the simulation model and run the simulation again.)

Figure 16.13 Distribution of
Days Required

You can answer the second question in two ways. First, you can calculate summary measures for days required and then back up from the due date. This is done in the range I22:J26. The formulas in column I are

=INT(RiskMean(Days_to_complete))

=RiskMin(Days_to_complete)

=RiskMax(Days_to_complete)

=RiskPercentile(Days_to_complete,0.05)

and

=RiskPercentile(Days_to_complete,0.95)

(The first uses the INT function to produce an integer.) You can then subtract each of these from the due date to obtain the potential starting dates in column J. Wozac should realize the pros and cons of these starting dates. For example, if the company wants to be 95% sure of meeting the due date, it should start production on August 2. In contrast, if Wozac starts production on September 21, there is only a 5% chance of meeting the due date.

Alternatively, you can get a more direct answer to the question by using @RISK's RiskTarget function. This allows you to find the probability of meeting the due date for *any* starting date, such as the trial dates in the range L22:L26. To do it, enter the formula

=RiskTarget(Days_to_complete,Due_date-L22)

in cell M22 and copy it down. This function returns the fraction of iterations where the (random) value in the first argument is less than or equal to the (fixed) value in the second argument. For example, you can see that 83.6% of the iterations have a value of days required less than or equal to 108, the number of days from August 15 to the due date.

What is our recommendation to Wozac? We suggest going with the 95th percentile—begin production on August 2. Then there is only a 5% chance of failing to meet the due date. But the table in the range L22:M26 also provides useful information. For each potential starting date, Wozac can see the probability of meeting the due date.

Using @RISK summary functions such as RiskMean, RiskPercentile, and others enables you to capture simulation results in the same work-sheet as the simulation model. These functions do not provide relevant results until the simulation is run.

Problems

Solutions for problems whose numbers appear within a colored box can be found in the Student Solution Files.

Level A

1. In the Miller bidding model, the possible profits vary from negative to positive for each of the 10 possible bids examined.
   a. For each of these, use @RISK's RiskTarget function to find the probability that Miller's profit is positive. Do you believe these results should have any bearing on Miller's choice of bid?
   b. Use @RISK's RiskPercentile function to find the 10th percentile for each of these bids. Can you explain why the percentiles have the values you obtain?

2. If the number of competitors in the Miller bidding model doubles, how does the optimal bid change?

3. Referring to the Miller bidding model, if the average bid for each competitor stays the same, but their bids exhibit less variability, does Miller's optimal bid increase or decrease? To study this question, assume that each competitor's bid, expressed as a multiple of Miller's cost to complete the project, follows each of the following distributions.
   a. Triangular with parameters 1.0, 1.3, and 2.4
   b. Triangular with parameters 1.2, 1.3, and 2.2
   c. Use @RISK's Define Distributions window to check that the distributions in parts **a** and **b** have the same mean as the original triangular distribution in the example, but smaller standard deviations. What is the common mean? Why is it not the same as the most likely value, 1.3?

4. In the Yakkon warranty model, the gamma distribution was used to model the skewness to the right of the lifetime distribution. Experiment to see whether the triangular distribution could have been used instead. Let its minimum value be 0, and choose its most likely and maximum values so that this triangular distribution has approximately the same mean and standard deviation as the gamma distribution in the example. (Use @RISK's Define Distributions window and trial and error to do this.) Then run the simulation and comment on similarities or differences between your outputs and the outputs in the example.

5. See how sensitive the results in the Yakkon warranty model are to the following changes. For each part, make the change indicated, run the simulation, and comment on any differences between your outputs and the outputs in the example.
   a. The cost of a new camera is increased to $450.
   b. The warranty period is decreased to one year.
   c. The terms of the warranty are changed. If the camera fails within one year, the customer gets a new camera for free. However, if the camera fails between 1 year and 1.5 years, the customer pays a pro rata share of the new camera, increasing linearly from 0 to full price. For example, if it fails at 1.2 years, which is 40% of the way from 1 to 1.5, the customer pays 40% of the full price.
   d. The customer pays $50 up front for an extended warranty. This extends the warranty to three years. This extended warranty is just like the original, so that if the camera fails within three years, the customer gets a new camera for free.

6. In the Wozac drug production model, we commented on the 95th percentile on days required and the corresponding date. If the company begins production on this date, then it is 95% sure to complete the order by the due date. We found this date to be August 2. Do you always get this answer? Find out by (1) running the simulation 10 more times, each with 1000 iterations, and finding the 95th percentile and corresponding date in each, and (2) running the simulation once more, but with 10,000 iterations. Comment on the difference between simulations (1) and (2) in terms of accuracy. Given these results, when would you recommend that production should begin?

7. In the Wozac drug production model, suppose you want to run five simulations, where the probability of passing inspection is varied from 0.6 to 1.0 in increments of 0.1. Use the RiskSimtable function appropriately to do this. Comment on the effect of this parameter on the key outputs. In particular, does the probability of passing inspection have a large effect on when production should start? (*Note:* When this probability is low, it might be necessary to produce more than 25 batches, the maximum built into the model. Check whether this maximum should be increased.)

16-3 Financial Models

There are many financial applications where simulation can be applied. Future cash flows, future stock prices, and future interest rates are some of the many uncertain variables financial analysts must deal with. In every direction they turn, they see uncertainty. In this section, we analyze a few typical financial applications that can benefit from simulation modeling.

16-3a Financial Planning Models

Many companies, such as GM, Eli Lilly, Procter & Gamble, and Pfizer, use simulation in their capital budgeting and financial planning processes. Simulation can be used to model the uncertainty associated with future cash flows. In particular, simulation can be used to answer questions such as the following:

- What are the mean and variance of a project's net present value (NPV)?
- What is the probability that a project will have a negative NPV?
- What are the mean and variance of a company's profit during the next fiscal year?
- What is the probability that a company will have to borrow more than $2 million during the next year?

The following example illustrates how simulation can be used to evaluate the financial success of a new car.

EXAMPLE

16.4 DEVELOPING A NEW CAR AT GF AUTO

General Ford (GF) Auto Corporation is developing a new model of compact car. This car is assumed to generate sales for the next five years. GF has gathered information about the following quantities through focus groups with the marketing and engineering departments.

- **Fixed cost of developing car.** This cost is assumed to be $600 million. The fixed cost is incurred at the beginning of year 1, before any sales are recorded.
- **Margin per car.** This is the unit selling price minus the variable cost of producing a car. GF assumes that in year 1, the margin will be $4000. Every other year, GF assumes the margin will decrease by 4%.[1]
- **Sales.** The demand for the car is the uncertain quantity. In its first year, GF assumes sales—number of cars sold—will be triangularly distributed with parameters 30,000, 55,000, and 65,000. Every year after that, the company assumes that sales will decrease by some percentage, where this percentage is triangularly distributed with parameters 5%, 8%, and 10%. GF also assumes that the percentage decreases in successive years are independent of one another.
- **Depreciation and taxes.** The company will depreciate its development cost on a straight-line basis over the lifetime of the car. The corporate tax rate is 21%.
- **Discount rate.** GF figures its cost of capital at 7%.

Given these assumptions, GF wants to develop a simulation model that will evaluate its NPV of after-tax cash flows for this new car over the five-year time horizon.

Objective

To simulate the cash flows from the new car model, from the development time to the end of its life cycle, so that GF can estimate the NPV of after-tax cash flows from this car.

Where Do the Numbers Come From?

There are many inputs to this problem. As we indicated, they are probably obtained from experts within the company and from focus groups of potential customers.

Solution

The variables for the model are shown in Figure 16.14. (See the file **New Car Development Big Picture.xlsx**.) This model is like most financial multiyear spreadsheet models. The completed model extends several years to the right, but most of the work is for the first year or two. From that point, you can copy to the other years to complete the model.

---

1 The margin decreases because the company assumes variable costs tend to increase through time, whereas selling prices tend to remain fairly constant through time.

Figure 16.14 Big Picture for GF Auto Simulation Model

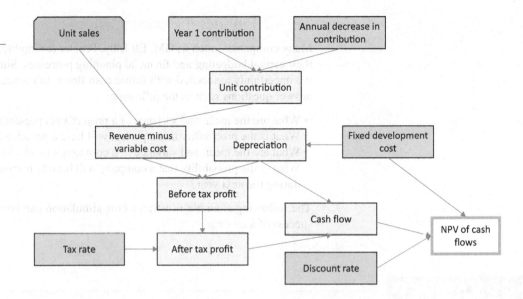

Developing the Simulation Model

The simulation model for GF appears in Figure 16.15. (See the file **New Car Development Finished .xlsx**.) It can be formed as follows.

New Car Development Model

1. **Inputs.** Enter the given inputs in the blue cells.
2. **Unit sales.** Generate first-year sales in cell B12 with the formula

   =RiskTriang(E5,F5,G5)

   Then generate the reduced sales in later years by entering the formula

   =B12*(1 − RiskTriang($E$6,$F$6,$G$6))

   in cell C12 and copying it across row 12. Note that each sales figure is a random fraction of the *previous* sales figure.

Figure 16.15 GF Auto Simulation Model

	A	B	C	D	E	F	G
1	New car simulation						
2							
3	Inputs				Parameters of triangular distributions		
4	Fixed development cost	$600,000,000				Min	Most likely	Max
5	Year 1 contribution	$4,000		Year 1 sales	30000	55000	65000
6	Annual decrease in contribution	4%		Annual decay rate	5%	8%	10%
7	Tax rate	21%					
8	Discount rate	7%					
9							
10	Simulation						
11	End of year	1	2	3	4	5	
12	Unit sales	56529	51303	46936	43585	41017	
13	Unit contribution	$4,000	$3,840	$3,686	$3,539	$3,397	
14	Revenue minus variable cost	$226,116,773	$197,004,495	$173,026,079	$154,246,551	$139,350,833	
15	Depreciation	$120,000,000	$120,000,000	$120,000,000	$120,000,000	$120,000,000	
16	Before tax profit	$106,116,773	$77,004,495	$53,026,079	$34,246,551	$19,350,833	
17	After tax profit	$83,832,251	$60,833,551	$41,890,602	$27,054,776	$15,287,158	
18	Cash flow	$203,832,251	$180,833,551	$161,890,602	$147,054,776	$135,287,158	
19							
20	NPV of cash flows	$89,240,670					

3. **Contributions.** Calculate the unit contributions in row 13 by entering the formulas

$$=B5$$

and

$$=B13*(1-\$B\$6)$$

in cells B13 and C13, and copying the latter across. Then calculate the contributions in row 14 as the product of the corresponding values in rows 12 and 13.

4. **Depreciation.** Calculate the depreciation each year in row 15 as the development cost in cell B4 divided by 5. This is exactly what "straight-line depreciation" means.

5. **Before-tax and after-tax profits.** To calculate the before-tax profit in any year, subtract the depreciation from total contribution, so each value in row 16 is the difference between the corresponding values in rows 14 and 15. The reason is that depreciation isn't taxed. To calculate the after-tax profits in row 17, multiply each before-tax profit by one minus the tax rate in cell B7. Finally, each cash flow in row 18 is the sum of the corresponding values in rows 15 and 17. Here depreciation is added back to get the cash flow.

Depreciation is subtracted to get before-tax profit, but it is then added back after taxes have been deducted.

6. **NPV.** Calculate the NPV of cash flows in cell B20 with the formula

$$=-B4+NPV(B8,B18:F18)$$

and designate it as an @RISK output cell (the only output cell). Here, we are assuming that the development cost is incurred right now, so that it isn't discounted, and that all other cash flows occur at the ends of the respective years. This allows the NPV function to be used directly.

Running the Simulation

Set the number of iterations to 1000 and the number of simulations to 1, and then run the simulation as usual.

Discussion of the Simulation Results

After running @RISK, you obtain the histogram in Figure 16.16. These results are somewhat comforting, but also a cause of concern for GF. On the bright side, the mean NPV is slightly more than $28 million, and there is some chance that the NPV could go well above that figure, even above $177 million. However, there is also a downside, as shown by the two sliders in the histogram. One slider has been placed over an NPV of 0. As the histogram indicates, there is a 65.9% chance of a positive NPV, but there is a 34.1% chance of it being negative. The second slider has been positioned at its default 5th percentile setting. Financial analysts often call this percentile the **value at risk at the 5% level**, or **VaR 5%**, because it indicates nearly the worst possible outcome. From this simulation, you can see that GF's VaR 5% is approximately a $111.77 million loss.

Figure 16.16 Histogram of NPV

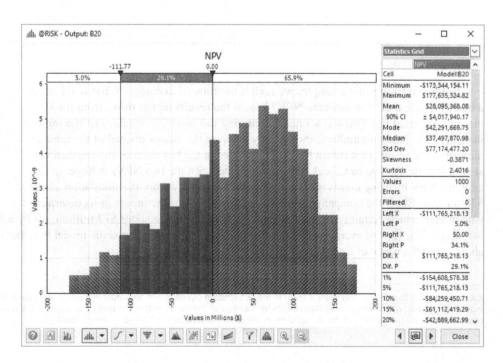

> The **value at risk at the 5% level**, or **VaR 5%**, is the 5th percentile of a distribution, and it is often used in financial models. It indicates nearly the worst possible outcome.

What is most responsible for this huge variability in NPV, the variability in first-year sales or the variability in annual sales decreases? This can be answered with @RISK's tornado graph, which lets you see which random inputs have the most effect on a specified output. (See Figure 16.17.) To get this graph, click the tornado button below the histogram in Figure 16.16 and select the Change in Output Mean option. This graph answers the question emphatically. Variability in first-year sales is by far the largest influence on NPV. It is very highly correlated with NPV. The annual decreases in sales are important, but they have much less effect on NPV. If GF wants to get a more favorable NPV distribution, it should do all it can to boost first-year sales—and make the first-year sales distribution less variable.

Figure 16.17 Tornado Graph for NPV

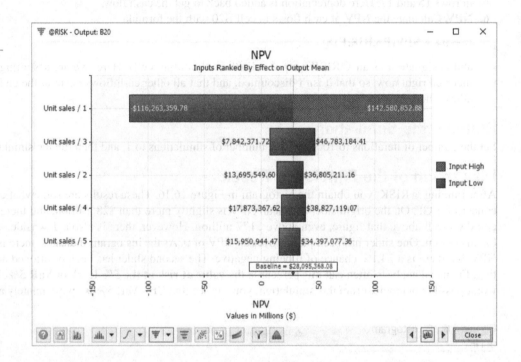

Before finishing this example, we revisit the flaw of averages. What if GF used a deterministic model to estimate NPV? Would the results match those from the simulation? We tried this two ways, once by entering the *most likely values* of the inputs instead of the random numbers, and once by entering the *means* instead of the random numbers. The results (not shown here) are available in the last sheet of the finished version of the file. As you can check, the difference between the two NPVs is huge. In this case, the NPV by using means is very close to the mean NPV from the simulation, about $28 million. But if the company used most likely values for the inputs in its deterministic model, which certainly seems sensible, the NPV would be about $77 million, off by a factor of more than two, another variation of the flaw of averages. Besides this problem, neither deterministic model provides even a hint that the company has about a 34.1% chance of a negative NPV.[2]

---

2 It turns out that the NPV in this model is *linear* in the two random inputs. When an output is linear in the inputs, the deterministic model using means of inputs *always* gives the correct mean output (aside from some randomness), so that the flaw of averages in the form from the previous chapter does not occur. Even so, a deterministic model still provides no indication of how bad or how good things could get.

> **Fundamental Insight**
>
> **The Mean Isn't Everything**
>
> Many discussions of simulation focus on the *mean* of an output variable. This makes sense, given the importance of EMV for decision making, as discussed in Chapter 6. After all, EMV is just the mean of a monetary output. However, analysts in many areas, including finance, are often at least as interested in the extreme values of an output distribution. For example, the VaR 5% discussed in this example indicates nearly how bad things could get if unlucky outcomes occur. If large amounts of money are at stake, particularly potential losses, companies might not want to focus only on the mean. They should be aware of potential disasters as well. Of course, simulation also shows the bright side, the extremes on the right that could occur if lucky outcomes occur. Managers shouldn't be so conservative that they focus only on the negative outcomes and ignore the upside potential.

16-3b Cash Balance Models

All companies track their cash balance over time. As specific payments come due, companies sometimes need to take out short-term loans to keep a minimal cash balance. The following example illustrates one such application.

EXAMPLE

16.5 MAINTAINING A MINIMAL CASH BALANCE AT ENTSON

The Entson Company believes that its monthly sales during the period from November of the current year to July of next year are normally distributed with the means and standard deviations given in Table 16.2. Each month Entson incurs fixed costs of $250,000. In March taxes of $150,000 and in June taxes of $50,000 must be paid. Dividends of $50,000 must also be paid in June. Entson estimates that its receipts in a given month are a weighted sum of sales from the current month, the previous month, and two months ago, with weights 0.2, 0.6, and 0.2. In symbols, if R_t and S_t represent receipts and sales in month t, then

$$R_t = 0.2S_{t-2} + 0.6S_{t-1} + 0.2S_t \tag{16.1}$$

The materials and labor needed to produce a month's sales must be purchased one month in advance, and the cost of these averages to 80% of the product's sales. For example, if sales in February are $1,500,000, then the February materials and labor costs are $1,200,000, but these must be paid in January.

Table 16.2 Monthly Sales (in Thousands of Dollars) for Entson		Nov.	Dec.	Jan.	Feb.	Mar.	Apr.	May	Jun.	Jul.
	Mean	1500	1600	1800	1500	1900	2600	2400	1900	1300
	Standard Deviation	70	75	80	80	100	125	120	90	70

At the beginning of January, Entson has $250,000 in cash. The company wants to ensure that each month's ending cash balance never falls below $250,000. This means that Entson might have to take out short-term (one-month) loans. For example, if the ending cash balance at the end of March is $200,000, Entson will take out a loan for $50,000, which it will then pay back (with interest) one month later. The interest rate on a short-term loan is 1% per month. At the beginning of each month, Entson earns interest of 0.5% on its cash balance. The company wants to use simulation to estimate the maximum loan it will need to take out to meet its desired minimum cash balance. Entson also wants to analyze how its loans will vary over time, and it wants to estimate the total interest paid on these loans.

Objective

To simulate Entson's cash flows and the loans the company must take out to meet a minimum cash balance.

Where Do the Numbers Come From?

Although there are many monetary inputs in the problem statement, they should all be easily accessible. Of course, Entson chooses the minimum cash balance of $250,000 as a matter of company policy.

Solution

The variables for this model appear in Figure 16.18. (See the file **Cash Balance Big Picture.xlsx**.) Clearly, there is a considerable amount of bookkeeping in this simulation, so it is a good idea to list the events in chronological order that occur each month. We assume the following:

- Entson observes its beginning cash balance.
- Entson receives interest on its beginning cash balance.
- Receipts arrive and expenses are paid (including payback of the previous month's loan, if any, with interest).
- If necessary, Entson takes out a short-term loan.
- The final cash balance is observed, which becomes next month's beginning cash balance.

Figure 16.18 Big Picture for Cash Balance Simulation Model

Developing the Simulation Model

The completed simulation model appears in Figure 16.19. (See the file **Cash Balance Finished.xlsx**.) It requires the following steps.

Cash Balance Model

1. **Inputs.** Enter the inputs in the blue cells. Note that loans are simulated (in row 42) only for the period from January to June of next year. However, sales figures are required (in row 28) in November and December of the current year to generate receipts for January and February. Also, July sales are required for next year to generate the material and labor costs paid in June.

2. **Actual sales.** Generate the sales in row 28 by entering the formula

   =RiskNormal(B6,B7)

   in cell B28 and copying across.

3. **Beginning cash balance.** For January of next year, enter the cash balance with the formula

   =B19

   in cell D31. Then for the other months, enter the formula

   =D43

   in cell E31 and copy it across row 31. This reflects that the beginning cash balance for one month is the final cash balance from the previous month.

Figure 16.19 Cash Balance Simulation Model

	A	B	C	D	E	F	G	H	I	J
1	Entson cash balance simulation									
2										
3	Inputs									
4	Distribution of monthly sales (normal)									
5		Nov	Dec	Jan	Feb	Mar	Apr	May	Jun	Jul
6	Mean	1500	1600	1800	1500	1900	2600	2400	1900	1300
7	St Dev	70	75	80	80	100	125	120	90	70
8										
9	Monthly fixed cost			250	250	250	250	250	250	
10	Tax, dividend expenses			0	0	150	0	0	100	
11										
12	Receipts in any month are of form: A*(sales from 2 months ago)+B*(previous month's sales)+C*(current month's sales), where:									
13		A	B	C						
14		0.2	0.6	0.2						
15										
16	Cost of materials and labor for next month, spent this month, is a percentage of product's sales from next month, where the percentage is:									
17		80%								
18										
19	Initial cash in January	250								
20	Minimum cash balance	250								
21										
22	Monthly interest rates									
23	Interest rate on loan	1.0%								
24	Interest rate on cash	0.5%								
25										
26	Simulation									
27		Nov	Dec	Jan	Feb	Mar	Apr	May	Jun	Jul
28	Actual sales	1516.008	1518.567	1809.091	1498.674	1952.505	2382.129	2391.557	1966.894	1443.801
29										
30	Cash, receipts									
31	Beginning cash balance			250.000	378.471	257.263	250.000	250.000	250.000	
32	Interest on cash balance			1.250	1.892	1.892	1.250	1.250	1.250	
33	Receipts			1576.160	1688.903	1651.523	1947.664	2298.090	2304.739	
34	Costs									
35	Fixed costs			250	250	250	250	250	250	
36	Tax, dividend expenses			0	0	150	0	0	100	
37	Material, labor expenses			1198.939	1562.004	1905.704	1913.245	1573.515	1155.041	
38	Loan payback (principal)				0.000	0.000	645.631	866.419	399.258	0.000
39	Loan payback (interest)				0.000	0.000	6.456	8.664	3.993	0.000
40										
41	Cash balance before loan			378.471	257.263	−395.631	−616.419	−149.258	647.697	
42	Loan amount (if any)			0.000	0.000	645.631	866.419	399.258	0.000	
43	Final cash balance			378.471	257.263	250.000	250.000	250.000	647.697	
44										
45	Maximum loan	866.419								
46	Total interest on loans	19.113								

All monetary values are in $1000s.

One user suggested that the formula for total interest in cell B46 should sum only through June, i.e., not include July. You could argue it either way, so feel free to change the formula in cell B46 if you like.

4. **Incomes.** Entson's incomes (interest on cash balance and receipts) are entered in rows 32 and 33. To calculate these, enter the formulas

=$B$24*D31

and

=SUMPRODUCT($B$14:$D$14,B28:D28)

in cells D32 and D33, and copy them across rows 32 and 33. This latter formula, which is based on Equation (16.1), multiplies the fixed weights in row 14 by the relevant sales and adds these products to calculate receipts.

5. **Expenses.** Entson's expenses (fixed costs, taxes and dividends, material and labor costs, and payback of the previous month's loan) are entered in rows 35 through 39. Calculate these by entering the formulas

=D9

=D10

=$B$17*E28

=D42

and

=D42*$B$23

in cells D35, D36, D37, E38, and E39, respectively, and copying these across rows 35 through 39. (For the loan payback, we are assuming that no loan payback is due in January.)

The loan amounts are determined by the random cash inflows and outflows and the fact that Entson's policy is to maintain a minimum cash balance.

6. **Cash balance before loan.** Calculate the cash balance before the loan (if any) by entering the formula

=SUM(D31:D33)−SUM(D35:D39)

in cell D41 and copying it across row 41.

7. **Amount of loan.** If the value in row 41 is below the minimum cash balance ($250,000), Entson must borrow enough to bring the cash balance up to this minimum. Otherwise, no loan is necessary. Therefore, enter the formula

=MAX($B$20−D41,0)

in cell D42 and copy it across row 42. (You could use an IF function, rather the MAX function, to accomplish the same result.)

8. **Final cash balance.** Calculate the final cash balance by entering the formula

=D41+D42

in cell D43 and copying it across row 43.

9. **Maximum loan, total interest.** Calculate the maximum loan from January to June in cell B45 with the formula

=MAX(D42:I42)

Then calculate the total interest paid on all loans in cell B46 with the formula

=SUM(E39:J39)

An @RISK output range, as opposed to a single output cell, allows you to obtain a summary graph that shows the whole simulated range at once. This range is typically a time series.

10. **Output range.** In the usual way, designate cells B45 and B46 as output cells. Also, designate the entire range of loans, D42:I42, as an output range. To do this, select this range and click the @RISK Add Output button. It will ask you for a name of the output. We suggest "Loans." Then a typical formula in this range, such as the formula for cell E42, will be

=RiskOutput("Loans",2)+MAX($B$20−E41,0)

This indicates that cell E42 is the second cell in the Loans output range.

Running the Simulation

Set the number of iterations to 1000 and the number of simulations to 1. Then run the simulation in the usual way.

Discussion of the Simulation Results

The summary results from the simulation are shown in Figure 16.20. They indicate that the maximum loan varies considerably, from a low of about $470,000 to a high of almost $1.5 million. The average is about $952,000. You can also see that Entson is spending close to $20,000 on average in interest on the loans, although the actual amounts vary considerably from one iteration to another.

You can also gain insights from the summary trend graph of the series of loans, shown in Figure 16.21. To obtain this graph, click the fourth button at the bottom of the Results Summary window in Figure 16.20. (This button is also available in any distribution graph window.) This graph clearly shows how the loans vary through time. The middle line is the expected loan amount. The inner bands extend to one standard deviation on either side of the mean, and the outer bands extend to the 5th and 95th percentiles. You can see that the largest loans are required in March and April.

Is it intuitively clear why the required loans peak in March and April? After all, why should Entson need money in months when its sales tend to be relatively high? There are two factors working here. First, Entson has to pay its costs early. For example, it has to pay 80% of its April sales for labor and material expenses in March. Second, most of its receipts arrive late. For example, 80% of its receipts from sales in March are not received until *after* March. Therefore, the answer to the question is that the timing and amounts of loans are fairly complex. Of course, this is why Entson builds a simulation model in the first place.

Figure 16.20 Summary
Measures for Cash Balance
Simulation

Figure 16.21 Summary Trend
Graph of Loans Through Time

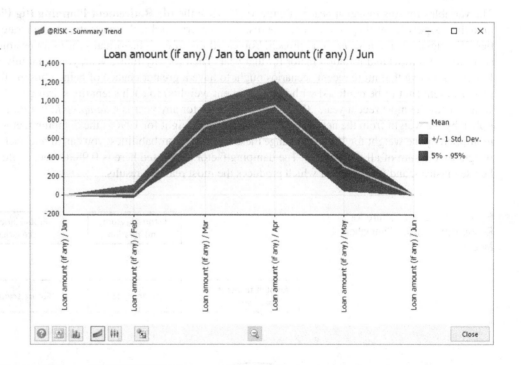

16-3c Investment Models

Individual investors typically want to choose investment strategies that meet some pre-specified goal. The following example is typical. Here, a person wants to meet a retirement goal, starting at an early age.

16.6 INVESTING FOR RETIREMENT

Attorney Sally Evans has just begun her career. At age 25, she has 40 years until retirement, but she realizes that now is the time to start investing. She plans to invest $1000 at the beginning of each of the next 40 years. Each year, she plans to put fixed percentages—the same each year—of this $1000 into stocks, Treasury bonds (T-bonds), and Treasury bills (T-bills). However, she is not sure which percentages to use. (We call these percentages *investment weights*.) She has historical annual returns from stocks, T-bonds, and T-bills from 1946 to 2007. These are listed in the file **Retirement Planning.xlsx**. This file also includes inflation rates for these years. For example, for 1993, the annual returns for stocks, T-bonds, and T-bills were 9.99%, 18.24%, and 2.90%, respectively, and the inflation rate was 2.75%. Sally would like to use simulation to help decide what investment weights to use, with the objective of achieving a large investment value, in *today's* dollars, at the end of 40 years.

Objective

To use simulation to estimate the value of Sally's future investments, in today's dollars, from several investment strategies in T-bills, T-bonds, and stocks.

Where Do the Numbers Come From?

Historical returns and inflation rates, such as those quoted here, are available on the Web. In fact, you might want to find more recent data than we have provided here.

Solution

The variables for this model appear in Figure 16.22. (See the file **Retirement Planning Big Picture.xlsx**.) The most difficult modeling aspect is settling on a way to use historical returns and inflation factors to generate *future* values of these quantities. We suggest using a *scenario* approach. You can think of each historical year as a possible scenario, where the scenario specifies the returns and inflation factor for that year. Then for any future year, you randomly choose one of these scenarios. It seems intuitive that more recent scenarios ought to have a greater chance of being chosen. To implement this idea, you can give a weight (not to be confused with the investment weights) to each scenario, starting with weight 1 for the most recent year, 2007. Then the weight for any year is a *damping factor* multiplied by the weight from the next year. For example, the weight for 1996 is the damping factor multiplied by the weight for 1997. To change these weights to probabilities, you can divide each weight by the sum of all the weights. The damping factor illustrated here is 0.98. Others could be used instead, and it is not clear which produces the most realistic results.

You can simulate future scenarios by randomly choosing past scenarios, giving higher probabilities to more recent scenarios.

Figure 16.22 Big Picture for Retirement Planning Simulation Model

The other difficult part of the solution is choosing "good" investment weights. This is really an optimization problem: find three weights that add to 1 and produce the largest mean final cash. (@RISK contains a powerful tool, RiskOptimizer, that solves this type of optimization–simulation problem, but we will not discuss it here.) This example illustrates several sets of weights, where some percentage is put into stocks and the remainder is split evenly between T-bonds and T-bills, and see which does best. You can try other sets if you like.

Without a tool like RiskOptimizer, you cannot find the "best" set of investment weights, but the simulation model lets you experiment with various sets of weights.

Developing the Simulation Model

The historical data and the simulation model (each with some rows hidden) appear in Figures 16.23 and 16.24. (Again, see the file **Retirement Planning Finished.xlsx**.) It can be developed as follows.

Investing for Retirement Model

1. **Inputs.** Enter the data in the blue regions of Figures 16.23 and 16.24.

Figure 16.23 Historical Data, Inputs, and Probabilities

◢	A	B	C	D	E	F	G
1	Planning for retirement						
2							
3	Historical data and probabilities						
4	Year	T-Bills	T-Bonds	Stocks	Inflation	ProbWts	Probability
5	1946	0.0035	−0.0010	−0.0807	0.1817	0.2916	0.0082
6	1947	0.0050	−0.0263	0.0571	0.0901	0.2976	0.0083
7	1948	0.0081	0.0340	0.0550	0.0271	0.3036	0.0085
8	1949	0.0110	0.0645	0.1879	−0.0180	0.3098	0.0087
9	1950	0.0120	0.0006	0.3171	0.0579	0.3161	0.0089
58	1999	0.0439	−0.0825	0.2089	0.0270	0.8508	0.0238
59	2000	0.0537	0.1666	−0.0903	0.0340	0.8681	0.0243
60	2001	0.0573	0.0557	−0.1185	0.0160	0.8858	0.0248
61	2002	0.0180	0.1512	−0.2198	0.0159	0.9039	0.0253
62	2003	0.0180	0.0038	0.2841	0.0227	0.9224	0.0258
63	2004	0.0218	0.0449	0.1070	0.0268	0.9412	0.0264
64	2005	0.0431	0.0287	0.0485	0.0339	0.9604	0.0269
65	2006	0.0488	0.0196	0.1563	0.0324	0.9800	0.0274
66	2007	0.0548	0.0488	0.1021	0.0285	1.0000	0.0280
67					Sums—>	35.7115	1.0000

2. **Weights.** The investment weights used for the model are in rows 10 through 12 of Figure 16.23. (For example, the first set puts 80% in stocks and 10% in each of T-bonds and T-bills.) You can simulate all three sets of weights simultaneously with a RiskSimtable and VLOOKUP combination as follows. First, enter the formula

= **RiskSimtable({1,2,3})**

in cell I16. Then enter the formula

= **VLOOKUP($I$16,LTable1,2)**

in cell J16 and copy it to cells K16 and L16. Then modify the formulas in these latter two cells, changing the last argument of the VLOOKUP to 3 and 4, respectively. For example, the formula in cell L16 should end up as

= **VLOOKUP($I$16,LTable1,4)**

The effect is that you can run three simulations, one for each set of weights in rows 10 through 12.

3. **Probabilities.** Enter value 1 in cell F66. Then enter the formula

= **$J$4*F66**

in cell F65 and copy it *up* to cell F5. Sum these values with the SUM function in cell F67. Then to convert them to probabilities (numbers that add to 1), enter the formula

= **F5/$F$67**

Figure 16.24 Retirement Simulation Model

	I	J	K	L	M	N	O	P	Q
3	**Inputs**								
4	Damping factor	0.98				**Range names used**			
5	Yearly investment	$1,000				LTable1	=Model!$I$10:$L$12		
6	Planning horizon	40	years			LTable2	=Model!$A$5:$E$66		
7						Weights	=Model!$J$16:$L$16		
8	**Alternative sets of weights to test**								
9	Index		T-Bills	T-Bonds	Stocks				
10	1		0.10	0.10	0.80				
11	2		0.20	0.20	0.60				
12	3		0.30	0.30	0.40				
13									
14	**Weights used**								
15	Index		T-Bills	T-Bonds	Stocks				
16	1		0.10	0.10	0.80				
17									
18	**Output from simulation below**								
19	Final cash (today's dollars)		$47,921						
20									
21					Column offset for lookup2				
22	**Simulation model**			2	3	4	5		
23	Future year	Beginning cash	Scenario	T-Bills	T-Bonds	Stocks	Inflation	Ending cash	Deflator
24	1	$1,000	1973	1.0693	0.9889	0.8534	1.0880	$889	0.919
25	2	$1,889	1992	1.0351	1.0805	1.0767	1.0290	$2,026	0.893
26	3	$3,026	2005	1.0431	1.0287	1.0485	1.0339	$3,165	0.864
27	4	$4,165	1968	1.0521	0.9974	1.1106	1.0472	$4,555	0.825
28	5	$5,555	1981	1.1471	1.0185	0.9509	1.0894	$5,428	0.757
29	6	$6,428	1968	1.0521	0.9974	1.1106	1.0472	$7,029	0.723
56	33	$102,516	1975	1.0580	1.0919	1.3720	1.0701	$134,562	0.194
57	34	$135,562	1958	1.0154	0.9390	1.4336	1.0176	$181,967	0.191
58	35	$182,967	1990	1.0781	1.0618	0.9683	1.0611	$180,887	0.180
59	36	$181,887	1961	1.0213	1.0097	1.2689	1.0067	$221,579	0.179
60	37	$222,579	2004	1.0218	1.0449	1.1070	1.0268	$243,116	0.174
61	38	$244,116	1951	1.0149	0.9606	1.2402	1.0587	$290,427	0.164
62	39	$291,427	1987	1.0547	0.9731	1.0523	1.0441	$304,431	0.158
63	40	$305,431	1970	1.0653	1.1210	1.0401	1.0549	$320,919	0.149

in cell G5 and copy it down to cell G66. Note how the probabilities for more recent years are considerably larger. When scenarios are selected randomly, recent years will have a greater chance of being chosen. (The SUM formula in cell G67 confirms that the probabilities sum to 1.)

4. **Scenarios.** Moving to the model in Figure 16.24, the goal is to simulate 40 scenarios in columns K through O, one for each year of Sally's investing. To do this, enter the formulas

=RiskDiscrete($A$5:$A$66,$G$5:$G$66)

and

=1+VLOOKUP($K24,LTable2,L$22)

in cells K24 and L24, and copy this latter formula to the range M24:O24. Then copy all of these formulas down to row 63. Make sure you understand how the RiskDiscrete and VLOOKUP functions combine to achieve the goal. (Also, check the list of range names used at the top of Figure 16.24.) The RiskDiscrete function randomly generates a year from column A, using the probabilities in column G. Then the VLOOKUP function captures the data from this year. (You add 1 to the VLOOKUP to get a value such as 1.08, rather than 0.08.) This is the key to the simulation. (By the way, do you see why Excel's RANDBETWEEN function isn't used to generate the years in column K? The reason is that this function makes all possible years equally likely, and the goal is to make more recent years *more* likely.)

5. **Beginning, ending cash.** The bookkeeping part is straightforward. Begin by entering the formula

=J5

in cell J24 for the initial investment. Then enter the formulas

=J24*SUMPRODUCT(Weights,L24:N24)

and

$$=\$J\$5 + P24$$

in cells P24 and J25 for ending cash in the first year and beginning cash in the second year. The former shows how the beginning cash grows in a given year. You should think it through carefully. The latter implies that Sally reinvests her previous money, plus she invests an additional $1000. Copy these formulas down columns J and P.

6. **Deflators.** You eventually need to deflate future dollars to today's dollars. The proper way to do this is to calculate deflators (also called deflation factors). Do this by entering the formula

$$=1/O24$$

in cell Q24. Then enter the formula

$$=Q24/O25$$

in cell Q25 and copy it down. The effect is that the deflator for future year 20, say, in cell Q43, is 1 divided by the product of all 20 inflation factors up through that year. (This is similar to discounting for the time value of money, but the relevant discount rate, now the inflation rate, varies from year to year.)

7. **Final cash.** Calculate the final value *in today's dollars* in cell K19 with the formula

$$=P63*Q63$$

Then designate this cell as an @RISK output cell.

Running the Simulation

Set the number of iterations to 1000 and the number of simulations to 3 (one for each set of investment weights to be tested). Then run the simulation as usual.

Discussion of the Simulation Results

Summary results appear in Figure 16.25. The first simulation, which invests the most heavily in stocks, is easily the winner. Its mean final cash, slightly more than $155,000 in today's dollars, is much greater than the means for the other two sets of weights. The first simulation also has a *much* larger upside potential (its 95th percentile is close to $368,000), and even its downside is slightly better than the others: Its 5th percentile is the best, and its minimum is only slightly worse than the minimum for the other sets of weights.

Figure 16.25 Summary Results for Retirement Simulation

Name	Cell	Sim#	Graph	Min	Mean	Max	Std Dev	5%	95%
Final cash	K19	1		$8,846.14	$155,486.90	$922,051.50	$112,539.50	$36,572.82	$367,883.10
Final cash	K19	2		$10,968.05	$105,956.60	$466,997.90	$59,434.02	$35,887.82	$213,030.90
Final cash	K19	3		$13,108.15	$72,557.41	$235,560.50	$31,191.41	$31,873.56	$130,136.20

(@RISK - Results Summary — Inputs= 41, Outputs= 1, Statistic Functions= 0, Iterations= 1000, Simulations= 3, Runtime= 00:00:03)

Nevertheless, the histogram for simulation 1 (put 80% in stocks), shown in Figure 16.26, indicates a lot of variability—and skewness—in the distribution of final cash. As in Example 16.4, the concept of value at risk (VaR) is useful. Recall that VaR 5% is defined as the 5th percentile of a distribution and is often the value investors worry about. Perhaps Sally should rerun the simulation with different investment weights, with an eye on the weights that increase her VaR 5%. Right now it is about $36,500—not too good considering that she invests $40,000 total. She might not like the prospect of a 5% chance of ending up with no more than this. We also encourage you to try running this simulation with other investment weights, both for the 40-year horizon and (after modifying the spreadsheet model slightly) for shorter time horizons such as 10 or 15 years. Even though the stock strategy appears to be best for a long horizon, it is not necessarily guaranteed to dominate for a shorter time horizon.

Figure 16.26 Histogram of
Final Cash with 80% in Stocks

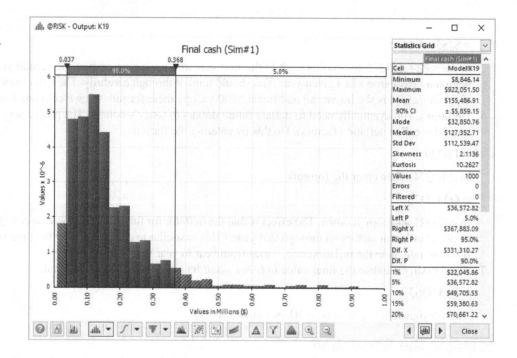

Problems

Level A

8. Rerun the GF Auto new car simulation model but now introduce uncertainty into the fixed development cost. Let it be triangularly distributed with parameters $500 million, $550 million, and $750 million. (You can check that the mean of this distribution is $600 million, the same as the cost given in the example.) Comment on the differences between your output and those in the example. Would you say these differences are important for the company?

9. Rerun the GF Auto new car simulation model but now use the RiskSimtable function appropriately to simulate discount rates of 5%, 7.5%, 10%, and 12.5%. Comment on how the output changes as the discount rate increases.

10. In the Entson cash balance model, the timing is such that some receipts are delayed by one or two months, and the payments for materials and labor must be made a month in advance. Change the model so that all receipts are received immediately, and payments made this month for materials and labor are 80% of sales *this* month (not next month). The period of interest is again January through June. Rerun the simulation, and comment on any differences between your outputs and those from the example.

11. In the Entson cash balance model, is the $250,000 minimum cash balance requirement really "costing" the company very much? Answer this by rerunning the simulation with minimum required cash balances of $50,000, $100,000, $150,000, and $200,000. Use the RiskSimtable function to run all simulations at once. Comment on the outputs from these simulations. In particular, comment on whether the company appears to be better off with a lower minimum cash balance.

12. Run the investing for retirement model with a damping factor of 1.0 (instead of 0.98), again using the same three sets of investment weights. Explain in words what it means, in terms of the simulation, to have a damping factor of 1. Then comment on the differences, if any, between your simulation results and those in the example.

13. The simulation output from the investing for retirement model indicates that an investment heavy in stocks produces the best results. Would it be better to invest *entirely* in stocks? Answer this by rerunning the simulation. Is there any apparent downside to this strategy?

14. Modify the investing for retirement model so that you use only the years 1975 to 2007 of historical data. Run the simulation for the same three sets of investment weights. Comment on whether your results differ in any important way from those in the example.

15. Rerun the investing for retirement model with a planning horizon of 10 years; 15 years; 25 years. For each, which set of investment weights maximizes the VaR 5% (the 5th percentile) of final cash in today's dollars? Does it appear that a portfolio heavy in stocks is better for long horizons but not for shorter horizons?

Level B

16. Change the GF Auto new car simulation model as follows. It is the same as before for years 1 through 5, including depreciation through year 5. However, the car might sell through year 10. Each year *after* year 5, the company examines sales. If fewer than 35,000 cars were sold that year, there is a 50% chance the car won't be sold after that year. Modify the model and run the simulation. Keep track of two outputs: NPV (through year 10) and the number of years of sales.

17. Based on Kelly (1956). You currently have $100. Each week you can invest any amount of money you currently have in a risky investment. With probability 0.4, the amount you invest is tripled (e.g., if you invest $100, you increase your asset position by $300), and, with probability 0.6, the amount you invest is lost. Consider the following investment strategies:

- Each week, invest 10% of your money.
- Each week, invest 30% of your money.
- Each week, invest 50% of your money.

Use @RISK to simulate 100 weeks of each strategy 1000 times. Which strategy appears to be best in terms of the maximum growth rate? (In general, if you can multiply your investment by M with probability p and lose your investment with probability $q = 1 - p$, you should invest a fraction $[p(M - 1) - q]/(M - 1)$ of your money each week. This strategy maximizes the expected growth rate of your fortune and is known as the *Kelly criterion*.) (*Hint*: If an initial wealth of I dollars grows to F dollars in 100 weeks, the weekly growth rate, labeled r, satisfies $F = (1 + r)^{100}*I$, so that $r = (F/I)^{1/100} - 1$.)

18. Amanda has 30 years to save for her retirement. At the beginning of each year, she puts $5000 into her retirement account. At any point in time, all of Amanda's retirement funds are tied up in the stock market. Suppose the annual return on stocks follows a normal distribution with mean 12% and standard deviation 25%. What is the probability that at the end of 30 years, Amanda will have reached her goal of having $1,000,000 for retirement? Assume that if Amanda reaches her goal *before* 30 years, she will stop investing. (*Hint*: Each year you should keep track of Amanda's beginning cash position—for year 1, this is $5000—and Amanda's ending cash position. Of course, Amanda's ending cash position for a given year is a function of her beginning cash position and the return on stocks for that year. To estimate the probability that Amanda meets her goal, use an

IF statement that returns 1 if she meets her goal and 0 otherwise.)

19. In the financial world, there are many types of complex instruments called derivatives that *derive* their value from the value of an underlying asset. Consider the following simple derivative. A stock's current price is $80 per share. You purchase a derivative whose value to you becomes known a month from now. Specifically, let P be the price of the stock in a month. If P is between $75 and $85, the derivative is worth nothing to you. If P is less than $75, the derivative results in a loss of $100*(75 - P)$ dollars to you. (The factor of 100 is because many derivatives involve 100 shares.) If P is greater than $85, the derivative results in a gain of $100*(P - 85)$ dollars to you. Assume that the distribution of the change in the stock price from now to a month from now is normally distributed with mean $1 and standard deviation $8. Let E be the expected gain/loss from this derivative. It is a weighted average of all the possible losses and gains, weighted by their likelihoods. (Of course, any loss should be expressed as a negative number. For example, a loss of $1500 should be expressed as $-$1500.) Unfortunately, this is a difficult probability calculation, but E can be estimated by an @RISK simulation. Perform this simulation with at least 1000 iterations. What is your best estimate of E?

20. Suppose you currently have a portfolio of three stocks, A, B, and C. You own 500 shares of A, 300 of B, and 1000 of C. The current share prices are $42.76, $81.33, and $58.22, respectively. You plan to hold this portfolio for at least a year. During the coming year, economists have predicted that the national economy will be awful, stable, or great with probabilities 0.2, 0.5, and 0.3, respectively. Given the state of the economy, the returns (one-year percentage changes) of the three stocks are independent and normally distributed. However, the means and standard deviations of these returns depend on the state of the economy, as indicated in the file **P16_20.xlsx**.

   a. Use @RISK to simulate the value of the portfolio and the portfolio return in the next year. How likely is it that you will have a negative return? How likely is it that you will have a return of at least 25%?

   b. Suppose you had a crystal ball where you could predict the state of the economy with certainty. The stock returns would still be uncertain, but you would know whether your means and standard deviations come from row 6, 7, or 8 of the file **P16_20.xlsx**. If you learn, with certainty, that the economy is going to be *great* in the next year, run the appropriate simulation to answer the same questions as in part **a**. Repeat this if you learn that the economy is going to be *awful*. How do these results compare with those in part **a**?

16-4 Marketing Models

There are many opportunities for marketing departments to use simulation. They face uncertainty in the brand-switching behavior of customers, the entry of new brands into the market, customer preferences for different attributes of products, the effects of advertising on sales, and so on. We examine several marketing applications of simulation in this section.

16-4a Customer Loyalty Models

What is a loyal customer worth to a company? This is an extremely important question for companies. Companies know that if customers become dissatisfied with the company's product, they are likely to switch and never return. Marketers refer to this customer loss as **churn**. The loss in profit from churn can be large, particularly because long-standing customers tend to be more profitable in any given year than new customers. The following example uses a reasonable model of customer loyalty and simulation to estimate the worth of a customer to a company. It is based on the excellent discussion of customer loyalty in Reichheld (1996).

EXAMPLE

16.7 LONG-TERM VALUE OF A CUSTOMER AT CCAMERICA

CCAmerica is a credit card company that does its best to gain customers and keep their business in a highly competitive industry. The first year a customer signs up for service typically results in a loss to the company because of various administrative expenses. However, after the first year, the profit from a customer is typically positive, and this profit tends to increase through the years. The company has estimated the mean profit from a typical customer to be as shown in column B of Figure 16.28 below. (See the file **Customer Loyalty.xlsx**.) For example, the company expects to lose $40 in the customer's first year but to gain $87 in the fifth year—provided that the customer stays loyal that long. For modeling purposes, we assume that the *actual* profit from a customer in a customer's *given* year of service is *normally* distributed with mean shown in Figure 16.28 and standard deviation equal to 10% of the mean. At the end of each year, the customer leaves the company, never to return, with probability 0.15, the *churn rate*. Alternatively, the customer stays with probability 0.85, the *retention rate*. The company wants to estimate the NPV of the net profit from any such customer who has just signed up for service at the beginning of year 1, at a discount rate of 8%, assuming that the cash flow occurs in the middle of the year.[3] It also wants to see how sensitive this NPV is to the retention rate.

Objective

To use simulation to find the NPV of a customer, and to see how this varies with the retention rate.

Where Do the Numbers Come From?

The numbers in column B of Figure 16.28 are undoubtedly averages, based on the historical records of many customers. To build in randomness for any *particular* customer, we need a probability distribution around the numbers in this figure. We arbitrarily chose a normal distribution centered on the historical average and a standard deviation of 10% of the average. These are educated guesses. Finally, the churn rate is a number very familiar to marketing people, and it can also be estimated from historical customer data.

Solution

The variables for this model appear in Figure 16.27. (See the file **Customer Loyalty Big Picture .xlsx**.) The idea is to keep simulating profits (or a loss in the first year) for the customer until the customer churns. We simulate 30 years of potential profits, but this could be varied.

Customer Loyalty Model

As usual, Excel's RAND function can be used inside an IF statement to determine whether a given event occurs.

Developing the Simulation Model

The simulation model appears in Figure 16.28. (See the file **Customer Loyalty Finished.xlsx**.) It can be developed with the following steps.

---

3 This assumption makes the NPV calculation slightly more complex, but it is probably more realistic than the usual assumption that cash flows occur at the *ends* of the years.

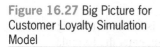

Figure 16.27 Big Picture for Customer Loyalty Simulation Model

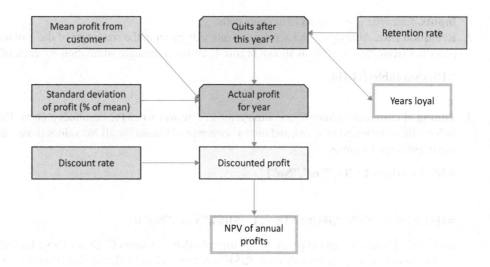

Figure 16.28 Customer Loyalty Model

	A	B	C	D	E	F	G	H	I	J
1	Customer loyalty model in the credit card industry									
2										
3	Inputs			Retention rates to try						
4	Retention rate	0.75		0.75	0.80	0.85	0.90	0.95		
5	Discount rate	0.08								
6	Stdev % of mean	10%								
7										
8										
9	Estimated means		Simulation				Outputs			
10	Year	Mean Profit(if still here)	Quits at end of year?	Actual profit	Discounted profit		NPV	$1,030.50		
11	1	−40.00	No	−41.50	−39.93		Years loyal	25		
12	2	66.00	No	66.84	59.55					
13	3	72.00	No	71.01	58.58		Means			
14	4	79.00	No	87.93	67.16		Simulation	Retention rate	NPV	Years loyal
15	5	87.00	No	92.98	65.76		1	0.75	$149.70	4.26
16	6	92.00	No	109.92	71.99		2	0.80	$184.67	4.92
17	7	96.00	No	100.17	60.74		3	0.85	$264.03	6.51
18	8	99.00	No	92.80	52.10		4	0.90	$388.32	9.25
19	9	103.00	No	82.43	42.86		5	0.95	$663.44	16.13
20	10	106.00	No	102.66	49.42					
21	11	111.00	No	109.56	48.83					
22	12	116.00	No	128.17	52.89					
23	13	120.00	No	95.80	36.61					
24	14	124.00	No	136.34	48.24					
25	15	130.00	No	109.77	35.96					
26	16	137.00	No	114.73	34.80					
27	17	142.00	No	117.20	32.92					
28	18	148.00	No	139.92	36.39					
29	19	155.00	No	156.15	37.60					
30	20	161.00	No	160.96	35.89					
31	21	161.00	No	145.97	30.14					
32	22	161.00	No	187.33	35.81					
33	23	161.00	No	152.59	27.01					
34	24	161.00	No	152.22	24.95					
35	25	161.00	Yes	159.68	24.23					
36	26	161.00		0.00	0.00					
37	27	161.00		0.00	0.00					
38	28	161.00		0.00	0.00					
39	29	161.00		0.00	0.00					
40	30	161.00		0.00	0.00					

1. **Inputs.** Enter the given inputs in the blue cells.
2. **Retention rate.** Although an 85% retention rate was given in the statement of the problem, it is useful to investigate retention rates from 75% to 95%, as shown in row 4. To run a separate simulation for each of these, enter the formula

   $=$ **RiskSimtable(D4:H4)**

   in cell B4.
3. **Timing of churn.** In column C, use simulation to discover when the customer churns. This column will contain a sequence of No values, followed by a Yes, and then a sequence of blanks (or all No values if the customer never churns). To generate these, enter the formulas

   $=$ **IF(RAND()<1−B4,"Yes","No")**

   and

   $=$ **IF(C11<>"No","",IF(RAND()<1−$B$4,"Yes","No"))**

   in cells C11 and C12, and copy the latter formula down column C. Study these formulas carefully to see how the logic works. Note that they do not rely on @RISK functions. Excel's RAND function can be used any time you want to simulate whether or not an event occurs.
4. **Actual and discounted profits.** Profits (or a loss in the first year) occur as long as there is not a blank in column C. Therefore, simulate the actual profits by entering the formula

   $=$ **IF(C11<>"",RiskNormal(B11,$B$6*ABS(B11)),0)**

   Careful discounting is required if cash flows occur in the middle of a year.

   in cell D11 and copying it down. (The absolute value function, ABS, is required in case any of the cash flows are negative. A normal distribution cannot have a *negative* standard deviation.) Then discount these appropriately in column E by entering the formula

   $=$ **D11/(1+$B$5)^(A11−0.5)**

   in cell E11 and copying it down. Note how the exponent of the denominator accounts for the cash flow in the *middle* of the year.
5. **Outputs.** Keep track of two outputs, the total NPV and the number of years the customer stays with the company. Calculate the NPV in cell H10 by summing the discounted values in column E. (They have already been discounted, so the NPV function is not needed.) To find the number of years the customer is loyal, count the number of No values plus the number of Yes values, that is, all nonblanks. Calculate this in cell H11 with the formula

   $=$ **COUNTIF(C11:C40,"No")+COUNTIF(C11:C40,"Yes")**

   Finally, designate both of cells H10 and H11 as @RISK output cells.

Running the Simulation

Set the number of iterations to 1000 and the number of simulations to 5 (one for each potential retention rate). Then run the simulation as usual.

Discussion of the Simulation Results

Summary results for all five retention rates appear in Figure 16.29. You can see that the mean NPV and the mean number of years loyal are quite sensitive to the retention rate.

Varying the retention rate can have a large impact on the value of a customer.

To follow up on this observation, you can use the RiskMean function to capture the means in columns I and J of the model sheet and then create line charts of them as a function of the retention rate. (See Figure 16.28, where years loyal is shown on a secondary axis.) These line charts show the rather dramatic effect the retention rate can have on the value of a customer. For example, if it increases from the current 85% to 90%, the mean NPV increases by about 47%. If it increases from 85% to 95%, the mean NPV increases by about 151%. In the other direction, if the retention rate decreases from 85% to 80%, the mean NPV decreases by about 30%. This is why credit card companies are so anxious to keep their customers.

Figure 16.29 Summary Results for Customer Loyalty Model

The following example is a variation of the customer loyalty example. We now investigate the effect of offering a customer an incentive to remain loyal.

EXAMPLE

16.8 THE VALUE OF A FREE MAINTENANCE AGREEMENT AT JAMESONS

Companies value loyal customers, and they sometimes go to great lengths to keep their customers loyal. This example investigates whether one such plan is worth its cost. We consider a nationwide company called Jamesons, which sells electronic appliances. Specifically, we will focus on sales of smart phones. To attract customers, the company is considering giving customers a free maintenance agreement with each purchase of a smart phone. The unit profit without free maintenance is currently $75. The company believes this will decrease to $60 with free maintenance. Their thinking is that about 5% of customers will actually use the free maintenance, and for each such customer, the company will lose about $300. Hence the average decrease in profit per purchaser is about $15.

Prior to this year, 50,000 customers were loyal to Jamesons and 100,000 customers were loyal to their competitors. (Loyalty is defined in terms of where the customer bought his or her last smart phone.) There are a number of uncertain quantities, and we assume they are all triangularly distributed. Their parameters (minimum, most likely, and maximum) are as follows. (1) The percentage of the 150,000 customers who purchase a smart phone in any given year has parameters 20%, 25%, and 40%. (2) The annual percentage change in unit profit has parameters 3%, 5%, and 6%. (3) In any year, the percentage of Jamesons' loyal customers who remain loyal has parameters 56%, 60%, and 66% if there is no free maintenance, and they increase to 60%, 64%, and 70% with free maintenance. (4) Similarly, the percentage of the competitors' loyal customers who switch to Jamesons has parameters 27%, 30%, and 34% if there is no free maintenance, and they increase to 32%, 35%, and 39% with free maintenance. These inputs are shown in the top section of Figure 16.31 below.

Jamesons is hoping that the decrease in unit profit from the free maintenance agreement will be more than offset by the higher loyalty percentages. Using a 15-year planning horizon, does the NPV of profits with a 8% discount rate confirm the company's hopes?

Objective

To use simulation to see whether it makes sense for Jamesons to give a free maintenance agreement to DVD player purchasers.

Where Do the Numbers Come From?

In the previous example, we discussed the switching rates, which would be estimated from extensive customer data. The other data in the problem statement are straightforward to obtain.

Solution

The variables for this model are shown in Figure 16.30. (See the file **Free Maintenance Big Picture.xlsx**.) The solution strategy is to compare two simulations, one without free maintenance and one with it. Because they are so similar, you can use RiskSimtable to run both simulations. We make one assumption that is common in marketing but might not be intuitive. We assume that only *purchasers* in a given year have any chance of switching loyalty in the next year. For example, if a customer is loyal to Jamesons and doesn't purchase a smart phone in a given year, this customer is automatically loyal to Jamesons in the next year.

Figure 16.30 Big Picture for Free Maintenance Simulation Model

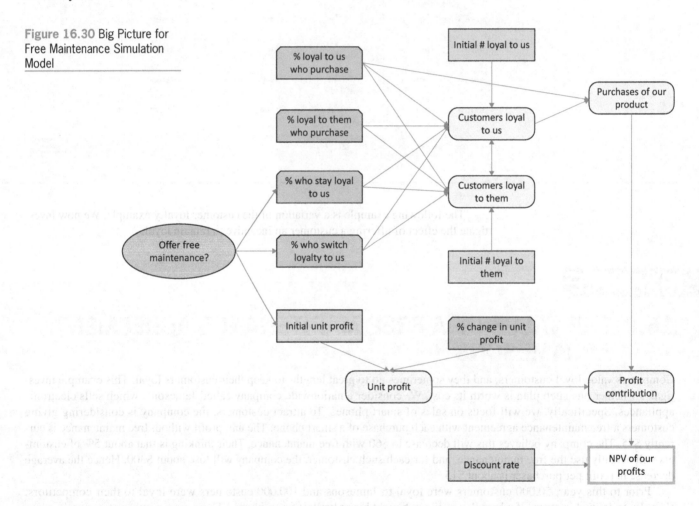

Developing the Simulation Model

The completed simulation model appears in Figure 16.31. (See the file **Free Maintenance 1 Finished.xlsx**.) It can be developed with the following steps.

1. **Inputs.** Enter the given inputs in the blue cells.
2. **Maintenance decision.** The current "no free maintenance" policy is labeled simulation #1 and the proposed "free maintenance" policy is labeled simulation #2, so enter the formula

   =RiskSimtable({1,2})

   in cell B21.

Free Maintenance Agreement Model

Figure 16.31 Free Maintenance Simulation Model

	A	B	C	D	E	F	G	H	I	J	K	L	M	N	O	P	Q
1	Free maintenance agreement - is it worth it?																
2																	
3	Common inputs					Inputs that depend on policy											
4	Loyal customers in previous year						Not free	Free									
5	To our brand	50000				Unit profit	$75	$60									
6	To their brand	100000															
7						% of our loyal customers who remain loyal (triangular distribution)											
8	% of potential customers who purchase in any year (triangular distribution)					Minimum	56%	60%									
9	Minimum	20%				Most likely	60%	64%									
10	Most likely	25%				Maximum	66%	70%									
11	Maximum	40%															
12						% of their loyal customers who switch to us (triangular distribution)											
13	Annual % growth in profit contribution (triangular distribution)					Minimum	27%	32%									
14	Minimum	3%				Most likely	30%	35%									
15	Most likely	5%				Maximum	34%	39%									
16	Maximum	6%															
17																	
18	Discount rate	8%															
19																	
20	Simulation																
21	Index of simulation	1															
22																	
23	Year	0	1	2	3	4	5	6	7	8	9	10	11	12	13	14	15
24	% loyal to us who purchase	21.3%	27.4%	23.2%	32.9%	34.0%	30.7%	39.3%	25.9%	33.0%	30.9%	26.9%	24.3%	32.7%	28.9%	25.1%	33.0%
25	% loyal to them who purchase	28.7%	26.6%	27.4%	24.1%	25.4%	32.5%	36.2%	22.8%	24.7%	33.5%	24.8%	30.7%	36.2%	31.5%	32.9%	28.6%
26	% who stay loyal to us		59.5%	59.4%	58.7%	59.5%	57.9%	63.0%	60.2%	62.0%	59.9%	57.7%	62.3%	61.9%	56.5%	65.3%	62.3%
27	% who switch loyalty to us		30.5%	28.2%	31.1%	28.7%	30.7%	31.1%	29.1%	32.1%	28.6%	27.9%	30.8%	27.2%	30.7%	30.7%	31.1%
28	Customers loyal to us	50000	54424	55550	58295	56886	56023	59166	59474	60250	58626	59494	60366	62275	63164	65235	67753
29	Customers loyal to them	100000	95576	94450	91705	93114	93977	90834	90526	89750	91374	90506	89634	87725	86836	84765	82247
30	Purchases of our product		14895	12862	19165	19327	17197	23277	15375	19874	18137	16032	14674	20356	18236	16365	22369
31	% change in unit profit			5.37%	3.89%	4.95%	5.61%	5.41%	3.93%	5.63%	5.05%	5.12%	5.83%	3.26%	4.17%	5.12%	4.69%
32	Unit profit		$75.00	$79.03	$82.10	$86.17	$91.00	$95.93	$99.70	$105.31	$110.63	$116.29	$123.07	$127.08	$132.38	$139.16	$145.69
33	Profit contribution		$1,117,157	$1,016,407	$1,573,477	$1,665,302	$1,564,988	$2,232,861	$1,532,883	$2,093,028	$2,006,493	$1,864,397	$1,805,893	$2,586,811	$2,414,209	$2,277,431	$3,258,973
34																	
35	NPV	$15,235,876															

In this version, different random percentages are generated for each year. (See the formulas in the green cells below). Also, note how the index in cell B21, along with VLOOKUPs and RiskSimtable functions), permit you to run two simulations, one without free maintenance and one with it.

3. **Percentages who purchase.** We assume that each year a random percentage of Jamesons' loyal customers and a random percentage of the competitors' loyal customers purchase a DVD player. Each of these is generated from the triangular distribution in rows 9–11, so enter the formula

= RiskTriang($B$9,$B$10,$B$11)

in cell B24 and copy it to the range B24:Q25.

4. **Percentage who stay or become loyal.** Each year a random percentage of the customers previously loyal to Jamesons remain loyal, and a random percentage of the competitors' previously loyal customers switch loyalty to Jamesons. Also, the distributions of these random percentages depend on the company's maintenance policy. Therefore, enter the formula

= IF($B$21 = 1,RiskTriang($G$8,$G$9,$G$10),RiskTriang($H$8,$H$9,$H$10))

in cell C26, enter the formula

= IF($B$21 = 1,RiskTriang($G$13,$G$14,$G$15),RiskTriang($H$13,$H$14,$H$15))

in cell C27, and copy these across their rows.

5. **Numbers of loyal customers.** Create links to cells B5 and B6 in cells B28 and B29. Then, remembering that only *purchasers* in a given year can switch loyalty, calculate the number of customers loyal to Jamesons in year 1 with the formula

= B28*((1-B24) + B24*C26) + B29*B25*C27

in cell C28 and copy it across row 28. Similarly, calculate the number of customers loyal to the competitors in year 1 with the formula

= B29*((1-B25) + B25*(1-C27)) + B28*B24*(1-C26)

in cell C29 and copy it across row 29. These are basic bookkeeping formulas. Jamesons' loyal customers are those who (1) were loyal and didn't purchase; (2) were loyal, purchased, and stayed loyal; and (3) weren't loyal, purchased, and switched loyalty. Similar logic holds for the competitors' loyal customers.

6. **Purchasers at Jamesons.** Calculate the number of purchasers at Jamesons in year 1 with the formula

= C24*C28

in cell C30 and copy it across row 30.

7. **Monetary outcomes.** These are straightforward. Start by entering the formula

=IF($B$21=1,G5,H5)

for unit profit in year 1 in cell C32. Then enter the formulas

=RiskTriang($B$14,$B$15,$B$16)

=C32*(1+D31)

and

=C32*C30

in cells D31, D32, and C33, respectively, and copy them across their rows. Finally, calculate the NPV with the formula

=NPV(B18,C33:Q33)

in cell B35, and designate this as an @RISK output cell.

Running the Simulation

Set up @RISK to run 1000 iterations and 2 simulations, one for each maintenance decision to be tested. Then run the simulation as usual.

Discussion of the Simulation Results

The summary measures for the two simulations appear in Figure 16.32. Using the current inputs, the free maintenance initiative does not look good. Every measure, except possibly the standard deviation, is worse with the free maintenance agreement (simulation 1) than without it (simulation 2). Evidently, the increase in loyal customers does *not* compensate for the decrease in unit profit. If Jamesons is reasonably confident about the inputs for this model, it should scrap the free maintenance idea. However, it might want to perform some sensitivity analysis on the decrease in unit profit or the increase in loyalty percentages (or both) to see when the free maintenance agreement starts looking attractive. We tried two possibilities. First, if the decrease in unit profit is only $7.50, not $15, and everything else remains the same, the two mean NPVs are very close, so the free maintenance agreement might be worth trying. Second, if the decrease in unit profit remains at $15, but all of the input percentages in the ranges H8:H10 and H13:H15 increase by five percentage points, the mean NPV with the free maintenance agreement is still slightly lower than the mean NPV without it. Evidently, the company can't take this big a hit in its profit margin unless it can convince a *lot* more customers to stay or become loyal.

Figure 16.32 Summary Measures for Comparing Two Decisions

There is an interesting modeling issue in this example. For each of the random quantities, we have generated a new random value each year. Would it be better to generate one random number from each triangular distribution and use it for each year? Would it make a difference in the results? The modified simulation appears in the file **Free Maintenance 2 Finished.xlsx**. The summary measures from this simulation appear in Figure 16.33. If we are interested in comparing the *mean* NPV with no free maintenance versus free maintenance, we get about the same comparison in either model. The main difference between Figures 16.32 and 16.33 is the variability. Are you surprised that the models with more random numbers in Figure 16.32 have much smaller standard deviations than those in Figure 16.33? Evidently, there is an averaging effect. When different random numbers are used for each year, the highs and lows tend to cancel out, resulting in lower variability in NPV.

Figure 16.33 Summary Results for Modified Model

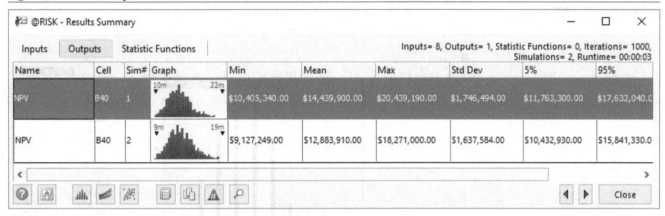

Name	Cell	Sim#	Graph	Min	Mean	Max	Std Dev	5%	95%
NPV	B40	1		$10,405,340.00	$14,439,900.00	$20,439,190.00	$1,746,494.00	$11,763,300.00	$17,632,040.0
NPV	B40	2		$9,127,249.00	$12,883,910.00	$18,271,000.00	$1,637,584.00	$10,432,930.00	$15,841,330.0

16-4b Marketing and Sales Models

We conclude this marketing section with a model of selling condos. The main issue is the timing of sales, and we demonstrate how a deterministic model of this timing can provide very misleading results.

EXAMPLE

16.9 SELLING CONDOS AT BLACKSTONE DEVELOPMENT

Blackstone Development Company has just finished building 120 high-end condos, each priced at $300,000. Blackstone has hired another company, Pletcher Marketing, to market and sell these condos. Pletcher will incur all of the marketing and maintenance costs, assumed to be $800 per unsold condo per month, and it will receive a 10% commission ($30,000) from Blackstone at the time of each condo sale. Because Blackstone wants these condos to be sold in a timely manner, it has offered Pletcher a $200,000 bonus at the end of the first year if at least half of the condos have been sold, and an extra $500,000 bonus at the end of the second year if all of the condos have been sold. Pletcher estimates that it can sell five condos per month on average, so that it should be able to collect the bonuses. However, Pletcher also realizes that there is uncertainty about the number of sales per month. How should this uncertainty be modeled, and will the resulting simulation model give different qualitative results than a deterministic model where exactly five condos are sold per month?

Objective

To develop a simulation model that allows us to see how the uncertain timing affects the monetary outcomes for Pletcher, and to compare this simulation model to a deterministic model with no uncertainty about the timing of sales.

Where Do the Numbers Come From?

The inputs are straightforward from Blackstone's agreement with Pletcher. The only difficulty is determining an appropriate probability model for the timing of sales, which we discuss next.

Solution

To make a fair comparison between a deterministic model with five sales per month and a simulation model with uncertainty in the timing of sales, we need a discrete distribution for monthly sales that has mean 5. One attractive possibility is to use the Poisson distribution discussed briefly in Chapter 5. It is discrete, and it has only one parameter, the mean. The Poisson distribution has one theoretical drawback in that it allows *all* nonnegative integers to occur, but this has no practical effect. As shown in Figure 16.34, the Poisson distribution with mean 5 has virtually no probability of values larger than, say, 15.

Developing the Simulation Model

The variables for the model appear in Figure 16.35. (See the file **Selling Condos Big Picture.xlsx**.) The deterministic model is straightforward and is not shown here. By selling a *sure* five condos per *Selling Condos Model*

Figure 16.34 Poisson
Distribution with Mean 5

Figure 16.35 Big Picture for Condo Selling Simulation Model

month, Pletcher sells all condos by the end of year 2, receives both bonuses, and realizes an NPV (including bonuses) of $2,824,333. However, this is not very realistic. The steps for creating a more realistic simulation model follow. (See Figure 16.36, with several hidden columns, and the file **Selling Condos Finished.xlsx**.) Because of the uncertain timing of sales, we cannot say when all 120 condos will be sold. It could be before 24 months or well after 24 months. Therefore, we model it through 40 months. (By experimenting, we found that all 120 condos will almost surely be sold in 40 months.)

1. **Inputs.** Enter the given inputs in the blue ranges.
2. **Random demands.** Generate the random demands for condos (the number of people who would like to buy) by entering the formula

   $=$**IF(B16>0,RiskPoisson($B$12),"")**

   in cell B15 and copying across to month 40. The IF function checks whether there are still any condos available in that month. If there aren't, a blank is recorded. Similar logic appears in many of the other formulas.

Figure 16.36 Condo Selling Simulation Model

	A	B	C	AB	AC	AD	AE	AF	AM	AN	AO
1	**Marketing and selling condos**										
2											
3	Condos to sell	120									
4	Unit marketing, maintenance cost	$800									
5	Commission per condo sale	$30,000									
6	Bonus if at least half sold in year 1	$200,000									
7	Extra bonus if all sold in 2 years	$500,000									
8	Discount rate (monthly)	0.8%									
9											
10	**Simulation model**										
11	Distribution of demand for condos each month (Poisson distributed)										
12	Mean demand per month	5									
13											
14	Month	1	2	27	28	29	30	31	38	39	40
15	Demand	4	5	7	1	6					
16	Condos left to be sold	120	116	10	3	2	0	0	0	0	0
17	Condos sold this month	4	5	7	1	2					
18	Maintenance cost	$92,800	$88,800	$2,400	$1,600	$0					
19	Commission from sales	$120,000	$150,000	$210,000	$30,000	$60,000					
20	Bonus at end of year 1										
21	Bonus at end of year 2										
22	Cash flow	$27,200	$61,200	$207,600	$28,400	$60,000					
23											
24	Months to sell out	29									
25	Total bonus received	$0									
26	NPV of cash flows	$1,991,401									

3. **Number remaining and sold.** In cell B16, enter a link to cell B3. In cell B17, find the number sold as the minimum of supply and demand with the formula

=IF(B16>0,MIN(B16,B15),"")

In cell C16, find the number remaining to be sold with the formula

=IF(B16>0,B16-B17,0)

Then copy the formulas in cells C16 and B17 across. Note that a 0, not a blank, is recorded in row 16 after all condos have been sold. This makes all the other IF functions work correctly.

4. **Monetary values.** Enter the formulas

=IF(B16>0,$B$4*(B16-B17),"")

=IF(B16>0,$B$5*B17,"")

and

=IF(B16>0,SUM(B19:B21)-B18,"")

in cells B18, B19, and B22, respectively, and copy these across. For the bonuses, enter the formulas

=IF(SUM(B17:M17)>=B3/2,B6,0)

and

=IF(SUM(B17:Y17)=B3,B7,0)

in cells M20 and Y21. These capture the all-or-nothing nature of the bonuses.

5. **Outputs.** Three interesting outputs are the number of months required to sell out, the total bonus earned, and the NPV of the cash flows, including bonuses. Calculate these in cells B24–B26 with the formulas

=COUNTIF(B16:AO16,">0")

=M20+Y21

and

=NPV(B8,B22:AO22)

Then designate them as @RISK output cells.

Running the Simulation

Set @RISK to run 1000 iterations for a single simulation. Then run the simulation in the usual way.

Discussion of the Simulation Results

Recall that the deterministic model sells out in 24 months, receives both bonuses, and achieves an NPV of about $2.82 million. As you might guess, the simulation model doesn't do this well. The main problem is that there is a fairly good chance that one or both bonuses will not be received. Distributions of the three outputs appear in Figures 16.37 through 16.39. Figure 16.37 shows that although 24 months is (nearly) the *most likely* number of months to sell out, there was at least one scenario where it took only 18 months and another where it took 32 months. Figure 16.38 shows the four possibilities for bonuses: receive neither, receive one or the other, or receive both. Unfortunately for Pletcher, the first three possibilities are fairly likely; the probability of receiving both bonuses is only about 0.37. Finally, the shape of the NPV distribution in Figure 16.39, with three separate peaks, is influenced heavily by the bonuses or lack of them. On average, the NPV is only about $2.38 million, *much* less than estimated by the deterministic model. This is still one more example—a dramatic one—of the flaw of averages.

Figure 16.37 Distribution of Months to Sell Out

Figure 16.38 Distribution of Total Bonus Received

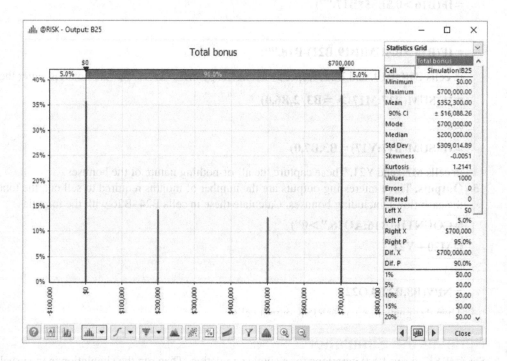

Figure 16.39 Distribution of NPV

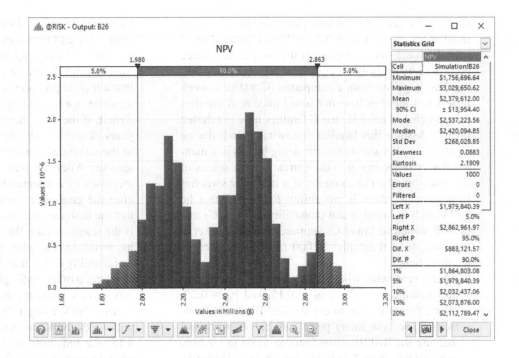

Problems

Level A

21. Suppose that Coke and Pepsi are fighting for the cola market. Each week each person in the market buys one case of Coke or Pepsi. If the person's last purchase was Coke, there is a 0.90 probability that this person's next purchase will be Coke; otherwise, it will be Pepsi. (You can assume that there are only two brands in the market.) Similarly, if the person's last purchase was Pepsi, there is a 0.80 probability that this person's next purchase will be Pepsi; otherwise, it will be Coke. Currently half of all people purchase Coke, and the other half purchase Pepsi. Simulate one year (52 weeks) of sales in the cola market and estimate each company's average weekly market share and each company's ending market share in week 52. Do this by assuming that the total market size is fixed at 100,000 customers. (*Hint*: Use the RiskBinomial function. However, if your model requires more RiskBinomial functions than the number allowed in the academic version of @RISK, remember that you can instead use the BINOM.INV function to generate binomially distributed random numbers. This takes the form =**BINOM.INV(n,p,RAND())**.)

22. Seas Beginning sells clothing by mail order. An important question is when to strike a customer from the company's mailing list. At present, the company strikes a customer from its mailing list if a customer fails to order from six consecutive catalogs. The company wants to know whether striking a customer from its list after a customer fails to order from four consecutive catalogs results in a higher profit per customer. The following data are available:

- If a customer placed an order the last time she received a catalog, then there is a 20% chance she will order from the next catalog.
- If a customer last placed an order one catalog ago, there is a 16% chance she will order from the next catalog she receives.
- If a customer last placed an order two catalogs ago, there is a 12% chance she will order from the next catalog she receives.
- If a customer last placed an order three catalogs ago, there is an 8% chance she will order from the next catalog she receives.
- If a customer last placed an order four catalogs ago, there is a 4% chance she will order from the next catalog she receives.
- If a customer last placed an order five catalogs ago, there is a 2% chance she will order from the next catalog she receives.

It costs $2 to send a catalog, and the average profit per order is $30. Assume a customer has just placed an order. To maximize expected profit per customer, would Seas Beginning make more money canceling such a customer after six nonorders or four nonorders?

23. Based on Babich (1992). Suppose that each week each of 300 families buys a gallon of orange juice from company A, B, or C. Let p_A denote the probability that a gallon produced by company A is of unsatisfactory quality, and define p_B and p_C similarly for companies B and C. If the last gallon of juice purchased by a family is satisfactory, the next week they will purchase a gallon of juice from the same company. If the last gallon of juice purchased by a family is not satisfactory, the family will purchase a gallon from a competitor. Consider a week in which A families have purchased juice A, B families have purchased juice B, and C families have purchased juice C. Assume that families that switch brands during a period are allocated to the remaining brands in a manner that is proportional to the current market shares of the other brands. For example, if a customer switches from brand A, there is probability $B/(B + C)$ that he will switch to brand B and probability $C/(B + C)$ that he will switch to brand C. Suppose that the market is currently divided equally: 10,000 families for each of the three brands.

a. After a year, what will the market share for each firm be? Assume $p_A = 0.10$, $p_B = 0.15$, and $p_C = 0.20$. (*Hint:* You will need to use the RiskBinomial function to see how many people switch from A and then use the RiskBinomial function again to see how many switch from A to B and from A to C. However, if your model requires more RiskBinomial functions than the number allowed in the academic version of @RISK, remember that you can instead use the BINOM.INV function to generate binomially distributed random numbers. This takes the form =**BINOM.INV(n,p,RAND())**.)

b. Suppose a 1% increase in market share is worth $10,000 per week to company A. Company A believes that for a cost of $1 million per year it can cut the percentage of unsatisfactory juice cartons in half. Is this worthwhile? (Use the same values of p_A, p_B, and p_C as in part a.)

Level B

24. The customer loyalty model in Example 16.7 assumes that once a customer leaves (becomes disloyal), that customer never becomes loyal again. Assume instead that there are two probabilities that drive the model, the retention rate and the *rejoin* rate, with values 0.75 and 0.15, respectively. The simulation should follow a customer who starts as a loyal customer in year 1. From then on, at the end of any year when the customer was loyal, this customer remains loyal for the next year with probability equal to the retention rate. But at the end of any year the customer is disloyal, this customer becomes loyal the next year with probability equal to the rejoin rate. During the customer's *n*th loyal year with the company, the company's mean profit from this customer is the *n*th value in the mean profit list in column B. Keep track of the same two outputs as in the example, and also keep track of the number of times the customer rejoins.

25. We are all aware of the fierce competition by mobile phone service companies to get our business. For

example, AT&T is always trying to attract Verizon's customers, and vice versa. Some even give away prizes to entice us to sign up for a guaranteed length of time. This example is based on one such offer. We assume that a mobile provider named Syncit is willing to give a customer a free laptop computer, at a cost of $300 to Syncit, if the customer signs up for a guaranteed two years of service. During that time, the cost of service to the customer is a constant $60 per month, or $720 annually. After two years, we assume the cost of service increases by 2% annually. We assume that in any year after the guaranteed two years, the probability is 0.7 that the customer will stay with Syncit. This probability is the retention rate. We also assume that if a customer has switched to another mobile service, there is always a probability of 0.1 that the customer will (without any free laptop offer) willingly rejoin Syncit. The company wants to see whether this offer makes financial sense in terms of NPV, using a 7% discount rate. It also wants to see how the NPV varies with the retention rate. Simulate a 15-year time horizon, both with and without the free offer, to estimate the difference. (For the situation without the free offer, assume the customer has probability 0.5 of signing up with Syncit during year 1.)

26. Suppose that GLC earns a $2000 profit each time a person buys a car. We want to determine how the expected profit earned from a customer depends on the quality of GLC's cars. We assume a typical customer will purchase 10 cars during her lifetime. She will purchase a car now (year 1) and then purchase a car every five years—during year 6, year 11, and so on. For simplicity, we assume that Hundo is GLC's only competitor. We also assume that if the consumer is satisfied with the car she purchases, she will buy her next car from the same company, but if she is not satisfied, she will buy her next car from the other company. Hundo produces cars that satisfy 80% of its customers. Currently, GLC produces cars that also satisfy 80% of its customers. Consider a customer whose first car is a GLC car. If profits are discounted at 7% annually, use simulation to estimate the value of this customer to GLC. Also estimate the value of a customer to GLC if it can raise its customer satisfaction rating to 85%, to 90%, or to 95%. You can interpret the satisfaction value as the probability that a customer will not switch companies.

27. Mutron Company is thinking of marketing a new drug used to make pigs healthier. At the beginning of the current year, there are 1,000,000 pigs that could use the product. Each pig will use Mutron's drug or a competitor's drug once a year. The number of pigs is forecast to grow by an average of 5% per year. However, this growth rate is not a sure thing. Mutron assumes that each year's growth rate is an independent draw from a normal distribution, with probability 0.95 that the growth rate will be between 3% and 7%. Assuming it enters the market, Mutron is not sure what its share of the market will be during year 1, so it models this with a triangular distribution. Its worst-case share is 20%, its most likely share is 40%, and its best-case share is 70%. In the absence of any *new* competitors entering this market (in addition to itself), Mutron believes its market share will remain the same in succeeding years. However, there are three potential entrants (in addition to Mutron). At the beginning of each year, each entrant that has not already entered the market has a 40% chance of entering the market. The year after a competitor enters, Mutron's market share will drop by 20% for each *new* competitor who entered. For example, if two competitors

enter the market in year 1, Mutron's market share in year 2 will be reduced by 40% from what it would have been with no entrants. Note that if all three entrants have entered, there will be no more entrants. Each unit of the drug sells for $2.20 and incurs a variable cost of $0.40. Profits are discounted by 8% annually.

a. Assuming that Mutron enters the market, use simulation to find its NPV for the next 10 years from the drug.

b. Again assuming that Mutron enters the market, it can be 95% certain that its *actual* NPV from the drug is between what two values?

16-5 Simulating Games of Chance

We realize that this is a book about business applications. However, it is instructive (and fun) to see how simulation can be used to analyze games of chance, including sports contests. Indeed, many analysts refer to Monte Carlo simulation, and you can guess where that name comes from—the gambling casinos of Monte Carlo.

16-5a Simulating the Game of Craps

Most games of chance are great candidates for simulation because they are, by their very nature, driven by randomness. In this section, we examine one such game that is extremely popular in the gambling casinos: the game of craps. In its most basic form, craps is played as follows. A player rolls two dice and observes the sum of the two sides turned up. If this sum is 7 or 11, the player wins immediately. If the sum is 2, 3, or 12, the player loses immediately. Otherwise, if this sum is any other number (4, 5, 6, 8, 9, or 10), that number becomes the player's *point*. Then the dice are thrown repeatedly until the sum is the player's point or 7. In case the player's point occurs before a 7, the player wins. But if a 7 occurs before the point, the player loses. The following example uses simulation to determine the properties of this game.

EXAMPLE

16.10 ESTIMATING THE PROBABILITY OF WINNING AT CRAPS

Joe Gamble loves to play craps at the casinos. He suspects that his chances of winning are less than fifty-fifty, but he wants to find the probability that he wins a single game of craps.

Objective
To use simulation to find the probability of winning a single game of craps.

Where Do the Numbers Come From?
There are no input numbers here, only the rules of the game.

Solution
The simulation is of a single game. By running this simulation for many iterations, you can find the probability that Joe wins a single game of craps. If his intuition is correct (and surely it must be, or the casino could not stay in business), this probability is less than 0.5.

Developing the Simulation Model

The simulation model is for a single game. (See Figure 16.40 and the file **Craps Finished.xlsx**. No "big picture" is provided for this model.) There is a subtle problem here: The number of tosses of the dice necessary to determine the outcome of a single game is unknown. Theoretically, the game could continue forever, with the player waiting for his point or a 7. However, it is extremely unlikely that more than, say, 40 tosses are necessary in a single game. (This can be shown by a probability argument not presented here.) Therefore, you can simulate 40 tosses and use only those that are necessary to determine the outcome of a single game. The steps required are as follows.

Figure 16.40 Simulation of Craps Game

	A	B	C	D	E	F	G	H	I	J
1	Craps Simulation									
2										
3	Simulated tosses									
4	Toss	Die 1	Die 2	Sum	Win on this toss?	Lose on this toss?	Continue?		Summary results from simulation	
5	1	6	4	10	0	0	Yes		Win? (1 if yes, 0 if no)	1
6	2	4	5	9	0	0	Yes		Number of tosses	6
7	3	1	4	5	0	0	Yes			
8	4	1	4	5	0	0	Yes		Pr(winning)	0.495
9	5	6	5	11	0	0	Yes		Expected number of tosses	3.344
10	6	4	6	10	1	0	No			
11	7	2	2	4						
12	8	6	2	8						
13	9	4	1	5						
14	10	3	6	9						

1. **Simulate tosses.** Simulate the results of 40 tosses in the range B5:D44 by entering the formula

   =RANDBETWEEN(1,6)

   in cells B5 and C5 and the formula

   =SUM(B5:C5)

   in cell D5. Then copy these to the range B6:D44. (Recall that the RANDBETWEEN function generates a random integer between the two specified values such that all values are equally likely, so it is perfect for tossing a die. You could also use @RISK's RiskIntUniform function, which works exactly like RANDBETWEEN.)

@RISK Function

RiskIntUniform

The @RISK function RiskIntUniform in the form =**RiskIntUniform(*N1,N2*)** works exactly like Excel's RANDBETWEEN function.

---

2. **First toss outcome.** Determine the outcome of the first toss with the formulas

   =IF(OR(D5=7,D5=11),1,0)

   =IF(OR(D5=2,D5=3,D5=12),1,0)

   and

   =IF(AND(E5=0,F5=0),"Yes","No")

   As in many spreadsheet simulation models, the concepts in this model are simple. The key is careful bookkeeping.

   in cells E5, F5, and G5, respectively. Note that the OR condition checks whether Joe wins right away (in which case a 1 is recorded in cell E5). Similarly, the OR condition in cell F5 checks whether he loses right away. In cell G5, the AND condition checks whether both cells E5 and F5 are 0, in which case the game continues. Otherwise, the game is over.

3. **Outcomes of other tosses.** Assuming the game continues beyond the first toss, Joe's point is the value in cell D5. Then he is waiting for a toss to have the value in cell D5 or 7, whichever occurs first. To implement this logic, enter the formulas

=IF(OR(G5="No",G5=""),"",IF(D6=$D$5,1,0))

=IF(OR(G5="No",G5=""),"",IF(D6=7,1,0))

and

=IF(OR(G5="No",G5=""),"",IF(AND(E6=0,F6=0),"Yes","No"))

in cells E6, F6, and G6, respectively, and copy these to the range E7:G44. The OR condition in each formula checks whether the game just ended on the previous toss or has been over for some time, in which case blanks are entered. Otherwise, the first two formulas check whether Joe wins or loses on this toss. If both of these return 0, the third formula returns Yes (and the game continues). Otherwise, it returns No (and the game has just ended).

4. **Game outcomes.** Keep track of two aspects of the game in @RISK output cells: whether Joe wins or loses and how many tosses are required. To find these, enter the formulas

=SUM(E5:E44)

and

=COUNT(E5:E44)

in cells J5 and J6, and designate each of these as an @RISK output cell. Note that both functions, SUM and COUNT, ignore blank cells.

5. **Simulation summary.** Although you can get summary measures in the various @RISK results windows after you run the simulation, it is useful to see some key summary measures right on the model sheet. To obtain these, enter the formula

=RiskMean(J5)

in cell J8 and copy it to cell J9. As the labels indicate, the RiskMean in cell J8, being an average of 0's and 1's, is just the fraction of iterations where Joe wins. The average in cell J9 is the average number of tosses until the game's outcome is determined.

Recall that the mean (or average) of a sequence of 0's and 1's is the fraction of 1's in the sequence. This can typically be interpreted as a probability.

Running the Simulation

Set the number of iterations to 10,000 (partly for variety and partly to obtain a more accurate result) and the number of simulations to 1. Then run the simulation as usual.

Discussion of the Simulation Results

After running @RISK, the summary results in cells J8 and J9 of Figure 16.40 (among others) are available. Our main interest is in the average in cell J8. It represents the best estimate of the probability of winning, 0.495. (It can be shown with a probability argument that the exact probability of winning in craps is 0.493.) You can also see that the average number of tosses needed to determine the outcome of a game was about 3.34. (The maximum number of tosses ever needed on these 10,000 iterations was 25.)

Perhaps surprisingly, the probability of winning in craps is 0.493, only slightly less than 0.5.

16-5b Simulating the NCAA Basketball Tournament

Each year the suspense reaches new levels as "March Madness" approaches, the time of the NCAA Basketball Tournament. Which of the 68 teams in the tournament will reach the "Sweet Sixteen," which will go on to the prestigious "Final Four," and which team will be crowned champion? The excitement at Indiana University is particularly high, given the strong basketball tradition here, so it has become a yearly tradition at IU (at least for the authors) to simulate the NCAA Tournament right after the brackets have been announced. We share that simulation in the following example.

EXAMPLE

16.11 MARCH MADNESS

At the time this example was written, the most recent NCAA Basketball Tournament was the 2018 tournament, won by Villanova. Of course, on the Sunday evening when the 68-team field was announced, we did not know which team would win. All we knew were the pairings (which teams would play which other teams) and the team ratings, based on Jeff Sagarin's nationally syndicated rating system. We now show how to simulate the tournament and keep a tally of the winners.

Objective

To simulate the NCAA basketball tournament and keep a tally on the number of times each team wins the tournament.

Where Do the Numbers Come From?

As soon as you learn the pairings for the *next* NCAA tournament, you can perform a Web search for "Sagarin ratings" to find the latest ratings.

Solution

We need to make one probabilistic assumption. From that point, it is a matter of "playing out" the games and doing the required bookkeeping. To understand this probabilistic assumption, suppose team A plays team B and Sagarin's ratings for these teams are, say, 85 and 78. Then Sagarin predicts that the actual point differential in the game (team A's score minus team B's score) will be the difference between the ratings, or 7.[4] We take this one step further. We assume that the *actual* point differential is normally distributed with mean equal to Sagarin's prediction, 7, and standard deviation 10. (Why 10? This is an estimate based on an extensive analysis of historical data. However, the spreadsheet model is set up so that you can change the standard deviation to a different value if you prefer.) Then if the actual point differential is positive, team A wins. If it is negative, team B wins.

We model the point spread as normally distributed, with mean equal to the difference between the Sagarin ratings and standard deviation 10.

Developing the Simulation Model

We provide only an outline of the simulation model. You can see the full details in the file **March Madness 2018.xlsx**. (This file includes the data for the 2018 tournament, but you can easily modify it for future tournaments.) The entire simulation is on a single Model sheet. Columns A through C list team indexes, team names, and Sagarin ratings. If two teams are paired in the first round, they are placed next to one another in the list. Also, all teams in a given region are listed together. (The regions are color-coded.) Columns H through N contain the simulation. The first-round results are at the top, the second-round results are below these, and so on. Winners from one round are automatically carried over to the next round with appropriate formulas. Selected portions of the model appear in Figure 16.41. This figure shows one possible scenario where Villanova did indeed win. We now describe the essential features of the model. (We didn't use @RISK in this model. We instead used Excel's built-in functions and a data table to replicate the results.)

March Madness Model

1. **Simulate rounds.** Jumping ahead to the fourth-round simulation in Figure 16.41, the winners from the previous round 3 are captured, and then the games in round 4 are simulated. The key formulas are in columns H and I. For example, the formulas in cells K137 and J137 are

   =VLOOKUP(F137,LTable,3)−VLOOKUP(F138,LTable,3)

   and

   =NORM.INV(RAND(),K137,$F$3)

   The first of these looks up the ratings of the two teams involved and subtracts to get the predicted point spread. The second formula simulates a point spread with the predicted point spread as its mean and the value in cell F3, 10, as its standard deviation. The rest of the formulas do the appropriate bookkeeping. You can view the details in the file.

2. **Outputs.** The model uses a data table to replicate the following outputs for each team: (1) whether the team wins the tournament, (2) whether the team reaches the final game, and (3) whether the team reaches the final four (the semi-finals). Then it shows tallies of these in tabular and graphical form. For example, after one run of 1000 replications, Villanova won the tournament 189 times, reached the final game 284 times, and reached the final four 437 times. They were clearly the favorite entering the tournament, and they backed it up by winning.

---

4 In general, there is also a home-court advantage, but we assume all games in the tournament are on "neutral" courts, so that there is no advantage to either team.

Figure 16.41 NCAA Basketball Simulation Model (Last Three Rounds Only)

	H	I	J	K	L	M	N	O
135	**Results of Round 4**							
136	Game	Indexes	Teams	Predicted	Simulated	Index of winner	Winner	Seed
137	1	5	Kentucky	1.42	7.13	5	Kentucky	5
138		11	Tennessee					
139	1	17	Xavier	−2.4	0.69	17	Xavier	1
140		32	North Carolina					
141	1	34	Villanova	9.89	14.44	34	Villanova	1
142		48	Arkansas					
143	1	58	Auburn	-8.59	−17.26	67	Duke	2
144		67	Duke					
145							Lowest seed to win	5
146	**Semifinals**							
147	Game	Indexes	Teams	Predicted	Simulated	Index of winner	Winner	Seed
148	1	5	Kentucky	−0.46	5.48	5	Kentucky	5
149		17	Xavier					
150	2	34	Villanova	1.38	4.06	34	Villanova	1
151		67	Duke					
152							Lowest seed to win	5
153	**Finals**							
154	Game	Indexes	Teams	Predicted	Simulated	Index of winner	Winner	Seed
155	1	5	Kentucky	−6.57	−11.58	34	Villanova	1
156		34	Villanova					
157								
158	**Winner**	34						

Problems

Level A

28. The game of Chuck-a-Luck is played as follows: You pick a number between 1 and 6 and toss three dice. If your number does not appear, you lose $1. If your number appears x times, you win $x. On the average, use simulation to find the average amount of money you will win or lose on each play of the game.

29. A *martingale* betting strategy works as follows. You begin with a certain amount of money and repeatedly play a game in which you have a 40% chance of winning any bet. In the first game, you bet $1. From then on, every time you win a bet, you bet $1 the next time. Each time you lose, you double your previous bet. Currently you have $63. Assuming you have unlimited credit, so that you can bet more money than you have, use simulation to estimate the profit or loss you will have after playing the game 50 times.

30. You have $5 and your opponent has $10. You flip a fair coin and if heads comes up, your opponent pays you $1. If tails comes up, you pay your opponent $1. The game is finished when one player has all the money or after 100 tosses, whichever comes first. Use simulation to estimate the probability that you end up with all the money and the probability that neither of you goes broke in 100 tosses.

Level B

31. Assume a very good NBA team has a 70% chance of winning in each game it plays. During an 82-game season what is the average length of the team's longest winning streak? What is the probability that the team has a winning streak of at least 16 games? Use simulation to answer these questions, where each iteration of the simulation generates the outcomes of all 82 games.

32. You are going to play the Wheel of Misfortune Game against the house. The wheel has 10 equally likely numbers: 5, 10, 15, 20, 25, 30, 35, 40, 45, and 50. The goal is to get a total as close as possible to 50 points without exceeding 50. You go first and spin the wheel. Based on your first spin, you can decide whether you want to spin again. (You can spin no more than twice.) After you are done, it is the house's turn. If your total is more than 50, the house doesn't need a turn; it wins automatically. Otherwise, the house spins the wheel. After its first spin, it can spin the wheel again if it wants. (The house can also spin no more than twice.) Then the winner is determined, where a tie goes to you. Use simulation to estimate your probability of winning the game if you and the house both use best strategies. What are the best strategies?

33. Consider the following card game. The player and dealer each receive a card from a 52-card deck. At the end of the game the player with the highest card wins; a tie goes to the dealer. (You can assume that Aces count 1, Jacks 11, Queens 12, and Kings 13.) After the player receives his card, he keeps the card if it is 7 or higher. If the player does not keep the card, the player and dealer swap cards. Then the dealer keeps his current card (which might be the player's original card) if it is 9 or higher. If the dealer does not keep his card, he draws another card. Use simulation with at least 1000 iterations to estimate the probability that the player wins. (*Hint*: See the file **P16_33.xlsx** to see a clever way of simulating cards from a deck so that the same card is never dealt more than once.)

34. Based on Morrison and Wheat (1984). When his team is behind late in the game, a hockey coach usually waits until there is one minute left before pulling the goalie out of the game. Using simulation, it is possible to show that coaches should pull their goalies much sooner. Suppose that if both teams are at full strength, each team scores an average of 0.05 goal per minute. Also, suppose that if you pull your goalie you score an average of 0.08 goal per minute and your opponent scores an average of 0.12 goal per minute. Suppose you are one goal behind with five minutes left in the game. Consider the following two strategies:

    • Pull your goalie if you are behind at any point in the last five minutes of the game; put him back in if you tie the score.

    • Pull your goalie if you are behind at any point in the last minute of the game; put him back in if you tie the score.

    Which strategy maximizes your probability of winning or tying the game? Simulate the game using 10-second increments of time. Use the RiskBinomial function to determine whether a team scores a goal in a given 10-second segment. This is reasonable because the probability of scoring two or more goals in a 10-second period is near zero.

35. You are playing tennis against a top tennis pro, and you have a 42% chance of winning each point. (You are *good*!)

    a. Use simulation to estimate the probability you will win a particular game. Note that the first player to score at least four points and have at least two more points than his or her opponent wins the game.

    b. Use simulation to determine your probability of winning a set. Assume that the first player to win six games wins the set if he or she is at least two games ahead; otherwise, the first player to win seven games wins the set. (We substitute a single game for the usual tiebreaker.)

    c. Use simulation to determine your probability of winning a match. Assume that the first player to win three sets wins the match.

16-6 Conclusion

We claimed in the previous chapter that spreadsheet simulation, especially together with an add-in like @RISK, is a powerful tool. After seeing the examples in this chapter, you should now appreciate how powerful and flexible simulation is. Unlike Solver optimization models, where you often make simplifying assumptions to achieve linearity, for example, you can allow virtually anything in simulation models. All you need to do is relate output cells to input cells with appropriate formulas, where any of the input cells can contain probability distributions to reflect uncertainty. The results of the simulation then show the distribution of any particular output. It is no wonder that companies such as GM, Eli Lilly, and many others are increasingly relying on simulation models to analyze their corporate operations.

Summary of Key Terms

TERM	EXPLANATION	EXCEL	PAGE
Gamma distribution	Right-skewed distribution of nonnegative values useful for many quantities such as the lifetime of an appliance		836
Value at risk at the 5% level (VaR 5%)	Fifth percentile of distribution of some output, usually a monetary output; indicates nearly the worst possible outcome		850
Churn	When customers stop buying a product or service and switch to a competitor's offering		864

Problems

Conceptual Questions

C.1. We have separated the examples in this chapter into operations, finance, marketing, and sports categories. List at least one other problem in each of these categories that could be attacked with simulation. For each, identify the random inputs, possible probability distributions for them, and any outputs of interest.

C.2. Suppose you are an HR (human resources) manager at a big university, and you sense that the university is becoming too top-heavy with full professors. That is, there do not seem to be as many younger professors at the assistant and associate levels as there ought to be. How could you study this problem with a simulation model, using current and/or proposed promotions, hiring, firing, and retirement policies?

C.3. You are an avid basketball fan, and you would like to build a simulation model of an entire game so that you could compare two different strategies, such as man-to-man versus zone defense. Is this possible? What might make this simulation model difficult to build?

C.4. Suppose you are a financial analyst and your company runs many simulation models to estimate the profitability of its projects. If you had to choose just two measures of the distribution of any important output such as net profit to report, which two would you choose? Why? What information would be missing if you reported only these two measures? How could they be misleading?

C.5. Software development is an inherently risky and uncertain process. For example, there are many examples of software that couldn't be "finished" by the scheduled release date—bugs still remained and features weren't ready. (Many people believe this was the case with Office 2007.) How might you simulate the development of a software product? What random inputs would be required? Which outputs would be of interest? Which measures of the probability distributions of these outputs would be most important?

C.6. Health care is continually in the news. Can (or should) simulation be used to help solve, or at least study, some of the difficult problems associated with health care? Provide at least two examples where simulation might be useful.

Level A

36. You now have $3000. You will toss a fair coin four times. Before each toss you can bet any amount of your money (including none) on the outcome of the toss. If heads comes up, you win the amount you bet. If tails comes up, you lose the amount you bet. Your goal is to reach $6000. It turns out that you can maximize your chance of reaching $6000 by betting either the money you have on hand or $6000 minus the money you have on hand, whichever is smaller. Use simulation to estimate the probability that you will reach your goal with this betting strategy.

37. You now have $10,000, all of which is invested in a sports team. Each year there is a 60% chance that the value of the team will increase by 60% and a 40% chance that the value of the team will decrease by 60%. Estimate the mean and median value of your investment after 50 years. Explain the large difference between the estimated mean and median.

38. Suppose you have invested 25% of your portfolio in four different stocks. The mean and standard deviation of the annual return on each stock are shown in the file **P16_38.xlsx**. The correlations between the annual returns on the four stocks are also shown in this file.
  a. What is the probability that your portfolio's annual return will exceed 20%?
  b. What is the probability that your portfolio will lose money during the year?

39. A ticket from Indianapolis to Orlando on Deleast Airlines sells for $150. The plane can hold 100 people. It costs Deleast $8000 to fly an empty plane. Each person on the plane incurs variable costs of $30 (for food and fuel). If the flight is overbooked, anyone who cannot get a seat receives $300 in compensation. On average, 95% of all people who have a reservation show up for the flight. To maximize expected profit, how many reservations for the flight should Deleast book? (*Hint*: The function RiskBinomial can be used to simulate the number who show up. It takes two arguments: the number of reservations booked and the probability that any ticketed person shows up.)

40. Based on Marcus (1990). The Balboa mutual fund has beaten the Standard and Poor's 500 during 11 of the last 13 years. People use this as an argument that you can beat the market. Here is another way to look at it that shows that Balboa's beating the market 11 out of 13 times is not unusual. Consider 50 mutual funds, each of which has a 50% chance of beating the market during a given year. Use simulation to estimate the probability that over a 13-year period the best of the 50 mutual funds will beat the market for at least 11 out of 13 years. This probability turns out to exceed 40%, which means that the best mutual fund beating the market 11 out of 13 years is not an unusual occurrence after all.

41. You have been asked to simulate the cash inflows to a toy company for the next year. Monthly sales are independent random variables. Mean sales for the months January through March and October through December are $80,000, and mean sales for the months April through September are $120,000. The standard deviation of each month's sales is 20% of the month's mean sales. Model the method used to collect monthly sales as follows:
  • During each month a certain fraction of new sales will be collected. All new sales not collected become one month overdue.

- During each month a certain fraction of one-month overdue sales is collected. The remainder becomes two months overdue.
- During each month a certain fraction of two-month overdue sales is collected. The remainder is written off as bad debt.

You are given the information in the file **P16_41.xlsx** from past months. Using this information, build a simulation model that generates the total cash inflow for each month. Develop a simple forecasting model and build the error of your forecasting model into the simulation. Assuming that there are $120,000 of one-month-old sales outstanding and $140,000 of two-month-old sales outstanding during January, you are 95% sure that total cash inflow for the year will be between what two values?

42. Consider a device that requires two batteries to function. If either of these batteries dies, the device will not work. Currently there are two new batteries in the device, and there are three extra new batteries. Each battery, once it is placed in the device, lasts a random amount of time that is triangularly distributed with parameters 15, 18, and 25 (all expressed in hours). When any of the batteries in the device dies, it is immediately replaced by an extra if an extra is still available. Use @RISK to simulate the time the device can last with the batteries currently available.

43. Consider a drill press containing three drill bits. The current policy (called *individual replacement*) is to replace a drill bit when it fails. The firm is considering changing to a *block replacement* policy in which all three drill bits are replaced whenever a single drill bit fails. Each time the drill press is shut down, the cost is $100. A drill bit costs $50, and the variable cost of replacing a drill bit is $10. Assume that the time to replace a drill bit is negligible. Also, assume that the time until failure for a drill bit follows an exponential distribution with a mean of 100 hours. Determine which replacement policy (block or individual replacement) should be implemented. (*Hint:* To generate an exponentially distributed time to failure, you can use =**RiskExpon(100)** or =−**100*LN(RAND())**. The latter uses only Excel functions, so it can be used to get around @RISK's 100-function limit in the academic version.)

44. Appliances Unlimited (AU) sells refrigerators. Any refrigerator that fails before it is three years old is replaced for free. Of all refrigerators, 3% fail during their first year of operation; 5% of all one-year-old refrigerators fail during their second year of operation; and 7% of all two-year-old refrigerators fail during their third year of operation.
   a. Use simulation to estimate the fraction of all refrigerators that will have to be replaced.
   b. It costs $500 to replace a refrigerator, and AU sells 10,000 refrigerators per year. If the warranty period were reduced to two years, how much per year in replacement costs would be saved?

45. The annual demand for Prizdol, a prescription drug manufactured and marketed by the NuFeel Company, is normally distributed with mean 50,000 and standard deviation 12,000. Assume that demand during each of the next 10 years is an independent random number from this distribution. NuFeel needs to determine how large a Prizdol plant to build to maximize its expected profit over the next 10 years. If the company builds a plant that can produce x units of Prizdol per year, it will cost $16 for each of these x units. NuFeel will produce only the amount demanded each year, and each unit of Prizdol produced will sell for $3.70. Each unit of Prizdol produced incurs a variable production cost of $0.20. It costs $0.40 per year to operate a unit of capacity.
   a. Among the capacity levels of 30,000, 35,000, 40,000, 45,000, 50,000, 55,000, and 60,000 units per year, which level maximizes expected profit? Use simulation to answer this question.
   b. Using the capacity from your answer to part **a**, NuFeel can be 95% certain that *actual* profit for the 10-year period will be between what two values?

46. A company is trying to determine the proper capacity level for its new electric car. A unit of capacity provides the potential to produce one car per year. It costs $10,000 to build a unit of capacity and the cost is charged equally over the next five years. It also costs $400 per year to maintain a unit of capacity (whether or not it is used). Each car sells for $14,000 and incurs a variable production cost of $10,000. The annual demand for the electric car during each of the next five years is believed to be normally distributed with mean 50,000 and standard deviation 10,000. The demands during different years are assumed to be independent. Profits are discounted at a 7.5% annual interest rate. The company is working with a five-year planning horizon. Capacity levels of 30,000, 40,000, 50,000, 60,000, and 70,000 are under consideration. You can assume that the company never produces more than demand, so there is never any inventory to carry over from year to year.
   a. Assuming that the company is risk neutral, use simulation to find the optimal capacity level.
   b. Using the answer to part **a**, there is a 5% chance that the *actual* discounted profit will exceed what value, and there is a 5% chance that the *actual* discounted profit will be less than what value?
   c. If the company is risk averse, how might the optimal capacity level change?

47. The DC Cisco office is trying to predict the revenue it will generate next week. Ten deals may close next week. The probability of each deal closing and data on the possible size of each deal (in millions of dollars) are listed in the file **P16_47.xlsx**. Use simulation to estimate total revenue. Based on the simulation, the company can be 95% certain that its total revenue will be between what two numbers?

Level B

48. A common decision is whether a company should buy equipment and produce a product in house or outsource production to another company. If sales volume is high enough, then by producing in house, the savings on unit costs will cover the fixed cost of the equipment. Suppose a company must make such a decision for a four-year time horizon, given the following data. Use simulation to estimate the probability that producing in house is better than outsourcing.

- If the company outsources production, it will have to purchase the product from the manufacturer for $18 per unit. This unit cost will remain constant for the next four years.
- The company will sell the product for $40 per unit. This price will remain constant for the next four years.
- If the company produces the product in house, it must buy a $400,000 machine that is depreciated on a straight-line basis over four years, and its cost of production will be $7 per unit. This unit cost will remain constant for the next four years.
- The demand in year 1 has a worst case of 10,000 units, a most likely case of 14,000 units, and a best case of 16,000 units.
- The average annual growth in demand for years 2–4 has a worst case of 10%, a most likely case of 20%, and a best case of 26%. Whatever this annual growth is, it will be the same in each of the years.
- The tax rate is 21%.
- Cash flows are discounted at 7% per year.

49. Consider an oil company that bids for the rights to drill in offshore areas. The value of the right to drill in a given offshore area is highly uncertain, as are the bids of the competitors. This problem demonstrates the "winner's curse." The winner's curse states that the optimal bidding strategy entails bidding a substantial amount below the company's assumed value of the product for which it is bidding. The idea is that if the company does not bid under its assumed value, its uncertainty about the actual value of the product will often lead it to win bids for products on which it loses money (after paying its high bid). Suppose Royal Conch Oil (RCO) is trying to determine a profit-maximizing bid for the right to drill on an offshore oil site. The actual value of the right to drill is unknown, but it is equally likely to be any value between $10 million and $110 million. Seven competitors will bid against RCO. Each bidder's (including RCO's) estimate of the value of the drilling rights is equally likely to be any number between 50% and 150% of the actual value. Based on past history, RCO believes that each competitor is equally likely to bid between 40% and 60% of its value estimate. Given this information, what fraction (within 0.05) of RCO's estimated value should it bid to maximize its expected profit? (*Hint:* You can use the RiskUniform function to model the actual value of the field and the competitors' bids.)

50. Suppose you begin year 1 with $5000. At the beginning of each year, you put half of your money under a mattress and invest the other half in Whitewater stock. During each year, there is a 50% chance that the Whitewater stock will double, and there is a 50% chance that you will lose half of your investment. To illustrate, if the stock doubles during the first year, you will have $3750 under the mattress and $3750 invested in Whitewater during year 2. You want to estimate your annual return over a 30-year period. If you end with F dollars, your annual return is $(F/5000)^{1/30} - 1$. For example, if you end with $100,000$, your annual return is $20^{1/30} - 1 = 0.105$, or 10.5%. Run 1000 replications of an appropriate simulation. Based on the results, you can be 95% certain that your annual return will be between which two values?

51. Mary Higgins is a freelance writer with enough spare time on her hands to play the stock market fairly seriously. Each morning she observes the change in stock price of a particular stock and decides whether to buy or sell, and if so, how many shares to buy or sell. Assume that on day 1, she has $100,000 cash to invest and that she spends part of this to buy her first 500 shares of the stock at the current price of $50 per share. From that point on, she follows a fairly simple "buy low, sell high" strategy. Specifically, if the price has increased three days in a row, she sells 25% of her shares of the stock. If the price has increased two days in a row (but not three), she sells 10% of her shares. In the other direction, if the price has decreased three days in a row, she buys up to 25% more shares, whereas if the price has decreased only two days in a row, she buys up to 10% more shares. The reason for the "up to" proviso is that she cannot buy more than she has cash to pay for. Assume a fairly simple model of stock price changes, as described in the file **P16_51.xlsx**. Each day the price can change by as much as $2 in either direction, and the probabilities depend on the previous price change: decrease, increase, or no change. Build a simulation model of this strategy for a period of 75 trading days. (You can assume that the stock price on each of the previous two days was $49.) Choose interesting @RISK output cells, and then run @RISK for at least 1000 iterations and report your findings.

52. You are considering a 10-year investment project. At present, the expected cash flow each year is $10,000. Suppose, however, that each year's cash flow is normally distributed with mean equal to *last* year's actual cash flow and standard deviation $1000. For example, suppose that the actual cash flow in year 1 is $12,000. Then year 2 cash flow is normal with mean $12,000 and standard deviation $1000. Also, at the end of year 1, your best guess is that each later year's expected cash flow will be $12,000.

a. Estimate the mean and standard deviation of the NPV of this project. Assume that cash flows are discounted at a rate of 7% per year.

b. Now assume that the project has an abandonment option. At the end of each year you can abandon the project for the value given in the file **P16_52.xlsx**. For example, suppose that year 1 cash flow is $4000. Then at the end of year 1, you expect cash flow for each remaining year to be $4000. This has an NPV of less than $62,000, so you should abandon the project and collect $62,000 at the end of year 1. Estimate the mean and standard deviation of the project with the abandonment option. How much would you pay for the abandonment option? (*Hint*: You can abandon a project at most once. So in year 5, for example, you abandon only if the sum of future expected NPVs is less than the year 5 abandonment value *and* the project has not yet been abandoned. Also, once you abandon the project, the actual cash flows for future years are zero. So in this case the future cash flows after abandonment should be zero in your model.)

53. Play Things is developing a new Miley Cyrus doll. The company has made the following assumptions:

- The doll will sell for a random number of years from 1 to 10. Each of these 10 possibilities is equally likely.
- At the beginning of year 1, the potential market for the doll is one million. The potential market grows by an average of 5% per year. The company is 95% sure that the growth in the potential market during any year will be between 3% and 7%. It uses a normal distribution to model this.
- The company believes its share of the potential market during year 1 will be at worst 20%, most likely 40%, and at best 50%. It uses a triangular distribution to model this.
- The variable cost of producing a doll during year 1 has a triangular distribution with parameters $8, $10, and $12.
- The current selling price is $20.
- Each year, the variable cost of producing the doll will increase by an amount that is triangularly distributed with parameters 4.5%, 5%, and 6.5%. You can assume that once this change is generated, it will be the same for each year. You can also assume that the company will change its selling price by the same percentage each year.
- The fixed cost of developing the doll (which is incurred right away, at time 0) has a triangular distribution with parameters $4, $6, and $12 million.
- There is currently one competitor in the market. During each year that begins with four or fewer competitors, there is a 20% chance that a new competitor will enter the market.
- Year *t* sales (for $t > 1$) are determined as follows.

Suppose that at the end of year $t - 1$, *n* competitors are present (including Play Things). Then during year *t*, a fraction $0.9 - 0.1n$ of the company's loyal customers (last year's purchasers) will buy a doll from Play Things this year, and a fraction $0.2 - 0.04n$ of customers currently in the market who did not purchase a doll last year will purchase a doll from Play Things this year. Adding these two provides the *mean* sales for this year. Then the *actual* sales this year is normally distributed with this mean and standard deviation equal to 7.5% of the mean.

a. Use @RISK to estimate the expected NPV of this project. Use a discount rate of 7%.

b. Use the percentiles in @RISK's output to find an interval such that you are 95% certain that the company's *actual* NPV will be within this interval.

54. An automobile manufacturer is considering whether to introduce a new model called the Racer. The profitability of the Racer depends on the following factors:

- The fixed cost of developing the Racer is triangularly distributed with parameters $3, $4, and $5, all in billions.
- Year 1 sales are normally distributed with mean 200,000 and standard deviation 50,000. Year 2 sales are normally distributed with mean equal to actual year 1 sales and standard deviation 50,000. Year 3 sales are normally distributed with mean equal to actual year 2 sales and standard deviation 50,000.
- The selling price in year 1 is $25,000. The year 2 selling price will be 1.05[year 1 price + $50 (% diff1)] where % diff1 is the number of percentage points by which actual year 1 sales differ from expected year 1 sales. The 1.05 factor accounts for inflation. For example, if the year 1 sales figure is 180,000, which is 10 percentage points below the expected year 1 sales, then the year 2 price will be 1.05[25,000 + 50(− 10)] = $25,725. Similarly, the year 3 price will be 1.05[year 2 price + $50(% diff2)] where % diff2 is the percentage by which actual year 2 sales differ from expected year 2 sales.
- The variable cost in year 1 is triangularly distributed with parameters $10,000, $12,000, and $15,000, and it is assumed to increase by 5% each year.

Your goal is to estimate the NPV of the new car during its first three years. Assume that the company is able to produce exactly as many cars as it can sell. Also, assume that cash flows are discounted at 7.5%. Simulate 1000 trials to estimate the mean and standard deviation of the NPV for the first three years of sales. Also, determine an interval such that you are 95% certain that the NPV of the Racer during its first three years of operation will be within this interval.

55. It costs a pharmaceutical company $40,000 to produce a 1000-pound batch of a drug. The average yield from a batch is unknown but the best case is 90% yield (that is, 900 pounds of good drug will be produced), the most likely case is 85% yield, and the worst case is 70% yield. The annual demand for the drug is unknown, with the best case being 22,000 pounds, the most likely case 18,000 pounds, and the worst case 12,000 pounds. The drug sells for $60 per pound and leftover amounts of the drug can be sold for $8 per pound. To maximize annual expected profit, how many batches of the drug should the company produce? You can assume that it will produce the batches only once, *before* demand for the drug is known.

56. A truck manufacturer produces the Off Road truck. The company wants to gain information about the discounted profits earned during the next three years. During a given year, the total number of trucks sold in the United States is $500,000 + 50,000G - 40,000I$, where G is the number of percentage points increase in gross domestic product during the year and I is the number of percentage points increase in the consumer price index during the year. During the next three years, Value Line has made the predictions listed in the file **P16_56.xlsx**. In the past, 95% of Value Line's G predictions have been accurate within 6%, and 95% of Value Line's I predictions have been accurate within 5%. You can assume that the actual G and I values are normally distributed each year.

At the beginning of each year, a number of competitors might enter the trucking business. The probability distribution of the number of competitors that will enter the trucking business is also given in the same file. Before competitors join the industry at the beginning of year 1, there are two competitors. During a year that begins with n competitors (after competitors have entered the business, but before any have left, and not counting Off Road), Off Road will have a market share given by $0.5(0.9)^n$. At the end of each year, there is a 20% chance that any competitor will leave the industry. The selling price of the truck and the production cost per truck are also given in the file. Simulate 1000 replications of the company's profit for the next three years. Estimate the mean and standard deviation of the discounted three-year profits, using a discount rate of 8% and Excel's NPV function. Do the same if the probability that any competitor leaves the industry during any year increases to 50%.

57. Suppose you buy an electronic device that you operate continuously. The device costs you $300 and carries a one-year warranty. The warranty states that if the device fails during its first year of use, you get a new device for no cost, and this new device carries exactly the same warranty. However, if it fails after the first year of use, the warranty is of no value. You plan to use this device for the next six years. Therefore, any time the device fails outside its warranty period, you will pay $300 for another device of the same kind. (We assume the price does not increase during the six-year period.) The time until failure for a device is gamma distributed with parameters $\alpha = 2$

and $\beta = 0.5$. (This implies a mean of one year.) Use @RISK to simulate the six-year period. Include as outputs (1) your total cost, (2) the number of failures during the warranty period, and (3) the number of devices you own during the six-year period.

58. Work the previous problem for a case in which the one-year warranty requires you to pay for the new device even if failure occurs during the warranty period. Specifically, if the device fails at time t, measured relative to the time it went into use, you must pay $300t$ for a new device. For example, if the device goes into use at the beginning of April and fails nine months later, at the beginning of January, you must pay $225. The reasoning is that you got 9/12 of the warranty period for use, so you should pay that fraction of the total cost for the next device. As before, however, if the device fails outside the warranty period, you must pay the full $300 cost for a new device.

59. Based on Hoppensteadt and Peskin (1992). The following model (the Reed–Frost model) is often used to model the spread of an infectious disease. Suppose that at the beginning of period 1, the population consists of five diseased people (called infectives) and 95 healthy people (called susceptibles). During any period there is a 0.05 probability that a given infective person will encounter a particular susceptible. If an infective encounters a susceptible, there is a 0.5 probability that the susceptible will contract the disease. An infective lives for an average of 10 periods with the disease. To model this, assume that there is a 0.10 probability that an infective dies during any given period. Use @RISK to model the evolution of the population over 100 periods. Use your results to answer the following questions. [*Hint*: During any period there is probability $0.05(0.50) = 0.025$ that an infective will infect a particular susceptible. Therefore, the probability that a particular susceptible is not infected during a period is $(1 - 0.025)^n$, where n is the number of infectives present at the end of the previous period.]

a. What is the probability that the population will die out?

b. What is the probability that the disease will die out?

c. On the average, what percentage of the population is infected by the end of period 100?

d. Suppose that people use infection "protection" during encounters. The use of protection reduces the probability that a susceptible will contract the disease during a single encounter with an infective from 0.50 to 0.10. Now answer parts **a** through **c** under the assumption that everyone uses protection.

60. Chemcon has taken over the production of Nasacure from a rival drug company. Chemcon must build a plant to produce Nasacure by the beginning of 2010. Once the plant is built, the plant's capacity cannot be changed. Each unit sold brings in $10 in revenue. The fixed cost (in dollars) of producing a plant that can produce x units per year of the drug is $5,000,000 + 10x$. This cost

is assumed to be incurred at the end of 2010. In fact, you can assume that all cost and sales cash flows are incurred at the ends of the respective years. If a plant of capacity x is built, the variable cost of producing a unit of Nasacure is $6 - 0.1(x - 1,000,000)/100,000$. For example, a plant capacity of 1,100,000 units has a variable cost of $5.90. Each year a plant operating cost of $1 per unit of capacity is also incurred. Based on a forecasting sales model from the previous 10 years, Chemcon forecasts that demand in year t, D_t, is related to the demand in the previous year, D_{t-1}, by the equation $D_t = 67,430 + 0.985D_{t-1} + e_t$, where e_t is normally distributed with mean 0 and standard deviation 29,320. The demand in 2009 was 1,011,000 units. If demand for a year exceeds production capacity, all demand in excess of plant capacity is lost. If demand is less than capacity, the extra capacity is simply not used. Chemcon wants to determine a capacity level that maximizes expected discounted profits (using a discount rate of 7.5%) for the time period 2010 through 2019. Use simulation to help it do so.

61. Tinkan Company produces one-pound cans for the Canadian salmon industry. Each year the salmon spawn during a 24-hour period and must be canned immediately. Tinkan has the following agreement with the salmon industry. The company can deliver as many cans as it chooses. Then the salmon are caught. For each can by which Tinkan falls short of the salmon industry's needs, the company pays the industry a $2 penalty. Cans cost Tinkan $1 to produce and are sold by Tinkan for $2 per can. If any cans are left over, they are returned to Tinkan and the company reimburses the industry $2 for each extra can. These extra cans are put in storage for next year. Each year a can is held in storage, a carrying cost equal to 20% of the can's production cost is incurred. It is well known that the number of salmon harvested during a year is strongly related to the number of salmon harvested the previous year. In fact, using past data, Tinkan estimates that the harvest size in year t, H_t (measured in the number of cans required), is related to the harvest size in the previous year, H_{t-1}, by the equation $H_t = H_{t-1}e_t$, where e_t is normally distributed with mean 1.02 and standard deviation 0.10.

Tinkan plans to use the following production strategy. For some value of x, it produces enough cans at the beginning of year t to bring its inventory up to $x + \hat{H}_t$, where $\hat{H}_t$ is the predicted harvest size in year t. Then it delivers these cans to the salmon industry. For example, if it uses $x = 100,000$, the predicted harvest size is 500,000 cans, and 80,000 cans are already in inventory, then Tinkan produces and delivers 520,000 cans. Given that the harvest size for the previous year was 550,000 cans, use simulation to help Tinkan develop a production strategy that maximizes its expected profit over the next 20 years. Assume that the company begins year 1 with an initial inventory of 300,000 cans.

62. You are unemployed, 21 years old, and searching for a job. Until you accept a job offer, the following situation occurs. At the beginning of each year, you receive a job offer. The annual salary associated with the job offer is equally likely to be any number between $20,000 and $100,000. You must immediately choose whether to accept the job offer. If you accept an offer with salary x, you receive $x per year while you work (assume you retire at age 70), including the current year. Assume that cash flows are discounted so that a cash flow received one year from now has a present value of 0.93. You decide to accept the first job offer that exceeds w dollars.
  a. Use simulation to determine the value of w (within $10,000) that maximizes the expected NPV of earnings you will receive the rest of your working life.
  b. Repeat part a, but now assume that you get a 3% raise in salary every year after the first year you accept the job.

63. A popular restaurant in Indianapolis does a brisk business, filling virtually all of its seats from 6 P.M. until 9 P.M. Tuesday through Sunday. Its current annual revenue is $2.34 million. However, it does not currently accept credit cards, and it is thinking of doing so. If it does, the bank will charge 4% on all receipts during the first year. (To keep it simple, you can ignore taxes and tips and focus only on the receipts from food and liquor.) Depending on receipts in year 1, the bank might then reduce its fee in succeeding years, as indicated in the file **P16_63.xlsx**. (This would be a one-time reduction, at the end of year 1 only.) This file also contains parameters of the two uncertain quantities, credit card usage (percentage of customers who will pay with credit cards) and increased spending (percentage increase in spending by credit card users, presumably on liquor but maybe also on more expensive food). The restaurant wants to simulate a five-year horizon. Its base case is not to accept credit cards at all, in which case it expects to earn $2.34 million in revenue each year. It wants to use simulation to explore other options, where it will accept credit cards in year 1 and then continue them in years 2–5 if the bank fee is less than or equal to some cutoff value. For example, one possibility is to accept credit cards in year 1 and then discontinue them only if the bank fee is less than or equal to 3%. You should explore the cutoffs 2% to 4% in increments of 0.5%. Which policy provides with the largest mean *increase* in revenue over the five-year horizon, relative to never using credit cards?

64. The Ryder Cup is a three-day golf tournament played every other year with 12 of the best U.S. golfers against 12 of the best European golfers. They play 16 team matches (each match has two U.S. golfers against two European golfers) on Friday and Saturday, and they play 12 singles matches (each match has a single U.S. golfer against a European golfer) on Sunday. Each match is either won or tied. A win yields 1 point for the winning team and 0 points for the losing team. A tie yields 0.5

point for each team. A team needs 14.5 points to win the Cup. If each team gets 14 points, the tournament is a tie, but the preceding winner gets to keep the Cup. In 1999, the U.S. was behind 10 points to 6 after the team matches. To win the Cup, the U.S. needed at least 8.5 points on Sunday, a very unlikely outcome, but they pulled off the miracle and won. Use simulation to estimate the probability of the U.S. scoring at least 8.5 points in the 12 singles matches, assuming all golfers in the tournament are essentially equal. Proceed as follows.

a. Use simulation to estimate the probability, call it h (for half), that a given match ends in a tie. To do this, you can assume that any of the 18 holes is tied with

probability 0.475 and won with probability 0.525. (These are the historical fractions of holes that have been tied and won in singles matches in the past few Ryder Cups.) Note that each match is "match play," so the only thing that counts on each hole is whether a golfer has fewer strokes than the other golfer—winning a hole by one stroke is equivalent to winning the hole by two or more strokes in match play. The player winning the most holes wins the match, unless they tie.

b. Run another simulation, using the estimated probability h as an input, to estimate the probability that the U.S. will score at least 8.5 points in the 12 singles matches.

CASE 16.1 College Fund Investment

Your next-door neighbor, Scott Jansen, has a 12-year-old daughter, and he intends to pay the tuition for her first year of college six years from now. The tuition for the first year will be $22,500. Scott has gone through his budget and finds that he can invest $3000 per year for the next six years. Scott has opened accounts at two mutual funds. The first fund follows an investment strategy designed to match the return of the S&P 500. The second fund invests in 3-month Treasury bills. Both funds have very low fees.

Scott has decided to follow a strategy in which he contributes a fixed fraction of the $3000 to each fund. An adviser from the first fund suggested that in each year he should invest 80% of the $3000 in the S&P 500 fund and the other 20% in the T-bill fund. The adviser explained that the S&P 500 has averaged much larger returns than the T-bill fund. Even though stock returns are risky investments in the short run, the risk should be fairly minimal over the longer six-year period. An adviser from the second fund recommended just the opposite: invest 20% in the S&P 500 fund and 80% in T-bills, because treasury bills are backed by the United States government. If you follow this allocation, he said, your average return will be lower, but at least you will have enough to reach your $22,500 target in six years.

Not knowing which adviser to believe, Scott has come to you for help.

Questions

1. The file **C16_01.xlsx** contains annual returns of the S&P 500 and 3-month Treasury bills from 1960. Suppose that in each of the next 72 months (six years), it is equally likely that any of the historical returns will occur. Develop a spreadsheet model to simulate the two suggested investment strategies over the six-year period. Plot the value of each strategy over time for a single iteration of the simulation. What is the total value of each strategy after six years? Do either of the strategies reach the target?

2. Simulate 1000 iterations of the two strategies over the six-year period. Create a histogram of the final fund values. Based on your simulation results, which of the two strategies would you recommend? Why?

3. Suppose that Scott needs to have $25,000 to pay for the first year's tuition. Based on the same simulation results, which of the two strategies would you recommend now? Why?

4. What other real-world factors might be important to consider in designing the simulation and making a recommendation?

CASE 16.2 Bond Investment Strategy

An investor is considering the purchase of zero-coupon U.S. Treasury bonds. A 30-year zero-coupon bond yielding 8% can be purchased today for $9.94. At the end of 30 years, the owner of the bond will receive $100. The yield of the bond is related to its price by the following equation:

$$P = \frac{100}{(1 + y)^t}$$

Here, P is the price of the bond, y is the yield of the bond, and t is the maturity of the bond measured in years. Evaluating this equation for $t = 30$ and $y = 0.08$ gives $P = 9.94$.

The investor is planning to purchase a bond today and sell it one year from now. The investor is interested in evaluating the *return* on the investment in the bond. Suppose, for example, that the yield of the bond one year from now is 8.5%. Then the price of the bond one year later will be

$9.39 [=100/(1 + 0.085)^{29}]$. The time remaining to maturity is $t = 29$ because one year has passed. The return for the year is -5.54% [= (9.39 − 9.94)/9.94].

In addition to the 30-year-maturity zero-coupon bond, the investor is considering the purchase of zero-coupon bonds with maturities of 2, 5, 10, or 20 years. All of the bonds are currently yielding 8.0%. (Bond investors describe this as a *flat yield curve*.) The investor cannot predict the future yields of the bonds with certainty. However, the investor believes that the yield of each bond one year from now can be modeled by a normal distribution with mean 8% and standard deviation 1%.

Questions

1. Suppose that the yields of the five zero-coupon bonds are all 8.5% one year from today. What are the returns of each bond over the period?

2. Using a simulation with 1000 iterations, estimate the expected return of each bond over the year. Estimate the standard deviations of the returns.

3. Comment on the following statement: "The expected yield of the 30-year bond one year from today is 8%. At that yield, its price would be $10.73. The return for the year would be 8% [= (10.73 − 9.94)/9.94]. Therefore, the average return for the bond should be 8% as well. A simulation isn't really necessary. Any difference between 8% and the answer in Question 2 must be due to simulation error."

PART 6
ADVANCED DATA ANALYSIS

CHAPTER 17

Data Mining

HOTTEST NEW JOBS: STATISTICS AND MATHEMATICS

The term *data analysis* has long been synonymous with the term *statistics,* but in today's world, with massive amounts of data available in business and many other fields such as health and science, data analysis goes beyond the more narrowly focused area of traditional statistics. But regardless of what it is called, data analysis is currently a hot topic and promises to get even hotter in the future. The data analysis skills you learn here, and possibly in follow-up quantitative courses, might just land you a very interesting and lucrative job.

This is exactly the message in a 2009 *New York Times* article, "For Today's Graduate, Just One Word: Statistics," by Steve Lohr. (A similar 2006 article, "Math Will Rock Your World," by Stephen Baker, was the cover story for *Business Week.* Both articles are available online by searching for their titles.) The statistics article begins by chronicling a Harvard anthropology and archaeology graduate, Carrie Grimes, who began her career by mapping the locations of Mayan artifacts in places like Honduras. As she states, "People think of field archaeology as Indiana Jones, but much of what you really do is data analysis." Since then, Grimes has leveraged her data analysis skills to get a job with Google, where she and many other people with a quantitative background are analyzing huge amounts of data to improve the company's search engine. As the chief economist at Google, Hal Varian, states, "I keep saying that the sexy job in the next 10 years will be statisticians. And I'm not kidding." The salaries for statisticians with doctoral degrees currently *start* at $125,000, and they will probably continue to increase. (The math article indicates that mathematicians are also in great demand.)

Why is this trend occurring? The reason is the explosion of digital data—data from sensor signals, surveillance tapes, Web clicks, bar scans, public records, financial transactions, and more. In years past, statisticians typically analyzed relatively small data sets, such as opinion polls with about 1000 responses. Today's massive data sets require new statistical methods, new computer software, and most importantly for you, more young people trained in these methods and the corresponding software. Several particular areas mentioned in the articles include (1) improving Internet search and online advertising, (2) unraveling gene sequencing information for cancer research, (3) analyzing sensor and location data for optimal handling of food shipments, and (4) the Netflix contest for improving the company's recommendation system.

The statistics article mentions three specific organizations in need of data analysts. The first is government, where there is an increasing need to sift through mounds of data as a first step toward dealing with long-term economic needs and key policy priorities. The second is IBM, which created a Business Analytics and Optimization Services group in April 2009. This group will use the more than 200 mathematicians, statisticians, and data analysts already employed by the company, but IBM intends to retrain or hire 4000 more analysts to meet its needs. The third is Google, which needs more data analysts to improve its search engine. You may think that today's search engines are unbelievably efficient, but Google knows they can be improved. As Ms. Grimes states, "Even an improvement of a percent or two can be huge, when you do things over the millions and billions of times we do things at Google."

Of course, these three organizations are not the only organizations that need to hire more skilled people to perform data analysis and other analytical procedures. It is a need faced by *all* large organizations. Various recent technologies, the most prominent by far being the Web, have given organizations the ability to gather massive amounts of data easily. Now they need people to make sense of it all and use it to their competitive advantage.

17-1 INTRODUCTION

Various types of data analysis, including the methods discussed in several previous chapters, are crucial to the success of most companies in today's data-driven business world. However, the sheer volume of available data often defies traditional methods of data analysis. Therefore, new methods—and accompanying software—have been developed under the name of data mining. **Data mining** attempts to discover patterns, trends, and relationships among data, especially nonobvious and unexpected patterns.[1] For example, an analysis might discover that people who purchase skim milk also tend to purchase whole wheat bread, or that cars built on Mondays before 10 A.M. on production line #5 using parts from supplier ABC have significantly more defects than average. This new knowledge can then be used for more effective management of a business.

The place to start is with a data warehouse. Typically, a **data warehouse** is a huge database that is designed specifically to study patterns in data. A data warehouse is not the same as the databases companies use for their day-to-day operations. A data warehouse should (1) combine data from multiple sources to discover as many relationships as possible, (2) contain accurate and consistent data, (3) be structured to enable quick and accurate responses to a variety of queries, and (4) allow follow-up responses to specific relevant questions. In short, a data warehouse represents a type of database that is specifically structured to enable data mining. Another term you might hear is data mart. A **data mart** is essentially a scaled-down data warehouse, or part of an overall data warehouse, that is structured specifically for one part of an organization, such as sales. Virtually all large organizations, and many smaller ones, have developed data warehouses or data marts in the past decade or two to enable them to better understand their business—their customers, their suppliers, and their processes.

Once a data warehouse is in place, analysts can begin to mine the data with a collection of methodologies and accompanying software. Some of the primary methodologies are classification analysis, prediction, cluster analysis, market basket analysis, and forecasting. Each of these is a large topic in itself, but some brief explanations follow.

- **Classification analysis** attempts to find variables that are related to a categorical (often binary) variable. For example, credit card customers can be categorized as those who pay their balances in a reasonable amount of time and those who don't. Classification analysis would attempt to find explanatory variables that help predict which of these two categories a customer is in. Some variables, such as salary, are natural candidates for explanatory variables, but an analysis might uncover others that are less obvious.
- **Prediction** is similar to classification analysis, except that it tries to find variables that help explain a continuous variable, such as credit card balance, rather than a categorical variable. Regression analysis, discussed Chapters 10 and 11, is one of the most popular prediction tools, but there are others not covered in this book.

---

1 The topics in this chapter are evolving rapidly, as is the terminology. Data mining is sometimes used as a synonym for **business analytics** or **data analytics**, although these latter terms are broader and encompass most of the material in this book. Another term gaining popularity is **big data**. This term is used to indicate the huge data sets often analyzed in data mining.

- **Cluster analysis** tries to group observations into clusters so that observations within a cluster are alike, and observations in different clusters are not alike. For example, one cluster for an automobile dealer's customers might be middle-aged men who are not married, earn over $150, 000, and favor high-priced sports cars. Once natural clusters are found, a company can then tailor its marketing to the individual clusters.
- **Market basket analysis** tries to find products that customers purchase together in the same "market basket." In a supermarket setting, this knowledge can help a manager position or price various products in the store. In banking and other settings, it can help managers to cross-sell (sell a product to a customer already purchasing a related product) or up-sell (sell a more expensive product than a customer originally intended to purchase).
- **Forecasting** is used to predict values of a time series variable by extrapolating patterns seen in historical data into the future. (This topic was covered in Chapter 12.) This is clearly an important problem in all areas of business, including the forecasting of future demand for products, forecasting future stock prices and commodity prices, and many others.

Not too long ago, data mining was considered a topic only for the experts. In fact, most people had never heard of data mining. Also, the required software was expensive and difficult to learn. Fortunately, this has been changing in recent years. Many people in organizations, not just the quantitative experts, have access to large amounts of data, and they have to make sense of it right away, not a year from now. Therefore, they must have some understanding of techniques used in data mining, and they must have software to implement these techniques.

Data mining is a huge topic. A thorough discussion, which would fill a large book or two, would cover the role of data mining in real business problems, data warehousing, the many data mining techniques that now exist, and the software packages that have been developed to implement these techniques. There is not nearly enough room to cover all of this here, so the goal of this chapter is more modest. We single out two of the most important problems tackled by data mining: classification and clustering. We discuss the problems themselves and several methods used to solve them. Fortunately, most (but not all) of these methods can be implemented in Excel, possibly with the Excel add-ins that are available with this book. You should be aware that much more powerful—and expensive and difficult-to-learn—software packages have been developed for classification, clustering, and other data mining problems, but the Excel methods discussed here will give you some insights into the possibilities.

It is worth noting that Microsoft's entry in the data mining software is its SQL Server Analysis Services (SSAS), which is part of its SQL Server database package. In parallel with what we present in this chapter, SSAS concentrates on two data mining problems: classification and clustering. There is also a Microsoft Data Mining Add-In, a "front end" for performing data mining in Excel, and we mention it in a few of the problems. However, for our purposes, this add-in has two drawbacks. First, although it is free (do a Web search for Microsoft Data Mining Add-In), it requires a connection to SSAS for the actual number-crunching, a connection most of you will not have. Second, it has evidently not been updated for Excel 2016, which makes us wonder whether Microsoft plans to continue this add-in.

17-2 Classification Methods

This section discusses one of the most important problems studied in data mining: classification. This is similar to the problem attacked by regression analysis—using explanatory variables to predict a dependent variable—but now the dependent variable is categorical. It usually has two categories, such as Yes and No, but it can have more than two categories, such as Republican, Democrat, and Independent. This problem has been analyzed with very different types of algorithms, some regression-like and others very different from regression, and this section discusses the most popular classification methods. Each of the methods has the same objective: to use data from the explanatory variables to classify each record (person, company, or whatever) into one of the known categories.

Before proceeding, it is important to discuss the role of **data partitioning** in classification and in data mining in general. Data mining is usually used to explore very large data sets, with many thousands or even millions of records. Therefore, it is very possible, and also very useful, to partition the data set into two or even three distinct subsets before the algorithms are applied. Each subset has a specified percentage of all records, and these subsets are typically chosen randomly. The first subset, usually with about 70% to 80% of the records, is called the **training** data set. The second subset, called the **testing** data set, usually contains the rest of the data. Each of these data sets should have *known* values of the dependent variable. Then the algorithm is trained with the data in the training data set. This results in a model that can be used for classification. The next step is to test this model on the testing data set. It is very possible that the model will work quite well on the training data set because this is, after all, the data set that was used to create the model. The real question is whether the model is flexible enough to make accurate classifications in the testing data set.

Most data mining software packages have utilities for partitioning the data. (For example, in the following subsections, you will see that the logistic regression procedure in StatTools does not yet have partitioning utilities, but the Palisade NeuralTools add-in for neural networks does have them.) The various software packages might use slightly different terms for the subsets, but the overall purpose is always the same, as just described. They might also let you specify a third subset, often called a **prediction** data set, where the values of the dependent variable are unknown. Then you can use the model to classify these unknown values. Of course, you won't know whether the classifications are accurate until you learn the actual values of the dependent variable in the prediction data set.

17-2a Logistic Regression

Logistic regression is a popular method for classifying individuals, given the values of a set of explanatory variables. It estimates the *probability* that an individual is in a particular category. As its name implies, logistic regression is somewhat similar to the usual regression analysis, but its approach is quite different. It uses a *nonlinear* function of the explanatory variables for classification.

Logistic regression is essentially regression with a binary (0–1) dependent variable. For the *two*-category problem (the only version of logistic regression discussed here), the binary variable indicates whether an observation is in category 0 or category 1. One approach to the classification problem, an approach that is sometimes actually used, is to run the usual multiple regression on the data, using the binary variable as the dependent variable. However, this approach has two serious drawbacks. First, it violates the regression assumption that the error terms are normally distributed. Second, the predicted values of the dependent variable can be between 0 and 1, less than 0, or greater than 1. If you want a predicted value to estimate a *probability*, then values less than 0 or greater than 1 make no sense.

Therefore, logistic regression takes a slightly different approach. Let X_1 through X_k be the potential explanatory variables, and create the linear function $b_0 + b_1 X_1 + \ldots + b_k X_k$. There is no guarantee that this linear function will be between 0 and 1, and hence that it will qualify as a probability. But the nonlinear function

$$1/(1+e^{-(b_0+b_1 X_1+\cdots+b_k X_k)})$$

is *always* between 0 and 1. In fact, the function $f(x) = 1/(1 + e^{-x})$ is an "S-shaped logistic" curve, as shown in Figure 17.1. For large negative values of x, the function approaches 0, and for large positive values of x, it approaches 1.

The logistic regression model uses this function to estimate the probability that any observation is in category 1. If p is the probability of being in category 1, the model

$$p = 1/(1+e^{-(b_0+b_1 X_1+\cdots+b_k X_k)})$$

is estimated. This equation can be manipulated algebraically to obtain an equivalent form:

$$Ln\left(\frac{p}{1-p}\right) = b_0 + b_1X_1 + \cdots + b_kX_k$$

This equation says that the natural logarithm of $p/(1-p)$ is a *linear* function of the explanatory variables. The ratio $p/(1-p)$ is called the **odds ratio**.

The odds ratio is a term frequently used in everyday language. Suppose, for example, that the probability p of a company going bankrupt is 0.25. Then the odds that the company will go bankrupt are $p/(1-p) = 0.25/0.75 = 1/3$, or "1 to 3." Odds ratios are probably most common in sports. If you read that the odds against Duke winning the NCAA basketball championship are 4 to 1, this means that the probability of Duke winning the championship is 1/5. Or if you read that the odds against Purdue winning the championship are 99 to 1, then the probability that Purdue will win is 1/100.

Figure 17.1 S-Shaped Logistic Curve

Logistic function: 1/(1+exp(−x))

The logarithm of the odds ratio, the quantity on the left side of the above equation, is called the **logit** (or **log odds**). Therefore, the logistic regression model states that the logit is a linear function of the explanatory variables. Although this is probably a bit mysterious and there is no easy way to justify it intuitively, logistic regression has produced useful results in many applications.

The numerical algorithm used to estimate the regression coefficients is complex, but the important goal for our purposes is to interpret the regression coefficients correctly. First, if a coefficient b is positive, then if its X increases, the log odds increases, so the probability of being in category 1 increases. The opposite is true for a negative b. So just by looking at the *signs* of the coefficients, you can see which explanatory variables are positively correlated with being in category 1 (the positive b's) and which are positively correlated with being in group 0 (the negative b's).

You can also look at the magnitudes of the b's to try to see which of the X's are "most important" in explaining category membership. Unfortunately, you run into the same problem as in regular regression. Some X's are typically of completely different magnitudes than others, which makes comparisons of the b's difficult. For example, if one X is income, with values in the thousands, and another X is number of children, with values like 0, 1, and 2, the coefficient of income will probably be *much* smaller than the coefficient of children, even though these two variables can be equally important in explaining category membership. We won't say more about the interpretation of the regression coefficients here, but you can find comments about them in the finished version of lasagna triers file discussed next.

In many situations, especially in data mining, the primary objective of logistic regression is to "score" members, given their X values. The score for any member is the estimated value of p, found by plugging into the logistic regression equation to get the logit and then solving algebraically to get *p*. (This is typically done automatically by the software package.) Those members who score highest are the most likely to be in category 1; those who score lowest are most likely to be in category 0. For example, if category 1 represents the responders to some direct mail campaign, a company might mail brochures to the top 10% of all scorers.

These scores can also be used to classify members. Here, a cutoff probability is required. All members who score below the cutoff are classified as category 0, and the rest are classified as category 1. This cutoff value is often 0.5, but any value can be used. This issue is discussed in more detail later in this section.

The following example illustrates how logistic regression is implemented in the StatTools add-in.

EXAMPLE

17.1 CLASSIFYING LASAGNA TRIERS WITH LOGISTIC REGRESSION

The **Lasagna Triers Logistic Regression.xlsx** file contains data on 856 people who have either tried or not tried a company's new frozen lasagna product. The categorical dependent variable, Have Tried, and several of the potential explanatory variables contain text, as shown in Figure 17.2. Some logistic regression software packages allow such text variables and implicitly create dummies for them, but StatTools requires all numeric variables. Therefore, the StatTools Dummy utility was used to create dummy variables for all text variables. (You could also do this with IF formulas.) Using the numeric variables, including dummies, how well is logistic regression able to classify the triers and nontriers?

Figure 17.2 Lasagna Data Set with Text Variables

	A	B	C	D	E	F	G	H	I	J	K	L	M
1	Person	Age	Weight	Income	Pay Type	Car Value	CC Debt	Gender	Live Alone	Dwell Type	Mall Trips	Nbhd	Have Tried
2	1	48	175	65500	Hourly	2190	3510	Male	No	Home	7	East	No
3	2	33	202	29100	Hourly	2110	740	Female	No	Condo	4	East	Yes
4	3	51	188	32200	Salaried	5140	910	Male	No	Condo	1	East	No
5	4	56	244	19000	Hourly	700	1620	Female	No	Home	3	West	No
6	5	28	218	81400	Salaried	26620	600	Male	No	Apt	3	West	Yes
7	6	51	173	73000	Salaried	24520	950	Female	No	Condo	2	East	No
8	7	44	182	66400	Salaried	10130	3500	Female	Yes	Condo	6	West	Yes
9	8	29	189	46200	Salaried	10250	2860	Male	No	Condo	5	West	Yes

Objective

To use logistic regression to classify users as triers or nontriers, and to interpret the resulting output.

Solution

A StatTools data set already exists (in the unfinished version of the file). It was used to create the dummy variables. To run the logistic regression, you select Logistic Regression from the StatTools Regression and Classification dropdown list. Then you fill out the usual StatTools dialog box as shown in Figure 17.3. At the top, you see two options: "with no Count Variable" or "with Count Variable." The former is appropriate here. (The latter is used only when there is a count of the 1's for each joint category, such as males who live alone.) The dependent variable is the dummy variable Have Tried Yes, and the explanatory variables are the original numeric variables (Age, Weight, Income, Car Value, CC Debt, and Mall Trips) and the dummy variables (Pay Type Salaried, Gender Male, Live Alone Yes, Dwell Type Condo, and Dwell Type Home). As in regular regression, one dummy variable for each categorical variable should be omitted.

The logistic regression output is much like regular regression output. There is a summary section and a list of coefficients, shown in Figure 17.4. The summary section is analogous to the ANOVA table in a regression output. The Improvement value indicates how much better the logistic regression classification is than a classification with no explanatory variables at all. The corresponding *p*-value indicates that this improvement is statistically significant at any of the usual significance levels, exactly like a small *p*-value in an ANOVA table.

Figure 17.3 StatTools Logistic
Regression Dialog Box

Figure 17.4 Summary and Coefficients in Logistic Regression Output

▲	A	B	C	D	E	F	G	H
1	*Logistic Regression for Have Tried Yes*							
2	*Summary Measures*							
3	Null Deviance	1165.604813						
4	Model Deviance	687.942884						
5	Improvement	477.661929						
6	p-Value	<0.0001						
7								
8		Coefficient	Standard Error	Wald Value	p-Value	Lower Limit	Upper Limit	Exp(Coef)
9	*Regression Coefficients*							
10	Constant	−2.540588	0.909698	−2.792781	0.0052	−4.323596	−0.757579	0.078820
11	Age	−0.069689	0.010808	−6.447602	<0.0001	−0.090873	−0.048504	0.932684
12	Weight	0.007033	0.003850	1.827036	0.0677	−0.000512	0.014579	1.007058
13	Income	0.000005	0.000004	1.260222	0.2076	−0.000003	0.000012	1.000005
14	Car Value	−0.000027	0.000020	−1.307318	0.1911	−0.000067	0.000013	0.999973
15	CC Debt	0.000078	0.000091	0.852025	0.3942	−0.000101	0.000257	1.000078
16	Mall Trips	0.687006	0.059764	11.495247	<0.0001	0.569868	0.804144	1.987754
17	Pay Type Salaried	1.332747	0.220913	6.032913	<0.0001	0.899758	1.765736	3.791445
18	Gender Male	0.255542	0.191544	1.334117	0.1822	−0.119884	0.630969	1.291162
19	Live Alone Yes	1.322630	0.283886	4.659013	<0.0001	0.766213	1.879047	3.753280
20	Dwell Type Condo	−0.080928	0.275087	−0.294191	0.7686	−0.620099	0.458243	0.922260
21	Dwell Type Home	0.176722	0.248864	0.710115	0.4776	−0.311051	0.664495	1.193299

The coefficient section is also analogous to the usual regression output. The Wald value is like the *t*-value, and each corresponding *p*-value indicates whether that variable could be excluded from the equation. In this case, Income, Car Value, CC Debt, Gender Male, and the two Dwell Type dummies could possibly be excluded. (You can check that if these variables are indeed excluded and the logistic regression is run again, very little changes.) The signs of the remaining coefficients indicate whether the probability of being a trier increases or decreases when these variables increase. For example, this probability decreases as Age increases (a minus sign), and it increases as Weight increases (a plus sign). Again, however, you have to use caution when interpreting the magnitudes of the coefficients. For example, the coefficient of Weight is small because Weight has values in the hundreds, and the coefficient of Live Alone Yes is much larger because this variable is either 0 or 1.

The Exp(Coef) column is easier to interpret. For example, as explained in the finished version of the file and in StatTools cell comments, if Live Alone Yes increases from 0 to 1—that is, a person who doesn't live alone is compared to a person who does live alone—the odds of being a trier increase by a factor of about 3.75. In other words, the people who live alone are much more likely to try the product. The other values in this column can be interpreted in a similar way, and you should be on the lookout for values well above 1 or well below 1.

Below the coefficient output, you see the classification summary shown in Figure 17.5. To create these results, StatTools plugs the explanatory values in each row into the logistic regression equation, which results in an estimate of the probability that the person is a trier. If this probability is greater than 0.5, the person is classified as a trier; if it is less than 0.5, the person is classified as a nontrier. The results show the number of correct and incorrect classifications. For example, 422 of the 495 triers, or 85.25%, are classified correctly as triers. The bottom summary indicates that 82.01% of all classifications are correct. However, how good is this really? It turns out that 57.83% of all observations are triers, so a naïve classification rule that classifies *everyone* as a trier would get 57.83% correct. The last number in the figure, 57.34%, represents the improvement of logistic regression over this naïve rule. Specifically, logistic regression is 57.34% of the way from the naïve 57.83% to a perfect 100%.

The last part of the logistic regression output, a small part of which is shown in Figure 17.6, lists all original data and the scores discussed earlier. For example, the first person's score is 75.28%. This is the probability estimated from the logistic regression equation that this person is a trier. Because it is greater than 0.5, this person is classified as a trier. However, this is

Figure 17.5 Classification Summary

	A	B	C	D
23		1	0	Percent
24	*Classification Matrix*			Correct
25	1	422	73	85.25%
26	0	81	280	77.56%
27				
28			Percent	
29	*Summary Classification*			
30	Correct		82.01%	
31	Base		57.83%	
32	Improvement		57.34%	

Figure 17.6 Scores for the First Few People

	M	N	O
34		Analysis	Original
35	Probability	Class	Class
36	75.28%	1	0
37	35.15%	0	1
38	7.65%	0	0
39	9.18%	0	0
40	60.22%	1	1
41	7.69%	0	0

one of the relatively few misclassifications. The first person is actually a nontrier. In the same way, explanatory values for *new* people, those whose trier status is unknown, could be fed into the logistic regression equation to score them. Then perhaps some incentives could be sent to the top scorers (or the middle scorers) to increase their chances of trying the product. The point is that logistic regression is then being used as a tool to identify the people most likely to be triers.

Before leaving this subsection, you have probably noticed that StatTools includes another classification procedure called **discriminant analysis**. This is a classical technique developed decades ago that is still sometimes used. It is somewhat similar to logistic regression and has the same basic goals. However, it is not as prominent in data mining discussions as logistic regression. Therefore, discriminant analysis is not discussed here.

17-2b Neural Networks

A **neural network** (or simply, **neural net**) methodology attempts to mimic the complex behavior of the human brain. It sends inputs (the values of explanatory variables) through a complex nonlinear network to produce one or more outputs (the values of the dependent variable). Methods for doing this have been studied by researchers in artificial intelligence and other fields for decades, and there are now many software packages that implement versions of neural net algorithms. Some people seem to believe that data mining is synonymous with neural nets. Although this is not true—data mining employs many algorithms that bear no resemblance to neural nets—the neural net methodology is one of the most popular methodologies in data mining. It can be used to predict a categorical dependent variable, as in this section on classification, and it can also be used to predict a numeric dependent variable, as in multiple regression.

The biggest advantage of neural nets is that they often provide more accurate predictions than any other methodology, especially when relationships are highly nonlinear. They also have a downside. Unlike methodologies like multiple regression and logistic regression, neural nets do not provide easily interpretable equations where you can see the contributions of the individual explanatory variables. For this reason, they are often called a "black box" methodology. If you want good predictions, neural nets often provide an attractive method, but you shouldn't expect to understand exactly how the predictions are made.

A brief explanation of how neural nets work helps to clarify this black box behavior. Each neural net has an associated network diagram, something like the one shown in Figure 17.7. This figure assumes two inputs and one output. The network also includes a "hidden layer" in the middle with two hidden nodes. Scaled values of the inputs enter the network at the left, they are weighted by the W values and summed, and these sums are sent to the hidden nodes. At the hidden nodes, the sums are "squished" by an *S*-shaped logistic-type function. These squished values are then weighted and summed, and the sum is sent to the output node, where it is squished again and rescaled. Although the details of this process are best left to software, small illustrative examples are available in the file **Neural Net Explanation.xlsm**. (The file, in the Finished Examples folder, is an .xlsm file because the logistic function is implemented with a macro, so make sure you enable macros.) There is one sheet for a one-input neural net and another for a two-input neural net. You can see how everything works by studying the cell formulas. However, the main insight provided by this file is that you can see how different sets of weights lead to very different nonlinear behaviors.

A neural net can have any number of hidden layers and hidden nodes, and the choices for these are far from obvious. Many software packages make these choices for you, based on rules of thumb discovered by researchers. Once the structure of the network is chosen, the neural net is "trained" by sending many sets of inputs—including the *same* inputs multiple times—through the network and comparing the outputs from the net with the known output values. Based on many such comparisons, the weights are repeatedly adjusted. This process continues until the weights stabilize or some other stopping criterion is reached. Depending on the size of the data set, this iterative process can take some time.

As research continues, the algorithms implemented with neural net software continue to change. The ideas remain basically the same, but the way these ideas are implemented, and even the results, can vary from one implementation to another.

StatTools does not implement neural nets, but another add-in in the Palisade suite, **NeuralTools**, does. The following continuation of the lasagna triers example illustrates its use.

Figure 17.7 Neural Net with Two Inputs and Two Hidden Nodes

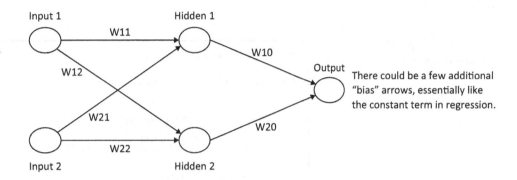

EXAMPLE

17.2 CLASSIFYING LASAGNA TRIERS WITH NEURAL NETS

Logistic regression provided reasonably accurate classifications for the lasagna triers data set. Can a neural net, as implemented in Palisade's NeuralTools add-in, provide comparable results?

Objective

To learn how the NeuralTools add-in works, and to compare its results to those from logistic regression.

Solution

The data for this version of the example are in the file **Lasagna Triers NeuralTools.xlsx**. There are two differences from the file used for logistic regression. First, no dummy variables are necessary. The NeuralTools add-in is capable of dealing directly with text variables. Second, there is a Prediction Data sheet with a second data set of size 250 to be used for prediction. Its values of the dependent Have Tried variable are unknown.

You launch NeuralTools just like StatTools, @RISK, or any of the other Palisade add-ins. This produces a NeuralTools tab and ribbon, as shown in Figure 17.8. As you can see, NeuralTools uses a Data Set Manager, just like StatTools. The only difference is that when you specify the data set, you must indicate the role of each variable in the neural net. The possible roles are Independent Numeric, Independent Categorical, Dependent Numeric, Dependent Categorical, Tag, and Unused. Except for Tag, which isn't used here, these have the obvious meanings. So the first step is to create two data sets, one for

Figure 17.8 NeuralTools Ribbon

File	Home	Insert	Page Layout	Formulas	Data	Review	View	Developer	NeuralTools

Data Set Manager · Data Viewer · Train · Test · Predict · Utilities · Help

Data · Neural Nets · Help

each sheet, with Have Tried as Dependent Categorical, Person as Unused, and the other variables as Independent Numeric or Independent Categorical as appropriate. (NeuralTools usually guesses the roles correctly.) We call these data sets Train/Test Data and Prediction Data, respectively.

To train the data in the Train/Test Data set, you activate the Data sheet and click Train on the NeuralTools ribbon to get a Training dialog box with three tabs. The Train tab shown in Figure 17.9 provides three basic options. The first option allows you to partition the data set into training and testing subsets. The default shown here is to set aside a random 20% of cases for testing. The second option is for predicting cases with missing values of the dependent variable. This is not relevant here because there are no such cases in the Data sheet. Besides, prediction will be performed later on the Prediction Data set. The third option is to calculate variable impacts. This is useful when you have a large number of potential explanatory variables. It lets you screen out the ones that appear to be least useful. You can check this option if you like. However, its output doesn't tell you, at least not directly, *how* the different explanatory variables affect the dependent variable.

Figure 17.9 Train Tab of Training Dialog Box

The Net Configuration tab shown in Figure 17.10 lets you select one of three options for the training algorithm. The PN/GRN (probabilistic neural net) algorithm is relatively new. It is fairly quick and it usually gives good results, so it is a good option to try, as is done here.[2] The MLF option (multilayer feedforward) algorithm is more traditional, but it is considerably slower. The Best Net Search tries both PN/GRN and various versions of MLF to see which is best, and it is quite slow.

The Runtime tab (not shown here) specifies stopping conditions for the algorithm. You can accept the defaults, and you can always stop the training prematurely if it doesn't seem to be making any improvement.

Once you click Next on any of the tabs, you will see a summary (not shown here) of the model setup. Then you can click its Train button to start the algorithm. You will see a progress monitor, and eventually you will see results on a new sheet, the most important of which are shown in Figure 17.11. (As in other Palisade add-ins, the results are stored by default in a new workbook. You can change this behavior from the Application Settings dialog box, available from the Utilities dropdown list.)

The top part shows classification results for the 80%, or 685, cases used for training. About 10% of the No values (row 31) were classified incorrectly, and about 6.5% of the Yes values (row 32) were classified incorrectly. The bottom part shows similar results for the 20%, or 171, cases used for testing. The incorrect percentages, about 24% and 16%, are not as good as for the

---

2 The abbreviation PN/GRN is a bit confusing. For classification problems, the algorithm is called probabilistic neural net (PNN). However, if the dependent variable is continuous, the same basic algorithm is called generalized regression neural net, which explains the GRN abbreviation.

Figure 17.10 Net
Configuration Tab of Training
Dialog Box

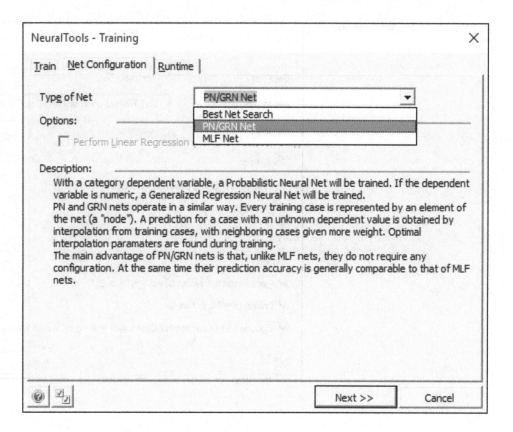

Figure 17.11 Selected Training
Results

	B	C	D	E
28	**Classification Matrix**			
29	(for training cases)			
30		No	Yes	Bad(%)
31	No	260	30	10.3448%
32	Yes	26	369	6.5823%
33				
34	**Classification Matrix**			
35	(for testing cases)			
36		No	Yes	Bad(%)
37	No	54	17	23.9437%
38	Yes	16	84	16.0000%

training set, but this is not unusual. Also, these results are slightly better than those from logistic regression, where about 18% of the classifications were incorrect. (Remember, however, that the data set wasn't partitioned into training and testing subsets for logistic regression.) These results are from an 80–20 random split of the original data. The results you get from a *different* random split will probably be different.

Now that the model has been trained, it can be used to predict the unknown values of the dependent variable in the Prediction Data set. To do so, you activate the Prediction Data sheet, click Predict on the NeuralTools ribbon, and then fill out the resulting dialog box as shown in Figure 17.12. If there are multiple trained nets, you can browse for the one you want to use in the Net to Use box. The Enable Live Prediction option provides real-time predictions: If values of the explanatory variables change for any cases in the prediction set, the predictions will update automatically.

After you click Next, you will see a Prediction Preview dialog box, and you can click its Predict button. At this point, NeuralTools runs each of the cases in the Prediction Data sheet through the trained net and displays the results next to

Figure 17.12 Prediction Dialog Box

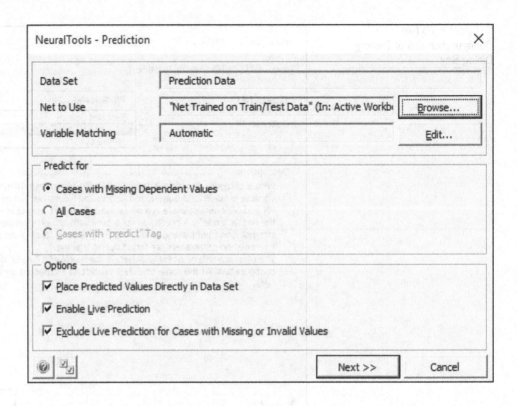

Figure 17.13 Prediction Results

	M	N	O	P	Q
1			Prediction Report: "Net Trained on		
2	Have Tried		Tag Used	Prediction	Prediction%
3	No		predict	No	89.89%
4	Yes		predict	Yes	84.00%
5	Yes		predict	Yes	64.31%
6	Yes		predict	Yes	65.33%
7	Yes		predict	Yes	92.13%
8	Yes		predict	Yes	99.47%
9	No		predict	No	54.20%
10	No		predict	No	74.65%
11	Yes		predict	Yes	99.47%

the prediction data. A few of these are shown in Figure 17.13. However, be careful about interpreting the Prediction% column. Unlike the StatTools logistic regression output, each percentage shown here is the probability that the prediction is *correct*, not the probability that the person is a trier. For example, the first person is classified as a nontrier, and there is 89.89% confidence that this classification is correct. Equivalently, the probability is only 10.11% that this person is a trier.

As indicated earlier, these results are live. For example, if you change the Live Alone and Mall Trips data for the first person to Yes and 8, respectively, you will see that the prediction changes to Yes, with very high confidence. This feature lets you experiment with explanatory data values to see their effect on the predictions. This doesn't explain exactly how the neural net "black box" is working, but it helps.

17-2c Naïve Bayes

The method discussed in this section is a simple and very different classification method from logistic regression and neural nets. It has the advantage of being fairly simple to implement in Excel, with no add-ins necessary. The idea is to find the conditional probabilities of given sets of explanatory X values, given that the dependent variable is 0, or given that it is 1. That is, you see how likely these X values are for the 0 category and how likely they are for the 1 category. These probabilities, which we'll label $P(X \mid 0)$ and $P(X \mid 1)$, are calculated from the observed training data for all observed sets of X values. Then for a new observation, you look up these probabilities for *its* explanatory X values. If its $P(X \mid 0)$ is larger than its $P(X \mid 1)$, it is classified as a 0. Otherwise, it is classified as a 1.

This is basically an application of Bayes' rule from Chapter 6, where the classification of a new observation is based on the posterior probability of 0 or 1, given its X values. This explains the word Bayes in the name of the method. But why naïve? This is due to the way the probabilities $P(X \mid 0)$ and $P(X \mid 1)$ are calculated from the training data. In any application, X is a set of explanatory values, such as male, lives alone, lives in a condo, and lives in the South neighborhood. So $P(X \mid 0)$ is the *joint* probability of these characteristics, given that the person is in the 0 category, and $P(X \mid 1)$ is similar for the 1 category. Normally, joint probabilities are difficult to estimate, but if we can assume probabilistic *independence* across characteristics, then a joint probability becomes much easier—it is the product of the individual characteristics. For example, the $P(X \mid 0)$ just mentioned becomes the product of $P(\text{male} \mid 0)$, $P(\text{lives alone} \mid 0)$, $P(\text{lives in a condo} \mid 0)$, and $P(\text{lives in the South neighborhood} \mid 0)$. Each of these is easy to estimate. For example, the estimate of $P(\text{male} \mid 0)$ is the proportion of people in the 0 category who are male.

It is naïve to assume independence across characteristics, and this assumption is not justified in most applications. Surprisingly, however, it often doesn't matter. The classifications from the naïve Bayes method are often quite good and comparable to more complex methods, despite the naïve independence assumption. The following example illustrates how the naïve Bayes method can be applied to the lasagna trier data.

EXAMPLE

17.3 CLASSIFYING LASAGNA TRIERS WITH NAÏVE BAYES

You have already seen how two algorithms, logistic regression and neural nets, provide reasonably accurate classifications for the lasagna trier data set. Does the naïve Bayes method provide comparable results?

Objective

To see how the naïve Bayes method can be implemented with Excel-only formulas and to compare its results to those from logistic regression and neural nets.

Solution

The data for this version of the example are in the file **Lasagna Triers Naïve Bayes.xlsx**. To calculate the probabilities $P(X \mid 0)$ and $P(X \mid 1)$ described above, the naïve Bayes method requires all explanatory variables to be categorical, with only a few possible values. In this data set, some of the explanatory variables such as Gender and Nbhd are already categorical, but others such as Age and Weight are numeric and essentially continuous. We rearranged the data so that all numeric variables are in contiguous columns (which made for easier copying), and we binned them into four categories, based on their quartiles. For example, the binned Age variable will be 1, 2, 3, or 4, depending on which quartile its Age value falls into. A sample of the resulting binned training data set appears in Figure 17.14. Actually, the training data set consists of only 700 of the 856 observations. We use the other 156 observations for testing, and the testing data set is binned similarly. For each set of X values, we need to calculate $P(X \mid 0)$ and $P(X \mid 1)$. Given the naïve independence assumption, each of these is a product of probabilities, and this product is usually *very* small. Therefore, it is customary to find the natural logs of the individual probabilities and use the fact that the log of a product is the sum of the logs. Figure 17.15 shows some of the calculations for the 0 category, where Have Tried is No. (See the file **Lasagna Triers Naive Bayes Finished.xlsx**. Columns AJ–AU to the right contain similar calculations for the 1 category, where Have Tried is Yes.) For example, the first person's binned age from Figure 17.14 is 4. Cell W4 then finds the log of the proportion of all people in the 0 category with binned age 4, using COUNTIFS and COUNTIF functions. Fortunately, the formula in cell W4 is copyable to the entire range W4:AG703, and a similar formula in cell AJ4 (replacing "No" with "Yes") is copyable to the range AJ4:AU703. Then the values in column AH (and column AU) are sums of these logs, meaning that they are the logs of the products of the individual probabilities. More simply, they are the logs of the estimated probabilities $P(X \mid 0)$ and $P(X \mid 1)$ required for classification.

Now we can use these probabilities for classification, either for the training data or the testing data. Some of the results for the training data appear in Figure 17.16. Each prediction in column N is based on a comparison of the total in column AH

Figure 17.14 Binned Training Data

	A	B	C	D	E	F	G	H	I	J	K	L	M
1													
2													
3	Person	Age	Weight	Income	Car Value	CC Debt	Mall Trips	Gender	Live Alone	Dwell Type	Pay Type	Nbhd	Have Tried
4	1	4	2	4	2	4	4	Male	No	Home	Hourly	East	No
5	2	2	3	2	2	2	3	Female	No	Condo	Hourly	East	Yes
6	3	4	2	2	3	2	1	Male	No	Condo	Salaried	East	No
7	4	4	4	1	1	3	2	Female	No	Home	Hourly	West	No
8	5	1	4	4	4	2	2	Male	No	Apt	Salaried	West	Yes
9	6	4	1	4	4	2	1	Female	No	Condo	Salaried	East	No
10	7	3	2	4	4	4	3	Female	Yes	Condo	Salaried	West	Yes
11	8	1	2	3	4	4	3	Male	No	Condo	Salaried	West	Yes
12	9	1	3	4	4	4	4	Male	No	Condo	Salaried	West	Yes
13	10	1	3	1	1	3	4	Female	Yes	Apt	Salaried	East	Yes

Figure 17.15 Estimated Log Probabilities for Training Data

	X	Y	Z	AA	AB	AC	AD	AE	AF	AG	AH
1	Log of conditional probabilities when Have Tried is No (training data only)										
2											
3	Age	Weight	Income	Car Value	CC Debt	Mall Trips	Gender	Live Alone	Dwell Type	Pay Type	Nbhd	Total Prob
4	=LN(COUNTIFS(B$4:B$703,B4,$M$4:$M$703,"No")/COUNTIF($M$4:$M$703,"No"))							−0.7588	−0.50749	−0.63154	−13.1283
5	LN(number) 35664	−1.39638	−1.331	−1.26963	−1.10532	−0.67656	−0.09832	−1.20063	−0.50749	−0.63154	−11.1468
6	−0.96425	−1.31842	−1.39638	−1.49575	−1.26963	−0.91295	−0.71001	−0.09832	−1.20063	−0.92132	−0.63154	−10.9192
7	−0.96425	−1.48094	−1.15715	−1.15715	−1.6061	−1.48094	−0.67656	−0.09832	−0.7588	−0.50749	−1.54156	−11.4292
8	−1.96277	−1.48094	−1.6061	−1.62291	−1.26963	−1.48094	−0.71001	−0.09832	−1.46634	−0.92132	−1.54156	−14.1608
9	−0.96425	−1.39638	−1.6061	−1.62291	−1.26963	−0.91295	−0.67656	−0.09832	−1.20063	−0.92132	−0.63154	−11.3006
10	−1.30599	−1.31842	−1.6061	−1.62291	−1.98687	−1.10532	−0.67656	−2.36824	−1.20063	−0.92132	−1.54156	−15.6539
11	−1.96277	−1.31842	−1.43776	−1.62291	−1.98687	−1.10532	−0.71001	−0.09832	−1.20063	−0.92132	−1.54156	−13.9059

Figure 17.16 Prediction Results for Training Data

	M	N	O	P	Q	R	S	T	U	V	W	X	Y
1											Log of conditional probabilities		
2													
3	Have Tried	Prediction	Correct?		Classification matrix						Age	Weight	Income
4	No	Yes	No				Actual				−0.96425	−1.31842	−1.6061
5	Yes	No	No					Yes	No	Total	−1.57331	−1.35664	−1.39638
6	No	No	Yes		Predicted	Yes	320	49	369		−0.96425	−1.31842	−1.39638
7	No	No	Yes			No	81	250	331		−0.96425	−1.48094	−1.15715
8	Yes	=IF(AH8>AU8,"No","Yes")				Total	401	299	700		−1.96277	−1.48094	−1.6061
9	No	N IF(logical_test, [value_if_true], [value_if_false])								−0.96425	−1.39638	−1.6061
10	Yes	Yes	Yes		Percentages of bad predictions						−1.30599	−1.31842	−1.6061
11	Yes	Yes	Yes				Yes	No	Total		−1.96277	−1.31842	−1.43776
12	Yes	Yes	Yes				20.2%	16.4%	18.6%		−1.96277	−1.35664	−1.6061
13	Yes	Yes	Yes								−1.96277	−1.35664	−1.15715

and the total in column AU, that is, $P(X \mid 0)$ versus $P(X \mid 1)$ for that row. (Actually, it is a comparison of their logs, but this is equivalent to a comparison of the probabilities.) If $P(X \mid 0)$ is larger, we predict No, and if $P(X \mid 1)$ is larger, we predict Yes. Finally, we check whether the prediction is correct in column O—that is, whether column N matches column M—and we tally the results in columns Q–U.

The calculations for the testing data set, shown in Figure 17.17, are entirely analogous except for one important difference. The log probabilities in columns W:AH and AJ:AU are based on the training data, not on the testing data. Essentially, the training data set is the "model" for this method, so predictions for the testing data (or new data) should be based on this model.

Figure 17.17 Prediction Results for Testing Data

	M	N	O	P	Q	R	S	T	U	V	W	X	Y
1											Log of conditional probabilities		
2													
3	Have Tried	Prediction	Correct?		Classification matrix						Age	Weight	Income
4	No	No	Yes			Actual					−1.30599	−1.39638	−1.43776
5	No	No	Yes				Yes	No	Total		−0.96425	−1.35664	−1.6061
6	No	No	Yes		Predicted	Yes	73	6	79		−1.96277	−1.35664	−1.39638
7	No	No	Yes			No	21	56	77		−0.96425	−1.48094	−1.6061
8	No	No	Yes			Total	94	62	156		−0.96425	−1.39638	−1.43776
9	Yes	Yes	Yes								−1.96277	−1.48094	−1.39638
10	Yes	Yes	Yes		Percentages of bad predictions						−0.96425	−1.48094	−1.6061
11	No	No	Yes				Yes	No	Total		−1.30599	−1.48094	−1.15715
12	Yes	Yes	Yes				22.3%	9.7%	17.3%		−1.57331	−1.39638	−1.39638
13	Yes	Yes	Yes								−1.96277	−1.31842	−1.6061

In any case, classification accuracy for the training data set in Figure 17.16 is similar to the classification accuracy for the testing data in Figure 17.17, and neither is very different from the logistic regression results in Figure 17.5 or the neural nets results in Figure 17.11.[3] In short, despite its simplicity, the naïve Bayes method is a worthy competitor to these much more complex classification methods.

We have based the classification on the *logarithm* of the conditional probabilities. This avoids very tiny probability estimates. However, this can also cause a problem. Suppose, for example, that some attribute value is *never* observed for the Yes category. Then the estimated probability of this attribute value, given Yes, is 0, and the log of 0 is undefined. This will show up as one or more errors in a log probability column. The easiest fix in this case is to not take logs. For example, there will be no LN functions as shown in Figure 17.15, and the total probability in column AH will be the *product* of the probabilities to its left, not the sum.

Before leaving this section, we mention that the naïve Bayes method can be used, in almost the same way illustrated here, for *text mining*. For example, imagine you have one set of tweets from Republican candidates and another set from Democrat candidates. Then you want to classify a new set of tweets as coming from Republicans or Democrats. In this case, the procedure is based on "bags of words." You parse each tweet into its individual words (ignoring common words like "the" and "and"), and these words become the X values for any tweet. For example, one word might be "overspending." Then the naïve Bayes method would find the log proportion of all Republican tweets that include

---

3 As usual, the results can depend on the training/testing split. You can see how sensitive the results are to this split in the file **Lasagna Triers Naïve Bayes Sensitivity.xlsm** (which contains a macro you will need to enable).

"overspending" (analogous to cell W4 in Figure 17.15) and the similar log proportion for Democrats. Finally, these log proportions of words would be used to classify new tweets exactly as in Figure 17.17. Admittedly, naïve Bayes is not the only classification method used for text mining, but it is simple and often surprisingly accurate.

17-2d Classification Trees

The first two classification methods discussed, logistic regression and neural networks, use complex nonlinear functions to capture the relationship between explanatory variables and a categorical dependent variables. The method discussed in this subsection, **classification trees** (sometimes called **decision trees**, not to be confused with the very different decision trees in Chapter 6), is also capable of discovering nonlinear relationships, but it is more intuitive. This method, which has many variations, has existed for decades, and it has been implemented in a variety of software packages. Unfortunately, it is not available in any of the software that accompanies this book, but the essential features of the method are explained here.

Referring to the lasagna data again, imagine that you have all 856 observations in a single box. If you choose one case randomly, there is considerable uncertainty about the Have Tried status of this person because the box is divided about 57% Yes to 43% No. The basic idea of classification trees is to split the box into two or more boxes so that each box is more "pure" than the original box, meaning that each box is more nearly Yes than No, or vice versa. There are many possible splits. For example, one possible split is on Mall Trips: those with fewer than 4 and those with 4 or more. You can check (with a pivot table) that the first box is divided 25.8% Yes to 74.2% No and the second box is divided 76.4% Yes to 23.6% No. Each of these boxes (or subsets, if you prefer) is purer than the original box, so this is a promising split.

Each of these boxes can now be split on another variable (or even the same variable) to make them even purer, and this splitting can continue. Eventually, the boxes are either sufficiently pure or they contain very few cases, in which case further splitting is not useful. This sounds simple enough, but the trick is to find the best splits and a good criterion for stopping. The details are implemented in different ways in different software packages.[4]

The attractive aspect of this method is that the final result is a set of simple rules for classification. As an example, the final tree might look like the one in Figure 17.18. (This is taken from Microsoft's SQL Server Analysis Services software.) Each box has a bar that shows the purity of the corresponding box, where blue corresponds to Yes values and red corresponds to No values. The first split, actually a three-way split, is on Mall Trips: fewer

Figure 17.18 Possible Classification Tree

---

4 We thought of including a version with Excel-only formulas, but the method does not lend itself well to Excel implementation. The simplicity of the method is obscured by the bulky Excel formulas. If you are interested, you can check one of our attempts in the file **Lasagna Triers Excel-Only Tree Method.xlsm**, which contains a macro you will have to enable.

than 4, 4 or 5, and at least 6. Each of these is then split in a different way. For example, when Mall Trips is fewer than 4, the split is on Nbhd West versus Nbhd not West. The splits you see here are the only ones made. They achieve sufficient purity, so the algorithm stops splitting after these.

Predictions are then made by majority rule. As an example, suppose a person has made 3 mall trips and lives in the East. This person belongs in the second box down on the right, which has a large majority of No values. Therefore, this person is classified as a No. In contrast, a person with 10 mall trips belongs in one of the two bottom boxes on the right. This person is classified as a Yes because *both* of these boxes have a large majority of Yes values. In fact, the last split on Age is not really necessary.

This classification tree leads directly to the following rules.

• If the person makes fewer than 4 mall trips:
  • If the person lives in the West, classify as a trier.
  • If the person doesn't live in the West, classify as a nontrier.
• If the person makes 4 or 5 mall trips:
  • If the person doesn't live in the East, classify as a trier.
  • If the person lives in the East, classify as a nontrier.
• If the person makes at least 6 mall trips, classify as a trier.

The ability of classification trees to provide such simple rules, plus fairly accurate classifications, has made this a very popular classification technique.

17-2e Measures of Classification Accuracy

Classification algorithms often provide probabilities of classifications, as well the classifications themselves. For example, a method might indicate that the probability of an observation being in the 1 category is 0.875. To use this probability to make a prediction, a cutoff value is required. If 0.5 is used as the cutoff, any observation with probability greater than or equal to 0.5 is classified as a 1, and any with probability less than 0.5 is classified as a 0. However, 0.5 is not necessarily the best cutoff value, and the tradeoffs for different cutoff values are discussed here.

Suppose a classification algorithm applied to a testing data set gives the results shown in Figure 17.19. (The specific algorithm is not important here, but if you are interested, the last two sheets of the file **Lasagna Triers Excel-Only Tree Method.xlsm** illustrate the typical calculations.) For example, the first observation is actually a No, and the algorithm estimates that its probability of being a Yes is 0.264. Of course, you would expect No values to get low probabilities and Yes values to get high probabilities.

Then a table of percentages can be calculated for various values of the cutoff value. Such a table appears in Figure 17.20. The columns shown here are typical, but you could calculate others. The terms **Precision**, **Specificity**, and **Sensitivity** are commonly used. They are defined as follows and are calculated as simple ratios from the data in Figure 17.19.

Figure 17.19 Prediction Probabilities from a Classification Algorithm

	M	N
5	Have Tried	Prob(Yes)
6	No	0.264
7	No	0.472
8	No	0.296
9	No	0.452
10	No	0.324
11	Yes	0.748
12	Yes	0.608
13	No	0.064
14	Yes	0.660
15	Yes	0.768

Figure 17.20 Accuracy
Measures for Various Cutoff
Values

	A	B	C	D	E
1	Cutoff for classification	Precision	True Negative Rate (Specificity)	False Positive Rate	True Positive Rate (Sensitivity)
2	0.05	0.603	0.000	1.000	1.000
3	0.10	0.618	0.065	0.935	1.000
4	0.15	0.644	0.161	0.839	1.000
5	0.20	0.664	0.242	0.758	0.989
6	0.25	0.697	0.355	0.645	0.979
7	0.30	0.722	0.435	0.565	0.968
8	0.35	0.783	0.597	0.403	0.957
9	0.40	0.830	0.710	0.290	0.936
10	0.45	0.884	0.823	0.177	0.894
11	0.50	0.937	0.919	0.081	0.787
12	0.55	0.973	0.968	0.032	0.755
13	0.60	0.971	0.968	0.032	0.702
14	0.65	0.966	0.968	0.032	0.596
15	0.70	0.957	0.968	0.032	0.479
16	0.75	0.941	0.968	0.032	0.340
17	0.80	1.000	1.000	0.000	0.255
18	0.85	1.000	1.000	0.000	0.170
19	0.90	1.000	1.000	0.000	0.096
20	0.95	1.000	1.000	0.000	0.021

- Precision: Of all testing rows predicted to be Yes—that is, P(Yes) is greater than or equal to the cutoff—the percentage where the dependent variable is Yes.
- Specificity (also called the true negative rate): Of all testing rows where the dependent variable is No, the percentage that are correctly classified—that is, P(Yes) is less than the cutoff.
- False positive rate (one minus the specificity): Of all testing rows where the dependent variable is No, the percentage that are incorrectly classified—that is, P(Yes) is greater than or equal to the cutoff.
- Sensitivity (also called the true positive rate): Of all testing rows where the dependent variable is Yes, the percentage that are correctly classified—that is, P(Yes) is greater than or equal to the cutoff.

Finally, it is common to graph the last two columns, the true positive rate versus the false positive rate, in a so-called **ROC curve**.[5] This curve appears in Figure 17.21. It is actually a scatterplot of the last two columns, with the dots connected. Clearly, we want a cutoff

Figure 17.21 ROC Curve

---

5 ROC stands for Receiver Operating Characteristic, a military term from World War II that has stuck.

where the false positive rate is low and the true positive rate (sensitivity) is high, so we want a point high and to the left on the curve. The circled points, corresponding to cutoff values around 0.5 to 0.6, seem to be the best. The important point is that the ROC curve provides a basis for choosing a good cutoff value. (The choice could also be based on the *costs* of misclassifications, but this is not discussed here.)

Another concept that often accompanies discussions of classification is **lift**. Imagine that you have a large population where 5% of the people, if they received one of your sales brochures, would actually purchase something from you. You have enough money to mail 10,000 sales brochures, and you naturally want to mail these to the people most likely to respond by making a purchase. If you randomly choose 10,000 people, you can expect to reach 500 purchasers (5% of 10,000) by luck alone. But if you use one of the classification techniques discussed here to *score* the people on their probability of purchasing, and you then mail brochures to the top 10,000 scorers, you ought to reach more—hopefully many more—than 500 purchasers. Lift is defined (loosely) as the increase in the number of purchasers you reach over the random mailing. (There is a very precise definition of lift, but the intuitive meaning given here will suffice.) Presumably, better classification methods provide a higher lift.

Many software packages provide a **lift chart**. This chart for the lasagna data is shown in Figure 17.22. You can think of the horizontal axis as the percentage of the population you mail to, and the vertical axis as the percentage of the triers you reach. In this data set, the 5% from the previous paragraph is replaced by about 57%, the percentage of triers total. The bottom line in the chart corresponds to the random mailing. If you mail to a random *x*% of the customers, you will reach about *x*% of the triers just by luck. At the other extreme, the top line is the perfect choice—it is when you have the perfect foresight to mail *only* to the triers, at least until there are no triers left (the flat part past 57%). The curve in between is from the classification method. As an example, if you mail to the top 31% of scorers, you will reach about 50% of the triers, not just 31% as in the random mailing. (From 31%, read up and to the left to get the 50%.) This is a reasonably good lift. Obviously, you want the middle curve to be as close as possible to the upper (perfect) line.

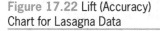

Figure 17.22 Lift (Accuracy) Chart for Lasagna Data

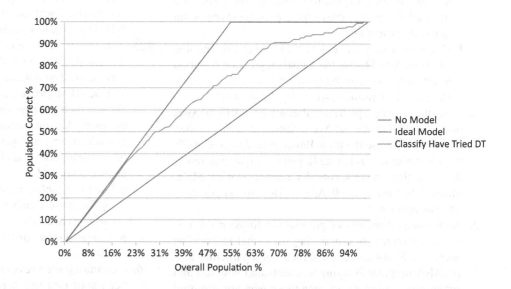

17-2f Classification with Rare Events

Classification methods are often used on data sets with rare events. As an example, suppose a company has data on millions of customers and is trying to classify them as either defaulting on credit card payments (Yes) or not (No). There is probably a very small percentage of Yes values in the data, maybe even less than 1%. In this case, unless special techniques are used, it is very likely that any classification algorithm in any software package will classify *everyone* as No. The algorithm can then claim that over 99% of its classifications are correct. This sounds good, but the predictions are worthless.

Fortunately, all is not lost. Most packages, including NeuralTools, accompany predictions of new observations with probabilities that the predictions are correct. So even if all of these probabilities are above 50%, you can still sort on the probability column to see the predictions that are least likely to be correct. Then if you are forced to choose some observations who will default on credit card payments, you can choose the ones with the highest probabilities of being classified as Yes.

In addition, some software packages allow you to **oversample**. In this case, you work with a training data set that contains *all* the Yes values (or at least most of them) and a small percentage of the No values. The resulting data set is more nearly 50–50 Yes and No, which gives the algorithm a better chance of "learning" what distinguishes No observations from Yes observations. Also, if the original data set is huge, this oversampled subset is still large enough for analysis.

Problems

Solutions for problems whose numbers appear within a colored box can be found in the Student Solution Files.

Level A

1. The file **P17_01.xlsx** contains data on 100 consumers who drink beer. Some of them prefer light beer, and others prefer regular beer. A major beer producer believes that the following variables might be useful in discriminating between these two groups: gender, marital status, annual income level, and age.
   a. Use logistic regression to classify the consumers on the basis of these explanatory variables. How successful is it? Which variables appear to be most important in the classification?
   b. Consider a new customer: Male, Married, Income $42,000, Age 47. Use the logistic regression equation to estimate the probability that this customer prefers Regular. How would you classify this person?

2. Using the same beer preference data in the file **P17_01.xlsx**, discretize the Income and Age variables according to their quartiles. Then use the naïve Bayes procedure to classify the 100 customers as having Regular or Light preference. Based on these results, consider a new customer: Male, Married, Income $42,000, Age 47. How would you classify this customer?

3. Admissions directors of graduate business programs constantly review the criteria they use to make admission decisions. Suppose that the director of a particular top-20 MBA program is trying to understand how she and her staff discriminate between those who are admitted to their program and those who are rejected. To do this, she collects data on each of the following variables for 100 randomly selected individuals who applied in the past academic year: whether the applicant graduated in the top 10% of his or her undergraduate class, whether the admissions office interviewed the applicant in person or over the telephone, the applicant's overall GMAT score (where the highest possible score is 800), and the applicant's undergraduate grade-point average (standardized on a four-point scale). These data are provided in the file **P17_03.xlsx**. How useful is logistic regression in discriminating between those who are admitted to this MBA program and those who are not on the basis of these variables?

4. Using the same admissions data in the file **P17_03.xlsx**, discretize the GMAT Score and Undergraduate GPA variables according to their quartiles. Then use the naïve Bayes procedure to classify the 100 applicants as Yes or No for admittance. (Remember that classifications can be based on the probabilities themselves, not necessarily their logs.) Based on these results, consider a new customer: in top 10% of undergraduate class, did not interview with admissions officer, GMAT 580, GPA 3.29. How would you classify this applicant?

5. A company that sells through a catalog and online through the Web has collected data on 10,000 potential customers. The data are in the file **P17_05.xlsx**. They include RFM (recency, frequency, and monetary) variables, which are popular in marketing research, as well as yes/no data on whether the person has received various advertising, and yes/no data on whether the person has made a catalog purchase or an online purchase in the latest time period.
   a. Use pivot tables to explore how or whether the Catalog Purchase variable in column I is influenced by the variables in columns B–H.
   b. Repeat part **a** for the Online Purchase variable in column J.

6. Continuing the previous problem, the same data have been split into two sets in the file **P17_06.xlsx**. The first 9500 observations are in the Training Data sheet, and the last 500 observations are in the Prediction Data sheet. In this latter sheet, the values in the Catalog Purchase and Online Purchase columns have been deleted. The purpose of this problem is to use NeuralTools to train a neural net with the data on the first sheet and then use this neural net to predict values on the second sheet. Proceed as follows.

a. Designate a NeuralTools data set for each sheet. The Customer and Catalog Purchase columns should be marked Unused, and the Online Purchase column should be marked Category Dependent. (The Catalog Purchase column is ignored in this problem.)

b. Use the NeuralTools Train option to train a neural net on the first data set, using the PNN algorithm. You can accept the option to set aside 20% of the 9500 observations for testing. Then interpret the outputs. In particular, can you tell how the neural net making its predictions?

c. Use the NeuralTools Predict option to predict Online Purchase for the observations in the Prediction Data sheet. What can you say about the resulting predictions? If you were forced to choose some people as most likely to make an online purchase, which people would you choose?

7. The file **P17_07.xlsx** contains data on 74 companies that have either gone bankrupt or haven't. The data set also contains data on five frequently quoted accounting ratios.

a. Create a pivot table that shows the average of each ratio, broken down by the Yes/No values in column G. Comment on which ratios seem to have an effect on whether a company goes bankrupt.

b. Use logistic regression to classify companies as bankrupt or not, using all five of the accounting ratios. Does this do a good job of classifying? Are any of the ratios insignificant?

c. Experiment with logistic regressions that use only two of the accounting ratios. Which pair classifies about as well as in part **b**, but with both ratios significant? Could the high p-values in part **b** be due to multicollinearity?

8. Using the same data as in the previous problem, use NeuralTools, with the PNN algorithm, to perform the classification. Even though there are only 74 companies, you can still use 20% of them for testing. Then at the end of the run, respond Yes to the sensitivity analysis. This lets you see how sensitive the percentage of bad predictions in the test data is to size or composition of the test data set. Comment on the results.

9. A classification algorithm was used to predict Yes/No values for a given training data set, and then the results were applied to 100 observations in a testing data set. The actual Yes/No values and the estimated probabilities of Yes for these 100 observations are listed in the file **P17_09.xlsx**. Calculate the same accuracy measures as in Figure 17.20 and create the corresponding ROC curve. Comment on how you would use it for future classifications.

Level B

10. The file **P17_10.xlsx** contains customer data on acceptance of products with various attributes. This is explained more fully in the file. There are three potential Yes/No dependent variables, Accept1, Accept2, and Accept3. To keep the outputs straight, it is a good idea to

store the results from the following three parts in separate files.

a. Use NeuralTools to classify the Accept1 dependent variable, ignoring Accept2 and Accept3. Try the PNN algorithm and then the MLF algorithm. Comparing their outputs, do they classify equally well? (Keep in mind that MLF takes a *lot* more computing time, but you can stop it prematurely if it doesn't seem to be making progress.)

b. Repeat part **a**, using Accept2 as the dependent variable and ignoring Accept1 and Accept3. You can skip the MLF algorithm for this part. However, respond Yes to run a sensitivity analysis at the end of the run. This lets you see how sensitive the percentage of bad predictions in the test data is to size or composition of the test data set. Comment on the results.

c. Repeat part **b**, using Accept3 as the dependent variable and ignoring Accept1 and Accept2.

11. The file **P17_11.xlsx** contains data on 178 wines. They are categorized into three types, labeled A, B, and C. The rest of the variables are numeric properties of the wines. Use NeuralTools to classify these wines. Use the PNN algorithm, and check the Variable Impact Analysis option in the Train dialog box. This ranks the variables on their impact, which provides some information on which variables might not be needed for the neural net. Then run the algorithm a second time, using only the top five variables in terms of their impact percentages. (In the Data Set Manager, mark the others Unused.) Comment on the results. Is the prediction accuracy much different without the deleted variables?

12. Continuing the previous problem, the file **P17_12.xlsx** contains the same wine data. Using a Microsoft Data Mining add-in (not discussed here), a decision tree classification was performed (with 0% of the cases held out for testing). You can see the resulting tree in the Tree sheet. Write out the corresponding decision rules implied by this tree. Then use a nested IF formula to make the classifications in column O of the Data sheet, and find the percentage of incorrect classifications. Would you say the decision tree is very accurate?

13. Neural nets (and NeuralTools) can also be used when the dependent variable is continuous, not categorical. In this case, the method is an alternative to multiple regression. The file **P17_13.xlsx** contains fairly old Boston housing data that appears frequently in data mining discussions. The original purpose was to use regression to see how the median value of a house (MEDVAL) depends on air quality, as measured by the variable NOX, after controlling for a number of other variables. The results of this regression appear in the Original Analysis sheet. As you can see on this sheet, the resulting RMSE (root mean square error) is about (in thousands of dollars). See if you can get better results with NeuralTools. Unlike the regression analysis, you don't need to create any nonlinear transformations—NeuralTools does this internally. Use the GRN algorithm, make sure the Perform Linear Regression option in the Net Configuration tab is *unchecked* and don't use any test cases. That is, use all of the cases for training. Discuss your results.

14. Continuing problem 6, there is another method that has been suggested when the dependent variable has only a small percentage of one category, in this case Y(yes). This is *oversampling*. To do this, you train the neural net on a subset that is more equally divided between Y and N values. This allows the net to "learn" better about the Y cases because it sees a much higher percentage of them. NeuralTools lets you do this fairly easily by creating a Tag variable, as explained in the file **P17_14.xlsx**. Then when you define the data set, you mark this variable as Tag. In general, each Tag value can be Train, Test,

or Predict, depending on how you want that case to be treated.

a. Run the PNN algorithm on the data in this file, using Online Purchase as the dependent variable, ignoring the Catalog Purchase variable, and using the given Tag variable. You will see in the Train dialog box how the Tag variable is recognized.

b. In the resulting output, you should see that the percentage of bad predictions for the training data is *larger* than the percentage of bad predictions for the testing data. However, using the classification matrices in the output, argue why this is actually misleading—that is, why the predictions are really *better* in the training data.

c. Are there any Y predictions for the prediction data (the last 500 rows)? What percentage?

17.3 Clustering Methods

In data mining terminology, the classification methods in the previous section are called **supervised** data mining methods. This term indicates that there is a dependent variable the method is trying to predict. In contrast, the clustering methods discussed in this section are called **unsupervised** data mining methods. Unsupervised methods have no dependent variable. Instead, they search for patterns and structure among all variables. *Clustering* is probably the most common unsupervised method, and it is the only one discussed here. However, another popular unsupervised method you might encounter is **market basket analysis** (also called **association analysis**), where patterns of customer purchases are examined to see which items customers tend to purchase together, in the same "market basket. " This analysis can be the basis for product shelving arrangements, for example.

Clustering, known in marketing circles as **segmentation**, tries to group entities (customers, companies, cities, or whatever) into similar clusters, based on the values of their variables. This method bears some relationship to classification, but the fundamental difference is that in clustering, there are no fixed groups like the triers and nontriers in classification. Instead, the purpose of clustering is to *discover* the number of groups and their characteristics, based entirely on the data.

Clustering methods have existed for decades, and a wide variety of clustering methods have been developed and implemented in software packages. The key to all of these is the development of a dissimilarity measure. Specifically, to compare two rows in a data set, you need a numeric measure of how dissimilar they are. Many such measures are used. For example, if two customers have the same gender, they might get a dissimilarity score of 0, whereas two customers of opposite genders might get a dissimilarity score of 1. Or if the incomes of two customers are compared, they might get a dissimilarity score equal to the squared difference between their incomes. The dissimilarity scores for different variables are then combined in some way, such as normalizing and then summing, to get a single dissimilarity score for the two rows as a whole.

Once a dissimilarity measure is developed, a clustering algorithm attempts to find clusters of rows where rows within a cluster are similar and rows in different clusters are dissimilar. Again, there are many ways to do this, and many variations appear in different software packages. For example, the package might let you specify the number of clusters ahead of time, or it might discover this number automatically.

Once an algorithm has discovered four clusters, for example, your job is to understand (and possibly name) these clusters. You do this by exploring the distributions of variables in different clusters. For example, you might find that one cluster is composed mostly of older women who live alone and have modest incomes, whereas another cluster is composed mostly of wealthy married men.

One of the most popular clustering algorithms is called **K-Means**, where K refers to the number of clusters. In this method, a "cluster center" is determined for each of the K clusters. Then using some measure of dissimilarity, or distance, each observation in the data set is assigned to the cluster it is closest to. The goal is to determine cluster centers such that observations in a given cluster are similar to one another, and observations in different clusters are dissimilar to one another. This becomes an optimization model for choosing the best cluster centers. You first choose a value of K and run the algorithm. Then you can experiment with different values of K.

Fortunately, the K-Means algorithm (at least one version of it) is fairly easy to implement with Excel-only formulas. This is illustrated in the following two examples.

EXAMPLE

17.4 CLUSTERING LARGE CITIES IN THE UNITED STATES

The file **City Clusters.xlsx** contains demographic data on 49 of the largest cities in the United States. Some of the data appear in the blue range of Figure 17.23. For example, Atlanta is 67% African American, 2% Hispanic, and 1% Asian. It has a median age of 31, a 5% unemployment rate, and a per-capita income of $22,000. The goal in this example is to group these 49 cities into four clusters of cities that are demographically similar. (You could then experiment with the number of clusters. For this discussion, the number is fixed at four.) The basic idea is to choose a city to anchor, or center, each cluster. Each city is then assigned to the nearest cluster center, where *nearest* is defined in terms of the six demographic variables. The objective is to minimize the sum of the distances from the 49 cities to their four cluster centers.

Figure 17.23 Demographic Data for Selected Cities

	A	B	C	D	E	F	G	H	I	J	K	L	M	N
13	City data								Standardized					
14	Index	City	PctAfrAmer	PctHispanic	PctAsian	MedianAge	UnempRate	PCIncome	PctAfrAmer	PctHispanic	PctAsian	MedianAge	UnempRate	PCIncome
15	1	Albuquerque	3	35	2	32	5	18	−1.179	1.239	−0.363	0.061	−0.751	−0.875
16	2	Atlanta	67	2	1	31	5	22	2.355	−0.764	−0.452	−0.440	−0.751	0.324
17	3	Austin	12	23	3	29	3	19	−0.682	0.510	−0.273	−1.442	−1.495	−0.575
18	4	Baltimore	59	1	1	33	11	22	1.913	−0.825	−0.452	0.562	1.480	0.324
19	5	Boston	26	11	5	30	5	24	0.091	−0.218	−0.093	−0.941	−0.751	0.924
20	6	Charlotte	32	1	2	32	3	20	0.423	−0.825	−0.363	0.061	−1.495	−0.275
21	7	Chicago	39	20	4	31	9	24	0.809	0.328	−0.183	−0.440	0.736	0.924
22	8	Cincinnati	38	1	1	31	8	21	0.754	−0.825	−0.452	−0.440	0.364	0.024
23	9	Cleveland	47	5	1	32	13	22	1.251	−0.582	−0.452	0.061	2.224	0.324
24	10	Columbus	23	1	2	29	3	13	−0.074	−0.825	−0.363	−1.442	−1.495	−2.375
25	11	Dallas	30	21	2	30	9	22	0.312	0.389	−0.363	−0.941	0.736	0.324
26	12	Denver	13	23	2	34	7	23	−0.627	0.510	−0.363	1.063	−0.008	0.624
27	13	Detroit	76	3	1	31	9	21	2.852	−0.704	−0.452	−0.440	0.736	0.024
28	14	El Paso	3	69	1	29	11	13	−1.179	3.303	−0.452	−1.442	1.480	−2.375
29	15	Fort Worth	22	20	2	30	9	20	−0.130	0.328	−0.363	−0.941	0.736	−0.275
30	16	Fresno	9	30	13	28	13	16	−0.847	0.935	0.624	−1.942	2.224	−1.475

Objective

To use Evolutionary Solver to find four cities to be used as cluster centers and to assign all other cities to one of these cluster centers.

Where Do the Numbers Come From?

The basic demographic data on cities are widely available. Note that the data used here are several years old, so the demographics may have changed slightly.

Solution

This example uses a variation of the usual K-means procedure (with K = 4) because its cluster centers are chosen from the existing 49 cities. In a typical K-means clustering, the cluster centers are not necessarily equal to any of the existing members, but the ideas are very similar. (Example 17.5 illustrates the more typical procedure.)

Regarding the data, if you use raw units, the percentages of African American and Hispanic will drive everything because these values are more spread out than the other demographic attributes. You can see this by calculating means and standard deviations of the characteristics. (See Figure 17.24, which also includes correlations between the attributes.) To remedy this problem, each demographic attribute is typically standardized by subtracting the attribute's mean and dividing the difference by the attribute's standard deviation. For example, the average city has 24.35% African Americans with a standard deviation of 18.11%. On a standardized basis, Atlanta is larger by $(67 - 24.35)/18.11 = 2.355$ standard deviations on the African-American attribute than a typical city. Working with standardized values for each attribute ensures that the analysis is unit-free. To create the standardized values shown in Figure 17.24, enter the formula

Figure 17.24 Summary Data for Demographic Attributes

	A	B	C	D	E	F	G
7		PctAfrAmer	PctHispanic	PctAsian	MedianAge	UnempRate	PCIncome
8	*One Variable Summary*	Data Set #1	Data Set #1	Data Set #1	Data Set #1	Data Set #1	Data Set #1
9	Mean	24.35	14.59	6.04	31.878	7.020	20.918
10	Std. Dev.	18.11	16.47	11.14	1.996	2.689	3.334
11							
12		PctAfrAmer	PctHispanic	PctAsian	MedianAge	UnempRate	PCIncome
13	*Correlation Table*	Data Set #1	Data Set #1	Data Set #1	Data Set #1	Data Set #1	Data Set #1
14	PctAfrAmer	1.000					
15	PctHispanic	−0.404	1.000				
16	PctAsian	−0.317	0.000	1.000			
17	MedianAge	0.010	−0.221	0.373	1.000		
18	UnempRate	0.308	0.341	−0.001	−0.007	1.000	
19	PCIncome	0.126	−0.298	0.374	0.480	0.014	1.000

=(C15-AVERAGE(C$15:C$63))/STDEV(C$15:C$63)

in cell I15 and copy it across to column N and down to row 63.

Developing the Spreadsheet Model
Now that all of the attributes have been standardized, you can develop the spreadsheet model as follows. It is shown in two parts in Figures 17.25 and 17.26.

Figure 17.25 Decision Variables and Objective Cell

	A	B	C	D	E	F	G	H
1	Clustering cities							
2								
3	Cluster centers and standardized values							
4		Column offset:	9	10	11	12	13	14
5	Cluster center	City index	PctAfrAmer	PctHispanic	PctAsian	MedianAge	UnempRate	PCIncome
6	San Francisco	43	−0.737	−0.036	2.060	2.065	−0.380	3.024
7	Philadelphia	35	0.864	−0.522	−0.273	0.562	0.736	0.624
8	Omaha	34	−0.627	−0.704	−0.452	0.061	−0.751	−0.275
9	Long Beach	23	−0.571	0.571	0.714	−0.941	0.364	0.024
10								
11	Sum of Distances	77.578						

1. **Lookup table.** One key to the model is to have an index (1 to 49) for the cities so that you can refer to them by index and then look up their characteristics with a VLOOKUP function. Therefore, name the range A15:N63 as LookupTable.
2. **Decision variables.** The only decision variable cells appear in the City_index range of Figure 17.25. They are the indexes of the four cities chosen as cluster centers. Enter any four integers from 1 to 49 in these cells.
3. **Corresponding cities and standardized attributes.** You can find the names and standardized attributes of the cluster centers with VLOOKUP functions. First, enter the function

=VLOOKUP(B6,LookupTable,2)

Figure 17.26 Other
Calculations for Cluster Analysis

	P	Q	R	S	T	U	V
13	Distances to centers					Assigned to	
14	To 1	To 2	To 3	To 4	Minimum	Index	Center
15	5.200	3.463	2.109	2.243	2.109	3	Omaha
16	5.487	2.371	3.083	3.646	2.371	2	Philadelphia
17	5.678	3.727	2.100	2.249	2.100	3	Omaha
18	5.193	1.367	3.472	3.616	1.367	2	Philadelphia
19	4.352	2.299	1.823	1.941	1.823	3	Omaha
20	4.897	2.517	1.295	2.941	1.295	3	Omaha
21	4.414	1.352	2.665	1.992	1.352	2	Philadelphia
22	4.998	1.280	1.873	2.306	1.280	2	Philadelphia
23	5.352	1.655	3.571	3.250	1.655	2	Philadelphia
24	7.044	4.356	2.747	3.581	2.747	3	Omaha
25	4.971	1.868	2.379	1.484	1.484	4	Long Beach
26	3.616	2.025	1.962	2.383	1.962	3	Omaha
27	6.013	2.320	3.828	3.885	2.320	2	Philadelphia
28	7.909	5.692	5.292	4.055	4.055	4	Long Beach
29	5.247	2.188	2.130	1.281	1.281	4	Long Beach
30	6.789	4.330	4.266	2.632	2.632	4	Long Beach
31	4.427	6.942	6.901	6.508	4.427	1	San Francisco

in cell A6 and copy it to the range A6:A9. Then enter the formula

=VLOOKUP($B6,LookupTable,C$4)

in C6 and copy it to the range C6:H9. Note, for example, that the standardized PctAfrAmer is the ninth column of the lookup table. This explains the column offset entries in row 4 of Figure 17.25.

4. **Distances to centers.** The next step is to see how far each city is from each of the cluster centers. Let z_i be standardized attribute i for a typical city, and let c_i be standardized attribute i for a typical cluster center. One way (but not the only way) to measure the distance from this city to this cluster center with the usual Euclidean distance formula

$$\text{Distance} = \sqrt{\sum_i (z_i - c_i)^2}$$

where the sum is over all six attributes. These distances appear in columns P through S of Figure 17.26. For example, the value in cell P15 is the distance from Albuquerque to the first cluster center (San Francisco), the value in Q15 is the distance from Albuquerque to the second cluster center (Philadelphia), and so on. These calculations can be performed in several equivalent ways. Probably the quickest way is to enter the formula

=SQRT(SUMXMY2($I15:$N15,$C$6:$H$6))

in cell P15 and copy it to the range P15:S63. (The function SUMXMY2 calculates the differences between the elements of the two range arguments and then sums the squares of these differences—exactly what is required.) The copied versions in columns Q, R, and S then have to be modified slightly. Each 6 in the second range argument needs to be changed to 7 in column Q, to 8 in column R, and to 9 in column S.

5. **Assignments to cluster centers.** Each city is assigned to the cluster center that has the smallest distance. Therefore, find the minimum distances in column T by entering the formula

=MIN(P15:S15)

in cell T15 and copying it down. Then you can identify the cluster index (1 through 4) and city name of the cluster center that yields the minimum with the MATCH function. Specifically, enter the formula

=MATCH(T15,P15:S15,0)

in cell U15 and copy it down. For example, the 2.109 minimum distance for Albuquerque corresponds to the third distance, so Albuquerque is assigned to the third cluster center. Finally, to get the *name* of the third cluster center, you can use the INDEX function. Enter the formula

=INDEX(Cluster_center,U15,l)

in cell V15 and copy it down. This formula returns the name in the second row and first (only) column of the Cluster_ center range (in Figure 17.25).

Excel Tip

INDEX

The function INDEX, using the syntax **INDEX(*Range,Row,Column*)**, is usually used to return the value in a given row and column of a specified range. For example, INDEX(*A5:C10,3,2*) returns the value in the third row and second column of the range *A5:C10,* that is, the value in cell *B7.* If the given range is a single row, the row argument can be omitted. If the given range is a single column, the column argument can be omitted.

---

6. **Sum of distances.** The objective is to minimize the sum of distances from all cities to the cluster centers to which they are assigned. Calculate this objective in cell B11 (in Figure 14.25) with the formula

=SUM(T15:T63)

Using Evolutionary Solver

The Solver dialog box should be set up as shown in Figure 17.27. Because the decision variable cells represent *indexes* of cluster centers, they must be integer-constrained, and suitable lower and upper limits are 1 and 49 (the number of cities). This problem is considerably more difficult to solve, so you should use Evolutionary Solver and allow plenty of time to search through a lot of potential solutions. (Actually, it finds the optimal solution very quickly, but then it runs a long time to *verify* that this solution is optimal.)

Figure 17.27 Solver Dialog Box for Cluster Model

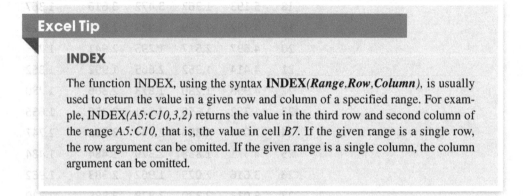

Discussion of the Solution

The solution in Figure 17.28, which uses Los Angeles, Memphis, Omaha, and San Francisco, is the best we found. You might find a slightly different solution, depending on your Solver settings and how long you let Solver run, but you should obtain a similar value in the objective cell. If you look closely at the cities assigned to each cluster center, this solution begins to make intuitive sense. The San Francisco cluster consists of rich, older, highly Asian cities. The Memphis cluster consists of highly African-American cities with high unemployment rates. The Omaha cluster consists of average income cities with few minorities. The Los Angeles cluster consists of highly Hispanic cities with high unemployment rates.

In cluster analysis, the number of clusters is typically unknown ahead of time. Some experimentation with the number of clusters is usually required.

Why four clusters? You could easily try three clusters or five clusters. However, when the number of clusters increases, the sum of distances will certainly decrease. In fact, you could obtain an objective value of 0 by using 49 clusters, one for each city, but this wouldn't provide any useful information. Therefore, to choose the "best" number of clusters, the typical approach is to stop adding clusters when the sum of distances fails to decrease by a substantial amount.

Figure 17.28 Clusters in the Solver Solution

	W	X	Y	Z	AA
13	**Clusters**				
14	Center:	Los Angeles	Memphis	Omaha	San Francisco
15		Dallas	Atlanta	Albuquerque	Honolulu
16		El Paso	Baltimore	Austin	San Francisco
17		Fort Worth	Chicago	Boston	Seattle
18		Fresno	Cincinnati	Charlotte	
19		Houston	Cleveland	Columbus	
20		Long Beach	Detroit	Denver	
21		Los Angeles	Memphis	Indianapolis	
22		Miami	New Orleans	Jacksonville	
23		NY	Oakland	Kansas City	
24		San Antonio	Philadelphia	Las Vegas	
25		San Diego	St. Louis	Milwaukee	
26		San Jose		Minneapolis	
27				Nashville	
28				Oklahoma City	
29				Omaha	
30				Phoenix	
31				Pittsburgh	
32				Portland	
33				Sacramento	
34				Toledo	
35				Tucson	
36				Tulsa	
37				Virginia Beach	

EXAMPLE

17.5 CLUSTERING CUSTOMERS FOR SHOES

The file **Shoe Sales Clusters.xlsx** contains data on 3000 transactions made by 250 customers. (See Figure 17.29.) Each transaction is for a dollar amount spent on one of five categories of shoes: athletic, dress, work, casual, or sandal. The goal is to find clusters of customers who have similar buying behavior. How can this be done in Excel?

Objective

To see how cluster analysis can be implemented in Excel to find clusters of customers with similar shoe-buying behavior.

Solution

We want to cluster *customers*, not transactions, so we need to transform the data set in Figure 17.29, where each row is a transaction, to a data set where each row is a customer. This can be done with COUNTIFS and SUMIFS functions (or with pivot

Figure 17.29 Shoe Transaction Data Set

	A	B	C	D
1	Transaction	CustID	Type	Spent
2	1	210	Sandal	29
3	2	7	Work	74
4	3	220	Dress	134
5	4	93	Athletic	150
6	5	66	Athletic	168
7	6	232	Dress	125
2998	2997	53	Athletic	67
2999	2998	136	Casual	27
3000	2999	173	Work	85
3001	3000	141	Work	276

tables), as shown in Figure 17.30. We have done this two ways, and either can be the basis for a cluster analysis. Both of these tables have 250 rows, one for each customer. The table on the left shows counts of transactions, broken down by shoe type. Its typical formula, in cell B3, is

=COUNTIFS(Data!$B$2:$B$3001, $A3, Data!$C$2:$C$3001, B$2)

The table on the right shows sums of amount spent, again broken down by shoe type. Its typical formula, in cell 13, is

=SUMIFS(Data!$D$2:$D$3001, Data!$B$2:$B$3001, $A3, Data!$C$2:$C$3001, I$2)

Figure 17.30 Pivot Tables for Customers

	A	B	C	D	E	F	G	H	I	J	K	L	M
1	Transaction counts							Dollar sums					
2	CustID	Athletic	Casual	Dress	Sandal	Work		CustID	Athletic	Casual	Dress	Sandal	Work
3	1	10	2	2	1	1		1	1257	77	719	42	184
4	2	0	7	1	3	1		2	0	499	190	160	170
5	3	0	1	9	0	0		3	0	42	1768	0	0
6	4	9	5	0	0	0		4	1862	381	0	0	0
7	5	9	2	0	1	2		5	1221	157	0	84	142
8	6	3	2	8	6	0		6	664	153	1612	320	0
9	7	1	1	1	1	8		7	61	74	117	82	914
10	8	0	3	1	4	2		8	0	221	214	260	361
11	9	1	2	3	1	7		9	348	279	600	70	651
12	10	1	5	1	0	10		10	124	244	322	0	1051
13	11	1	5	8	6	2		11	55	159	1215	297	159
14	12	0	3	6	1	1		12	0	188	1094	94	144

The finished version of the file shows two cluster analyses, one based on each of these tables. We will focus only on the transaction counts here, but both cluster analyses lead to similar results.

The counts in the first table are then copied to another sheet, shown in Figure 17.31. Each row corresponds to a customer, and each column from B to F represents an "attribute" for the cluster analysis. Typically, the attribute columns can be of very different magnitudes (although this isn't the case here), so it is again useful to standardize them in some way. For illustration, we have expressed each as a percentage of the maximum value in its column. These percentages appear in columns G to K. This isn't the only way to standardize, but it has the attractive property that each standardized value is between 0 and 1.

Figure 17.31 Customer Counts and Standardized Counts

	A	B	C	D	E	F	G	H	I	J	K
1	Transaction counts						% of max in column				
2											
3	CustID	Athletic	Casual	Dress	Sandal	Work	Athletic%	Casual%	Dress%	Sandal%	Work%
4	1	10	2	2	1	1	0.833333	0.2	0.142857	0.125	0.076923
5	2	0	7	1	3	1	0	0.7	0.071429	0.375	0.076923
6	3	0	1	9	0	0	0	0.1	0.642857	0	0
7	4	9	5	0	0	0	0.75	0.5	0	0	0
8	5	9	2	0	1	2	0.75	0.2	0	0.125	0.153846
9	6	3	2	8	6	0	0.25	0.2	0.571429	0.75	0
10	7	1	1	1	1	8	0.083333	0.1	0.071429	0.125	0.615385
11	8	0	3	1	4	2	0	0.3	0.071429	0.5	0.153846
12	9	1	2	3	1	7	0.083333	0.2	0.214286	0.125	0.538462
13	10	1	5	1	0	10	0.083333	0.5	0.071429	0	0.769231

Next we perform the K-Means procedure, shown in Figure 17.32. We have somewhat arbitrarily chosen K = 4, so that four clusters will be used. (We ask you in the problems to rerun the analysis with other values of K.) We need four cluster centers, listed in columns T to X. Each cluster center is a set of attribute values, and because of the way we standardized, each of these attribute values should be between 0 and 1. *Any* values can be used initially; Solver will eventually be used to find the "best" cluster centers. (Again, this contrasts with the previous example, where we required each cluster center to be one of the existing 49 cities.) For any given cluster centers, we find the "distance" from each customer's standardized attributes to each cluster center. Various distance measures are used in cluster analysis, but we will again use the popular Euclidean (straight-line) distance measure: the square root of the sum of squared differences. There are several ways to implement this in Excel, but we have used a combination of the SUMXMY2 (sum of squared X minus Y values) and the OFFSET function. The formula in cell L4, which can be copied down and across, is

Figure 17.32 K-Means Procedure

	L	M	N	O	P	Q	R	S	T	U	V	W	X
1	Distances to cluster centers							Cluster centers (decision variable cells)					
2								ClusterID	Athletic	Casual	Dress	Sandal	Work
3	1	2	3	4	Min Dist	Cluster		1	0.057971	0.239528	0.415672	0.238348	0.046336
4	0.83124	0.905869	0.231257	0.946315	0.231257	3		2	0.034539	0.327508	0.067711	0.072579	0.474255
5	0.594565	0.62393	0.83213	0.249242	0.249242	4		3	0.634545	0.25512	0.057822	0.074008	0.043852
6	0.365238	0.783538	0.881122	0.884916	0.365238	1		4	0.052704	0.528175	0.097712	0.544528	0.05719
7	0.882321	0.881141	0.289896	0.892381	0.289896	3							
8	0.823199	0.798835	0.1855	0.888152	0.1855	3		Total distance	68.61493				
9	0.571518	1.000115	0.934662	0.645384	0.571518	1							
10	0.689405	0.277164	0.81076	0.82009	0.277164	2							

=SQRT(SUMXMY2($G4:$K4,OFFSET($T$2,L$3,0,1,5)))

The range G4:K4 contains the standardized attributes for this particular customer, and the OFFSET function uses the indexes in row 3 to return the attributes for the appropriate cluster center. Then each customer is assigned to the cluster with the minimum distance. The formulas in cells P4 and Q4 are

=MIN(L4:O4)

and

=MATCH(P4,L4:O4,0)

The total distance over all customers in cell T8, the sum of the values in column P, is then the objective to be minimized. The Solver setup appears in Figure 17.33. The decision variable cells are the cluster centers, and they are constrained to be between 0 and 1. We have again used the Evolutionary method instead of the GRG Nonlinear method. This is a highly nonlinear (and nonsmooth) problem, and the Evolutionary method is more reliable.

The last step is to make sense of the clusters. To do this, it is useful to return to the transaction data, but with cluster IDs attached. This is shown in Figure 17.34. (Each cluster ID in column E is based on a lookup of the CustID in the table in Figures 17.31 and 17.32.) Then a table of transaction counts and an associated chart can be created, as shown in Figure 17.35. Each value in the table represents the number of transactions for a given shoe type made by customers in a given cluster. The typical formula, in cell B3, is

=SUMIF('Cluster by Count'!$Q$4:$Q$253,$A3,'Cluster by Count'!B$4:B$253)

(Again, these counts could be found more easily with pivot tables.)

It is particularly useful to use a chart of the stacked column type, where each piece of each column represents that cluster's percentage of all transactions made by that cluster. As described in the text box, the "meaning" of the clusters is then quite apparent. The shoe company could assign other customers (that is, other than these 250) to the given clusters, based on their past buying behavior. Then it could devise specific promotions for each cluster and target market to customers based on their cluster membership.

Figure 17.33
Solver Dialog Box
for Finding Optimal
Cluster Centers

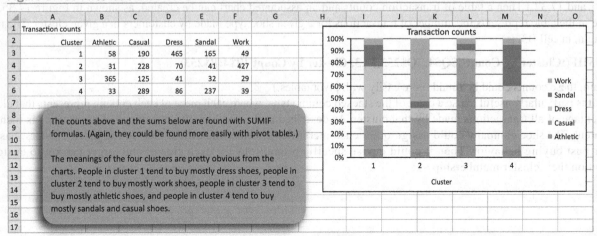

Solver Parameters ☒

Set Objective: $STS8

To: ○ Max ● Min ○ Value Of: 0

By Changing Variable Cells:
$TS3:$X$6

Subject to the Constraints:
$TS3:$X$6 <= 1

Add
Change
Delete
Reset All
Load/Save

☑ Make Unconstrained Variables Non-Negative

Select a Solving Method: Evolutionary   Options

Solving Method
Select the GRG Nonlinear engine for Solver Problems that are smooth nonlinear. Select the LP Simplex engine for linear Solver Problems, and select the Evolutionary engine for Solver problems that are non-smooth.

Help   Solve   Close

Figure 17.34
Transaction Data with
Cluster IDs

	A	B	C	D	E
1	Transaction	CustID	Type	Spent	Count Cluster
2	1	210	Sandal	29	1
3	2	7	Work	74	2
4	3	220	Dress	134	1
5	4	93	Athletic	150	1
6	5	66	Athletic	168	3
7	6	232	Dress	125	1
8	7	132	Work	72	2
9	8	82	Casual	102	4
10	9	72	Work	66	2
11	10	99	Casual	74	2

Figure 17.35 Pivot Table and Pivot Chart of Transaction Counts

	A	B	C	D	E	F
1	Transaction counts					
2	Cluster	Athletic	Casual	Dress	Sandal	Work
3	1	58	190	465	165	49
4	2	31	228	70	41	427
5	3	365	125	41	32	29
6	4	33	289	86	237	39

The counts above and the sums below are found with SUMIF formulas. (Again, they could be found more easily with pivot tables.)

The meanings of the four clusters are pretty obvious from the charts. People in cluster 1 tend to buy mostly dress shoes, people in cluster 2 tend to buy mostly work shoes, people in cluster 3 tend to buy mostly athletic shoes, and people in cluster 4 tend to buy mostly sandals and casual shoes.

A difficult issue in cluster analysis is finding the distance between two rows of attributes. We solved this fairly easily in the previous example because all attributes contain positive numeric values. We standardized these to values between 0 and 1 and then used the Euclidean distance measure. But what if some attributes are text, such as Male/Female or Democrat/Republican/Independent? How can you measure the "distance" between a Democrat male earning $60,000 and a Republican female earning $80,000? Let's just say that various distance measures have been proposed. You are asked to explore some possibilities in one of the problems.

Problems

Level A

15. The file **P17_15.xlsx** contains the following information about the top 25 MBA programs (according to the 1997 Business Week Guide): percentage of applicants accepted, percentage of accepted applicants who enroll, mean GMAT score of enrollees, mean undergraduate GPA of enrollees, annual cost of school (for state schools, this is the cost for out-of-state students), percentage of students who are minorities, percentage of students who are non-U. S. residents, and mean starting salary of graduates (in thousands of dollars). Use these data and the method of Example 17.4 to divide the top 25 schools into four clusters. Then interpret your clusters.

16. The file **P17_16.xlsx** contains various data on 325 metropolitan cities in the United States. Cell comments in row 1 explain some of the variables. A Microsoft Data Mining add-in (not discussed here) was used to cluster these cities, with the results shown in the file. There are four clusters, cluster membership is listed in column V of the Data sheet, and the composition of clusters is in the Categories Report sheet. Study this report carefully, and then write a short report about the clusters. Does the clustering make sense? Can you provide descriptive, meaningful names for the clusters?

17. Continuing problem 11, the file **P17_17.xlsx** contains the same wine data. Instead of trying to use a classification algorithm to classify wines into the three known types (A, B, and C), it is interesting to see if a clustering algorithm can *discover* these known categories. The file contains the results of two runs of a Microsoft Data Mining Detect Categories algorithm (not discussed here). Of course, neither uses the Type variable in column A. The first run didn't specify the number of categories, and the add-in found 7, with category membership in column O of the Data sheet. The second run specified the number of categories as 3, with category membership in column P of the Data sheet. Analyze the results closely. Do either (or both) of the runs seem to discover the known A, B, and C types?

Level B

18. Using the data in the file **P17_18.xlsx**, the same data as in Problem 16, use the method in Example 17.5 to find four clusters of cities. Note that there are two text variables, Crime_Trend and Unemployment_Threat. You can ignore them for this problem. Write a short report about the clusters you find. Does the clustering make sense? Can you provide descriptive, meaningful names for the clusters?

19. Using the data in the file **P17_11.xlsx**, the same data as in Problem 17, use the method in Example 17.5 to find three clusters of wine types. (Of course, don't use the Type variable when creating clusters.) Write a short report about the clusters you find. Does the clustering agree with the Type variable?

20. This problem lets you see how dissimilarity, the key to clustering, might be calculated and then used for prediction. The file **P17_20.xlsx** contains data for 10 people. The value of Amount Spent for person 10 is unknown, and the ultimate purpose is to use the data for the first 9 people to predict Amount Spent for person 10. To do so, a common "nearest neighbor" approach is used. You find the three most similar people to person 10 and then use the average of their Amount Spent values as a prediction for person 10. Proceed as follows.
    a. For each of the five attributes, Gender to Marital Status, fill in the corresponding yellow boxes as indicated. Each box shows how dissimilar each person is to each other person, based on a single attribute only. The box for Gender has been filled in to get you started.
    b. These yellow values can be combined in at least three ways, as indicated by the cell comments above the orange boxes. Fill in these orange boxes.
    c. Find the dissimilarity between each person and person 10 in three ways in the blue box at the top, following the cell comment in cell 12.
    d. Use Excel's RANK function in the green box to rank the dissimilarities in the blue box.
    e. Find three predictions of Amount Spent for person 10, each an average of Amount Spent for the three most similar people to person 10. There will be *three* predictions because each set of rankings in the green box can lead to a different set of three nearest neighbors.

17.4 Conclusion

Data mining is a huge topic, and its importance is becoming increasingly important in business and other areas. Admittedly, data analysis has played an important role for many years, but large data sets are now more common than ever before, and better algorithms, better software, and better technology in general are now available to mine large data sets. The discussion in this chapter provides only a glimpse of the variety of problems data mining can attack and the types of methods it can employ. Indeed, an increasing number of books on data mining, some highly technical and others much less technical, are being written.[6] Finally, it is important to realize that data mining is only part, although a very important part, of "business analytics." For example, business analytics often uses the insights from data mining to optimize a system. The optimization aspect is not usually included in the realm of data mining, but data mining as a first step often enables an intelligent optimization.

Summary of Key Terms

TERM	EXPLANATION	EXCEL	PAGE
Data mining	Variety of methods used to discover patterns in data sets, usually large data sets		772
Data warehouse	Specially constructed database that can be used for data mining		772
Data mart	Scaled-down data warehouse for a particular business function or department		772
SQL Server Analysis Services (SSAS)	Part of SQL Server (Microsoft's server-based database package) that performs data mining analysis		775
Classification methods	Methods for predicting a dependent categorical variable from given explanatory variables		774
Data partitioning	Dividing large data set into training and testing subsets so that algorithms trained on one set can be tested on the other	Available in NeuralTools, not in StatTools	774
Logistic regression	Classification method where the logit is estimated as a linear function of the explanatory variables	StatTools Regression & Classification group	775
Odds ratio	Ratio of p to $1-p$, where p is the probability of a given category		775
Logit	Logarithm of the odds ratio		776
Neural network (or neural net)	Complex nonlinear method for classification or prediction, attempts to mimic the human brain		779
NeuralTools	Add-in in the Palisade DecisionTools suite, used for implementing neural nets	NeuralTools tab	780
Classification Trees (or Decision Trees)	Classification method that splits sets of cases so that subsets become purer in terms of composition of categories		788
Lift	Data mining term, the ability to determine the most likely responders to a mail campaign, for example		791

---

6 To appreciate how big this topic is becoming, just watch TV ads by IBM and other companies. You might also want to read two recent books: *In the Plex*, by Levy and Ganser, Simon & Schuster, 2011; and *Big Data*, by Mayer-Schonberger and Cukier, Eamon Dolan/Houghton Mifflin Harcourt, 2013. The former, mostly about the many ways data mining is used at Google, is mind-blowing.

Key Terms (continued)

TERM	EXPLANATION	EXCEL	PAGE
Supervised versus unsupervised data mining methods	Supervised methods try to predict a dependent variable; unsupervised methods don't have a dependent variable		795
Clustering (or segmentation)	Unsupervised method, tries to attach cases to categories (clusters), with high similarity within categories and high dissimilarity across categories		795
Market basket analysis (or association analysis)	Where patterns of customer purchases are examined to see which items customers tend to purchase together, in the same "market basket."		795

Problems

Conceptual Questions

C.1. How does the general classification problem discussed in Section 17-3 differ from the general problem analyzed with regression, and why does standard regression not work for the classification problem?

C.2. What is the main purpose of logistic regression, and how does it differ from the type of regression, discussed in Chapters 10 and 11?

C.3. Suppose that a term in a logistic regression equation is 0.687*MallTrips, as in Figure 17.17. Explain, exactly what this means.

Level A

21. The lasagna data discussed in the chapter is repeated in the file **17_21.xlsx**. Instead of trying to classify a dependent variable, Have Tried, this file shows the result of clustering. Specifically, a Microsoft Data Mining Detect Categories algorithm (not discussed here) was used, arbitrarily specifying the number of categories as 3. Also, the Have Tried variable was treated just like all of the other variables. Using the results in the Categories_Report sheet, what can you say about the composition of the categories the algorithm found? How might you "name" these categories?

22. The file **P17_22.xlsx** contains the following data on 84 people: annual income, amount invested in the stock market, and a 0-1 variable on whether they subscribe to the Wall Street Journal.
  a. Use logistic regression to classify these people on whether they are subscribers. How accurate are the classifications?
  b. Repeat part **a** but use neural networks (with no data partition). Is this method more accurate for this data set than logistic regression?

23. The file **P17_23.xlsx** contains data on 80 (fictional) houses, including their selling prices, although the selling price is missing for the first house. It turns out that

C.4. Suppose you are trying to classify a variable where 96% of its observations equal 0 and only 4% equal 1. You run a logistic reg-ression, and the classification table shows that 97% of the classifications are correct. Why might this large percentage still not be cause for celebration?

C.5. What are the strengths and drawbacks of neural nets versus classification trees?

C.6. Clustering algorithms always start with a dissimilarity measure. Why it is not always obvious how to develop such a measure?

when the dependent variable is numeric, NeuralTools can compare a linear regression with a neural net. If the regression has a lower RMSE than the neural net on the test cases, then the regression equation is used for prediction; otherwise, the neural net is used for prediction. Run NeuralTools on this data set. In the Training dialog box, accept all the defaults, including the option to Perform Linear Regression on the Net Configuration tab, but check the Place Predicted Values Directly in Data Set option on the Train tab. You will get a prediction of the selling price of the first house on the Data sheet. Can you explain, in detail, how this prediction is calculated?

Level B

24. This problem (originally created by Palisade) is a test of a neural net's ability to learn. The file **P17_24.xlsx** contains data on three numbers, two operations, and two results. The first two numbers are combined with Operation1 (add or subtract) to produce Result1. That is, Result1 is either Number1 + Number2 or Number1 − Number2. Then the third number and Result1 are combined with Operation2 (add, subtract, or multiply) to produce Result2. That is, Result2 is either Result1 + Number3, Result1 − Number3, or Result1 * Number3.

The question is whether a neural net, with a numeric dependent variable, can discover the pattern and accurately predict Result2. Note that the value of Result2 is missing for the first three observations. You can figure out these three values, but can a neural net?

a. Use NeuralTools to perform the prediction, using columns A–F as predictors. Specifically, accept all the defaults in the Training dialog box, but check the Place Predicted Values Directly in Data Set option. (At the end of the run, you can respond No to the sensitivity analysis.) In this case, NeuralTools performs linear regression, as in Chapters 10 and 11, with dummies for the Operation variables, *and* it compares this with a neural net. Now "bad" predictions are defined as those off by at least 30%, and RMSE is a measure of overall accuracy. Comment on how well the neural net predicts and how it compares to linear regression. How accurate are its predictions of the three missing values?

b. There are currently only 1000 observations. Create a new file with these 1000 observations plus 9000 more tacked on to the bottom and repeat part **a** on this larger data set. The question is whether a neural net trained on more data is more accurate. (For the new data, generate uniformly distributed random numbers in columns A–C, generate "add" or "subtract" in column D with probability 0.5 each, generate "add" or "subtract" or "multiply" in column E with probability 1/3 each, and calculate columns F and G accordingly. Then copy all the new data and paste it over itself as values before using NeuralTools.)

25. The file **P17_25.xlsx** contains Gender, Age, Education, and Success (Yes/No) data of 1000 people. The purpose is to see how a classification tree method can use the first three variables to classify Success. You start with 564 Yes values and 436 No values. This is quite diverse (close to 50–50), and as explained in the file, it has a diversity index of 0.9836, the highest being 1. The question you are asked to explore is which splits you should make to reduce this diversity index—that is, to make the subsets purer. Directions are given in the file. (The method suggested is only one variation of splitting and measuring diversity in classification trees. When a Microsoft Data Mining add-in (not discussed here) is used on this data set, it finds an extremely simple rule: Classify as Yes if Education is UG or G, and classify as No if Education is HS. This is probably slightly different from what your method will find.)

CASE   17.1 Houston Area Survey

The Kinder Institute at Rice University in Houston has surveyed people in the Houston area for several decades on a multitude of issues. An explanation of the research, along with a "codebook" for the survey questions through the years, is available in the file **Houston Area Survey Codebook (1982-2014).pdf**. A subset of the data from the most recent survey in 2014 is available in the file **C17_01.xlsx**. This file contains data on about 1750 responders on over 80 variables (survey questions).

An explanation of the variables is included in the Variables sheet. These variables have been color-coded according to several broad topics and categories within these topics. This sheet lists the survey questions and the possible responses. Most of the questions have only a few possible responses, such as Male/Female or Better off/About the same/ Worse off, but a few have numeric responses with many possible values.

In the full data set from 2014, there were many more variables, but about a third of them were deleted to produce the Excel file for this case. Many of the deleted variables had a large number of missing values, which made them unsuitable for our purposes. However, a few of the remaining variables also have some missing values. In addition, most of the remaining variables have several RF/DK values. These correspond to "Refused to answer" or "Didn't know" responses.

The last two columns of the Variables sheet indicate the number of RF/DK and Blank cells for each variable.

The last sheet in the file contains a simple pivot table for your convenience. It lets you see the counts of possible responses for any of the questions. In this way, you can quickly get some insights into the data.

In terms of real-world surveys of this type, this Excel file is not at all large. It has "only" about 1750 rows and about 80 columns. Still, this data set is large enough to raise the questions, "What data mining questions should I ask" or "Where do I begin?" We won't provide answers to these questions. The only guidelines we will provide are the following:

1. Use pivot tables (or PowerPivot) to find interesting breakdowns of the data.
2. Choose a dependent variable with only two possible values and a set of explanatory variables (which doesn't need to be *all* of the potential variables). Then use one or more classification methods to "explain" the dependent variable.
3. Use a subset (of your choosing) to run a cluster analysis on the data. You can choose the number of clusters. Once you have created the clusters, try to explain what each one is all about.

REFERENCES

Afshartous, D. "Sample Size Determination for Binomial Proportion Confidence Intervals: An Alternative Perspective Motivated by a Legal Case." *The American Statistician* 62, no. 1 (2008): 27–31.

Allen, J.D., R. Tobin, and A. Calderan. "Verizon Optimizes Work Center Locations to Reduce Installation and Repair Operations Costs." *Interfaces* 47, no. 2 (2017): 111–121.

Appleton, D., J. French, and M. Vanderpump. "Ignoring a Covariate: An Example of Simpson's Paradox." *The American Statistician* 50 (1996): 340–341.

Armstrong, S. "Research on Forecasting: A Quarter-Century Review, 1960–1984." *Interfaces* 16, no. 1 (1986): 89–103.

Babich, P. "Customer Satisfaction: How Good Is Good Enough?" *Quality Progress* 25 (1992): 65–68.

Balson, W., J. Welsh, and D. Wilson. "Using Decision Analysis and Risk Analysis to Manage Utility Environmental Risk." *Interfaces* 22, no. 6 (1992): 126–139.

Bean, J., C. Noon, and G. Salton. "Asset Divestiture at Homart Development Company." *Interfaces* 17, no. 1 (1987): 48–65.

Bean, J., C. Noon, S. Ryan, and G. Salton. "Selecting Tenants in a Shopping Mall." *Interfaces* 18, no. 2 (1988): 1–10.

Berger, P., and R. Maurer. *Experimental Design.* Belmont, CA: Duxbury, 2002.

Blyth, C. "On Simpson's Paradox and the Sure-Thing Principle." *Journal of the American Statistical Association* 67 (1972): 364–366.

Brinkley, P., D. Stepto, J. Haag, K. Liou, K. Wang, and W. Carr. "Nortel Redefines Factory Information Technology: An OR-Driven Approach." *Interfaces* 28, no. 1 (1998): 37–52.

Camm, J., M. Fry, and J. Shaffer. "A Practitioner's Guide to Best Practices in Data Visualization." *Interfaces* 47, no. 6 (2017): 473–488.

Carreyrou, J. *Bad Blood.* Knopf, 2018.

Cawley, J., and P. Sommers, "Voting Irregularities in the 1995 Referendum on Quebec Sovereignty." *Chance* 9, no. 4 (Fall 1996): 29–30.

Collie, R., and B. Jelen. *Power Pivot Alchemy.* Uniontown, OH: Holy Macro! Books, 2014.

Deming, E., *Out of the Crisis.* Cambridge, MA: MIT Center for Advanced Engineering Study, 1986.

DeVor, R., T. Chang, and J. Sutherland. *Statistial Quality Design and Control.* New York: Macmillan, 1992.

Ferrari, A., and M. Russo. *The Definitive Guide to DAX.* Redmund, WA: Microsoft Press, 2015.

Ferrari, A., and M. Russo. *Analyzing Data with Microsoft Power BI and Power Pivot for Excel.* Redmund, WA: Microsoft Press, 2017.

Hammond, J., R. Keeney, and H. Raiffa. *Smart Choices.* Harvard Business Review Press, 2015.

Herrnstein, R., and C. Murray. *The Bell Curve.* Free Press, 1994.

Hoppensteadt, F., and C. Peskin. *Mathematics in Medicine and the Life Sciences.* New York: Springer-Verlag, 1992.

Howard, R. "Decision Analysis: Practice and Promise." *Management Science* 34, no. 6 (1988): 679–695.

Huntsinger, G., R. Burk, T. Trainor. "The US Army Projects the Effect of Merit Pay on Payroll Growth." *Interfaces* 42, no. 4 (2012): 395–405.

Hutton, D., M. Brandeau, and S. So. "Doing Good with OR: Supporting Cost-Effective Hepatitis B Interventions." *Interfaces* 41, no. 3 (2011): 289–300.

Inman, R., M. Frick, T. Hitchman, R. Muiter, J. Owen, and G. Takasaki. "Optimizing New-Vehicle Inventory at General Motors." *Interfaces* 45, no. 5 (2017): 396–410.

Kelly, J. "A New Interpretation of Information Rate." *Bell System Technical Journal* 35 (1956): 917–926.

Kirkwood, C. "An Overview of Methods for Applied Decision Analysis." *Interfaces* 22, no. 6 (1992): 28–39.

Kutner, M. H., C. J. Nachtsheim, J. Neter, and W. Li. *Applied Linear Statistical Models.* 5th ed. New York: McGraw-Hill/Irwin, 2005.

LeBlanc, L., M. Bartolacci, and T. Grossman. "Increasing Productivity and Minimizing Errors in Operations Research Spreadsheet Models." *Interfaces* 47, no. 3 (2018): 260–269.

Levine, E., J. Tisch, A. Tasso, and M. Joy. "The New York City Police Department's Domain Awareness System." *Interfaces* 47, no. 1 (2017): 70–84.

Levy, P., and S. Lemeshow. *Sampling of Populations: Methods and Applications.* 4th ed. New York: Wiley, 2008.

Lindsey, G. "Statistical Data Useful for the Operation of a Baseball Team." *Operations Research* 7, no. 2 (1959): 197–207.

Love, R., and J. Hoey. "Management Science Improves Fast Food Operations." *Interfaces* 20, no. 2 (1990): 21–29.

Marcus, A. "The Magellan Fund and Market Efficiency." *Journal of Portfolio Management* (Fall 1990): 85–88.

McDaniel, S., and L. Kinney. "Ambush Marketing Revisited: An Experimental Study of Perceived Sponsorship Effects on Brand Awareness, Attitude Toward the Brand, and Purchase Intention." *Journal of Promotion Management* 3 (1996): 141–167.

Metters, R., C. Queenan, M. Ferguson, L. Harrison, J. Higbie, S. Ward, B. Barfield, T. Farley, H. A. Kuyumcu, and A. Duggasani. "The Killer Application of Revenue Management: Harrah's Cherokee Casino & Hotel." *Interfaces* 38, no. 3 (2008): 161–175.

Morrison, D., and R. Wheat. "Pulling the Goalie Revisited." *Interfaces* 16, no. 6 (1984): 28–34.

Patterson, S. *The Quants.* Random House, 2010.

Power Pivot Alchemy, 2014.

Press, S.J. "Sample-Audit Tax Assessment for Businesses: What's Fair?" *Journal of Business & Economic Statistics* 13, no. 3 (1995): 357–359.

Reichheld, F. *The Loyalty Effect.* Boston, MA: Harvard Business School Press, 1996.

Roselka, R. "The New Mantra: MVT." *Forbes* (March 11, 1996): 114–118.

Sagaert, Y. E. A., N. Kourentzes, and B. Desmet. "Temporal Big Data for Tactical Sales Forecasting in the Tire Industry." *Interfaces* 48, no. 2 (2018): 121–129.

Savage, S., S. Scholtes, and D. Zweidler. "*Probability Management, Part 1.*" OR/MS Today, Feb 2006.

Savage, S., S. Scholtes, and D. Zweidler. "*Probability Management, Part 2.*" OR/MS Today, Feb 2006.

Schmidt, S., and R. Launsby. *Understanding Industrial Designed Experiments*. 4th ed. Colorado Springs: Air Academy Press, 1994.

Schnarrs, S., and J. Bavuso. "Extrapolation Models on Very Short-Term Forecasts." *Journal of Business Research* 14 (1986): 27–36.

Sonderman, D., and P. Abrahamson. "Radiotherapy Design Using Mathematical Programming." *Operations Research* 33, no. 4 (1985): 705–725.

Stephen Baker. "Math Will Rock Your World."

Stephens-Davidowitz, S. *Everybody Lies: Big Data, New Data, and What the Internet Can Tell Us About Who We Really Are*. HarperCollins Publishers, 2017.

Steve Lohr. "For Today's Graduate, Just One Word: Statistics."

Taleb, N. N. *The Black Swan*. Random House, 2007.

Tandon, R., A. Chakraborty, G. Srinivasan, M. Shroff, A. Abdullah, B. Shamasundar, R Sinha, S. Subramanian, D. Hill, and P. Dhore. "Hewlett Packard: Delivering Profitable Growth for HPDirect.com Using Operations Research." *Interfaces* 43, no. 1 (2013): 48–61.

Thomas J. Stanley, and William D. Danko. *"The Millionaire Next Door."* Longstreet Press, 1996.

Westbrooke, I. "Simpson's Paradox: An Example in a New Zealand Survey of Jury Composition." *Chance* 11, no. 2 (1998): 40–42.

Winston, W. L. *Operations Research: Applications and Algorithms*. 4th ed. Belmont, CA: Duxbury Press, 2003.

INDEX

ISBN-13: 978-0-357-10996-0
ISBN-10: 0-357-10996-1

90000

9 780357 109960